Design of
Enzyme Inhibitors as Drugs

Design of Enzyme Inhibitors as Drugs

Edited by

Merton Sandler

Professor of Chemical Pathology,
University of London

and

H. John Smith

Senior Lecturer in Medicinal Chemistry,
University of Wales

OXFORD   NEW YORK   TOKYO
OXFORD UNIVERSITY PRESS
1989

Oxford University Press, Walton Street, Oxford OX2 6DP

Oxford New York Toronto
Delhi Bombay Calcutta Madras Karachi
Petaling Jaya Singapore Hong Kong Tokyo
Nairobi Dar es Salaam Cape Town
Melbourne Auckland
and associated companies in
Berlin Ibadan

Oxford is a trade mark of Oxford University Press

Published in the United States
by Oxford University Press, New York

British Library Cataloguing in Publication Data

Design of enzyme inhibitors as drugs.
1. Man. Enzymes. Inhibitors: Drugs
I. Sandler, Merton   II. Smith, H.
John, 1930–
615'.7
ISBN 0–19–261537–8

Library of Congress Cataloging in Publication Data

Design of enzyme inhibitors as drug/edited by
Merton Sandler and H. John Smith.
1. Enzyme inhibitors–Therapeutic use—Testing.   2. Enzyme
inhibitors—Structure-activity relationships.   I. Sandler, Merton.
II. Smith, H. J., 1930–
[DNLM: 1. Chemistry, Pharmaceutical.   2. Enzyme Inhibitors.
QU 143 D457]
RM666.E548D47   1989   615'.75—dc 19   88-1432
ISBN 0–19–261537–8

Set by Macmillan India
Printed in Great Britain
at the University Printing House, Oxford
by David Stanford
Printer to the University

Preface

At first sight, it may seem strange and paradoxical that a drug can exert a beneficial effect by impairing a particular body function. And yet, when enzyme inhibitors are used as drugs, that is precisely what we design them to do! Increasingly, in recent years, drugs have been developed which work by inhibiting a selected target enzyme in a metabolic chain—for a variety of reasons, which will become clear when the chapters which follow are consulted.

Although specialized aspects of this topic have been reviewed earlier in more limited compilations, comprehensive coverage in one volume has not previously been attempted. Such a book seemed badly overdue in this rapidly advancing field of drug design. Accordingly, we decided to provide a wide overview of the main target enzymes and their known inhibitors and, within this framework of knowledge, to demonstrate how the drug designer uses all available information to develop a specific therapeutic agent. Paramount in our minds was the need to tackle the subject in interdisciplinary fashion so as to appeal to the widest range of biological interests. Thus, chemical and biochemical data concerning inhibitor structures and the way these compounds inhibit are presented, together with pharmacological and clinical material on their toxicity, bioavailability, and pharmacokinetics. Another prominent aspect of the text relates to modern computerized techniques of drug design such as QSAR and molecular graphics. This topic has been dealt with in a general introductory manner and built on in particular chapters where appropriate. The authors of each of the chapters which follow are acknowledged world experts and it is a pleasure to express our gratitude to them for their willing cooperation.

London   M. S.
Cardiff   H. J. S.
July 1987

Contents

Contributors

Norman Aldridge, The Robens Institute of Environmental Health and Safety, University of Surrey, Guildford, Surrey GU2 5XH, UK.

D. P. Baccanari, Wellcome Research Laboratories, Research Triangle Park, NC 27709, USA.

L. L. Bennett, Jr., Kettering-Meyer Laboratories, Southern Research Institute, 2000 Ninth Avenue South, P.O. Box 55305, Birmingham, AL 35255, USA.

Philippe Bey, Merrell Dow Research Institute, Cincinnati Center, Ohio 45025, USA.

F. N. Bolkenius, Merrell Dow Research Institute, Strasbourg Center, 16 rue d'Ankara, 67084, Strasbourg Cedex, France.

Angela Brodie, Department of Pharmacology and Experimental Therapeutics, University of Maryland School of Medicine, 655 West Baltimore Street, Baltimore, MD 21201, USA.

R. W. Carrell, Laboratory of Molecular Biology, Medical Research Council Centre, University Medical School, Hills Road, Cambridge CB2 2QH, UK.

P. Charlier, Service de Microbiologie appliquée aux sciences pharmaceutiques, Faculté de Médecine, Université de Liège, Institute de Chimie, B6, B-4000 Sart Tilman (Liège 1), Belgium.

David A. Cooney, National Cancer Institute, National Institutes of Health, Bethesda, MD 20205, USA.

Dr James K. Coward, Department of Medical Chemistry, College of Pharmacology, The University of Michigan, 428 Church Street, Ann Arbor, MI 48109-1065, USA.

J. Coyette, Service de Microbiologie appliquée aux sciences pharmaceutiques, Faculté de Médecine, Université de Liège, Institute de Chimie, B6, B-4000 Sart Tilman (Liège 1), Belgium.

Charles Danzin, Merrell Dow Research Institute, Strasbourg Center, 16 Rue d'Ankara, F-67084 Strasbourg Cedex, France.

J. C. Dearden, Department of Pharmaceutical Chemistry, School of Pharmacy, Liverpool Polytechnic, Byrom Street, Liverpool L3 3AF, UK.

O. Dideberg, Service de Microbiologie appliquée aux sciences pharmaceutiques, Faculté de Médecine, Université de Liège, Institute de Chimie, B6, B-4000 Sart Tilman (Liège 1), Belgium.

G. Dive, Service de Microbiologie appliquée aux sciences pharmaceutiques, Faculté de Médecine, Université de Liège, Institute de Chimie, B6, B-4000 Sart Tilman (Liège 1), Belgium.

C. Duez, Service de Microbiologie appliquée aux sciences pharmaceutiques, Faculté de Médecine, Université de Liège, Institute de Chimie, B6, B-4000 Sart Tilman (Liège 1), Belgium.

J. Dusart, Service de Microbiologie appliquée aux sciences pharmaceutiques, Faculté de Médecine, Université de Liège, Institute de Chimie, B6, B-4000 Sart Tilman (Liège 1), Belgium.

J. M. Frère, Service de Microbiologie appliquée aux sciences pharmaceutiques, Faculté de Médecine, Université de Liège, Institute de Chimie, B6, B-4000 Sart Tilman (Liège 1), Belgium.

Lloyd J. Frick, Wellcome Research Laboratories, Research Triangle Park, NC 27709, USA.

P. M. George, Chemical Pathologist, The Princess Margaret Hospital, Christchurch, New Zealand.

Jean-Marie Ghuysen, Service de Microbiologie appliquée aux sciences pharmaceutiques, Faculté de Médecine, Université de Liège, Institute de Chimie, B6, B-4000 Sart Tilman (Liège 1), Belgium.

William J. Greenlee, Department of Drug Metabolism, Merck, Sharp & Dohme Research Laboratories, Division of Merck & Co. Inc. West Point, PA 19486, USA.

Arnulf Hache, Zentralinstitut für Molekularbiologie, Akademie der Wissenschaften der DDR, Robert-Rössle-Straße 10, 1115 Berlin-Buch, DDR (East Germany).

Gerry Higgs, Department of Mediator Pharmacology, The Wellcome Research Laboratories, Beckenham, Kent BR3 3BS, UK.

G. H. Hitchings, Wellcome Research Laboratories, Research Triangle Park, NC 27709, USA.

W. H. Hörl, Abteilung Innere Medizin IV, Medizinische Universitätsklinik, Hungstetter Straße 55, 7800 Freiburg IBR FRG.

B. Joris, Service de Microbiologie appliquée aux sciences pharmaceutiques, Faculté de Médecine, Université de Liège, Institute de Chimie, B6, B-4000 Sart Tilman (Liège 1), Belgium.

Michel Jung, Merrell Dow Research Institute, Strasbourg Center, 16 rue d'Ankara, F-67084 Strasbourg Cedex, France.

Thomas W. Kensler, Division of Experimental Pathology and Toxicology, The Johns Hopkins University School of Hygiene and Public Health, 615 North Wolfe Street, Baltimore, MD 21205, USA.

L. F. Kuyper, Wellcome Research Laboratories, Research Triangle Park, NC 27709, USA.

J. Lamotte-Brasseur, Service de Microbiologie appliquée aux sciences pharmaceutiques, Faculté de Médecine, Université de Liège, Institute de Chimie, B6, B-4000 Sart Tilman (Liège 1), Belgium.

M. Leyh-Bouille, Service de Microbiologie appliquée aux sciences pharmaceutiques, Faculté de Médecine, Université de Liège, Institute de Chimie, B6, B-4000 Sart Tilman (Liège 1), Belgium.

Sven Lindskog, Department of Biochemistry, University of Umeå, S-901 87 Umeå, Sweden.

F. Markwardt, Institut für Pharmakologie und Toxikologie, Medizinische Akademie Erfurt, Nordhäuser Straße 74, 5060 Erfurt, DDR (East Germany).

Ian A. McDonald, Merrell Dow Research Institute, Cincinnati Center, Ohio 45025, USA.

Rudolph Megges, Zentralinstitut für Molekularbiologie, Akademie der Wissenschaften der DDR, Robert-Rössle-Straße 10, 1115 Berlin-Buch, DDR (East Germany).

J. A. Montgomery, Kettering-Meyer Laboratories, Southern Research Institute, 2000 Ninth Avenue South, P. O. Box 55305, Birmingham, AL 35255, USA.

A. C. T. North, The Astbury Department of Biophysics, The University of Leeds, Leeds LS2 9JT, UK.

M. Nuygen-Distèche, Service de Microbiologie appliquée aux sciences pharmaceutiques, Faculté de Médecine, Université de Liège, Institute de Chimie, B6, B-4000 Sart Tilman (Liège 1), Belgium.

Michael Palfreyman, Merrell Dow Research Institute, Cincinnati Center, OH 45025, USA.

James C. Powers, Department of Chemistry, Georgia Institute of Technology, Atlanta, GA 30332, USA.

Rex F. Pratt, Associate Professor of Chemistry, Department of Chemistry, Hall-Atwater Laboratories, Middletown, CT 06457, USA.

Walter C. Prozialeck, Department of Physiology and Pharmacology, Philadelphia College of Osteopathic Medicine, Philadelphia, Pennsylvania, USA.

D. S. Reeves, Southmead Health Authority, Department of Medical Microbiology, Division of Pathology, Southmead Hospital, Westbury-on-Trym, Bristol BS10 5NB, UK.

K. R. H. Repke, Zentralinstitut für Molekularbiologie, Akademie der Wissenschaften der DDR, Robert-Rössle-Straße 10, 1115 Berlin-Buch, DDR (East Germany).

Jill Roberts-Lewis, Division of Neuropsychopharmacology, Department of Pharmacology, The Medical College of Pennsylvania, 3300 Henry Avenue, Philadelphia, PA 19129, USA.

M. Sandler, Department of Chemical Pathology, Queen Charlotte's Hospital, Goldhawk Road, London W6 OXG, UK.

Werner Schönfeld, Zentralinstitut für Molekularbiologie, Akademie der Wissenschaften der DDR, Robert-Rössle-Straße 10, 1115 Berlin-Buch, DDR (East Germany).

Jean-Charles Schwartz, Unité de Neurobiologie, Centre Paul Broca de l'Inserm, 2 ter, rue d'Alésia, 75014 Paris, France.

Nikolaus Seiler, Merrell Dow Research Institute, Strasbourg Center, 16 rue d'Ankara, 67084 Strasbourg Cedex, France.

Elliot Shaw, Friedrich Miescher-Institut, P.O. Box 2543, CH-4002 Basel, Switzerland.

H. J. Smith, UWIST, King Edward VII Avenue, Cardiff CF1 3NU, UK.

Jörg Stürzebecher, Institut für Pharmakologie und Toxikologie, Medizinische Akademie Erfurt, Nordhäuser Straße 74, 5060 Erfurt, DDR (East Germany).

Keith F. Tipton, Biochemistry Department, University of Dublin, Trinity College, Dublin 2, Ireland.

E. H. Ulm, Department of Drug Metabolism, Merck, Sharp & Dohme Research Laboratories, Division of Merck & Co. Inc., West Point, PA 19486, USA.

Sir John Vane, FRS, The William Harvey Research Institute, St Bartholomews Hospital Medical College, Charterhouse Square, London ECIM 6BQ, UK.

Jürgen Weiland, Zentralinstitut für Molekularbiologie, Akademie der Wissenschaften der DDR, Robert-Rössle-Straße 10, 1115 Berlin-Buch, DDR (East Germany).

Benjamin Weiss, Division of Neuropsychopharmacology, Department of Pharmacology, The Medical College of Pennsylvania, 3300 Henry Avenue, Philadelphia, PA 19129, USA.

L. O. White, Department of Medical Microbiology, Division of Pathology, Southmead Hospital, Westbury-on-Trim, Bristol BS10 5NB, UK.

Per J. Wistrand, Department of Medical Pharmacology, Uppsala University Biomedical Centre, Box 593, S-751 24 Uppsala, Sweden.

Richard V. Wolfenden, Department of Biochemistry and Nutrition, The University of North Carolina at Chapel Hill School of Medicine, Faculty Laboratory Office Building 231H, Chapel Hill, NC 27514, USA.

Morris Zimmerman, Box 7116, Wachtung, NJ 07060, USA.

Abbreviations

AADC	L-aromatic amino acid 1-decarboxylase (EC 4.1.1.28)
ACE	angiotensin-converting enzyme (peptidylpeptide carboxyhydrolase, EC 3.4.15.1)
4-acetoxyA	4-acetoxyandrostene-3,17-dione
AChE	acetylcholinesterase (acetylcholine acetyl hydrolase, EC 3.1.1.7)
Ade	adenine
Ado	adenosine
AICAR	phosphoribosylaminoimidazole carboxamide
AICAR TF-ase	AICAR formyltransferase (EC 2.1.2.3)
Ala-T	alanine aminotransferase
AMCA	tranexamic acid
amido-PRT	amidophosphoribosyl transferase (EC 2.4.2.14)
AMP-DA	adenosine-5'-monophosphate deaminase (EC 3.5.4.6)
α-NAPAP	$N\alpha$-(2-napthylsulphonylglycyl)-4-amidinophenylalanine
AOAA	aminooxyacetic acid
APPA	4-amidinophenylpyruvic acid
araA	9-β-D-arabinofuranosyladenine
ARDS	adult respiratory distress syndrome
ATCase	L-aspartate transcarbamoylase (EC 2.1.3.2)
ATD	1,4,6-androstene-3,6,17-trione
A-trione	4-androstene-3,6,17-trione
BP	blood pressure
CA	carbonic anhydrase (EC 4.2.1.1)
CAPP	norchlorpromazine isothiocyanate
CM	calmodulin
CoF	coformycin
COMT	catechol-O-methyltransferase (EC 2.1.1.6)
CONV	5-chloropentanoic acid
CPA	carboxypeptidase A
CPB	carboxypeptidase B
CPS II	carbamoyl phosphate synthetase II (EC 2.7.2.9)
CPZ	chlorpromazine
CSF	cerebrospinal fluid

CTP	cystidine-5′-triphosphate
CuAO	copper-containing amine oxidases
cyclic AMP	cyclic 3′,5′-adenosine monophosphate
DAO	diamine oxidase (EC 1.4.3.6)
DAPA	Nα-dansyl-L-arginine-4-ethylpiperidineamide
DBH	3,4 dihydroxyphenylethylamine ascorbate; O_2 oxidoreductase (β-hydroxylating) (dopamine-β-hydroxylase; dopamine-β-monooxygenase, EC 14.7.11)
dCF	2′-deoxycoformin
D,D-peptidases	D-alanyl-D-alanine transpeptidases/carboxypeptidases
DDTHF	5,10 dideazatetrahydrofolate
DFMO	α-difluoromethylornithine
DHEA	dehydroepiandrosterone
DHFR	dihydrofolate reductase (5,6,7,8-terahydrofolate: $NADP^+$ oxidoreductase, EC 1.5.1.3)
DHOase	L-dihydroorotase (EC 3.5.2.3)
DHOdeHase	L-dihydroorotate dehydrogenase (EC 3.5.2.3)
DHT	dihydroxytestosterone
DMBA	7,12-dimethylbenz(a)anthracene
DOC	11-hydroxycorticosterone
dopa	3,4-dihydroxyphenylalanine
DPG	diphosphoglycerate
dTMPS	thymidylate synthetase
EACA	ε-aminocaproic acid
ETYA	tetraynoic analogue of arachidonic acid
e. p. r.	electron paramagnetic resonance
F-araA	9-β-D-arabinofuranosyl-2-fluoroadenine
FdUMP	5-fluoro-2′-deoxyuridylate
FGARP	5′-phosphoribosylglycinamide (EC 6.3.5.3)
FH_2	dihydrofolate
FH_4	tetrahydrofolate
FOY	ε-guanidinocaproic acid (gabexate mesilate)
FU	fluorouracil
GABA-T	GABA transaminase (4-aminobutyric acid: 2-oxo-glutarate aminotransferase, EC 2.6.1.19)
GAD	L-glutamate carboxy-lyase (glutamate decarboxylase, EC 4.1.1.5)

GAR TFase	phosphoribosylglycinamide formyltransferase (EC 2.1.2.2)
GlcNAc	N-acetylglucosamine
Hcy	homocysteine
HDC	L-histidine carboxy-lyase (histidine decarboxylase, EC 4.1.1.22)
HETE	hydroxyeicosatetraenoic acid
HPETE	hydroperoxyeicosatetraenoic acid
3-HSD	Δ^5-3β-hydroxysteroid dehydrogenase
HTC cells	rat hepatoma tissue culture cells
IAHQ	N-[p-{[(2-amino-4-hydroxy-6-quinazolinyl) amino]methyl}benzoyl]-L-glutamic acid
IMP-DHO	inosine monophosphate dehydrogenase (EC 1.1.1.205)
IPF	idiopathic pulmonary fibrosis
m^{6}a	N^6-methyladenosine
4-MA	17β-N,N-diethylcarbamoyl-4-methyl-4-aza-5α-androst-3-one (DMAA)
4-MAPC	sodium 4-methyl-3-oxo-4-aza-5α-pregnane-20(S)carboxylate
MAO	monoamine oxidase (EC 1.4.3.4)
MeMPR	6-(methylthio)purine ribonucleotide
MIX	1-methyl-3-isobutylxanthine
MP	6-mercaptopurine
MPA	mycophenolic acid
MPRP	6-mercaptopurine ribonucleotide
MR	molar refractivity
mRNA	messenger ribonucleic acid
MSA	multi-substrate adduct
MTA	5'-deoxy-5'-methylthioadenosine
MTT	7-deaza MTA
MTRP	5-deoxy-5-methylthioribose phosphate
MurNAc	N-acetylmuramic acid
Na$^+$,K$^+$-ATPase	Na$^+$,K$^+$-transporting adenosine triphosphatase (EC 3.6.1.37)
NDGA	nordihydro-guaiaretic acid
NEM	N-methylmaleimide
n.m.r.	nuclear magnetic resonance
NTE	neuropathy target esterase

OAT	ornithine aminotransferase (EC 2.6.1.13)
4-OHA	4-hydroxyandrostene-3,17-dione
OMPdeCase	orotidine-5′-monophosphate decarboxylase (EC 4.1.1.23)
OPRTase	orotate phosphoribosyl transferase (EC 2.1.3.2)
Orn-DC	L-ornithine-1-carboxylase (EC 4.1.1.17)
pAB	*para*-aminobenzoic acid
PALA	*N*-(phosphonacetyl)-*L*-aspartic acid
pAMBA	*para*-aminomethylbenzoic acid
PAO	polyamine oxidase
PAPT	putrescine aminopropyl transferase (spermidine synthase—EC 2.5.1.16)
PBP	penicillin binding protein
PG	prostaglandin
pHBCN	[ring-^{3}H] *para*-hydroxybenzyl cyanide
pHMN	*para*-hydroxymandelonitrile
PMN	polymorphonuclear
PMSG	pregnant mare's serum gonadotrophin
PRA	plasma renin activity
PRPP	5′-phosphoribosyl pyrophosphate
PTH	parathyroid hormone
QSAR	quantitative structure–activity relationship
RAS	renin–angiotensin–aldosterone system
RCS	rabbit aorta contracting substance
RDPR	ribonucleotide diphosphate reductase (EC 1.17.4.1)
SADATO	*S*-adenosyl-1,8-amino-3-thiooctane
SADATAD	*S*-adenosyl-1,12-diamino-8-aza-3-thiooctane
SAH	*S*-adenosyl homocysteine
SAHase	*S*-adenosyl homocysteine hydrolase (EC 3.3.1.1)
SAICAR	phosphoribosylaminoimidazole succino-carboxamide
SAM	*S*-adenosyl methionine
SAM-DC	*S*-adenosyl methionine decarboxylase (EC 4.1.1.50)
SAPT	spermidine aminopropyl transferase (spermine synthase—EC 2.5.1.22)
SEM	standard error of the mean
SIBA	5′-isobutylthioadenosine
SRS-A	slow-reacting substance of anaphylaxis

STH	c^7S-adenosylhomocysteine
T	testosterone
TG	6-thioguanine
TGDA	2-tetradecylglycidic acid
TS	thymidylate synthetase (EC 2.1.1.45)
TX	thromboxane
u.v.	ultra-violet

1

Introduction to the use of enzyme inhibitors as drugs

Merton Sandler and H. John Smith

1.1 Introduction

A number of drugs in clinical use exert their action by inhibiting a specific enzyme, the target enzyme, present either in tissues of the individual under treatment or in those of an invading organism. This chapter serves to introduce aspects of the art of designing enzyme inhibitors as useful or potentially useful drugs: it is slanted towards surveying underlying concepts; it concerns itself with target enzyme selection; and it offers guidelines for choosing an appropriate inhibitor for the biochemical system under study.

1.2 Basic concept and its application

The basis for using enzyme inhibitors as drugs is that inhibition of a suitably selected target enzyme leads to a build-up in concentration of substrate(s) and a corresponding decrease in concentration of the metabolite(s), one of which leads to a useful clinical response. The different ways of achieving this end, in principle at least, are summarized in Fig. 1.1. In practice, the position may be more complex, as discussed in later chapters of this book.

Consider situation (a) (see Fig. 1.1), where the target enzyme exerts a degradative role on a substrate and, not being part of a metabolic chain, acts in isolation, where:

(1) the substrate, gives a required response (agonist), then enzyme inhibition leads to its accumulation and accentuation of that response; or where

1

(a)
A
E
B
Inhibitor
(b)
A
E1
B
E2
C
E3
D
E4
E
(Metabolite)
Inhibitor
(c)
A
E1
B
E2
C
E3
D
E4
E
(Metabolite)
Co factor
Y
X
E
Inhibitor
(d)
A
E1
B
E2
C
E3
D
E4
E
(Metabolite)
Co factor Z
+
inhibitor
E2Z' Inhibitor'
Dead-end complex
(e)
A
E1
B
E2
C
E3
D
E4
E
(Metabolite)
Inhibitor (1)
Inhibitor (2)
(f)
A
E1
B—CH3
(Metabolite)
SAM
Inhibition
SAH
SAH ase
Products
Inhibitor
(g)
A
Metabolizing enzyme
Inert product(s)
(Agonist)
Co-drug(inhibitor)

Fig. 1.1. Summary of different ways of achieving the basic concept.

(2) the metabolite, has an action judged to be clinically undesirable or too pronounced, then enzyme inhibition reduces its concentration with a decreased (desired) response.

In Fig. 1.1(b), where the target enzyme is part of a biosynthetic pathway consisting of a sequence of enzymes with their specific substrates and coenzymes, the aim is to prevent the overall production of a metabolite that either

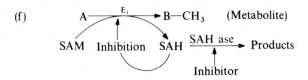

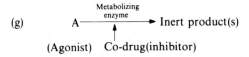

gives a clinically unwanted response or is essential to bacterial or cancerous growth. Careful selection of the target enzyme in the pathway is required to achieve this end, as we discuss later.

An alternative way [Fig. 1.1(c)] of decreasing overall metabolite production in a biosynthetic chain is to inhibit a target enzyme responsible for regeneration of a cofactor in the form required for one of the chain enzymes to function. Variations on this theme (d) are that the cofactor may be left in either a non-usable form or non-replaceable, non-usable form (Table 1.1).

Combination chemotherapy involves the use of two inhibitors simultaneously on a metabolic chain [Fig. 1.1(e)]. It is employed with the aim of achieving a greater therapeutic effect than by application of either inhibitor alone, when dosage is limited by host toxicity or when resistant bacterial strains have emerged. The best known combination (Garrod *et al.* 1969) is the antibacterial mixture of trimethoprim [dihydrofolate reductase (DHFR) inhibitor] and the sulphonamide, sulphamethoxazole (dihydropteroate synthetase inhibitor). However, not all combinations are synergistic or additive but may be antagonistic within a metabolic network (Grindey *et al.* 1975).

In enhancement of product inhibition [Fig. 1.1(f)], product build-up progressively decreases the activity of an enzyme on its substrate. This build-up is achieved by inhibiting an enzyme that disposes of the product. *S*-adenosylhomocysteine (SAH), the product of methylating enzymes using *S*-adenosylmethionine (e.g. COMT) and an inhibitor of these enzymes, is removed by the hydrolytic action of its hydrolase (SAHase). Inhibitors of SAHase are being designed that should allow a build-up of the product, SAH, leading to a useful clinical effect (Chiang 1984).

A more subtle application [Fig. 1.1(g)] of enzyme inhibitors in therapy has been to use them as co-drugs to protect an administered drug with a required action from the effects of a metabolizing enzyme. Inhibition of the metabolizing target enzyme permits higher plasma levels of the administered drug to persist, so prolonging its biological half-life and either preserving its effect or resulting in less frequent administration. Examples are given in Table 1.2.

1.3   Development of a rationale for target enzyme selection

The ways in which a target enzyme has been pinpointed as a suitable candidate for *in vivo* inhibition are varied and not always based on logical design. Occasionally, drugs in current use for one therapeutic purpose have exhibited side-effects indicative of potential usefulness for another, subsequent work establishing that the newly-discovered drug effect is due to inhibition of a target enzyme. Although the drug may possess minimal therapeutic usefulness in its new-found role, it does constitute an important 'lead' compound for the development of analogues with improved clinical characteristics. Sulphanilamide, used as an antibacterial drug, exhibited acidosis as a side-effect due to its inhibition of renal carbonic anhydrase (Schwartz 1949). This observation led to

Table 1.1 Decrease in overall metabolite production by modifying metabolic enzyme cofactor regeneration

Cofactor	Metabolic enzyme	Inhibitor	Enzyme inhibited	Notes	Reference
THF	Thymidylate synthetase	Trimethoprim* (& others)	Dihydrofolate reductase (DHFR)	Inhibition of DHFR prevents conversion of DHF →THF essential for thymidylate enzyme	Burchall and Hitchings 1965 Hitchings *et al.* 1950
Pyridoxal phosphate	GABA transaminase	Gabaculine[†]	—	Dead end complex	Rando 1977
THF	Thymidylate synthetase	5-fluorouracil[†]	—	Dead end complex	Santi *et al.* 1978
NAD	SAHase	2-deoxyadenosine[†]	—	Enzyme-bound NAD converted to NADH	Abeles *et al.* 1982

* Reversible, competitive.
† Mechanism-based inactivators.

Table 1.2 Examples of administration of inhibitors as co-drugs to protect an administered drug from metabolic degradation

Co-drug	Administered drug	Target enzyme	Clinical role of administered drug	Reference
Clavulanic acid sulbactam	Penicillin (β-lactamase sensitive)	β-lactamase	Antibiotic	Howarth et al. 1976 Reading and Cole 1977 English et al. 1978; Calderwood et al. 1982.
Benserazide Carbidopa	L-dopa	AADC	Treatment of Parkinson's disease	Burkard et al. 1962; Sletzinger et al. 1963.
Selegiline (L-)deprenyl	L-dopa	MAO B	Treatment of Parkinson's disease	Sandler and Stern 1982
Allopurinol	6-mercaptopurine	Xanthine oxidase	Cancer chemotherapy	Elion et al. 1963a Elion et al. 1963b
Tetra hydrouridine	Ara-C	Pyrimidine nucleoside deaminase	Cancer chemotherapy	Camiener 1968; Neil et al. 1970
5-diazouracil	5-fluorouracil	Dihydrouracil dehydrogenase	Cancer chemotherapy	Cooper and Greer 1970 Copper et al. 1972

the development, first, of the diuretic acetazolamide, and subsequently the chlorothiazide group of diuretics. The anticonvulsant aminoglutethimide was withdrawn from the market due to inhibition of the cholesterol side-chain cleavage enzyme involved in steroid biosynthesis, which led to a 'medical adrenalectomy' (Cash *et al.* 1967; Dexter *et al.* 1967). Aminoglutethimide (in conjunction with supplementary hydrocortisone) is now used for the treatment of oestrogen receptor-positive breast cancer is post-menopausal women because of its ability to inhibit aromatase, another enzyme in the biosynthetic pathway (Santen *et al.* 1978). Other more potent aromatase inhibitors have subsequently been developed, e.g. 4-hydroxyandrostenedione.

Iproniazid, used as a drug in the treatment of tuberculosis, was noted to have a central nervous stimulant effect (Zeller *et al.* 1952) associated with its inhibitory effect on MAO. More potent inhibitors of MAO, such as phenelzine, tranylcypromine, selegiline [(−)-deprenyl], and clorgyline have since been developed.

Many drugs introduced into therapy for a particular purpose, following detection of biological activity by screening experiments with animal tissues, whole animals, bacteria, or protozoa, have subsequently been shown to exert their action by inhibition of a specific enzyme in the animal or parasite. This knowledge has helped in the development of clinically more useful drugs, not only by reducing screening tests for drug activity to the isolated pure or partially purified target enzyme concerned, but also by introducing a more logical design approach as described below.

In the foregoing paragraphs, the pinpointing of a target enzyme in a fortuitous manner has removed from the design arena the necessity of selecting the enzyme and has focused attention on design of the inhibitor. However, starting from first principles, the rational design of an enzyme inhibitor for a particular disease or condition presents a more challenging task to the drug designer, since it involves selection of a suitable target enzyme as a first step in the process. The *a priori* examination of the biochemical or physiological processes responsible for a disease or condition, where these are known or can be guessed at, may point to a suitable target enzyme in its biochemical environment (see Section 1.4.2.1), the inhibition of which would rationally be expected to lead to alleviation or removal of the disease or condition. Should sufficient information be available about the target enzyme with regard to the structure of its substrates, mechanism of catalysis, structure of active site, or even its topography, then design should eventually give a 'lead' compound. Should little be known about the target enzyme, then sometimes an inspired guess can be made regarding the nature and relevant positioning of binding and catalytic areas, by comparison with the structure of a related enzyme where these factors are well known (e.g. ACE and carboxypeptidase A; Cushman *et al.* 1980).

For mechanism-based inactivators, a knowledge of the mechanism for the modification of the normal substrate is essential in suggesting a 'lead' compound and understanding its mechanism of action. Manipulative changes, such as the introduction of a difluoromethyl, olefinic, or acetylenic group in a substrate, leading to successful inactivation of a particular target enzyme, can sometimes be applied with success to other related target enzymes (pyridoxal phosphate-dependent enzymes; GABA-T, Orn-DC, AADC; Jung *et al.* 1980) or even unrelated enzymes (aromatase; Johnston *et al.* 1984).

Once a 'lead' compound for a target enzyme has been discovered, then structural modification of the molecule, incorporating such changes as interspatial distances between groups/atoms, fixed conformations in cyclic systems, isosteric replacements, introduction of bulky hydrophobic groups, etc., is carried out to obtain analogues with improved clinical properties, attention being paid to potency, pharmacokinetics, and side-effects.

Structural design changes are increasingly being aided by the modern techniques of computer graphics and QSAR (quantitative structure–activity relationships), involving linear free-energy relationships, and using sophisticated statistics and computer software (see Chapter 2).

1.4 Criteria for selection of target enzyme and inhibitor type

1.4.1 Types of inhibitors

The type of inhibitor selected for a particular target enzyme may be important in producing a useful clinical effect, for reasons to be discussed later. A brief summary of the different types follows, with a detailed discussion of each in Chapter 2.

Enzyme-inhibiting processes may be divided into two main classes, *reversible* and *irreversible*, depending upon the manner in which the inhibitor (or inhibitor residue) is attached to the enzyme. Reversible inhibition occurs when the inhibitor is bound to the enzyme through a suitable combination of van der Waals', electrostatic, hydrogen bonding, and hydrophobic attractive forces, the extent of the binding being determined by the equilibrium constant K_i, for breakdown of the EI or EIS complex for classical inhibitors (although the situation may be more complex for slow-binding and slow, tight-binding inhibitors, Morrison 1982). In irreversible inhibition reactions, after initial binding of the inhibitor (or substrate) to the enzyme, a covalent bond is formed between a functional group on the enzyme and the inhibitor (eqn. (1.1); active site-directed irreversible inhibition) or reactive residue formed from the substrate (eqn. 1.2; mechanism-based enzyme inactivation).

$$E + I \underset{}{\overset{K_i}{\rightleftharpoons}} EI \xrightarrow{k_2} E\!-\!I \qquad (1.1)$$

$$E + S \rightleftharpoons ES \xrightarrow{k_{cat}} EX \xrightarrow{k_{inh}} E\!-\!I \qquad (1.2)$$
$$\Updownarrow$$
$$E + X \text{ (product)}$$

Reversible inhibitors may be competitive, non-competitive, uncompetitive, or of mixed type, depending upon their point of entry into the enzyme–substrate reaction scheme (Webb 1963). Nearly all reversible inhibitors that have been designed as potential drugs, as well as drugs in current use, are competitive inhibitors. Notable exceptions are the cardiac glycosides, which are non-competitive inhibitors of Na^+,K^+-ATPase. One reason for this is that competitive inhibitors of the enzyme bear some resemblance to the substrate, since they bind at the same site, and this knowledge has provided a starting point in design, whereas the other types of inhibitor bind elsewhere on the enzyme and need not resemble the substrate, so removing an obvious design aspect. However, in the future, design of inhibitors that bind in a different manner to the substrate should be possible from a consideration of the potential binding surfaces revealed by crystallographic studies on a pure enzyme. This approach has been used to improve binding of known competitive inhibitors that form a suitable enzyme–inhibitor (EI) complex (e.g. methotrexate and DHFR; see Krohn 1984).

A special type of competitive inhibitor is a transition-state (multi-substrate) analogue. This is a stable compound that resembles in structure the substrate portion(s) of the enzymic transition state for chemical change. Even an analogue crudely resembling the transition state should bind to the enzyme very strongly, since the affinity of the enzyme for the transition state (Lindquist 1975) is extremely large (10^8–10^{14} fold greater) compared with that for the substrate(s). Values for this difference in affinity have been reported in the range 10^2–10^5, perhaps reflecting imperfect analogues (Lindquist 1975).

Compounds producing irreversible enzyme inhibition fall into two groups. Active-site-directed (affinity labelling) inhibitors possess a reactive function which, after binding of the inhibitor to the enzyme surface, forms a covalent bond with a functional group at or near the active site of the enzyme. Mechanism-based inactivators (k_{cat} inhibitors, suicide substrates) do not carry a biologically reactive functional group but, by acting as substrates, are modified by the target enzyme to a moiety containing a reactive function that subsequently forms a covalent bond with a group on the target enzyme. In rare instances, a dead-end complex is formed, with a substrate residue covalently bound to the enzyme (e.g. 5-fluorouracil and thymidylate synthetase; Santi *et al.* 1978) or a mechanism-based inactivator is modified by its target enzyme to give a residue that binds non-covalently but tightly to the enzyme, e.g. allopurinol and xanthine oxidase (Massey *et al.* 1970).

1.4.2   Inhibitor selection—general considerations

What criteria should be used to design the best type of inhibitor for a target enzyme in a particular *in vivo* biochemical system in order to produce the most acceptable clinical response? In general, the most important considerations determining selection are: (1) biochemical environment of the target enzyme; (2) specificity of action not associated with toxic or undesirable side-effects.

1.4.2.1 *Biochemical environment of the target enzyme*

In a chain of reactions in a steady-state, where the initial substrate, A, does not undergo a change in concentration as a consequence of changes effected elsewhere in the chain, then any type of *reversible* inhibitor that inhibits the first step of the chain will effectively block that sequence of reactions (Webb 1963; Grindey *et al.* 1975). This also applies to the first reaction following a branching point in a divergent chain if the alternative route is the major reaction, thus maintaining a constant flux of the common substrate. Inhibitors acting at later points in the chain will have quite different effects. If the reaction $B \xrightarrow{E_2} C$ [eqn (1.3)] is considered, competitive inhibition

$$A \xrightarrow[v_1]{E_1} B \xrightarrow[v_2]{E_2} C \xrightarrow[v_3]{E_3} D \xrightarrow[v_4]{E_4} E \text{ (metabolite)} \tag{1.3}$$

of E_2 will initially decrease the rate of formation of C but the concentration of B will rise, due to a difference between its rate of formation and rate of consumption. Eventually the original velocity (v_2) of the step will be re-established. Although a competitive inhibitor does not cause a sustained inhibition in the rate of formation of C (or D and E), it does cause an increase in the substrate concentration of the enzyme inhibited. Such an increase may have secondary effects on the chain due to product inhibition (by B on E_1) or product reversal $(A \rightleftharpoons B)$. If the step $C \xrightarrow{E_3} D$ is considered, where E_3 is the target enzyme, then feedback inhibition by C on E_1 is a further effect. Either of these effects can lead to a slowing of the overall pathway by slowing v_1. Thus a single inhibitor with a single site of action could cause multiple effects when it acts on an enzyme that is a member of a regulated steady-state system. Consequently, the selection of a target enzyme within a metabolic chain which does not inhibit the first step may lead successfully to translation of *in vitro* results to the *in vivo* situation due to these additional changes. Needless to say, such a selection procedure approach is based on an element of chance, unless the chain has been exhaustively studied. In this connection, Grindey *et al.* (1975) have quantitatively analysed the effects of two inhibitors on the same enzyme (one or two substrates) or two different enzymes in a sequence, taking into account feedback effects and using different types of inhibitors. Successful application of these concepts and development of basic models for combinations of drugs in the tetrahydrofolate (THF) synthetic pathway and in DNA biosynthesis led them to conclude that concerted inhibition by two agents within specific metabolic networks can yield synergistic, additive, or antagonistic interactions, depending on the type of reversible inhibitor, its site of action within the network, and the structure of the metabolic chain being inhibited.

Another factor to be considered, which may be overriding, is whether or not the chain is under hormonal control. Where the metabolite produced by a chain is a hormone, e.g. oestradiol, testosterone, cortisone, depletion of its plasma level by inhibition of its synthesis may lead to stimulation of the hypothalamus–pituitary–organ axis, causing the release of another hormone to accelerate the synthetic pathway. This action restores the plasma hormone to near normal levels, reversing the effect of the inhibitor. An example of this process is the release of luteinizing hormone (LH) as the result of falling oestrogen levels after administration of aminoglutethimide to women in the luteal phase. LH reverses the aromatase block and leads to increased oestrogen plasma levels due to a 'rebound' effect (Salhanick 1982).

As is apparent from the previous discussion, the view that the overall rate in a linear chain can be depressed only by inhibiting the rate-limiting reaction, i.e. the one with lowest velocity at saturation with its substrate, is a general misconception (Webb 1963). The overall rate is determined to a great extent by the concentration of the initial substrate and intermediates; thus, the first enzyme will often be rate-limiting, irrespective of its potential rate, due to low substrate concentration.

Lack of success in decreasing overall metabolite production by competitive reversible inhibition of an enzyme in the metabolic chain, which is not the first, is well illustrated by studies on inhibitors of the noradrenalin biosynthetic pathway (Bartholini and Pletscher 1975; von Euler 1972). The inhibitors were intended to decrease production of noradrenalin (agonist), with an associated reduction in the blood pressure of hypertensive patients. One of the enzymes in the biosynthesis of noradrenalin from tyrosine is dopa decarboxylase (AADC), the enzyme catalysing the conversion of dopa to dopamine. Many reversible inhibitors, although active *in vitro* against this enzyme, failed to lower noradrenalin production *in vivo*—although they may slow decarboxylation of dopa in peripheral tissues (Jung *et al.* 1980). α-monofluoromethyldopa is a mechanism-based inactivator of AADC and produces a metabolite that irreversibly inhibits and decreases the level of the enzyme by >99 per cent, with a near complete depletion of catecholamine levels in the brain, heart, and kidney (Jung *et al.* 1979).

Examination of the list of successful competitive inhibitors with a clinical use (Table 1.3), together with a consideration of the biochemical environment of the target enzyme, indicates that in many instances the target enzyme plays a degradative role on a substrate produced by an unrelated metabolic chain, i.e. the target enzyme functions in isolation from the chain producing its substrate. In the conversion $A \xrightarrow{E_1} B$, where the pool of the substrate A is relatively constant, due to homeostatic control or for other reasons (e.g. carbon dioxide), or where A has reached a maximal concentration (e.g. acetylcholine after nerve stimulation), thereby promoting a useful clinical effect, inhibition of E_1 by reversible inhibitors will not be antagonized by substrate build-up with reversal of the inhibition. Of course, irreversible inhibition (carbamates–AChE) is more effective in this situation, since although the presence of substrate slows the 'irreversible' reaction, the reaction is progressive and nears completion (Aldridge and Reiner 1972).

Transition-state analogues as a group are usually many times more potent than their classical reversible inhibitor counterparts (Lienhard 1972). Such increased potency can be exploited where, assuming similar pharmacokinetic properties, a classical inhibitor is unable to penetrate a cellular membrane sufficiently to produce an effective inhibitor concentration. For design of multi-substrate analogues for enzymes catalysing reactions involving two substrates, a knowledge is required of whether the reaction involves a ternary complex, or sequential transfer of substrates to the enzyme surface (ping–pong mechanism; Cleland 1970), since different transition state structures are involved in each case. Other tight-binding inhibitors are known that do not resemble the transition state and can have a half-life for the off (dissociation) rate in terms of days or months. Several of these are useful drugs, e.g. coformycin, methotrexate, and allopurinol. However, tight binding where the dissociation from the EI complex takes days is not distinguishable in effect from covalent bonding (Walsh 1984) and this type of inhibitor may be included in the following discussion.

Irreversible inhibition progressively decreases the titre of the target enzyme to a low level and the biochemical environment of the enzyme is unimportant, as intimated earlier. A list of drugs in use which act in this manner is given in Table 1.4. However, the production of inhibited enzyme must be faster than the generation of new enzyme by resynthesis to maintain the target enzyme titre at a low level (Smith 1978). Consequently, for active-site-directed irreversible inhibitors, the inhibitor concentration and potency (k_2/K_i) are important factors in determining their *in vivo* suitability. For mechanism-based inactivators, not only is the turnover rate of the enzyme important because of enzyme resynthesis, [and this may be 10^3–10^5 slower than for natural substrates (Rando 1984)], but, the partitioning between the product molecules released and the inhibition event should favour the latter. Ideally every turnover should result in inhibition [eqn (1.2)] so as to conserve drug so that a lower dose regimen is required and increased specificity is achieved (see later). Obviously, the greater the chemical reactivity of the reactive entity, the less chance exists for escape from the active site (Walsh 1984).

1.4.2.2 *Specificity and toxicity*

Inhibitors used in therapy must show specificity towards the target enzyme, since inhibition of closely related enzymes with different biological roles [e.g. trypsin-like enzymes: thrombin, plasmin, kallikrein (Kettner and Shaw 1979)] or reaction with constituents essential for the well-being of the body (e.g. DNA, glutathione, liver P-450 metabolizing enzymes) could lead to serious side-effects.

The problem of specificity of inhibitor action is exacerbated when the target enzyme is common to the host's normal cells as well as to cancerous or parasitic cells. On rare occasions, nature has helped to solve this problem either by providing host parasitic cells with different isoenzymes [e.g. DHFR, that of the parasite being more susceptible to carefully designed inhibitors (Burchall and Hitchings 1965)] or by the existence of a biochemical lesion. The sulphonamide

Table 1.3 Some reversible inhibitors used clinically (after Smith and Williams 1983)

Drug	Enzyme inhibited	Clinical use
Allopurinol	Xanthine oxidase	Gout
Acetazolamide, Methazolamide, Dichlorphenamide, Ethoxzolamide	Carbonic anhydrase II	Glaucoma, anticonvulsant
Sulthiame	Carbonic anhydrase	Anticonvulsant (epilepsy)
Indomethacin, ibuprofen, naproxen	Prostaglandin synthetase	Anti-inflammatory
Cardiac glycosides	Na^+, K^+-ATPase	Cardiac disorders
6-mercaptopurine Azathioprine	Riboxyl amidotransferase	Anti-cancer therapy
Captopril Enalapril Cilazapril	Angiotensin-converting enzyme	Antihypertensive agent
Sodium valproate	Succinic semi-aldehyde dehydrogenase	Epilepsy
Idoxuridine	Thymidine kinase and thymidylate kinase	Anti-viral agent
Cytosine arabinoside (Ara-C) 5-fluoro-2,5-anhydrocytosine arabinoside	DNA, RNA polymerases	Anti-viral and anti-cancer agent
N-(phosphonoacetyl)-L-aspartate (PALA)	Aspartate transcarbamylase	Anti-cancer agent
Trimethoprim Methotrexate Pyrimethamine	Dihydrofolate reductase	Anti-bacterial, anti-cancer, and anti-protozoal agent
Pyridostigmine	Acetylcholinesterase	Glaucoma, myasthenia gravis

Biphenquinate	L-dihydroorotate dehydrogenase	Anti-cancer agent
Aminoglutethimide	Aromatase	Oestrogen-mediated breast cancer
Omeprazole	H^+,K^+-ATPase	Anti-ulcer agent
Gabexate mesylate (FOY), camostat mesylate	Trypsin and related enzymes	Pancreatitis and hyperproteolytic states
ε-aminocaproic acid (EACA); p-aminomethylbenzoic acid (pAMBA); tranexamic acid (AMCA)	Plasmin	Antifibrinolytic agent
Toloxatone	MAO A	Antidepressant
Meglutol	Cholesterol synthetic enzyme	Hypolipidemic
Nitrefazole	Aldehyde dehydrogenase	Alcoholism
Miconazole, clotrimazole, ketoconazole, ticonazole	Sterol 14α-demethylase of fungi	Antimycotic
Benserazide	AADC (peripheral)	Co-drug with L-dopa for Parkinson's disease
Sorbinil	Aldose reductase inhibitor	Diabetes mellitus complications

Table 1.4 Some active site-directed irreversible inhibitors and mechanism-based inactivators used clinically (after Smith and Williams 1983)

Drug	Enzyme inhibited	Clinical use
Sulphonamides	Dihydropteroate synthetase	Antibacterial
Iproniazid, phenelzine, isocarboxazid, tranylcypromine.	MAO	Antidepressant
Selegiline [(−)-deprenyl]	MAO B	Co-drug with L-dopa for Parkinson's disease
Neostigmine, eserine, dyflos, benzpyrinium, ecothiopate	Acetylcholinesterase	Glaucoma, myasthenia gravis
Penicillins, cephalosporins cephamycins, carbapenems, monobactams	Transpeptidase	Antibiotics
Organo-arsenicals	Pyruvate dehydrogenase	Antiprotozoal agents
O-carbamyl-D-serine	Alanine racemase	Antibiotic
D-cycloserine	Alanine racemase	Antibiotic
Azaserine	Formylglycinamide ribonucleotide aminotransferase	Anti-cancer
γ-vinyl GABA (vigabatrin)	GABA transaminase	Epilepsy
Clavulanic acid, sulbactam	β-lactamase	Adjuvant to penicillin antibiotic
Carbidopa	AADC (peripheral)	Co-drug with L-dopa for Parkinson's disease
4-hydroxyandrostenedione	Aromatase	Oestrogen-mediated breast cancer
Chloramphenicol	Peptidyl transferase	Antibiotic
α-difluoromethylornithine, E-2-(fluoromethyl) dehydroornithine	L-ornithine decarboxylase	Trypanosomal and other parasitic diseases
Aspirin	Prostaglandin synthetase	Anti-inflammatory
5-fluorouracil	Thymidilate synthetase	Anti-inflammatory
Disulfiram	Aldehyde dehydrogenase	Alcoholism
Acetohydroxamic acid	Bacterial urease	Chronic urea-splitting urinary infections

target enzyme, dihydropteroate synthetase, is absent in the host cell, since the cell utilizes preformed folic acid, which the susceptible bacterial cell cannot use and must synthesize using this enzyme. In cancer, the normal and cancerous cells contain the same form of the target enzyme, DHFR, but the faster rate of growth of the tumour cells makes them more susceptible to the effects of an inhibitor (Grindey *et al.* 1975). Side-effects of such inhibitors on normal tissue are quite apparent and are only acceptable because of the seriousness of the disease.

Active-site-directed irreversible inhibitors are reactive agents and, apart from the target enzyme, would also be expected to react with other tissue constituents containing amino or thiol groups, with potentially serious side-effects. The concentration of such constituents may be many orders of magnitude higher than that of the inhibitor. Thus, a reaction of this kind at a turnover rate much lower than that for inhibition of the enzyme could, because of a mass action effect, deplete plasma inhibitor levels before the inhibition reaction is complete (Smith 1978).

Mechanism-based inactivators do not possess a biologically reactive functional group until after they have been modified by the target enzyme and, consequently, would be expected to demonstrate high specificity of action and low incidence of adverse reactions; it is this feature which has encouraged their active application in inhibitor design studies. However, for this situation to be realized in practice, the reactive entity developed at the surface of the target enzyme must react at a faster rate than the rate at which it dissociates from the enzyme surface as a reactive rather than an inert product (Rando 1984). Otherwise, the reactive species will diffuse away and react elsewhere, with potentially serious side-effects.

1.4 Summary

The design and development of new drugs for existing diseases is increasingly concerned with enzyme inhibitors, as will become apparent by the coverage given in subsequent chapters of this book as well as in current journals dealing with aspects of biochemistry, pharmacology, enzyme inhibition, and medicinal chemistry. Very considerable progress has been made in this area over the last few years, especially with the advent of the mechanism-based inactivators and the re-emergence of interest in competitive reversible inhibitors, heralded by the use of peptide inhibitors for peptide-metabolizing enzymes (Cushman *et al.* 1980; Schwartz *et al.* 1985). Further expansion is to be expected.

In this chapter, we have summarized the concepts and general guidelines laid down for the successful application of this approach, based on theory and rationalization of experience. It is to be hoped that continued application of these concepts to new systems, followed by critical evaluation of their validity, will lead to their consolidation, expansion, or re-interpretation, with subsequent benefit to future developments in the field.

References

Abeles, R. H., Fish, S., and Lapinskas, B. (1982). S-adenosyl homocysteinase: mechanism of inactivation by 2'-deoxyadenosine and interaction with other nucleosides. *Biochemistry*, **21**, 5557–62.

Aldridge, W. N. and Reiner, E. (1972). *Enzyme inhibitors as substrates. Interactions of esterases with esters of organophosphorus and carbamic acids*, pp. 1–328. North-Holland, Amsterdam.

Bartholini, G. and Pletscher, A. (1975). Decarboxylase inhibitors. *Pharmacol. Ther.*, **B1**, 407–21.

Burchall, J. J. and Hitchings, G. H. (1965). Inhibitor binding analysis of dihydrofolate reductases from various species. *Mol. Pharmacol.*, **1**, 126–36.

Burkard, W. P., Gey, K. F., and Pletscher, A. (1962). A new inhibitor of decarboxylase of aromatic amino acids. *Experientia*, **18**, 411–12.

Calderwood, S. B., Gardella, A., Philippon, A. M., Jacoby, G. A., and Moellering, R. C. (1982). Effects of azlocillin in combination with clavulanic acid, sulbactam and N-formimidoyl thienamycin against β-lactamase producing, carbenicillin-resistant *Pseudomonas aeruginosa*. *Antimicrob. Agents Chemother.*, **22**, 266–71.

Camiener, G. W. (1968). Studies of the enzymatic deamination of aracytidine. V. Inhibition *in vitro* and *in vivo* by tetrahydrouridine and other reduced pyrimidine nucleosides. *Biochem. Pharmacol.*, **17**, 1981–91.

Cash, R., Brough, A. J., Cohen, M. N. P., and Satoh, P. S. (1967). Aminoglutethimide (Elipten-Ciba) as an inhibitor of adrenal steroidogenesis: mechanism of action and therapeutic trial. *J. Clin. Endocrinol. Metab.*, **27**, 1239–48.

Chiang, P. K. (1984). S-adenosylhomocysteine hydrolase as a pharmacological target for the inhibition of transmethylation. In *Advances in experimental medicine and biology. Purine metabolism in man IV Part B. Biochemical, immunological and cancer research* (ed. C. H. M. M. De Bruyn, H. A. Simmonds, and M. M. Muller), pp. 199–203, Plenum, New York.

Cleland, W. W. (1970). Steady state kinetics. In *The enzymes* (3rd edn) (ed. P. D. Boyer), Vol. 2, pp. 1–66. Academic Press, New York.

Cooper, G. M. and Greer, S. (1970). Irreversible inhibition of dehalogenation of 5-iodouracil by 5-diazouracil and reversible inhibition by 5-cyanouracil. *Cancer Res.*, **30**, 2937–41.

Cooper, G. M., Dunning, W. F., and Green, S. (1972). Role of catabolism in pyrimidine utilisation for nucleic acid synthesis *in vivo*. *Cancer Res.*, **32**, 390–7.

Cushman, D. W., Ondetti, M. A., Cheung, H. S., Sabo, E. F., Antonaccio, M. J., and Rubin, B. (1980). Angiotensin-converting enzyme inhibitors. In *Enzyme inhibitors as drugs* (ed. M. Sandler), pp. 231–47. Macmillan, London.

Dexter, R. N., Fishman, L. M., Ney, R. L., and Liddle, G. W. (1967). Inhibition of adrenal corticosteroid synthesis by aminoglutethimide: studies of the mechanism of action. *J. Clin. Endocrinol. Metab.*, **27**, 473–80.

Elion, G. B., Callahan, S., Rundles, R. W., and Hitchings, G. H. (1963a). Relation between metabolic fates and antitumour activities of thiopurines. *Cancer Res.*, **23**, 1207–1217.

Elion, G. B., Callahan, S., Nathan, H., Bieber, S., Rundles, R. W., and Hitchings, G. H. (1963b). Potentiation by inhibition of drug degradation: 6-substituted purines and xanthine oxidase. *Biochem. Pharmacol.*, **12**, 85–93.

English, A. R., Retsema, J. A., Girard, A. E., Lynch, J. E., and Barth, W. E. (1978). CP-45, 899, a β-lactamase inhibitor that extends the antibacterial spectrum of β-lactams. Initial bacteriological characterisation. *Antimicrob. Agents Chemother.*, **14**, 414–19.

Garrod, L. P., James, D. G., and Lewis, A. A. G. (eds.), (1969). The synergy of trimethoprim and sulphonamides. *Postgrad. Med. J. Suppl.*, **45**(11), 7–104.

Grindey, G. B., Moran, R. G., and Werkheiser, W. C. (1975). Approaches to the rational combination of antimetabolites for cancer chemotherapy. In *Drug design* (ed. E. J. Ariens) Vol. V, pp. 169–249. Academic Press, New York.

Howarth, T. T., Brown, A. G., and King T. J. (1976). Clavulanic acid, a novel β-lactam isolated from *Streptomyces clavuligerus*. X-ray crystal-structure analysis. *J. Chem. Commun.*, 266–67.

Hitchings, G. H., Elion, G. B., Falco, E. A., Russell, P. B., Sherwood, M. B., and Vanderwerff, H. (1950). Antagonists of nucleic acid derivatives, I. The *Lactobacillus casei* model: *J. Biol. Chem.*, **183**, 1–9.

Johnston, J. O., Wright, C. L., and Metcalf, B. W. (1984). Biochemical and endocrine properties of a mechanism-based inhibitor of aromatase. *Endocrinology (Baltimore)*, **115**, 776–85.

Jung, M. J., Palfreyman, M. G., Wagner, J., Bey, P., Ribereau-Gayon, G., Zraika, M., and Koch-Weser, J. (1979). Inhibition of monoamine synthesis by irreversible blockade of aromatic amino acid decarboxylase with α-monofluoromethyldopa. *Life Sci.*, **24**, 1037–42.

Jung, M. J., Koch-Weser, J., and Sjoerdsma, A. (1980). Biochemistry and pharmacology of enzyme-activated irreversible inhibitors of some pyridoxal phosphate-dependent enzymes. In *Enzyme inhibitors as drugs* (ed. M. Sandler), pp. 95–114. Macmillan, London.

Kettner, C. and Shaw, E. (1979). D-Phe–Pro–ArgCH$_2$Cl–a selective affinity label for thrombin. *Thromb. Res.*, **14**, 969–973.

Krohn, A. (1984). The use of molecular graphics in the design of enzyme inhibitors. In *Second SCI–RSC medicinal chemistry symposium* (ed. J. C. Emmett), pp. 109–23. The Royal Society of Chemistry, London.

Lienhard, G. E. (1972). Transition state analogs as enzyme inhibitors. *Ann. Rep. Med. Chem.*, **7**, 249–58.

Lindquist, R. N. (1975). The design of enzyme inhibitors. Transition state analogs. In *Drug design* (ed. E. J. Ariens), Vol. V, pp. 23–80. Academic Press, New York.

Massey, V., Komai, H., Palmer, G., and Elion, G. B. (1970). On the mechanism of inactivation of xanthine oxidase by allopurinol and other pyrazolo [3,4-*d*] pyrimidines. *J. Biol. Chem.*, **245**, 2837–44.

Neil, G. L., Moxley, T. E., and Manak, R. C. (1970). Enhancement by tetrahydrouridine of 1-β-D-arabsinofuranosylcytosine (cytarabine) oral activity in L1210 leukemic mice. *Cancer Res.*, **30**, 2166–72.

Morrison, J. F. (1982). The slow-binding and slow, tight-binding inhibition of enzyme-catalysed reactions. *Trends Biochem. Sci.*, **7**, 102–5.

Rando, R. R. (1977). Mechanism of the irreversible inhibition of γ-aminobutyric acid–α-ketoglutaric acid transaminase by the neurotoxin gabaculine. *Biochemistry*, **16**, 4604–10.

Rando, R. R. (1984). Mechanism-based enzyme inactivators. *Pharmacol. Rev.*, **36**, 111–42.

Reading, C. and Cole, M. (1977). Clavulanic acid: a beta-lactamase-inhibiting beta-lactam from *Streptomyces clavuligerus*. *Antimicrob. Agents Chemother.*, **11**, 852–7.

Salhanick, H. A. (1982). Basic studies on aminoglutethimide. *Cancer Res.*, **42S**, 3315–21.

Sandler, M. and Stern, G. M. (1982). Deprenyl in Parkinson's disease. In *Neurology 2. Movement disorders* (ed. C. D. Marsden and S. Fahn), pp. 166–73. Butterworth Scientific, London.

Santen, R. J., Santner, S., Davis, B., Veldhuis, J., Samojlik, E., and Ruby, E. (1978).

Aminoglutethimide inhibits extraglandular estrogen production in postmenopausal women with breast carcinoma. *J. Clin. Endocrinol. Metab.*, **47**, 1257–65.

Santi, D. V., Wataya, Y., and Matsuda, A. (1978). Approaches to the design of mechanism-based inhibitors of pyrimidine metabolism. In *Enzyme-activated irreversible inhibitors* (ed. N. Seiler, M. J. Jung, and J. Koch-Weser), pp. 291–303, Elsevier-North Holland, Amsterdam.

Schwartz, W. B. (1949). The effect of sulfanilamide on salt and water excretion in congestive heart failure. *New Engl. J. Med.*, **240**, 173–77.

Schwartz, J.-C., Costentin, J., and Lecomte, J. M. (1985). Pharmacology of enkephalinase inhibitors. *Trends Pharmacol. Sci.*, **6**, 472–6.

Sletzinger, M., Chemerda, J. M., and Bollinger, F. W. (1963). Potent decarboxylase inhibitors. Analogs of methyldopa. *J. Med. Chem.*, **6**, 101–3.

Smith, H. J. (1978). Perspectives in the design of small molecule enzyme inhibitors as useful drugs. *J. Theor. Biol.*, **73**, 531–8.

Smith, H. J. and Williams, H. (1983). Design of enzyme inhibitors (anti-metabolites) as drugs. In *Introduction to the principles of drug design* (ed. J. Smith and H. Williams), pp. 84–131. Wright, P. S. G., Bristol.

Von Euler, U. S. (1972). Synthesis, uptake and storage of catecholamines in adrenergic nerves; the effect of drugs. *Catecholamines* (eds. H. Blaschko and E. Muscholl), pp. 186–230. Springer, Heidelberg.

Walsh, C. T. (1984). Suicide substrates, mechanism-based inactivators: recent developments. *Ann. Rev. Biochem.*, **53**, 493–535.

Webb, J. L. (1963). Inhibition in multienzyme systems. In *Enzyme and metabolic inhibitors*, Vol. I, pp. 319–2. Academic Press, New York.

Zeller, E. A., Barsky, J., Fouts, J. R., Kirchheimer, W. F., and Van Orden, L. S. (1952). Influence of isonicotinic acid hydrazide and 1-isonicotinoyl-2-isopropylhydrazine on bacterial and mammalian enzymes. *Experientia*, **8**, 349–50.

2

General approaches to the design of inhibitors

Section 2A

Substrate and transition-state analogue inhibitors

Lloyd Frick and Richard Wolfenden

2A.1   Introduction

When an enzyme converts a substrate to a product, a preliminary enzyme–substrate complex is formed that decomposes to products relatively slowly. This model is based on observations that rates of enzyme reactions approach a limiting value with increasing substrate concentration, and that unreactive analogues of substrates often serve as competitive inhibitors, with enzyme affinities comparable with the apparent affinities of substrates. Malonic acid, an inhibitor of succinate dehydrogenase, appears to have been the compound that inspired the concept of competitive inhibition (Quastel and Wooldridge 1928), and was later useful in uncovering the existence of the tricarboxylic acid cycle. For a discussion of the history of this concept, and some of the vast array of

19

substrate analogue inhibitors that arose from the earlier work, the reader is referred to the comprehensive monograph by Webb (1966).

In addition to their well-recognized affinities for substrates, enzymes have a special property that is indispensable for catalysis: an exceptionally high affinity for altered substrates in the transition state for substrate transformation. Pauling (1946) appears to have been the first to realize that this might serve as a basis for inhibitor design. Jencks (1966) was able to identify several such inhibitors from the literature, and coined the term 'transition-state analogue'. Wolfenden (1969a) developed a simple thermodynamic argument to support the inevitability of this relationship [scheme (2A.1)], and put it to an experimental test in designing a powerful inhibitor of triosephosphate isomerase, 2-phospho-glycollate. Using this equation, it can be shown that an enzyme increases the rate of a chemical reaction to the same extent that it binds the altered substrate in the transition state more tightly than it binds the substrate. A similar derivation was performed for enzymes acting on two or more substrates, as shown in scheme (2A.2). Inspection of the equations shown in schemes (2A.1) and (2A.2) suggests a straightforward way of determining the enzyme's affinity for the altered substrate in the transition state: the ratio of the spontaneous rate of reaction to the k_{cat}/K_m is equal to the K_{TX}. Data on k_{cat}/K_m are abundant, but rates of the corresponding uncatalysed reactions have seldom been determined.

Scheme 2A.1

$$S \xrightarrow{k_{non}} P \qquad\qquad S \underset{}{\overset{K_S^{\ddagger}}{\rightleftharpoons}} S^{\ddagger} \longrightarrow P$$

$$ES \xrightarrow{k_{cat}} E+P \qquad ES \underset{}{\overset{K_{ES}^{\ddagger}}{\rightleftharpoons}} ES^{\ddagger} \longrightarrow E+P$$

$$\boxed{\dfrac{K_{ES}^{\ddagger}}{K_S^{\ddagger}} = \dfrac{k_{cat}}{k_{non}}} \qquad \text{where } k_{cat} = \text{turnover number of enzyme,}$$
$$k_{non} = \text{rate constant of non-enzymatic reaction}$$

$$
\begin{array}{ccc}
E+S & \overset{K_S^{\ddagger}}{\rightleftharpoons} & E+S^{\ddagger} \longrightarrow P \\
\updownarrow K_S & & \updownarrow K_{TX} \\
ES & \underset{K_{ES}^{\ddagger}}{\rightleftharpoons} & ES^{\ddagger} \longrightarrow P
\end{array}
\qquad
K_{TX} = \dfrac{K_S \cdot K_S^{\ddagger}}{K_{ES}^{\ddagger}}
$$

$$\dfrac{K_{TX}}{K_S} = \dfrac{k_{non}}{k_{cat}}$$

Scheme 2A.2

$$R + S \xrightarrow{k_{non}} P \qquad\qquad R + S \overset{K^{\ddagger}_{R,S}}{\rightleftharpoons} RS^{\ddagger} \longrightarrow P$$

$$ERS \xrightarrow{k_{cat}} E + P \qquad ERS \overset{K^{\ddagger}_{ERS}}{\rightleftharpoons} ERS^{\ddagger} \longrightarrow E + P$$

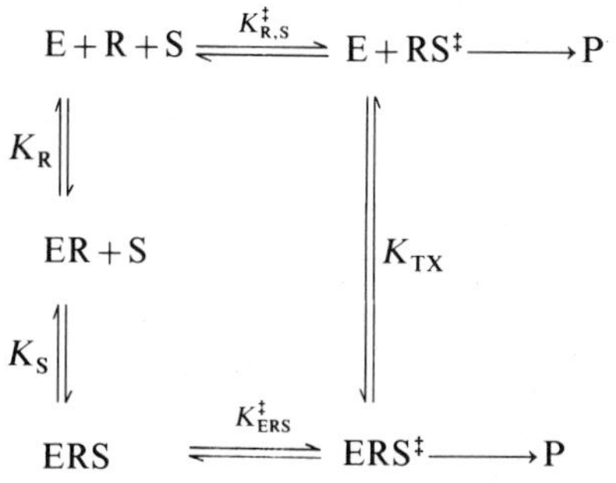

$$E + R + S \overset{K^{\ddagger}_{R,S}}{\rightleftharpoons} E + RS^{\ddagger} \longrightarrow P$$

$$K_R \Big\updownarrow \qquad\qquad \Big\updownarrow$$

$$ER + S \qquad\qquad K_{TX}$$

$$K_S \Big\updownarrow \qquad\qquad \Big\updownarrow$$

$$ERS \overset{K^{\ddagger}_{ERS}}{\rightleftharpoons} ERS^{\ddagger} \longrightarrow P$$

$$K_{TX} = \frac{K_R \cdot K_S \cdot K^{\ddagger}_{R,S}}{K^{\ddagger}_{ERS}} = \frac{k_{non} \cdot K_R \cdot K_S}{k_{cat}}$$

Several that have been determined are presented in Table 2A.1, along with the rate enhancements and deduced affinity of enzymes for the corresponding transition states. These affinities are seen to be very high indeed, surpassing 10^{-18} M for alkaline phosphatase.

Direct comparison of rates, as in Table 2A.1, is actually likely to lead to underestimation of an enzyme's affinity for the transition state. The non-enzymatic reaction inevitably proceeds by the pathway with the lowest available energy of activation, and this may be more rapid than any pathway that would resemble the reaction on the enzyme more closely; the enzyme's ability to stabilize the transition state for the reaction *as it occurs on the enzyme* will have been underestimated accordingly. Alternatively, the enzyme reaction may be limited by a physical process (such as a change in conformation or the release of products). In such a case, it is necessary to suppose that all chemical steps are faster than this physical process, and that the enzyme stabilizes the chemical transition state more than the enzymatic rate would suggest. Again, the enzyme's binding affinity for the chemical transition state will have been underestimated (Wolfenden 1972). In enzyme reactions that proceed by double displacement, the enzyme itself is part of the transition state, so that comparisons of enzymatic and non-enzymatic rates become problematic. Lienhard (1973) has suggested a way out of this dilemma, wherein a substance having the

Table 2A.1 Minimal affinities of enzymes for transition states

Enzyme	$k_{non}(s^{-1})$	k_{cat}/K_m^a $(M^{-1}s^{-1})$	$K_{TX}(M)$
Alkaline phosphatase	1.0×10^{-15b}	5.7×10^3	2×10^{-19}
Acetylcholine esterase	1.1×10^{-8c}	1.6×10^8	7×10^{-17}
Adenosine deaminase	1.8×10^{-10}	1.4×10^7	8×10^{-17}
Deoxycytidylate deaminase	9.2×10^{-11}	1.5×10^6	6×10^{-17}
Cytidine deaminase	3.2×10^{-10}	7.5×10^5	4×10^{-16}
Urease	3.0×10^{-10}	2.3×10^5	1×10^{-15}
Triosephosphate isomerase	4.3×10^{-6}	9.1×10^6	5×10^{-13}
Chorismate mutase	2.6×10^{-5}	1.1×10^6	2×10^{-11}
Carbonic anhydrase	3.7×10^{-2}	1.2×10^8	3×10^{-11}

[a] When calculating k_{cat}, it was assumed that all subunits were equally active.
[b] Estimated by extrapolation to neutral pH.
[c] From the rate of ethyl acetate hydrolysis.

same functional group as the enzyme (e.g. an alcohol in place of a serine protease) takes part in the non-enzymatic reaction. By comparing the rate constant for this reaction with the rate constant for the enzyme reaction, one may calculate an equilibrium constant for transfer of the altered substrate in the · transition state from the alcohol to the enzyme.

2A.2   Sources of transition-state affinity

The special affinity of enzymes for altered substrates in the transition state provides an attractive rationale for inhibitor and drug design, and the early successes of this approach (see Appendix) have led to a keener appreciation of its subtleties and limitations. Transition states are characterized by incompletely formed bonds and awkward geometries and no real compound is likely to resemble in detail this least stable of structures on the pathway from substrates to products. Transition-state analogues are therefore more likely to resemble high-energy intermediates along the reaction pathway than the transition state itself, and it is therefore not possible to tell whether an inhibitor is binding as a poor analogue of a very tightly bound transition state, or as a somewhat better analogue of a somewhat less tightly bound high-energy intermediate. Nonetheless, the affinity of an enzyme for the altered substrate in the transition state is so great that capturing even a small fraction of it would result in an exceedingly potent inhibitor.

Similar difficulties arise in attempting to distinguish between the important group of inhibitors known as multi-substrate analogues and transition-state analogues. The very great reduction in entropy gained by combining multiple binding determinants in a single molecule can result in tight binding regardless of the chemical nature of the transition state (Jencks 1975). Since the transition state will necessarily have binding determinants in common with each of several substrates, any transition-state analogue inhibitor of a multi-substrate enzyme is also a potential multi-substrate analogue. When examination of the structure of the inhibitor indicates that ambiguity of this kind exists, it may be of special interest to vary the conditions of the assay or the structure of the inhibitor in such a way that k_{cat} and K_m are independently altered. Transition-state analogues should exhibit variation in K_i that reflects changes in *either* k_{cat} or K_m, whereas substrate and multi-substrate analogues should reflect variations in K_m only.

It is evident that although the theoretical basis for transition-state affinity is relatively simple, there are difficulties in estimating its magnitude in a quantitative sense, so that the theory of transition state analogy is more useful as a qualitative principle in guiding the design of potent inhibitors than as a method of estimating the exact affinity expected of any real inhibitor that may be prepared. When a promising inhibitor has been obtained, its structure can be varied to enhance inhibitory or pharmacological properties. An evolutionary process of this kind took place in the development of inhibitors of angiotensin-converting enzyme (see Chapter 3). Early work had shown that benzylsuccinic acid was an effective inhibitor of carboxypeptidase A (another zinc-containing enzyme), probably because it resembled the products of substrate hydrolysis immediately after peptide bond cleavage (Byers and Wolfenden 1972). Reasoning that the enzyme–inhibitor complex was stabilized by interactions between one of the carboxylic acid groups and the active-site zinc, Cushman *et al.* (1977) developed inhibitors with a thiol group at the analogous position (capable of forming even tighter complexes with zinc) and equipped with other binding determinants to satisfy the specificity requirements of the converting enzyme. The resulting compound, captopril, has proven effective in the clinical control of hypertension. Enalapril, a dicarboxylic acid whose design more closely resembles that of benzylsuccinate, also shows great promise as an antihypertensive agent (Patchett *et al.* 1980).

2A.3   Uses of transition-state analogues in enzymology

Transition-state analogues are stable, so that their complexes with enzymes can be examined directly by chemical and physical methods. It is not always clear at the outset which of several reaction mechanisms is employed by a particular enzyme and information about the structure of enzyme–inhibitor complexes can be helpful in deciding between alternative mechanisms. Any potent inhibitor, although it may be stable in free solution, interacts very strongly with active site of an enzyme. Because binding of the inhibitor may involve its removal from solvent water, juxtaposition to acids or bases, or to groups on the enzyme with enhanced reactivity, inhibition may occur by an unexpected route. The inhibition of β-galactosidase by D-galactal, for example (Fig. 2A.1), was first suspected to be due to its resemblance to a half-chair oxonium ion intermediate

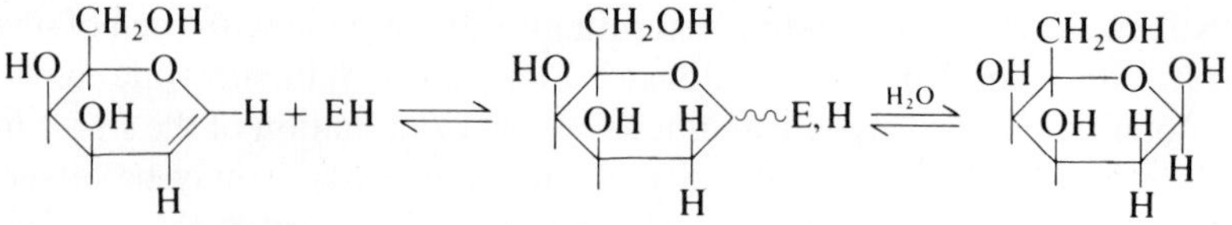

Fig. 2A.1 Interaction of galactal with galactosidase.

in the hydrolysis galactosides (Lee 1969). Galactal was later found instead to be a poor, but very tightly bound, substrate of the enzyme, being slowly converted to 2-deoxygalactose via hydrolysis of a presumed covalent adduct formed by Michael addition of an active site nucleophile as shown in Fig. 2A.1 (Wentworth and Wolfenden 1974). These results pointed to a double-displacement mechanism for the enzyme, rather than the carbonium ion mechanism that had been suspected originally.

As this illustration suggests, some inhibitors can serve as analogues of intermediates formed by several alternative mechanisms. Many hydrolases for carboxylic acid derivatives, for example, are reversibly inhibited by substrate derivatives with activated carbonyl groups, such as aldehydes (Westerik and Wolfenden 1971, 1974; Thompson 1973; Andersson *et al.* 1982; Frick and Wolfenden 1985) and halomethyl ketones (Kettner *et al.* 1974; Hammock *et al.* 1982; Gelb *et al.* 1985). Several of these compounds were initially designed to inhibit enzymes that proceeded by double-displacement mechanisms. Aldehyde groups, for example, were expected to react with sulphur or oxygen nucleophiles at the active site to form a covalent adduct resembling tetrahedral intermediates formed during nucleophilic attack on the peptide bond. However, these carbonyl compounds were sufficiently activated by the proximity of electron-withdrawing amido or amino functions to exist in solution largely as their covalent hydrates or *gem*-diols. The hydrates resemble tetrahedral intermediates that could arise during direct attack of water on the peptide bond. Because alternative mechanisms of inhibition exist, these inhibitors are unusually versatile, but their inhibitory activity does not by itself provide an indication of mechanism. If the structure of the enzyme–inhibitor complex can be determined, the result is likely to be helpful in establishing the mechanism of catalysis. Thus, a proteinase might bind an aldehyde as a hydrate analogous in structure to an intermediate in direct attack by water on the peptide substrate; as an enzyme hemiacetal or thiohemiacetal analogous in structure to tetrahedral intermediates in formation and breakdown of an acyl enzyme intermediate; or as the free aldehyde if the active site is sterically restricted or hydrophobic. The form in which an aldehyde is bound by a specific enzyme can be determined from secondary deuterium isotope effects on aldehyde binding (Lewis and Wolfenden 1977; Andersson *et al.* 1985), n.m.r. spectroscopy (Lowe and Nurse 1977; Clark *et al.* 1977, Chen *et al.* 1979; Gamcsik *et al.* 1983; Malthouse *et al.* 1985), X-ray diffraction from single enzyme crystals (Brayer *et al.* 1979; Christianson and

Lipscomb 1985), and solvent deuterium isotope effects on aldehyde binding (Bone and Wolfenden 1985).

A good deal of attention has been devoted to the observation that inhibition by transition-state analogues is often remarkably slow (see Wolfenden 1976). However, it now appears likely that instances where the onset of inhibition is much slower than the diffusion-controlled limit are due to the particular circumstances of the enzyme–inhibitor interaction and do not reflect a general phenomenon associated with some aspect of transition-state analogue inhibitors. Indeed several inhibitors, such as phosphonoacetohydroxamate, an inhibitor of enolase, and 3-nitro-2-hydroxypropionate, an inhibitor of fumarase, are bound at or near the diffusion-controlled limit, although their status as transition-state analogues seems secure (Anderson et al. 1984).

Transition-state analogue inhibitors have now been designed for enzymes acting on all classes of biological compounds, so that investigators can often adapt an earlier idea to their purpose. In what follows, some representative transition-state analogues have been grouped into several classes, emphasizing their charge, hydrophobicity, multi-substrate character, reactivity with nucleophiles, or ability to bind to metals. Only a small fraction of those that have been reported are mentioned here. For an extended list of transition state and multi-substrate analogue inhibitors, using the IUPAC method of classification, the reader is referred to the Appendix.

2A.4 Multi-substrate analogues

In many enzymes, an important part of the catalytic process seems to be the concentration and orientation of substrates at the active site. Page and Jencks (1971) have estimated that binding of two substrates in their ground states could in principle lead to rate enhancements as large as 10^8. For the same reason, the entropic advantage of combining the binding determinants of two molecules into one molecule could enhance its binding affinity by a factor as large as 10^8, relative to the product of the association constants of the individual molecules. One way of looking at this is to suppose that much of the energy barrier limiting the reaction rate represents the rareness of productive encounter of the several substrates. The two substrates, bound together at the active site, can be considered to represent a kind of high-energy intermediate characterized by low entropy, rather than chemical activation. Once the substrates have been brought into close apposition according to such a mechanism, there would be a reduced energy barrier to their subsequent chemical transformation. Multi-substrate analogues that also incorporate characteristics of the chemical step can capture some of the additional affinity that normally promotes this step. Although the relative contributions of 'entropic' and 'chemical' factors cannot be assessed by merely comparing the binding affinities of multi-substrate analogues, the minimal affinity expected in the ideal case can be predicted from scheme (2A.2) (Wolfenden 1972).

One of the more attractive features of multi-substrate analogues is their conceptual simplicity: the structure of the substrates and their likely orientation to each other can usually be guessed. Even if the binding affinity of a multi-substrate analogue falls far short of theoretical predictions, it is likely to exceed the combined affinities of the substrates individually. An early example was pyridoxylalanine, an inhibitor of pyridoxamine–pyruvate transaminase prepared by reducing the aldimine formed by condensation of alanine with pyridoxal (Dempsey and Snell 1963). The reduced aldimine contains a tetrahedral carbon at the point of junction, and may resemble the collected substrates during the approach of the amine of alanine towards the carbonyl group of pyridoxal (see Fig. 2A.2). Carbinolamine formation does not appear to be rate-limiting in transamination reactions, so that it may not be necessary for intermediates with a tetrahedral configuration to be stabilized by the enzyme (Raso and Stollar 1975). Phosphonoacetyl-L-aspartate (Fig. 2A.2), another multi-substrate analogue, is an inhibitor of aspartate transcarbamoylase (Collins and Stark 1971). This compound, made by condensing the azide of phosphonoacetic acid with diethyl aspartate, exhibits an affinity for the enzyme resembling those of the two substrates combined. It makes no allowance for the sp_3 hybridization that develops at the carbamoyl carbon during nucleophilic attack by aspartate, and is thus more reasonably considered a multi-substrate analogue than a transition-state analogue. Several adducts of NADH have been considered to resemble the configuration of the two substrates immediately before hydride transfer, and serve as specific inhibitors of the appropriate

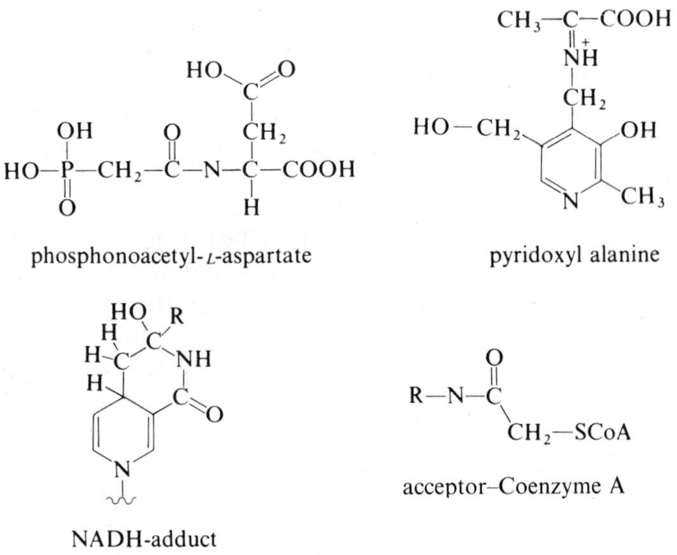

phosphonoacetyl-L-aspartate

pyridoxyl alanine

NADH-adduct

acceptor–Coenzyme A

Fig. 2A.2 Structures of some multi-substrate analogues.

dehydrogenases (Fig. 2A.2, Everse *et al.* 1971). Acetyltransferases can be strongly inhibited by joining coenzyme A to the acceptor by a two-carbon linkage (Chase and Tubbs 1969); and a potent inhibitor of histone and spermidine acetylase was recently synthesized by alkylating coenzyme A with bromoacetic acid and condensing the product with spermidine (Fig. 2A.2, Cullis *et al.* 1982).

Another kind of multi-substrate analogue, Ap_5A, is formed by joining ATP to ADP through their terminal phosphoryl groups (Lienhard and Secemski 1973). This compound proves to be highly effective as an inhibitor of adenylate kinase, compared with Ap_4A, although this shorter analogue is closer to the combined length of the two substrates for the enzyme, AMP and ATP. Bone *et al.* (1986) have recently demonstrated that nucleoside and nucleotide kinases are strongly inhibited by analogues that are slightly longer than the combined substrates. It seems probable that the substrates 'sit down' on the enzyme at a small distance from each other, allowing binding interactions to be maximized in the transition state, in which bonds to the migrating phosphoryl group are longer than stable covalent bonds.

These compounds appear to resemble collected substrates rather than chemical intermediates, and none are bound more than two orders of magnitude more tightly than the product of the apparent molar dissociation constants of the substrates they resemble. Their affinity can thus be accounted for in terms of multi-substrate character. This is not the case for an important class of hydrolase inhibitors that incorporate the elements of water as well as the scissile substrate (Fig. 2A.3). These inhibitors, many of them natural products, include pepstatin, an inhibitor of pepsin (Umezawa *et al.* 1970); coformycin and a methanol photoadduct of purine nucleoside, inhibitors of adenosine deaminase (Evans and Wolfenden 1970; Nakamura *et al.* 1974); bestatin, an inhibitor of aminopeptidases (Nishizawa *et al.* 1977); and tetrahydrouridine and a hydroxy-diazepinone, inhibitors of cytidine deaminase (Cohen and Wolfenden 1971; Marquez *et al.* 1980). These compounds are bound four to seven orders of magnitude more tightly than substrates, and their structures, containing sp_3-hybridized carbon atoms at positions analogous to the carbon atom at which water attack occurs in substrates, indicate that they should be considered as transition-state analogues rather than substrate analogues. Adenosine deaminase appears to stabilize a transition state that occurs very early during the chemical reaction, before the leaving group has experienced appreciable bond cleavage (Wolfenden 1969b). It is therefore of special interest that the seven-membered diazepinol ring of coformycin is puckered in such a way that the hydroxyl group is positioned on an axis that is nearly normal to the face of the ring (Nakamura *et al.* 1974). Thus, although the hydroxyl group is attached to a tetrahedral carbon atom, it resembles a water molecule approaching the ring perpendicularly.

To compare the affinities of these hydrolase inhibitors with those of the individual substrates, it would be desirable to know the affinity of the enzymes for both substrates, one of which is water. No method is available for determi-

bestatin

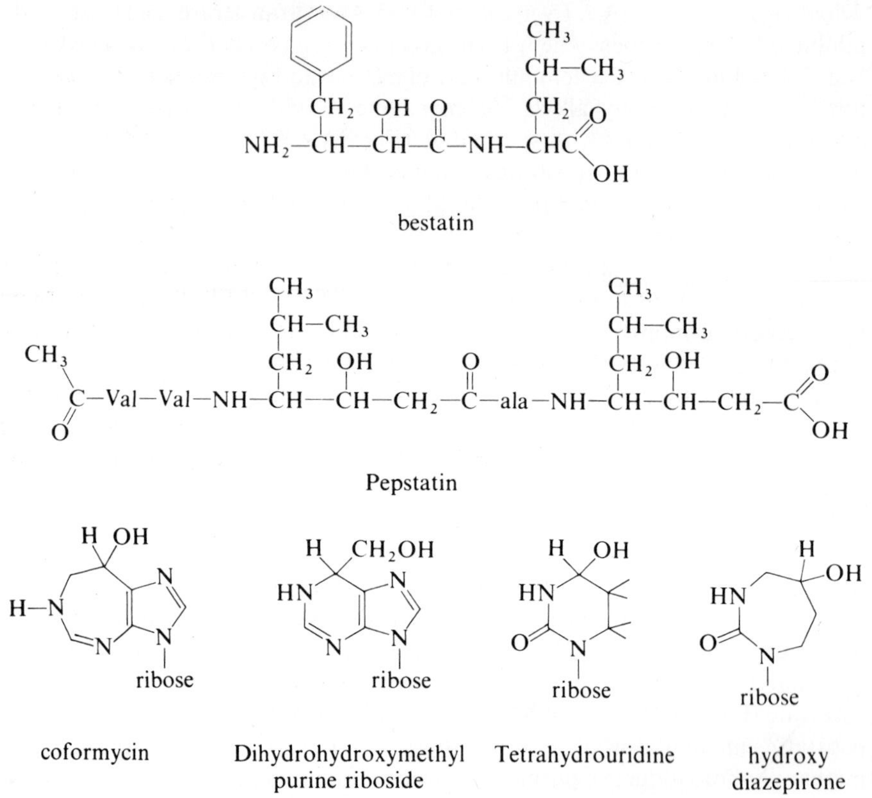

Pepstatin

| coformycin | Dihydrohydroxymethyl purine riboside | Tetrahydrouridine | hydroxy diazepirone |

Fig. 2A.3 Structures of potent hydrolase inhibitors.

ning the K_m of substrate water directly, but Dale *et al.* (1985) have estimated a K_m of approximately 10 M for water as a substrate of almond glucosidase, based on extrapolation from the behaviour of alcohols as alternative substrates. This large K_m value, if typical of hydrolases in general, suggests that relatively little is to be gained by constructing a simple multi-substrate analogue incorporating the elements of water. The exceptional affinities of these inhibitors suggests that they should be considered transition-state analogues.

2A.5   Analogues of ionic intermediates: anions

The activities of some enzymes can be attributed to their ability to abstract a proton from the substrate. Stabilization of the resulting ionic high-energy intermediate plays a key role in the catalytic process. Triosephosphate isomerase, an early target of analogue design, was found to be strongly inhibited by 2-phosphoglycollate, analogous in structure to a suspected enediolate intermediate in the enzyme-catalysed reaction (Wolfenden 1969a; Hartman *et al.* 1975).

The effect of pH on the K_i was consistent with binding of a dianionic species. Carbon and phosphorus nuclear magnetic resonance studies of the enzyme–inhibitor complex showed, however, that the inhibitor was actually bound as the trianionic species, implying that the enzyme underwent an obligatory proton uptake concomitant with inhibitor binding (Campbell *et al.* 1978). The position of the resonance of the carboxylate carbon of the inhibitor suggested hydrogen bonding to the enzyme, probably to the group responsible for proton uptake in the normal reaction.

Nitro-substitution has been used to generate carbanions intended to mimic carbanionic intermediates in several lyase-catalysed reactions: 3-nitropropionate for isocitrate lyase (Schloss and Cleland 1982); nitro analogues of citrate and isocitrate for aconitase (Schloss *et al.* 1980); 3-nitro-2-aminopropionate for aspartase (Porter and Bright 1980); and N^6-(L-2-carboxyethyl-2-nitroethyl)-adenosine for adenylosuccinate lyase. In these inhibitors, the nitronate form of the carbanion appears to resemble the *aci*-carbonate carbanionic intermediate (Fig. 2A.4).

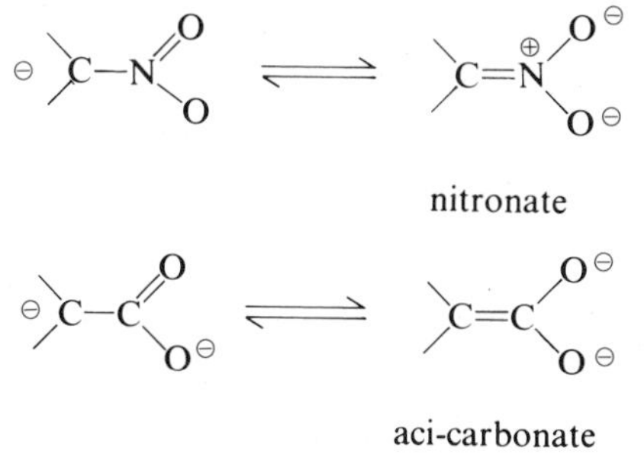

nitronate

aci-carbonate

Fig. 2A.4 Structural similarity between nitronates and *aci*-carbonates.

Barbituric acid ribonucleoside 5′-phosphate was found to be an excellent inhibitor of orotidylate decarboxylase from yeast, presumably because one of the canonical forms resembles a 6-carbanionic intermediate formed during the decarboxylation step of the enzymatic reaction (Levine *et al.* 1980).

2A.6   Analogues of ionic intermediates: cations

Cationic intermediates have been suggested for a number of enzymes involved in alkyl transfer reactions. A number of glycosidases, for example, are strongly inhibited by 1-aminosugars that presumably resemble carbonium ion intermediates (Lai and Axelrod 1973). Secemski and Lienhard (1971), reasoning that lactone derivatives of substrates might resemble such intermediates in charge distribution and ring structure, prepared such a derivative by oxidation of chitotetraose with iodine, and showed that it was substantially more tightly bound than the substrate. Many glucosidases are strongly inhibited by nojirimycin, a natural product in which the ring oxygen is replaced by nitrogen (Fig. 2A.5): it has been suggested that a dehydrated form of the inhibitor may be the active species (Reese *et al.* 1971). However, Dale *et al.* (1985) have shown that nojirimycin may bind to an inactive ionic species of almond glucosidase, and thus may not be a transition-state analogue.

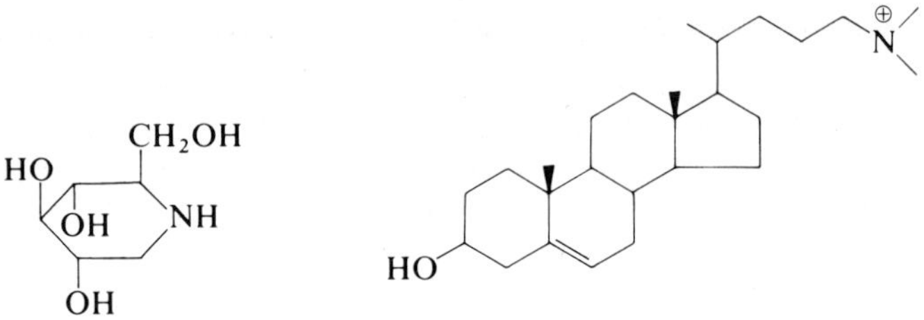

nojirimycin   25-azacholesterol

Fig. 2A.5 Cationic transition state analogues.

Sterol methyl transferases are thought to act by nucleophilic attack by electrons in a double bond of the substrate on the methyl function of S-adenosyl methionine. The methylated intermediate possesses a positive charge on an adjacent, tertiary carbon, and when this carbon is replaced by nitrogen, potent inhibition results (Fig. 2A.5; Oehlschlager *et al.* 1984). Another enzyme involved in sterol biosynthesis, squalene synthetase, is believed to generate a carbonium ion adjacent to a cyclopropane ring by scission of a pyrophosphate group. Rearrangement of this intermediate and hydride transfer lead to squalene. An azasterol prepared by Sandifer *et al.* (1982) serves as a strong inhibitor.

2A.7   Analogues of hydrophobic intermediates

When charged reactants form products via an uncharged transition state, organic solvents tend to enhance the rate of reaction. Lienhard and his associates (Crosby and Lienhard 1970; Gutowski and Lienhard 1976) have shown that pyruvate dehydrogenase enhances the rate of decarboxylation of pyruvate by a factor of 10^5–10^6; whereas conducting the non-enzymatic reaction in ethanol resulted in a 10^4–10^5 enhancement of rate over that observed in water. This increase in the non-enzymatic rate was ascribed to the greater stability of the neutral resonance form of the reactive ylide ('active acetaldehyde') in the organic solvent, and it was suggested that much of the transition state stabilization of pyruvate dehydrogenase was due to the hydrophobic nature of its active site. Keto or thioketo substitution at C-2 of the thiamine ring resulted in compounds with sp^2 hybridization at C-2, causing the ring nitrogen atom to lose its positive charge, thus lowering its affinity for water (Fig. 2A.6). Tested against pyruvate decarboxylase, these substances proved to be highly effective inhibitors. Another uncharged thiamine analogue has been prepared by sodium borohydride reduction of the cofactor (Lowe *et al.* 1983). Although this procedure results in complete reduction of the thiazole ring to yield a tetrahydro derivative, the compound exhibits an affinity for the enzyme comparable with the affinities of the sulphur and oxygen derivatives. The importance of the neutrality of the thiazolidine nitrogen is underscored by the relatively modest inhibition of pyruvate decarboxylase observed with methylacetylphosphonate, a phosphonate analogue of pyruvate. This compound forms an adduct at C-1 of thiamine pyrophosphate, but the reaction does not proceed further. Despite the resemblance of this multi-substrate analogue to the pyruvate–thiamine intermediate, it is not bound as tightly by the enzyme as a comparison of the dissociation constants of pyruvate and thiamine would lead one to expect for a multi-substrate analogue (Kluger and Pike 1977).

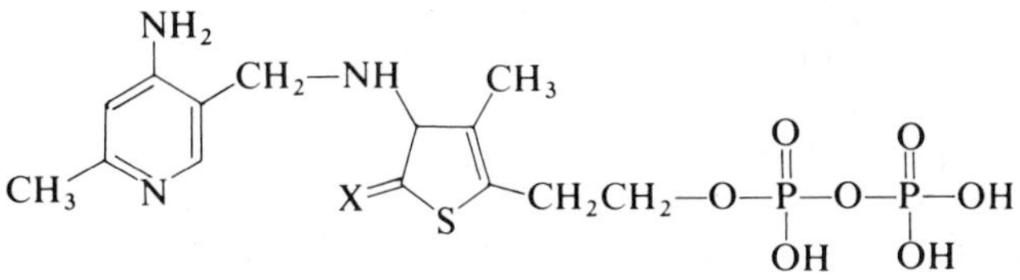

X = O; Thiamin thiazolone
X = S : Thiamin Thiothiazolone

Fig. 2A.6 Hydrophobic analogues of thiamine pyrophosphate.

Several inhibitors of polyamine biosynthesis are considered to owe their effectiveness at least in part to hydrophobicity. These inhibitors, which can also be considered multi-substrate analogues, were synthesised by alkylation of thioamines by 5'-deoxy-5'-chloroadenosine. The strong inhibitory activity of these compounds was much reduced when they were methylated with methyl iodide to form the methyl sulphonium salt. Tang *et al.* (1980) suggested that these findings could be reconciled with a mechanism involving charge dispersal in the transition state, relative to the fully charged ground state.

2A.8 Electrophilic transition-state analogues

Many hydrolytic enzymes act by a double displacement mechanism that entails an enzyme-bound intermediate formed by attack of an enzyme nucleophile on the scissile bond of the substrate. Such enzymes are readily inhibited by substrate-like electrophiles that lack a good leaving group, but can undergo nucleophilic attack to form stable enzyme–inhibitor complexes with an sp_3-hybridized carbon atom. For esterases and peptidases, activated carbonyl compounds such as amidoaldehydes (Westerik and Wolfenden 1971; Thompson 1973) and haloketones (Gelb et al. 1985) are effective inhibitors. Carbonyl groups of peptide aldehydes are often bound by proteases as hemiacetals as discussed earlier, but it remains to be determined whether the hemiacetal hydroxyl group forms an oxyanion in the active site. Trivalent boron derivatives also add oxygen nucleophiles readily, affording a basis for strong inhibition of such enzymes as chymotrypsin (Koehler and Lienhard 1971) and acetylcholinesterase (Koehler and Hess 1974). Sugar derivatives unsaturated at the 1–2 position, termed 'glucals', are electrophilic species that act as Michael acceptors, adding enzyme nucleophiles across the double bond, as was described earlier (p. 23) for β-galactosidase and galactal.

2A.9   Inhibitors that interact with active-site metals

Zinc ions occur frequently at the active sites of enzymes. In hydrolytic enzymes, zinc may activate water molecules and form stable mono- or bidentate complexes with tetrahedral intermediates in substrates hydrolysis. Analogues incorporating functional groups that can form strong coordinate bonds with zinc have been shown to be excellent inhibitors of zinc hydrolases such as carboxypeptidase, angiotensin converting enzyme, thermolysin, and leucine aminopeptidase. In crystalline complexes of N-carboxymethyl dipeptides with thermolysin, carbonyl oxygen atoms of the inhibitor are found to be associated with the active site zinc (Monzingo and Matthews 1984). An interesting inhibitor of enolase was discovered by Anderson et al. (1984), while attempting to synthesize nitrocarbon inhibitors of enolase. This compound, phosphonoacetohydroxamate, does not resemble the aci-carbonate intermediate, but the hydroxyl group of its hydroxamate moiety is isosteric with the hydroxyl group at the C-3 carbon of the substrate. The hydroxyl groups of these compounds are believed to bind Mg^{2+} when they form complexes with the enzyme.

2A.10   Transition-state analogues as drugs

Transition-state analogues are unusually potent reversible inhibitors, and because the transition state is uniquely characteristic of any enzyme reaction, transition state analogues are expected to be highly specific in their action. In contrast, ordinary substrate analogues are expected to affect the two or more enzymes that are usually involved in formation and breakdown of the corresponding substrate. For these reasons, transition-state analogues represent attractive targets for drug design.

We have already alluded to early successes of Squibb and Merck investigators in developing clinically useful inhibitors of human angiotensin converting enzyme. An important dividend of this work has been to show that a variety of forms of hypertension respond to inhibition of this single enzyme (for recent reviews, see Ondetti and Cushman 1984, and Patchett and Cordes 1985).

Inhibitors of enzymes involved in purine and pyrimidine metabolism have attracted interest as potential antineoplastic agents. Adenosine deaminase acts on *ara*-adenosine, other adenine ribonucleosides, and even thio-inosine, to inactivate these chemotherapeutic agents. It appears possible that inhibitors of this enzyme, such as coformycin, may be useful in combined therapy, although coformycin by itself is toxic and leads to immunosuppression (for review, see Agarwal 1982). Phosphonoacetyl-L-aspartate (see Fig. 2A.2), a multi-substrate analogue inhibitor of aspartate transcarbamomylase and the pyrimidine biosynthetic pathway, appears to be considerably less effective *in vivo* than had been anticipated (Kensler *et al.* 1981), possibly due to problems arising from hydrolysis of the inhibitor, substrate accumulation, and the operation of pyrimidine salvage pathways.

2A.11   Appendix

Potential transition state and multi-substrate analogues

Oxidoreductases

alcohol dehydrogenase EC 1.1.1.1	NAD adduct (Everse *et al.* 1971)
lactate dehydrogenase EC 1.1.1.27	NAD adduct, oxalate (Novoa *et al.* 1959), oxalylethyl-NADH (Kapmeyer *et al.* 1976)
malate dehydrogenase EC 1.1.1.37	NAD adduct (Everse *et al.* 1971)
progesterone 5α-reductase EC 1.1.1.145	4-aza-4-methyl-5α-pregnane-3,20-dione (Bertics *et al.* 1984)
lactate oxidase EC 1.1.3.2	oxalate (Nova *et al.* 1959)
glyceraldehyde 3-phosphate dehydrogenase EC 1.2.1.12	threose 2,4-diphosphate (Fluharty and Ballou 1958)
pyruvate dehydrogenase EC 1.2.7.1	thiamine thiazolone and thiamine thio- thiazolone pyrophosphates (Gutowski and Lienhard 1976), tetrahydrothiamine pyro- phosphate (Lowe *et al.* 1983), acetylphosphon- ate (Kluger and Pike 1977)
alanine dehydrogenase EC 1.4.1.1	oxalylethyl-NADH (Kapmeyer *et al.* 1976)
glutamate dehydrogenase EC 1.4.1.2	NAD adduct (Everse *et al.* 1971)

dihydrofolate reductase EC 1.5.1.3	methotrexate (Werkheiser 1961)
glutathione peroxidase EC 1.11.1.9	mercaptosuccinate (Chaudiere *et al.* 1984)
protocatechuate oxygenase EC 1.13.11.3	2-hydroxyisonicotinic acid N-oxide (May *et al.* 1982).
lactate monooxygenase EC 1.13.12.4	oxalate (Ghisla and Massey 1975), malonate (Ghisla and Massey 1977)

Transferases

Δ^{24} sterol methyltransferase EC 2.1.1.41	25-azacholesterol (Oehlschlager *et al.* 1984)
thymidylate synthetase EC 2.1.1.45	1-(β-D-2'-deoxyribofuranosyl) 8-azapurin- 2-one 5'-monophosphate (Kalman and Goldman 1981), multi-substrate analogue (Srinivasan *et al.* 1984)
spermidine synthase EC 2.1.1.53	S-adenosyl-3-thio-1,8-diaminooctane (Tang *et al.*1980)
SAM: sterol C-24- methyltransferase transcarboxylase EC 2.1.3.1	24-methyl-25-azacycloartanol (Narula *et al.* 1981) oxalate (Northrop and Wood 1969)
aspartate transcarbamylase EC 2.1.3.2	phosphonoacetylaspartate (Collins and Stark 1971)
ornithine transcarbamylase EC 2.1.3.3	phosphonoacetylornithine (Mori *et al.* 1977; Hoogenraad 1978)
carnitine acetyltransferase EC 2.3.1.7	O-(2-(S-coenzyme A)acetyl)carnitine (Chase and Tubbs 1969)
spermidine (histone) acetyltransferase EC 2.3.1.48	N-(2-(S-coenzyme A)acetyl)spermidine amide (Cullis *et al.* 1982)
gentamycin acetyltransferase EC 2.3.1.59	N-(2-(S-coenzyme A)-acetyl)gentamycin (Williams and Northrop 1979)
gamma-glutamyl transpeptidase EC 2.3.2.2	serine–borate complex (Tate and Meister 1978)
glycogen phosphorylase EC 2.4.1.1	1,5-gluconolactone (Tu *et al.* 1971; Gold *et al.* 1971)
riboflavin synthase EC 2.5.1.9	6,7-dioxolumazine (Al-Hassan *et al.* 1980)
squalene synthase EC 2.5.1.21	ammonium analogue of carbocation (Sandifer *et al.* 1982)
pyridoxamine–pyruvate transaminase EC 2.6.1.2	pyridoxylalanine (Dempsey and Snell 1963)

hexokinase
   EC 2.7.1.1

chromium-ATP (Danenberg and Cleland 1975)

adenosine kinase
   EC 2.7.1.20

Ap_4A (Bone et al. 1986)

thymidine kinase
   EC 2.7.1.21

Ap_5T (Bone et al. 1986)

pyruvate kinase
   EC 2.7.1.40

oxalate (Reed and Morgan 1974)

alkyl-dihydroxyacetone
   phosphate synthase
   EC 2.7.1.84

2(3)-palmitoyl-1,2,3-trihydroxyeicosane
   1-phosphate (Hixson and Wolfenden 1981)

creatine kinase
   EC 2.7.3.2

nitrate (Milner-White and Watts 1971)

arginine kinase
   EC 2.7.3.3

nitrate (Buttlaire and Cohn 1974a)

adenylate kinase
   EC 2.7.4.3

Ap_5A (Lienhard and Secemski 1973)

pyruvate–water dikinase
   EC 2.7.9.2

oxalate (Narindrasorasak and Bridger 1978)

coenzyme A transferase
   EC 2.8.3.5

succinomonohydroxamic acid
   (Pickart and Jencks 1979)

Hydrolases

carboxylesterase
   EC 3.1.1.1

benzil (Berndt et al. 1977a), ethylphenyl-
   glyoxalate (Berndt et al. 1977b)

acetylcholinesterase
   EC 3.1.1.7

boronate (Koehler and Hess 1974), fluoroketone
   (Brodbeck et al. 1979; Gelb et al. 1985)

cholinesterase
   EC 3.1.1.8

diphenyl boric acid (Garner et al. 1984)

juvenile hormone esterase

fluoroketones (Hammock et al. 1982)

alkaline phosphatase
   EC 3.1.3.1

vanadate (Lopez et al. 1976)

acid phosphatase
   EC 3.1.3.2

tungstate, molybdate (Van Etten et al. 1974)

arylsulphatase A
   EC 3.1.6.1

sulphite (Roy 1955)

ribonuclease
   EC 3.1.27.5

uridine–vanadate (Lindquist et al. 1973)

α-amylase
   EC 3.2.1.1

D-malto-bionolactone (Laszlo et al. 1978)

O-glycosyl glycosidase
   EC 3.2.1.10

acarbose (Schmidt et al. 1977)
   bis(hydroxymethyl) dihydroxy-pyrrolidine
   (Schindler and Sharon 1976)

lysozyme
EC 3.2.1.17

lactone (Everse *et al.* 1971), $\Delta^{2,3}$-2-acetamido-2-deoxyglucose (Card and Hitz 1985)

neuraminidase
EC 3.2.1.18

2-deoxy-2,3-dehydro-*N*-acetylneuraminic acid (Miller *et al.* 1978)

β-glucosidase
EC 3.2.1.21

1-aminoglucoside (Lai and Axelrod 1973), *δ*-gluconolactone (Santos and Terra 1985)

galactosidases, *α* & *β*
EC 3.2.1.22, 3.2.1.23

1-aminogalactoside (Lai and Axelrod 1973), galactal (Wentworth and Wolfenden 1974)

N-acetylglucosaminidase
EC 3.2.1.30

NAG-lactone (Lee 1969)

α-L-arabinofuranosidase
EC 3.2.1.55

L-arabino-1,4-lactone (Fielding *et al.* 1981)

AMP nucleosidase
EC 3.2.2.4

formycin 5′-phosphate (de Wolf *et al.* 1979)

leucine aminopeptidase
EC 3.4.11.1

amino aldehydes (Andersson *et al.* 1982), bestatin (Umezawa *et al.* 1976), amastatin (Rich *et al.* 1984), α-aminohydroxamates (Chan *et al.* 1982)

pyroglutamyl-peptide hydrolase
EC 3.4.11.8.

oxoprolinal (Friedman *et al.* 1985)

angiotensin-converting enzyme
EC 3.4.15.1

captopril (Cushman *et al.* 1977), enalapril (Patchett *et al.* 1980), fluoroketone (Brodbeck *et al.* 1979), aminoalcohol (Gordon *et al.* 1985), 2-mercaptoacetyldipeptides (Holmquist and Vallee, 1979), ketodimethylpeptides (Gordon *et al.* 1984), α-aminoketodimethyl peptides (Gordon *et al.* 1985)

carboxypeptidase A
EC 3.4.17.1

benzylsuccinate (Byers and Wolfenden 1972), L-2-phosphoryloxy-3-phenylpropionic acid (Cushman *et al.* 1977), dipeptide phosphoramidates (Jacobsen and Bartlett 1981), 2-benzyl-3-formylpropionate, 2-mercaptoacetyldipeptides (Holmquist and Vallee 1979), 3-phosphono-proprionic acid (Grobelny *et al.* 1985), α-bromoketones (Galardy and Kortylewicz 1985)

carboxypeptidase B
EC 3.4.17.2

benzylsuccinate (McKay and Plummer 1978)

carboxypeptidase N
EC 3.4.17.7

2-mercaptomethyl-3-guanidinoethylthiopropionate (Plummer and Ryan 1981), phosphonodipeptide (Yamauchi *et al.* 1985)

chymotrypsin
EC 3.4.21.1

aldehyde (Breaux and Bender 1975), 1-acetamido-2-phenylethaneboronic acid (Koehler and Lienhard 1971)

elastase EC 3.4.21.11	acetyl-Pro-Ala-Pro-Alaninal (Thompson 1973)
subtilisin EC 3.4.21.14	benzeneboronic acid (Lindquist and Terry 1974)
papain EC 3.4.22.2	acetyl-Phe-glycinal (Westerik and Wolfenden 1971)
ficin EC 3.4.22.3	acetyl-Phe-glycinal (Lewis and Wolfenden 1977)
pepsin EC 3.4.23.1	pepstatin (Umezawa et al. 1970), methyl-pepstatin and statone (Rich et al. 1985) fluoroketone (Gelb et al. 1985), phosphinic acid dipeptide (Bartlett and Keyer 1984)
renin EC 3.4.23.4	reduced peptide (Szelke et al. 1982)
collagenase EC 3.4.24.3	Isomylphosphonyl peptide (Galardy and Grobelny 1983)
thermolysin EC 3.4.24.4	N-carboxymethyl dipeptides (Maycock et al. 1981), phosphonamidates (Bartlett and Marlowe 1983), dipeptide and 2-mercapto-acetyldipeptides (Holmquist and Valllee 1979), hydroxamates (McKay and Plummer 1978; Nishino and Powers 1978)
neutral metalloendopeptidase EC 3.4.24.11	N-carboxymethylpeptides (Almenoff and Orlowski 1983), 2-mercapto-acetyldipeptides (Holmquist and Vallee 1979)
asparaginase EC 3.5.1.1	aspartate semialdehyde (Westerik and Wolfenden 1974
amidase EC 3.5.1.4	acetaldehyde–ammonia (Findlater and Orsi 1973)
guanine deaminase EC 3.5.4.3	(1,2,6)-thiadiazine-1,1-dioxides (Meyer and Skibo 1979)
adenosine deaminase EC 3.5.4.4	1,6-dihydro-6-hydroxymethyl purine riboside (Evans and Wolfenden 1970), coformycin (Sawa et al. 1967)
cytidine deaminase EC 3.5.4.5	tetrahydrouridine (Cohen and Wolfenden 1971), phosphapyrimidine (Ashley and Bartlett 1984); 1,3 diazepin-2-ol-ribonucleoside (Marquez et al. 1980)
AMP deaminase EC 3.5.4.6	coformycin-5'-phosphate (Frieden et al. 1979)
dCMP deaminase EC 3.5.4.12	tetrahydrouridine 5'-phosphate (Maley and Maley 1971)

phosphonatase
    EC 3.11.1.1

phosphite + acetaldehyde (Lanauze *et al.* 1970)

cholesterol 5,6-oxide hydrolase

5,6α-iminocholestanol (Nashed *et al.* 1985)

Lyases

oxaloacetate decarboxylase
    EC 4.1.1.3

oxalate (Schmitt *et al.* 1966)

acetoacetate decarboxylase
    EC 4.1.1.4

acetopyruvate (Tagaki *et al.* 1968), acetoacetone
    (Fridovich 1968)

orotidylate decarboxylase
    EC 4.1.1.23

1-(5'-phospho-β-D-ribosyl) barbituric acid
    (Potvin *et al.* 1978)

RUDP carboxylase
    EC 4.1.1.39

carboxyribitol diphosphate (Wishnick *et al.*
    1970); carboxyarabinitol diphosphate
    (Pierce *et al.* 1980)

aldolase, yeast
    EC 4.1.2.13

phosphoglycolohydroxamate (Collins 1974)

tryptophan synthase
    EC 4.1.2.20

2,3-dihydrotryptophan (Phillips *et al.* 1984)

isocitrate lyase
    EC 4.1.3.1

3-nitropropionate (Schloss and Cleland 1982)

phenylalanine-ammonia lyase
    EC 4.1.3.5

L-2-aminooxy-3-phenylpropionic acid
    (Hanson 1981)

citrate synthase
    EC 4.1.3.7

carboxymethyl-CoA and oxaloacetate (Bayer *et
    al.* 1981)

tryptophanase
    EC 4.1.99.1

2,3-dihydrotryptophan (Phillips *et al.* 1984)

fumarase
    EC 4.2.1.2

3-nitro-2-hydroxypropionate (Porter and Bright
    1980)

enolase
    EC 4.2.1.11

aminoethylpyruvate 2-phosphate (Spring and
    Wold 1971), phosphonoacetohydroxamate
    (Anderson *et al.* 1984)

crotonase
    EC 4.2.1.17

acetoacetyl-CoA (Waterson and Hill 1972)

aconitase
    EC 4.2.1.3

nitro analogues of citrate and isocitrate (Schloss
    et al. 1980)

aspartase
    EC 4.3.1.1

3-nitro-2-aminopropionate (Porter and Bright
    1980)

argininosuccinate lyase
    EC 4.3.2.1

fluorofumarate; difluorofumarate (Garrard
    et al. 1983)

adenylosuccinate lyase
    EC 4.3.2.2

N^6-(L-2-carboxyethyl-2-nitroethyl)-AMP (Porter
    et al. 1983)

glyoxalase
    EC 4.4.1.5

3-hydroxy-2-methyl-4H-pyran-4-one,
    isoascorbate (Douglas and Nadvi 1979)

Isomerases

proline racemase EC 5.1.1.4	pyrrole (Cardinale and Abeles 1968), pyrroline 2-carboxylates (Keenan and Alworth 1974)
triosephosphate isomerase EC 5.3.1.1	2-phospho-glycolate (Hartman *et al.* 1975), 2-phospho-glycolohydroxamate (Collins 1974)
ribose 5-phosphate isomerase EC 5.3.1.6	4-phosphoerythronate (Woodruff and Wolfenden 1979)
glucose 6-phosphate isomerase EC 5.3.1.9	5-phosphoarabinonate (Chirgwin and Noltmann 1973)
arabinose 5-phosphate isomerase EC 5.3.1.13	4-phosphoerythronate (Bigham *et al.* 1984)
steroid-delta-isomerase EC 5.3.3.1	17β-dihydroequinalin (Wang *et al.* 1963)
chorismate mutase EC 5.4.99.7	oxabicylo-[3.3.1]-nonene (Bartlett and Johnson 1985); 2-aza-2,3-dihydrosqualene (Duriatti *et al.* 1985)

Ligases

aminoacyl-tRNA synthetases EC 6.3.1	aminoalkyladenylates (Cassio *et al.* 1967), aminophosphonyl adenylates (Biryukov *et al.* 1978)
glutamine synthetase EC 6.3.1.2	methionine sulphoximine phosphate (Rowe *et al.* 1969)
pyruvate carboxylase EC 6.4.1.4	oxalate (Mildvan *et al.* 1966)
γ-glutamylcysteine synthetase EC 6.3.2.2	buthionine sulphoximine phosphate (Griffith 1982)

References

Agarwal, R. (1982). Inhibitors of adenosine deaminase. *Pharmacol. Ther.*, **17**, 399–429.

Al-Hassan, S. S., Kulick, R. J., Livingstone, D. B., Suckling, C. J., and Wood, H. C. S. (1980). Specific enzyme inhibitors in vitamin biosynthesis. Part 3. The synthesis and inhibitory properties of some substrates and transition state analogues of riboflavin synthase. *J. Chem. Soc. Perkin I*, 2645–56.

Almenoff, S., and Orlowski, M. (1983). Membrane-bound kidney neutral metalloendopeptidase: interaction with synthetic substrates, natural peptides and inhibitors. *Biochemistry*, **22**, 590–99.

Anderson, V. E., Weiss, P. M., and Cleland, W. W. (1984). Reaction intermediate analogues for enolase. *Biochemistry*, **23**, 2779–86.

Andersson, L., Isley, T. C., and Wolfenden, R. (1982). α-aminoaldehydes: transition-state analogue inhibitors of leucine aminopeptidase. *Biochemistry*, **21**, 4177–80.

Andersson, L., MacNeela, J. P., and Wolfenden, R. (1985). Use of secondary isotope effects and varying pH to investigate the mode of binding of inhibitory amino aldehydes by leucine aminopeptidase. *Biochemistry*, **24**, 330–3.

Ashley, G. W. and Bartlett, P. A. (1984). Inhibition of *Escherichia coli* cytidine deaminase by a phosphopyrimidine nucleoside. *J. Biol. Chem.*, **259**, 13621–7.

Bartlett, P. A. and Johnson, C. R. (1985). An inhibitor of chorismate mutase resembling the transition-state conformation. *J. Am. Chem. Soc.*, **107**, 7792–3.

Bartlett, P. A. and Keyer, W. B. (1984). Phosphinic acid dipeptide analogues: potent, slow binding inhibitors of aspartic peptidases. *J. Am. Chem. Soc.*, **106**, 4282–3.

Bartlett, P. A. and Marlowe, C. K. (1983). Phosphonamidates as transition-state analogue inhibitors of thermolysin. *Biochemistry*, **22**, 4618–24.

Bayer, E., Bauer, B., and Eggerer, H. (1981). Evidence from inhibitor studies for conformational changes of citrate synthase. *Eur. J. Biochem.*, **120**, 155–60.

Berndt, M. C., de Jersey, J., and Zerner, B. (1977a). Inhibition of chicken liver carboxylesterase (EC 3.1.1.1) by benzils. Direct spectrophotometric evidence for the reversible formation of active-site hemiketal adducts. *J. Am. Chem. Soc.*, **99**, 8332–4.

Berndt, M. C., de Jersey, J., and Zerner, B. (1977b). Ethyl phenylglyoxylate, a simultaneous inhibitor and substrate of chicken liver carboxylesterase (EC 3.1.1.1). Enzyme-catalyzed fragmentation of (E)-benzil monoxime O-2,4-dinitrophenyl ether. *J. Am. Chem. Soc.*, **99**, 8334–5.

Bertics, P. J., Edman, C. F., and Karavolas, H. J. (1984). Potent inhibition of the hypothalamic progesterone 5α-reductase by a 5α-dihydroprogesterone analog. *J. Biol. Chem.*, **259**, 107–11.

Bigham, E. C., Gragg, C. E., Hall, W. R., Kelsey, J. E., Mallory, W. R., Richardson, D. C., Benedict, C., and Ray, P. H. (1984). Inhibition of arabinose 5'-phosphate isomerase— an approach to the inhibition of bacterial lipopolysaccharide biosynthesis. *J. Med. Chem.*, **27**, 717–26.

Biryukov, A. I., Ishmuratov, B. K., and Khomutov, R. M. (1978). Transition-state analogs of aminoacyl adenylates. *FEBS Lett.*, **91**, 249–52.

Black, M. J., and Jones, M. E. (1984). Characterization and significance of carbamyl-phosphate phosphatase. *Cancer Res.*, **44**, 4336–76.

Bone, R. and Wolfenden, R. (1985). Solvent isotope effects on formation of protease complexes with inhibitory aldehydes, with an appendix on the determination of deuterium fractionation factors by NMR. *J. Am. Chem. Soc.*, **107**, 4772–7.

Bone, R., Cheng, Y. C., and Wolfenden, R. (1986). Inhibition of thymidine kinase by P^1 (adenosine-5')-P^5 (thymidine-5')-pentaphosphate. *J. Biol. Chem.*, **261**, 5731–5.

Brayer, G. D., Delbaere, L. T. J., James, M. N. G., Bauer, C. A., and Thompson, R. C. (1979). Crystallographic and kinetic investigations of the covalent complex formed by a specific tetrapeptide aldehyde and the serine protease from *Streptomyces griseus*. *Proc. Nat. Acad. Sci., USA*, **76**, 96–100.

Breaux, E. J. and Bender, M. L. (1975). Binding of specific and non-specific aldehyde substrate analogs to α-chymotrypsin. *FEBS Lett.*, **56**, 81–4.

Brodbeck, U., Schweikert, K., Gentinetta, R., and Rottenberg, M. (1979). Fluorinated aldehydes and ketones acting as quasi-substrate inhibitors of acetylcholinesterase. *Biochim. Biophys. Acta*, **567**, 357–69.

Buttlaire, D. H., and Cohn, M. (1974a). Interaction of manganous ion, substrates, and anions with arginine kinase. *J. Biol. Chem.*, **249**, 5733–40.

Buttlaire, D. H., and Cohn, M. (1974b). Characterization of the active site structures of arginine kinase–substrate complexes. *J. Biol. Chem.*, **249**, 5741–8.

Byers, L. D., and Wolfenden, R. (1972). A potent reversible inhibitor of carboxypeptidase A. *J. Biol. Chem.*, **247**, 606–8.

Campbell, I. D., Jones, R. B., Kiener, P. A., Richards, E., Waley, S. G. and Wolfenden, R. (1978). The form of 2-phosphoglycollic acid bound by triose-phosphate isomerase. *Biochem. Biophys. Res. Commun.*, **83**, 347–52.

Card, P. J., and Hitz, W. D. (1985). Synthesis of 2(R),5(R)-bis(hydroxymethyl)-3(R),4(R)dihydroxypyrrolidine—a novel glycosidase inhibitor. *J. Org. Chem.*, **50**, 891–3.

Cardinale, G. J., and Abeles, R. H. (1968). Purification and mechanism of action of proline racemase. *Biochemistry*, **7**, 3970–8.

Cassio, D., Lemoine, F., Waller, J. P., Sandrin, E., and Boissonas, R. A. (1967). Selective inhibition of aminoacyl ribonucleic acid synthetases by aminoalkyl adenylates. *Biochemistry*, **6**, 827–36.

Chan, W. W-C., Dennis, P., Demmer, W., and Brand, K. (1982). Inhibition of leucine aminopeptidase by amino acid hydroxamates. *J. Biol. Chem.*, **257**, 7955–7.

Chase, J. F. A. and Tubbs, P. K. (1969). Conditions for the self-catalysed inactivation of carnitine acetyltransferase. *Biochem. J.*, **111**, 225–35.

Chaudiere, J., Wilhemsen, E. C., and Tappel, A. L. (1984). Mechanism of selenium–glutathione peroxidase and its inhibition by mercaptocarboxylic acids and other mercaptans. *J. Biol. Chem.*, **259**, 1043–50.

Chen, R., Gorenstein, D. G., Kennedy, W. P., Lowe, G., Nurse, D., and Schultz, R. M. (1979). Evidence for hemiacetal formation between N-acyl-L-phenylalanials and α-chymotrypsin by cross-saturation nuclear magnetic resonance spectroscopy. *Biochemistry*, **18**, 921–6.

Chirgwin, J. M., and Noltmann, E. A. (1973). 5-phosphoarabonate as a potential 'transition-state analogue', for phosphoglucose isomerase. *Fed. Proc. Fed. Am. Soc. Exp. Biol.*, **32**, 667.

Christianson, D. W., and Lipscomb, W. N. (1985). Binding of a possible transition-state analogue to the active site of carboxypeptidase A. *Proc. Nat. Acad. Sci. USA*, **82**, 6840–4.

Clark, P. J., Lowe, G. and Nurse, D. (1977). Detection of enzyme-bound intermediates by cross-saturation in nuclear magnetic resonance spectroscopy. Investigation of papain-N-benzoylaminoacetaldehyde complex. *J. Chem. Soc. Chem. Commun.*, 451–3.

Cohen, R. M., and Wolfenden, R. (1971). Cytidine deaminase from *Escherichia coli*. *J. Biol. Chem.*, **246**, 7561–5.

Collins, K. D. (1974). An activated intermediate analogue. The use of phosphoglycolo-hydroxamate as a stable analogue of a transiently occurring dihydroxyacetone phosphate-derived enolate in enzymatic catalysis. *J. Biol. Chem.*, **249**, 136–42.

Collins, K. D., and Stark, G. R. (1971). Aspartate transcarbamylase. Interaction with the transition-state analogue N-(phosphonoacetyl-L-aspartate. *J. Biol. Chem.*, **246**, 6599–605.

Crosby, J., and Lienhard, G. E. (1970). Mechanisms of thiamine-catalyzed reactions. A kinetic analysis of the decarboxylation of pyruvate by 3,4-dimethylthiazolium ion in water and in ethanol. *J. Am. Chem. Soc.*, **92**, 5707–16.

Cullis, P. M., Wolfenden, R., Cousens, L. S., and Alberts, B. M. (1982). Inhibition of histone acetylation by N-[2-(S-coenzyme A)acetyl] spermidine amide, a multisubstrate analog. *J. Biol. Chem.*, **257**, 12165–9.

Cushman, D. W., Cheung, H. S., Sabo, E. F., and Ondetti, M. A. (1977). Design of potent competitive inhibitors of angiotensin-converting enzyme. Carboxyalkanoyl and mercaptoalkanoyl amino acids. *Biochemistry*, **16**, 5484–91.

Dale, M. P., Ensley, H. E., Kern, K., Sastry, K. A. R., and Byers, L. D. (1985). Reversible inhibitors of β-glucosidase. *Biochemistry*, **24**, 3530–9.

Danenberg, K. D. and Cleland, W. W. (1975). Use of chromium-adenosine triphosphate and lyxose to elucidate the kinetic machanism and coordination state of the nucleotide substrate for yeast hexokinase. *Biochemistry*, **14**, 28–39.

Dempsey, W. B., and Snell, E. E. (1963). Pyridoxamine–pyruvate transaminase. II. Characteristics of the enzyme. *Biochemistry*, **2**, 1414–19.

Douglas, K. T., and Nadvi, I. N. (1979). Inhibition of glyoxylase I—possible transition-state analog inhibitor approach to potential anti-neoplastic agents. *FEBS Lett.*, **106**, 393–6.

Duriatti, A., Bouvier-Nave, P., Benveniste, P., Schuber, F., Delprino, L., Balliano, G., and Cattel, L. (1985). *In vitro* inhibition of animal and higher-plant 2,3 oxidosqualene-sterol cyclases by 2-aza-2,3-dihydrosqualene and derivatives, and by other ammonium-containing molecules. *Biochem. Pharmacol.*, **34**, 2765–77.

Evans, B., and Wolfenden, R. (1970). A potential transition-state analog for adenosine deaminase. *J. Am. Chem. Soc.*, **92**, 4751–2.

Everse, J., Zoll, E. C., Kahan, L., and Kaplan, N. O. (1971). Addition products of diphosphopyridine nucleotides with substrates of pyridine nucleotide-linked dehydrogenases. *Bioorg. Chem.*, **1**, 207–33.

Fielding, A. H., Sinnott, M. L., Kelly, M. A., and Widows, D. (1981). Product stereochemistry and some inhibitors of the α-arabinofuranosidases of *Monilinia fructigena*. *J. Chem. Soc. Perkin I*, 1013–14.

Findlater, J. D., and Orsi, B. A. (1973). Transition-state analogs of an aliphatic amidase. *FEBS Lett.*, **35**, 109–111.

Fluharty, A. L., and Ballou, C. E. (1958). D-threose 2,4-diphosphate inhibition of D-glyceraldehyde 3-phosphate dehydrogenase. *J. Biol. Chem.*, **234**, 2517–22.

Frick, L. and Wolfenden, R. (1985). Mechanistic implications of the inhibition of peptidases by aminoaldehydes and bestatin. *Biochim. Biophys. Acta*, **829**, 311–18.

Fridovich, I. (1968). A study of the interaction of acetoacetic decarboxylase with several inhibitors. *J. Biol. Chem.*, **243**, 1043–51.

Frieden, C., Gilbert, H. R., Miller, W. H., and Miller, R. L. (1979). Adenylate deaminase: potent inhibitor by 2′ deoxycoformycin 5′-phosphate. *Biochem. Biophys. Res. Commun.*, **91**, 278–83.

Friedman, T. C., Kline, T. B., and Wilk, S. (1985). 5-Oxoprolinal: transition-state aldehyde inhibitor of pyroglutamyl-peptide hydrolase. *Biochemistry*, **24**, 3907–13.

Galardy, R. E., and Grobelny, D. (1983). Inhibition of collagenase from *Clostridium histolyticum* by phosphoric and phosphonic amides. *Biochemistry*, **22**, 4556–61.

Galardy, R. E., and Kortylewicz, Z. P. (1985). α-bromo ketone substrate analogues are powerful reversible inhibitors of carboxypeptidase A. *Biochemistry*, **24**, 7607–7612.

Gamcsik, M. P., Malthouse, J. P. G., Primrose, W. U., Mackenzie, N. E., Boyd, A. S. F., Russell, R. A., and Scott, A. I. (1983). Structure and stereochemistry of tetrahedral inhibitor complexes of papain by direct n.m.r. observation. *J. Am. Chem. Soc.*, **105**, 6324–5.

Garner, C. W., Little, G. W., and Pelley, J. W. (1984). Serum-cholinesterase inhibition by boronic acids. *Biochim. Biophys. Acta*, **790**, 91–3.

Garrard, L. J., Mathis, J. M., and Raushel, F. M. (1983). Substrate-induced inactivation of arginosuccinate lyase by monofluorofumarate and difluorofumarate. *Biochemistry*, **22**, 3729–35.

Gelb, M. H., Svaren, J. P., and Abeles, R. H. (1985). Fluoroketone inhibitors of hydrolytic enzymes. *Biochemistry*, **24**, 1813–17.

Ghisla, S., and Massey, V. (1975). Mechanism of inactivation of the flavoenzyme lactate oxidase by oxalate. *J. Biol. Chem.*, **250**, 577–84.

Ghisla, S., and Massey, V. (1977). Studies on the mechanism of action of the flavoenzyme lactate oxidase. *J. Biol. Chem.*, **252**, 6729–35.

Gold, A. M., Legrand, E., and Sanchez, G. R. (1971). Inhibition of muscle phosphorylase α by 5-gluconolactone. *J. Biol. Chem.*, **246**, 5700–6.

Gordon, E. M., Natarajan, S., Pluscec, J., Weller, H. N., Godfrey, J. D., Rom, M. B., Sabo, E. F., Engebrecht, J., and Cushman, D. W. (1984). Ketomethyldipeptides 2. Effect of modifications of the α-aminoketon portion on inhibition of angiotensin converting enzyme. *Biochem. Biophys. Res. Commun.*, **124**, 148–55.

Gordon, E. M., Godfrey, J. D., Pluscec, J., von Langen, D., and Natarajan, S. (1985). Design of peptide derived amino-alcohols as transition-state analog inhibitors of angiotensin converting enzyme. *Biochem. Biophys. Res. Commun.*, **126**, 419–26.

Griffith, O. W. (1982). Mechanism of action, metabolism, and toxicity of buthionine sulfoximine and its higher homologs, potent inhibitors of glutamine synthesis. *J. Biol. Chem.*, **257**, 13704–12.

Grobelny, D., Goli, U. B., and Galardy, R. E. (1985). 3-phosphoropropionic acids inhibit carboxypeptidase-A as multisubstrate analogs or as transition-state analogs. *Biochem. J.*, **232**, 15–19.

Gutowski, J. A., and Lienhard, G. E. (1976). Transition state analogs for thiamin pyrophosphate-dependent enzymes *J. Biol. Chem.*, **251**, 2863–6.

Hammock, B. D., Wing, K. D., McLaughlin, J., Lovell, V. M., and Sparks, T. C. (1982). Trifluoromethylketones as possible transition-state analog inhibitors of juvenile hormone esterase. *Pestic. Biochem. Physiol.*, **17**, 76–88.

Hanson, K. R. (1981). Phenylalanine–ammonia lyase—mirror-image packing of D-phenylalanine and L-phenylalanine and D-transition and L-transition state analogs into the active site. *Arch. Biochem. Biophys.*, **211**, 575–88.

Hartman, F. C., La Muraglia, G. M., Tomozawa, Y., and Wolfenden, R. (1975). The influence of pH on the interaction of inhibitors with triosephosphate isomerase and determination of the pK_a of the active-site carboxyl group. *Biochemistry*, **14**, 5274–79.

Hixson, S. and Wolfenden, R. (1981). Inhibitors of ether lipid biosynthesis. *Biochem. Biophys. Res. Commun.*, **101**, 1064–70.

Holmquist, B., and Vallee, B. L. (1979). Metal-coordinating substrate analogs as inhibitors of metalloenzymes. *Proc. Nat. Acad. Sci. USA*, **76**, 6216–20.

Hoogenraad, N. J. (1978). Synthesis and properties of Δ-*N*-(phosphonoacetyl)-L-ornithine-transition-state analog inhibitor of ornithine transcarbamylase. *Arch. Biochem. Biophys.*, **188**, 137–44.

Jacobsen, N. E. and Bartlett, P. A. (1981). A phosphonamidate dipeptide analogue as an inhibitory carboxypeptidase A. *J. Am. Chem. Soc.*, **103**, 654–7.

Jencks, W. P. (1966). Strain and conformation change in enzymatic catalysis. In *Current aspects of biochemical energetics* (ed. N. O. Kaplan and E. P. Kennedy), pp. 273–298. Academic Press, New York.

Jencks, W. P. (1975). Binding energy, specificity, and enzymic catalysis—the Circe effect. *Adv. Enzymol.*, **43**, 219–410.

Kalman, T. I. and Goldman, D. (1981). Inactivation of thymidylate synthetase by a novel mechanism-based enzyme inhibitor: 1-(β-D-2'-deoxyribofuranosyl)-8-azapurin-2-one 5'-monophosphate. *Biochem. Biophys. Res. Commun.*, **102**, 682–9.

Kapmeyer, H., Pfleiderer, G., and Trommer, W. E. (1976). A transition state analogue for two pyruvate metabolizing enzymes, lactate dehydrogenase and alanine dehydrogenase. *Biochemistry*, **15**, 5024–8.

Keenan, M. V., and Alworth, W. L. (1974). The inhibition of proline racemase by a transition state analogue: Δ-1-pyrroline-2-carboxylate. *Biochem. Biophys. Res. Commun.*, **57**, 500–4.

Kensler, T. W., Mutter, G., Hankerson, J. G., Reck, L. J., Harley, C., Han, N., Ardalan, B., Cysyk, R. L., Johnson, R. K., Jayaram, H. N., and Cooney, D. A. (1981). Mechanism of resistance of variants of the Lewis lung-carcinoma to *N*-(phosphonoacetyl) aspartic acid. *Cancer Res.*, **41**, 894–904.

Kettner, C., Glover, G. I., and Prescott, J. M. (1974). Kinetics of inhibition of *Aeromonas* aminopeptidase by leucine methyl ketone derivatives. *Arch. Biochem. Biophys.*, **165**, 739–43.

Kluger, R. and Pike, D. C. (1977). Active site generated analogues of reactive intermediates in enzymic reactions. Potent inhibition of pyruvate dehydrogenase by a phosphonate analogue of pyruvate. *J. Am. Chem. Soc.*, **99**, 4504–6.

Koehler, K. A., and Hess, G. P. (1974). A new, specific and reversible bifunctional alkylborinic acid inhibitor of acetylcholinesterase. *Biochemistry*, **13**, 5345–50.

Koehler, K. A., and Lienhard, G. E. (1971). 2-phenylethaneboronic acid, a possible transition-state analog for chymotrypsin. *Biochemistry*, **10**, 2477–83.

Lai, H. L. and Axelrod, B. (1973). 1-aminoglycosides, a new class of specific inhibitors of glycosidases. *Biochem. Biophys. Res. Commun.*, **54**, 463–8.

Lanauze, J. M., Rosenberg, H., and Shaw, D. C. (1970). The enzymic cleavage of the carbon–phosphorus bond: purification and properties of phosphonatase. *Biochim. Biophys. Acta*, **212**, 332–50.

Laszlo, E., Hollo, J., Hoschke, A., and Sarosi, G. (1978). Active center of amylolytic enzymes. 1. Study by means of lactone inhibition of role of a half-chain glycosyl conformation at active-center of amylolytic enzymes. *Carbohydrate Res.*, **61**, 387–94.

Lee, Y. C. (1969). Inhibition of β-D-galactosidases by D-galactal. *Biochem. Biophys. Res. Commun.*, **35**, 161–7.

Levine, H. L., Brody, R. S., and Westheimer, F. H. (1980). Inhibition of orotidine-5′-phosphate decarboxylase by 1-(5′-phospho-β-D-ribofuranosyl) barbituric acid, 6-azauridine 5′-phosphate and uridine 5′-phosphate. *Biochemistry*, **19**, 4993–9.

Lewis, C. A., and Wolfenden, R. (1977). Thiohemiacetal formation by inhibitory aldehydes at the active site of papain. *Biochemistry*, **16**, 4890–5.

Lienhard, G. E. (1973). Enzymatic catalysis and transition state theory. *Science*, **180**, 149–54.

Lienhard, G. E., and Secemski, I. I. (1973). P^1,P^5-di(adenosine-5′)pentaphosphate, a potent multisubstrate inhibitor of adenylate kinase. *J. Biol. Chem.*, **248**, 1121–3.

Lindquist, R. N., and Terry, C. (1974). Inhibition of subtilisin by boronic acids, potential analogs of tetrahedral reaction intermediates. *Arch. Biochem. Biophys.*, **160**, 135–44.

Lindquist, R. N., Lynn, J. L., Jr., and Lienhard, G. E. (1973). Possible transition-state analogs for ribonuclease. The complexes of uridine with oxovanadium (IV) ion and vanadium (V) ion. *J. Am. Chem. Soc.*, **95**, 8762–8.

Lopez, V., Stevens, T., and Lindquist, R. N. (1976). Vanadium ion inhibition of alkaline phosphatase-catalyzed phosphate ester hydrolysis. *Arch. Biochem. Biophys.*, **175**, 31–8.

Lowe, G. and Nurse, D. (1977). Evidence for hemiacetal formation between α chymotrypsin and hydrocinnamaldehyde by cross-saturation nuclear magnetic resonance spectroscopy. *J. Chem. Soc. Chem. Commun.*, 815–817.

Lowe, P. N., Leeper, F. J., and Perham, R. N. (1983). Stereoisomers of tetrahydrothiamin pyrophosphate, potent inhibitors of the pyruvate dehydrogenase multienzyme complex from *Escherichia coli*. *Biochemistry*, **22**, 150–7.

McKay, T. J., and Plummer, T. H. (1978). By-product analogues for bovine carboxypeptidase B. *Biochemistry*, **17**, 401–5.

Maley, F., and Maley, G. F. (1971). Tetrahydrodeoxyuridylate: a potent inhibitor of deoxyuridylate deaminase. *Arch. Biochem. Biophys.*, **144**, 723–9.

Malthouse, J. P. G., Primrose, W. U., MacKenzie, N. E., and Scott, A. I. (1985). ^{13}C n.m.r. study of the ionizations within a trypsin–chloromethyl ketone inhibitor complex. *Biochemistry*, **24**, 3478–87.

Marquez, V. E., Liu, P. S., Kelley, J. A., Driscoll, J. S. and McCormack, J. J. (1980). Synthesis of 1,3-diazepin-2-one nucleosides as transition state inhibitors of cytidine deaminase. *J. Med. Chem.*, **23**, 713–15.

May, S. W., Oldham, C. D., Mueller, P. W., Padgette, S. R., and Sowell, A. L. (1982). Protocatechuate 3,4-dioxygenase. *J. Biol. Chem.*, **257**, 12746–51.

Maycock, A. L., De Sousa, D. M., Payne, L. G., ten Broeke, J., Wu, M. T. and Patchett, A. A. (1981). Inhibition of thermolysin by *N*-carboxymethyl dipeptides. *Biochem. Biophys. Res. Commun.*, **102**, 963–9.

Meyer, R. B., and Skibo, E. B. (1979). Synthesis of fused (1,2,6) thiadiazine 1,1-dioxides as potential transition-state analog inhibitors of xanthine-oxidase and guanase. *J. Med. Chem.*, **22**, 944–8.

Mildvan, A. S., Scrutton, M. C., and Utter, M. F. (1966). Pyruvate carboxylase VII. A possible role for tightly bound manganese. *J. Biol. Chem.*, **241**, 3488–98.

Miller, C. A., Wang, P., and Flashner, M. (1978). Mechanism of *Arthrobacter sialophilus* neuraminidase: the binding of substrates and transition state analogs. *Biochem. Biophys. Res. Commun.*, **83**, 1479–87.

Milner-White, E. J., and Watts, D. C. (1971). Inhibition of adenosine 5'-triphosphate–creatine phosphotransferase by substrate–anion complexes. *Biochem. J.*, **122**, 727–40.

Monzingo, A. F., and Matthews, B. W. (1984). Binding of *N*-carboxymethyl dipeptide inhibitors to thermolysin determined by X-ray crystallography: a novel class of transition-state analogues for zinc peptidases. *Biochemistry*, **23**, 5724–9.

Mori, M., Aoyagi, K., Tatibana, M., Ishikawa, T., and Ishii, H. (1977). Nδ-(phosphonoacetyl)-L-ornithine, a potent transition state analogue inhibitor of ornithine carbamoyltransferase. *Biochem. Biophys. Res. Commun.*, **76**, 900–4.

Nakamura, H., Koyama, G., Iitaka, Y., Ohno, M., Yagisawa, N., Kondo, S., Maeda, K., and Umezawa, H. (1974). Structure of coformycin, an unusual nucleoside of microbial origin. *J. Am. Chem. Soc.*, **96**, 4327–8.

Narindrasorasak, S., and Bridger, W. A. (1978). Probes of structure of phosphoenolpyruvate synthetase-effects of a transition-state analog on enzyme conformation. *Can. J. Biochem.*, **56**, 816–19.

Narula, A. S., Rahier, A., Benveniste, D., and Schuber, F. (1981). 24-methyl-25-azacycloartanol, an analogue of a carbonium ion high-energy intermediate, is a potent inhibitor of (*S*)-adenosyl-L-methionine: sterol C-24-methyltransferase in higher plant cells. *J. Am. Chem. Soc.*, **103**, 2408–9.

Nashed, N. T., Michaud, D. P., Levin, W., and Jerina, D. M. (1985). Properties of liver microsomal cholesterol 5,6-oxide hydrolase. *Arch. Biochem. Biophys.*, **241**, 149–62.

Nishino, N., and Powers, J. C. (1978). Peptide hydroxamic acids as inhibitors of thermolysin. *Biochemistry*, **17**, 2846–50.

Nishizawa, R., Saino, T., Takita, T., Suda, H., Aoyagi, T., and Umezawa, H. (1977). Synthesis and structure–activity relationships of bestatin analogs, inhibitors of aminopeptidase B. *J. Med. Chem.*, **20**, 510–15.

Northrop, D. B., and Wood, H. G. (1969). Transcarboxylase VII. Exchange reactions and kinetics of oxalate inhibition. *J. Biol. Chem.*, **244**, 5820–7.

Novoa, W. B., Winer, A. D., Glaid, A. J., and Schwert, G. W. (1959). Lactic dehydrogenase V. Inhibition by oxamate and by oxalate. *J. Biol. Chem.*, **234**, 1143–8.

Oehlschlager, A. C., Angus, R. H., Pierce, A. M., Pierce, H. D., Jr., and Srinivasan, R. (1984). Azasterol inhibition of Δ^{24}-sterol methyltransferase in *Saccharomyces cerevisia*. *Biochemistry*, **23**, 3582–9.

Ondetti, M. A. and Cushman, D. W. (1984). Angiotensin-converting enzyme inhibitors—biochemical properties and biological actions. *CRC Crit. Rev. Biol.*, **16**, 381–441.

Page, M. I. and Jencks, W. P. (1971). Entropic contributions to rate accelerations in enzymic and intramolecular reactions and the chelate effect. *Proc. Nat. Acad. Sci. USA*, **68**, 1678–83.

Patchett, A. A. and Cordes, E. H. (1985). The design and properties of *N*-carboxyalkyldipeptide inhibitors of angiotensin-converting enzyme. *Adv. Enzymol.*, **57**, 1–84.

Patchett, A. A., Harris, E., Tristam, E. W., Wyvratt, M. J., Wu, M. T., Taub, D., Peterson, E. R., Ikeler, T. J., and ten Broeke, J. (1980). A new class of angiotensin-converting enzyme inhibitors. *Nature*, **288**, 280–3.

Pauling, L. (1946). Molecular architecture and biological reactions. *Chem. Eng. News*, **24**, 1375–7.

Phillips, R. S., Miles, E. W., and Cohen, L. A. (1984). Interaction of trytophan synthase, tryptophanase, and pyridoxal phosphate with oxindoyl-L-alanine and 2,3-dihydro-2-tryptophan: support for an indolenine intermediate in tryptophan metabolism. *Biochemistry*, **23**, 6228–34.

Pickart, C. M. and Jencks, W. P. (1979). Formation of stable anhydrides from CoA transferase and hydroxamic acids. *J. Biol. Chem.*, **254**, 9120–9.

Pierce, J., Tolbert, N. E., and Barker, R. (1980). Interaction of ribulosebisphosphate carboxylase/oxygenase with transition-state analogues. *Biochemistry*, **19**, 934–42.

Plummer, T. H. and Ryan, T. J. (1981). A potent mercapto by-product analogue inhibitor for human carboxypeptidase N. *Biochem. Biophys. Res. Commun.*, **98**, 448–54.

Porter, D. J. T. and Bright, H. J. (1980). 3-carbanionic substrate analogues bind very tightly to fumarase and aspartase. *J. Biol. Chem.*, **255**, 4772–80.

Porter, D. J. T., Rudie, N. G., and Bright, H. J. (1983). Nitro analogs of substrates for adenylosuccinate synthetase and adenylosuccinate lyase. *Arch. Biochem. Biophys.*, **255**, 157–63.

Potvin, B. W., Stern, H. J., May, S. R., Lam, G. R., and Krooth, R. S. (1978). Inhibition by barbituric acid and its derivatives of enzymes in rat brain which participate in synthesis of pyrimidime ribotides. *Biochem. Pharmacol.*, **27**, 655–65.

Quastel, J. H. and Wooldridge, W. R. (1928). LXXXIV. Some properties of the dehydrogenating enzymes of bacteria. *Biochem. J.*, **22**, 689–702.

Raso, V. and Stollar, B. D. (1975). The antibody–enzyme analogy. Comparison of enzymes and antibodies specific for phosphopyridoxyltyrosine. *Biochemistry*, **14**, 591–599.

Reed, G. H. and Morgan, S. D. (1974). Kinetic and magnetic resonance studies of the interaction of oxalate with pyruvate kinase. *Biochemistry*, **13**, 3537–41.

Reese, E. T., Parrish, F. W., Ettlinger, M. (1971). Nojirimycin and D-glucono-1,5-lactone as inhibitors of carbohydrases. *Carbohydrate Res.*, **18**, 381–8.

Rich, D. H., Moon, B. J., and Harbeson, S. (1984). Inhibition of aminopeptidase by amastatin and bestatin derivatives—effect of inhibitor structure on slow-binding processes. *J. Med. Chem.*, **27**, 417–422.

Rich, D. H., Bernatowicz, M. S., Agarwal, N. S., Kawai, M., and Salituro, F. G. (1985). Inhibition of aspartic acid protease by pepstatin and 3-methylstatine derivatives of pepstatin. Evidence for collected-substrate enzyme inhibition. *Biochemistry*, **24**, 3165–73.

Rowe, W. B., Ronzio, R. A., and Meister, A. (1969). Inhibition of glutamine synthetase by methionine sulfoximine. Studies on methionine sulfoximine phosphate. *Biochemistry*, **8**, 2674–80.

Roy, A. B. (1955). The sulphatase of ox liver. 2. The purification and properties of sulphatase A. *Biochem. J.*, **55**, 653–61.

Sandifer, R. M., Thompson, M. D., Gaughan, R. G., and Poulter, C. D. (1982). Squalene synthetase. Inhibition by an ammonium analogue of a carbocationic intermediate in the conversion of presqualene pyrophosphate to squalene. *J. Am. Chem. Soc.*, **104**, 7376–8.

Santos, C. D. and Terra, W. R. (1985). Physical properties, substrate specificities, and a probable mechanism for a β-D-glucosidase (cellobiase) from midgut cells of the cassava hornworm (*Erinnyis ello*). *Biochim. Biophys. Acta*, **831**, 179–85.

Sawa, T., Fukagawa, Y., Homma, I., Takeuchi, T., and Umezawa, H. (1967). Mode of inhibition of coformycin on adenosine deaminase. *J. Antibiot.*, **201**, 227–31.

Schindler, M. and Sharon, N. (1976). A transition state analog of lysozyme catalysis prepared from the bacterial cell wall tetrasaccharide. *J. Biol. Chem.*, **251**, 4330–5.

Schloss, J. V. and Cleland, W. W. (1982). Inhibition of isocitrate lyase by 3-nitropropionate, a reaction-intermediate analogue. *Biochemistry*, **21**, 4420–7.

Schloss, J. V., Porter, D. J. T., Bright, H. J., and Cleland, W. W. (1980). Nitro analogues of citrate and isocitrate as transition-state analogues for aconitase. *Biochemistry*, **19**, 2358–62.

Schmidt, D., Frommer, W., Junge, B., Müller, L., Wingender, W., Truscheit, E., and Schäfer, D. (1977). α-glucosidase inhibitors—new complex oligosaccharides of microbial origin. *Naturwissenschaften*, **64**, 535–6.

Schmitt, A., Bottke, I., and Siebert, G. (1966). Eigenschaften einer Oxalacetat-Decarboxylase aus Dorschmuskulatur, *Hoppe-Seyler's Z. Physiol. Chem.*, **347**, 18–34.

Secemski, I. I., and Lienhard, G. E. (1971). The role of strain in catalysis by lysozyme. *J. Am. Chem. Soc.*, **93**, 3549–50.

Spring, T. G. and Wold, F. (1971). Studies on two high-affinity enolase inhibitors. Reaction with enolases. *Biochemistry*, **10**, 4655–60.

Srinivasan, A., Amarnath, V., Broom, A. D., Zou, F. C., and Cheng, Y. -C. (1984). A potent multisubstrate analog inhibitor of human thymidylate synthetase. *J. Med. Chem.*, **27**, 1710–17.

Szelke, M., Leckie, B., Hallett, A., Jones, D. M., Sueiras, J., Atrash, B., and Lever, A. F. (1982). Potent new inhibitors of human renin. *Nature*, **299**, 555–7.

Tagaki, W., Guthrie, J. P., and Westheimer, F. H. (1968). Acetoacetate decarboxylase. Reaction with acetopyruvate. *Biochemistry*, **7**, 905–13.

Tang, K. C., Pegg, A. E., and Coward, J. K. (1980). Specific and potent inhibition of spermidine synthase by the transition-state analog, *S*-adenosyl-3-thio-1,8-diaminooctane. *Biochem. Biophys. Res. Commun.*, **96**, 1371–7.

Tate, S. S. and Meister, A. (1978). Serine–borate complex as a transition-state inhibitor of γ-glutamyl transpeptidase. *Proc. Nat. Acad. Sci. USA*, **75**, 4806–9.

Thompson, R. C. (1973). Use of peptide aldehydes to generate transition-state analogs of elastase. *Biochemistry*, **12**, 47–51.

Tu, J. I., Jacobson, G. R., and Graves, D. J. (1971). Isotopic effects and inhibition of polysaccharide phosphorylase by 1,5-gluconolactone. Relationship to the catalytic mechanism. *Biochemistry*, **10**, 1229–36.

Umezawa, H., Aoyagi, T., Morishima, H., Matzusaki, M., Hamada, H., and Takeuchi, T. (1970). Pepstatin, a new pepsin inhibitor produced by *Actinomycetes*. *J. Antibiot.*, **23**, 259–62.

Umezawa, H., Aoyagi, H., Suda, H., Hamada, M., and Takeuchi, T. (1976). Bestatin, an inhibitor of aminopeptidase-B, produced by actinomycetes. *J. Antibiot.*, **29**, 97–9.

Van Etten, R. L., Waymack, P. P., and Rehkop, D. M. (1974). Transition metal ion inhibition of enzyme-catalyzed phosphate ester displacement reactions. *J. Am. Chem. Soc.*, **96**, 6782–5.

Wang, S., Kawahara, F. S., and Talalay, D. (1963). The mechanism of the Δ^5-3-ketosteroid isomerase reaction: absorption and fluorescence spectra of enzyme–steroid complexes. *J. Biol. Chem.*, **238**, 576–85.

Waterson, R. M. and Hill, R. L. (1972). Enoyl coenzyme A hydratase (crotonase). *J. Biol. Chem.*, **247**, 5258–65.

Webb, J. L. (1966). *Enzyme and metabolic inhibitors.* Academic Press, New York.

Wentworth, D. F. and Wolfenden, R. (1974). Slow binding of D-galactal, a 'reversible' inhibitor of bacterial β-galactosidase. *Biochemistry*, **13**, 4715–20.

Werkheiser, W. C. (1961). Specific binding of 4-amino folic acid analogues by folic acid reductase. *J. Biol. Chem.*, **236**, 888–93.

Westerik, J. O., and Wolfenden, R. (1971). Aldehydes as inhibitors of papain. *J. Biol. Chem.*, **247**, 8195–7.

Westerik, J. O. and Wolfenden, R. (1974). Aspartic-β-semialdehyde: a potent inhibitor of *Escherichia coli* L-asparaginase. *J. Biol. Chem.*, **249**, 6351–3.

de Wolf, W. E., Fullin, F. A., and Schramm, V. L. (1979). The catalytic site of AMP nucleosidase. *J. Biol. Chem.*, **254**, 10868–75.

Wolfenden, R. (1969a). Transition state analogues for enzyme catalysis. *Nature*, **223**, 704–5.

Wolfenden, R. (1969b). On the rate-determining step in the action of adenosine deaminase. *Biochemistry*, **8**, 2409–15.

Wolfenden, R. (1972). Analog approaches to the structure of the transition state in enzyme reactions. *Accounts Chem. Res.*, **5**, 10–18.

Wolfenden, R. (1976). Analog inhibitors and enzyme catalysis. *Ann. Rev. Biophys. Bioeng.*, **5**, 271–305.

Williams, J. W. and Northrop, D. B. (1979). Synthesis of a tight-binding multisubstrate analog inhibitor of gentamycin acetyltransferase 1. *J. Antibiot.*, **32**, 1147–54.

Wishnick, M., Lane, M. D., and Scrutton, M. C. (1970). The interaction of metal ions with ribulose 1,5-diphosphate carboxylase from spinach. *J. Biol. Chem.*, **245**, 4939–47.

Woodruff, W. W. and Wolfenden, R. (1979). Inhibition of ribose-5-phosphate isomerase by 4-phosphoerythronate. *J. Biol. Chem.*, **254**, 5866–7.

Yamauchi, K., Ohtsuki, S., and Kinoshita, M. (1985). Phosphonodipeptides containing (2-aminoethyl)phosphoric acid (cilatine)—transition state analog inhibitors of carboxylpeptidase A. *Biochim. Biophys. Acta*, **827**, 275–82.

Section 2B

Active-site-directed irreversible inhibitors

Elliot Shaw

2B.1   Introduction

The development of active-site-directed inhibitors had the goal of identifying groups essential for enzyme function by making a covalent alteration that could be located by protein chemistry (Schoellmann and Shaw 1962; Ong *et al.* 1965). For this purpose, the substrate of an enzyme is provided with an added, reactive chemical function. After formation of a normal enzyme–substrate complex in a reversible phase, a covalent bond joins the substrate analogue to the active centre. This irreversibly inactivates the enzyme and alters an amino acid side chain for subsequent identification. This procedure is also described as *affinity labelling*. Many applications have been reviewed (Shaw 1970; Jakoby and Wilchek 1977). Reactive groups incorporated into substrates to promote covalent interaction include the haloacyl group, haloketone, diazomethyl ketone, epoxide, sulphonyl fluoride, unsaturation, disulphide bonds, photosensitive groups, and others. This chapter is arranged by chemical category to provide examples of each type.

For drug design, the virtues of this approach are that it offers a rational way of developing biologically active molecules once a useful target enzyme has been selected. Secondly, the irreversibility of the inhibition offers a probable means of obtaining very effective drugs since displacement by normal metabolites is impossible. Many useful drugs are now recognized to be irreversible enzyme inhibitors although discovered by other means, and their effectiveness is very probably due to this property.

In this review are also included some covalent bond-forming inhibitors such as carbonyl compounds or reagents that form esters or disulphide bonds; these reactions may be eventually reversible but the derivative is long-lived compared to a readily reversible enzyme–inhibitor complex. Irreversible inhibitors acting by affinity-labelling are occasionally criticized as being too non-specific and likely to lead to undesirable side-reactions. A variation has been introduced in which a reactive function is generated at the active centre. This has been achieved most readily with enzymes using coenzymes such as pyridoxal phosphate, which generate a reactive species *in situ*. Such inhibitors are referred to as *suicide inhibitors* or *mechanism-based inhibitors* (Abeles and Maycock 1976; Walsh 1984; see Chapter 2C).

2B.2   General characteristics

2B.2.1   Kinetic characterization of inhibitors

Active-site-directed irreversible inhibitors typically show a time-dependent inhibition. A mixture of the enzyme and inhibitor is incubated and an aliquot assayed periodically with dilution by substrate adequate to displace complexed enzyme and thus measure residual available activity.

$$E + I \rightleftharpoons \text{complex} \xrightarrow{k_2} E\text{—}I \tag{2B.1}$$

If $[I] > [E]$, the residual activity loss follows apparent first-order kinetics and k_{app} may be calculated from $0.693/t_{1/2}$; $t_{1/2}$ is the half-time for inactivation taken from a first order plot of activity loss versus time. The presence of a substrate or competitive inhibitor in the reaction mixture can slow this inactivation by competition for the free enzyme. This may be used merely as diagnostic evidence that a change is taking place at the active centre, or to slow down the reaction to a rate more convenient for measurement. In this case the K_i or K_s of the third component enters into the kinetic analysis. The analysis most commonly used is that of Kitz and Wilson (1962); k_{app} for inactivation is measured at a number of inhibitor concentrations and a double reciprocal plot constructed. A positive intercept on the $1/k_{app}$ axis indicates the reciprocal of a limiting velocity, k_2, due to complex formation. Since the slope of the line is K_i/k_2, from this value and k_2, one can calculate K_i (the horizontal intercept gives the value of $-1/K_i$). In rapid inactivations when the inhibitor concentration may not greatly exceed that of the enzyme, this approach is not valid. In these cases it is advisable to carry out the inactivation in the presence of substrate that permits the inhibitor concentration to be varied over a reasonably wide range. The desired kinetic constants can be derived by the method of Hart and O'Brien (1973) or related ones (Tian and Tsou 1982; Walker and Elmore 1984). In many cases investigators are content to observe the inactivation without carrying out a kinetic characterization. To compare the reactivity of inhibitors, it is common to compare the inactivation rates they cause, that is the second-order rate constant derived from the experimental observations, $k_{app}/[I]$. Care should be taken to choose inhibitor concentrations at which saturation effects are not encountered, i.e. where the ratio, $k_{app}/[I]$, is more or less constant.

2B.2.2 Protein chemistry

Typically, active-site-directed irreversible inhibitors form covalent bonds in a stoichiometric manner with active enzyme (or subunit) on a particular amino acid side chain. These properties are best demonstrated with a radioactive inhibitor with which covalent bond formation and stoichiometry can be readily established. Determination of the nature and location of altered side-chains requires the generation of peptides and their fractionation, accompanied by radioactivity determination. This is most efficiently achieved in the study of an enzyme whose sequence is known. A structural analysis of native and modified enzymes may be carried out in parallel. Many such studies are cited below. The covalent bond introduced by the inhibitor must be stable enough to survive prolonged proteolytic digestions and fractionation procedures. With alkylated histidines, this is no problem. Alternatively, if an ester of glutamic or aspartic acid is generated by the inhibitor, it may be advisable to carry out a second derivatization. For example, the ester may be cleaved with hydroxylamine and the resultant hydroxamic acid degraded to diamino butyric or -propionic acid (Harris and Wilson 1983). Unanticipated cross-linking may occur—as in the case of triosephosphate isomerase inactivated by chloroacetol phosphate, in which the phosphate was later displaced by a tyrosine phenolic group—unless the carbonyl group of the reagent has first been reduced by borohydride (De La Mare *et al.* 1972). Thiol groups modified by affinity-labelling reagents of the sulphonyl fluoride type remain in an active form as thiolsulphonate esters, which may undergo intramolecular displacement with adjacent thiols, generating a disulphide bond (Colman 1983). Fortunately, these complications are not common.

2B.3   Specific acylation, sulphonylation, phosphorylation

2B.3.1   Prostaglandin synthetase

The anti-inflammatory action of aspirin has been traced to a selective acetylation of this enzyme (cyclooxygenase). The salicylic acid portion of the drug allows specific recognition by the enzyme and provides an active ester. The salicylic acid portion is not covalently transferred to the enzyme (Hack *et al.* 1984), whereas the acetyl portion is. The site of acetylation has been identified as a serine residue (Van der Ouderaa *et al.* 1980). An extended sequence of 22 amino acids encompassing this residue has been identified in the enzyme from the sheep vesicular gland and very likely consists of an active centre region of the enzyme (Roth *et al.* 1983).

2B.3.2   Serine proteinases

These function by covalent catalysis with temporary transfer of the carboxylic acid part of the susceptible peptide bond to the serine at the active centre. Normal acyl enzymes quickly hydrolyse. However, certain features may prolong the life of an acyl enzyme, such as steric hinderance to hydrolysis or lowered chemical reactivity.

The guanidino-benzoyl group (1) is analogous to an arginyl residue, and when introduced into trypsin-like enzymes from the nitrophenyl ester, undergoes a. slow deacylation for which the half-time, in the case of plasmin, is measured in hours (Chase and Shaw 1969), perhaps for steric reasons. Acrosin, a trypsin-like enzyme from sperm, is a target for irreversible inhibitors as a possible approach to contraception, since the active protease is required for fertilization. Active esters of guanidinobenzoate inactivate the protease in the intact acrosome (Muller-Esterl *et al.* 1983). Various phenols likely to be more physiologically tolerated than *p*-nitrophenol are under investigation (Kaminski *et al.* 1986), and these may be useful in other transfer reactions [cf. also acyl imidazoles (Walker and Elmore 1984)]. Deacylation is retarded for electronic reasons when an acyl residue is carbamate-derived. In peptide analogues, this may be taken advantage of by the use of aza-amino acids (2) (Elmore and Smyth 1968; Powers *et al.* 1977); cf. also acetylcholine esterase results as summarized by Aldridge and

Reiner (1972). A number of heterocyclic structures have been used to obtain acyl enzymes of a deactivated nature. For example, isatoic anhydride (3) stoichiometrically reacts with chymotrypsin, leading ultimately to anthraniloyl chymotrypsin (Moorman and Abeles 1982) but has no effect on trypsin. However, the 7-aminomethyl derivative satisfies the specificity of trypsin and related enzymes and inactivates the latter but not chymotrypsin (Gelb and Abeles 1986). The 1-benzyl derivative (4) is more specific and inactivates thrombin at inhibitor concentrations that have no effect on trypsin and plasmin. After 13 h at 25°C, 30 per cent of thrombin activity is restored by a slow deacylation.

2B.3.3 β-lactamase

This enzyme has a serine residue at the active centre and many inactivators function by stable acyl enzyme formation (Knott-Hunziker et al. 1982). In most cases, this is the result of changes that take place in the acyl residue after interaction with the enzyme, i.e. the inhibitors are mechanism-based (Fisher and Knowles 1980). However, the inactivation of TEM-1 β-lactamase by 6-acetyl-methylene penicillanic acid (5) may be a case of relatively stable acyl enzyme formation without additional alteration (Arisawa and Adam 1983).

The sulphonyl fluoride group was introduced into a number of substrates by Baker (1967) to anchor them to a side-chain adjacent to the active centre of an enzyme, not a catalytically important one. More recently this group has been extensively used as a means to link nucleotides covalently to binding sites on proteins. Thus, 5'-*p*-fluorosulphonyl-benzoyladenosine labels ATP and other nucleotide binding sites in a variety of enzymes, as reviewed by Colman (1983).

Selective phosphorylation has been little studied. However, Lamden and Bartlett (1983) reported the properties of phosphonic acid analogues of amino acids. For example, the phenylalanine analogue shown (6) was extremely effective in inactivating chymotrypsin.

2B.4   Displacement reactions

The most extensively used method of forming a covalent bond with an enzyme side-chain is by displacement of X from $-CH_2-CH_2X$, $-NH-\overset{\overset{O}{\|}}{C}-CH_2X$, or $-CH_2-\overset{\overset{O}{\|}}{C}-CH_2X$. X has most often been Br and, to a lesser extent, Cl. A great variety of applications of such reagents in affinity labelling have been made with purified enzymes. The simplicity of the system and the ability to control reaction conditions often permit a very selective labelling and provide useful structural information. Such results (some are given below) illustrate the versatility possible in developing active-site-directed enzyme inhibitors but neglect some features important in drug design. The more reactive bond-forming groups, such as bromomethyl ketone, are likely to invite many side-reactions in a complex cellular environment. Some recent attention has been given to the possibility of achieving alkylation by displacing fluoride ion from $-CH_2F$. Such a process is normally a very slow one and therefore not likely to be a source of side reactions, but perhaps may be susceptible to promotion by a proximity effect in affinity-labelling.

2B.4.1   Serine and cysteinyl proteinases

The properties of peptide-derived chloromethyl ketones have been well explored *in vitro* as inactivators of serine proteinases in which the peptide part can direct the reagent to proteases of different specificities such as chymotrypsin, trypsin, and elastase (see also Chapter 18C and D). Even within a class, for example trypsin-like proteinases, considerable selectivity can be achieved by variation in amino acid sequence (Kettner and Shaw 1981). The selectivity arises from variations in affinity in the reversible phase of action, which controls the amount of inhibitor–enzyme complex present. The rate of covalent bond formation, k_2, changes much less from one complex to another (Kettner and Shaw 1978). Protein chemistry indicates alkylation of the active centre histidine, as in (7). For

7   8   9

the purpose of enhancing affinity of the peptide portion, various extended side-chains not encountered in proteins may be helpful (Ganu and Shaw 1986; Walker *et al.* 1985). Chloromethyl ketones also inactivate thiol proteases (Bender and Brubacher 1966).

Peptidyl fluoromethyl ketones have not been available until recently due to earlier synthetic difficulties (Rasnick 1985; Rauber *et al.* 1986; Imperiali and Abeles 1986). In some cases mono-, di-, and trifluoro derivatives have been prepared (Imperiali and Abeles 1986). The expectation was that such derivatives might inhibit serine and thiol proteinases merely by forming a stable adduct without displacement, as in (**8**). Such adducts are formed by peptidyl aldehydes and thiol proteinases (Lowe and Nurse 1977) and were also encountered in the inactivation of acetylcholinesterase by a trifluoromethyl ketone derivative of a substrate analogue (Brodbeck *et al.* 1979). On the other hand, a displacement reaction might occur as with the chloro- and bromomethyl ketones. In the case of serine proteinases this is typically promoted by the active centre histidine residue (Schoellmann and Shaw 1962). The remainder of the inhibitor also has the final configuration of a hemiketal (**9**), involving the active centre serine. This was shown by the determination of the structure of the derivative formed on inactivation of substitution by Phe-Ala-LysCH$_2$Cl and other chloromethyl ketones in the crystallographic studies of Poulos *et al.* (1976). The formation of a similar structure on inactivation of trypsin by tos-LysCH$_2$Cl was revealed by n.m.r. studies (Malthouse *et al.* 1985). Hemiketal formation may precede the displacement reaction (McMurray and Dyckes 1986). It appears that the fluorinated inhibitors will fall into two groups, depending on the degree of substitution by fluorine. The di- and trifluoromethyl ketones form stable ad-ducts with serine proteases (Imperiali and Abeles 1986) and bind more tightly than the parent methyl ketones. Since they are hydrated, they could be viewed as transition-state analogues (see Chapter 2A). The monofluoro derivatives on the other hand undergo a displacement reaction. This was observed by Rauber *et al.* (1986) in the inactivation of chymotrypsin by Cbz–PheCH$_2$F, which provided a characteristic time-dependence of inactivation and loss of histidine. Similar findings were made by Imperiali and Abeles (1986). This work has been extended to trypsin and plasmin with Ala-Phe-LysCH$_2$F, which showed saturation kinetics, as expected, but in comparison with chloromethyl ketones the rate of covalent bond formation was about an order of magnitude slower. However, fluoromethyl ketones may provide useful reagents for the inactivation of serine proteinases *in vivo*, since their chemical reactivity is greatly reduced. The rate of alkylation of glutathione at pH 7.4, 37°C, is about 1/500th that of a chloromethyl ketone (Angliker *et al.* 1987).

In the case of the cysteinyl proteinases, the peptidyl fluoromethyl ketones have almost the same reactivity as the chloromethyl ketones (Rasnick 1985; Rauber *et al.* 1986), presumably due to the greater nucleophilicity of the thiol group compared with the histidine in serine proteinases. These side-chains are the sites of alkylation in the respective proteinase classes. Comparison of the rate of alkylation of the thiol group of glutathione with that obtained with enzyme by these fluoromethanes shows that a proximity effect within the enzyme–inhibitor complex is responsible for a rate enhancement of about 10^8.

2B.4.2 Triosephosphate dehydrogenase

Evidence that fluoride might be displaceable by protein side-chains was indicated by earlier work. Halohydroxyacetone phosphates with the general structure X—CH$_2$—$\overset{\displaystyle O}{\overset{\|}{C}}$—CH$_2OP_3^-$, analogues of dihydroxyacetonephosphate, inactivate triosephosphate dehydrogenase by formation of an ester bond with an active centre glutamate residue (Hartman 1971; De La Mare *et al.* 1972). The derivatives with X = I, Br or Cl, do not diminish in activity in that order presumably because the large bulk of the iodine atom at the enzyme surface increases the distance from the displacing carboxylate ion, an interesting difference between chemistry in solution and on a protein surface. This work was extended to the fluoro analogue by Silverman *et al.* (1975) and a slow inactivation of triosephosphate dehydrogenase was also observed, at about 0.1 per cent of the rate of the chloro analogue.

2B.4.3 Isopentyl diphosphate: dimethylallyl diphosphate isomerase

This enzyme is irreversibly inhibited by fluorinated derivatives of the substrates IPP (**10**) and DMAPP (**11**), which are allyl fluorides FIPP (**12**) and FDMAPP (**13**). The latter are rapid and effective inactivators for which the $k_{\text{inact.}}$ are 0.22 and 0.4 min^{-1} and K_i are 9×10^{-8} and 6×10^{-7} M—, respectively, at pH 7.0, 37°C (Muehlbacher and Poulter 1985). When radioactive forms of the inhibitors were used, the radioactivity remained attached to the protein under denaturing conditions. The chemistry remains to be clarified.

2B.4.4 Dihydrofolate reductase

Although available inhibitors bind tightly to this enzyme, partial enzyme function may supply product at a rate adequate to support growth. For improved antitumour action, irreversible inhibitors have been sought. The iodoacetyl-containing derivative (14) was tested as an inactivator of the enzyme from *Lactobacillus casei*. Crystallography reveals that a histidine in the side-chain binding region may be available for alkylation. The affinity of the analogue was high since a concentration of 4.5×10^{-9}M displaced 50 per cent of the labelled, enzyme-bound methotrexate. Irreversible alkylation was slow, $t_{1/2}$ being about 2 hs with 1×10^{-7}M inhibitor (Rosowsky *et al.* 1982). A smaller halogen might be more reactive (cf. triosephosphate isomerase above).

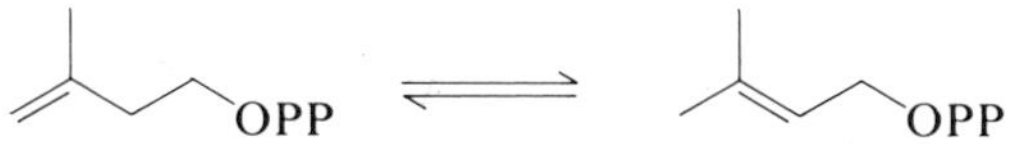

IPP

10

DMAPP

11

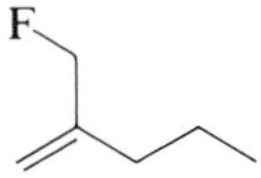

FIPP

12

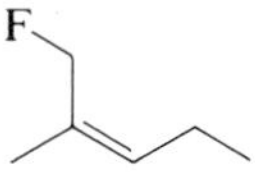

FDMAPP

13

An alkylating analogue of trimethoprim, that is 2,4-diamino-5-[3,5-dimethoxy-4(4-bromoacetamidophenylmethoxy)benzyl]pyrimidine (15) was only a reversible inhibitor of dihydrofolate reductase from *Escherichia coli* (Roth *et al.* 1981), but inactivated the enzyme from *Neisseria gonorrhoeae*, known to be different and with poor affinity for reversible inhibitors (Tansik *et al.* 1984). Thus alkylation offered a practical approach to effective inhibition. In the reversible phase K_i is 1×10^{-8}M. In the presence of NADPH, a time-dependent inactivation ensued, with $k_{app} = 0.025$ min^{-1}. Radio-labelled inhibitor showed a stoichiometric alkylation of His-25. An inhibitor which is irreversible for dihydrofolate from one source and reversible for another is an interesting example of specific inactivation.

2B.4.5 Chloramphenicol acetyltransferase

The antibiotic activity of chloramphenicol is destroyed by an enzymatic acetylation of its primary hydroxyl. This derivative spontaneously isomerizes to the

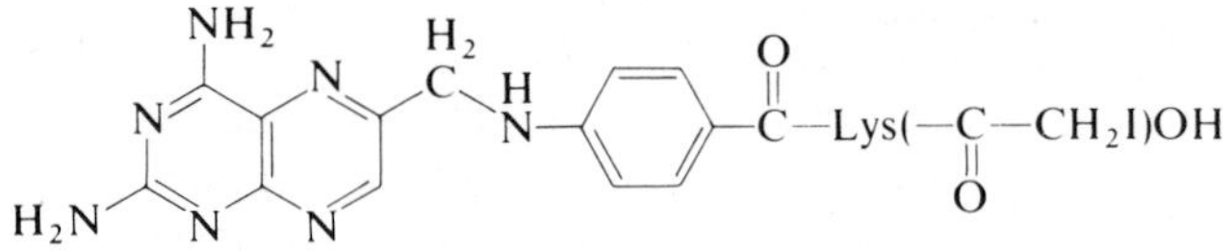

14

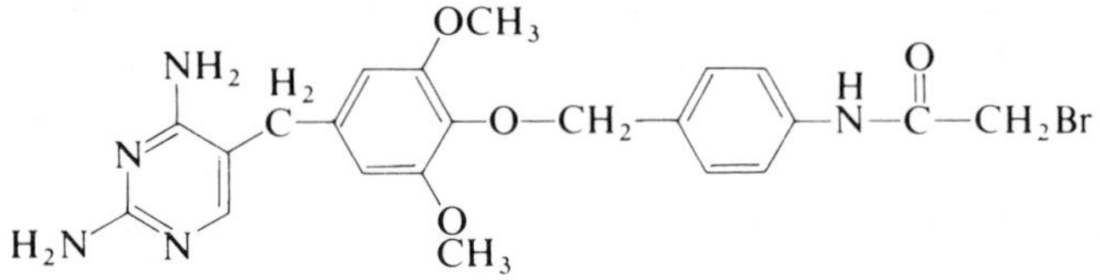

15

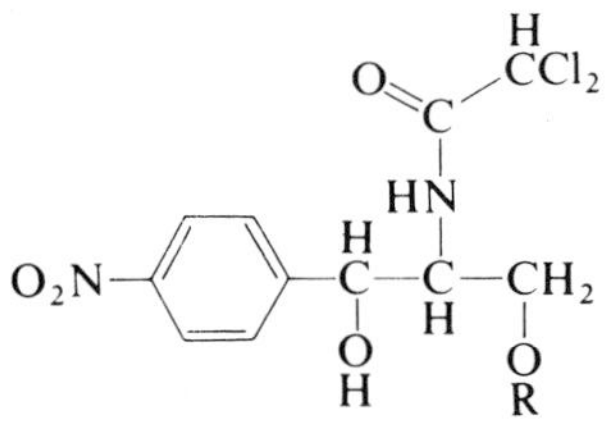

16

R = H—chloroamphenicol
R = bromoacetyl—inhibitor

acetate of the secondary hydroxyl and the primary one may be reacetylated (Shaw 1983). 3-(bromoacetyl)chloroamphenicol (**16**) was found to be a very effective affinity label for the transacetylase (Kleanthous *et al.* 1985). The second-order rate constant for the inactivation was 30×10^3 $M^{-1}s^{-1}$. The kinetic characteristics were not amenable to demonstration of complex formation, i.e. the action was rapid, and with an initial concentration of 0.24×10^{-6} M, $t_{1/2}$ was less than 2 min. However, protection by substrate leaves no doubt that the active centre of the enzyme was being irreversibly alkylated. It was shown that N_3 of His-189 was the site of reaction. Chloroamphenicol bromoacetate was somewhat unstable but was considered the prototype of a new class of agents of potential value in antibacterial chemotherapy with chloramphenicol, since the acetyltransferase is a product of resistant organisms.

2B.4.6　Fatty acid synthase

3-chloropropionyl-coenzyme A rapidly inactivates the synthase from rat mammary gland. Inhibitor labelled in either the chloropropionyl chain or the CoA phosphorus revealed that only the former was transferred to the enzyme, about one acyl group per active site (Miziorko *et al.* 1986). Evidence was obtained for a sequential reaction involving acylation (thioester formation) followed by an alkylation with displacement of Cl^-. This produced cross-linked protomers. Earlier haloacyl CoA analogues described probably suffered from too high a reactivity and non-specific alkylations.

2B.4.7 Oestradiol 17β-dehydrogenase

Oestradiol 17β-dehydrogenase from human placenta has been studied with a number of steroid bromoacetates that probe the active centre of the enzyme. 3-bromoacetoxy-oestrone and 12β-bromoacetoxy-4-oestrene-3,17-dione (Chin et al. 1982) label a histidine residue in the sequence Leu-Ala-His-Ser-Lys, thought to be in the region binding the A-ring of the steroid (Murdock et al. 1983). Other derivatives, such as 3-methoxyestriol-16-(bromoacetate), alkylate histidines in an adjacent peptide sequence which is considered to provide D-ring binding (Murdock et al. 1986). The inhibitors act very slowly but are being developed to obtain structural information rather than for eventual physiological use.

2B.4.8 Displacement of groups other than halide

Displacement of thiophenol derivatives from arylmercaptopurine nucleosides and nucleotides is indicated by the observations of Fasold et al. (1977).

2B.4.8.1 *ATPase* (F_1)

ATPase (F_1) is irreversibly inhibited by the reactive ATP analogue 6-[(3-carboxy-4-nitrophenyl)thio]-9β-D-ribofuranosylpurine 5'-triphosphate (Nbs^{6}ITP) by a combination of covalent and firmly bound inhibitor molecules (Hulla et al. 1978). The irreversible modification is thought to involve displacement by some group other than —SH (Koepsell et al. 1982).

2B.4.8.2 Δ^5-3-*oxosteroid isomerase*

The observations of Penning (1985) on the inactivation of Δ^5-3-oxosteroid isomerase (from *Pseudomonas testosteroni*) by 2-cyanoprogesterone suggest displacement of cyanide from a cyanoketone with properties of an active-site-directed process.

2B.5 Carbonyl compounds

Under displacement reactions, it was noted that carbonyl reactivity could be influenced by adjacent fluoro substituents. Displacement from monofluoro ketones was observed, but stable adducts were the end-product of di- and trifluoro methyl derivatives and serine proteases. Normally reversible carbonyl addition reactions may, in the case of enzymes, become essentially irreversible due to accumulated interactions that stabilize the product. The carbonyl-containing reagents may be hydrated and therefore possibly act as transition state analogues in some cases (see Chapter 2A).

Cleavage of ribosides and ribonucleotides having free 2′ and 3′ —OH groups with periodate provides a dialdehyde derivative often useful in affinity-labelling. Occasionally, reduction is necessary to obtain irreversibility (Colman 1983), but not always.

2B.5.1   6-phosphogluconate dehydrogenase

This enzyme is strongly inhibited in a time-dependent manner by the dialdehyde from NADP with $K_i = 3 \times 10^{-6}$ M, but not from NAD (Rippa *et al.* 1975), the inhibition being reversed by dilution.

2B.5.2   *S*-adenosylhomocysteine hydrolase

SAHase is stoichiometrically inactivated by oxidized adenosine, $K_i = 2.4 \times 10^{-9}$ M, and activity is not reversed by dialysis unless amine-containing buffers are used (Patel-Thombre and Borchardt 1985).

2B.5.3   Succinyl CoA synthetase

This enzyme is irreversibly inactivated by oxidized ADP and remains so in spite of dialysis (Nishimura *et al.* 1983).

2B.5.4   Dihydrofolate reductase

Johanson and Henken (1985) took note of the presence of arginines near the binding region for the *p*-aminobenzoyl-Glu bond in the crystal structures of the reductases from *E. coli* and *L. casei*. Predictions could be made from computer graphic modelling in which arginine in the enzyme from either source would combine with the glyoxal-containing analogue (**17**). This behaved as an active-site-directed ligand, modifying the arginines as predicted (in borate buffer). Although not of therapeutic application, this study is an encouraging model.

2B.6   Diazomethyl ketones

2B.6.1   Amido transferases

The diazomethyl ketone group as an alkylating function for enzymes was first appreciated in the work of Buchanan (1973) on the mechanism of action of the antibiotic azaserine, which was shown to be a glutamine analogue. An essential —SH group of an amido transferase involved in purine biosynthesis is alkylated by azaserine.

2B.6.2   Cysteinyl proteinases

Diazomethyl ketones derived from peptides are very effective inactivators of this class of proteases. First observed with papain and Cbz-PheCHN$_2$ (Leary *et al.* 1977), it has been shown by Green and Shaw (1981) that among proteases, only members of the cysteinyl class are inactivated and that alterations in the peptide portion greatly influence selectivity. Some derivatives at nanomolar concentrations inactivate cathepsin B (Shaw *et al.* 1983).

2B.7   Epoxides

2B.7.1   Carnitine palmitoyl transferase

2-tetradecylglycidic acid, TDGA (**18**) has been developed (Tutwiler *et al.* 1981) as an inhibitor of fatty acid oxidation acting on carnitine palmitoyltransferase,

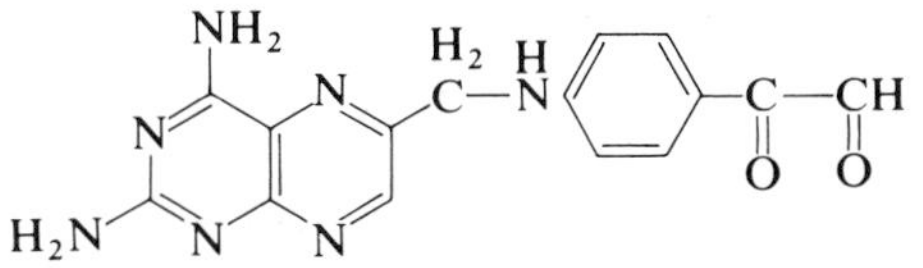

17

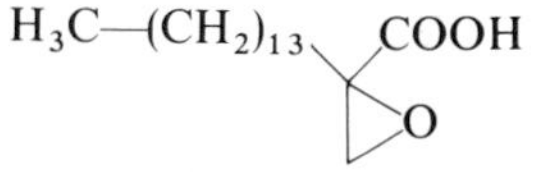

18

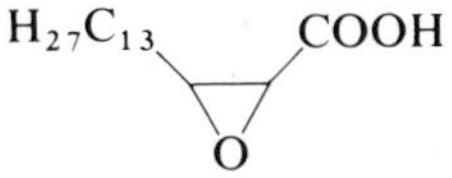

19

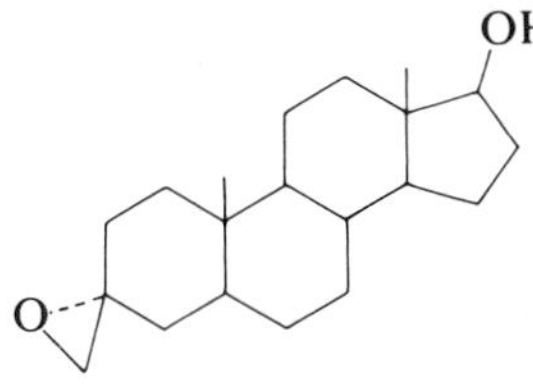

20

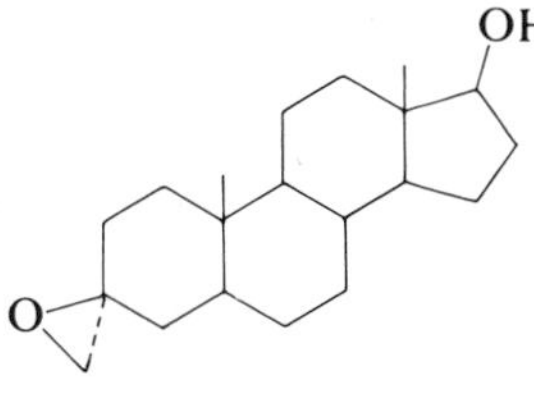

α

21

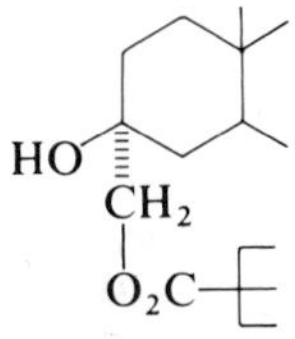

β

22

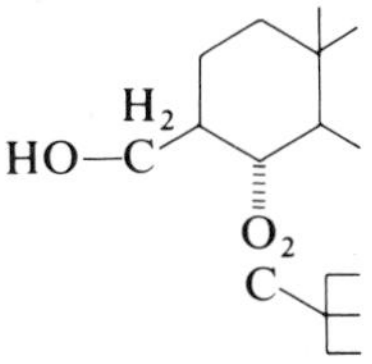

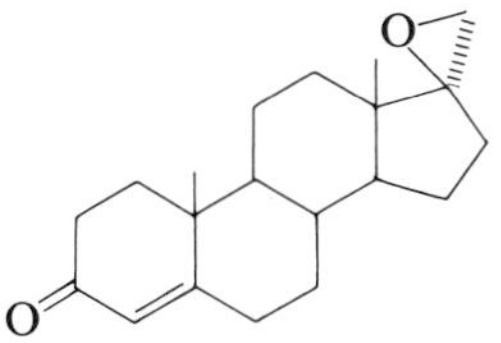

24

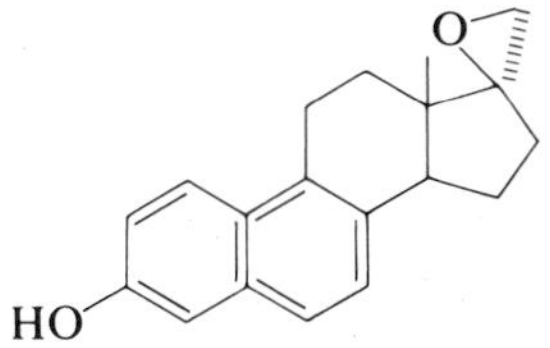

25

23

which catalyses the formation of palmitoyl carnitine from palmitoyl CoA and carnitine. This enzyme is thought to be a regulatory site for control of fatty acid oxidation. TDGA is converted to the acyl-CoA analogue by acyl-CoA synthases and this product inactivates carnitine palmitoyl transferase from rat liver mitochondria (Kiorpes *et al.* 1984). The K_i value is about 3×10^{-7} M. This mechanism is thought to account for the *in vivo* hypoglycaemic action of TDGA, since the repression of fatty acid oxidation may stimulate glucose utilization. The related structure (19) is not converted to a CoA derivative and lacks hypoglycaemic action. Covalent bond formation to a protein but not yet to a particular amino acid has been demonstrated.

2B.7.2 Δ^5-3-ketosteroid isomerase

The enzyme from *Pseudomonas testosteroni* has been the target of steroidal oxiranes as irreversible inhibitors. The enzyme catalyses a migration of the double bond to the Δ^5 position. The α-isomer of spiro-3-oxiranyl-5α-androstan-17β-ol (20) is a competitive inhibitor of the enzyme, with $K_i = 21$ μM but the β-isomer (21) causes a time-dependent inactivation with a K_i value of 1.7×10^{-5} M (Pollack *et al.* 1979), and 1.13 mol of inhibitor becomes bound per monomer subunit (Bevins *et al.* 1984). Two peptides were obtained on tryptic digest in similar amounts, each with a different derivative of the inhibitor bound by an ester linkage. Two steroid derivatives were identified after hydrolysis, indicating that inactivation had resulted in the formation of the two esters shown (22, 23; E = enzyme). The free alcohol group contains the epoxide oxygen atom. Each peptide portion was the same, from the N-terminal region, and Asp-38 was the likely altered side-chain.

Similar observations were made with 17β-oxiranes (Bevins *et al.* 1980) as stoichiometric inactivators of Δ^5-3-ketosteroid isomerase. With (24), comparable amounts of tryptic peptides with ester-bound steroid were obtained, originating from Asp-38 (Kayser *et al.* 1983). In inactivation by (25), the proportions of derivatives formed were unequal, that is 9:1 (Bantia *et al.* 1985). Asp-38 was shown to be involved in the major ester. The structure of the steroid derivatives liberated from the peptide form indicated that the alpha side of the steroid was interacting with the enzyme, as in the case of the 3β-oxiranes described above, suggesting that the steroid derivatives have two binding modes. Since the enzymatic reaction involves the A ring, affinity-labelling by the 3-β-oxiranes is rational, but the action of the 17β-oxiranes must involve 'backward binding' to account for esterification of the same aspartic acid by both reagents.

2B.7.3   Cysteinyl proteinases

A natural product, E-64, isolated from mould as a thiol proteinase inhibitor, has been shown by Hanada *et al.* (1978) to be the epoxide, *N*-[*N*-(L-trans carboxyoxiran-2-carbonyl)-L-leucyl]agmatine (26). The epoxide group is responsible for a rapid irreversible and stoichiometric inactivation of lysosomal thiol proteinases (Barrett *et al.* 1982), as well as calcium-activated thiol proteinases (Parkes *et al.* 1985). In both cases E-64 can be used as an enzyme titrant. The peptidyl portion may be varied by synthesis (Tamai *et al.* 1981), with

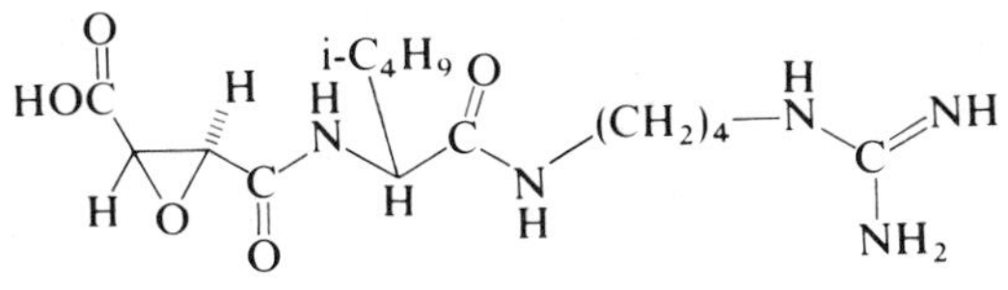

26

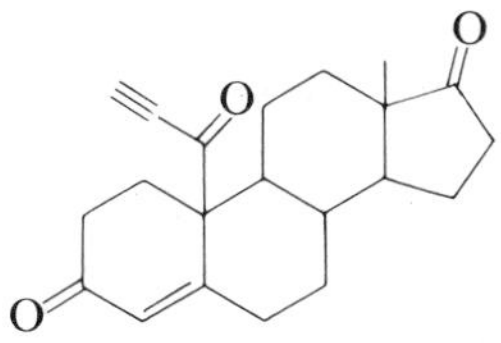

27

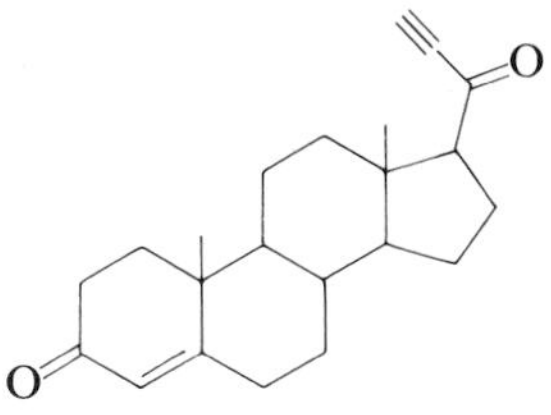

28

modulation of activity, undoubtedly promoting binding to the proteinase active centre, probably to the part referred to as the 'departing group' region.

2B.8 Unsaturation

N-ethylmaleimide has long been used as a diagnostic reagent in enzymology to detect an essential —SH group due to rapid, irreversible addition across the double bond. Occasionally, other side-chains found in proteins react. Proximity effects could readily promote this type of result. A triple bond in conjugation can also participate in Michael additions (Diapoh and Olomucki 1982).

2B.8.1 Δ^5-3-oxosteroid isomerase

The enzyme from *P. testosteroni* is inactivated by the keto-acetylene containing steroids (**27**) and (**28**) (Penning *et al.* 1981). For (**27**), K_i is 6.6×10^{-5} M and k_2 is 12.5×10^{-3} s^{-1}. For compound (**28**), $K_i = 1.45 \times 10^{-5}$ M, but k_2 is only 0.13×10^{-3} s^{-1}. The chemistry of the reaction has not been clarified.

2B.8.2 $17\beta,20\alpha$-hydroxysteroid dehydrogenase

The acetylenic ketone (**27**) was also studied with this enzyme from human placenta, for which it is a substrate in the presence of NADH (Tobias *et al.* 1982). However, in the absence of the cofactor, it covalently inactivates in a process for which K_i is 1.9×10^{-4} M and k_2 is 9.5×10^{-2} s^{-1} at pH 9.2. The enzyme has two activities; it is a 17β-oestradiol dehydrogenase and a 20α-hydroxysteroid dehydrogenase. Both activities were lost simultaneously during affinity-labelling. The α-isomer of the acetylenic alcohol corresponding to (**28**) was oxidized by the enzyme if NAD$^+$ was present, generating the affinity alkylator and producing a slow inactivation.

In another study, this enzyme was shown to convert 16-methylene oestradiol to 16-methylene oestrone. This unsaturated ketone inactivates the enzyme rather slowly at pH 7, but more rapidly at pH 9.2. At the highest pH, a stoichiometric reaction was found, with $K_i = 2.61 \times 10^{-4}$ M and $k_2 = 8 \times 10^{-4}$ s^{-1}. 16-methylene oestradiol thus generates the affinity-labelling ketone enzymatically in the presence of NAD$^+$ (Thomas *et al.* 1985).

2B.9　Modification of —SH groups by disulphide exchange and analogous displacements

The conversion of a catalytically essential thiol group to an inactive disulphide by an exchange reaction,

$$E{-}SH + R{-}S{-}S{-}R' \rightleftharpoons E{-}S{-}S{-}R + HS{-}R' \qquad (2B.2)$$

is amenable to active-site-directed facilitation as shown below. Since the reaction is reversible by thiols, it may look unpromising for drug design. However, it should be rewarding to study structural features that diminish reversibility or that provide high affinity as a means of obtaining essentially irreversible inactivations.

2B.9.1　Cyclic AMP-dependent protein kinase

The presence of thiol groups on the catalytic subunit possibly involved in the catalysis mechanism suggested the synthesis of a reagent capable of a specific disulphide exchange reaction. A peptide analogous to the region of substrate containing a serine to be phosphorylated was synthesized, but the serine residue was replaced by a half-cysteine residue activated as the 3-nitro-2-pyridine-sulphenyl derivative (Bramson *et al.* 1982). The latter was displaced by the kinase and the peptide portion became attached as anticipated. One of the reagents had $K_i = 4 \times 10^{-5}$ M and $k_2 = 0.25$ s^{-1}.

2B.9.2　CoA-dependent enzymes

The disulphide of CoA inactivates these enzymes, but on oxidation of the disulphide a more reactive form of the reagent was obtained, a thiosulfonate, which has a better departing group (Nishimura *et al.* 1982). This derivative was shown to be effective in forming a mixed disulphide with clostridial phospho-transacetylase and pigeon muscle carnitine acetyltransferase. A similar derivative, but employing a more reactive departing group, the alkoxycarbonylthio-, has been used to inactivate malate thiokinase (Hersh and Surendranather 1982). A somewhat different approach using a less reactive derivative is instructive. S-dimethylarsino-CoA is not strictly a disulphide derivative, but the —S—As— bond is cleaved by thiol groups. The CoA analogue inactivates phosphotransacetylase but not carnitine acetyltransferase, nor citrate synthetase (Duhr *et al.* 1983). From model reactions and the use of labelled reagents, it was concluded that in this case the dimethylarsino group was transferred to the enzyme, not the coenzyme portion of the reagent. Reactivation was not possible with mercaptoethanol or other thiols.

2B.10 Concluding comments

The results described in the limited selection above, obtained with a variety of enzyme targets, demonstrate the ability of chemists to design reagents that covalently inactivate, usually in a stoichiometric combination. These studies have been largely carried out with purified enzymes and therefore the possibilities for side-reactions were not so great as they would be in a biological environment containing a much higher concentration of nucleophiles. For *in vivo* applications it seems advisable to concentrate on the development of reagents with a greatly diminished reactivity that can be enhanced by the proximity effects produced within enzyme–inhibitor complexes. This may require, in some cases, a better geometrical fit to improve proximity and thus to develop the highest potential of affinity labelling.

References

Abeles, R. H. and Maycock, A. L. (1976). Suicide enzyme inactivators. *Acc. Chem. Res.*, **9**, 313–19.

Aldridge, W. N. and Reiner, E. eds. (1972). Kinetics of reaction of β-esterases with carbamates. In *Enzyme inhibitors as substrates*. Chapter 8, pp. 123–45. North-Holland, Amsterdam.

Angliker, H., Wikstrom, P., Rauber, P., and Shaw, E. (1987). The synthesis of lysyl fluoromethanes and their properties as inhibitors of trypsin, plasmin, and cathepsin B. *Biochem. J.*, **241**, 871–5.

Arisawa, M. and Adam, S. (1983). Mechanism of inactivation of β-lactamase by 6-acetylmethylene penicillanic acid. *Biochem. J.*, **211**, 447–54.

Baker, B. R. (1967). *Design of active-site-directed irreversible enzyme inhibitors*. Wiley, New York.

Bantia, S., Bevins, C. L., and Pollack, R. M., (1985). Mechanism of inactivation of 3-oxosteroid Δ^5-isomerase by 17β-oxiranes. *Biochemistry*, **24**, 2606–9.

Barrett, A. J., Kembhavi, A. A., Brown, M. A., Kirschke, H., Knight, C. G., Tamai, M., and Hanada, K. (1982). L-*trans*-epoxysuccinyl-leucylamido (4-guanidino)butane (E-64) and its analogues as inhibitors of cysteine proteinases including cathepsins B, H, and L. *Biochem. J.*, **201**, 189–98.

Bender, M. and Brubacher, L. J. (1966). The kinetics and mechanism of papain-catalyzed hydrolyses. *J. Am. Chem. Soc.*, **88**, 5880–9.

Bevins, C. L., Kayser, R. H., Pollack, R. M., Ekiko, D. B., and Sadoff, S. (1980). Irreversible active-site-directed inhibition of Δ^5-3-keto-steroid isomerase by steroidal 17-β-oxiranes. Evidence for two modes of binding in steroid–enzyme complexes. *Biochem. Biophys. Res. Commun.*, **95**, 1131–7.

Bevins, C. L., Bantia, S., Pollack, R. M., Bounds, P. L. and Kayser, R. H. (1984). Modification of an enzyme carboxylate residue in the inhibition of 3-oxo-Δ^5-steroid isomerase by (3S)-spiro[5-androstane-3,2′-oxirane]-17β-ol. Implications for the mechanism of action. *J. Am. Chem. Soc.*, **106**, 4957–62.

Brodbeck, U., Schweik, R. Gentinetta, M. and Rottenburg, M. (1979). Fluorinated aldehydes and ketones acting as quasi-substrate inhibitors of acetylcholinesterase. *Biochim. Biophys. Acta*, **567**, 357–69.

Bramson, H. N., Thomas, N., Matsueda, R, Nelson, N. C., Taylor, S. S., and Kaiser, E. T. (1982). Modification of the catalytic subunit of bovine heart cAMP-dependent protein kinase with affinity labels related to peptide substrates. *J. Biol. Chem.*, **257**, 10575–81.

Buchanan, J. M. (1973). The amidotransferases. *Adv. Enzymol.*, **39**, 91–183.

Chase, T. Jr. and Shaw, E. (1969). Comparison of the esterase activities of trypsin, plasmin, and thrombin on guanidinobenzoate esters. Titration of the enzymes. *Biochemistry*, **8**, 2214–24.

Chin. C.-C., Murdock, G. L., and Warren, J. C. (1982). Identification of two histidyl residues in the active site of human placental estradiol 17β-dehydrogenase. *Biochemistry*, **21**, 3322–6.

Colman, R. F. (1983). Affinity labeling of purine nucleotide sites in proteins. *Ann. Rev. Biochem.*, **52**, 67–91.

De La Mare, S., Coulson, A. F. W., Knowles, J. R., Priddle, J. D., and Offord, R. E. (1972). Active-site labeling of triose phosphate isomerase. The reaction of bromohydroxyacetone phosphate with a unique glutamic residue and the migration of the label to tyrosine. *Biochem. J.*, **129**, 321–31.

Diapoh, J. and Olomucki, M. (1982). The use of the acetylenic function for direct chemical modification of proteins. *Bioorg. Chem.*, **11**, 463–77.

Duhr, E. F., Owens, M. S., and Barden, R. E. (1983). Irreversible inhibition of phosphotransacetylase by *S*-dimethylarsino-CoA. *Biochim. Biophys. Acta*, **749**, 84–90.

Elmore, D. T. and Smyth, J. J. (1968). A new method of determining the absolute molarity of solutions of trypsin and chymotrypsin by using *p*-nitrophenyl N^2-acetyl-N^1-benzylcarbazate. *Biochem. J.*, **107**, 103–7.

Fasold, H., Hulla, F. W., Ortanderl, F. and Rack, M. (1977). Aromatic thioethers of purine nucleotides. *Meth. Enzymol.*, **46**, 289–95.

Fisher, J. F. and Knowles, J. R. (1980). The inactivation of β-lactamase by mechanism-based reagents, in *Enzyme inhibitors as drugs* (ed. M. Sandler), pp. 209–18. Macmillan, London.

Ganu, V. and Shaw, E. (1987). Improved inactivators of plasmin. *Thrombosis Res.*, **45**, 1–6.

Gelb, M. H. and Abeles, R. H. (1986). Substituted isatoic anhydrides: selective inactivators of trypsin-like serine proteases. *J. Med. Chem.*, **29**, 585–9.

Green, G. D. J. and Shaw, E. (1981). Peptidyl diazomethyl ketones are specific inactivators of thiol proteinases. *J. Biol. Chem.*, **256**, 1923–8.

Hack, N., Carey, F., and Crawford, N. (1984). The inhibition of platelet cyclo-oxygenase by aspirin is associated with the acetylation of a 72kDa polypeptide in the intracellular membranes. *Biochem. J.*, **223**, 105–111.

Hanada, K., Tamai, M., Ohmura, S., Sawada, J., Seki, T., and Tanaka. I. (1978). Studies on thiol protease inhibitors. Part II. Structure and synthesis of E-64, a new thiol protease inhibitor. *Agric. Biol. Chem.*, **42**, 529–36.

Harris, R. B. and Wilson, I. B. (1983). Glutamic acid is an active site residue of angiotensin I-converting enzyme. *J. Biol. Chem.*, **258**, 1357–62.

Hart, G. J. and O'Brien, R. D. (1973). Recording spectrophotometric method for determination of dissociation and phosphorylation constants for the inhibition of acetylchlolinesterase by organophosphates in the presence of substrate. *Biochemistry*, **12**, 2940–45.

Hartman, F. C. (1971). Haloacetol phosphates. Characterization of the active site of rabbit muscle triose phosphate isomerase. *Biochemistry*, **10**, 146–54.

Hersh, L. B. and Surendranather, K. K. (1982). Reaction of malate thiokinase with methoxycarbonyl-CoA disulphide. *J. Biol. Chem.*, **257**, 11633–8.

Hulla, F. W., Hockel, M., Rack, M., Risi, S., and Dose, K. (1978). Characterization and affinity labeling of nucleotide binding sites of bacterial plasma membrane adenosine triphosphatase (F$_1$). *Biochemistry*, **17**, 823–8.

Imperiali, B. and Abeles, R. H. (1986). Inhibition of serine proteases by peptidyl fluoromethyl ketones. *Biochemistry*, **25**, 3760–7.

Jakoby, W. B. and Wilchek, M. (eds.) (1977). Affinity labeling, *Methods in Enzymology*, Vol. 46, Academic Press, New York.

Johanson, R. A. and Henkin, J. (1985). Affinity labelling of dihydrofolate reductase with an antifolate glyoxal. *J. Biol. Chem.*, **260**, 1465–74.

Kaminski, J. M., Bauer, L., Mack, S. R., Anderson, R. A., Jr., Waller, D. P., and Zaneveld, L. J. D. (1986). Synthesis and inhibition of human acrosin and acute toxicity of aryl 4-guanidinobenzoates. *J. Med. Chem.*, **29**, 514–19.

Kayser, R. H., Bounds, P. L., Bevins, C. L., and Pollack, R. M. (1983). Affinity alkylation of bacterial Δ^5-3-ketosteroid isomerase. *J. Biol. Chem.*, **258**, 909–15.

Kettner, C. and Shaw, E. (1978). The synthesis of peptides of arginine chloromethyl ketone. The selective inactivation of plasma kallikrein. *Biochemistry*, **17**, 4778–84.

Kettner, C. and Shaw, E. (1981). Inactivation of trypsin-like enzymes with peptides of arginine chloromethyl ketone, in *Meth. Enzymol.*, **80**, 826–41.

Kiorpes, T. C., Hoerr, D., Ho, W., Weaner, L. E., Inman, M. G., and Tutwiler, G. F. (1984). Identification of 2-tetradecylglycidyl coenzyme A as the active form of methyl 2-tetradecylglycidate (methyl palmoxirate) and its characterization as an irreversible, active site-directed inhibitor of carnitine palmitoyltransferase A in isolated rat liver mitochondria. *J. Biol. Chem.*, **259**, 9750–5.

Kitz, R. and Wilson, I. B. (1962). Esters of methanesulfonic acid as irreversible inhibitors of acetylcholinesterase. *J. Biol. Chem.*, **237**, 3245–9.

Kleanthous, C., Cullis, P. M., and Shaw, W. (1985). 3-(bromoacetyl)-chloramphenicol, an active site directed inhibitor for chloramphenicol acetyltransferase. *Biochemistry*, **24**, 5307–13.

Knott-Hunziker, V. Peturson, S., Jayatilake, G. S., Waley, S. G., Jaurin, B., and Grunstrom, T. (1982). Active sites of β-lactamases. *Biochem. J.*, **201**, 621–7.

Koepsell, H., Hulla, F. W. and Fritzsch, G. (1982). Different classes of nucleotide binding sites in the (Na$^+$ + K$^+$)-ATPase studied by affinity labelling and nucleotide-dependent SH-group modifications. *J. Biol. Chem.*, **257**, 10733–41.

Lamden, L. A. and Bartlett, P. A. (1983). Aminoalkylphosphonofluoridate derivatives. *Biochem. Biophys. Res. Commun.*, **112**, 1085–90.

Leary, R., Larsen, D., Watanabe, H. and Shaw, E. (1977). Diazomethyl ketone substrate derivatives as active-site-directed inhibitors of thiol proteases. *Biochemistry*, **16**, 5857–61.

Lowe, G. and Nurse, D. (1977). Evidence for hemiacetal formation between α-chymotrypsin and hydrocinnamaldehyde by cross-saturation nuclear magnetic resonance spectroscopy. *J. Chem. Soc. Chem. Commun.*, 815–816.

McCurray, J. S. and Dyckes, D. F. (1986). Evidence for hemiketals as intermediates in the inactivation of serine proteinases with halomethyl ketones. *Biochemistry*, **25**, 2298–2301.

Malthouse, J. P. G., Primrose, W. U., MacKenzie, N. E. and Scott, A. I. (1985). ^{13}C NMR study of the ionizations within a trypsin–chloromethyl ketone inhibitor complex. *Biochemistry*, **24**, 3478–87.

Miziorko, H. M., Behnke, C. E., Ahmad, P. M., and Ahmad, F. (1986). Active site directed inactivation of rat mammary gland fatty acid synthase by 3-chloropropionyl coenzyme A. *Biochemistry*, **25**, 468–73.

Moorman, A. R. and Abeles, R. H. (1982). A new class of serine protease inactivators based on isatoic anhydride. *J. Am. Chem. Soc.*, **104**, 6785–6.

Muehlbacher, M. and Poulter, C. D. (1985). Isopentenyl diphosphate: dimethylallyl diphosphate isomerase. Irreversible inhibition of the enzyme by active-site-directed covalent attachment. *J. Am. Chem. Soc.*, **107**, 8307–8.

Muller-Esterl, W., Wendt, V., Leidl, W., Dann, O., Shaw, E., Wagner, G., and Fritz, H. (1983). Intra-acrosomal inhibition of boar acrosin by synthetic proteinase inhibitors *J. Reprod. Fert.*, **67**, 13–18.

Murdock, G. L., Chin, C.-C., Offord, R. E., Bradshaw, R. A., and Warren, J. C. (1983). Human placental estradiol 17β-dehydrogenase. Identification of a single histidine residue affinity-labeled by both 3-bromo-acetoxyestrone and 12-bromoacetoxy-4-estrene-3,17-dione. *J. Biol. Chem.*, **258**, 11460–4.

Murdock, G. L., Chin, C. -C., and Warren, J. C. (1986). Human placental estradiol 17β-dehydrogenase; sequence of a histidine-bearing peptide in the catalytic region *Biochemistry*, **25**, 641–6.

Nishimura, J. S., Mitchell, T, Hill, K. A., and Collier, G. E. (1982). Coenzyme A thiosulfonate (coenzyme A disulfide-*S,S*-dioxide), an affinity analog of coenzyme A. *J. Biol. Chem.*, **257**, 14896–902.

Nishimura, J. S., Mitchell, T., Collier, G. E., Matula, J. M., and Ball, D. J. (1983). Affinity labeling of succinyl-CoA synthetase from *Escherichia coli* by the 2′,3′-dialdehyde derivative of adenosine 5′-diphosphate. *Eur. J. Biochem.*, **136**, 83–7.

Ong, E. B., Shaw, E., and Schoellmann, G. (1965). The identification of the histidine residue at the active center of chymotrypsin. *J. Biol. Chem.*, **240**, 694–8.

Parkes, C., Kembhavi, A. A., and Barrett, A. J. (1985). Calpain inhibition by peptide epoxides. *Biochem. J.*, **230**, 509–16.

Patel-Thombre, U. and Borchardt, R. T. (1985). Adenine nucleoside dialdehydes: potent inhibitors of bovine liver *S*-adenosylhomocysteine hydrolase. *Biochemistry*, **24**, 1130–36.

Penning, T. M. (1985). Irreversible inhibition of Δ^5-3-oxosteroid isomerase by 2-substituted progesterones. *Biochem. J.*, **226**, 469–76.

Penning, T. M., Covey, D. F., and Talalay, P. (1981). Inactivation of Δ^5-3-oxo steroid isomerase with active-site-directed acetylenic steroids. *Biochem. J.*, **193**, 217–27.

Pollack, R. M., Kayser, R. H., and Bevins, C. L. (1979). An active-site-directed irreversible inhibitor of Δ^5-3-ketosteroid isomerase. *Biochem. Biophys. Res. Commun.*, **91**, 783–90.

Poulos, T. L., Alden, R. A., Freer, S. T., Birktoft, J. J., and Kraut, J. (1976). Polypeptide halomethyl ketones bind to serine proteases as analogs of the tetrahedral intermediate. *J. Biol. Chem.*, **251**, 1097–103.

Powers, J. C., Gupton, B. F., Harley, A. D., Nishino, N., and Whitley, R. J. (1977). Specificity of porcine pancreatic elastase, human leukocyte elastase, cathepsin G. Inhibition with peptide chloromethyl ketones. *Biochim. Biophys. Acta*, **485**, 156–6.

Rasnick, D. (1985). Synthesis of peptide fluoromethyl ketones and the inhibition of human cathepsin B. *Anal. Biochem.*, **149**, 461–5.

Rauber, P., Angliker, H., Walker, B. and Shaw, E. (1986). The synthesis of peptidylfluoromethanes and their properties as inhibitors of serine proteinases and cysteinyl proteinases. *Biochem. J.*, **239**, 633–40.

Rippa, M., Signorini, M., Signori, R., and Dallocchio, F. (1975). A new powerful inhibitor specific for the TPN binding site of 6-phosphogluconate dehydrogenase. *FEBS Lett.*, **51**, 281–3.

Rosowsky, A., Wright, J. E., Ginty, C., and Uren, J. (1982). Methotrexate analogues. 15. A methotrexate analog designed for active-site-directed irreversible inactivation of dihydrofolate reductase. *J. Med. Chem.*, **25**, 960–4.

Roth, B., Aig, E., Rauckman, B. S., Strelitz, J. Z., Phillips, A. P., Ferone, R., Bushby, S. R. M., and Sigel, C. W. (1981). 2,4-diamino-5-benzylpyrimidines and analogues as antibacterial agents. 5. 3′,5′-dimethoxy-4′-substituted-benzyl analogues of trimethoprim. *J. Med. Chem.*, **24**, 933–41.

Roth, G. J., Machuga, E. T., and Ozols, J. (1983). Isolation and structure of the aspirin-modified, active-site region of prostaglandin synthetase. *Biochemistry*, **22**, 4672–5.

Schoellmann, G. and Shaw, E. (1962). A new method for labeling the active center of chymotrypsin. *Biochem. Biophys. Res. Commun.*, **7**, 36–40.

Shaw, E. (1970). The selective chemical modification of proteins. *Physiol. Rev.*, **50**, 244–96.

Shaw, E., Wikstrom, P., and Ruscica, J. (1983). An exploration of the primary specificity site of cathepsin B. *Arch. Biochem. Biophys.*, **222**, 424–9.

Shaw, W. V. (1983). Chloramphenicol acetyltransferase: enzymology and molecular biology. *CRC Crit. Rev. Biochem.*, **14**, 1–46.

Silverman, J. B., Babiarz, P. S., Mahajan, K. P., Buschek, J., and Fondy, T. P. (1975). 1-Halo analogs of dihydroxyacetone 3-phosphate. The effects of the fluoro analog on cytosolic glycerol-3-phosphate dehydrogenase and triosephosphate isomerase. *Biochemistry*, **14**, 2252–8.

Tamai, M., Hanada, K., Adachi, T., Oguma, K., Kashiwagi, K., Ohmura, S., and Ohzeki, M. (1981). Papain inhibitions by optically active E-64 analogs. *J. Biochem. (Tokyo)*, **90**, 225–57.

Tansik, R. L., Averett, D. R., Roth, B., Paterson, S. J., Stone, D., and Baccanari, D. P. (1984). Species-specific irreversible inhibition of *Neisseria gonorrhoeae* dihydrofolate reductase by a substituted 2,4-diamino-5-benzylpyrimidine. *J. Biol. Chem.*, **259**, 12299–305.

Thomas, J. L., LaRochelle, M. C., Asibey-Berko, E., and Strickler, R. C. (1985). Reactivation of human placental 17β,20α-hydroxysteroid dehydrogenase affinity alkylated by estrone 3-(bromoacetate): topographic studies with 16α-(bromoacetoxy)estradiol 3-(methyl ether). *Biochemistry*, **24**, 5361–7.

Tian, W.-X. and Tsou, C.-L. (1982). Determination of the rate constant of enzyme modification by measuring the substrate reaction in the presence of the modifier. *Biochemistry*, **21**, 1028–32.

Tobias, B., Covey, D. F. and Strickler, R. (1982). Inactivation of human placental 17β-estradiol dehydrogenase and 20α-hydroxysteroid dehydrogenase with active site-directed 17β-propynyl-substituted progestin analogs. *J. Biol. Chem.*, **257**, 2783–86.

Tutwiler, G. F., Ho, W., and Mohrbacher, R. J. (1981). 2-tetradecylglycidic acid., *Meth. Enzymol.*, **72**, 533–51.

Van der Ouderaa, F. J., Buytenhek, M., Nugteren, D. H., and Van Dorp, D. A. (1980). Acetylation of prostaglandin endoperoxide synthetase with acetylsalicylic acid. *Eur. J. Biochem.*, **109**, 1–8.

Walker, B. and Elmore, D. T. (1984). The irreversible inhibition of urokinase, kidney-cell plasminogen activator, plasmin and β-trypsin by 1-(N-6-amino-n-hexyl)carbamoylimidazole. *Biochem. J.*, **221**, 277–80.

Walker, B., Wikstrom, P., and Shaw, E. (1985). Evaluation of inhibitor constants and alkylation rates for a series of thrombin affinity labels. *Biochem. J.*, **230**, 645–50.

Walsh, C. T. (1984). Suicide substrates, mechanism-based enzyme inactivators: recent developments. *Ann. Rev. Biochem.*, **53**, 493–535.

2C.1   Introduction

A mechanism-based enzyme inhibitor is a compound that is not intrinsically highly reactive but is converted by a specific enzyme to a reactive species, which then reacts with a group on its surface leading to irreversible inhibition. Such inhibitors differ from active-site-directed inhibitors (see Chapter 2B) in that their reactivity results from a specific transformation effected by the enzyme itself, whereas in active-site-directed inhibition the enzyme is assumed to play an essentially passive role after the formation of the enzyme–inhibitor complex. Mechanism-based inhibition can also be distinguished from lethal synthesis mechanisms, in which an enzyme catalyses the formation of a product which then acts as an inhibitor of another enzyme.

The interaction of an enzyme with a mechanism-based inhibitor thus involves an initial formation of a non-covalent enzyme–inhibitor complex, analogous to the formation of the Michaelis–Menten enzyme–substrate complex, followed by a part of the normal catalytic cycle of the enzyme to generate the active species, which then reacts covalently with a group on the enzyme surface. Such behaviour should result in a very high degree of inhibitor specificity, and the lack of intrinsic reactivity should minimize the possibility of undesirable 'side-reactions' between the inhibitor and other tissue components.

Mechanism-based inhibitors are also known as suicide inhibitors, k_{cat} inhibitors or enzyme-activated irreversible inhibitors. Specific examples of such inhibitors are dealt with in other chapters of this book and in several reviews

(Seiler et al. 1978; Walsh 1983; Rando 1984; Silverman and Hoffman 1984). The purpose of the present chapter is to discuss the general behaviour of these compounds and methods for analysing their interactions with enzymes.

2C.2 Irreversible inhibition mechanisms

This section will be restricted to the treatment of irreversible inhibition. Such inhibition is time-dependent and not freely reversible by procedures such as dilution, dialysis, or gel filtration. The behaviour of reversible inhibitors has been discussed in detail elsewhere (see e.g. Dixon and Webb 1979; Tipton 1980; Tipton and Fowler 1984).

2C.2.1 Non-specific inhibitors

These react with groups on the enzyme surface without the formation of a specific non-covalent enzyme–inhibitor complex. Their reaction can thus be represented by the general equation (see Aldridge 1950):

$$E + I \xrightarrow{k} E{-}I \qquad (2C.1)$$

where E—I represents the irreversibly inhibited species resulting from the reaction between the enzyme E and the inhibitor I.

The time-course of the reaction would be expected to be second-order. However if the inhibitor concentration is sufficiently high for it to be unchanged during the reaction, i.e. the inhibitor concentration is much higher than that of the enzyme, *pseudo*-first-order conditions will apply and the time-course of the reaction will be described by the equation:

$$\frac{dx}{dt} = k \cdot i \qquad (2C.2)$$

where x and i are the concentrations of E—I and inhibitor, respectively. Integration of this equation yields

$$\ln x = \ln e - \ln(e{-}x) = k \cdot i \cdot t \qquad (2C.3)$$

where e represents the total enzyme concentration.

Since the progress of such reactions is frequently followed by measuring the loss of enzyme activity, this relationship may be conveniently expressed in the form

$$\ln \frac{A_t}{A_0} = -k \cdot i \cdot t \qquad (2C.4)$$

or

$$\log_{10} \frac{A_t}{A_0} = \frac{-t}{2.303} k \cdot i \qquad (2C.5)$$

where A_t represents the activity remaining after time t and A_0 represents the initial activity.

Thus a graph of $\log_{10}$ fractional activity remaining against time will be linear with a slope of $-k \cdot i/2.303$ (Fig. 2C.1) and the slopes of the lines obtained will be a linear function of the inhibitor concentration [see Fig. 2C.2(a)]. Some more complex mechanisms of non-specific inhibition that can lead to non-linear plots of $\log_{10}$ activity against time have been considered by Ray and Koshland (1961) and Rakitzis (1977).

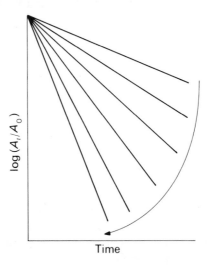

Fig. 2C.1 First-order inactivation of an enzyme according to eqn (2C.5) or eqn (2C.12). The arrow indicates increasing inhibitor concentrations.

2C.2.2 Specific irreversible inhibitors

These differ from those discussed above in that a specific non-covalent enzyme–inhibitor complex is formed and enzyme inhibition subsequently occurs by reaction within this complex. Such a mechanism, which applies to mechanism-based inhibitors and active-site-directed irreversible inhibitors, can be represented in its simplest possible form by the equation:

$$E + I \underset{k_{-1}}{\overset{k_{+1}}{\rightleftharpoons}} E.I. \xrightarrow{k_{+2}} E{-}I \tag{2C.6}$$

where E.I represents the non-covalent enzyme–inhibitor complex and E—I the irreversibly-inhibited species.

The behaviour of such systems has been analysed by Kitz and Wilson (1962). Under conditions where the inhibitor concentration is much greater than that of

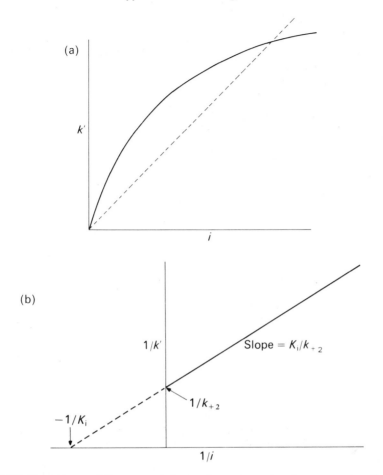

Fig. 2C.2 Dependence of the apparent first-order rate constant for enzyme inactivation on inhibitor concentration. (a) The solid line shows the dependence given by a specific irreversible inhibitor following the mechanisms given in eqn (2C.6). The broken line shows the dependence for a non-specific inhibitor, eqn (2C.1). (b) A double-reciprocal plot for a specific irreversible inhibitor.

the enzyme, and the rate of formation of the irreversibly inhibited species from the non-covalent complex is slow relative to the breakdown of that complex to free enzyme and inhibitor ($k_{+2} \ll k_{-1}$), a quasi-equilibrium will exist and the following relationships will apply:

$$x = e/(1 + K_i/i) \qquad (2C.7)$$

and

$$\frac{dy}{dt} = k_{+2}x \qquad (2C.8)$$

where y and x represent the concentrations of E—I and E.I, respectively, e is the total enzyme concentration, and K_i is the dissociation constant for the non-covalent complex.

$$K_i = k_{-1}/k_{+1} \tag{2C.9}$$

Combination of eqns (2C.7) and (2C.8) yields on integration

$$k't = \ln e - \ln(e - x) \tag{2C.10}$$

where the apparent first-order rate constant k' is given by the relationship:

$$k' = \frac{k_{+2}}{1 + K_i/i}. \tag{2C.11}$$

Equation (2C.10) can be rewritten in terms of activity loss as:

$$\log_{10} \frac{A_t}{A_0} = \frac{-t}{2.303} k'. \tag{2C.12}$$

Thus the loss of activity will be first-order with respect to time (see Fig. 2C.1) but a graph of the apparent first-order rate constant (k') against the inhibitor concentration will be hyperbolic, tending to a maximum value at high inhibitor concentrations [Fig. 2C.2(a)]. A double-reciprocal plot, or similar transformation (see e.g. Dixon and Webb 1979) of these data, can then be used to determine K_i and k_{+2} [Fig. 2C.2(b)]. The value of k' may also be calculated from the time taken for inhibition to reach 50 per cent, $t_{1/2}$, since $k' = 0.693/t_{1/2}$.

A more general treatment of the mechanism shown in eqn (2C.6) has been given by Malcolm and Radda (1970), who showed that if steady-state conditions were assumed, the relationships shown in eqns (2C.11) and (2C.12) were valid if K_i was replaced by the steady-state constant, K_m^i, where

$$K_m^i = \frac{k_{-1} + k_{+2}}{k_{+1}}. \tag{2C.13}$$

Brocklehurst (1979) and Cornish-Bowden (1979) have shown that, despite claims to the contrary (Childs and Bardsley 1975), the quasi-equilibrium mechanism considered by Kitz and Wilson (1962) will be valid for most systems. In cases where k_{+2} is not very much less than k_{-1} the treatment of Malcolm and Radda (1970) would be appropriate. In the extreme case, where $k_{+2} \gg k_{-1}$ neither of these treatments would be applicable but the time-dependence of the reaction would show significant deviation from first-order behaviour (Cornish-Bowden 1979). If the values of k_{+2} and k_{-1} are both relatively large, it may be difficult in practice to observe saturation kinetics because at inhibitor concentrations approaching K_i the rate of reaction may be too fast to measure accurately. Such behaviour has been reported for the inhibition of acetylcholinesterase by diisopropylfluorophosphonate (Main 1964). In such cases it is possible to determine the apparent bimolecular rate constant, k_{+2}/K_i, for inhibitor binding from the slope of the plot shown in Fig. 2C.2(b). However, it is necessary to be sure that the inhibition really is of the specific, rather than non-specific, type if eqn (2C.12) is used in this way, since the dependence on inhibitor concentration will be hard to distinguish from that predicted by eqn (2C.5). In the case of the inhibition of acetylcholinesterase mentioned above, specific inhibition was assumed because other, less rapidly reacting inhibitors in this class did give rise to saturation kinetics (Main 1964). A more realistic reaction scheme describing the interactions between an enzyme and mechanism-based inhibitor might be:

$$E + I \underset{k_{-1}}{\overset{k_{+1}}{\rightleftharpoons}} E.I. \xrightarrow{k_{+2}} E.I^* \xrightarrow{k_{+3}} E\!-\!I \qquad (2C.14)$$

where the non-covalent enzyme–inhibitor complex (E.I) is transformed into an activated species (E.I*), which then reacts to produce the irreversibly inhibited species.

Steady-state analysis of such a mechanism will give relationships identical to eqns (2C.10) and (2C.12), but the constants are rather more complex. Thus eqn (2C.11) becomes:

$$k' = \frac{k_{+2}k_{+3}/(k_{+2}+k_{+3})}{1 + K_m^i/i} \qquad (2C.15)$$

where:

$$K_m^i = \frac{k_{-1}k_{+3} + k_{+2}k_{+3}}{k_{+1}(k_{+2}+k_{+3})}. \qquad (2C.16)$$

If $k_{+2} \ll k_{+3}$, these relationships simplify to eqns (2C.11) and (2C.13).

If the time-dependent inhibition is relatively slow, it may also be possible to determine the inhibitory action due to non-covalent binding. A simple study of the effects of the inhibitor on the initial rate of substrate transformation, without any enzyme–inhibitor preincubation, will allow the inhibitor type and K_i value to be determined by standard procedures (see e.g. Dixon and Webb 1979). Since mechanism-based inhibitors function in part as substrates, they would be expected to be competitive inhibitors with respect to the corresponding substrate. Agreement between the K_i value determined in this way with that calculated by the method of Kitz and Wilson (1962) would provide evidence that the simple quasi-equilibrium mechanism was valid.

In determining the kinetics of inhibition from the time-course of inactivation [eqns (2C.11) and (2C.12)], it should be noted that the equations are derived in terms of the irreversible component of the inhibition, whereas an assay of the activity remaining is likely to determine both the non-covalent (reversible) and irreversible inhibition. The former component can be minimized by dilution of the enzyme–inhibitor mixture before assay, to lower the free inhibitor concentration and cause dissociation, and also by determining the activity in the presence of a sufficiently high substrate concentration to displace the reversibly bound inhibitor.

2C.2.3   The effects of substrate concentration

As mentioned above, a mechanism-based inhibitor would be expected to act as a competitive inhibitor with respect to the corresponding substrate. A simple scheme representing such behaviour can be written as (Malcolm and Radda 1970):

$$ES \underset{k_{+3}S}{\overset{k_{-3}}{\rightleftharpoons}} E \underset{k_{-1}}{\overset{k_{+1}I}{\rightleftharpoons}} E.I \overset{k_{+2}}{\longrightarrow} E\text{---}I. \qquad (2C.17)$$

In the presence of a constant amount of substrate, this system will obey eqn (2C.12), where k' is given by:

$$k' = \frac{k_{+2}}{1 + K_i(1 + s/K_s)/i} \qquad (2C.18)$$

where s represents the substrate concentration and K_s is the enzyme–substrate dissociation constant, k_{-3}/k_{+3}. Thus determination of k' at a series of fixed substrate concentrations will allow K_s to be determined from a graph of $1/k'$ against s (see also Connolly and Trayer 1979). Graphical analysis of this equation is discussed further in Section 2C.2.4 [see Fig. 2C.4(a–d)].

The above equations have assumed that the substrate is not transformed by the enzyme. If the enzyme-catalysed reaction does take place, the dissociation constant K_s in eqn (2C.18) must be replaced by the steady-state Michaelis constant $(k_{-3} + k_{+4})/k_{+3}$, where k_{+4} represents the rate constant for decomposition of the enzyme–substrate complex into free enzyme plus products (see Section 2C.2.4).

Many enzyme-catalysed reactions involve two or more substrates. The second substrate may or may not be required for the enzyme-catalysed transformation required to activate the mechanism-based inhibitor. For example in the inactivation of monoamine oxidase by acetylenic inhibitors, the generation of the enzyme-bound active species involves a dehydrogenation reaction that does not require the second substrate, oxygen (Singer 1979) and no substrate addition is required for the mechanism-based inhibition of many pyridoxal-phosphate-requiring enzymes (see Metcalfe *et al.* 1978; Silverman and Hoffman 1984). In contrast, the inhibition of glutamine synthetase by methionine sulphoximine requires the presence of the coenzyme, either ATP or ADP, necessary for inhibitor binding. This inhibitor is an analogue of glutamate and, as would be expected, that substrate protects against inhibition competitively (Meister 1978). Similarly, NAD^+ is required for the binding of cyclopropanonehydrate to aldehyde dehydrogenase (Wiseman *et al.* 1980). The second substrate, NAD^+, is required not only for the binding of the mechanism-based inhibitor 3-ethylthioallyl alcohol to alcohol dehydrogenase, but also as a hydrogen acceptor in the reaction leading to the generation of the reactive species (MacInnes *et al.* 1981). Even in cases where the second substrate is not required for inhibitor binding or transformation, its presence may affect the rate of inhibition by affecting the apparent K_i value in a manner that will depend on the catalytic mechanism obeyed (see Tsou 1988).

Protection by either or both substrates may occur in the case of non-specific inhibition and might be expected to occur if the inhibitor were reacting with a group at the active site. Thus the observation of substrate protection is not sufficient, alone, to distinguish between specific and non-specific inhibition.

2C.2.4 Time-courses of substrate protection

In the presence of a mechanism-based inhibitor, the time-course of the reaction monitored by substrate disappearance or product formation will be non-linear because the amount of active enzyme is decreasing with time [see Fig. 2C.3(a)]. After all reaction has ceased, addition of more substrate will not result in further reaction, as would be the case if the reaction had ceased because of substrate depletion or approach to the equilibrium of the reaction. However, addition of a further sample of the enzyme would restart the reaction.

The kinetic analysis of such progress curves has been considered by Tsou and his colleagues (Tian and Tsou 1982; Tsou et al. 1985; Liu and Tsou 1986; Tsou 1988) and by Forsberg and Puu (1984). Under conditions where the substrate and inhibitor concentrations are much greater than that of the enzyme, the time-course of product formation can be described by the general equation:

$$P_t = P_\infty(1 - e^{-k't})$$ (2C.19)

where P_t is the product concentration at any time t, and P_∞ is the final product concentration when the reaction has ceased.

This equation can be integrated and rearranged to give:

$$\ln(P_\infty - P_t) = \ln P_\infty - k't$$ (2C.20)

which is a similar relationship to that shown in eqn (2C.10). A graph of $\ln(P_\infty - P_t)$ versus t will thus be linear with a slope of $-k'$ and an intercept on the vertical axis of $\ln P_\infty$ [Fig. 2C.3(b)]. Alternatively, if $\log_{10}$ is plotted the relationship becomes:

$$\log_{10}(P_\infty - P_t) = \log_{10} P_\infty - k't/2.303$$ (2C.21)

The meaning of the apparent first-order rate constant, k', will depend on the mechanism of inhibition. For the specific inhibition mechanism (Tsou et al. 1985):

$$E + I \underset{k_{-1}}{\overset{k_{+1}}{\rightleftharpoons}} E.I \xrightarrow{k_{+2}} E$$

$$+$$

$$S \qquad\qquad (2C.22)$$

$$k_{+3} \updownarrow k_{-3}$$

$$ES \xrightarrow{k_{+4}} E + P$$

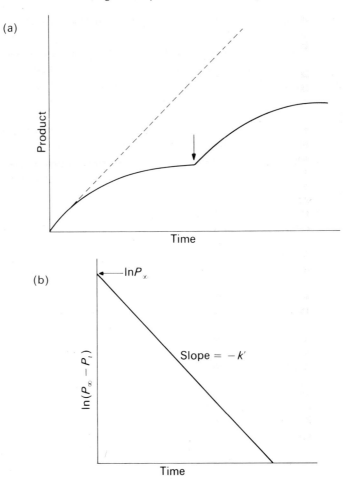

Fig. 2C.3 The effects of the presence of an irreversible inhibitor on the rate of an enzyme-catalysed reaction. (a) Solid line, product formation in the presence of a time-dependent inhibitor. At the point indicated by the arrow a further addition of enzyme was made. Similar behaviour is given by mechanism-based inhibitors that also act as substrates (eqn 2C.29) if the product derived from the inhibitor is monitored directly. The broken line represents the formation of product in the absence of inhibitor. (b) Determination of the apparent first-order rate constant for inactivation from the time-course of product formation according to eqn (2C.20).

The relationship is identical to eqn (2C.18):

$$k' = \frac{k_{+2}}{1 + (K_i/i)[1 + (s/K_m)]} \tag{2C.23}$$

Thus a graph of $1/k'$ against $1/i$ will give a family of straight lines at different substrate concentrations, each with a slope of $(1 + s/K_m)K_i/k_{+2}$, that intersect at a common point corresponding to $1/k_{+2}$ [Fig. 2C.4(a)]. If the slopes of these lines are then plotted against s, the resulting linear plot will intersect the baseline at $-K_m$ [Fig. 2C.4(b)]. A graph of $1/k'$ against s will also be linear, but in this case both the slopes and vertical axis intercepts will depend on the inhibitor concentration [Fig. 2C.4(c)]. The lines will intersect at a point above the horizontal axis corresponding to $-K_m$. A graph of the intercepts on the vertical axis against $1/i$ will be linear with an intercept on the baseline of $-1/K_i$ and a vertical-axis intercept of $1/k_{+2}$ (Fig. 2C.4(d)].

Tsou et al. (1985) also presented equations for the time courses for reaction in the presence of a non-specific inhibitor. As mentioned above there is no *a priori* reason to assume that substrate will protect in these cases, and Tsou et al. (1985) presented equations for competitive, non-competitive, and uncompetitive substrate effects. All these cases can be distinguished from the specific case because a graph of i/k' versus i will be independent of the inhibitor concentration. For example, in the non-specific case where substrate protects competitively:

$$E\!-\!I \xleftarrow{\;k_{+3}I\;} E \underset{k_{-1}}{\overset{k_{+1}S}{\rightleftharpoons}} ES \xrightarrow{\;k_{+2}\;} E+P \qquad (2C.24)$$

(a)

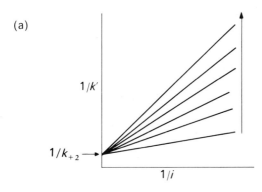

(b)

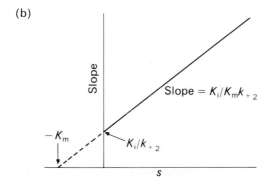

(c)

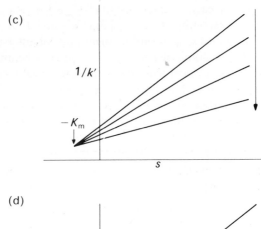

(d)

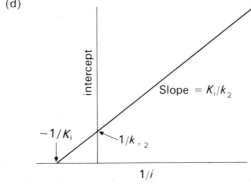

Fig. 2C.4 Determination of the kinetic parameters for the effects of a specific irreversible inhibitor on substrate transformation according to eqns (2C.22) and (2C.23) and also eqns (2C.17) and (2C.18). (a) Double-reciprocal plot of the dependence of the apparent rate constant on the inhibitor concentration. The arrow indicates the direction of increasing substrate concentration. The slopes of the lines are $(1 + s/K_m)K_i/k_{+2}$. (b) Plot of the slopes of the lines in (a) against the substrate concentration. (c) Graphs of the reciprocal apparent first-order rate constant against substrate concentration. The arrow shows the direction of increasing inhibitor concentration. Each line has a slope of $K_i/(K_m \cdot k_{+2} \cdot i)$ and intersects the vertical axis at a value of $(1 + K_i/i)/k_{+2}$. (d) Plot of the vertical axis intercepts of (c) against the reciprocal of the inhibitor concentration.

the apparent rate constant, k', will be given by:

$$\frac{i}{k'} = \frac{s}{K_m}\frac{1}{k_{+3}} + \frac{1}{k_{+3}}.$$

(2C.25)

In contrast eqn (2C.23) can be rearranged to give

$$\frac{i}{k'} = \frac{K_i}{k_{+2}}\left(1 + \frac{s}{K_m}\right) + \frac{i}{k_{+2}}$$

(2C.26)

and thus i/k' will be a linear function of i with a slope of $1/k_{+2}$.

Walker and Elmore (1984) have also considered the behaviour of the system represented by eqn (2C.22). They stressed the necessity for the substrate concentration to remain essentially unchanged during the inhibitory process if valid data were to be obtained. Their recommendation was that conditions should be chosen so that not more than 1 per cent of the substrate was converted to product before the enzyme was completely inhibited. For the system described by eqns (2C.19)–(2C.23), they showed that the amount of product formed at completion of the inhibitory reaction was given by:

$$P_\infty = k_{+4} K_i s e / k_{+2} K_m i \tag{2C.27}$$

and thus the product of this equation and that for the apparent first-order rate constant (eqn 2C.23) becomes:

$$k' P_\infty = k_{+4} e / [1 + (1 + i/K_i)(K_m/s)]. \tag{2C.28}$$

Thus these equations can be used for determining K_i and k_{+4} if the total enzyme concentration is known and K_m and k_{+4} are determined from separate experiments in the absence of the inhibitor. Alternatively, graphical procedures similar to those discussed previously can be used to determine the constants from eqn (2C.28).

2C.3 Mechanism-based inhibitors as substrates

Since at least part of the catalytic action of the enzyme is required in order to generate the reactive species it is possible that a mechanism-based inhibitor may also act as a substrate for the enzyme. In such a case the reaction may be represented by the scheme (Waley 1980):

$$E + I \underset{k_{-1}}{\overset{k_{+1}}{\rightleftharpoons}} E.I \xrightarrow{k_{+2}} E.I^* \xrightarrow{k_{+4}} E\text{—}I \tag{2C.29}$$

$$\downarrow k_{+3}$$

$$E + P$$

where the initial non-covalent enzyme–inhibitor complex (E.I) is converted to an activated species (E.I*), which can then either react within the complex to produce the irreversibly inhibited enzyme or break down to yield free enzyme and products (P).

If it is possible to follow the reaction by monitoring product formation, a time-course similar to that shown in Fig. 2C.3(a) will be obtained. When product formation has ceased, the reaction cannot be restarted by the addition of more inhibitor, or any other substrate for the enzyme, if the inhibitor was in sufficient excess to give complete enzyme inhibition. However, the reaction can be restarted by addition of more enzyme.

The ratio between rate constants, r, which is given by

$$r = k_{+3}/k_{+4}, \tag{2C.30}$$

has been termed the *partition ratio* by Waley (1980, 1985), and represents the ratio between the number of productive turnovers and those leading to enzyme inactivation.

The monoamine oxidase inhibitor MD 780236 has been shown, for example, to follow the mechanism represented by eqn (2C.29), where the value of r was calculated to be about 530 (Tipton *et al.* 1933a). In contrast, no significant formation of product can be detected during the inhibition of the same enzyme by the acetylenic inhibitors clorgyline, $(-)$-deprenyl, and pargyline, indicating that k_{+3} is close to zero and that the model represented by eqn (2C.6) or (2C.14) is applicable (Fowler *et al.* 1982). Clavulanate and β-iodopenicillanate have also been shown to inhibit β-lactamases by a similar mechanism (Frère *et al.* 1982a, b), although in the case of the former compound alternative pathways of product formation also exist.

Under conditions where the amount of inhibitor is in sufficient excess to give complete inhibition, the amount of product formed will be $r \cdot e$, where e represents the initial enzyme concentration. These conditions will apply when the initial inhibitor concentration is greater than $(1+r)e$, where $(1+r)$ represents the number of molecules of inhibitor required to inactivate one molecule of enzyme (the molar proportion for inactivation) (Tatsunami *et al.* 1981; Waley 1985). If the inhibitor concentration is less than $(1+r)e$ the amount of product formed will be given by $r \cdot e_i$, where e_i represents the concentration of inhibited enzyme. From these relationships it can be seen that under these conditions the amount of active enzyme remaining (e_r) will be given by the relationship:

$$e_r = e - i/(1+r). \tag{2C.31}$$

From this it follows that

$$\frac{e_r}{e} = 1 - \frac{i}{(1+r)e}. \tag{2C.32}$$

Thus from a graph of the fractional activity remaining against the ratio of the initial concentration of the inhibitor to that of the enzyme, the value of $(1+r)$ will be given by the intercept on the abscissa (Tatsunami *et al.* 1981; Knight and Waley 1985; Waley 1985).

Equations describing the time-courses of such reactions have been presented by Waley (1980, 1985) and by Tatsunami *et al.* (1981). The analysis of such systems depends on whether the rate of loss of enzyme activity, the decrease in activity towards a substrate added with the inhibitor, the appearance of the product derived from the inhibitor, or the disappearance of the inhibitor is measured, and the full equations can be somewhat cumbersome.

A practical approach to analysing the data has been proposed by Waley (1985). The time-course for enzyme inactivation by the mechanism shown in eqn (2C.29) can be written as

$$t = N \cdot \ln(1 - M \cdot z) - N' \cdot \ln(1 - Z) \tag{2C.33}$$

where z represents the fractional inhibition of the enzyme (e_i/e) and the values of the other constants are given in Table 2C.1 (Waley 1935). Of these constants the first-order rate constant for inactivation (k_{in}) and the apparent Michaelis constant (K') are important, in addition to r, for characterizing the system. The corresponding first-order rate constant for substrate will be given by $r \cdot k_{in}$.

Table 2C.1 Symbols, definitions, and relationships of mechanism-based inhibitors following eqns (2C.29)–(2C.37)

Symbol	Definition	Dimension of parameter
k_{in}	$\dfrac{k_{+2}k_{+4}}{k_{+2}+k_{+3}+k_{+4}}$	1/time
K'	$\left(\dfrac{k_{-1}+k_{+2}}{k_{+1}}\right)\left(\dfrac{k_{+3}+k_{+4}}{k_{+2}+k_{+3}+k_{+4}}\right)$	Concentration
r	$\dfrac{k_{+3}}{k_{+4}}$	Dimensionless
M	$(1+r)\cdot\dfrac{e}{i}$	Dimensionless
z	e_i/e	Dimensionless
u	i_t/i	Dimensionless
N	$K'/\{k_{in}(1-M)i\}$	Time
N'	$(1/k_{in})+K'/\{k_{in}(1-M)i\}$	Time
	Relationships	
$M<1$	$z_\infty=1$	$u_\infty=1-M$
$M>1$	$z_\infty=1/M$	$u_\infty=0$
$z=(1-u)/M$	$u=1-M\cdot z$	$P=r\cdot e\cdot z$

Adapted, with permission, from Waley (1985).

If the time-course of activity loss is determined and the time for 50 per cent inactivation (the half-time, $t_{1/2}$) is measured, eqn (2C.33) can be simplified by setting $z=0.5$:

$$i\cdot t_{1/2}=\left(\frac{\ln(2-M)}{1-M}\right)\frac{K'}{k_{in}}+\frac{\ln 2}{k_{in}}\cdot i. \qquad (2C.34)$$

Thus if $i\cdot t_{1/2}$ is plotted against i under conditions where the ratio i/e is kept constant, the values of K' and k_{in} may be determined [Fig. 2C.5(a)].

If the rate of formation of the product formed from the mechanism-based inhibitor is followed, the relationships discussed above show that z in

(a)

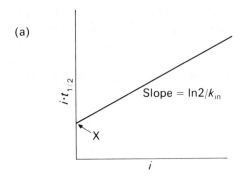

(b)

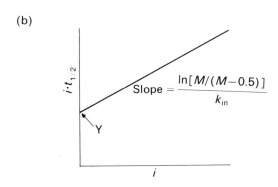

Fig. 2C.5 Kinetics of a mechanism-based inhibitor that also acts as a substrate. (a) Graph of the product of the half-time of the reaction leading to activity loss and the initial inhibitor concentration, under conditions where the ratios of the initial inhibitor and enzyme concentrations is kept constant, according to eqn (2C.34). The intercept, X, is given by $X = [\ln(2-M)/(1-M)]K'/k_{in}$. (b) Similar graph to that shown in (a) for the case in which inhibitor disappearance is followed (eqn 2C.36). The intercept, Y, is given by $Y = \dfrac{\ln[M/(2M-1)]}{(1-M)}\cdot\dfrac{K'}{k_{in}}$. The symbols are defined in Table 2C.1.

eqn (2C.33) can be replaced by $P/r \cdot e$ and thus the eqn (2C.34) will be applicable if the time for 50 per cent formation of product is determined.

If the disappearance of the inhibitor is determined, this may be simply related to product formation if the enzyme concentration is known or the relationship:

$$t = N \cdot \ln u - N' \cdot \ln[(u+M-1)/M] \qquad (2C.35)$$

may be used where $u = i_t/i$, the ratio of the inhibitor concentration after time t to that present initially. In terms of the time taken for half of the total observed inhibitor depletion to occur, the equation becomes:

$$i \cdot t_{1/2} = \frac{\ln[M/(2M-1)]}{1-M} \cdot \frac{K'}{k_{in}} + \frac{\ln[M/(M-0.5)]}{k_{in}} \cdot i \qquad (2C.36)$$

and thus a graph of $i \cdot t_{1/2}$ is plotted against i under conditions where the ratio i/e is constant; the values of k_{in} and K' can then be determined as shown in Fig. 2C.5B.

If the rate of loss of activity towards an added substrate is monitored, the time at which the rate has fallen to half that observed in the absence of the inhibitor can be determined as $t_{1/2}$ in eqn (2C.34). The apparent values of K' obtained, K'_{app}, may be related to the true value by the equation:

$$K'_{app} = K'(1 + s/K_m) \qquad (2C.37)$$

where s is the initial concentration of the monitoring substrate, which is assumed not to change significantly during the course of the reaction, and K_m is the Michaelis constant for that substrate. Should significant substrate depletion occur during the time period of the inhibitory reaction, the mean value may be used (Waley 1985; Lee and Wilson 1971). Difficulties in accurately estimating the half-time by this procedure may be overcome if on-line computer data analysis is used. Alternatively Waley (1985) has discussed procedures for doing this.

2C.4 Possible complications

Although the equations presented above can be readily applied to the analysis of enzyme inhibition in ideal circumstances, there are a number of possible complications that should be considered.

2C.4.1 Instability

The procedures described above have assumed the enzyme to be stable in the absence of the inhibitor. In cases where the loss of activity is determined by assaying the activity remaining after a series of fixed times, a control experiment in which the enzyme is incubated under identical conditions but in the absence of inhibitor may be used to correct for any loss of activity of the enzyme alone. However, a number of enzymes are stabilized against denaturation by the presence of their substrates and this procedure cannot exclude the possibility that the mechanism-based inhibitor itself may stabilize the enzyme.

Analysis of the time-courses of substrate or inhibitor transformation also assumes that product formation is linear with time in the absence of the inhibitor. There are several possible reasons for non-linearity in the progress curves of enzyme-catalysed reactions, some of which may be prevented by changing the assay conditions (see e.g. Dixon and Webb 1979; Tipton 1985). Selwyn (1965) has proposed a simple test for determining whether enzyme inactivation is occurring during an assay, and this should be applied before attempts are made to analyse reaction progress curves in the presence of a mechanism-based inhibitor.

Problems can also be encountered if the inhibitor is unstable under the assay conditions so that its concentration is decreasing with time. Preincubation of the inhibitor in the reaction medium for various times before addition of the enzyme will result in different observed rates of inactivation if this is occurring. If the decay of the inhibitor is a first-order process governed by a rate constant $\bar{k}$, the rate equation governing the loss of enzyme activity for non-specific inhibition (eqn 2C.1) becomes (Purdie and Heggie 1970; Ashani *et al.* 1972; Rakitzis 1974, 1984):

$$\ln \frac{A_t}{A_0} = \frac{k}{\bar{k}} \cdot i(e^{-\bar{k}t} - 1) \tag{2C.38}$$

whereas for specific inhibition (eqn 2C.6), the corresponding equation becomes (Purdue and Heggie 1970; Rakitzis 1974, 1984):

$$\ln \frac{A_t}{A_0} = \frac{k_{+2}}{k} \ln \frac{K_i + i e^{-\bar{k}t}}{K_i + i} . \tag{2C.39}$$

One approach to determining the kinetic constants in these equations has been to incubate the enzyme and inhibitor for a sufficient time for complete disappearance of the latter to occur before the activity remaining is determined (Purdie and Heggie 1970; Ashani *et al.* 1972; Rakitzis 1974, 1978, 1981). Under those conditions eqns (2C.38) and (2C.39) can be solving by setting t equal to infinity and in the case of eqn (2C.39) also assuming that the initial inhibitor concentration is much greater than K_i. This procedure has however been criticized by Topham (1985), who pointed out that, in addition to the undesirability of the extended incubation periods that might be necessary, the assumption that the concentration of inhibitor at any given time was governed solely by its rate of decomposition was invalid in neglecting the consumption of inhibitor by the enzyme. Simulation of progress curves for specific (eqn 2C.6) and non-specific (eqn 2C.1) inhibition by an unstable inhibitor has recently been used to demonstrate that this approach can indeed give erroneous results, particularly at relatively high enzyme concentrations (Topham 1986).

An alternative approach is to rearrange eqn (2C.38) to give (Topham 1984):

$$\ln \frac{A_t}{A_0} = -k \cdot i \cdot t' \tag{2C.40}$$

where

$$t' = (1 - e^{\bar{k}t}) / \bar{k} \tag{2C.41}$$

and thus, if the rate constant for decomposition of the inhibitor can be determined from a separate experiment, k may be found from a graph of the fractional activity remaining against t'.

In the case of systems obeying eqn (2C.39) it can be shown that when i is much greater than K_i, and hence $i \cdot e^{-\bar{k}t} \gg K_i$, it will simplify to (Purdie and Heggie 1970; Topham 1986).

$$\ln \frac{A_t}{A_0} = -k_{+2} t \tag{2C.42}$$

and thus k_{+2} can be determined graphically. If $\bar{k}$ is known, a separate experiment in which the initial inhibitor concentration is not much greater than K_i can then be used to determine the latter constant, since (Topham 1986):

$$\left(\frac{A_t}{A_0}\right)^{\bar{k}/k_{+2}} = \frac{K_i}{K_i+i} + \frac{1}{K_i+i} \cdot i \cdot e^{-\bar{k}t} \tag{2C.43}$$

and thus a graph of $(A_t/A_0)^{\bar{k}/k_{+2}}$ against $i \cdot e^{-\bar{k}t}$ will give K_i directly as the ratio of the intercept on the ordinate to the slope.

2C.4.2 Reversibility

The mechanism of action of mechanism-based inhibitors assumes that inhibition, resulting from the formation of a covalent adduct between the inhibitor and enzyme, is irreversible. However, the bond may not be completely stable and it is possible that the adduct may slowly break down to regenerate the free enzyme. In the case of specific inhibition, this may be represented as (see e.g. Aldridge and Reiner 1972; O'Brien (1968):

$$E+I \underset{k_{+1}}{\overset{k_{+1}}{\rightleftharpoons}} E.I \xrightarrow{k_{+2}} E{-}I \xrightarrow{k_{+3}} E+\text{Product}. \tag{2C.44}$$

Clearly, it will depend on the relative rate of breakdown of the enzyme–inhibitor adduct whether the compound is regarded as a poor substrate or as an inhibitor.

For kinetic studies an operational definition of irreversibility is used, which defines the inhibitor as being irreversible if it does not dissociate from the enzyme significantly during the time period of the kinetic studies. Slower breakdown of the irreversibly inhibited species may be investigated by greatly decreasing the concentration of free inhibitor, for example by dilution or dialysis, and assaying at intervals for regain of enzyme activity. In the case of the inhibition of monoamine oxidase by allylamine, the process has been shown to be irreversible but the presence of substrate results in reactivation of the enzyme (Rando and Eigner 1977). Silverman and Hoffman (1984) have also discussed a number of cases in which the inhibitor generated by the action of the enzyme may bind very tightly but non-covalently to it.

Time-dependence of the inhibitory process has often been used to show that it is irreversible. However, reversible inhibitors that have extremely high affinities for the enzyme, and processes in which the formation of reversibly inhibited species depends on a slow conformational change may also show time dependence (see Tipton and Fowler 1984).

2C.4.3 Other mechanisms

Baker (1967) pointed out that a mechanism in which an inhibitor inactivates by a bimolecular (non-specific) mechanism (eqn 2C.1) but is also capable of binding to the enzyme reversibly according to the scheme

$$\text{E.I} \underset{k+1}{\overset{k-1}{\rightleftharpoons}} \text{E}+\text{I} \xrightarrow{k} \text{E—I} \tag{2C.45}$$

would give rise to an equation of the same form as eqn (2C.10), where the apparent first-order rate constant k' would be given by (cf. eqn 2C.11):

$$k' = \frac{k \cdot K_i}{1 + K_i/i}. \tag{2C.46}$$

Thus, this mechanism gives identical kinetic behaviour to that predicted by inactivation according to the specific inhibition shown in eqn (2C.6). However, the effects of added substrate might allow a distinction to be made if one of the two inactivation processes shown in eqn (2C.45) did not involve interaction at the substrate binding site. Plapp (1983) has also discussed a number of criteria that may be useful in distinguishing this mechanism from specific inhibition.

Branlant et al. (1981) have extended the scheme shown in eqn (2C.45) to include the interaction of the non-covalent enzyme–inhibitor complex with a second molecule of inhibitor to give an irreversibly inhibited species:

$$\text{I—E.I} \xleftarrow{k_2} \text{E.I} \underset{k+1}{\overset{k-1}{\rightleftharpoons}} \text{E}+\text{I} \xrightarrow{k} \text{E—I.} \tag{2C.47}$$

In this case the apparent rate constant for irreversible inhibition will be a complex function of the inhibitor concentration, and a plot of the reciprocal of this constant against the reciprocal of the inhibitor concentration will be non-linear according to the equation:

$$\frac{1}{k'} = \frac{K_i + i}{k \cdot K_i \cdot i + k_{+2} \cdot i^2}. \tag{2C.48}$$

A reaction mechanism in which the product was a potent inhibitor of the enzyme might lead to progress curves that were difficult to distinguish from those given by the mechanism shown in eqn (2C.29). However, in this case addition of a system, such as another enzyme, that removed the product continuously should prevent inhibition. A similar behaviour would be observed if the curvature of the reaction were due to the approach to equilibrium of a reversible reaction. If the product were to be an irreversible inhibitor of the enzyme catalysing its formation, a lag-time might be observed if it was released from the active site prior to irreversible inhibition.

2C.5　The uses of derived constants

The specific constants derived from the analysis of the kinetic behaviour of mechanism-based inhibitors can be of particular value in inhibitor design. The efficiency of inhibition will depend on the affinity of the enzyme and inhibitor, governed by the constant K_i, and the rate of reaction within the non-covalent complex to form the irreversibly inhibited species. Thus a knowledge of the values of these constants for a range of inhibitors can be of value in optimizing their design.

Many mechanism-based inhibitors have been found not to be completely specific for a single enzyme. For example, a number of mechanism-based inhibitors derived from 4-aminobutyrate are inhibitors of a number of amino-transferases in addition to 4-aminobutyrate aminotransferase (see Jung 1978) and, although a high degree of inhibition of one or other of the two forms of monoamine oxidase (see Tipton *et al.* 1983b) is observed with mechanism-based inhibitors, no compound has yet been developed that is absolutely specific as a mechanism-based inhibitor of only one form. Selectivity of inhibition for one of two enzymes will depend on differences in the K_i values for non-covalent binding and/or the rate constant for irreversible inhibition. In the case of the monoamine oxidase inhibitor clorgyline, it has been shown that both these factors contribute to its selectivity towards the A-form of that enzyme, whereas in the case of the B-form-selective inhibitor pargyline, the selectivity appears to be largely due to the compound having a greater affinity for non-covalent binding to that form of the enzyme (Fowler *et al.* 1982). A comparison of two other monoamine oxidase inhibitors, AGN1133 (J508) and AGN1142, has suggested that the former may show a greater affinity for non-covalent binding to the A-form of the enzyme but a greater reactivity, within the non-covalent complex, with the B-form (Tipton *et al.* 1982, 1983b).

Although K_i will not represent a simple dissociation constant under steady-state conditions (see eqns 2C.13–16), it can be seen that at very low inhibitor concentrations eqns (2C.11) or (2C.15) and (2C.16) simplify to:

$$k' = \frac{k_{+2}}{K_i} \cdot i \tag{2C.49}$$

and eqn (2C.16) simplifies to eqn (2C.13). Thus the ratio k_{+2}/K_i will represent the apparent rate constant for the combination of enzyme and inhibitor. This relationship will hold whether equilibrium or steady-state conditions apply and also in conditions where the inhibitor also acts as a substrate (Section 2C.3). It thus provides an important measure of enzyme–inhibitor interaction that does not require any assumptions about the existence of a quasi-equilibrium.

2C.6 Conclusions

From the above considerations it is possible to summarize a number of specific properties of mechanism-based inhibitors:

1. Inhibition is first-order with respect to time and the rate of inactivation shows saturation kinetics with respect to inhibitor concentration.

2. Inhibition involves interaction with the active site of the enzyme and thus substrate will protect competitively.

3. The inhibitor is not intrinsically reactive, but is converted to a reactive form by the action of the enzyme, inhibition occurring by subsequent reaction within the complex. There should be a stoichiometric relationship between the number of enzyme active sites modified by the inhibitor and the activity loss.

A fourth criterion, that inactivation is irreversible, is usually added but, as discussed earlier, this does not exclude a slow reactivation of the enzyme due to instability of the adduct formed. In addition, Silverman and Hoffman (1984) have given a number of examples where a mechanism-based process results in the formation of a very tightly but non-covalently bound inhibitor. If the rate of dissociation of the inhibitor is very slow relative to the time course of the experiments, the kinetic behaviour in such cases will not be distinguishable from the behaviour of inhibitors that are truly irreversible (Cha 1976).

Some of the aspects summarized above are shared with other types of enzyme inhibitors, such as the active-site-directed irreversible inhibitors discussed in Chapter 2B, but it is their combination, and particularly the specific involvement of the catalytic function of the enzyme (see Point 3 above), that gives rise to the high degree of selectivity and the potential pharmacological importance of these compounds.

Acknowledgements

I am grateful to the Medical Research Council of Ireland for the support of a research grant and to Drs C. M. Topham, C. L. Tsou, and S. G. Waley for helpful discussion and comments.

References

Aldridge, W. N. (1950). Some properties of specific cholinesterase with particular reference to the mechanism of inhibition by diethyl *p*-nitrophenyl thiophosphate (E 605) and analogues. *Biochem., J.*, **46**, 451–60.

Aldridge, W. N. and Reiner, E. (1972). *Enzyme inhibitors as substrates*. North Holland, Amsterdam.

Ashani, Y., Wins, P., and Wilson, I. B. (1972). The inhibition of cholinesterase by diethylphosphorochloridate. *Biochim. Biophys. Acta*, **284**, 427–34.

Baker, B. R. (1967). *Design of active-site-directed irreversible enzyme inhibitors*, pp. 123–124. Wiley, New York.

Branlant, G., Tritch, D., and Biellmann, J.-F. (1981). Evidence for the presence of anion recognition sites in pig liver aldehyde reductase. Modification by phenyl glyoxal and *p*-carboxyphenyl glyoxal of an arginyl residue close to the substrate-binding site. *Eur. J. Biochem.*, **116**, 505–12.

Brocklehurst, K. (1979). The equilibrium assumption is valid for the kinetic treatment of most time-dependent protein-modification reactions. *Biochem. J.*, **181**, 775–8.

Cha, S. (1976). Tight-binding inhibitors—III. A new approach for the determination of competition between tight-binding inhibitors and substrates-inhibition of adenosine deaminase by conformycin. *Biochem. Pharmacol.*, **25**, 2695–702.

Childs, R. E. and Bardsley, W. G. (1975). Time-dependent inhibition of enzymes by active-site directed reagents. A theoretical treatment of the kinetics of affinity labelling. *J. Theor. Biol.*, **53**, 381–94.

Connolly, B. A. and Trayer, I. P. (1979). Affinity labelling of rat-muscle hexokinase type II by a glucose-derived alkylating agent. *Eur. J. Biochem.*, **93**, 375–83.

Cornish-Bowden, A. (1979). Validity of a 'steady-state' treatment of inactivation kinetics. *Eur. J. Biochem.*, **93**, 383–5.

Dixon, M. and Webb, E. C. (1979). *Enzymes.* Longman, London.

Forsberg, A. and Puu, G. (1984). Kinetics of the inhibition of acetylcholinesterase from electric eel by some organophosphates and carbamates. *Eur. J. Biochem.*, **140**, 153–6.

Fowler, C. J., Mantle, T. J., and Tipton, K. F. (1982). The nature of the inhibition of rat liver monoamine oxidase types A and B by the acetylenic inhibitors clorgyline, l-deprenyl and pargyline. *Biochem. Pharmacol.*, **31**, 3555–61.

Frère, J.-M., Dormans, C., Lenzini, V. M., and Duyckaerts, C. (1982a). Interaction of clavulanate with the β-lactamase of *Streptomyces albus* G and *Actinomadura* R39. *Biochem. J.*, **207**, 429–436.

Frère, J.-M., Dormans, C., Duyckaerts, C., and De Graeve, J. (1982b). Interaction of β-iodopenicillanate with the β-lactamase of *Streptomyces albus* G and *Actinomadura* R39. *Biochem. J.*, **207**, 437–44.

Jung, M. J. (1978). *In vivo* biochemistry of GABA transaminase inhibition. In *Enzyme activated irreversible inhibitors* (ed. N. Seiler, M. J. Jung, and J. Koch-Weser), pp. 135–48. Elsevier-North Holland, Amsterdam.

Kitz, R., and Wilson, I. B. (1962). Esters of methane sulfonic acid as irreversible inhibitors of acetylcholinesterase. *J. Biol. Chem.*, **237**, 3245–49.

Knight, G. C. and Waley, S. G. (1985). Inhibition of class C β-lactamases by (1′R, 6R)-6-(1′hydroxy)-benzylpenicillanic acid S,S-dioxide. *Biochem. J.*, **225**, 435–9.

Lee, Y.-J. and Wilson, I. B. (1971). Enzymic parameters. Measurement of V and K. *Biochim. Biophys. Acta*, **242**, 519–22.

Liu, W. and Tsou, C. L. (1986). Determination of rate constants for the irreversible inhibition of acetylcholine esterase by continuously monitoring the substrate reaction in the presence of the inhibitor. *Biochim. Biophys. Acta*, **870**, 185–90.

McInnes, I., Schorstein, D. E., Suckling, C. J., and Wrigglesworth, R. (1981). Latent inhibitors. Part 2. Allylic inhibitors of alcohol dehydrogenase. *J. Chem. Soc. Perkin Trans.*, **1**, 1103–8.

Main, A. R. (1964). Affinity and phosphorylation constants for the inhibition of esterases by organophosphates. *Science*, **144**, 992–3.

Malcolm, A. D. B. and Radda, G. K. (1970). The reaction of glutamate dehydrogenase with 4-iodoacetamido salicylic acid *Eur. J. Biochem.*, **15**, 555–61.

Meister, A. (1978). Inhibition of glutamine synthetase and γ-glutamyl cysteine synthetases by methionine sulfoximine and related compounds. In *Enzyme-activated irreversible inhibitors* (ed. N. Seiler, M. J. Jung, and J. Koch-Weser), pp. 187–210. Elsevier-North Holland, Amsterdam.

Metcalf, B. W., Lippert, B., and Casara, P. (1978). Enzyme-activated irreversible inhibition of transaminases. In *Enzyme-activated irreversible inhibitors* (ed. N. Seiler, M. J. Jung, and J. Koch-Weser), pp. 123–33. Elsevier-North Holland, Amsterdam.

O'Brien, R. D. (1968). Kinetics of the carbamylation of cholinesterase. *Mol. Pharmacol.*, **4**, 121–30.

Plapp, B. V. (1983). Application of affinity labelling for studying structure and function of enzymes. In *Contemporary enzyme kinetics and mechanism* (ed. D. L. Purich), pp. 321–51, Academic Press, New York.

Purdie, J. E. and Heggie, R. M. (1970). The kinetics of the reaction of *N*,*N*-dimethyl-2-phenylaziridinium ion with bovine erythrocyte acetylcholinesterase. *Can. J. Biochem.*, **48**, 244–50.

Rakitzis, E. T. (1974). Kinetics of irreversible enzyme inhibition by an unstable inhibitor. *Biochem. J.*, **141**, 601–3.

Rakitzis, E. T. (1977). The kinetics of irreversible enzyme inhibition: cooperative effects. *J. Theor. Biol.*, **67**, 49–52.

Rakitzis, E. T. (1978). Kinetics of irreversible enzyme inhibition by an unstable inhibitor: cooperative effects. *J. Theor. Biol.*, **75**, 239–43.

Rakitzis, E. T. (1981). Kinetics of irreversible enzyme inhibition by an unstable inhibitor. *Biochem. J.*, **199**, 462–3.

Rakitzis, E. T. (1984). Kinetics of protein modification reactions. *Biochem. J.*, **217**, 341–51.

Rando, R. R. (1984). Mechanism-based enzyme inactivators. *Pharmacol. Rev.*, **36**, 111–42.

Rando, R. R. and Eigner, A. (1977). The pseudoirreversible inhibition of monoamine oxidase by allylamine. *Mol. Pharmacol.*, **13**, 1005–13.

Ray, W. J. and Koshland, D. E. (1961). A method for characterizing the type and numbers of groups involved in enzyme action *J. Biol. Chem.*, **236**, 1973–9.

Seiler, N., Jung, M. J., and Koch-Weser, J. (1978). *Enzyme-activated irreversible inhibitors.* Elsevier-North Holland, Amsterdam.

Selwyn, M. J. (1965). A simple test for inactivation of an enzyme during assay. *Biochim. Biophys. Acta*, **105**, 193–5.

Silverman, R. B. and Hoffman, S. J. (1984). The organic chemistry of mechanism based enzyme inhibition: a chemical approach to drug design. *Med. Res. Rev.*, **4**, 415–47.

Singer, T. P. (1979). Active site-directed irreversible inhibition of monoamine oxidase. In *Monoamine oxidase: structure, function and altered functions* (ed. T. P. Singer, R. W. Von Korff, and D. L. Murphy), pp. 7–24. Academic Press, New York.

Tatsumani, S., Yago, N., and Hosoe, M. (1981). Kinetics of suicide substrates. Steady-state treatments and computer-aided exact solutions. *Biochim. Biophys. Acta*, **662**, 226–35.

Tian, W. X. and Tsou, C. L. (1982). Determination of the rate constants of enzyme modification by measuring the substrate reaction in the presence of the modifier. *Biochemistry*, **21**, 1028–32.

Tipton, K. F. (1980). Kinetics and enzyme inhibition studies. In *Enzyme inhibitors as drugs* (ed. M. Sandler), pp. 1–23. Macmillan, London.

Tipton, K. F. (1985). Enzyme assays and kinetic studies. In *Techniques in the life sciences. B1/11 Supp. Protein and enzyme biochemistry* (ed. K. F. Tipton), pp. B113/1–B113/61. Elsevier, Ireland.

Tipton, K. F. and Fowler, C. J. (1984). The kinetics of monoamine oxidase inhibitors in relation to their clinical behavior. In *Monoamine oxidase and disease* (ed. K. F. Tipton, P. Dostert, and M. Strolin Benedetti), pp. 27–40, Academic Press, London.

Tipton, K. F., McCrodden, J. M., Kalir, A. S., and Youdim, M. B. H. (1982). Inhibition of rat liver monoamine oxidase by α-methyl- and *N*-propargyl-amine derivatives. *Biochem. Pharmacol.*, **31**, 1251–5.

Tipton, K. F., Fowler, C. J., McCrodden, J. M., and Strolin, Benedetti, M. (1983a). The enzyme-activated irreversible inhibition of type-B monoamine oxidase by 3-{-4-[(3-chlorophenyl)methoxy]phenyl}-5-[(methylamino)methyl]-2-oxazolidinone   methane sulphonate (compound MD 780236) and the enzyme-catalysed oxidation of this compound as competing reactions. *Biochem. J.*, **209**, 235–42.

Tipton, K. F., O'Carroll, A.-M., Mantle, T. J., and Fowler, C. J. (1983b). Factors involved in the selective inhibition of monoamine oxidase. *Mod. Probl. Pharmacopsychiat.*, **19**, 15–30.

Topham, C. M. (1985). Chemical modification of enzymes: reaction with an unstable inhibitor. *Biochem. J.*, **227**, 1025–26.

Topman, C. M. (1988). Computer simulation of the kinetics of irreversible enzyme inhibition by an unstable inhibitor. *Biochem. J.*, **240**, 817–20.

Tsou, C. L. (1988). Kinetics of substrate reactions during irreversible modification of enzyme activity. *Meth. Enzymol.*, in press.

Tsou, C. L., Tian, W. X., and Zhao, K. Y. (1985). Kinetics of irreversible modification of enzyme activity. In *Molecular architecture of proteins and enzymes.*, pp. 15–30., Academic Press, New York.

Waley, S. G. (1980). Kinetics of suicide substrates. *Biochem. J.*, **185**, 771–3.

Waley, S. G. (1985). Kinetics of suicide substrates: practical procedures for determining parameters. *Biochem. J.*, **277**, 843–9.

Walker, B. and Ellmore, D. T. (1984) The irreversible inhibition of urokinase, kidney-cell plasminogen activator, plasmin and β-trypsin by 1-(N-6-amino-N-hexyl)carbamoylimidazole. *Biochem. J.*, **221**, 277–80.

Walsh, C. T. (1983). Suicide substrates: mechanism-based enzyme inactivators with therapeutic potential. *Trends Biochem. Sci.*, **8**, 254–7.

Wiseman, J. S., Tayrien, G., and Abeles, R. H. (1980). Kinetics of cyclopropanone hydrate with yeast aldehyde dehydrogenase: a model for enzyme–substrate interaction. *Biochemistry*, **19**, 4222–31.

Section 2D

Potential of molecular graphics in the computer-aided design of inhibitors

A C T North

2D.1   Introduction

The use of molecular models is well established. It is particularly necessary in

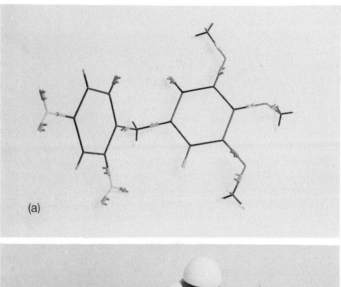

Fig. 2D.1 The trimethoprim (TMP) molecule illustrated by (a) a skeletal model, (b) a space-filling model, (c) a 'ball-and-spoke' model, (d) a skeletal representation on a calligraphic display, and (e) a space-filling representation on a raster display.

the study of macromolecules such as proteins and nucleic acids, for which a three-dimensional representation is essential for a proper appreciation of the spatial arrangement of functional groups and for an assessment of the significant interactions between pairs of molecules. Computer graphics provide an inherently precise and flexible approach to modelling molecular structures.

The most familiar use of molecular models is to illustrate known structures. An extension of this is the initial investigation of substances of as yet unknown

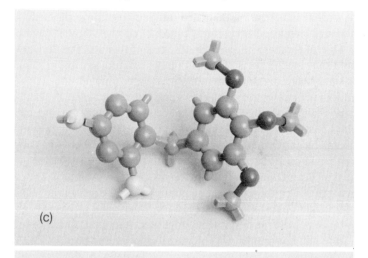

(c)

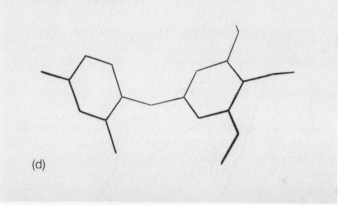

(d)

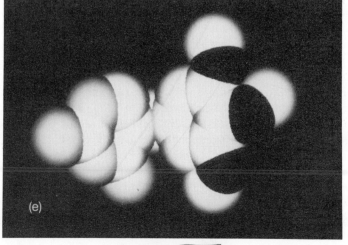

(e)

three-dimensional structure by the use of models that are sufficiently precise to ensure that any proposed structures conform to the known laws of stereochemistry. One of the best-known applications of this was the derivation of the structure of DNA on the basis of the rather sparse information present in X-ray fibre diagrams. Molecular models are widely used in building detailed three-dimensional structures of proteins from crystallographically-derived electron-density maps which, although sufficiently accurate, are lacking in detail because of the limited resolution of the data; detail is effectively provided by the known stereochemical constraints placed by the models upon the relative positions of atoms. Another application is in the interpretation of n.m.r. spectra, so permitting the distance and angular information derivable from the spectra to be transformed into three-dimensional structures.

Molecular models can take a variety of forms: skeletal models [Fig. 2D.1(a)] show the covalent links joining atoms together, but the atoms themselves are indicated only as the points of intersection between bonds. This form of representation allows the stereochemistry to be defined and the positions of atoms to be measured very precisely, but it gives a very uninformative and, indeed, misleading impression of the space occupied by atoms. Space-filling models [Fig. 2D.1(b)] give a clear indication of atomic volumes and of the shapes of molecular surfaces but, as the centres of atoms lie within the components, they cannot be positioned accurately and, while the atoms of the outer surface can be seen readily, they obscure those buried within the molecule. Between these two extremes fall 'ball-and-spoke' models (Figure 2D.1c), but they represent neither the accurate positions of atom centres nor the shapes of surfaces, although they are very valuable for didactic purposes.

A major problem with any kind of conventional 'hardware' model lies in the difficulty of supporting a large structure sufficiently rigidly and the tendency of components to come apart.

A revolutionary advance in molecular modelling has come through the ability to interface computers to display devices, so that molecular components represented precisely within the computer by their coordinates may be illustrated in a variety of styles on the display screen. An important adjunct is an input device to the computer so that the model can be changed readily by the operator. While parameters to be altered can be input via a conventional computer keyboard, a much more natural and effective interaction between operator and computer can be achieved by 'analog' input devices such as rotatable knobs or joysticks (see Fig. 2D.2). These not only permit the whole molecule to be rotated or translated, but can also allow molecules to be built up from components and their conformations to be adjusted by rotations about bonds, analogously to the assembly and manipulation of a hardware model from atomic components. This interactive use of computer displays requires a rapid response from the computer so that movement of the model appears not to lag appreciably behind movement of the control. Because of 'retention of

Fig. 2D.2 Leeds computer display system and its controlling keyboard—note the rotatable knobs for interactive control by the user.

vision', a response time of 1/50 or 1/25 s appears to be instantaneous and to give smooth movement.

The principal merits of computer graphics for molecular modelling may be summarized as follows.

1. Flexibility, including:
   (a) the ability to use different forms of representation, e.g. skeletal, space-filling or diagrammatic, either singly or in combination;
   (b) the ability to select relevant parts of the molecule for detailed examination, displaying only those of current interest, whether they lie on the surface or in the centre of the molecule;
   (c) the ability to vary stereochemical parameters such as bond lengths or inter-bond angles (which would require the construction of a new set of components for hardware models).

2. Precision. Atomic coordinates and molecular geometries may be held within the computer as precisely as required.

3. Comparison of different molecules, e.g. a family of drugs, by superimposing their representations on the screen, so allowing similarities and differences to be visualized much more readily than with conventional models, which have to be placed side-by-side.

4. Computation of structure-related properties can be carried out for any functions that can be derived from the atomic coordinates, e.g. interaction energies between pairs of molecules. A particular advantage is gained if these calculations can be made in 'real time', which effectively means within the 1/50 or 1/25-s interval between successive display frames. The calculated quantity then appears to vary continuously as the molecular geometry is changed.

5. Use of colour either to colour-code atom types in the conventional way or to represent properties such as electrostatic potential or surface hydrophobicity—this feature gives colour displays a very great advantage over monochrome systems.

2D.2 Display hardware

There are two essentially different ways of drawing a picture from a list of the coordinates of the features that are to be displayed.

In calligraphic (or vector) displays, the picture is made up from a number of straight lines. The computer program selects the lines, evaluates their end-points and sends the required coordinates either in pairs or as a list to the display processor, which converts the coordinates into voltages that are applied to the deflector plates of the cathode ray tube; the beam is thus moved in a straight line between the two end-points [Fig. 2D.3(a)]. A further item of data from the computer specifies the colour to be used and the brightness of the line, allowing also the beam to be switched off while it is deflected, a feature required when a line does not begin from the end of the preceding one. A very common requirement is for the picture to be rotated and/or translated so that the molecule may be seen from a different standpoint from that implied by the coordinates stored in the computer. This may be achieved by operating on the coordinates by a rotation/translation matrix while they are 'on the way' to being displayed. This operation, which can also scale the picture to fit conveniently on the screen, can either be carried out by software within the computer or by a special hardware unit. Such hardware is to be found on more powerful (and expensive) systems and it has a number of advantages in addition to speed; for example, the control knobs used to vary parameters can feed directly into the rotation hardware, thus bypassing the computer. Additional processing operations can be incorporated, such as front- and back-clipping, which cuts off all features that lie outside a slab of specified thickness along the viewing direction.

In the alternative type of display, the CRT beam traverses the tube in a raster, as in a television set. The picture is composed of an array of pixels (picture elements), for example 1200 wide and 1000 high. Each feature of the structure to be displayed is converted into the corresponding pixels, a number being placed in the appropriate element of an array (the pixel store), specifying the colour to be drawn. As the beam scans over the tube, the pixel store array is read synchronously and its value used to control the colour and brightness of the

(a) CALLIGRAPHIC (VECTOR)

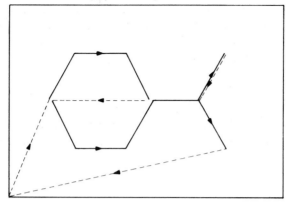

(b) RASTER

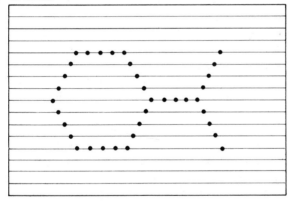

Fig. 2D.3 Comparison of calligraphic (a) and raster (b) display generation. In (a) the CRT beam is moved along the vectors making up the diagram, with intensity switched off (broken line) when successive vectors are not contiguous; in (b) the beam scans the screen in a raster and is intensified whenever its position corresponds to a point in the 'pixel' array that has been set 'on'. In practice, the beam size is large enough for adjacent points to coalesce.

displayed pixel [Fig. 2D.3(b)]. Loading of the pixel store, given the coordinates of the ends of vectors or the centres and radii of circles, may be accomplished by software or special-purpose hardware. As with calligraphic displays, rotation, translation, scaling, and clipping may be incorporated by software or hardware.

It should be apparent from these brief descriptions that the raster systems require an extra store (the pixel array) and an extra stage of processing (converting features into the corresponding pixels) compared to calligraphic displays (Fig. 2D.4). The latter have therefore tended to predominate and still

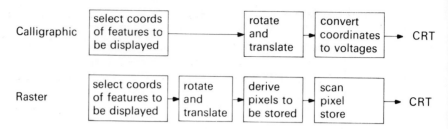

Fig. 2D.4 Schematic diagram showing the successive operations entailed in the generation of pictures on calligraphic and raster systems.

have an unrivalled capacity for drawing large numbers of vectors, as required for skeletal models [Fig. 2D.1(d)] and contour maps. However, the increasing speed of computer circuits and decreasing cost of computer memory have improved the performance and price of raster displays and they have an important advantage in their ability to display solid areas of colour without a speed penalty, as the time for the picture to be scanned is constant and independent of the amount of detail in it. By contrast, with calligraphic displays solid areas require a very large number of vectors, and there is a limit to the number of vectors that can be drawn without the refresh rate being reduced, with consequent flickering of the picture. At the present time, the two types must be considered as complementary, calligraphic displays being pre-eminent with pictures comprising many discrete elements (particularly vectors), and raster systems being advantageous for showing coloured areas as in space-filling models [Fig. 2D.1(e)].

The situation may well change fairly soon, as further increases in performance and decreases in price can be expected for raster systems. (This forecast made at the time of writing (February, 1986) is indeed proving correct.) An important reason for the latter expectation is that the circuits of raster-type tubes are similar to those in television sets, and moves to introduce high resolution domestic television should lead, through mass-production, to cheap raster systems with high performance, whereas calligraphic systems will probably continue to be restricted to scientific research and low-volume industrial applications.

So far, we have been discussing the advanced systems suitable for interactive modelling in specialist laboratories, costing £40 000 or more. Present day microcomputers, costing only a few hundred pounds, can nevertheless produce quite presentable pictures, but they lack both resolution and the processor capacity required for interactive manipulations. Technical developments may well reduce the price gap between the simple and advanced hardware, bringing molecular graphics systems into much wider use.

The effective study of molecular structures and interactions, particularly if the latter are to be placed on a quantitative basis by calculation of interaction energies, requires both a display system and a computer; an important matter that we have not yet discussed is the division of responsibility between the two. At one extreme, both the computational work and most of the picture processing could be carried out on the computer; for the approach to be viable, it would be essential for users to have virtually instantaneous access to the computer. At the other extreme, the display would be part of a 'work-station' with all the special-purpose hardware required for picture manipulation and for building up complex pictures from defined fragments. This greatly reduces the demand on the computer, so that a much lower-level of response could be tolerated. The choice is likely to be determined largely by the other uses to which the main computer is to be put and by the number of people concerned with molecular modelling, as well as the ever-changing prices of computing equipment.

There is one respect in which present-day molecular graphics systems are inferior to molecular models—the image on the screen can only be two-dimensional. Various palliatives are used to overcome this deficiency:

1. 'Depth-cueing', i.e. variation in the brightness of the image depending on the distance of the feature from the observer. This is not a very powerful aid.

2. Rotation or rocking of the image. This is effective but it is difficult to examine details of structure or interactions in a continuously moving picture.

3. Stereoscopic systems; these are very effective but it must be appreciated that a significant proportion of people do not have the facility of good stereoscopic vision. For those who do, several different types of system are available:

   (a) The red/green anaglyph system. Unfortunately, if red and green are being used to provide stereoscopic information, the images cannot use the full range of colour desirable for the visualization of structures and properties.
   (b) Split-screen stereo in which two images are displayed separately on the two halves of the screen, with an optical device being used to help merge them. This reduces the size of the largest possible image and it is difficult for more than one person at a time to view the image.
   (c) Tachistoscopic systems in which the two images are displayed alternately and viewed through shutters synchronized so that each eye sees only one image. Probably the most satisfactory devices of this kind employ spectacles in which the two 'lenses' are liquid crystal cells that can be made alternately transparent and opaque (Fig. 2D.5) (Harris et al. 1985). A possible improvement is to put the liquid crystal cell on the face of the CRT screen, with the observer wearing passive polarizing spectacles, but this advance requires the manufacture of very large liquid crystal cells with stable performance.

2D.3 Computer display software

While there are several adequate hardware systems that can be bought 'off-the-shelf', there is no single software package that can meet all the requirements for

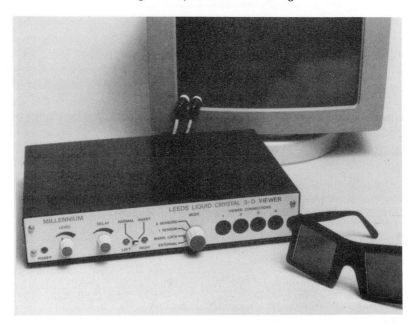

Fig. 2D.5 A stereoscopic viewing system. The CRT displays the left-eye and right-eye views alternately. Photopickups read fiducial marks from the screen and transmit signals to the controller, which drives the spectacle 'lenses' in synchrony with the display.

drug design. Developments in software have originated in two effectively different research schools. Protein crystallographers have developed programs with the principal aim of displaying large polymeric molecules made up from a limited number of types of component (amino acids), each of well-known structure, and of manipulating the molecular conformation to fit the crystallographically derived electron-density distributions. Extensions of this approach permit the display of non-standard fragments and the calculation of interaction energies involving electrostatic and van der Waals' forces, though not generally 'in real time'. Probably the most widely used program of this kind is FRODO, originally written by Jones (1978), and subsequently much modified by others to run on a variety of machines and to incorporate additional features.

The alternative approach has been used by chemists interested in the structures of small molecules such as drugs and inhibitors, whose programs were aimed initially at building up molecules from small chemical groups. These fragment-building programs are interfaced to molecular mechanics routines, which use standard force-fields to determine the minimum-energy conformation of the structure that has been sketched out, or, alternatively, to quantum mechanics programs that have essentially the same objective of deriving the most probable molecular conformation, together with its electronic charge distribution.

An additional interface made by many of these programs is with structure data-bases. Foremost among these is the Cambridge crystallographic data-base (Allen *et al.* 1979), a carefully checked compilation of the three-dimensional structures of small molecules, which can be searched to find the preferred conformations (or range of conformations) of molecular fragments as they occur in known, accurately-determined crystal structures. Other information that can be extracted from this data-base includes preferred hydrogen bonding geometries. Another source of information is the Brookhaven Protein Data Bank (Bernstein *et al.* 1977), which contains the coordinates of many of the proteins whose three-dimensional structures have been determined. The accuracy of these coordinates is difficult to specify, partly because further refinement of many of the structures is still in progress, partly because many proteins clearly have well-defined very stable cores but more flexible surface loops. Workers who are not experienced in protein crystallography would therefore be well-advised to consult the source of the coordinates before advancing any revolutionary theories based on them.

Some of the graphics programs have been aimed particularly at providing representations of molecular structures with high impact and clarity, often simplifying the diagrams in a cartoon-like fashion, for example to bring out the helical, sheet, and coil elements in the structure (e.g. Lesk and Hardman 1982) (Fig. 2D.6). Such programs are particularly valuable in the comparison of structures and in the study of conformational changes. Another use is in interpreting the results of molecular dynamics simulations of molecular vibration modes by means of time-lapse photography of a succession of pictures. Space-filling models require the very time-consuming removal of all features hidden by others nearer to the observer and it is not generally possible to make conformational changes or alter the viewing direction 'in real time'. Computer graphics representations of space-filling models thus have a double disadvantage—the first that interior features are hidden, the second that changes can only be made slowly.

Methods have, however, been devised to show surface shape semi-transparently. One way is to draw a three-dimensional contour of the surface of the 'chicken-wire' type, surrounding the skeletal diagram (Fig. 2D.7), (Barry and North 1971). The approach pioneered by Connolly (Langridge *et al.* 1981) is to draw a number of dots on the van der Waals' radius surface around each atom, each dot being a very short vector (Fig. 2D.8). With either of these methods, the picture can be rotated as a whole quite satisfactorily. It is often valuable to use clipping so that only a small part of the depth of the molecule is shown. It is more difficult to make conformational adjustments, since this requires re-computation of the surfaces of adjacent atoms when their lines of intersection change, but computer methods are being developed for this. The van der Waals' surface is not in fact the most helpful, as it contains many invaginations and

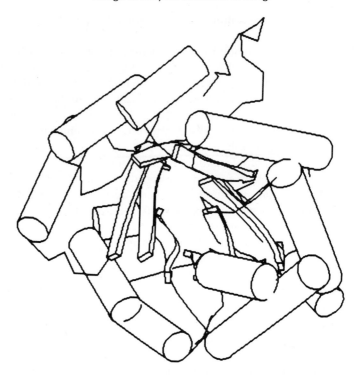

Fig. 2D.6 A 'cartoon' representation of a protein structure, in which α-helical regions are represented by cylinders and β-strands by flat arrows.

internal holes that are inaccessible. A more useful surface is the 'accessible surface' defined by Lee and Richards (1971) and generated by the computational analogue of rolling a ball (representing, say, a solvent molecule) over the van der Waals' surface of the molecule (Fig. 2D.9). The resultant surface defines the parts of the molecules that are available to interact with others; internal holes are only shown if they are large enough to entrap other molecules.

As explained earlier, the molecular surface can be coloured whether it is depicted in the area-filled form available on a raster graphics system or whether by the Connolly type of transparent representation on a calligraphic display. The colours can be chosen to indicate atomic species (as with conventional molecular models) or properties such as electrostatic potential. An excellent example of this showed clearly the variation in potential over the surface of the enzyme superoxide dismutase, which is such as to draw the small, negatively charged superoxide radical towards the active site of the enzyme (Getzoff *et al.* 1983). Nakamura *et al.* (1985) have demonstrated that when an enzyme (the host) interacts with a ligand (the guest), the potential on the surface of the guest due to its own atoms is largely complementary to the potential distribution on

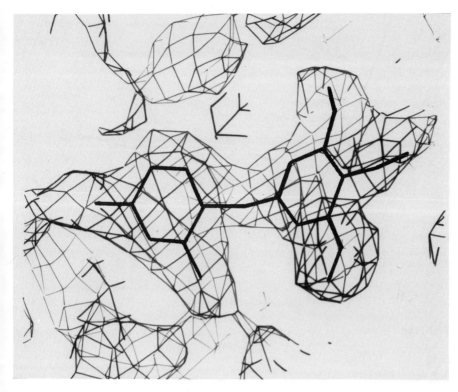

Fig. 2D.7 Molecular model showing the covalent bond structure of TMP with the van der Waals' surface indicated by a 'chicken-wire' mesh.

the surface of the guest due to the host atoms. Such coloured displays are most informative; unfortunately they are too complex to be reproduced here in monochrome.

2.D.4 Study of molecular interactions

Three-dimensional structural studies by X-ray crystallography, supported by complementary methods that can be applied in the solution state such as n.m.r. spectroscopy, leave no doubt that the specificity of interactions between enzymes and their substrates or inhibitors rests on a complementarity of structural features. These include an overall complementarity of surface shape, together with the juxtaposition of specific interacting groups such as hydrogen-bond donors and acceptors, and of pairs of hydrophobic surface patches. Although in some cases there may be gross conformational changes in an enzyme during the course of catalysis, particularly if two or more substrate molecules are concerned, the binding of single ligands normally involves comparatively small chan-

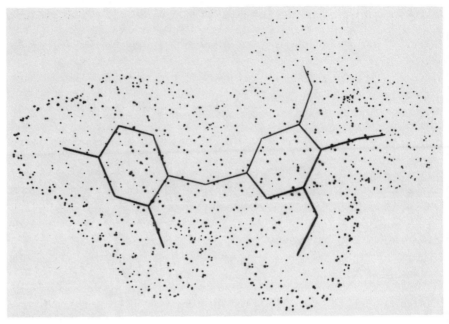

Fig. 2D.8 An alternative method of representing the surface by dots on the calligraphic display.

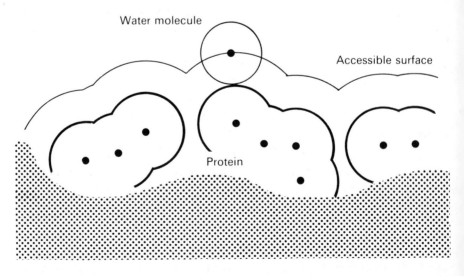

Fig. 2D.9 Generation of the solvent-accessible surface of a molecule, effectively achieved by rolling a sphere (representing a solvent molecule) over the van der Waals' surface.

ges from the free conformation, though these may be subtle and important, such as the distortion of a substrate towards its transition-state conformation.

A useful starting point is the assumption that the complementarity can be recognized when the molecules are each in their uncomplexed conformations, which are expected to be those of minimum free energy. The formation of the Michaelis complex might well involve small mutual distortions, with the binding energy more than offsetting the increases of conformational free energy entailed. Rather grosser changes may occur in the formation of a productive enzyme–substrate complex, in which the transition state may entail severe local distortions in conformational geometry and/or electronic configuration. The design of drugs that are to act by inhibiting specific enzymes or receptors thus requires a knowledge only of the conformations of the free molecules, whereas a drug that is intended to elicit a productive response must be able to adopt the transition-state geometry and cause its receptor to do likewise.

In attempting to design drugs complementary to receptors of known structure, it is moderately straightforward to calculate the enthalpic contributions to the free energy of binding, although the difficulty of assessing the permittivity (dielectric constant) appropriate for calculation of electrostatic effects presents problems. Even more difficult is allowing properly for desolvation energies and, as Fersht and his colleagues (Fersht *et al.* 1985) have shown by protein engineering, the introduction of an extra apparently favourable interaction may actually lead to less favourable ligand binding if it also increases the energy required to strip solvent molecules from the interacting surfaces. Account should also be taken of the reduction of entropy that occurs when two molecules coalesce. One component of this is due to the loss of conformational entropy that occurs when a flexible molecule has its mobility restricted on binding to another. A further stratagem in enhancing the free energy of ligand binding is thus to rigidify the ligand (with its principal reactive groups in the correct arrangement for productive binding) so as to reduce its entropy loss on binding.

In considering the applications of computer graphics to drug design, we may distinguish between two situations:

(1) when the three-dimensional structure of the receptor is unknown; and

(2) when it is known, as in the case of inhibitors of vital enzymes, the structures of which have been determined crystallographically.

In both cases, it must always be recognized that the 'design' of a geometrically appropriate molecule does not guarantee an effective drug—for pharmacological activity the drug has first to be delivered to the correct site. The assumption behind the rational approach to drug design based on molecular structure is, first, that there is no point in carrying out costly animal or clinical trials on substances with molecular structures that are inappropriate from the outset and, second, that a knowledge of the molecular shape and disposition of functional groups may well suggest radically new molecular families with the required properties, rather than just small variations of a 'lead' compound.

2D.5   Modelling drugs for receptors of unknown structure

The approach is to compare compounds that are known to have similar effects. Such comparison of molecular structures is greatly facilitated by the ability of computer graphics to superimpose pictures of molecular structures, and the first stage is to obtain a relative orientation of the molecules that maximizes correspondence between the overall shapes, the positions of functional groups, and the distribution of charge. Marshall and his colleagues (Marshall *et al.* 1979) have shown the value of the concept of the 'union' of the molecular volumes, which indicates the shape of the space that must be available on the receptor for productive binding. Comparison of inactive compounds with active ones commonly shows that the inactive ones occupy additional space that is unavailable on the receptor (Fig. 2D.10). Such comparison of a family of active and related inactive compounds is thus able to indicate not only the spatial disposition of functional groups important for activity (and hence to map the disposition of complementary groups on the receptor) but also to map the shape of the binding site, i.e. that volume that is excluded in total by all active compounds but which may overlap the additional volumes required by inactive compounds.

One further point should be made; ligands may well be conformationally distorted from their free forms on binding to a receptor and the complementary conformation of the binding site may require a mutual distortion of two or more ligands to give the best spatial correspondence between their effective functional groups. This may be obtained by a minimization procedure that permits energetically small conformational changes that significantly improve the matching of features. Alternatively, the display may be used (Fig. 2D.11) to map the positions available to rotameric functional groups of the ligand so as to show the range of conformations within which the active conformation must lie (Hassall *et al.* 1982).

2D.6   Modelling drugs for receptors of known structure

While comparison of active and inactive substances may give valuable leads to new drugs even without knowledge of the receptor structure, the approach is clearly more powerful when the three-dimensional structure of the receptor is available. As membrane-bound receptors have generally defied crystallization so far, the method has been tried with ligands that act by inhibiting metabolically important soluble enzymes.

A widely studied example is angiotensin-converting enzyme (ACE), controlled inhibition of which is desired for the control of blood pressure. Unfortunately, the three-dimensional structure of ACE is not yet known, but a reasonable model for it can be made as a result of its homology to other Zn-containing enzymes such as thermolysin (Hassall *et al.* 1982; Smith *et al.* 1984), the structures of which have been determined (Holmes and Matthews 1982). This exemplifies what is likely to prove an invaluable finding from protein structural

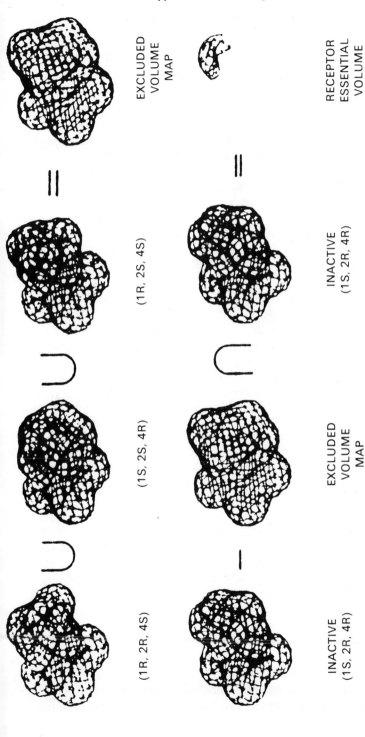

Fig. 2D.10 Unions of volumes of three active compounds (top line) to map the total receptor volume available for drug binding. In the lower line, comparison of the excluded volume with the volume required by an inactive compound yields an additional volume that is required by the inactive compound and is presumed to be part of the receptor itself, thus preventing the inactive compound from binding (from Marshall *et al.* 1979). Adapted with permission from ACS. Symposium Series 112, pp. 205–226. Copyright 1979, American Chemical Society.

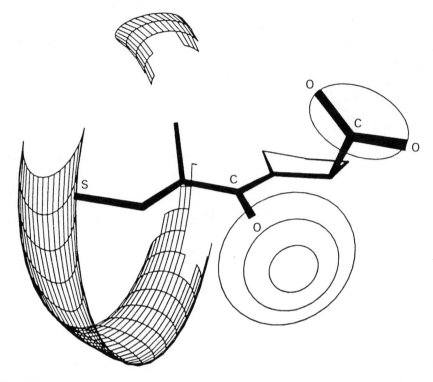

Fig. 2D.11 Mapping the proposed binding site for captopril, an inhibitor of ACE. The mesh on the left hand part of the figure shows the range of positions for the sulphur atom as single bonds are rotated through conformations of low energy. The circular contours (bottom right) indicate the locus of hydrogen-bond donors on the binding site that could interact with the carbonyl oxygen of captopril. The hoop (top right) shows the range of positions accessible to the carboxylate group which would interact with a positive charge on the receptor (from Hassall *et al.* 1982). Adapted with permission from *FEBS Lett.* (1982) **147**, 175–9.

studies—proteins appear to belong to families, the members of which have structural similarities, either of the whole molecule or of domains (molecular components that are folded essentially independently). Such similarities are generally presumed to arise by evolutionary divergence from an ancestral precursor. It is now clear that homology in three-dimensional structure may be retained despite wide divergence in amino-acid sequence and function.

At the present time, the amino-acid sequences of several thousand proteins are known, whereas the three-dimensional structures of less than 200 proteins have been determined. This imbalance is likely to increase as modern sequencing methods are increasingly fast and can succeed with minute quantities of material, compared to X-ray crystallography. The prediction of three-dimensional structure from sequence is as yet restricted essentially to the conformation of local features. Nevertheless, the combination of sensitive methods for the detection of weak homology with secondary-structure prediction seems likely to be fruitful in building models for many proteins of known sequence but unknown three-dimensional structure. The development of data-bases of protein sequences and structural data is important if protein homologies are to be exploited.

In the case of thermolysin and ACE, workers at the Squibb laboratories used a relatively unsophisticated two-dimensional approach to design a clinically useful ACE inhibitor, captopril (Ondetti *et al.* 1977), a molecule that incorporates functional groups that mimic essential groups of the natural substrate, angiotensin I. Not only is its similarity to thermolysin sufficient to enable a model of the active-site region of ACE to be built but also knowledge of the modes of binding of a series of thermolysin inhibitors was used by the Merck group to derive the structural features expected for ACE ligands (Smith *et al.* 1984). Study of the conformational changes that occur in thermolysin substrates during catalysis has enabled the latter authors to design inhibitors that are transition-state analogues. Workers at Roche Products (Hassall *et al.* 1982) also have endeavoured to make more effective ACE inhibitors by varying their functional groups and restricting the conformational flexibility while aiming at the same time to design molecules that can be synthesized more readily.

Goodford and his colleagues (Beddell *et al.* 1976) have used a knowledge of the binding site of haemoglobin for its allosteric effector, diphosphoglycerate (DPG), to synthesize potent effectors of a quite different chemical structure to DPG, and they and the Leeds group have shown (Chabot *et al.* 1981; North 1982) that the calculated binding energies for this system correlate well with the observed effects.

One of the most widely studied biological systems that has been subjected to computer-assisted molecular modelling concerns dihydrofolate reductase

Table 2D.1 Relative ability of three drugs to inhibit dihydrofolate reductase from three different species. The table lists the concentrations ($\times 10^8$ M) required to give 50 per cent inhibition of DHFR. It shows, for example, that trimethoprim effectively inhibits the bacterial enzyme, but not the human

	Enzyme source		
Inhibitor	Human liver	*E. coli*	*Plasmodium berghei*
Methotrexate	9	0.1	0.07
Trimethoprim	30 000	0.5	7.0
Pyrimethamine	180	2500	0.05

(DHFR), a key enzyme in the biosynthesis of nucleic acid and amino acid precursors, principally through the reduction of dihydrofolate (FH$_2$) to tetrahydrofolate (FH$_4$). A number of clinically useful drugs have already been developed, and are employed as anti-cancer agents (methotrexate, MTX), antibacterials (trimethoprim, TMP), and anti-malarials (pyrimethamine). The latter two drugs rely on exploiting the subtle differences between human DHFR and the DHFRs of bacteria and the malarial parasite, so as to exert a selective inhibitory effect (Table 2D.1), which damages the parasite cells without harming the host. The objective of the structural studies has been to improve this

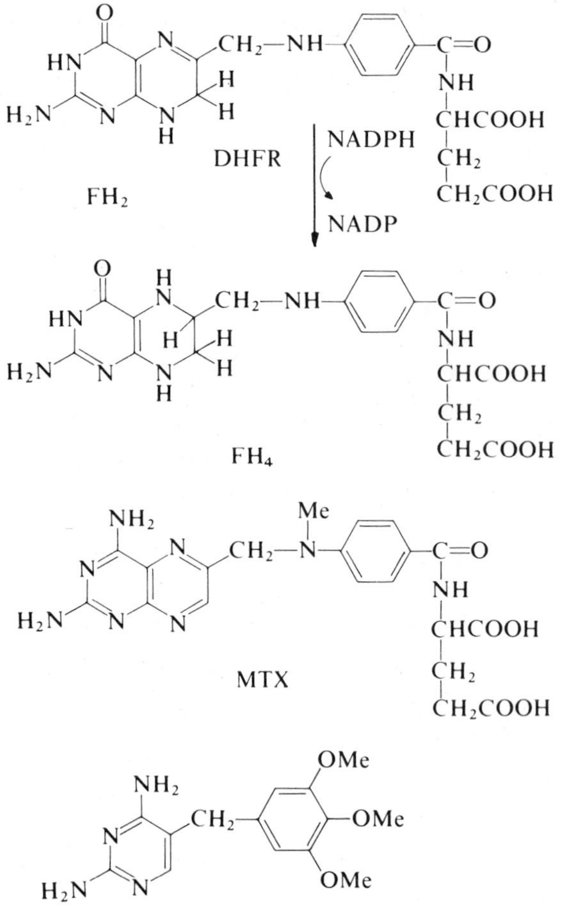

Fig. 2D.12 The substrate (dihydrofolate, FH$_2$), product (tetrahydrofolate, FH$_4$), and inhibitors (methotrexate, MTX and trimethoprim, TMP) of dihydrofolate reductase DHFR.

selectivity and develop more effective inhibitors that can be synthesized readily and used at lower concentrations.

MTX is clearly a close analogue of FH_2 (Fig. 2D.12), although the replacement of the carbonyl oxygen by an amino group on the diaminopyrimidine ring leads to a difference in polarity of the ring; consequently when MTX binds to the enzyme (at least at certain pH ranges), the ring is rotated through 180° to what would be a non-productive mode of binding for FH_2. TMP and pyrimethamine are smaller molecules, lacking the long glutamate tail of MTX and FH_2.

Both the Leeds group (Chabot *et al.* 1981; North 1982) and the Roche group (Kröhn 1983) have used molecular graphics to model the binding of TMP to bacterial DHFRs, the three-dimensional structures of both *Lactobacillus casei* and *Escherichia coli* DHFR having been determined by Kraut, Matthews, and their colleagues (Matthews *et al.* 1977, 1978). The minimum energy conformation for TMP bound to *E. coli* DHFR and its mode of binding were predicted by the Leeds group (Fig. 2D.13); the predictions were subsequently confirmed crystallographically (Baker *et al.* 1981) and the Roche workers have reported similar results (Kröhn 1983).

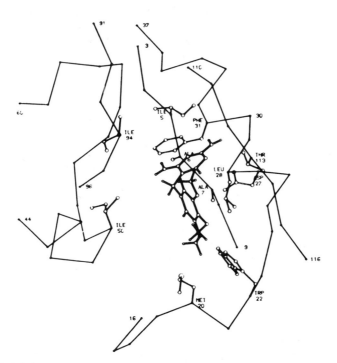

Fig. 2D.13 Minimum energy conformation of TMP and its preferred mode of binding to *E. coli* DHFR as deduced by computer graphics (Chabot *et al.* 1981; North 1982). Parts of the Cα backbone of the enzyme are shown, together with side-chains that make significant interactions with the inhibitor.

The Roche group observed the empty channel between the trimethoxybenzene ring of TMP and an arginine side-chain of the enzyme which interacts with the glutamate tails of FH_2 and MTX (Fig. 2D.14). They have therefore synthesized a series of derivatives of TMP with carboxyalkyl tails of varying lengths. These new derivatives show both enhanced DHFR inhibition and greater selectivity for the bacterial enzyme, though unfortunately they are apparently unable to penetrate bacterial cell walls.

The Leeds group has also investigated a series of TMP derivatives substituted at the 3', 4', and 5' positions of the phenyl ring and found a generally satisfactorily proportionality of the calculated enthalpies of binding to the observed inhibition constants (Fig. 2D.15). Comparison of the calculated interactions of several other compounds also placed them in the correct order compared to experimentally observed binding (Potterton *et al.* 1983).

The calculated enthalpies referred to have so far ignored solvent effects (and thus correspond to interactions *in vacuo*) and are too large compared to the observed free energies of binding (which include also entropy changes). The explanation for the success in predicting rank orders of binding appears to be that the factors that have been excluded give effects proportional, though of opposite sense, to those included in the calculations. This is not too surprising. Desolvation effects can be thought of as being partly general, dependent on the change of interfacial surface area between the solute molecules and the solvent, and partly specific, dependent on the removal of individual water molecules

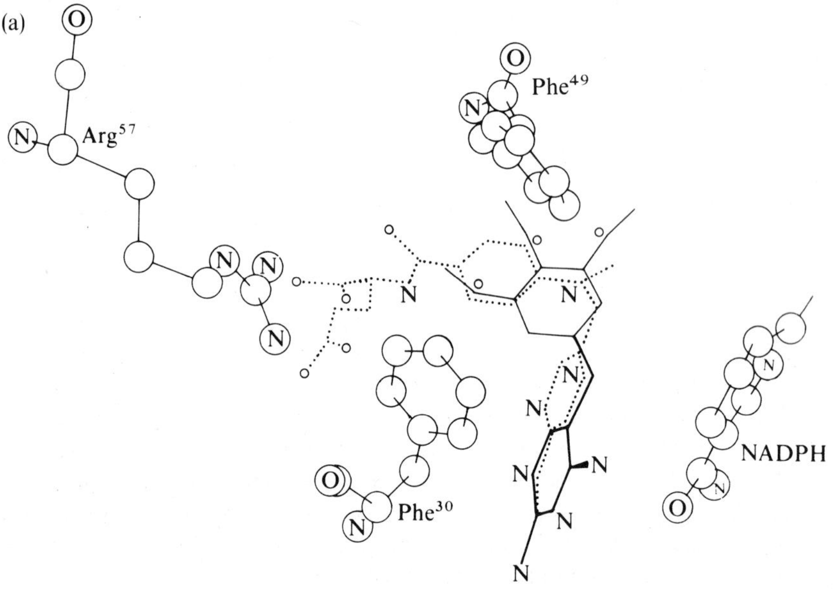

(b)

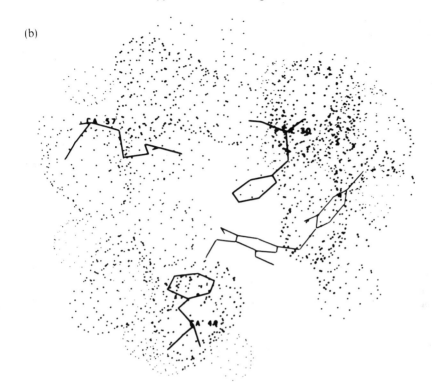

Fig. 2D.14 Interaction between the glutamate tail of MTX (dotted lines) and arginine 57 of DHFR, showing the unoccupied channel in the complex between DHFR and TMP (solid lines). (a) Diagrammatic representation (from Kröhn 1983); (b) from computer graphics screen with volume of enzyme atoms represented by dotted surfaces. Note that the two diagrams are from different view points—the unoccupied channel runs in (b) from the trimethoxybenzene ring of TMP towards the arginine side-chain (top left of figure).

Figure 2D.14(a) reproduced with permission from second SCI-RSC Medicinal Chemistry Symposium, ed. J. C. Emmett. Copyright 1983, Royal Society of Chemistry.

from the H-bonding groups to which they are attached. The first of these effects would be proportional to the areas of contact between ligand and enzyme, to which the van der Waals' energies included in the calculation also will be roughly proportional. The second would tend to be proportional to the number of H-bonds between ligand and enzyme, though of lower strength because of the better fit between the two solute molecules as compared to the arrangement of the water shell around each individually. As far as entropy changes are concerned, they are likely to be of similar magnitude for the binding of a series of ligand molecules of generally similar size and flexibility.

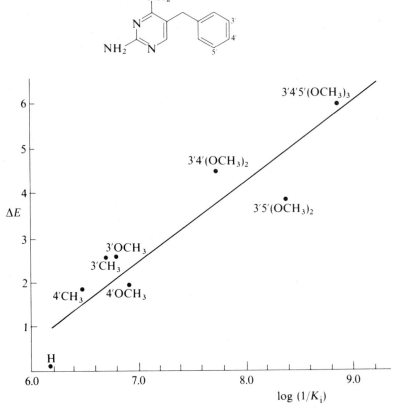

Fig. 2D.15 A series of DHFR inhibitors, based on benzylpyrimidine substituted at the 3',4', and 5' positions. Calculated enthalpies of binding (ΔE) for the benzylpyrimidine derivatives plotted against their experimentally observed inhibition constants, K_i (Hansch *et al.* 1982; Baccanari *et al.* 1982).

The extra complications entailed in a better modelling of solvent and entropic effects will doubtless be incorporated in future studies but it is encouraging to note that even when these factors are neglected, the correct ranking of members of a family of ligands shows the computer graphics approach to be a valuable aid in assessing the effects of the structural changes on binding and, hence, on potency.

The method used by the Leeds group and others is essentially a two-stage one (Fig. 2D.16). In the first stage, carried out interactively, the research worker uses his or her chemical knowledge ro recognize possible modes of interaction between ligand and receptor site and then steers the ligand towards a favourable mode. This may require conformational changes of ligand and receptor, in particular moving mobile receptor side-chains out of the way—this is an

STAGE 1—Interactive

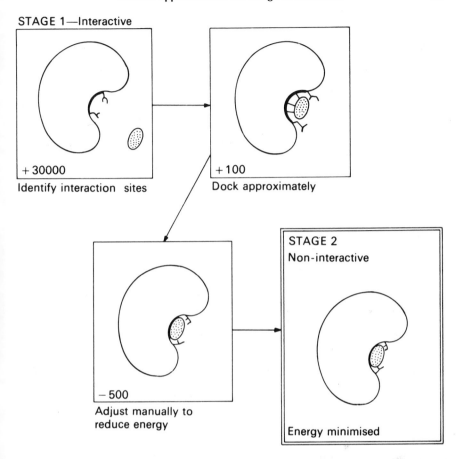

Fig. 2D.16 Two-stage approach to the use of computer graphics in 'docking' a ligand into a protein binding site. First, the user examines the ligand and protein separately in order to identify complementary features; then he or she moves the ligand into the binding site, which may necessitate moving protein side-chains out of the way; further adjustments are then made to position and conformation to optimize the fit, guided by the 'real-time' calculation of interaction energies (figure in bottom left of screen); with the correct binding site thus located interactively, the second stage comprises an automatic refinement, carried out by an off-line molecular mechanics program, at the end of which the final minimum-energy conformation is drawn on the screen.

important reason why a direct automatic energy minimization method will often be unable to move the ligand out of local energy minima into the global minimum. The Leeds graphics system (North *et al.* 1980) is able to compute energies arising from about 20 pairwise interactions in 'real time', and this aids the research worker in comparing alternative binding modes and aligning the molecules in an optimal fashion. In the second stage, the coordinates found interactively (which should have selected the correct global minimum) are then used as input to an automatic minimization program, which carries out final adjustment and derives the energy associated with the optimal configuration. Even with the automatic refinement procedure, usually carried out in an 'off-line' computer, it is instructive to store the coordinates from each cycle and then display them graphically in order to check the steps undergone during the refinement process.

2D.7 Concluding remarks

The combination of computers with graphical displays enables scientists to work with the precision they need and to utilize the most highly developed sense, vision, to make informed judgements of the effects of changing molecular conformations and chemical functional groups on enhancing drug–receptor interactions and selectivity of binding.

From the number of high-performance molecular graphics systems recently installed, both in universities and pharmaceutical laboratories, it seems clear that the value of the method is widely accepted. The approach is still very new and it will doubtless be several years yet before drugs designed by these methods have successfully completed clinical trials and become generally known.

References

Allen, H. A., Bellard, S., Brice, M. C., Cartwright, B. A., Doubleday, A., Higgs, H., Hummelink, T., Hummelink-Peters, B. G., Kennard, O. Motherwell, W. D. S., Rodgers, J. R., and Watson D. G. (1979). The Cambridge crystallographic data centre: computer-based search, retrieval, analysis and display of information. *Acta Crystallogr.*, **B35**, 2331–9.

Baccanari, D. P., Daluge, S., and King, R. W. (1982). Inhibition of dihydrofolate reductase: effect of reduced nicotinamide adenine dinucleotide phosphate on the selectivity and affinity of diaminobenzyl pyrimidines. *Biochemistry*, **21**, 5068–75.

Baker, D. J., Beddell, C. R., Champness, J. N., Goodford, P. J., Norrington, F. E. A., Smith, D. R., and Stammers, D. K. (1981). The binding of trimethoprim to bacterial dihydrofolate reductase. *FEBS Lett.*, **126**, 49–52.

Barry, C. D. and North A. C. T. (1971). The use of a computer-controlled display system in the study of molecular conformations. *Cold Spring Harbor Symp. Quant. Biol.*, **36**, 577–84.

Beddell, C. R., Goodford, P. J., Norrington, F. E., Wilkinson, S., and Wootton, R. (1976). Compounds designed to fit a site of known structure in human haemoglobin. *Br. J. Pharmacol.*, **57**, 201–9.

Bernstein, F. C., Koetzle, T. F., Williams, G. J. B., Meyer, E. F., Brice, M. D., Rodgers, J. R., Kennard, O., Shimanouchi, T., and Tasumi, M. (1977). The protein data bank: a computed-based archival file for macromolecular structures. *J. Mol. Biol.*, **112**, 535–42.

Chabot, A. A., Geddes, A. J., North, A. C. T., and Potterton, E. A. (1981). Examples of the use of interactive computer graphics with real-time energy calculations in studies of protein–ligand interactions and in drug design. *Acta Crystallogr.*, **A37**, C340.

Fersht, A. R., Shi, J.-P, Knill-Jones, J., Lowe, D. M., Wilkinson, A. J., Blow, D. M., Brick,

P., Carter, P., Waye, M. M. Y., and Winter, G. (1985). Hydrogen-bonding and biological specificity analysed by protein engineering. *Nature (London)*, **314**, 235–8.

Getzoff, E., Tainer, J. A., Weiner, P. K., Kollman, P. A., Richardson, J. S., and Richardson, D. C. (1983). Electrostatic recognition between superoxide and copper, zinc superoxide dismutase, *Nature (London)*, **306**, 287–90.

Hansch, C., Lai, R-C., Blaney, J. M., and Langridge, R. (1982). Comparison of the inhibition of *E. coli* and *L. casei* DHFR by 2,4-diamino-5 (substituted-benzyl) pyrimidnies: QSAR, X-ray crystallorgaphy and computer graphics in S.A. analysis. *J. Med. Chem.*, **25**, 777–84.

Harris, M. R., Geddes, A. J., and North, A. C. T. (1985). A versatile stereo viewing system for use with colour graphics displays. In *Colour in information technology and visual displays*. Institute of Electronic and Radio Engineers, Publication no. 61, pp. 75–80.

Hassall, C. H., Kröhn, A., Moody, C. J., and Thomas W. A. (1982). The design of a new group of angiotensin-converting enzyme inhibitors. *FEBS Lett.*, **147**, 175–9.

Holmes, M. A. and Matthews, B. W. (1982). Structure of thermolysin refined at 1.6Å resolution *J. Mol. Biol.*, **160**, 623–39.

Jones, T. A. (1978). A graphics model building and refinement system for macromolecules. *J. Appl. Crystallogr.*, **11**, 268–72.

Kröhn, A. (1983). The use of molecular graphics in the design of enzyme inhibitors. In *Second SCI–RSC medicinal chemistry smposium* (ed. J. C. Emmett). Royal Society of Chemistry, London.

Langridge, R., Ferrin, T., Kuntz. I., and Connolly, M. (1981). Real-time color graphics in studies of molecular interactions. *Science*, **211**, 661–6.

Lee, B. and Richards, F. M. (1971). The interpretation of protein structures: estimation of static accessibility. *J. Mol. Biol.*, **55**, 379–400.

Lesk, A. M. and Hardman, K. (1982). Computer-generated schematic diagrams of protein structures. *Science*, **216**, 539–40.

Marshall, G. R., Barry, C. D., Bosshard, H. E., Dammkoehler, R. A., and Dunn, D. A. (1979). Conformational parameter in drug design—active analog approach. *A.C.S. Symposium Series*, **112**, 205–26.

Matthews, D. A., Alden, R. A., Bolin, J. T., Freer, S. T., Hamlin, R., Xuong, N., Kraut, J., Poe, M., Williams, M. N., and Hoogsteen, K. (1977). Dihydrofolate reductase: X-ray structure of the binary complex with methotrexate. *Science*, **197**, 452–5.

Matthews, D. A., Alden, R. A., Bolin, J. T., Filman, D. J., Freer, S. T., Hamlin, R., Hol, G. J., Kisliuk, R. L., Pastore, E. J., Plante, L. T., Xuong, N., and Kraut, J. 1978). Dihydrofolate reductase from *L. casei*: X-ray structure of the enzyme–methotrexate–NADPH complex. *J. Biol. Chem.*, **253**, 6946–54.

Nakamura, H., Komatsu, K., Nakagawa, S., and Umeyama, H. (1985). Visualization of electrostatic recognition by enzymes for their ligands and cofactors. *J. Mol. Graphics*, **3**, 2–11.

North, A. C. T. (1982). Use of interactive computer graphics in studying molecular structures and interactions. *Chem. Ind.*, 3 April, pp. 221–225.

North, A. C. T., Denson A. K., Evans, A. C., Ford, L. O., and Willoughby, T. V. (1980). The use of an interactive computer graphics system in the study of protein conformations. In *Biomolecular structure, conformation, function and evolution* (ed. R. Srinivasan), Vol. 1, pp. 59–72. Pergamon Press, London.

Ondetti, M. A., Rubin, B., and Cushman, D. W. (1977). Design of specific inhibitors of angiotensin-converting enzyme: new class of orally active antihypertensive agents. *Science*, **196**, 441–4.

Potterton, E. A., Geddes, A. J., and North, A. C. T. (1983) Attempts to design inhibitors of dihydrofolate reductase using interactive computer graphics with real-time energy calculations. In *Pteridine and folic acid derivatives* (ed. J. A. Blair), pp. 299–303. de Gruyter, Berlin.

Smith, G. M., Hangauer, D. G., Andose, J. D., Bush, B. L., Fluder, E. M., Gund, P., and McIntyre, E. F. (1984). Intermolecular modelling methods in drug design/modelling the mechanism of peptide cleavage by thermolysin. *Drug. Inf. J.*, **18**, 167–78.

Section 2E

Quantitative structure–activity studies of enzyme inhibition

John C. Dearden

2E.1   Introduction

It is axiomatic that the response of an organism to an administered compound must be a function of the chemical structure of the compound. More specifically, the response will depend on the nature, strength, and extent of the interaction of the compound with the receptor site that triggers the response. Ultimately, all those factors are controlled by the behaviour of the outer electrons of a molecule, and one day it may be possible to predict, say, a good angiotensin-converting enzyme inhibitor solely from a consideration of electron behaviour. Such predictions are a long way off, and for the present we have to make do with predicting biological response from a consideration of structural and physico-chemical properties (which themselves, of course, are dependent on electronic behaviour).

In very broad terms, three factors—lipophilic, electronic and steric—predominate in controlling the effect that a chemical compound exerts on an organism.

Lipophilicity, characterized by, for example, the octanol–water partition coefficient P, reflects the ability of a compound to penetrate lipid membranes, and thus to reach the active site. It can also play a role in receptor binding if hydrophobic interactions are important.

Electronic factors govern the nature and strength of receptor binding. They can be represented by, for example, the Hammett substituent constant σ, or dipole moment, or calculated atomic charges. In *in vivo* studies, they can also control metabolism and hence can affect the rate at which the active species arrives at the receptor site.

Steric factors are important in receptor binding, particularly if the receptor is in the cleft of an enzyme so that only molecules of certain size and shape are able to reach and fit into the receptor. Steric effects can also play a part in metabolism, by hindering access of attacking species to a reacting molecule.

Medicinal chemists have for many decades been aware of the operation of these and other characteristics, and have used them to good effect in drug and pesticide design. Many such applications have been qualitative, in that, for example, chloro substitution is adjudged to confer chemical stability, or that fluoro is isosteric with methyl. Such qualitative strategies are limited because they cannot easily predict optimal or maximal biological activity. How much better if the relevant characteristics can be quantified, so that the variation in biological activity within (usually) a congeneric series of compounds can be described mathematically.

The first successful quantitative structure–activity relationship (QSAR) was developed by Hansch *et al.* (1962) for a series of 20 phenoxyacetic acid herbicides:

$$\log 1/C = 4.08\pi - 2.14\pi^2 + 2.78\sigma + 3.36 \qquad (2\mathrm{E}.1)$$

In this equation C represents the concentration of compound inducing a 10 per cent growth of *Avena* coleoptiles in 24 h, π is a hydrophobic substituent constant defined as $\log(P_X/P_H)$ where X represents a derivative and H the parent compound, and σ is the Hammett substituent constant, representing the electron-directing effect of a substituent. The presence of the π^2 term, together with its negative coefficient, indicates that biological activity passes through a maximum as lipophilicity varies, and that such variation can be described by a parabola. This biphasic relationship of activity to lipophilicity is very common (Hansch and Clayton 1972), and has a number of explanations. In terms of the transport of a xenobiotic, which involves a number of *in vivo* partitioning steps through lipid and aqueous compartments of an organism, it most probably arises from the inability of hydrophilic compounds to pass easily from aqueous to lipid phase, and the corresponding inability of very lipophilic compounds to pass readily from lipid to aqueous phase; consequently the optimal lipophilicity for transport to and from the active site is of intermediate value. The exact value can be obtained by differentiating the QSAR with respect to $\log P$ or π and setting equal to zero. In terms of receptor binding, the concept of optimal lipophilicity probably relates to the ability of a substituent to interact with a hydrophobic binding site; a polar group will not be attracted to such a binding site, while a strongly lipophilic group may be too tightly bound, or may, by virtue of its size or shape, impinge on an adjacent polar region of the binding site.

The generalized 'Hansch' equation may be written as:

$$\log 1/C = a\pi + b\pi^2 + cE + dS + e \tag{2E.2}$$

where E represents an electronic parameter and S a steric parameter. Other terms may be substituted or added, as appropriate.

Although it is usual to describe the biphasic variation of activity with a parameter such as $\log P$ or π by a parabola (i.e. a quadratic equation), other mathematical expressions have been so used. Probably the most useful of these is the bilinear equation of Kubinyi (1976):

$$\log(1/C) = a \log P - b(\beta P + 1) + c \tag{2E.3}$$

This equation has the advantage over the quadratic equation that it can cope with different gradients on the two sections of the biphasic relationship.

A QSAR such as eqn (2E.1) can be used for two purposes: to predict active compounds and to throw light on mechanism of action to map a receptor. Examples will be discussed below.

There is by now a very extensive literature on QSAR studies of enzyme inhibitors. This review therefore does not seek to be comprehensive; it is, however, hoped that the examples given encompass the main developments in the field. Examples are, on the whole, restricted to isolated enzyme studies, except where comparison with whole-cell or whole-organism studies is believed to be important.

2E.2   Early work

Following Hansch's pioneering work on QSARs, it was to be expected that attention would soon be turned to enzyme inhibition. Neely (1965) reported a correlation of the rate constant of inhibition of cholinesterase by a series of phenylphosphoramidates with the infra-red stretching frequency of the O-phenyl bond, which must represent an electronic effect. Purcell et al. (1966) found that 75 per cent of the inhibition of cholinesterase by N-alkyl-substituted amides could be accounted for by partition. Corral et al. (1966), on the other hand, observed that the inhibitory effects of dialkyl aryl phosphates on cholinesterase were affected largely by electron-directing effects and size of substituents.

Interestingly, Martin (1981) reported that in 1959 she had attempted QSAR analysis of monoamine oxidase (MAO) inhibition by pargyline using $\log P$, pK_a, molecular weight, and solubility, but that no useful correlations could be obtained.

There is little doubt, however, that the first definitive work on the QSAR of enzyme inhibition came from the Hansch group, which has continued to lead in this field ever since. Hansch and Fujita (1964), in a paper covering QSAR studies on many different biological systems, reported what is probably the first published QSAR for enzyme inhibition, relating to the inhibitory effect of phenyl diethyl phosphates on fly-head acetylcholinesterase:

$$\log 1/I_{50} = 2.59\sigma + 4.29 \tag{2E.4}$$

$$n = 12 \qquad r = 0.906 \qquad s = 0.620$$

The inference to be drawn from this equation is that the variation in inhibitory activity is largely electronically controlled. However, the sample size is rather small, and more detailed work on larger data-sets often indicates that more variables, and position-dependence of substitution, are necessary to describe the inhibitory effect of a series of compounds on an enzyme.

Hansch and Deutsch (1966) analysed the cholinesterase inhibitory effects of several series of compounds. For 4-substituted methyl carbamates, they developed the following equation:

$$\log 1/C = 0.714\pi - 0.868\sigma + 3.486 \tag{2E.5}$$

$$n = 23 \qquad r = 0.839 \qquad s = 0.399$$

whereas for 4-substituted diphenyl phosphates they found

$$\log 1/C = 0.251\pi + 3.858\sigma + 4.214 \tag{2E.6}$$

$$n = 6 \qquad r = 0.957 \qquad s = 0.572.$$

Equation (2E.5) does not give a particularly good correlation, accounting for only 70 per cent of the variation in inhibitory activity ($r^2 = 0.704$). Equation (2E.6) is statistically dubious, since Topliss and Costello (1972) have shown that at least five data points per independent variable are necessary to reduce the risk of chance correlations to a low level. This misuse of multiple regression analysis continues to dog QSAR studies even now.

Another problem of multiple regression is collinearity; two variables that are highly correlated should not be used in the same equation. Recent papers often include a table of collinearities of the various parameters used in the correlation analysis.

Assuming, however, that eqns (2E.5) and (2E.6) are valid, what can be deduced from them? Firstly, for both series of compounds, inhibition is affected by hydrophobic and electronic factors, but there the similarity ends. The regression coefficients on the π term are quite different; π is generally taken (Hansch *et al.* 1977a) to model partitioning into enzymic space, with concomitant desolvation. A coefficient of <1 probably reflects partial desolvation, which in turn could indicate interaction with a loose hydrophobic pocket or even a flat hydrophobic surface. Thus the diphenyl phosphates probably bind to a different, looser hydrophobic pocket than do the methyl carbamates. The coefficients on the electronic term are even more different; eqn (2E.5) says that electron-donating substituents encourage binding of the methyl carbamates, while eqn (2E.6) indicates that electron-attracting substituents encourage binding of the diphenyl phosphates, and that moreover this binding dominates the interaction, since the regression coefficient is extremely high, and also because σ alone is well-correlated with inhibitory activity:

$$\log 1/C = 3.451\sigma + 4.461 \tag{2E.7}$$

$$n = 6 \qquad r = 0.954 \qquad s = 0.507.$$

The binding of inhibitors into pockets or clefts in enzymes suggests that size and/or shape of molecules should be important. Kutter and Hansch (1969) used the Taft steric constant E_s to help correlate the inhibitory effects of some N-(phenoxyethyl)cyclopropyl amines on MAO:

$$pI_{50} = 0.702\,E_s + 1.640\sigma + 0.198\pi + 4.153 \tag{2E.8}$$

$$n = 18 \qquad r = 0.945 \qquad s = 0.330.$$

Leaving out three outliers (which might, of course, yield some important structure–activity information) they improved this to:

$$pI_{50} = 0.766\,E_s + 1.752\sigma + 0.180\pi + 3.996 \tag{2E.9}$$

$$n = 15 \qquad r = 0.976 \qquad s = 0.203.$$

Kutter and Hansch used calculated values of E_s (some of which seem very strange; e.g. $E_{S_{3\text{-Me}}} = 1.24$, $E_{S_3,\ 5\text{-Me}} = 0.00$, $E_{S_4\text{-Me}} = 2.48$); eqns (2E.8) and (2E.9) indicate that an increase in substituent size increases inhibitory activity, which could mean that the conformation of the enzyme is being changed sterically, causing reduced activity. Kutter and Hansch make the following comment:

The fit of drugs onto or into macromolecules is not an all-or-none situation which the 'lock-and-key' theory often conjures up. The present results are hard to explain without assuming that the binding or partial insertion of groups of molecules of moderate size on or into a macromolecular pouch is, at least over a limited range, a continuous linear process. Since the free energy change involved parallels so closely that for simple shielding of an ester group in a hydrolytic process, one would assume a great deal of flexibility in the macromolecular receptor site.

In similar vein, McCammon *et al.* (1977) envisage a fluid-like interior of proteins, with the molecule able to wander over a range of conformations that are in the neighbourhood of the X-ray structure but not identical with it.

Since about 1970 QSAR studies of enzyme inhibition have burgeoned. Some enzymes in particular have been the subject of extensive study, and we shall look at some of these in turn.

2E.3 Studies of specific enzymes

2E.3.1 Cholinesterase

Not surprisingly, much work on cholinesterase inhibition has been directed towards insecticidal activity (see p. 294). Fujita *et al.* (1970) found that the antiacetylcholinesterase activity of β-pyridylmethylamino compounds could be described by:

$$pI_{50} = -0.225 \, \Sigma\pi - 2.619 \, \Sigma\sigma^* + 2.996 \qquad (2E.10)$$

$$n = 19 \qquad r = 0.916 \qquad s = 0.397$$

where σ^* is the Taft substituent constant for aliphatic substitution. For comparison, the *in vivo* activities of the compounds against house fly are given by:

$$\log(1/LD_{50}) = -0.265 \, \Sigma\pi - 1.661 \, \Sigma\sigma^* + 0.281 \, n_H + 0.517 \qquad (2E.11)$$

$$n = 19 \qquad r = 0.838 \qquad s = 0.259$$

where n_H is the number of hydrogens on the conjugate NH_4^+ ion.

Surprisingly, the regression coefficients on π are similar for the two correlations; often it is found that hydrophobicity is important only in the *in vivo* situation, reflecting transport to the active site. For example, Hansch and Fujita (1964) found, for phenyl diethyl phosphates against fly-head acetylcholinesterase:

$$\log 1/I_{50} = 2.59\sigma + 4.29 \qquad (2E.4)$$

$$n = 12 \qquad r = 0.906 \qquad s = 0.620$$

while against the house fly they found:

$$\log(1/ED_{50}) = 0.256\pi + 2.420\sigma - 0.600 \qquad (2E.12)$$

$$n = 8 \qquad r = 0.987 \qquad s = 0.228.$$

Miyagawa and Fujita (1982) found both steric and hydrogen-bonding effects to be important in the binding of *m*-substituted benzyltrimethylammonium salts to electric eel acetylcholinesterase:

$$\log 1/K_i = 0.958\pi + 0.442 \, E_s + 1.119 \, HB + 3.827 \qquad (2E.13)$$

$$n = 13 \qquad r = 0.922 \qquad s = 0.190$$

where HB is an indicator variable having the value of 1 for hydrogen-bonding substituents and 0 for others.

In a detailed study of phenyl *N*-methyl carbamates against the house fly and its acetylcholinesterase, Kamoshita *et al.* (1979) found that they had to employ position-specific parameters to order to obtain a good QSAR:

$$\log 1/K_d = 1.410\pi_2 + 1.132\pi_3 + 0.963\sigma_+^0 - 1.582\sigma_-^0 + 1.121 \, HB_1$$
$$+ 0.354 \, HB_2 + 4.114 \qquad (2E.14)$$

$$n = 77 \qquad r = 0.965 \qquad s = 0.241$$

where the subscripts on π represent the position of substitution, σ_+^0 is a modified Hammett constant intended to eliminate reinforcing resonance effects for o- and electron-withdrawing p-substituents, σ_-^0 is that for m- and less electron-withdrawing p-substituents, HB_1 is an indicator variable having the value of 1 for hydrogen-bonding substituents save m-OR, for which $HB_2 = 1$.

This equation is very similar to that found for inhibition of bovine erythrocyte acetylcholinesterase (Nishioka *et al.* 1977). Correlation of *in vivo* results against the house fly gave:

$$\log(1/LD_{50}) = 0.288\pi_{2,3} - 0.125\pi_4 + 1.047\sigma_+^0 - 0.607\sigma_-^0 + 0.671\,HB_1$$
$$+ 0.339\,HB_2 + 8.471 \tag{2E.15}$$
$$n = 42 \qquad r = 0.940 \qquad s = 0.127.$$

It would be tempting to ascribe the differences between the *in vitro* and *in vivo* correlations to transport and distribution. However, the authors then carried out a correlation analysis on the differences between the *in vitro* and *in vivo* activities:

$$\log 1/K_d - \log 1/LD_{50} = 1.168\pi_2 + 0.855\pi_3 + 0.294\pi_4 - 0.650\sigma_-^0$$
$$+ 0.634\,HB_1 - 4.426 \tag{2E.16}$$
$$n = 41 \qquad r = 0.947 \qquad s = 0.228$$

The fact that the π terms are still position-specific indicates that the difference between *in vitro* and *in vivo* activity is not merely in terms of transport and distribution, but occurs also at the enzyme level; the authors speculate that this might be due to *in vivo* inhibition of the ali-esterase in the fly body.

It happens that Goldblum *et al.* (1981) have also investigated the inhibition of fly-head acetylcholinesterase by phenyl N-methyl carbamates, and they derived an equation containing 12 independent variables:

$$pI_{50} = 0.557\,MR_{3,4,5} + 1.558\,MR_2 - 0.611\,E_{s_3} - 0.940\,(\Sigma\sigma_{o,p}^- + \sigma_m)^2$$
$$+ 1.431\,CHG - 0.227\,MR_2^2 - 5.236\,F_{2,6}^2 + 3.465\,F_{2,6}$$
$$+ 0.659\,RGMR - 0.618\,HB - 0.052\,MR_3^2 - 0.563\,E_{s_2}\cdot E_{s_6} + 3.458 \tag{2E.17}$$
$$n = 269 \qquad r = 0.892 \qquad s = 0.485$$

where σ^- is a modified Hammett constant relating to negative centre generation, F is the Swain–Lupton field parameter, RGMR is the molar refractivity of certain parts of ring substituents, and CHG is an indicator variable having the value of 1 for charged substituents.

Equations (2E.14 and 2E.17) stand in quite marked contrast to each other. Of course the dependent variable is different in each case, being a binding constant in eqn (2E.14) and a measure of inhibitory activity in eqn (2E.17), but each must reflect binding to the enzyme. Equation (2E.14) places emphasis on hydrophobic and electronic effects, whereas eqn (2E.17) includes no hydrophobicity term, but instead says that bulk and electronic terms dominate the inhibition. This example shows the risks that can arise in trying to learn something of the receptor from QSAR studies alone. Indeed, Hansch *et al.* (1984) have commented that 'practicing QSAR is somewhat like a blind man defining an object or a room by exploring it with his hands; eventually, a good image can be developed'. They go on to extol the use of crystallographic studies and molecular graphics in conjunction with QSAR: 'the use of crystallography is somewhat like giving sight to the blind man: one can immediately "see" what sort of ligands (it) would be foolish to make from, say, the steric or hydrophobic point of view and which ligands would be good bets to test'.

Some comment on the use of molar refractivity (MR) is appropriate here, as Hansch and co-workers have used MR widely in their enzyme QSAR studies. Essentially MR is a measure of molar volume, although it is often not collinear with, for example, E_s. MR also contains a polarizability component, and thus may reflect the operation of dispersion forces (Pauling and Pressman 1945). Binding through dispersion forces might not require desolvation (Franks 1975) as does hydrophobic binding (Hansch *et al.* 1977a).

2E.3.2   Dehydrogenase

As early as 1967, Wedding, Hansch, and Fukuoto related inhibition of malate dehydrogenase by phenols to hydrophobic and electronic effects:

$$\log 1/K_i = 1.46\pi - 0.33\pi^2 - 0.47\sigma + 0.73\sigma^2 + 1.55 \tag{2E.18}$$
$$n = 23 \qquad r = 0.868 \qquad s = 0.338.$$

The use of the σ^2 term is most unusual; the authors had several suggestions as to its significance, for example that several steps are involved in the inhibition, one becoming limiting when σ is negative and another when σ is positive.

Coats and his co-workers have studied dehydrogenase inhibition extensively, showing the importance of MR in correlating inhibitory activity. In an investigation of 7-substituted 4-hydroxyquinoline-3-carboxylic acids, Shah and Coats (1977) found, for inhibition of malate dehydrogenase:

$$\log 1/C = 0.70\,\text{MR} + 2.29 \tag{2E.19}$$
$$n = 13 \qquad r = 0.939 \qquad s = 0.315.$$

However, for inhibition of ascites cells they observed:

$$pI_{50} = 0.46\pi + 3.22 \tag{2E.20}$$
$$n = 14 \qquad r = 0.933 \qquad s = 0.280.$$

That is, while molecular bulk controls enzyme binding, transport probably controls cellular inhibition.

In a later, more detailed multivariate principal components analysis of three dehydrogenases and ascites cells, Dove *et al.* (1985) found two principal components, the first of which (x_1) accounted for 69 per cent of the variance:

$$x_1 = 0.20\mu + 0.81 \, B_4 - 2.85 \tag{2E.21}$$
$$n = 8 \qquad r = 0.902 \qquad s = 0.305$$

where μ is dipole moment and B_4 is the Sterimol maximum width parameter, a steric term (Verloop et al. 1976).

This component they attributed to enzyme binding. However, for ascites cell inhibition alone they found:

$$pI_{50} = 0.39\pi - 0.12\mu + 3.71 \tag{2E.22}$$
$$n = 8 \qquad r = 0.949 \qquad s = 0.190.$$

Since this is completely different from eqn (2E.21), the authors conclude that none of the three dehydrogenases examined was the primary target in the inhibition of Ehrlich ascites respiration by these compounds.

Coats et al. (1982) tested 4-hydroxyquinoline-3-carboxylic acids against three dehydrogenases:

Skeletal muscle lactate dehydrogenase
$$pI_{50} = 0.36 \, MR + 2.79 \tag{2E.23}$$
$$n = 11 \qquad r = 0.96 \qquad s = 0.20.$$

Cytoplasmic malate dehydrogenase
$$pI_{50} = 0.32 \, MR + 2.65 \tag{2E.24}$$
$$n = 11 \qquad r = 0.90 \qquad s = 0.28.$$

Mitochondrial malate dehydrogenase
$$pI_{50} = 0.62 \, MR + 2.40 \tag{2E.25}$$
$$n = 11 \qquad r = 0.96 \qquad s = 0.35.$$

Clearly, skeletal lactate and cytoplasmic malate dehydrogenase are inhibited in virtually identical manner by these compounds, whereas mitochondrial malate dehydrogenase is much more susceptible to whatever MR represents (bulk and/or dispersion forces). The authors suggest that the mitochondrial malate dehydrogenase binding site, or a portion of it, may be more flexible and more lipophilic than the binding sites of the other enzymes.

Using a much larger number of compounds, Yashimoto and Hansch (1976) found somewhat different correlations:

Lactate dehydrogenase
$$\log 1/C = 0.0803 \, MR_{1, 5, 6, 8} + 0.487 \, I_1 - 0.114 \, I_2 + 3.853 \tag{2E.26}$$
$$n = 79 \qquad r = 0.836 \qquad s = 0.173$$

where I_1 and I_2 are indicator variables for the presence of 5-$(CH_2)_n C_6 H_5$ and 1-H respectively.

Malate dehydrogenase
$$\log 1/C = 0.699\pi_5 + 0.290 \text{ MR}_{6, 7, 8} - 1.121 I_1 + 3.156 \qquad (2E.27)$$
$$n = 75 \qquad r = 0.943 \qquad s = 0.385$$

where I_1 is an indicator variable for the presence of 5-$O(CH_2)_nOC_6H_5$.

Although the correlations of eqns (2E.26) and (2E.27) are not so good as those of eqns (2E.23) and (2E.24), the much larger sample size and the use of position-specific substituent constants and indicator variables mean that Yashimoto and Hansch's equations probably give better activity predictions and more information about the receptors.

2E.3.3   Dihydrofolate reductase

More QSAR studies have been made of dihydrofolate reductase (DHFR) inhibition than of any other enzyme, undoubtedly as a result of its importance in bacterial metabolism and in cancer cells. Blaney *et al.* (1984) have recently published a comprehensive review on the subject. Space permits of only a few examples of the work in this area.

Hansch *et al.* (1977b) quantified the selectivity of quinazolines as DHFR inhibitors by comparing the QSARs for mammalian and bacterial DHFR inhibition:

Rat liver DHFR
$$\log 1/C = 0.81 \text{ MR}_6 - 0.064 \text{ MR}_6^2 + 0.78 \, \pi_5 - 0.73 \, I_1 - 2.14 \, I_2$$
$$- 0.54 \, I_3 - 1.39 \, I_4 + 0.78 \, I_6 - 0.20 \text{ MR}_6 \cdot I_1 + 4.92 \qquad (2E.28)$$
$$n = 101 \qquad r = 0.961 \qquad s = 0.441$$

where I_1, I_2, I_3, I_4, and I_6 are indicator variables for the presence of 2-OH or SH, 2-H, 4-OH or SH, selected bridges between position 5 and an aryl group, and 6-SO_2Ar respectively.

S. faecium DHFR
$$\log 1/C = 1.125 \, \pi_5 - 1.103 \text{ MR}_5 - 2.385 \, I_1 - 4.092 \, I_2 - 2.368 \, I_3$$
$$+ 8.255 \qquad (2E.29)$$
$$n = 67 \qquad r = 0.926 \qquad s = 0.672$$

where the indicator variables have the same meaning as for eqn (2E.28).

Equation (2E.29) is considerably different from eqn (2E.28), particularly in respect of the susceptibility of the 6-position to the influence of bulk. Thus these equations could be used to design selective inhibitors.

Chen *et al.* (1979) have obtained similar equations; they also point out that simple multiple regression does not always yield good QSARs, because of, for example, interdependence of variables and non-additivity of group contributions. They discuss the use of cluster analysis, factor analysis, and discriminant analysis as alternatives to multiple regression in QSAR.

In addition to quinazolines, two other classes of compound, the triazines and the pyrimidines, have been widely investigated through QSAR as DHFR inhibitors.

Hansch and co-workers have made detailed comparisons of DHFR from different sources, as an aid both to receptor-mapping and to developing selectively active inhibitors. The following examples are of triazines containing a 3-substituent in the phenyl ring:

Human DHFR (Hathaway *et al.* 1984)

$$\log 1/K_{i_{app}} = 1.07\,\pi'_3 - 1.10\,\log(\beta\cdot 10^{\pi'_3} + 1) + 0.50\,I + 0.82\sigma + 6.07 \qquad (2E.30)$$

$$n = 60 \qquad r = 0.890 \qquad s = 0.308 \qquad \pi'_0 = 2.10 \qquad \log\beta = -0.577$$

where π' indicates that π_Y in substituents $CH_2SC_6H_4Y$, $OCH_2C_6H_4Y$, and $SCH_2C_6H_4Y$ is set to zero, and I indicates the presence of those substituents.

Chicken liver DHFR (Hansch *et al.* 1984)

$$\log 1/K_{i_{app}} = 1.01\,\pi'_3 - 1.16\,\log(\beta\cdot 10^{\pi'_3} + 1) + 0.86\,\sigma + 6.33 \qquad (2E.31)$$

$$n = 59 \qquad r = 0.906 \qquad s = 0.286 \qquad \pi'_0 = 1.89 \qquad \log\beta = -1.08$$

Bovine liver DHFR (Guo *et al.* 1981)

$$\log 1/K_{i_{app}} = 1.10\,\pi'_3 - 1.23\,\log(\beta\cdot 10^{\pi'_3} + 1) + 0.61\,\sigma + 7.08 \qquad (2E.32)$$

$$n = 38 \qquad r = 0.914 \qquad s = 0.277 \qquad \pi'_0 = 1.72 \qquad \log\beta = 0.789.$$

Murine leukaemia L5178YR-C_3 DHFR (Guo *et al.* 1981)

$$\log 1/K_{i_{app}} = 1.19\,\pi'_3 - 1.38\,\log(\beta\cdot 10^{\pi'_3} + 1) + 0.50\,I + 0.90\,\sigma + 6.20 \qquad (2E.33)$$

$$n = 38 \qquad r = 0.935 \qquad s = 0.289 \qquad \pi'_0 = 1.56 \qquad \log\beta = -0.750.$$

L. casei DHFR (Hansch *et al.* 1984)

$$\log 1/K_{i_{app}} = 0.83\,\pi'_3 - 0.91\,\log(\beta\cdot 10^{\pi'_3} + 1) + 0.71\,I + 4.60 \qquad (2E.34)$$

$$n = 38 \qquad r = 0.961 \qquad s = 0.244 \qquad \pi'_0 = 2.69 \qquad \log\beta = -1.68.$$

The equations for vertebrate DHFR are remarkably consistent, which does not augur well for the use of these compounds against leukaemia. The QSAR for bacterial DHFR is quite different, but the small intercept (4.60) shows these triazines to be much less active against bacterial than against vertebrate DHFR.

The pyrimidines are the most widely studied class of DHFR inhibitors, due undoubtedly to the success of the antimicrobial agent trimethoprim. Again, differences can be seen between mammalian and bacterial DHFR:

Bovine liver DHFR (Li *et al.* 1982a)

$$\log 1/K_{i_{app}} = 0.48\,\pi_{3,\,5} - 1.25\,\log(\beta\cdot 10^{\pi_{3,5}} + 1) + 0.13\,MR_4$$
$$+ 0.24\,\sigma + 5.43 \qquad (2E.35)$$

$$n = 42 \qquad r = 0.875 \qquad s = 0.227 \qquad \pi_0 = 1.52 \qquad \log\beta = -1.98.$$

Human DHFR (Li *et al.* 1982b)

$$\log 1/K_{i_{app}} = 0.59\,\pi_{3,\,5} - 0.63\,\log(\beta\cdot 10^{\pi_{3,5}} + 1) + 0.19\,\pi_4 + 0.19\,MR_3$$
$$+ 0.30\,\sigma + 4.03 \qquad (2E.36)$$

$$n = 38 \qquad r = 0.879 \qquad s = 0.266 \qquad \pi_0 = 1.94 \qquad \log\beta = -0.82.$$

L. casei DHFR (Hansch *et al.* 1982)

$$\log 1/K_i = 0.31\,\pi_{3,4} - 0.91\log(\beta \cdot 10^{\pi_{3,4}} + 1) + 0.89\,MR'_{3,4}$$
$$-0.22\,\sigma_R^- + 5.31 \tag{2E.37}$$
$$n = 42 \qquad r = 0.889 \qquad s = 0.214 \qquad \pi_0 = 1.05 \qquad \log\beta = -1.34$$

where MR′ indicates that any substituent value of MR above 0.79 (scaled from true by 0.1) is given the value of 0.79. This has implications for the size of the MR-related pocket on the enzyme.

E. coli DHFR (Hansch *et al.* 1982)

$$\log 1/K_i = 0.43\,\pi_{3,4,5} - 0.88\log(\beta \cdot 10^{\pi_{3,4,5}} + 1) + 1.23\,MR'_{3,5}$$
$$+0.80\,MR'_4 - 0.45\,\sigma_R^- + 5.81 \tag{2E.38}$$
$$n = 43 \qquad r = 0.923 \qquad s = 0.273 \qquad \pi_0 = 0.64 \qquad \log\beta = -0.67.$$

Electronic effects are opposite in the mammalian and bacterial QSARs, and the coefficients on MR are quite different. Furthermore, the optimal π values (π_0) are much lower for bacterial DHFR. These differences are exemplified by the case of trimethoprim itself, which is some 100 000 times more active against *E. coli* DHFR than against human DHFR.

Seydel and co-workers have studied extensively the QSAR of DHFR inhibition by sulphonamides and have emphasized the importance of electronic parameters. Seydel and Schaper (1980) found, for one series of compounds:

$$\log I_{50} = 0.48\,pK_a - 0.33\,I - 2.47 \tag{2E.39}$$
$$n = 18 \qquad r = 0.97 \qquad s = 0.08$$

where I is an indicator variable for *o*- and *m*-substitution.

The corresponding equation for whole-cell activity was:

$$\log MIC = 0.68\,pK_a - 0.24\,I - 4.78 \tag{2E.40}$$
$$n = 18 \qquad r = 0.95 \qquad s = 0.14.$$

The two equations are quite similar, with no transport term being required in eqn (2E.40), but the intercepts show that whole-cell activities are some 200 times higher than against the isolated enzyme, suggesting that DHFR is not the primary target of these compounds in the cell.

2E.3.4 Other enzymes

Numerous other enzymes, among them MAO, chymotrypsin, papain, glyoxalase, guanine deaminase, and DNA polymerase, to name but a few, have been the subject of QSAR investigations. For reasons of space, only a few of these can be commented upon.

Dunn and Hodnett (1977) found that rat Novikoff tumour and human ribonucleoside diphosphate reductase (RDR) gave similar QSARs against α-(N)-formylheteroaromatic thiosemicarbazones, save that the compounds were some

500 times more active against the tumour enzyme, which has implications for the design of selective antitumour agents.

Rat Novikoff tumour RDR

$$pI_{50} = 9.40 - 1.78 \, MR_5 \tag{2E.41}$$
$$n = 10 \qquad r = 0.93 \qquad s = 0.33.$$

Human RDR

$$pI_{50} = 6.70 - 1.81 \, MR_5 \tag{2E.42}$$
$$n = 13 \qquad r = 0.80 \qquad s = 0.37.$$

In a study related to anti-inflammatory drugs, Habicht and Brune (1983) examined the inhibition of prostaglandin E_2 release by salicylates, benzoates, and phenols. They developed the following QSAR:

$$pI_{50} = 0.078 \, MR - 1.632 \, I_1 + 0.669 \, I_2 - 0.516 \, I_4 - 0.898 \, I_5 + 3.489 \tag{2E.43}$$
$$n = 59 \qquad r = 0.87 \qquad s = 0.53$$

where I_1, I_2, I_4, and I_5 are indicator variables for benzoates, phenols, salicylates with lipophilic substituents, and salicylates substituted in the 4 or 6 position, respectively.

As with so many other enzymes, inhibition of prostaglandin synthetase seems to be controlled by steric or bulk effects, as modelled by MR.

Wright and Gambino (1984) investigated the QSARs of 6-anilinouracils as inhibitors of both susceptible and resistant *B. subtilis* DNA polymerase III. They observed some differences:

Enzyme from susceptible organism

$$pK_i = 1.00 \, \pi_3 + 0.71 \, \pi_4 + 3.87 \, MR_3 - 2.30 \, MR_3^2 + 2.86 \, MR_4$$
$$- 2.18 \, MR_4^2 + 2.50 \tag{2E.44}$$
$$n = 37 \qquad r = 0.942 \qquad s \text{ not given.}$$

Enzyme from resistant organism

$$pK_i = 1.26 \, \pi_3 + 1.13 \, \pi_4 + 2.51 \, MR_3 - 1.67 \, MR_3^2 + 3.48 \, MR_4$$
$$- 2.42 \, MR_4^2 + 2.39 \tag{2E.45}$$
$$n = 37 \qquad r = 0.948 \qquad s \text{ not given.}$$

Interestingly, the intercepts of the two equations are very close, indicating that the differences in resistance to inhibition reside in the differences in position-specific hydrophobic and bulk effects. This leads to the speculation that it should be relatively easy to design compounds that will inhibit enzyme from the resistant mutant.

Naeff *et al.* (1985) have examined by QSAR the difference between free and Sepharose-immobilised xanthine oxidase inhibited by 6-(4-substituted phenyl)-pteridine-4-ones:

Free xanthine oxidase

$$-\log K_i = -0.599 \, B_1 + 0.011 \, MR^2 - 0.191 \, MR + 1.596 \qquad (2E.46)$$

$$n = 13 \qquad r = 0.93 \qquad s = 0.21.$$

Immobilized xanthine oxidase

$$-\log K_i' = -0.262 \, B_1 - 0.418 \, \pi + 0.005 \, MR^2 - 0.076 \, MR + 0.645 \qquad (2E.47)$$

$$n = 13 \qquad r = 0.93 \qquad s = 0.14$$

where B_1 is the Sterimol minimum width parameter (Verloop *et al.* 1976).

The π term in eqn (2E.47) reflects the partitioning between bulk solution and the Sepharose matrix to which the enzyme is attached. The change in regression coefficients presumably can be taken to indicate that immobilization has altered the enzyme conformation to some extent.

Finally in this section, another indication is given of the need to consider *in vivo* as well as isolated enzyme inhibition, if effective drugs and pesticides are to be designed. Dary and Cutkamp (1984) found that mitochondrial ATPase was inhibited by DDT congeners according to the following equation:

$$pI_{50} = 0.59 \, \Sigma\pi - 0.70 \times 10^{-3} \, \Sigma V^2 - 0.91 \qquad (2E.48)$$

$$n = 13 \qquad r = 0.875 \qquad s = 0.502$$

where V is the van der Waals' radius of the substituent.

In vivo studies of the compounds against *Musca domestica* gave:

$$\log(1/LD_{50}) = 1.04 \, \Sigma\pi - 2.51 \, \Sigma R - 0.38 \, \Sigma F - 3.50 \qquad (2E.49)$$

$$n = 17 \qquad r = 0.956 \qquad s = 0.221$$

where R and F are the Swain–Lupton resonance and field parameters respectively.

The regression coefficient on $\Sigma\pi$ in eqn (2E.49) indicates complete desolvation into hydrophobic space, and suggests that partitioning rather than binding is dominant. The presence of electronic terms in eqn (2E.49) is unusual, and perhaps reflects polar interactions on the random walk to the receptor site, which would reduce potency.

2E.4   Other parameters

Since Hansch and co-workers developed the QSAR approach to biological activity, and since they have led the QSAR study of enzyme inhibition, it is not surprising that most other workers have used what has become known as Hansch analysis, and have tended to use the same or similar parameters. There have, nevertheless, been some rather different approaches.

Kier and Hall (1976) developed the topological index known as molecular connectivity, which is readily calculated from a knowledge of the structural formula of a compound. The number of non-hydrogen links formed by each atom is noted, and the product obtained of these numbers for atoms at each end of a bond; the reciprocal square root of this product is calculated, and the sum of these values obtained for all non-hydrogen links in the molecule. The resulting index is termed the first-order molecular connectivity ($^1\chi$). Corrections for multiple bonds and heteroatoms can also be made, to give a valence-corrected index (χ^v). χ values across two or more bonds can be calculated to give higher-order terms. Molecular connectivity has been shown to correlate with numerous other parameters, including lipophilicity, but higher-order terms in particular, reflecting branching, can be considered to be steric in nature. There are, however, two important drawbacks to the use of connectivity indices in drug design. First, they have no physical significance, so that inferences concerning mode of action or binding cannot be drawn; secondly, good QSARs can be obtained generally only when substituents are alkyl or halogen.

van't Riet *et al.* (1980) correlated the inhibition of ribonucleotide reductase by benzohydroxamic acids with molecular connectivity:

$$pC = 2.36\ ^3\chi_p - 3.98\ ^0\chi^v + 0.97\,(^1\chi^v)^2 + 9.20 \tag{2E.50}$$
$$n = 28 \qquad r = 0.943 \qquad s = 0.21.$$

Gupta *et al.* (1983) found a simple correlation of the inhibition of, *inter alia*, skeletal muscle lactate dehydrogenase by 4-hydroxyquinoline-3-carboxylic acids with χ:

$$pI_{50} = 0.41\ ^1\chi^v + 2.78 \tag{2E.51}$$
$$n = 11 \quad r = 0.96 \qquad s = 0.20.$$

The correspondence of this equation with eqn (2E.23) is quite remarkable, and confirms that χ may be used as a steric parameter, for this series of substituents at least. Whether or not such a correspondence would be observed if polar substituents were included is open to question.

Testa and Purcell (1978) used the Cartesian coordinates of molecules as steric parameters, and were able to correlate the binding of sulphonamides to carbonic anhydrase:

$$\log AC = 0.0308\ V_s + 1.08\ \text{DIST} \tag{2E.52}$$
$$n = 34 \qquad r = 0.997 \qquad s = 0.554$$

where AC is the affinity constant of binding, V_s is the volume of the substituent, and DIST is the sulphur–carbon distance. Hansch *et al.* (1985) have, however, criticized the Testa and Purcell study, pointing out that both electronic and hydrophobic effects are important in the binding of sulphonamides to carbonic anhydrase.

Akahane *et al.* (1984) included solvent-accessible surface area among the parameters they examined to correlate the inhibition of thromboxane synthetase by pyridine derivatives:

$$\text{Inhibitory potency} = 0.0623\ \text{DIS}^2 - 2.443\ \text{SA} - 3.879\ \text{SA(N, O)}$$
$$- 1.604\ B_2^z + 0.547\ I + 8.218 \tag{2E.53}$$
$$n = 27 \qquad r = 1.000 \qquad s\ \text{not given}$$

where DIS is molecular length, SA is solvent-accessible surface area, SA(N, O) is that for N and O atoms, B_2^α is the Sterimol B_2 parameter for a substituent in the α-position of the pyridine ring, and I is an indicator variable for hydrogen-donor substitution at the β-position.

Simon and co-workers have developed the minimal steric distance (MSD) or minimal topological distance (MTD) method of assessing steric contributions to biological activity (Simon *et al.* 1984). The MTD is defined as the number of unsuperimposable atoms when a molecule is superimposed atom by atom upon a standard that is presumed to be close to an ideal fit to its receptor (e.g. the most potent inhibitor). In practice, the standard may have to be changed as the investigation proceeds.

Crăescu (1980) found, for a series of hydrazides inhibiting rat liver mitochondrial MAO:

$$A = 6.985 - 0.430 \text{ MTD} \tag{2E.54}$$

$$n = 23 \qquad r = 0.952 \qquad s = 0.175.$$

As with other steric parameters, MTD often needs to have other parameters included in order to obtain a good correlation. Crăescu (1980) reports the following correlation for the inhibition of beef liver mitochondrial MAO by α-carbolines:

$$A = 3.631 - 0.367 \text{ MTD} + 0.624\pi + 0.400 \, \sigma + 0.662 \, E_s \tag{2E.55}$$

$$n = 12 \qquad r = 0.981 \qquad s = 0.136.$$

Hopfinger has devised a shape parameter that can be used in QSARs. The compounds in a data set are energy-minimized to determine the most stable conformations. Then, as with the MTD method, a reference compound is selected with which the shapes of all the other congeners can be compared. A so-called overlap volume (V_o) is thus obtained, and this or $S_o (= V_o^{2/3})$ is used in the QSAR. Mabilia *et al.* (1985) found that V_o could effectively describe the variation in binding of benzylpyrimidine DHFR inhibitors:

$$\log 1/K_{i_{app}} = 0.0413 \, V_o - 0.396 \tag{2E.56}$$

$$n = 18 \qquad r = 0.98 \qquad s = 0.15.$$

In a direct comparison of molecular shape analysis with the Hansch approach, Hopfinger (1981) developed the following correlation for DHFR inhibition by 2,4-diaminotriazines:

$$\log 1/I_{50} = 1.384 \, S_o - 0.02127 \, S_o^2 + 0.434 \, \Sigma\pi - 0.574 \, D_4$$
$$- 0.294 \, D_4^2 - 15.66 \tag{2E.57}$$

$$n = 27 \qquad r = 0.953 \qquad s = 0.44$$

where D_4 is an intermolecular shape descriptor to account for the low activity of two congeners.

The equation derived by Dietrich *et al.* (1979) for the same data set is:

$$\log 1/I_{50} = 1.05\,\pi_3 - 1.21\,\log(\beta \cdot 10^{\pi_3} + 1) + 6.64 \tag{2E.58}$$

$$n = 28 \qquad r = 0.955 \qquad s = 0.210.$$

Useful as the molecular shape analysis approach is, it has to be said that eqn (2E.58) is to be preferred over eqn (2E.57) because it contains fewer parameters, the standard error is much less, and the parameters have (to this reviewer at least) more physical meaning in relation to receptor mapping and the design of good inhibitors.

A Japanese group has developed a so-called substituent entropy constant σ_s^0 which they have tested on the same data set as used in eqns (2E.57) and (2E.58). Kawaki *et al.* (1982) obtained the following correlation:

$$\log 1/C = -25.29(\sigma_{s2}^0)^2 + 7.04\,\sigma_{s3,4}^0 + 3.22|\sigma_i|_{3,4} + 3.68|\sigma_\pi|_{3,4} + 6.37 \tag{2E.59}$$

$$n = 21 \qquad r = 0.981 \qquad s = 0.09$$

where σ_i and σ_π are substituent enthalpy constants. The authors claim several advantages using σ_s^0, compared with the Hansch and Hopfinger approaches, namely that the number of independent variables is reduced, and that the physicochemical meaning of the parameter is explicit. These claims remain open to doubt.

The use of *de novo* constants (constants generated from the biological data), although quite widespread in QSAR, has received only little attention in enzyme studies. The best-known approach to the use of *de novo* constants is that of Free and Wilson (1964); Hansch *et al.* (1975) used a modified Free–Wilson approach to study the inhibition of DHFR by 2,4-diamino-5-(3,4-dichlorophenyl)-6-substituted pyrimidines. Although Free–Wilson analyses do not generally result in equations, the approach adopted in this case enabled the different substitution patterns to be handled as indicator variables, yielding the following equation:

$$\log 1/C = 0.365I_1 - 1.013I_8 - 0.784I_9 + 0.419I_{13} - 0.220I_{15}$$
$$+ 0.513I_{20} + 0.674I_4 \cdot I_8 + 7.174 \tag{2E.60}$$

$$n = 105 \qquad r = 0.903 \qquad s = 0.229.$$

A total of 27 indicator variables were examined, only the above seven being found to be significant.

Numerous attempts have been made to utilize quantum chemical indices in QSARs, and this approach has naturally included enzyme inhibition. Testa (1980) found that the inhibition of cytochrome P-450-mediated aniline hydroxylation by alcohols could be quantified using a combination of theoretical indices and log P:

$$pI_{50} = 0.402E_{HOMO} + 1.66\log P - 0.471(\log P)^2 - 1.35\,BULK_{lat} + 4.93$$
$$n = 21 \qquad r = 0.895 \qquad s = 0.293 \tag{2E.61}$$

where E_{HOMO} is the energy of the highest occupied molecular orbital, and $BULK_{lat}$ is a lateral bulk parameter.

Lukovits (1983) obtained the following correlation for the inhibition of phenylethanolamine N-methyltransferase by benzylamines:

$$pI_{50} = -0.22 q_1 - 0.10 \Sigma'_q + 0.18 \mu - 0.09 \mu_x - 0.20 \mu_y$$
$$- 0.12 \Delta E + 0.15 \varepsilon_{HOMO} - 0.22 \varepsilon_{LEMO} \tag{2E.62}$$
$$n = 22 \qquad r = 0.84 \qquad s = 0.57$$

where q_1 is charge density at atom 1 of the benzene ring calculated by CNDO/2 or Hückel, Σ'_q is the sum of charges at atoms 2–6 of the benzene ring, μ is dipole moment, μ_x and μ_y are orthogonal components of μ, ΔE is singlet excitation energy and ε_{HOMO} and ε_{LEMO} are the energies of the highest occupied and lowest empty molecular orbitals respectively.

Superdelocalizability has been employed by Miertus and Filipovic (1982) to correlate the inhibitory action of 2-formylpyridines against ribonucleoside diphosphate reductase from human H.Ep-2 cells:

$$pI_{50} = 41.76 + 60.01 S^E_{1,8,12} \tag{2E.63}$$
$$n = 10 \qquad r = 0.901$$

where $S^E_{1,8,12}$ is the sum of electrophilic superdelocalizabilities at atoms 1,8, and 12.

$$pI_{50} = -2.5 + 18.6 S^N_7 \tag{2E.64}$$
$$n = 10 \qquad r = 0.914$$

where S^N_7 is the nucleophilic superdelocalizability at position 7.

Abdul-Ahab and Webb have published several studies of calculated indices correlating with enzyme inhibition. For example, they report (Abdul-Ahab and Webb 1982) that the inhibitory effects of a series of 2,4-diamino-5-benzylpyrimidines against *E. coli* DHFR can be described by:

$$pC_{50} = 7.64 F^E(C_{11}) - 5.13 E(C_8 - C_9) - 182.3 \tag{2E.65}$$
$$n = 10 \qquad r = 0.997 \qquad s = 0.08$$

where $F^E(C_{11})$ is the frontier electron density at C_{11} and $E(C_8-C_9)$ is the bond energy between C_8 and C_9.

The use of quantum chemical indices is leading us towards the ultimate goal of being able to predict activities solely from a consideration of electron behaviour. Nevertheless, it has to be said that, at the present time at least, correlations involving such indices are less easy to interpret than are those using indices of lipophilicity or steric bulk, for example. In addition, the problems of designing more effective compounds are probably greater using quantum chemical indices or parameters such as molecular connectivity.

2E.5   Distance geometry

All the above approaches to QSARs of enzyme inhibition involve relating the biological data to selected theoretical, structural, or physicochemical parameters to yield a multiple regression equation. An entirely different approach, known as distance geometry, has been developed by Crippen (1979), in which a number of binding points of, say, inhibitor to enzyme are postulated for each inhibitor molecule; upper and lower bounds of interatomic distances are calculated over all sterically allowed conformations. Then a plausible binding mode is chosen, in which the binding of atoms to each site point on the receptor is specified. Using these and other constraints (Ghose and Crippen 1982), binding energies are calculated and compared with experimentally observed values. One of the important features of the method is that the ligand is allowed to be flexible, so that different modes of binding can be accommodated. Ghose and Crippen (1983) found that, using nine site points, they could correlate the calculated and observed inhibition data for 33 triazines and 15 quinazolines against rat liver DHFR with $r = 0.892$ and $s = 0.596$. The model was then used to predict the inhibitory activities of a further 91 compounds, with $r = 0.790$ and $s = 0.907$. The site geometry was found to compare well with the known crystal structure of a triazine bound to chicken liver DHFR. The distance geometry approach thus offers a useful alternative to Hansch analysis in mapping enzyme receptor sites and designing bioactive compounds.

A somewhat similar approach has been developed by Höltje (1975), who has calculated, using the monopole bond polarizability method, binding energies of cyclopropylamines to a model of the receptor site in MAO. The calculated binding energies were found to correlate well ($r = 0.938$) with pI_{50} values for a series of 12 compounds. Höltje and Simon (1984) obtained similarly good results for a series of sulphonamides inhibiting carbonic anhydrase-C.

2E.6   QSAR and molecular graphics

The quote given earlier (see p. 127) from Hansch et al. (1984) indicated that crystallography and molecular graphics could add, as it were, another dimension to QSAR. QSAR does indeed enable one to 'map' a receptor, or at least to learn sufficient about it so that new compounds—even new classes of compound can be designed that will interact with the receptor to generate an appropriate response. But QSAR is literally searching in the dark, without the added dimension of visualization. The human brain is designed to deal very efficiently with visual information, and to see an enzyme receptor-site depicted on a screen is instantly to know much about that site. If, in addition to the backbone structure of the enzyme, the 'flesh' can be put on in the form of a dot surface, say, then the actual shape of the receptor can be seen. If, further, one can use depth-cueing or stereo-images to give a three-dimensional effect, and if areas of the receptor can be coloured appropriately (e.g. red for hydrophobic regions, blue for polar areas), then the impact can be quite overwhelming. Add to this the ability to change conformation, and to cause inhibitor and receptor to interact, all in real time, and it can perhaps be understood why molecular graphics is at the present time having such a powerful impact (see Chapter 2D).

In recent years, Hansch and co-workers have been stressing the advantages that can come from using both QSAR and molecular graphics together in receptor-mapping studies (see, for example, Li *et al.* 1982a; Hansch *et al.* 1982, 1985). Li *et al.* (1982b) compared, *inter alia*, the inhibition of chicken liver DHFR and *E. coli* DHFR by a series of 5-(X-benzyl)-2,4-diaminopyrimidines.

Chicken liver DHFR

$$\log 1/K_{i_{app}} = 0.55 \ \pi_{3,4,5} + 0.20 \ \mathrm{MR}_3 - 0.42 \ \log(\beta \cdot 10^{\pi_{3,4,5}} + 1$$
$$+ 0.32 \ \Sigma\sigma + 4.46 \tag{2E.66}$$

$$n = 39 \qquad r = 0.900 \qquad s = 0.241 \qquad \log \beta = -0.22.$$

E. coli DHFR

$$\log 1/K_{i_{app}} = 0.75 \ \pi_{3,4,5} + 1.36 \ \mathrm{MR}'_{3,5} + 0.88 \ \mathrm{MR}'_4$$
$$- 1.07 \ \log(\beta.10^{\pi_{3,4,5}} + 1) + 6.20 \tag{2E.67}$$

$$n = 43 \qquad r = 0.903 \qquad s = 0.290 \qquad \pi_0 = 0.25 \qquad \log \beta = -0.12.$$

These equations are different in a number of ways. First, the *E. coli* DHFR receptor shows a very different response to bulk. The MR terms are highly position-sensitive, and the prime means that any increase of MR above a value of 0.79 (scaled × 0.1) has no effect; that is, the remainder of the substituent does not appear effectively to contact the enzyme. Secondly, polar effects, represented by $\Sigma\sigma$, play no part in binding to the bacterial enzyme.

A molecular graphics study of the enzyme-trimethoprim complexes indicated a number of important differences that are not apparent from the QSARs. First, the bound trimethoprim conformation is quite different in the two cases; secondly, and probably linked to this, the conformation of an appreciable part of the receptor is different (see p. 345). For example, there is a much more non-polar environment around the benzyl side-chain of trimethoprim in chicken liver DHFR than in *E. coli* DHFR. These differences undoubtedly account for the fact, shown by the QSARs, that binding to the chicken liver enzyme is controlled much more by π than by MR, whereas the reverse is true for the *E. coli* enzyme. The 4-position of trimethoprim bound to *E. coli* DHFR points away from the active site towards solvent, so that there is but little opportunity for contact with the surface of the active site. A similar situation arises for the 3- and 5-positions. This explains the need to use MR' in the bacterial equation.

Thus graphics and QSAR can profitably be used together to build up a more comprehensive picture of the active site, and consequently to permit better design of more active inhibitors.

2E.7   Conclusions

One of the questions that is often asked about QSAR is: 'how many drugs or pesticides have been designed by QSAR?' The question is a little unfair, and rather like asking how many drugs have been designed by n.m.r. spectroscopy. It is true that in the early days of QSAR, overenthusiastic claims were made for its potential in drug design. But it is now accepted as one of numerous tools that the drug designer has at his or her disposal. There are indeed a few examples of marketable compounds having been designed largely by the use of QSAR (Fujita 1984); there are also many (largely unpublished) instances of QSAR contributing in some way towards the design of a drug (see, for example, Ganellin 1983 and Hopfinger 1985).

So far as enzyme inhibitors are concerned, it is clear that QSAR studies have contributed and are continuing to contribute greatly to our knowledge of receptor sites on enzymes. Recent work with large numbers of congeners of inhibitors has shown that generally the receptor has fairly specific requirements regarding the lipophilicity, bulk, and position of substituents on an inhibitor, and rather less specific requirements regarding electronic effects. This means that in many cases it is relatively easy to design a potent inhibitor. Whether such a compound will be active *in vivo*, and will also be without damaging side-effects, is sometimes a very different matter. Examples have been given in which the whole-cell or *in vivo* correlation is very different from that obtained with the isolated enzyme.

It would appear to be important, from the drug aspect, that isolated enzyme and *in vivo* studies go hand in hand. Many examples of such combined studies already exist, but more are needed.

The symbiosis of QSAR and molecular graphics, although only of recent origin, is already giving new insights into the nature of enzyme receptors and the way that they interact with inhibitors. Much more is anticipated from this and other related approaches, such as those of Weinstein (Weinstein *et al.* 1983) and Marshall (1983).

This review of QSAR of enzyme inhibition has of necessity been brief. A number of reviews of various aspects of the subject have been published (Hansch and Coats 1970; Hansch 1975; Grieco *et al.* 1978; Hansch 1979, 1980; Seydel and Schaper 1980; Blaney *et al.* 1984) to which the reader may wish to turn for more detail. In addition, there are several books (Martin 1978; Dearden 1983; Kuchař 1984; Mager 1984; Franke 1984; Seydel 1985) on more general aspects of quantitative structure–activity relationships, as well as many review articles too numerous to mention.

References

Abdul-Ahab, P. G. and Webb, G. A. (1982). An interpretation of some substituent effects in a series of dihydrofolate reductase inhibitors. *Eur. J. Med. Chem.*, **17**, 219–21.
Akahane, K., Momose, D., Iizuka, K., Miyamoto, T., Hayashi, M., Iwase, K., and

Moriguchi, I. (1984). Structure–activity study of pyridine derivatives inhibiting thromboxane synthetase. *Eur. J. Med. Chem.*, **19**, 85–8.

Blaney, J. M., Hansch, C., Silipo, C., and Vittoria, A. (1984). Structure-activity relationships of dihydrofolate reductase inhibitors. *Chem. Rev.* **84**, 333–407.

Chen, B.-K., Horváth, C., and Bertino, J. R. (1979). Multivariate analysis and quantitative structure-activity relationships. Inhibition of dihydrofolate reductase and thymidylate synthetase by quinazolines. *J. Med. Chem.*, **22**, 483–91.

Coats, E. A., Shah, K. J., Milstein, S. R., Genther, C. S., Nene, D. M., Roesener, J., Schmidt, J., Pleiss, M., Wagner, E., and Baker, J. K. (1982). 4-hydroxyquinoline-3-carboxylic acids as inhibitors of cell respiration. 2. Quantitative structure–activity relationship of dehydrogenase enzyme and Ehrlich ascites tumor cell inhibitions. *J. Med. Chem.*, **25**, 57–63.

Corral, C., González, E., Municio, A. M., and Ribera, A. (1966). Anticholinesterases. Influence of electronic and steric factors on the biological activity of dialkyl aryl phosphates. *An. Real Soc. Esp. Fis. Quim.*, **62B**, 503–14.

Crăescu, C. T. (1980). Quantitative structure–activity relationships using minimal topological distance parameters in some series of monoamine oxidase inhibitors. *Rev. Roum. Biochim.*, **17**, 11–21.

Crippen, G. M. (1979). Distance geometry approach to rationalizing binding data. *J. Med. Chem.*, **22**, 988–97.

Dary, C. C. and Cutkamp, L. K. (1984). Physicochemical structure–activity relationship of DDT congeners and the inhibition of mitochondrial ATPase. *Pestic. Sci.*, **15**, 443–54.

Dearden, J. C., ed. (1983). *Quantitative approaches to drug design.* Elsevier, Amsterdam.

Dietrich, S. W., Smith, R. N., Fukunga, J. Y., Olney, M., and Hansch, C. (1979). Dihydrofolate reductase inhibition by 2,4-diaminotriazines: a structure–activity study. *Arch. Biochem. Biophys.*, **194**, 600–11.

Dove, S., Coats, E., Scharfenberg, P., and Franke, R. (1985). 7-substituted-4-hydroxyquinoline-3-carboxylic acids as inhibitors of dehydrogenase enzymes and of the respiration of Ehrlich ascites tumor cells: multivariate analysis and quantitative structure–activity relationship for polar substituents. *J. Med. Chem.*, **28**, 447–51.

Dunn, W. J. and Hodnett, E. M. (1977). Structure–activity relationships for inhibition of ribonucleoside diphosphate reductase by α-(N)-formylheteroaromatic thiosemicarbazones. *Eur. J. Med. Chem.*, **12**, 113–16.

Franke, R. (1984). *Theoretical drug design methods.* Elsevier, Amsterdam.

Franks, F. (1975). The hydrophobic interaction. In *Water: a comprehensive treatise* (ed. F. Franks), Vol. 4, pp. 1–94. Plenum Press, New York.

Free, S. M. and Wilson, J. W. (1964). A mathematical contribution to structure–activity studies. *J. Med. Chem.*, **7**, 395–9.

Fujita, T. (1984). The role of QSAR in drug design. In *Drug design: fact or fantasy?* (ed. G. Jolles and K. R. H. Wooldridge), pp. 19–32. Academic Press, London.

Fujita, T., Yamamoto, I., and Nakajima, M. (1970). Analysis of the structure–activity relationship of nicotine-like insecticides using substituent constants. In *Biochemical toxicology of insecticides* (ed. R. D. O'Brien and I. Yamamoto), pp. 21–32. Academic Press, New York.

Ganellin, C. R. (1983). Dynamic structure–activity analysis exemplified with H_2 receptor histamine antagonists. In *Quantitative approaches to drug design* (ed. J. C. Dearden), pp. 239–51. Elsevier, Amsterdam.

Ghose, A. K. and Crippen, G. M. (1982). Quantitative structure–activity relationships by distance geometry: quinazolines as dihydrofolate reductase inhibitors. *J. Med. Chem.*, **25**, 892–9.

Ghose, A. K. and Crippen, G. M. (1983). Combined distance geometry analysis of dihydrofolate reductase inhibition by quinazolines and triazines. *J. Med. Chem.*, **26**, 996–1010.

Goldblum, A., Yoshimoto, M., and Hansch, C. (1981). Quantitative structure–activity relationship of phenyl *N*-methylcarbamate inhibition of acetylcholinesterase. *J. Agric. Food Chem.*, **29**, 277–88.

Grieco, C., Silipo, C., and Vittoria, A. (1978). Correlation analysis in the study of enzyme–ligand interactions. *Farmaco Ed. Sci.*, **33**, 382–400.

Guo, Z., Dietrich, S. W., Hansch, C., Dolnick, B. J., and Bertino, J. R. (1981). A comparison of the inhibition of bovine and murine leukemia dihydrofolate reductase by 4,6-diamino-1,2-dihydro-2,2-dimethyl-1-(3-phenyl)-5-triazines. *Mol. Pharmac.*, **20**, 649–56.

Gupta, S. P., Prabhakar, Y. S., and Handa, A. (1983). QSAR studies on 4-hydroxy-quinoline-3-carboxylic acids as inhibitors of cell respiration using molecular connectivity and van der Waals' volume. *Res. Commun. Chem. Pathol. Pharmacol.*, **42**, 455–62.

Habicht, J. and Brune, K. (1983). Inhibition of prostaglandin E_2 release by salicylates, benzoates and phenols: a quantitative structure–activity study. *J. Pharm. Pharmacol.*, **35**, 718–28.

Hansch, C. (1975). Enzyme study as a source of strategy in drug design. In *Advances in pharmacology and chemotherapy* (ed. S. Garattini, A. Goldin, F. Hawking, and I. J. Kopin), Vol. 13, pp. 45–82. Academic Press, New York.

Hansch, C. (1979). The interaction of ligands with enzymes. A starting point in drug design. *Farmaco Ed. Sci.*, **34**, 729–42.

Hansch, C. (1980). Computer-assisted enzyme studies in drug design. In *The use of alternatives in drug research* (ed. A. N. Rowan and C. J. Stratman), pp. 1–13. Macmillan, London.

Hansch, C. and Clayton, J. M. (1972). Lipophilic character and biological activity of drugs II. The parabolic case. *J. Pharm. Sci.*, **62**, 1–21.

Hansch, C. and Coats, E. (1970). α-chymotrypsin: a case study of substituent constants and regression analysis in enzymic structure–activity relationships. *J. Pharm. Sci.*, **59**, 731–43.

Hansch, C. and Deutsch, E. W. (1966). The use of substituent constants in the study of structure–activity relationships in cholinesterase inhibitors. *Biochim. Biophys. Acta.*, **126**, 117–28.

Hansch, C. and Fujita, T. (1964). ρ–σ–π analysis. A method for the correlation of biological activity and chemical structure. *J. Am. Chem. Soc.*, **86**, 1616–26.

Hansch, C., Maloney, P. P., Fujita, T., and Muir, R. M. (1962). Correlation of biological activity of phenoxyacetic acids with Hammett substituent constants and partition coefficients. *Nature (London)*, **194**, 178–80.

Hansch, C., Silipo, C., and Steller, E. E. (1975). Formulation of *de novo* substituent constants in correlation analysis: inhibition of dihydrofolate reductase by 2,4-diamino-5-(3,4-dichlorophenyl)-6-substituted pyrimidines. *J. Pharm. Sci.*, **64**, 1186–91.

Hansch, C., Grieco, C., Silipo, C., and Vittoria, A. (1977a). Quantitative structure–activity relationships of chymotrypsin–ligand interactions. *J. Med. Chem.*, **20**, 1420–35.

Hansch, C., Fukunaga, J. Y., Jow, P. Y. C., and Hynes, J. B. (1977b). Quantitative structure–activity relationships of antimalarial and dihydrofolate reductase inhibition by quinazolines and 5-substituted benzyl-2,4-diaminopyrimidines. *J. Med. Chem.*, **20**, 96–102.

Hansch, C., Hathaway, B. A., Guo, Z., Selassie, C. D., Dietrich, S. W., Blaney, J. M., Langridge, R., Volz, K. W., and Kaufman, B. T. (1984). Crystallography, quantitative structure–activity relationships and molecular graphics in a comparative analysis of the inhibition of dihydrofolate reductase from chicken liver and *Lactobacillus casei* by 4,6-diamino-1,2-dihydro-2,2-dimethyl-1-(substituted phenyl)-*s*-triazines. *J. Med. Chem.*, **27**, 129–43.

Hansch, C., McClarin, J., Klein, T., and Langridge, R. (1985). A quantitative structure–activity relationship and molecular graphics study of carbonic anhydrase inhibitors. *Mol. Pharmacol.*, **27**, 493–8.

Hathaway, B. A., Guo, Z., Hansch, C., Delcamp, T. J., Susten, S. S., and Freisheim, J. H. (1984). Inhibition of human dihydrofolate reductase by 4,6-diamino-1,2-dihydro-2,2-dimethyl-1-(substituted phenyl)-*s*-triazines. A quantitative structure–activity relationship analysis. *J. Med. Chem.*, **27**, 144–9.

Höltje, H.-D. (1975). Theoretical study of structure–activity relationships in a series of monoamine oxidase-inhibiting cyclopropyl amines. *Arch. Pharm.*, **308**, 438–44.

Höltje, H.-D. and Simon, H. (1984). Theoretical investigations of interactions between drug molecules and models of receptor sites. 4. The interaction complex between sulfonamides and human erythrocyte carbonic anhydrase-C. *Arch. Pharm.*, **317**, 506–16.

Hopfinger, A. J. (1981). A general QSAR for dihydrofolate reductase inhibition by 2,4-diaminotriazines based upon molecular shape analysis. *Arch. Biochem. Biophys.*, **206**, 153–63.

Hopfinger, A. J. (1985). Computer-assisted drug design. *J. Med. Chem.*, **28**, 1133–9.

Kamoshita, K., Ohno, I., Fujita, T., Nishioka, T., and Nakajima, M. (1979). Quantitative structure–activity relationships of phenyl *N*-methylcarbamates against the house fly and its acetylcholinesterase. *Pestic. Biochem. Physiol.*, **11**, 83–103.

Kawaki, H., Takagi, T., Iwata, A., and Sasaki, Y. (1982). The substituent entropy constant σ_s^0 used in the quantitative structure–activity relationship investigation of dihydrofolate reductase inhibition by Baker triazines. *Chem. Pharm. Bull. Tokyo*, **30**, 750–1.

Kier, L. B. and Hall, L. H. (1976). *Molecular connectivity in chemistry and drug research.* Academic Press, New York.

Kubinyi, H. (1976). Quantitative structure–activity relationships IV. Non-linear dependence of biological activity on hydrophobic character: a new model. *Arzneim-Forsch.*, **26**, 1991–7.

Kuchař, M. (ed.) (1984). *QSAR in design of bioactive compounds.* Prous, Barcelona.

Kutter, E. and Hansch, C. (1969). Steric parameters in drug design: monoamine oxidase inhibitors and antihistamines. *J. Med. Chem.*, **12**, 647–52.

Li, R., Hansch, C., and Kaufman, B. T. (1982a). Comparison of the inhibitory action of 5-(substituted benzyl)-2,4-diaminopyrimidines on dihydrofolate reductase from chicken liver with that from bovine liver. *J. Med. Chem.*, **25**, 435–40.

Li, R., Hansch, C., Matthews, D., Blaney, J. M., Langridge, R., Delcamp, T. J., Susten, S. S., and Freisheim, J. H. (1982b). A comparison by QSAR, crystallography, and computer graphics of the inhibition of various dihydrofolate reductases by 5-(X-benzyl)-2,4-diaminopyrimidines. *Quant. Struct. Activ. Relat.*, **1**, 1–7.

Lukovits, I. (1983). Quantitative structure–activity relationships employing independent quantum chemical indices. *J. Med. Chem.*, **26**, 1104–9.

Mabilia, M., Pearlstein, R. A., and Hopfinger, A. J. (1985). Molecular shape analysis and energetics-based intermolecular modelling of benzylpyrimidine dihydrofolate reductase inhibitors. *Eur. J. Med. Chem.*, **20**, 163–74.

McCammon, J. A., Gelin, B. R., and Karplus, M. (1977). Dynamics of folded proteins. *Nature (London)*, **267**, 585–90.

Mager, P. P. (1984). *Multidimensional pharmacochemistry.* Academic Press, Orlando.

Marshall, G. R. (1983). Computer graphics and receptor modelling. In *Quantitative approaches to drug design* (ed. J. C. Dearden), pp. 129–36. Elsevier, Amsterdam.

Martin, Y. C. (1978). *Quantitative drug design.* Marcel Dekker, New York.

Martin, Y. C. (1981). A practitioner's perspective on the role of quantitative structure–activity analysis in medicinal chemistry. *J. Med. Chem.*, **24**, 229–37.

Miertus, S. and Filipovic, P. (1982). Relationship between electronic structure and biological activity of 2-formylpyridine thiosemicarbazones. *Eur. J. Med. Chem.*, **17**, 145–8.

Miyagawa, H. and Fujita, T. (1982). Quantitative structure–activity study for inhibition of acetylcholinesterase by *m*-substituted benzyltrimethylammonium salts. *Farmaco Ed. Sci.*, **37**, 797–804.

Naeff, H. S. D., van der Plas, H. C., Tramper, J., and Müller, F. (1985). Synthesis and quantitative structure–activity relationship (QSAR) analysis of some novel xanthine oxidase inhibitors: 6-(*para*-substituted phenyl)-pteridine-4-ones. *Quant. Struct. Activ. Relat.*, **4**, 161–6.

Neely, W. B. (1965). The use of molecular orbital calculations as an aid to correlate the structure and activity of cholinesterase inhibitors. *Mol. Pharmacol.*, **1**, 137–44.

Nishioka, T., Fujita, T., Kamoshita, K., and Nakajima, M. (1977). Mechanism of inhibition reaction of acetylcholinesterase by phenyl *N*-methylcarbamates. Separation of hydrophobic, electronic, hydrogen bonding and proximity effects of aromatic substituents. *Pestic. Biochem. Physiol.*, **7**, 107–21.

Pauling, L. and Pressman, D. (1945). The serological properties of simple substances. IX. Hapten inhibition of precipitation of antisera homologous to the *o*-, *m*-, and *p*-azophenylarsonic acid groups. *J. Am. Chem. Soc.*, **67**, 1003–12.

Purcell, W. P., Beasley, J. G., Quintana, R. P., and Singer, J. A. (1966). Application of partition coefficients, electric moments, electronic structures and free-energy relationships to the interpretation of chloinesterase inhibition. *J. Med. Chem.*, **9**, 297–303.

Seydel, J. K. (ed.) (1985). *QSAR and strategies in the design of bio-active compounds.* VCH, Weinheim.

Seydel, J. K. and Schaper, K.-J. (1980). Quantitative structure–activity relationships as applied to enzyme inhibitors. In *Enzyme inhibitors as drugs* (ed. M. Sandler), pp. 53–71. Macmillan, London.

Shah, K. J. and Coats, E. A. (1977). Design, synthesis and correlation analysis of 7-substituted 4-hydroxyquinoline-3-carboxylic acids as inhibitors of cellular respiration. *J. Med. Chem.*, **20**, 1001–6.

Simon, Z., Chiriac, A., Holban, S., Ciubotaru, D., and Mihalas, G. I. (1984). *Minimum steric difference.* Wiley, New York.

Testa, B. (1980). Structural and electronic factors governing the inhibition of cytochrome-P450-mediated aniline hydroxylation by alcohols—a molecular orbital and quantitative structure–activity relationship study. In *Enzyme inhibitors* (ed. U. Brodbeck), pp. 75–83. Verlag Chemie, Weinheim.

Testa, B. and Purcell, W. P. (1978). A QSAR study of sulfonamide binding to carbonic anhydrase as test of steric models. *Eur. J. Med. Chem.*, **13**, 509–14.

Topliss, J. G. and Costello, R. J. (1972). Chance correlations in structure–activity studies using multiple regression analysis. *J. Med. Chem.*, **15**, 1066–9.

van't Riet, B., Kier, L. B., and Elford, H. L. (1980). Structure–activity relationships of benzohydroxamic acid inhibitors of ribonucleotide reductase. *J. Pharm. Sci.*, **69**, 856–7.

Verloop, A., Hoogenstraaten, W., and Tipker, J. (1976). Development and application of new steric substituent parameters in drug design. In *Drug design* (ed. E. J. Ariëns) vol. 7, pp. 165–207. Academic Press, New York.

Wedding, R. T., Hansch, C., and Fukuoto, T. R. (1967). Inhibition of malate dehydrogenase by phenols and the influence of ring substituents on their inhibitory effectiveness. *Arch. Biochem. Biophys.*, **121**, 9–21.

Weinstein, H., Osman, R., Topiol, S., and Venazi, C. A. (1983). Molecular determinants for biological mechanisms: model studies of interaction in carboxypeptidase. In *Quantitative approaches to drug design* (ed. J. C. Dearden), pp. 81–90. Elsevier, Amsterdam.

Wright, G. E. and Gambino, J. J. (1984). Quantitative structure–activity relationships of 6-anilinouracils as inhibitors of *Bacillus subtilis* DNA polymerase III. *J. Med. Chem.*, **27**, 181–5.

Yashimoto, M. and Hansch, C. (1976). Correlation analysis of Baker's studies on enzyme inhibition. 2. Chymotrypsin, trypsin, thymidine phosphorylase, uridine phosphorylase, thymidylate synthetase, cytosine nucleoside deaminase, dihydrofolate reductase, malate dehydrogenase, glutamate dehydrogenase, lactate dehydrogenase, and glyceraldehyde-phosphate dehydrogenase. *J. Med. Chem.*, **19**, 71–98.

3

Inhibitors of the renin–angiotensin system enzymes

Edgar H. Ulm and William J. Greenlee

3.1   Introduction

Since the discovery of angiotensin and the enzymes responsible for its formation, the therapeutic potential for inhibitors of these enzymes has been apparent. Angiotensin II is the most potent vasoconstrictor known. If a hypertensive state exists where the renin–angiotensin–aldosterone system (RAS) is responsible, any intervention which reduces angiotensin II availability to receptors could act to lower blood pressure. Possible modes of intervention are inhibition of renin release, renin inhibition, angiotensin-converting enzyme (ACE) inhibition, and angiotensin receptor antagonism. All of these approaches have received the attention of those looking for drugs, but the most successful to date has been the specific inhibition of ACE. Inhibitors of the converting enzyme have reached the market and are finding increasing acceptance for the treatment of mild to severe hypertension and congestive heart failure. It is the purpose of this chapter to draw from examples of the successful commercial development of ACE inhibitors and the promising advances made with renin inhibitors, elements of the process of enzyme inhibitor discovery/design that might be utilized with other systems possessing therapeutic potential.

. For those interested in the rich history of the elucidation of the renin–angiotensin–aldosterone system and its importance in blood pressure control and salt–water balance, the following volumes are recommended: Braun-Menendez *et al.* (1946); Page and McCubbin (1968); and Page and Bumpus (1974).

Many excellent reviews present detailed descriptions of the physiology of the renin-angiotensin-aldosterone system and the development of ACE inhibitors (Cushman *et al.* 1980; Sweet and Blaine 1984; Reid 1985; Patchett and Cordes 1985; Peach 1977). These will provide the reader with access to the primary literature in these fields. Renin inhibitors on the other hand are not so advanced and so we will reference this subject more thoroughly.

3.1.1   Renin–angiotensin pathway and physiology

As illustrated in Fig. 3.1, the initial substrate in the angiotensin pathway is an α-2-globulin synthesized in the liver and found in the general circulation. Renin, synthesized and released by the kidneys in response to decreased renal perfu-

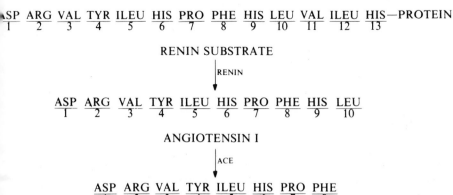

Fig. 3.1. Biochemical pathway of the renin–angiotensin system.

sion, cleaves the amino terminal decapeptide from angiotensinogen to yield angiotensin I. ACE, both in the plasma and on the outer membrane of endothelial cells, catalyses the removal of the carboxy terminal dipeptide to form angiotensin II. This short-lived octapeptide acts via its receptors to constrict the vasculature, to stimulate the release of aldosterone from the adrenals and, in a direct negative feedback loop, to inhibit the further release of renin from the kidney. Angiotensin II is also known to stimulate both drinking behaviour and salt appetite by acting on brain regions within and outside the blood–brain barrier. When injected into the brain ventricles of rats, angiotensin II increases blood pressure and drinking behaviour.

In addition to the sites of origin and action outlined here, evidence exists for the occurrence of the renin–angiotensin system in other tissues as well. However, its precise role in the arterial wall or in the central nervous system, for example, remains controversial.

Historically, it was the observation of Tigerstedt and Bergman (1898) that hypertension could be induced in dogs by injection of kidney extracts which eventually led to the characterization of the renin–angiotensin system. A variety of stimuli act upon the kidney to control the release of renin into the blood-stream, e.g. the blood pressure in the afferent arteriole, sodium concentration in the distal tubule, renal sympathetic nerve activity and angiotensin II concentrat-ion. Release of renin from the kidney and the subsequent cascade of events act to ensure adequate renal function (Fig. 3.2). Angiotensin II-induced vasoconstric-tion raises systemic pressure, as does the angiotensin II-stimulated release of aldosterone. The latter acts to conserve sodium, thereby tending to increase vascular volume. As noted above, in a direct feedback loop, angiotensin II inhibits renin release and, indirectly, increases renal perfusion pressure, which also acts physiologically to reduce renin release.

3.2   Renin

Theoretically, renin, as the first enzyme in the renin-angiotensin cascade, is the site where therapeutic control should be most effective. Its inhibition interferes with the formation of angiotensin I and, because angiotensinogen is the only naturally occurring substrate of renin, no additional effects on other systems would be expected. Development of renin inhibitors has lagged behind that of ACE inhibitors in part because of the strict recognition requirements of renin, the minimal substrate of which is an octapeptide.

3.2.1   Properties of renin (EC 3.4.99.19)

Renin is found in the plasma and has been identified in other tissues within the body. As its name implies, the highest concentrations of this enzyme are in the kidney, specifically within the granules of the juxtaglomerular cells. Concentrat-ions of renin in the blood are quite variable, depending on the physiological

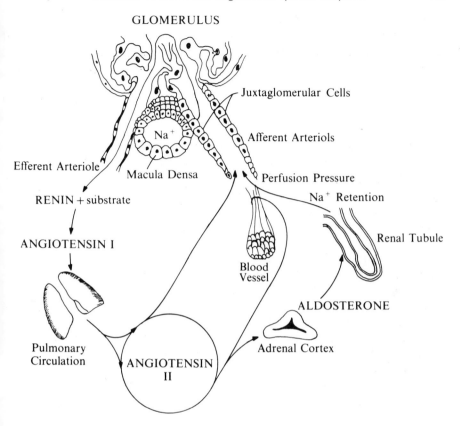

GLOMERULUS

Fig. 3.2. Increases in angiotensin II result in decreases in renin release by direct feedback inhibition, by direct vasoconstriction resulting in increased blood pressure, and indirectly through retention of sodium by direct effects on the macula densa and through stimulation of aldosterone release. Sodium retention tends to increase extracellular volume, which thereby increases blood pressure. (From Oparil, S. and Haber, E. Reprinted by permission from the *New England Journal of Medicine* (1974) **291**, 393.)

state of the organism. As one would expect of an enzyme that is important in controlling a homeostatic process, renin is rapidly turned over, with the $t_{1/2}$ for clearance of exogenously administered renin estimated at 13 min in rats (Nakamura *et al.* 1984).

Renin is a glycoprotein formed as inactive pre-pro-renin which, based on the sequence of the human gene, consists of 403 amino acid residues, including a 66-residue amino-terminal pre-pro-peptide (Imai *et al.* 1983; Hobart *et al.* 1984). The enzyme formed in the kidney appears to be a mixture of fully active renin and renin associated with a large polypeptide inhibitor. Inactive renin can be activated by a number of manipulations including limited proteolysis of the inhibitor. Although these multiple forms, and the glycoprotein nature of renin have not made its purification an easy task, homogeneous renin has been purified from a variety of sources including human kidney (Slater *et al.* 1978; Galen *et al.* 1979; Yokosawa *et al.* 1980), dog kidney (Dzau *et al.* 1979), hog kidney (Corvol *et al.* 1977), rat kidney (Matoba *et al.* 1978) and the mouse submaxillary gland (Cohen *et al.* 1972).

Renin is an aspartic proteinase, but differs from the other members of this class (e.g. pepsin, cathepsin D, gastricin and the fungal proteinases, penicillopepsin, endothiopepsin, and rhizopus pepsin) in two very important respects. First, renin possesses good enzymatic activity at physiological pH, whereas, the other aspartic proteinases demonstrate by their pH optima the basis for their pseudonym—acid proteinases. Second, renin has a remarkably narrow substrate specificity, limited to a single bond in angiotensinogen, whereas, the other members of the class have little in the way of specificity. The human substrate scissile bond is Leu-Val, while it is Leu-Leu for other mammals. Even this minimal substrate difference is significant, in that while the human enzyme will cleave human and other mammalian substrates, only human renin will cleave human substrate (i.e. the renins of other species do not cleave human substrate). A variety of renin assays are used to determine activities of inhibitors. Among these are human kidney renin (HKR) assays, which use partially or extensively purified enzyme and human angiotensinogen; other mammalian angiotensinogens and synthetic peptides have been used as substrates. In human plasma renin assays, cleavage of endogenous substrate by endogenous enzyme is measured by radioimmunoassay. A variety of assay conditions (pH, presence of other proteinase inhibitors, detection method) have been reported. As a result, comparisons between literature IC_{50} values are difficult; the literature references cited in this chapter should be consulted when differences in IC_{50} values are interpreted.

The aspartic proteinases share the functional presence of carboxyl residues in the active site, many common structural features (where these are known), and striking sequence homology. Tang (1979) described many of these similarities, and additional work, particularly with respect to the sequence homologies, has further strengthened the relationships (Imai *et al.* 1983; Sogawa *et al.* 1983; Panthier *et al.* 1982). Although the three-dimensional structure of renin has not been determined, the structures of related aspartic proteinases show the active site aspartic acids centred in a long cleft, capable of binding at least eight amino acids. A stereochemical analysis of the catalytic mechanism of penicillopepsin, based on an X-ray structure of an enzyme–inhibitor complex, has been reported (James and Sielecki 1985).

3.2.2   *In vitro* inhibition of renin

Development of renin inhibitors has evolved from knowledge of substrate sequence, mechanistic hypotheses based on structural information drawn from several aspartic proteinases, and the discovery of pepstatin, a naturally occurring inhibitor of this class of proteinases. In the last five years, renin inhibitor design has yielded several classes of potent inhibitors, the best of which are active at the nanomolar level. Steady progress has been made toward smaller inhibitors more likely to represent effective thereapeutic agents. Inhibition of renin has been achieved with renin antibodies, substrate analogues, and transition-state analogues.

3.2.3 Renin antibodies

Inhibitory renin antibodies provided the first evidence that interference in the action of the renin–angiotensin system had thereapeutic potential (Wakerlin 1958). Although these first renin antibodies were impure, polyclonal, monoclonal, and FAB antibodies prepared recently using purified renins have shown potent ($K_i = 0.01$–1.0 nM) renin inhibition (Burton et al. 1982; Galen et al. 1983, 1984; Dzau et al. 1984; Wood et al. 1986) and hypotensive effects when administered i.v. to salt-depleted monkeys (see below).

3.2.4 Substrate analogues and other peptide inhibitors

Work on substrate analogues as renin inhibitors has influenced later work with transition state inhibitors. Early substrate analogues, based on residues 10–13 of angiotensinogen, were renin-stable inhibitors with K_i values in the millimolar range (Kokubu et al. 1968). Burton and colleagues began with the minimum substrate sequence (Table 3.1, **1**), as determined by Skeggs et al. (1968), and synthesized decapeptide **2**, which they named RIP (renin inhibitory peptide). The N-terminal proline and C-terminal lysine of **2** increase water solubility, and the substitution of Phe-Phe for Leu-Leu prevents cleavage by renin (Burton et al. 1980; Cody et al. 1980). More recently, this approach has led to a shortened sequence, Phe-Phe(4-I)-Val-Tyr-Lys (RI-103), reported to be as potent as RIP (Burton et al. 1983). An interesting discovery is that peptides derived from the prosegment of human prorenin are competitive inhibitors of human renin, the best being Boc-Leu-Lys-Arg-Met-Pro-OCH$_3$, with an IC$_{50}$ of 16.6 μM (Cumin et al. 1985).

3.2.5 Transition-state inhibitors of renin

The design of enzyme inhibitors that resemble the transition state for the enzyme-catalysed reaction has been described by Wolfenden (1972). The transition state is the molecular arrangement of highest free energy along the reaction pathway. It is believed that the acceleration of reactions brought about by enzymes is a result of tight binding and stabilization of the transition-state species by the enzyme, and thus it is expected that inhibitors whose designs approximate the transition state will bind more tightly than substrates or products. Using the transition-state inhibitor approach, Szelke and co-workers

Table 3.1. Inhibitors of human renin

	6	7	8	9	10	11	12	13
Minimum Substrate (**1**)	His-	Pro-	Phe-	His-	Leu-	Leu-	Val-	Tyr
Human sequence	His-	Pro-	Phe-	His-	Leu-	Val-	Ile-	His

Inhibitor	Structure	IC_{50}(nM)
RIP (**2**)	Pro-His-Pro-Phe-His-Phe-Phe- Val-Tyr-Lys	(2 000)
H-142 (**3**)	Pro-His-Pro-Phe-His-Leu$\overset{R}{-}$Val -Ile-His-Lys	10
H-261 (**4**)	Boc-His-Pro-Phe-His-Leu$\overset{OH}{-}$Val -Ile-His	0.70
U-17 038 (**5**)	Boc-Pro-Phe-(N-Me)His-Leu$\overset{OH}{-}$Val -Ile-NH-CH$_2$(4-pyr)	0.39
6	Boc-Phe-His-Cal$\overset{R}{-}$Val NH-2(S)-methylbutyl	(8.6)
7	t-BuCOCH$_2$CH(CH$_2$Ph)CO-His-Cal$\overset{OH}{-}$Val -NH-CH$_3$	(2)
Pepstatin A (**8**)	Iva-Val-Val-Sta -Ala-Sta	22 000
SR 42 128 (**9**)	Iva-Phe-Nle-Sta -Ala-Sta	28
SCRIP (**10**)	Iva-His-Pro-Phe-His-Sta -Leu-Phe-NH$_2$	16
CGP-29 287 (**11**)	Z-Arg-Arg-Pro-Phe-His-Sta -Ile-His-Lys(Boc)-OCH$_3$	1.0
ES-305 (**12**)	BNMA-His-Sta -NH-2(S)-methylbutyl	9.2
ACRIP (**13**)	Iva-His-Pro-Phe-His-ACHPA -Leu-Phe-NH$_2$	0.17
14	Boc-Phe-His-ACHPA -NH-2(S)-methylbutyl	(4)
RRM-188 (**15**)	Z-[3-(1-naphthyl)]Ala-His-Leu-al	(80)

A-60707 (**16**)

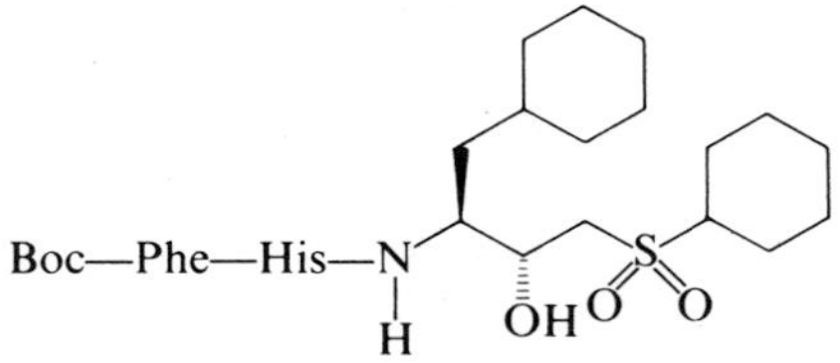

Boc—Phe—His—N—H

(2.5)

KRI-1230 (**17**)

His—N—H

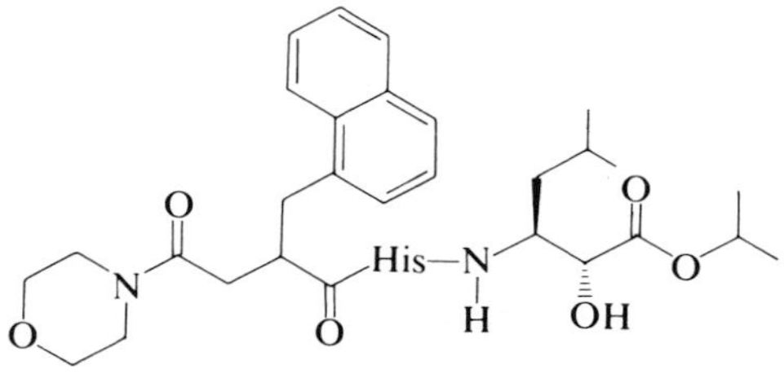

7.8

References and abbreviations in text: Cal = 3-cyclohexylalanine; Boc = t-butoxycarbonyl; Z = carbobenzoxy; Iva = isovaleroyl. Moieties replacing scissile bond are underlined; R indicates reduced bond, OH indicates hydroxy isostere (Fig. 3.3). IC_{50} values are for plasma resin assays; those in parentheses are for human kidney renin assays.

Table 3.2. Inhibitors of angiotensin converting enzyme

pGlu-Trp-Pro-Arg-Pro-Glu-Ile-Pro-Pro
Teprotide (**18**)

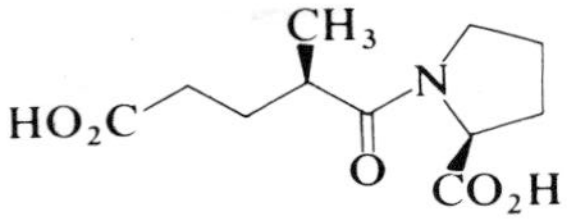

(**19**)

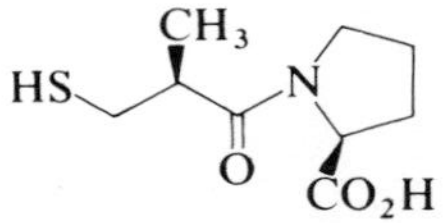

Captopril (**20**)

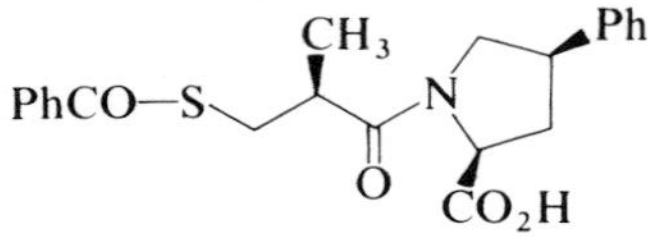

Zofenopril (**21**)

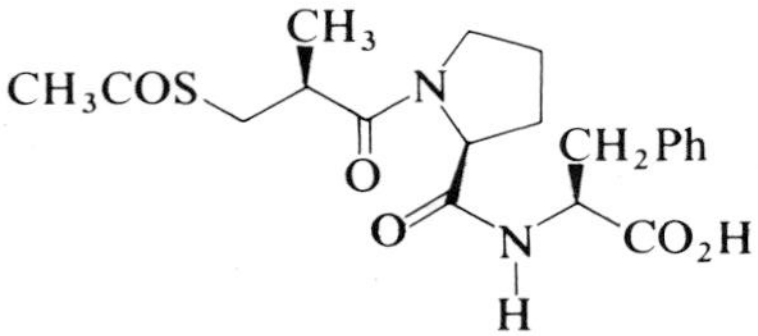

Alacipril (**22**)

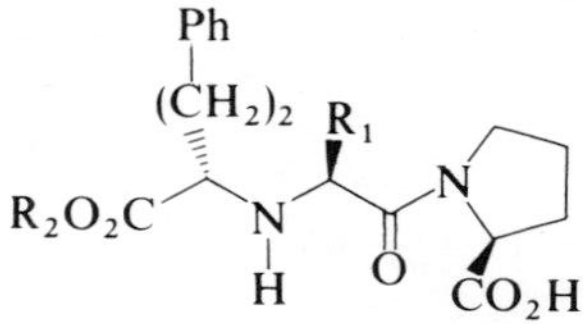

Spatial structure for **23**, **24**, **25**

Enalapriat (**23**) $R_1 = -CH_3$
                    $R_2 = -H$

Enalapril (**24**) $R_1 = -CH_3$
                    $R_2 = -C_2H_5$
                    Maleate Salt

Lisinopril (**25**) $R_1 = -(CH_2)_4NH_2$
                     $R_2 = -H$

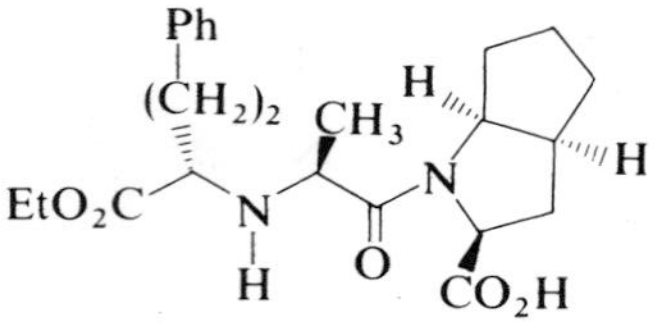

Ramipril (**26**)

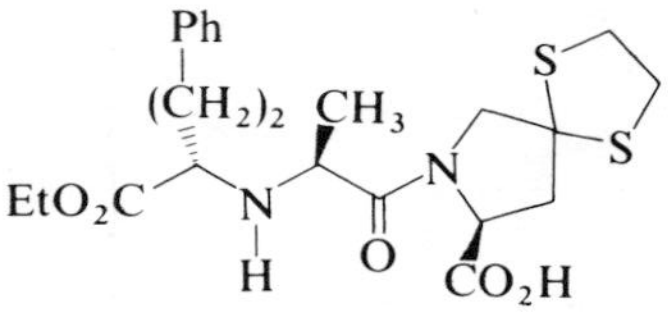

Spiropril (**27**)

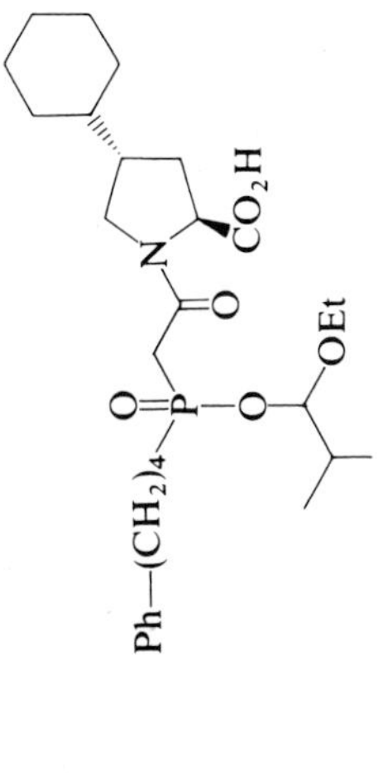

SQ 29 852 **(29)**

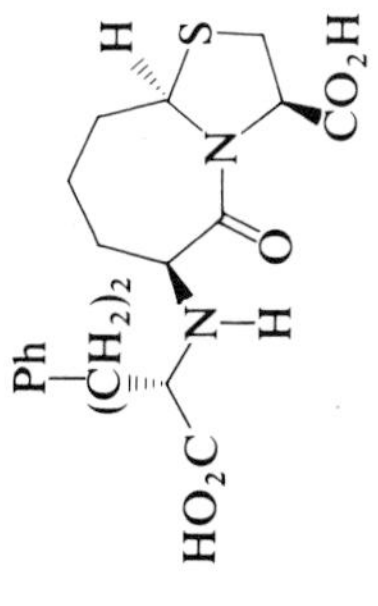

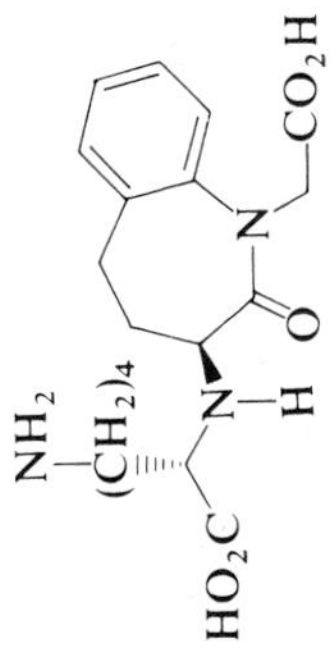

CGS 16617 **(31)**

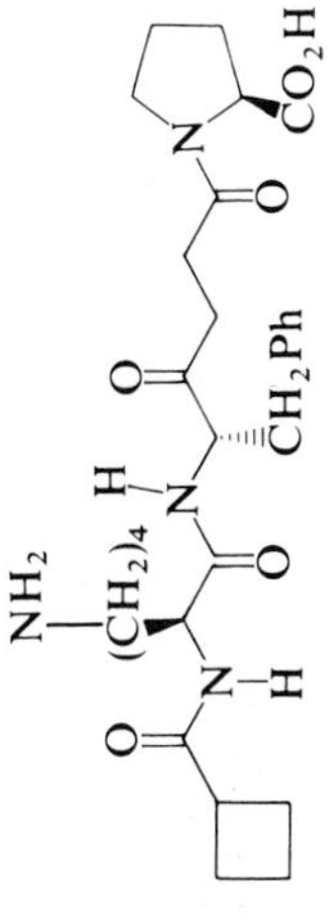

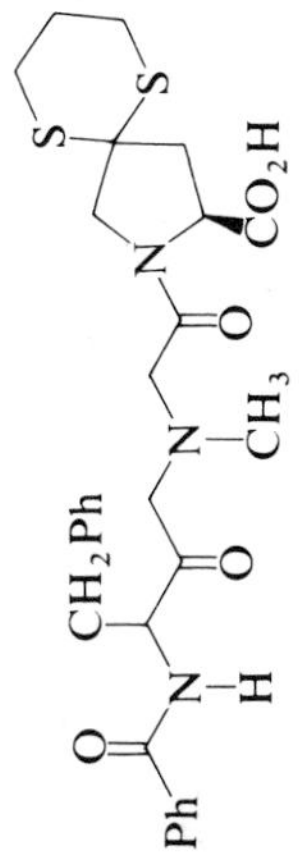

(33)

Fosenopril **(28)**

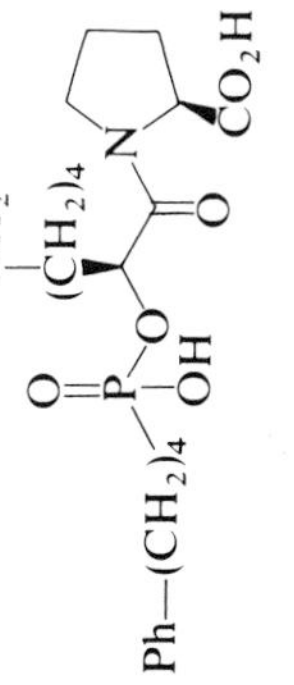

Cilazapril **(30)**

(32)

Table 3.2. (*continued*)

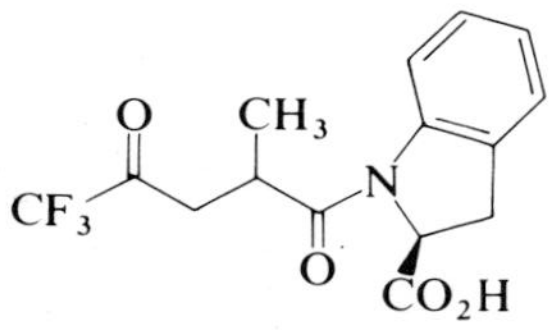

(34)

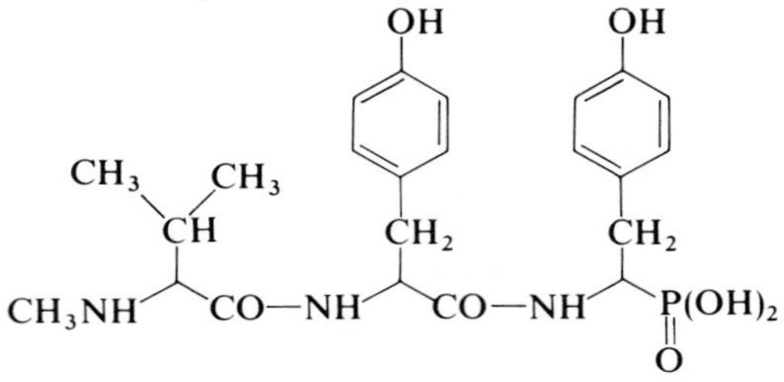

(35)

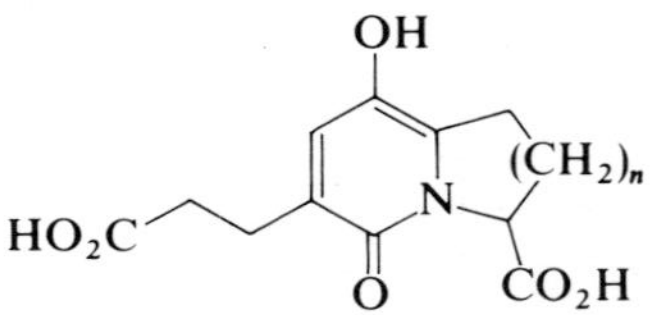

(36) *n* = 1
(37) *n* = 2

have designed potent inhibitors of renin in which the scissile bond of substrate analogues is replaced by either a 'reduced peptide' bond ($-CH_2NH_2-$) or a 'hydroxy isostere' ($-CHOHCH_2-$) as illustrated in Fig. 3.3 Both functionalities are intended to mimic the tetrahedral intermediate for the peptide bond hydrolysis, a structure that is presumed to approximate that of the transition state. The effectiveness of the first design is illustrated by the potent 'reduced peptide' inhibitor (Table 3.1, 3) (Szelke *et al.* 1985); that of the second by inhibitors 4 (Szelke 1985; Szelke *et al.* 1985) and 5 (Thaisrivongs *et al.* 1986a). Inhibitors 6 (Plattner *et al.* 1986) and 7 (Rasetti *et al.*, 1986) are lower molecular weight representatives of these two classes.

The naturally occurring aspartic proteinase inhibitor pepstatin A (8) (Umezawa *et al.* 1970) is an exceedingly potent ($K_i = 0.05$ nM) inhibitor of pepsin (Workman and Burkitt 1979), but a much weaker inhibitor (Table 3.1) of human renin (Boger *et al.* 1983). The central statine [4(S)-amino-3(S)-hydroxy-6-methylheptanoic acid] element of pepstatin A (Fig. 3.3) has been proposed to serve as a mimic of the transition state for hydrolysis (Marciniszyn *et al.* 1976) or, alternatively, as a 'collected substrate' analogue (Rich 1985). Derivatives of pepstatin with increased solubility have been prepared as inhibitors of human

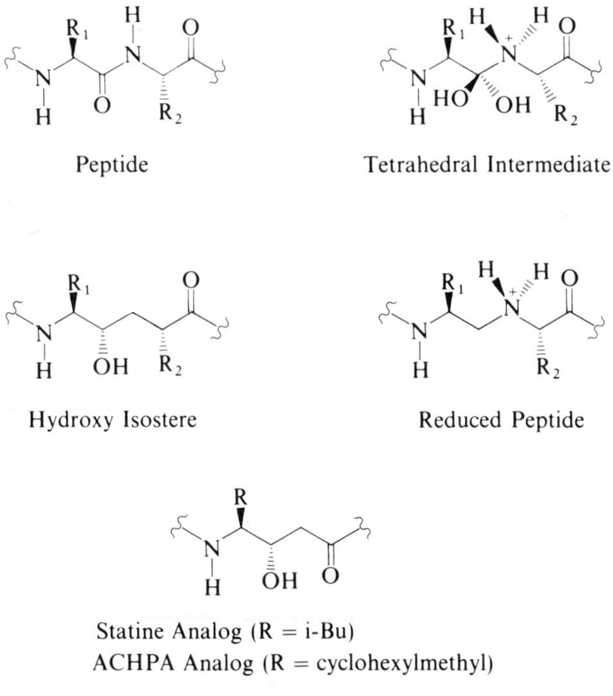

Peptide

Tetrahedral Intermediate

Hydroxy Isostere

Reduced Peptide

Statine Analog (R = i-Bu)
ACHPA Analog (R = cyclohexylmethyl)

Fig. 3.3. Stereochemical relationship of peptide bond and tetrahedral intermediate for hydrolysis to hydroxy isostere, reduced peptide and statine (ACHPA) analogue.

renin, the best being pepstatin-Glu with a K_i of 5.8 μM (Eid *et al.* 1981). More recently, the Sta-Ala-Sta sequence has been incorporated into highly potent pentapeptides such as **9** (Guegan *et al.* 1986).

Since renin is a highly specific proteinase, Boger and co-workers incorporated statine into the angiotensinogen sequence hoping to find more potent renin inhibitors (Boger *et al.* 1983). Powers *et al.* (1977), noting similarities between the structure of pepstatin and substrates of aspartic proteinases, suggested that statine might replace both amino acids around the cleavage site, a conclusion also reached by Boger *et al.* (1983) using molecular modeling methods (see below). Peptides such as **10** (statine-containing, renin-inhibitory peptide— SCRIP), synthesized on the basis of this hypothesis, are potent inhibitors of human renin and are selective for renin versus other aspartic proteinases (Boger *et al.* 1983). Incorporation of statine modelled as a single amino acid replacement gave less potent inhibitors. Inhibitors such as **11** have demonstrated that IC_{50} values of 1 nM can be obtained in the statine series (Wood *et al.* 1985). Inhibitors containing an analogue of statine ('aminostatine'), where the statine hydroxyl is replaced by an amino group, show no advantage in potency (Jones *et al.* 1985; Arrowsmith *et al.* 1986). A favourable ionic interaction with the active-site aspartic acids might be balanced by the energy required for desolvation of the ammonium group as inhibitor binds to renin.

Considerable progress toward lower molecular weight inhibitors has been made. Statine-containing renin inhibitors with high potency include the dipeptide inhibitor **12**, which incorporates the BNMA (bis-napthylmethylacetyl group) (Kokubu *et al.* 1986). Boger and co-workers used molecular modelling (see below) to predict that inhibitors containing the statine analogue ACHPA [4(*S*)-amino-5-cyclohexyl-3(*S*)-hydroxypentanoic acid] would have increased potency. The ACHPA-containing analogue ACRIP (**13**) corresponding to SCRIP was in fact more potent (Boger *et al.* 1985a) and many recently reported renin inhibitor designs have featured the cyclohexyl modification. ACHPA-containing inhibitors as small as tripeptide **14** are highly potent (Sham *et al.* 1986). In another approach to increased potency, analogues of statine and ACHPA bearing 2*R* or 2*S* alkyl substituents have been prepared and incorporated into peptide inhibitors in order to replace the S'_1 side-chain, which is absent when statine or ACHPA are used as dipeptide mimics. Although replacement of statine in a large peptide inhibitor (*i*Bu-His-Pro-Phe-Phe-Sta-Leu-Phe-NH$_2$) by 2*R*- and 2*S*-isobutyl substituted statines gave no increase in potency (Veber *et al.* 1984), incorporation of a 2-allyl substituent into smaller inhibitors such as the unsubstituted ACHPA-containing tripeptide **14** did yield more potent inhibitors (Stein *et al.* 1986).

Peptide aldehydes such as **15**, which utilize binding sites only to the amino terminal side of the cleavage site, have been reported to be potent inhibitors of renin (Fehrentz *et al.* 1984; Kokubu *et al.* 1984). This potency could be explained if they bind in the hydrated form and, as such, mimic the transition state for substrate cleavage. Inhibitors of pepsin (Gelb *et al.* 1985) and renin

(Thaisrivongs *et al.* 1986b) that incorporate a difluorinated ketone analogue of statine (difluorostatone) are believed to bind as ketone hydrates. The fact that these are more potent against renin than peptide aldehydes may reflect the fact that they make binding interactions on both sides of the cleavage site. Additional transition-state inhibitors designs incorporate a C-terminal hydroxysulphone element (Table 3.1, **16**) (Dellaria *et al.* 1987) and a shortened statine (norstatine) ester (**17**) (Miyazaki *et al.* 1986); others utilize diol (Hanson *et al.* 1985) or amino alcohol (Ryono *et al.* 1985; Dann *et al.* 1986) elements.

3.2.6   The role of molecular modelling in renin inhibitor design

Models of mouse renin (Blundell *et al.* 1983) and human renin (Sibanda 1984; Sibanda *et al.* 1984; Carlson *et al.* 1985; Akahane *et al.* 1985) have been derived from their known primary sequences and the X-ray crystal structures of related aspartic proteinases. Preliminary X-ray crystallographic data on mouse submaxillary gland renin and inhibitor complexes has been reported by Navia *et al.* (1984). An X-ray crystal structure of a complex of pepstatin with the aspartic proteinase from *Rhizopus chinensis* (Bott *et al.* 1982) was used by Boger to derive the statine derivative ACHPA and to predict the activity of two classes of cyclic statine-containing inhibitors (Boger 1985a). X-ray structures have also been described for a complex of inhibitor **3** with endothiapepsin (Hallett *et al.* 1985) and of a pepstatin analogue (Iva-Val-Val-Sta-OEt) with penicillopepsin (James and Sielecki 1985). Although other contributions of molecular modelling to renin inhibitor design are anticipated, they must at present be based on proposed models. Exact molecular modelling of renin inhibitors awaits completion of an X-ray structure of renin with an inhibitor bound to it.

3.2.7   *In vivo* inhibition of renin

The *in vivo* use of renin antibodies to inhibit renin has been discussed by Haber (1985). *In vivo* studies of peptide-based inhibitors of renin have been reviewed by Boger (1985b) and by Hofbauer and Wood (1985). Effective inhibition of plasma renin activity (PRA) and lowering of blood pressure (BP) have been obtained in renin-dependent models, including primates, with administration of inhibitor by infusion or i.v. bolus. Duration of action is usually quite short but is often seen to increase with a larger dose of inhibitor. In comparisons in salt-depleted animals of the hypotensive effects of renin inhibitors versus those of ACE inhibitors, either little difference (Leckie *et al.* 1983), or a slightly greater effect for an ACE inhibitor (Oldham *et al.* 1984; Blaine *et al.* 1985), has been reported. The latter result is consistent with the hypothesis that ACE inhibitors may also potentiate bradykinin and other hypotensive peptides. Two renin inhibitors, **2** and **3** (Table 3.1) have been studied in humans. Compound **2** administered by infusion showed effective lowering of BP in sodium-depleted monkeys, but in several salt-depleted humans it produced hypotension accompanied by brady-cardia at the highest dose (0.5 mg kg^{-1} min^{-1}) (Haber 1985). Infusions of **3** into sodium-deficient humans (17 μg^{-1} kg^{-1} min^{-1}) produced a normal lowering of blood pressure with no change in heart rate (Webb *et al.* 1983).

Inhibition of the RAS brings about release of renin from the kidney by suppressing the negative feedback mechanism mediated by angiotensin II (Blair-West *et al.* 1971) and this has been of concern with regard to the potential use of renin inhibitors as therapeutic agents. However, in marmosets the maximum level of renin (presumed steady state) was the same whether renin or ACE was blocked (Hofbauer *et al.* 1985). Moreover, Blaine *et al.* (1984) found no 'break-through' of the inhibitory effect of **10** by newly released renin during a 48-hour infusion into sodium-deficient dogs.

Moving from *in vitro* inhibitors to agents which will act *in vivo*, preferably after oral administration, presents additional problems of design. To be success-ful as a drug, a renin inhibitor must be specific for renin, survive numerous proteinases in the gastrointestinal tract to pass across the gut wall intact and possess pharmacokinetic properties that will ensure a reasonable duration of action at an acceptable dose. Clinically useful inhibitors of renin should not inhibit other proteinases, including pepsin and cathepsin D. High specificity for human renin has been reported with statine-containing inhibitors and with others, even for inhibitors as small as **12** (Kokubu *et al.* 1986) and **15** (Fehrentz *et al.* 1984). The presence of an aromatic amino acid (or an equivalent, as in **12**) at the Phe(8) position and the presence of His(9) appear to be important deter-minants for this specificity. Amide bonds involving the statine moiety have been shown to be stable toward cleavage *in vivo* (Boger *et al.* 1985b) but a pancreatic homogenate was found to cleave the Phe(8)-His(9) bond of **14**. Stabilization of this bond was achieved by replacement of Phe(8) with *p*-methoxyphenylalanine, but duration of action for the resulting inhibitor was not increased (Dellaria *et al.* 1987). The presence of D-Pro in the inhibitor Iva-His-D-Pro-Phe-His-Sta-Leu benzylamide prevents cleavage of the Phe-His bond (Boger *et al.* 1985b). Inhibitor **12**, in which the labile bond has been eliminated, is stable to pro-teinases (Miyazaki *et al.* 1986). A potent inhibitor with a metabolically stable *N*-methylated Phe(8)-His(9) bond (**5**) was recently reported (Thaisrivongs *et al.* 1986a).

As yet, only a few reports of renin inhibitors with oral activity have appeared. High doses (100 mg kg^{-1}) of **11** reduced PRA and BP after oral administration to salt-deficient marmosets, but both had returned to pre-treatment levels within 2 h (Wood *et al.* 1985). Inhibitor **5**, when administered orally to salt-depleted monkeys (50 mg kg^{-1}), produced a drop in BP and PRA which persisted for over 5 h (Pals *et al.*, 1986). Oral administration of **17** to monkeys (30 mg kg^{-1}) reduced PRA and BP for 6 h, after a 1 h induction period, presumably due to a slow rate of absorption (Miyazaki *et al.* 1986). Recently, oral activity in marmosets was reported for **7**, at a dose of 10 mg kg^{-1}; duration of action was about 2 h (Rasetti *et al.* 1986).

The high oral doses required for activity, coupled with short duration of action after i.v. administration of all but high doses, suggest that both low oral absorption and rapid elimination or inactivation of inhibitor represent major limitations to bioavailability. Although proteolytic cleavage may be partially responsible, biliary excretion of intact inhibitor contributes to their rapid disappearance. After i.v. administration of the stabilized statine-containing inhibitor (Iva-His-D-Pro-Phe-His-Sta-Leu benzylamide), 63 per cent of inhibitor appeared undegraded in bile within 2 h (Boger *et al.* 1985b). Factors determining whether or not a drug is eliminated in the bile are poorly defined. In humans, biliary excretion of drugs becomes increasingly likely as molecular weight rises above a 'threshold' of 500 (Klaassen and Watkins 1984). All potent renin inhibitors reported to date have molecular weights exceeding this 'threshold' (e.g. inhibitor **17**, $M_r = 649$). If current inhibitor designs, as exemplified in Table 3.1, fail to yield potent inhibitors of lower molecular weight, other approaches, such as adjustment of physical properties (solubility, lipophilicity, ionic state) may be necessary to address the problem of biliary excretion. Although examples of orally effective drugs with high molecular weight exist (e.g. erythromycin, cyclosporin, reserpine), they provide little guidance about how the problem of biliary excretion should be addressed.

Renin inhibitors have become interesting pharmacological tools for study of the renin–angiotensin system. Development of orally effective inhibitors will make it possible to study their long-term antihypertensive effects and will allow their clinical value and possible advantages over ACE inhibitors to be investigated.

3.3   Angiotensin-converting enzyme

Angiotensin-converting enzyme, or more properly dipeptidyl carboxypeptidase (peptidyldipeptide hydrolase), is a widely distributed peptidase that bears close relationships to three very well characterized zinc metalloproteinases, carboxypeptidase A and B (CPA and CPB), and thermolysin. The properties of ACE, and the development of potent specific inhibitors of its action, have been the subjects of a number of excellent reviews (Ondetti and Cushman 1981; Soffer 1981; Johnston 1984; Patchett and Cordes 1985). Presented here will be those features of ACE which, in retrospect, have been important in the discovery of inhibitors that are now useful therapeutic agents. There is no doubt that the interest these agents have generated and the information which has become available through their study has added immeasurably to our knowledge of the intimate details of the enzyme's mechanism.

3.3.1   Properties of ACE (EC 3.4.15.1)

Like CPA, CPB, and thermolysin, ACE bears a single zinc atom at the active centre. It has long been known that chelators inhibit the action of ACE

(Soffer 1981) and that addition of metals back to the inhibited enzyme restores its activity. Lung and plasma angiotensin-converting enzymes ($M_r = 130\,000$–$140\,000$) consist of a single polypeptide of approximately 95 KDa, with the remainder accounted for by carbohydrate. Except for carbohydrate content, the plasma enzyme and the lung enzyme are identical, which suggests that the plasma activity is due to enzyme that has been released from the endothelium. Comparison of the immunological and physical properties of the slightly smaller rabbit testis ACE with those for the enzyme from the rabbit lung, strongly suggests that these two represent separate gene products.

The conversion of AI to AII is typical of the reactions catalysed by ACE; a dipeptide is cleaved from the unblocked C-terminus of a polypeptide chain. This chloride-ion-dependent reaction is similar to that catalysed by CPA and CPB except that the carboxypeptidases catalyse removal of a single amino acid from their substrates. Modification studies with active-site reagents have identified arginine, glutamic acid, and tyrosine residues in the active site of ACE, similar to the active sites of the carboxypeptidases and thermolysin. Structural and mechanistic information about CPA played an important role in design of ACE inhibitors.

As with renin, the three-dimensional structure of ACE has not been determined, primarily because the high carbohydrate content and size of the enzyme make preparation of suitable crystals difficult. Although a detailed understanding of the mechanism and substrate specificity of ACE are not yet available, evidence does exist that substrates bind in an extended cleft in the enzyme surface (Angus *et al.* 1973; Harris *et al.* 1981) and that amino acid side-chain interactions in sub-sites S_3, S_2, S_1, S_1' and S_2' make important contributions to rate of cleavage (notation of Schechter and Berger 1967).

Unlike renin, ACE is rather non-specific, and this represents a potential therapeutic advantage for renin inhibitors compared with ACE inhibitors. ACE will accept substrates as small as acylated tripeptides, but does not readily cleave substrates with C-terminal dicarboxylic acids or a penultimate proline. These and other determinants of specificity have been summarized by Soffer (1981). Although ACE usually requires that the C-terminus of a substrate be unblocked, tripeptidyl carboxypeptidase activity with des-Arg-9-bradykinin (Inokuchi and Nagamatsu 1981) and substance P (Cascieri *et al.* 1984; Skidgel *et al.* 1983) has been described. In the latter case, the cleaved tripeptide is Gly-Leu-Met-NH$_2$. ACE activity against the vasodilator, bradykinin (Arg-Pro-Pro-Gly-Phe-Ser-Pro-Phe-Arg), which provides the basis for another name for the enzyme-kininase II, may be of physiological importance for some antihypertensive activity and some infrequent side-effects of ACE inhibitors.

Synthetic substrates and their use in *in vitro* assays for ACE activity have been reviewed by Patchett and Cordes (1985). The varieties of assays (e.g. different substrates and controls) used to determine *in vitro* activities for inhibitors make comparisons between literature IC_{50} values difficult; literature references cited in this chapter should be consulted for interpretation of small differences in IC_{50} values.

3.3.2 *In vitro* inhibition of ACE

The path to drugs that act by inhibition of ACE began with characterization of natural substrates and inhibitors. This information, coupled with insights into the catalytic mechanism of related zinc metalloproteinases, has allowed Ondetti, Cushman, and co-workers at Squibb, Patchett and co-workers at Merck, and others in industry and academia, to design orally active inhibitors that have a high potency.

3.3.3 Naturally occurring peptide inhibitors

The first potent inhibitors of ACE were provided by snake venom peptides (reviewed by Ondetti and Cushman 1981). These early inhibitors, most notably the nonapeptide teprotide (Table 3.2, **18**), permitted study of the pharmacological, toxicological, and thereapeutic consequences of ACE inhibition. Teprotide was not orally active but its efficacy and safety led to optimism that the design of smaller, peptide-based inhibitors with potential for increased bioavailability was possible. In fact, the pentapeptide BPP_{5a} (pGlu-Lys-Trp-Ala-Pro) had an IC_{50} of 0.05 μM against ACE (Cushman *et al.* 1973). Inhibition of ACE, both by tripeptides such as Phe-Ala-Pro ($IC_{50} = 1.4\,\mu$M) and by dipeptide products of cleavage (Cheung *et al.* 1980) was also found.

Given the broad specificity of ACE, it is not surprising that a growing number of peptides that serve as substrates and inhibitors have been reported. Methionine and leucine enkephalin, substance P, ACTH, and a metabolite of TRH (pGlu-His-Pro) are substrates and competitive inhibitors of ACE with K_i values in the micromolar range. The octapeptide [des-pro^3]-bradykinin (Arg-Pro-Gly-Phe-Ser-Pro-Phe-Arg), is an exceedingly potent inhibitor ($K_i = 0.0045$ nM) of ACE (Okuda and Arakawa 1984). Des-Leu^{10} angiotensin I is a potent inhibitor ($K_i = 0.31\,\mu$M), and may be an endogenous regulator of ACE (Snyder and Wintroub 1985). Ancovenin, a peptide composed of 16 amino acid residues with three disulphide linkages, is a potent inhibitor (Wakamiya *et al.* 1985).

3.3.4 Sulphur-containing inhibitors

The development of captopril by Squibb built upon the extensive structure activity relationships revealed in the study of the snake venom peptides and the hypothesis that ACE is structurally and mechanistically similar to CPA (reviewed by Cushman *et al.* 1977; Cushman and Ondetti 1980; Ondetti and Cushman 1981). This hypothesis led to the prediction that inhibitor designs successful against CPA could be adapted for inhibition of ACE. The Squibb group took particular interest in the reports of Byers and Wolfenden (1972, 1973) that D-2-benzylsuccinic acid was a potent 'biproduct' inhibitor of carboxypeptidase A ($K_i = 0.45\,\mu$M). By mimicking the C-terminal Ala–Pro sequence derived from the snake venom peptides, they obtained inhibitors such as 2-methylglutarylproline (Table 3.2, **19**) ($IC_{50} = 4.9\,\mu$M). Introduction of a thiol function for chelation to the active-site zinc atom of ACE then yielded captopril (**20**), the first potent ($IC_{50} = 23$ nM), orally active ACE inhibitor and the first to be approved for use as an antihypertensive. This success, achieved in a remarkably short time, was a milestone in rational drug design.

Squibb's success with captopril led to extensive structure–activity studies, both at Squibb and elsewhere (for recent reviews, see Ondetti and Cushman 1982; Petrillo and Ondetti 1982; Wyvratt and Patchett 1985). Thus far, all thiol-containing inhibitors derived from the captopril design give data consistent with an active-site model, whose interactions with captopril are outlined in Fig. 3.4 (discussed in detail by Petrillo and Ondetti 1982). Among the properties being sought in new captopril analogues are increased potency and longer duration of action. Several inhibitors now in clinical trial appear to have achieved these goals. One is zofenopril (**21**), a stable pro-drug ester of a potent ($IC_{50} = 8$ nM) captopril analogue, which incorporates a 4-substituted proline (Powell *et al.* 1983). Another is alacipril (**22**), a carboxyl modified analogue, which is metabolized largely to captopril (Kono 1983). Both drugs are reported to have longer duration of action than captopril.

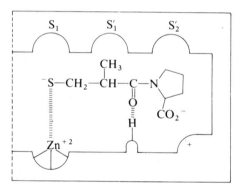

Fig. 3.4. Binding interactions between captopril and ACE as hypothesized by Petrillo and Ondetti (1982). (From Wyvratt and Patchett, 1985. Reprinted from *Medicinal Research Reviews* by permission of John Wiley & Sons, Inc., copyright 1985)

3.3.5 *N*-carboxyalkyl dipeptides

The design of enalaprilat by the Merck group (Patchett *et al.* 1980) drew upon the same body of knowledge as did that of captopril. Like captopril, the Merck *N*-carboxyalkyl dipeptide inhibitors were derived from 2-benzylsuccinic acid, the biproduct inhibitor of CPA (Byers and Wolfenden 1972, 1973). Since biproduct inhibitors are believed to derive their potency from incorporating into a single molecule both products of the enzyme-catalysed reaction (in this case, amino and carboxyl fragments), the Merck group reasoned that it should be possible to make an inhibitor such as **19** more potent by making it structurally more similar to a dipeptide. Thus the inhibitor (*N*-carboxymethyl-L-Ala-L-Pro) was synthesized, and although it was only moderately active ($IC_{50} = 1 \mu M$), extension of this series eventually led to enalaprilat (**23**), which had high affinity for ACE ($IC_{50} = 1.2$ nM). Proposed binding interactions between enalaprilat and ACE (Wyvratt and Patchett 1985) are outlined in Fig. 3.5. A key contribution to the activity of enalaprilat is believed to be made by binding of the phenethyl group in the S_1 subsite of ACE, although potent inhibitors with smaller (e.g. n-propyl) and even charged (aminobutyl) S_1 side-chains have been reported.

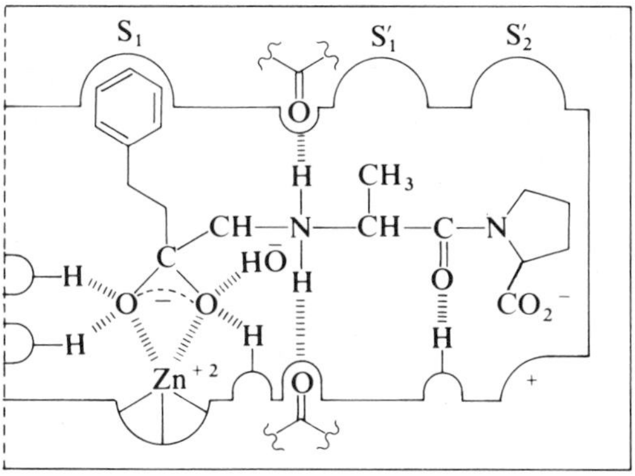

Fig. 3.5. Binding interactions between enalaprilat and ACE as hypothesized by Wyvratt and Patchett (1985) (Reprinted from *Medicinal Research Reviews* by permission of John Wiley & Sons, Inc., copyright 1985)

Enalaprilat was not well-absorbed after oral dosing, a property considerably improved by development of the ethyl ester enalapril (**24**) (Patchett *et al.* 1980; Tocco *et al.* 1982; Gross *et al.* 1984). Not only is enalapril better absorbed, but after *in vivo* hydrolysis to enalaprilat, it maintains sufficiently high plasma concentrations over time to allow once or twice-a-day dosing in humans. Enalapril is prepared as a crystalline maleate salt, a material less prone to formation of diketopiperazine (Wyvratt *et al.* 1984). Enalapril maleate was the second ACE inhibitor approved for use as an antihypertensive. During the development of enalapril, the lysine analogue lisinopril (Table 3.2, **25**), one of some 300 analogues prepared, was found to have potency against ACE similar to that of enalaprilat. Lisinopril, currently in clinical trial, was found to have acceptable oral activity without converting it into a pro-drug ester. The extent of its absorption is intermediate between enalaprilat and enalapril, but its absorption continues over a longer period, giving lisinopril a longer duration of action than a comparable dose of enalapril (Ulm et al. 1982).

Since enalapril lacks the sulphhydryl group present in captopril, it was expected to be pharmaceutically more stable and have less tendency to produce rash and loss of taste, which are side-effects reported especially for high doses of captopril. These characterisitcs have made N-carboxyalkyl dipeptides the subject of intensive structure–activity studies (Wyvratt and Patchett 1985) leading to the development of several new N-carboxyalkyl dipeptides, currently under clinical investigation. The clinical effectiveness, potency, and duration of action of several of these have been reviewed by Brunner et al. (1985). With the efficacy and safety of enalapril demonstrated, effort has been directed towards design of analogues with longer duration of action and decreased renal excretion (for use where renal function is impaired). These and other potential clinical goals for new ACE inhibitors have been discussed by Mackaness (1985). Many new inhibitors incorporate lipophilic proline surrogates, and although these do not produce a substantial increase in in vitro potency, several with interesting in vivo properties have been reported. A notable example is ramipril (Table 3.2, **26**), now in phase III clinical trials, which was reported to have a particularly long in vivo duration of action, inhibiting ACE (approximately 45 per cent of controls) 72 h after a single 3.2 mg oral dose (Witte et al. 1983). Both ramipril (Eckert et al. 1984) and zofenopril (Dean et al. 1984) have shown reduced renal excretion in rats. Spirapril, SCH 33 844 (**27**), a potent ($K_i = 0.74$ nM for diacid form) and long-acting inhibitor currently in phase II clinical trials, is largely excreted via the bile (Sybertz et al. 1986; Weber et al. 1986). It is likely that extensive clinical studies will be required to establish whether or not these and other properties will provide important clinical advantages relative to enalapril.

3.3.6   Phosphorus-based inhibitor designs

Inhibition of thermolysin by phosphoramidon and the crystallographic analysis of the thermolysin–phosphoramidon complex provided a model for the design of ACE inhibitors incorporating a hydroxyphosphinyl moiety as a mimic of the transition state for peptide bond hydrolysis. Reports of inhibition of ACE with phosphoramide, phosphonamide, phosphonic acid/ester, and phosphinic acid-based inhibitors have appeared (Galardy 1982; Petrillo and Ondetti 1982; Thorsett et al. 1982; Galardy 1982). Work on phosphinic acid-based inhibitors at Squibb has led to fosenopril (**28**), an orally active inhibitor with a prodrug ester, which is currently under clinical investigation. The free phosphinic acid form of fosenopril has ACE inhibitory activity similar to that of captopril (Petrillo 1984). A potent ($IC_{50} = 36$ nM) phosphorus-containing inhibitor SQ 29 852 (**29**), which shows oral activity without a pro-drug ester (Karenewsky et al. 1986), is in phase I clinical trial. This third group of potent, orally active ACE inhibitors may provide variations in the basic properties of ACE inhibitors.

3.3.7 Additional inhibitor designs

Important contributions in understanding the requirements for inhibition of ACE have been made by the many modifications of the basic inhibitor designs outlined above. Conformationally restricted lactam inhibitors have been described in the captopril and enalapril series (Parsons *et al.* 1983; Thorsett *et al.* 1983, 1986; Wyvratt *et al.* 1983; Hassall *et al.* 1984; Attwood *et al.* 1986) but none yet in the phosphorus inhibitor series. While lactam inhibitors are not substantially more active *in vitro* than is enalapril, they may offer other favourable properties. Cilazapril (**30**), now in phase III clinical trial, was reported to have improved absorption and duration of action in rats (Natoff *et al.* 1985). The lactam inhibitor CGS16617 (**31**), which is orally active without prodrug esterification (Stanton *et al.* 1985), is in phase I clinical trial.

Several current inhibitor designs differ in important respects from the major series discussed above. Among these are the peptide ketone inhibitors developed by Almquist *et al.* (1985). A particularly potent example is ketone **32** ($IC_{50} = 3$ nM). Although good oral absorption has been achieved with this ketone series, a high rate of biliary excretion limits their bioavailability. Keto-methylene dipeptides such as **33** ($IC_{50} = 1$ nM) (Gordon *et al.* 1984; Natarajan *et al.* 1984), and fluorinated ketones exemplified by **34** ($K_i = 12$ nM) (Gelb *et al.* 1985) have been reported. In both cases, the inhibitory species is believed to result from addition of water or an enzyme nucleophile to the ketone. Oral activity has not yet been reported in these two series.

3.3.8 Role of molecular modelling in ACE inhibitor design

Molecular modelling has not played a major role thus far in *de novo* design of therapeutically relevant inhibitors, since neither a crystal structure nor an amino acid sequence is yet available for ACE. Applications of molecular modelling to ACE inhibitor design did not begin until after the discovery of captopril, and construction of a three-dimensional picture of the active site of ACE has become a possibility only now, when *in vitro* activities for many hundreds of inhibitors in the two series, including conformationally restricted analogues, are available. Although detailed modelling, which could assist in the design of new inhibitors of ACE, has not yet been possible, recent conformational studies, especially those of lactam inhibitors and other conformationally restricted inhibitors (Weller *et al.* 1984), have aided understanding of the mode of binding of ACE inhibitors.

The structural and mechanistic analogies drawn between ACE and CPA, and their contributions to inhibitor design, have been mentioned. Thermolysin, an enzyme well-studied by X-ray crystallography, provides a second model enzyme for ACE. An X-ray crystal structure of a complex of an *N*-carboxyalkyl dipeptide inhibitor with thermolysin has been determined (Monzingo and Matthews 1984). Hangauer *et al.* (1985) used this structure, in conjunction with molecular modelling, to design thermolysin inhibitors with increased potency, but more potent ACE inhibitor designs have not yet resulted.

3.3.9   Inhibitors from natural sources

The pivotal role that the snake venom peptides played in establishing the clinical value of ACE inhibitors and the contribution of the naturally-occuring phosphormidon to the development of phosphorus-based ACE inhibitors have been mentioned. The continuing search for novel ACE inhibitors from natural sources has yielded several interesting structures, as reviewed recently by Cohen (1985). In addition to the peptides mentioned above, recently reported naturally occurring inhibitors include bicyclic lactams **36** and **37** (Table 3.1) (O'Connor and Nakatsukasa 1983; Hunt *et al.* 1984), and the tripeptide phosphonic acid 15B2 (**35**) ($IC_{50} = 91$ nM) (Kido *et al.* 1984). If **35** binds to ACE, as do other phosphorus-based inhibitors, it is the first potent inhibitor to utilize binding sites only toward the amino terminal side of the cleavage site i.e. does not bind in S_1' or S_2'. It is expected that screening of natural products will yield other ACE inhibitors with novel structures.

3.4   From inhibitor to drug

To this point, discussions have centred around the design of inhibitors of renin and ACE from a largely academic point of view. As intensive, arduous, and complex as this process is, turning a potent inhibitor into a drug requires a monumental interdisciplinary effort, which can be accomplished only at great expense. In today's world, this means engaging the research and development resources of a pharmaceutical company. In this chapter we can only make mention of the essential contributions of process chemists in taking a bench-scale synthesis and reshaping it into a efficient plant scale operation, of formulation chemists who select the excipients in order to obtain a tablet that reliably delivers the drug and possesses a long shelf life, of toxicologists who establish the safety of the compound to humans, and of the clinical pharmacologists who determine the safety and efficacy of the drug in patients.

From the many hundreds of very potent ACE inhibitors known to exist in the collections of pharmaceutical houses, only a small number will become marketed drugs, since besides being effective and safe, a drug must appear profitable to its manufacturer. In drug marketing, the first entity introduced generally captures and maintains the lion's share of the market, unless a subsequently introduced entity is preceived by the medical community to have clear advantages over the first. Given the excellent track records to date for first captopril and later enalapril, each new ACE inhibitor can expect to garner an ever smaller share of total sales. It is often market forecasters and financial analysts, not its inventors, who decide whether a compound is developed.

For many companies, to be first to market with a drug that inhibits renin is a goal that promises great rewards. Persistent, insightful basic research into inhibitor design and the details of enzyme catalysis by many groups and individuals had led to the current state of development of renin inhibitors, and to the successful use of ACE inhibitors in the treatment of hypertension and congestive heart failure. Renin inhibitors must still overcome some obstacles in order for a drug to emerge but the success of the ACE inhibitors in clearing some of the same hurdles in encouraging.

Acknowledgements

We are indebted to Drs J. S. Boger, D. G. Hangauer, A. A. Patchett, E. D. Thorsett, and M. J. Wyvratt for their review and discussion of this chapter, to Carol Klekotka and Karen Messick for typographical and bibliographic assistance, and to John Wiley & Sons, Inc. and the *New England Journal of Medicine* for permission to reprint Figs. 3.2, 3.4, and 3.5.

References

Akahane, K., Umeyama, H., Nakagawa, S., Moriguchi, I., Hirose, S., Izuka, K., and Murakami, K. (1985). 3-dimensional structure of human renin. *Hypertension*, **7**, 3–12.

Almquist, R. G., Jennings-White, C., Chao, W.-R., Steeger, T., Wheeler, K., Rogers, J., and Mitoma, C. (1985). Synthesis and biological-activity of pentapeptide analogs of the potent angiotensin converting enzyme–inhibitor 5(S)-benzamido-4-oxo-6-phenyl-hexanoyl-L-proline. *J. Med. Chem.*, **28**, 1062–6.

Angus, C. W., Lee, H.-J., and Wilson, I. B. (1973). Substrate specificity of hog plasma angiotensin-converting enzyme. *Biochim. Biophys. Acta*, **309**, 169–74.

Arrowsmith, R. J., Carter, K., Dann, J. G., Davies, D. E., Harris, C. J., Morton, J. A., Lister, P., Robinson, J. A., and Williams, D. J. (1986). Novel renin inhibitors—synthesis of aminostatine and comparison with statine-containing analogs. *J. Chem. Soc. Chem. Commun.*, 755–7.

Attwood, M. R., Hassall, C. H., Krohn, A., Lawton, G., and Redshaw, S. (1986). The design and synthesis of the angiotensin-converting enzyme-inhibitor cilazapril and related bicyclic compounds. *J. Chem. Soc. Perkin Trans. I*, 1011–19.

Blaine, E. H., Nelson, B. J., Seymour, A. A., Schorn, T. W., Sweet, C. S., Slater, E. E., Nussberger, J., and Boger, J. (1985). Comparison of renin and converting enzyme-inhibition in sodium-deficient dogs. *Hypertension*, **7** (Suppl 1), 166–71.

Blaine, E. H., Schorn, T. W., and Boger, J. (1984). Statine-containing renin inhibitor—dissociation of blood-pressure lowering and renin inhibition in sodium-deficient dogs. *Hypertension*, **6**, (Suppl 1), 111–18.

Blair-West, J. R., Coghlan, J. P., Denton, D. A., Funder, J. W., Scoggins, B. A., and Wright, R. D. (1971). Inhibition of renin secretion by systemic and intrarenal angiotensin infusion. *Am. J. Physiol.*, **220**, 1309–15.

Blundell, T. L., Sibanda, B. L., and Pearl, L. (1983). Three-dimensional structure, specificity and catalytic mechanism of renin. *Nature (London)*, **304**, 273–5.

Boger J. (1985a). Renin inhibitors. Design of angiotensinogen transition-state analogs containing statine. In *Aspartic proteinases and their inhibitors* (ed. V. Kostka), pp. 401–20. Walter de Gruyter, Berlin.

Boger, J. (1985b). Renin inhibition. In *Annual reports in medicinal chemistry* (ed. D. M. Bailey), Vol. 20, pp. 257–66. Academic Press, New York.

Boger, J., Bennett, C. D., Payne, L. S., Ulm, E. H., Blaine, E. H., Homnick, C. F., Schorn, T. W., LaMont, B. I., and Veber, D. F. (1985b). Design of proteolytically stable, peptidal renin inhibitors and determination of their fate *in vivo. Regul. Pept.*, (Suppl 4), pp. 8–13.

Boger, J., Lohr, N. S., Ulm, E. H., Poe, M., Blaine, E. H., Fanelli, G. M., Lin, T.-Y., Payne, L. S., Schorn, T. W., LaMont, B. I., Vassil, T. C., Stabilito, I. I., Veber, D. F., Rich, D. H., and Bopari, A. S., (1983). Novel renin inhibitors containing the amino acid statine. *Nature (London)*, **303**, 81–4.

Boger, J., Payne, L. S., Perlow, D. S., Lohr, N. S., Poe, M., Blaine, E. H., Ulm, E. H., Schorn, T. W., LaMont, B. I., Lin, T.-Y., Kawai, M., Rich, D. H., and Veber, D. F. (1985). Renin inhibitors—syntheses of subnanomolar, competitive, transition-state analog inhibitors containing a novel analog of statine. *J. Med. Chem.*, **28**, 1779–90.

Bott, R., Subramanian, E., and Davies, D. R. (1982). Three-dimensional structure of the complex of the *Rhizopus chinensis* carboxyl proteinase and pepstatin at 2.5-Å resolution. *Biochemistry*, **21**, 6956–62.

Braun-Menendez, E., Fasciolo, J. C., Leloir, L. F., Munoz, J. M., and Taquini, A. C. (1946). Renin. In *Renal hypertension*, pp. 113–17. Charles C. Thomas, Springfield, Ill.

Brunner, H. R., Nussberger, J., and Waeber, B., (1985). The present molecules of converting enzyme inhibitors. *J. Cardiovasc. Pharmacol.*, **7**, S2–11.

Burton, J., Cody, R. J. Jr., Herd, J. A., and Haber, E. (1980). Specific-inhibition of renin by an angiotensinogen analog—studies in sodium depletion and renin-dependent hypertension. *Proc. Natl. Acad. Sci. USA*, **77**, 5476–9.

Burton, J., Slater, E. E., Corvol, P., Menard J., and Hartley, L. H. (1982). Use of anti-human renin antisera to inhibit renin in primates. *Clin. Exp. Hypertension Theor. Pract.*, **A4**, 322–4.

Burton, J., Hyun H., and TenBrink, R. (1983). The design of substrate analog renin inhibitors. In *Peptides, structure and function. Proceedings of the eighth american peptide symposium* (ed. V. J. Hruby and D. H. Rich), pp. 559–67. Pierce Chemical, Rockford, IL.

Byers, L. D. and Wolfenden, R. (1972). A potent reversible inhibitor of carboxypeptidase A. *J. Biol. Chem.*, **247**, 606–8.

Byers, L. D. and Wolfenden, R. (1973). Binding of the by-product analog benzylsuccinic acid by carboxypeptidase A. *Biochemistry*, **12**, 2070–8.

Carlson, W., Karplus, M., and Haber, E. (1985). Construction of a model for the 3-dimensional structure of human renal renin. *Hypertension*, **7**,13–26.

Cascieri, M. A., Bull, H. G., Mumford, R. A., Patchett, A. A., Thornberry, N. A., and Liang, T. (1984). Carboxyl-terminal tripeptidyl hydrolysis of substance-P by purified rabbit lung angiotensin-converting enzyme and the potentiation of substance-P activity *in vivo* by captopril and MK-422. *Mol. Pharmacol.*, **25**, 287–93.

Cheung, H. S., Wang, F. L., Ondetti, M. A., Sabo, E. F., and Cushman, D. W. (1980). Binding of peptide substrates and inhibitors of angiotensin-converting enzyme. Importance of the COOH-terminal dipeptide sequence. *J. Biol. Chem.*, **255**, 401–7.

Cody, R. J., Burton, J., Evin, G., Poulsen, K., Herd, J. A., and Haber, E. (1980). A substrate analog inhibitor of renin that is effective *in vivo. Biochem. Biophys. Res. Commun.*, **97**, 230–5.

Cohen, M. L. (1985). Synthetic and fermentation-derived angiotensin-converting enzyme inhibitors. *Ann. Rev. Pharmacol. Toxicol.*, **25**, 307–23.

Cohen, S., Taylor, J. M., Murakami, K., Michelakis, A. M., and Inagami, T. (1972).

Isolation and characterization of renin-like enzymes from mouse submaxillary glands. *Biochemistry*, **11**, 4286–93.

Corvol, P. DeVaux, C., Ito, T., Sicard, P., Ducloux, J., and Menard, J. (1977). Large scale purification of hog renin. Physicochemical characterization. *Circ. Res.*, **41**, 616–22.

Cumin, F., Evin, G., Fehrentz, J.-A., Seyer, R., Castro, B., Menard, J., and Corvol, P. (1985). Inhibition of human renin by synthetic peptides derived from its prosegment. *J. Biol. Chem.*, **260**, 9154–7.

Cushman, D. W. and Ondetti, M. A. (1980). Inhibitors of angiotensin-converting enzyme. In *Progress in medicinal chemistry* (ed. G. P. Ellis and G. B. West), Vol. 17, pp. 41–104. Elsevier/North-Holland Biomedical Press, New York.

Cushman, D. W., Pluscec, J., Williams, N. J., Weaver, E. R., Sabo, E. F., Kocy, O., Cheung, H. S., and Ondetti, M. A. (1973). Inhibition of angiotensin-converting enzyme by analogs of peptides from *Bothrops jararaca* venom. *Experientia*, **29**, 1032–5.

Cushman, D. W., Cheung, H. S., Sabo, E. F., and Ondetti, M. A. (1977). Design of potent competitive inhibitors of angiotensin-converting enzyme. Carboxyalkanoyl and mercaptoalkanoyl amino acids. *Biochemistry*, **16**, 5484–91.

Cushman, D. W., Ondetti, M. A., Cheung, H. S., Sabo, E. F., Antonaccio, M. J., and Rubin, B. (1980). Angiotensin-converting enzyme inhibitors. In *Enzyme inhibitors as drugs* (ed. M. Sandler) pp. 231–47, Macmillan, London.

Dann, J. G., Stammers, D. K., Harris, C. J., Arrowsmith, R. J., Davies, D. E., Hardy, G. W., and Morton, J. A. (1986). Human renin — a new class of inhibitors. *Biochem. Biophys. Res. Commun.*, **134**, 71–7.

Dean, A. V., Kripalani, K. J., and Migdalof, B. H. (1984). Disposition of SQ-26 991 (Zofenopril) and SQ-26 900, new angiotensin converting enzyme (ACE) inhibitors, in rats. *Fed. Proc. Fed. Am. Soc. Exp. Biol.*, **43**, 349.

Dellaria, J. F., Maki, R. G., Bopp, B. A., Cohen, J., Kleinert, H. D., Luly, J. R., Merits, I., Plattner, J. J., and Stein, H. H. (1987). Optimization and *in vivo* evaluations of a series of small, potent and specific renin inhibiters containing a novel Leu-Val replacement. *J. Med. Chem.*, **30**, 2137–44.

Dzau, V. J., Slater, E. E., and Haber, E. (1979). Complete purification of dog renal renin. *Biochemistry*, **18**, 5224–8.

Dzau, V. J., Kopelman, R. I., Barger A. C., and Haber, E. (1984). Comparison of renin-specific IGG and antibody fragments in studies of blood-pressure regulation. *Am. J. Physiol.*, **246**, H404–9.

Eckert, H. G., Badian, M. J., Gantz, D, Kellner, H. M., and Volz, M. (1984). Pharmacokinetics and biotransformation of 2-(N-((S)-1-ethoxycarbonyl-3-phenylpropyl)-L-alanyl)-(1S,3S,5S)-2-azabicyclo (3.3.0)octane-3-carboxylic acid (HOE 498) in rat, dog and man. *Arzneim. Forsch.*, **34**, 1435–47.

Eid, M., Evin, G., Castro, B., Menard, J., and Corvol, P. (1981). New renin inhibitors homologous with pepstatin. *Biochem. J.*, **197**, 465–71.

Fehrentz, J.-A., Heitz, A., Castro, B., Cazaubon, C., and Nisato, D. (1984). Aldehydic peptides inhibiting renin. *FEBS Lett.*, **167**, 273–6.

Galardy, R. E. (1982). Inhibition of angiotensin converting enzyme by phosphoramidates and polyphosphates. *Biochemistry*, **21**, 5777–81.

Galardy, R. E., Kontoyiannidou-Ostrem, V., and Kortylewicz, Z. P. (1983). Inhibition of angiotensin converting enzyme by phosphonic amides and phosphonic acids. *Biochemistry*, **22**, 1990–5.

Galen, F. X., Devaux, C., Guyenne, T., Menard, J., and Corvol, P. (1979). Multiple forms of human renin. Purification and characterization. *J. Biol. Chem.*, **254**, 4848–55.

Galen, F. X., Devaux, C., Soubrier, F., Pau, B., Menard J., and Corvol, P. (1983).

Application of human renin antibodies. In *Selected topics in clinical enzymology* (ed., D. M. Goldberg and M. Werner), pp. 169–80. Walter de Gruyter, New York.

Galen, F. X., Devaux, C., Atlas, S., Guyenne, T., Menard, J., Corvol, P., Simon, D., Cazaubon, C. Richer, P. Badouaille, G. Richaud, J. P., Gros, P., and Pau, B. (1984). New monoclonal-antibodies directed against human renin—powerful tools for the investigation of the renin system. *J. Clin. Invest.*, **74**, 723–35.

Gelb, M. H., Svaren, J. P. and Abeles, R. H. (1985). Fluoro ketone inhibitors of hydrolytic enzymes. *Biochemistry*, **24**, 1813–17.

Gordon, E. M., Natarajan, S., Pluscec, J., Weller, H. N., Godfrey, J. D., Rom, M. B., Sabo, E. F., Engebrecht, J., and Cushman, D. W. (1984). Ketomethyldipeptides. 2. Effect of modifications of the alpha-aminoketone portion on inhibition of angiotensin converting enzyme. *Biochem. Biophys. Res. Commun.*, **124**, 148–55.

Gross, D. M., Sweet, C. S., Ulm, E. H., Backlund, E. P., Morris, A. A., Weitz, D., Bohn, D. L., Wenger, H. C., Vassil, T. C., and Stone, C. A. (1984). Effect of *N*-[(*S*)-1-carboxy-3-phenylpropyl]-L-Ala-L-Pro and its ethyl ester (MK-421) on angiotensin converting enzyme *in vitro* and angiotensin I pressor response *in vivo*. *J. Pharmacol. Exp. Ther.*, **216**, 552–7.

Guegan, R., Diaz, J., Cazaubon, C., Beaumont, M., Carlet, C., Clement, J., Demarne, H., Mellet, M., Richaud, J.-P., Segondy, D., Vedel, M., Gagnol, J.-P., Roncucci, R., Castro, B., Corvol, P., Evin, G., and Roques, B. P. (1986). Pepstatin analogs as novel renin inhibitors. *J. Med. Chem.*, **29**, 1152–9.

Haber, E. (1985). Will renin inhibitors influence decision-making in antihypertensive therapy? *J. Hypertension*, **3**, (Suppl 2), S71–80.

Hallett, A., Jones, D. M., Atrash, B., Szelke, M., Leckie, B. J., Beattie, S., Dunn, B. M., Valler, M. J., Rolph, C. E., Kay, J., Foundling, S. I., Wood, S. P., Pearl, L. H., Watson, F. E., and Blundell, T. L. (1985). Inhibition of aspartic proteinases by transition state substrate analogues. In *Aspartic proteinases and their inhibitors* (ed. V. Kostka), pp. 467–78. Walter de Gruyter, Berlin.

Hangauer, D. G., Ondeyka, D., Bull, H., Thornberry, N., Greenlee, W., Patchett, A., Ulm. E., and LaMont, B. (1985). Use of enzyme crystal-structures and computer-graphics for inhibitor design. Thermolysin as a model for angiotensin converting enzyme. *Abstracts 190th American Chemical Society National Meeting*, Chicago, IL., MEDI 50. American Chemical Society, Washington, D.C.

Hanson, G. J., Baran, J. S, Lindberg, T., Walsh, G. M., Papaioannou, S. E., Babler, M., Bittner, S. E., Yang, P.-C., and Corobbo, M. D. (1985). Dipeptide glycols—a new class of renin inhibitors. *Biochem. Biophys. Res. Commun.*, **132**, 155–61.

Harris, R. B., Ohlsson, J. T., and Wilson, I. B. (1981). Purification of human serum angiotensin I-converting enzyme by affinity chromatography. *Anal. Biochem.*, **111**, 227–34.

Hassall, C. H., Krohn, A., Moody, C. J. and Thomas, W. A. (1984). The design and synthesis of new triazolo, pyrazolo-pyridazine, and pyridazo-pyridazine derivatives as inhibitors of angiotensin converting enzyme. *J. Chem. Soc. Perkin Trans. I*, 155–64.

Hobart, P. M., Fogliano, M., O'Connor, B. A., Schaefer, I. M., and Chirgwin, J. M. (1984). Human renin gene-structure and sequence-analysis. *Proc. Nat. Acad. Sci. USA*, **81**, 5026–30.

Hofbauer K. G. and Wood, J. M. (1985). Inhibition of renin: recent immunological and pharmacological advances. *Trends. Pharmacol. Sci.*, 173–7.

Hofbauer, K. G., Wood, J. M., Gulati, N., Heusser, C., and Menard, J. (1985). Increased plasma-renin during renin inhibition-studies with a novel immunoassay. *Hypertension*, **7** (Suppl 1), 61–5.

Hunt, A. H., Mynderse, J. S., Maciak, G. M. Jones, N. D., Samlaska, S., and Fukuda, D. S. (1984). Structure elucidation of A58365A and A58365B, angiotensin converting enzyme-inhibitors produced by *Streptomyces chromofuscus*. *Abstracts 187th National Meeting, American Chemical Society*, St. Louis, MO, PHYS 145. American Chemical Society, Washington, D.C.

Imai, T. Miyazaki, H., Hirose, S, Hori, H., Hayashi, T., Kageyama, R., and Ohkubo, H. (1983). Cloning and sequence analysis of cDNA for human renin precursor. *Proc. Nat. Acad. Sci. USA*, **80**, 7405–9.

Inokuchi, J.-I. and Nagamatsu, A. (1981). Tripeptidyl carboxypeptidase activity of kininase II (angiotensin-converting enzyme). *Biochim. Biophys. Acta*, **662**, 300–7.

James, M. N. and Sielecki, A. R. (1985). Stereochemical analysis of peptide-bond hydrolysis catalyzed by the aspartic proteinase penicillopepsin. *Biochemistry*, **24**, 3701–13.

Johnston, C. I. (1984). Angiotensin converting enzyme inhibitors. In *Handbook of hypertension: clinical pharmacology of antihypertensive drugs* (ed. A. E. Doyle), Vol. 5, pp. 272–311. Elsevier Science Publishers, Amsterdam.

Jones, M., Sueiras-Diaz, J., Szelke, M., Leckie, B., and Beattie, S. (1985). Renin inhibitors containing the novel amino-acid 3-amino-deoxystatine. In *Peptides, structure and function. Proceedings of the ninth American peptide symposium* (eds. C. M. Deber, V. J. Hruby, and K. D. Kopple), pp. 759–62. Pierce Chemical, Rockford, IL.

Karenewsky, D. S., Badia, M. C., Cushman, D. W., DeForrest, J. M., Duggan, M. E., Loots, M. J., Perri, M. G., Petrillo, E. W. Jr., Powell, J. R., and Ryono, D. E. (1986). Novel orally active inhibitors of angiotensin-converting enzyme. *Abstracts 192nd National Meeting, American Chemical Society*, Anaheim, CA, MEDI 8. American Chemical Society, Washington, D.C.

Kido, Y., Hamakado, T., Anno, M., Miyagawa, E., and Motoki, Y. Wakamiya, T., and Shiba, B. (1984). Isolation and characterization of 15B2, a new phosphorus containing inhibitor of angiotensin-I converting enzyme produced by *Actinomadura sp. J. Antibiot.*, **37**, 965–9.

Klaassen, C. D. and Watkins J. B. III (1984). Mechanisms of bile formation, hepatic-uptake, and biliary-excretion. *Pharmacol. Rev.*, **36**, 1–67.

Kokubu, T., Ueda, E., Fujimoto, S., Hiwada, K., Kato, A., Akutsu, H., Yamamura, Y., Saito, S., and Mizoguchi, T. (1968). Peptide inhibitors of the renin–angiotensin system. *Nature, Lond.*, **217**, 456–9.

Kokubu, T., H. Hiwada, K., Y. Sato, Y., Iwata, T., Imamura, Y., Matsueda, R., Yabe, Y., Kogen, H., Yamazaki, M., Iijima Y., and Baba, Y. (1984). Highly potent and specific inhibitors of human renin. *Biochem. Biophys. Res. Commun.*, **118**, 929–33.

Kokubu, T., Hiwada, K., Nagae, A., Murakami, E., Morisawa, Y., Yabe, Y., Koike, H. and Iijima, Y. (1986). Statine-containing dipeptide and tripeptide inhibitors of human renin. *Hypertension*, **8**, Suppl. II, 1–5.

Kono, T. (1983). Effects of a new angiotensin-converting enzyme inhibitor, 1-(D-3-acetylthio-2-methylpropanoyl)-L-propyl-L-phenylalanine [Du-1219], in normal men. *Jap. Arch. Intern. Med.*, **30**, 415–20.

Leckie, B., Szelke, M., Hallett, A., Huges, M., Lever, A. F., McIntyre, G., Morton, J. J., and Tree, M. (1983). Peptide inhibitors of renin. *Clin. Exp. Hypertension Theor. Pract.*, **A5**, 1221–36.

Mackaness, G. B. (1985). The future of angiotensin-converting enzyme-inhibitors. *J. Cardiovasc. Pharmacol.*, **7**, S30–4.

Marciniszyn, J. Jr., Hartsuck, J. A., and Tang, J. (1976). Mode of inhibition of acid proteases by pepstatin. *J. Biol. Chem.*, **251**, 7088–94.

Matoba, T., Murakami, K., and Inagami, T. (1978). Rat renin: purification and characterization. *Biochim. Biophys. Acta*, **526**, 560–71.

Miyazaki, M., Toda, N., Etoh, Y., Kubota, T., and Iizuka, K. (1986). Newly synthesized, potent human renin inhibitor. *Jap. J. Pharmacol.*, **40**, 70P.

Monzingo, A. F. and Matthews, B. W. (1984). Binding of *N*-carboxymethyl dipeptide inhibitors to thermolysin determined by X-ray crystallography—a novel class of transition-state analogs for zinc peptidases. *Biochemistry*, **23**, 5724–9.

Nakamura, N., Iwao, H., Ikemoto, F., and Yamamoto, K. (1984). Renal metabolism in mice of exogenously administered ^{125}I-labelled renin. *J. Hypertension*, **2**, 241–8.

Natoff, I. L., Nixon, J. S., Francis, R. J., Klevans, L. R., Brewster, M., Budd, J., Patel, A. T., Wenger, J., and Worth, E. (1985). Biological properties of the angiotensin-converting enzyme-inhibitor cilazapril. *J. Cardiovasc. Pharmacol.*, **7**, 569–80.

Natarajan, S., Gordon, E. M., Sabo, E. F., Godfrey, J. D., Weller, H. N., Pluscec, J., Rom, M. B., and Cushman, D. W. (1984). Ketomethyldipeptides. 1. A new class of angiotensin converting enzyme-inhibitors. *Biochem. Biophys. Res. Commun.*, **124**, 141–7.

Navia, M. A., Springer, J. P., Poe, M., Boger, J., and Hoogsteen, K. (1984). Preliminary X-ray crystallographic data on mouse submaxillary-gland renin and renin–inhibitor complexes. *J. Biol. Chem.*, **259**, 12714–17.

O'Connor, S. C. and Nakatsukasa, W. M. (1983). Process for enzyme inhibitors. US Patents 4 404 281 and 4 404 282.

Okuda, M. and Arakawa, K. (1984). Potent inhibition of converting enzyme by (Des-Pro3)-bradykinin or converstatin. *Clin. Exp. Hypertension*, **A6**, 912.

Oldham, A. A., Arnstein, M. J. A., Major, J. S., and Clough, D. P. (1984). *In vivo* comparison of the renin inhibitor H77 with the angiotensin-converting enzyme-inhibitor captopril. *J. Cardiovasc. Pharmacol.*, **6**, 672–7.

Ondetti, M. A. and Cushman, D. W. (1981). Inhibitors of angiotensin-converting enzyme. In *Biochemical regulation of blood pressure* (ed. R. L. Soffer), pp. 165–204. Wiley, New York.

Ondetti, M. A. and Cushman, D. W. (1982). Enzymes of the renin–angiotensin system and their inhibitors. *Ann. Rev. Biochem.*, **51**, 283–308.

Page, I. H. and Bumpus, F. M., eds. (1974). *Angiotensin*. Springer, New York.

Page, I. H. and McCubbin, J. W. (1968). *Renal hypertension*. Year Book Medical Publishers, Chicago, Ill.

Pals, D. T., Thaisrivongs, S., Lawson, J. A., Kati, W. M., Turner, S. R., DeGraaf, G. L., Harris, D. W., and Johnson, G. A. (1986). An orally active inhibitor of renin. *Hypertension*, **8**, 1105–12.

Panthier, J. J., Foote, S., Chambraud, B., Strosberg, A. D., Corvol, P., and Rougeon, F. (1982). Complete amino acid sequence and maturation of the mouse submaxillary gland renin precursor. *Nature. Lond.*, **298**, 90–2.

Parsons, W. H., Davidson, J. D., Taub, D., Aster, S. D., Thorsett, E. D., and Patchett, A. A. (1983). Benzolactams. A new class of converting enzyme inhibitors. *Biochem. Biophys. Res. Commun.*, **117**, 108–13.

Patchett, A. A. and Cordes, E. H. (1985). The design and properties of *N*-carboxyalkyldipeptide inhibitors of angiotensin-converting enzyme. *Adv. Enzymol.*, **57**, 1–84.

Patchett, A. A., Harris, E., Tristram, E. W., Wyvratt, M. J., Wu, M. T., Taub, D., Peterson, E. R., Ikeler, T. J., tenBroeke, J., Payne, L. G., Ondeyka, D. L., Thorsett, E. D., Greenlee, W. J., Lohr, N. S., Hoffsommer, R. D., Joshua, H., Ruyle, W. V., Rothrock, J. W., Aster, S. D., Maycock, A. L., Robinson, F. M., Hirschmann, R., Sweet, C. S., Ulm, E. H., Gross, D. M., Vassil, T. C., and Stone, C. A. (1980). A new class of angiotensin-converting enzyme inhibitors. *Nature*, **288**, 280–3.

Peach, M. J. (1977). Renin–angiotensin system: biochemistry and mechanisms of action. *Physiol. Rev.*, **57**, 313–70.

Petrillo, E. W. Jr. (1984). New orally active phosphinic acid angiotensin converting enzyme inhibitors. Abstract 18th Middle Atlantic Regional Meeting, American Chemical Society, Newark, NJ, No. 41. American Chemical Society, Washington, D.C.

Petrillo, E. W. and Ondetti, M. A. (1982). Angiotensin-converting enzyme inhibitors: medicinal chemistry and biological actions. *Med. Res. Rev.*, **2**, 1–41.

Plattner, J. J., Greer J., Fung, A. K. L., Stein, H., Kleinert, H. D., Sham, H. L., Smital, J. R., and Perun, T. J. (1986). Peptide analogs of angiotensinogen effect of peptide-chain length on renin inhibition. *Biochem. Biophys. Res. Commun.*, **139**, 982–90.

Powell, J. R., Rubin, B., Cushman, D. W., Krapcho, J., and Antonaccio, M. J. (1983). Antihypertensive activity of SQ26 900; a new potent long lasting analog of captopril. Abstracts International Society of Hypertension, 1st European Meeting on Hypertension, Milan, Italy, No. 355.

Powers, J. C., Harley, A. D., and Myers, D. V. (1977). Subsite specificity of porcine pepsin. In *Acid proteases—structure function and biology* (ed. J. Tang), pp. 141–57. Plenum, New York.

Rasetti, V., Stanton, J., Buhlmayer, P., Fuhrer, W., Goshke, R., and Wood, J. (1986). Renin inhibitors containing only one natural amino acid. Abstracts, Ninth International Symposium on Medicinal Chemistry (EFMC), West Berlin, p. 130.

Reid, I. A. (1985). The renin–angiotensin system and body function. *Arch. Intern. Med.*, **145**, 1475–9.

Rich, D. H. (1985). Pepstatin-derived inhibitors of aspartic proteinases—a close look at an apparent transition-state analog inhibitor. *J. Med. Chem.*, **28**, 263–73.

Ryono, D. E., Free, C. A., Neubeck, R., Sammaniego, S. G., Godfrey, J. D., and Petrillo, E. W. Jr. (1985). Potent inhibitors of hog and human renin containing an amino alcohol dipeptide surrogate. In *Peptides, structure and function. proceedings of the ninth American peptide symposium* (eds. C. M. Deber, V. J. Hruby, and K. D. Kopple), pp. 739–42. Pierce Chemical, Rockford, IL.

Schechter, I. and Berger, A. (1967). On the size of the active site in proteases. I. Papain. *Biochem. Biophys. Res. Commun.*, **27**, 157–62.

Sham, H., Rempel, C., Plattner, J., Stein, H., Cohen, J., and Perun, T. J. (1986). Renin inhibitors—tripeptides incorporating 2-substituted statine analogs which display potent and specific-inhibition of human renin. *Abstracts 191st National Meeting of the American Chemical Society*, New York, NY, MEDI 8. American Chemical Society, Washington, D.C.

Sibanda, B. L. (1984). Computer-graphics modeling and the specificity of renins. *Biochem. Soc. Trans.*, **12**, 953–6.

Sibanda, B. L., Blundell, T., Hobart, P. M., Fogliano, M., Bindra, J. S., Dominy, B. W., and Chirgwin, J. M. (1984). Computer-graphics modeling of human renin—specificity, catalytic activity and intron–exon junctions. *FEBS Lett.*, **174**, 102–11.

Skeggs, L., Lentz, K. Kahn, J., and Hochstrasser, H. (1968). Kinetics of the reaction of renin with nine synthetic peptide substrates. *J. Exp. Med.*, **128**, 13–34.

Skidgel, R. A., Johnson, A. R., Ashton, J. H., and Erdos, E. G. (1983). Inactivation of substance-P and neurotensin by converting enzyme and enkephalinase. *Circulation*, **68(II)**, 349.

Slater, E. E., Cohn, R. C., Dzau, V. J., and Haber, E. (1978). Purification of human renal renin. *Clin. Sci. Mol. Med.*, **55**, 117–20.

Snyder, R. A. and Wintroub, B. U. (1985). Inhibition of angiotensin-converting enzyme by des-leu^{10}-angiotensin-I—a potential mechanism of endogenous angiotensin-converting enzyme regulation. *Biochim. Biophys. Acta*, **871**, 1–5.

Soffer, R. L. (1981). Angiotensin-converting enzyme. In *Biochemical regulation of blood pressure* (ed. R. L. Soffer), pp. 123–64. Wiley, New York.

Sogawa, K., Fujii-Kuriyama, Y., Mizukami, Y., Ichihara, Y., and Takahashi, K. (1983). Primary structure of human pepsinogen gene. *J. Biol. Chem.,* **258**, 5306–11.

Stanton, J. L., Gruenfeld, N., Babiarz, J. E., Ackerman, M. H., Friedmann, R. C., Yuan, A. M., and Macchia, W. (1983). Angiotensin converting enzyme inhibitors: N-substituted monocyclic and bicyclic amino acid derivatives. *J. Med. Chem.,* **26**, 1267–76.

Stein, H., Cohen, J., Tricarico, K., Sham, H., Rempel, C., Perun, T., and Plattner, J., (1986). Proteolytic and species specificities of substituted statine-containing renin inhibitors. *Fed. Proc. Fed. Am. Soc. Exp. Biol.,* **45**, 869.

Sweet, C. S. and Blaine, E. H. (1984). Angiotensin-converting enzyme and renin inhibitors. In *Cardiovascular pharmacology* (ed. M. J. Antonaccio), pp. 119–54. Raven Press, New York.

Sybertz, E. J., Watkins, R. W., Ahn, H. S., Baum. T., LaRocca, P., Patrick, J., and Leitz, F. (1986). Pharmacological, metabolic, and toxicological profile of Spiropril (SCH33844), a new angiotensin converting enzyme inhibitor. Abstracts International Society of Hypertension 11th Scientific Meeting, Heidelberg, West Germany, No. 0057.

Szelke, M. (1985). Chemistry of renin inhibitors. In *Aspartic proteases and their inhibitors* (ed. V. Kostka), pp 421–41. Walter de Gruyter, Berlin.

Szelke, M., Tree, M., Leckie, B. J., Jones, D. M., Atrash, B., Beattie, S., Donovan, B., Hallett, A., Hughes, M., Lever, A. F., Morton, J., and Sueiras-Diaz, J. (1985). A transition-state analog inhibitor of human renin (H-261)—test *in vitro* and a comparison with captopril in the anesthetized baboon. *J. Hypertension,* **3**, 13–18.

Tang, J. (1979). Evolution in the structure and function of carboxyl proteases. *Mol. Cell. Biochem.,* **26**, 93–109.

Thaisrivongs, S., Pals, D. T., Harris, D. W., Kati, W. M., and Turner, S. R. (1986a). Design and synthesis of a potent and specific renin inhibitor with a prolonged duration of action *in vivo. J. Med. Chem.,* **29**, 2088–93.

Thaisrivongs, S., Pals, D. T., Kati, W. M., Turner, S. R., Thomasco, L. M., and Watt, W. (1986b). Design and synthesis of potent and specific renin inhibitors containing difluorostatine, difluorostatone, and related analogs. *J. Med. Chem.,* **29**, 2080–7.

Thorsett, E. D., Harris, E. E., Peterson, E. R., Greenlee, W. J., Patchett, A. A., Ulm, E. H., and Vassil, T. C. (1982). Phosphorus-containing inhibitors of angiotensin-converting enzyme. *Proc. Nat. Acad. Sci. USA,* **79**, 2176–80.

Thorsett, E. D., Harris, E. E., Aster, S., Peterson, E. R., Taub, D., Patchett, A. A., Ulm, E. H., and Vassil, T. C. (1983). Dipeptide mimics. Conformationally restricted inhibitors of angiotensin-converting enzyme. *Biochem. Biophys. Res. Commun.,* **111**, 166–71.

Thorsett, E. D., Harris, E. E., Aster, S. D., Peterson, E. R., Snyder, J. P., Springer, J. P., Hirshfield, J., Tristram, E. W., Patchett, A. A., Ulm, E. H., and Vassil, T. C. (1986). Conformationally restricted inhibitors of angiotensin converting enzyme-synthesis and computations. *J. Med. Chem.,* **29**, 251–60.

Tigerstedt, R. and Bergman, P. G. (1898). Niere and Kreislauf. *Skand. Arch. Physiol.,* **8**, 223–72.

Tocco, D. J., deLuna, F. A., Duncan, A. E. W., Vassil, T. C., and Ulm, E. H. (1982). The physiological disposition and metabolism of enalapril maleate in laboratory animals. *Drug Metab. Dispos.,* **10**, 15–19.

Ulm, E. H., Hichens, M., Gomez, H. J., Till, A. E., Hand, E., Vassil, T. C., Bolliaz, J., Brunner, H. R., and Schelling, J. L. (1982). Enalapril maleate and a lysine analogue (MK-521): disposition in man. *Br. J. Clin. Pharmacol.,* **14**, 357–62.

Umezawa, H. Aoyagi, T., Morishima, H., Matsuzaki, M., Hamada, M., and Takeuchi, T.

(1970). Pepstatin, a new pepsin inhibitor produced by *Actinomycetes*. *J. Antibiot.*, **23**, 259–62.

Veber, D. F., Bock, M. G., Brady, S. F., Ulm, E. H., Cochran, D. W., Smith, G. M., LaMont, B. I., Dipardo, R. M., Poe, M., Freidinger, R. M., Evans, B. E., and Boger, J. (1984). Renin inhibitors containing 2-substituted statine. *Biochem. Soc. Trans.*, **12**, 956–9.

Wakamiya, T, Ueki, Y., Shiba, T., Kido, Y., and Motoki, Y. (1985). The structure of ancovenin, a new peptide inhibitor of angiotensin-I converting enzyme. *Tetrahedron Lett.*, **26**, 665–8.

Wakerlin, G. E. (1958). Antibodies to renin as proof of the pathogenesis of sustained renal hypertension. *Circulation*, **17**, 653–7.

Webb, D. J., Cumming, A. M. M., Leckie, B. J., Lever, A. F., Morton, J. J., Robertson, J. I. S., Szelke, M., and Donovan, B. (1983). Reduction of blood pressure in man with H-142: a potent new renin inhibitor. *Lancet*, 1486–7.

Weber, M. A., Ferraresi, R. W., and Poorvin, D. (1986). Evaluation of a new angiotensin converting enzyme inhibitor, spirapril, in mild to moderate essential hypertension. *J. Hypertension.*, **4** (Suppl 16), S171–3.

Weller, H. N., Gordon, E. M., Rom, M. B., and Pluscec, J. (1984). Design of conformationally constrained angiotensin-converting enzyme-inhibitors. *Biochem. Biophys. Res. Commun.*, **125**, 82–9.

Witte, P. U., Metzger, H., and Irmisch, R. (1983). Pharmacodynamics of a new orally active long acting angiotensin converting enzyme inhibitor (HOE 498) in healthy subjects. *IRCS Med. Sci.*, **11**, 1053–5.

Wolfenden, R. (1972). Analog approaches to the structure of the transition state in enzyme reactions. *Accounts Chem. Res.*, **5**, 10–18.

Wood, J. M., Gulati, N., Forgiarini, P., Fuhrer, W. and Hofbauer, K. G. (1985). Effects of a specific and long-acting renin inhibitor in the marmoset. *Hypertension*, 7, 797–803.

Wood, J. M., Heusser, C, Gulati, N., Forgiarini, P., and Hofbauer, K. G. (1986). Monoclonal-antibodies against human renin—blood-pressure effects in the marmoset. *Hypertension*, **8**, 600–5.

Workman, R. J. and Burkitt, D. W. (1979). Pepsin inhibition by a high specific activity radioiodinated derivative of pepstatin. *Arch. Biochem. Biophys.*, **194**, 157–64.

Wyvratt, M. J. and Patchett, A. A. (1985). Recent developments in the design of angiotensin-converting enzyme-inhibitors. *Med. Res. Rev.*, **5**, 483–531.

Wyvratt, M. J., Tischler, M. H., Ikeler, T. J., Springer, J. P., Tristram, E. W., and Patchett, A. A. (1983). Bicyclic inhibitors of angiotensin-converting enzyme. In *Peptides: structure and function. Proceedings of the eighth American peptide symposium* (eds. V. J. Hruby and D. H. Rich), pp. 551–4. Pierce Chemical Rockford, Ill.

Wyvratt, M. J., Tristram, E. W., Ikeler, T. J., Lohr, N. S., Joshua, H., Springer, J. P., Arison, B. H., and Patchett, A. A. (1984). Reductive amination of ethyl 2-oxo-4-phenylbutanoate with L-alanyl-L-proline—synthesis of enalapril maleate. *J. Org. Chem.*, **49**, 2816–9.

Yokosawa, H., Holladay, L. A., Inagami, T., Haas, E., and Murakami, K. (1980). Human renal renin. Complete purification and characterization. *J. Biol. Chem.*, **255**, 3498–502.

4

β-lactamase inhibitors

R. F. Pratt

4.1   Introduction

The β-lactamases are a group of bacterial enzymes that catalyse the hydrolysis of β-lactam antibiotics (Scheme 4.1). Since the hydrolysed β-lactam has no antibiotic activity, the β-lactamases represent a source of bacterial resistance against β-lactam antibiotics, and thus are clinically important. The effectiveness of β-lactamase-mediated resistance has increased markedly over the 40 years since the introduction of β-lactam antibiotics into clinical practice, through evolutionary selection processes in β-lactam-challenged bacteria, such that β-lactamases currently represent the most prevalent mode of resistance to these antibiotics. The β-lactamases have been recently reviewed extensively from a number of points of view (see, for example, the monograph by Hamilton-Miller and Smith 1979 and subsequent reviews by Sykes and Bush 1982; Bush and Sykes 1984; Coulson 1985; Fink 1985), and hence no detailed overview of their general properties seems necessary here.

In order to overcome bacterial resistance to the β-lactam antibiotics, two general strategies have been followed by medicinal chemists. The first, and to date the much more extensively pursued, is that of avoidance. The β-lactamase problem is avoided by the design of β-lactam antibiotics that are poor or non-substrates of β-lactamases. The second strategy is that of β-lactamase inacti-

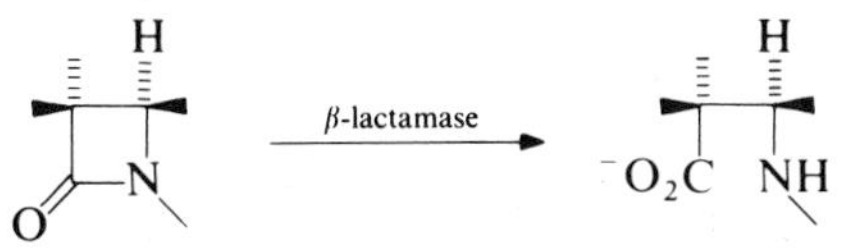

Scheme 4.1

vation. In principle, the inactivating agent could be the antibiotic itself, or it could be a separate molecule, administered in synergy with a β-lactamase-sensitive antibiotic. Since the design of a molecule that would be optimally effective under a wide range of circumstances, both as a β-lactamase inhibitor and as an antibiotic is, at the very least, difficult, and may be impossible, most published thought to date has been in the direction of specialized β-lactamase inhibitors that can be administered with antibiotics of the desired specificity. This search has led, as will be made clear below, to a now impressive series of β-lactamase inhibitors, many of which are extremely potent.

In tandem with the search for inhibitors, much has been done over the last ten years towards the elucidation of the mechanism of action of β-lactamases. These two lines of inquiry can of course be tightly correlated, and often are for most dramatic progress. In the particular case of the β-lactamases for example, very little was known about the mechanism of β-lactamase catalysis before the discovery of the first two or three mechanism-based inhibitors. Knowledge of the mechanisms of catalysis and inhibition thereby gained then led to further inhibitor design. This cycle is of course becoming widely employed in inhibitor and drug development.

Several excellent reviews of β-lactamase inhibitors, again from a variety of points of view, have appeared over the last few years (for example, those of Cole 1979, 1984; Bush and Sykes 1983; Cartwright and Waley 1983; Knowles 1983, 1985; Fisher 1984; Fink 1985). The present review is designed to give an overview of the different *kinds* of mechanisms of β-lactamase inhibition that have emerged, and an attempt is made to classify them usefully. There is little or no discussion of the détailed specificity of these reagents against particular β-lactamases, nor of their synergistic effects on β-lactam antibiotic efficiency, *in vitro* or *in vivo*, although a final section summarizes the current clinical position. The discussion of inhibitor mechanisms is preceded by short sections on the classification of β-lactamases and on their mechanisms of catalysis.

4.2 Classification of β-lactamases

β-lactamases have been classified in a number of different ways. The most meaningful from the point of view of a chemist—although not perhaps for a medicinal (Richmond and Sykes 1973; Sykes 1982) or clinical (Neu 1985b) microbiologist—is that on the basis of catalytic mechanism. In the absence of direct mechanistic studies, the most readily obtained reliable indicator of mechanistic homology is probably the amino acid sequence. Sequence homology will generally translate into three-dimensional structural homology, active site structural homology, and hence mechanistic homology. Thus the maximum number of mechanistic variants can be determined from a classification based on amino acid sequence; only an upper limit is obtained, since non-homologous structural groups may be mechanistically homologous through a process of convergent evolution.

On the basis of primary structure, Ambler (1980) recognized two classes of β-lactamases, class A and class B. Class A is now known to contain the gram-positive bacterial enzymes of *Bacillus cereus* (β-lactamases I and, probably, III—Connolly and Waley 1983; Nielsen and Lampen 1983), *Staphylococcus aureus*, and *Bacillus licheniformis*, and the TEM plasmid enzymes TEM-1 and TEM-2, which are commonly found in gram negative bacteria. Recent partial sequence data suggest that the K1 β-lactamase of *Klebsiella aerogenes* is also a member of this class (Emanuel *et al.* 1986). Class B contains only the zinc-requiring β-lactamase II of *B. cereus*. Subsequently, a third class, C, was recognized (Jaurin and Grundstrom 1981), which has now been rigorously shown to contain the ampC β-lactamase of *Escherichia coli*, the P99 enzyme of *Enterobacter cloacae* (Joris *et al.* 1984) and an important β-lactamase from *Pseudomonas aeruginosa* (Knott-Hunziker *et al.*, 1982a). DNA probes indicate that this class of enzyme is widely spread through the chromosomes of gram negative bacteria (Bergstrom *et al.* 1982, 1983). No further classes have been declared but there are strong indications that the zinc-requiring L1 β-lactamase of *Pseudomonas maltophilia* (Bicknell and Waley 1985a) and the OXA-2 plasmid β-lactamase (Dale *et al.* 1985) may represent further classes, again on the basis of sequence data.

4.3   Mechanisms of β-lactamase catalysis

Investigations of the details of interactions of mechanism-based inhibitors (Fisher *et al.* 1978; Charnas *et al.* 1978; Pratt and Loosemore 1978; Loosemore *et al.* 1980; Cohen and Pratt 1980; Knott-Hunziker *et al.* 1979a, 1979b, 1980; Cartwright and Coulson 1979; Fisher *et al.* 1980a; Kiener *et al.* 1980) and, later, of substrates (Anderson and Pratt 1981, 1983; Cartwright and Fink 1982) with class A β-lactamases indicated that these enzymes catalyse β-lactam hydrolysis by a double displacement mechanism involving a covalent acyl-enzyme intermediate. The primary nucleophile of the active site of the *B. cereus* β-lactamase I was identified as a specific serine hydroxyl group (Knott-Hunziker *et al.* 1979b; Cohen and Pratt 1980). This identification was subsequently confirmed with this and other class A enzymes (Fisher *et al.* 1981; Cartwright and Fink 1982; Clarke *et al.* 1983; Heckler and Day 1983; Hilhorst *et al.* 1984; Coulson 1985). Thus a minimal mechanism for class A β-lactamase catalysis is that shown in Scheme 4.2. Similar studies show that this mechanism also applies to class C β-lactamases (Knott-Hunziker *et al.* 1982b; Joris *et al.* 1984), indicating perhaps (but see below) a case of convergent evolution. It seems likely that during

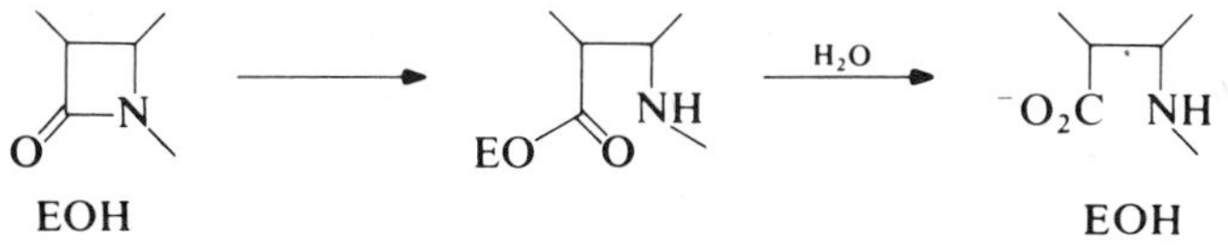

Scheme 4.2

turnover of typical *β*-lactam substrates by class C *β*-lactamases deacylation, i.e. the hydrolysis of the acyl-enzyme, is usually rate-determining (Knott-Hunziker *et al.* 1982b), whereas acylation may commonly be rate-determining with class A *β*-lactamases (Fisher 1984; Bicknell and Waley 1985a).

It is not possible now, if it ever was, to review *β*-lactamases without some mention of the other enzymes with which *β*-lactams specifically interact, the bacterial cell wall biosynthetic D-alanyl-D-alanine (abbreviated D,D-) transpeptidases/carboxypeptidases (abbreviated peptidases). These enzymes are almost certainly the primary site of action of the *β*-lactams as antibiotics (for comprehensive reviews see Ghuysen *et al.* 1979; Georgopapadakou and Sykes, 1983; Waxman and Strominger 1983; Frère and Joris 1985; see Chapter 17). They resemble *β*-lactamases in possessing at the active site a nucleophilic serine hydroxyl group that is acylated by *β*-lactams, but differ in that they are unable to catalyse the hydrolysis of this acyl-enzyme efficiently, and are thus inhibited by *β*-lactams. The natural substrates of these enzymes are D-alanyl-D-alanine peptides, which they are thought to cleave in a double displacement type of mechanism, analogous to that of Scheme 4.1, but where the terminal residue, D-alanine, is lost on formation of the acyl enzyme. *β*-lactams are thought to inactivate these enzymes through a combination of their non-covalent affinity for the active site, derived from a modest resemblance in shape and charge distribution to D-alanyl-D-alanine, their powerful acylating ability when bound, and their neutralization of the deacylation mechanism (Ghuysen *et al.* 1979; Boyd 1982; Waxman and Strominger 1983; Lamotte-Brasseur *et al.* 1984).

In view of the structural similarities between the substrates of these two classes of enzymes (the D,D-peptidases and the *β*-lactamases) and the ability of *β*-lactams to acylate the D,D-peptidases, Tipper and Strominger (1965) proposed, some 20 years ago, that *β*-lactamases might be descendants of early D,D-peptidases, evolved to meet the challenge of naturally occurring *β*-lactams. In this evolutionary process, the ability to catalyse *β*-lactam acyl-enzyme hydrolysis would be gained, while the ability to be acylated by and cleave peptides would be lost. The latter change could be as important as the former, since it would prevent *β*-lactamases, which are usually produced by bacteria in much larger quantities than D,D-peptidases, from interfering with cell wall biosynthesis. *β*-lactamases, in fact, have low non-covalent affinity for D-alanyl-D-alanine peptides and do not catalyse their hydrolysis to any significant extent (Pratt *et al.* 1980; Pratt and Govardhan 1984). The major difference between *β*-lactams and peptides, which excludes the latter as β-lactamase substrates, and which would thus probably have been exploited in the evolutionary process, is that of chemical reactivity towards nucleophiles. Acyclic depsipeptides, structural mimics of D-alanyl-D-alanine peptides but possessing the chemical reactivity of bicyclic β-lactams towards nucleophiles, are in fact β-lactamase substrates (Pratt and Govardhan 1984). Thus the hypothetical active site evolution would include a decrease in the nucleophilicity of the serine hydroxyl group or, conversely perhaps, loss of an electrophilic (general acid, for example) catalytic group necessary for nucleophilic attack on peptides.

The perceived strength of the protein structural evidence for such an evolutionary process has waxed and waned as the amount of sequence data has increased; currently these data appear to be ambiguous (Spratt 1983; Waxman and Strominger 1983; Broome-Smith *et al.* 1985; Coulson 1985; Keck *et al.* 1985; Nicholas *et al.* 1985). The class A β-lactamase sequences are highly homologous, as are the class C sequences, but homology between these groups, and between these and the (*E. coli*) DD-peptidase sequences, is very limited, and restricted to a region closely adjacent to the active-site serine. This would suggest that if all these serine enzymes did diverge from a common ancestor, the separation must have occurred in the far distant past (Maruyama *et al.* 1983); convergent evolution is perhaps just as likely on this evidence. From the point of view of essential functional groups, it seems that, apart from the nucleophilic serine, no residue is completely conserved (again however, see below). Even the much-noted lysine, two residues beyond the active site serine, Ser-X-Y-Lys, appears unnecessary in one case, the D, D-peptidase of *Actinomadura R39* (Duez *et al.* 1981).

Fresh insight into this problem has very recently been afforded by a comparison, from X-ray crystallographic results, of the three-dimensional arrangement of secondary structural elements in the class A *B. licheniformis* β-lactamase and the *Streptomyces R61* DD-peptidase (Kelly *et al.* 1986). Although in the region of the active site serine there is marked homology between the two amino acid sequences, this similarity decreases in other areas, a finding in agreement with those referred to above. Nonetheless, the number and arrangement of secondary structural elements is very similar. The extra length of the larger peptidase (M_r 37 400 vs 29 500 for the β-lactamase), which has often posed problems for evolutionary speculation, appears mainly in the loops joining the conserved secondary elements. On the basis of this result, it appears likely that the question of tertiary structural homology will be more important than primary structural homology in comparisons of these enzymes. Further, it is now seen to be still possible that all the serine D,D-peptidases and β-lactamases may have the same basic tertiary structure and perhaps also the same active site components (taking into account the functional difference between D,D-peptidases and β-lactamases). The structural basis for the difference between D,D-peptidases and β-lactamases may well emerge from inspection of the high-resolution structures of the *B. licheniformis* β-lactamase and the *R61* D, D-peptidase when they become available

(Kelly *et al.* 1985). Preliminary crystallographic data from Phillips and co-workers (Samraoui *et al.* 1986) suggest that the *β*-lactamase I of *B. cereus* also has a tertiary structure similar to that of the above enzymes.

The mechanism of action of the class B *β*-lactamase II of *B. cereus* must be quite different from those of the serine enzymes described above. For example, the mechanism-based inhibitors of the serine enzymes, discussed in detail below, appear to have little effect on *B. cereus* *β*-lactamase II. All evidence suggests that it is a zinc metalloenzyme (Abraham and Waley 1979), quite probably analogous to carboxypeptidase A. A careful and detailed cryoenzymological study by Bicknell and Waley (1985b) detected intermediates in the catalytic pathway, but none of them appeared to be covalent. This information, combined with the discovery of a catalytically essential glutamate residue (Little *et al.* 1986), yielded the proposed mechanism of Scheme 4.3 where, in a manner completely analogous to that widely accepted for the zinc proteases (Hangauer *et al.* 1984; Fersht 1985), the carboxylate group acts as a general base catalyst of nucleophilic attack by water on the scissile peptide carbonyl group of the substrate, which is activated by coordination to the zinc ion.

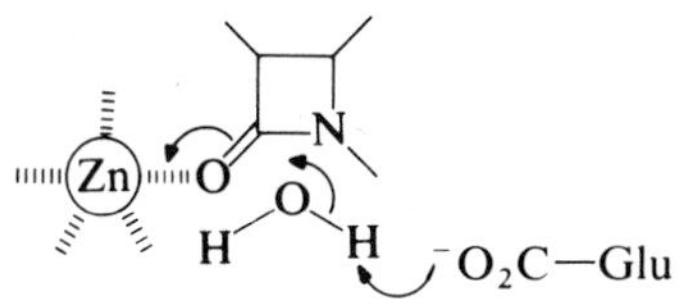

Scheme 4.3

4.4 *β*-lactamase inhibitor mechanisms

Although the search for *β*-lactamase inhibitors began quite soon after the discovery of *β*-lactamases (Reid *et al.* 1946; Behrens and Garrison 1950), it was not until relatively recently, some 10 years ago, that generally effective and specific inhibitors were found. In retrospect this seems due, on the one hand, to the fact that no general classes of molecules that bind strongly to *β*-lactamase active sites (other than bicyclic *β*-lactams) have been discovered, and on the other, to the fact that *β*-lactams with appropriate inhibitory functionality are difficult to synthesize—the synthetic methodology has not available until recently. It has turned out (and this is probably related to the above points) that the recently developed inhibitors are all mechanism-based, that is, as described in detail in Chapter 2C, they are substrates containing additional *functionality*, which acts during turnover so as to divert normal enzyme—substrate intermediates into less labile forms.

Over the time period that has elapsed since mechanism-based inhibitors (suicide inhibitors) were first recognized (Bloch 1969; Rando 1974; Maycock and Abeles 1976), it has become clear that several sub-classes of this mode of inhibition exist, differing in the manner in which the final inert complex is reached. Since the β-lactamase inhibitors appear to span these sub-classes widely, an attempt is made below to classify them. The inhibitors discussed, it should be noted, function in the ways described only against the serine class A and class C β-lactamases. No comparably effective specific inhibitors have yet been found for the class B enzyme, although the discovery of a second zinc metallo-β-lactamase (Saino *et al.* 1982; Bicknell and Waley 1985a), and one that is clinically significant in that it catalyses the hydrolysis of *N*-formimidoyl-thienamycin, for example, may stimulate activity in this area. The recent advances in the design of zinc protease inhibitors (see, for example, Blumberg and Tauber 1983 and references therein; Charlier *et al.* 1984) should be a useful guide in this regard. The other general statement that can be made at the outset concerning the mechanism of action of these mechanism-based inhibitors of class A and C β-lactamases is that they all involve diversion of normal acyl-enzyme intermediates into less labile acyl enzymes; the inhibited enzymes thus have substrate fragments covalently bound to them.

The inhibitory mechanisms can be divided first into 'active' and 'passive' classes. In the former category, a normal intermediate is diverted into a reactive (and abnormally so) complex, which then rapidly rearranges into the inert complex, whereas in the latter, a normal intermediate partitions directly into the inert complex. These two classes can then be subdivided on the basis of whether the rearrangement leading to inert complex involves covalent or non-covalent chemistry; the latter will of course commonly, although not invariably involve protein conformational changes. These mechanisms are shown in comparison with that for turnover of a normal substrate in Table 4.1.

In these reaction schemes ES, ES', EI, and EI' represent intermediates in the normal turnover of substrate S and mechanism-based inhibitor I, EI'' represents a complex with a covalently altered (beyond the normal) inhibitor but still attached to the enzyme in the normal way (i.e. as S is in ES', and I in EI'), E—II'' represents a complex with the altered inhibitor covalently bound to the enzyme in an (additional) abnormal way, (EI'')' and (EI')' refer to complexes whose inert nature is dictated by non-covalent interactions (i.e. by conformational changes of enzyme, substrate or both), P represents the product(s) of normal turnover, and P(I) the products from the rearranged inhibitor. In each case the inert complex whose accumulation leads to enzyme inhibition is in italics, and the possibilities are included of its reversion to the normal intermediate EI', and of its slow breakdown to product(s) and free enzyme. The effectiveness of the inhibitor will be determined in each case by the rate of formation of EI', the relative rates of turnover of the inert complex and the normal complex, and the relative amounts of the inert and normal complexes at steady state, i.e. by the partition ratio of EI' between normal turnover and formation of the inert complex (Walsh 1978, 1984). Usually the activated complexes, EI'', of classes 1(a) and 1(b) will not accumulate and thus their breakdown to products, although theoretically possible, is not included in the schemes. Significant mechanistic

Table 4.1 A classification of mechanism-based inhibitors

Substrate

$$E + S \rightleftharpoons ES \rightleftharpoons ES' \rightarrow E + P$$

Mechanism-based inhibitors

1(a) Active covalent

$$E + I \rightleftharpoons EI \rightleftharpoons EI' \rightarrow E + P$$
$$\downarrow \uparrow$$
$$EI'' \rightleftharpoons E\text{-}I'' \rightarrow E + P(I)$$

1(b) Active non-covalent

$$E + I \rightleftharpoons EI \rightleftharpoons EI' \rightarrow E + P$$
$$\downarrow \uparrow$$
$$EI'' \rightleftharpoons (EI'')' \rightarrow E + P(I)$$

2(a) Passive covalent

$$E + I \rightleftharpoons EI \rightleftharpoons EI' \rightarrow E + P$$
$$\downarrow \uparrow$$
$$EI'' \rightarrow E + P(I)$$

2(b) Passive non-covalent

$$E + I \rightleftharpoons EI \rightleftharpoons EI' \rightarrow E + P$$
$$\downarrow \uparrow$$
$$(EI')' \rightarrow E + P$$

---

possibilities not shown explicitly are those variants of Class 1 where the activation step is non-covalent in nature rather than covalent, although 1(b) of this type would be difficult to distinguish from 2(b). In mechanisms of Class 1(b), it is possible that the non-covalent change leading to the inert intermediate might be concerted with the activation step, but even if so, the result would be different from that of 2(a) in that the inert nature of the complex would still result from the non-covalent changes rather than the covalent.

The mechanisms of action of the recently discovered inhibitors of the class A and C *β*-lactamases will now be discussed within the framework of the above classification scheme.

4.4.1 Active covalent [Class 1(a)]

This sub-class includes most of the 'classic' mechanism-based inhibitors originally recognised and developed by, for example, Rando (1974), Abeles (Maycock and Abeles, 1976) and Walsh (1978, 1984), where the substrate rearranges during turnover into a chemically reactive form which then covalently modifies the enzyme. Although this type of inhibitor still dominates the literature on mechanism-based inhibitors, there is yet to be an example of this type that specifically inhibits *β*-lactamases. It seems likely though that a combination of two recent events, the successful design of such inhibitors for serine proteinases

(Walsh 1984), and the demonstration that monocyclic β-lactams (Pratt et al. 1980) and acyclic depsipeptides (Pratt and Govardhan 1984) are β-lactamase substrates, will stimulate further attempts to produce one of these. The monocyclic β-lactam, **1** (Scheme 4.4), for example, was designed to be such (Zrihen et al. 1983) but apparently did not covalently inhibit a variety of β-lactamases.

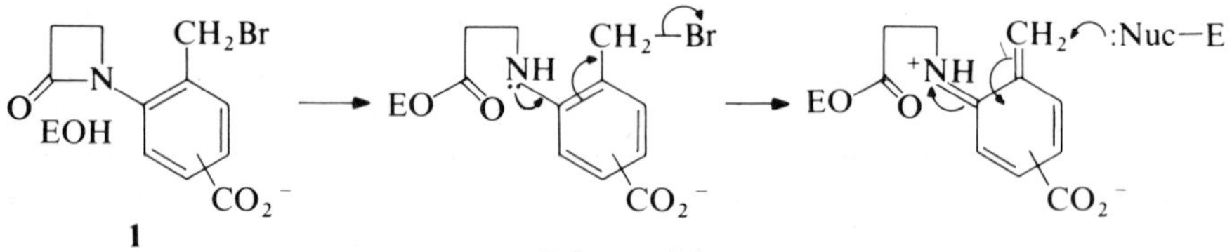

Scheme 4.4

4.4.2   Active non-covalent [Class 1(b)]

There are two important groups of molecules that inhibit β-lactamases and which seem to come under this rubric. The first of these to be subjected to mechanistic scrutiny was the olivanic acids, **2** (Scheme 4.5), which may well be paradigmatic for all penems and carbapenems. Knowles and co-workers (Charnas and Knowles 1981a; Easton and Knowles 1982) have demonstrated that the progressive inhibition of the TEM β-lactamase by certain olivanic acid derivatives was due to diversion, by covalent rearrangement, of the normal Δ^2-pyrroline intermediate **3** into the tautomeric and thermodynamically more stable Δ^1-pyrroline **4** (Scheme 4.5). Since there is no obvious reason why **4** should deacylate by ester hydrolysis much more slowly than **3**, i.e. there appears no difference in the intrinsic reactivity of the esters, the difference must lie with the enzyme, which must be somehow different in **3** and **4**. Hence the enzyme and substrates (water is the second substrate) must have undergone relative motion during the conversion of **3** to **4**, yielding a less effective orientation of functional groups in **4**. The effectiveness of penems and carbapenems as β-lactamase inhibitors, i.e. the partition ratio of **3** in favour of **4** and/or the relative hydrolytic lability of **3** and **4**, appears to be a strong function of the nature and stereochemistry of the C-6 substituent (Fisher 1984).

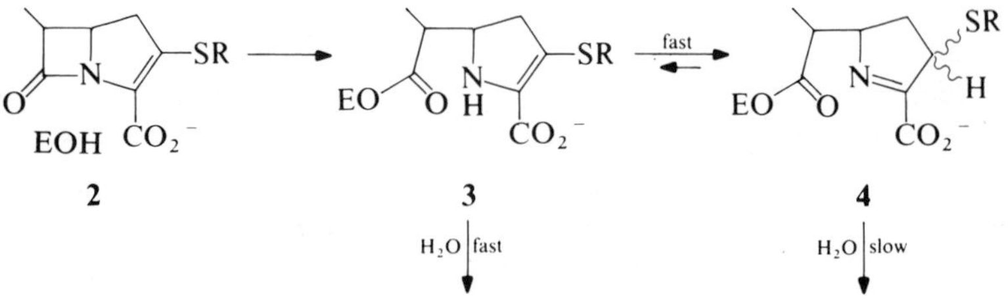

Scheme 4.5

An analogous situation appears to obtain in cephalosporins **5** and cephamy-cins **6** (Scheme 4.6). Clinically important members of these groups of antibiotics generally have a heteroatom and leaving group, X, at $C_{3'}$, often acetoxy, pyridinium, or, more recently, heteroarylthio. One purpose of this is to activate, by electron withdrawal, the β-lactam carbonyl group to nucleophilic attack by D,D-peptidases. It has been known for some time that the final product of alkaline and β-lactamase catalysed hydrolysis of these compounds is the ex-omethylene compound **7**, i.e. that elimination of the 3'-leaving group accompan-ies β-lactam hydrolysis (Hamilton-Miller et al. 1970a, b) (Scheme 4.6). Until recently, it was believed (Boyd 1982) that departure of the leaving group was concerted with β-lactam ring opening. It is now clear however (Faraci and Pratt 1984; Pratt and Faraci 1986) that these two steps are not, in general, concerted, and that **8** usually occurs as an intermediate. Consequently there are potentially two types of acyl-enzymes, **9** and **10** (Scheme 4.7), which may occur on reaction of class A and C β-lactamases with cephalosporins, and which, in principle, should deacylate at different rates. A detailed study of the kinetics and mech-anism of interaction of cephalosporins with the S. aureus β-lactamase led to the reaction sequence of Scheme 4.7 (Faraci and Pratt 1985). Here the initially formed acyl enzyme, **9**, partitions between hydrolysis, completing turnover, and elimination of the 3'-substituent, yielding **10**, which also hydrolyses. The impor-tant result in this case is that **10** is some 10^3 times more inert to hydrolysis than **9**, possessing a half-life of around 10 min at 20°C. An enzyme diverted to **10** is thus transiently inhibited. This finding probably explains the early observations, which in part led to the rapid development of cephalosporins, that cephalothin

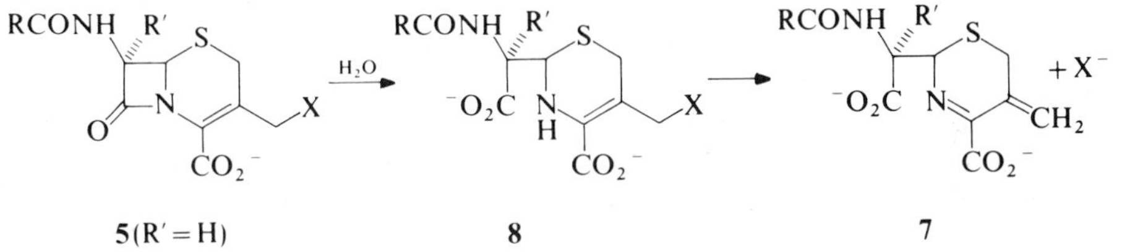

5(R' = H)
6(R' = OMe)

8

7

Scheme 4.6

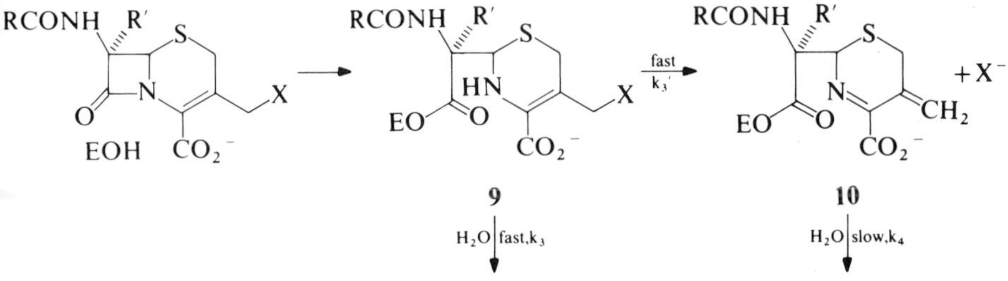

9

10

Scheme 4.7

and cephaloridine were effective antibiotics against β-lactamase-producing *S. aureus* (Wick 1972).

There appears to be clear structural analogy between the inert complex **10** and the carbapenem-derived **4**; in the former case also the reason for the inert nature of **10** must lie with the enzyme active site structure. It might be noted finally that the elimination reactions of **8** and **9** can be reversed by nucleophilic addition to **7** and **10** (Pratt and Faraci 1986; Faraci and Pratt 1987) leading, in the latter instance, to reactivation of the enzyme via **9**.

According to Scheme 4.7,

$$k_{cat} = k_4(1 + k_3/k_3') = k_4(1 + n) \tag{4.1}$$

where n is the partition ratio in favour of hydrolysis. Clearly, for the most effective inhibition, n should be as small as possible. The value of n should be decreased by an increase in k_3', the elimination rate constant, and/or by a decrease in k_3, the hydrolysis rate constant. The following evidence suggests that n does vary predictably in this way:

1. An increase in k_3' could reasonably be generated by making X a better leaving group. In the above-mentioned study with the *S. aureus* β-lactamase, n values for three pyridine leaving groups of decreasing pK_a and thus increasing leaving group ability were 100 (pK_a 6.8), 11 (pK_a 5.1), and 1 (pK_a 4.3). In contrast, k_3 did not significantly vary between these compounds. For the better leaving group, acetoxy, $n = 0$, and the diversion to **10** is complete ($k_{cat} = k_4$).

2. A decrease in k_3 can be brought about by modification of the C-7 substituents. A well-known case in point is cefoxitin, **6** (X = OCONH$_2$) which was shown by Knowles and co-workers (Fisher *et al.* 1980a) to form an acyl enzyme, whose slow hydrolysis is rate-determining to turnover, with the TEM β-lactamase. We have examined in more detail the role of the 3'-substituent in the stability of this complex (Faraci and Pratt 1986a). The accumulating intermediate had structure **10** (R' = OMe); the carbamoyloxy group, another good leaving group, had been eliminated. More importantly, when a leaving group was not present, as in descarbamoyloxycefoxitin, **6** (X = H), the acyl enzyme did not accumulate, i.e. acylation was rate-determining. The data showed that although the 7α-OMe group slowed down both acylation and deacylation of the enzme, it was elimination of the 3'-leaving group that led to accumulation of the acyl enzyme, and thus to transient inhibition of the enzyme. A similar picture emerged from a study of these compounds in reaction with the *S. aureus* β-lactamase.

Class C β-lactamases appear to respond in the same fashion qualitatively, although certainly not quantitatively, to these mechanism-based inhibitors and thus may have, as suggested above, analogous catalytic mechanisms to those of the class A enzymes. One might expect then that the elimination of 3'-leaving groups from acyl-enzymes formed on interaction of class C *β*-lactamases with cephalosporins or cephamycins would also increase the lifetimes of these species. This effect should be readily determinable since it seems likely, as mentioned above, that deacylation is generally rate-determining to turnover by class C *β*-lactamases. Certainly, carbapenems are known to be generally effective progressive inhibitors of class C *β*-lactamases (Fisher 1984), presumably via the mechanism described above. Also it is known that many of the third generation cephalosporins form tight, inert complexes with class C *β*-lactamases (Bush *et al.* 1982; Labia 1982; Then and Angehrn 1982; Labia *et al.* 1983, 1984). In at least one case, that of moxalactam, the complex has been proven to be a covalent one, presumably an acyl enzyme (Murakami and Yoshida 1985).

A further interesting point is the question as to whether these mechanisms of inhibition are relevant to the D,D-peptidases, since these enzymes also, of course, form stable acyl enzymes with carbapenems and cephalosporins. To this point we have recently shown, in the case of the soluble *Streptomyces R61* D,D-peptidase, that good 3'-leaving groups (acetate, pyridine, heteroarylthiolate) are in fact eliminated after enzyme acylation, i.e. the stable covalent complexes have structure **10**. Furthermore, as with *β*-lactamases, although to a lesser extent, deacylation of the R61 adduct **10** is slower than that of structure **9**, where the latter was generated from cephalosporins without 3'-leaving groups (Faraci and Pratt 1986b). Thus the effectiveness of cephalosporins as antibiotics might be affected by the presence or otherwise of a leaving group at C-3'. Boyd (1984) has, in fact, gathered biodata which suggest that, other things being equal, cephalosporins with 3'-leaving groups are more effective than those without.

4.4.3 Passive covalent [Class 2(a)]

This group includes the now classic, first group of specific *β*-lactamase inhibitors, and the only ones yet to achieve significant commercial development purely as *β*-lactamase inhibitors (see below)—clavulanic acid and its analogues, the 6*β*-halopenicillanic acids, and the penicillin sulphones. The prototype molecules here were clavulanic acid itself, a natural product (Brown *et al.* 1976), and two synthetic compounds, 6*β*-bromopenicillanic acid (Pratt and Loosemore 1978; Knott-Hunziker *et al.* 1979a) and penicillanic acid sulfone (English *et al.* 1978). The mechanism of action of these compounds (Fisher *et al.* 1978, 1980b; Cohen and Pratt 1980; Hill *et al.* 1980) can be encompassed by Scheme 4.8. The initially formed acyl enzyme **11** is thought to partition between normal turnover (a) and rearrangement into inert structures (b). The latter probably involves the opening of the heteroazolidine ring to yield **12**, followed by irreversible trapping of the leaving group X^-, thus allowing rearrangement into the hydrolytically more inert vinylogous carbamate system **13**. In the case of clavulanic acid, $X^-(O^-)$ is trapped by ketonization of the enolate resulting from oxazolidine ring opening; in the case of 6*β*-bromopenicillanic acid, $X^-(S^-)$ is trapped by its nucleophilic displacement of bromide from the C-6 position to form a stable

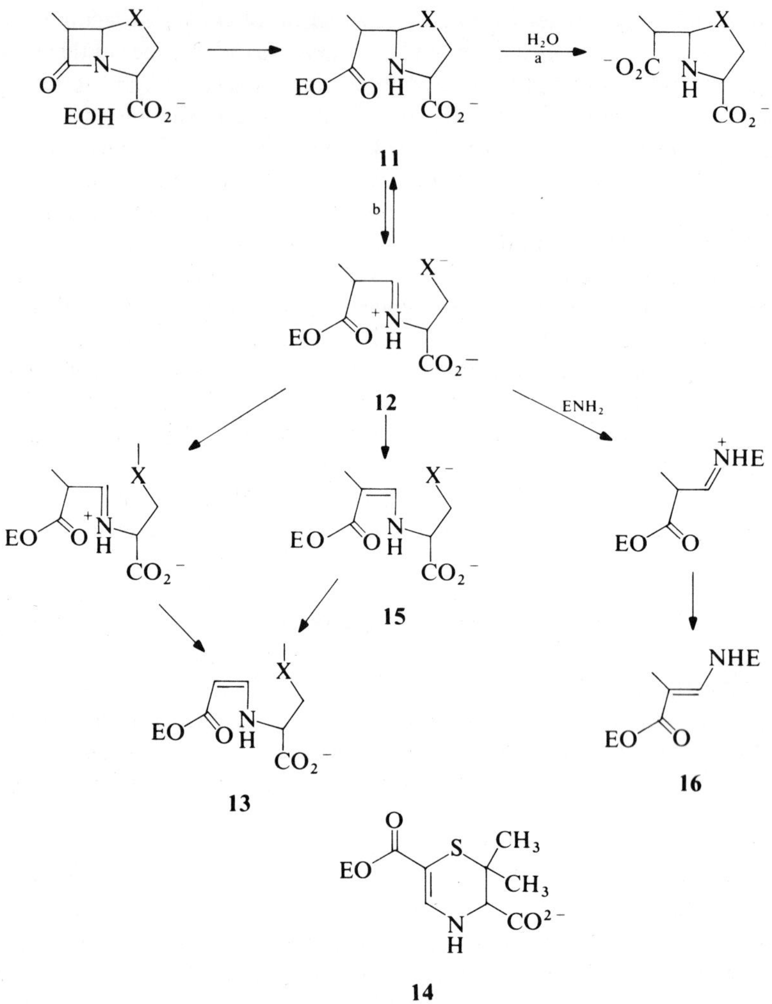

Scheme 4.8

dihydrothiazine **14**; and in the case of the sulphones, $X^-(SO_2^-)$ is stable in the open form, **15**.

The vinylogous carbamates are well characterised by distinctive absorption spectra. They are transiently stable in the case of clavulanic acid (with the TEM β-lactamase for example, the half-life is about three min at pH 7 and at 30°C (Fisher *et al.* 1978) and penicillanic acid sulphone [about 13 s under the same conditions (Kemal and Knowles 1981)] but apparently completely inert in the case of 6β-bromopenicillanic acid [and β-lactamase I of *B. cereus* (Pratt and Loosemore 1978)] where reversion to **11** is not possible. Although the formation of these transiently inhibited complexes may be sufficient, in general, to seriously discommode *β*-lactamases *in vivo*, the structures of clavulanic acid and penicillanic acid sulphone also provide for a less easily reversible mode of inactivation. In separate, but slower pathways of diversion of **11**, involving fragmentation of the inhibitor molecules (Charnas *et al.* 1978; Charnas and Knowles 1981b; Fisher *et al.* 1981; Kemal and Knowles 1981; Brenner and Knowles 1984a), hydrolytically inert species are produced whose nature is not completely defined. One of these, common to both clavulanic acid and penicillanic acid sulphone, is thought to have the structure **16** and thus to arise by a transamination reaction of **12** with an enzymic amine, presumably of lysine. This mode of inhibition would of course place these compounds in the 'active covalent', Class 1(a) group, but, in general, as seen with 6*β*-bromopenicillanic acid for example, these slower reactions are not essential to significant *β*-lactamase inhibition. Other *β*-lactamases appear to behave qualitatively very similarly with these reagents (Durkin and Viswanatha 1978; Reading and Hepburn 1979; Reading and Farmer 1981; Labia *et al.* 1980; Frère *et al.* 1982a, b; Sawai and Tsukamoto 1982).

A variety of other clavulanate (see for example Bentley *et al.* 1981; Newall 1981; Brooks *et al.* 1984) and penicillin sulphone (see for example Fisher *et al.* 1981; Mezes *et al.* 1982; Foulds *et al.* 1984; Hall *et al.* 1984; Dmitrienko *et al.* 1985; Gottstein *et al.* 1985) analogues have been synthesized which, by and large, appear to behave similarly to the prototypes. They do, in general, have different *β*-lactamase specificities; the partitioning of **11** and **12** between the various pathways and thus the effectiveness of the inhibitor is a strong function of the inhibitor structure and the enzyme. 6*β*-halopenicillanic acid analogues with different leaving groups at C-6 have not been explored as extensively as the above variants (Kemp *et al.* 1980; Hamanaka 1984; Sheehan *et al.* 1984).

Another group of inhibitors that are probably best classified here are the 6-methylenepenams and 6-methylenecarbapenams, which include the naturally occurring asparenomycins **17** (Murakami *et al.* 1982), and two synthetic molecules, 6-acetylmethylenepenicillanic acid **18** (Arisawa and Then 1982, 1983) and 6-methoxymethylenepenicillanic acid **19** (Brenner and Knowles 1984b). Several structural features of these molecules lead to the formation of the inert acyl-enzymes (Scheme 4.9). First, the rehybridization of the carbon atoms at C-6 and C-7 on formation of the initial acyl enzyme **20** on *β*-lactam ring opening, yields an acrylate ester that is sufficiently deactivated towards hydrolysis to make deacylation rate-determining to turnover of **18** and **19** by the TEM *β*-lactamase. Second, as clearly demonstrated in the case of **17** (Brenner and Knowles 1984b),

17 **18** **19**

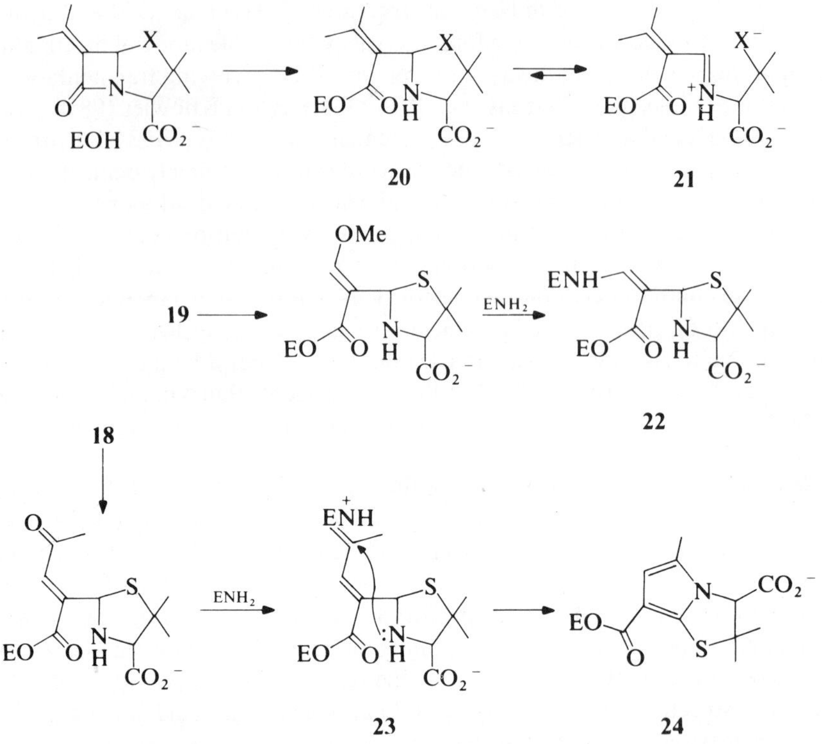

Scheme 4.9

further stabilization of the acyl enzyme can be achieved by its diversion to the open chain form **21**. This is analogous to Scheme 4.8, where the open form is stabilized by extended conjugation. Both **18** and **19** also have reactive functionality that can interact with protein amine groups, and both are proposed to form cross-linked complexes, **22** and **23** respectively, in this way. Since this functionality is not unveiled as part of the reaction mechanism, it probably should not be considered as part of a mechanism-based pathway (although it might become correctly positioned as part of the mechanism). Compound **18** can undergo further intramolecular rearrangement (Scheme 4.9) to an even more stable acyl enzyme **24** (Arisawa and Adam 1983). The asparenomycins combine the inhibitory equipment of the 6-methylenepenams with that of the olivanic acids and presumably may make use of aspects of both inhibitory mechanisms, yielding **25** or **26** as very refractory acyl enzymes.

It is likely that many of these acyl enzymes, derived from extensive rearrangement, are inert for non-covalent (conformational) reasons [cf. Class 1(b)] as well as covalent. Another general point that should be made is that stereoelectronic factors are clearly important in many of these rearrangements (Boyd 1982;

HO SR EO O N H CO_2^-

HO SR EO O N H CO_2^-

25   **26**

Crackett and Stoodley 1984; Stoodley 1985); these factors of course may be influenced by steric interactions with the protein.

4.4.4 Passive non-covalent [Class 2(b)]

The prevalence of this type of inhibition of β-lactamases appears to correlate with certain long known and much discussed features (Citri and Pollock 1966; Citri 1971, 1973, 1981; Pain and Virden 1979) of class A β-lactamases—their marked, and perhaps extreme, conformational flexibility, and the low energy barriers that seem to exist between the active conformation(s) and less active or inactive forms. Single-site mutations of class A β-lactamases, for example, often appear to lead to conformationally disturbed enzymes of reduced activity (Craig et al. 1985; Dalbadie-McFarland et al.1986; Schultz and Richards 1986). These inactive conformations also appear to be inducible by substrates and seem most readily accessible at the acyl enzyme stage (Virden et al. 1975, 1978; Pain and Virden 1979; Kiener et al. 1980; Frère 1981; Faraci and Pratt 1986a), and thus are perhaps promoted by conformational changes normally accompanying acylation or required for subsequent deacylation (cf. D,D-peptidases). Alternatively, this flexibility might represent the efforts of an enzyme attempting to accomodate its active site to the widest possible range of β-lactams.

The substrates best able to induce these conformational transitions (A type substrates; Citri et al. 1976) appear to be penicillins with bulky and/or rigid (Samuni and Meyer 1978; Blanpain et al. 1980) substituents at C-6. The classical examples include, for example, methicillin, cloxacillin, and quinacillin. Such compounds produce acyl enzymes that partition to an inert conformation (Virden et al. 1975, 1978; Kiener et al. 1980). That the protein conformation in these accumulating intermediates is different to, or at least more mobile than, the original, is well documented by the increases in the protein susceptibility to heat, denaturants, proteases, and chemical modifying reagents (Citri 1971, 1973) and by changes in physical properties such as peptide proton exchange rates (Kiener and Waley 1977). In the case of the S. aureus enzyme, Pain and co-workers have proposed that the conformational inactivation results from inter-domain motion (Carrey and Pain 1978; Pain and Virden 1979; Carrey et al. 1984). This proposal is perhaps supported by the recent observations of Fink and co-workers (Fink *et al.* 1987) who have isolated the inert complex of cloxacillin and *B. cereus* β-lactamase I and found that its circular dichroism and fluorescence emission spectra were indistinguishable from those of the native enzyme. There is also reason to believe that in some cases the conformational changes may persist beyond deacylation, i.e. there is the appearance of hysteresis (Citri 1971, 1973; Samuni and Citri 1975, 1979; Citri *et al.* 1984).

Conformational restriction of the enzyme, by antibodies (Citri 1971, 1973; Pain and Virden 1979) or by chemical cross-linking (Klemes and Citri 1979, 1980) can slow down or eliminate these inactivating transitions. In this regard, it might be noted that mechanism-based inhibitors in general may be sensitive to conformational restriction, since they typically involve structural changes at the active site beyond those produced by normal substrates. We have shown for example (B. George and R. F. Pratt, in preparation) that the partitioning of the initial acyl enzymes generated on reaction of 6β-bromopenicillanic acid and quinacillin sulphone with *B. cereus* β-lactamase I can be redirected in favour of hydrolysis rather than inactivation by conformational restriction.

Another particular structural feature capable of inducing conformational changes in class A β-lactamases is the 7α-OMe substituent in cephalosporins (cephamycins). Cefoxitin, as described previously in this review, forms a relatively stable acyl enzyme on interaction with the TEM β-lactamase. Citri and co-workers (Citri and Zyk 1982; Citri *et al.* 1984) have shown that the conformation of the protein in this acyl enzyme is significantly different from that in the free enzyme. Although it is the combination of the 7α-OMe substituent and the departure of the 3′-leaving group that leads to the accumulation of the acyl enzyme, it is the former rather than the latter structural feature that is responsible for the conformational transition (Faraci and Pratt 1986a). The same conclusion was reached with the *S. aureus* β-lactamase. This work (Faraci and Pratt 1986a) also showed that the conformational change induced by the 7α-OMe group of cefoxitin did occur at the acyl-enzyme stage rather than in the Michaelis complex, and hence inhibitors like cefoxitin really can be seen as mechanism-based, where unexpected (by the enzyme) non-covalent (rather than the classical covalent) interactions lead to inactivation.

The question of the conformational sensitivity of class C β-lactamases has not yet been investigated to anywhere near the extent it has been with respect to the class A enzymes. Nevertheless, there are indications that class C enzymes may be inactivated by non-covalent interactions in an analogous fashion. For example, cloxacillin is a very powerful inhibitor of class C β-lactamases by virtue of the stable acyl enzyme formed (Knott-Hunziker *et al.* 1982a; Joris *et al.* 1984). Similarly, many of the newer β-lactams with bulky oximino-containing side chains, e.g. cefotaxime and cefmenoxime (Labia *et al.* 1984) and the monobactam aztreonam (Bush *et al.* 1982) bind strongly to these enzymes; so too do the 6α-methoxypenicillin, temocillin (Jules and Neu 1982), and the cephamycins, cefoxitin and moxalactam (Bush *et al.* 1982; Labia 1982; Murakami and Yoshida 1985). Closer investigation of these phenomena should reveal the extent of the conformational lability of class C β-lactamases.

4.5 Inhibition by functional-group-specific reagents

These reagents were much less influential in the elucidation of *β*-lactamase mechanisms than they were with many other enzymes. Early experiments with the class A *β*-lactamases (Pain and Virden 1979; Durkin and Viswanatha 1980) gave no indication of overt functionality. In retrospect, the borate inhibition (Dobozy *et al.* 1971; Kiener and Waley 1978) might have been more confidently interpreted in terms of serine, but the relative (to serine proteases) ineffectiveness of phosphoryl and sulphonyl fluorides (Pain and Virden 1979) was not reassuring. (More recently a slow inactivation of both class A and C *β*-lactamases by the latter reagents has been described; Bush *et al.* 1982).

Of the other functional group reagents, perhaps only those directed against amines appear to give any reasonably consistent indication of specific inhibition of the class A *β*-lactamases (Davies and Virden 1978; Schenkein and Pratt 1980; Grace *et al.* 1987) although no specific residue has been pinpointed. With regard to lysine, it might be recalled that several of the mechanism-based reagents discussed above are thought to cross-link the enzyme through lysine, and absorption spectra support this idea (Brenner and Knowles 1984a). The Ser-X-Y-Lys motif remains enticing, particularly since Richards and co-workers (J. R. Richards, personal communication) have demonstrated by site-specific mutagenesis that lysine in this position is essential for *β*-lactamase activity by the TEM-1 *β*-lactamase. It should finally be noted that all evidence suggests that histidine is not a functional active site residue; only a carboxylate seems to remain as a possibility (Waley 1975; Durkin and Viswanatha 1980; Anderson and Pratt 1983; Hardy *et al.* 1984). The class C *β*-lactamases appear not to have been significantly probed with functional group reagents, but the precedent is not encouraging. Thus the question of accessory functionality at the active sites of class A and C *β*-lactamases remains open, and may well remain so until a crystal structure emerges.[†]

4.6 Clinical indications

To date, very little calculated advantage has been taken of specifically designed *β*-lactamase inhibitors in clinical practice. The strategy of *β*-lactamase avoidance, described in the introduction, has dominated the pharmaceutical scene. It should be noted however that a number of antibiotics, developed as poor *β*-lactamase substrates, appear in restrospect, as described above, to be mechanism-based inhibitors of certain *β*-lactamases, and no doubt, in some circumstances at least, derive some of their antibiotic effectiveness from this fact, e.g. cloxacillin, cephalothin, cefoxitin, moxalactam, thienamycin, and aztreonam.

Subsequent to the discovery of effective *β*-lactamase inhibitors which are not themselves antibiotics, certain pharmaceutical companies have devoted consi-

---

[†] *Note added in proof.* The very recently published crystal structures of the *S. aureus* (Herzberg, O. and Moult, J. (1987); *Science* **236**, 694–701) and *Streptomyces albus G* (Dideberg, O. *et al.* (1987); *Biochem. J.*, **245**, 911–13) class A *β*-lactamases indicate the presence of two conserved lysine residues and one glutamate in the vicinity of the active site.

derable effort and resources into developing the most promising of these into synergists for β-lactamase sensitive antibiotics. Currently the longest track record is possessed by clavulanic acid, which, in combination with amoxicillin, is distributed as 'Augmentin', and indicated for formerly amoxicillin-resistant infections by *S. aureus, Haemophilus influenzae, Neissevia gonorrhoeae,* and *Branhamella catarrhalis.* In order to extend the range of 'Augmentin', particularly in the direction of *Bacteroides fragilis, Klebsiella pneumoniae* and *P. aeruginosa,* a combination of clavulanic acid with ticarcillin is also reaching maturity as 'Timentin' (see, for example, the proceedings of a symposium on the subject; Neu 1985a).

Pencillanic acid sulphone, in combination with ampicillin as 'Sultamicillin', has apparently been undergoing serious clinical trials in Japan [see, for example, supplement 2 of *Chemotherapy* (Tokyo), Vol. 33 (1985)] and it seems that 6β-bromopenicillanic acid, in various combinations with ampicillin (Baltzer *et al.* 1980; Von Daehne *et al.,* 1983, 1985) is being tested in Europe. These combinations appear to have a similar *in vivo* spectrum to the corresponding clavulanic acid combination although they may be less effective against certain gram negative organisms (and their class C β-lactamases), such as *Enterobacter* and *Pseudomonas* species, because of the lower permeability of the β-lactamase inhibitors through the outer membranes (Wise *et al.* 1981; Coleman *et al.* 1983; Hunter 1984; Neu 1985b); there is, however, contrary opinion on this point of comparison of 6β-bromopenicillanic acid combinations with 'Augmentin' (W. Von Daehne and J. Keiding, personal communication).

Although there are still very few data from the marketplace bearing on the long-term position of specialized β-lactamase inhibitors, the progress of 'Augmentin' suggests that they might have a place. In view of the great difficulties and enormous cost facing the developer of totally new broad spectrum antibiotics (consider the thienamycin saga, for example; Kahan *et al.* 1983), it may well be that the pharmacokinetics of antibiotic mixtures and antibiotic/β-lactamase inhibitor mixtures might appear more and more the lesser evil, even in the near future. Furthermore, β-lactamase inhibitors are still in a very early stage of development clinically, where variants of even the current top three drugs have not been thoroughly assessed. Aspirants, however, do have to face most of the same barriers that the antibiotics themselves do. Already, for example, some inhibitors, such as simple penems, clavems, and 6-acetylmethyl-enepenicillanic acid (**18**), appear to fail on the criterion of stability, which is perhaps not surprising in view of the functional complexity of these molecules; even clavulanic acid itself lies close to the usable limit in this respect. Nevertheless, the compounds already available (or obtainable from them by logical extension) appear to be capable, if skilfully developed, and if they are in fact needed to assist the β-lactamase resistant β-lactams, of essentially eliminating β-lactamase-mediated resistance. As that stage approaches, however, the other modes of resistance to β-lactam antibiotics (Parr and Bryan 1984) will have more firmly captured our attention.

Acknowledgements

The author is grateful to Drs A. L. Fink, J. R. Knox, J. H. Richards, and S. G. Waley for access to manuscripts prior to publication.

References*

Abraham, E. P. and Waley, S. G. (1979). *β*-lactamases from *Bacillus cereus*. In *Beta-lactamases* (ed. J. M. T. Hamilton-Miller and J. T. Smith), pp. 330–5. Academic Press, New York.

Ambler, R. P. (1980). The structure of *β*-lactamases. *Phil. Trans. R. Soc.*, **B289**, 321–31.

Anderson, E. G. and Pratt, R. F. (1981). Pre-steady state *β*-lactamase kinetics. Observation of a covalent intermediate during turnover of a fluorescent cephalosporin by the *β*-lactamase of *Staphylococcus aureus* PCl. *J. Biol. Chem.*, **256**, 11401–4.

Anderson, E. G. and Pratt, R. F. (1983). Pre-steady state *β*-lactamase kinetics. The trapping of a covalent intermediate and the interpretation of pH-rate profiles. *J. Biol. Chem.*, **258**, 13120–6.

Arisawa, M. and Adam, S. (1983). Mechanism of inactivation of TEM-1 *β*-lactamase by 6-acetylmethylenepenicillanic acid. *Biochem. J.*, **211**, 447–54.

Arisawa, M. and Then, R. L. (1982). 6-acetylmethylenepenicillanic acid (RO 15–1903), a potent *β*-lactamase inhibitor I. Inhibition of chromosomally and R-factor mediated *β*-lactamases. *J. Antibiot.*, **35**, 1578–83.

Arisawa, M. and Then, R. L. (1983). Inactivation of TEM-1 *β*-lactamase by 6-acetylmethylenepenicillanic acid. *Biochem. J.*, **209**, 609–13.

Baltzer, B., Binderup, E., Von Daehne, W., Godtfredsen, W. O., Hansen, K., Nielsen, B., Soerensen, H., Vangedal, S. (1980). Mutual prodrugs of *β*-lactam antibiotics and *β*-lactamase inhibitors. *J. Antibiot.*, **33**, 1183–92.

Behrens, O. K. and Garrison, L. (1950). Inhibitors for penicillinase. *Arch. Biochem. Biophys.*, **27**, 94–98.

Bentley, P. H., Berry, P. D., Brooks, G., Gilpin, M. L., Hunt, E., and Zomaya, I. I. (1981). Synthesis and structure–activity relationships of totally synthetic clavulanic acid analogues. In *Recent advances in the chemistry of β-lactam antibiotics* (ed. G. I. Gregory), pp. 175–83. Royal Society of Chemistry, London.

Bergstrom, S., Olsson, O., and Normark, S. (1982). Common evolutionary origin of chromosomal *β*-lactamase genes in Enterobacteria. *J. Bacteriol.*, **150**, 528–34.

Bergstrom, S., Lindberg, F. P., Olsson, O., and Normark, S. (1983). Comparison of the overlapping frd and ampC operons of *Escherichia coli* with the corresponding sequences in other gram-negative bacteria. *J. Bacteriol.*, **155**, 1297–1305.

Bicknell, R. and Waley, S. G. (1985a). Single turnover and steady-state kinetics of hydrolysis of cephalosporins by *β*-lactamase I from *Bacillus cereus*. *Biochem. J.*, **231**, 83–8.

Bicknell, R. and Waley, S. G. (1985b). Cryoenzymology of *Bacillus cereus* *β*-lactamase II. *Biochemistry*, **24**, 6876–87.

Bicknell, R., Emanuel, J., Gagnon, J., and Waley, S. G. (1985). The production and molecular properties of the zinc *β*-lactamase of *Pseudomonas maltophilia* IID 1275. *Biochem. J.*, **129**, 791–7.

Blanpain, P. C., Nagy, J. B., Laurent, G. H., and Durant, F. V. (1980). A multifaceted approach to the study of the side-chain conformation in *β*-lactamase-resistant penicillins. *J. Med. Chem.*, **23**, 1283–92.

Bloch, K. (1969). Enzymatic synthesis of monounsaturated fatty acids. *Acc. Chem. Res.*, **2**, 193–202.

Blumberg, S. and Tauber, Z. (1983). Inhibition of metalloendopeptidases by 2-mercap-toacetyl-dipeptides. *Eur. J. Biochem.*, **136**, 151–4.

Boyd, D. B. (1982). Theoretical and physicochemical studies on β-lactam antibiotics. In *Chemistry and biology of β-lactam antibiotics* (ed. R. B. Morin and M. Gorman), Vol. 1, pp. 437–545. Academic Press, New York.

Boyd, D. B. (1984). Electronic structures of cephalosporins and penicillins. 15. Inductive effect of the 3-position side chain in cephalosporins. *J. Med. Chem.*, **27**, 63–6.

Brenner, D. G. and Knowles, J. R. (1984a). 6-(methoxymethylene) penicillanic acid: inactivator of RTEM β-lactamase from *Escherichia coli*. *Biochemistry*, **23**, 5839–46.

Brenner, D. G. and Knowles, J. R. (1984b). Penicillanic acid sulfone: nature of irreversible inactivation of RTEM β-lactamase from *Escherichia coli*. *Biochemistry*, **23**, 5833–9.

Brooks, G., Bruton, G., Finn, M. J., Harbridge, J. B., Harris, M. A., Howarth, T. J., Hunt, E., Stirling, I., and Zomaya, I. I. (1984). The chemistry of clavulanic acid and its derivatives. In *Recent advances in the chemistry of β-lactam antibiotics* (ed. A. G. Brown and S. M. Roberts), pp. 222–41. Royal Society of Chemistry, London.

Broome-Smith, J. K., Edelman, A., Yousif, S., and Spratt, B. G. (1985). The nucleotide sequences of the pon A and pon B genes encoding penicillin-binding proteins 1A and 1B of *Escherichia coli* K12. *Eur. J. Biochem.*, **147**, 437–46.

Brown, A. G., Butterworth, D., Cole, M., Hanscomb, G., Hood, J., Reading, C., and Rolinson, G. N. (1976). Naturally occurring β-lactamase inhibitors with antibacterial activity. *J. Antibiot.*, **29**, 668–9.

Bush, K. and Sykes, R. B. (1983). β-lactamase inhibitors in perspective. *J. Antimicrob. Chemother.*, **11**, 97–107.

Bush, K. and Sykes, R. B. (1984). Interaction of β-lactam antibiotics with β-lactamases as a cause for resistance. In *Antimicrobial drug resistance* (ed. L. E. Bryan), pp. 1–31. Academic Press, Orlando, Fl.

Bush, K., Freudenberger, J. S., and Sykes, R. B. (1982). Interaction of azthreonam and related monobactams with β-lactamases from gram-negative bacteria. *Antimicrob. Agents. Chemother.*, **22**, 414–20.

Carrey, E. A. and Pain, R. H. (1978). Conformation of a stable intermediate on the folding pathway of Staphylococcus aureus penicillinase. *Biochim. Biophys. Acta*, **533**, 12–22.

Carrey, E. A., Virden, R., and Pain, R. H. (1984). The reversible deactivation of β-lactamase from *Staphylococcus aureus* by quinacillin and cephaloridine and its modification by antibodies. *Biochim. Biophys. Acta*, **785**, 104–10.

Cartwright, S. J. and Coulson, A. F. W. (1979). A semi-synthetic penicillinase inactivator. *Nature Lond.*, **278**, 360–61.

Cartwright, S. J. and Fink, A. L. (1982). Isolation of a covalent intermediate in β-lactamase I catalysis. *FEBS Lett.* **137**, 186–8.

Cartwright, S. J. and Waley, S. G. (1983). β-lactamase inhibitors *Med Res. Rev.*, **3**, 341–82.

Charlier, P., Dideberg, O., Jamoulle, J.-C., Frère, J.-M., Ghuysen, J.-M., Dive, G., and Lamotte-Brasseur, J. (1984). Active-site-directed inactivators of the Zn^{2+}-containing D-alanyl-D-alanine cleaving carboxypeptidase of Streptomyces albus G. *Biochem. J.*, **219**, 763–772.

Charnas, R. L. and Knowles, J. R. (1981a). Inhibition of the RTEM β-lactamase from *Escherichia coli*. Interaction of enzyme with derivatives of olivanic acid. *Biochemistry*, **20**, 2732–7.

Charnas, R. L. and Knowles, J. R. (1981b). Inactivation of RTEM β-lactamase from *Escherichia coli* by clavulanic acid and 9-deoxyclavulanic acid. *Biochemistry*, **20**, 3214–19.

Charnas, R. L., Fisher, J., and Knowles, J. R. (1978). Chemical studies on the inactivation of *Escherichia coli* RTEM β-lactamase by clavulanic acid. *Biochemistry*, **17**, 2185–9.

Citri, N. (1971). Penicillinase and other *β*-lactamases. In *The enzymes*, (ed. P. D. Boyer) 3rd ed, Vol. 4, pp. 23–46. Academic Press, London.

Citri, N. (1973). Conformational adaptability in enzymes. *Adv. Enzymol.*, **37**, 397–648.

Citri, N. (1981). Recognition of penicillins by *β*-lactamase: the role of the side chain. In *Beta-lactam antibiotics* (ed. S. Mitsuhashi), pp. 225–32. Japan Science Society Press, Tokyo.

Citri, N. and Pollock, M. R. (1966). The biochemistry and function of *β*-lactamase (penicillinase). *Adv. Enzymol.*, **28**, 237–323.

Citri, N. and Zyk, N. (1982). Interaction of the pBR 322-coded RTEM *β*-lactamase with substrates. Evidence for specific conformational transitions. *Biochem. J.*, **201**, 425–7.

Citri, N., Samuni, A., and Zyk, N. (1976). Acquisition of substrate-specific parameters during the catalytic reaction of penicillinase. *Proc. Nat. Acad. Sci. USA* **73**, 1048–52.

Citri, N., Kalkstein, A., Samuni, A., and Zyk, N. (1984). Conformational adaption of RTEM *β*-lactamase to cefoxitin. *Eur. J. Biochem.*, **144**, 333–8.

Clarke, A. J., Mezes, P. S., Vice, S. F., Dmitrienko, G. I., and Viswanatha, T. (1983). Inactivation of *Bacillus cereus* 569/H *β*-lactamase I by 6-*β*-(trifluoromethanesulfonyl) amidopenicillanic acid sulfone and its *N*-methyl derivative. *Biochim. Biophys. Acta*, **748**, 389–97.

Cohen, S. A. and Pratt, R. F. (1980). Inactivation of *Bacillus cereus* *β*-lactamase I by 6-*β*-bromopenicillanic acid: mechanism. *Biochemistry*, **19**, 3996–4003.

Cole, M. (1979). Inhibition of *β*-lactamases. In *Beta-lactamases* (ed. J. M. T. Hamilton-Miller and J. T. Smith), pp. 205–89. Academic Press, New York.

Cole, M. (1984). *β*-lactamase inhibitors: biochemical properties and bacteriological application. In *Antimicrobial. Agriculture: Proceedings, Fourth International Symposium on Antibiotics and Agriculture: Benefits Malefits* (ed. M. Woodbine), pp. 5–29. Butterworth, London.

Coleman, K., Hunter, P. A., and Kenig, M. (1983). Comparative *β*-lactamase inhibitory and synergistic properties of 6-*β*-halogenated penams and clavulanic acid. In *Proceedings of the 13th International Congress on Chemotherapy* (ed. K. H. Spitzy and K. Karrer), Vol. 2, pp. 89/4689/51. Egermann, Vienna.

Connolly, A. K. and Waley, S. G. (1983). Characterisation of the membrane *β*-lactamase in *Bacillus cereus* 569/H/9. *Biochemistry*, **22**, 4647–51.

Coulson, A. (1985). *β*-lactamases: molecular studies. *Biotech. Genet. Eng. Rev.*, **3**, 219–53.

Crackett, P. H. and Stoodley, R. J. (1984). Some observations regarding *β*-lactam-cleavage reactions of penicillanate 1,1-dioxides and related compounds. *Tetrahedron Lett.*, **25**, 1295–8.

Craig, S., Hollecker, M., Creighton, T. E., and Pain, R. H. (1985). Single amino acid mutations block a late step in the folding of *β*-lactamase from *Staphylococcus aureus. J. Mol. Biol.*, **185**, 681–7.

Dalbadie-McFarland, G., Neitzel, J. J. and Richards, J. H. (1986). Active-site mutants of *β*-lactamase: use of an inactive double mutant to study requirements for catalysis. *Biochemistry*, **25**, 332–8.

Dale, J. W., Godwin, D., Mossakowska, D., Stephenson, P., and Wall, S. (1985). Sequence of the OXA2 *β*-lactamase: comparison other penicillin-reactive enzymes. *FEBS Lett.*, **191**, 39–44.

Davies, M. S. and Virden, R. (1978). The inactivation of penicillinase by methyl acetimidate. *Biochem. Soc. Trans.*, **6**, 1222–3.

Dmitrienko, G. I., Copeland, C. R., Arnold, L., Savard, M. E., Clarke, A. J., and Viswanatha, T. (1985). Inhibition of *β*-lactamase I by 6-*β*-sulfonamidopenicillanic acid sulfones: evidence for conformational change accompanying the inhibition process. *Bioorg. Chem.*, **13**, 34–46.

Dobozy, O., Mile, I. Ferencz, I., and Csanyi, V. (1971). Effect of electrolytes on the activity and iodine sensitivity of penicillinase from *Bacillus cereus*. *Acta Biochim. Biophys. Acad. Sci. Hung.*, **6**, 97–105.

Duez, D., Joris, B., Frère, J.-M., Ghuysen, J.-M., and von Beeumen, J. (1981). The penicillin-binding site in the exocellular DD-carboxypeptidase–transpeptidase of Actinomadura R39. *Biochem. J.*, **193**, 83–6.

Durkin, J. P. and Viswanatha, T. (1978). Clavulanic acid inhibition of β-lactamase I from Bacillus cereus 569/H. *J. Antibiot.*, **31**, 1162–9.

Durkin, J. P. and Viswanatha, T. (1980). Bacillus cereus 569/H β-lactamase I: structure–function relationship. *Carlsberg Res. Commun.*, **45**, 411–20.

Easton, C. J. and Knowles, J. R. (1982). Inhibition of the RTEM β-lactamase from *Escherichia coli*. Interaction of the enzyme with derivatives of olivanic acid. *Biochemistry*, **21**, 2857–62.

Emanuel, E. L., Gagnon, J., and Waley, S. G. (1986). Structural and kinetic studies on β-lactamase K1 from *Klebsiella aerogenes*. *Biochem. J.*, **234**, 343–7.

English, A. R., Retsema, J. A., Girard, A. E., Lynch, J. E., and Barth, W. E. (1978). CP-45, 899, a beta-lactamase inhibitor that extends the antibacterial spectrum of beta-lactams: initial bacteriological characterization. *Antimicrob. Agents. Chemother.*, **14**, 414–19.

Faraci, W. S. and Pratt, R. F. (1984). Elimination of a good leaving group from the 3′-position of a cephalosporin need not be concerted with β-lactam ring opening: TEM-2 β-lactamase catalysed hydrolysis of PADAC and of cephaloridine. *J. Am. Chem. Soc.*, **106**, 1489–90.

Faraci, W. S. and Pratt, R. F. (1985). Mechanism of inhibition of the PC1 β-lactamase of Staphylococcus aureus by cephalosporins: importance of the 3′-leaving group. *Biochemistry*, **24**, 903–10.

Faraci, W. S. and Pratt, R. F. (1986a). Mechanism of inhibition of the RTEM-2 β-lactamase by cephamycins: relative importance of the 7α-methoxy group and the 3′-leaving group. *Biochemistry*, **25**, 2934–41.

Faraci, W. S. and Pratt, R. F. (1986b). Interactions of cephalosporins with the *Streptomyces* R61 DD-transpeptidase/carboxypeptidase. Influence of the 3′-substituent. *Biochem. J.*, **238**, 309–2.

Faraci. W. S. and Pratt, R. F. (1987). Nucleophilic reactivation of the PC1 β-lactamase of *Staphylococcus aureus* and of the D,D-peptidase of *Streptomyces* R61 after their inactivation by cephalosporins and cephamycins. *Biochem. J.*, **246**, 651–58.

Fersht, A. (1985). *Enzyme structure and mechanism*, (2nd edn.), pp. 416–422. W. H. Freeman, New York.

Fink, A. L. (1985). The molecular basis of β-lactamase catalysis and inhibition. *Pharm. Res.*, 55–61.

Fink, A. L., Behner, K. M. and Tan, A. K. (1987). Kinetic and structural characteristics of reversible inactivated β-lactamase. *Biochemistry*, **26**, 4248–58.

Fisher, J. (1984). β-Lactams resistant to β-lactamases. In *Antimicrobial drug resistance* (ed. L. E. Bryan), pp. 33–79. Academic Press, Orlando, FL.

Fisher, J., Charnas, R. L., and Knowles, J. R. (1978). Kinetic studies on the inactivation of *Escherichia coli* RTEM β-lactamase by clavulanic acid. *Biochemistry*, **17**, 2180–4.

Fisher, J., Belasco, J. G., Khosla, S., and Knowles, J. R. (1980a). β-lactamase proceeds via an acyl-enzyme intermediate. Interaction of the *Escherichia coli* RTEM enzyme with cefoxitin. *Biochemistry*, **19**, 2895–901.

Fisher, J., Belasco, J. G., Charnas, R. L., Khosla, S., and Knowles, J. R. (1980b). β-lactamase inactivation by mechanism-based reagents. *Phil. Trans. R. Soc.*, **B289**, 309–19.

Fisher, J., Charnas, R. L., Bradley, S. M., and Knowles, J. R. (1981). Inactivation of the RTEM β-lactamase from *Escherichia coli*. Interaction of penam sulfones with enzyme. *Biochemistry*, **20**, 2726–31.

Foulds, C. D., Kosmirak, M., O'Sullivan, A. C., and Sammes, P. G. (1984). On the design of new β-lactamase inhibitors. In *Recent advances in the chemistry of β-lactam antibiotics* (ed. A. G. Brown and S. M. Roberts), pp. 255–65. Royal Society of Chemistry, London.

Frère, J.-M. (1981). Interaction between serine β-lactamase and class A substrates: a kinetic analysis and a reaction pathway hypothesis. *Biochem. Pharmacol.*, **30**, 549–52.

Frère, J.-M. and Joris, B. (1985). Penicillin-sensitive enzymes in peptidoglycan biosynthesis. *CRC Crit. Rev. Microbiol.*, **11**, 299–396.

Frère, J.-M., Dormans, C., Lenzini, V. M., and Duyckaerts, C. (1982a). Interaction of clavulanate with the β-lactamases of Streptomyces albus G and Actinomadura R39. *Biochem. J.*, **207**, 429–36.

Frère, J.-M., Dormans, C., Duyckaerts, C., and DeGraeve, J. (1982b). Interaction of β-iodopenicillanate with β-lactamases of *Streptomyces* albus G and Actinomadura R39. *Biochem. J.*, **207**, 437–44.

Georgopapadakou, N. H. and Sykes, R. B. (1983). Bacterial enzymes interacting with β-lactam antibiotics. *Handbook Exp. Pharmacol.*, (ed. A. L. Demain and N. A. Solomon) **67** (II), 1–77, Springer-Verlag, Berlin.

Ghuysen, J.-M., Frère, J.-M., Leyh-Bouille, M., Coyette, J., Dusart, J., and Nguyen-Distèche, M. (1979). Use of model enzymes in the determination of the mode of action of penicillins and Δ^3-cephalosporins. *Ann. Rev. Biochem.*, **48**, 73–101.

Gottstein, W. J., Haynes, U. J., and McGregor, D. N. (1985). Synthesis and β-lactamase inhibitory properties of 2β-[(acyloxy)methyl]-2-methyl-penam-3α-carboxylic acid 1,1-dioxides. *J. Med. Chem.*, **28**, 518–22.

Grace, M. E., Schenkein, D. P. and Pratt, R. F. (1987). Kinetics and mechanism of inactivation of the RTEM-2 β-lactamase by phenylpropynal. Identification of the characteristic chromophore. *J. Biol. Chem.*, **262**, 16778–85.

Hall, T. W., Maiti, S. N., Micetich, R. G., Spevak, P., Yamabe, S., Ishida, N., Kajitani, M., Tanaka, M., and Yamasaki, T. (1984). YTR-830 and related active β-lactamase inhibitors. In *Recent advances in the chemistry of β-lactam antibiotics* (ed. A. G. Brown and S. M. Roberts), pp. 242–54. Royal Society of Chemistry, London.

Hamanaka, E. S. (1984). β-lactamase inhibiting 6-β-sulfonyloxypenieillanic acid derivatives. U.S. Pat. 4 486 411 (*Chem. Abst.*, **102**, 184903).

Hamilton-Miller, J. M. T., Newton, G. G. F., and Abraham, E. P. (1970a). Products of aminolysis and enzymic hydrolysis of cephalosporins. *Biochem. J.*, **116**, 371–4.

Hamilton-Miller, J. M. T., Richards, E., and Abraham, E. P. (1970b). Changes in proton-magnetic-resonance spectra during aminolysis and enzymic hydrolysis of cephalosporins. *Biochem. J.*, **116**, 385–96.

Hamilton-Miller J. M. T. and Smith, J. T., ed (1979). *Beta-lactamases*. Academic Press, New York.

Hangauer, D. G., Monzingo, A. F., and Matthews, B. W. (1984). An interactive computer graphics study of thermolysin-catalysed peptide cleavage and inhibition by *N*-carboxymethyl dipeptides. *Biochemistry*, **23**, 5730–41.

Hardy, L. W., Nishida, C. H., and Kirsch, J. F. (1984). Anomalous pH dependence of the reactions of carbenicillin and sulbenicillin with *Bacillus cereus* β-lactamase I. Influence of the α-substituent charge on the kinetic parameters. *Biochemistry*, **23**, 1288–94.

Heckler, T. G. and Day, R. A. (1983). *Bacillus cereus* 569/H penicillinase serine-44 acylation by diazotized 6-aminopenicillanic acid. *Biochim. Biophys. Acta*, **745**, 292–300.

Hilhorst, I. M., Dmitrienko, G. I., Viswanatha, T., and Lampen, J. O. (1984). *Bacillus licheniformis* 749/C β-lactamase inactivated by 6-β-(trifluoromethanesulfonyl)-amidopenicillanic acid sulfone. *J. Protein Chem.*, **3**, 275–86.

Hill, H. A. O., Sammes, P. G., and Waley, S. G. (1980). Active sites of β-lactamases from *Bacillus cereus. Phil. Trans. R. Soc.*, **B289**, 333–44.

Hunter, P. A. (1984). Properties affecting the clinical potential of new compounds. *Pharm. Weekblad.*, **119**, 650–7.

Jaurin, B. and Grundstrom, T. (1981). Ampc cephalosporinase of *Escherichia coli* K12 has a different evolutionary origin from that of β-lactamases of the penicillinase type. *Proc. Nat. Acad. Sci. USA*, **78**, 4897–901.

Joris, B., Dusart, J., Frère, J.-M. Van Beeumen, J., Emanuel, E. L., Petursson, S., Gagnon, J., and Waley, S. G. (1984). The active site of the P99 β-lactamase from *Enterobacter cloacae. Biochem. J.*, **223**, 271–4.

Jules, K. and Neu, H. (1982). Antibacterial activity and β-lactamase stability of temocillin. *Antimicrob. Agents Chemother.*, **22**, 453–60.

Kahan, F. M., Kropp, H., Sundelof, J. G., and Birnbaum, J. (1983). Thienamycin: development of imipenem–cilastatin. *J. Antimicrob. Chemother.*, **12**, (Suppl. D), 1–35.

Keck, W., Glauner, B., Schwarz, U., Broome-Smith, J. K., and Spratt, B. G. (1985). Sequences of the active-site peptides of three of the high-M_r penicillin-binding proteins of Escherichia coli K12. *Proc. Nat. Acad. Sci. USA*, **82**, 1999–2003.

Kelly, J. A., Knox, J. R., Moews, P. C., Hite, G. J., Bartolone, J. B., Zhao, H., Joris, B., Frère, J.-M., and Ghuysen, J.-M. (1985). 2.8Å structure of penicillin-sensitive D-alanyl carboxypeptidase-transpeptidase from *Streptomyces* R61 and complexes with β-lactams. *J. Biol. Chem.*, **260**, 6449–58.

Kelly, J. A., Dideberg, O., Charlier, P., Wery, J. P., Libert, M., Moews, P. C., Knox, J. R., Duez, C., Fraipont, Cl., Joris, B., Dusart, J., Frère, J.-M., and Ghuysen, J.-M. (1986). On the origin of bacterial resistance to penicillin: comparison of a β-lactamase and a penicillin target. *Science*, **231**, 1429–31.

Kemal, C. and Knowles, J. R. (1981). Penicillanic acid sulfone: interaction with RTEM β-lactamase from *Escherichia coli* at different pH values. *Biochemistry*, **20**, 3688–95.

Kemp, J. E. G., Closier, M. D., Narayanaswami, S., and Stefaniak, M. H. (1980). Nucleophilic S_N2 displacements on penicillin-6-and cephalosporin-7-triflates; 6-β-iodopenicillanic acid, a new β-lactamase inhibitor. *Tetrahedron Lett.*, **21**, 2991–4.

Kiener, P. A. and Waley, S. G. (1977). Substrate-induced deactivation of penicillinases. Studies of β-lactamase I by hydrogen exchange. *Biochem. J.*, **165**, 279–85.

Kiener, P. A. and Waley, S. G. (1978). Reversible inhibitors of penicillinases. *Biochem. J.*, **169**, 197–204.

Kiener, P. A., Knott-Hunziker, V., Petursson, S., and Waley, S. G. (1980). Mechanism of substrate-induced inactivation of β-lactamase I. *Eur. J. Biochem.*, **109**, 575–80.

Klemes, Y. and Citri, N. (1979). Catalytic and conformational properties of cross-linked derivatives of penicillinase. *Biochim. Biophys. Acta*, **567**, 401–9.

Klemes, Y. and Citri, N. (1980). Cross-linking preserves conformational changes induced in penicillinase by its substrates. *Biochem. J.*, **187**, 529–32.

Knott-Hunziker, V., Orlek, B. S., Sammes, P. G., and Waley, S. G. (1979a) 6-β-bromopenicillanic acid inactivates β-lactamase I. *Biochem. J.*, **177**, 365–7.

Knott-Hunziker, V., Waley, S. G., Orlek, B. S., and Sammes, P. G. (1979b). Penicillinase active sites: labelling of serine-44 in β-lactamase I by 6-β-bromopenicillanic acid. *FEBS Lett.*, **99**, 59–61.

Knott-Hunziker, V., Orlek, B. S., Sammes, P. G., and Waley, S. G. (1980). Kinetics of inactivation of β-lactamase I by 6-β-bromopenicillanic acid. *Biochem. J.*, **187**, 797–802.

Knott-Hunziker, V., Petursson, S., Jayatilake, G. S., Waley, S. G., Jaurin, B., and Grundstrom, T. (1982a). Active site of *β*-lactamases. The chromosomal *β*-lactamases of *Pseudomonas aeruginosa* and *Escherichia coli*. *Biochem. J.*, **201**, 621–7.

Knott-Hunziker, V., Petursson, S., Waley, S. G., Jaurin, B., and Grundstrom, T. (1982b). The acyl-enzyme mechanism of *β*-lactamase action. The evidence for class C *β*-lactamases. *Biochem. J.*, **207**, 315–22.

Knowles, J. R. (1983). Anti-*β*-lactamase agents. *Antibiotics*, **6**, 90–107.

Knowles, J. R. (1985). Penicillin resistance: the chemistry of *β*-lactamase inhibition. *Acc. Chem. Res.*, **18**, 97–104.

Labia, R. (1982). Moxalactam: an oxa-*β*-lactam antibiotic that inactivates *β*-lactamases. *Rev. Infect. Dis.*, **4**, S529–35.

Labia, R., Lelievre, V., and Peduzzi, J. (1980). Inhibition kinetics of three R-factor-mediated *β*-lactamases by a new *β*-lactam sulfone (CP 45899). *Biochim. Biophys. Acta*, **611**, 351–7.

Labia, R., Morand, A., and Peduzzi, J. (1983). Cefotetan and *β*-lactamases II. An unusual property: the inactivation of some *β*-lactamases by cefotetan. *J. Antimicrob. Chemother.*, **11** (Suppl. A), 153–7.

Labia, R., Morand, A., Verchere-Beaur, C., and Bryskier, A. (1984). Affinity of cefmenoxime for beta-lactamase: an analysis. *Am. J. Med.*, **77** (Suppl. 6A), 25–27.

Lamotte-Brasseur, J., Dive, G., and Ghuysen, J.-M. (1984). On the structural analogy between D-alanyl-D-alanine terminated peptides and *β*-lactam antibiotics. *Eur. J. Med. Chem. Chim. Ther.* **19**, 319–30.

Little, C., Emanuel, E. L., Gagnon, J., and Waley, S. G. (1986). Identification of an essential glutamic acid residue in *β*-lactamase II from *Bacillus cereus*. *Biochem. J.*, **233**, 465–9.

Loosemore, M. J., Cohen, S. A., and Pratt, R. F. (1980). Inactivation of *Bacillus cereus β*-lactamase I by 6-*β*-bromopenicillanic acid: kinetics. *Biochemistry*, **19**, 3990–6.

Maruyama, I. N., Yamamoto, A., Maruyama, T., and Hirota, Y. (1983). The fine architecture and function of the gene coding for the PBP-3 of *Escherichia coli*. In *The target of penicillin* (ed. R. Hakenbeck, J.-V. Holtje, and H. Labischinski), pp. 393–402. De Gruyter, Berlin.

Maycock, A. and Abeles, R. (1976). Suicide enzyme inactivators. *Acc. Chem. Res.*, **9**, 313–9.

Mezes, P. S. F., Clarke, A. J., Dmitrienko, G. I., and Viswanatha, T. (1982). The inactivation of *Bacillus cereus* 569/H *β*-lactamase by 6-*β*-(trifluoromethanesulfonyl)amidopenicillanic acid sulfone: pH dependence and stoichiometry. *J. Antibiot.*, **35**, 918–20.

Murakami, K., Doi, M., and Yoshida, T. (1982). Asparenomycins A, B and C, new carbapenem antibiotics V. Inhibition of *β*-lactamases. *J. Antibiot.*, **35**, 39–45.

Murakami, K. and Yoshida, T. (1985). Covalent binding of moxalactam to cephalosporinase of *Citrobacter freundii*. *Antimicrob. Agents Chemother.*, **27**, 727–32.

Neu, H. C. (1985a). Beta-lactamase inhibition: therapeutic advances. 1985; Fort Landerdale. In *Am. J. Med.*, **79** (Suppl. 5B), 1–196, (ed. H. C. Neu). The American Journal of Medicine, New York.

Neu, H. C. (1985b). Contributions of beta-lactamases to bacterial resistance and mechanisms to inhibit beta-lactamases. *Am. J. Med.*, **79** (Suppl. 5B), 2–12.

Newall, C. E. (1981). Clavems, penems and ethylidenepenams derived from clavulanic acid. In *Recent advances in the chemistry of *β*-lactam antibiotics* (ed. G. I. Gregory), pp. 151–169. Royal Society of Chemistry, London.

Nicholas, R. A., Suzuki, H., Hirota, Y., and Strominger, J. L. (1985). Purification and sequencing of the active site tryptic peptide from penicillin-binding protein 1b of *Escherichia coli*. *Biochemistry*, **24**, 3448–53.

Nielsen, J. B. K. and Lampen, J. O. (1983). β-lactamase III of *Bacillus cereus* 569: membrane lipoprotein and secreted protein. *Biochemistry*, **22**, 4652–6.

Pain, R. H. and Virden, R. (1979). The structural and conformational basis of β-lactamase activity. In *Beta-lactamases* (ed. J. M. T. Hamilton-Miller and J. T. Smith), pp. 141–80. Academic Press, New York.

Parr, Jr., T. R. and Bryan, L. E. (1984). Nonenzymatic resistance to β-lactam antibiotics and resistance to other cell wall synthesis inhibitors. In *Antimicrobial drug resistance* (ed. L. E. Bryan), pp. 81–111. Academic Press, Orlando, FL.

Pratt, R. F. and Faraci, W. S. (1986). Direct observation by ^{1}H NMR of cephalosporoate intermediates in aqueous solution during the hydrazinolysis and the β-lactamase-catalysed hydrolysis of cephalosporins with 3′-leaving groups: kinetics and equilibria of the 3′-elimination reaction. *J. Am. Chem. Soc.*, **108**, 5328–33.

Pratt, R. F. and Govardhan, C. P. (1984). β-lactamase-catalysed hydrolysis of acyclic depsipeptides and acyl transfer to specific amino acid acceptors. *Proc. Nat. Acad. Sci. USA*, **81**, 1302–6.

Pratt, R. F. and Loosemore, M. J. (1978). 6-β-bromopenicillanic acid, a potent β-lactamase inhibitor. *Proc. Nat. Acad. Sci. USA*, **75**, 4145–9.

Pratt, R. F., Anderson, E. G., and Odeh, I. (1980). Certain monocyclic β-lactams are β-lactamase substrates: nocardicin A and desthiobenzyl-penicillin. *Biochem. Biophys. Res. Commun.*, **93**, 1266–73.

Rando, R. (1974). Chemistry and enzymology of k_{cat} inhibitors. *Science*, **185**, 320–4.

Reading, C. and Farmer, T. (1981). The inhibition of β-lactamases from gram-negative bacteria by clavulanic acid. *Biochem. J.*, **199**, 779–87.

Reading, C. and Hepburn, P. (1979). The inhibition of staphylococcal β-lactamase by clavulanic acid. *Biochem. J.*, **179**, 67–76.

Reid, R. D., Felton, L. C., and Pittroff, M. A. (1946). Prolongation of penicillin activity with penicillinase-inhibiting compounds. *Proc. Soc. Exp. Biol. Med.*, **63**, 438–43.

Richmond, M. H. and Sykes, R. B. (1973). β-lactamases of gram-negative bacteria and their possible physiological role. *Adv. Microb. Physiol.*, **9**, 31–88.

Saino, Y., Kobayashi, F., Inoue, M., and Mitsuhashi, S. (1982). Purification and properties of an inducible penicillin β-lactamase isolated from *Pseudomonas maltophilia*. *Antimicrob. Agents Chemother.*, **22**, 564–70.

Samraoui, B., Sutton, B. J., Todd, R. J., Artymiuk, R. P., Waley, S. G., and Phillips, D. C. (1986). Tertiary structural similarity between a class A β-lactamase and a penicillin-sensitive D-alanyl carboxypeptidase–transpeptidase. *Nature, Lond.*, **320**, 378–80.

Samuni, A. and Citri, N. (1975). Biphasic kinetics induced by modified substrates of penicillinases. *Biochem. Biophys. Res. Commun.*, **62**, 7–11.

Samuni, A. and Citri, N. (1979). How specific is the effect of penicillins on the conformation of penicillinase? An experimental model. *Mol. Pharmacol.*, **16**, 250–5.

Samuni, A. and Meyer, A. Y. (1978). Conformation patterns in penicillins and the penicillin–penicillinase interaction. *Mol. Pharmacol.*, **14**, 704–9.

Sawai, T. and Tsukamoto, K. (1982). Cefoxitin, *N*-formimidoyl thienamycin, clavulanic acid and penicillanic acid sulfone as suicide inhibitors for different types of β-lactamases produced by gram-negative bacteria. *J. Antibiot.*, **35**, 1594–1602.

Schenkein, D. P. and Pratt, R. F. (1980). Phenylpropynal, a specific irreversible non-β-lactam inhibitor of β-lactamases. *J. Biol. Chem.*, **255**, 45–8.

Schultz, S. C. and Richards, J. H. (1986). Site-saturation studies of β-lactamase: production and characterisation of mutant β-lactamases with all possible amino acid substitutions at residue 71. *Proc. Nat. Acad. Sci. USA*, **83**, 1588–92.

Sheehan, J. C., Chacko, E., Commons, T. J., Lo, Y. S., Ponzi, D. R., and Schwabacher, A. (1984). *In vitro* biological activities of 6-isosteric penicillins and 7-isosteric cephalosporins. *J. Antibiot.*, **37**, 1441–8.

Spratt, B. G. (1983). Penicillin-binding proteins and the future of *β*-lactam antibiotics. *J. Gen. Microbiol.*, **129**, 1247–60.

Stoodley, R. J. (1985). Synthesis of novel bicyclic *β*-lactam derivatives. In *Recent advances in the chemistry of β-lactam antibiotics* (ed. A. G. Brown and S. M. Roberts), pp. 183–2. The Royal Society of Chemistry, London.

Sykes, R. B. (1982). The classification and terminology of enzymes that hydrolyse *β*-lactam antibiotics. *J. Infect. Dis.*, **145**, 762–5.

Sykes. R. and Bush, K. (1982). Physiology, biochemistry and inactivation of *β*-lactamases. In *Chemistry and biology of β-lactam antibiotics* (ed. R. B. Morin and M. Gorman), Vol. 3, pp. 155–207. Academic Press, New York.

Then, R. L. and Angehrn, P. (1982). Trapping of nonhydrolysable cephalosporins by cephalosporinases in *Enterobacter cloacae* and *Pseudomonas aeruginosa* as a possible resistance mechanism. *Antimicrob. Agents Chemother.*, **21**, 711–17.

Tipper, D. J. and Strominger, J. L. (1965). Mechanism of action of penicillins: a proposal based on their structural similarity to acyl-D-alanyl-D-alanine. *Proc. Nat. Acad. Sci. USA*, **54**, 1133–41.

Virden, R., Bristow, A., and Pain, R. H. (1975). The active site of penicillinase from *Staphylococcus aureus* PCl. Isolation of a specific covalent complex with the substrate quinacillin. *Biochem. J.*, **149**, 397–401.

Virden, R., Bristow, A., and Pain, R. H. (1978). Reversible inhibition of penicillinase by quinacillin: evaluation of mechanisms involving two conformational states of the enzyme. *Biochem. Biophys. Res. Commun.*, **82**, 951–6.

Von Daehne, W., Nielsen, B., and Roholt, I. (1983). *In vivo* evaluation of pivampicillin 6-*β*-bromopenicillinate (VD 2085), a novel broad-spectrum oral antibiotic. In *Proceedings of the 13th International Congress on Chemotherapy* (ed. K. H. Spitzy and K. Karrer), Vol. 3, pp. 55/1–6. Egermann, Vienna.

Von Daehne, W., Nielsen, B., and Roholt, I. (1985). Mutual prodrugs of ampicillin and 6-*β*-halopenicillanic acids. In *Proceedings of the 14th International Congress on Chemotherapy, Antimicrobial Section 2* (ed. J. Ishigami), pp. 1280–1. University of Tokyo Press, Tokyo.

Waley, S. G. (1975). The pH-dependence and group modification of *β*-lactamase I. *Biochem. J.*, **149**, 547–51.

Walsh, C. (1978). Chemical approaches to the study of enzymes catalyzing redox transformations. *Ann. Rev. Biochem.*, **47**, 881–931.

Walsh, C. (1984). Suicide substrates, mechanism-based enzyme inactivators: recent developments. *Ann. Rev. Biochem.*, **53**, 493–535.

Waxman, D. J. and Strominger, J. L. (1983). Penicillin-binding proteins and the mechanism of action of *β*-lactam antibiotics. *Ann. Rev. Biochem.*, **52**, 825–69.

Wick, W. E. (1972). Biological evaluation. In *Cephalosporins and penicillins* (ed. E. H. Flynn). pp. 496–531. Academic Press, New York.

Wise, R., Andrews, J. M., and Patel, N. (1981). 6-*β*-bromo-and 6-*β*-iodopenicillanic acid, two novel *β*-lactamase inhibitors. *J. Antimicrob. Chemother.*, **7**, 531–6.

Zrihen, M., Labia, R., and Wakselman, M. (1983). Substituted *N*-arylazetidinones, potential inhibitors of *β*-lactamases. *Eur. J. Med. Chem. Chim. Ther.*, **18**, 307–14.

---

* Review covers literature to end of 1985.

5

Enkephalinase inhibitors as drugs

Jean-Charles Schwartz

5.1   Introduction

In 1974, Kerr and Kenny isolated from membranes of rabbit kidney microvilli a metallo-peptidase cleaving large peptides such as insulin or glucagon, which was thereafter designated 'neutral proteinase from kidney brush borders' (EC 3.4.24.11). In following years, although its presence in intestinal microvilli was established, its widespread occurrence in many tissues, including brain, was not unravelled and its functional role remained elusive (Kenny 1977).

Following the discovery of opioid peptides the search for peptidases responsible for turning off the signals conveyed by these neurotransmitters began in several laboratories (reviewed by Schwartz *et al.* 1981; Hersh 1982; McKelvy 1983). Malfroy *et al.* (1978) detected in cerebral membranes an enzyme activity, designated 'enkephalinase', able to cleave the Gly^3–Phe^4 amide bond of enkephalins and suggested that it might be physiologically implicated in their metabolism. This view was strengthened when Thiorphan, a selective and potent inhibitor, was developed and shown to possess naloxone-reversible antinociceptive activity (Roques *et al.* 1980) as well as the ability to protect endogenous enkephalins from extensive degradation (Patey *et al.* 1981). Using a sensitive radiometric assay, enkephalinase activity was detected not only in brain but also in lung (Swerts *et al.* 1979a, b) and a variety of peripheral organs including the kidney and pituitary (Llorens and Schwartz 1981). Almenoff *et al.* (1981)

originally suggested that a metalloendopeptidase from pituitary membranes was identical with both enkephalinase and the neutral proteinase from kidney brush borders, a view soon confirmed (Malfroy and Schwartz 1982a, b; Fulcher *et al.* 1982). More recently, the purified enzyme was shown to hydrolyse a variety of messenger peptides and its role in their physiological inactivation was suggested, although this remains to be experimentally proven (reviewed by Schwartz *et al.* 1985a; Turner *et al.* 1985). This short historical background shows that enkephalinase inhibitors can be regarded as a new class of agents able to facilitate enkephalinergic (and possibly other peptidergic) transmissions. It also explains how the enzyme numbered EC 3.4.24.11, although apparently a single molecular entity found in various tissues, is commonly referred to as 'neutral proteinase from kidney brush borders' (name recommended by the Enzyme Commission but obviously inappropriate), 'neutral metalloendopeptidase', 'thermolysin-like peptidase', 'endopeptidase 24-11' or 'enkephalinase'. We have adopted the last trivial designation, which refers to its sole physiological function hitherto established, by analogy with the trivial name 'angiotensin-converting enzyme', which commonly designates peptidyl dipeptidase (EC 3.4.15.1).

5.2 Properties and localization of enkephalinase

5.2.1 Purification and physicochemical properties

The enzyme has been purified to homogeneity, in most cases starting from the kidney cortex e.g. from rabbits (Kerr and Kenny 1974; Almenoff and Orlowski 1984), rats (Malfroy and Schwartz 1982a, b, 1984) or humans (Gafford *et al.* 1983) in view of the high enzyme content of this tissue (0.1–0.5 per cent of total proteins). The preliminary preparation of a microsomal fraction containing renal brush borders constitutes an efficient purification step. Enkephalinase has also been purified completely from bovine pituitaries (Orlowski and Wilk 1981) and pig brain (Relton *et al.* 1983) and partially from rat (Gorenstein and Snyder 1979; Rush and Hersh 1982; Hersh 1984) and rabbit brain (Almenoff and Orlowski 1984). Being an integral membrane glycoprotein, enkephalinase has first to be released, a step accomplished in the early studies by toluene–trypsin treatments whereas, in more recent studies, it has been solubilized by detergents such as Triton X-100 or deoxycholate. In addition to the usual purification steps such as ion-exchange chromatography or gel filtration, more specific steps have included affinity chromatography on phenylsepharose (Almenoff and Orlowski 1984) or lectin columns (Malfroy and Schwarts *et al.* 1982a, b, 1984; Hersh 1984) and immunoadsorption (Relton *et al.* 1983).

The molecular weight of the enzyme from various sources appears to be in the range of 87 000–95 000 (Na-dodecylsulphate polyacrylamide gel electrophoresis), the lower value corresponding to the cerebral enzyme. The size of the latter might be slightly lower due to differences in glycosylation (Relton *et al.* 1983) and slight differences in its kinetic and immunological properties as compared with the renal enzyme have also been suggested (Almenoff and Orlowski 1984). The presence of four distinct forms in rat brain was also suggested, based upon differences in charge and carbohydrate content but not in catalytic activity (Hersh 1984). The optimal pH toward a variety of substrates is around 7.0 and the purified enzyme does not lose appreciable activity when stored at 4 °C for several months.

The renal enzyme contains one atom of Zn and 7.2 per cent of sugar residues (Kenny 1977). The importance of the Zn atom in catalysis is shown by the complete inhibition of the enzyme activity by chelating agents (EDTA, o-phenanthroline) as well as by the 1000-fold increase in inhibitory potency of dipeptides in which a Zn-chelating group is introduced (Schwartz et al. 1981). Following extraction of the Zn atom by chelating agents, the activity of the enzyme in cerebral membranes can be restored by several divalent metals, among which Co^{2+} is especially effective (Schwartz et al. 1982a, b).

5.2.2 Substrate specificity

The specificity of the purified kidney enzyme was initially studied using large substrates such as the insulin B chain (30 residues) corticotropin (24 residues), or glucagon (29 residues) and the importance of its endopeptidase activity was underlined: hence its designation 'neutral proteinase from brush borders' (Kenny 1977). In the insulin B chain, the internal bonds most readily cleaved were those involving the amino group of hydrophobic residues, such as Phe, Tyr, Leu, and Val. In contrast, initial specificity studies performed on cerebral membranes before isolation of the enzyme and realization that it was identical (or closely similar) to the renal enzyme, indicated the importance not only of the hydrophobic residue in P'_1 (according to the nomenclature proposed by Schechter and Berger 1967) but also of a free carboxylate in P'_1 pointing to its preferential dipeptidylcarboxypeptidase activity (Schwartz et al. 1981). Now, following the determination of patterns of attack and relative rates of hydrolysis of a large range of natural and model peptides (see main references in Table 5.1), the substrate specificity of the enzyme can be summarized as follows.

The main specificity determinants seem to be a hydrophobic residue in P'_1 followed by a residue in P'_2. When this P'_1 residue is in the C-terminal position, the bond is not cleaved, i.e. the enzyme cannot function as a pure carboxypeptidase. However, its amidation allows hydrolysis to occur at a relatively slow rate, e.g. in cholecystokinin (Table 5.1) or in YGGF-NH$_2$ but not YGGF (Malfroy and Schwartz 1984). Amidation (or esterification) of the P'_2 residue, e.g. in enkephalinamides or substance P, reduces the catalytic efficiency, as shown by the reduction in the specificity constant, i.e. the ratio of K_{cat}/K_M, by one order of magnitude. Extension of the peptide chain in the C-terminal side of the P'_2 residue progressively reduces the specificity constant as illustrated in the series of opioid peptides. (Met[5])enkephalin is the best substrate, whereas the Gly[3] Phe[4] bond of the heptapeptide is more slowly cleaved and those of dynorphins, neo-

Table 5.1 Hydrolysis of biologically active peptides by purified enkephalinase

Peptides	Bonds hydrolysed	Specificity Constants[a] (K_{cat}/K_M)	References
Opioid peptides			
(Leu⁵)enkephalin	YGG↓FL	100	Malfroy and Schwartz 1984
(Met⁵)enkephalin	YGG↓FM	300	Malfroy and Schwartz 1984
(D-Ala², Met⁵) enkephalinamide	YdAG↓FM—NH₂	5	Malfroy and Schwartz 1984
Enkephalin hepta- peptide	YG↓GFMRF	21	Schwartz *et al.* 1984
Dynorphin (1–9)	YG↓GFLRRIR	<3	Schwartz *et al.* 1984
Dynorphin (1–13)	YGGFLRRIRPKLK	n.h.	Hersh 1984
α-neoendorphin	YFFFLRYPK	n.h.	Hersh 1984
β-neoendorphin	YGGFLRKYP	n.h.	Hersh 1984
β-endorphin (31 amino acids)	YGGFM . . .	n.h.	Schwartz *et al.* 1984
Other messenger peptides			
Cholecystokinin-8	DYMGWM↓DF—NH₂	10	Zuzel *et al.* 1985
Cholecystokinin-4	WM↓DF—NH₂	3	Zuzel *et al.* 1985
Substance P	RPKPQQF↓F↓G↓LM—NH₂	362[b]	Matsas *et al.* 1983
Chemotactic peptide	f↓MLF	100	Connelly *et al.* 1985
Bradykinin	RPPGF↓SPFR	63	Gafford *et al.* 1983
Angiotensin II	DRVYI↓HPF	24	Gafford *et al.* 1983
Neurotensin	pELYENLPR↓R↓PYIL	n.d.	Chercler *et al.* 1984

n.h. = not hydrolysed; n.d. = not determined

[a] Specificity constants relative to that of (Leu⁵) enkephalin (= 100). The value of the latter, determined with rat kidney enkephalinase purified to homogeneity, was 90 μM⁻¹ min⁻¹ (Malfroy and Schwartz 1984).

[b] The authors did not indicate to which bond cleavage this value refers.

endorphins, and β-endorphin are hardly cleaved at all. In other words, the enzyme functions better as a dipeptidylcarboxypeptidase than as an endopeptidase, a feature attributed to the salt-linking of an Arg residue in its active site by a free carboxylate in P'_2 of substrates (Malfroy and Schwartz 1982a, b, 1984, 1985). The P_1, P_2, P_3 etc. residues seem less important specificity determinants than the P'_1 and P'_2 residues, but optimal residues appear to be Phe in P_2 and Gly (or Ala) in P_1 (Pozsgay *et al.* 1985), which may account for the unexpectedly high hydrolysis rate of substance P (Matsas *et al.* 1983) in which this sequence occurs.

5.2.3   Methods of assay

Initially the kidney enzyme was assayed with $[^{125}I]$ iodoinsulin B chain as substrate, by evaluating the release of trichloroacetic acid-soluble radioactivity (Kenny 1977). Obviously this assay is not selective, since the substrate is also cleaved by several endopeptidases and the fragments initially formed can serve as secondary substrates for other peptidases such as aminopeptidases, leading to an overestimation of enkephalinase activity in non-purified tissue extracts (Malfroy and Schwartz 1984). Initially the cerebral enzyme was assayed with (^3H) enkephalins as substrates, isolating $[^3H]$ YGG, the characteristic product of the reaction, by TLC or HPLC (Malfroy *et al.* 1978, 1979). This assay is rather tedious and must be performed in the presence of inhibitors of other enkephalin-degrading peptidases, e.g. mainly aminopeptidases. A more convenient substrate is $[^3H]$ (D-Ala^2, Leu^5)enkephalin (now commercially available at CEN, Saclay, France) because it is largely aminopeptidase-resistant and the product, (^3H)YdAG, is readily isolated by polystyrene bead chromatography (Llorens *et al.* 1982). This substrate can be replaced by $[^3H]$(D-Ala^2, Met^5)enkephalinamide in a similar assay (Malfroy and Schwartz 1985). Two-step spectrophotometric or fluorometric assays using substrates such as glutaryl-Ala-Ala-Phe-naphthylamide (Almenoff *et al.* 1981) or succinyl-Ala-Ala-Phe-aminomethylcoumarin (Mumford *et al.* 1981; Spillantini *et al.* 1984; Schwartz *et al.* 1984) are also rather convenient ones, although they require secondary release of the absorbing or fluorescent moiety by added aminopeptidases. One-step fluorometric assays, based on disappearance of intramolecular quenching, have been proposed (Florentin *et al.* 1984; Rush *et al.* 1984) but the substrates are not yet commercially available.

When any of these assays is used with non-purified tissue extracts, it is advisable to perform parallel blank incubations in the presence of an inhibitor such as Thiorphan or phosphoramidon.

5.2.4   Tissue localization

The widespread distribution of enkephalinase among peripheral organs (Llorens and Schwartz 1981) and brain regions (Malfroy *et al.* 1978) has been established mainly using enzyme activity assays. More recently, monoclonal (Schwartz *et al.* 1984, 1985b; Pollard *et al.* 1984) and polyclonal (Erdös *et al.* 1985) antibodies, as well as autoradiography with a [^{3}H] inhibitor (Waksman *et al.* 1985; Pollard *et al.* 1984) have allowed cytochemical localization of the enzyme. A monoclonal antibody has also been used in an immunoradiometric assay (Gee *et al.* 1985). Enkephalinase activity has been characterized in various mammalian species including humans (Llorens *et al.* 1982) and seems also to be present in electric organs of Torpedos (Altstein *et al.* 1984; Turner and Dowdall 1984).

Although soluble forms have been characterized in human plasma and cerebrospinal fluid (Spillantini *et al.* 1984; Schwartz *et al.* 1984), enkephalinase is mainly found in membranes. In kidney microvilli, it appears as an integral amphipathic protein anchored in the membrane by a relatively short region close to one end (Fulcher and Kenny 1983). Other epithelial membranes contain high enkephalinase activity, including the intestinal mucosa (Kenny 1977), the ependymal cells in brain (Schwartz *et al.* 1985b) and the placental syncytiotrophoblast (Johnson *et al.* 1984).

Membrane fractions from other peripheral tissues displaying high enkephalinase activity include the lungs, in which it seems to be localized in the bronchial epithelium (Swerts *et al.* 1979; Schwartz *et al.* 1985b); the male genital tract, in which it is abundant in testis, prostate (luminal epithelium), and epididymis (Llorens and Schwartz 1981; Erdös *et al.* 1985); and endocrine or exocrine glands like the pituitary, adrenal, and salivary glands (Llorens and Schwartz 1981; Almenoff *et al.* 1981). In brain, the regional distribution of enkephalinase is highly heterogeneous and parallels to a large extent that of enkephalins, with the highest levels in pallidum, striatum, and substantia nigra (Malfroy *et al.* 1978, 1979; Llorens *et al.* 1982). It seems to be present on neuronal membranes, being enriched in synaptic membranes fractions (Altstein and Vogel 1980; De la Baume *et al.* 1981) and decreased following administration of neurotoxins (Malfroy *et al.* 1979).

In addition its localization in glial membranes seems possible from its detection in primary cultures of astrocytes from rat brain (Lentzen and Palenker 1983), whereas it was not detected in a neuroblastoma cell line (Palenker *et al.* 1984).

5.2.5 Functional role

The participation of a given peptidase in physiological processes seems to be governed by two main factors; its substrate specificity, which dictates the nature of peptides that can be cleaved; and its cellular localization, which ultimately determines which peptides will meet it *in vivo*.

The rather broad biochemical specificity of enkephalinase, (mainly directed toward short peptides with aromatic residues) together with its widespread tissue distribution suggest that it may have multiple functions. Being an ecto-enzyme located in the membrane of epithelial cells in contact with several extracellular fluids, it may potentially participate in the metabolism (activation or inactivation) of a variety of peptides.

Its presence in kidney and intestinal microvilli suggests that it may act on short peptides in tubular and digestive fluids and thereby participate in the release of amino acids that can subsequently be transported into the circulation. However, this hypothesis has never been tested. Its presence in other tissues, particularly in brain synaptic membranes, points to its participation in the physiological inactivation of released neuropeptides, i.e. its functioning as a 'neuropeptidase' (Schwartz *et al.* 1981). However, enkephalinase does not appear to participate *in vivo* in the breakdown of any other neuropeptide that it is able to cleave in the test tube (Zuzel *et al.* 1985) and its role cannot be predicted from purely biochemical considerations. A series of additional factors presumably determine which neuropeptide will be hydrolysed *in vivo*:

(1) the actual extracellular neuropeptide concentration in the synaptic cleft;
(2) the local concentration and anatomical localization of the peptidase relative to peptidergic terminals and corresponding postsynaptic receptors;
(3) the properties, abundance, and localization of other candidate peptidases also able to cleave the neuropeptide.

Obviously these factors cannot be easily evaluated but the use of enkephalinase inhibitors has clearly established that the enzyme plays a key role in the inactivation of endogenous opioid peptides released from enkephalin neurons in the CNS. As detailed in the next section (pharmacology of enkephalinase inhibitors), this conviction is based upon three series of observations with inhibitors, which (i) protect endogenous enkephalins released from brain slices, (ii) *in vivo* strongly reduce the level of the endogenous tripeptide YGG, a metabolite of enkephalins, and (iii) mimic a large number of opioid effects *in vivo*.

Corresponding evidence is still lacking for any other neuropeptide that the enzyme is able to cleave in the test tube. It therefore, remains to be established whether its function is that of a general neuropeptidase or of a specific enkephalin-degrading peptidase.

5.3   Enkephalinase inhibitors

5.3.1   Rational design of active-site-directed inhibitors

5.3.1.1   *Mechanism*

The rational design of enkephalinase inhibitors has greatly benefited from the earlier development of inhibitors of several related zinc metallopeptidases such as carboxypeptidases, ACE, and thermolysin (Cushman and Ondetti 1981). Our understanding of the mechanisms of active-site binding of these competitive inhibitors largely derives from X-ray crystallographic studies of carboxypeptidase A or thermolysin (Quiocho and Lipscomb 1971; Kester and Matthews

1977; Holmes and Matthews 1981), which suggested the existence of close similarities in the active site of various zinc-metallopeptidases, their respective catalytic mechanisms, and the mode of interaction with inhibitors. Enkephalinase inhibitors all seem to belong to the class of biproduct analogues (Byers and Wolfenden 1973), i.e. molecules combining the modes of binding of the two products of the hydrolysis of the susceptible amide bond of substrates. Potent inhibitors of zinc metallopeptidases can be developed by incorporating in the same molecule:

(1) a peptide backbone satisfying the main interactions with the subsites surrounding the scissile amide bond; and

(2) an efficient zinc-binding ligand mimicking the putative interaction of the carbonyl of the scissile amide bond.

Because several efficient zinc-binding groups had been previously identified, the task of developing potent and selective enkephalinase inhibitors has mainly consisted in the precise characterization of the structure of amino-acid residues positioned in close proximity to the scissile bonds and preferred for selective binding with the corresponding sub-sites of the enzyme. The main enkephalinase sub-sites (S_1' and S_2') were first characterized by systematically evaluating the influence of corresponding P_1' and P_2' residues on the inhibitory potencies of a series of dipeptides (Llorens et al. 1980). The conclusions drawn from this study have been thereafter largely confirmed with corresponding dipeptide derivatives containing various zinc-binding groups.

5.3.1.2 *Influence of the P_1' amino-acid residue*

The hydrolysis of natural substrates (Table 5.1) suggests that the specificity of enkephalinase is mainly governed by a putative S_1' 'hydrophobic pocket', apparently similar to that of carboxypeptidase A or thermolysin, i.e. able to accommodate aromatic or, to a lesser extent, hydrophobic aliphatic residues. This was systematically shown (Llorens et al. 1980) by the large (over 100-fold) differences in inhibitory potencies of dipeptides of the general formula X-Ala, of which the most potent are those in which X = Phe, Tyr, Trp or, to a lesser extent, Ile or Pro (Table 5.2).

This essential feature and the mode of interaction of dipeptides with the active site was confirmed with corresponding dipeptide derivatives containing thiol (Roques et al. 1980; Gordon et al. 1983; Fournié-Zaluski et al. 1984a), carboxylate (Fournié-Zaluski et al. 1980; Mumford et al. 1982; Murthy et al. 1984) or hydroxamate (Hudgin et al. 1981) as zinc-binding groups. The requirement of a hydrophobic P_1' residue is also satisfied by the Leu residue in phosphoramidon (Kenny 1977). Finally, the 'hydrophobic pocket' being apparently absent in the active site of ACE, inhibitors with an aromatic residue in P_1' display a clear-cut preference towards enkephalinase. As an example, the IC_{50} value of the dipeptide Tyr–Ala is 1 μM on enkephalinase (Llorens et al. 1980) and 469 μM on ACE (Cushman and Ondetti 1981).

Table 5.2 Inhibitory potency of various dipeptides on enkephalinase activity from mouse striatum

X-Ala	IC_{50} (μM)	Phe-Y or Tyr-Y	IC_{50} (μM)
Phe-Ala	1	Phe-Ala	1
Tyr-Ala	1	retro-Phe-Ala	10
Trp-Ala	2	Phe-Gly	5
Ile-Ala	10	Phe-Ser	100
Pro-Ala	10	Phe-Phe	5
Val-Ala	36	Phe-Trp	5
Met-Ala	100	Phe-Val	10
Thr-Ala	100	Phe-Ile	10
Ala-Ala	100	Phe-Leu	20
Ser-Ala	100	Phe-Ser	30
Glu-Ala	> 100	Phe-Asp	> 100
Asp-Ala	> 100	Phe-Pro	> 100
Lys-Ala	> 100	Tyr-Arg	> 100
Ser-Ala	> 100	Tyr-Lys	> 100

Values taken from Llorens-Cortes *et al.* (1980).

5.3.1.3 *Influence of the P'_2 residue*

Among a series of dipeptides of the general formula Phe–Y (or Tyr–Y), the most potent were those with Y residues without (Gly) or with short (Ala) side-chains but the presence of an aromatic or a large hydrophobic aliphatic residue allows retention of rather good affinity for the enzyme (Table 5.2). In contrast, the presence of a charged P'_2 residue reduces the inhibitory potency (Llorens *et al.* 1980). These features have been generally confirmed with inhibitors containing a zinc-binding group, particularly in the series of thiol derivatives (Gordon *et al.* 1983). Whereas the positive influence of P'_2 aromatic residues is similar in enkephalinase and ACE, the latter differs by a strong preference for Pro residues in this position. This feature accounts for the low inhibitory potency towards enkephalinase of commonly used ACE inhibitors that contain a C-terminal Pro (Swerts *et al.* 1979a, b).

5.3.1.4 *Influence of the peptide bond between P'_1 and P'_2 residues*

N-methylation of the amide bond of the dipeptides Phe-Gly (leading to Phe-Sar), Phe-Ala, or Phe-Leu reduces their inhibitory potency by about 100-fold (Table 5.2 and Llorens *et al.* 1980) and a similar modification in enkephalins also leads to a marked loss in affinity for enkephalinase, since the inhibition constant of (MePhe[4], Met[5]) enkephalin is 40 times higher than that of (Met[5]) enkephalin (Fournié-Zaluski *et al.* 1979). In contrast, the inversion of the peptide bond of Phe-Ala reduces its inhibitory potency only about 10-fold (Table 5.2). The same modification introduced in Thiorphan, a thiol derivative of the dipeptide Phe-Gly, also leads to a modest loss in inhibitory potency, a feature attributed to the structural analogy between one isomer of the retropeptide and the 'natural' peptide (Roques *et al.* 1983).

5.3.1.5 *Influence of a free carboxylate on the P'_2 residue*

As for substrates, the presence of a free terminal carboxylate in P'_2 has a favourable influence on the affinity of various inhibitors. Amidation of this group in Thiorphan (Malfroy and Schwartz 1982, 1984) or a close analogue (Gordon *et al.* 1983) reduces potency about 10-fold, whereas its replacement by a primary alcohol group in the latter compound leads to a drastic loss of potency. Even more marked losses result from amidation or esterification of this C-terminal carboxylate in the series of substituted *N*-carboxymethyl dipeptides (Mumford *et al.* 1982). These features are attributable to the interaction of the free carboxylate with a positively charged guanidinium group at the active site (Malfroy and Schwartz 1982a, 1985).

5.3.1.6 *Influence of stereochemistry*

The inversion of either the P'_1 or P'_2 residue in dipeptides markedly reduces their inhibitory potency (Llorens *et al.* 1980). However, quite unexpectedly, the absolute configuration of the P'_1 residue is of limited importance in thiol derivatives, suggesting that a good deal of flexibility exists within the region of the active site of enkephalinase (but not of ACE) encompassing the S'_1 subsite and zinc ion (Gordon *et al.* 1983; Fournié-Zaluski *et al.* 1984a; Mendelsohn *et al.* 1985).

5.3.1.7 *Influence of the Zn-binding group*

Amino acids or short peptides fulfilling the essential binding requirements of various metallopeptidases and containing terminal thiol, carboxyl, phosphoramidate, or hydroxamate zinc-coordinating groups constitute potent inhibitors of these enzymes (Cushman and Ondetti 1981). The first compound designed along the lines of this scheme was Thiorphan, which displays nanomolar potency towards enkephalinase, significantly less potency (by two orders of magnitude) towards ACE, and negligible potency towards aminopeptidases or thermolysin (Roques *et al.* 1980). It has been followed by a number of other thiol (Fournié-Zaluski *et al.* 1980, 1984a; Gordon *et al.* 1983), *N*-carboxymethyl (Fournié-Zaluski *et al.* 1980; Mumford *et al.* 1982), phosphoramidate (Altstein *et al.* 1981, 1983; Elliott *et al.* 1985) or hydroxamate (Blumberg *et al.* 1981; Hudgin *et al.* 1981; Roques *et al.* 1981; Bouboutou *et al.* 1984) derivatives, among which the best compounds also display nanomolar potencies towards enkephalinase. Some hydroxamate derivatives, among which kelatorphan (Fig. 5.1) seems the most potent, display negligible affinity towards ACE but significantly inhibit other metallopeptidases like dipeptidylaminopeptidases and, to a lesser extent, aminopeptidases (Blumberg *et al.* 1981; Bouboutou *et al.* 1984).

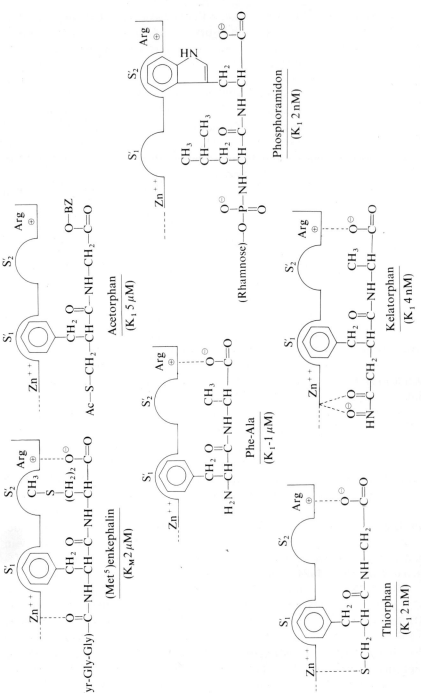

Fig. 5.1. A model of the active site of enkephalinase with modes of binding of substrates and inhibitors

The position of the Zn-binding group in inhibitors seems critical, the potency being optimal in compounds in which it is separated by a single carbon from the chiral centre of the P'_1 residue.

5.3.1.8   *Acetorphan, a parenterally active inhibitor*

The introduction of hydrophobic zinc-binding groups in dipeptides leads to inhibitors with a limited ability to penetrate the brain. For example the effects of Thiorphan on the CNS only occur at dosages as high as $50-100\,mg/kg^{-1}$ (Roques *et al.* 1980) and central effects of inhibitors were mostly established following their intracerebroventricular administration.

Recently acetorphan, a diester derivative of Thiorphan, was devised as a 'prodrug' (Lecomte *et al.* 1986a, b). Although this compound is approximately 1000 times less potent than Thiorphan on the purified enzyme, it becomes nearly as potent when preincubated with cerebral membranes where splitting of the thioester and ester groups occurs. This illustrates the importance of the Zn- and Arg-binding functions. Being a lipophilic molecule, acetorphan easily enters the brain following its parenteral administration and locally generates Thiorphan, thereby producing central effects at dosages around $1\,mg/kg^{-1}$.

5.3.2   Pharmacology of enkephalinase inhibitors

5.3.2.1   *Protection of endogenous neuropeptides by enkephalinase inhibitors*

Obviously, enkephalinase inhibitors prevent to some extent the hydrolysis of numerous exogenous messenger peptides by any biological preparation (e.g. synaptic membranes) containing the peptidase, but the critical issue is whether they do modify the metabolism of *endogenous* neuropeptides. This was first studied by evaluating the effect of inhibitors on recovery of endogenous neuropeptides released by depolarization of brain slices. This model has the important advantage of maintaining the tissue organization, namely the topographic relationship between neuronal stores of peptides and their potential synaptic inactivation systems. With either (Met^5)enkephalin or cholecystokinin, extensive hydrolysis takes place within the preparation: less than 20 per cent of the immunoreactivity released from K^+-depolarized tissues reaches the incubation medium in intact form. In the case of the enkephalins, Thiorphan (Patey *et al.* 1981) or other enkephalinase inhibitors (Altstein *et al.* 1983) enhance recovery about twofold, but complete recovery is obtained only in the co-presence of an aminopeptidase M inhibitor, suggesting a critical role for the two corresponding peptidase activities (De la Baume *et al.* 1983; Giros *et al.* 1986a, b). In contrast in the case of cholecystokinin, a rather good substrate for enkephalinase (Deschodt-Lanckman and Strosberg 1983), these peptidase inhibitors do not significantly improve the recovery, suggesting that other enzymes are involved (Zuzel *et al.* 1985).

In vivo, enkephalinase inhibitors do not significantly modify steady-state enkephalin levels in the brain, presumably because the alternative aminopeptidase metabolic pathway is implicated (Schwartz 1983). However, they markedly and rapidly reduce the cerebral levels of the tripeptide YGG, which appears to represent an endogenous opioid peptide metabolite (Llorens-Cortes *et al.* 1985a, b, 1986). This is suggested by its mainly extraneuronal localization in the brain, its regional distribution (which parallels that of enkephalin neurons), its decrease following lesions of these neurons, and its formation following release of enkephalins from depolarized brain slices (Llorens-Cortes *et al.* 1985a, 1986; Giros *et al.* 1986b). So far the effects of enkephalinase inhibitors on the metabolism of other *endogenous* neuropeptides have not been reported.

5.3.2.2   *Analgesic activity of enkephalinase inhibitors*

Thiorphan not only potentiates the antinociceptive activity of exogenous enkephalins but also decreases responses to various noxious stimuli in a naloxone-reversible manner (Roques *et al.* 1980; Chipkin *et al.* 1982a, b; Greenberg and O'Keefe 1982). Similar effects are observed with other enkephalinase inhibitors, including Phe-Ala (Borin *et al.* 1983), phosphoramidon (Rupreht *et al.* 1983), retro-thiorphan (Roques *et al.* 1983), kelatorphan (Fournié-Zaluski *et al.* 1984b), and acetorphan (Kayser and Guilbaud 1983; Lecomte *et al.* 1986a, b).

These effects are weaker than those of exogenous opioids, but become comparable when aminopeptidase activity is also inhibited (Zhang *et al.* 1982; Chaillet *et al.* 1983). They are also more selective, being only observed in some animal tests (e.g. hot-plate jump, writhing, vocalization) but not in others on which exogenous opioids are active (e.g. hot-plate licking, tail flick) (Kayser and Guilbaud 1983; Schwartz *et al.* 1982c; Costentin *et al.* 1986).

Because this dissociated pattern mirrors that of pronociceptive activity of opiate receptor antagonists, it may reflect the selective participation of endogenous opioids in the control of a limited number of nociceptive reflexes. In agreement with this view, Thiorphan becomes analgesic in the tail-flick test in rats previously submitted to a 'stressful' treatment purported to evoke endogenous opioid release (Chipkin *et al.* 1982a).

Presumably relevant is the fact that the firing of rat thalamus neurones, elicited by various noxious stimuli, is significantly prevented by parenteral acetorphan, an effect largely blocked by naloxone. However, the receptive field enlargement of 'non-noxious' thalamic neurones, also observed with the drug, is resistant to naloxone (Kayser *et al.* 1984). In contrast acetorphan does not affect the activity of dorsal horn convergent neurones in the anaesthetized rat (Villanueva *et al.* 1985).

The possibility that the antinociceptive activity of enkephalinase inhibitors is not related to inhibition of the enzyme has been raised in view of a lack of correlations between the two properties among a limited series of compounds (Murthy *et al.* 1984; Mendelsohn *et al.* 1985). However the fact that some weak inhibitors exerted antinociceptive actions, possibly through a non-opioid mechanism (naloxone reversibility was not tested), does not constitute strong evidence: obviously not all analgesics act through enkephalinase inhibition.

Interestingly, mice chronically treated with acetorphan for 2–3 weeks do not display tolerance to the antinociceptive activity of the drug (Lecomte *et al.* 1986a, b).

Finally, acetorphan was found in a controlled study to exert mild, but statistically significant, analgesia in a group of patients undergoing a painful neuroradiological test (Floras *et al.* 1983).

5.3.2.3 *Other actions of enkephalinase inhibitors*

Besides analgesia, enkephalinase inhibitors elicit a variety of opioid-like effects which are, in general, prevented by opiate–receptor antagonists. For instance they accelerate the turnover of striatal dopamine or cortical serotonin but decrease that of cortical noradrenalin (Wood 1982; Llorens and Schwartz 1984; Lecomte *et al.* 1986a, b). Phosphoramidon suppresses the increased susceptibility to seizure induced by REM sleep deprivation, whereas its effect is inverse in normal mice; both effects, which mimic those of exogenous opioids, are completely prevented by naloxone (Ukponmwan and Dzoljic 1984). Like opioid agents and tricyclic antidepressants, Thiorphan or acetorphan display naloxone-reversible 'antidepressant' properties in the mouse 'behavioural despair' test (Ben Natan *et al.* 1984; Lecomte *et al.* 1986a, b).

In cats, Thiorphan inhibits, in a naloxone-reversible manner, the reflex contractions of the urinary bladder (Hisamitsu and De Groat 1984). Acetorphan displays a pronounced, naloxone-reversible, antidiarrhoeal activity in the castor oil test (Lecomte *et al.* 1986b) and inhibits cholera-toxin-induced intestinal hypersecretion (L. Bueno, personal communication). However, it does not significantly affect the delay of intestinal transit, as evaluated in the charcoal meal test on which opiate receptor agonists are active (Marcais-Collado *et al.* 1987). Thiorphan (i.c.v.) enhances the colonic motor response to feeding (Fioramenti *et al.* 1985) and decreases gastric acid secretion (Chicau-Chovet *et al.* 1985).

In contrast with these various opioid-like effects, enkephalinase inhibitors do not elicit any marked cardiovascular or respiratory effects and are not recognized in the morphine-cue test (Buxton *et al.* 1982). In addition, chronically treated rodents challenged with naloxone do not develop the typical opiate withdrawal syndrome (Bean and Vaught 1984; Lecomte *et al.* 1986b).

5.3.2.4 *Therapeutic applications*

Little can be said on this matter at this early stage of utilization of enkephalinase inhibitors. An obvious potential application suggested by the first published clinical trial of acetorphan is as an analgesic agent (Floras *et al.* 1983). The analgesia observed in this trial was of limited extent, presumably because the second pathway in enkephalin breakdown, i.e. cleavage of the Tyr^1–Gly^2 bond by aminopeptidases (Schwartz 1983), was not inhibited. Co-inhibition of both pathways is presumably required to elicit strong analgesia.

In addition, since the opioid peptides, in brain and in peripheral tissues, have many actions other than control of pain messages (control of mood, autonomic or endocrine functions, etc.), it is likely that enkephalinase inhibitors may find wider applications, especially if it appears that they affect the metabolism of other neuronal or hormonal peptides.

5.4 Conclusions

Once more, the present review illustrates how selective inhibitors of a given enzyme might constitute powerful research tools to establish the functional role of this enzyme. In the case of enkephalinase they have allowed the establishment of its participation in the metabolism of opioid peptides. In addition, they have provided researchers with a new means of modifying enkephalinergic transmission in brain and peripheral organs. Moreover, there are already some indications that they may constitute a new class of pharmacological agents, with potential clinical applications in pain treatment and possibly other therapeutic fields.

References

Almenoff, J. and Orlowski, M. (1984). Biochemical and immunological properties of a membrane-bound brain metalloendopeptidase: comparison with thermolysin-like kidney neutral metalloendopeptidase. *J. Neurochem.*, **42**, 151–7.

Almenoff, J., Wilk, S., and Orlowski, M. (1981). Membrane bound pituitary metalloendopeptidase: apparent identity of enkephalinase. *Biochem. Biophys. Res. Commun.*, **102**, 206–14.

Altstein, M. and Vogel, Z. (1980). On the inactivation of enkephalin by enkephalinase. In *Neurotransmitters and their receptors* (ed. V. Z. Littauer), pp. 497–507. Wiley, New York.

Altstein, M., Blumberg, S., and Vogel, Z. (1981). Phosphoryl-Leu-Phe: a potent inhibitor of enkephalin degradation by enkephalinase *Eur. J. Pharmacol.*, **76**, 299–303.

Altstein, M., Bachar, E., Vogel, Z., and Blumberg, S. (1983). Protection of enkephalins from enzymatic degradation utilizing selective metal-chelating inhibitors. *Eur. J. Pharmacol.*, **91**, 353–61.

Altstein, M., Dudai, Y., and Vogel, Z. (1984). Enkephalin degrading enzymes are present in the electric organ of *Torpedo californica*. *FEBS Lett.*, **166**, 183–8.

Bean, A. J. and Vaught, J. L. (1984). Physical dependence produced by chronic intercerebroventricular infusion of D-Arg kyotorphin or thiorphan to rats. *Eur. J. Pharmacol.*, **105**, 333–7.

Ben Natan, L., Chaillet, P., Lecomte, J-M., Marcais, H., Uchida, G., and Costentin, J. (1984). Involvement of endogenous enkephalins in the mouse 'behavioural despair' test. *Eur. J. Pharmacol.*, **97**, 301–4.

Blumberg, S., Vogel, Z., and Altstein, M. (1981). Inhibition of enkephalin-degrading enzymes from rat brain and of thermolysin by amino acid hydroxamates. *Life Sci.*, **28**, 301–6.

Borin, G., Giusti, P., and Cima, L. (1983). Analgesic properties of N-terminal substituted phenylalanyl-alanine. *Life Sci.*, **33**, 1575–80.

Bouboutou, R., Waksman, G., Devin, J., Fournie-Zaluski, M-C., and Roques, B. P. (1984). Bidentate peptides: highly potent new inhibitors of enkephalin degrading enzymes. *Life Sci.*, **35**, 1023–30.

Buxton, D. A., Priestley, T., Shaw, J. S., and Turnbull, M. J. (1982). Failure of the enkephalinase inhibitor thiorphan to produce the narcotic cue. *Br. J. Pharmacol.*, **75**, 105.

Byers, L. D. and Wolfenden, R. (1973). Binding of the by product analogue benzylsuccinyl acid by carboxypeptidase A. *Biochemistry*, **12**, 2070–8.

Chaillet, P., Marcais-Collado, H., Costentin, J., Yi. C. C., De la Baume, S., and Schwartz, J.-C. (1983). Inhibition of enkephalin metabolism by, and antinociceptive activity of, bestatin, an aminopeptidase inhibitor. *Eur. J. Pharmacol.*, **86**, 329–36.

Checler, F., Emson, P. C., Vincent, J.-P., and Kitabgi, P. (1984). Inactivation of neurotensin by rat brain synaptic membranes. Cleavage at the Pro^{10}–Tyr^{11} bond by endopeptidase 24.11 (enkephalinase) and a peptidase different from proline-endopeptidase. *J. Neurochem.*, **43**, 1295–301.

Chicau-Chovet, M., Dubrasquet, M., Chariot, J., Lecomte, J.-M., and Roze, C. (1985). Enkephalinase inhibitors decrease pentagastrin-stimulated gastric acid secretion in rats and cats. Possible involvement of endogenous enkephalins. In *Regulatory peptides in digestive, nervous and endocrine systems* (ed. M. J. M. Lewin and S. Bonfils), pp. 345–9. Elsevier, Amsterdam.

Chipkin, R. E., Latranyi, M. B., and Iorio, L. C. (1982a). Potentiation of stress-induced analgesia (SIA) by thiorphan and its block by naloxone. *Life Sci.*, **31**, 1189–92.

Chipkin, R. E., Iorio, L. C., Barnett, A., Berger, J., and Billard, W. (1982b). *In vitro* and *in vivo* effects of thiorphan: an inhibitor of enkephalinase A. *Adv. Biochem. Psychopharmacol.*, **33**, 235–42.

Connelly, J. C., Skidgel, R. A., Schulz, W. W., Johnson, A. R., and Erdos, E. G. (1985). Neutral endopeptidase 24.11 in human neutrophils: cleavage of chemotatic peptide. *Proc. Nat. Acad. Sci. USA*, **82**, 8737–41.

Costentin, J., Vlaiculescu, A., Chaillet, P., Ben Natan, L., Aveaux, D., and Schwartz, J.-C. (1986). Dissociated effects of inhibitors of enkephalin metabolising peptidases or naloxone on various nociceptive responses. *Eur. J. Pharmacol.*, **123**, 37–44.

Cushman, D. W. and Ondetti, M. A. (1981). Specific inhibitors of zinc metallopeptidases. In *Topics in molecular pharmacology* (ed. A. S. V. Burgen and G. C. K. Roberts), pp. 127–68. Elsevier, Amsterdam.

De La Baume, S., Patey, G., and Schwartz, J.-C. (1981). Subcellular distribution of enkephalin-dipeptidyl carboxypeptidase (enkephalinase) in rat brain. *Neuroscience*, **6**, 315–21.

De la Baume, S., Yi, C. C., Schwartz, J.-C., Chaillet, P., Marcais-Collado, H., and Costentin, J. (1983). Participation of both 'enkephalinase' and aminopeptidase activities in the metabolism of endogenous enkephalins. *Neuroscience*, **8**, 143–51.

Deschodt-Lanckman, M. and Strosberg, D. (1983). *In vitro* degradation of the C-terminal octapeptide of cholecystokinin by "enkephalinase A". *FEBS Lett.*, **152**, 109–13.

Elliott, R. L., Marks, N., Berg, M. J., and Portoghese, P. S. (1985). Synthesis and biological evaluation of phosphoramidate peptide inhibitors of enkephalinase and angiotensin-converting enzyme. *J. Med. Chem.*, **28**, 1208–16.

Erdös, E. G., Schulz, W. W., Gafford, J. T., and Defeudini, R. (1985). Neutral metalloendopeptidase in human male genital tract. Comparison to angiotensin-I-converting enzyme. *Lab. Invest.*, **52**, 437–47.

Fioramenti, J., Bueno, L., and Fargeas, M. J. (1985). Enhancement of colonic motor response to feeding by central endogenous opiates in the dog. *Life Sci.*, **36**, 2509–14.

Floras, P., Bidabe, A. M., Caille, J. M., Simonnet, G., Lecomte, J.-M., and Sabathie, M. (1983). Double-blind study of effects of enkephalinase inhibitor on adverse reactions to myelography. *Am. J. Neuroradiol.*, **4**, 653–5.

Florentin, D., Sassi, A., and Roques, B. P. (1984). A highly sensitive fluorometric assay for 'enkephalinase': a neutral metalloendopeptidase that releases tyrosine–glycine–glycine from enkephalins. *Anal. Biochem.*, **141**, 62–9.

Fournié-Zaluski, M. C., Perdrisot, R., Gacel, G., Swerts, J. P., Roques, B. P., and Schwartz, J.-C. (1979). Inhibitory potency of various peptides on enkephalinase activity from mouse striatum. *Biochem. Biophys. Res. Commun.*, **91**, 130–35.

Fournié-Zaluski, M.-C., Llorens, C., Gacel, G., Malfroy, B., Swerts, J. P., Lecomte, J.-M., Schwartz, J.-C., and Roques, B. P. (1980). Synthesis and biological properties of highly potent enkephalinase inhibitors. In *Peptides* (ed. K. Brunfeldt), pp. 476–81. Scriptor, Copenhagen.

Fournié-Zaluski, M.-C., Lucas, E., Waksman, G., and Roques, B. P. (1984a). Differences in the structural requirements for selective interaction with neutral metalloendopeptidase (enkephalinase) or angiotensin-converting enzyme. Molecular investigation by use of new thiol inhibitors. *Eur. J. Biochem.*, **139**, 267–74.

Fournié-Zaluski, M.-C., Chaillet, P., Bouboutou, R., Coulaud, A., Cherot, P., Waksman, G., Costentin, J., and Roques, B. P. (1984b). Analgesic effects of kelatorphan, a new highly potent inhibitor of multiple enkephalin degrading enzymes. *Eur. J. Pharmacol.*, **102**, 525–8.

Fulcher, I. S. and Kenny, A. J. (1983). Proteins of the kidney microvillar membrane. The amphipathic forms of endopeptidase purified from pig kidneys. *Biochem. J.*, **211**, 743–53.

Fulcher, I. S., Matsas, R., Turner, A. J., and Kenny, A. J. (1982). Kidney neutral endopeptidase and the hydrolysis of enkephalin by synaptic membranes show similar sensitivity to inhibitors. *Biochem. J.*, **203**, 519–22.

Gafford, J. T., Skidgel, R. A., Erdos, E. G., and Hersh, L. B. (1983). Human kidney 'enkephalinase': a neutral metalloendopeptidase that cleaves active peptides. *Biochemistry*, **22**, 3265–71.

Gee, N. S., Bowes, M. A., Buck, P., and Kenny, A. J. (1985). An immunoradiometric assay for endopeptidase 24.11 shows it to be a widely distributed enzyme in pig tissues. *Biochem. J.*, **22**, 119–26.

Giros, B., Gros, C., Solhonne, B., and Schwartz, J.-C. (1986a). Characterization of aminopeptidases responsible for the inactivation of endogenous (Met[5]) enkephalin in brain slices using peptidase inhibitors and aminopeptidase M antibodies. *Mol. Pharmacol.*, **29**, 281–7.

Giros, B., Llorens-Cortes, C., Gros, C., and Schwartz, J.-C. (1986b) The endogenous tripepetide Tyr-Gly-Gly as a possible metabolite of opioid peptides in rat brain: identification, regional distribution, effect of lesions and formation in depolarised slices. *Peptides*, **7**, 669–78.

Gordon, E. M., Cushman, D. W., Tung, R., Cheung, H. S., Wang, F. L., and Delaney, N. G. (1983). Rat brain enkephalinase: characterization of the active site using mercaptopropanoyl amino acid inhibitors, and comparison with angiotensin-converting enzyme. *Life. Sci.*, **33**, 113–6.

Gorenstein, C. and Snyder, S. H. (1979). Two distinct enkephalinases: solubilization, partial purification and separation from angiotensin-converting enzyme. *Life Sci.*, **25**, 2065–70.

Greenberg, R. and O'Keefe, E. H. (1982). Thiorphan potentiation of stress-induced analgesia in the mouse. *Life Sci.*, **31**, 1185–8.

Hersh, L. B. (1982). Degradation of enkephalins: the search for an enkephalinase. *Mol. Cell. Biochem.*, **47**, 35–43.

Hersh, L. B. (1984). Reaction of opioid peptides with neutral endopeptidase ('enkephalinase'). *J. Neurochem.*, **43**, 487–93.

Hisamitsu, T. and De Groat, W. C. (1984). The inhibitory effect of opioid peptides and morphine applied intrathecally and intracerebroventricularly on the micturition reflex in the cat. *Brain Res.*, **298**, 51–65.

Holmes, M. A. and Matthews, B. W. (1981). Binding of hydroxamic acid inhibitors to crystalline thermolysin suggests a pentacoordinate zinc intermediate in catalysis. *Biochemistry*, **20**, 6912–20.

Hudgin, R. L., Charleson, S. E., Zimmerman, M., Mumford, R., and Wood, P. L. (1981). Enkephalinase: selective peptide inhibitors. *Life Sci.*, **29**, 2953–601.

Kayser, V. and Guilbaud, G. (1983). The analgesic effects of morphine, but not those of the enkephalinase inhibitor thiorphan, are enhanced in arthritic rats. *Brain Res.*, **267**, 131–8.

Kayser, V., Benoist, J.-M., Gautron, M., and Guilbaud, G. (1984). Effects of ES 52, an enkephalinase inhibitor, on responses of ventrobasal thalamic neurons in rats. *Peptides*, **5**, 1159–65.

Kenny, A. J. (1977). Proteinases associated with cell membranes. In *Proteinase in mammalian cells and tissues* (ed. A. J. Barrett), pp. 393–444. Elsevier, Amsterdam.

Kerr, M. A. and Kenny, A. J. (1974). The molecular weight and properties of a neutral metallo-endopeptidase from rabbit kidney brush border. *Biochem. J.*, **137**, 489–95.

Kester, W. R. and Matthews, B. W. (1977). Crystallographic study of the binding of dipeptide inhibitors to thermolysin: implications for the mechanism of catalysis. *Biochemistry*, **16**, 2506–16.

Lecomte, J.-M., Costentin, J., Vlaiculescu, A., Chaillet, P., Marcais-Collado, H., Llorens-Cortes, C., Leboyer, M., and Schwartz, J.-C. (1986a). Pharmacology of acetorphan and other 'enkephalinase' inhibitors. In *Innovative approaches in drug research* (ed. A. F. Harms), pp. 315–30. Elsevier, Amsterdam.

Lecomte, J.-M., Costentin, J., Vlaiculescu, A., Chaillet, P., Marcais-Collado, H., Llorens-Cortes, C., Leboyer, M., and Schwartz, J.-C. (1986b). Pharmacological properties of acetorphan, a parenterally active 'enkephalinase' inhibitor. *J. Pharmacol. Exp. Ther.*, **237**, 937–44.

Lentzen, H. and Palenker, J. (1983). Localization of the thiorphan-sensitive endopeptidase, termed enkephalinase A, on glial cells. *FEBS Lett.*, **153**, 93–7.

Llorens-Cortes, C. and Schwartz, J.-C. (1981). Enkephalinase activity in rat peripheral organs. *Eur. J. Pharmacol.*, **69**, 113–6.

Llorens-Cortes, C. and Schwartz, J.-C. (1984). Changes in turnover of cerebral monoamines following inhibition of enkephalin metabolism by Thiorphan and bestatin. *Eur. J. Pharmacol.*, **104**, 369–74.

Llorens-Cortes, C., Gacel, G., Swerts, J. P., Perdrisot, R., Fournié-Zaluski, M. C., Schwartz, J.-C., and Roques, B. P. (1980). Rational design of enkephalinase inhibitors: substrate specificity of enkephalinase studied from inhibitory potency of various dipeptides. *Biochem. Biophys. Res. Commun.*, **96**, 1710–16.

Llorens-Cortes, C., Malfroy, B., Schwartz, J.-C., Gacel, G., Roques, B. P., Roy, J., Morgat, J.-L., Javoy-Agid, F., and Agid Y. (1982). Enkephalin dipeptidyl carboxypeptidase (enkephalinase) activity: selective radioassay, properties and regional distribution in human brain. *J. Neurochem.*, **39**, 1081–9.

Llorens-Cortes, C., Gros, C., and Schwartz, J.-C. (1985a). Study of endogenous Tyr–Gly–Gly, a putative enkephalin metabolite, in mouse brain: validation of radioimmunoassay, localisation and effects of peptidase inhibitors. *Eur. J. Pharmacol.*, **119**, 183–91.

Llorens-Cortes, C., Schwartz, J.-C. and Gros, C. (1985b). Detection of the tripeptide Tyr–Gly–Gly, a putative enkephalin metabolite in brain, using a sensitive radioimmunoassay. *FEBS Lett.*, **189**, 325–8.

Llorens-Cortes, C., Gros, C., and Schwartz, J.-C. (1986). Steady-state level and turnover rate of the tripeptide Tyr–Gly–Gly as indexes of striatal enkephalin release *in vivo* and their reduction during pentobarbital anesthesia. *Proc. Nat. Acad. Sci. USA*, **83**, 6226–30.

McKelvy, J. F (1983). Enzymatic degradation of brain peptides. In *Brain peptides* (ed. D. T. Krieger, M. J. Brownstein, and J. B. Martin), pp. 117–34. Wiley, New York

Malfroy, B. and Schwartz, J.-C. (1982a). Properties of 'enkephalinase' from rat kidney: comparison of dipeptidylcarboxypeptidase and endopeptidase activities. *Biochem. Biophys. Res. Commun.*, **106**, 276–85.

Malfroy, B. and Schwartz, J.-C. (1982b). Purification and substrate specificity of rat kidney 'enkephalinase'. *Life Sci.*, **31**, 1745–8.

Malfroy, B. and Schwartz, J.-C. (1984). Enkephalinase from rat kidney. Purification, characterization, and study of substrate specificity. *J. Biol. Chem.*, **259**, 14365–70.

Malfroy, B. and Schwartz, J.-C. (1985). Comparison of dipeptidyl carboxypeptidase and endopeptidase activities in the three enkephalin-hydrolysing peptidases: "angiotensin-converting enzyme", thermolysin and 'enkephalinase'. *Biochem. Biophys. Res. Commun.*, **130**, 372–7.

Malfroy, B., Swerts, J.-P., Guyon, A., Roques, B. P., and Schwartz, J.-C. (1978). High affinity enkephalin-degrading peptidase in brain is increased after morphine. *Nature (London)*, **276**, 523–6.

Malfroy, B., Swerts, J.-P., Llorens, C., and Schwartz, J.-C. (1979). Regional distribution of a high-affinity enkephalin-degrading peptidase ('enkephalinase') and effects of lesions suggest localization in the vicinity of opiate receptors in brain. *Neurosci. Lett.*, **11**, 329–34.

Marcais-Collado, H., Uchida, G., Costentin, J., Schwartz, J.-C., and Lecomte, J.-M. (1987). Naloxone-reversible antidiarrheal effects of enkephalinase inhibitors. *Eur. J. Pharmacol.*, **144**, 125–32.

Matsas, R., Fulcher, I. S., Kenny, J. A., and Turner, A. J. (1983). Substance P and Leu enkephalin are hydrolyzed by an enzyme in pig caudate synaptic membranes that is identical with the endopeptidase of kidney microvilli. *Proc. Nat. Acad. Sci. USA*, **80**, 3111–5.

Mendelsohn. L. G., Johnson, B. G., Scott, W. L., and Frederickson, R. C. A. (1985). Thiorphan and analogs: lack of correlation between potency to inhibit 'enkephalinase A' *in vitro* and analgesic potency *in vivo*. *J. Pharmacol. Exp. Ther.*, **234**, 386–90.

Mumford, R. A., Pierschala, P. A., Strauss, A. W., and Zimmerman, M. (1981). Purification of a membrane-bound metalloendopeptidase from porcine kidney that degrades peptide hormones. *Proc. Nat. Acad. Sci. USA*, **78**, 6623–7.

Mumford, R. A., Zimmerman, M., Ten Broeke, J., Taub, D., Joshua, H., Rothrock, J. W., Hirshfield, J. M., Springer, J. P., and Patchett, A. A. (1982). Inhibition of porcine kidney 'enkephalinase' by substituted-*N*-carboxymethyl dipeptides. *Biochem. Biophys. Res. Commun.*, **109**, 1303–9.

Murthy, L. R., Glick, S. D., Almenoff, J. A., Wilk, S., and Orlowski, M. (1984). Inhibitors of an enkephalin degrading membrane-bound metalloendopeptidase: analgesic properties and effects on striatal enkephalin levels. *Eur. J. Pharmacol.*, **102**, 305–13.

Orlowski, M. and Wilk, S. (1981). Purification and properties of a membrane-bound metalloendopeptidase from bovine pituitaries. *Biochemistry*, **20**, 4942–50.

Palenker, J., Lentzen, H., and Brandt, V. (1984). Enkephalin degradation by enkephalinergic neuroblastoma cells. Involvement of angiotensin-converting enzyme. *Naunyn Schmiedebergs. Arch. Pharmacol.*, **325**, 214–7.

Patey, G., De la Baume, S., Schwartz, J.-C., Gross, C., Roques, B. P., Fournié-Zaluski, M. C., and Soroca-Lucas, E. (1981). Selective protection of methionine enkephalin released from brain slices by enkephalinase inhibition. *Science*, **212**, 1153–5.

Pollard, H., De la Baume, S., Bouthenet, M. L., and Schwartz, J.-C. (1987). Characterisation of two probes for the localisation of enkephalinase in rat brain: [^{3}H] Thiorphan and a [^{125}I] labelled, monoclonal antibody. *Eur. J. Pharmacol.*, **133**, 155–60.

Poszgay, M., Michaud, C. and Orlowski, M. (1985). The active site of endopeptidase-24.11: substrate and inhibitor studies. *Biochem. Soc. Trans.*, **13**, 44–7.

Quiocho, F. A. and Lipscomb, W. N. (1971). Carboxypeptidase A: a protein and an enzyme. *Adv. Protein Chem.*, **25**, 1–48.

Relton, J. M., Gee, N. S., Matsas, R., Turner, A. J., and Kenny, A. J. (1983). Purification of endopeptidase-24.11 ('enkephalinase') from pig brain by immunoadsorbent chromatography. *Biochem. J.*, **215**, 519–23.

Roques, B. P., Fournié-Zaluski, M. C., Soroca, E., Lecomte, J.-M., Malfroy, B., Llorens, C., and Schwartz, J.-C. (1980). The enkephalinase inhibitor thiorphan shows antinociceptive activity in mice. *Nature (London)*, **288**, 286–8.

Roques, B. P., Schwartz, J.-C., and Lecomte, J.-M. (1981). Nouveaux dérivés d'aminoacides et leur application thérapeutique, French Patent. No. 812 3488.

Roques, B. P., Lucas-Soroca, E., Chaillet, P., Costentin, J., and Fournié-Zaluski, M. C. (1983). Complete differentiation between enkephalinase and angiotensin-converting enzyme inhibition by retro-thiorphan. *Proc. Nat. Acad. Sci. USA*, **80**, 3178–82.

Rupreht, J., Ukponmwan, O. E., Admiraal, P. V., and Dzoljic, M. R. (1983). Effect of phosphoramidon—a selective enkephalinase inhibitor—on nociception and behaviour. *Neurosci. Lett.*, **41**, 331–5.

Rush, R. S. and Hersh, L. B. (1982). Multiple molecular forms of rat brain enkephalinase. *Life. Sci.*, **31**, 445–51.

Rush, R. S., Mitas, M., Powers, J. C., Tanaka, T., and Hersh, L. B. (1984). Fluorogenic substrates for the enkephalin-degrading neutral endopeptidase (enkephalinase). *Archs. Biochem. Biophys.*, **231**, 390–9.

Schechter, I. and Berger, A. (1967). On the size of the active site in proteases. *Biochem. Biophys. Res. Commun.*, **27**, 157–62.

Schwartz, J.-C. (1983). Metabolism of enkephalins and the concept of neuropeptidase. *Trends Neurosci.*, **6**, 45–8.

Schwartz, J.-C., Malfroy, B., and De La Baume, S. (1981). Biological inactivation of enkephalins and the role of enkephalin-dipeptidyl-carboxypeptidase ('enkephalinase') as neuropeptidase. *Life Sci.*, **29**, 1715–40.

Schwartz, J.-C., De La Baume, S., Llorens, C., Malfroy, B., Soroca, E., Fournié-Zaluski, M. C., Roques, B. P., Morgat, J.-L., Roy, J., Javoy-Agid, F., and Agid, Y. (1982a). Enkephalin dipeptidyl carboxypeptidase ('enkephalinase') assay, properties and distribution in human brain and exploration of the active site. *Adv. Biochem. Psychopharmacol.*, **33**, 225–34.

Schwartz, J.-C., De La Baume, S., Llorens, C., Malfroy, B., Soroca, E., Fournié-Zaluski, M. C., Roques, B. P., Morgat, J.-L., Roy, J., Lecomte, J.-M., Javoy-Agid, F., and Agid, Y. (1982b). Role of 'enkephalinase' (enkephalin dipeptidylcarboxypeptidase) as synaptic neuropeptidase. In *Advances in pharmacology and therapeutics* (ed. H. Yoshida, Y. Hagihara, and S. Ebashi), Vol. 1, pp. 17–27. Pergamon Press, Oxford.

Schwartz, J.-C., De La Baume, S., Yi, C. C., Chaillet, P., Marcais-Collado, H., and Costentin, J. (1982c). Enkephalin metabolism in brain and its inhibition. *Prog. Neuropsychopharmacol. Biol. Psychiat.*, **6**, 665–71.

Schwartz, J.-C., Giros, B., Gros, C., Llorens, C., and Malfroy, B. (1984). Metabolism of enkephalins and its inhibition. In *Proceedings of the Ninth IUPHAR Congress on Pharmacology* (ed. J. F. Mitchell, W. Paton, and P. Turner), Vol. 3, pp. 277–283, Macmillan, Oxford.

Schwartz, J.-C., Costentin, J., and Lecomte, J.-M. (1985a). Pharmacology of enkephalinase inhibitors. *Trends Pharmacol. Sci.*, **6**, 472–6.

Schwartz, J.-C., Gros, C., Giros, B., Llorens, C., Malfroy, B., Rose, C., Zuzel, K., Pollard, H., and Pachot, I. (1985b). Ectopeptidases responsible for the inactivation of enkephalins. In *Cellular biology of ectoenzymes* (ed. G. W. Kreutzberg, M. Reddington, and H. Zimmerman), pp. 272–84. Springer, Berlin.

Spillantini, M. G., Fanciullacci, M., Michelacci, S. and Sicuteri, F. (1984). Enkephalinase activity in both plasma and CSF of patients with idiopathic headache: effect of captopril administration. *IRCSJ. Med. Sci.*, **12**, 102–3.

Swerts, J.-P., Perdrisot, R., Malfroy, B., and Schwartz, J.-C. (1979a). Is 'enkephalinase' identical with "angiotensin-converting enzyme"? *Eur. J. Pharmacol.*, **53**, 209–10.

Swerts, J.-P., Perdrisot, R., Patey, G., De La Baume, S., and Schwartz, J.-C. (1979b). Enkephalinase is distinct from brain 'angiotensin-converting enzyme'. *Eur. J. Pharmacol.*, **57**, 279–81.

Turner, A. J. and Dowdall, M. J. (1984). The metabolism of neuropeptides. Both phosphoramidon- and captopril-sensitive metallopeptidases are present in the electric organ of *Torpedo marmorata. Biochem. J.*, **224**, 255–9.

Turner, A. J., Matsas, R., and Kenny, A. J. (1985). Are there neuropeptide-specific peptidases? *Biochem. Pharmacol.*, **34**, 1347–56.

Ukponmwan, O. E. and Dzoljic, M. R. (1984). Enkephalinase inhibition antagonizes the increased susceptibility to seizure induced by REM sleep deprivation. *Psychopharmacology*, **83**, 229–32.

Villanueva, L., Cadden, S., Chitour, D., and Le Bars, D. (1985). Failure of ES 52, a highly potent enkephalinase inhibitor, to affect nociceptive transmission by rat dorsal horn convergent neurones. *Brain Res.*, **333**, 156–60.

Waksman, G., Bouboutou, R., Devin, J., Besselièvre, R., Fournié-Zaluski, M. C., and Roques, B. P. (1985). Binding of the bidentate inhibitor ^{3}H HACBo–Gly to the rat brain neutral endopeptidase 'Enkephalinase'. *Biochem. Biophys. Res. Commun.*, **131**, 262–8.

Wood, P. L. (1982). Phasic enkephalinergic modulation of nigrostriatal dopamine metabolism: potentiation with enkephalinase inhibitors. *Eur. J. Pharmacol.*, **82**, 119–20.

Zhang, A. Z., Yang, H. Y., and Costa, E. (1982). Nociception, enkephalin content and dipeptidyl carboxypeptidase activity in brain of mice treated with exopeptidase inhibitors. *Neuropharmacology*, **21**, 625–30.

Zuzel, K. A., Rose, C., and Schwartz, J.-C. (1985). Assessment of the role of 'enkephalinase' in cholecyctokinin inactivation. *Neuroscience*, **15**, 149–58.

6

Monoamine oxidase inhibitors

Ian A. McDonald, Philippe Bey, and

Michael G. Palfreyman

6.1 Introduction

Clinically useful inhibitors of monoamine oxidase (MAO, EC 1.4.3.4., mono-amine:O_2 oxido-reductase—flavin-containing) have a long history, which began with astute clinical observations of the central mood-elevating effects of iproniazid (Selikoff et al. 1952). The subsequent association of these effects to the inhibition of MAO (Zeller et al. 1952) heralded the development of numerous inhibitors that were enthusiastically proclaimed for the treatment of depression. This popularity, however, was short-lived when the appearance of serious side-effects, coupled with the introduction of tricyclic antidepressants, rapidly relegated them to drugs of second choice.

The recent resurgence of interest in the design, development, and clinical evaluation of MAO inhibitors can be attributed to a better understanding of the enzyme's characteristics, largely due to the development of very selective in-hibitors (Fowler and Ross 1984). Well-controlled clinical studies with these selective inhibitors have shown them to be useful in a variety of affective disorders (Quitkin et al. 1979) and, in certain cases, in Parkinson's disease (see Rinne 1983). Despite these encouraging results, which have excited specialists in the field, the one factor that still makes clinicians wary of using these drugs is the risk of dangerous hypertensive reaction with tyramine-containing foods—the so-called 'cheese effect'. As a result, most new developments in the area have been directed towards ways of overcoming this potentially serious side-effect. The purpose of this chapter is to examine research efforts that have been directed towards this goal.

The breakthrough came in the early 1970s when it was suggested (Johnston 1968; Knoll and Magyar 1972) and later confirmed (Cawthorn and Breakefield 1979; Denney et al. 1982) that MAO is in fact two closely related enzymes, designated type A (clorgyline sensitive) and type B (L-deprenyl sensitive). A complete definition of MAO-A and B can be found in Murphy et al. (1984). Once the distribution of each form of the enzyme had been established, it became possible to rationalize both the therapeutic efficacy of these inhibitors and the 'cheese effect'. In humans, MAO-A is predominantly located in the outer mitochondrial membrane of aminergic neurones but is also found in the gut and placenta, while MAO-B is the form found exclusively in platelets and is the major form present in liver and glial cells (Murphy et al. 1984). Circumstances leading to the 'cheese effect', therefore, are believed to arise when peripheral MAO-A is inhibited, especially the enzyme located in the gastrointestinal tract and the sympathetic nerve terminals (Ilett et al. 1980).

Currently, basic research aimed at finding clinically trouble-free MAO inhibitors broadly encompasses four areas of activity. Historically, the first approach has been the development of selective inhibitors of MAO-B. The rationale for the therapeutic use of such inhibitors will be presented later in the chapter. Another objective has been to develop short-acting, reversible MAO-A selective inhibitors. The concept behind this idea is that with reversible inhibitors, in contrast to irreversible ones such as clorgyline, dangerous interactions with food would be minimal and short-lasting. A third approach has been to combine an inhibitor of amine uptake with an MAO inhibitor (either in one molecule or as separate entities). Tyramine has to be taken up into nerve terminals by the amine pump before it can release noradrenalin, so blocking its uptake would theoretically prevent the 'cheese reaction'. Finally, the ideal approach for treating mental disease with MAO inhibitors would be to develop site-selective inhibitors, especially those with preference for the brain. This chapter will focus primarily on MAO-B and site-selective inhibitors, although comments will be directed towards the combined use of uptake/MAO inhibitors. Reversible MAO type A inhibitors have been the subject of many reviews (see Tipton et al. 1984; Fowler and Ross 1984; Strolin Benedetti and Dostert 1985) and will only be discussed here in connection with site selectivity.

6.2   Selective MAO-B inhibitors

6.2.1   Pharmacology and therapeutic potential in Parkinson's disease

When L-deprenyl was reported by Knoll and Magyar (1972) to inhibit selectively the B form of MAO, the therapeutic potential of such a compound appeared somewhat limited because the two monoamines most likely to be implicated in depression, noradrenalin and serotonin, were believed to be preferentially degraded by MAO-A (Murphy *et al.* 1984). Subsequently it was shown by Sandler's group (Glover *et al.* 1977) and confirmed by others (Reynolds *et al.* 1980; Riederer *et al.* 1981) that dopamine is predominantly metabolized by MAO-B in humans, a finding that rationalized the use of a selective MAO-B inhibitor in the dopamine deficiency syndrome, Parkinson's disease. Although the consequences of the 80–90 per cent reduction in the dopamine content of the basal ganglia of Parkinsonian patients are not amenable to improvement by L-deprenyl therapy alone (Csanda *et al.* 1983), when combined with L-dopa and carbidopa a large number of clinical trials have revealed that there is a beneficial effect on the pharmacokinetics of the dopamine formed from L-dopa (Schachter *et al.* 1980; Presthus and Hajba 1983). L-Deprenyl is particularly useful in end-of-dose dyskinesia and in the control of the on–off phenomenon frequently seen in patients receiving L-dopa/carbidopa medication (Wajsbort *et al.* 1982; see Rinne 1983).

The aetiological events which eventually result in Parkinson's disease have not yet been unravelled. In this context, the recent revelation that 1-methyl-4-phenyl-1,2,3,6-tetrahydropyridine (MPTP), a contaminant of a pethidine-related 'designer drug', is transformed by MAO-B into a neurotoxin that selectively destroys nigrostriatal dopamine neurones, resulting in clinical signs that are indistinguishable from Parkinson's disease (see Burks 1985) has attracted considerable attention. The MAO-B selective inhibitors L-deprenyl, pargyline (Cohen *et al.* 1985), AGN 1135 (Heikkila *et al.* 1985), RO 16-6491 (Kettler *et al.* 1985), and MDL 72145 (Bradbury *et al.* 1986) have been used to block the metabolic activation of MPTP in animals. The interest generated by the biochemical and pathological effects of MPTP has resurrected the dormant hypothesis that the neuronal degeneration seen in Parkinson's disease is due to environmental factors. The observation that L-deprenyl increases the life expectancy of Parkinsonian patients (Birkmayer *et al.* 1983) and the prediction that MAO-B inhibition can improve the quality of life in senescence (Knoll 1985) may also be relevant to this hypothesis.

6.2.2 Therapeutic potential in depression

Whereas L-deprenyl is now marketed in some countries for use in Parkinson's disease, its efficacy as an antidepressant is still controversial (Mendis *et al.* 1981). Although several studies have claimed a good response amongst depressed patients (Mann and Gershon 1980; Mendlewicz and Youdim 1983; Quitkin *et al.* 1984) we and others (Liebowitz *et al.* 1985) feel that the clinical data are difficult to interpret in terms of MAO-B inhibition alone because of the relatively high non-selective doses of inhibitor used in the studies. For instance, post-mortem analyses of brain from patients who only received the usual low therapeutic regimen of 10 mg day^{-1} of L-deprenyl for treatment of their Parkinson's disease showed greater than 70 per cent MAO-A inhibition in numerous brain regions after chronic inhibitor therapy (Riederer and Reynolds 1980). Several studies in depression have used considerably higher doses. To complicate matters further, the fact that L-deprenyl is rapidly and quantitatively metabolized to amphetamine and methamphetamine must be taken into consideration (Reynolds *et al.* 1979; Karoum *et al.* 1982; Elsworth *et al.* 1982). In another approach, Birkmayer and Reiderer and their group (Birkmayer *et al.* 1984) recently demonstrated in a large open study that L-deprenyl (10 mg day^{-1}) combined with phenylalanine (250 mg day^{-1}) resulted in improvement in 70 per cent of the depressed patients. This bioprecursor approach, which relies on L-deprenyl to prevent the degradation of increased amounts of phenethylamine generated from the amino acid, merits further evaluation in a double-blind study. A similar study has been reported with 5-hydroxytryptophan and L-deprenyl (Mendelwicz and Youdim 1981), though the logic of using a selective MAO-B inhibitor with a bioprecursor that results in the formation of a predominantly MAO A-substrate is not immediately apparent.

So far as the 'cheese effect' is concerned, selective inhibitors of MAO-B appear to be very safe. The outstanding feature of the many studies conducted with L-deprenyl is the clear demonstration that MAO-B inhibition does not *per se* lead to interactions with tyramine or tyramine-containing foods (Elsworth *et al.* 1978; Pickar *et al.* 1981). This has been confirmed in volunteers with the MAO B-selective allylamine, MDL 72145 (Alken *et al.* 1984).

6.2.3   Design of MAO-B selective inhibitors

All potent, irreversible inactivators of MAO fall into well-defined chemical classes, the major ones being propargylamines, fluoroallylamines, cyclopropylamines, allenic amines, and hydrazines. These compounds can be considered as enzyme-activated, mechanism-based, K_{cat}, or suicide inhibitors of MAO. This classification indicates that the compounds *per se* are chemically inert, but once accepted by MAO as pseudo substrates oxidation begins as usual, leading to the formation of chemically reactive intermediates within the active centre of the enzyme. Subsequent covalent interaction with an enzyme or cofactor (flavin) residue leads to irreversible inhibition. These substances usually inactivate MAO-A and MAO-B equally well, though in some cases selectivity for one form or the other is apparent. The most important MAO-B selective enzyme-activated inhibitors are listed in Fig. 6.1 and Table 6.1.

Recently two reversible inhibitors, (*R*)-MD 240928 (Dostert *et al.* 1983) and RO 16-6491 (Kettler *et al.* 1985), which show selectivity for MAO-B, have been described. Interestingly, the enantiomer of MD 240928, (*S*)-MD 240931, is an irreversible inhibitor *in vivo*.

Of the many hundreds of MAO inhibitors reported in the literature very few have actually been rationally designed. Once the potential of the hydrazine and later the propargyl group to inhibit MAO was described these groups were

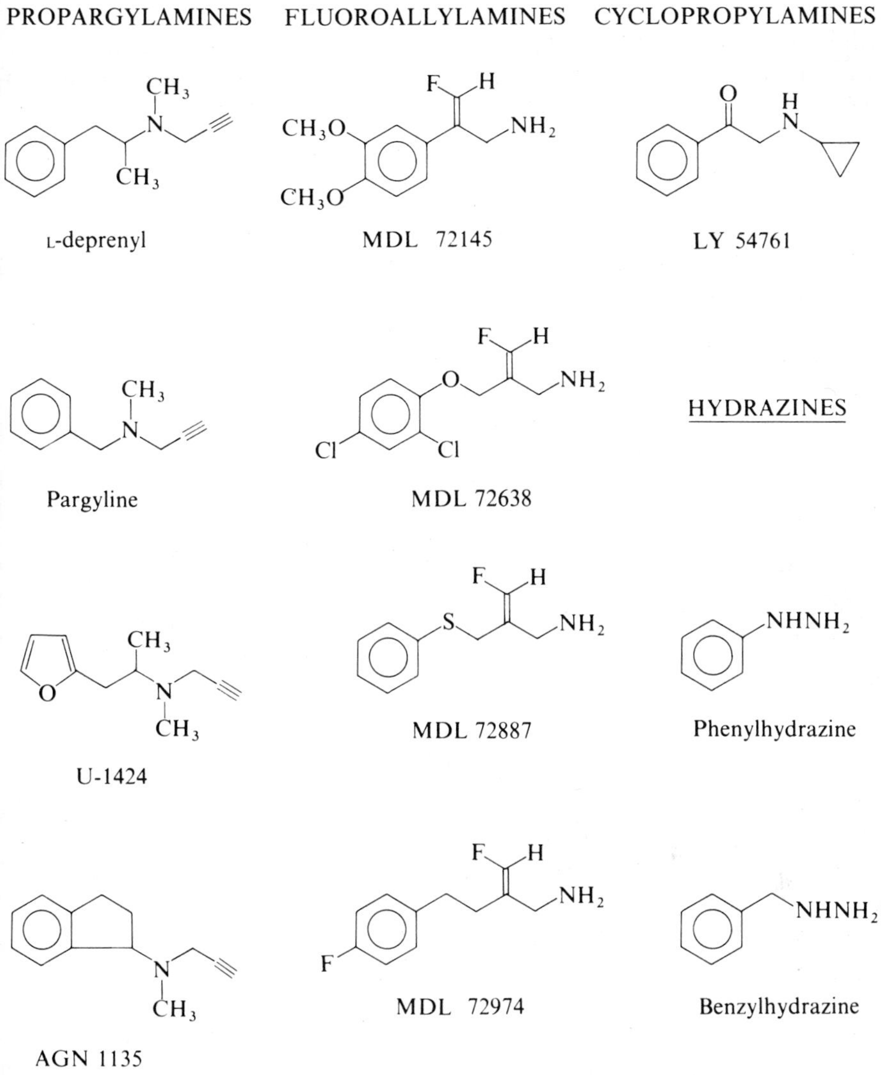

PROPARGYLAMINES   FLUOROALLYLAMINES   CYCLOPROPYLAMINES

L-deprenyl   MDL 72145   LY 54761

Pargyline   MDL 72638   HYDRAZINES

U-1424   MDL 72887   Phenylhydrazine

AGN 1135   MDL 72974   Benzylhydrazine

Fig. 6.1. MAO-B selective irreversible inhibitors.

incorporated randomly into a wide range of molecules often leading to active compounds and very occasionally to selective ones. One of these, the prototype MAO-B selective inhibitor, L-deprenyl, has been taken by Knoll and his group (Knoll *et al.* 1978) as a starting point for an extensive structure–activity relationship study; their results are summarized in Fig. 6.2.

A more recent approach has been to design rationally enzyme-activated inhibitors that are structural analogues of a known substrate of the enzyme.

Table 6.1 MAO-B selectivity of some irreversible inhibitors. Selectivity is determined either from the ratio of IC_{50} values (left hand column) or from the ratio of inhibitor concentrations required to inhibit both forms of the enzyme at the same rate (right hand column)

Name	$\dfrac{IC_{50}\ MAO\text{-}A}{IC_{50}\ MAO\text{-}B}$	Selectivity Time*	$\dfrac{[I]^A\dagger}{[I]^B}$	Reference
L-deprenyl	16	20	100	Kalir *et al.* (1981); McDonald *et al.* (1985)
Pargyline	80	20	—	Kalir *et al.* (1981)
AGN 1135	100	30	100	Tipton *et al.* (1982); Palfreyman, McDonald and Zreika (unpublished)
U-1424	>L-deprenyl			Knoll *et al.* (1978)
MDL 72145	43	15	100	McDonald *et al.* (1985)
MDL 72638	23	15	200	Palfreyman, McDonald and Zreika (unpublished)
MDL 72887	230	15	>1000	Palfreyman, McDonald and Zreika (unpublished)
MDL 72974	190	15	200	Palfreyman, McDonald and Zreiker (unpublished)
LY 54761	10	30	—	Murphy *et al.* (1978)
Phenylhydrazine	50	10	—	Roth *et al.* (1981)
Benzylhydrazine	15	10	—	Roth (1979)

* Pre-incubation time.

† Where $K_{app}^A = K_{app}^B$.

With an understanding of, or at least an educated guess at, the chemistry involved in the enzyme-catalysed reaction, the substrate is modified to incorporate a latent chemically reactive entity in the hope that the enzyme will accept the molecule as a pseudo-substrate as described above. The development of the fluoroallylamine inhibitors was based on such a premise (McDonald *et al.* 1985; Zreika *et al.* 1984), in which the potential of simple allylamine derivatives reported previously as weak inhibitors of the enzyme (Rando and Eigner 1977) was exploited. It was proposed that if the MAO-mediated oxidation process could be described by Scheme (6.1), the corresponding β-fluoromethylene analogues would inhibit the enzyme (Scheme 6.2). In this case such an approach turned out to be very fruitful. For example, the first compound prepared in the series, (E)-2-(3,4-dimethoxyphenyl)-3-fluoroallylamine (MDL 72145), was found to be a potent and selective MAO-B inhibitor. Of the approximately 70 compounds prepared in this series to date, many have been found to be potent

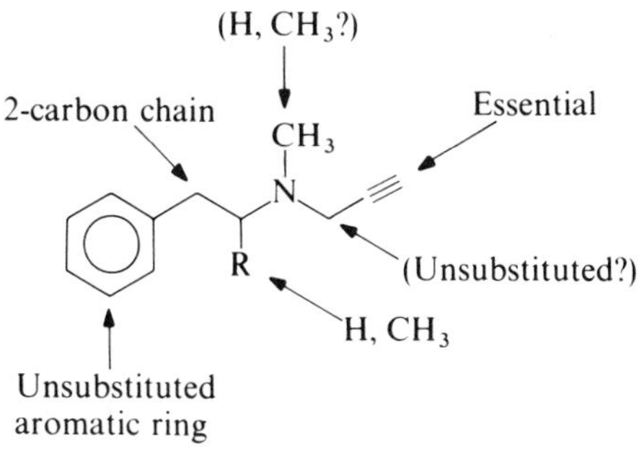

Fig. 6.2. Structure–activity relationship in the L-deprenyl series.

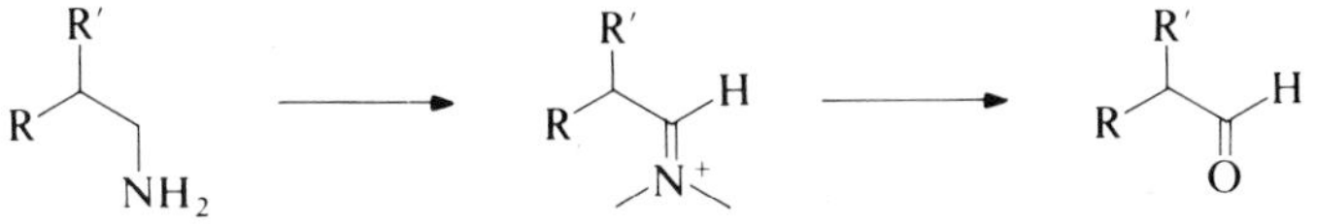

Scheme 6.1

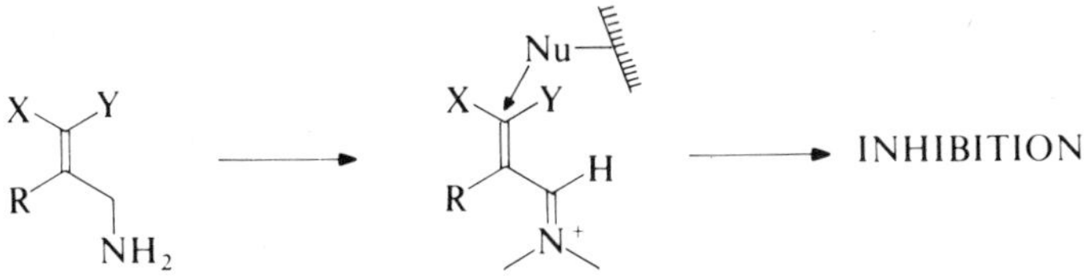

Scheme 6.2

MAO-B selective inhibitors. A selection of these compounds can be found in Fig. 6.1 and Table 6.1, the most interesting ones from a structure–activity point of view being MDL 72638 and MDL 72887.

The design of MDL 72638 was based on the structure of clorgyline in the expectation that the aromatic ring–nitrogen atom distance in clorgyline was related to its MAO-A selectivity (Knoll *et al.* 1978; Kalir *et al.* 1981). The fact that MDL 72638 is a very potent selective inhibitor of MAO-B (McDonald *et al.* 1986b) was quite unexpected and may have important implications concerning the geometry of the active centre of MAO-B. The sulphide, MDL 72887, was also found to be a potent compound but this time the selectivity for MAO-B was extremely high, approaching that seen with clorgyline for MAO-A. These compounds are time-dependent inhibitors of MAO, displaying pseudo first-order kinetics over several half-lives. When the kinetic data are analysed according to the methods of Kitz and Wilson (1962), it can be seen that selectivity results from a better affinity for the B form of the enzyme (K_i) and especially from a much faster rate of inactivation (ζ_{50}). The structure–activity relationship in this series is summarized in Fig. 6.3.

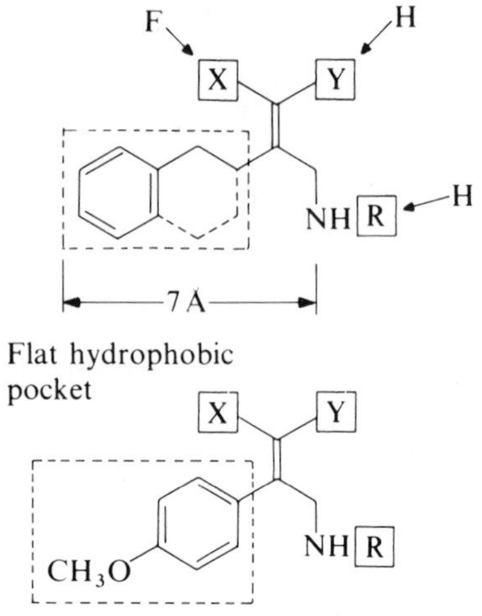

Fig. 6.3. Structure–activity relationship in the fluoroallylamine series. The arrowed atoms are required for maximum potency for both MAO-A and MAO-B whereas the flat hydrophobic pocket is optimal for MAO-B.

The approach summarized in Schemes (6.1) and (6.2) can successfully lead to the discovery of potent MAO inhibitors but cannot predict with certainty the selectivity of a particular inhibitor. For example, while a good correlation exists between the MAO-B substrate 4-methoxyphenethylamine (Suzuki *et al.* 1980) and the 100-fold greater MAO-B selective inhibitor (*E*)-2-(4-methoxyphenyl)-3-fluoroallylamine (McDonald *et al.* 1985), and probably also with 3,4-dimethoxyphenethylamine (Houslay and Tipton 1974) and MDL 72145, this does not always apply to other families of MAO inhibitors. If we compare for instance, the MAO-B substrate phenethylamine and the reversible MAO-A inhibitor amphetamine, or L-deprenyl and amphetamine the relationship does not hold at all. Clearly, other factors must play a role in this respect.

6.3   Combined amine uptake/MAO inhibitors

For tyramine to release noradrenalin and hence produce the 'cheese effect', it must first be taken up into sympathetic nerve endings in the periphery via the amine carrier (Trendelenburg 1972). Thus, the use of an uptake blocker in combination with an MAO inhibitor could logically be expected to minimize the problem. *A priori*, the two properties could be included either in one molecule (Fig. 6.4) or as two separate drugs. Several groups, including our own, have investigated these ideas.

6.3.1   Design of combined amine uptake/MAO inhibitors

Although the idea of a combined inhibitor is conceptually attractive, it has been difficult to achieve in practice due to several inherent problems. The first is a

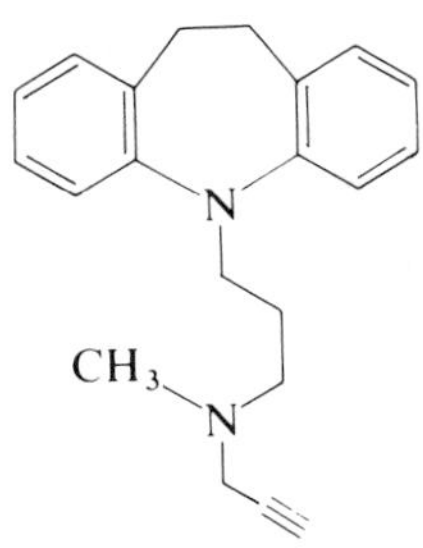

Fig. 6.4. Compounds possessing MAO inhibitory and amine uptake blocking properties.

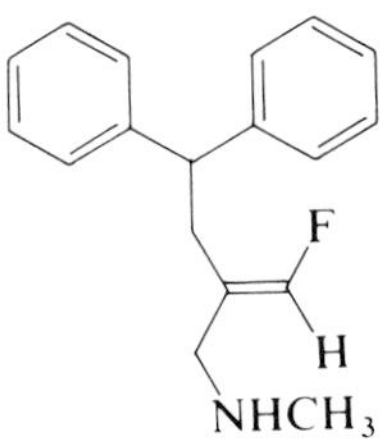

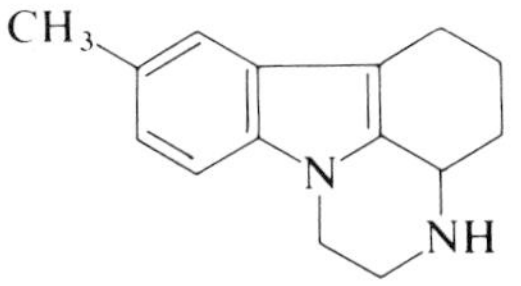

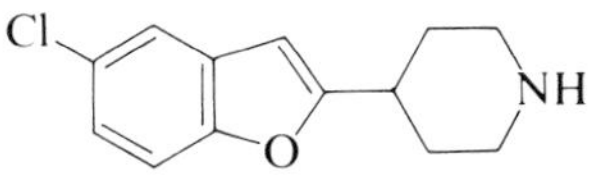

problem of pharmacokinetics; ideally such properties should be very similar for both actions. In most cases, the effect of irreversible inhibitors of MAO remains long after they have been cleared from the body, in contrast with the uptake inhibitory components, which depart with the molecule. At best, short-term protection against tyramine is all that can be achieved. If competitive, rather than irreversible MAO inhibition is incorporated into the molecule, the duration of action of the two effects might be expected to be better equilibrated. This has indeed been claimed for two experimental compounds, pirlindole and CGP 4718 A (Fig. 6.4). Although pirlindole apparently does affect the oxidative deamination of tyramine (Mashkovsky and Andrejeva 1981), it is in reality a very weak inhibitor of MAO relative to its potency as an uptake inhibitor. On the other hand CGP 4718 A, which preferentially blocks 5-HT uptake and is a more potent inhibitor of MAO-A, does produce short-lasting tyramine potentiation, particularly after oral administration (Bieck *et al.* 1984; Waldmeier *et al.* 1984).

The second problem may be the more serious, and relates to the apparent incompatibility of structural requirements for potent MAO inhibition compared with potent uptake inhibition. The tricyclic MAO inhibitor K-Y 1349 (Kaliv *et al.* 1981; Fig. 6.4) and the benzhydryl derivative MDL 72662 (Palfreyman, McDonald and Richards, unpublished results; Fig. 6.4) illustrate this point. MAO prefers non-bulky, fairly planar groups in proximity to the amine functionality, whereas amine uptake blockers are generally bulky and often puckered molecules, e.g. the tricyclic aromatics or various freely rotating benzhydryl derivatives (Maxwell and White 1978). Furthermore, the relative location of MAO and the amine carrier should be taken into account. MAO is situated on intracellular *mitochondrial* outer membranes, whereas the uptake site is on the *neuronal* outer membrane. Whether good uptake blockers possessing MAO inhibitory properties could reach the intraneuronal enzyme is an open question.

Perhaps the best option is to use two separate compounds, the individual properties of which can be independently optimized to achieve overall compatible pharmacokinetics. This approach has been tested in the clinic by Pare (Pare *et al.* 1982; Kline *et al.* 1982) and others (White and Simpson 1981) with encouraging results both in terms of efficacy and safety. Although 'polypharmacology' of this nature may not suit the purists, if the clinical results are positive, such approaches are worth pursuing.

6.4   Site-selective inhibitors of MAO

If it can be safely assumed that MAO inhibitors exert their therapeutic effect in depression through a central mechanism and that the majority of side-effects arise from inhibition of the peripheral enzyme, the ideal inhibitor would be one that acts exclusively in the brain. In recent years, some progress has been made in this direction as a result of two conceptually different approaches.

6.4.1   Design of site-selective inhibitors of MAO

The first site-selective inhibitor arose from a research effort directed towards the discovery of short-acting, potent, reversible MAO inhibitors, which culminated in the development of amiflamine (Ask *et al.* 1982b). In common with most amphetamine derivatives, amiflamine is a potent MAO-A selective inhibitor but, more interestingly, it preferentially inhibits the degradation of serotonin *in vivo*. Subsequently it was demonstrated in a series of elegent experiments that the inhibitor is actively taken up into serotonergic neurones, resulting in substantial increases in serotonin levels in the brain (Ask *et al.* 1982a, b, 1985). It was anticipated that this preference would lead to good antidepressant effects and that the reversible nature of the inhibitor would avoid problems with ingested tyramine. Unfortunately, as with some other reversible MAO-A selective inhibitors, this was not the case; the 'cheese effect' still appeared to be an unavoidable problem at therapeutically effective doses (Rosell 1985).

Our research group in Strasbourg has tackled the problem along different lines. We have synthesized several 'dual-enzyme activated' inhibitors and shown that almost exclusive irreversible inhibition of the brain (neuronal) enzyme can be achieved with these substances under certain circumstances. In this case, the dual-enzyme activated inhibitors rely on a biosynthetic enzyme in the same metabolic pathway to generate *in situ* an enzyme-activated inhibitor of the target enzyme, MAO.

In contrast to α-substituted phenethylamine and phenylalanine derivatives, the chemistry and biology of β-substituted derivatives is a largely unexplored area. Having shown that β-fluoromethylenephenethylamine analogues are potent inhibitors of MAO (McDonald et al. 1985), we felt that if the corresponding ring-hydroxylated phenylalanine derivatives are substrates for L-aromatic amino acid decarboxylase (AADC), it would be possible to have MAO inhibition close to sites of high AADC content—i.e. in aminergic neurones (Fig. 6.5). Going one step further, the concomitant administration of a peripherally acting inhibitor of AADC, such as carbidopa, would block much of the decarboxylation of the amino acid bioprecursor outside the brain and have the effect of increasing the ratio of brain-to-periphery MAO inhibition. Ultimately, this ratio could approach the ideal situation—good brain but poor peripheral inhibition—so that the chances of adverse reactions would be minimized at therapeutically effective doses.

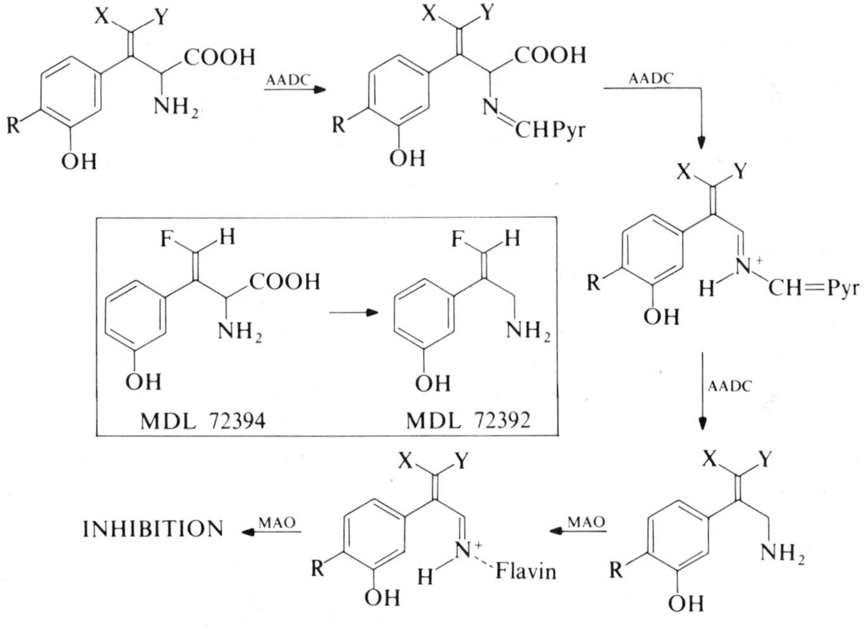

Fig. 6.5. Dual enzyme-activated inhibition of MAO.

Of the compounds synthesized to date, (E)-β-fluoromethylene-m-tyrosine (MDL 72394) appears to be the most promising (McDonald et al. 1986a). It is an excellent substrate of AADC, both in vitro (McDonald et al. 1984) and in vivo (Palfreyman et al. 1985), and it is not an inhibitor of the enzyme that could have been anticipated on mechanistic grounds. As expected, only the L-isomer is decarboxylated, in agreement with the specificity of AADC. In animal experiments, we find that prior treatment with peripherally-acting AADC inhibitors, such as carbidopa or α-monofluoromethyldopa (low doses), largely restricts MAO inhibition to the brain. This can also be inferred from experiments demonstrating that such combined treatment results in a greatly reduced propensity to augment the cardiovascular effects of tyramine compared with the effects seen when MDL 72394 is given alone (Palfreyman et al. 1983, 1985).

The fact that brain AADC is located predominantly in monoamine-containing nerves suggested that this aromatic amino acid bioprecursor approach would direct MAO inhibition to the desired site. In a series of experiments, this hypothesis has been verified (Mely et al. 1984a, b; Palfreyman et al. 1985; Sleight et al. 1985). Furthermore, it is also apparent that MDL 72394 is a substrate for the amino acid transport system from the blood to the brain (Palfreyman et al. 1985). These attributes are probably related to the structural analogy of MDL 72394 with L-tyrosine and thus may explain the surprising potency of this compound as an MAO inhibitor. Doses as low as 62.5 μg kg^{-1} p.o., given daily for 5 days with carbidopa (10 mg kg-day^{-1} p.o.), result in substantial inhibition of rat brain MAO and significant increases in the concentrations of noradrenalin and serotonin, yet only produce minimal potentiation of the cardiovascular effects of tyramine (Palfreyman et al. 1983, 1984, 1985).

These bioprecursor MAO inhibitors cannot readily be classified as MAO-A or B selective in the usual sense. While it is true that MDL 72394 is metabolized to the slightly MAO-A selective inhibitor MDL 72392, it is important to be aware that either form of MAO, in proximity to high concentrations of AADC, is likely to be inhibited, despite such selectivity. For this reason, we prefer to consider such compounds as site-selective rather than MAO-A or B selective, as the case may be.

Although the rat was employed for most of the early evaluation of MDL 72394, it was clear that it would be difficult to predict accurately from these experiments what effects would be seen with this compound in humans. The reason is that, in contrast to humans, the rat has high decarboxylase activity in peripheral tissues. We therefore performed critical experiments in the dog, the decarboxylating capacity of which more closely resembles that of humans (Sasahara et al. 1980). Preliminary experiments conducted by Davies and collaborators (Davies 1984; Davies et al. 1984), using their isolated intestinal loop preparation (Ilett et al. 1980), suggested that it was possible to get substantial inhibition of MAO in the brain with minimal inhibition of intestinal enzyme, following repeated oral treatment of dogs with MDL 72394. We have extended these experiments in intact dogs with the aim of assessing the potential for augmentation of the cardiovascular effects of both oral and intravenous tyramine (DiFrancesco et al. 1986). For purposes of comparison, the same experiments were performed with tranylcypromine. Briefly summarized, the results from these experiments (Table 6.2) strongly indicate that the MDL 72394/carbidopa regimen does not lead to conditions that can provoke the 'cheese effect', although substantial levels of MAO inhibition are attained in the

Table 6.2 Effects of MDL 72394, alone or combined with carbidopa, and tranylcypromine on MAO activity and tyramine potentiation in the dog.

Oral treatment (mg/kg-day^{-1} × 4 p.o)	MAO activity (% control, $n = 4$)				Tyramine potentiation[b]	
	Brain cortex		Duodenum	Liver		
	(MAO-A)	(MAO-B)	(MAO-A)	(MAO-B)	i. v.	Oral
MDL 72394 (0.1) plus carbidopa (2)	48 ± 7^a	36 ± 3^a	121 ± 1	80 ± 7	1.2	1
MDL 72394 (0.5)	25 ± 1^a	14 ± 3^a	26 ± 9^a	11 ± 3^a	1.9	4
Tranylcypromine (2)	3 ± 0.2^a	1 ± 0.2^a	4 ± 1^a	3 ± 1^a	3.4	> 30

[a] $P < 0.05$ (ANOVA).
[b] Ratio relative to control determined from dose–response curves to intravenous (10–100 μg kg^{-1}) or oral (0.3–10 mg kg^{-1}) tyramine using the mean arterial blood pressure/heart rate as the cardiovascular index (see Dollery *et at.* 1983).

brain. Indeed, MDL 72394 alone produces only small potentiation of the cardiovascular effects of tyramine, in distinct contrast to the situation seen with tranylcypromine. If, as seems to be the case, the human capacity to decarboxylate is similar to that of the dog, it is likely that this new MAO inhibitor will have little propensity to potentiate tyramine. This would, therefore, overcome one of the major obstacles restricting the use of these potentially valuable drugs.

6.5 Perspectives

Some of the examples discussed in this chapter illustrate the advantages of designing enzyme-activated inhibitors based on close structural analogues of naturally occurring substrates of the enzyme. Not only can these compounds function as irreversible inhibitors but, in the most favourable cases, they may be able to take advantage of other biological processes (such as transport) to achieve site selectivity. Moreover, certain of these inhibitors have the potential to mimic the physiological effects of the natural substrate on which they are based. For example, (E)-β-(3,4-dihydroxyphenyl)-3-fluoroallylamine (MDL 72434) is a full dopamine agonist, as well as a potent inhibitor of MAO with 10-fold selectivity for the A-form.

What does the future hold for MAO inhibitors? It would appear that a good understanding of the clinical implications of selective MAO-B inhibition is close at hand with the advent of such compounds as L-deprenyl, AGN 1135, and MDL 72145. The development of MAO inhibitors for use in depression without accompanying problems with hypertensive crises would appear to be a significant step nearer with the development of MDL 72394.

Finally, there exists another family of amine oxidases in addition to the flavin-dependent MAO discussed in this chapter; these are the Cu^{2+}-dependent enzymes. It is conceivable that careful design of substrate analogues of these enzymes will also lead to selective inhibitors and ultimately to the unravelling of the complexities concerning their distribution and functional roles.

References

Alken, R. G., Palfreyman, M. G., Brown, M. J., Davies, D. S., Lewis, P. J., and Schechter, P. J. (1984). Selective inhibition of MAO type B in normal volunteers by MDL 72145. *Br. J. Clin. Pharmacol.*, **17**, 615P–16P.

Ask, A.-L., Fagervall, I., and Ross, S. B. (1982a). Evidence for a selective inhibition by FLA 336(+) of the monoamine oxidase in serotonergic neurons in the rat brain. *Acta Pharmacol. Toxicol.*, **51**, 395–6.

Ask, A.-L., Högberg, K., Schmidt, L., Kiessling, H., and Ross, S. B. (1982b). (+)-4-dimethylamino-2,α-dimethylphenethylamine [FLA 336 (+)], a selective inhibitor of monoamine oxidase in the rat brain. *Biochem. Pharmacol.*, **31**, 1401–6.

Ask, A.-L., Fagervall, I., Florvall, L., Ross, S. B., and Ytterborn, S. (1985). Inhibition of monoamine oxidase in 5-hydroxytryptaminergic neurons by substituted *p*-aminophenylalkylamines. *Br. J. Pharmacol.*, **85**, 683–90.

Bieck, P. R., Cremer, G., Antonin, K. H., Schick, C., and Nilsson, E. (1984). Assessment of peripheral effects of the new monoamine oxidase/5-HT uptake inhibitor CGP 4718 A in a healthy man. *J. Pharm. Pharmacol.*, **36**, 69W.

Birkmayer, W., Knoll, J., Riederer, P., and Youdim, M. B. H. (1983). (−)-deprenyl leads to prolongation of L-dopa efficacy in Parkinson's disease. *Mod. Probl. Pharmacopsychiat.*, **19**, 170–6.

Birkmayer, W., Riederer, P., Linauer, W., and Knoll, J. (1984). L-deprenyl plus L-phenylalanine in the treatment of depression. *J. Neural Transmiss.*, **59**, 81–7.

Bradbury, A. J., Costall, B., Jenner, P. G., Kelly, M. E., Marsden, C. D., and Naylor, R. J., (1986). The effect of 1-methyl-4-phenyl-1,2,3,6-tetrahydropyridine (MPTP) on striatal and limbic catecholamine neurones in white and black mice. *Neuropharmacology*, **25**, 897–904.

Burks, T. F., ed. (1985). Current concepts in dopamine neurotoxic features of MPTP. *Life Sci.*, **36**, 199–254.

Cawthorn, R. M. and Breakefield, X. O. (1979). Differences in A and B forms of monoamine oxidase revealed by limited proteolysis and peptide mapping. *Nature (London)*, **281**, 692–4.

Cohen, G., Pasik, P., Cohen, B., Leist, A., and Mytilineou C. (1985). Pargyline and deprenyl prevent the neurotoxicity of 1-methyl-4-phenyl-1,2,3,6-tetrahydropyridine (MPTP) in monkeys. *Eur. J. Pharmacol.*, **106**, 209–10.

Csanda, E., Tarczy, M., Takats, A., Mogyoros, I., Koves, A., and Katona, G. (1983). L-deprenyl in the treatment of Parkinson's disease. *J. Neural Transmiss.* (Suppl. 19), 283–90.

Davies, D. S. (1984). Pharmacokinetic and concentration-effect relationships of reversible and irreversible inhibitors. In *Monoamine oxidase and disease* (ed. K. F. Tipton, P. Dostert, and M. Strolin Benedetti). pp. 167–172. Academic Press, London.

Davies, D. S., Yasuhara, H., Boobis, A. R., and George, C. F. (1984). The effects of reversible and irreversible inhibitors of monoamine oxidase on tyramine deamination by the dog intestine. In *Monoamine oxidase and disease* (ed. K. F. Tipton, P. Dostert, and M. Strolin Benedetti) pp. 443–8. Academic Press, London.

Denney, R. M., Fritz, R. R., Patel, N. T., and Abell, C. W. (1982). Human liver MAO-A and MAO-B separated by immunoaffinity chromatography with MAO-B-specific monoclonal antibody. *Science*, **215**, 1400–3.

DiFrancesco, G. F., Palfreyman, M. G., Spedding, M., and Zreika, M. (1986). Inhibition of MAO in the dog by MDL 72394 with minimal tyramine potentiation. *Br. J. Pharmacol.*, **89**, 685P.

Dollery, C. T., Brown, M. J., Davies, D. S., Lewis, P. J., and Strolin Benedetti, M. (1983). Oral absorption and concentration–effect relationship of tyramine with and without cimoxatone, a type-A specific inhibitor of monoamine oxidase. *Clin. Pharmacol. Ther.*, **34**, 651–61.

Dostert, P., Strolin Benedetti, M., and Guffroy, C. (1983). Different stereoselective inhibition of monoamine oxidase-B by the R- and S-enantiomers of MD 78236. *J. Pharm. Pharmacol.*, **35**, 161–5.

Elsworth, J. D., Glover, V., Reynolds, G. P., Sandler, M., Lees, A. J., Phuapradit, P., Shaw, K. M., Stern, G. M., and Kumar, P. (1978). Deprenyl administration in man: a selective monoamine oxidase B inhibitor without the "cheese effect." *Psychopharmacology*, **57**, 33–8.

Elsworth, J. D., Sandler, M., Lees, A. J., Ward, C., and Stern, G. M. (1982). The contribution of amphetamine metabolites of (−)-deprenyl to its antiparkinsonian properties. *J. Neural Transmiss.*, **54**, 105–10.

Fowler, C. J. and Ross, S. B. (1984). Selective inhibitors of monoamine oxidase A and B: biochemical, pharmacological, and clinical properties. *Med. Res. Rev.*, **4**, 323–58.

Glover, V., Sandler, M., Owen, F., and Riley, C. J. (1977). Dopamine is a monoamine oxidase B substrate in man. *Nature (London)*, **265**, 80–1.

Heikkila, R. E., Duvoisin, R. G., Finberg, J. P. M., and Youdim, M. B. H. (1985). Prevention of MPTP-induced neurotoxicity by AGN-1133 and AGN-1135, selective inhibitors of monoamine oxidase-B. *Eur. J. Pharmacol.*, **116**, 313–17.

Houslay, M. D. and Tipton, K. F. (1974). A kinetic evaluation of monoamine oxidase activity in rat liver mitochondrial outer membrane. *Biochem. J.*, **139**, 645–52.

Ilett, K. F., George, C. F., and Davies, D. S. (1980). The effect of monoamine oxidase inhibitors in 'first pass' metabolism of tyramine in dog intestine. *Biochem. Pharmacol.*, **29**, 2551–6.

Johnston, J. P. (1968). Some observations upon a new inhibitor of monoamine oxidase in brain tissue. *Biochem. Pharmacol.*, **17**, 1285–97.

Kalir, A., Sabbagh, A., and Youdim, M. B. H. (1981). Selective acetylenic 'suicide' and reversible inhibitors of monoamine oxidase types A and B. *Br. J. Pharmacol.*, **73**, 55–64.

Karoum, F., Chuang, L.-W., Eisler, T., Calne, D. B., Liebowitz, M. R., Quitkin, M. D., Klein, D. F., and Wyatt, R. J. (1982). Metabolism of (−)-deprenyl to amphetamine and methamphetamine may be responsible for deprenyl's therapeutic benefit: a biochemical assessment. *Neurology*, **32**, 503–9.

Kettler, R., Keller, H. H., Bonetti, E. P., Wyss, P. C., and Da Prada, M. (1985). RO 16–6491: a new highly selective and reversible MAO-B inhibitor. *J. Neurochem.*, **44**, S94C.

Kitz, R. and Wilson, I. B. (1962). Esters of methanesulfonic acid as irreversible inhibitors of acetylcholinesterase. *J. Biol. Chem.*, **237**, 3245–9.

Kline, N. S., Pare, C. M. B., Hallstrom, C., and Cooper, T. B. (1982). Amitriptyline protects patients on MAOIs from tyramine reactions. *J. Clin. Psychopharmacol.*, **2**, 434–5.

Knoll, J. (1985). The facilitation of dopaminergic activity in the aged brain by (−)-deprenyl. A proposal for a strategy to improve the quality of life in senescence. *Mech. Aging Dev.*, **30**, 109–22.

Knoll, J. and Magyar, K. (1972). Some puzzling pharmacological effects of monoamine oxidase inhibitors. *Adv. Biochem. Psychopharmacol.*, **5**, 393–408.

Knoll, J., Ecsery, Z., Magyar, K., and Satory, E. (1978). Novel (−)-deprenyl-derived selective inhibitors of B-type monoamine oxidase. The relation of structure to their action. *Biochem. Pharmacol.*, **27**, 1739–47.

Liebowitz, M. R., Karoum, F., Quitkin, F. M., Davies, S. O., Schwartz, D., Levitt, M., and Linnoila, M. (1985). Biochemical effects of L-deprenyl in atypical depressives. *Biol. Psychiat.*, **20**, 558–65.

McDonald, I. A., Lacoste, J. M., Bey, P., Wagner, J., Zreika, M., and Palfreyman, M. G. (1984). (*E*)-β-(Fluoromethylene)-*m*-tyrosine: a substrate for aromatic L-amino acid decarboxylase liberating an enzyme-activated irreversible inhibitor of monoamine oxidase. *J. Am. Chem. Soc.*, **106**, 3354–6.

McDonald, I. A., Lacoste, J. M., Bey, P., Palfreyman, M. G., and Zreika, M. (1985). Enzyme-activated irreversible inhibitors of monoamine oxidase: phenylallylamine structure-activity relationships. *J. Med. Chem.*, **28**, 186–93.

McDonald, I. A., Lacoste, J. M., Bey, P., Wagner, J., Zreika, M., and Palfreyman, M. G. (1986a). Dual enzyme-activated irreversible inhibition of monoamine oxidase. *Bioorg. Chem.*, **14**, 103–18.

McDonald, I. A., Palfreyman, M. G., Zreika, M., and Bey, P. (1986). (*Z*)-2-(2,4-dichlorophenoxy)methyl-3-fluoroallylamine (MDL 72638): a clorgyline analogue with surprising selectivity for monoamine oxidase type B. *Biochem. Pharmacol.*, **35**, 349–51.

Mann, J. and Gershon, S. (1980). L-deprenyl, a selective monoamine oxidase type-B inhibitor in endogenous depression. *Life Sci.*, **26**, 877–82.

Mashkovsky, M. D. and Andrejeva, N. I. (1981). Pharmacological properties of 2,3,3a,4,5,6-hexahydro-8-methyl-1*H*-pyrazino [3,2,1-j,k]carbazol hydrochloride (pirlindole), a new antidepressant. *Arzneim.-Forsch. Drug Res.*, **31**, 75–9.

Maxwell, R. A. and White, H. L. (1978). Tricyclic and monoamine oxidase inhibitor antidepressant: structure–activity relationships. In *Handbook of psychopharmacology* (ed. L. L. Iversen, S. D. Iversen, and S. H. Snyder), Vol. 14, pp. 83–155. Plenum Press, New York.

Mely, Y., Palfreyman, M. G., Sleight, A. J., and Zreika, M. (1984a). Selective activation of the monoamine oxidase inhibiting prodrug MDL 72394 by AADC of central monoamine neurons. *Br. J. Pharmacol.*, **83**, 355P.

Mely, Y., Palfreyman, M. G., and Zreika, M. (1984b). *In vitro* evidence for the Neuronal selectivity of the MAO inhibiting prodrug, MDL 72394. *J. Pharm. Pharmacol.*, **36**, 39W.

Mendlewicz, J. and Youdim, M. B. H. (1981). A selective MAO-B inhibitor (L-deprenil) and 5-HTP as antidepressant therapy. In *Monoamine oxidase inhibitors: the state of the art* (ed. M. B. H. Youdim and E. S. Paykel), pp. 177–188. Wiley, New York.

Mendlewicz, J. and Youdim, M. B. H. (1983). L-deprenil, a selective monoamine oxidase type B inhibitor, in the treatment of depression: a double blind evaluation. *Br. J. Psychiat.*, **142**, 508–11.

Mendis, N., Pare, C. M. B., Sandler, M., Glover, V., and Stern, G. (1981). (−)-deprenyl in the treatment of depression. In *Monoamine oxidase inhibitors: the state of the art* (ed. M. B. H. Youdim and E. S. Paykel), pp. 171–6. Wiley, New York.

Murphy, D. L., Donnelly, C. H., Richelson, E., and Fuller, R. W. (1978). N-substituted cyclopropylamines as inhibitors of MAO-A and -B forms. *Biochem. Pharmacol.*, **27**, 1767–9.

Murphy, D. L., Garrick, N. A., Aulakh, C. S., and Cohen, R. M. (1984). New contributions from basic science to understanding the effects of monoamine oxidase inhibiting antidepressants. *J. Clin. Psychiat.*, **45**, 37–43.

Palfreyman, M. G., McDonald, I. A., Zreika, M., and Fozard, J. (1983). MDL 72394: a site-selective inhibitor of monoamine oxidase (MAO). *Prog. Neuro. Psychopharmacol. Biol. Psychiat.*, (Suppl.), Abst. 369.

Palfreyman, M. G., McDonald, I. A., Zreika, M., and Fozard, J. (1984). MDL 72394: the prodrug approach to brain selective MAO inhibition. In *Monoamine oxidase and disease* (ed. K. F. Tipton, P. Dostert, and M. Strolin Benedetti), pp. 561–2. Academic Press, London.

Palfreyman, M. G., McDonald, I. A., Fozard, J., Mely, Y., Sleight, A. J., Zreika, M., Wagner, J., Bey, P., and Lewis, P. J. (1985). Inhibition of monoamine oxidase selectively in brain monoamine nerves using the bioprecursor (E)-β-fluoromethylene-m-tyrosine (MDL 72394), a substrate for aromatic L-amino acid decarboxylase. *J. Neurochem.*, **45**, 1850–60.

Pare, C. M. B., Hallstrom, C., Kline, N., and Cooper, T. B. (1982). Will amitriptyline prevent the 'cheese' reaction of monoamine oxidase inhibitors? *Lancet*, **ii**, 183–6.

Pickar, D., Cohen, R. M., Jimerson, D. C., and Murphy, D. L. (1981). Tyramine infusions and selective monoamine oxidase inhibitor treatment. I. Changes in pressor sensitivity. *Psychopharmacology*, **74**, 4–7.

Presthus, J. and Hajba, A. (1983). Deprenyl (selegiline) combined with L-dopa and a decarboxylase inhibitor in the treatment of Parkinson's disease. *Acta Neurol. Scand. Suppl.*, **95**, 127–33.

Quitkin, F. M., Liebowitz, M. R., Stewart, J. W., McGrath, P. J., Harrison, W., Rabkin, J. G., Markowitz, J., and Davies, S. O. (1984). l-deprenyl in atypical depressives. *Arch. Gen. Psychiat.*, **41**, 777–81.

Quitkin, F., Rifkin, A., and Klein, D. F. (1979). Monoamine oxidase inhibitors: a review of antidepressant effectiveness. *Arch. Gen. Psychiat.*, **36**, 749–60.

Rando, R. R. and Eigner, A. (1977). The pseudoirreversible inhibition of monoamine oxidase by allylamine. *Mol. Pharmacol.*, **13**, 1005–13.

Reynolds, G. P., Riederer, P., and Rausch, W. -D. (1980). Dopamine metabolism in human brain: effect of monoamine oxidase inhibition *in vitro* by (−) deprenyl and (+) and (−) tranylcypromine. *J. Neural Transmiss.*, (Suppl. **16**), 173–8.

Reynolds, G. P., Riederer, P., and Sandler, M. (1979). 2-phenylethylamine and amphetamine in human brain: effects of L-deprenyl in Parkinson's disease. *Biochem. Soc. Trans.*, **7**, 143–5.

Riederer, P. and Reynolds, G. P. (1980). Deprenyl is a selective inhibitor of brain MAO-B in the long-term treatment of Parkinson's disease. *Br. J. Clin. Pharmacol.*, **9**, 98–9.

Riederer, P., Reynolds, G. P., and Youdim, M. B. H. (1981). Selectivity of MAO inhibitors in human brain and their clinical consequences. In *Monoamine oxidase inhibitors: the state of the art* (ed. M. B. H. Youdim and E. S. Paykel), pp. 63–76. Wiley, New York.

Rinne, U. K. (ed.) (1983). A new approach to the treatment of Parkinson's disease. *Acta Neurol. Scand.* (Suppl. **95**), 1–144.

Rosell, S. (1985). Problems in ASTRA's R&D. Cited in *Scrip*, **982**, 23.

Roth, J. A. (1979). Benzylhydrazine—a selective inhibitor of human and rat brain monoamine oxidase. *Biochem. Pharmacol.*, **28**, 729–32.

Roth, J. A., Eddy, B. J., Pearce, L. B., and Mulder, K. M. (1981). Phenylhydrazine: selective inhibition of human brain type B monoamine oxidase. *Biochem. Pharmacol.*, **30**, 945–50.

Sasahara, K., Nitanai, J., Habata, T., Morioka, T., and Nahajima, E. (1980). Dosage form design for improvement of bioavailability of levodopa II: Bioavailability of marketed levodopa preparations in dogs and Parkinsonian patients. *J. Pharm. Sci.*, **69**, 261–5.

Schachter, M., Marsden, C. D., Parkes, J. D., Jenner, P., and Testa, B. (1980). Deprenyl in the management of response fluctuations in patients with Parkinson's disease on levodopa. *J. Neurol. Neurosurg. Psychiat.*, **43**, 1016–21.

Selikoff, I. J., Robitzek, E. H., and Ornstein, G. G. (1952). Toxicity of hydrazine derivatives of isonicotinic acid in chemotherapy of human tuberculosis (preliminary report). *Q. Bull. Sea View Hosp.*, **13**, 17–26.

Sleight, A. J., Redfern, P. H., and Palfreyman, M. G. (1985). Pharmacological evidence for the neuronal selectivity of the MAO inhibiting prodrug, MDL 72394. *Br. J. Pharmacol.*, **86**, 480P.

Strolin Benedetti, M., and Dostert, P. (1985). Stereochemical aspects of MAO interactions: reversible and selective inhibitors of monoamine oxidase. *Trends Pharmacol. Sci.*, **6**, 246–51.

Suzuki, O., Matsumoto, Y., and Oya, M. (1980). Methoxyphenylethylamines as substrates for type A and type B monoamine oxidase. Experientia, **36**, 895–7.

Tipton, K. F., McCrodden, J. M., Kalir, A. S., and Youdim, M. B. H. (1982). Inhibition of rat liver monoamine oxidase by α-methyl- and N-propargyl-amine derivatives. *Biochem. Pharmacol.*, **31**, 1251–5.

Tipton, K. F., Dostert, P., and Strolin Benedetti, M. (eds.) (1984). *Monoamine oxidase and disease.* Academic Press, London.

Trendelenburg, H. (1972). Classification of sympathomimetic amines. In *Handbook of experimental pharmacology* (ed. H. Blaschko and E. Muscholl). Vol. 23, pp. 336–62. Springer, Berlin.

Wajsbort, J., Kartmazov, K., Oppenheim, B., Barkey, R., and Youdim, M. B. H. (1982). The clinical and biochemical investigation of L-deprenyl in Parkinson's disease with special reference to the 'on-off' effect. *J. Neural Transmiss.*, **55**, 201–15.

Waldmeier, P. C., Tipton, K. F., Bernasconi, R., Felner, A. E., Baumann, P. A., and Maitre, L. (1984). CGP 4718A, a new potential antidepressant with a dual mode of action. *Eur. J. Pharmacol.*, **107**, 79–89.

White, K. and Simpson, G. (1981). Combined MAOI–tricyclic antidepressant treatment: a reevaluation. *J. Clin Psychopharmacol.*, **1**, 264–82.

Zeller, E. A., Barsky, J., Fouts, J. R., Kirchheimer, W. F., and van Orden, L. S. (1952). Influence of isonicotinic acid hydrazide (INH) and 1-isonicotinyl-2-isopropyl hydrazide (IIM) on bacterial and mammalian enzymes. Experientia, **8**, 349–50.

Zreika, M., McDonald, I. A., Bey, P., and Palfreyman, M. G. (1984). MDL 72145, an enzyme-activated irreversible inhibitor with selectivity for monoamine oxidase type B. *J. Neurochem.*, **43**, 448–54.

7

Polyamine oxidase inhibitors

F. N. Bolkenius and N. Seiler

7.1 Introduction

There is considerable confusion concerning the enzymes that oxidize the poly-amines, spermidine and spermine. Basically two types of enzymes are involved:

1. Copper-containing amine oxidases (CuAO) oxidatively deaminate terminal (primary) amino groups of the polyamines to the corresponding aldehydes. The best known among these enzymes is bovine serum amine oxidase, which has been purified to homogeneity and extensively characterized (Mondovi et al. 1983). CuAO also exist in tissues (small intestine is especially rich). In contrast with the serum enzyme, which deaminates the aminopropyl moiety exclusively, both terminal amino groups of spermidine are oxidized, to form (in a concerted reaction with an aldehyde dehydrogenase) putreanine and isoputreanine lactam (Seiler et al. 1982). Spermine is converted into N^8-(2-carboxyethyl)spermidine and spermic acid. These tissue oxidases have not yet been characterized. It is not known whether one enzyme oxidizes both primary amino groups, or whether two or more enzymes are involved in this reaction. We cannot even exclude the possibility intestinal diamine oxidase (DAO) is responsible for these reactions (Seiler et al. 1983).

In addition, an enzyme that is capable of oxidizing both the diamines (putrescine and cadaverine) and the polyamines, spermidine and spermine, was reported by Gahl et al. (1982) to occur in human pregnancy serum.

2. A flavin enzyme, for which the designation polyamine oxidase (PAO) has been suggested (Hölttä 1977), splits the C–N bond of spermidine and spermine between the secondary nitrogen and the aminopropyl moiety to form putrescine

245

and spermidine, respectively. This chapter is exclusively devoted to this tissue enzyme.

7.2   Polyamine oxidase

PAO has been purified to homogeneity from rat liver. Its average molecular weight is 60 kDa. FAD is tightly bound as prosthetic group and there is some evidence that Fe^{2+} may be a cofactor (Höltta 1983). Isoenzymes are not known. Like monoamine oxidase (MAO), with which it has a number of common features, PAO needs O_2 as electron acceptor and forms H_2O_2 (Fig. 7.1), but unlike MAO, it is not localized in mitochondria. In liver and kidney, it was found within the peroxisomes (Höltta 1977; Beard et al. 1985). Its subcellular localization has not yet been established in other organs, but it is found in virtually all tissues (Seiler et al. 1980).

Although spermidine and spermine are substrates in vitro, there is strong evidence that N^1-acetylspermidine and N^1-acetylspermine are the natural substrates of PAO (Bolkenius and Seiler 1981) and in fact there is no evidence that spermidine or spermine are oxidized by PAO under physiological conditions (Mamont et al. 1981; Bolkenius et al. 1985). With a K_M of 0.6 μM, N^1-acetylspermine is the substrate with the highest affinity for the enzyme, followed by N^1-acetylspermidine ($K_M = 14$ μM) (Bolkenius and Seiler 1981).

The reactions in which PAO participates are shown in Fig. 7.2. The acetyltransferase (acetyl CoA:spermidine/spermine N^1-acetyltransferase) is an inducible enzyme (Pegg and Erwin 1985; Pegg et al. 1985). It regulates the rate of polyamine degradation along this pathway (Della Ragione and Pegg 1982). Because one polyamine is converted into another and the reaction products, spermidine and putrescine, can be re-utilized for de novo synthesis of spermine and spermidine respectively, this reaction sequence was called the interconversion pathway (Seiler et al. 1981). Formally, it is the inversion of the synthetic reactions. We assume that the interconversion reaction is responsible for the physiological turnover of the polyamines (Seiler and Bolkenius 1985; Seiler et al. 1985).

Morgan (1985) has recently described an amine oxidase in human pregnancy serum with characteristics that are compatible with the assumption that it is a PAO according to our definition. It remains to be shown whether the enzyme of Gahl et al. (1982) and that of Morgan are identical or not.

7.3   Inhibitors of polyamine oxidase

7.3.1   Inhibitors acting on cofactors

Evidence for Fe^{2+} as a cofactor of PAO came from the observation that the iron chelators α,α-dipyridyl, 8-hydroxyquinoline, and o-phenanthroline are inhibitors of this enzyme (Höltta 1977). The fact that quinacrine (N^4-(6-chloro-2-

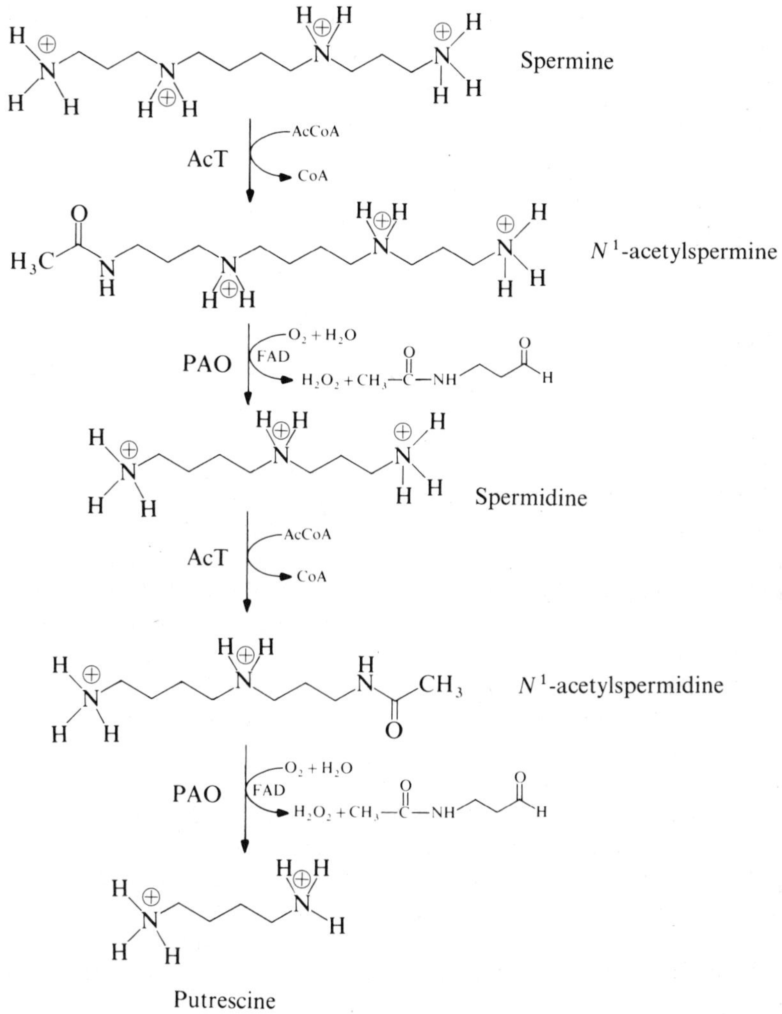

Fig. 7.1. Reaction scheme of polyamine catabolism. AcT: acetyl CoA:spermidine/spermine N^1-acetyltransferase. PAO:polyamine oxidase. FAD: flavine–adenine dinucleotide. AcCoA: acetyl coenzyme A.

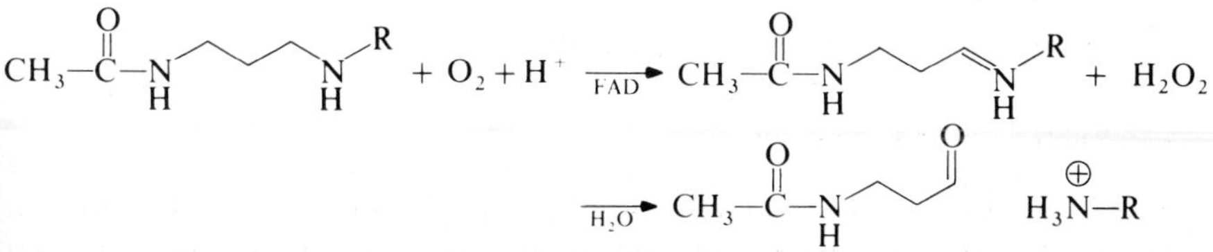

Fig. 7.2. Oxidative cleavage of N^1-acetylpolyamines by PAO.

methoxy-9-acridinyl)-N^1,N^1-diethyl-1,4-pentanediamine) effectively inhibited PAO suggested FAD as Cofactor (Höltta 1977).

Both types of inhibitors are evidently not specific for PAO, but also inhibit other Fe^{2+}- and FAD-dependent enzymes, such as MAO. Their value as a tool in the elucidation of the significance of PAO is, therefore, restricted.

7.3.2 Specific, irreversible inhibitors

7.3.2.1 *Structural considerations*

From the fact that N^1-acetylspermidine, N^1-acetylspermine, and N^1,N^{12}-diacetylspermine are substrates of PAO, but not N^1,N^8-diacetylspermidine (Bolkenius and Seiler 1981), it has been assumed that essential features of substrates of PAO are the following:

(1) the presence of positive charges on both putrescine nitrogens;
(2) the absence of a positive charge on the aminopropyl moiety.

From the analogies between MAO and PAO, and the fact that pargyline (N-methyl-N-benzylpropargylamine) is a weak inhibitor of PAO (Höltta 1977), despite the structural differences between pargyline and substrates of PAO, it was concluded that putrescine analogues with unsaturated, non-charged substituents on the nitrogen atoms are potential inactivators of PAO. 2-propynyl- (Taylor *et al.* 1960), 2-propenyl- (Rando and Eigner 1977) and 2,3-butadienyl-amines (Krantz *et al.* 1979) are known to be enzyme-activated irreversible inhibitors of MAO. By analogy with these prototypes, a number of putrescine derivatives were prepared (Bey *et al.* 1985), summarized in Table 7.1. It appears from the data in this table that, indeed, all β-unsaturated N-alkyl derivatives of putrescine are inhibitors of PAO, although with greatly differing potencies. The propynyl derivatives were the weakest in the series, and were therefore not considered for further examination. The most potent inhibitors were the allenic amines N-(2,3-butadienyl)-1,4-butanediamine (MDL 72468), N-methyl, N'-(2,3-butadienyl)-1,4-butanediamine (MDL 72521) and N,N'-bis(2,3-butadienyl)-1,4-butane-diamine (MDL 72527).

In these and other cases, substitution of the second nitrogen by a methyl group or a second 2,3-butadienyl residue enhanced the affinity (Table 7.1), by analogy with the higher affinity of N^1,N^{12}-diacetylspermine ($K_M = 5$ μM), as compared with N^1-acetylspermidine ($K_M = 14$ μM) (Bolkenius and Seiler 1981). Another advantage of substitution of both nitrogens is that the compound is protected from oxidative deamination by DAO (F.N. Bolkenius, unpublished results).

In the case of MAO inhibitors, the order of potency is reversed: propargylic amines are more potent than allylic or allenic amines (Krantz *et al.* 1979). The reason for this difference is not known; however, one may speculate that geometric factors play a role.

Table 7.1 Structural formulae and kinetic parameters of inhibitors of polyamine oxidase

MDL No.		$K_1 (\mu M)$	$\tau_{1/2}$ (min)
72333		425	260
72335		313	100
72348[a]		13	30
72431[a]		4	9
72468		0.7	1
72521		0.3	0.5
72527		0.1	2.2

All compounds were crystallized as dihydrochlorides.
The apparent dissociation constant (K_1) and the half-life of the enzyme under saturating conditions ($\tau_{1/2}$) were calculated according to Kitz and Wilson (1962) (see caption to Fig. 7.4).
[a] 'Pseudo-irreversible' inhibitors (according to the definition of Rando and Eigner 1977).

Assuming that the stretched lipophilic arm of N^1-acetylspermidine (i.e. the 3-acetamidopropyl moiety) is bound in a lipophilic pocket within the active site of the enzyme, it appears, from the comparison of models, that the 2,3-butadienyl derivative of putrescine has a more appropriate geometry for this type of interaction than the allylic and propargylic residues (Fig. 7.3).

That N^8-acetylspermidine is not a substrate of PAO may be explained by the size and flexibility of the 4-acetamidobutyl-residue, which it is assumed does not fit into the suggested lipophilic pocket. The smaller distance between the two positively charged nitrogens in the case of N^8-acetylspermidine, as compared with the putrescine derivatives, is presumably of minor importance: the monoa-

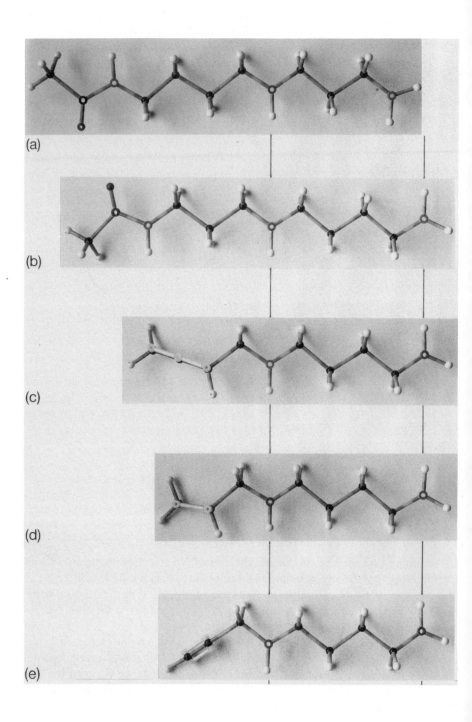

(a)

(b)

(c)

(d)

(e)

cetyl derivative of N-(3-aminopropyl)-1,3-diaminopropane and N,N'-bis(3-aminopropyl)-1,3-diaminopropane, lower homologues of spermidine and spermine, are substrates of PAO (Bolkenius and Seiler 1981; Bolkenius et al. 1985).

7.3.2.2 In vitro properties of PAO inactivators

Inactivation of PAO by the compounds in Table 7.1 was time- and dose-dependent, and followed pseudo first-order kinetics. Figure 7.4 shows the experimental inactivation curves of hog liver PAO by the allenic amines. The kinetic data in Table 7.1 were calculated from these and analogous curves.

Studies of the mechanism of reaction of PAO with N-substituted putrescines have not yet been carried out, but the available information is compatible with the assumption that the 2,3-butadienyl derivatives are enzyme-activated, irreversible inhibitors of PAO (Seiler et al. 1978). Neither extensive dialysis nor incubation of the inactivated enzyme with a substrate, such as N^1,N^{12}-diacetylspermine, reactivated PAO (Table 7.2).

The presence of substrate decreased the rate of enzyme inactivation. This suggested that inhibitors and substrate compete for the active site of the enzyme, a view supported by the observation that, in short-term incubations, N-(2-propenyl)-putrescine (MDL 72348) seemed to behave like a competitive inhibitor ($K_1 = 40$ μM), and a certain portion of the compound was split to form putrescine, as is expected of a substrate. Analogously, MDL 72431 formed N-methylputrescine. These reaction products were, however, not detected in the case of the allenic amines, owing to the rapid inactivation of the enzyme.

It was mentioned above that PAO which has been inactivated by the allenic amines could not be reactivated. Dialysis alone was also insufficient for reactivation of PAO, after inactivation by any of the compounds of Table 7.1. However, if inactivation of the enzyme had been achieved with N-methyl, N'-(2-propenyl) putrescine (MDL 72431), it could be fully reactivated by incubation for 2 h with substrate (Table 7.2). Similarly, reactivation of PAO is observed in MDL 72431-treated HTC cells upon exogenous addition of the substrate, N^1-acetylspermine. This behaviour resembles the reaction of MAO with allylamine, which was characterized as 'pseudo-irreversible inhibition' (Rando and Eigner 1977).

For the determination of residual enzyme activity after preincubation with the inactivator, the experimental procedure requires the incubation of partly inactivated enzyme with substrate. Partial reactivation during this step will

---

Fig. 7.3. Orbit molecular models of: (a) N^8-acetylspermidine; (b) N^1-acetylspermidine; (c) MDL 72468 [N-(2,3-butadienyl)-1,4-butanediamine]; (d) MDL 72348 [N-(2-propenyl)-1,4-butanediamine]; (e) MDL 72333 [N-(2-propynyl)-1,4-butanediamine]. The models are arranged so that the nitrogen atoms of the putrescine moieties are connected by vertical lines.

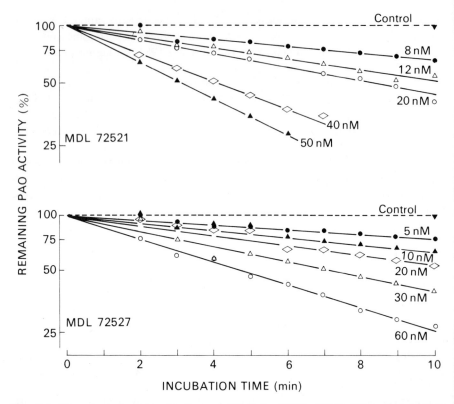

Fig. 7.4. Time-dependent inactivation of PAO by MDL 72521 [N-methyl-N'-(2,3-butadienyl)-putrescine]) and MDL 72527 [N,N'-bis(2,3-butadienyl)-putrescine].

Partially purified PAO from pig liver (specific activity 2.2 nmol N^1-acetylspermidine formed per mg protein per h from N^1,N^{12}-diacetylspermine under saturating conditions) was used. After preincubation of PAO with inhibitor, the residual enzyme activity was determined after 20-fold dilution, by following H_2O_2 formation according to Snyder and Hendley (1968). Kinetic data were calculated from the inactivation rates according to Kitz and Wilson (1962).

invariably affect the kinetic parameters, which are calculated from the experimental data. The values given in Table 7.1 for MDL 72348 and 72431, and presumably those for MDL 72333 and MDL 72335, are therefore only upper limits of the actual kinetic parameters.

7.3.2.3 *Specificity of the allenic amines MDL 72521 and 72527*

Both allenic amines, MDL 72521 and 72527, are specific for PAO. At 1 mM they do not inhibit the following enzymes: MAO, DAO, ornithine decarboxylase (Orn-DC), S-adenosylmethionine decarboxylase (SAM-DC), acetyl CoA: spermidine/spermine N^1-acetyltransferase, spermidine synthase, spermine synthase. Only N^8-acetylspermidine deacetylase is reversibly inhibited; (MDL 72521:

Table 7.2 Irreversibility of PAO-inactivation by *N*-substituted putrescine derivatives

Treatment	PAO-activity (per cent control)		
	MDL 72431	MDL 72521	MDL 72527
A	39 ± 3	0.9 ± 1.3	1.4 ± 1.3
B	108 ± 1	4.2 ± 0.4	3.6 ± 0.4

A: Incubation of hog liver PAO with 0.2 mM inactivator (3 h; 30°C) and subsequent dialysis against 50 mM borate buffer, pH 9.0 (24 h; two solvent changes).
B: Treatment as in A, followed by incubation with 0.8 mM N^1,N^{12}-diacetylspermine (2 h; 37°C) and dialysis.
MDL 72431: *N*-methyl,*N'*-(2-propenyl)-1,4-butanediamine. 2HCl.
MDL 72521: *N*-methyl,*N'*-(2,3-butadienyl)-1,4-butanediamine. 2HCl.
MDL 72527: *N*,*N'*-bis(2,3-butadienyl)-1-4-butanediamine. 2HCl.

$ID_{50} = 55$ μM at 80 μM N^8-acetylspermidine; Bolkenius *et al.* 1985). However, exposure of cultured rat hepatoma tissue culture (HTC) cells to MDL 72521 in doses sufficient to inactivate PAO completely does not cause any accumulation of N^8-acetylspermidine, although an accumulation can be observed if the deacetylase is inhibited by 7-amino-2-heptanone (Mamont *et al.* 1984). Similarly, daily administration of MDL 72527 (20 mg kg^{-1}) did not produce any signs of deacetylase inhibition such as enhancement of N^8-acetylspermidine concentration in tissues of mice (Bolkenius *et al.* 1985) or in the urine of rats (Seiler *et al.* 1985), suggesting that these compounds are suitable tools for elucidating the physiological role of PAO.

7.4 Some biochemical consequences of polyamine oxidase inhibition

As is demonstrated by the observations described below, the allenic amines are suitable for the complete inactivation of PAO in an intact animal, and MDL 72521 and MDL 72527 are about equipotent *in vivo* in peripheral tissues of mice and rat. A single intraperitoneal dose of 10 mg kg^{-1} or greater is sufficient to inactivate at least 90 per cent of the PAO activity in liver (within 30 min) for about 24 h. Thereafter, a gradual reactivation of the enzyme is observed. In liver, 50 per cent of the normal PAO activity is regained after 3 to 4 days (Bolkenius *et al.* 1985). It is not known whether this period is identical with the biological half-life of PAO, although it is compatible with other observations that suggest a slow turnover of this enzyme (Seiler *et al.* 1980). *N*,*N'*-bis(2,3-butadienyl)1,4-butanediamine (MDL 72527) is about 20 times more effective than MDL 72521 in inhibiting PAO in mouse brain ($ID_{50} = 0.25$ mg kg^{-1} and 5 mg kg^{-1}, respectively) probably because of its higher lipophilicity. Thus it is the compound of choice for the complete inactivation of PAO in an intact animal.

What consequences are to be expected from the inactivation of PAO? It is suggested by the reaction scheme (Fig. 7.2) that concentrations of the substrates, N^1-acetylspermidine and N^1-acetylspermine, are elevated at the rate of their formation, and concentrations of the reaction products, spermidine and putrescine, decrease proportionately to the quantitative role of the PAO catalysed formation of these compounds. (This is disregarding the possibility that compensatory changes of enzyme activity in other pathways of putrescine and spermidine formation (ODC, SAM-DC), or feedback inhibition of acetyltransferase, may affect the observable changes.)

In principle the expectations outlined above were fulfilled in practice. If HTC cells were exposed to MDL 72521 in doses $\geqslant 10\ \mu$M, they accumulated N^1-acetylspermine and N^1-acetylspermidine in a time- and dose-dependent manner. Putrescine and spermidine concentrations were, however, not significantly, lowered, due to the high rate of ornithine decarboxylation and spermidine formation from putrescine by the normal biosynthetic route (Mamont et al. 1984). Repeated doses of 20 mg kg^{-1} MDL 72527 given to mice caused a significant increase in levels of N^1-acetylspermidine and N^1-acetylspermine, and a decrease in putrescine concentrations in all organs. Spermidine concentration decreased significantly in brain and testes. But on the whole, the observed concentration changes were small, except in brain, which accumulated close to 60 nmol g^{-1} N^1-acetylspermidine (Bolkenius et al. 1985).

The explanation for these facts is that N^1-acetylspermidine is effectively excreted in the urine. In rats, which were treated with 20 mg kg^{-1} MDL 72521, the amount of urinary N^1-acetylspermidine increased from $0.24 \pm 0.03\ \mu$mol per 24 h to $3.1 \pm 0.4\ \mu$mol per 24 h. This value corresponds to about 60 per cent of the total polyamines in urine and demonstrates the quantitative significance of the interconversion pathway (Seiler et al. 1985). In addition to excretion, N^1-acetylspermidine undergoes oxidative deamination in vivo (Seiler et al. 1983) and N^1-acetylspermine is prone to undergo the same catabolic reaction. [N^1-acetylspermine is not a urinary excretion product, and products of its catabolism have not yet been demonstrated directly. It is likely that its elimination from the body occurs after oxidative deamination to N^1-acetyl-N^8-(2-carboxyethyl)spermidine. The hydrolysis product of this amino acid has been found in urine (Nakajima et al. 1980).]

Complete inactivation of PAO in rat HTC cells did not affect cellular growth rates, in spite of the accumulation of N^1-acetylspermidine and N^1-acetylspermine (Mamont et al. 1984). The most conspicuous observation was that even daily administration of 20 mg kg^{-1} MDL 72527 for 6 weeks did not produce any obvious toxic or behavioural effects in mice (Bolkenius et al. 1985), suggesting that the presence of active PAO is not essential for normal growth and behaviour. As was demonstrated above, the body is capable of disposing of the substrates of PAO, and the amounts of putrescine and spermidine normally formed by this enzyme seem dispensable.

7.5 Conclusions

N,N'-bis(2,3-butadienyl)putrescine (MDL 72527) and N-methyl,N'-(2,3-butadienyl)putrescine (MDL 72521) are potent and specific inactivators of PAO. Although their mode of action has not yet been studied in detail, one can expect on the basis of the observed kinetic properties that they are enzyme-activated irreversible inhibitors (suicide inactivators).

Treatment of animals with these compounds produced metabolic effects that are in full agreement with the polyamine interconversion scheme and, in fact, provide strong evidence for this new metabolic concept.

That the PAO inhibitors did not produce any obvious pharmacological effects, despite the ubiquitous occurrence and usually high activity of PAO in all tissues, is a remarkable fact. One may conclude from this finding that PAO inhibitors are unlikely to be useful other than as tools in the exploration of metabolic and dynamic aspects of the polyamines. However, this conclusion may be premature. Not only is our knowledge of polyamine metabolism incomplete, but more importantly, our experience with these new enzyme inhibitors is fragmentary, and needs considerable expansion. Since the brain is nearly a closed system as far as polyamine metabolism is concerned, and since polyamine interconversion and putrescine formation from spermidine is quantitatively of greater importance in brain than in other organs (Seiler and Bolkenius 1985; Antrup and Seiler 1980), the exploration of potential central effects of the new inhibitors seems of special interest. Perhaps there are more analogies between MAO and PAO than just those that seem to be suggested by the mechanistic similarities of these two oxidases.

References

Antrup, H. and Seiler, N. (1980). On the turnover of polyamines spermidine and spermine in mouse brain and other organs. *Neurochem. Res.*, **5**, 123–43.

Beard, M. E., Baker, R., Conomos, P., Pugatch, D., and Holtzman, E. (1985). Oxidation of oxalate and polyamines by rat peroxisomes. *J. Histochem. Cytochem.*, **33**, 460–4.

Bey, P., Bolkenius, F. N., Seiler, N., and Casara, P. (1985). N-2,3-butadienyl-1,4-butanediamine derivatives: potent irreversible inactivators of mammalian polyamine oxidase *J. med. Chem.*, **28**, 1–2.

Bolkenius, F. N. and Seiler, N. (1981). Acetylderivatives as intermediates in polyamine catabolism. *Int. J. Biochem.*, **13**, 287–92.

Bolkenius, F. N., Bey, P., and Seiler, N. (1985). Specific inhibition of polyamine oxidase *in vivo* is a method for the elucidation of its physiological role. *Biochim. Biophys. Acta*, **838**, 69–76.

Della Ragione, F. and Pegg, A. E. (1982). Purification and characterization of spermidine/spermine N^1-acetyltransferase from rat liver. *Biochemistry*, **21**, 6152–8.

Gahl, W. A., Vale, A. M., and Pitot, H. C. (1982). Spermidine oxidase in human pregnancy serum. *Biochem. J.*, **20**, 161–6.

Hölttä, E. (1977). Oxidation of spermidine and spermine in rat liver: purification and properties of polyamine oxidase. *Biochemistry*, **16**, 91–100.

Höltta, E. (1983). Polyamine oxidase (rat liver). *Meth. Enzymol.*, **94**, 306–11.

Kitz, R. and Wilson, B. (1962). Esters of methanesulfonic acid as irreversible inhibitors of acetylcholinesterase. *J. Biol. Chem.*, **237**, 3245–9.

Krantz, A., Kokel, B., Sachdeva, Y. P., Salach, J., Claesson, A., and Sahlberg, C. (1979). Allenic amines as inactivators of mitochondrial monoamine oxidase. In *Drug action and design: mechanism-based enzyme inhibitors* (ed. T. Kalman), pp. 145–74. Elsevier/North-Holland, New York.

Mamont, P. S., Seiler, N., Siat, M., Joder-Ohlenbusch, A.-M., and Knödgen, B. (1981). Metabolism of acetyl derivatives of polyamines in cultured polyamine-deficient rat hepatoma cells. *Med. Biol.*, **59**, 347–53.

Mamont, P. S., Bolkenius, F., Seiler, N., Bey, P., and Kolb, M. (1984). Biochemical consequences of polyamine oxidase and N^8-acetylspermidine deacetylase inhibition in cultured rat hepatoma (HTC) cells. Abstract No. 6, International Conference on Polyamines, Budapest, Hungary.

Mondovi, B., Turini, P., Befani, O., and Sabatini, S. (1983). Purification of bovine plasma amine oxidase. *Meth. Enzymol.*, **94**, 314–18.

Morgan, D. M. L. (1985). Human pregnancy-associated polyamine oxidase: partial purification and properties. *Biochem. Soc. Trans.*, **13**, 351–2.

Nakajima, T., Noto, T., and Kato, N. (1980). Isolation and identification of polyamine metabolites in urine of animals. *Physiol. Chem. Phys.*, **12**, 401–10.

Pegg, A. E. and Erwin, B. G. (1985). Induction of spermidine/spermine N^1-acetyltransferase in rat tissues by polyamines. *Biochem. J.*, **231**, 285–9.

Pegg, A. E., Erwin, B. G., and Persson, L. (1985). Induction of spermidine/spermine N^1-acetyltransferase by methylglyoxal-bis(guanylhydrazone). *Biochim. Biophys. Acta*, **842**, 111–18.

Rando, R. and Eigner, A. (1977). The pseudoirreversible inhibition of monoamine oxidase by allylamine. *Mol. Pharmacol.*, **13**, 1005–13.

Seiler, N. and Bolkenius, F. N. (1985). Polyamine reutilization and turnover in brain. *Neurochem. Res.*, **10**, 529–44.

Seiler, N., Jung, M. J., and Koch-Weser, J. (eds.) (1978). *Enzyme-activated irreversible inhibitors*. Elsevier/North-Holland Biomedical Press, Amsterdam.

Seiler, N., Bolkenius, F. N., Knödgen, B., and Mamont, P. (1980). Polyamine oxidase in rat tissues. *Biochim. Biophys. Acta*, **615**, 480–8.

Seiler, N., Bolkenius, F. N., and Rennert, O. M. (1981). Interconversion, catabolism and elimination of the polyamines. *Med. Biol.*, **59**, 334–46.

Seiler, N., Knödgen, B., and Haegele, K. (1982). N-(3-aminopropyl)pyrroli-din-2-one, a product of spermidine catabolism *in vivo*. *Biochem. J.*, **208**, 189–97.

Seiler, N., Knödgen, B., Bink, G., Sarhan, S., and Bolkenius, F. (1983). Diamine oxidase and polyamine catabolism. *Adv. Polyamine Res.*, **4**, 135–54.

Seiler, N., Bolkenius, F. N., and Knödgen, B. (1985). The influence of catabolic reactions on polyamine excretion. *Biochem. J.*, **225**, 219–26.

Snyder, S. H. and Hendley, E. D. (1968). A simple and sensitive fluorescence assay for monoamine oxidase and diamine oxidase. *J. Pharmacol. Exp. Ther.*, **163**, 386–92.

Taylor, J. D., Wykes, A. A., Gladish, Y. C., and Martin, W. B. (1960). New inhibitor of monoamine oxidase. *Nature, Lond.*, **187**, 941–2.

8

New developments in enzyme-activated irreversible inhibitors of pyridoxal phosphate-dependent enzymes of therapeutic interest

Michel J. Jung and Charles Danzin

8.1   Introduction

Since the last review of the field (Jung *et al.* 1980), a number of new enzyme-activated irreversible inhibitors of pyridoxal phosphate-dependent enzymes have been described, and the biochemical and pharmacological effects of such compounds are now better understood. After a general introduction on the different types of inhibitors used, this chapter will deal with the following enzymes: 4-aminobutyrate: 2-oxoglutarate aminotransferase (EC 2.6.1.19, GABA-T); L-glutamate carboxy-lyase (EC 4.1.1.15, GAD); L-aromatic amino acid carboxy-lyase (EC 4.1.1.28, AADC); L-ornithine carboxy-lyase (EC 4.1.1.17, Orn-DC); and L-histidine carboxy-lyase (EC 4.1.1.22, HDC).

8.2   Enzyme-activated irreversible inhibitors of pyridoxal phosphate-dependent enzymes

Pyridoxal phosphate-dependent enzymes catalyse a variety of reactions on α- and ω-amino acids:

(1) transamination to the corresponding α-ketoacid; racemization of the α-centre (L-enantiomer $\rightleftharpoons$ D-enantiomer);

(2) decarboxylation to the parent amine;

(3) C-α—C-β bond breaking as in serine hydroxymethyl transferase (EC 2.1.2.1) or threonine aldolase (EC 4.1.2.5);

(4) elimination of leaving groups on C-β and C-γ; oxidative deamination on ω-amino acids such as 4-aminobutyric acid (GABA), 3-aminopropionic acid (β-Ala), ornithine, and lysine.

The first step (Fig. 8.1) in all these reactions is the formation of a Schiff base between the amino group of the entering substrate and the aldehyde function of the cofactor. Usually this Schiff-base formation occurs by addition of the amino group to the C=N bond existing, in the absence of substrate, between pyridoxal phosphate and a lysine side-chain of the protein. To explain the diversity of reactions catalysed with pyridoxal phosphate, it has been suggested by Dunathan (1966) that a part of the reaction specificity is achieved by control of the conformation around the C-α—N bond of the substrate–cofactor complex so as to orient the bond at C-α, which is to be broken perpendicular to the plane of the conjugated Π system. Either by hydrogen abstraction (transamination, racemization) or by decarboxylation, a negative charge is developed on the α-carbon atom, which may be delocalized over the whole conjugated cofactor system. Normally, this charge is quenched by protonation either on the α-carbon (decarboxylation, racemization) or on the carbon of the methylene part of the cofactor (transamination).

To apply such a mechanism to the design of inhibitors of these enzymes, it appeared desirable to divert the electron flux from its normal pathway, or to use

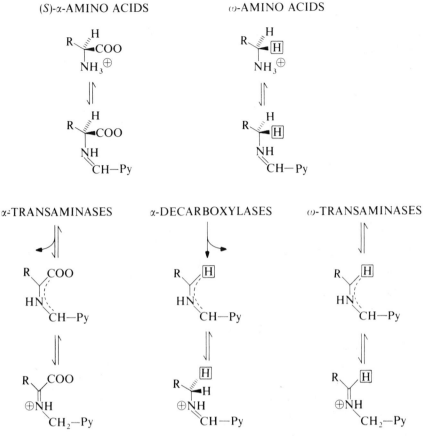

Fig. 8.1. General mechanism of pyridoxal phosphate-dependent (S)-α-amino acid α-transaminases and α-decarboxylases, and ω-amino acid ω-transaminases.

the normal flux to generate reactive species, or to direct it in such a way that a stable substrate–cofactor entity having a high affinity for the enzyme active-site is formed. In addition, owing to the principle of reversibility of enzyme-catalysed reaction, inhibitors can be designed as analogues of either the product or substrate of the enzymic reaction. Specific examples of these different possibilities will be discussed in the following sections. Selected examples given in Fig. 8.2 illustrate such hypothetical mechanisms.

In earlier work (Seiler et al. 1978b and references cited therein), it was believed that the enamines or vinylimines generated could function as alkylating agents and react irreversibly with a nucleophile of the enzyme active site [Fig. 8.3(a)]. However, more recently, another mechanism has been demonstrated for the inhibition of aspartate aminotransferase (EC 2.6.1.1) and GAD by serine-O-sulphate (Ueno et al. 1982; Likos et al. 1982) and of alanine racemase (EC 5.1.1.1)

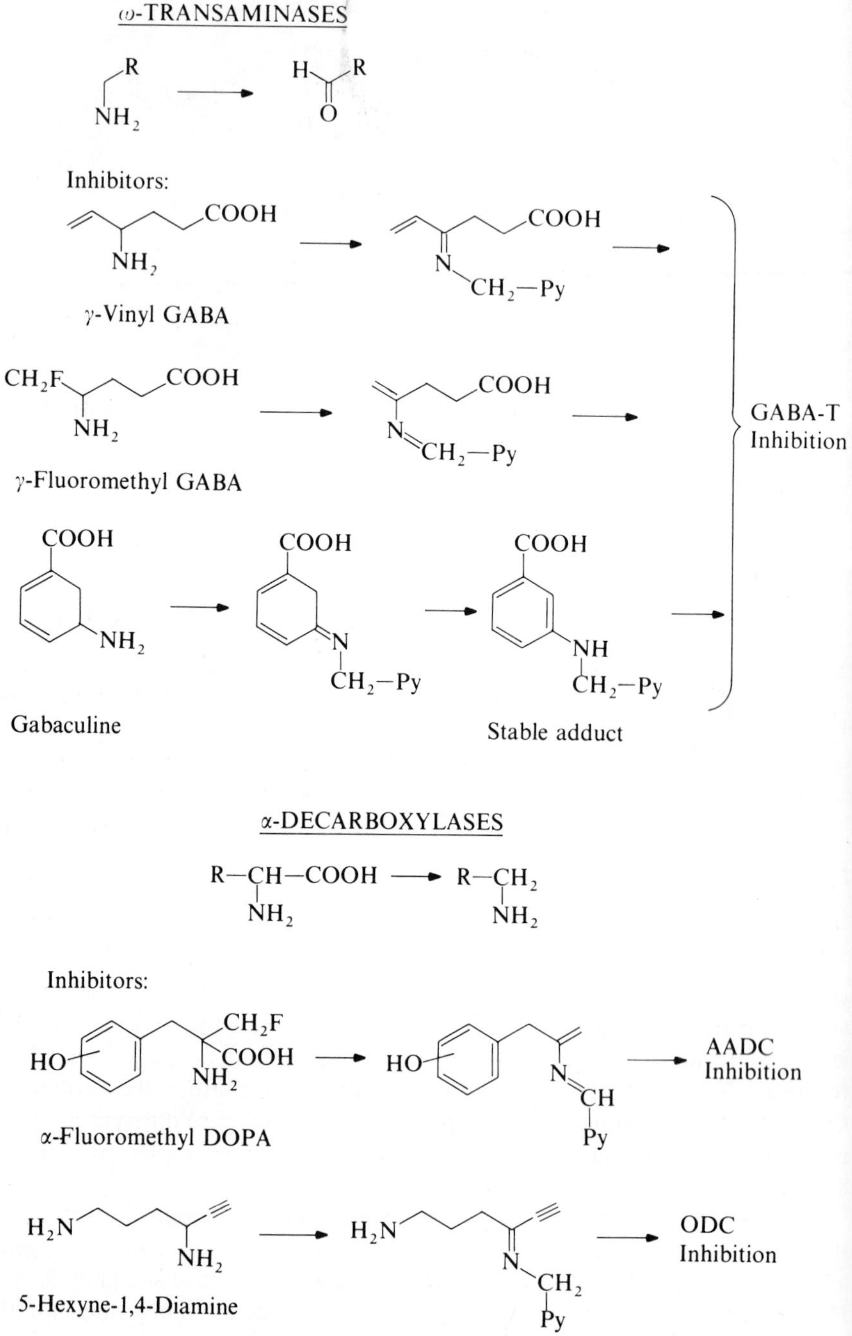

Fig. 8.2. Examples of enzyme-activated irreversible inhibitors of ω-transaminases and α-decarboxylases.

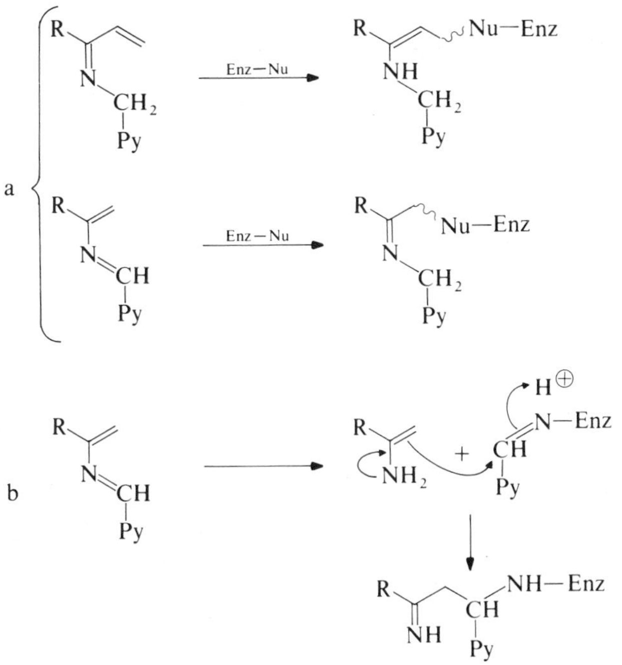

Fig. 8.3. Possible mechanisms of pyridoxal phosphate-dependent enzyme inactivation by enamines and vinylamines generated from enzyme-activated irreversible inhibitors.

by β-haloalanines and O-acetylserine (Badet *et al.* 1984; Roise *et al.* 1984). This mechanism [Fig. 8.3(b)] demands that the enamines dissociate from the cofactor, which then recombines with the lysine of the active site; the enamine reacts thereafter with this complex in an electrophilic manner, yielding a stable enzyme–inhibitor–cofactor complex. In most of the examples given through this review, the exact mechanism has not been worked out in detail, generally due to a lack of sufficient enzyme.

The interaction of such inhibitors with their target-enzyme is characterized by a time-dependent inhibition that is not normally reversed by dialysis (for a discussion see Kalman and Yalowich 1979). Different analyses of the kinetics of inactivation have been published (see more particularly Kitz and Wilson 1962; Cornish-Bowden 1979; Waley, 1980; 1985). However, even the most complete and complex analyses agree with the simple steady-state hypothesis:

$$E+I \underset{k_{-1}}{\overset{k_1}{\rightleftharpoons}} EI \underset{k_{-2}}{\overset{k_2}{\rightleftharpoons}} EI^* \overset{k_3}{\longrightarrow} E_i. \qquad (8.1)$$
$$\downarrow k_4$$
$$E+P$$

Assuming that k_4 is negligible (i.e. the partition ratio $k_3/k_4 \gg 1$, as has been proven experimentally in many of the cases cited later) and combining k_2, k_{-2}, and k_3 into a single constant (since under usual conditions there is no easy access to the individual rate constants), then eqn (8.1) can be simplified and becomes:

$$E + I \underset{k_{-1}}{\overset{k_1}{\rightleftarrows}} \quad EI \xrightarrow{k_2'} E_i. \tag{8.2}$$

For $[I] \gg [E_0]$, the equations to be solved for the rate of inhibition are:

$$[E_0] = [E] + [EI] + [E_i] \tag{8.3}$$

$$[I][E]/[EI] = (k_{-1} + k_2')/k_1 = K_I \tag{8.4}$$

$$\frac{d(E_i)}{dt} = k_2' EI \tag{8.5}$$

and the solution is:

$$\ln \frac{(E_0) - (E_i)}{(E_0)} = -k_2' t/(1 + K_I/[I]) \tag{8.6}$$

Equation (8.6) is the equation of the family of first-order rate constants of inactivation. If $t_{1/2}$ is the time of half-inactivation of enzyme at a given $[I]$, and $\tau_{1/2}$ the time of half-inactivation of enzyme at infinite concentration of I (i.e. $\tau_{\frac{1}{2}} = \ln 2/k_2'$), one can derive eqn (8.7):

$$t_{1/2} = \tau_{1/2}(1 + K_I/[I]) \tag{8.7}$$

Equations (8.6) and (8.7) predict that the inhibition should be pseudo first-order and saturable; K_I and $\tau_{1/2}$ (and k_2') are accessible by plotting $t_{1/2}$ as a function of $[I]^{-1}$.

Other means which have been used to ascertain the inhibition mechanism are:

1. A study of primary deuterium isotope effects (Metcalf et al. 1978; Lippert et al. 1980; Danzin et al. 1982).

2. The use of an inhibitor labelled with a radioactive isotope, and measurement either of loss of radioactivity, after $^{14}CO_2$ liberation if 1-^{14}C amino acids are used as substrates for decarboxylases (Maycock et al. 1980), or of incorporation of radioactivity into the inhibited protein and liberation of inorganic halide concomitant with decarboxylation or transamination (Jung et al. 1978; Lippert et al. 1980; Maycock et al. 1980; Pritchard et al. 1981).

3. A spectroscopic analysis of pyridoxal phosphate transformation during the inactivation (Jung et al. 1978; Likos et al. 1982; Badet et al. 1984; Roise et al. 1984).

4. A study of the stereochemistry of inactivation which should be in agreement with the known properties of the enzyme (Jung et al. 1978; Bouclier et al. 1979; Maycock et al. 1980; Silverman and Levy 1981a; Danzin and Jung 1984; Danzin et al. 1984).

5. Ultimately, and only in rare cases, analysis of modified amino acid residues in the inhibited protein (Gehring et al. 1977), or characterization of the pyri-

doxal phosphate-inhibitor complex (Rando 1977; Metcalf and Jung 1979; Likos *et al.* 1982; Ueno *et al.* 1982).

8.3 Inhibitors of GABA transaminase (GABA-T)

γ-aminobutyric acid (GABA) is widely accepted as the main inhibitory neuro-transmitter in the mammalian central nervous system (CNS) (Krnjevic 1974; Roberts 1974). A number of disorders of the mammalian CNS, among which epilepsy has a leading place, have been claimed to be associated with a deficiency in GABA neurotransmission (Roberts 1974; Tower 1976). Among the different approaches likely to correct such a deficiency, inhibition of GABA metabolism holds a privileged place (for review, see Jung 1982). In this section, we will review those inhibitors that have been previously described and then discuss briefly recent literature on the clinical efficiency of γ-vinyl GABA (Vigabatrin), the most widely used of these inhibitors.

8.3.1 GABA-T inhibitors bearing an unsaturated function

γ-acetylenic and γ-vinyl GABA (see Table 8.1 for formulae) have already been discussed in a previous review (Jung et al. 1980). Very little new information on the mechanism of action has become available since that time. In summary, γ-acetylenic GABA is a time-dependent inhibitor of GABA-T; it also inhibits, however, glutamate decarboxylase (GAD) both *in vitro* and *in vivo* and ornithine aminotransferase (EC 2.6.1.13, OAT), at least *in vitro*. Concerning the stereo-chemical features of these inhibitions, the (S)-enantiomer of γ-acetylenic GABA, at low concentrations, inhibits GABA-T and OAT. The (R)-enantiomer inhibits bacterial GAD, in agreement with the proposed mechanism of decarboxylases. However, the (S)-enantiomer of γ-acetylenic GABA inhibits GAD of mammal-ian origin. The implications of this lack of stereospecificity have been discussed recently (Danzin and Jung 1984; Danzin et al. 1984). γ-vinyl GABA was found to be more selective since it has no noticeable effect on alanine aminotransferase (EC 2.6.1.2, Ala-T), GAD, and OAT; its (S)-enantiomer, essentially, is respons-ible for GABA-T inhibition. The therapeutic potential of γ-vinyl GABA will be discussed in the next section.

More recently, three groups have described the synthesis of α-allenyl de-rivatives of amines and amino acids (Casara *et al.* 1984; Castelhano and Krantz 1984; Hiemstra *et al.* 1984). The racemate of γ-allenyl GABA, and the (S)-enantiomer [prepared from (S)-γ-acetylenic GABA] are indeed selective time-dependent inhibitors of GABA-T. (R,S)-γ-allenyl GABA is slightly more potent than (R,S)-γ-vinyl GABA since 0.1 mM of the former inhibits GABA-T at the same rate as 0.25 mM of the latter. The same ratio of potency is observed *in vivo*. The enzyme selectivity of γ-allenyl GABA is the same as that for γ-vinyl GABA (Jung *et al.* 1984a).

Kinetic constants of this class of GABA-T inhibitors are summarized in Table 8.1.

Table 8.1 Kinetic constants of GABA-T inhibitors bearing an unsaturated function

GABA analogues	Kinetic constants		$t_{1/2}$ at 1mM (min)	References
	K_I(mM)	$\tau_{1/2}$(min)		
(structure: $HC\equiv C$–CH(NH$_2$)–CH$_2$–COOH)	N.D.	N.D.	15	Bey et al. (1981)
(structure: CH$_2$=CH–CH(NH$_2$)–CH$_2$–COOH)	N.D.	N.D.	33	Bey et al. (1981)
(structure: $HC\equiv C$–CH(NH$_2$)–CH$_2$–CH$_2$–COOH)	0.008	6	6	Lippert et al. (1980)
(structure: CH$_2$=CH–CH(NH$_2$)–CH$_2$–CH$_2$–COOH)	no saturation kinetics		1	Lippert et al. (1977)
(structure: CH$_2$=CH–CH(NH$_2$)–CH=CH–COOH)	no saturation kinetics		5	Bey et al. (1986)
(structure: CH$_2$=C=CH–CH(NH$_2$)–CH$_2$–COOH)	no saturation kinetics		0.5	Jung et al. (1984a)

8.3.2 GABA-T inhibitors bearing a leaving group

The first irreversible inhibitor of GABA-T to be described, was ethanolamine-O-sulphate (Fowler and John 1972). Much of the *in vivo* work was done using intracerebroventricular injection. However, more recently it was realized that the compound is also active by systemic routes, if given at sufficiently high doses.

In a series of papers, Silverman and Levy (1980a, b, 1981a) described the inactivation of GABA-T by halomethyl derivatives of GABA. They synthesized these compounds in a sequence of steps leading from (S)-glutamate to γ-hydroxymethyl GABA, and then to halomethyl GABA, the halogen being either F, Cl, or Br. The fluoromethyl derivative is the best time-dependent inhibitor ($K_I=0.4$ mM, $k_{cat}=0.50$ min^{-1}), followed by the chloromethyl derivative ($K_I=13$ mM, $k_{cat}=0.55$ min^{-1}). The bromomethyl derivative is too unstable to be useful, although it produces a time-dependent inhibition. It is worth noting that the k_{cat} values for both fluoromethyl and chloromethyl derivatives are very similar; this could mean that the rate-determining step of the inactivation process occurs after elimination of the halide. Interestingly, when the halogen substituent is introduced in the chain instead of the terminal methyl group, the corresponding 3-halo GABA derivatives are good substrates of GABA-T but do not lead to enzyme inactivation, although the halide is eliminated as before (Silverman and Levy 1981b). This is reminiscent of the behaviour of 2,3-dehydro GABA, which is an excellent substrate of GABA-T and does not inactivate the enzyme (Johnston *et al.* 1979; Silverman *et al.* 1986).

A second group of workers (Bey *et al.* 1981) studied the structure–activity relationship for mammalian GABA-T inactivation as a function of the chain length of ω-amino acids, and the degree and position of fluorine substitutions. The results modified and completed from the original publication, are reported in Table 8.2. Several conclusions can be drawn from this work: trifluoromethyl derivatives do not produce GABA-T inactivation; moreover, while there is not a great difference in the kinetic constants of inactivation between mono- and difluorinated analogues of β-alanine, the monofluoromethyl derivatives have better affinities and produce a more rapid inactivation of the enzyme than the difluoromethyl derivatives in the GABA and homo-GABA series. Within the β-alanine series, the nature and position of the halogen also proved to be important: the β-chlorofluoromethyl derivative is less active than the β-difluoromethyl analogue (Schirlin *et al.* 1987), while 2,4-difluoro-3-aminobutyric acid is less active than the 4,4-difluoro analogue at concentrations lower than 1 mM and more active at concentrations greater than 2 mM. Furthermore, it is interesting to note that 4-keto-5-fluoropentanoic acid, i.e. the theoretical product of transamination of γ-fluoromethyl GABA, is a good time-dependent inhibitor of GABA-T, but only when the holo enzyme is in the pyridoxamine form (Lippert *et al.* 1982). Unexpectedly, from the *in vitro* structure activity relationship, the effects on brain GABA metabolism in mice were in the following order of decreasing potency: β-difluoromethyl β-alanine = 2-fluoro, 4-fluoro, 3-amino butyric acid > β-monofluoromethyl β-alanine = γ-monofluoromethyl GABA > γ-difluoromethyl GABA = γ-vinyl GABA. The difference in potency to achieve half-maximal elevation of brain GABA is almost 100-fold between β-difluoromethyl β-alanine and γ-vinyl GABA. However, it was disappointing that β-difluoromethyl-β-alanine showed unexplained delayed toxicity even after a single administration. Therefore this compound was not further developed.

8.3.3   Formation of a stable complex with the cofactor

It cannot be ruled out that the compounds described in the two previous sections inhibit GABA-T by a mechanism similar to that described by Metzler and collaborators (Likos *et al.* 1982; Ueno *et al.* 1982) for the inhibition of aspartate aminotransferase, and by Walsh and collaborators (Badet *et al.* 1984; Roise *et al.* 1984) for the inhibition of alanine racemase by β-fluoroalanine [see above, Fig. 8.3(b)], so that all the above compounds may belong to the present

Table 8.2 Kinetic constants of GABA-T inhibitors bearing in leaving group

GABA-T inhibitors	Kinetic constants			References
	K_I (mM)	$\tau_{1/2}$ (min)	$t_{1/2}$ at 1mM (min)	
β-alanine derivatives				
CH$_2$F–CH(NH$_2$)–CH$_2$–COOH	1.7	1.0	4.5	Bey *et al.* (1981)
CHF$_2$–CH(NH$_2$)–CH$_2$–COOH	2.0	2.0	6.5	Bey *et al.* (1981)
CH$_2$F–CF(NH$_2$)–CH$_2$–COOH	no saturation kinetics		8	Bey *et al.* (1981)
CHFCl–CH(NH$_2$)–CH$_2$–COOH	10	2.0	45	Schirlin *et al.* (1987)
CF$_3$–CH(NH$_2$)–CH$_2$–COOH	no time-dependent inhibition at 1 mM			Schirlin *et al.* (1987)
CHF$_2$–CH(NH$_2$)–CH$_2$–COOH	no time-dependent inhibition at 1 mM			Schirlin *et al.* (1987)
CHF$_2$–CH(NH$_2$)–CH$_2$–COOH	N.D.	N.D.	6.0	Schirlin *et al.* (1987)
GABA derivatives				
CH$_2$F–CH(NH$_2$)–CH$_2$–CH$_2$–COOH	2.0	1.8	5.0	Bey *et al.* (1981)
CH$_2$F–CH(NH$_2$)–CH=CH–COOH	0.2	3.6	4.0	Bey *et al.* (1986)
CHF$_2$–CH(NH$_2$)–CH$_2$–CH$_2$–COOH	20	1.8	40	Bey *et al.* (1981)
CF$_3$–CH(NH$_2$)–CH$_2$–CH$_2$–COOH	no time-dependent inhibition at 1 mM			Bey *et al.* (1981)

Table 8.2   (*Continued*)

GABA-T inhibitors	K_I(mM)	$\tau_{1/2}$ (min)	$t_{1/2}$ at 1 mM (min)	References
Kinetic constants				

Homo-GABA derivatives

CH₂F— ... —COOH / NH₂ structure

| 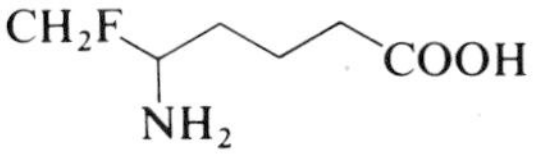 | 4.7 | 2.1 | 11.5 | Bey *et al.* (1981) |

CHF₂— ... —COOH / NH₂ structure

| 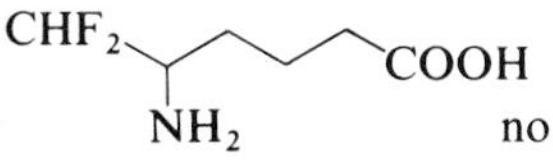 | no saturation kinetics | | 40 | Bey *et al.* (1981) |

section. One series of compounds, however, deserves special notice here: these are inhibitors based on the aromatization concept.

In 1976, Kobayashi and co-workers (Kobayashi *et al.* 1976) found that 5-amino-1,3-cyclohexadienylcarboxylic acid, a natural product isolated from *Streptomyces toyocaensis* is a potent inhibitor of GABA-T. One has to credit R. R. Rando, and also one of the reviewers of his first paper about this compound (Rando 1977) for guessing and demonstrating the mechanism of action of this compound, named gabaculine (see Fig. 8.2) by the former authors. It was demonstrated that gabaculine forms a Schiff base as a normal substrate of GABA-T. Once transaminated, the intermediate rapidly aromatizes to form the *m*-anthranilic acid derivative tightly bound at the active site, resulting in the inactivation of the enzyme. This mechanism could apply to the two other double-bond isomers of gabaculine, i.e. 3-amino-1,5-cyclohexadienyl carboxylic acid and 3-amino-1,4-cyclohexadienyl carboxylic acid. The first of these two compounds was synthesized by our group and found to be equipotent to gabaculine both *in vitro* and *in vivo* (Metcalf and Jung 1979). The other was synthesized by Danishefsky and Hershenson (1979). No data on biological activity of this compound are available, to our knowledge.

In medicinal chemistry, heterocyclic rings such as thiophene and furan are often considered to be isosteric with a phenyl ring. 4-amino-4,5-dihydro-2-thiophene carboxylic acid and 4-amino-4,5-dihydrofuran carboxylic acid (Lippert *et al.* 1985), like the dihydrophenyl analogues of GABA discussed previously are potent time-dependent inhibitors of mammalian brain GABA-T both *in vitro* and *in vivo*. The most potent inhibitory species is the (*S*)-enantiomer, as for γ-acetylenic and γ-vinyl GABA. A dose of 5 mg kg⁻¹ of either compound elevates brain GABA levels eighth fold over control values, 24 h after administration.

The gabaculine analogues have anticonvulsant effects in several models of physically or chemically induced seizures in animals (Schechter *et al.* 1979). As occurred for the fluorinated GABA-T inhibitors (see above), development did not go beyond animal pharmacology. Corresponding information on the heterocyclic analogues is not yet available.

8.3.4 Clinical effects of γ-vinyl GABA (vigabatrin)

The correlation between brain GABA level elevation after γ-vinyl GABA administration and increases of free and conjugated GABA in CSF has been investigated thoroughly in animals (Böhlen *et al.* 1979; Palfreyman *et al.* 1984). The elevation of GABA in CSF has been used to monitor biochemical efficacy of γ-vinyl GABA in humans (Grove *et al.* 1981).

Huntington's disease has been claimed to be associated with deficient GABA-ergic function due to degeneration of neurons in the globus pallidus and in the nigrostriatal axis. However, neither γ-acetylenic GABA (Tell *et al.* 1981) nor γ-vinyl GABA (Scigliano *et al.* 1984) had any beneficial effect in patients with Huntington's disease.

In an open study, it was found that γ-vinyl GABA improved the psychological symptoms in four out of five patients suffering from catatonic or hebephrenoca-tatonic schizophrenia (Lambert *et al.* 1983). This is certainly a lead worth pursuing in the future.

Involuntary hyperkinetic movements, such as those seen in tardive dyskinesia, may be influenced by GABA-ergic drugs. Indeed, γ-vinyl GABA reduced tardive dyskinesia in psychotic patients, but had little effect on psychiatric features and worsened Parkinsonian symptoms (Lambert *et al.* 1982; Korsgaard *et al.* 1983).

So far, however, the most promising indications for γ-vinyl GABA are in epilepsy. A number of open or controlled studies performed in different centres on drug-resistant epileptic patients, not controlled by currently available therapy, have led to the provisional conclusion that additional therapy with γ-vinyl GABA ($1-3$ g day^{-1}) reduced seizures by over 50 per cent in more than half the population studied (Rimmer and Richens 1984; *Lancet* Editorial 1985). More importantly, in controlled patients followed for up to 32 months, there was no sign of tolerance development (Pedersen *et al.* 1985).

During long-term toxicity studies ($6-16$ months), it was found that micro-vacuoles appeared in the brain of rodents and dogs (Rimmer and Richens 1984). The mechanism of such microvacuole formation is presently under investigation. A clinical correlation has not been found in human trials. Extremely sensitive measures for conduction alterations due to demyelinization or ischaemic damage, such as auditory and visual evoked potentials and encephalograms, do not show any changes, even after one year of γ-vinyl GABA administration (Hammond and Wilder 1985). So the clinical relevance of the microvacuoles seen in animal toxicity studies is uncertain.

8.4   Inhibitors of glutamate decarboxylase (GAD)

The recognition of 4-aminobutyric acid (GABA) as a major inhibitory neuro-transmitter in the mammalian central nervous system (CNS) is well documented (Krnjevic 1974; Roberts 1974). Inhibition of GABA transaminase (GABA-T), the primary catabolic enzyme for GABA, significantly elevates GABA concentrations in the brain (see this chapter, and for earlier review, see Palfreyman *et al.* 1981). In animals, the main benefit of augmented GABA in CNS is an anticonvulsant effect (Schechter *et al.* 1977). Conversely, inhibition of glutamate decarboxylase (GAD) and the concomitant reduction of GABA levels in CNS produce convulsions (see Reingold and Orlowski 1979, and references cited therein). Compounds that inhibit GAD centrally have no clear therapeutic use in mammals.

However, recent evidence has led to the suggestion that GABA may also be a neurotransmitter in the vertebrate peripheral autonomic nervous system (Jessen *et al.* 1979). In this respect, GABA may regulate intestinal motility (Ong and Kerr 1983), cardiovascular function (De Feudis, 1981, 1982), endocrine pancreatic function (Cavagnini *et al.* 1982; Kawai and Unger 1983) and movements of oviduct muscle (Erdö *et al.* 1984; Fernandez *et al.* 1984). While the major pathway for GABA formation in CNS involves L-glutamate decarboxylation, catalysed by GAD, other pathways that play an important role in the synthesis of GABA in peripheral tissues have been proposed (Seiler and Eichentopf 1975; White 1981). Nevertheless, it is noteworthy that high GAD activities have been demonstrated in myenteric plexus (Jessen *et al.* 1979; Ong and Kerr 1983, and references cited therein), in rat pancreatic islets and human insulinoma (Okada *et al.* 1976), as well as in the rat oviduct mucosa and in nerves innervating the oviduct (Murashima and Kato 1986). Therefore specific and potent inhibitors of GAD, with a selective effect in peripheral tissues, would be useful tools for further investigation of the role of GABA in these tissues. Moreover, such inhibitors would permit the investigation of the role of GAD in host-dependent microorganisms such as *Mycobacterium leprae*, in which this enzyme has been characterized (Prabhakaran *et al.* 1983) and in nematodes, such as *Ascaris suum*, in which GABA is a possible inhibitory transmitter at neuromuscular junctions (del Castillo *et al.* 1964; Kass *et al.* 1980).

8.4.1   Carbonyl trapping agents and competitive inhibitors

A number of compounds that inhibit GAD *in vitro* have been described. Carbonyl-trapping agents and competitive inhibitors of the enzyme have been reviewed by Metcalf (1979). Reversible formation of a Schiff base between the α-amino function of the α-amino acid substrates and the carbonyl group of the pyridoxal phosphate cofactor is an obligatory step in the reaction of pyridoxal phosphate-dependent enzymes. Functional groups, such as hydrazine or hydroxyamine, which can form bonds with the carbonyl function of the cofactor that are more stable than those of the normal Schiff base, have been used successfully to design potent inhibitors of GAD. In particular, aminooxyacetic acid (AOAA; Kuriyama *et al.* 1966; Wu and Roberts 1974), glutamic acid γ-hydrazide (Tapia *et al.* 1975), and *N*-hydroxyglutamate (Cooper and Griffith 1979), markedly inhibit GAD *in vitro*. However these compounds also inhibit several other pyridoxal phosphate-dependent enzymes. A variety of mercapto-carboxylic acids are potent competitive inhibitors of mammalian GAD, the most potent being the convulsant agent 3-mercaptopropionic acid ($K_1 = 1.8$ μM) (Wu and Roberts 1974; Taberner *et al.* 1977). However, these compounds also inhibit GABA-T. Interestingly, it has been suggested that the mercaptocarboxylic acids inhibit GAD by combining with the pyridoxal phosphate–lysine Schiff base (Wu and Roberts 1974). 4,5-dihydroxyisophthalic acid, produced by a *Streptomyces* species, has been found to be the most potent competitive inhibitor of brain GAD known to date ($K_1 = 0.18$ μM, K_m for L-glutamate = 3.6 mM; Endo *et al.* 1978).

8.4.2   Enzyme-activated irreversible inhibitors

More recently, with the development of the concept of substrate-induced irreversible inhibition of enzymes, several compounds that inactivate GAD have been reported. The first example of such a mechanism of GAD inhibition has been described for 2-keto-4-pentenoic acid, a metabolite of the convulsant agent allylglycine (Reingold and Orlowski 1979). The active reagent appears to be the dienolate of 2-keto-4-pentenoate, acting as a nucleophile. The probable active-site electrophile could be the imine function of the Schiff base formed by pyridoxal phosphate and a lysine residue of GAD (Walsh 1982). At the same time, Chrystal *et al.* (1979) reported the irreversible inhibition of brain GAD by (*E*)-2-(methyl)dehydroglutamic acid ($K_1 = 6.6.10^{-4}$ M; $\tau_{1/2} = 10$ min). The α-methyl group of the compound prevents its transamination and, therefore, the inactivation of transaminases by this molecule. It is worth noting that (*E*)-2-(methyl)dehydroglutamic acid does not inhibit bacterial GAD. Conversely, α-(fluoromethyl)glutamic acid is a potent enzyme-activated irreversible inhibitor of *Escherichia coli* GAD ($K_1 = 2.8$ μM; $\tau_{1/2} = 2$ min), but only a weak inhibitor of the mammalian enzyme, even at millimolar concentrations (Kollonitsch *et al.* 1978; Kuo and Rando 1981).

While no attempt to separate enantiomers of α-(fluoromethyl)glutamic acid has been made, it was presumed that only the (*S*)-isomer would produce inactivation of GAD (Kuo and Rando 1981). This assumption is germane to the fact that all pyridoxal phosphate-dependent α-L-amino acid decarboxylases studied have been shown to introduce a *pro-R* hydrogen in the reaction product, i.e. to function with retention of configuration (for review, see Floss and Vederas 1982). Owing to the reversibility of enzyme-catalysed reactions, the pyridoxal phosphate-dependent α-L-amino acid decarboxylases should be able to abstract specifically the α-*pro-R* hydrogen from their reaction product, i.e. from the amine formed after decarboxylation of the substrate. Stereospecific abstraction of an α-proton seems indeed to be involved in the inactivation of bacterial GAD by (R)-4-aminohex-5-ynoic acid (Jung *et al.* 1978). However, removal of the α-proton from L-serine-O-sulphate, which has a chirality opposite to that of (R)-4-aminohex-5-ynoic acid, was also implied in the inactivation of bacterial GAD (Likos *et al.* 1982). Moreover, mammalian GAD has been shown to be inactivated *in vitro* only by the (S)-enantiomer of 4-aminohex-5-ynoic acid (Bouclier *et al.* 1979). This lack of stringent stereospecificity, or even specificity opposite to that expected, was, in fact, demonstrated in the inactivation of several other pyridoxal phosphate-dependent enzymes (for review, see Danzin and Jung 1984). These observations are explained either by assuming a common ancestor for these enzymes, lacking stringent stereospecificity, or by invoking a misplacement of the cofactor–inhibitor complex within the active site, which would modify the stereochemistry of catalysis (Danzin and Jung 1984).

In a recent paper, Marquet and collaborators have reported stereochemical data about decarboxylation of the *threo* and *erythro* isomers of (2R)-3-fluoroglutamate by *E. coli* GAD (Vidal-Cros *et al.* 1985). The *threo* isomer is decarboxylated into optically active 4-amino-3-fluorobutyrate, whereas the *erythro* isomer loses its fluorine atom during the reaction, yielding succinic semialdehyde after hydrolysis of the unstable intermediate enamine. Inactivation of the enzyme does accompany the loss of the fluorine atom from the *erythro* isomer, while a reactive aminoacrylate should be formed in the active site (Vidal-Cros *et al.* 1985).

Although a potent and specific enzyme-activated irreversible inhibitor of mammalian GAD which does not penetrate in the brain has not yet been found, the considerable progress accomplished in the design of enzyme inactivators should make such a compound available in the next few years.

8.5   Inhibitors of aromatic amino acid decarboxylase (AADC)

Aromatic amino acid decarboxylase (EC 4.1.1.28, AADC) catalyses the decarboxylation of a number of aromatic amino acids, among which 3,4-dihydroxyphenylalanine (dopa) and 5-hydroxytryptophan appear to be the most important so far in mammalian pharmacology. It is still a question of debate whether AADC describes a single enzyme or a class of isoenzymes (for review see Jung 1986). The enzyme has been purified from hog kidney; it has a molecular weight of 110 000 and consists of two subunits, which are probably non-identical as there is only one pyridoxal phosphate molecule per dimer. This pyridoxal phosphate is strongly bound to the enzyme; however, exogenous pyridoxal phosphate stimulates enzyme activity by a poorly understood mechanism.

Inhibitors of AADC have been sought since the discovery of its role in the synthesis of biogenic amines in central and peripheral neurons. More recently, the enzyme has been found in neurons not containing any of the classical biogenic amines (Jaeger *et al.* 1983). We may speculate that its role there, if any, is to generate amines that are not conventionally considered as vertebrate neurotransmitters, e.g. tyramine, tryptamine, or phenethylamine. In addition, AADC plays a role in insects for the synthesis of octopamine and of the sclerotizing agent N-acetyldopamine (Turnbull *et al.* 1980). Little is known about the molecular properties of the insect enzyme, and the discussion will concentrate here on properties and inhibitors of the classical mammalian enzyme found in neurones.

8.5.1   α- and β-alkyl amino acids as inhibitors of AADC

α-methyl dopa, a well known antihypertensive agent, is decarboxylated by AADC at one hundreth the rate of dopa and therefore behaves as a competitive inhibitor. In addition, for every 50 turnovers of α-methyl dopa an abnormal decarboxylation-dependent transamination takes place (protonation on the methylene carbon atom of pyridoxal phosphate instead of the α-carbon of the substrate), resulting in the pyridoxamine phosphate form of the holoenzyme (O'Leary and Baughn 1977).

Rigid analogues of dopa in which the α-carbon atom is linked to the aromatic nucleus, forming five- or six- membered rings, behave essentially as competitive inhibitors, with no evidence of decarboxylation (Cannon *et al.* 1974). The same seems to hold for α,β-cyclopropyl analogues of *m*-tyrosine whereas the corresponding analogue of dopa is apparently unstable (Bernabé *et al.* 1979).

8.5.2   α-substituted-unsaturated derivatives of amino acids

The synthesis and study of the biochemical properties of α-vinyl and α-ethynyl dopa have been reported by two separate groups (Metcalf and Jund 1977; Taub and Patchett 1977; Maycock *et al.* 1979; Ribereau-Gayon *et al.* 1979). α-ethynyl dopa and α-vinyl dopa produce a rapid but partial inhibition of AADC within a few minutes. This rapid inhibition is followed by a slower time-dependent inactivation of the enzyme. $^{14}CO_2$ is still released from $[1-^{14}C]$ -ethynyl dopa during the second phase of inhibition. However, no significant amine formation could be detected by HPLC (Ribereau-Gayon *et al.* 1979) but the method may not have been sufficiently sensitive. Therefore the mechanism of AADC inhibition by α-substituted-unsaturated derivatives of dopa appears to be complex and no sound explanation has been proposed so far to account for the biphasic pattern of inhibition. Due to the poor activity of these compounds *in vivo* (Ribereau-Gayon *et al.* 1979), they have not been further developed.

β-methylene *m*-tyrosine was synthesized as a potential irreversible inhibitor of AADC (Chari and Wemple 1979), but was found not to inhibit the enzyme. These authors missed the opportunity to test the compound as a substrate of AADC. Scientists at our Institute, while working on enzyme-activated irreversible inhibitors MAO (see Chapter 6, this volume) predicted that β-methylene or β-fluoromethylene derivatives of the substrates of AADC could serve as substrates of the enzyme *in vivo*, thus generating locally potent inhibitors of MAO. This concept of a cleverly designed bioprecursor of an enzyme inhibitor allowed inhibitions of MAO-A exclusively in the brain (McDonald *et al.* 1984; Palfreyman *et al.* 1985; Jung *et al.* 1985). (*E*)-*β*-fluoromethylene-*m*-tyrosine is presently undergoing clinical trials.

8.5.3   α-substituted-unsaturated derivatives of amines

It has been reported that 5-hydroxytryptamine inhibits AADC in a time-dependent manner with formation of 5-hydroxyindoleacetaldehyde (Borri Voltattorni and Minelli 1980). Other amines do not behave in the same manner. It is not known at present whether α-hydrogen abstraction from serotonin is compatible with the stereochemistry demanded by the reversibility principle of enzyme-catalysed reactions (for discussion, see Danzin and Jung 1984, and references cited therein). This principle had been thought to explain the inhibition of bacterial GAD by (*R*)-*γ*-acetylenic GABA (Jung *et al.* 1978). Therefore, α-vinyl and α-ethynyl dopamine have been synthesized and, indeed, were found to be time-dependent inhibitors of AADC (Maycock *et al.* 1978). The inactivation is slow and at least as complex as that observed for the corresponding amino acids.

8.5.4   α-halomethyl amino acids

α-chloromethyl, α-monofluoromethyl, and α-difluoromethyl derivatives of dopa are time-dependent inhibitors of AADC (Bey 1978). As AADC has a broad spectrum of acceptance of substrates regarding ring substitutions, a study of structure–activity relationship has been carried out on the mono- and difluoromethyl derivatives (Jung 1986). As a general rule for this enzyme, the mono-fluorinated compounds are more active than the difluorinated derivatives. Regarding ring substitutions, the 3,4-dihydroxy derivative is equipotent with the 2,3- and 2,5-dihydroxy compounds, and with the 3-hydroxy analogues. The *o*-tyrosine derivative is somewhat less potent, while the derivative of *p*-tyrosine is almost inert (see below). α-fluoromethyl-5-hydroxy tryptophan is comparable to α-difluromethyl dopa, i.e. about 10 times weaker than α-monofluoromethyl dopa.

A thorough investigation of the inhibition of AADC by the latter compound has been reported (Maycock *et al.* 1980). The time-dependent inhibition, which does not follow pseudo first-order kinetics, is irreversible and independent of exogenous pyridoxal phosphate. During one turnover of inhibitor by the enzyme, one equivalent of CO_2 and F^- are released and inhibitor binds stoichiometrically to the enzyme–cofactor complex. It cannot be decided yet whether inhibition occurs through enzyme alkylation [Fig. 8.3(a)] or through reaction with pyridoxal phosphate [Fig. 8.3(b)]. Similarly [ring 2,5,6-^{3}H]-α-difluoromethyl dopa is incorporated into the inhibited enzyme and the radio-label cannot be removed by acid precipitation (Ribereau-Gayon *et al.* 1980).

In vivo, α-monofluoromethyl dopa (MFMD) is sufficiently potent to block biogenic amine synthesis at a step that is normally not rate-limiting (Jung *et al.* 1979). During extensive *in vivo* investigations, it was realized that serotonin synthesis was also blocked (Bey *et al.* 1980) by this compound. This lack of specificity relates to the similarity of the enzyme in the two types of neurones (they may even be identical), and to the uptake of MFMD by catecholaminergic as well as serotoninergic neurons. α-monofluoromethyl-*p*-tyrosine, which is inert as an AADC inhibitor (see above), is converted by the action of tyrosine hydroxylase (EC 1.14.16.2) into MFMD both *in vitro* and *in vivo* (Jung *et al.* 1984b). In addition to a strict selectivity on catecholaminergic structures, α-monofluoromethyl-*p*-tyrosine also offers the advantage that its biochemical effectiveness will depend on the state of tyrosine hydroxylase induction (Hornsperger 1984).

For comparison, the properties of α-monofluoromethyltryptophan were also investigated. This compound is a good substrate of tryptophan hydroxylase (EC 1.14.16.4), like its tyrosine counterpart for tyrosine hydroxylase; however, *in vivo* its effects are not significant, probably because α-monofluoromethyl-5-hydroxytryptophan is itself a poor inhibitor of AADC (Hornsperger 1984).

8.5.5 α-halomethyl amine derivatives

α-monofluoromethyl dopamine is a potent irreversible inhibitor of AADC (Maycock *et al.* 1980). The inhibitory species is the (*R*)-enantiomer, in agreement with a mechanism based on the reversibility of enzyme reaction (see above). There is a stoichiometric incorporation of tritiated-ring α-monofluoromethyldopamine into the inhibited enzyme. It must be noticed, however, that at equal concentrations, the inhibition by α-monofluoromethyldopamine is slower than by α-monofluoromethyl dopa. This could mean that hydrogen abstraction catalysed by AADC is slower than decarboxylation, all other things being equal.

8.5.6 Pharmacological potential of AADC inhibitors

α-methyl dopa is a commercial drug for reducing blood pressure. Its mechanism of action is mediated by AADC, but not because α-methyl dopa is an inhibitor of the enzyme, rather because it is a substrate. It is unlikely that the abortive transamination (see above) is of any consequence *in vivo*, as pyridoxal phosphate is present at sufficient concentration. However, α-methyldopamine formed by decarboxylation is hydroxylated in the β-position to α-methylnoradrenalin, a weak sympathomimetic agent (Sjoerdsma 1982).

α-methylhydrazino dopa (carbidopa) and N^1-seryl-N^2-(2,3,4 trihydroxybenzyl) hydrazine (benserazide), although not discussed in this section, deserve a comment here. These compounds are potent pseudo-irreversible inhibitors *in vitro* and *in vivo*, functioning probably by binding to pyridoxal phosphate (Bartholini and Pletscher 1975). They have no effect on endogenous catecholamine synthesis, but do protect however exogenous dopa against decarboxylation. As they penetrate the CNS poorly, they are used in combination with L-dopa for the treatment of Parkinsonism and serve a dual more, to avoiding peripheral formation of dopamine and allowing more L-dopa to reach the brain, where it can be decarboxylated to dopamine.

α-difluoromethyl dopa is comparable to carbidopa in its biological effects in mammals. It inhibits brain AADC only at concentrations greater than 500 mg kg^{-1} while effectively protecting exogenous dopa against decarboxylation in the periphery at doses of 50–200 mg kg^{-1}.

α-monofluoromethyl dopa has a completely different spectrum of action. This compound inhibits AADC centrally almost as effectively as in the peripheral tissues, and to an extent where decarboxylation becomes rate-limiting. The resulting depletion of catecholamines and indoleamines produces antihypertensive effects, which can be reversed by i.v. infusion of dopamine (Fozard *et al.* 1981). α-monofluoromethyltyrosine (administered as the methyl ester) has similar effects. The antihypertensive action of these compounds can be accounted for by their peripheral effects. The consequences of central regulation of amine synthesis remain to be determined.

8.6   Inhibitors of histidine decarboxylase (HDC)

HDC catalyses the decarboxylation of histidine to histamine, an important autacoid and perhaps a neurotransmitter in mammals. A potent inhibitor of HDC should allow the depletion of histamine from all its pools whether they have a rapid or slow turnover. Therefore, such a compound should be useful in studying the physiological and pharmacological role of these different histamine stores.

To the knowledge of the authors, only a few irreversible inhibitors of mammalian HDC have been reported in the literature: α-chloromethylhistidine (Lippert *et al.* 1979), α-monofluoromethylhistidine and α-monofluoromethylhistamine (Kollonitsch *et al.* 1978), α-trifluoromethylhistamine (Metcalf *et al.* 1984), and α-ethynylhistamine (Holbert and Metcalf 1984). The most potent of these compounds is α-monofluoromethylhistidine. Therefore we will briefly review what has been reported on the other compounds and describe, in more detail, the biological effects of α-monofluoromethylhistidine.

8.6.1   α-chloromethylhistidine

HDC prepared from foetal rat liver, or from hamster placenta, was inhibited in time-dependent manner by α-chloromethylhistidine. For instance, at 0.1 mM α-chloromethylhistidine, half-inactivation of the enzyme occurred within 3–4 min.

At this concentration, no inhibition of AADC, or of *Lactobacillus* 30a HDC (a pyruvate-enzyme instead of a pyridoxal phosphate-dependent enzyme) could be detected; (Lippert *et al.* 1979). The compound also irreversibly blocks HDC in rat stomach: a dose of 200 mg kg^{-1} inhibits the enzyme by 90 per cent. The inhibition is of short duration, probably due to new HDC synthesis. α-chloro-methylhistidine has anti-secretory properties in the pylorus-ligated rat (Lippert *et al.* 1979).

8.6.2   α-monofluoromethylhistamine

This compound was reported in the original publication by the Merck group, describing their range of α-fluoromethyl derivatives of amines and amino acids (Kollonitsch *et al.* 1978). These authors claimed that both the (*R*)- and (*S*)-enantiomers of α-monofluoromethyl histamine inhibit HDC from foetal rat liver in a time-dependent manner. Using (*R, S*)-monofluoromethylhistamine synthesized in our centre, we found no inhibition of hamster placenta enzyme at concentrations up to 1 mM (M. Bouclier and M. J. Jung, unpublished).

8.6.3   α-trifluoromethylhistamine

While trifluoromethyl derivatives of GABA or β-alanine were found to have no time-dependent effect on GABA-T (Bey *et al.* 1981), and α-trifluoromethylpu-trescine did not inhibit Orn-DC irreversibly (Sjoerdsma and Schechter 1984; C. Danzin, unpublished results), α-trifluoromethylhistamine has been reported to act as an enzyme-activated irreversible inhibitor of HDC from hamster placenta (Metcalf *et al.* 1984). The kinetics of the time-dependent inhibition are biphasic, with a rapid onset followed by either a slower phase at 10^{-5} M or a plateau at 10^{-4} M (25 per cent enzyme activity remaining) and at 10^{-3} M (10 per cent enzyme activity remaining). The inhibited enzyme seems to reactivate upon dilution and dialysis. α-trifluoromethylhistamine could fall into the category of slow-on and slow-off binding inhibitors as no evidence of hydrogen abstraction and fluorine elimination could be demonstrated.

The compound is also active *in vivo*. A dose of 100 mg kg^{-1} inhibits rat stomach HDC by 80 per cent and the inhibition lasts at least 3 h. However, no effect on gastric secretion in the pylorus-ligated rat, used as a model of gastric secretion, was observed (Metcalf *et al.* 1984).

8.6.4   α-ethynylhistamine

An irreversible component has been observed in the inhibition of HDC from hamster placenta with α-ethynylhistamine. However, the inactivation process does not follow pseudo first-order kinetics, as was observed with α-trifluoro-methylhistamine (Holbert and Metcalf 1984). No data regarding *in vivo* effects of α-ethynylhistamine are available so far.

8.6.5   α-monofluoromethylhistidine

Kollonitsch et al. (1978) published the first report on time-dependent inhibition of HDC by α-monofluoromethylhistidine in vitro. The first use in vivo of the inhibitor was reported shortly afterwards (Garbarg et al. 1980).

The mechanism of inhibition of HDC by (S)-α-monofluoromethylhistidine was investigated using HDC extensively purified from foetal rats (Kubota et al. 1984; Wada et al. 1984). The inactivation follows pseudo first-order kinetics, goes to completion and is not reversed by dialysis. At 10^{-5} M (S)-α-monofluoromethylhistidine, the time for half-inactivation of the enzyme is approximately 20 min. The apo-enzyme is not inhibited by 100-fold higher concentrations of the compound. Kinetic constants of the inactivation process have been measured ($K_1 = 8.3 \mu M$; $\tau_{1/2} = 4$ min). Using [ring 4-^{3}H]-(S)-α-monofluoromethylhistidine, Kubota et al. (1984) demonstrated a correlation between the extent of incorporation of radioactivity into HDC and the degree of inactivation of the enzyme. When the enzyme is totally inactivated, the incorporation corresponds to 1 mol of tritiated (S)-α-monofluoromethylhistidine per subunit of HDC. α-monofluoromethylhistamine, the product of a normal decarboxylation was not found in the reaction mixture. Similarly, absence of amine formation had been shown by Maycock et al. (1980) when α-monofluoromethyl dopa was incubated with AADC. [1-^{14}C]-(S)-α-monofluoromethylhistidine did not incorporate radioactivity into the inactivated HDC, indicating liberation of CO_2. From the measurements of the CO_2 released and the incorporation of tritiated inhibitor into the enzyme, a ratio of 2.8 was found, indicating that the mechanism of inhibition is very efficient. Furthermore, Wada et al. (1984) reported that, after incubation of HDC with ring [4-^{3}H]-(S)-α-monofluoromethylhistidine, and radioactivity associated with the protein in SDS gel electrophoresis, i.e. under denaturing conditions, is retained only after sodium borohydride reduction of the inactivated enzyme. These authors concluded that this observation is in agreement with the mechanism described in Scheme 8.3(b).

α-monofluoromethylhistidine has been used in a number of in vivo situations. It could, for instance, be demonstrated that single doses of the compound reduce the basal level of gastric HDC as well as the enzyme activity induced by pentagastrin but have little effect on mucosal histamine content. However, the induction of gastric secretion by pentagastrin was significantly shortened (Bouclier et al. 1983a). In a model of stress ulceration, the effects of α-monofluoromethylhistidine on central (hypothalamic) and gastric mucosal histamine metabolism were compared to those of cimetidine, the well known H_2 antagonist (Bouclier et al. 1983b). Cimetidine did not change the induction of gastric and hypothalamic HDC activity, nor the elevation of histamine content in the hypothalamus. α-monofluoromethylhistidine, by contrast, blocked these biochemical changes. Interestingly, both compounds produced a similar protection against gastric ulceration.

Histamine is present in pools with different rates of renewal, and HDC is a fairly inducible enzyme and has a rapid turnover. In an attempt to see whether whole body histamine could be depleted by prolonged HDC inhibition, α-monofluoromethylhistidine was given by continous infusion via osmotic mini-pumps (Bouclier *et al.* 1983c). For instance, 5 mg kg^{-1} h^{-1} of α-monofluoro-methylhistidine for 3 weeks depletes histamine in hypothalamus by 94 per cent, in gastric mucosa by 75 per cent, in thymus by 56 per cent, in liver by 44 per cent, and in heart by 38 per cent. This treatment produced no apparent behavioural change in animals; for instance, body temperature, pH of stomach washing, and body weight were not modified. In a similar experiment giving the compound i.p. once daily, the effects were similar although less marked: after administration of 250 mg kg^{-1} day^{-1} of α-monofluoromethylhistidine for 13 weeks to male rats, there was no change of histamine concentration in plasma, but a 50 per cent reduction of histamine in diaphragm and ear (mast cells pools) and a 60 per cent reduction in stomach (Duggan *et al.* 1984). Unexpectedly, the same treatment produced more marked effects in female animals (Duggan *et al.* 1984). The need for a constant presence of α-monofluoromethylhistidine for maximal depletion of histamine, especially in mast cells, was also demonstrated in another study (Lagunoff *et al.* 1985).

In W/W^v mutant mice lacking mast cells, a single administration of α-monofluoromethyl histidine totally depletes central histamine for 24 hr, while in congeneic normal mice, the decrease is only 50 per cent (Maeyama *et al.* 1983). This selective effect on histamine with a rapid turnover may be related to the suppression of muricidal behaviour in rats by α-monofluoromethyl histidine (Onodera and Ogura 1985). Prolonged depletion of hypothalamic histamine by daily injection of α-monofluoromethylhistidine had no gross effect on the growth of body and brain and did not affect the development of other neuro-transmitter systems (Slotkin *et al.* 1983). Thus, α-monofluoromethylhistidine is likely to be a very useful tool for the study of the neuropharmacology of histamine.

In the periphery, α-monofluoromethylhistidine blocks histamine synthesis in basophil cells in culture (Woldemussie and Beaven 1985), in human peripheral blood leucocytes *in vitro* and *in vivo* (Tung *et al.* 1985), in mouse skin exposed to tetradecanoylphorbol acetate (Watanabe *et al.* 1981), and in a gastric carcinoma of the African rodent *Mastomys natalensis* (Hosoda *et al.* 1985). These biochemical effects raise the prospect that α-monofluoromethylhistidine may be useful in inflammation, immunology, and control of proliferative conditions. Indeed, it has been reported that the compound inhibits the development of tumours induced by hepatoma tissue culture cells in Buffalo rats, of EMT6 sarcomas, and of Lewis lung carcinoma in mice (Bartholeyns and Bouclier, 1984). The cyto-static mechanism of α-monofluoromethylhistidine could be due to a similarity in roles for newly formed histamine and polyamines in cell proliferation. Alternatively, it could be more complex and may result from a stimulated cellular immune response.

The study of α-monofluoromethylhistidine is still in its infancy. For the first time, there exists the means to block new histamine formation selectively and, provided the dosage regimen is appropriate, to decrease significantly and perhaps deplete whole body histamine pools.

8.7   Inhibitors of ornithine decarboxylase (Orn-DC)

Considerable knowledge has accumulated during the last few years on the regulatory functions of the naturally occurring polyamines putrescine, spermidine, and spermine in cellular growth and differentiation (for reviews, see Jänne *et al.* 1978; Williams-Ashman and Canellakis 1979; Heby 1981; Pegg and McCann 1982; Tabor and Tabor 1984; see also Chapter 21). This progress was mainly achieved by studying the biochemical and pharmacological consequences of polyamine deficiency in prokaryotes and eukaryotes. This deficiency has been achieved either by mutation (Tabor *et al.* 1980, 1983; Morris 1981; Paulus *et al.* 1982) or by specific inhibition of the biosynthetic enzymes.

In eukaryotes, the *de novo* synthesis of putrescine, the precursor of spermidine and spermine, involves the decarboxylation of ornithine catalyzed by the pyridoxal phosphate-dependent enzyme ornithine decarboxylase (Orn-DC) (for review, see Pegg and Williams-Ashman 1981). This enzyme is present in very small amounts in quiescent cells; its activity can be increased dramatically within a few hours of exposure to a variety of trophic hormones or agents that stimulate cell growth and division. Orn-DC has a very short biological half-life; its activity is finely modulated by the cellular content of putrescine and spermidine through several 'repression' mechanisms, one of them involving an inhibitory protein called *antizyme*.

As polyamine synthesis was believed to be a prerequisite for cell proliferation, Orn-DC became a logical target for inhibition to reduce or block cell growth. Several investigators have taken advantage of the mechanism of 'repression' of Orn-DC activity by polyamines by using putrescine analogues. For example 1,3-diamino propane and 1,3-diamino-2-propanol are very effective in decreasing Orn-DC activity and putrescine concentration in cultured cells and in various rat tissues (for review see Heby and Jänne 1981). However rapid metabolism, lack of specificity of action, and toxicity make these putrescine analogues unsuitable for use as potential therapeutic agents (Höltta *et al.* 1981). A more straightforward approach consists in achieving direct Orn-DC inhibition by means of specific reversible or irreversible inhibitors.

8.7.1   Reversible inhibitors

The first publication dealing with Orn-DC inhibitors appeared in 1972 (Skinner and Johansson 1972). During the period 1972–1978, a range of ornithine and putrescine derivatives were synthesized as potential reversible inhibitors of Orn-DC. They formed the subject of several reviews (Williams-Ashman *et al.* 1976;

Stevens and Stevens 1980; Mamont *et al* 1980; Heby and Jänne 1981) and important information regarding the topography of the active site of Orn-DC was obtained from their dissociation constants (Bey *et al.* 1978). Although some of the reversible inhibitors of Orn-DC proved to be useful tools to deplete polyamine concentrations in cells in culture, they were neither sufficiently potent to cause a significant decrease of spermidine and spermine concentration *in vivo* nor sufficiently specific to be devoid of undesirable secondary pharmacological effects (Mamont *et al.* 1980; Höltta *et al.* 1981). The competitive inhibitors have, in addition, the major drawback of increasing Orn-DC not only because proteolytic degradation is decreased (Harik *et al.* 1974; McCann *et al.* 1977), but also because enzyme synthesis is stimulated (Persson *et al.* 1985). Due to these effects, administration of such compounds leads to an accumulation of Orn-DC. When the concentration of inhibitor in the body falls because of metabolic clearance, reactivation of the enzyme results in an 'overshoot' of putrescine production. These different problems prompted the search for irreversible inhibitors of Orn-DC. The design of specific irreversible inhibitors of Orn-DC has been closely associated with the development of the concept of substrate-induced irreversible inhibition of enzymes (Rando 1974; Abeles and Maycock 1976; Walsh 1977, 1982, 1984; Seiler *et al.* 1978b).

8.7.2   Irreversible inhibitors based on the ornithine structure

The ornithine analogue α-difluoromethylornithine (DFMO) is one of the first and most studied irreversible inhibitors of Orn-DC. Since its discovery (Bey 1978; Metcalf *et al.* 1978), more than 600 publications have reported on its biochemical effects on cultured eukaryotic cells, microorganisms, plants, animal tissues, and human diseases (for reviews, see Mamont *et al.* 1978; Seiler *et al.* 1978a; Koch-Weser *et al.* 1981; Sjoerdsma 1981; Bitonti *et al.* 1983; Sjoerdsma and Schechter 1984; Heby 1985). The proposed mechanism of action for DFMO involves enzymatic decarboxylation of the compound after formation of the Schiff base with pyridoxal phosphate with concomitant elimination of fluoride ion (Bey 1978; Metcalf *et al.* 1978). The resulting α-β-unsaturated imine, being a Michael acceptor, could then alkylate a nucleophile of the enzyme active site. Alternatively, the fluoroenamine liberated after hydrolysis could react as a nucleophile and alkylate the imine function of the Schiff base formed between the liberated pyridoxal phosphate and a lysine residue of Orn-DC, as discussed previously [Scheme 8.3(b)].

DFMO produces a time-dependent inhibition of Orn-DC *in vitro* ($K_1 = 39\,\mu M$; $\tau_{1/2} = 3.1\,min$) and enzyme activity is not restored by dialysis (Metcalf *et al.* 1978).

In rats, DFMO produces a rapid and dose-dependent decrease of Orn-DC activity in several tissues, the enzyme of ventral prostate being the most affected by the compound (Danzin *et al.* 1979a). Repeated intraperitoneal injections of DFMO, or administration of the compound in solution in water (usually

$20\,\mathrm{g}\,\mathrm{l}^{-1}$ as the sole drinking fluid of animals, cause marked decreases of putrescine, and, to a lesser extent, of spermidine concentrations in several tissues, but barely affect spermine concentrations (Danzin *et al.* 1979a; Wagner *et al.* 1982).

The low toxicity of DFMO is worth reporting. The LD_{50} of this drug is higher than 5 g kg^{-1} of body weight, in mice (Prakash *et al.* 1978) and in rats (C. Danzin, unpublished). Treatment of rats with a daily dose of $2\,\mathrm{g}\,\mathrm{kg}^{-1}$ of body weight, either by intraperitoneal injections or by administration of the compound in solution in the drinking water of animals, for several weeks results in a low reduction in gain of body weight (Seiler *et al.* 1978a; Dowling *et al.* 1985).

DFMO has dramatic antitumor effects in numerous rodent models (Koch-Weser *et al.* 1981; Pegg and McCann 1982; Heby 1985). More spectacularly, it has a dramatic curative effect in animals infected by various strains of parasitic protozoa such as *Trypanosoma brucei brucei* (Bacchi *et al.* 1980) or *Eimeria tenella* (Hanson *et al.* 1982). Based on these observations, the antineoplastic and antiprotozoal actions of DFMO have been extended considerably and include clinical results (Schechter *et al.* 1987; Sjoerdsma and Schechter 1984).

Other ornithine analogues such as α-monofluoromethyl ornithine (Bey 1978; Kollonitsch *et al.* 1978) and α-ethynyl ornithine (Danzin *et al.* 1981) decrease Orn-DC in rat tissues. However, they are somewhat less effective than DFMO in this respect (Danzin *et al.* 1981). Among a series of ornithine analogues recently synthesized in our Institute (Bey *et al.* 1983), (*E*)-2-(fluoromethyl) dehydroornithine has been found to be an enzyme-activated irreversible inhibitor of Orn-DC that is 10 times more potent than DFMO *in vitro*. This compound, however, does not demonstrate better efficiency than DFMO in decreasing Orn-DC activity in rat tissues (Mamont *et al.* 1986), suggesting that it is poorly absorbed. In order to improve the effectiveness of (*E*)-2-(fluoromethyl) dehydroornithine, esters of the compound have been synthesized as potential prodrugs (Mamont *et al.* 1986). The use of ester derivatives is based on the ubiquitous distribution of non-specific esterases (Krisch 1971). Due to increased cellular concentrations and effective intracellular hydrolysis, the methyl and ethyl-esters are 10 times more effective in decreasing Orn-DC activity than the parent amino acid or DFMO in animal tissues. Moreover, these esters produce a particularly long-lasting Orn-DC inhibition. Interestingly, (*E*)-2-(fluoromethyl)-dehydroornithine methyl ester is more active than DFMO against mouse trypanosomiasis (Bitonti *et al.* 1985) and in blocking exoerythrocytic schizogony of *Plasmodium berghei* in mice (Hollingdale *et al.* 1985). These effects warrant further study of the methyl ester in other animal models of protozoal infection.

8.7.3 Irreversible inhibitors based on the putrescine structure

5-hexyne-1,4-diamine, another potent enzyme-activated irreversible inhibitor of mammalian Orn-DC, was discovered at the same time as DFMO (Metcalf *et al.*

1978; Danzin *et al.* 1979b). It was soon discovered that this putrescine analogue also inhibits 4-aminobutyrate aminotransferase (GABA-T) *in vivo* and increases the levels of the neurotransmitter 4-aminobutyric acid (GABA) in brain, thus producing secondary pharmacological effects (Danzin *et al.* 1979c). These effects are due to the oxidation of 5-hexyne-1,4-diamine to 4-aminohex-5-ynoic acid, a potent irreversible inhibitor of GABA-T (Jung *et al.* 1977). The first step of this metabolic pathway is catalysed by mitochondrial monoamine oxidase (MAO) (Danzin *et al.* 1979c, 1983a). Taking advantage of the fact that α-branched primary amines are very poor substrates of MAO (Blaschko 1952; Silverman 1984), 6-heptyne-2,5-diamine has been synthesized as both a racemic mixture and as the four individual stereoisomers (Casara *et al.* 1985). *In vitro* studies have demonstrated that most of the Orn-DC inhibitory activity lies in the (2R, 5R)-stereoisomer (Danzin *et al.* 1983b; Casara *et al.* 1985). *In vivo*, (2R, 5R)-6-heptyne-2,5-diamine is 10 times more potent than DFMO and as effective as the esters of (E)-2-(fluoromethyl) dehydroornithine in inhibiting Orn-DC. However, the duration of action of MAP is not longer than that of DFMO. Like DFMO, (2R, 5R)-6-heptyne-2,5-diamine has marginal toxicity in mice and rats at effective doses. The 50 per cent lethal dose values are higher than $1\,\mathrm{g\,kg^{-1}}$ of body weight for both i.v. and p.o. routes of administration (Bartholeyns *et al.* 1984). Surprisingly, (2R, 5R)-6-heptyne-2,5-diamine appears to be more effective than DFMO in animal models of neoplasms (Bartholeyns *et al.* 1984), but less active in treating mouse trypanosomiasis (Sjoerdsma and Schechter 1984; Bitonti *et al.* 1985).

Other putrescine analogues found to be effective in irreversibly inhibiting Orn-DC *in vitro* and *in vivo* are α-monofluoromethylputrescine and α-difluoromethylputrescine, but they are substantially less potent than (2R, 5R)-6-heptyne-2,5-diamine. Furthermore, like 5-hexyne-1,4-diamine, they are oxidized *in vivo* to the corresponding acids and produce GABA-T inhibition (Danzin *et al.* 1982). The dehydroputrescine analogues *trans*-hex-2-en-5-yne-1,4-diamine (Metcalf *et al.* 1978) and (E)-2-(fluoromethyl)dehydroputrescine (Bey *et al.* 1983) are very potent Orn-DC inhibitors *in vitro* and *in vivo*, but because of their significant toxicity, the action of these compounds has not been explored further in animals (C. Danzin, unpublished results).

8.8   Conclusions

In this review, we have tried to demonstrate the advantages of enzyme-activated irreversible inhibitors over classical competitive inhibitors with regard to duration of action and selectivity. Two classes of compound are undergoing clinical evaluation, GABA-T inhibitors (essentially γ-vinyl GABA) and Orn-DC inhibitors [DFMO and E-(2)-(fluoromethyl) dehydroornithine as antiprotozoal agents, and (2R, 5R)-6-heptyne-2,5-diamine as an antitumour agent]. Inhibitors of AADC, such as α-monofluoromethyl dopa, and of HDC, such as α-monofluoromethylhistidine, are interesting pharmacological tools and may prove to possess therapeutic utility in the future.

We think that the reasonable success shown here justifies applying this type of approach to the search for inhibitors of other classes of enzyme.

References

Abeles, R. H. and Maycock, A. L. (1976). Suicide enzyme inactivators. *Acc. Chem. Res.*, **9**, 313–19.

Bacchi, C. J., Nathan, H. C., Hutner, S. H., McCann, P. P., and Sjoerdsma, A. (1980). Polyamine metabolism: a potential therapeutic target in trypanosomes. *Science*, **210**, 332–4.

Badet, B., Roise, D., and Walsh, C. T. (1984). Inactivation of the *dadB Salmonella typhirium* alanine racemase by D- and L-isomers of β-substituted alanines: Kinetics, stoichiometry, active site peptide sequencing, and reaction mechanism. *Biochemistry*, **23**, 5188–94.

Bartholeyns, J. and Bouclier, M. (1984). Involvement of histamine in growth of mouse and rat tumors: antitumoral properties of monofluoromethylhistidine, an enzyme-activated irreversible inhibitor of histidine decarboxylase. *Cancer Res.*, **44**, 639–645.

Bartholeyns, J., Mamont, P., and Casara, P. (1984). Antitumor properties of (2*R*, 5*R*)-6-heptyne-2,5-diamine, a new potent enzyme-activated irreversible inhibitor of ornithine decarboxylase, in rodents. *Cancer Res.*, **44**, 4972–7.

Bartholini, G. and Pletscher, A. (1975). Decarboxylase inhibitors. *Pharmacol. Ther.*, **B1**, 407–21.

Bernabé, M. Cuevas, O., and Fernandez-Alvarez, E. (1979). Dérivés du cyclopropane. V. Préparation d'acides amino-1 aryl-2 cyclopropanecarboxyliques et résultats préliminaires de leur interaction avec la dopadécarboxylase. *Eur. J. Med. Chem.*, **14**, 33–45.

Bey, P. (1978). Substrate-induced irreversible inhibition of α-amino acid decarboxylases. In *Enzyme-activated irreversible inhibitors* (ed. N. Seiler, M. J. Jung, and J. Koch-Weser), pp. 27–41. Elsevier/North-Holland Biomedical Press, Amsterdam.

Bey, P., Danzin, C., Van Dorsselear, V., Mamont, P., Jung, M., and Tardif, C. (1978). Analogues of ornithine as inhibitors of ornithine decarboxylase. New deductions concerning the topography of the enzyme's active site. *J. Med. Chem.*, **21**, 50–5.

Bey, P., Jung, M. J., Koch-Weser, J., Palfreyman, M. G., Sjoerdsma, A., Wagner, J., and Zreika, M. (1980). Further studies on the inhibition of monoamine synthesis by monofluoromethyldopa. *Br. J. Pharmacol.*, **70**, 571–6.

Bey, P., Jung, M. J., Gerhart, F., Schirlin, D., Van Dorsselaer, V., and Casara, P. (1981). ω-fluoromethyl analogues of ω-amino acids as irreversible inhibitors of 4-amino-butyrate: 2-oxoglutarate aminotransferase. *J. Neurochem.*, **37**, 1341–44.

Bey, P., Gerhart, F., Van Dorsselaer, V., and Danzin, C. (1983). α-(fluoromethyl)-dehydroornithine and α-(fluoromethyl)dehydroputrescine analogues as irreversible inhibitors of ornithine decarboxylase. *J. Med. Chem.*, **26**, 1551–6.

Bey, P., Gerhart, F., and Jung, M. J. (1986). Synthesis of γ-(fluoromethyl)dehydro GABA and γ-(vinyl) dehydro GABA: Potential irreversible inhibitors of GABA-T. *J. Org. Chem.*, **51**, 2835–8.

Bitonti, A. J., Kallio, A., McCann, P. P., and Sjoerdsma, A. (1983). Inhibition of bacterial polyamine biosynthesis and consequent effects on cell proliferation. *Adv. Polyamine Res.*, **4**, 495–506.

Bitonti, A. J., Bacchi, C. J., McCann, P. P., and Sjoerdsma, A. (1985). Catalytic irreversible inhibition of *Trypanosoma brucei brucei* ornithine decarboxylase by substrate and product analogs and their effects on murine trypanosomiasis. *Biochem. Pharmacol.*, **34**, 1773–7.

Blaschko, H. (1952). Amine oxidase and amine metabolism. *Pharmacol. Rev.*, **4**, 415–58.

Böhlen, P., Huot, S., and Palfreyman, M. G. (1979). The relationship between GABA concentrations in brain and cerebrospinal fluid. *Brain Res.*, **167**, 297–305.

Borri Voltattorni, C., and Minelli, A. (1980). Inactivation of DOPA decarboxylase activity by serotonin. *Bull. Mol. Biol. Med.*, **5**, 52–60.

Bouclier, M., Jung, M. J., and Lippert, B. (1979). Stereochemistry of reactions catalysed by mammalian-brain L-glutamate 1-carboxy-lyase and 4-aminobutyrate: 2-oxoglutarate aminotransferase. *Eur. J. Biochem.*, **98**, 363–8.

Bouclier, M., Jung, M., and Gerhart, F. (1983a). Inhibition of histamine biosynthesis and gastric function in the rat: effect of a pentagastrin-induced gastric acid secretion. *Agents Actions*, **13**, 241–6.

Bouclier, M., Jung, M. J., and Gerhart, F. (1983b). Histamine receptor blockade (H2) versus inhibition of histamine synthesis in stress ulceration in rats. *Eur. J. Pharmacol.*, **90**, 129–32.

Bouclier, M., Jung, M. J., and Gerhart, F. (1983c). Effect of prolonged inhibition of histidine decarboxylase on tissue histamine concentrations. *Experientia*, **39**, 1303–5.

Cannon, J. G., O'Donnell, J. P., Rosazza, J. P., and Poppin, C. R. (1974). Rigid amino acids related to α-methyldopa. *J. Med. Chem.*, **17**, 565–8.

Casara, P. Jund, K., and Bey, P. (1984). General synthetic access to α-allenyl amines and α-allenyl-α-aminoacids as potential enzyme-activated irreversible inhibitors of PLP dependent enzymes. *Tetrahedron Lett.*, **25**, 1891–4.

Casara, P., Danzin, C., Metcalf, B., and Jung, M. (1985). Stereospecific synthesis of (2R, 5R)-hept-6-yne-2,5-diamine: a potent and selective enzyme-activated irreversible inhibitor of ornithine decarboxylase (ODC). *J. Chem. Soc. Perkin Trans. I*, 2201–7.

Castelhano, A. L. and Krantz, A. (1984). Allenic amino acids. 1. Synthesis of γ-allenic GABA by a novel aza-cope rearrangement. *J. Am. Chem. Soc.*, **106**, 1877–9.

Cavagnini, F., Pinto, M. Dubini, A., Invitti, C., Cappelletti, G., and Polli, E. E. (1982). Effects of gamma-aminobutyric acid (GABA) and muscimol on endocrine pancreatic function in man. *Metabolism*, **31**, 73–7.

Chari, R. V. J. and Wemple, J. (1979). A simple, efficient synthesis of β-methylene phenylalanine. A new approach to the preparation of β,γ-unsaturated α-amino acid enzyme substrate analogs. *Tetrahedron Lett.*, 111–114.

Chrystal, E., Bey, P., and Rando, R. R. (1979). The irreversible inhibition of brain L-glutamate-1-decarboxylase by (2RS, 3E)-2-methyl-3,4-didehydroglutamic acid. *J. Neurochem.*, **32**, 1501–7.

Cooper, A. J. L. and Griffith, O. W. (1979). N-hydroxyamino acids. Irreversible inhibitors of pyridoxal 5'-phosphate enzymes and substrates of D- and L-amino acid oxidases. *J. Biol. Chem.*, **254**, 2748–53.

Cornish-Bowden, A. (1979). Validity of a 'steady-state' treatment of inactivation kinetics. *Eur. J. Biochem.*, **93**, 383–5.

Danishefsky, S. and Hershenson, F. M. (1979). Regiospecific synthesis of isogabaculine. *J. Org. Chem.*, **44**, 1180–1.

Danzin, C. and Jung, M. J. (1984). Lack of stringent stereospecificity in the inactivation of pyridoxal phosphate-dependent enzymes by suicide-substrates. In *Chemical and biological aspects of vitamin B_6 catalysis* (ed. A. E. Evangelopoulos), Part A, pp. 377–385. Alan Liss, New York.

Danzin, C., Jung, M. J., Grove, J., and Bey, P. (1979a). Effect of α-difluoromethylornithine, an enzyme-activated irreversible inhibitor of ornithine decarboxylase, on polyamine levels in rat tissues. *Life Sci.*, **24**, 519–24.

Danzin, C., Jung, M. J., Metcalf, B. W., Grove, J., and Casara, P. (1979b). Decrease of polyamine levels in rat tissues by 5-hexyne-1,4-diamine, an enzyme-activated irreversible inhibitor of ornithine decarboxylase. *Biochem. Pharmacol.*, **28**, 627–31.

Danzin, C., Jung, M. J., Seiler, N., and Metcalf, B. W. (1979c). Effect of 5-hexyne-1,4-diamine on brain 4-aminobutyric acid metabolism in rats and mice. *Biochem. Pharmacol.*, **28**, 633–9.

Danzin, C., Casara, P., Claverie, N., and Metcalf, B. W. (1981). α-ethynyl and α-vinyl analogues of ornithine as enzyme-activated inhibitors of mammalian ornithine decarboxylase. *J. Med. Chem.*, **24**, 16–20.

Danzin, C., Bey, P., Schirlin, D., and Claverie, N. (1982). α-monofluoromethyl and α-difluoromethyl putrescine as ornithine decarboxylase inhibitors: *In vitro* and *in vivo* biochemical properties. *Biochem. Pharmacol.*, **31**, 3871–8.

Danzin, C., Casara, P., Claverie, N., and Grove, J. (1983a). Effects of the enantiomers of 5-hexyne-1,4-diamine on ODC, GAD, and GABA-T activities in the rat. *Biochem. Pharmacol.*, **32**, 941–2.

Danzin, C., Casara, P., Claverie, N., Metcalf, B. W., and Jung, M. J. (1983b). (2R, 5R)-6-heptyne-2,5-diamine, an extremely potent inhibitor of mammalian ornithine decarboxylase. *Biochem. Biophys. Res. Commun.*, **116**, 237–43.

Danzin, C., Claverie, N., and Jung, M. J. (1984). Stereochemistry of the inactivation of 4-aminobutyrate: 2-oxoglutarate aminotransferase and L-glutamate 1-carboxy-lyase by 4-aminohex-5-ynoic acid enantiomers. *Biochem. Pharmacol.*, **33**, 1741–6.

De Feudis, F. V. (1981). GABA and 'neuro-cardiovascular' mechanisms. *Neurochem. Int.*, **3**, 113–22.

De Feudis, F. V. (1982). GABA—an inhibitory neurotransmitter that is involved in cardiovascular control. *Pharmacol. Res. Commun.*, **14**, 567–75.

Del Castillo, J., de Mello, W. C., and Morales, T. (1964). Inhibitory action of γ-aminobutyric acid (GABA) on *Ascaris* muscle. *Experientia*, **20**, 141–3.

Dowling, R. H., Hosomi, M., Stace, N. H., Lirussi, F., Miazza, B., Levan, H., and Murphy, G. M. (1985). Hormones and polyamines in intestinal and pancreatic adaptation. *Scand. J. Gastroenterol.*, **20** (Suppl. 112), 84–95.

Duggan, D. E., Hooke, K. F., and Maycock, A. L. (1984). Inhibition of histamine synthesis *in vitro* and *in vivo* by S-α-fluoromethylhistidine. *Biochem. Pharmacol.*, **33**, 4003–9.

Dunathan, H. C. (1966). Conformation and reaction specificity in pyridoxal phosphate enzymes. *Proc. Nat. Acad. Sci. USA*, **55**, 712–16.

Endo, A., Kitahara, N., Oka, H., Miguchi-Fukazawa, Y., and Terahara, A. (1978). Isolation of 4,5-dihydroxyisophthalic acid, an inhibitor of brain glutamate decarboxylase, produced by a *Streptomyces* species. *Eur. J. Biochem.*, **82**, 257–9.

Erdö, S. L., Riesz, M., Karpati, E., and Szporny, L. (1984). GABA-B receptor-mediated stimulation of the contractility of isolated rabbit oviduct. *Eur. J. Pharmacol.*, **99**, 333–6.

Fernandez, I., Orensanz, L. M., and de Ceballos, M. L. (1984). GABA modulation of cholinergic transmission in rat oviduct. *Life Sci.*, **35**, 357–64.

Floss, H. G. and Vederas, J. C. (1982). Stereochemistry of pyridoxal phosphate-catalysed reactions. In *Stereochemistry* (ed. C. Tamm) pp. 161–99. Elsevier Biomedical Press, Amsterdam.

Fowler, L. J. and John, R. A. (1972). Active-site directed irreversible inhibition of rat brain 4-aminobutyrate aminotransferase by ethanolamine-O-sulphate *in vitro* and *in vivo*. *Biochem. J.*, **130**, 569–73.

Fozard, J. R., Möhring, J., Palfreyman, M. G., and Koch-Weser, J. (1981). Mechanism of the antihypertensive action of D,L-α-monofluoromethyldopa: Implications for the role of the sympathetic nervous system in maintenance of elevated blood pressure in spontaneously hypertensive rats. *J. Cardiovasc. Pharmacol.*, **3**, 1038–49.

Garbarg, M. Barbin, G., Rodergas, E., and Schwartz, J. C. (1980). Inhibition of histamine synthesis in brain by α-fluoromethylhistidine, a new irreversible inhibitor: *in vitro* and *in vivo* studies. *J. Neurochem.*, **35**, 1045–52.

Gehring, H., Rando, R. R., and Christen, P. (1977). Active-site labeling of aspartate aminotransferases by the β,γ-unsaturated amino acid vinylglycine. *Biochemistry*, **16**, 4832–6.

Grove, J., Schechter, P. J., Tell, G., Koch-Weser, J., Sjoerdsma, A., Warter, M., Marescaux, C., and Rumbach, L. (1981). Increased gamma-aminobutyric acid (GABA), homocarnosine, and beta-alanine in cerebrospinal fluid of patients treated with gamma-vinyl GABA (4-amino-hex-5-ynoic acid). *Life Sci.*, **28**, 2431–9.

Hammond, E. J. and Wilder, B. J. (1985). Gamma-vinyl GABA. *Gen. Pharmacol.*, **16**, 441–7.

Hanson, W. L., Bradford, M. M., Chapman, W. L. Jr., Waits, V. B., McCann, P. P., and Sjoerdsma, A. (1982). α-difluoromethylornithine: a promising lead for preventive chemotherapy of coccidiosis. *Am. J. Vet. Res.*, **43**, 1651–3.

Harik, S. I., Hollenberg, M. D., and Snyder, S. H. (1974). Ornithine decarboxylase turnover slowed by α-hydrazinoornithine. *Mol. Pharmacol.*, **10**, 41–7.

Heby, O. (1981). Role of polyamines in the control of cell proliferation and differentiation. *Differentiation*, **19**, 1–20.

Heby, O. (1985). Ornithine decarboxylase as target of chemotherapy. *Adv. Enzyme Regul.*, **24**, 103–24.

Heby, O. and Jänne, J. (1981). Polyamine antimetabolites: biochemistry, specificity, and biological effects of inhibitors of polyamine synthesis. In *Polyamines in biology and medicine* (ed. D. R. Morris and L. J. Marton), pp. 243–310. Marcel Dekker, New York.

Hiemstra, H., Fortgens, H. P., and Speckamp, W. N. (1984). Lewis acid induced reactions of propargyl trimethyl silane with ω-ethoxy lactams: synthesis of γ-allenyl-GABA. *Tetrahedron Lett.*, **25**, 3115–18.

Holbert, G. W. and Metcalf, B. W. (1984). Synthesis of α-ethynylhistamine, an inactivator of histidine decarboxylase. *Tetrahedron*, **40**, 1141–44.

Hollingdale, M. R., McCann, P. P., and Sjoerdsma, A. (1985). *Plasmodium berghei*: effects of inhibitors of ornithine decarboxylase on the exoerythrocytic stage. *Exp. Parasitol.*, **60**, 111–17.

Hölttä, E., Korpela, H., and Hovi, T. (1981). Several inhibitors of ornithine and adenosylmethionine decarboxylases may also have antiproliferative effects unrelated to polyamine depletion. *Biochim. Biophys. Acta*, **677**, 90–102.

Hornsperger, J. M. (1984). Hydroxylation de l'α-fluoromethyltyrosine *in vitro* et *in vivo*: effets sur la synthèse des amines biogènes. Thèse de Doctorat d'Etat, Université Louis Pasteur, Strasbourg.

Hosoda, S., Saito, T., Kumazawa, H., Watanabe, T., and Wada, H. (1985). Marked inhibition of histamine formation in transplantable histamine-producing gastric carcinoid of *Mastomys natalensis* by (S)-α-fluoromethylhistidine and its potent antiulcer effect on tumor-bearing hosts. *Biochem. Pharmacol.*, **34**, 4327–9.

Jaeger, C. B., Teitelman, G., Joh, T. H., Albert, V. R., Park, D. H., and Reis, D. J. (1983). Some neurons of the rat central nervous system contain aromatic-L-amino-acid decarboxylase but not monoamines. *Science*, **219**, 1233–5.

Jänne, J., Pösö, H., and Raina, A. (1978). Polyamines in rapid growth and cancer. *Biochim. Biophys. Acta*, **473**, 241–93.

Jessen, K. R., Mirsky, R., Dennison, M. E., and Burnstock, G. (1979). GABA may be a neurotransmitter in the vertebrate peripheral nervous system. *Nature (London)*, **281**, 71–4.

Johnston, G. A. R., Allan, R. D., Kennedy, S. M. E., and Twitchin, B. (1979). Systematic study of GABA analogues of restricted conformation. In *GABA-neurotransmitters, Alfred Benzon Symposium 12* (ed. P. Krogsgaard-Larsen, J. Scheel-Krüger, and H. Kofod) pp. 149–64. Munksgaard, Copenhagen.

Jung, M. J. (1982). GABA-transaminase inhibitors and neuronal function. In *Neurotransmitter interaction and compartmentation* (ed. H. F. Bradford), pp. 329–44. Plenum, New York.

Jung, M. J. (1986). Substrates and inhibitors of aromatic amino acid decarboxylase. *Bioorg. Chem.*, **14**, 429–43.

Jung, M. J., Lippert, B., Metcalf, B. W., Schechter, P. J., Böhlen, P., and Sjoerdsma, A. (1977). The effect of 4-amino-hex-5-ynoic acid (γ-acetylenic GABA, γ-ethynyl GABA), a catalytic inhibitor of GABA-transaminase, on brain GABA metabolism. *J. Neurochem.*, **28**, 717–23.

Jung, M. J., Metcalf, B. W., Lippert, B., and Casara, P. (1978). Mechanism of the stereospecific irreversible inhibition of bacterial glutamic acid decarboxylase by (R)-(−)-4-aminohex-5-ynoic acid, an analogue of 4-aminobutyric acid. *Biochemistry*, **17**, 2628–32.

Jung, M. J., Palfreyman, M. G., Wagner, J., Bey, P., Ribereau-Gayon, G., Zreika, M., and Koch-Weser, J. (1979). Inhibition of monoamine synthesis by irreversible blockade of aromatic amino acid decarboxylase with α-monofluoromethyldopa. *Life Sci.*, **24**, 1037–42.

Jung, M. J., Koch-Weser, J., and Sjoerdsma, A. (1980). Biochemistry and pharmacology of enzyme-activated irreversible inhibitors of some pyridoxal phosphate-dependent enzymes. In *Enzyme inhibitors as drugs* (ed. M. Sandler), pp. 95–114. Macmillan, Basingstoke.

Jung, M. J., Heydt, J-G., and Casara, P. (1984a). γ-allenyl GABA, a new inhibitor of 4-aminobutyrate aminotransferase. Comparison with other inhibitors of this enzyme. *Biochem. Pharmacol.*, **22**, 3717–20.

Jung, M. J., Hornsperger, J. M., Gerhart, F. and Wagner, J. (1984b). Inhibition of aromatic amino acid decarboxylase and depletion of biogenic amines in brain of rats treated with α-monofluoromethyl p-tyrosine: similarities and differences from the effects of α-monofluoromethyldopa. *Biochem. Pharmacol.*, **33**, 327–30.

Jung, M. J., Hornsperger, J. M., McDonald, I. A., Fozard, J. R., and Palfreyman, M. G. (1985). Bio-precursor approach to site-selective enzyme inhibition. In *Drug targetting* (ed. P. Buri and A. Gumma), pp. 165–78. Elsevier, Amsterdam.

Kalman, T. I. and Yalowich (1979). Survival and recovery: the reversibility of covalent drug–enzyme interactions. In *Drug action and design: mechanism-based inhibitors* (ed. T. I. Kalman), pp. 75–91. Elsevier-North Holland, Amsterdam.

Kass, I. S., Wang, C. C., Walrond, J. P., and Stretton, O. W. (1980). Avermectin B_1a, a paralyzing anthelmintic that affects interneurons and inhibitory motoneurons in *Ascaris*. *Proc. Nat. Acad. Sci. USA*, **77**, 6211–15.

Kawai, K. and Unger, R. H. (1983). Effects of γ-aminobutyric acid on insulin, glucagon, and somatostatin release from isolated perfused dog pancreas. *Endocrinology*, **113**, 111–13.

Kitz, R. and Wilson, I. B. (1962). Esters of methanesulfonic acid as irreversible inhibitors of acetylcholinesterase *J. Biol. Chem.*, **237**, 3245–9.

Kobayashi, K. Miyazawa, S., Terahara, A., Mishima, H., and Kurihara, H. (1976). Gabaculine: γ-aminobutyrate aminotransferase inhibitor of microbial origin. *Tetrahedron Lett.*, 537–540.

Koch-Weser, J., Schechter, P. J., Bey, P., Danzin, C., Fozard, J. R., Jung, M. J., Mamont, P. S., Seiler, N., Prakash, N. J., and Sjoerdsma, A. (1981). Potential of ornithine decarboxylase inhibitors as therapeutic agents. In *Polyamines in biology and medicine* (ed. D. R. Morris and L. J. Marton), pp. 437–53, Marcel Dekker, New York.

Kollonitsch, J. Patchett, A. A., Marburg, S., Maycock, A. L., Perkins, L. M., Doldouras, G. A., Duggan, D. E., and Aster, S. D. (1978). Selective inhibitors of biosynthesis of aminergic neurotransmitters. *Nature (London)*, **274**, 906–8.

Korsgaard, S., Casey, D. E., and Gerlach, J. (1983). Effect of gamma vinyl GABA in tardive dyskinesia. *Psychiat. Res.*, **8**, 261–9.

Krisch, K. (1971). Carboxylic ester hydrolases. In *The enzymes* (3rd edn) (ed. P. D. Boyer), Vol. 5, pp. 43–69. Academic Press, New York.

Krnjevic, K. (1974). Chemical nature of synaptic transmission in vertebrates. *Physiol. Rev.*, **54**, 418–540.

Kubota, H., Hayashi, H., Watanabe, T., Taguchi, Y., and Waba, H. (1984). Mechanism of inactivation of mammalian L-histidine decarboxylase by (S)-α-fluoromethylhistidine. *Biochem. Pharmacol.*, **33**, 983–90.

Kuo, D. and Rando, R. R. (1981). Irreversible inhibition of glutamate decarboxylase by α-(fluoromethyl) glutamic acid. *Biochemistry*, **20**, 506–11.

Kuriyama, K., Roberts, E., and Rubinstein, M. K. (1966). Elevation of γ-aminobutyric acid in brain with amino-oxyacetic acid and susceptibility to convulsive seizures in mice: a quantitative re-evaluation. *Biochem. Pharmacol.*, **15**, 221–36.

Lagunoff, D., Ray, A., and Rickard, A. (1985). Effect on mast cell histamine of inhibiting histamine formation *in vivo* with α-fluoromethylhistidine. *Biochem. Pharmacol.*, **34**, 1205–09.

Lambert, P. A., Cantiniaux, P., Channes, J. P., Tell, G., Schechter, P. J., and Koch-Weser, J. (1982). Essai thérapeutique du gamma-vinyl GABA, un inhibiteur de la GABA-transaminase, dans les dyskinesies tardives induites par les neuroleptiques. *L'Encéphale*, **8**, 371–6.

Lambert, P., Chabannes, J., Cantiniaux, P., Schechter, P. J., and Tell, G. (1983). Effects du gamma-vinyl GABA *per os* dans cinq cas de schizophrenie hébéphreno-catatonique. *L'Encéphale*, **9**, 145–9.

Lancet Editorial (1985). New drugs for epilepsy. *Lancet*, **i**, 198–200.

Likos, J. J., Ueno, H., Feldhaus, R. W., and Metzler, D. E. (1982). A novel reaction of the coenzyme of glutamate decarboxylase with L-serine O-sulfate. *Biochemistry*, **21**, 4377–86.

Lippert, B., Metcalf, B. W., Jung, M. J., and Casara, P. (1977). 4-aminohex-5-enoic acid, a selective catalytic inhibitor of 4-aminobutyrate aminotransferase in mammalian brain. *Eur. J. Biochem.*, **74**, 441–5.

Lippert, B., Bey, P., Van Dorsselaer, V., Vevert, J. P., Danzin, C., Ribereau-Gayon, G., and Jung, M. J. (1979). Selective irreversible inhibition of mammalian histidine decarboxylase by α-chloromethyl histidine. *Agents Actions*, **9**, 38–9.

Lippert, B., Jung, M. J., and Metcalf, B. W. (1980). Biochemical consequences of reactions catalyzed by GAD and GABA-T. *Brain Res. Bull.*, **5**, 375–9.

Lippert, B., Metcalf, B. W., and Resvick, R. J. (1982). Enzyme-activated irreversible inhibition of rat and mouse brain 4-aminobutyric acid α-ketoglutarate transaminase by 5-fluoro-4-oxo-pentanoic acid. *Biochem. Biophys. Res. Commun.*, **108**, 146–52.

Lippert, B., Resvick, R., Burkhart, J., Holbert, G., Adams, J., and Metcalf, B. W. (1985). Aromatization: a driving force for inhibition of pyridoxal phosphate-dependent enzymes. *Fed. Proc. Fed. Am. Soc. Exp. Biol.*, **44**, 1399.

McCann, P. P., Tardif, C., Duchesne, M. C., and Mamont, P. S. (1977). Effect of α-methylornithine on ornithine decarboxylase activity of rat hepatoma cell in culture. *Biochem. Biophys. Res. Commun.*, **76**, 893–99.

McDonald, I. A., Lacoste, J. M., Bey, P., Wagner, J., Zreika, M., and Palfreyman, M. G. (1984). (*E*)-β-(fluoromethylene)-*m*-tyrosine: a substrate for aromatic L-amino acid decarboxylase liberating an enzyme-activated irreversible inhibitor of monoamine oxidase. *J. Am. Chem. Soc.*, **106**, 3354–6.

Maeyama, K., Watanabe, T., Yamatodani, A., Taguchi, Y., Kambe, H., and Wada, H. (1983). Effect of α-fluoromethylhistidine on the histamine content of the brain of W:W^v mice devoid of mast cells: turnover of brain histamine. *J. Neurochem.*, **41**, 128–34.

Mamont, P. S., Duchesne, M-Ch., Joder-Ohlenbusch, A. M., and Grove, J. (1978). Effects of ornithine decarboxylase inhibitors on cultured cells. In *Enzyme-activated irreversible inhibitors* (ed. N. Seiler, M. J. Jung, and J. Koch-Weser), pp. 43–54. Elsevier/North-Holland, Biomedical Press, Amsterdam.

Mamont, P. S., Bey, P., and Koch-Weser, J. (1980). Biochemical consequences of drug-induced polyamine deficiency in mammalian cells. In *Polyamines in biomedical research* (ed. J. M. Gaugas), pp. 147–65. Wiley, Chichester.

Mamont, P. S., Danzin, C., Kolb, M., Gerhart, F., Bey, P., and Sjoerdsma, A. (1986). Marked and prolonged inhibition of mammalian ornithine decarboxylase *in vivo* by esters of (*E*)-2-(fluoromethyl) dehydroornithine. *Biochem. Pharmacol.*, **35**, 159–65.

Maycock, A. L., Aster, S. D., and Patchett, A. A. (1978). Studies with inhibitors of aromatic amino acid decarboxylase. In *Enzyme-activated irreversible inhibitors* (ed. N. Seiler, M. J. Jung, and J. Koch-Weser), pp. 211–20, Elsevier/North Holland, Amsterdam.

Maycock, A. L., Aster, S. D., and Patchett, A. A. (1979). Suicide inactivation of decarboxylases. In *Drug action and design: mechanism-based inhibitors* (ed. T. I. Kalman), pp. 115–29, Elsevier/North Holland, Amsterdam.

Maycock, A. L., Aster, S. D., and Patchett, A. A. (1980). Inactivation of 3-(3,4-dihydrophenyl) alanine decarboxylase by 2-(fluoromethyl)-3-(3,4-dihydrophenyl)-alanine. *Biochemistry*, **19**, 709–18.

Metcalf, B. W. (1979). Inhibitors of GABA metabolism. *Biochem. Pharmacol.*, **28**, 1705–12.

Metcalf, B. W. and Jund, K. (1977). Synthesis of β,γ-unsaturated amino acids as potential catalytic irreversible enzyme inhibitors. *Tetrahedron Lett.*, 3689–92.

Metcalf, B. W. and Jung, M. J. (1979). Molecular basis for the irreversible inhibition of 4-aminobutyric acid: 2-oxoglutarate and L-ornithine: 2-oxoacid aminotransferases by 3-amino-1,5-cyclohexadienyl carboxyl acid (isogabaculine). *Mol. Pharmacol.*, **16**, 539–45.

Metcalf, B. W., Bey, P., Danzin, C., Jung, M. J., Casara, P., and Vevert, J. P. (1978). Catalytic irreversible inhibition of mammalian ornithine decarboxylase (EC 4.1.1.17) by substrate and product analogues. *J. Am. Chem. Soc.*, **100**, 2551–3.

Metcalf, B. W., Holbert, G. W., and Lippert, B. (1984). α-trifluoromethylhistamine: a mechanism-based inhibitor of mammalian histidine decarboxylase. *Bioorg. Chem.*, **12**, 91–7.

Morris, D. R. (1981). *In vivo* studies on the role of putrescine and spermidine in *Escherichia coli*. In *Polyamines in biology and medicine* (ed. D. R. Morris and L. J. Marton), pp. 223–42. Marcel Dekker, New York.

Murashima, Y. L. and Kato, T. (1986). Distribution of γ-aminobutyric acid and glutamate decarboxylase in the layers of rat oviduct. *J. Neurochem.*, **46**, 166–72.

Okada, Y., Taniguchi, H., and Shimada, C. (1976). High concentration of GABA and high glutamate decarboxylase activity in rat pancreatic islets and human insulinoma. *Science*, **194**, 620–2.

O'Leary, M. H. and Baughn, R. L. (1977). Decarboxylation-dependent transamination catalysed by mammalian 3,4-dihydroxyphenylalanine decarboxylase. *J. Biol. Chem.*, **252**, 7168–73.

Ong, J. and Kerr, D. I. B. (1983). GABA A- and GABA B-receptor mediated modification of intestinal motility. *Eur. J. Pharmacol.*, **86**, 9–17.

Onodera, K. and Ogura, Y. (1985). Muricidal suppression by histidine and its antagonism by α-fluoromethylhistidine in thiamine deficient rats. *Jap. J. Psychopharmacol.*, **5**, 11–17.

Palfreyman, M. G., Schechter, P. J., Buckett, W. R., Tell, G. P., and Koch-Weser, J. (1981). The pharmacology of GABA-transaminase inhibitors. *Biochem. Pharmacol.*, **30**, 817–24.

Palfreyman, M. G., Grove, J., and Schechter, P. J. (1984). Does CSF GABA reflect brain GABA function? European Winter Brain Research Conference, Courchevel, France, 11–17 March. Abstract of the Proceedings.

Palfreyman, M. G., McDonald, I. A., Fozard, J. R., Mely, Y., Sleight, A. J. Zreika, M., Wagner, J., Bey, P., and Lewis, P. J. (1985). Inhibition of monoamine oxidase selectively in brain monoamine nerves using the bioprecursor (E)-β-fluoromethylene-m-tyrosine (MDL 72394), a substrate for aromatic L-amino acid decarboxylase. *J. Neurochem.*, **45**, 1850–60.

Paulus, T. S., Kiyono, P., and Davis, R. H. (1982). Polyamine-deficient *Neurospora crassa* mutants and synthesis of cadaverine. *J. Bacteriol.*, **152**, 291–7.

Pedersen, S. A., Klosterkov, P., Gram, L., and Dam, M. (1985). Long-term study of gamma-vinyl GABA in the treatment of epilepsy. *Acta Neurol. Scand.*, **72**, 295–8.

Pegg, A. E. and Williams-Ashman, H. G. (1981). Biosynthesis of putrescine. In *Polyamines in biology and medicine* (ed. D. R. Morris and L. J. Marton), pp. 3–42. Marcel Dekker, New York.

Pegg, A. E. and McCann, P. P. (1982). Polyamine metabolism and function. *Am. J. Physiol.*, **243**, C212–21.

Persson, L. Oredson, S. M., Anehus, S., and Heby, O. (1985). Ornithine decarboxylase inhibitors increase the cellular content of the enzyme: implications for translational regulation. *Biochem. Biophys. Res. Commun.*, **131**, 239–45.

Prabhakaran, K., Harris, E. B., and Kirchheimer, W. F. (1983). Glutamic acid decarboxylase in *Mycobacterium leprae*. *Arch. Microbiol.*, **134**, 320–3.

Prakash, N. J., Schechter, P. J., Grove, J., and Koch-Weser, J. (1978). Effect of α-difluoromethylornithine, an enzyme-activated irreversible inhibitor of ornithine decarboxylase, on L1210 leukemia in mice. *Cancer Res.*, **38**, 3059–62.

Pritchard, M. L., Seely, J. E., Pösö, H., Jefferson, L. S., and Pegg, A. E. (1981). Binding of radioactive α-difluoromethylornithine to rat liver ornithine decarboxylase. *Biochem. Biophys. Res. Commun.*, **100**, 1597–603.

Rando, R. R. (1974). Chemistry and enzymology of k_{cat} inhibitors. *Science*, **185**, 320–4.

Rando, R. R. (1977). Mechanism of the irreversible inhibition of γ-aminobutyric acid α-ketoglutaric acid transaminase by the neurotoxin gabaculine. *Biochemistry*, **16**, 4604–10.

Reingold, D. F. and Orlowski, M. (1979). Inhibition of brain glutamate decarboxylase by 2-keto-4-pentenoic acid, a metabolite of allylglycine. *Biochem. Pharmacol.*, **32**, 907–13.

Ribereau-Gayon, G., Danzin, C., Palfreyman, M. G., Aubry, M., Wagner, J., Metcalf, B. W., and Jung, M. J. (1979). *In vitro* and *in vivo* effects of α-acetylenic DOPA and α-vinyl DOPA on aromatic L-amino acid decarboxylase. *Biochem. Pharmacol.*, **28**, 1331–35.

Ribereau-Gayon, G., Palfreyman, M. G., Zraika, M., Wagner, J., and Jung, M. J. (1980). Irreversible inhibition of aromatic-L-amino acid decarboxylase by α-difluoromethyl-DOPA and metabolism of the inhibitor. *Biochem. Pharmacol.*, **29**, 2465–9.

Rimmer, E. M. and Richens, A. (1984). Double-bind study of gamma-vinyl GABA in patients with refractory epilepsy. *Lancet*, **i**, 189–90.

Roberts, E. (1974). γ-aminobutyric acid and nervous system function—a perspective. *Biochem. Pharmacol.*, **23**, 2637–49.

Roise, D., Soda, K., Yagi, T., and Walsh, C. T. (1984). Inactivation of the *Pseudomonas striata* broad specificity amino acid racemase by D- and L-isomers of β-substituted alanines: kinetics, stoichiometry, active site peptide, and mechanistic studies. *Biochemistry*, **23**, 5195–201.

Schechter, P. J., Tranier, Y., Jung, M. J., and Böhlen, P. (1977). Audiogenic seizure protection by elevated brain GABA concentration in mice: effects of γ-acetylenic GABA and γ-vinyl GABA, two irreversible GABA-T inhibitors. *Eur. J. Pharmacol.*, **45**, 319–28.

Schechter, P. J., Tranier, Y., and Grove, J. (1979). Gabaculine and isogabaculine: *in vivo* biochemistry and pharmacology in mice. *Life Sci.*, **24**, 1173–82.

Schechter, P. J., Barlow, J. L. R. and Sjoerdsma, A. (1987). Clinical aspects of inhibition of ornithine decarboxylase with emphasis on therapeutic trials of eflornitine (DFMO) in cancer and protozoan diseases. In *Inhibition of polyamine metabolism* (ed. P. P. McCann, A. E. Pegg, and A. Sjoerdsma), pp. 345–65, Academic Press, Orlando, Fl.

Schirlin, D., Baltzer, S., Heydt, J.-G., and Jung, M. J. (1987). Irreversible inhibition of GABA-T by halogenated analogues of β-alanine. *J. Enzyme Inhibition*, **1**, 243–58.

Scigliano, G., Giovanni, P., Girotti, F., Grassi, M. P., Caraceni, T., and Schechter, P. J. (1984). Gamma-vinyl GABA treatment of Huntington's disease. *Neurology*, **34**, 94–6.

Seiler, N. and Eichentopf, B. (1975). 4-aminobutyrate in mammalian putrescine catabolism. *Biochem. J.*, **152**, 201–10.

Seiler, N., Danzin, C., Prakash, N. J., and Koch-Weser, J. (1978a). Effects of ornithine decarboxylase inhibitors *in vivo*. In *Enzyme-activated irreversible inhibitors* (ed. N. Seiler, M. J. Jung, and J. Koch-Weser), pp. 57–71. Elsevier-North Holland, Biomedical Press, Amsterdam.

Seiler, N., Jung, M. J., and Koch-Weser, J., ed. (1978b). *Enzyme-activated irreversible inhibitors*. Elsevier–North Holland, Biomedical Press, Amsterdam.

Silverman, R. B. (1984). Effect of α-methylation on inactivation of monoamine oxidase by N-cyclopropylbenzylamine. *Biochemistry*, **23**, 5206–13.

Silverman, R. B. and Levy, M. A. (1980a). Syntheses of (S)-5-substituted 4-aminopentanoic acids: a new class of γ-aminobutyric acid transaminase inactivators. *J. Org. Chem.*, **45**, 815–18.

Silverman, R. B. and Levy, M. A. (1980b) Irreversible inactivation of pig brain γ-aminobutyric acid-α-ketoglutarate transaminase by 4-amino-5-halopentanoic acids. *Biochem. Biophys. Res. Commun.*, **95**, 250–5.

Silverman, R. B. and Levy, M. A. (1981a). Mechanism of inactivation of γ-aminobutyric acid-α-ketoglutaric acid aminotransferase by 4-amino-5-halopentanoic acids. *Biochemistry*, **20**, 1197–203.

Silverman, R. B. and Levy, M. A. (1981b). Substituted 4-aminobutanoic acids. *J. Biol. Chem.*, **256**, 11565–8.

Silverman, R. B., Durkee, S. C., and Invergo, B. J. (1986). 4-amino-2-(substituted methyl)-

2-butenoic acids: substrates and potent inhibitors of γ-aminobutyric acid aminotransferase. *J. Med. Chem.*, **29**, 764–70.

Sjoerdsma, A. (1981). Suicide enzyme inhibitors as potential drugs. *Clin. Pharmacol. Ther.*, **30**, 3–22.

Sjoerdsma, A. (1982). Methyldopa. *Br. J. Clin. Pharmacol.*, **13**, 45–9.

Sjoerdsma, A. and Schechter, P. J. (1984). Chemotherapeutic implications of polyamine biosynthesis inhibition. *Clin. Pharmacol. Ther.*, **35**, 287–300.

Skinner, W. A. and Johansson, J. G. (1972). Ornithine analogs as potential ornithine decarboxylase inhibitors 1. N-substituted ornithine derivatives. *J. Med. Chem.*, **15**, 427–8.

Slotkin, T. A., Slepetis, R. J., Weigel, S. J., and Whitmore, W. L. (1983). Effects of α-fluoromethylhistidine (FMH), an irreversible inhibitor of histidine decarboxylase, on development of brain histamine and catecholamine systems in the neonatal rat. *Life. Sci.*, **32**, 2897–903.

Stevens, L. and Stevens, E. (1980). Inhibitors of the biosynthesis of putrescine, spermidine and spermine. In *Polyamines in biomedical research* (ed. J. M. Gaugas), pp. 167–83. Wiley, Chichester.

Taberner, P. V., Pearce, M. J., and Watkins, J. C. (1977). The inhibition of brain glutamate decarboxylase by some structural analogues of L-glutamic acid. *Biochem. Pharmacol.*, **26**, 345–9.

Tabor, C. W. and Tabor, H. (1984). Polyamines. *Ann. Rev. Biochem.*, **53**, 749–90.

Tabor, H., Hafner, E. W., and Tabor, C. W. (1980). Construction of an *Escherichia coli* strain unable to synthesize putrescine, spermidine, or cadaverine: characterization of two genes controlling lysine decarboxylase. *J. Bacteriol.*, **144**, 952–6.

Tabor, C. W., Tabor, H., and Tyagi, A. K. (1983). Biochemical and genetic studies of polyamines in *Saccharomyces cerevisiae*. *Adv. Polyamine Res.*, **4**, 467–78.

Tapia, R., Sandoral, M. E., and Contreras, P. (1975). Evidence for a role of glutamate decarboxylase activity as a regulatory mechanism of cerebral excitability. *J. Neurochem.*, **24**, 1283–5.

Taub, D. and Patchett, A. A. (1977). Synthesis of α-ethynyl-3,4-dihydroxyphenylalanine and α-vinyl-3,4-dihydroxyphenylalanine. *Tetrahedron Lett.*, 2745–8.

Tell, G., Böhlen, P., Schechter, P. J., Koch-Weser, J., Agid, Y., Bonnet, A. M., Coquillat, G., Chazot, G., and Fischer, C. (1981). Treatment of Huntington disease with γ-acetylenic GABA, an irreversible inhibitor of GABA-transaminase: increased CSF GABA and homocarnosine without clinical amelioration. *Neurology*, **31**, 207–11.

Tower, D. B. (1976). GABA and seizures: clinical correlates in man. In *GABA in nervous system function* (ed. E. Roberts, T. B. Chase, and D. B. Tower), pp. 461–78. Raven Press, New York.

Tung, A. S., Blake, J. T., Roman, I. J., Vlasses, P. H., Ferguson, R. K., and Zweerink, H. J. (1985). *In vivo* and *in vitro* inhibition of human histidine decarboxylase by (S)-α-fluoromethylhistidine. *Biochem. Pharmacol.*, **34**, 3509–15.

Turnbull, I. F., Pyliotis, N. A., and Howells, A. J. (1980). The effects of DOPA decarboxylase inhibitors on the permeability and ultrastructure of the larval cuticle of the Australian sheep blowfly *Lucilia cuprina*. *J. Insect Physiol.*, **26**, 525–32.

Ueno, H., Likos, J. J., and Metzler, D. E. (1982). Chemistry of the inactivation of cytosolic aspartate aminotransferase by serine-O-sulfate. *Biochemistry*, **21**, 4387–93.

Vidal-Cros, A., Gaudry, M., and Marquet, A. (1985). Interaction of L-*threo* and L-*erythro* isomers of 3-fluoroglutamate with glutamate decarboxylase from *Escherichia coli*. *Biochem. J.*, **229**, 675–8.

Wada, H., Watanabe, T., Maeyama, K., Taguchi, Y., and Hayashi, H. (1984). Mammalian histidine decarboxylase and its suicide substrate α-fluoromethylhistidine. In *Chemical and biological aspects of vitamin B₆ catalysis* (ed. A. E. Evangelopoulos), Part A, pp. 245–254, Alan Liss, New York.

Wagner, J., Danzin, C., and Mamont, P. (1982). Reversed-phase ion-pair liquid chromatographic procedure for the simultaneous analysis of S-adenosylmethionine, its metabolites and the natural polyamines. *J. Chromatogr.*, **227**, 349–68.

Waley, S. G. (1980). Kinetics of suicide substrates. *Biochemistry*, **185**, 771–3.

Waley, S. G. (1985). Kinetics of suicide substrates—practical procedures for determining parameters. *Biochem. J.*, **227**, 843–9.

Walsh, C. (1977). Recent developments in suicide substrates and other active site-directed inactivating agents of specific target enzymes. *Horizons Biochem. Biophys.*, **3**, 36–55.

Walsh, C. (1982). Suicide substrates: mechanism-based enzyme inactivators. *Tetrahedron*, **38**, 871–909.

Walsh, C. T. (1984). Suicide substrates, mechanism-based enzyme inactivators: recent developments. *Ann. Rev. Biochem.*, **53**, 493–535.

Watanabe, T., Taguchi, Y., Sasaki, K., Tsuyama, K., and Kitamura, Y. (1981). Increase in histidine decarboxylase activity in mouse skin after application of the tumor promoter tetradecanoylphorbol acetate. *Biochem. Biophys. Res. Commun.*, **100**, 427–32.

White, H. L. (1981). Glutamate as a precursor of GABA in rat brain and peripheral tissues. *Mol. Cell. Biochem.*, **39**, 253–9.

Williams-Ashman, H. G. and Canellakis, Z. N. (1979). Polyamines in mammalian biology and medicine. *Perspect. Biol. Med.*, **22**, 421–53.

Williams-Ashman, H. G., Corti, A., and Tadolini, B. (1976). On the development of specific inhibitors of animal polyamine biosynthetic enzymes. *Ital. J. Biochem.*, **25**, 5–32.

Woldemussie, E. and Beaven, M. A. (1985). α-fluoromethyl histidine: kinetics of uptake and inhibition of histamine synthesis in basophil (2H3) cell cultures. *Mol. Pharmacol.*, **28**, 191–9.

Wu, J.-Y. and Roberts, E. (1974). Properties of brain L-glutamate decarboxylase: inhibitor studies. *J. Neurochem.*, **23**, 759–67.

Cholinesterase and esterase inhibitors and reactivation of organophosphorus inhibited esterases

W. N. Aldridge

9.1   Introduction

The use of the word 'drug' in the title of this volume, *Design of enzyme inhibitors as drugs*, would seem to restrict the scope of this chapter. There are relatively few examples of the use of organophosphorus compounds or carbamates for direct therapeutic purposes. The organophosphorus compounds were first synthesized as nicotine substitutes and, subsequently, because of their high mammalian toxicity, became candidate chemical warfare agents. From this unpromising start, they were developed into pesticides which, in addition to their efficiency as insecticides, were acceptable since they were readily biodegradable. Thus, as a group, the anticholinesterases have been used for purposes of great benefit to humankind—to kill off insects and increase the agricultural yields of crops and also to reduce the number of insects and parasites that are vectors of human disease.

The early and developing knowledge of the mechanism of the interaction of organophosphorous compounds with the cholinesterases will be described, as will the nucleophilic reactivators, which were among the earliest rationally designed therapeutic agents. The mechanism of interaction of organophosphorus compounds with esterases was the forerunner of many anti-catalytic-centre directed inhibitors. The range of enzymes includes esterases that are present in mammalian tissues in large (in terms of molecular concentration) amounts and are found in many different catalytic proteins. Their differing substrate patterns in different tissues and even differing cellular sites within tissues may provide a means whereby pro-drugs may be targeted.

Where known, the mechanism of toxicity will be briefly described so that those wishing to use this class of compound for therapeutic purposes may be able to eliminate the undesirable biological properties. For extensive reviews see Aldridge and Reiner 1972; Heath 1961; Koelle 1963; Heilbronn 1967; O'Brien 1960; Reiner 1975; Aldridge 1980).

9.2   General principles

Once a hypothesis for the mechanism of action of a compound with a particular enzyme is available, new and more active compounds may be synthesized. The development of new covalent compounds that interact covalently with enzymes is not, even with a good hypothesis, an entirely rational process. It is usually possible to predict that a particular structure will be an inhibitor, but how good it will be often awaits further experiments. It is still very difficult to predict with any precision the rate of reaction of a compound with an enzyme. Drugs are intended for the treatment of animals and humans, and distribution and pharmacokinetics may have a decisive influence on efficacy. The relationship between measurements *in vitro* and effects or efficacy in the whole animal and cross-species variations are still challenging problems.

9.3   Inhibition of esterases

9.3.1   Mechanism

The mechanism of interaction of organophosphorus compounds with esterases is well established and is shown diagramatically in Fig. 9.1. The process is entirely analogous to the enzyme–substrate reaction (Aldridge and Reiner 1972; Aldridge 1981). In detailed kinetic studies evidence for K_a, the analogue of K_m in the substrate reaction, has been produced as well as k_{+2} and k_{+3}, the phosphorylation and hydrolysis constants. Thus the organophosphorus compounds are substrates for esterases.

Covalent interaction with the catalytic centre of esterases requires that the substrate and the inhibitor possess a hydrolysable bond, a tertiary structure that fits into the catalytic centre so that the bond to be hydrolysed is in the right

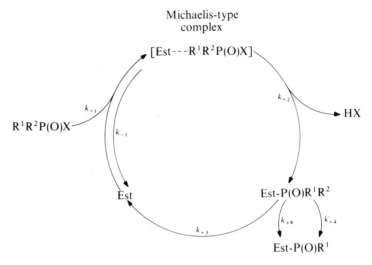

Fig. 9.1. Diagrammatic representation of the reaction of esterases with organophospho-rus compounds. Est = serine or B-esterase. The reaction pathway also holds for carba-mates and sulphonates (Aldridge 1981).

juxtaposition to the reacting groups in the enzyme. Whether a compound is considered as a substrate or an inhibitor depends mainly on the stability of the phosphorylated or acylated enzyme. There is a continuous spectrum from good substrate through a slowly hydrolysed substrate and poor inhibitor to powerful inhibitor.

The structures of some covalent inhibitors are shown in Fig. 9.2. Included are the organo derivatives of phosphoric, phosphonic, and phosphinic acids. The bonding of alkyl, aryl, or other groups to the phosphorus atom may be via an oxygen, nitrogen, or sulphur atom (Fig. 9.2, **1**, **2**, **3**). Other compounds carbamyl-ate, carbonylate or sulphonate the catalytic centre (**4**, **5**, **6**). When all of the above structures react with B- or serine esterases a group (X in Fig. 9.2) is released into the medium. Other structures such as the saligenin phosphates, the benzoxazin-ones, and the isocyanates (**7**, **8**, **9**) do not possess a leaving group and reaction depends on ring-opening or direct interaction. Included in Fig. 9.2 are the fluoroketones, even though they do not yield an enzyme derivative with a covalent bond to the hydroxyl of serine. They are considered to form stable hemiketals with the serine. These hemiketals are dissociable, but the dissociation constants are so low that they merit especial mention. For the covalent in-hibitors, the hydrolysability of the bond leading to the release of X (**1–6**) or to ring-opening (**7** and **8**) is a guide to how good an inhibitor with a particular structure is, but only within a range of homologous structures.

Often, particular characteristics in the structure of compounds lead to active inhibitors (Aldridge 1981). These include, for example, a preference for two

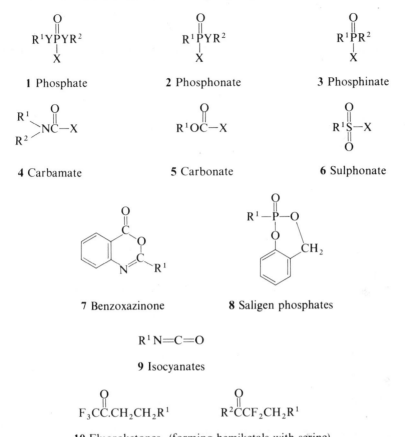

1 Phosphate

2 Phosphonate

3 Phosphinate

4 Carbamate

5 Carbonate

6 Sulphonate

7 Benzoxazinone

8 Saligen phosphates

$$R^1 N=C=O$$

9 Isocyanates

$$F_3CC.CH_2CH_2R^1 \qquad R^2CCF_2CH_2R^1$$

10 Fluoroketones (forming hemiketals with serine)

Fig. 9.2. Structures of inhibitors of serine or B-esterases. Literature references are as follows: **1–4, 6**, Aldridge and Reiner 1972; **5**, Bender and Wedler 1972; **7**, Hedstrom *et al.* 1984; Abeles and Weidman, 1984; **8**, Toia and Casida, 1979; **9**, Krupka 1974; **10**, Gelb *et al.* 1985.

In structures **1** and **2**, Y may be O, S, or N atoms.

aromatic groups for both substrates and inhibitors of chymotrypsin, a positive charge for cholinesterase, and a two-phase system with a lipid–water interface for lipase. Acetylcholinesterase does not accept inhibitors containing negative charges in the molecule and the converse is true for liver esterase.

Various constants can be derived from the reaction shown in Fig. 9.1. The derivations are essentially similar to those for enzyme–substrate reactions but the meaning of the constants so derived may be different. K_a is $(k_{-1}+k_{+2})/k_{+1}$ when k_{+3} is small as for most inhibitors. The analogous operational constant for substrates is the Michaelis constant, K_m, which is $k_{+3}(k_{-1}+k_{+2})/k_{+1}(k_{+2}+k_{+3})$. When k_{+2} is of comparable magnitude to k_{-1} then K_a is defined as stated above and can only be regarded as analogous to a dissociation or affinity constant if k_{+2} is small compared to k_{-1}. This is sometimes ignored. Many of the derivations also require that the concentration of inhibitor is in large excess to the concentration of the enzyme. This is often the case but for some very active inhibitors may not be so. These matters are fully discussed by Aldridge and Reiner (1972). In a recent paper (Forsberg and Gertrud 1984), it has been shown for the reaction of various organophosphorus inhibitors and carbamates with electric eel cholinesterase that k_{+2} varies only from 0.06 to 0.91 s^{-1} whereas K_a has a far greater range (1.1×10^{-3} to 8.2×10^{-7} M), the implication being that the main determinant of activity is the affinity for the enzyme (Forsberg and Gertrud 1984). No general relationship between k_{+2} and K_a was found. This is to be expected since, as for substrates, the rate of the acylation step will be dependent on fit in the catalytic centre in relation to the reacting groups in the enzyme, on the intrinsic chemical hydrolysability of the bond to be broken, and on the interpretation of the meaning of K_a, i.e. how close it approximates to a dissociation constant .

In all cases where K_a has or can be determined, the phosphorylated group in the catalytic centre is serine. For chymotrypsin inhibited by phenylmethanesulphonyl fluoride, there is indirect evidence that the sulphonyl group is attached to serine. There is no direct evidence that in carbamylated esterases the carbamyl group is attached to serine due to instability during the isolation procedures. Perhaps it may be possible to answer this question with other inhibitors which produce more stable carbamylated esterases. For example, butyl isocyanate is a powerful inhibitor of the cholinesterases, presumably producing a butylcarbamylated enzyme (Krupka 1974). For the interaction of substrates with esterases, there is of course no direct evidence that the acyl group is attached to serine, the main evidence being analogy with inhibitors. Thus, it is a good working hypothesis that for all esterases that are inhibited by organophosphorus compounds and related compounds, the acyl groups from both inhibitors and substrates become attached to one unusually reactive serine in the catalytic centre. Such esterases are called B- or serine esterases. Another class of esterases is known that are not inhibited and hydrolyse the inhibitor. These are called A-esterases (Aldridge 1953a, b). This group of esterases is not well characterized and the mechanism of catalysis is not established. Interest in one enzyme of this class, first described in 1951, which hydrolyses paraoxon (diethyl 4-nitrophenyl phosphate) to release 4-nitrophenol, has been stimulated since it has been shown to be associated with the rather common genetically-determined disease cystic fibrosis (Eiberg et al. 1985). In future studies, the function of this enzyme may now be established and work to establish its catalytic mechanism may be stimulated.

Mammalian tissues possess many as yet ill-defined A- and B-esterases. If it is assumed that, at reasonable concentrations, organophosphorus compounds only interact with esterases, it can readily be demonstrated using radio-labelled inhibitors that the amount of known enzymes can only account for a small proportion of the radio-labelled protein (Aldridge 1981). There is no doubt that these esterases could be separated and characterized with the application of sensitive analytical methodology and selective inhibition using principles established long ago (Aldridge and Reiner 1972).

As known for substrates, allosteric interactions of inhibitors have been demonstrated that influence reaction rates with acylating inhibitors (Aldridge and Reiner 1972; Radic *et al.* 1984; Reiner 1986).

9.3.2   Properties of the inhibited enzymes

The magnitude of k_{+3} determines the rate of completion of a substrate cycle and the hydrolysis of 1 mol of the inhibitor. The complete cycle is a complete description of the reactions of carbamates, sulphonates, and phosphinates (Fig. 9.1). For other organophosphorus compounds, when groups are attached to the phosphorus via other atoms and not by phosphorus–carbon bonds, another reaction can take place. This 'ageing reaction' is so called because it is relatively slow when compared with the initial inhibitory process. For two phosphylated cholinesterases (pinacolyl methylphosphonyl acetylcholinesterase and di-isopropyl phosphorylcholinesterase from horse serum) it has been shown by unambiguous chemical methods that the reaction consists of the release of one of the groups attached to the phosphorus atom, e.g. pinacolyl or di-isopropyl. In the former case, the reaction is certainly via a carbonium ion mechanism. Even for phosphorylated and phosphonylated acetylcholinesterases, another mechanism is possible when the phosphorus–oxygen–carbon bond is broken between the phosphorus and oxygen bonds. Ageing of di-isopropyl phosphorylated atropine esterase, chymotrypsin, or subtilisin in $H_2 {}^{18}O$ resulted in the isolation of isopropanol from the medium with a ${}^{18}O/{}^{16}O$ ratio equal to that of the medium. The oxygen in the released isopropanol must have come from the water solvent and therefore P—O—C bond has broken between C and O. In these experiments, propene was also detected but the amounts found varied (chymotrypsin 1.2 per cent, subtilisin 3.8 per cent, atropine esterase 11.3 per cent; Van der Drift 1983).

Several methods are available to measure the extent and rate of the ageing reaction. Chemical methods may be used and involve the degradation of the inhibited enzyme, usually with alkali followed by the determination of the di- or mono-organophosphorus acids. Sometimes the primary released group has been determined. A recent publication (Van der Drift 1983) describes the use of ${}^{31}P$-n.m.r. to follow the change to an ionized phosphorus-containing moiety attached to the protein. Most of the above methods rely on a highly radio-labelled inhibitor (by ${}^{32}P$ or by ${}^{3}H$ or ${}^{14}C$ in the carbon-containing groups) and for an enzyme preparation purified free from other B-esterases. The most commonly used method for less purified preparations employs nucleophilic reactivators and determines regenerated activity at different times after incubation with inhibitor. The method requires that the un-aged inhibited enzyme is readily reactivated by nucleophiles; interpretation is sometimes a problem when aging is slow and when controls require sizeable corrections to the experimental data.

The ageing of neuropathy target esterase (NTE) differs from all other esterases examined (Johnson 1982). Not only is the reaction rapid for many inhibited NTEs but also the released group becomes attached to the protein. It seems likely that the point of attachment is to the protein molecule containing the catalytic centre but it could be to another protein in the neighbourhood. The mechanism of this ageing reaction is not known but is of considerable interest because of the involvement of NTE in the development of delayed neuropathy (see later). The nature of the group in the protein to which the phosphorus and the released groups becomes attached and any clue as to the mechanisms of ageing is unknown. It is not known whether the alcohol group or only the carbon part of it is transferred. If the latter is general, then the reaction may be somewhat analogous to the glutathione transferase process if it is assumed that aging with di-isopropyl-, dimethyl-, and diaryl-derivatives is by the same mechanism. In conclusion, much research is required to understand the mechanism of the ageing reaction of a range of esterases inhibited by different inhibitors. From a practical point of view, ageing prevents therapy with nucleophilic reactivators of poisoning by organophosphorus compounds. Mono-organophosphylated acetylcholinesterase is stable and return of enzyme activity in animals and in humans requires the synthesis of new esterase protein.

9.3.3   Stereoisomers of organophosphorus compounds

Since inhibition of esterases is an enzyme–substrate reaction with some of the steps very slow, it is expected that, as for substrates, the chirality of atoms in inhibitors will affect the rate of reaction of various stereoisomers. Examples of chiral organophosphorus inhibitors are shown in Fig. 9.3.

A complete review of the literature will not be presented here; references are provided for those wishing to read further (Aaron et al. 1958; Boter and Van Dijk 1969; Boter and Ooms 1967; De Jong and Van Dijk 1972; Keijer and Wolring 1969; Ooms and Boter 1965; Ooms and Van Dijk 1966; Wustner and Fukuto 1974; Johnson et al. 1986). However, the recent development of methods for the separation of stereoisomers and their determination has led to an increase of research in this area. The inhibition of esterases by Soman (Fig. 9.3) which possesses two chiral atoms will be used to illustrate the principles. Methods for the synthesis, separation, and determination of the four isomers have been developed (Benschop et al. 1981a, b; Nordgren et al. 1985). Inhibition of acetylcholinesterase by the $P_{(-)}$ isomers ($C_{(-)}P_{(-)}$ and $C_{(+)}P_{(-)}$; for nomenclature of isomers see Fig. 9.3) is at least 3.6×10^4 times faster than for the $P_{(+)}$ isomers and toxicity follows the same ratio (Benschop et al. 1984a, b). In contrast, the hydrolysis by A-esterases present in plasma shows a specificity for the $P_{(+)}$ stereoisomers (Benschop et al. 1981a, b, 1984a; Nordgren et al. 1984) and, in vivo, their disposal is much more rapid than the $P_{(-)}$ stereoisomers (De

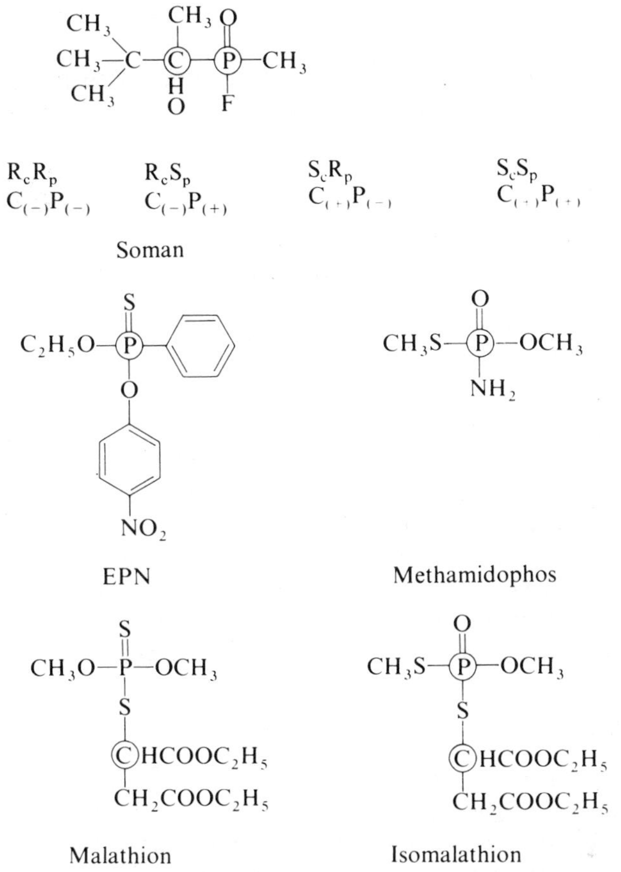

CH₃—C(CH₃)(CH₃)—C(CH₃)(H)—P(O)(OF)—CH₃ (structure)

R_cR_p R_cS_p S_cR_p S_cS_p
$C_{(-)}P_{(-)}$ $C_{(-)}P_{(+)}$ $C_{(+)}P_{(-)}$ $C_{(+)}P_{(+)}$

Soman

C_2H_5O—P(=S)(—C₆H₅)—O—C₆H₄—NO₂ (structure)

CH_3S—P(=O)(—OCH₃)—NH₂ (structure)

EPN   Methamidophos

CH_3O—P(=S)(—OCH₃)—S—CH(COOC₂H₅)—CH₂COOC₂H₅ (structure)

CH_3S—P(=O)(—OCH₃)—S—CH(COOC₂H₅)—CH₂COOC₂H₅ (structure)

Malathion   Isomalathion

Fig. 9.3. Structures of chiral organophosphorus compounds. For nomenclature of Soman stereoisomers see Nordgren *et al.* 1985. The chiral centres are circled.

Jong and Van Dijk 1984; Nordgren *et al.* 1985). Rates of aging also differ with the different stereoisomers (Keijer and Wolring 1969).

The ability of stereoisomers of Soman to inhibit neuropathy target esterase (NTE) and cause delayed neuropathy has been examined. Although the question whether particular stereoisomers cause delayed neuropathy is not yet clearly answered (Willems *et al.* 1984; Johnson *et al.* 1985a), it has been established that they do react with NTE *in vitro*. In contrast to the major differences in their rates of reaction with acetylcholinesterase, all four stereoisomers inhibit NTE with a difference of only 10-fold in the rate constants for the different isomers. However, both $P_{(-)}$ stereoisomers produced a phosphonylated enzyme which spontaneously reactivated and only the $C_{(-)}P_{(+)}$ isomer-inhibited enzyme aged within 18 h (Johnson *et al.* 1985b). It will be interesting if these unexpected results are associated with other unusual properties of this esterase (NTE; see discussion on ageing).

In summary, it is clear that stereospecificity around the phosphorus atom greatly influences the rate of reaction with B-esterases, the properties of the inhibited enzymes, and hydrolysis by some A-esterases. Stereospecificity around other atoms in the molecule may be important, particularly when detoxification involves reaction at some site distant from the phosphorus atom as in malathion (Hassan and Dauterman 1968).

9.3.4   Reactivation of inhibited enzymes by nucleophilic reagents

The use of knowledge of the mechanisms of reaction of organophosphorus compounds with acetylcholinesterase in the development of rational therapeutic drugs for the treatment of poisoning has been a success story (Hobbiger 1963; 1968). Of the hydroxamic acids, oximes, quaternized pyridine-2-aldoximes, and bis-pyridinium aldoximes, the latter are the most effective reactive agents *in vitro* and *in vivo* (Hobbiger *et al.* 1960; Erdmann 1976; Simeon *et al.* 1979; Schoene *et al.* 1983). The mechanism is known and is illustrated in Fig. 9.4. The reactivation of phosphylated esterases in the case of chymotrysin and trypsin shows a direct relationship between pK of the reactivator and the reactivating potency (Cohen and Erlanger 1960; Cohen *et al.* 1962). In other words, the dissociation constant of the nucleophile is an expression of its affinity for protons, and this is analogous to its affinity for the positively charged phosphorus. For reactivation of phosphylated acetylcholinesterase, the above relationship does not hold; it is assumed that other structural requirements such as a positively charged nitrogen or other atom in the nucleophile are important. It is now accepted that the rate of reactivation of inhibited acetylcholinesterase is dependent upon the structure and the pK of the nucleophilic reagent, the structure of the phosphorus-containing group attached to the esterase, the asymmetric centres in either this group attached to esterases or in the nucleophilic reagent, and upon the stability and inhibitory potency of the phosphorylated oximes generated during the reaction. Many phosphorylated oximes are powerful inhibitors of acetylcholinesterases, some having rate constants as high as $3 \times 10^{7} \, \mathrm{l \, mol^{-1} \, min^{-1}}$ (Schoene 1976).

Fluoride has been known for some time as an effective reactivator of phosphylated esterases (Heilbronn 1965; Clothier and Johnson 1979, 1980). It has been used extensively for the study of the ageing reaction of NTE and it seems probable that it will prove to be an effective experimental tool for the study of many different inhibited esterases. As shown in Fig. 9.4, the mechanism is expected to be the reaction of fluoride with the phosphylated esterase to form the original, catalytically active enzyme, and an organophosphoryl fluoridate, both of which are, like the oximes, active inhibitors. It has been shown recently (De Jong and Van Dijk 1984) that when carboxylesterase from rat plasma is

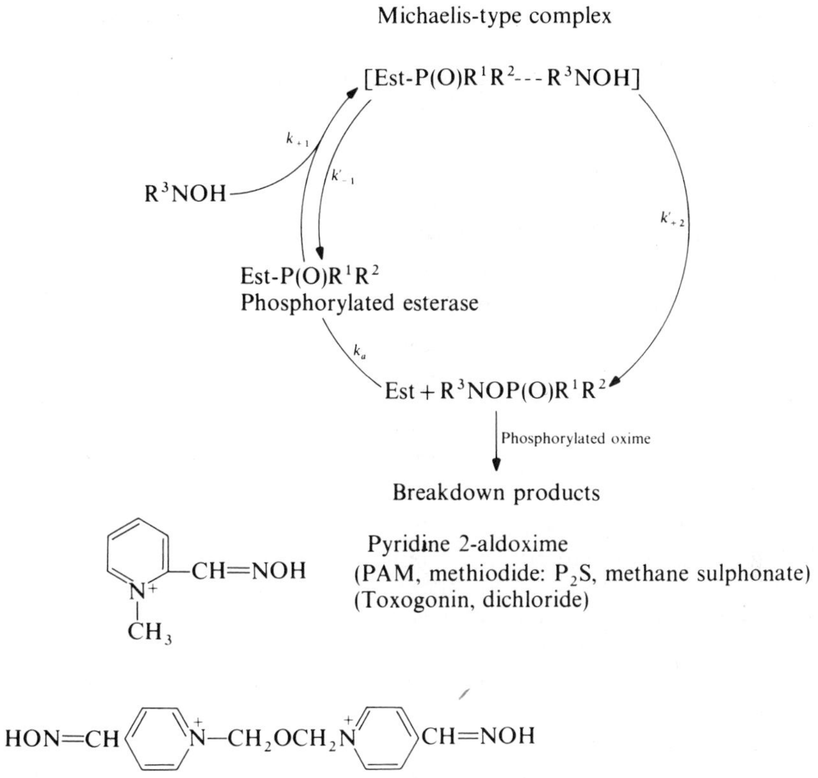

Michaelis-type complex

$[\text{Est-P(O)R}^1\text{R}^2\text{---R}^3\text{NOH}]$

k_{+1}

k'_{-1}

R^3NOH

k'_{+2}

Est-P(O)R^{1}R^2
Phosphorylated esterase

k_a

Est + R^{3}NOP(O)R^{1}R^2

Phosphorylated oxime

Breakdown products

Pyridine 2-aldoxime
—CH=NOH   (PAM, methiodide: P$_2$S, methane sulphonate)
(Toxogonin, dichloride)

HON=CH〈 〉N—CH$_2$OCH$_2$N〈 〉CH=NOH

Fig. 9.4. Diagrammatic representation of the mechanism of reactivation of phosphylated esterases by nucleophilic oximes or hydroxamic acids. Est = serine or B-esterases;
R^3NOH = substituted oxime or hydroxamic acid. The reaction of phosphylated oxime
with esterase has been abbreviated to one step (k_a), although it should strictly be as in
Fig. 9.1.

inhibited by Soman $P_{(-)}$ enzyme derivatives are formed; reactivation by incubation with sodium fluoride yields $P_{(-)}$ Soman.

Pre-treatment of animals with carbamates such as eserine renders them able
to tolerate much higher doses of an otherwise lethal organophosphate (for
discussion, see Aldridge 1980). It was postulated that the mechanism involved a
complex readjustment of the reaction rates of the various steps of the interaction
of acetylcholine, carbamate, and organophosphate with acetylcholinesterase
and the rate(s) of disposal of the organophosphate. A theoretical approach to
this complex problem has been published by Green (1983), who agrees with this
conclusion but points out that a crucial issue is the amount or activity of
acetylcholinesterase (presumably at various sites, the relative importance of
which may vary in different species of animal) necessary to maintain life.

Although the broad outlines of the mechanisms of reactivation of acetylcholinesterase by nucleophilic reagents is understood, no sound method has been devised for prediction from *in vitro* techniques of the therapeutic value of particular compounds. The foregoing discussion has underlined the complexity of the situation *in vitro*, but *in vivo* many more reactions will contribute to therapeutic efficiency, particularly processes leading to the disposal of the reformed organophosphate. In recent studies of bis-quaternary oximes, unexpected activity was noted in compounds that possess no oxime group (Schoene *et al.* 1983). Using isolated diaphragm of rat, guinea pig and marmoset, results were obtained which suggest that differences seen between the preparations from the different species may be due to processes that include enzyme reactivation, direct action of the reactivator on the acetylcholine receptor, and adaptation (French *et al.* 1983).

9.4 Bioactivation

Many organophosphorus compounds that are toxic by virtue of their inhibition of acetylcholinesterase are not active inhibitors when added to the enzyme *in vitro*. Many pesticides are in this class and are bioactivated, usually by the cytochrome P-450 drug-processing systems. Most of the compounds are oxidized in the liver but other tissues may play a significant role for some compounds. Examples of several bioactivation routes are shown in Fig. 9.5, together with relevant references. For a detailed discussion of bioactivation processes, see Anders (1985).

9.5 Detoxification

The routes of disposal and detoxification of organophosphorus compounds involve oxidative, hydrolytic, and transfer enzyme systems. Most of the reactions, either singly or by the sequential action of two processes (e.g. oxidation followed by hydrolysis) lead to an organophosphorus compound containing a negative charge. This effectively increases its water solubility and excretion, and in the case of cholinesterase removes its inhibiting ability. For other enzymes, this need not be the case, e.g. bis-4-nitrophenyl phosphate is a good inhibitor of liver carboxyl esterases.

The reactions leading to the inhibition of esterases (Fig. 9.1) lead to the loss of one molecule of inhibitor for each molecule of enzyme inhibited. For most carboxyl esterases no function is known, except perhaps a general scavenging purpose to remove esters available from exogenous and endogenous sources. Thus, for a powerful organophosphorus inhibitor, reaction with carboxyl esterases can be detoxification pathway. The conditions for effective detoxification are that the carboxylesterase should be present with a high activity and low catalytic centre activity (i.e. a high molar concentration of enzyme protein), associated with a rapid rate of resynthesis of new protein. This has been

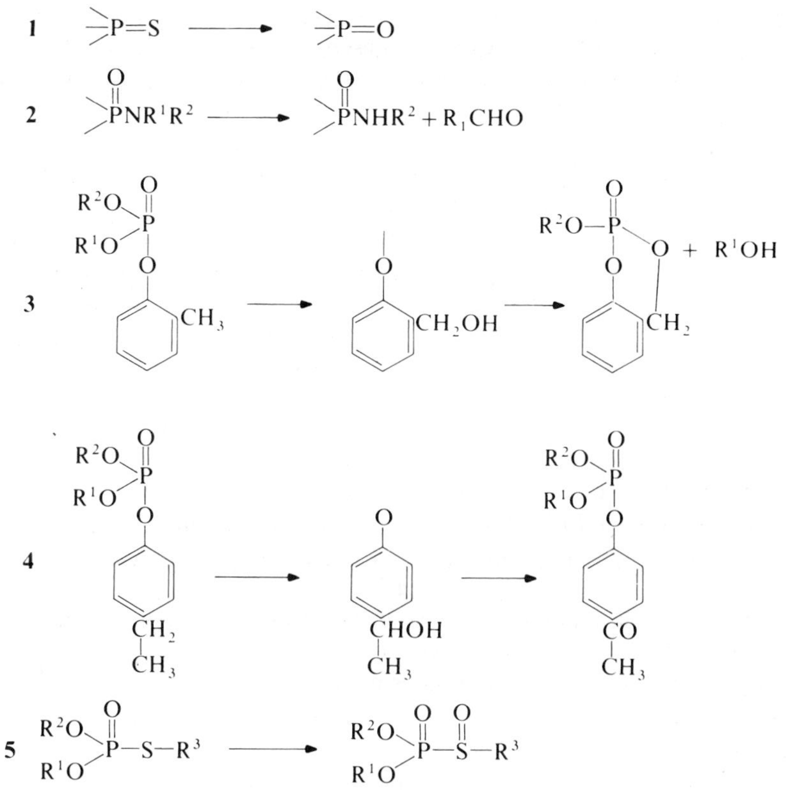

1 $>P=S \longrightarrow >P=O$

2 $>P(=O)NR^1R^2 \longrightarrow >P(=O)NHR^2 + R_1CHO$

3 (figure: phosphate ester with R^2O, R^1O and aryl–CH_3 group $\longrightarrow$ aryl–CH_2OH $\longrightarrow$ cyclic product $+ R^1OH$)

4 (figure: phosphate ester with R^2O, R^1O and aryl–CH_2CH_3 $\longrightarrow$ aryl–$CHOH\,CH_3$ $\longrightarrow$ aryl–$CO\,CH_3$)

5 $R^2O,R^1O\text{-}P(=O)\text{-}S\text{-}R^3 \longrightarrow R^2O,R^1O\text{-}P(=O)\text{-}S(=O)\text{-}R^3$

Fig. 9.5. Examples of routes of bioactivation of organophosphorus compounds. Literature references are: **11**, Neal 1985; **12**, Arthur and Casida 1958; **13**, Eto *et al.* 1962; **14**, Eto *et al.* 1971; **15**, Wing *et al.* 1984.

established for the organophosphorus inhibitor Sarin and the carboxyl esterase in rat plasma (Fonnum and Sterri 1981; Clement 1984; Fonnum *et al.* 1985). It is probable that such a detoxification role for esterases and even cholinesterases may be important in exposure to low concentrations of organophosphorus compounds and carbamates.

9.6 Mechanisms of toxicity

9.6.1 Acute toxicity

No discussion is necessary of the mechanisms of acute toxicity, which is due to accumulation of acetylcholine following the prevention of its physiological destruction (Hobbiger 1968). Species differences still remain to be explained, and different anticholinesterases can produce a range of symptomatology and variations on the expected syndrome (e.g. symptoms arising from the central effects rather than from inhibition of acetylcholinesterase in the periphery). Repeated and prolonged inhibition of acetylcholinesterase may produce muscle necrosis in experimental animals (for discussion of the literature see Dettbarn 1984).

9.6.2   Delayed neuropathy

The mechanism of the initiation of delayed neuropathy caused by some organo-phosphorus compounds has been established, but the subsequent biological or biochemical changes that lead to the dying-back lesion, particularly in the long nerves in the peripheral and central nervous system, is not understood. The response appears to be a general one in most mammalian species, although the chicken and humans appear to be very sensitive. A protein that is an esterase, since it hydrolyses ester substrates at a rapid rate, is present in the nervous system, and its esteratic activity is inhibited when it is phosphorylated. This in itself is not sufficient for the development of the disease, for unless a second step (the aging reaction) takes place, involving the release of a group attached to the phosphorus atom (cf. Fig. 9.1; k_{+4}), the symptoms of the disease do not appear until 10–14 days later in chickens or after up to 3 weeks in humans. As pointed out previously (see discussion on the ageing reaction, Section 9.3.2), this esterase is probably unique because the released group is transferred to another site, presumably close to the catalytic centre. If the esterase reacts with an inhibitor to produce an inhibited esterase that does not age, then the disease not only does not develop, but chickens so treated are resistant to other neuropathic com-pounds. Phosphinates, carbamates, and sulphonates produce inhibited NTE that cannot age. This hypothesis provides a good explanation for the structure–activity relationships found from administration of the compounds to adult hens. The hypothesis is now being extended to include stereoisomers of organophosphates and phosphinates (Johnson et al. 1985a, b, 1986). For a detailed discussion of these findings see the reviews by Johnson (1975a, b, 1982).

Because the initiating target is known, it has been possible to begin to answer some of the problems of prediction of results in humans from results obtained in experiments on animals. Provided the structure of the compound is known, a simple measurement of the inhibitory power of the proximal toxin (some compounds are bioactivated) for neurotoxic esterase will indicate the potential for producing disease. Usually one day after dosing hens, measurement of residual NTE will provide much information about the toxic hazard and whether repeated exposure is likely to cause the disease; existing tests take six weeks and rely on the observation of hens and histology of the spinal cord. Testing of phosphinates, carbamates, and sulphonates for their potential to cause delayed neuropathy can now cease, since it is known that they cannot take part in all the reactions necessary for the development of the disease. Species differences can be examined by a comparison of brain tissue of animals and humans (Lotti and Johnson 1978; 1980). The consequences of chronic exposure and the question of whether there is a threshold for inhibition of NTE can now be answered in a logical way. Thus, although from a single acute dose 80 per cent inhibition of NTE is required to produce disease, 50 per cent inhibition can be tolerated for several weeks with no clinical signs (Lotti and Johnson 1980). NTE is now known to be present in tissues other than the nervous system (Williams and Johnson 1981); amongst these tissues are the spleen and leucocytes. Measurement of the inhibition of leucocyte NTE is now being evaluated as a monitoring system in humans for exposure to potentially neuropathic organophosphorus compounds (Lotti 1983).

9.7   Other potential toxic reactions

9.7.1   Carcinogenesis and mutagenesis

It is perhaps natural that the organophosphates in use as pesticides should be suspected, since they are often alkyl phosphates, of having a potential to cause cancer or mutation. The compound which has been examined most in this regard is dichlorvos (*O,O*-dimethyl *O*-dichlorovinyl phosphate). Although positive at high concentrations in some bacterial tests for mutagenesis (ICPEMC Publication 1980), there have been few convincing results from experiments in which animals have been exposed to the compound (International Symposium 1981). It has been concluded from a variety of experimental approaches that the risk is extremely small (International Symposium 1981). This is a matter of some importance because metrifonate, by its non-enzymic conversion to dichlorvos *in vivo*, produces a rather prolonged exposure to the compound when patients are treated for *Schistoma haematobium* infections (Davis and Bailey 1969; Plestina *et al.* 1972; Aldridge 1980; WHO 1985).

9.7.2   Toxicity to the lung

Because of the large-scale accident during a malaria eradication programme in Pakistan during which many spray-men were poisoned due to the potentiation of the toxicity of Malathion by an impurity (Isomalathion; see Fig. 9.3), interest has been focused on other impurities in commercial pesticides (Aldridge *et al.* 1979; 1986). Trialkyl phosphorothioates are present in many thiono organophosphates and the trimethyl and triethyl series have been shown to cause delayed death due to respiratory failure consequent on lung damage. The primary cellular target is the type 1 pneumocyte, followed by a massive increase in lung weight due to fluid in the alveoli and proliferation of type 2 pneumocytes (Dinsdale *et al.* 1982, 1984). The structure of the active compounds is shown in Fig. 9.6. A sulphur atom is required in the molecule between the alkyl group and the phosphorus (Verschoyle and Cabral 1982). Trialkyl phosphates do not cause lung toxicity. One compound containing sulphur atoms, SSS—Et(O) (see Fig. 9.6 for nomenclature), does not produce lung damage, probably because its high solubility in lipids makes it impossible to maintain a sufficient concentration in the lung. Most of the methyl and ethyl series of compounds mix with body water

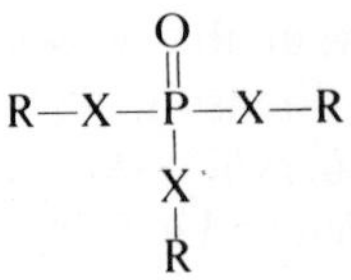

$$R-X-\overset{\overset{\displaystyle O}{\|}}{\underset{\underset{\displaystyle R}{|}}{P}}-X-R$$

R = CH$_3$ or C$_2$H$_5$

where each of the three atoms denoted by X have the combination OOS, OSS, SSS

Style of abbreviation: OSS—Me(O), where atom in parentheses is double-bonded to phosphorus

Trialkyl phosphorothioates (thiolates)

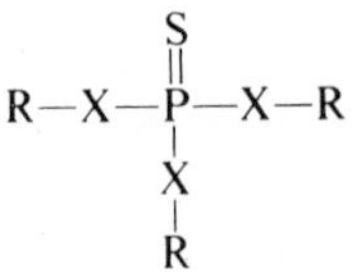

$$R-X-\overset{\overset{\displaystyle S}{\|}}{\underset{\underset{\displaystyle R}{|}}{P}}-X-R$$

R = CH$_3$

where each of the three atoms denoted by X have the combination OOO, OOS

Style of abbreviation: OOS—Me(S), where atom in parentheses is double-bonded to phosphorus

Trialkyl phosphorothionates

Fig. 9.6. Structures of compounds causing lung damage and the thionates that protect against this damage.

and produce a uniform concentration in blood and tissues. They are rapidly removed from the bloodstream due to metabolism by both oxidative processes involving the cytochrome P-450 drug-processing systems and by glutathione transferases (Aldridge *et al.* 1984, 1985). Administration of thiono compounds such as OOO—Me(S) and OOS—Me(S), either before or with the trialkyl phosphorothioates, prevents the development of lung damage. These thiono compounds selectively inhibit the cytochrome P-450 systems in the lung while leaving those in the liver almost unaffected. From these observations, and other evidence, it seems certain that the trialkyl phosphorothioates themselves do not cause damage to the type 1 pneumocytes but have to be bioactivated by oxidative systems in the lung. The metabolites responsible have not yet been identified (Aldridge *et al.* 1986; Nemery 1986).

In a follow-up of the structure–activity relationships for the protective activity of thiono compounds, it has been shown that several currently used organophosphorus pesticides are extremely active and cause inhibition of the cytochrome P-450 systems in the lung at doses 100 times less than those causing toxicity due to inhibition of acetylcholinesterase (Aldridge *et al.* 1986; Verschoyle, unpublished observations).

9.8   Conclusions

The main uses of the anticholinesterases are as insecticides and pesticides for agricultural purposes and for vector control (International Conference 1971). As such they have saved many lives and prevented much disease. Metrifonate [*O,O*-dimethyl-(1-hydroxy-2,2,2-trichloroethyl)phosphonate] has been widely used for the treatment of *S. haematobium* infections. Quaternary carbamates have been useful for the amelioration of the symptoms of myaesthenia gravis. Several anticholinesterase carbamates and organophosphorus compounds are used for the control of intraocular pressure in glaucoma. Eserine (physostigmine) has also been used for the restoration of the vital functions after poisoning with drugs influencing cholinergic receptors.

Although there are relatively few direct uses of the anticholinesterases as drugs for the treatment of disease in humans, their study and then elucidation of the mechanisms of their biological effects provide a model for other drugs acting on other systems. Because they produce covalently bound adducts with enzymes, the primary targets necessary for the initiation of their biological activity, and because they interact with these targets to give relatively stable derivatives, the relative importance of other systems to the overall toxicity in the whole animal may be quantitatively evaluated. For example, by the influence of drug-metabolizing systems in different species, the determination of structure–activity relationships at the target, and dose–response relationships in terms of the absorbed dose instead of a less exact measure of dose administered by a variety of routes.

References

Aaron, H. S., Michal, H. O., Witton, B., and Millar, J. J. (1958). The stereochemistry of asymmetric phosphorus compounds. II. Stereospecificity of the irreversible inactivation of cholinesterase by the enantiomorphs of an organophosphorus inhibitor. *J. Am. Chem. Soc.*, **80**, 456–8.

Abeles, R. H. and Weidman, B. (1984). Mechanism of inactivation of chymotrypsin by 5-butyl-3H-1,3-oxazine-2,6-dione. *Biochemistry*, **23**, 2373–6.

Aldridge, W. N. (1953a). Serum esterases. 1. Two types of esterase (A & B) hydrolysing *p*-nitrophenyl acetate, propionate and butyrate and a method for their determination. *Biochem. J.*, **53**, 110–17.

Aldridge, W. N. (1953b). Serum esterases. 2. An enzyme hydrolysing diethyl *p*-nitrophenyl phosphate (E600) and its identity with the A-esterases of mammalian sera. *Biochem. J.*, **53**, 117–24.

Aldridge, W. N. (1980). Acetylcholinesterase and other esterase inhibitors. In *Enzyme inhibitors as drugs* (ed. M. Sandler), pp. 115–25. Macmillan, London.

Aldridge, W. N. (1981). Organophosphorus compounds: molecular basis for their biological properties. *Sci. Prog. (London)*, **67**, 131–47.

Aldridge, W. N. and Reiner, E. (1972). *Enzyme inhibitors as substrates*. Interaction of esters with esters of organophosphorus and carbamic acids, pp. 1–328. North Holland, Amsterdam.

Aldridge, W. N., Miles, J. W., Mount, D. L., and Verschoyle, R. D. (1979). The toxicological properties of impurities in malathion. *Arch. Toxicol.*, **42**, 95–106.

Aldridge, W. N., Verschoyle, R. D., and Peal, J. A. (1984). *O,S,S*-trimethyl phosphorodithioate and *O,O,S*-trimethyl phosphorothioate: pharmacokinetics in rats and effect of pretreatment with compounds affecting drug processing systems. *Pestic. Biochem. Physiol.*, **21**, 265–74.

Aldridge, W. N., Grasdalen, H., Aarstad, K., Street, B. W., and Norkov, T. (1985). Trialkylphosphorothioates and glutathione *S*-transferases. *Chem. Biol. Interactions*, **54**, 243–56.

Aldridge, W. N., Dinsdale, D., Nemery, B., and Verschoyle, R. D. (1986). Toxicology of impurities in malathion potentiation of malathion toxicity and lung toxicity caused by trialkyl phosphorothioates. In *Selectivity and molecular mechanisms of toxicity* (ed. F. De Matteis and E. Lock). pp. 265–94. Macmillan, London.

Anders, M. W. (ed.) (1985). Bioactivation of foreign compounds. In *Biochemical pharmacology and toxicology monographs*, pp. 1–555. Academic Press., Orlando, FL.

Arthur, B. W. and Casida, J. E. (1958). Biological and chemical oxidation of tetramethyl phosphorodiamidic fluoride (Dimefox). *J. Econ. Entomol.*, **51**, 49–56.

Bender, M. L. and Wedler, F. C. (1972). Phosphate and carbonate ester 'aging' reactions with α-chymotrypsin. Kinetics and mechanism. *J. Am. Chem. Soc.*, **94**, 2101–9.

Benschop, H. P., Berends, F., and De Jong, L. P. A. (1981a). GLC-analysis and pharmacokinetics of the four stereoisomers of Soman. *Fundam. Appl. Toxicol.*, **1**, 177–82.

Benschop, H. P., Konings, C. A. G., and De Jong, L. P. A. (1981b). Gas chromatographic separation of the four stereoisomers of 1,2,2-trimethylpropyl methylphosphonofluoridate (Soman). Stereospecificity of *in vitro* 'detoxification' reactions. *J. Am. Chem. Soc.*, **103**, 4260–2.

Benschop, H. P., Konings, C. A. G., Van Genderen, J., and De Jong, L. P. A. (1984a). Isolation, *in vitro* activity and acute toxicity in mice of four stereoisomers of Soman. *Fundam. Appl. Toxicol.*, **4**, S84–95.

Benschop, H. P., Konings, C. A. G., Van Genderen, J., and De Jong, L. P. A. (1984b). Isolation, anticholinesterase properties and acute toxicity in mice of the four stereoisomers of the nerve gas Soman. *Toxicol. Appl. Pharmacol.*, **72**, 61–74.

Boter, H. L. and Ooms, A. J. J. (1967). Stereospecificity of hydrolytic enzymes in their reaction with optically active organophosphorus compounds. II. The inhibition of aliesterases, acetylesterases, chymotrypsin and trypsin by *S*-alkyl *p*-nitrophenyl methylphosphonothiolates. *Biochem. Pharmacol.*, **16**, 1563–9.

Boter, H. L. and Van Dijk, C. (1969). Inhibition of acetylcholinesterase and butyrylcholinesterase by enantiomeric forms of sarin. *Biochem. Pharmacol.*, **18**, 2403–7.

Clothier, B. and Johnson, M. K. (1979). Rapid aging of neurotoxic esterase after inhibition by di-isopropyl phosphorofluoridate. *Biochem. J.*, **177**, 549–58.

Clothier, B. and Johnson, M. K. (1980). Reactivation and aging of neurotoxic esterase inhibited by a variety of organophosphorus esters. *Biochem. J.*, **185**, 739–47.

Clement, J. G. (1984). Role of aliesterase in organophosphorus poisoning. *Fundam. Appl. Toxicol.*, **4**, S96–105.

Cohen, W. and Erlanger, B. F. (1960). Studies on the reactivation of diethylphosphoryl-chymotrypsin. *J. Am. Chem. Soc.*, **82**, 3928–34.

Cohen, W., Lache, M., and Erlanger, B. F. (1962). The reactivation of diethylphosphoryl trypsin. *Biochemistry*, **1**, 686–93.

Davis, A. and Bailey, D. R. (1969). Metrifonate in urinary schistosomiasis. *Bull. WHO*, **41**, 209–24.

De Jong, L. P. A. and Van Dijk, C. (1972). Inhibition of acetylcholinesterases by the enantiomers of isopropyl *S*-2-trimethylammoniumethyl methylphosphonothioate iodide. Affinity and phosphorylation constants. *Biochim. Biophys. Acta*, **268**, 680–9.

De Jong, L. P. A. and Van Dijk, C. (1984). Formation of soman (1,2,2-trimethylpropyl methylphosphonyl fluoridate) via fluoride induced reactivation of soman-inhibited aliesterase in rat plasma. *Biochem. Pharmacol.*, **33**, 663–9.

Dettbarn, W. D. (1984). Pesticide induced muscle necrosis: mechanisms and prevention. *Fundam. Appl. Toxicol.*, **4**, S18–26.

Dinsdale, D., Verschoyle, R. D., and Cabral, J. R. P. (1982). Cellular responses to trialkyl phosphorothioate induced injury to the lung. *Arch. Toxicol.*, **51**, 79–89.

Dinsdale, D., Verschoyle, R. D., and Ingham, J. E. (1984). Ultrastructural change in rat Clara cells induced by a single dose of *O,S,S*-trimethyl phosphorodithioate. *Arch. Toxicol.*, **56**, 59–65.

Eiberg, H., Mohr, J., Schmiegelow, K., Nielsen, L. S., and Williamson, R. (1985). Linkage relationships of paraoxonase (PON) with other markers: indication of PON-cystic fibrosis synteny. *Clin. Genet.*, **28**, 265–71.

Erdmann, W. D. (1976). Success and failure of oxime therapy in acute poisoning by organophosphorus compounds. In *Medical protection against chemical warfare agents*, pp. 46–52. Stockholm International Peace Research Institute, Almqvist & Wiksell International, Stockholm.

Eto, M., Casida, J. E., and Eto, T. (1962). Hydroxylation and cyclisation reaction involved in the metabolism of trio-*o*-cresylphosphate. *Biochem. Pharmacol.*, **11**, 337–52.

Eto, M., Abe, M., and Takahara, H. (1971). Metabolism of tri-*p*-ethylphenylphosphate and neurotoxicity of the metabolites. *Agric. Biol. Chem.*, **35**, 929–40.

Fonnum, F. and Sterri, S. H. (1981). Factors modifying the toxicity of organophosphorus compounds including Soman and Sarin. *Fundam. Appl. Toxicol.*, **1**, S143–7.

Fonnum, F., Sterri, S. H., Aas, P., and Johnsen, H. (1985). Carboxylesterases. Importance for detoxification of organophosphorus anticholinesterases and trichothecenes. *Fundam. Appl. Toxicol.*, **5**, S29–38.

Forsberg, A. and Gertrud, P. U. U. (1984). Kinetics for the inhibition of acetylcholinesterase for the electric eel by some organophosphates and carbamates. *Eur. J. Biochem.*, **140**, 153–6.

French, M. C., Wetherall, J. R., and White, P. D. T. (1983). The reversal by oximes and their de-oximomethyl analogues of neuromuscular block produced by soman. *Eur. J. Pharmacol.*, **91**, 399–409.

Gelb, M. H., Svaren, J. P., and Abeles, R. H. (1985). Fluoro ketone inhibitors of hydrolytic enzymes. *Biochemistry*, **24**, 1813–17.

Green, A. L. (1983). A theoretical kinetic analysis of the protective action exerted by eserine and other carbamate anticholinesterases against poisoning by organophosphorus compounds. *Biochem. Pharmacol.*, **11**, 1717–21.

Hassan, A. and Dauterman, W. C. (1968). Studies on the optically active isomers of *O,O*-diethyl malathion and *O,O*-diethyl malaoxon. *Biochem. Pharmacol.*, **17**, 1431–9.

Heath, D. F. (1961). *Organophosphorus poisons; anticholinesterases and related compounds*, pp. 1–403. Pergamon Press, Oxford.

Hedstrom L., Moorman, A. R., Dobbs, J., Abeles, R. H. (1984). Inactivation of chymotrypsin by benzoxazinones. *Biochemistry*, **23**, 1753–9.

Heilbronn, E. (1965). Action of fluoride on cholinesterase. II. *In vitro* reactivation of cholinesterases inhibited by organophosphorus compounds. *Biochem. Pharmacol.*, **14**, 1363–73.

Heilbronn, E., ed. (1967). *Structures and reactions of DFP sensitive enzymes*, pp. 1–200. Research Institute of National Defence, Stockholm.

Hobbiger, F. (1963). Reactivation of phosphorylated acetylcholinesterase. In *Cholinesterases and anticholinesterase agents* (ed. G. B. Koelle), pp. 921–88; Springer, Berlin.

Hobbiger, F. (1968). Anticholinesterases. In *Recent advances in pharmacology* (ed. J. M. Robson and R. S. Stacey), pp. 291–310. Churchill, London.

Hobbiger, F., Pitman, M., and Sadler, P. W. (1960). Reactivation of phosphorylated acetocholinesterases by pyridinium aldoximes and related compounds. *Biochem. J.*, **75**, 363–72.

IARC (1979). Monographs on the evaluation of the carcinogenic risk of chemicals to humans. *Dichlorvos*, **20**, 97–127.

International Symposium (1981). Metrifonate and dichlorvos. Theoretical and practical aspects. *Acta Pharmacol. Toxicol.*, **49**, Suppl. 5, pp. 1–136.

ICPEMC (International Commission for Protection Against Environmental Mutagens and Carcinogens) (1980). Publication No. 5. An evaluation of the genetic toxicity of Dichlorvos. *Mutation Res.*, **76**, 297–309.

International Conference (1971). Alternative insecticides for vector control. *Bull. WHO*, **44**, 1–470.

Johnson, M. K. (1975a). The delayed neuropathy caused by some organophosphorus esters: mechanism and challenge. *Crit. Rev. Toxicol.*, **3**, 289–316.

Johnson, M. K. (1975b). Organophosphorus esters causing delayed neurotoxic effects. Mechanism of action and structure–activity studies. *Arch. Toxicol.*, **34**, 259–88.

Johnson, M. K. (1982). The target for the initiation of delayed neurotoxicity by organophosphorus esters: biochemical studies and toxicological applications. *Rev. Biochem. Toxicol.*, **4**, 141–212.

Johnson, M. K., Willems, J. L., De Bisschop, H. C., Read, D. J., and Benschop, H. P. (1985a). Can Soman cause delayed neuropathy? *Fundam. Appl. Toxicol.*, **5**, S180–1.

Johnson, M. K., Read, D. J., and Benschop, H. P. (1985b). Interaction of the four stereoisomers of soman (pinacolyl methylphosphonofluoridate) with acetylcholinesterase and neuropathy target esterase of hen brain. *Biochem. Pharmacol.*, **34**, 1945–51.

Johnson, M. K., Read, D. J., and Yoshikawa, H. (1986). The effect of steric factors on the interaction of some phenylphosphonates with acetylcholinesterase and neuropathy target esterase of hen brain. *Pestic. Biochem. Physiol.*, **25**, 133–42.

Keijer, J. H. and Wolring, G. Z. (1969). Stereospecific aging of phosphorylated cholinesterases. *Biochim. Biophys. Acta*, **185**, 465–8.

Koelle, G. B. (ed.) (1963). *Cholinesterases and anticholinesterase agents*. Springer, Berlin.

Krupka, R. M. (1974). On the anticholinesterase activity of Benomyl. *Pestic. Sci.*, **5**, 211–16.

Lotti, M. (1983). Lymphocyte neurotoxic esterase. A biochemical monitor of organophosphorus induced delayed neuropathy in man. *Adv. Biosci.*, **45**, 101–8.

Lotti, M. and Johnson, M. K. (1978). Neurotoxicity of organophosphorus pesticides: predictions can be based on *in vitro* studies with hen and human tissue. *Arch. Toxicol.*, **41**, 215–21.

Lotti, M. and Johnson, M. K. (1980). Neurotoxic esterase in human nervous tissue. *J. Neurochem.*, **34**, 747–9.

Neal, R. A. (1985). Thiono-sulphur compounds. In *Bioactivation of foreign compounds* (ed. M. W. Anders), pp. 519–40. Academic Press, Orlando.

Nemery, B. (1986). The effect of O,O,S-trimethyl phosphorothioate on the lung. Thesis. Council for National Academic Awards.

Nordgren, I., Lundgren, G., Puu, G., and Holmstedt, B. (1984). Stereoselectivity of enzymes involved in the toxicity and detoxification of soman. *Arch. Toxicol.*, **55**, 70–5.

Nordgren, I., Lundgren, G., Puu, G., Karten, B., and Holmstedt, B. (1985). Distribution and elimination of the stereoisomers of Soman and their effect on brain acetylcholine. *Fundam. Appl. Toxicol.*, **5**, S252–9.

O'Brien (1960). *Toxic phosphorus esters. Chemistry, metabolism and biological effects*, pp. 1–434. Academic Press, New York.

Ooms, A. J. J., and Boter, H. L. (1965). Stereospecificity of hydrolytic enzymes in their reaction with optically active organophosphorus compounds. I. The reaction of cholinesterase and paraoxonase with S-alkyl p-nitrophenyl methylphosphonothiolates. *Biochem. Pharmacol.*, **14**, 1839–46.

Ooms, A. J. J. and Van Dijk, C. (1966). Reaction of organophosphorus compounds with hydrolytic enzymes. III. Inhibition of chymotrypsin and trypsin. *Biochem. Pharmacol.*, **15**, 1361–77.

Plestina, R., Davis, A., and Bailey, D. R. (1972). Effect of metrifonate on blood cholinesterases in children during treatment of schistosomiasis. *Bull. WHO*, **46**, 747–59.

Radic, Z., Reiner, E., and Simeon, V. (1984). Binding sites on acetylcholinesterase for reversible ligands and phosphorylating agents. A theoretical model tested on haloxon and physostigmine. *Biochem. Pharmacol.*, **33**, 671–7.

Reiner, E. (ed.) (1975). Cholinesterases and cholinesterase receptors. *Croat. Chem. Acta*, **47**, 163–505.

Reiner, E. (1986). Inhibition of acetylcholinesterase by 4,4′-bipyridine and its effect upon phosphonylation of the enzyme. *Croat. Chem. Acta*, in press.

Schoene, K. (1976). Kinetic studies on chemical reactions between acetylcholinesterase, toxic organophosphates and pyridinium oximes. In *Medical protection against chemical warfare agents*, pp. 89–100. Stockholm International Peace Research Institute, Almqvist & Wiksell International, Stockholm.

Schoene, K., Steinhauses, J. and Oldiges, H. (1983). Reactivation of soman inhibited acetylcholinesterase *in vitro* and protection against soman *in vivo* by bis pyridinium 2-aldoximes. *Biochem. Pharmacol.*, **32**, 1649–51.

Simeon, V., Wilhelm, K., Granor, A., Besarovic-Lazarev, S., Buntic, A., Fajdetic, A., and Binefeld, Z. (1979). 1,3-bispyridinium-dimethylether mono and dioximes: synthesis, reactivating potency and therapeutic effect in experimental poisoning by organophosphorus compounds. *Arch. Toxicol.*, **41**, 301–6.

Toia, R. F. and Casida, J. E. (1979). Phosphorylation, aging and possible alkylation reactions of saligenin cyclic phosphorus esters with α-chymotrypsin. *Biochem. Pharmacol.*, **28**, 211–16.

Van der Drift, A. C. M. (1983). Physico-chemical characterisation of atropine esterase from *Pseudomonas putida*. Thesis, University of Utrecht, pp. 1–205.

Verschoyle, R. D. and Cabral, J. R. P. (1982). Investigation of the acute toxicity of some trimethyl and triethyl phosphorothioates with particular reference to those causing lung damage. *Arch. Toxicol.*, **51**, 221–31.

WHO (1985). The control of schistosomiasis. Technical Report Series No. 728, 1–113.

Williams, D. G. and Johnson, M. K. (1981). Gel electrophoretic identification of hen brain neurotoxic esterase, labelled with tritiated di-isopropyl phosphorofluoridate. *Biochem. J.*, **199**, 323–33.

Willems, J. L., Nicaise, M., and De Bisschop, H. C. (1984). Delayed neuropathy by the organophosphorus nerve agents soman and tabun. *Arch. Toxicol.*, **55**, 76–77.

Wing, K. D., Glickman, A. H., and Casida, J. E. (1984). Phosphorothiolate pesticides and related compounds: oxidative bioactivation and aging of the inhibited acetylcholinesterase. *Pestic. Biochem. Physiol.*, **21**, 22–30.

Wustner, D. A. and Fukuto, T. R. (1974). Affinity and phosphorylation constants for the inhibition of cholinesterases by the optical isomers of *o*-2-butyl *S*-2 (dimethylammonium) ethyl ethylphosphonothioate hydrogen oxalate. *Pestic. Biochem. Physiol.*, **4**, 365–76.

10

Inhibitors of enzymes of the arachidonic acid metabolic pathways

Gerry Higgs and John Vane

10.1 Introduction

Arachidonic acid is a twenty-carbon polyunsaturated fatty acid, one of a group of essential fatty acids first identified in the 1930s. At about the same time, Von Euler (1937) gave the name 'prostaglandin' to an activity detected in semen, which contracted uterine smooth muscle. More than 30 years later it was discovered that prostaglandins are derived from arachidonic acid and other polyunsaturated fatty acids (Van Dorp *et al.* 1964; Bergstrom *et al.* 1964). The potent biological properties of prostaglandins and their involvement in a number of physiological and pathological processes has concentrated interest on the enzymes that metabolize arachidonic acid. We now know that there are several enzymes that catalyse the conversion of arachidonic acid to prostaglandins, thromboxanes, hydroxy acids, and leukotrienes. A key step in the realization of the importance of arachidonic acid metabolism was the demonstration that the large group of non-steroid anti-inflammatory drugs, of which aspirin is the prototype, act selectively to inhibit the biosynthesis of prostaglandins (Vane 1971; Smith and Willis 1971; Ferreira *et al.* 1971). In this chapter, we shall discuss the relationship between inhibition of arachidonic acid metabolism and therapeutic effects. We shall also attempt to show how increased knowledge of lipid peroxidation has revealed enzyme targets for the development of new drugs.

10.2   The products of arachidonic acid peroxidation

The development of highly sensitive techniques of analytical biochemistry permitted Bergstrom and his colleagues in 1960 to elucidate the structure of two so-called primary prostaglandins (Bergstrom and Sjovall 1960a, b). These were designated prostaglandin (PG)E and PGF according to their partition between *E*ther and phosphate (Swedish *F*osfat) buffer. Since then, subsequent prostaglandins have been named on an alphabetical basis and to date there are subdivisions from PGA to PGJ. Prostaglandins E and F were shown to be 20-carbon cyclized fatty acids and their structural similarity to the essential polyunsaturated fatty acids led to the proposal that arachidonic acid and other 20-carbon fatty acids are the precursors of prostaglandins (Bergstrom *et al.* 1964; Van Dorp *et al.* 1964). It is now known that arachidonic acid (eicosatetraenoic acid) is the major source of prostaglandins in mammalian tissues.

Prostaglandins derived from arachidonic acid contain two double bonds (Fig. 10.1); hence PGD_2, PGE_2, etc. Prostaglandins derived from eicosatrienoic acid ($C20:3\omega6$) or eicosapentaenoic acid ($C20:5\omega3$) contain one or three double bonds and are denoted PGD_1, PGE_1, or PGD_3, PGE_3, respectively.

The availability of pure prostaglandins for use as standards in biological experiments was a strong impetus for the investigation of the role of prostaglandins in physiological and pathological processes. It became apparent, however, that there were a number of biologically active substances derived from arachidonic acid which could not be matched by the primary prostaglandins. For example, in 1969, Piper and Vane detected a labile substance in the effluent of isolated perfused lungs during anaphylactic challenge. This substance contracted the rabbit aorta and was also released by infusions of arachidonic acid (Vargaftig and Dao Hai 1972; Palmer *et al.* 1973), suggesting that the activity was due to an unstable intermediate in the synthesis of prostaglandins. The predicted intermediates were isolated and their structure elucidated by Samuelsson and his colleagues in 1974 (Hamberg and Samuelsson 1974). They found that arachidonic acid was converted to two cyclic endoperox-

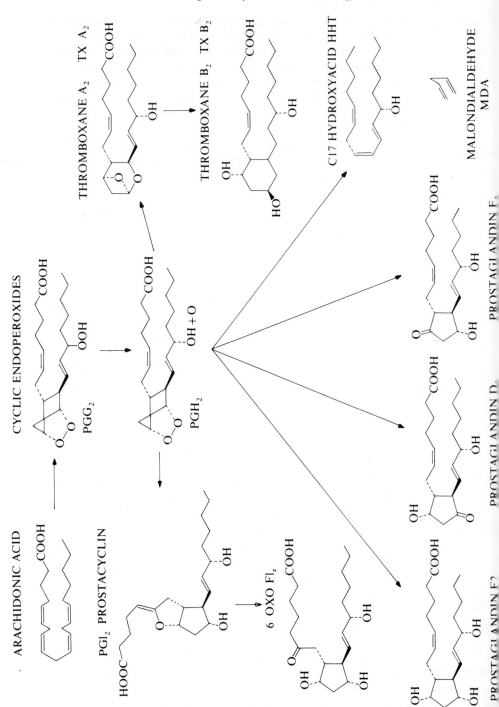

ides (PGG$_2$ and PGH$_2$; Fig. 10.1), which stimulated platelet aggregation. There were doubts, however, as to whether the endoperoxides could explain the rabbit aorta contracting activity originally detected by Piper and Vane. The Swedish group then found that PGG$_2$ and PGH$_2$ could be converted to a non-prostanoic compound with an oxane ring which, because of its potent activity in aggregating platelets (*throm*bocytes), was called thromboxane A$_2$ (TXA$_2$; Fig. 10.1; Hamberg *et al.* 1975). TXA$_2$ accounts for the activity of rabbit aorta contracting substance.

The discovery of thromboxane and its potential importance in platelet function and thrombosis led to the search for thromboxane synthetase in various tissues. Platelets were an abundant source of the enzyme that converted the endoperoxides to TXA$_2$ (Needleman *et al.* 1976) but vascular tissue was unable to generate thromboxane. In fact, the study of arachidonic acid metabolism in blood vessels resulted in a new discovery. Instead of producing a vasoconstrictor and aggregatory substance, aortic tissues generated a powerful vasodilator substance, which was also a potent inhibitor of platelet aggregation (Moncada *et al.* 1976). This substance was later shown to be a bicyclic prostaglandin (prostacyclin; PGI$_2$; Fig. 10.1) which, like TXA$_2$, is unstable and could be generated from PGG$_2$ or PGH$_2$. Thromboxane A$_2$ degrades to TXB$_2$ with a half-life of 30s. Prostacyclin degrades to 6-oxo-PGF$_{1\alpha}$ with a half-life of 2–3 min (Fig. 10.1). TXA$_2$ and 6-oxo-PGE$_{1\alpha}$ are stable and relatively inactive. Thus, the endoperoxides occupy a pivotal position in the production of prostaglandins, thromboxane, and prostacyclin. The metabolism of endoperoxides is determined by the tissues in which they are generated. In normal tissues the primary prostaglandins (PGE, F, and D; Fig. 10.1) are sometimes relatively minor products of fatty acid oxygenation, although in injury and inflammation PGE$_2$ is a major metabolite (Higgs *et al.* 1984a).

The production of prostaglandins depends on the release of arachidonic acid from membrane phospholipids by the acyl hydrolase phospholipase A$_2$. Molecular oxygen is then incorporated into the unsaturated fatty acid in a dioxygenase reaction. Peroxidation occurs at C11 and C15 followed by ring closure between C8 and C12. This process is catalysed by cyclooxygenase. Peroxidation of the fatty acid may, however, occur at other carbon atoms in the molecule. These reactions, which are catalysed by lipoxygenases, are not followed by ring formation and give rise to straight-chain hydroperoxyeicosatetraenoic acids (HPETEs), which can then be converted to hydroxyeicosatetraenoic acids (HETEs; Fig. 10.2).

In the absence of cyclooxygenase, peroxidation at C11 or C15 leads to the production of 11-HETE or 15-HETE, but in 1974 a separate lipoxygenase pathway which produces 12-HETE, was discovered in platelets, (Hamberg and Samuelsson 1974). Later, polymorphonuclear leucocytes (PMNs) were found to contain a 5-lipoxygenase (Borgeat *et al.* 1976). As well as producing 5-HETE, the leucocyte 5-lipoxygenase initiates the formation of a family of compounds that have in common a conjugated triene structure and because of their source are called the leukotrienes (Murphy *et al.* 1979). 5-HPETE is converted to the 5,6 epoxide of arachidonic acid [leukotriene A_4 (LTA_4); Fig. 10.2], which can be converted to the 5,12-dihydroxy acid LTB_4. Alternatively, the addition of glutathione to the epoxide by glutathione-S-transferase results in the formation of LTC_4. The removal of glutamate from LTC_4 by γ-glutamyl transpeptidase gives LTD_4, which is further metabolized to LTE_4 with the loss of glycine. The addition of glutamate to LTE_4, giving cysteine–glutamate at C6, results in LTF_4 (for review see Samuelsson 1983).

The leukotrienes do not contain a cyclopentane ring or an oxane ring and so they retain the same number of double bonds as their precursor fatty acids. This explains the numerical suffix given to the leukotrienes: LTA_3 is derived from eicosatrienoic acid, LTA_4 from arachidonic acid (eicosatetraenoic acid) and LTA_5 from eicosapentaenoic acid. The cyclooxygenase and lipoxygenase pathways represent the major routes for the oxidative metabolism of arachidonic acid, although cytochrome P450 also produces biologically active products from arachidonic acid (Schwartzmann *et al.* 1985). The various groups of prostaglandins, thromboxanes, leukotrienes, and hydroxy acids that retain the 20-carbon backbone are collectively known as the *eicosanoids*.

10.3   The enzymes of arachidonic acid metabolism

10.3.1   Cyclooxygenase

The enzyme that initiates prostaglandin synthesis has been variously called 'prostaglandin synthetase', 'cyclooxygenase' and 'prostaglandin endoperoxide synthetase', and is designated EC 1.14.99.1. The term prostaglandin was originally coined because Von Euler (1937) believed that the biological activity he detected in semen was derived from the prostate. We now know that a wide range of mammalian tissues can generate prostaglandin endoperoxides, and of the isolated cell preparations that have been studied only the enucleate red blood cells are deficient in the enzyme.

The association of prostaglandins with male reproductive organs led to the use of ovine and bovine seminal vessels as a source of prostaglandin synthetase. These tissues were rich in the enzyme and partial purification revealed that activity was located on cellular membranes in the microsomal fraction (Van der Ouderaa *et al.* 1977; Hemler *et al.* 1976; Miyamoto *et al.* 1976). The purified cyclooxygenase contained no phospholipid and was identified as a glycoprotein containing mannose and N-acetylglucosamine. There is evidence that the native enzyme exists as a dimer of about 130 kDa, whereas the purified enzyme migrates on polyacrylamide gel electrophoresis as a single protein of 69 000 daltons. Lands and his colleagues demonstrated both haem and non-haem iron in the holoenzyme (Helmer *et al.* 1976) but others were unable to detect any metal ions in association with the apoenzyme (Van der Ouderaa *et al.* 1977). It is

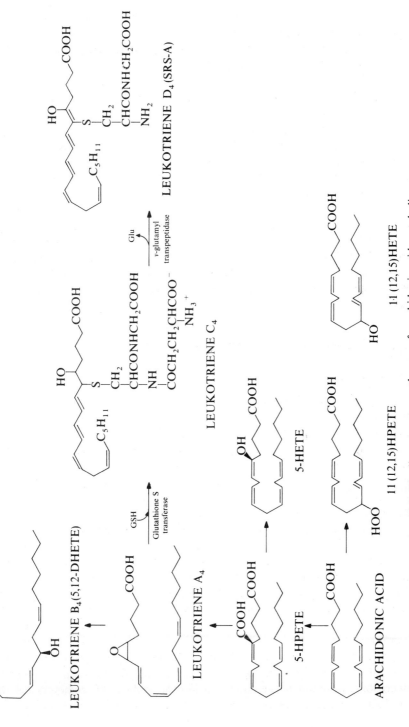

Fig. 10.2. The lipoxygenase pathways of arachidonic acid metabolism.

generally accepted, however, that haem iron is necessary for activity and haematin has been found bound to the enzyme (Van der Ouderaa *et al.* 1979).

Platelets have also been used to purify and characterize cyclo-oxygenase. Roth and Majerus (1975) reported that the inhibition of platelet aggregation by aspirin correlated with the acetylation of a protein corresponding to cyclooxygenase. The use of aspirin labelled with ^{3}H in the acetyl group provided a marker for purification procedures, which showed that aspirin covalently acetylates a serine residue at the active site of the enzyme. These experiments have important implications for understanding the mechanism of action of cyclooxygenase inhibitors.

There is a high degree of substrate specificity for cyclooxygenase, which has a markedly greater affinity for C20 unsaturated fatty acids than for C19 or C21 acids (Van Dorp 1967). Similarly there is a greater affinity for C20:4ω6 than C20:3ω6 or C20:5ω3.

Purified cyclooxygenase catalyses two enzymatic processes, the incorporation of oxygen in a dioxygenase step to form PGG_2 and the subsequent peroxidation to PGH_2 (Fig. 10.1). The reaction is initiated by the stereospecific abstraction of hydrogen at C13 followed by oxygen attack at C11 and C15 and ring closure between C8 and C12 in a concerted reaction (Hamberg and Samuelsson 1967). Use of $^{18}O_2$ indicated that the oxygen atoms in the C9 and C11 substituents on the cyclopentane ring of the primary prostaglandins were derived from the same molecule of oxygen. The oxygen at C-15 is also derived from molecular oxygen. Because primary prostaglandins cannot be produced from 15-HPETE, it was proposed that peroxidation at C-11 was the first step in prostaglandin synthesis, leading to an 11-peroxy intermediate in the formation of the cyclic endoperoxides. These biochemical mechanisms have been extensively reviewed by Samuelsson *et al.* (1978).

10.3.2   Prostaglandin isomerases

The primary prostaglandins can be formed by non-enzymic degradation of the endoperoxides, but the formation of PGE_2 and PGD_2 can also be catalysed by isomerases (Ogino *et al.* 1977; Christ-Hazelhof and Nugteren, 1979). There is little evidence for a PGF isomerase and it is most likely that $PGF_{2\alpha}$ is formed by reductive cleavage of the endoperoxide in the presence of reducing agents. The nature of the isomerases has not been well characterized, although in one report PGD_2 synthetase was purified and found to be identical to serum albumin (Ogino *et al.* 1977). The use of cofactors such as glutathione in studies of prostaglandin synthesis *in vitro* has resulted in the formation of primary prostaglandins that are not necessarily the natural products of the endoperoxide. For example, in the original investigation of prostaglandin synthesis in microsomal fractions of seminal vesicles, the addition of cofactors led to the production predominantly of PGE and PGF, whereas we now know that in the absence of cofactors the major arachidonate metabolite in this tissue is prosta-cyclin (Cottee *et al.* 1977).

10.3.3 Prostacyclin synthetase

Prostacyclin is the major arachidonic acid metabolite produced by vascular tissue and there is a gradient of prostacyclin production across the blood vessel wall. The endothelium has the highest and the adventitia the lowest capacity for prostacyclin production (Moncada *et al.* 1977b). This appears to be due more to a active cyclo-oxygenase in the endothelium than to a lack of prostacyclin synthetase in the outer layers of the blood vessel wall (Smith *et al.* 1983). Prostacyclin synthetase is also present in non-vascular smooth muscle from the lung, uterus, bladder and intestine but could not be demonstrated in cardiac or skeletal muscle (Smith *et al.* 1983).

The stable product of prostacyclin, 6-oxo-$PGF_{1\alpha}$ had been detected in intestinal tissue before the discovery of prostacyclin itself (Pace-Asciak 1976). This led to the suggestion that a 6,9-oxocyclase pathway of endoperoxide metabolism existed. Prostacyclin synthetase has been purified using monoclonal antibodies and is a haem-containing protein of about 52 000 daltons (Smith *et al.* 1983). Prostacyclin production proceeds by polarization of the 9–11 endoperoxide and the formation of a 6,9 epoxy derivative giving rise to a bicyclic structure (Fig. 10.1). This is accompanied by loss of hydrogen from C6.

10.3.4 Thromboxane synthetase

Thromboxane production was first detected in aggregating platelets (Hamberg *et al.* 1975) and the microsomal fraction of platelet homogenates was later shown to contain an enzyme that converts prostaglandin endoperoxides to thromboxane (Needleman *et al.* 1976). Similarly, various preparations of leucocytes make predominantly thromboxane (Morley *et al.* 1979). The suggestion that TXA_2 production in leucocyte preparations comes from contaminating platelets is not well based (see below). Thromboxane production has been reported in many tissues (Johnson *et al.* 1983), but the presence of thromboxane synthetase in circulating platelets and leucocytes indicates that some of this activity may be due to contaminating blood.

The wide distribution of cyclooxygenase complicates the identification of the source of product. In one series of experiments, however, the participation of different cells in thromboxane production was clearly elucidated. Thromboxane concentrations were measured in the serum from clotted blood and in inflammatory exudates taken from the same animals (Higgs *et al.* 1983). Following the depletion of circulating platelets, TXB_2 was undetectable in the serum but unchanged in the exudates. Conversely, when the animals were made neutropenic, serum thromboxane levels were not reduced whereas TXB_2 in the exudates was reduced to less than 10 per cent of control values. These observations indicate that platelets are the source of TXA_2 in clotting blood but do not contribute to TXA_2 production in inflammation, while neutrophils (PMNs) appear to be the major source of TXA_2 in acute inflammation.

Thromboxane synthetase from platelet microsomes has been solubilized and partially purified (Ho *et al.* 1976; Hammarstrom and Falardeau 1977; Yoshimoto *et al.* 1977). The purification of the enzyme paralleled the purification of cytochrome P450 and this, coupled with evidence that thromboxane synthetase inhibitors interact with cytochrome P450, has led to the proposal that cytochrome P450 plays a part in the conversion of prostaglandin endoperoxides to TXA_2 (Ullrich and Haurand 1983).

The enzyme-catalysed conversion of PGH_2 to TXA_2 is initiated by heterolytic cleavage and polarization of the endoperoxide. The cation formed after protonation at C9 can then rearrange to form either TXA_2 or HHT (plus malondialdehyde, MDA; Fig. 10.1). Partially purified thromboxane synthetase from platelets produces similar amounts of TXB_2 and HHT (Hammarstrom and Falardeau 1977; Yoshimoto *et al.* 1977), suggesting that HHT is a product of enzyme activity. In other situations, however, HHT is produced in the absence of enzyme and the significance of its production in conjunction with TXB_2 is not fully understood (Hamberg and Samuelsson 1967).

10.3.5   Arachidonate lipoxygenases

Lipoxygenases are common in plants but similar enzymes had not been detected in mammalian tissues until the discovery of 12-lipoxygenase in platelets and 5-lipoxygenase in leucocytes. Lipoxygenase activity has been found in the cytoplasmic and particulate fractions of platelets from a number of species, including humans. Most is known about the soluble enzyme, which resolves on gel filtration into two components of 100 000 and 160 000 Da (Siegel *et al.* 1980a). The smaller molecule produces mainly 12-HPETE whilst the larger molecule produces both 12-HPETE and 12-HETE. This has prompted the suggestion that the larger component may represent a complex between a 12-lipoxygenase and a peroxidase. Platelet lipoxygenase has a higher affinity for arachidonic acid and other 20-carbon unsaturated fatty acids than for linoleic acid, the preferred substrate of plant enzymes. Lipoxygenases catalyse the abstraction of a hydrogen radical from the methylene group of a pentadiene in the fatty acid chain and this step resembles the initiation of the cyclooxygenase pathway. The activated pentadiene is then vulnerable to oxygen attack across either of the double bonds. In common with plant enzymes, mammalian lipoxygenases require iron (Aharony *et al.* 1981). Although the nature of the peroxidase is not well characterized, there is evidence that reduced glutathione is an important cofactor (Chang *et al.* 1982).

In leucocytes, the major lipoxygenase pathway results in the formation of 5-HPETE. This can be converted by a peroxidase to 5-HETE but a mixture of more polar products, including the 5,12-dihydroxy acid LTB_4, is also formed.

This raised the possibility of a double lipoxygenation mechanism, but further investigation revealed a novel enzymatic pathway. The incorporation of isotopically labelled molecular oxygen at C5 is consistent with a 5-lipoxygenase reaction, but the discovery that oxygen at C12 was derived from water ruled out a second lipoxygenase step. This indicated that LTB_4 is formed by hydrolysis of an intermediate. The intermediate has now been identified as a 5,6 epoxide of arachidonic acid (LTA_4), which can be formed by dehydration of 5-HPETE (Borgeat and Samuelsson 1979).

The substrate specificity of 5-lipoxygenase is different from that of the platelet enzyme, requiring double bonds at the 5,8, and 11 positions and not being so dependent upon chain length (Jakschik et al. 1980). In addition, the 5-lipoxygenase differs from the 12-lipoxygenase in its calcium dependence. There is some evidence that calcium interacts with inactive monomers of the 5-lipoxygenase ($M_r = 90\,000$) to give an activated dimer ($M_r = 180\,000$; Parker and Aykent 1982). The conversion of LTA_4 to LTB_4 is enzymatic, and an epoxide hydrolase has been identified in the cytoplasm (Maycock et al. 1982). This is in contrast to the enzymes that convert LTA_4 to the peptido-leucotrienes, glutathione-S-transferase and α-glutamyl transpeptidase, which are particulate (Jakschik and Kuo, 1983).

10.4 The role of eicosanoids in disease

Many eicosanoids were initially detected by virtue of their potent biological activities and often this has been the result of studying pathological processes. For example, slow-reacting substance of anaphylaxis (SRS-A; Feldberg and Kellaway 1938) and rabbit aorta contracting substance (RCS; Piper and Vane 1969) were detected in models of anaphylaxis. These substances were later identified as the peptido-leukotrienes (Murphy et al. 1979) and thromboxane A_2 (Hamberg et al. 1975), respectively. In fact, it has been through the investigation of disease processes such as asthma, inflammation, and thrombosis that our knowledge of arachidonic acid peroxidation and the subsequent production of eicosanoids has progressed.

Eicosanoids are produced in pathological processes and they have biological activities that contribute to the pathology. The most convincing evidence that eicosanoids are mediators of disease, however, comes not only from their ability to mimic the effects of the disease but also from the demonstration that compounds that selectively interfere with eicosanoid synthesis have therapeutic effects. For many years the mechanism of action of aspirin and other non-steroid anti-inflammatory drugs was ill-defined. The discovery that this large group of drugs acts by inhibiting cyclo-oxygenase has provided a unifying explanation of their therapeutic actions and has firmly established certain prostaglandins as important mediators of inflammatory disease (for review, see Higgs et al. 1984a).

The discovery of alternative enzyme pathways that produce thromboxanes and leukotrienes, with thrombotic, inflammatory, and bronchoconstrictor properties not shared by the prostaglandins, has led to a vigorous search for new enzyme inhibitors as potential therapeutic agents.

10.4.1 Inflammatory properties of cyclooxygenase products

Phospholipase is activated when tissues are subjected to mechanical, chemical or immunological stimulation. This liberates arachidonic acid as a substrate for cyclooxygenase and as inflammation is the response of living tissue to injury, prostaglandin production always accompanies the inflammatory response. Prostaglandin E_2 is the predominant eicosanoid detected in inflammatory conditions ranging from experimental acute oedema and sunburn through to chronic arthritis in humans. Because inflammation is one of the few conditions in which PGE_2 is a major product of cyclooxygenase, it is possible that the process of inflammation directs the enzymatic pathway towards this product.

Prostaglandin E_2 is a potent dilator of vascular smooth muscle accounting for the characteristic vasodilation and erythema (redness) seen in acute inflammation (Solomon *et al.* 1968). The effect of vasodilation is to increase the flow of blood through inflamed tissues and this augments the extravasation of fluid (oedema) caused by agents that increase vascular premeability such as bradykinin and histamine (Williams and Peck 1977). Prostaglandin E_2 also acts synergistically with other mediators to produce inflammatory pain. Without having any direct pain-producing activity, PGE_2 sensitizes receptors on afferent nerve endings to the actions of bradykinin and histamine (Ferreira 1972). Thirdly, PGE_2 is a potent pyretic agent and its production in bacterial and viral infections contributes to the fever associated with these diseases (Saxena *et al.* 1979).

Many other cyclooxygenase products have been detected in inflammatory lesions. These include $PGF_{2\alpha}$, PGD_2, prostacyclin, and TXB_2, but usually they are present at less than a quarter of the concentrations of PGE_2. Of these products, prostacyclin is probably the most important in terms of inflammatory signs. Prostacyclin has a similar vasodilator potency to PGE_2 and is a more potent hyperalgesic agent than PGE_2 (Higgs *et al.* 1978). It is likely, therefore, that both PGE_2 and prostacyclin contribute to the development of inflammatory erythema and pain. Inhibition of the formation of these products of cyclo-oxygenase by aspirin-like drugs accounts for their anti-inflammatory, analgesic, and anti-pyretic actions (Vane 1971).

10.4.2 Inflammatory properties of lipoxygenase products

There is little evidence that lipoxygenase products are important mediators of vascular changes in inflammation, although hydroperoxides of arachidonic acid cause erythema (Ferreira 1972) and LTB_4, LTC_4, and LTD_4 cause transient weal and flare reactions in human skin (Lewis *et al.* 1982). It is not clear, however, if these are direct effects or whether they are mediated through the production of other agents.

Leukotriene B_4 and 12-HETE are the only lipoxygenase products to have been consistently detected in inflammation (Hammarstrom et al. 1975; Rae et al. 1982; Simmons et al. 1983), although other leukotrienes and hydroxy acids may be found when more sensitive assays have been developed. It is likely that the major contribution of LTB_4 and 12-HETE to inflammation is through an effect on leucocytes. Turner et al. (1975) found that platelet lipoxygenase products were chemotactic for PMNs. The leucocyte product 5-HETE is more potent than the platelet product 12-HETE, and the 5,12-dihydroxy acid LTB_4 is even more potent (Ford-Hutchinson et al. 1980; Palmer et al. 1980). It seems, therefore, that 5-lipoxygenase activity in migrating leucocytes represents a local control mechanism to amplify the recruitment of inflammatory cells to damaged tissues. This hypothesis is supported by the observation that a compound that inhibits the synthesis of LTB_4 in inflammation also reduces the accumulation of PMNs (Higgs et al. 1979).

Cyclooxygenase products are not chemotactic and do not play a major role in leucocyte activation. For this reason, aspirin-like drugs have little effect on leucocyte function and it has been proposed that this is why they do not arrest the progress of chronic inflammatory disorders. Inhibition of both cyclo-oxygenase and lipoxygenase became, therefore, an attractive target for novel anti-inflammatory drugs with potential advantages over conventional non-steroid anti-inflammatory agents (Higgs et al. 1979).

10.4.3   The role of cyclooxygenase products in cardio-thrombotic diseases

The study of arachidonic acid metabolism in platelets led to the isolation and identification of prostaglandin endoperoxides and thromboxanes. These unstable substances account for the vasoconstrictor activity (RCS) originally detected by Piper and Vane (1969), but they also aggregate platelets. Thromboxane A_2 is considerably more potent than the endoperoxides and was, therefore, proposed as a mediator of thrombotic diseases.

These observations provided a molecular basis for the clinical investigations of aspirin in syndromes associated with platelet activation, based on the assumption that inhibition of platelet activity would reduce thromboembolism through the inhibition of TXA_2 production. In well-controlled clinical trials, aspirin has been shown to be of benefit in the prevention of transient ischaemic attack and stroke (Fields et al. 1977; Aspirin Myocardial Infarction Study Research Group 1980), the prevention of death and non-fatal myocardial infarction in unstable angina (Lewis et al. 1983; Cairns et al. 1984), and the prevention of coronary graft occlusion (Chesebro et al. 1982, 1984). The analysis of combined data from six trials indicated a 21 per cent reduction in reinfarction rate and a 16 per cent reduction in cardiovascular mortality rate in patients treated with aspirin (Mustard et al. 1983). Aspirin and other cyclo-oxygenase inhibitors can only be expected to be effective when TXA_2 plays a major role in thrombus development, but many platelet aggregation agonists act by thromboxane-independent mechanisms. Aspirin has little effect on thrombosis when ADP release, thrombin generation, or fibrin formation are major factors. It is likely, therefore, that the effects of aspirin treatment will be optimized when diseases in which TXA_2-induced platelet activation is the dominant feature can be accurately diagnosed.

The search for thromboxane synthetase in vascular tissues led to the discovery of prostacyclin, which has opposing actions to TXA_2. The potent anti-aggregating and vasodilator properties of prostacyclin are important defensive mechanisms in the control of intravascular thrombosis and blood pressure. Furthermore, the balance between prostacyclin and TXA_2 production may be a key factor in the maintenance of homeostasis (for review see Moncada and Vane 1978).

Some doubts remain about the efficacy of aspirin in cardiovascular diseases because, as a cyclooxygenase inhibitor, it prevents the formation of prostacyclin as well as thromboxane. As a consequence, selective inhibition of thromboxane synthetase has been identified as a potential therapeutic target and a number of compounds with this property have been developed (Johnson et al. 1983). These compounds do not inhibit the synthesis of endoperoxides and this has the advantage over cyclooxygenase inhibitors of not inhibiting prostacyclin production; indeed prostacyclin production is increased through increased availability of endoperoxide precursor. Selective inhibition of TXA_2 and enhanced prostacyclin production have been reported after administration of thromboxane synthetase inhibitors to humans (Fitzgerald et al. 1985). The efficacy of these compounds in human disease has, however, been disappointing. No improvement was seen in patients with Raynaud's phenomenon or severe peripheral vascular disease (Ettinger et al. 1984; Luderer et al. 1984). In addition, there was no change in the time to exercise-induced angina despite an 80 per cent inhibition of thromboxane production (Reuben et al. 1983). Long-term dosing studies with thromboxane synthetase inhibitors have not, however, been reported in patients with primary cardiac disease. The failure of these drugs may be because the endoperoxides alone are sufficient to induce platelet activation, or alternatively, because thromboxane is only of minor importance in the diseases so far investigated. Thromboxane antagonists are also of interest and it could be that a combination of a thromboxane synthetase inhibitor and a thromboxane antagonist would have the best therapeutic potential.

10.4.4   Leukotrienes in diseases of the airways

The release of slow-reacting substances in immediate hypersensitivity reactions has been studied for many years and the bronchoconstrictor properties of SRS-A are well-documented (Austen 1978). The peptide-substituted leukotrienes, which account for the SRS activity, are two to three orders of magnitude more potent than histamine as bronchoconstrictors and contractors of isolated airway smooth muscle, although LTC_4 and LTD_4 are more potent than LTE_4. There is considerable species variation in response to the leukotrienes, with human and guinea-pig respiratory smooth muscle being more sensitive than rat, cat, or dog airways. LTE_4 is generally less potent but has a longer duration of action than LTC_4 or LTD_4 (Piper 1984). As well as bronchoconstrictor action, there is some evidence that leukotrienes also stimulate the secretion of mucus and thereby might impair airway clearance (Ahmed et al. 1981).

Leukotrienes contract isolated preparations of tracheal, bronchial, and paren-chymal smooth muscle, but experiments in vivo indicate that they have a selective action on the small airways. LTC_4 and LTD_4 induce a preferential reduction in compliance and are relatively less effective in reducing specific airway conduc-tance (Drazen et al. 1980). When administered to normal volunteers, LTC_4 and LTD_4 caused coughing, bronchoconstriction, wheezing, tightness of the chest, and a reduction in expiratory maximum air flow rate (Holroyde et al. 1981; Weiss et al. 1982).

It is clear, therefore, that leukotrienes can cause some of the symptoms of respiratory distress associated with bronchial asthma, and this coupled with the observation that sputum collected from asthmatics contains leukotrienes (Kay 1983; Zakrzewski et al. 1985) strengthens the argument that leukotrienes are important mediators of respiratory pathology. Furthermore, leukotrienes C, D, and E have been detected in nasal washes of allergic patients following antigen challenge (Creticos et al. 1984). There is preliminary evidence that the leukotriene antagonist FPL 55712 substantially inhibits LTC_4-induced bronchoconstriction and cough (Holroyde et al. 1981), although when administered to chronic asthmatics, FPL 55712 was only weakly active (Lee et al. 1981). Some of the most convincing evidence that leukotrienes contribute importantly to allergic bron-choconstriction was provided by Patterson and his colleagues (1981). They showed that a lipoxygenase inhibitor reversed or significantly attenuated the pulmonary changes induced by antigen challenge in the monkey (Fig. 10.3).

The release of leukotrienes, prostaglandins, and other anaphylactic mediators from the lung could result in effects on the heart and cardiovascular system. LTC_4 and LTD_4 exert vasoconstrictor effects in the coronary circulation and it has been proposed that they may contribute to myocardial ischaemia and angina (Piper 1984).

10.5   Enzyme inhibitors

10.5.1   Inhibition of cyclooxygenase

The inhibition of prostaglandin synthesis by aspirin-like anti-inflammatory drugs has been demonstrated in a wide variety of cell types and tissues ranging from whole animals and humans to microsomal enzyme preparations. Cyclooxy-

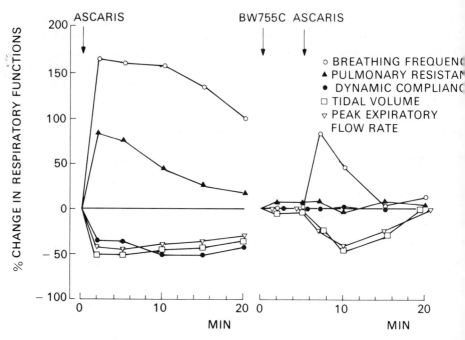

Fig. 10.3. The effect of BW755C on *Ascaris*-induced changes in respiratory function in a rhesus monkey (Patterson *et al.* 1981). The curves on the left of the figure show the changes induced by *Ascaris* challenge in an untreated animal. The curves on the right show the effects of challenging the same animal 5 min after aerosol treatment with BW755C ($10\,\mathrm{mg\,ml^{-1}}$).

genase is inhibited by preventing the abstraction of hydrogen from C-13 and, therefore, blocking peroxidation at C-11 and C-15. This action is highly specific, for similar abstraction and peroxidation reactions at other points in the fatty acid molecule are not inhibited. Furthermore, these drugs do not prevent the generation of prostaglandins from cyclic endoperoxides.

Within two years of the discovery that non-steroid anti-inflammatory drugs inhibit prostaglandin synthesis, several classes of inhibitors had been identified (Flower 1974). A more recent reviewer lists no fewer than 12 major chemical series known directly to affect prostaglandin production and concludes 'It is remarkable that in the short span of time since the first observations with aspirin and indomethacin, such a variety of chemical structures have been identified as inhibitors of prostaglandin synthesis' (Shen 1979).

This diverse group of chemicals has been broadly classified to exhibit three types of inhibition: reversible competitive, irreversible, and reversible non-competitive (Lands 1981). Examples of reversible competitive inhibitors are fatty acids, closely related to the substrate, which have a comparable affinity for the enzyme but are not converted to oxygenated products. The anti-inflammatory drug ibuprofen (Fig. 10.4), has a binding affinity for cyclooxygenase similar to that of the substrate arachidonic acid, and this explains why ibuprofen inhibits the enzyme (Rome and Lands 1975). Aspirin (Fig. 10.4) itself is an irreversible inhibitor, which covalently acetylates a serine residue in the active site of the enzyme (Roth and Majerus 1975). This mechanism does not, however, explain the action of other inhibitors such as indomethacin and flurbiprofen (Fig. 10.4).

SELECTIVE CYCLO-OXYGENASE INHIBITORS (NON-STEROID ASPIRIN-LIKE DRUGS)

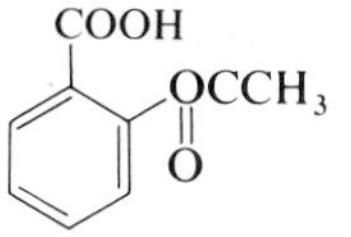

ASPIRIN

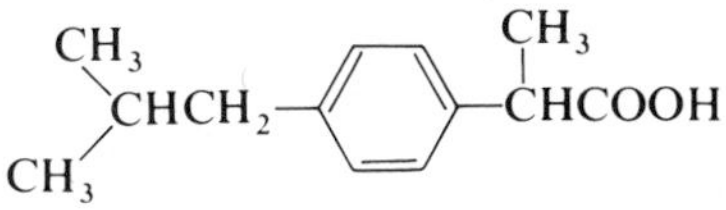

IBUPROFEN

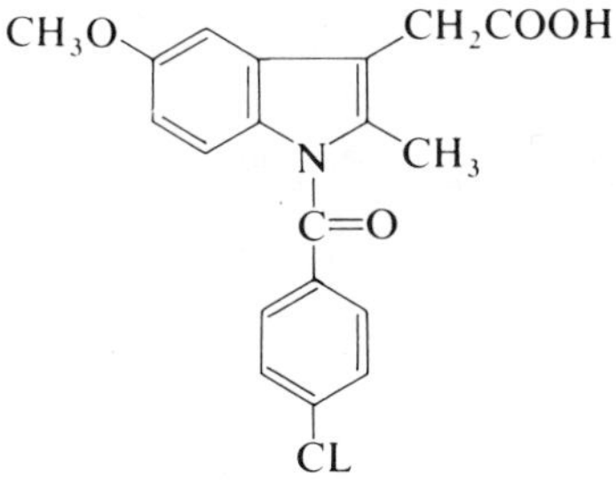

INDOMETHACIN

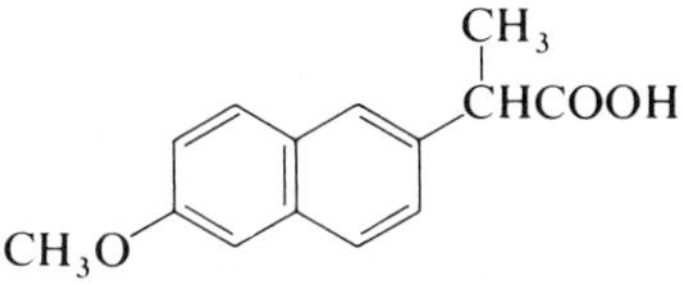

NAPROXEN

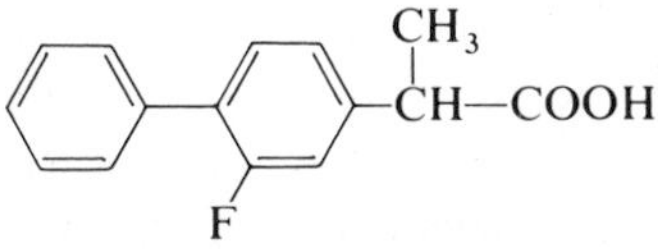

FLURBIPROFEN

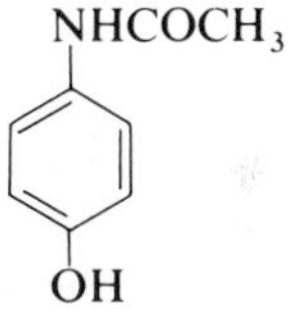

PARACETAMOL

SELECTIVE THROMBOXANE
SYNTHETASE INHIBITOR

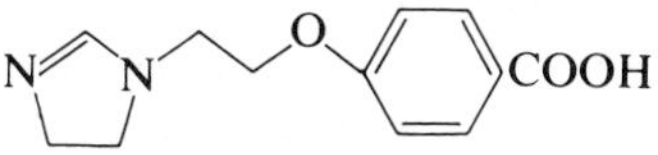

DUAL CYCLO-OXYGENASE AND
LIPOXYGENASE INHIBITOR

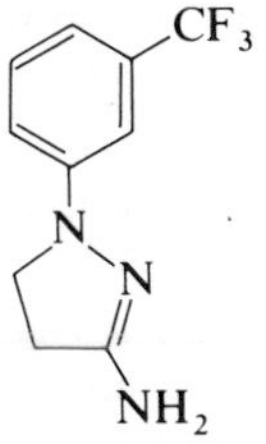

DAZOXIBEN

BW 755C

Fig. 10.4. Inhibitors of arachidonic acid metabolism.

A model for the active site of cyclooxygenase has been proposed, based upon conformational analysis of aryl acidic non-steroid anti-inflammatory drugs (Gund and Shen 1977). The carboxyl function of these compounds is said to mimic the terminal carboxyl of arachidonic acid and the planar, hydrophobic groups bind to the enzyme to prevent hydrogen abstraction at C-13. The presence of an aryl halogen has also been recognized as enhancing this activity (Rome and Lands 1975). An alternative view is that propionic acids such as naproxen (Fig. 10.4) act as structural analogues of the cyclic endoperoxides rather than arachidonic acid itself (Appleton and Brown 1979). Inhibition by these drugs is stereospecific as a number of α-methyl arylacetic acids with the $S(+)$ configuration are active but their $R(-)$ enantiomers are not (Shen 1979). This difference also applies to their anti-inflammatory activity *in vivo*. It is generally accepted that the majority of these drugs compete with the substrate for enzyme binding and are competitive irreversible inhibitors.

The induction period required to initiate cyclooxygenase activity is reduced by addition of hydroperoxy acids and this has led to the concept that the peroxide tone in inflamed tissues may determine enzyme activity (Lands 1981). It has been proposed that a continual presence of lipid peroxide induces a free-radical chain reaction that sustains cyclooxygenase activity. This can be blocked by the addition of radical scavengers or anti-oxidants, which act as reversible non-competitive inhibitors. The analgesic drug paracetamol (Fig. 10.4) may block prostaglandin synthesis by this mechanism (Lands *et al.* 1976), although in lower concentrations it stimulates prostaglandin biosynthesis.

10.5.2   Inhibition of cyclooxygenase *in vivo*

In humans, aspirin blocks cyclooxygenase activity in platelets within an hour of oral administration (Smith and Willis 1971) and this observation has been confirmed in several species. Because aspirin irreversibly acetylates the enzyme and platelets are unable to generate new enzyme, inhibition of platelet cyclooxygenase lasts for the lifetime of the cell. This results in effects on platelet function for several days after a single dose of aspirin.

Aspirin is significantly more potent in inhibiting cyclooxygenase *in vitro* than salicylate (Vane 1971), but the anti-inflammatory potency of the two drugs is similar, as is their ability to reduce urinary output of prostaglandin metabolites (Hamberg 1972). This can be explained by aspirin acting as a pro-drug for salicylate, which is, after all, why aspirin was originally synthesized (Dreser 1899). Aspirin acts directly on blood cells such as platelets and leucocytes but has little effect on peripheral tissues, as most of the drug is hydrolysed to salicylate before leaving the hepatic portal circulation (Pedersen and Fitzgerald 1984). Following large oral doses of aspirin, the drug can be detected in the plasma of peripheral blood and even in the peripheral tissues, but aspirin concentrations are rapidly exceeded (50 to 100-fold) by salicylate concentrations (Henderson *et al.* 1986). After 1–2 h aspirin is undetectable in the periphery, but

Table 10.1   Concentrations of aspirin and salicylate in peripheral blood plasma of rats 0.5–6h after a single oral dose of aspirin $(200\,mg/kg^{-1})$. Each value is the mean of five values ± 1 sem (Henderson *et al.* 1986)

Time (h)	ASPIRIN (μg/ml)	SALICYLATE (μg/ml)
0.5	1.32 $\pm$ 0.46	108.99 $\pm$ 15.49
1	0.19 $\pm$ 0.10	115.84 $\pm$ 14.75
2	0.08 $\pm$ 0.08	127.44 $\pm$ 10.06
6	0	57.56 $\pm$ 4.09

salicylate persists for more than 6 h (Table 10.1). During this time the synthesis of prostaglandins at a peripheral site of inflammation is reduced and this correlates with anti-inflammatory activity. It is likely, therefore, that the anti-inflammatory activity of orally dosed aspirin or salicylate is due to the inhibition of prostaglandin production in the inflamed tissues by salicylate (Henderson *et al.* 1986).

There is a good correlation between the relative potencies of aspirin-like drugs in reducing prostaglandin concentrations in inflammatory exudates and their inhibition of inflammatory oedema (Table 10.2). Furthermore, in groups of patients with arthritis receiving aspirin-like drugs, the mean concentration of

Table 10.2   The effect of non-steroid anti-inflammatory drugs on prostaglandin E_2 (PGE_2) synthesis and carrageenin-induced oedema in the rat (for methodology see Higgs *et al.* 1980). The relative potency of each drug is expressed in relation to naproxen, which is arbitrarily designated unity.

NON-STEROID ANTI-INFLAMMATORY DRUG	RELATIVE POTENCY *IN VIVO*	
	INHIBITION OF PGE_2 SYNTHESIS	INHIBITION OF OEDEMA
SODIUM SALICYLATE	0.02	0.10
ASPIRIN	0.07	0.11
FENCLOFENAC	0.05	0.22
ALCLOFENAC	0.35	0.40
BENOXAPROFEN	1.2	0.40
PHENYLBUTAZONE	0.39	0.73
IBUPROFEN	0.20	0.85
NAPROXEN	1.0	1.0
SULINDAC	0.7	4.8
DICLOFENAC	5.5	5.4
INDOMETHACIN	7.3	5.4
KETOPROFEN	64.7	8.5
FLURBIPROFEN	34.4	25.9

cyclo-oxygenase products in synovial fluids is only one tenth of the concentrations in fluids from untreated patients (Higgs *et al.* 1974; Trang *et al.* 1977) and this is associated with symptomatic relief.

10.5.3 Inhibition of thromboxane synthesis

The development of selective thromboxane synthetase inhibitors has been seen as a means of removing an important activator of platelets while maintaining the production of prostacyclin, which inhibits platelet activation. The search for thromboxane synthetase inhibitors has been dominated by the discovery in 1977 that imidazole has a selective effect on the enzyme and only reduces cyclo-oxygenase activity at high concentrations (Moncada *et al.* 1977a). Since then, interest has focused on 1-substituted derivatives of imidazole (e.g. dazoxiben; Fig. 10.4) and 3-substituted derivatives of pyridine (Tai and Yuan 1978; Tai *et al.* 1980) although endoperoxide analogues are also effective thromboxane synthetase inhibitors (Gorman 1980). By varying the position and length of the side chain and introducing planar hydrophobic groups, compounds with four orders of magnitude greater potency than imidazole have been synthesized. Furthermore, a 10 000-fold selectivity in inhibiting thromboxane synthetase over cyclo-oxygenase has been achieved (Johnson *et al.* 1983).

In the clinic, selective inhibition of thromboxane production, coupled with enhanced prostacyclin generation, has been demonstrated after oral administration of dazoxiben (Fig. 10.4) to humans (Fitzgerald *et al.* 1985). As mentioned earlier, however, this has not resulted in significant therapeutic activity in the diseases so far investigated. Compounds of longer duration of action may be required to test the hypothesis that this type of drug is efficacious in human disease.

10.5.4 Inhibition of lipoxygenase

Lipoxygenase activity can result in at least six different HPETEs. The aspirin-like drugs prevent abstraction of hydrogen at C13 and therefore, inhibit the production of 11-HPETE and 15-HPETE as well as the cyclized prostaglandins (Siegel *et al.* 1980b). However, these drugs have little or no inhibitory action on lipoxygenase reactions at other points in the molecule. For example, concentrations of indomethacin that completely block cyclooxygenase, increase production of 5-HETE in leucocytes (Randall *et al.* 1980).

The first class of inhibitors of mammalian lipoxygenase to be described was the acetylenic analogues of arachidonic acid. These compounds contain triple bonds in place of double bonds and so hydrogen abstraction and subsequent peroxidation cannot occur. The tetraynoic analogue of arachidonic acid (ETYA) inhibits both cyclooxygenase and lipoxygenase (Hamberg and Samuelsson 1974), whereas the monoynoic derivatives, 5,6-, 11,12-, or 14,15-dehydro-arachidonic acid, block selectively peroxidation in the 5,11, or 15 positions respectively

Corey and Munroe 1982; Corey and Park 1982). These acetylenic analogues compete with the natural substrate for enzyme binding and inhibit the enzyme because they cannot be peroxidized. Other substrate analogue inhibitors have been described, such as the hydroxy-amide derivative of arachidonic acid (Corey *et al.* 1984), and the inhibitory mechanism of this compound may involve chelation of iron in the enzyme.

There are numerous reports of substances that are structurally unrelated to arachidonic acid and are potent and selective 5-lipoxygenase inhibitors *in vitro*. These include the anti-oxidant nordihydro-guaiaretic acid (NDGA; Hamberg 1976) which also inhibits other lipoxygenases and cyclooxygenase at higher doses. An interesting group of inhibitors has been described among the naturally occurring flavonoids. Quercetin, esculetin, and baicalein have a high degree of selectivity for inhibiting 5-lipoxygenase and baicalein is one of the most potent inhibitors yet reported (Sekiya and Okuda 1982; Sekiya *et al.* 1982). Other natural product inhibitors are retinol (Vitamin A; Bray 1984) and caffeic acid (Koshihara *et al.* 1984). Some plant extracts that have been used in medicine for centuries contain these substances, suggesting that their therapeutic activity may be in part due to the inhibition of lipoxygenase.

Despite a wealth of compounds known to inhibit 5-lipoxygenase *in vitro*, little has been reported about their activity *in vivo*. Indeed, ETYA and NDGA have no effects after systemic administration (Higgs and Mugridge 1982), most probably because they are rapidly metabolized. Benoxaprofen inhibits 5-lipoxygenase in isolated leucocytes (Harvey *et al.* 1983), but has no effect on the production of LTB_4 in experimental inflammation (Salmon *et al.* 1984). Its anti-inflammatory properties correlate closely with its reduction of cyclo-oxygenase activity *in vivo*.

The evidence to support the hypothesis that lipoxygenase inhibitors may have important therapeutic effects is confined at present to experiments with dual inhibitors of cyclo-oxygenase and lipoxygenase. The most widely studied of these is the phenyl-pyrazoline BW755C (Fig. 10.4; Higgs *et al.* 1979) which inhibits both pathways of arachidonic acid metabolism in a wide range of isolated tissues (for review, see Higgs *et al.* 1984a). *In vivo*, BW755C causes dose-dependent reductions in the concentrations of PGE_2 and LTB_4 in inflammatory exudates, whereas aspirin, indomethacin, and flurbiprofen inhibit only PGE_2 (Salmon *et al.* 1983). Inhibition of LTB_4 production by BW755C is associated with reduced leucocyte migration, in contrast with the effects of aspirin, which does not inhibit LTB_4 production or leucocyte accumulation.

A dual inhibitor of prostaglandin and leukotriene synthesis such as BW755C may extend the therapeutic value of aspirin-like drugs by limiting leucocyte mobilization. This may be useful in chronic inflammatory conditions in which the release of lysosomal enzymes from these migrating cells contributes to tissue damage and necrosis (Davis and Allison 1978). In some types of chronic degenerative disease such as rheumatoid arthritis, the control of leucocytes could be an important factor in limiting tissue damage. BW755C reduces tissue damage and necrosis in experimental models of inflammation (Higgs *et al.* 1984b) and myocardial infarction (Lucchesi *et al.* 1982; Mullane and Moncada 1982) and in both those models the effect is accompanied by a reduction in leucocyte numbers in the affected tissues.

In most experimental models of anaphylaxis, indomethacin and other selective cyclooxygenase inhibitors enhance antigen-induced responses. BW755C, however, blocks the anaphylactic contractions of isolated lung tissue (Everitt *et al.* 1979) and reduces bronchoconstriction in isolated perfused lungs (Nijkamp and Ramakers 1980). In a model of IgE-mediated asthma in monkeys, BW755C abolishes *Ascaris*-induced changes in pulmonary resistance and dynamic compliance (Patterson *et al.* 1981; Fig. 10.3). Because aspirin-like drugs have no therapeutic value in anaphylaxis, a selective lipoxygenase inhibitor is an obvious target for drug development.

We do not know the mechanism of enzyme inhibition by BW755C but it is most probably of the anti-oxidant or radical scavenging type (Marnett *et al.* 1982). If this is so, the compound will fall into Lands' category of reversible noncompetitive inhibitors (Lands 1981), possibly acting by removing lipid peroxide radicals, which are necessary for enzyme activity. In this context, it is interesting that BW755C does not prevent the physiological production of prostacyclin (which is cytoprotective) in the gastric mucosa, whereas in the same animals it abolishes PGE_2 production in inflamed tissues (Whittle *et al.* 1980). It is possible that anti-oxidants such as BW755C are most effective in tissues where there is sufficient damage to generate a high level of peroxides. Such a mechanism would result in a targetting of drug activity to injured tissues with obvious therapeutic benefits and reduced toxic effects. Progressive *N*-alkylation of the primary amino group in BW755C has led to a series of pyrazolines with increased potency and increased selectivity in inhibiting 5-lipoxygenase (Copp *et al.* 1984).

10.6   Other enzyme targets

The release of arachidonic acid from cell membrane phospholipids is brought about by phospholipases and their activity is suppressed by the anti-inflammatory corticosteroids. This inhibitory activity is mediated by the release of a protein variously called macrocortin (Blackwell *et al.* 1980), lipomodulin (Hirata *et al.* 1980) and renocortin (Cloix *et al.* 1983). This protein has now been named lipocortin (DiRosa *et al.* 1984) and has been sequenced and synthesized by genetic engineering techniques (Wallner *et al.* 1986). Inhibitors of phospholipase, based either on lipocortin or on smaller synthetic chemicals, could well have importance as therapeutic agents in the treatment of inflammation and asthma.

10.7   Summary

The selective inhibition of cyclooxygenase by the large group of aspirin-like non-steroid anti-inflammatory drugs explains their therapeutic activity. The elucidation of other pathways of oxidative metabolism of arachidonic acid has revealed new targets for the development of drugs with potentially greater therapeutic activity in the treatment of inflammation, cardio-thrombotic diseases, and asthma.

References

Aharony, D., Smith, J. B., and Silver, M. J. (1981). Inhibition of platelet lipoxygenase by toluene-3,4 dithiol and other ferric iron chelators. *Prostaglandins Med.*, **6**, 237–42.

Ahmed, T., Greenblatt, D. W., Birch, S., Marchette, B., and Wanner, A. (1981). Abnormal mucociliary transport in allergic patients with antigen-induced bronchospasm: role of slow reacting substance of anaphylaxis. *Ann. Rev. Resp. Dis.*, **124**, 110–14.

Appleton, R. A. and Brown, K. (1979). Conformational requirements at the prostaglandin cyclo-oxygenase receptor site: a template for designing non-steroidal anti-inflammatory drugs. *Prostaglandins*, **18**, 29–34.

Aspirin Myocardial Infarction Study Research Group (1980). A randomized controlled trial of aspirin in persons recovering from myocardial infarction. *J. Am. Med. Ass.*, **243**, 661–9.

Austen, K. F. (1978). Homeostasis of effector systems which can also be recruited for immunologic reactions. *J. Immunol.*, **121**, 793–805.

Bergstrom, S. and Sjovall, J. (1960a). The isolation of prostaglandin F from sheep prostate glands. *Acta. Chim. Scand.*, **14**, 1693–701.

Bergstrom, S. and Sjovall, J. (1960b). The isolation of prostaglandin E from sheep prostate glands. *Acta. Chim. Scand.*, **14**, 1701–9.

Bergstrom, S., Danielsson, H., and Samuelsson, B. (1964). The enzymatic formation of prostaglandin E_2 from arachidonic acid. Prostaglandins and related factors, 32. *Biochim. Biophys. Acta.*, **90**, 207–10.

Blackwell, G. J., Carnuccio, R., DiRosa, M., Flower, R. J. Parente, L., and Persico, P. (1980). Macrocortin: a polypeptide causing the anti-phospholipase effect of glucocorticoids. *Nature (London)*, **287**, 147–9.

Borgeat, P., Hamberg, M., and Samuelsson, B. (1976). Transformation of arachidonic acid and dihomo-γ-linolenic acid by polymorphonuclear leucocytes. *J. Biol. Chem.*, **251**, 7816–20.

Borgeat, P. and Samuelsson, B. (1979). Arachidonic acid metabolism in polymorphonuclear leukocytes: unstable intermediate in formation of dihydroxy acids. *Proc. Nat. Acad. Sci. USA*, **76**, 3213–17.

Bray, M. A. (1984). Retinoids are potent inhibitors of the generation of rat leukocyte leukotriene B_4-like activity *in vitro*. *Eur. J. Pharmacol.*, **98**, 61–7.

Cairns, J., Gent, M., Singer, J., Finnie, K., Froggatt, G., Holder, D., Jablonsky, G., Kostuk, W., Melendez, L., Myers, M., Sackett, D., Sealey, B., and Tanzer, P. (1984). A study of aspirin and/or sulfinpyrazone in unstable angina. *Circulation*, **70**: (Suppl. II), 415 (abst.).

Chang, W.-C., Nakao, J., Orimo, H. and Murota, S.-I. (1982). Effects of reduced glutathione on the 12-lipoxygenase pathways in rat platelets. *Biochem. J.*, **202**, 771–6.

Chesebro, J. H., Clements, I. P., Fuster, V., Elveback, L. R., Smith, H. C., Bardsley, W. T., Frye, R. L., Holmes, D. R., Vlietstra, R. E., Pluth, J. R., Wallace, R. B., Puga, F. J., Orszulak, T. A., Pehler, J. M., Schaff, H. V., and Danielson, G. K. (1982). A platelet inhibitor drug trial in coronary artery bypass operations. Benefit of perioperative dipyridamole and aspirin therapy on early postoperative vein graft patency. *New Engl. J. Med.*, **307**, 73–8.

Chesebro, J. H., Fuster, V., Elveback, L. R., Clements, I. P., Smith, H. C., Holmes, D. R., Bardsley, W. T., Pluth, J. R., Wallace, R. B., Puga, F. J., Orszulak, T. A., Piehler, J. M., Danielson, G. K., Schaff, H. V., and Frye, R. L. (1984). Effects of dipyridamole and aspirin on late vein-graft patency after coronary bypass operations. *New. Engl. J. Med.*, **310**, 209–14.

Christ-Hazelhof, E. and Nugteren, D. H. (1979). Purification and characterisation of prostaglandin endoperoxide D-isomerase, a cytoplasmic glutathione-containing enzyme. *Biochim. Biophys. Acta*, **572**, 43–51.

Cloix, J. F., Colard, O., Rothhut, B., and Russo-Marie, F. (1983). Characterisation and partial purification of renocortins:two polypeptides formed in renal cells causing the anti-phospholipase-like action of glucocorticoids. *Br. J. Pharmacol.*, **79**, 313–21.

Copp, F. C., Islip, P. J., and Tateson, J. E. (1984). 3-N-substituted-amino-1-[3-(trifluoromethyl phenyl]-2-pyrazolines have enhanced activity against arachidonate 5-lipoxygenase and cyclo-oxygenase. *Biochem. Pharmacol.*, **33**, 339–40.

Corey, E. J. and Munroe, J. E. (1982). Irreversible inhibition of prostaglandin and leukotriene biosynthesis from arachidonic acid by 11,12-dehydro- and 5,6-dehydro-arachidonic acids respectively. *J. Am. Chem. Soc.*, **104**, 1752–4.

Corey, E. J. and Park. H. (1982). Irreversible inhibition of the enzymic oxidation of arachidonic acid to 15 (hydroperoxy)-5,8,11(Z), 13(E)-eicosatetraenoic acid (15-HPETE) by 14,15-dehydroarachidonic acid. *J. Am. Chem. Soc.*, **104**, 1750–2.

Corey, E. J., Cashman, J. R., Kantner, S. S., and Wright, S. W. (1984). Rationally designed potent competitive inhibitors of leukotriene biosynthesis. *J. Am. Chem. Soc.*, **106** 1503–4.

Cottee, F., Flower, R. J., Moncada, S., Salmon, J. A., and Vane, J. R. (1977). Synthesis of 6-keto-PGF$_{1\alpha}$ by ram vesicle microsomes. *Prostaglandins*, **14**, 413–23.

Creticos, P. S., Peters, S. P., Adkinson, Jr. N. F., Naclerio, R. M., Hayes, E. C., Norman, P. S., and Lichtenstein, L. M. (1984). Peptide leukotriene release after antigen challenge in patients sensitive to ragweed. *New Engl. J. Med.*, **310**, 1626–30.

Davis, P. and Allison, A. C. (1978). The release of hydrolytic enzymes from phagocytic and other cells participating in acute and chronic inflammation. In: *Inflammation* (ed. J. R. Vane and S. H. Ferreira), pp. 267–94. Springer, Berlin.

Di Rosa, M., Flower, R. J., Hirata, F., Parente, L., and Russo-Marie, F. (1984). Anti-Phospholipase proteins. *Prostaglandins*, **28**, 441–2.

Drazen, J. M., Austen, K. F., Lewis, R. A., Clark, D. A., Goto, G., Marfat, A., and Corey, E. J. (1980). Comparative airway and vascular activities of leukotrienes C-1 and D *in vivo* and *in vitro*. *Proc. Nat. Acad. Sci. USA.* **77**, 4354–8.

Dreser, H. (1899). Pharmakologisches über Aspirin (Acetylsalicylsäure). *Pflügers Arch. Gesante Physiol. Menschen Tiere*, **76**, 306–18.

Ettinger, W. H., Wise, R. R., Schaffhauser, D., and Wigley, F. M. (1984). Controlled double blind trial of dazoxiben and nifedipine in the treatment of Raynaud's phenomenon. *Am. J. Med.*, **77**, 451–6.

Everitt, B. J., Bentley, J. A., Spiegel, W. D., and Porter, N. A. (1979). Inhibition of anaphylactic and arachidonic acid-induced contractions of guinea-pig isolated trachea by a cyclo-oxygenase and lipoxygenase inhibitor. *Pharmacologist*, **21**, 153.

Feldberg, W. and Kellaway, C. H. (1938). Liberation of histamine and formation of lysolecithin-like substance by cobra venom. *J. Physiol.*, **94**, 187–226.

Ferreira, S. H. (1972). Prostaglandins, aspirin-like drugs and analgesia. *Nature (London)*, **240**, 200–3.

Ferreira, S. H., Moncada, S., and Vane, J. R. (1971). Indomethacin and aspirin abolish prostaglandin release from the spleen. *Nature (London)*, **231**, 237–9.

Fields, W. S., Lemak, N. A., Frankowski, R. F., and Hardy, R. J. (1977). Controlled trial of aspirin in cerebral ischaemia. *Stroke*, **8**, 301–14.

Fitzgerald, G. A., Reilly, I. A. G., and Pedersen, A. K. (1985). The biochemical Pharmacology of thromboxane synthase inhibition in man. *Circulation*, **72**, 1194–201.

Flower, R. J. (1974). Drugs which inhibit prostaglandin biosynthesis. *Pharmacol. Rev.*, **26**, 33–67.

Ford-Hutchinson, A. W., Bray, M. A., Doig, M. V., Shipley, M. E., and Smith, M. J. H. (1980). Leukotriene B_4, a potent chemokinetic and aggregatory substance relased from polymorphonuclear leukocytes. *Nature (London)*, **286**, 264–5.

Gorman, R. R. (1980). Biochemical and pharmacological evaluation of thromboxane synthetase inhibitors. *Adv. Prost. Thromb. Res.*, **6**, 417–25.

Gund, P. and Shen, T. Y. (1977). A model for the prostaglandin synthetase cyclooxygenation site and its inhibition by anti-inflammatory arylacetic acids. *J. Med. Chem.*, **20**, 1146–52.

Hamberg, M. (1972). Inhibition of prostaglandin synthesis in man. *Biochem. Biophys. Res. Commun.*, **49**, 720–6.

Hamberg, M. (1976). On the formation of thromboxane B_2 and 12L-hydroxy-5,8,10,14-eicosatetraenoic acid (12ho-20:4) in tissues from the guinea pig. *Biochim. Biophys. Acta.*, **431**, 651–4.

Hamberg, M. and Samuelsson, B. (1967). On the mechanism of the biosynthesis of prostaglandins E_1 and $F_{1\alpha}$. *J. Biol. Chem.*, **242**, 5336–43.

Hamberg, M. and Samuelsson, B. (1974). Prostaglandin endoperoxides. Novel transformations of arachidonic acid in human platelets. *Proc. Nat. Acad. Sci. USA*, **71**, 3400–4.

Hamberg, M., Svensson, J., and Samuelsson, B. (1975). Thromboxanes: a new group of biologically active compounds derived from prostaglandin endoperoxides. *Proc. Nat. Acad. Sci. USA*, **72**, 2994–8.

Hammarstrom, S. and Falardeau, P. (1977). Resolution of prostaglandin endoperoxide synthase and thromboxane synthase of human platelets. *Proc. Nat. Acad. Sci. USA.*, **74**, 3691–5.

Hammarstrom, S., Hamberg, M., Samuelsson, B., Duell, E. A., Stawiski, M, and Voorhees, J. J. (1975). Increased concentrations of non-esterified arachidonic acid, 12L-hydroxy-5,8,10,14-eicosatetraenoic acid, prostaglandin E_2 and prostaglandin $F_{2\alpha}$ in epidermis of psoriasis. *Proc. Nat. Acad. Sci. USA.*, **72**, 5130–4.

Harvey, J., Parish, H., Ho, P. P. K., Boot, J. R., and Dawson, W. (1983). The preferential inhibition of 5-lipoxygenase product formation by benoxaprofen. *J. Pharm. Pharmac.*, **35**, 44–5.

Hemler, M., Lands, W. E. M., and Smith, W. L. (1976). Purification of the cyclooxygenase that forms prostaglandins. Demonstration of two forms of iron in the holoenzyme. *J. Biol. Chem.*, **251**, 5575–9.

Henderson, B., Higgs, G. A., Salmon, J. A., and Vane, J. R. (1986). Is aspirin a pro-drug for salicylate? *Br. J. Pharmacol.*, **88**: 400P.

Higgs, E. A., Moncada, S., and Vane, J. R. (1978). Inflammatory effects of prostacyclin (PGI_2) and 6-oxo-$PGF_{1\alpha}$ in the rat paw. *Prostaglandins*, **16**, 153–62.

Higgs, G. A. and Mugridge, K. G. (1982). The effects on carrageenin-induced inflammation of compounds which interfere with arachidonic acid metabolism. *Br. J. Pharmacol.*, **76**, 284P.

Higgs, G. A., Vane, J. R., Hart, F. D., and Wojtulewski, J. A. (1974). Effects of anti-inflammatory drugs on prostaglandins in rheumatoid arthritis. In *Prostaglandin synthetase inhibitors*, (ed. H. J. Robinson and J. R. Vane), pp. 165–73. Raven Press, New York.

Higgs, G. A., Flower, R. J., and Vane, J. R. (1979). A new approach to anti-inflammatory drugs. *Biochem. Pharmacol.*, **28**, 1959–61.

Higgs, G. A., Eakins, K. E., Mugridge, K. G., Moncada, S., and Vane, J. R. (1980). The effects of non-steroid anti-inflammatory drugs on leukocyte migration in carrageenin-induced inflammation. *Eur. J. Pharmacol.*, **66**, 81–6.

Higgs, G. A., Moncada, S., Salmon, J. A., and Seager, K. (1983). The source of Prostaglandins and thromboxane in experimental inflammation. *Br. J. Pharmacol.*, **79**, 863–8.

Higgs, G. A., Moncada, S., and Vane, J. R. (1984a). Eicosanoids in inflammation. *Ann. Clin. Res.*, **16**, 287–99.

Higgs, G. A., Mugridge, K. G., Moncada, S., and Vane, J. R. (1984b). Inhibition of tissue damage by the arachidonate lipoxygenase inhibitor BW755C. *Proc. Nat. Acad. Sci. USA*, **81**, 2890–2.

Hirata, F., Schiffmann, E., Venkatasubramanian, K., Salomon, D., and Axelrod, J. (1980). A phospholipase A$_2$ inhibitory protein in rabbit neutrophils induced by glucocorticoids. *Proc. Nat. Acad. Sci. USA*, **77**, 2533–6.

Ho, P. P. K., Walters, P., and Sullivan, H. R. (1976). Biosynthesis of thromboxane B$_2$: assay, isolation and properties of the enzyme in human platelets. *Prostaglandins*, **12**, 951–70.

Holroyde, M. C., Altounyan, R. E. C., Cole, M., Dixon, M., and Elliott, E. V. (1981). Bronchoconstriction produced in man by leukotrienes C and D. *Lancet*, **2**, 17–18.

Jakschik, B. A. and Kuo, C. G. (1983). Subcellular localisation of leukotriene-forming enzymes. *Adv. Prost. Thromb. Leuk. Res.*, **11**, 141–5.

Jakschik, B. A., Sams, A. R., Sprecher, H., and Needleman, P. (1980). Fatty acid structural requirements for leukotriene biosynthesis. *Prostaglandins*, **20**, 401–10.

Johnson, M., Carey, F., and McMillan, R. M. (1983). Alternative pathways of arachidonate metabolism: prostaglandins, thromboxane and leukotrienes. *Essays Biochem.*, **19**, 40–141.

Kay, A. B. (1983). The sputum in bronchial asthma. In *Asthma* (ed. T. J. H. Clark and S. Godfrey), pp. 99–110. Chapman and Hall, London.

Koshihara, Y., Neichi, T., Murota, S-I., Lao, A-N, Fukimoto, Y., and Tatsuno, T. (1984). Caffeic acid is a selective inhibitor for leukotriene biosynthesis. *Biochim. Biophys. Acta*, **792**, 92–7.

Lands, W. E. M. (1981). Actions of anti-inflammatory drugs. *Trends Pharmacol. Sci.*, **2**, 78–80.

Lands, W. E. M., Cook, H. W., and Rome, L. H. (1976). Prostaglandin biosynthesis: Consequences of oxygenase mechanism upon *in vitro* assays of drug effectiveness. *Adv Prost. Thromb. Res.*, **1**, 7–17.

Lee, T. H., Walport, M. J., Wilkinson, A. H., Turner-Warwick, M., and Kay, A. B. (1981). Slow reacting substance of anaphylaxis antagonist, FPL 55712 in chronic asthma *Lancet*, **2**, 304–5.

Lewis, R. A., Austen, K. F., Drazen, J. M., Soter, N. A., Figueiredo, J. C., and Corey, E. J (1982). Structure, function and metabolism of leukotriene constituents of SRS-A. *Adv Prost. Thromb. Leuk. Res.*, **10**: 137–51.

Lewis, H. D., Davis, J. W., Archibald, D. G., Steinke, W. E., Smitherman, T. C. Dougherty, J. E., Schnaper, H. W., Le Winter, M. M., Linares, E., Pouget, J. M. Sabhatwal, S. C., Chesler, E., and De Mots, H. (1983). Protective effects of aspirin against acute myocardial infarction and death in man with unstable angina. *New. Engl J. Med.*, **309**, 396–403.

Lucchesi, B. R., Jolly, S. R., Baslie, M. B., and Abrams, G. D. (1982). Protection of ischaemic myocardium by BW755C. *Fed. Proc. Fed. Am. Soc. Exp. Biol.*, **41**, 1737.

Luderer, J. R., Nicholas, G. G., Neumyer, M. M., Riley, D. L., Vary, J. E., Garcia, G., and Schneck, D. W. (1984). Dazoxiben, a thromboxane synthetase inhibitor in Raynaud's phenomenon. *Clin. Pharmacol. Ther.*, **36**, 105–15.

Marnett, L. J., Siedlik, P. H., and Fung, L. W. M. (1982). Oxidation of phenidone and BW755C by prostaglandin endoperoxide synthetase. *J. Biol. Chem.*, **257**, 6957–64.

Maycock, A. L., Anderson, M. S., De Sousa, D. M., and Kuehl, F. A. (1982). Leukotriene A_4: preparation and enzymic conversion in a cell free system to leukotriene B_4. *J. Biol. Chem.*, **257**, 13911–14.

Miyamoto, T., Ogino, N., Yamamoto, S., and Hayaishi, O. (1976). Purification of prostaglandin endoperoxide synthetase from bovine vesicular gland microsomes. *J. Biol. Chem.*, **251**, 2629–36.

Moncada, S. and Vane, J. R. (1978). Pharmacology and endogenous roles of prostaglandin endoperoxides, thromboxane A_2 and prostacyclin. *Pharmacol. Rev.*, **30**, 293–331.

Moncada, S., Gryglewski, R. J., Bunting, S., and Vane, J. R. (1976). An enzyme isolated from arteries transforms prostaglandin endoperoxides to an unstable substance that inhibits platelet aggregation. *Nature (London)*, **263**, 663–5.

Moncada, S., Bunting, S., Mullane, K., Thorogood, P., Vane, J. R., Raz, A., and Needleman, P. (1977a). Imidazole; a selective inhibitor of thromboxane synthetase. *Prostaglandins*, **13**, 611–18.

Moncada, S., Herman, A. G., Higgs, E. A., and Vane, J. R. (1977b). Differential formation of prostacyclin (PGX or PGI_2) by layers of the arterial wall. An explanation for the anti-thrombotic properties of vascular endothelium. *Throm. Res.*, **11**, 323–44.

Morley, J., Bray, M. A., Jones, R. W., Nugteren, D. H., and Van Dorp, D. A. (1979). Prostaglandin and thromboxane production by human and guinea-pig macrophages and leukocytes. *Prostaglandins*, **17**, 730–6.

Mullane, K. M. and Moncada, S. (1982). The salvage of ischaemic myocardium by BW755C in anaesthetised dogs. *Prostaglandins*, **24**, 255–66.

Murphy, R. C., Hammarstrom, S., and Samuelsson, B. (1979). Leukotriene C: a slow-reacting substance from murine mastocytoma cells. *Proc. Nat. Acad. Sci. USA*, **76**, 4275–9.

Mustard, J. F., Kinlough-Rathbone, R. L., and Packham, M. A. (1983). Aspirin in the treatment of cardiovascular disease: a review. *Am. J. Med.*, **74**, 43–9.

Needleman, P., Moncada, S., Bunting, S., Vane, J. R., Hamberg, M., and Samuelsson, B. (1976). Identification of an enzyme in platelet microsomes which generates thromboxane A_2 from prostaglandin endoperoxides. *Nature (London)*, **261**, 558–60.

Nijkamp, F. P. and Ramakers, A. G. M. (1980). Prevention of anaphylactic bronchoconstriction by a lipoxygenase inhibitor. *Eur. J. Pharmacol.*, **62**, 121–2.

Ogino, N., Miyamoto, T., Yamamoto, S., and Hayaishi, O. (1977). Prostaglandin endoperoxide E isomerase from bovine vesicular gland microsomes, a glutathione-requiring enzyme. *J. Biol. Chem.*, **252**, 890–5.

Pace-Asciak, C. R. (1976). Isolation, structure and biosynthesis of 6-keto-$PGF_{1\alpha}$ in the rat stomach. *J. Am. Chem. Soc.*, **98**, 2348–9.

Palmer, M. A., Piper, P. J. and Vane, J. R. (1973). Release of rabbit aorta contracting substance (RCS) and prostaglandins induced by chemical or mechanical stimulation of guinea-pig lungs. *Br. J. Pharmacol.*, **49**, 226–42.

Palmer, R. J., Stepney, R., Higgs, G. A., and Eakins, K. E. (1980). Chemokinetic activity of arachidonic acid lipoxygenase products on leukocytes from different species. *Prostaglandins*, **20**, 411–18.

Parker, C. W. and Aykent, S. (1982). Calcium stimulation of the 5-lipoxygenase from RBL-1 cells. *Biochem. Biophys. Res., Commun.*, **109**, 1011–16.

Patterson, R., Pruzansky, J. L., and Harris, K. E. (1981). An agent which releases basophil and mast cell histamine but blocks cyclo-oxygenase and lipoxygenase metabolism of arachidonic acid inhibits IgE mediated asthma in rhesus monkeys. *J. Allergy Clin. Immunol.*, **67**, 444–9.

Pedersen, A. K. and Fitzgerald, G. A. (1984). Dose-related kinetics of aspirin. Presystemic acetylation of platelet cyclo-oxygenase. *New. Engl. J. Med.*, **311**, 1206–11.

Piper, P. J. (1984). Leukotrienes. In *Development of Anti-asthmatic drugs* (ed. D. R. Buckle and H. Smith), pp. 55–72. Butterworths, London.

Piper, P. J. and Vane, J. R. (1969). The release of additional factors in anaphylaxis and its antagonism by anti-inflammatory drugs. *Nature (London)*, **223**, 29–35.

Rae, S. A., Davidson, E. M., and Smith, M. J. H. (1982). Leukotriene B$_4$, an inflammatory mediator in gout. *Lancet*, **ii**, 1122–4.

Randall, R. W., Eakins, K. E., Higgs, G. A., Salmon, J. A., and Tateson, J. E. (1980). Inhibition of arachidonic acid cyclo-oxygenase and lipoxygenase activities of leukocytes by indomethacin and compound BW755C. *Agents Actions*, **10**, 553–5.

Reuben, S. R., Kuan, P., Cairns, T., and Gysle, O. H. (1983). Effect of dazoxiben and exercise performance in chronic stable angina. *Br. J. Clin. Pharmacol.*, **15** (Suppl. 1), 835.

Rome, L. H. and Lands, W. E. M. (1975). Structural requirements for time-dependent inhibition of prostaglandin biosynthesis by anti-inflammatory drugs. *Proc. Nat. Acad. Sci. USA*, **72**, 4863–5.

Roth, G. J. and Majerus, P. W. (1975). The mechanism of the effect of aspirin on human platelets. 1. Acetylation of a particulate fraction protein. *J. Clin. Invest.*, **56**, 624–32.

Salmon, J. A., Simmons, P. M., and Moncada, S. (1983). The effects of BW755C and other anti-inflammatory drugs on eicosanoid concentrations and leukocyte accumulation in experimentally-induced acute inflammation. *J. Pharm. Pharmacol.*, **35**, 808–13.

Salmon, J. A., Higgs, G. A., Tilling, L., Moncada, S., and Vane, J. R. (1984). Mode of action of benoxaprofen. *Lancet*, **1**, 848.

Samuelsson, B. (1983). Leukotrienes: mediators of immediate hypersensitivity reactions and inflammation. *Science*, **220**, 568–75.

Samuelsson, B., Goldyne, M., Granstrom, E., Hamberg, M., Hammarstrom, S., and Malmsten, C. (1978). Prostaglandins and thromboxanes. *A. Rev. Biochem.*, **47**, 997–1029.

Saxena, P. N., Beg, M. M. A., Singhal, K. C., and Ahmad, M. (1979). Prostaglandin-like activity in the cerebrospinal fluid of febrile patients. *Indian J. Med. Res.*, **79**, 495–8.

Schwartzmann, M., Ferreri, N. R., Carroll, M. A., Songa-Mize, E., and McGiff, J. C. (1985). Renal cytochrome P450-related arachidonate metabolite inhibits (Na$^+$ + K$^+$) ATPase. *Nature (London)*, **314**, 620–2.

Sekiya, K. and Okuda, H. (1982). Selective inhibition of platelet lipoxygenase by baicalein. *Biochem. Biophys. Res. Commun.*, **105**, 1090–5.

Sekiya, K., Okuda, H., and Arichi, S. (1982). Selective inhibition of platelet lipoxygenase by esculetin. *Biochim. Biophys. Acta*, **713**, 68–72.

Shen, T. Y. (1979). Prostaglandin synthetase inhibitors. In *Anti-inflammatory drugs* (ed. J. R. Vane and S. H. Ferreira), pp. 305–47. Springer, Berlin.

Siegel, M. I., McConnell, R. T., Porter, N. A., and Cuatrecasas, P. (1980a). Arachidonate metabolism via lipoxygenase and 12-L-hydroperoxy-5,8,10,14-eicosatetraenoic acid peroxidase sensitive to anti-inflammatory drugs. *Proc. Nat. Acad. Sci. USA*, **77**, 308–12.

Siegel, M. I., McConnell, R. T., Porter, N. A., Selph, J. L., Truax, J. F., Vinegar, R., and Cuatrecasas, P. (1980b). Aspirin-like drugs inhibit arachidonic acid metabolism via lipoxygenase and cyclo-oxygenase in rat neutrophils from carrageenin pleural exudates. *Biochem. Biophys. Res. Commun.*, **92**, 688–95.

Simmons, P. M., Salmon, J. A., and Moncada, S. (1983). The release of leukotriene B_4 during experimental inflammation. *Biochem. Pharmacol.*, **32**, 1353–9.

Smith, J. B. and Willis, A. L. (1971). Aspirin selectively inhibits prostaglandin production in human platelets. *Nature (London)*, **231**, 235–7.

Smith, W. L., DeWitt, D. L., and Day, J. S. (1983). Purification, quantitation and localisation of PGI_2 synthase using monoclonal antibodies. *Adv. Prost. Thromb. Leuk. Res.*, **11**, 87–92.

Solomon, L. M., Juhlin, L., and Kirschenbaum, M. B. (1968). Prostaglandins on cutaneous vasculature. *J. Invest. Derm.*, **51**, 280–2.

Tai, H-H. and Yuan, B. (1978). On the inhibitory potency of imidazole and its derivatives on thromboxane synthetase. *Biochem. Biophys. Res., Commun.*, **80**, 236–42.

Tai, H-H, Tai, C. L., and Lee, N. (1980). Selective inhibition of thromboxane synthetase by pyridine and its derivatives. *Arch. Biochem. Biophys.*, **203**, 758–63.

Trang, L. E., Granstrom, E., and Lovgren, O. (1977). Levels of prostaglandin $F_{2\alpha}$ and E_2 and thromboxane B_2 in joint fluid in rheumatoid arthritis. *Scand. J. Rheumatol.*, **6**, 151–4.

Turner, S. R., Tainer, J. A., and Lynn, W. S. (1975). Biogenesis of chemotactic molecules by the arachidonate lipoxygenase system of platelets. *Nature (London)*, **257**, 680–1.

Ullrich, V. and Haurand, M. (1983). Thromboxane synthetase as a cytochrome P450 enzyme. *Adv. Prost. Thromb. Leuk. Res.*, **11**, 105–10.

Van der Ouderaa, F. J., Buytenhek, M., Nugteren, D. H., and Van Dorp, D. A. (1977). Purification and characterisation of prostaglandin endoperoxide synthetase from sheep vesicular glands. *Biochim. Biophys. Acta.*, **487**, 315–31.

Van der Ouderaa, F. J., Buytenhek, M., Slikkerveer, F. J., and Van Dorp, D. A. (1979). On the haemoprotein character of prostaglandin endoperoxide synthetase. *Biochim. Biophys. Acta*, **572**, 29–42.

Van Dorp, D. A. (1967). Aspects of the biosynthesis of prostaglandins. *Prog. Biochem. Pharmacol.*, **3**, 71–82.

Van Dorp, D. A., Beerthuis, R. K., Nugteren, D. H., and Vonkeman, H. (1964). The biosynthesis of prostaglandins. *Biochim. Biophys. Acta.*, **90**, 204–7.

Vane, J. R. (1971). Inhibition of prostaglandin synthesis as a mechanism of action for the aspirin-like drugs. *Nature (London)*, **231**, 232–5.

Vargaftig, B. B. and Dao Hai, N. (1972). Selective inhibition by mepacrine of the release of 'rabbit aorta contracting substance' evoked by the administration of bradykinin. *J. Pharm. Pharmacol.*, **24**, 159–61.

Von Euler, U. S. (1937). On the specific vasodilating and plain muscle stimulating substance from accessory genital glands in man and certain animals (prostaglandin and vesiglandin). *J. Physiol.*, **88**, 213–34.

Wallner, B. P., Mattaliano, R. J., Hession, C., Cate, R. L., Tizard, R., Sinclair, L. K., Foeller, C., Chow, E. P., Browning, J. L., Ramachandran, K. L., and Pepinsky, R. B. (1986). Cloning and expression of human lipocortin, a phospholipase A_2 inhibitor with potential anti-inflammatory activity. *Nature (London)*, **320**, 77–81.

Weiss, J. W., Drazen, J. M., Coles, N., McFadden, E. R., Weller, P. W., Corey, E. J., Lewis, R. A., and Austen, K. F. (1982). Bronchoconstrictor effects of leukotriene C in humans. *Science*, **216**, 196–8.

Whittle, B. J. R., Higgs, G. A., Eakins, K. E., Moncada, S., and Vane, J. R. (1980). Selective inhibition of prostaglandin production in inflammatory exudates and gastric mucosa. *Nature (London)*, **284**, 271–3.

Williams, T. J. and Peck, M. J. (1977). Role of prostaglandin-mediated vasodilatation in inflammation. *Nature (London)*, **270**, 530–2.

Yoshimoto, T., Yamamoto, S., Okuma, M., and Hayaishi, O. (1977). Solubilisation and resolution of thromboxane synthesising system from microsomes of bovine blood platelets. *J. Biol. Chem.*, **252**, 5871–4.

Zakrzewski, J. T., Barnes, N. C., Piper, P. J., and Costello, J. R. (1985). Quantitation of leukotrienes in asthmatic sputum. *Br. J. Clin. Pharmacol.*, **19**, 574P.

11

Selective inhibitors of dihydrofolate reductases

G. H. Hitchings, L. F. Kuyper, and D. P. Baccanari

11.1   Introduction

The marketing of co-trimoxazole in 1968, followed by trimethoprim (**1**, TMP), and the continued interest in methotrexate (**2**, MTX) and related substances, together with the expanding information concerning the composition and functions of tetrahydrofolate-containing cofactors (see e.g. Hitchings 1983), stimulated intensive studies on dihydrofolate reductase (DHFR).

It is the chief purpose of this paper to focus on the developing knowledge of the intimate structure and functioning of the enzyme that may be useful in the purposeful design of new inhibitors. It is now clear that the intimate structure of the enzyme is vastly more variable than was conceivable a decade ago. Pairwise homologies of the order of 25 per cent can be expanded to *c.* 50 per cent by considering closely related amino acid residues, such as Leu and Ile, as equivalents. One is nevertheless left with a surprisingly large range of size and composition for isofunctional enzymes. These differences may be grist to the mill of the drug designer.

11.2   General properties of DHFR

Numerous DHFR have been extensively studied, and it would be impossible to describe succinctly all their properties in this short chapter. The purpose of this section is to present an overview of the enzyme and to make some generalizations that are useful in understanding the specificity of enzyme–inhibitor interactions. Some exceptions to these generalizations and a more comprehensive listing of data can be found in a recent review by Blakley (1984).

Large amounts of homogeneous DHFR, often in the hundreds of mg range, have been needed to study the molecular basis of catalysis and inhibition. Animal liver (but not human liver) and cultured mammalian cell lines are good sources of vertebrate DHFR (Kamen *et al.* 1985). In contrast, levels of DHFR in bacteria are normally low, but preparative amounts of the enzyme have been obtained from inhibitor-resistant, mutant strains of *Diplococcus pneumoniae*, *Escherichia coli*, *Lactobacillus casei*, *Streptococcus faecium* (see Blakley 1984), and *Neisseria gonorrhoeae* (Baccanari *et al.* 1984). In these cases, the induced TMP or MTX resistance is the result of overproduction of the normal chromosomal enzyme. More recently, the DHFR genes from *E. coli*, *L. casei*, and human cells have been cloned and sequenced (Smith and Calvo 1980; Andrews *et al.* 1985 and Masters and Attardi 1983). MTX affinity chromatography is still the method of choice for purifying DHFR.

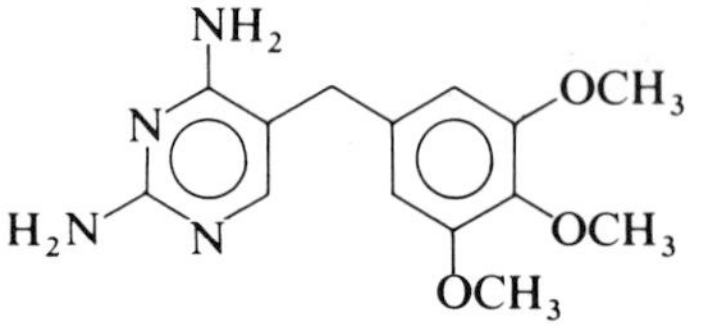

1 (TMP)

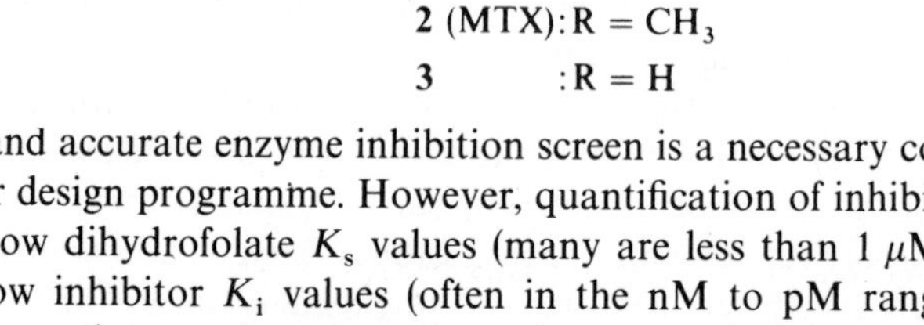

2 (MTX): R = CH_3

3   : R = H

A simple and accurate enzyme inhibition screen is a necessary component of any inhibitor design programme. However, quantification of inhibition is complicated by low dihydrofolate K_s values (many are less than 1 μM), substrate inhibition, low inhibitor K_i values (often in the nM to pM range), multiple protein conformations, and rate transients that occur during the enzyme assay (see Hitchings and Baccanari 1984; Blakley 1984). In spite of these difficulties, there are a number of methods available for quantifying inhibitor affinity. For example, DHFR utilizes a random Bi–Bi reaction mechanism (Burchall 1970), and the dissociation constant (K_d) of an inhibitor from the ternary complex with enzyme and NADPH should be equivalent to the kinetic constant K_i determined at saturating NADPH concentrations (Spector and Cleland 1981). Direct measurements of enzyme affinity constants include the determination of K_d values by n.m.r. (Roberts et al. 1974), equilibrium dialysis (Baccanari et al. 1982) and fluorescence titrations (Perkins and Bertino 1966), whereas determinations of inhibitor dissociation rate constants (k_{off}) have often served as an indirect measure of affinity. In the latter case, it is assumed that differences in relative K_d values are dependent only upon differences in inhibitor k_{off} values (Weber 1975). In general though, medicinal chemists have circumvented these problems by basing their inhibitor design strategies and QSAR determinations on measurements of IC_{50} values (Cheng and Prusoff 1973). IC_{50} determinations allow the use of substrate concentrations sufficiently high to avoid substrate depletion; dihydrofolate Michaelis constants need not be rigorously determined, and reaction rates can be measured after most velocity transients and protein conformational changes have occurred. Although this methodology usually gives a reliable ranking of DHFR affinity for TMP analogues, some inhibitors require a more detailed kinetic analysis. For example, MTX and aminopterin (3) bind with such high affinity that their IC_{50} values are roughly equivalent to half the concentration of enzyme in the assay mixture (Cha 1975; Williams and Morrison 1979). In addition, IC_{50} values are not true inhibition constants. The ratios of IC_{50} values for two enzymes are equivalent to K_i ratios only when the assays are performed under the same conditions and the enzymes have identical K_s values. The range of dihydrofolate K_s values reported for various bacterial and mammalian DHFR varies from about 0.05 to 15 μM (Blakley 1984). Therefore IC_{50} ratios do not reflect actual differences in inhibitor binding. For example, the average ratio of TMP IC_{50} values between mammalian DHFR (from rat liver and human liver) and the enzyme from pathogenic bacteria (E. coli, Staphlococcus aureus, and Proteus vulgaris) is 35 000 (Burchall 1974). Yet when binding affinities are estimated from ternary dissociation rate constants, less than a 3000-fold difference was observed between the E. coli and mouse lymphoma SR1 enzymes (Baccanari et al. 1982). These data indicate that ratios of IC_{50} values tend to overestimate the species specificity of DHFR for TMP. A similar conclusion was reached by Cocco et al. (1983), when they showed that the ratio of ternary TMP K_d values, measured directly by fluorescence techniques, for the bovine and L. casei enzymes is 375 and that the K_d ratio between the bovine and S. faecium enzymes is 100.

11.3 DHFR structure and ligand binding site

In the past 10 years, considerable advances have been made in understanding DHFR catalysis and inhibitor binding, and the most useful information has come from correlating physical and kinetic properties with amino acid sequences and protein conformations. The amino acid sequences of DHFR from numerous bacterial and vertebrate sources are known (see Blakley 1984 for a compilation and references). In general, there is much greater homology (76 per cent) among the DHFR from vertebrate sources than there is among the bacterial reductases (13 per cent). Only 10 per cent of the residues were identical in all the sequences considered by Lai *et al.* (1982). The amino acid sequences of DHFR from *L. casei, E. coli, N. gonorrhoeae,* and chicken liver are shown in Table 11.1 and will be discussed in more detail in a later section.

The structural characteristics of DHFR and its interactions with NADPH and various inhibitors have been thoroughly described (see Freisheim and Matthews 1984), but a brief summary of the overall DHFR structure will be presented as the framework of a more detailed discussion of differential inhibitor affinity.

DHFR has been classified by Richardson (1981) as a doubly wound mixed β-sheet in which the central eight-stranded β-sheet is protected on either side by two alpha helices. The twisted β-sheet is clearly seen in the simplified representation of the structure in Fig. 11.1. In keeping with the nomenclature suggested by Matthews *et al.* (1977), the individual strands of the β-sheet are designated A–H in order of their occurrence in the linear protein sequence. Each helix is assigned the letter of the β-strand that it precedes in the sequence.

A deep cleft exists on the enzyme surface between alpha helices B and C, and this cavity serves as the binding site for the diaminopyrimidine-type inhibitors and presumably the substrate dihydrofolic acid. The nicotinamide portion of the cofactor also binds in this cleft, in a position to transfer its hydride equivalent to the adjacent substrate. The diphosphate bridge of the cofactor is draped over the edge of the β-sheet in a shallow groove between the amino termini of alpha helices C and F, and the adenine moiety binds in a niche on the other side of the sheet.

This general description of DHFR applies to each of the four different isozymes for which three-dimensional structures are known (*E. coli*, Matthews *et al.* 1977; *L. casei*, Matthews *et al.* 1978; chicken, Volz *et al.* 1982; mouse, Stammers *et al.* 1983). As in other isozyme families, overall structure is preserved in spite of large deviations in linear sequence. The extent of homology among the four isozymes is less than 30 per cent for each pair except for the two vertebrate enzymes, which are 76 per cent homologous. Differences due to insertions or deletions of amino acid residues occur primarily in random chain or loop regions at the periphery of the enzyme structure.

The central portion of the inhibitor binding cleft of DHFR is lined with hydrophobic residues and is flanked at both ends by polar regions. Several hydrogen bonding sites are located at one end, deep within the cleft. The most important of these is a carboxyl group from an aspartate residue in the bacterial enzymes and a glutamate in the enzymes of vertebrate origin. The guanidinium moiety of an intact arginine residue is found at the other end. Although near the exterior surface of the enzyme, this guanidinium group is buried in a hydrophobic pocket. The sequestered nature of these two ionizable functions is suggestive of their potential importance to ligand binding.

The function of the polar–hydrophobic–polar character of the binding cleft can be illustrated by the *L. casei* DHFR ternary complex with MTX (Bolin *et al.* 1982; Filman *et al.* 1982). This structure, refined at 1.7 Å resolution, is shown in Plate 11.1. The 2,4-diaminopyrimidine moiety of the inhibitor is linked to the enzyme through five hydrogen bonds. The pyrimidine ring is protonated at N-1 and interacts ionically with the carboxyl group of Asp-26. The hydrogen at N-1 and one of the hydrogens of the 2-amino group serve as hydrogen-bond donors in that interaction. The other hydrogen of the 2-amino group is associated with a buried water molecule that has been observed in each of the refined DHFR structures. The backbone carbonyl oxygens of Leu-4 and Ala-97 provide hydrogen-bonding sites for the 4-amino group of the inhibitor. In addition, the 8-N of the pyrazine ring is apparently hydrogen-bonded to an active-site water molecule. Non-polar residues, such as Leu-19, Leu-27, Phe-30, Phe-49, and Leu-54, surround the central hydrophobic portion of the inhibitor, with the phenyl rings of MTX and residues 30 and 49 steeply inclined to one another in face-to-edge orientations. The α-carboxyl group of the polar glutamate end of MTX forms a salt bridge with the buried guanidinium ion of Arg-57, and the γ-carboxyl group is hydrogen bonded to His-28 on the exterior surface of the enzyme.

Since there is no crystallographic information available on folate binding, our current understanding of the stereochemistry of DHFR catalysis is actually an amalgamation of results from several studies. Pastore and Friedkin (1962) showed that a hydride is transferred from the A side of the NADPH nicotinamide ring to dihydrofolate. Small molecule X-ray crystallography and n.m.r. have been used to establish the absolute configuration at C-6 of tetrahydrofolates (Fontecilla-Camps *et al.* 1979; Charlton *et al.* 1985). These data, in light of the observed relative orientation of MTX and NADPH in the enzyme active site, suggest that the binding of dihydrofolate involves a 180° flip of the pteridine ring compared to MTX (Hitchings and Roth 1980; Freisheim and Matthews 1984). In this binding model, it is proposed that the active-site carboxyl group is hydrogen bonded to the 2-amino group and the N-3 nitrogen of dihydrofolate and that this carboxyl group indirectly transfers a proton to N-5, perhaps via a water molecule. Kinetic studies with the *E. coli* enzyme support the concept that the Asp-27 is important for catalysis (Baccanari *et al.* 1981; Stone and Morrison, 1983, 1984). In a more recent report, Howell *et al.* (1986) described the kinetics of a variant Asn-27 *E. coli* DHFR generated by site-directed mutagenesis of the wild-type enzyme. This proved to be a powerful technique for studying structure–function relationships. Measurement of the kinetic parameters of the enzymes as a function of pH provided direct evidence that Asp-27 is required for protonation of bound substrate but is not essential for hydride transfer. A number of different site-directed mutations of *E. coli* DHFR have been made,

Table 11.1. Amino acid sequences of DHFR from selected organisms.

The table is an aligned sequence alignment; each residue is given as its position number (superscript) followed by the one‑letter amino‑acid code. "—" marks an alignment gap. Rows: **Ec** (E. coli), **Lc** (L. casei), **Ng**, **Cl**.

	Aligned sequence (position‑residue)
Ec	— — ^{1}M ^{2}I ^{3}S ^{4}L ^{5}I ^{6}A ^{7}A ^{8}L ^{9}A ^{10}V ^{11}D ^{12}R ^{13}V ^{14}I ^{15}G ^{16}M ^{17}E ^{18}N ^{19}A ^{20}M ^{21}P ^{22}W — ^{23}N ^{24}L ^{25}P ^{26}A ^{27}D ^{28}L ^{29}A ^{30}W ^{31}F ^{32}K ^{33}R ^{34}N ^{35}T ^{36}L ^{37}N ^{38}K ^{39}P ^{40}V ^{41}I ^{42}M ^{43}G ^{44}R ^{45}H ^{46}T ^{47}W ^{48}E ^{49}S ^{50}I ^{51}G ^{52}R ^{53}P ^{54}L ^{55}P ^{56}G ^{57}R ^{58}K ^{59}N ^{60}I ^{61}I ^{62}L ^{63}S ^{64}S ^{65}Q ^{66}P — ^{67}G ^{68}T ^{69}D ^{70}D ^{71}R ^{72}V ^{73}T ^{74}W ^{75}V ^{76}K ^{77}S ^{78}V ^{79}D ^{80}E ^{81}A ^{82}I ^{83}A ^{84}A ^{85}C ^{86}G ^{87}D ^{88}V ^{89}P ^{90}E ^{91}I
Lc	— — — ^{1}T ^{2}A ^{3}F ^{4}L ^{5}W ^{6}A ^{7}Q ^{8}N ^{9}R ^{10}N ^{11}G ^{12}L ^{13}I ^{14}G ^{15}K ^{16}D ^{17}G ^{18}H ^{19}L ^{20}P ^{21}W — ^{22}H ^{23}L ^{24}P ^{25}D ^{26}D ^{27}L ^{28}H ^{29}Y ^{30}F ^{31}R ^{32}A ^{33}Q ^{34}T ^{35}V ^{36}G ^{37}K ^{38}I ^{39}M ^{40}V ^{41}V ^{42}G ^{43}R ^{44}R ^{45}T ^{46}Y ^{47}E ^{48}S ^{49}F ^{50}P ^{51}K ^{52}R ^{53}P ^{54}L ^{55}P ^{56}E ^{57}R ^{58}T ^{59}N ^{60}V ^{61}V ^{62}L ^{63}T ^{64}H ^{65}Q ^{66}E ^{67}D ^{68}Y ^{69}Q ^{70}A ^{71}Q ^{72}G ^{73}A ^{74}V ^{75}V ^{76}V ^{77}H ^{78}D ^{79}V ^{80}A ^{81}A ^{82}V ^{83}F ^{84}A ^{85}Y ^{86}A ^{87}K ^{88}Q ^{89}H ^{90}L ^{91}D ^{92}Q ^{93}E ^{94}L
Ng	^{1}M ^{2}L ^{3}K ^{4}I ^{5}T ^{6}I ^{7}I ^{8}A ^{9}A ^{10}C ^{11}A ^{12}E ^{13}N ^{14}L ^{15}C ^{16}I ^{17}G ^{18}A ^{19}G ^{20}N ^{21}A ^{22}M ^{23}P ^{24}W — ^{25}H ^{26}I ^{27}P ^{28}E ^{29}D ^{30}F ^{31}A ^{32}F ^{33}F ^{34}K ^{35}Q ^{36}R ^{37}M ^{38}K ^{39}I ^{40}K ^{41}P ^{42}V ^{43}I ^{44}E ^{45}G ^{46}K ^{47}N ^{48}N ^{49}E ^{50}E ^{51}S ^{52}L ^{53}P ^{54}V ^{55}K ^{56}P ^{57}L ^{58}P ^{59}G ^{60}R ^{61}R ^{62}N ^{63}I ^{64}V ^{65}I ^{66}S ^{67}R ^{68}Q ^{69}A ^{70}D ^{71}Y ^{72}C ^{73}A ^{74}A ^{75}G ^{76}A ^{77}E ^{78}E ^{79}V ^{80}A ^{81}S ^{82}L ^{83}E ^{84}V ^{85}A ^{86}L ^{87}A ^{88}L ^{89}C ^{90}A ^{91}G ^{92}G ^{93}C ^{94}E ^{95}A
Cl	^{1}V ^{2}R ^{3}S ^{4}L ^{5}N ^{6}S ^{7}I ^{8}V ^{9}A ^{10}V ^{11}C ^{12}Q ^{13}N ^{14}M ^{15}G ^{16}I ^{17}G ^{18}K ^{19}D ^{20}G ^{21}N ^{22}L ^{23}P ^{24}W ^{25}P ^{26}P ^{27}L ^{28}R ^{29}N ^{30}E ^{31}Y ^{32}K ^{33}Y ^{34}F ^{35}Q ^{36}R ^{37}M ^{38}L ^{39}P ^{40}K ^{41}P ^{42}V ^{43}I ^{44}E ^{45}G ^{46}K ^{47}Q ^{48}N ^{61}P ^{62}E ^{63}K ^{64}N ^{65}N ^{66}P ^{67}L ^{68}K ^{69}D ^{70}R ^{71}N ^{72}N ^{73}I ^{74}V ^{75}L ^{76}S ^{77}R ^{78}E ^{79}L ^{80}K ^{81}E ^{82}A ^{83}P ^{84}K ^{92}S ^{93}L ^{94}D ^{95}D ^{96}D ^{97}L ^{98}A ^{99}L ^{100}L ^{101}L ^{102}S ^{103}P ^{104}P ^{105}L ^{106}K ^{107}S ^{108}K ^{109}V ^{110}D ^{111}M ^{112}V

Ec 92M 93V 94I 95G 96G 97G 98R 99V 100Y 101E 102Q 103F 104L — — 105P 106K 107A 108Q 109K 110L 111Y 112L 113T 114H 115I 116D 117A

Lc 95V 96I 97A 98G 99G 100A 101Q 102I 103I 104T 105A 106Q 107K 108M — — 108D 109V 110V 111D 112T 113L 114L 115V 116I 117R 118L 119A 120G

Ng 96V 97I 98M 99G 100G 101A 102I 103I 104Y 105G 106Q 107A 108M — 109P 110L 111A 112T 113D 114L 115R 116I 117T 118E 119V 120D 121L

Cl 113W 114I 115V 116G 117G 118T 119A 120V 121Y 122K 123A 124A 125M 126E 127K 128P 129I 130N 131H 132R 133L 134F 135V 136T 137R 138I 139L 140H

Ec 118Q 119V 120E 121G 122D 123T 124H 125F 126P 127D 128Y 129E 130P 131D 132D 133W 134E 135S 136V 137F 138S — — — 139E

Lc 121S 122F 123E 124G 125D 126T 127K 128M 129I 130P 131L 132N 133W 134D 135D 136F 137T 138K 139V 140S 141S — — — 142R

Ng 122S 123V 124E 125G 126D 127A 128F 129F 130P 131E 132I 133D 134R 135T 136H 137W 138R 139E 140A 141E 142R 143T 144E — 145R

Cl 141E 142F 143E 144S 145D 146T 147F 148F 149P 150E 151I 152D 153Y 154K 155D 156F 157K 158L 159L 160T 161E 162Y 163P 164G 165V 166P 167A 168D

Ec 140F 141H 142D 143A 144D 145A 146Q 147N 148S 149H 150S 151Y 152C 153F 154E 155I 156L 157E 158R 159R

Lc 143T 144V 145E 146D 147T 148N 149P 150A 151L 152T 153H 154T 155Y 156E 157V 158W 159Q 160K 161K 162A

Ng 146R 147V 148S 149S 150K 151G — — 152V 153A 154Y 155F 156F 157V 158H 159Y 160L 161G 162K

Cl 169I 170Q 171E 172E 173D 174G — — 175I 176Q 177Y 178K 179F 180E 181V 182Q 183Q 184K 185S 186V 187L 188A 189Q

Ec = E. coli, Lc = L. casei, Ng = N. gonorrhoeae, Cl = Chicken Liver

A - Alanine, R - Arginine, N - Asparagine, D - Aspartic Acid, C - Cysteine, Q - Glutamine, E - Glutamic Acid, G - Glycine, H - Histidine, I - Isoleucine, L - Leucine, K - Lysine, M - Methionine, F - Phenylalanine, P - Proline, S - Serine, T - Threonine, W - Tryptophan, Y - Tyrosine, V - Valine.

Sequence alignment for the Ec, Lc, and Cl enzymes follows that of Volz et al. (1982) which was based on the corresponding three-dimensional structures. Alignment of the Ng sequence was based on maximal homology.

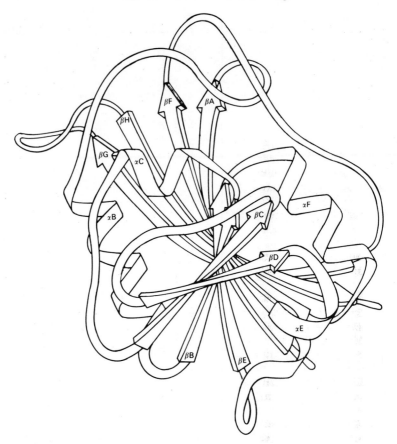

Dihydrofolate reductase

Fig. 11.1. Ribbon drawing of *L. casei* DHFR from Richardson (1981). Reproduced by permission of J. S. Richardson and Academic Press.

and they can potentially provide an unambiguous interpretation of the function of each mutated residue in the protein sequence (Villafranca *et al.* 1983; Chen *et al.* 1985).

11.4   DHFR selectivity for TMP

11.4.1   Structural basis for selectivity

Although the binding of inhibitor to enzyme is a complex process in which solvent can play an important part, inhibitor selectivity is ultimately dependent on differences in composition and geometry of the isozyme active sites. X-ray crystallography is providing an opportunity to begin to understand those

Plate 11.1   The active site region of *L. casei* DHFR in ternary complex with MTX and NADPH (Bolin *et al.* 1982). Protein and ligands are represented by non-hydrogen atoms: hydrogens are shown only for the five water molecules. Colour coding for the protein and water molecules is by atom type: C, green; H, white; N, blue; O, red. MTX and NADPH are shown in pink. Hydrogen bonds are indicated by the dotted lines and shown only for selected active-site interactions. Selected amino acid residues are labelled using the one-letter code (see Table 11.1 for key).

Plate 11.2   Comparison of the active-site regions of the *E. coli* (yellow) and chicken liver DHFR (blue). Atomic coordinates are from the respective ternary complexes with TMP (Matthews *et al.* 1985a; Champness *et al.* 1986). The two structures were superimposed by a least squares procedure (Corey and Bentley 1984) on the PROPHET computer system (Raub 1974), using only those alpha carbon pairs that were within 1.0 Å of each other after a superposition in which all possible pairs of sequence-aligned (see Table 11.1) alpha carbon pairs were used. Selected amino acid residues are labelled using the one-letter code (see Table 11.1 for key). The TMP structure has been deleted for clarity.

Plate 11.3   Binding geometry comparison of TMP (green) in ternary complex with chicken liver DHFR (blue; Matthews *et al.* 1985a) versus TMP (orange) in ternary complex with DHFR from *E. coli* (yellow; Champness *et al.* 1986). Superposition was accomplished as described in the legend of Plate 11.2. Hydrogen bonds between TMP and its binding site are indicated by dotted lines. Selected amino acid residues are labelled using the one-letter code (see Table 11.1 for key).

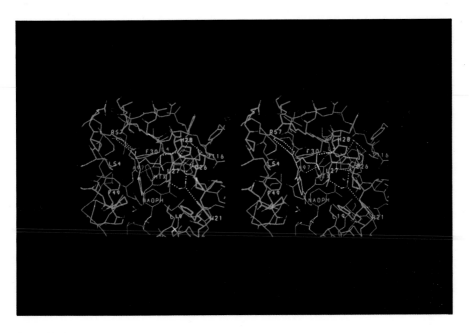

Plate 11.1

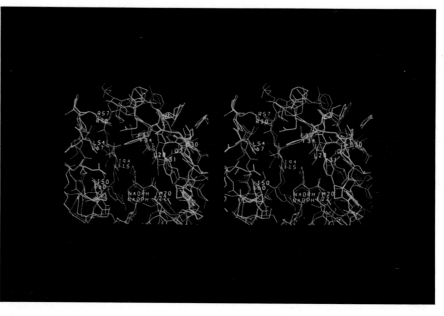

Plate 11.2

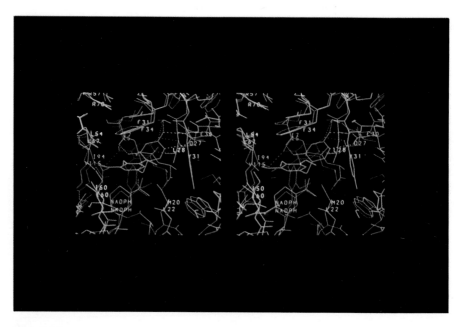

Plate 11.3

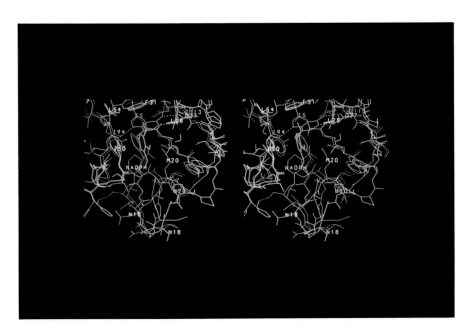

Plate 11.4

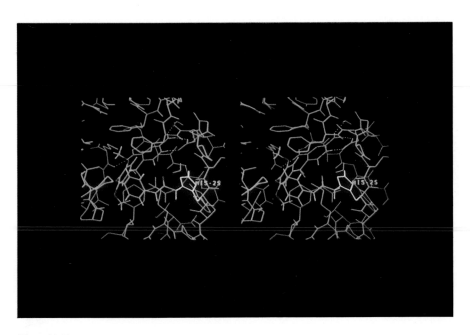

Plate 11.5

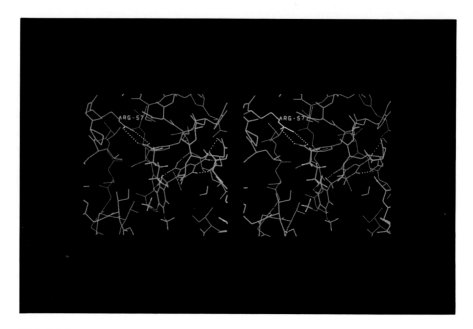

Plate 11.6

Plate 11.4 Comparison of the TMP binding sites of the *E. coli* DHFR binary (blue; Matthews *et al.* 1985a) and ternary (yellow; Champness *et al.* 1986) complexes. For clarity, only TMP from the binary complex is shown and is coloured green along with its associated hydrogen bonds. Selected amino acid residues are labelled using the one-letter code (see Table 11.1 for key).

Plate 11.5 Hypothetical model of DHFR (blue) from *N. gonorrhoeae* in covalent complex with compound **4**. Histidine-25, the site of covalent attachment, is labelled and highlighted. Compound **4** is colour-coded by atom type as described in Plate 11.1. All hydrogen atoms of compound **4** are shown, but for the protein only those hydrogens attached to heteroatoms are shown. Hydrogen bonds to the inhibitor are indicated by the dotted lines.

Plate 11.6 X-ray crystal structure of *E. coli* DHFR (blue) in complex with compound **5** (colour-coded by atom type, see Plate 11.1 for key; Kuyper *et al.* 1985). Hydrogen bonds between the inhibitor and its binding site are indicated by the dotted lines. The carboxy group of the inhibitor interacts ionically with the side chain of arginine-57 (highlighted). Protein hydrogen atoms are shown for heteroatoms only.

differences and their significance to ligand selectivity. A careful analysis by Matthews *et al.* (1985a, b) of several chicken and *E. coli* X-ray structures provides considerable insight into the structural basis for selectivity. Quantitative assessment of structural differences between these two enzymes was made by comparing calculated distances between corresponding pairs of atoms. This analysis shows that residues on opposite sides of the inhibitor binding cleft in chicken DHFR are about 1.5–2.0 Å further apart than the structurally homologous residues in the *E. coli* enzyme. A visual comparison of the chicken and *E. coli* isozyme structures is shown in Plate 11.2, where it can be seen that the distance between Leu-28 and Ile-50 in the *E. coli* enzyme is significantly less than that of the corresponding residues (Tyr-31 and Ile-60, respectively) of chicken DHFR. This relatively subtle structural difference is apparently largely responsible for the 3000-fold difference in affinity for TMP.

Residue composition of the two active sites is very similar. However, the presence of Tyr-31 in the chicken enzyme versus Leu-28 in *E. coli* DHFR is considered to be a significant difference with respect to TMP selectivity. Model-building experiments by Matthews *et al.* (1985b) suggest that because of the wider binding cleft and the presence of tyrosine at position 31, the chicken enzyme cannot favourably accommodate the trimethoxybenzyl moiety of TMP while maintaining optimal interactions with the diaminopyrimidine ring. This is in contrast to the binding to TMP of *E. coli* DHFR, in which the smaller cleft provides a very favourable binding site for the benzyl group that also allows for good positioning of the pyrimidine ring. A comparison of these two very different binding geometries is shown in Plate 11.3. In the chicken DHFR structure, the benzyl group of TMP is held in the upper part of the cleft where, presumably, hydrophobic interactions are maximized. This favourable location for the benzyl group is occupied at the expense of a less than optimal location for the pyrimidine ring. That ring is forced deeper into the cleft and can no longer donate a hydrogen bond from its 4-amino group to the carbonyl of Val-115. The overall effect is a relatively weak affinity compared to that of the *E. coli* enzyme.

11.4.2   Importance of cooperativity to selectivity

As mentioned above, the kinetic mechanism of DHFR is a random Bi–Bi reaction (Burchall 1970). The two non-competing substrates bind independently to the free enzyme, but the occupancy of one site usually alters the ligand affinity of the other (Weber 1975) and often results in a higher affinity in the ternary complex. This mutual enhancement in ligand binding is commonly called *cooperativity*. With DHFR, substrate cooperative effects are small, in the range of two-fold, for dihydrofolate and NADPH (Smith *et al.* 1979; Stone and Morrison 1982), but larger and more variable effects have been observed with inhibitors. For example, NADPH alters the binding affinity of DHFR for MTX as much as 100-fold for the L1210 enzyme (Kamen *et al.* 1983), 675-fold for the *L. casei* enzyme (Birdsall *et al.* 1980) and 6000-fold for the *S. faecium* enzyme

(Williams *et al.* 1979). It is not known if these differences in the magnitude of cooperativity reflect true enzyme variability or differences in methodology.

Cooperativity appears to be an important factor in the efficacy of TMP as an antibacterial agent. For example, Baccanari *et al.* (1982) studied the dissociation of TMP and a number of close structural analogues in binary and ternary complex with DHFR from *E. coli*, *L. casei*, and mouse lymphoma cells. Ligand affinity was assessed by a combination of techniques including enzyme inhibition assays, equilibrium constant measurements, and determinations of inhibitor k_{off} rates; the data showed that NADPH had a profound effect on the affinity of some of the enzyme–inhibitor complexes. In general, NADPH increased the inhibitor affinity of the bacterial enzymes, and this cooperative effect varied with the degree of methoxy substitution (up to 230-fold for TMP with Form 2 *E. coli* DHFR). The relative antibacterial activities of the compounds against *E. coli* varied significantly and were in direct proportion to their ternary complex affinity for *E. coli* DHFR. Markedly different results were observed with the mouse enzyme. All the diaminobenzylpyrimidines were relatively weak inhibitors, and none showed more than a five-fold cooperative effect. In separate studies, Cocco *et al.* (1983) used protein fluorescence titrations to show that the bovine liver, *S. faecium*, and *L. casei* enzymes have ratios of binary to ternary TMP dissociation constants of 17, 55, and 450, respectively. If these results are representative of other DHFR, the combination of high bacterial enzyme cooperativity and poor mammalian enzyme cooperativity helps TMP to be a potent and species-specific antibacterial agent.

The reciprocal nature of TMP–NADPH cooperativity is illustrated by comparing the k_{off} values of NADPH and TMP from binary and ternary complexes. For the *L. casei* enzyme, the k_{off} of NADPH decreases 135-fold in the presence of TMP (Birdsall *et al.* 1980), whereas the k_{off} of TMP decreases 100-fold in the presence of NADPH (Baccanari *et al.* 1982).

Combinations of enzyme kinetics, n.m.r. spectroscopy, and X-ray crystallography are being used to study cooperativity and inhibitor binding. Stopped-flow kinetics and analyses of reaction progress curves have shown that a considerable portion of the strong affinity of MTX (Williams *et al.* 1979; Blakley and Cocco 1985) and TMP (Williams *et al.* 1980) arises from isomerizations occurring after the inhibitors initially bind in the ternary complex. These transformations must alter the conformation of the enzyme, the bound ligand, or both, but the structures of the intermediate enzyme–inhibitor complexes are not known. However, since the isomerization reactions are rapid, the conformation observed by X-ray crystallography is probably the physiologically relevant one.

Some insight into the molecular basis of cooperativity has been gained from X-ray crystallographic studies. Champness *et al.* (1986) have recently reported the X-ray structure of the *E. coli* DHFR–NADPH–TMP ternary complex and have compared it to the corresponding enzyme–inhibitor binary complex. The superimposed active-site regions of those two structures are shown in Plate 11.4. The two protein structures are very similar except in the vicinity of residues 15–21. That loop of protein interacts directly with the cofactor in the ternary complex, and its conformation is apparently strongly influenced by that interaction. Inspection of the two structures suggests that binding of the inhibitor is enhanced in the ternary complex in part because of the conformational change induced by NADPH. In particular, the side chain of Met-20 is moved into direct contact with TMP. Direct contact between cofactor and inhibitor must also contribute to cooperativity. Similar proposals have been made by Matthews *et al.* (1985a) based on a hypothetical model of the *E. coli* DHFR ternary complex.

In the X-ray structure of chicken DHFR–NADPH–TMP, TMP adopts a conformation very different from that observed in the corresponding *E. coli* DHFR complex (see Plate 11.3), and Champness *et al.* (1986) suggest that the lower cooperativity observed for TMP binding to vertebrate DHFR might be due to the fewer contacts between inhibitor, enzyme, and cofactor as compared to the analogous *E. coli* complex.

11.5 Receptor-based inhibitor design

11.5.1 Irreversible inhibitors

The different chemical classes of reversible DHFR inhibitors show broad species specificity (see Roth 1983). For example, diaminobenzylpyrimidines generally have high affinity for bacterial dihydrofolate reductases and low affinity for the vertebrate enzymes, whereas the opposite is true for the diaminodihydrotriazines (Hitchings and Burchall 1966). However, affinity labels or active-site-directed irreversible inhibitors have recently demonstrated a level of DHFR specificity that is not constrained by phylogenetic boundaries. An affinity label interacts with the enzyme via a two-step process. It first reversibly binds to the catalytic site. This fixes the position of the inhibitor functional group, often in a region adjacent to the active site, where variability of amino acid residues may occur. If a reactive amino acid is within the proximity of the functional group, a covalent linkage can then result.

The bromoacetamidophenoxy analogue of TMP, compound **4** (BAPP), was designed as a potential affinity label by Roth *et al.* (1981). In a kinetic study of its inhibitory action, the enzymes from *N. gonorrhoeae*, *L. casei*, *S. faecium*, *E. coli*, SR-1 rodent lymphoma and chicken liver were all reversibly inhibited, but only the *L. casei* and gonococcal enzymes showed the additional covalent component (Tansik *et al.* 1984). Aminoacid sequence determinations of enzymes covalently linked to radio-labelled BAPP showed that the modified gonococcal protein residue is His-25 (Tansik *et al.* 1984), and the modified *L. casei* protein residue is His-22 (D. Baccanari, unpublished results). These are equivalent positions in amino acid sequence alignments of the two enzymes (see Table 11.1). The corresponding residues in the *E. coli*, *S. faecium* and vertebrate enzymes are the less reactive residues asparagine, arginine, and proline, respectively.

                        4 (BAPP)   **5**

A three-dimensional model of the *L. casei* enzyme with compound **4** covalently bound to His-22 has been derived using the X-ray crystal structure of the *L. casei* DHFR–NADPH–MTX ternary complex (Chan *et al.* 1985). Models were constructed in which compound **4** was covalently linked to either the delta or epsilon nitrogen of the three active-site histidine residues, His-18, His-22, and His-28. Energy-minimized models (see Chapter 2D) were produced from each of the initial structures using molecular mechanics procedures, and the resulting energies predicted the delta nitrogen of His-22 to be the site of covalent attachment, in agreement with the sequencing results described above. A similar model of the gonococcal enzyme, shown in Plate 11.5, was constructed by fitting the amino acid side chains of the gonococcal enzyme to the backbone conformation of the *L. casei* DHFR X-ray structure, using energy-minimization techniques. Compound **4** was modelled into this hypothetical active site in a manner similar to that described for the *L. casei* DHFR complex. Since *N. gonorrhoeae* DHFR has not yet been crystallized, this model might serve as a starting point for the design of new, high-affinity antigonococcal agents.

Additional DHFR affinity labels have been shown to interact with the chicken liver, *E. coli*, and/or *L. casei* enzymes, and in each case the residue modified agreed with predictions made from X-ray crystallographic data (Freisheim *et al.* 1983; Johanson and Henkin 1985). For example, the iodoacetyllysine analogue of MTX is a tight-binding inhibitor of the *L. casei* enzyme that can covalently interact with either of the imidazole nitrogen atoms of His-28 (Freisheim *et al.* 1983). These data suggest that the imidazole side chain of His-28 can assume at least two orientations in the enzyme–inhibitor complex. An interesting observation was made concerning the interactions of the *L. casei* and *E. coli* DHFR with a glyoxal analogue of aminopterin (Johanson and Henkin 1985). Each enzyme has an arginine residue at position 52 which, based on the X-ray crystal structure of the *E. coli* enzyme, would be predicted to be covalently modified by inhibitor. However, the X-ray crystal structure of the *L. casei* enzyme suggests a different result. In this case Arg-31, rather than Arg-52, appears to be in the better position to react with the glyoxal moiety of the inhibitor. When each nzyme was reacted with radio-labelled inhibitor, separation of their CNBr leavage products gave results that agreed with the crystallography and proved hat the functional role of invariant Arg-52 is not conserved.

1.5.2   Reversible inhibitors

Vith the accumulation of such a wealth of information regarding the structure nd function of DHFR comes the expectation of rational inhibitor design. An xample of such work has been recently reported in which analogues of TMP vere designed based on the three-dimensional structure of *E. coli* DHFR Kuyper *et al.* 1982, 1985).

Using molecular models of the enzyme a series of compounds, exemplified by ompound **5**, were devised to interact ionically with the guanidinium group of Arg-57. Affinity up to 55-fold greater than that of TMP was observed for several f these inhibitors, supporting the proposed mode of binding for this class of nhibitor. X-ray crystallographic studies of *E. coli* DHFR binary complexes with 'MP and compound **5** confirmed the predicted binding geometries and the nteraction with Arg-57. Plate 11.6 depicts the X-ray structure of compound **5**, he most active inhibitor in the series, in complex with *E. coli* DHFR and lustrates the association between the inhibitor and Arg-57 (Kuyper *et al.* 1982, 985). The design and synthesis of an inhibitor related to compound **5**, in which sulphonamide moiety serves as the acidic functionality, has also been reported Hyde *et al.* 1983). X-ray crystallographic analysis of its complex with *E. coli* DHFR shows that it too interacts with Arg-57.

In a closely analogous but independent effort to design DHFR inhibitors sing the three-dimensional enzyme structure, Kompis and Then (1984) (see also Birdsall *et al.* 1984) prepared a series of TMP analogues designed to interact onically with His-28 and Arg-57 of *L. casei* DHFR. Increased enzyme affinity of p to 1000-fold was observed for these compounds.

1.6   Tools for inhibitor design

he abundance of inhibitor binding data and structural information available or DHFR has been used in a number of ways for developing techniques f rational inhibitor design and analysis such as classical QSAR, distance eometry, and molecular graphics (see Blaney *et al.* 1984). The most obvious pproach to the design of novel inhibitors is the utilization of the three-imensional structures of the enzyme. In our experience, simple fitting of nolecular models of enzyme and hypothetical inhibitors can generate a large umber of potential synthetic targets. However, a key problem is the evaluation f those ideas so that only the best candidates are pursued at the bench. Ideally, ne would like to be able to predict quantitatively the DHFR affinity, or at least elative affinity, of any hypothetical inhibitor. Considering the complexities involved in the binding of inhibitor to enzyme in aqueous solution, this goal is not easily attainable. Computational methodology is, however, being developed toward that end.

Treatment of macromolecular systems using theoretical methods such as molecular mechanics and molecular dynamics has become increasingly practicable over the past several years. These methods, in conjunction with high-resolution crystal structures, show promise of providing the kind of quantitative insight into enzyme–inhibitor interactions that are needed for efficient inhibitor design. For example, Kuyper (1985) has used molecular mechanics to simulate the interactions involved in the binding of a series of closely related TMP analogues to *E. coli* DHFR. Differences in the calculated interaction energies for the series of enzyme–inhibitor complexes correlated well with the corresponding experimental binding constants. Complications due to the effects of solvent were apparently minimal because of the close similarity of the inhibitors. Such methodology would hopefully be useful for predicting the enzyme affinity of related but novel inhibitors. For inhibitors that differ significantly in solvent-related interactions, the work of Blaney *et al.* (1982) suggests means of estimating affinity contributions due to solvation effects.

Although much more costly in computer time, molecular dynamics techniques offer the potential of calculating differences in free energy of enzyme–inhibitor complexes in solution (Tembe and McCammon 1984; Brünger *et al.* 1985; Lybrand *et al.* 1985). With the ever-decreasing cost of computer power, these techniques will certainly become practical in the near future and will hopefully be usefully applicable to inhibitor design.

11.7   Epilogue

Dihydrofolate reductase has played a central role in a drama, still unfolding, that encompasses major discoveries in intermediary metabolism, enzymology, and chemotherapy. Figure 11.2 identifies some of the types and objectives of investigative work that have kept this performer center stage for more than four decades.

The diversity among the isofunctional enzymes from differing sources that was detected before 1950 as 'non-classical' inhibitors were discovered, was substantiated by 'inhibitor analysis'. Residual scepticism dissolved as one after another specific DHFR were purified to homogeneity and amino acid sequences were determined. To the astonishing variability among enzymes from microorganisms and the not unexpected homogeneity among those from mammalian sources, X-ray crystallography studies of enzyme–ligand complexes brought the further unforeseen finding that a wide range of basic compositions could result in very similar conformations.

As little by little the bonds of attachment of substrates and subtler details of structure have been revealed by new techniques, the opportunities for rational

EVENTS IN THE HISTORY OF DHFR

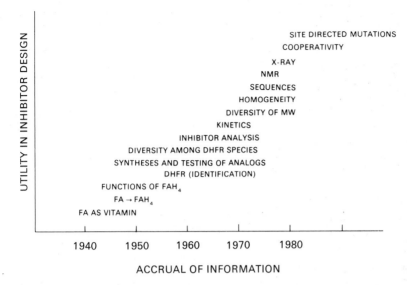

Fig. 11.2. Approaches contributing to information about the intimate structure and mechanism of action of dihydrofolate reductase. Each new probe is placed in its approximate position on a time scale. The ordinate is intended to indicate the accumulation of information and the availability of tools yielding new insights.

design of selective inhibitors have multiplied. It has been the purpose of this paper to point the way to this end primarily by precept but also by examples currently regarded as only the beginning.

Acknowledgements

Atomic coordinates of *L. casei* and chicken liver DHFR were generously provided by Drs D. Matthews and J. Kraut. The *E. coli* DHFR structures were supplied by Drs J. Champness, D. Stammers, and C. Beddell. We are indebted to J. Bentley for developing the computer program for the Evans and Sutherland PS330 graphics system that was used to display the stereo pictures shown in the colour plates of this chapter.

References

Andrews, J., Clore, G. M., Davies, R. W., Gronenborn, A. M., Gronenborn, B., Kalderon, D., Papadopoulos, P. C., Schäfer, S., Sims, P. F. G., and Stancombe, R. (1985). Nucleotide sequence of the dihydrofolate reductase gene of methotrexate-resistant *Lactobacillus casei. Gene*, **35**, 217–22.

Baccanari, D. P., Stone, D., and Kuyper, L. (1981). Effect of a single amino acid substitution on *Escherichia coli* dihydrofolate reductase catalysis and ligand binding. *J. Biol. Chem.*, **256**, 1738–47.

Baccanari, D. P., Daluge, S., and King, R. W. (1982). Inhibition of dihydrofolate reductase: effect of reduced nicotinamide adenine dinucleotide phosphate on the selectivity and affinity of diaminobenzylpyrimidines. *Biochemistry*, **21**, 5068–75.

Baccanari, D. P., Tansik, R. L., Paterson, S. J., and Stone, D. (1984). Characterization and amino acid sequence of *Neisseria gonorrhoeae* dihydrofolate reductase. *J. Biol. Chem.*, **259**, 12291–8.

Birdsall, B., Burgen, A. S. V., and Roberts, G. C. K. (1980). Binding of coenzyme analogues to *Lactobacillus casei* dihydrofolate reductase: Binary and ternary complexes. *Biochemistry*, **19**, 3723–31.

Birdsall, B., Feeney, J., Pascual, C., Roberts, G. C. K., Kompis, I., Then, R. L., Müller, K., and Kroehn, A. (1984). A ^{1}H NMR study of the interactions and conformations of rationally designed brodimoprim analogues in complexes with *Lactobacillus casei* dihydrofolate reductase. *J. Med. Chem.*, **27**, 1672–6.

Blakley, R. L. (1984). Dihydrofolate reductase. In '*Folates and pterins*' (ed. R. L. Blakley and S. J. Benkovic), Vol. 1, pp. 191–253. Wiley, New York.

Blakley, R. L. and Cocco, L. (1985). Role of isomerization of initial complexes in the binding of inhibitors to dihydrofolate reductase. *Biochemistry*, **24**, 4772–7.

Blaney, J. M., Weiner, P. K., Dearing, A., Kollman, P. A., Jorgensen, E. C., Oatley, S. J., Burridge, J. M., and Blake, C. C. F. (1982). Molecular mechanics simulation of protein–ligand interactions: binding of thyroid hormone analogues to prealbumin. *J. Am. Chem. Soc.*, **104**, 6424–34.

Blaney, J. M., Hansch, C., Silipo, C., and Vittoria, A. (1984). Structure–activity relationships of dihydrofolate reductase inhibitors. *Chem. Rev.*, **84**, 333–407.

Bolin, J. T., Filman, D. J., Matthews, D. A., Hamlin, R. C., and Kraut, J. (1982). Crystal structures of *Escherichia coli* and *Lactobacillus casei* dihydrofolate reductase refined at 1.7Å resolution. I. General features and binding of methotrexate. *J. Biol. Chem.*, **257**, 13650–62.

Brünger, A. T., Brooks, C. L. III, and Karplus, M. (1985). Active site dynamics of ribonuclease. *Proc. Nat. Acad. Sci. USA*, **82**, 8458–62.

Burchall, J. J. (1970). Purification and properties of dihydrofolate reductase from *Escherichia coli*. In *Chemistry and biology of pteridines* (ed. L. Iwai, M. Goto and K. Iwanamie) pp. 351–5, International Academic Printing, Tokyo.

Burchall, J. J. (1974). Trimethoprim and pyrimethamine. In *Antibiotics: Mechanism of action antimicrobial and antitumor agents* (ed. J. W. Corcoran and F. E. Hahn), Vol. III, pp. 304–320. Springer, New York.

Cha, S. (1975). Tight-binding inhibitors. I. Kinetic behavior. *Biochem. Pharmacol.*, **24**, 2177–85.

Champness, J. N., Stammers, D. K., and Beddell, C. R. (1986). Crystallographic investigation of the cooperative interaction between trimethoprim, reduced cofactor and dihydrofolate reductase. *FEBS Lett.*, **199**, 61–7.

Chan, J. H., Kuyper, L. F., and Roth, B. (1985). Molecular mechanics modeling of a covalent complex between *L. casei* dihydrofolate reductase and an active-site directed irreversible inhibitor: prediction of attachment site and three-dimensional structure. 189th National Meeting of the American Chemical Society, Miami Beach, FL, 28 April–3 May; see *Abstracts of papers*, MEDI 87. American Chemical Society, Washington, DC.

Charlton, P. A., Young, D. W., Birdsall, B., Fenney, J., and Roberts, G. C. K. (1985). Stereochemistry of reduction of the vitamin folic acid by dihydrofolate reductase. *J. Chem. Soc. Perkin Trans. I*, 1349–53.

Chen, J.-T., Mayer, R. J., Fierke, C. A., and Benkovic, S. J. (1985). Site-specific mutagenesis of dihydrofolate reductase from *Escherichia coli*. *J. Cell. Biochem.*, **29**, 73–82.

Cheng, Y.-C., and Prusoff, W. H. (1973). Relationship between the inhibition constant (K_i) and the concentration of inhibitor which causes 50 per cent inhibition (I_{50}) of an enzymatic reaction. *Biochem. Pharmacol.*, **22**, 3099–108.

Cocco, L., Roth, B., Temple, Jr., C., Montgomery, J. A., London, R. E., and Blakely, R. L. (1983). Protonated state of methotrexate, trimethoprim, and pyrimethamine bound to dihydrofolate reductase. *Arch. Biochem. Biophys.*, **226**, 567–77.

Cory, M., and Bentley, J. (1984). MATCHMOL, an interactive computer graphics procedure for superposition of molecular models. *J. Mol. Graphics*, **2**, 39–42.

Filman, D. J., Bolin, J. T., Matthews, D. A., and Kraut, J. (1982). Crystal structures of *Escherichia coli* and *Lactobacillus casei* dihydrofolate reductase refined at 1.7Å resolution. II. Environment of bound NADPH and implications for catalysis. *J. Biol. Chem.*, **257**, 13663–72.

Fontecilla-Camps, J. C., Bugg, C. E., Temple, Jr., C., Rose, J. D., Montgomery, J. A., and Kisliuk, R. L. (1979). Absolute configuration of biological tetrahydrofolates: a crystallographic determination. *J. Am. Chem. Soc.*, **101**, 6114–15.

Freisheim, J. H. and Matthews, D. A. (1984). The comparative biochemistry of dihydrofolate reductase. In *Folate antagonists as therapeutic agents* (ed. F. M. Sirotnak, J. J. Burchall, W. B. Ensminger, and J. A. Montgomery), Vol. 1, pp. 69–131. Academic Press, New York.

Freisheim, J. H., Susten, S. S., Delcamp, T. J., Rosowsky, A., Wright, J. E., Kempton, R. J., Blankenship, D. T., Smith, P. L., and Kumar, A. A. (1983). Structure, function and affinity labeling studies of dihydrofolate reductase. In *Chemistry and biology of pteridines* (ed. J. A. Blair), pp. 223–7. Walter de Gruyter, New York.

Hitchings, G. H. (1983). Functions of tetrahydrofolate and the role of dihydrofolate reductase in cellular metabolism. In *Inhibition of folate metabolism in chemotherapy* (ed. G. H. Hitchings), pp. 11–23. Springer, New York.

Hitchings, G. H. and Burchall, J. J. (1966). Species differences among dihydrofolate reductase. *Fed. Proc. Fed. Am. Soc. Exp. Biol.*, **25**, 881–3.

Hitchings, G. H. and Roth, B. (1980). Dihydrofolate reductase as targets for selective inhibitors. In *Enzyme inhibitors as drugs* (ed. M. Sandler), pp. 263–80. Macmillan, Basingstoke.

Hitchings, G. H., and Baccanari, D. P. (1984). Design and synthesis of folate antagonists as antimicrobial agents. In *Folate antagonists as therapeutic agents* (ed. F. M. Sirotnak, J. J. Burchall, W. B. Ensminger, and J. A. Montgomery), Vol. 1, pp. 151–72. Academic Press, New York.

Howell, E. E., Villafranca, J. E., Warren, M. S., Oatley, S. J., and Kraut, J. (1986). Functional role of aspartic acid-27 in dihydrofolate reductase revealed by mutagenesis. *Science*, **231**, 1123–8.

Hyde, R. M., Paterson, R. A., Beddell, C. R., Champness, J. N., Stammers, D. K., Baker, D. J., Goodford, P. J., Kuyper, L. F., Ferone, R., Roth, B., and Elwell, L. P. (1983). The activity of sulfonamide-substituted benzylpyrimidines against dihydropteroate synthase, dihydrofolate reductase, and bacterial cell cultures. In *Chemistry and biology of pteridines* (ed. J. A. Blair), pp. 505–9. Walter de Gruyter, New York.

Johanson, R. A., and Henkin, J. (1985). Affinity labeling of dihydrofolate reductase with an antifolate glyoxal. *J. Biol. Chem.*, **260**, 1465–74.

Kamen, B. A., Whyte-Bauer, W., and Bertino, J. R. (1983). A mechanism of resistance to methotrexate. NADPH but not NADH stimulation of methotrexate binding to dihydrofolate reductase. *Biochem. Pharmacol.*, **32**, 1837–41.

Kamen, B. A., Nylen, P. A., Whitehead, V. M., Abelson, H. T., Dolnick, B. J., and Peterson, D. W. (1985). Lack of dihydrofolate-reductase in human tumor and leukemia cells *in vivo. Cancer Drug Delivery*, **2**, 133–8.

Kompis, I. and Then, R. L. (1984). Rationally designed brodimoprim analogues: Synthesis and biological activities. *Eur. J. Med. Chem. Chim. Ther.*, **19**, 529–34.

Kuyper, L. F. (1985). Molecular mechanics modeling of dihydrofolate reductase-inhibitor complexes: Correlation between calculated energy and observed affinity, 189th National Meeting of the American Chemical Society, Miami Beach, FL, April 28–May 3; See 'Abstracts of Papers'; American Chemical Society: Washington, DC; Abstr. MEDI 88.

Kuyper, L. F., Roth, B., Baccanari, D. P., Ferone, R., Beddell, C. R., Champness, J. N., Stammers, D. K., Dann, J. G., Norrington, F.E.A., Baker, D. J., and Goodford, P. J. (1982). Receptor-based design of dihydrofolate reductase inhibitors: comparison of crystallographically determined enzyme binding with enzyme affinity in a series of carboxy-substituted trimethoprim analogues. *J. Med. Chem.*, **25**, 1120–2.

Kuyper, L. F., Roth, B., Baccanari, D. P., Ferone, R., Beddell, C. R., Champness, J. N., Stammers, D. K., Dann, J. G., Norrington, F. E. A., Baker, D. J., and Goodford, P. J. (1985). Receptor-based design of dihydrofolate reductase inhibitors: comparison of crystallograpically determined enzyme binding with enzyme affinity in a series of carboxy-substituted trimethoprim analogues. *J. Med. Chem.*, **28**, 303–11.

Lai, P.-H., Pan, Y.-C. E., Gleisner, J. M., Peterson, D. L., Williams, K. R., and Blakley, R. L. (1982). Structure of dihydrofolate reductase: primary sequence of the bovine liver enzyme. *Biochemistry*, **21**, 3284–94.

Lybrand, T. P., Ghosh, I., and McCammon, J. A. (1985). Hydration of chloride and bromide anions: determination of relative free energy by computer simulation. *J. Am. Chem. Soc.*, **107**, 7793–4.

Masters, J. N. and Attardi, G. (1983). The nucleotide sequence of the cDNA coding for the human dihydrofolic acid reductase. *Gene*, **21**, 59–63.

Matthews, D. A., Alden, R. A., Bolin, J. T., Freer, S. T., Hamlin, R., Xuong, N., Kraut, J., Poe, M., Williams, M., and Hoogsteen, K. (1977). Dihydrofolate reductase: X-ray structure of the binary complex with methotrexate. *Science*, **197**, 452–5.

Matthews, D. A., Alden, R. A., Bolin, J. T., Filman, D. J., Freer, S. T., Hamlin, R., Hol, W. G. J., Kisliuk, R. L., Pastore, E. J., Plante, L. T., Xuong, N., and Kraut, J. (1978). Dihydrofolate reductase from *Lactobacillus casei*: X-ray structure of the enzyme–methotrexate–NADPH complex. *J. Biol. Chem.*, **253**, 6946–54.

Matthews, D. A., Bolin, J. T., Burridge, J. M., Filman, D. J., Volz, K. W., Kaufman, B. T., Beddell, C. R., Champness, J. N., Stammers, D. K., and Kraut, J. (1985a). Refined crystal structures of *Escherichia coli* and chicken liver dihydrofolate reductase containing bound trimethoprim. *J. Biol. Chem.*, **260**, 381–91.

Matthews, D. A., Bolin, J. T., Burridge, J. M., Filman, D. J., Volz, K. W., and Kraut, J. (1985b). Dihydrofolate reductase. The stereochemistry of inhibitor selectivity. *J. Biol. Chem.*, **260**, 392–9.

Pastore, E. J., and Friedkin, M. (1962). The enzymatic synthesis of thymidylate. II.

Transfer of tritium from tetrahydrofolate to the methyl group of thymidylate. *J. Biol. Chem.*, **237**, 3802–10.

Perkins, J. P. and Bertino, J. R. (1966). Dihydrofolate reductase from the L1210R murine lymphoma: fluorometric measurements of the enzyme with coenzymes, substrates and inhibitors. *Biochemistry*, **5**, 1005–12.

Raub, W. F. (1974). The PROPHET system and resource sharing. *Fed. Proc. Fed. Am. Soc. Exp. Biol.*, **33**, 2390–2.

Richardson, J. S. (1981). The anatomy and taxonomy of protein structure. *Adv. Protein Chem.*, **34**, 167–339.

Roberts, G. C. K., Feeney, J., Burgen, A. S. V., Yuferov, V., Dann, J. G., and Bjur, R. (1974). Nuclear magnetic resonance studies of the binding of substrate analogs and coenzyme to dihydrofolate reductase from *Lactobacillus casei*. *Biochemistry*, **13**, 5351–7.

Roth, B. (1983). Selective inhibitors of bacterial dihydrofolate reductase: structure–activity relationships. In *Handbook of experimental pharmacology* (ed. G. H. Hitchings), Vol. 64, pp. 107–27. Springer, New York.

Roth, B., Aig, E., Rauckman, B. S., Strelitz, J. Z., Phillips, A. P., Ferone, R., Bushby, S. R. M., and Sigel, C. W. (1981). 2,4-diamino-5-benzylpyrimidines and analogues as antibacterial agents. 5.3′,5′-dimethoxy-4′-substituted-benzyl analogues of trimethoprim. *J. Med. Chem.*, **24**, 933–41.

Smith, D. R. and Calvo, J. M. (1980). Nucleotide sequence of the *E. coli* gene coding for dihydrofolate reductase. *Nucleic Acids Res.*, **8**, 2255–74.

Smith, S. L., Patrick, P., Stone, D., Phillips, A. W., and Burchall, J. J. (1979). Porcine liver dihydrofolate reductase: Purification, properties and amino acid sequence. *J. Biol. Chem.*, **254**, 11475–484.

Spector, T. and Cleland, W. W. (1981). Meanings of K_i for conventional and alternate-substrate inhibitors. *Biochem. Pharmacol.* **30**, 1–7.

Stammers, D. K., Champness, J. N., Dann, J. G., and Beddell, C. R. (1983). The three-dimensional structure of mouse L1210 dihydrofolate reductase. In *Chemistry and biology of pteridines* (ed. J. A. Blair), pp. 567–71. Walter de Gruyter, New York.

Stone, S. R. and Morrison, J. F. (1982). Kinetic mechanism of the reaction catalyzed by dihydrofolate reductase from *Escherichia coli*. *Biochemistry*, **21**, 3757–65.

Stone, S. R., and Morrison, J. F. (1983). The pH-dependence of the binding of dihydrofolate and substrate analogues to dihydrofolate reductase from *Escherichia coli*. *Biochim. Biophys. Acta*, **745**, 247–58.

Stone, S. R., and Morrison, J. F. (1984). Catalytic mechanism of the dihydrofolate reductase reaction as determined by pH studies. *Biochemistry*, **23**, 2753–8.

Tansik, R. L., Averett, D. R., Roth, B., Paterson, S. J., Stone, D., and Baccanari, D. P. (1984). Species-specific irreversible inhibition of *Neisseria gonorrhoeae* dihydrofolate reductase by a substituted 2,4-diamino-5-benzylpyrimidine. *J. Biol. Chem.*, **259**, 12299–305.

Tembe, B. L., and McCammon, J. A. (1984). Ligand–receptor interaction. *Comput. Chem.*, **8**, 281–5.

Villafranca, J. E., Howell, E. E., Voet, D. H., Strobel, M. S., Ogden, R. C., Abelson, J. N., and Kraut, J. (1983). Directed mutagenesis of dihydrofolate reductase. *Science*, **222**, 782–8.

Volz, K. W., Matthews, D. A., Alden, R. A., Freer, S. T., Hansch, C., Kaufman, B. T., and

Kraut, J. (1982). Crystal structure of avian dihydrofolate reductase containing phenyl-triazine and NADPH. *J. Biol. Chem.*, **257**, 2528–36.

Weber, G. (1975). Energetics of ligand binding to proteins. *Adv. Protein Chem.*, **24**, 1–83.

Williams, J. W., and Morrison, J. F. (1979). The kinetics of reversible tight-binding inhibition. *Meth. Enzymol.*, **63**, 437–67.

Williams, J. W., Morrison, J. F. , and Duggleby, R. C. (1979). Methotrexate, a high-affinity pseudosubstrate of dihydrofolate reductase. *Biochemistry*, **18**, 2567–73.

Williams, J. W., Duggleby, R. G., Cutler, R. and Morrison, J. F. (1980). The inhibition of dihydrofolate reductase by folate analogues: structural requirements for slow- and tight-binding inhibition. *Biochem. Pharmacol.*, **29**, 589–95.

12

The antibacterial sulphonamides

L. O. White and D. S. Reeves

12.1 Historical background

At the turn of the century, Paul Ehrlich, impressed by the specificity of antibodies and their ability to fix to parasites, or 'seek them out like magic bullets' and not to attach themselves to host tissues, turned his attention to the idea of looking for chemical 'magic bullets' (Ehrlich 1909). He was particularly interested in dyes because of their ability to stain different cell types selectively, and put forward the idea of their binding to specific chemoreceptors. In the search for magic bullets he formulated two important concepts:

(1) the need to synthesize and test numerous chemical derivatives of a parent compound;

(2) the need to test a compound's ability to cure experimental infections rather than its power merely to kill microorganisms *in vitro*.

Ehrlich showed clearly that compounds may be inactive *in vitro* but active *in vivo*. For example, an 8 per cent solution of arsanilic acid (atoxyl) did not kill trypanosomes *in vitro* but did cure trypanosomal infections in mice because it was metabolized to a dimer at least 100 000 times more active. In addition, because mice varied in their ability to metabolize atoxyl, Ehrlich was able to

363

demonstrate that the dimer was considerably more toxic to mice than the parent compound (Ehrlich 1909). A derivative of atoxyl (compound 606) was later found to be extremely active against *Treponema pallidum*; it revolutionized the treatment of syphilis, and was named Salvarsan.

None of Ehrlich's compounds were of value in treating bacterial infections, but his ideas paved the way for the discovery and development of the first really effective specific antibacterial chemotherapeutic agents, the sulphonamides.

12.1.1   Prontosil and sulphanilamide

Domagk (1935) tested a number of azo dye compounds against *Streptococci* both *in vitro* and in a mouse model. Sulphachrysoidine [prontosil red, Fig. 12.1(a)], inactive *in vitro*, was extremely effective in the treatment of streptococcal infection in mice. It was also relatively non-toxic to mice. The compound could be administered orally or subcutaneously and when tested clinically was found to be effective against life-threatening streptococcal infections in humans (Klee and Römer 1935; Schreus 1935). Domagk's daughter was possibly the first person to be saved from death by prontosil when she developed streptococcal septicaemia from a wound in the hand caused by a knitting needle.

(a) prontosil red H_2NO_2S—⟨ ⟩—$N{=}N$—⟨ ⟩—NH_2
                                                    |
                                                  NH_2

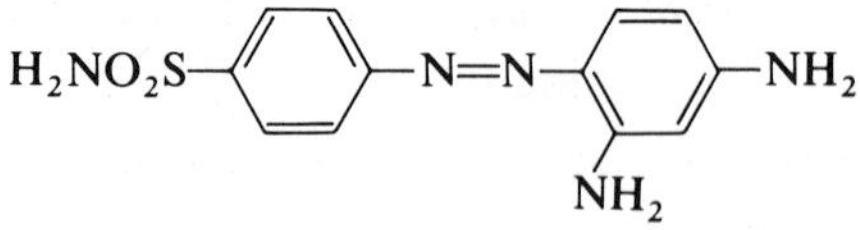

(b) sulphanilamide H_2NO_2S—⟨ ⟩—NH_2

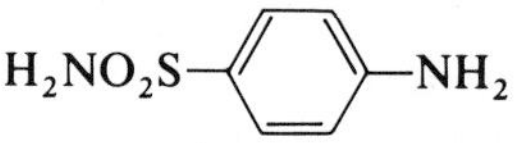

(c) *para*-amino benzoic acid $HOOC$—⟨ ⟩—NH_2

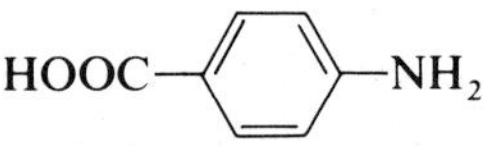

Fig. 12.1.

Prontosil thus revolutionized the treatment of a bacterial infection with an otherwise very high mortality rate. Its fame was however short-lived;Tréfouël *et al.* (1935) soon demonstrated that prontosil is metabolized and that the active antibacterial compound is sulphanilamide [Fig. 12.1(b)]. This discovery led to the synthesis and testing of numerous sulphonamide derivatives by the pharmaceutical industry for two reasons:

1. Unlike prontosil red, sulphanilamide had been known for many years and was not under patent. Thus virtually anyone could market it.

2. Sulphanilamide is the colourless part of the prontosil red molecule, suggesting that the testing of dye derivatives for antibacterial properties should now be extended to colourless sulphonamides.

One of the earliest post-sulphanilamide sulphonamides to be marketed was sulphapyridine (M & B 693). This achieved great clinical success against a number of bacterial infections, notably pneumococcal pneumonia, but was soon superseded by other derivatives with greater potency and reduced toxicity.

12.2 The sulphonamides

The major antibacterial sulphonamide derivatives for human clinical use are listed in Table 12.1. These are all compounds substituted in the N^1 position and almost all substituents are heterocyclic. An unsubstituted *p*-amino group is essential for antibacterial activity. N^4-substituted derivatives are only active if the *p*-amino group is obtainable by hydrolysis. Changes or substitutions in the benzene ring cause loss or reduction of activity (Seydel 1968). Apart from being more active than sulphanilamide, the compounds in Table 12.1 differ little between themselves with regard to antibacterial activity, and the chemical modifications to the SO_2NH_2 group essentially produced improvements in toxicity and solubility, and changes in pharmacokinetics and metabolism.

12.2.1 The antibacterial activity of sulphonamides

The *p*-amino group confers antibacterial activity to sulphonamide derivatives. Potency of antibacterial agents is normally measured *in vitro* by seeding a series of tubes or plates of nutrient medium with increasing concentrations of the drug, inoculating each with the organism under test, and then determining the lowest concentration of drug which prevents the growth of the organism. This is referred to as the MIC (minimum inhibitory concentration). Testing the sensitivity of bacteria to sulphonamides can be very misleading because the results are dramatically affected by medium composition and the initial density of bacteria (inoculum size) (Waterworth 1978). These problems may explain why the antibacterial properties of sulphanilamide were never appreciated until it was found to be a metabolite of prontosil red. By careful standardization of conditions, the *in vitro* activity of sulphonamides can be compared (Niepp 1964; Garrod *et al.* 1973). In general, all sulphonamides are broad-spectrum agents, acting against a number of gram negative and gram positive pathogens. These include most streptococci, pneumococci, staphylococci, *Clostridium welchii*, meningococci, gonococci, *Haemophilus*, *Bordatella*, and several members of the Enterobacteriaceae. Notable exceptions are *Streptococcus faecalis*, *Pseudomonas*, and *Mycobacterium tuberculosis*, which are resistant. Garrod *et al.* (1973) concluded that sulphacetamide and sulphadimidine had relatively low activity and sulphadiazine, sulphafurazole, and sulphamethoxazole were the most active. *In vitro* activity does not, however, necessarily correlate well with efficacy *in vivo* (Niepp 1964). *In vitro* activity may correlate with lipid solubility and pK_a (Struller 1968).

Table 12.1   Some clinically important sulphonamides, in chronological order

$$R—NHSO_2 \underset{1}{} \text{⟨ring⟩} \underset{4}{}—NH_2$$

Name	R	Half-life (h)	N^4 acetylation (per cent)	Hydroxylation (per cent)
Sulphanilamide	H	?	20	—
Sulphacetamide		12	?	—
Sulphathiazole		4	10	—
Sulphadiazine		17	25	20
Sulphadimidine		7	80	—
Sulphacarbamide	$-\overset{\text{O}}{\underset{}{\text{C}}}-NH_2$	2	?	?
Sulphamethisole		2.5	5	—
Sulphamethoxypyridazine		37	15	—
Sulphadimethoxine		40	10	75
Sulphamethoxazole		11	50	30

Table 12.1 Some clinically important sulphonamides, in chronological order

Name	R	Half-life (h)	N^4 acetylation (per cent)	Hydroxylation (per cent)
Sulphametopyrazine	OCH$_3$ (ring structure)	65	—	—
Sulphadoxine	OCH$_3$ OCH$_3$ (ring structure)	150	5	—

12.2.2 Sulphonamide–trimethoprim synergy

Co-trimoxazole is a combination of sulphamethoxazole with trimethoprim, a folate antagonist. It is claimed that this combination acts synergistically against many pathogens, although this claim has been disputed (Lacey 1979). The supposed mode of action of this synergism is discussed later. A large proportion of the sulphonamide prescribed today in the developed countries is as co-trimoxazole or similar sulphonamide/trimethoprim combinations.

12.2.3 Solubility

A big problem with early sulphonamides was poor solubility in water and acid urine of both parent drug and possible metabolites. Crystallization of sulphon-amides in the renal tubules (crystalluria) is a potential complication of therapy which may cause pain, haematuria, and even stop urine production. Patients should maintain a high fluid intake and take sodium bicarbonate or sodium citrate to keep the urine alkaline. Relatively more soluble derivatives, for example sulphafurazole and sulphamethisazole, are now available. An alterna-tive approach was the use of triple sulphonamide mixtures, such as sulphadia-zine plus sulphamerazine and either sulphathiazole (Lehr 1948) or sulphadimi-dine (Yow 1955), based on the fact that the solubility of one sulphonamide is not affected by the presence of the other two but the antibacterial effect is additive.

12.2.4 Pharmacokinetics

Sulphonamides are usually administered orally, are well absorbed, and reach peak blood concentrations within 2–4 h. Parenteral versions of some com-pounds (usually as the sodium salt) such as sulphadiazine sulphadimidine, and sulphamethoxazole (in co-trimoxazole) are available. Sulphonamides are bound to serum proteins to a greater or lesser extent, the longer-acting derivatives usually being more protein bound, although there is no fixed correlation between protein binding and serum half-life (Rieder 1963). There is a correlation between protein binding and molecular weight (Struller 1968). Drugs such as phenylbutazone and ethyldicoumarol can displace sulphonamides from binding sites. Alternatively sulphonamides can displace bilirubin (see below under 'toxicity').

The serum half-life of different sulphonamide derivatives varies tremendously (Table 12.1) and derivatives are often classified as short, medium, long, or very long-acting. The view that early sulphonamides were short-acting and later derivatives were long-acting is not accurate; sulphadiazine and sulphamerazine, both early compounds, have respective half-lives of 17 and 24 h. The effect of this was not appreciated when these drugs were introduced and overdosage, resulting in accumulation and toxic effects, was common (Domagk 1957). The half-life of a sulphonamide depends on rate of excretion and metabolism and whether reabsorption occurs. A long half-life is related to the presence of methoxy groups; replacement of the methyl groups of sulphadimidine (Table 12.1) with methoxy groups to give 2-sulphanilamido-4,6-dimethoxy pyrimidine increases the half life over five-fold; the replacement of the methoxy groups of sulphadimethoxime with methyl groups to give sulphisomidine reduces the half life over five-fold (Struller 1968). No short-acting derivatives in clinical usage contain methoxy groups. Sulphonamides are almost entirely excreted by the kidneys, partly by glomerular filtration and partly by tubular secretion; the extent of these processes varies with the sulphonamide. There is also some tubular reabsorption (varies with derivative). There is, consequently, a risk of drug accumulation in patients with impaired renal function.

Almost all sulphonamides are metabolized (reviewed by Vree and Hekster 1985; see Table 12.1.) N-acetyltransferases may acetylate at the N^4 position. Most are acetylated to a fixed extent. For some, however, urinary pH is important; for example, sulphamethoxazole is excreted more rapidly in alkaline urine and is therefore less extensively acetylated (Vree et al. 1979). Other sulphonamides (e.g. sulphadiazine, sulphamerazine, sulphadimidine) show a bimodal distribution of acetylation because of different acetylator phenotypes; fast acetylators may possess a second enzyme, which will only acetylate these derivatives (Vree et al. 1983b; Weber et al. 1968). Trends in the degree of acetylation can be correlated with the composition of the N^1 constituent (Vree et al. 1983b). Desacetylation may also occur. In patients with no renal function, sulphonamides like sulphamethoxazole or sulphametrole, which produce acetyl metabolites, show a rapid decline in serum concentration followed by a less rapid decline, which parallels a decline in the acetyl metabolite concentration. The 'parent' drug in this second phase is produced by deacetylation of the acetyl metabolite (Vree et al. 1983a). The best sulphonamide for use in renal failure is probably one which is acetylated/deacetylated to a very small degree, e.g. sulphamethisole.

Sulphonamides may also be hydroxylated, deaminated, sulphonated, and conjugated with glucuronic acid to a greater or lesser degree. Dihydropteroate metabolites produced by the conjugation of a sulphonamide and pteridine by dihydropteroate synthetase have also been reported and will be discussed below (Section 12.2.5).

12.2.5 Mode of action

Although initially nothing was known of the mode of action of sulphanilamide, it soon became apparent that sulphonamides were not general cell poisons. They were essentially bacteriostatic rather than bacteriocidal in that they prevented bacterial growth as opposed to killing the bacteria. When sulphonamide was added to a medium in which bacteria were growing, there was a delay of a few generations before growth stopped, this delay being longer in complex media than in simple media. A low molecular weight extract of bacterial cells was found to inhibit sulphonamide activity (Stamp 1939; Green 1940), and sulphonamides were relatively ineffective clinically in purulent open wounds, suggesting their inactivation or inhibition (see Woods 1962). Consequently, the idea that sulphonamides might act by interfering with the activity of some essential bacterial metabolite, vitamin, or growth factor was investigated.

In 1939 at the Middlesex Hospital, Woods began to purify the anti-sulphonamide factor from yeast extract. A bioassay was used; dilutions of extract or purified fractions were added to a minimal growth medium inoculated with *Streptococcus haemolyticus*, which contained enough sulphanilamide (M/3000) to inhibit the organisms' growth. Chemical tests on the partially purified factor that overcame the sulphonamide inhibition in this bioassay suggested that it contained an aromatic nucleus, an amino group and an acidic (possibly carboxylic acid) group. The kinetics of inhibition suggested that it was competitive and that one molecule of antagonist would inhibit many molecules of sulphanilamide. Woods (1940) considered that sulphanilamide and the antagonist were probably chemically similar and, since it was commercially available, tested *para*-aminobenzoic acid (*p*AB) [Fig. 12.1(c)] in his bioassay. At the time *p*AB had no known biological function but it proved to be highly active. A concentration of $1.2–5.8 \times 10^{-8}$ M *p*AB would antagonize 3.03×10^{-4} M sulphanilamide. Sulphapyridine, approximately five times as antibacterially active as sulphanilamide, required five times as much *p*AB for complete antagonism. Other compounds, including the isomers *o*AB and *m*AB, were inactive. Novocaine (a diethylamino ethyl ester of *p*AB) was active after a short delay and was presumably hydrolysed to *p*AB.

At this time, the role of *p*AB in metabolism was not known. Once it became established that, (a) folic acid and related compounds were essential growth factors for many organisms including bacteria (Angier *et al.* 1946), (b) *p*AB formed part of the folate molecule (Stokstad *et al.* 1948), (c) sulphonamides inhibited *in vivo* synthesis of compounds with folate activity and that *p*AB competitively interfered with this (Nimmo-Smith *et al.* 1948; Lascelles and Woods 1952, 1954), and (d) folate-requiring organisms are resistant to sulphon-amides (Lampen and Jones 1946, 1947; Lascelles *et al.* 1954), it seemed likely that sulphonamides inhibited bacterial growth by inhibiting the synthesis of folic acid from *p*AB and a precursor (see Fig. 12.2).

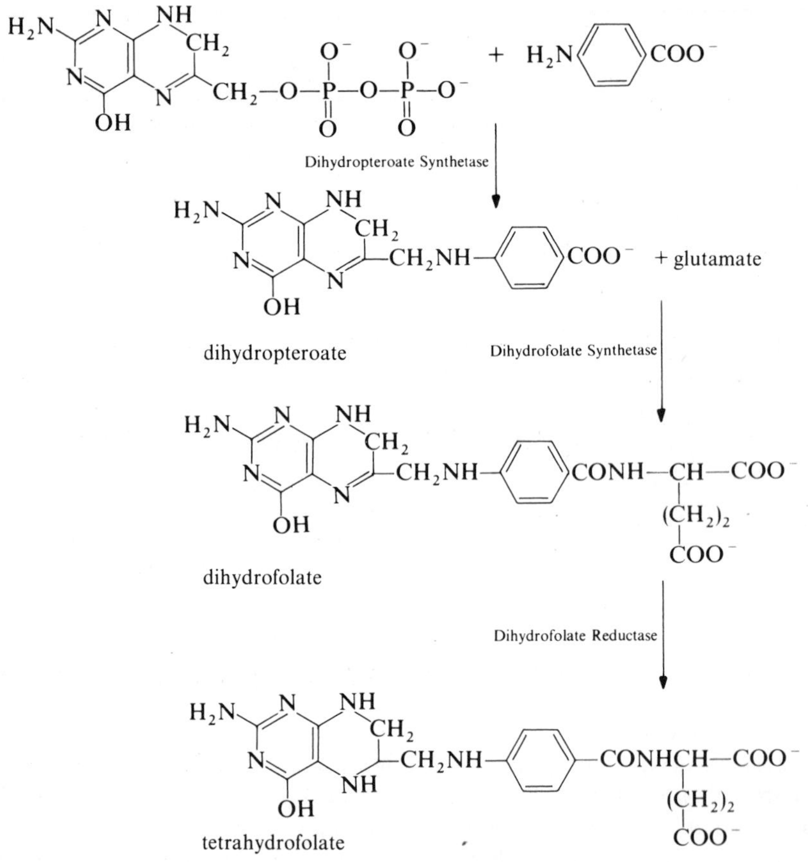

Fig. 12.2.

Brown *et al.* (1961) demonstrated that cell-free extracts of *E. coli* contained an enzyme requiring ATP and magnesium that synthesized dihydropteroate from *p*AB and hydroxymethyldihydropteridine, and that the dihydropteroate would combine with glutamate to give dihydrofolate. A similar enzyme pathway was found in *Lactobacillus arabinosus* (Shiota 1959). Sulphonamides inhibited the enzyme system to a greater or lesser degree (Table 12.2). The inhibition was

Table 12.2

	Enzyme inhibition[a]	Growth inhibition[a]
Sulphanilamide	20.0	21 500
Sulphapyridine (M & B 693)	3.8	1 400
Sulphacetamide	7.0	2 900
Sulphathiazole	0.7	250
Sulphadiazine	1.9	270
Sulphabenzamide	0.9	1 100
Sulphaguanidine	5.0	16 300
Sulphanilic acid	2.5	NONE

[a] Ratio of sulphonamide to *p*AB to achieve 50 per cent inhibition of enzyme activity or growth (from Brown 1962).

partly competitive and partly *p*AB-irreversible, the sulphonamide acting as a substrate and thus depleting the pteridine precursor by forming a sulphonamide–pteroate product (Brown 1962).

Bock *et al.* (1974) demonstrated that growing *E. coli* synthesized the same sulphonamide–pteroate analogue, N^4(7,8 dihydro-6-pterinylmethyl) sulphamethoxazole (Figure 12.3), from ^{35}S-sulphamethoxazole, as did the cell-free enzyme system using 7,8 dihydro-6-hydroxymethylpterin as a substrate.

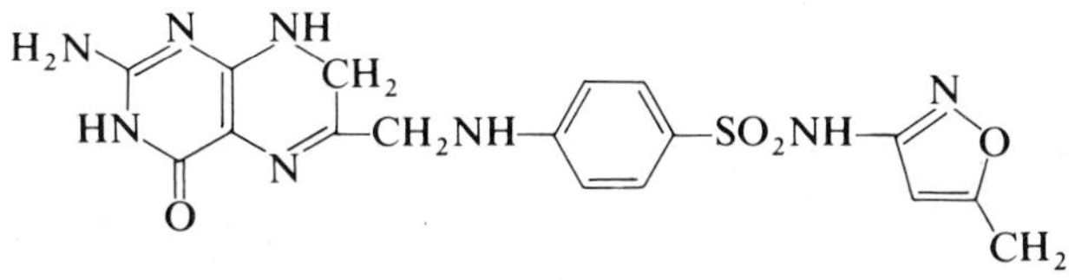

Fig. 12.3. N^4 (7,8 dihydro-6-pterinylmethyl) sulphamethoxazole.

Sulphonamide–pterin metabolites are not themselves antibacterial (Roland *et al.* 1979) but inhibit dihydropteroate synthetase and other enzymes in the tetrahydrofolate pathway but not dihydrofolate reductase.

A sulphonamide's ability to inhibit growth does not always correlate well with its ability to inhibit dihydropteroate synthesis (Table 12.2). Sulphanilic acid for example inhibits the enzyme but has no growth-inhibiting activity. This discrepancy is presumed to be due to differences in cell uptake (Brown 1962). Most clinically-important sulphonamide derivatives are considerably more active enzyme inhibitors than sulphanilamide. This is because the introduction of weakly basic groups into SO_2NH_2 makes it, on the basis of ionization and dissociation properties, more like the COOH group of *p*AB (Bell and Roblin 1942).

Richey and Brown (1969) purified the *E. coli* enzyme system and showed that it comprised:

(1) a 2-amino-4-hydroxy-6-hydroxymethyl dihydropteridine pyrophosphokinase (EC 2.7.6.3) requiring magnesium and ATP, which formed a pteridine pyrophosphate; and

(2) a dihydropteroate synthetase (EC 2.5.1.15), which formed dihydropteroate from *p*AB and the pteridine pyrophosphate.

The system required magnesium, had a K_m for *p*AB of 2.5×10^{-6} M, and a molecular weight of approximately 50 000. Roland *et al.* (1979) found that the K_m values for *p*AB and some sulphonamides for dihydropteroate synthetase were similar to their K_i values, a property typical of competitive inhibitors, which are alternative substrates.

12.2.6 Basis of selective toxicity

Sulphonamides restrict bacterial growth by inhibiting dihydropteroate synthetase, an enzyme not present in humans, who require pre-formed folate in their diet. Most bacteria are impermeable to folate and must synthesize it. This is the basis of the selective toxicity of sulphonamides.

At the time of the discovery of prontosil and sulphanilamide, their action as inhibitors of a mammalian enzyme, carbonic anhydrase, was unknown (Mann and Keilin 1940). Thus, sulphanilamide inhibits at least two unrelated enzymes, one bacterial and one mammalian. The reason why it retains its 'selective toxicity' (but see below, sulphonamide toxicity) is that over 99 per cent of carbonic anhydrase activity must be inhibited to obtain a physiological response (Maren 1984) and normal doses of sulphanilamide fail to achieve this effect. Thus, sulphanilamide gave birth to two families of sulphonamide derivatives, antibacterial agents with substituted SO_2NH_2 groups and an unsubstituted *para*-NH_2 group, and carbonic anhydrase inhibitors characterized by their requirement for an unsubstituted SO_2NH_2 group (Maren 1984; see also Chapter 20). Interestingly, prontosil is now used as a specific stain for isoenzymes of carbonic anhydrase (Siffert *et al.* 1983), teaching us that 'magic bullets' do not necessarily hit the expected target.

12.2.7 Synergy between sulphonamides and trimethoprim

Trimethoprim is an inhibitor of dihydrofolate reductase (EC 1.5.1.3) an enzyme in the pathway synthesizing tetrahydrofolate, like dihydropteroate synthetase (Fig. 12.2). Both mamalian and bacterial cells possess this enzyme but trimethoprim is 80 000 times more active against the bacterial version (Buchall 1979) and this is the basis of its selective toxicity (see Chapter 11). *In vitro* tests show that a combination of trimethoprim and sulphonamide is synergistic against many bacteria, i.e. the combination is much more antibacterial than either drug alone

(Bushby 1973). This synergy is ascribed to sequential blocking of the same pathway or consideration of the reactions as cyclic rather than linear (Buchall 1979). Evidence that sulphonamides can also inhibit dihydrofolate reductase has been put forward (Poe 1976); however, the exact nature of the synergy may be very complex. Sulphonamide inhibition of dihydropteroate synthetase is both competitive and irreversible, as the enzyme both exhibits product inhibition and sulphonamide–pteridine metabolites inhibit it and later enzymes in the pathway (Roland et al. 1979).

12.2.8 Sulphonamide resistance

Soon after the sulphonamides were introduced, resistant forms of *Neisseria gonorrhoeae* appeared and now resistant strains of all normally-sensitive pathogens occur (Garrod et al. 1973). The incidence varies from 20 to 40 per cent or more, depending on the species (Hamilton-Miller 1979). In our hospital (Southmead, Bristol), 33 per cent of urinary and 23 per cent of systemic coliforms isolated in 1985 were resistant (unpublished data).

Genes encoding antibiotic resistance can either be chromosomal or located on transmissible DNA plasmids. Some plasmids may carry resistance to several different antibiotics (Foster 1983). Some sulphonamide resistance genes are located within transposons, units of DNA that can transfer between plasmids and between plasmid and chromosome with little regard for sequence homology (Jacoby 1985). Plasmid-mediated resistance can rapidly spread to new bacterial hosts and most clinically significant antibiotic resistance is plasmid-mediated.

Some sulphonamide-resistant bacteria appear less permeable to the drug (Akiba and Yokota 1962; Wise and Abou-Donia 1975; Nagate et al. 1978), but whether this finding is a significant contribution to resistance is doubtful (Wise and Abou-Donia 1975; Smith and Amyes 1984). Mutation to thymine auxotrophy creates sulphonamide resistance, since thymine synthesis is a major task of tetrahydrofolate metabolism. Although infections with such mutants have been documented, this form of resistance probably has little clinical significance (Then 1982).

The most common resistance mechanisms involve alteration in the sulphonamide sensitivity of an organism's dihydropteroate synthetase. Laboratory-induced mutants of *Streptococcus pneumoniae* produce an altered synthetase with a greatly increased K_i for sulphonamide but with only a slightly altered K_m for pAB (Ortiz 1970; Wolf and Hotchkiss, 1963). Ho et al. (1974) obtained similar results with naturally occurring resistant mutants of *N. gonorrhoeae* and *N. meningitidis*; these showed a direct relationship between the MIC and the K_i/K_m ratio. Plasmid-encoded resistance in *E. coli* has been shown to be mediated by at least two synthetase enzymes distinct from the chromosomal enzyme (Svedberg and Skold 1980; Foster 1983). Type I enzyme is very thermolabile and is encoded by such plasmids as R1, R6, and R388. Type II enzyme is thermostable and is found on small non-conjugative plasmids such as RSF 1010 and pJPl.

Both enzymes are smaller than the chromosomal enzyme (M_r 40 000) and have an approximately 10 000-fold lower affinity for sulphonamide. Interestingly, earlier failure to detect new enzyme in some cases of plasmid-mediated resistance (Nagate et al. 1978) could be due to there being only small amounts of labile type I enzyme present. The enzyme on R388 could only be demonstrated after cloning to produce gene amplification. Types I and II are genetically distinct from the chromosomal enzyme and from one another. Only 10–50 per cent of the enzyme activity in plasmid-carrying bacteria is resistant to sulphonamide; the chromosomal enzyme is presumably still actively depleting the precursor pool and inactivating sulphonamide by synthesizing sulphonamide–pteroate metabolites. It is believed that types I and II are produced constitutively and that II could be regulated by catabolite repression, but this has not been investigated (Foster 1983).

12.2.9 Toxicity

Compared with most other currently available antibacterial drugs, the sulphonamides show a high incidence of side-effects. Early experiences were reviewed by Lane et al. (1953) and Weinstein et al. (1960), and the more recent situation is summarized by Garrod et al. (1981) and Hughes (1986). Although numerous side-effects have been documented, the most serious arise from poor solubility, hypersensitivity reactions, and idiosyncratic effects.

Poor solubility was a problem with the early compounds but, as mentioned above, has been circumvented by the use of triple sulphonamide mixtures. Hypersensitivity reactions, caused by the serum protein-conjugated sulphonamide acting as a hapten, are common. The incidence of adverse reactions with some topical preparations was so high that they are no longer used. Eosinophilia, rash, and drug fever occurred in about 3 per cent of patients treated with sulphisoxazole or sulphamethoxazole, and more serious reactions such as hepatic necrosis, vasculitis, agranulocytosis, thrombocytopenia, and Stevens–Johnson syndrome have been reported. Stevens–Johnson syndrome (a potentially fatal condition of fever, malaise, and severe erythema multiforme) has been particularly associated with long-acting derivatives, such as sulphamethoxypyridazine (O'Carroll et al. 1966).

Neutropenia is commonly associated with sulphonamide therapy. Transient neutropenia in children treated with co-trimoxazole for minor infections, such as of the urinary tract or otitis media, may be as high as 35 per cent (Hughes 1986). Also of interest is the unexplained observation that side-effects of co-trimoxazole are much more common in AIDS patients than in others (Hughes 1986). The reason for this is not known. However, there is very recent evidence that the lymphocytes of patients who show adverse reactions to sulphonamides are more susceptible to the effects of some (unidentified) cytotoxic metabolite (Lancet Editorial 1986). It is generally considered that the side-effects of co-trimoxazole therapy are attributable to sulphamethoxazole rather than trimethoprim and, although this is not proven (Ball 1986), there is now considerable movement towards replacing co-trimoxazole with trimethoprim alone for many indications (Reeves 1982). Idiosyncratic haemolytic anaemia, associated with sulphonamide oxidation of haemoglobin to methaemoglobin, is a recognized complication of low incidence, more common in patient groups with inherited glucose-6-phosphate dehydrogenase deficiency, such as negroes.

As mentioned earlier, sulphonamides can displace bilirubin from plasma protein binding sites. For this reason, it is contra-indicated in late pregnancy since elevated tissue levels of foetal bilirubin can result and give rise to kernicterus.

Some toxic manifestations of sulphonamides have had interesting and useful repercussions. Sulphanilamide-induced metabolic acidosis helped lead to the drug's recognition as a carbonic anhydrase inhibitor. Hypoglycaemia induced by sulphonamide derivatives led to the development of sulphonylurea antidiabetic agents and sulphaguanidine-induced goitre in rats led to the development of thiouracil and related antithyroid drugs.

12.3   Concluding remarks

The antibacterial sulphonamides revolutionized the treatment of life-threatening bacterial infections. They have now been with us for 50 years. They have been shown to act by specifically inhibiting a bacterial enzyme, dihydropteroate synthetase. The sulphonamide story teaches us several lessons about specific enzyme inhibitors as drugs. First, the breakthrough compound, prontosil red, proved to be an inactive pro-drug. Its active metabolite, sulphanilamide, was a double-ended 'magic bullet', inhibiting both bacterial dehydropteroate synthetase and mammalian carbonic anhydrase. The numerous antibacterial derivatives of sulphanilamide were more active enzyme inhibitors, showing improved pharmacokinetics and solubility, and improved resistance to metabolic inactivation or toxicity. Bacteria soon became resistant to the action of sulphonamides by either chromosomal mutation or the acquisition of a second sulphonamide-resistant dihydropteroate synthetase. The toxicity problem with sulphonamides has never been overcome, idiosyncratic and hypersensitivity reactions being associated with all their derivatives.

References

Akiba, T. and Yokota, T. (1962). Studies on the mechanism of transfer of drug resistance in bacteria. 18. Incorporation of ^{35}S-sulphathiazole into cells of the multiply-resistant strain and artificial sulphonamide-resistant strain of E. coli. Med. Biol., 63, 155–9.

Angier, R. B., Boothe, J. H., Hutchings, B. L., Mowat, J. H., Semb, J., Stokstad, E. L. R., SubbaRow, Y., Waller, C. W., Cosulich, D. B., Fahrenbach, M. J., Hultquist, M. E., Kuh, E., Northey, E. H., Seeger, D. R., Sickels, J. P., and Smith, J. M. (1946). Structure and synthesis of the liver L. casei factor. Science, 103, 667–9.

Ball, P. (1986). Toxicity of sulphonamide–diaminopyrimidine combinations: implications for future use. *J. Antimicrob. Chemother.*, **17**, 694–6.

Bell, P. H. and Roblin, R. O. (1942). Studies in chemotherapy VII. A theory of the relation of structure to activity of sulphanilamide compounds. *J. Am. Chem. Soc.*, **64**, 2905–17.

Bock, L., Miller, G., Schaper, K. J., and Seydel, J. K. (1974). Sulphonamide structure–activity relationships in a cell-free system. 2. Proof for the formation of a sulphona-mide-containing folate analog. *J. Med. Chem.*, **17**, 23–8.

Brown, G. M. (1962). The biosynthesis of folic acid. II. Inhibition by sulphonamides. *J. Biol. Chem.*, **237**, 536–40.

Brown, G. M., Weisman, R. A., and Molnar, D. A. (1961). The biosynthesis of folic acid. I. Substrate and cofactor requirements for enzymatic synthesis by cell free extracts of *Escherichia coli*. *J. Biol. Chem.*, **236**, 2534–43.

Buchall, J. J. (1979). The development of the diaminopyrimidines. *J. Antimicrob. Chemother.*, **5** (Suppl. B), 3–14.

Bushby, S. R. M. (1973). Trimethoprim-sulfamethoxazole: *in vitro* microbiological aspects. *J. Infect. Dis.*, **128**, 5442–62.

Domagk, G. (1935). Ein Beitrag zur Chemotherapie der bakteriellen Infektionen. *Dtsch. Med. Wsch.*, **61**, 250–3.

Domagk, G. (1957). Twenty-five years of sulfonamide therapy. *Ann. N. Y. Acad. Sci.*, **69**, 380–4.

Ehrlich, P. (1909). Uber moderne Chemotherapie. Vortrag gehalten in der X. Tagung der Deutschen Dermatologischen Gesellschaft. In *Beiträge zur experimentellen Pathologie und Chemotherapie*, pp. 167–202. Akademische Verlagsgesellschaft m.b.H., Leipzig.

Foster, T. O. (1983). Plasmid-determined resistance to antimicrobial drugs and toxic metal ions in bacteria. *Microbiol. Rev.*, **47**, 361–409.

Garrod, L. P., Lambert, H. P, and O'Grady, F. (1973). Sulphonamides. In *Antibiotics and chemotherapy*. (4th edn), pp. 12–28. Churchill Livingstone, Edinburgh.

Garrod, L. P., Lambert, H. P., and O'Grady, F. (1981). Sulphanomides. In *Antibiotics and chemotherapy*. (fifth edn), pp. 11–25. Churchill Livingstone, Edinburgh.

Green, N. H. (1940). The mode of action of sulphanilamide with special reference to a bacterial growth-stimulating factor ('P' factor) obtained from *Br. abortus* and other bacteria. *Br. J. Exp. Path.*, **21**, 38–64.

Hamilton-Miller, J. M. T. (1979). Mechanisms and distribution of bacterial resistance to diaminopyrimidines and sulphonamides. *J. Antimicrob. Chemother.*, **5** (Suppl. B), 61–73.

Ho, R. I., Corman, L., Morse, S. A., and Artenstein, M. S. (1974). Alterations in dihydropteroate synthetase in cell-free extracts of sulphanilamide-resistant *Neisseria meningitidis* and *Neisseria gonorrhoeae*. *Antimicrob. Agents Chemother.*, **5**, 388–392.

Hughes, W. T. (1986). Trimethoprim and sulphonamides. In *The antimicrobial agents annual*—1. (ed. P. K. Peterson and J. Verhoef), pp. 197–204. Elsevier, Amsterdam.

Jacoby, G. A. (1985). Genetics and epidemiology of resistance. *Symp. Soc. Gen. Microbiol.*, **38**, 185–218.

Klee, P. and Römer, M. (1935). Prontosil bei Streptokokken-Erkrankungen. *Dtsch. Med. Wsch.*, **61**, 253–5.

Lacey, R. W. (1979). Mechanism of action of trimethoprim and sulphonamides: relevance to synergy *in vivo*. *J. Antimicrob. Chemother.*, **5** (Suppl. B), 75–83.

Lampen, J. O. and Jones, M. J. (1946). The antagonism of sulphonamide inhibition of certain lactobacilli and enterococci by pteroylglutamic acid and related compounds. *J. Biol. Chem.*, **166**, 435–48.

Lampen, J. O. and Jones, M. J. (1947). The growth-promoting and antisulfonamide activity of *p*-aminobenzoic acid, pteroylglutamic acid, and related compounds for *Lactobacillus arabinosus* and *Streptobacterium plantarum*. *J. Biol. Chem.*, **170**, 133–46.

Lancet Editorial (1986). Hypersensitivity to sulphonamides—a clue? *Lancet*, **ii**, 958–9.

Lane, S. L., Kutscher, A. H., and Segall, R. (1953). Unusual toxic reactions to sulphonamide and antibiotic therapy. *Ann. Allergy*, **11**, 615–32.

Lascelles, J. and Woods, D. D. (1952). The synthesis of 'folic acid' by *Bacterium coli* and *Staphylococcus aureus* and its inhibition by sulphonamides. *Br. J. Exp. Pathol.* **33**, 288–303.

Lascelles, J., Cross, M. J., and Woods, D. D. (1954). The folic acid and serine nutrition of *Leuconostoc mesenteroides P60* (*Streptococcus equinus P60*). *J. Gen. Microbiol.*, **10**, 267–84.

Lehr, D. (1948). Prevention of renal damage by use of mixtures of sulphonamides. *Br. Med. J.*, **ii**, 934–46.

Mann, T. and Keilin, D. (1940). Sulphanilamide as a specific inhibitor of carbonic anhydrase. *Nature (London)*, **146**, 164–5.

Maren, T. H. (1984). Carbonic anhydrase: The middle years 1945–1960, and introduction to pharmacology of sulphonamides. *Ann. N. Y. Acad. Sci.*, **429**, 10–17.

Nagate, T., Inoue, M. Inoue, K., and Mitsuhashi, S. (1978). Plasmid-mediated sulphanilamide resistance. *Microbiol. Immunol.*, **22**, 367–75.

Niepp, L. (1964). *Antibacterial chemotherapy with sulphonamides in experimental chemotherapy 2*. (ed. R. J. Schnitzer and F. Hawking), pp. 169–248. Academic Press, New York.

Nimmo-Smith, R. H., Lascelles, J., and Woods, D. D. (1948). The synthesis of 'folic acid' by *Streptobacterium plantarum* and its inhibition by sulphonamides. *Br. J. Exp. Pathol.*, **29**, 264–81.

O'Carroll, O. M., Bryan, P. A., and Robinson, R. J. (1966). Stevens–Johnson syndrome associated with long-acting sulphonamides. *J. Am. Med. Ass.*, **195**, 691–3.

Ortiz, P. (1970). Dihydrofolate and dihydropteroate synthesis by partially purified enzymes from wild-type and sulphonamide resistant *Pneumococcus. Biochemistry*, **9**, 355–61.

Poe, M. (1976). Antibacterial synergism: a proposal for chemotherapeutic potentiation between trimethoprim and sulphamethoxazole. *Science*, **194**, 533–5.

Reeves, D. S. (1982). Sulphonamides and trimethoprim. *Lancet*, **ii**, 370–3.

Richey, D. P. and Brown, G. M. (1969). The biosynthesis of folic acid. IX. Purification and properties of the enzymes required for the formation of dihydropteroic acid. *J. Biol. Chem.*, **244**, 1582–92.

Rieder, J. (1963). Physikalisch-chemische und biologische Untersuchungen und Sulphonamiden. *Arzneimittel-Forsch.*, **13**, 81–103.

Roland, S., Ferone, R., Harvey, R. J., Styles, V. L., and Morrison, R. W. (1979). The characteristics and significance of sulphonamides as substrates for *Escherichia coli* dihydropteroate synthetase. *J. Biol. Chem.*, **254**, 10337–45.

Schreus, T. (1935). Chemotherapie des Erysipels und anderer Infektionen mit Prontosil. *Dtsch. Med. Wsch.*, **61**, 255–6.

Seydel, J. K. (1968). Sulphonamides, structure–activity relationship, and mode of action. *J. Pharm. Sci.*, **57**, 1455–78.

Shiota, T. (1959). Enzymic synthesis of folic acid-like compounds by cell-free extracts of *Lactobacillus arabinosus. Arch. Biochem. Biophys.*, **80**, 155–61.

Siffert, W., Teske, W., Gartner, A., and Gros, G. (1983). The use of prontosil for the visualisation of carbonic anhydrase bands in polyacrylamide gels. Application to the carbonic anhydrase isozymes of erythrocytes and white skeletal muscle of the rabbit. *J. Biochem. Biophys. Meth.*, **8**, 331–8.

Smith, J. T. and Amyes, S. G. B. (1984). Bacterial resistance to antifolate chemotherapeutic agents mediated by plasmids. *Br. Med. Bull.*, **40**, 42–6.

Stamp, T. C. (1939). Bacteriostatic action of sulphanilamide *in vitro*. *Lancet*, **ii** 10–17.

Stokstad, E. L. R., Hutchings, B. L., Mowat, J. H., Boothe, J. H., Waller, C. W., Angier, R. B., Semb, J., and SubbaRow, Y. (1948). The degradation of the fermentation *Lactobacillus casei* factor. I. *J. Am. Chem. Soc.*, **70**, 5–9.

Struller, T. (1968). Long-acting and short-acting sulphonamides. Recent developments. *Antibiot. Chemother.*, **14**, 179–215.

Syedberg, G. and Skold, O. (1980). Characterization of different plasmid-borne dihydropteroate synthases mediating bacterial resistance to sulfonamides. *J. Bacteriol.*, **142**, 1–7.

Then, R. L. (1982). Mechanisms of resistance to trimethoprim, the sulphonamides and trimethoprim–sulphamethoxazole. *Rev. Infect. Dis.*, **4**, 261–9.

Tréfouël, J., Tréfouël, J., Nitti, F., and Bovet, D. (1935). Activité du *p*-aminophénylsulfamide sur les infections streptococciques expérimentales de la souris et du lapin. *C. R. Soc. Biol.*, **120**, 756–8.

Vree, T. B. and Hekster, Y. A. (1985). *Pharmacokinetics of sulphonamides revisited*. Karger, Basel.

Vree, T. B., Hekster, Y. A., Damsma, J. E., Van der Kleijn, E., and O'Reilly, W. J. (1979). Pharmacokinetics of N_1-acetyl and N_4 acetylsulphamethoxazole in man. *Clin. Pharmacokin.*, **4**, 310–19.

Vree, T. B. Hekster, Y. A., and Van Dalen, R. (1983a). Some consequences of drug choice and dosage regimen for patients with impaired kidney function. *Drug Intell. Clin. Pharm.*, **17**, 267–73.

Vree, T. B., Hekster, Y. A., Tijhuis, M. W., Baakman, M., Janssen, T. J., and Termond, E. F. S. (1983b). The effect of the molecular structure of closely related N_1-substituents of sulphonamides on the pathways of elimination in man. *Pharm. Weekbl. Sci. Ed.*, **5**, 49–56.

Waterworth, P. (1978). Quantitative methods for bacterial sensitivity testing. In *Laboratory methods in antimicrobial chemotherapy*. (ed. Reeves, D. S., Philips, I., Williams, J. D. and Wise, R.), pp. 31–40. Churchill Livingstone, Edinburgh.

Weber, W. W., Cohen, S. N., and Steinberg, M. S. (1968). Purification and properties of *N*-acetyltransferase from mammalian liver. *Ann. N. Y. Acad. Sci.*, **151**, 734–41.

Weinstein, L., Madoff, M. A., and Samet, C. M. (1960). The sulphonamides. *New Engl. J. Med.*, **263**, 793–800.

Wise, E. M. and Abou-Donia, M. M. (1975). Sulfonamide resistance mechanism in *Escherichia coli*: R plasmids can determine sulfonamide-resistant dihydropteroate syntheses. *Proc. Nat. Acad. Sci. USA*, **72**, 2621–5.

Wolf, B. and Hotchkiss, R. D. (1963). Genetically modified folic acid synthesizing enzymes of *Pneumococcus*. *Biochemistry*, **2**, 145–50.

Woods, D. D. (1940). The relation of *p*-aminobenzoic acid to the mechanism of the action of sulphanilamide. *Br. J. Exp. Path.*, **21**, 74–90.

Woods, D. D. (1962). The biochemical mode of action of sulphonamide drugs. *J. Gen. Microbiol.*, **29**, 687–702.

Yow, E. M. (1955). A re-evaluation of sulphonamide therapy. *Ann. Int. Med.*, **43**, 323–32.

13

Inhibitors of the *de novo* pyrimidine pathway

Thomas W. Kensler and David A. Cooney

13.1   Characteristics of pyrimidine biosynthetic enzymes

The requirement for pyrimidines is ubiquitously distributed throughout the spectrum of living organisms and can be fulfilled by two synthetic pathways: a *de novo* route and a salvage pathway. Uridine-5′-monophosphate (UMP) is a common product of these two pathways. The *de novo* pathway is generally considered to consist of six enzymes: carbamyl phosphate synthetase II (CPS II); L-aspartate transcarbamylase (ATCase); L-dihydroorotase (DHOase); L-dihydroorotate dehydrogenase (DHO deHase); orotate phosphoribosyl transferase (OPRTase); and orotidine-5′-monophosphate decarboxylase (OMP deCase). Several excellent reviews of this pathway appear in the recent literature (Shambaugh 1979; Jones 1980). The main components of the pyrimidine ring are derived from L-aspartic acid and L-glutamine, while the ribosyl and phosphoryl moieties are transferred from phosphoribosyl pyrophosphate (Fig. 13.1). So far as is known, this 'geneology' of the pyrimidine ring is universal and serves to underscore the intimate inter relationship of the dicarboxylic amino acids and their amides with nucleic acid biosynthesis. The salvage pathway, by contrast, utilizes preformed nucleosides or bases in the biosynthesis of pyrimidine nucleotides (Levine *et al.* 1974). Two additional enzymes, namely, thymidylate synthetase (TS) and cytidylate synthetase (CTP synthetase), catalyse modification of

379

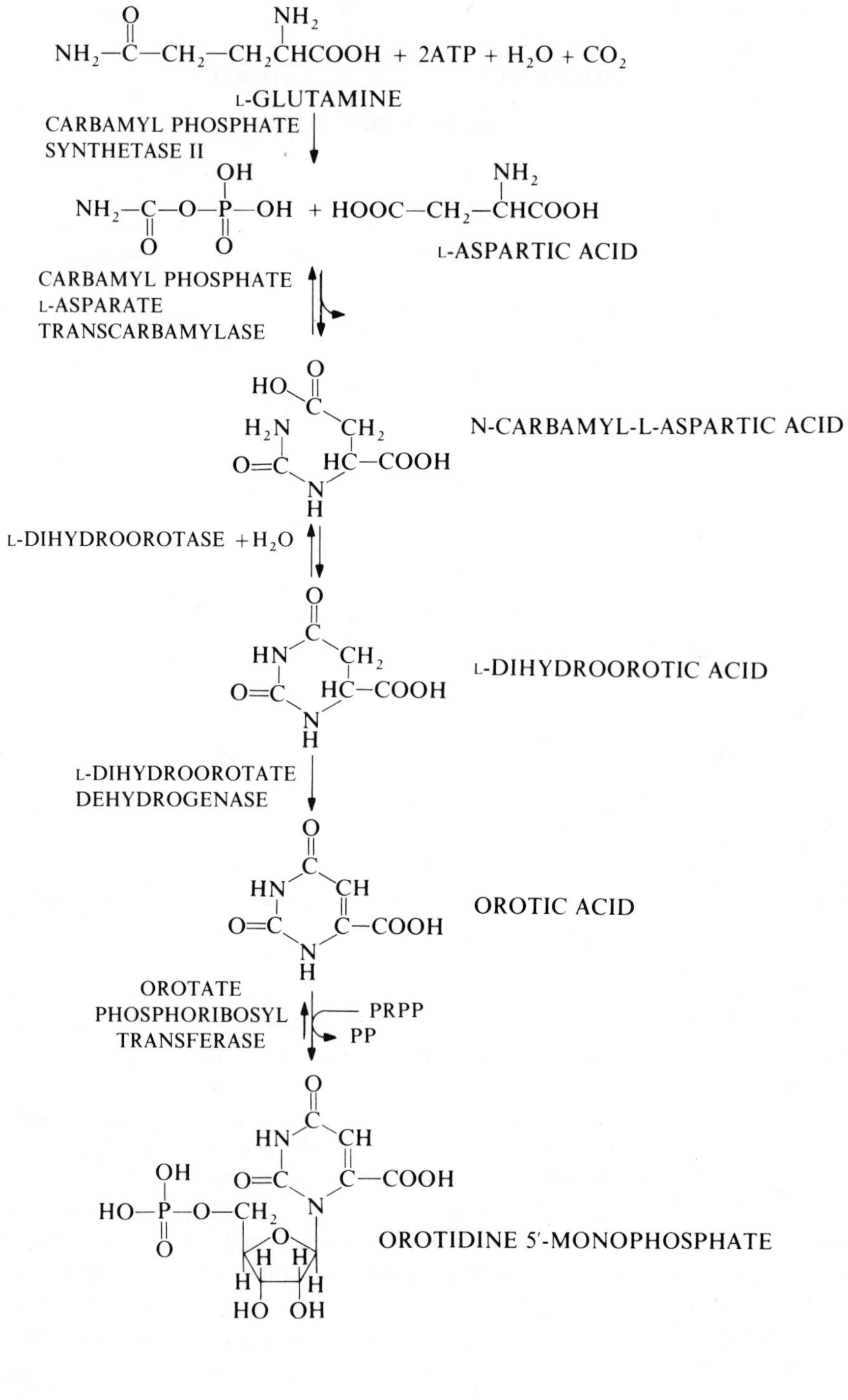

$$NH_2-\overset{\overset{\textstyle O}{\|}}{C}-CH_2-CH_2\overset{\overset{\textstyle NH_2}{|}}{C}HCOOH + 2ATP + H_2O + CO_2$$

L-GLUTAMINE

CARBAMYL PHOSPHATE
SYNTHETASE II

$$NH_2-\overset{\overset{\textstyle }{}}{\underset{\underset{\textstyle O}{}}{C}}-O-\overset{\overset{\textstyle OH}{|}}{\underset{\underset{\textstyle O}{}}{P}}-OH + HOOC-CH_2-\overset{\overset{\textstyle NH_2}{|}}{C}HCOOH$$

L-ASPARTIC ACID

CARBAMYL PHOSPHATE
L-ASPARATE
TRANSCARBAMYLASE

N-CARBAMYL-L-ASPARTIC ACID

L-DIHYDROOROTASE $+H_2O$

L-DIHYDROOROTIC ACID

L-DIHYDROOROTATE
DEHYDROGENASE

OROTIC ACID

OROTATE
PHOSPHORIBOSYL   PRPP
TRANSFERASE   PP

OROTIDINE 5'-MONOPHOSPHATE

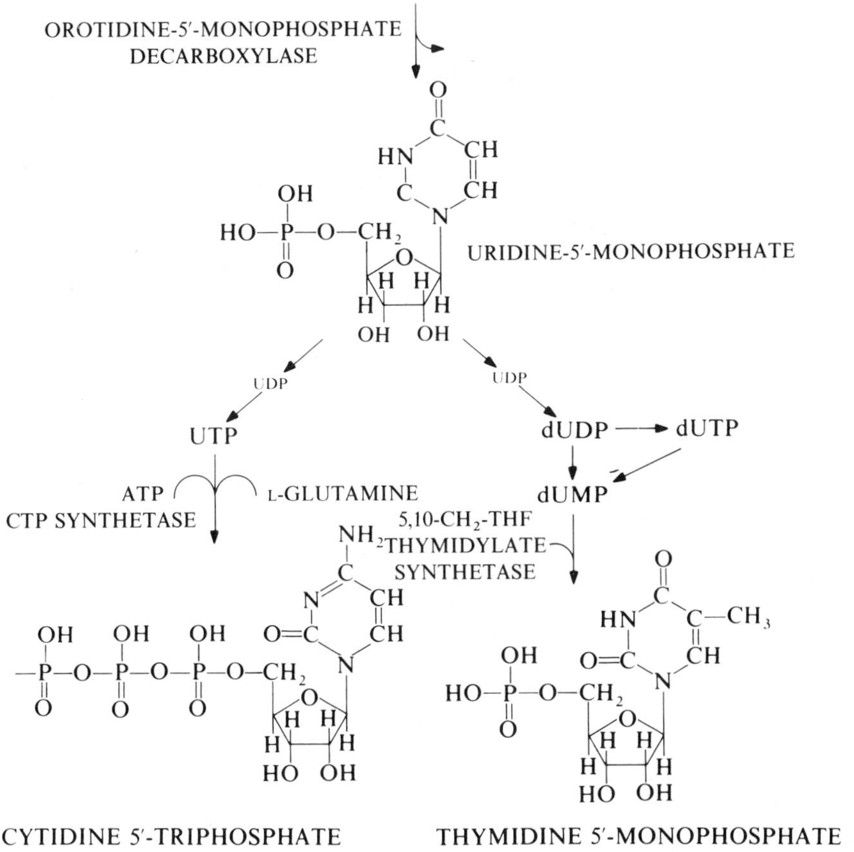

Fig. 13.1. Pyrimidine biosynthetic pathway. The specific activities of the enzymes of *de novo* pyrimidine biosynthesis are quite variable in mammalian cells (Kensler *et al.* 1988); however, the relative rates of these enzymes, under optimal substrate concentrations, show considerable homology. Thus, for illustrative purposes, the specific activities of the pyrimidine biosynthetic enzymes in P388 leukaemia, a widely-used transplantable murine tumour line, are listed as follows in units of nmol activity per mg protein per h: CPS II, 6; ATCase, 715; DHOase, 205; DHO deHase, 14; OPRTase, 12; OMP deCase, 27; TS, 0.5; and CTP synthetase, 5.

the pyrimidine ring to yield the two other major pyrimidine nucleotides, cytidine-5'-triphosphate (CTP) and thymidine-5'-monophosphate (TMP) (Buchanan 1973; Dunlap 1978; Weinfeld *et al.* 1978).

The intracellular localization of the six catalytic activities of the *de novo* pyrimidine biosynthetic pathway appear to be optimized to ensure efficient flux or to permit breaking of output in response to physiological needs (Shoaf and Jones 1973). CPS II, ATCase, and DHOase exist as a large cytosolic multienzyme complex (*pyrl-3*). The proximity of consecutive catalysts serves to channel products from one active site to another without undue dilution by or diffusion into the ambient cytoplasmic milieu. In essence, this complex is an enzymatic assembly line. The fourth enzyme of the pathway, DHO deHase, is particulate and is sequestered on the outer face of the inner mitochondrial membrane. Thus, this enzyme is ideally sited to exert regulatory control over the velocity of pyrimidine ring assembly because both its substrate and product must diffuse across the mitochondrial membrane. Another cytosolic multienzyme complex (*pyr5,6*), composed of OPRTase and OMP deCase, effects the last two steps of pyrimidine biosynthesis, producing UMP as the final product for use as such or for further transformation into cytidine and thymidine nucleotides. A more rigorous discussion of the factors influencing rates of reaction for the individual enzymes, as well as overall flux through this pathway, can be found elsewhere (Kensler and Cooney 1981). It should be noted here, however, that the pyrimidine biosynthetic pathway is subject to complex regulation by its products and substrates; as a result, physiological or drug-induced alterations in the levels of these regulators can provoke important changes in the *de novo* output of UMP. Inasmuch as the specific activities of five of the six enzymes of the central pathway are similar and low (Fig. 13.1, caption), only that of ATCase being disproportionately vigorous, it is apparent that the system is an attractive one in terms of pharmacological intervention.

13.2 Chemotherapeutic activities of inhibitors of the *de novo* pyrimidine biosynthetic pathway

A substantial number of compounds have been described that exert inhibitory activity on one or more of the pyrimidine biosynthetic enzymes *in vitro* (for a more detailed review see Kensler and Cooney 1981). However, two subsequent requirements, efficacy *in vivo* and manageable host toxicity, have precluded admission of all but a few of these drugs into clinical trials. The cytoreductive chemotherapeutic activity of the principal inhibitors of *de novo* pyrimidine biosynthesis against transplantable murine tumours customarily used for the screening of new oncolytic drugs has been reviewed elsewhere (Kensler *et al.* 1988). Table 13.1 summarizes the kinetic and clinical features of representative inhibitors of pyrimidine biosynthesis.

13.2.1 Inhibitors of carbamyl phosphate synthetase II

Inasmuch as the synthesis of carbamyl phosphate is a critical, and one of the rate-limiting steps in pyrimidine biosynthesis (Mori and Tatibana 1978) (Fig. 13.1), the role of inhibitors of CPS II merits attention, particularly in view of the fact that the substrates of CPS II are involved in many other cellular reactions and thus will not accumulate to toxic levels behind a blockade, as can occur later in this pathway. Regrettably, no specific inhibitor of this *L*-glutamine (**1**)-utilizing amidotransferase is at present available. Nonetheless, L-glutamine

Table 13.1 Kinetic and clinical features of representative inhibitors of pyrimidine biosynthesis

Enzyme target and drug	Kinetic features			Therapeutic activity against murine tumours[a]	Clinical features	
	K_i	Type of inhibition	Enzyme source		Best sites of activity	Principal toxicities
Carbamyl phosphate synthetase II						
Azaserine				L1210, P388	No activity	Gastrointestinal
DON				L1210, P388	No activity	Gastrointestinal
CONV				No activity	Not tested	
Acivicin	105 μM	Competitive: L-glutamine (irreversible)	Lewis lung	L1210, P388, M5076	Non-small Cell Lung	Myelosuppression, neurological, G. I.
L-aspartate transcarbamylase						
Phosphonacetic acid	500 μM	Competitive: carbamyl phos.	*E. coli*	B16	No activity	
PALA	20 nM	Competitive: carbamyl phos.	Lewis lung	Lewis lung, Colon 26, M5076, Glioma 26, Ehrlich ascites, B16	Melanoma	Stomatitis, G. I., diarrhoea, skin, neurological
L-dihydroorotase						
5-Fluoroorotate	24 μM	Competitive: Carbamyl asp.	Ehrlich ascites	L1210	Not tested	
5-Aminoorotate	28 μM	Competitive: Carbamyl asp.	Ehrlich ascites	P388	Not tested	
5-Methylorotate	36 μM	Competitive: Carbamyl asp.	Ehrlich ascites	No activity	Not tested	
Sulphadiazine	200 μM	Non-competitive: Carbamyl asp.	*Z. oroticum*	No activity	No activity	

Table 13.1 Kinetic and clinical features of representative inhibitors of pyrimidine biosynthesis

Enzyme target and drug	K_i	Kinetic features		Therapeutic activity against murine tumours[a]	Clinical features	
		Type of inhibition	Enzyme source		Best sites of activity	Principal toxicities
L-dihydroorotate dehydrogenase						
Lapachol	2 μM	Uncompetitive: Dihydroorotate	L1210	No activity	No activity	
Dichloroallyl lawsone	27 nM	Uncompetitive: Dihydroorotate	L1210	No activity	No activity	
Dihydro-5-azaorotate				No activity	Not tested	
Orotate phosphoribosyl transferase or/and orotidine-5'-monophosphate transferase						
Allopurinol				No activity	No activity	
Barbituric acid				No activity	No activity	
Barbiturate-5'-monophosphate	4 nM	Competitive: OMP	Rat brain	Not tested	Not tested	
6-azauridine				L1210		
6-azauridine-5'-monophosphate	100 nM	Competitive: OMP	Ehrlich ascites	Not tested	Not tested	
6-uracilsulphonic acid	7 μM	Competitive: Orotic acid	Yeast	No activity	Not tested	
Pyrazofurin				No activity	Multiple Myeloma	Stomatitis, skin, myelosuppression
Pyrazofurin-5'-monophosphate	5 nM	Competitive: OMP	L5178Y	Not tested	Not tested	

Thymidylate synthetase

	Requires	anabolism				
5-fluorouracil				L1210, P388, L5178Y, Lewis lung, Colon 26	Colorectal, Breast	Stomatitis, G. I., myelosuppression
5-F-dUMP	1.4 nM	Competitive: dUMP	L1210	L1210	Not tested	
5-Br-dUMP	1.4 μM	Competitive: dUMP	L. casei	Not tested	Not tested	
5-Cl-dUMP	190 μM	Competitive: dUMP	L. casei	Not tested	Not tested	
5-nitro-dUMP	29 nM	Competitive: dUMP	L. casei	Not tested	Not tested	
Methotrexate	300 nM	Competitive: Methylene THF	L1210	L1210	Choriocarcinoma, breast, leukaemia	Myelosuppression, stomatitis, G. I.
IAHQ	5 μM	Non-Competitive: dUMP	L1210	L1210, P388		
CB3717	1 nM	Competitive: Methylene THF	L1210	L1210	Ovarian, breast, hepatomas	Myelosuppression, rashes, liver
Cytidine 5'-triphosphate synthetase						
3-deazauridine	5 μM	Competitive: UTP	Calf liver	L1210	No activity	Myelosuppression, 'mucositis', fever
Acivicin	1.1 μM	Competitive: L-glutamine (irreversible)	Rat hepatoma	supra	supra	supra
Cyclopentenyl cytosine	1 μM	Unknown	P388	L1210	Not tested	

[a] Experimental therapeutic activity is defined as either > 90 per cent tumour inhibition or > 75 per cent increase in lifespan in mice bearing the indicated tumours; no activity refers to <75 per cent increase in lifespan in mice bearing L1210 leukaemia.

$$
\begin{array}{ccccc}
\text{NH}_2 & & \text{H—C=N=N} & \text{Cl} & \text{H—C=N=N} \\
| & & | & | & | \\
\text{C=O} & \text{Cl}\diagdown\ \text{N} & \text{C=O} & \text{CH}_2 & \text{C=O} \\
| & & | & | & | \\
\text{CH}_2 & \qquad\quad \text{O} & \text{CH}_2 & \text{C=O} & \text{O} \\
| & & | & | & | \\
\text{CH}_2 & \qquad\text{—H} & \text{CH}_2 & \text{CH}_2 & \text{CH}_2 \\
| & \text{H—C—NH}_2 & | & | & | \\
\text{H—C—NH}_2 & | & \text{H—C—NH}_2 & \text{H—C—NH}_2 & \text{H—C—NH}_2 \\
| & \text{COOH} & | & | & | \\
\text{COOH} & & \text{COOH} & \text{COOH} & \text{COOH}
\end{array}
$$

L-GLUTAMINE	ACIVICIN	DON	CONV	AZASERINE
(1)	**(2)**	**(3)**	**(4)**	**(5)**

antagonists are inhibitors of this enzymic target (Livingston *et al.* 1970; Jayaram *et al.* 1975), including acivicin (**2**), L-6-diazo-5-oxo-norvaline (DON) (**3**), L-2-amino-4-oxo-5-chloropentanoic acid (CONV) (**4**), and azaserine (**5**). Acivicin engenders inhibition of CPS II that, over time, becomes effectively irreversible, presumably through alkylation at the L-glutamine binding site (Tso *et al.* 1980). Additionally, acivicin exerts pronounced inhibition of flux through the *de novo* pyrimidine pathway in murine tumours (Kensler *et al.* 1981b). Therapeutically, acivicin is highly active against murine leukaemias, but also exhibits modest activity against several solid tumours (Kensler *et al.* 1988). By contrast, most other representatives of this class of agent show activity against only the leukaemias. Azaserine, the first highly inhibitory L-glutamine antagonist to be discovered and isolated, exemplifies this point.

Since the L-glutamine antagonists exert actions at plural sites, it is difficult to ascertain whether inhibition of one enzymic step, such as CPS II, is a principal—as opposed to contributory—cause of the antitumour activity seen. The fact that these agents are (contrary to expectation) most active against tumours with comparatively rich endowments of CPS II (Kensler and Cooney 1981) might be taken to suggest that these drugs are oncolytic principally because of activities at a site or sites other than the inaugural enzyme of pyrimidine biosynthesis. Azaserine, DON, and acivicin have all been given phase I trials in humans, but with disappointing therapeutic results (Kisner *et al.* 1983). Moreover, all produced severe gastrointestinal toxicities, ranging from glossitis to proctitis, and so were poorly tolerated in their clinical tests.

13.2.2   Inhibitors of L-aspartate transcarbamylase

Mammalian ATCase is not particularly sensitive to feedback or product inhibition by pyrimidines. Indeed, the most effective inhibitors of this enzyme are analogues of the two substrates and, in particular, of the transition-state intermediate in the reaction. PALA (*N*-(phosphonacetyl)-L-aspartic acid) (**6**) is a recently devised pyrimidine biosynthesis inhibitor and, in certain regards, the most distinctive. PALA was synthesized as a stable analogue of the transition-state intermediate (**7**) in the reaction catalysed by ATCase (Collins and Stark

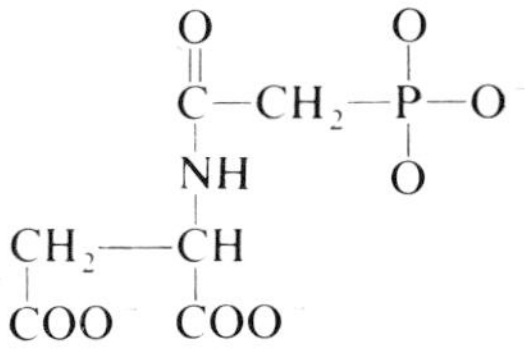

$$\underset{\substack{\text{COO} \quad \text{COO} \\ | \qquad | \\ \text{CH}_2\text{---CH} \\ | \\ \text{NH}}}{\overset{\substack{\text{O} \qquad \text{O} \\ || \qquad || \\ \text{C---CH}_2\text{---P---O} \\ \qquad\qquad |}}{}}$$

PALA

(6)

CARBAMYL PHOSPHATE

L-ASPARTIC ACID

POSSIBLE TRANSITION-STATE
INTERMEDIATE

N-CARBAMYL-L-
ASPARTIC ACID

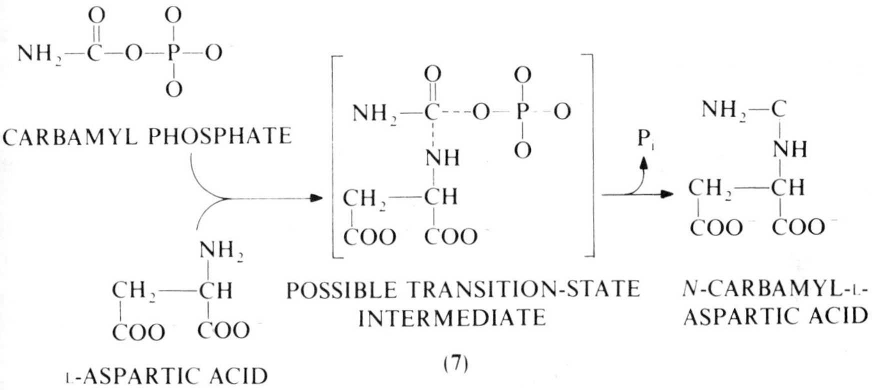

(7)

1971) and, as such, combines the structural features of the two natural substrates, carbamyl phosphate and L-aspartic acid. Transition-state analogues offer attractive potentials as metabolic inhibitors because they can bind to their target enzymes with high affinity and specificity. In this instance, as well as is known, ATCase is the only enzyme directly affected by PALA. PALA produces competitive inhibition with carbamyl phosphate as the variable substrate, but is non-competitive with respect to L-aspartic acid. The apparent K_i versus carbamyl phosphate is reported to be between 10^{-8} and 10^{-10} M for enzyme prepared from a variety of mammalian cell types (Hoogenraad 1974; Kempe *et al.* 1976; Jayaram *et al.* 1979; Kensler *et al.* 1980, 1981a). Not only is inhibition potent, it is also persistent *in vivo*. Although enzyme inhibition by PALA is reversible, ATCase from mouse spleen, tumours, and human leukocytes is inhibited for up to two weeks after PALA administration (Yoshida *et al.* 1974; Jayaram and Cooney 1979; Jayaram *et al.* 1979; Kensler *et al.* 1980). This effect is probably a reflection of the slow terminal elimination phase of the drug (Ardalan *et al.* 1981). As far as is known, PALA is not metabolized. Because of its inhibitory potency, this agent has been subjected to uniquely intensive across-the-board screening. PALA is highly active in the treatment of many solid transplantable rodent tumours, but is ineffective against the leukemias and most of the ascitic tumours. The observation that the specific activities of ATCase are lower in solid tumours than in the more rapidly-developing leukaemias provides support for the generalization that tumours with low levels of this *de novo* biosynthetic capability are likely to be most susceptible to the cytotoxic actions of PALA (Jayaram *et al.* 1979).

Despite its outstanding activity against solid transplantable murine tumours, the clinical performance of PALA has been disappointing. Although not myelosuppressive, dose-limiting toxicities in the skin and gastrointestinal tract are observed. Mild neurotoxicity has also been reported. Throughout intensive phase and I and II trials, the drug has failed to exhibit any material activity as a single agent against human neoplasia (Von Hoff *et al.* 1979). Nevertheless, because PALA is an antimetabolite of well-defined specificity and because of the striking oncolytic effects achieved when PALA is used in conjunction with acivicin in animal models (or, in other words, when concerted inhibition was inflicted on both the first and second steps of the *de novo* pathway) (Kensler *et al.* 1981b; Loh and Kufe 1981), it is anticipated that PALA will assume a role in combination chemotherapeutic strategies intended for the control of cancer in humans.

Porter *et al.* (1969) have evaluated a series of carbamyl phosphate analogues as inhibitors of ATCase from *Escherichia coli*. All analogues with a phosphate or phosphate dianion were competitive inhibitors, albeit not potent. For example, *N,N'*-dimethylcarbamyl phosphate, *N*-methylcarbamyl phosphate, acetylphosphate, and phosphonacetic acid have K_is in the 0.1 to 0.5×10^{-3} range. Natural analogues of L-aspartic acid, such as β-methylaspartate, as well as dicarboxylic acids, particularly succinate and maleate, also inhibit the bacterial enzyme (Porter *et al.* 1969); however, none of these latter agents have significant therapeutic properties.

13.2.3   Inhibitors of L-dihydroorotase

Studies on the regulation of mammalian DHOase and, in particular, the generation of effective and specific inhibitors are notably lacking. Thus, not only are allosteric repressants lacking in the case of DHOase, but there is also a shortage of specific or active-site-directed inhibitors of this enzyme. Christopherson and Jones (1980) have presented a very systematic evaluation of the inhibitory effects of 5-substituted analogues of orotate against mammalian DHOase *in vitro*. However, only two moderately potent substrate analogues have been identified as chemotherapeutic: 5-fluoroorotate and 5-aminoorotate, which are active against several transplantable murine leukaemias (Kensler and Cooney 1981). It should be noted, however, that 5-fluoroorotate is metabolized in part to 5-fluorodeoxyuridine-5'-monophosphate, a metabolite that very probably makes a major contribution to the antileukaemic effects, which follow administration of this substrate analogue. Plainly, L-dihydroorotase is a target awaiting attack by interested medicinal chemists.

13.2.4   Inhibitors of L-dihydroorotate dehydrogenase

Inhibition of the mitochondrial enzyme involved in *de novo* pyrimidine biosynthesis, DHO deHase, is accomplished by two general classes of compounds.

In common with most other enzymes in this pathway, DHO deHase is subject to product inhibition; orotic acid and some of its analogues are effective inhibitors, particularly dihydro-5-azaorotic acid. However, this compound is therapeutically inactive against several murine tumours. Additionally, naphthoquinones have been recently identified as potent inhibitors of DHO deHase. These drugs may act as analogues of the cofactor, ubiquinone, and serve as electron acceptors that alter electron flow. One such quinone, lapachol (**8**) inhibits DHO deHase from mouse liver mitochondria non-competitively with L-dihydroorotate as substrate, the apparent K_i being 2.1×10^{-6} M (Bennett *et al.* 1979). However, lapachol is without antitumour activity in humans, apparently because gastrointestinal toxicity becomes dose-limiting at sub-therapeutic plasma concentrations (Loo *et al.* 1978). Dichloroallyl lawsone (**9**), a close congener of

LAPACHOL

(**8**)

DICHLOROALLYL LAWSONE

(**9**)

lapachol, inhibits DHO deHase with a K_i of 2.7×10^{-8} M (Bennett *et al.* 1979). Despite this 100-fold increase in potency, lapachol is roughly five times more cytotoxic than dichloroallyl lawsone to cultured L1210 cells, and exhibits substantial activity in the L1210 and P388 leukaemias, against which dichloroallyl lawsone is inactive. Conversely, against solid tumours, dichloroallyl lawsone has greater activity and a better therapeutic index than lapachol. Dichloroallyl lawsone produces a vastly more profound and persistent reduction of uridine nucleotides than its more cytotoxic congener. These disparate observations suggest that attributes of these agents other than inhibition of DHO deHase might play a role in their cytotoxicities. Two such attributes are their abilities to interrupt cellular respiration or to generate free radicals capable of damaging DNA and other biomolecules. It is relevant to add that dichloroallyl lawsone is not myelosuppressive in humans, and shows little gastrointestinal toxicity; however, high doses in primates induce acute cardiotoxicity, a feature which has sharply limited the clinical application of the drug (McKelvey *et al.* 1979).

Of great interest is the recent observation of Dexter *et al.* (1985) that biphenquinate[6-fluoro-2-(2'-fluoro-1,1'-biphenyl-4-yl)-3-methyl-4-quinoline-carboxylic acid], a synthetic, lipophilic molecule, has good therapeutic activity against human colon, breast, and lung xenographs growing in nude mice, and also produces a strong depression in the levels of the pyrimidine nucleotides of tumours treated with the agent. This depression has recently been attributed to profound inhibition of DHO deHase in these neoplasms (Chen *et al.* 1986).

Kinetic analyses with partially purified preparations of DHO deHase show that biphenquinate engenders substantial (50 per cent) inhibition of this enzyme at concentrations as low as 1 ng ml^{-1}. Phase I clinical trials with this experimental drug are underway in Europe (1986) and Phase II trials are scheduled in the United States.

13.2.5   Inhibitors of orotate phosphoribosyl transferase and/or orotidylate decarboxylase

OPRTase exists as a soluble multi-enzyme complex with OMP deCase in mammalian cells. As a result, it becomes difficult to segregate the actions of inhibitors of one enzyme from the other. A number of orotate analogues have been described as inhibitors of OPRTase; many are also substrates for the enzyme and can form fraudulent nucleotides which, in turn, are potent inhibitors of OMP deCase. By contrast, potent inhibitors of OPRTase are scarce.

The first antagonists of OPRTase to be described were the 6-uracilsulphonic acids. 6-uracilsulphonic acid ($K_i = 7 \times 10^{-6}$ M), 6-uracilsulphonamide ($K_i = 3.9 \times 10^{-4}$ M), and 6-uracil methyl sulphone ($K_i = 7.1 \times 10^{-4}$ M) are competitive inhibitors of yeast OPRTase (Holmes 1956). No anabolism of these compounds to phosphate derivatives has been demonstrated. The rationale for the synthesis of these compounds was based on the established antimetabolic activity of sulphonic acids, sulphonamides, and substituted sulphones analogous to certain naturally occurring carboxylic acids; in this instance the acid was orotic acid. These orotic acid analogues inhibited microbial growth (Holmes and Welch 1956) but showed limited carcinostatic activity due to host toxicity (Jaffee and Cooper 1958). 5-substituted analogus of orotate have also been evaluated. 5-fluoroorotate is a good inhibitor of enzyme prepared from mouse Ehrlich ascites cells: 50 μM 5-fluoroorotate inhibited activity by 75 per cent (Traut and Jones 1977a, b). This agent is also an excellent competitive substrate for yeast OPRTase (Dahl et al. 1959). Synthetic pyrimidine and purine analogues, which after monophosphorylation are extremely potent OMP deCase inhibitors (see below), are in general inhibitors of OPRTase, i.e. allopurinol (10), oxipurinol (11), 6-azauridine (12), 6-azauracil, barbituric acid, and 5-azaorotate (Rubin et al. 1964; Traut and Jones 1977 a, b; Potvin et al. 1978). The activity of these base analogues is not particularly profound, although with 5-azaorotate notable potency is observed ($K_i = 5 \times 10^{-7}$ M) (Rubin et al. 1964). In large measure the impact of these OPRTase inhibitors on pyrimidine biosynthesis is likely to be a consequence of subsequent anabolism to highly potent ribotide inhibitors of the adjacent enzyme, OMP deCase.

Two potent antimetabolites are available for the inhibition of OMP deCase, involved in the last step in the assembly of the pyrimidine ring—6-azauridine and pyrazofurin (13). Both agents are phosphorylated *in vivo* to 5'-monophosphate derivatives through the actions of uridine/cytidine and adenosine kinases, respectively, and it is these anabolites that strongly impede the decarboxylation

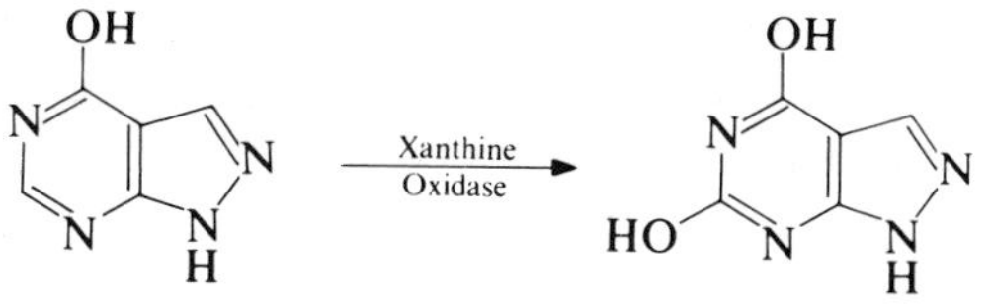

ALLOPURINOL
(10)

OXIPURINOL
(11)

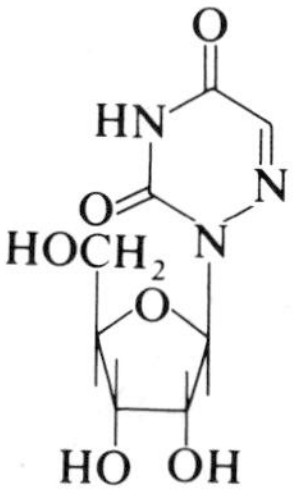

6-AZAURIDINE
(12)

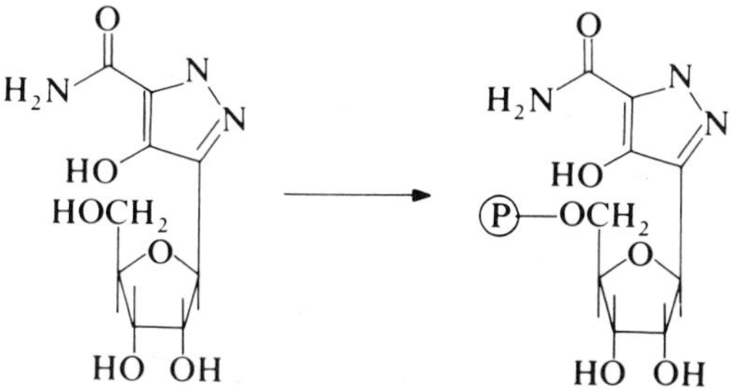

PYRAZOFURIN
(13)

PYRAZOFURIN-5'-MONOPHOSPHATE
(14)

of orotidine-5'-monophosphate (Cadman *et al.* 1978; Dix *et al.* 1979). The 5'-monophosphate derivative of pyrazofurin (14) is a competitive inhibitor of purified OMP deCase with an apparent K_i of 5×10^{-9} M. Both 6-azauridine and pyrazofurin exhibit fairly good antileukaemic activity *in vivo* and show modest activity against the two most widely used transplantable solid tumours, the Lewis lung carcinoma and the B16 melanoma. Clinical trials have demonstrated that neither agent exhibits prominent antitumour activity in humans, although 6-azauridine has been used clinically for the management of neoplasms such as chronic myelogenous and acute leukaemias (Hernandez *et al.* 1969; Ohnuma *et al.* 1977; Cadman *et al.* 1978).

Pyrazofurin also blocks the *de novo* synthesis of purines by inhibiting 4-aminoimidazole carboximide ribose monophosphate formyl transferase with a K_i of 3×10^{-5} M (Worzalla and Sweeney 1980). Pyrazofurin increases the excretion of 4-aminoimidazole carboximide in rats, indicating that this action occurs *in vivo*. However, the oncolytic effect of this drug on hepatoma cells in culture can be reversed by addition of uridine, suggesting that this antipurine action does not contribute, in an important manner, to cytotoxicity (Olah *et al.* 1980).

13.2.6 Inhibitors of thymidylate synthetase

Thymidylate synthetase (dTMPS) catalyses the conversion of 2'-deoxyuridylate (dUMP) to thymidylate (dTMP) with concomitant transfer and reduction of the one-carbon unit of 5,10-methylene tetrahydrofolate. Since the action of dTMPS provides the only *de novo* source of thymidine, it is a pivotal enzyme in the synthesis of DNA; although its activity is elevated in proliferating tissues, in absolute terms it is generally the lowest of the eight enzymes involved in pyrimidine biosynthesis. For this reason dTMPS has become a popular target for inhibitors with potential antineoplastic activity. Compounds explored with success to date fall into two distinct categories; the 5-substituted deoxyuridylates and the antifolates. Strong emphasis has been placed on the development of mechanism-based inhibitors of dTMPS. These inhibitors, exemplified by the fluoropyrimidines, bind reversibly to the active site, and then undergo events parallel to the steps of the normal catalytic reaction, ultimately leading to the formation of a covalent enzyme–inhibitor complex (Fig. 13.2).

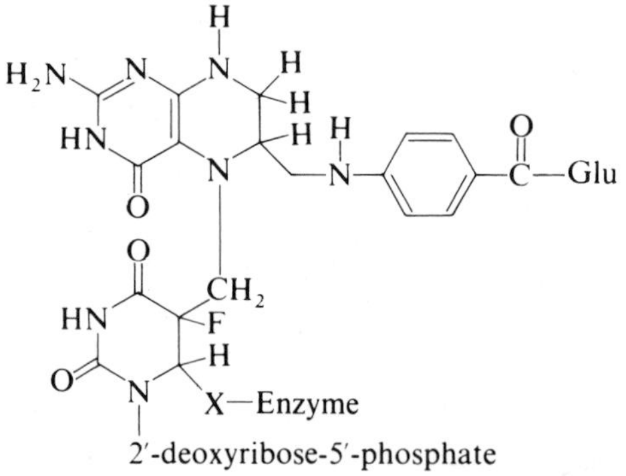

Fig. 13.2. Diagrammatic representation of the covalent ternary complex between dTMP synthetase (enzyme), FdUMP, and methylene tetrahydrofolate.

Fluorouracil (FU) (**15**) was designed by Heidelberger (Heidelberger *et al.* 1957, 1958) with precisely such activation in mind. FU is a potent antineoplastic used clinically against cancer of the breast and colon. *In vivo* FU is converted to its active metabolite, 5-fluoro 2'-deoxyuridylate (FdUMP) (**16**), which has a K_i of 14×10^{-9} M against dTMPS from the L1210 leukaemia (Santi 1981). This compound serves as a competitive inhibitor of dTMPS but its potency is sharply

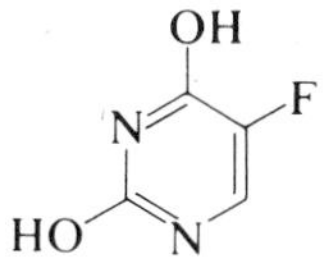

5-FLUROURACIL (5-FU)

(15)

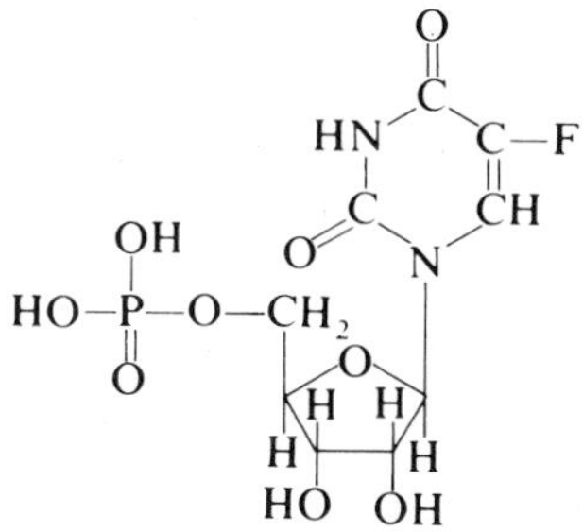

FdUrd-5'-P (5-FdUMP)

(16)

diminished in the presence of high levels of dUMP, the normal substrate. In fact, one of the problems with ongoing FU treatment is the development of large dUMP pools by the tumour cells, which effectively circumvent blockade of the enzyme. A second complication can arise from the fact that adequate concentrations of the folate cofactor are required to stabilize the complex of enzyme and substrate. If for any reason (e.g. cachexia, anorexia, or frank folate deficiency) these concentration requirements are not met, FdUMP binding remains non-covalent and only weakly inhibitory ($K_i \approx 10^{-5}$ M). Lastly, it should be pointed out that, in addition to inhibiting dTMPS, FU has also been shown to exert cytotoxicity as a consequence of its incorporation into nucleic acids.

Other active analogues of FdUMP include 5-bromo-dUMP, 5-chloro-dUMP, and related molecules with substituents on carbon atom 5 (Santi 1981 and references therein). These analogues presumably act through the same mechanism as FdUMP. Recently, however, newer dUMP derivatives have been synthesized and have been shown to work independently of the presence of folate cofactor. These substances, of which 5-nitro-dUMP is the prototype, have strong electron-withdrawing substituents in the 5'-position of the substrate ring (Fig. 13.3), and therefore do not require the folate for stabilization of the ternary complex (Matsuda 1978). Indeed, binding of these compounds is at least five times stronger than that of FdUMP in the absence of cofactor. Such drugs merit consideration for use in combination with the classical antifolates.

The fluoropyrimidines and related analogues provide mechanism-based inhibitors that have been shown to be effective against a number of tumours. FU, the most commonly used, is highly cytotoxic. Unfortunately, 5-nitrouracil is therapeutically inactive; this inactivity has been attributed to the fact that the compound is not metabolized to 5-nitro-dUMP at sufficiently fast rate to accumulate and compete with the natural substrate. Moreover, unlike the nucleotides of FU, 5-nitrouracil is not incorporated into RNA. Nevertheless, if further developments are made to increase the metabolism or affinity of this class of compounds for the enzyme and to keep dUMP levels down, then the 5-substituted uridylates may offer promise as antimetabolites.

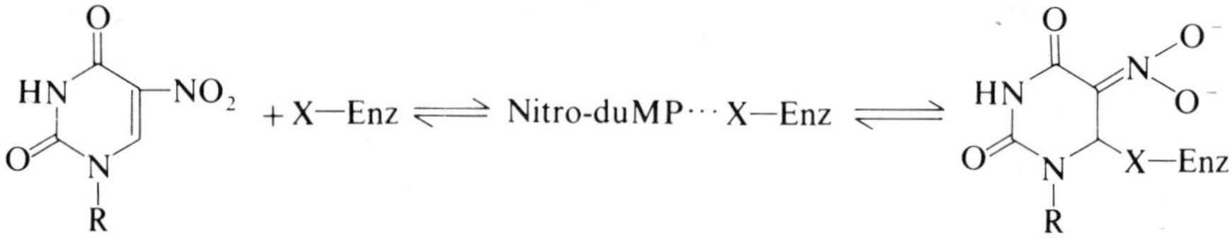

Fig. 13.3. Proposed mechanism of interaction of nitro-dUMP with dTMP synthetase (enz): R = 2′-deoxyribose-5′-phosphate; X = nucleophilic group.

Another method of blockade of the dTMPS system is the use of the antifolates, such as methotrexate (MTX) (**17**). MTX has been used effectively against a

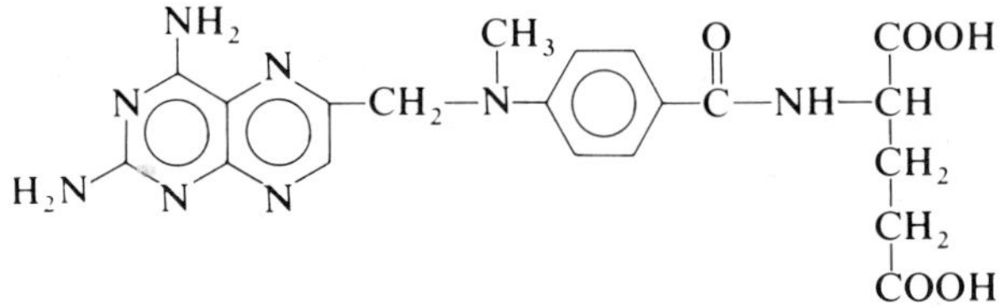

METHOTREXATE (MTX)

(**17**)

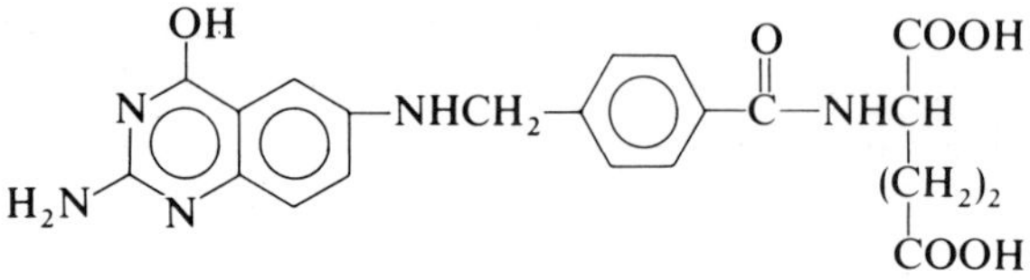

IAHQ (H338)

(**18**)

number of tumours including osteosarcoma, choriocarcinoma, leukaemia, and breast tumours. However, its toxicity to normal tissues and the rapid emergence of resistance are obstacles to its clinical effectiveness. MTX inhibits dihydrofolate reductase as well as directly binding to dTMPS, creating a double blockade of dTMP synthesis. Additionally, MTX in combination with the fluoropyrimidines can work antagonistically or synergistically. Inhibition of the dihydrofolate reductase system reduces the amount of folate cofactor and therefore decreases FdUMP binding and subsequent toxicity. However, high doses of MTX promote binding by stabilizing the complex much as the true cofactor does. In addition, MTX provokes an increase in PRPP levels, which increases the conversion of FU to its active species FdUMP.

Fernandez *et al.* (1983) have developed a number of newer MTX analogues, which show strong antineoplastic activity. The prototypical compound in this series is IAHQ (*N*-[*p*-{[(2-amino-4-hydroxy-6-quinazolinyl)amino]methyl}-benzoyl]-L-glutamic acid) (**18**). IAHQ shows activity versus dihydrofolate reductase, but more importantly, it non-competitively binds dTMPS at a site different from that of dUMP. The development of such compounds seems promising in that no metabolic activation is required and high dUMP levels do not reverse the inhibition. Moreover, the concentrations required to inhibit dTMPS are pharmacologically attainable. IAHQ has been show to be active against experimental adenocarcinoma of the colon and several murine leukaemias.

Jones *et al.* (1980) have described the synthesis of another second-generation antifolate, CB3717 (*N*-(4-{*N*-[(2-amino-4-hydroxy-6-quinazolinyl)methyl]prop-2-ynlamino}benzoyl]-L-glutamic acid) (**19**); this quinazoline inhibitor of dTMPS

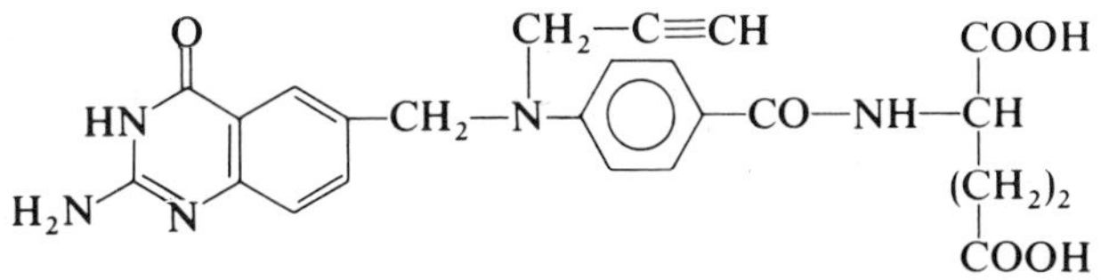

CB 3717

(**19**)

exhibits a K_i value of about 1×10^{-9} M. It is curative in the L1210 leukaemia model, is apparently well-tolerated by the host animals, and has entered clinical trials. It has been speculated that the comparatively low toxicity of CB3717 may be due to the fact that—unlike most other antifolates, most notably MTX and its polyglutamates—it does not inhibit *de novo* purine biosynthesis at the two folate-requiring steps, glycinamide ribonucleotide and 5-aminoimidazole-4-carboxamide ribonucleotide transformylases (Matherly *et al.* 1986). Certainly, in molar terms, this quinazoline is among the most potent molecules of those considered in this review.

13.2.7 Inhibitors of cytidine 5'-triphosphate synthetase

Using ATP for energy and L-glutamine as a nitrogen donor, CTP synthetase catalyses the conversion of uridine 5'-triphosphate into the corresponding nucleotide of cytidine. The enzyme is an attractive target for chemotherapeutic attack because of its comparatively low specific activity in the *de novo* pathway (Fig. 13.1, caption). Although a number of inhibitors of CTP synthetase have been identified, in this review only three prototypical inhibitors will be discussed, 3-deazauridine, (**20**) a veteran of the chemotherapeutic pharmacopeia, cyclopentenyl cytosine (**21**), a new synthetic achievement in which the ribofuranose ring is replaced by the reactive cyclopentenyl group, and acivicin, described earlier as a potent antagonist of L-glutamine.

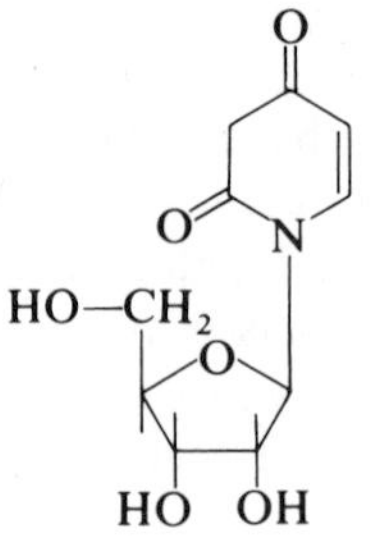

3-DEAZAURIDINE
(20)

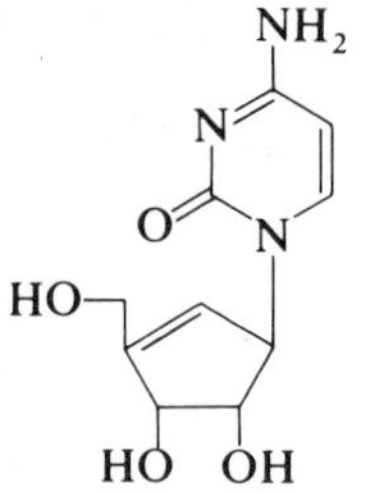

CYCLOPENTENYL CYTOSINE
(21)

3-deazauridine was developed as an anticancer drug, principally because of its activity against the L1210 and P388 murine leukaemias, systems in which nine daily intraperitoneal injections of 100 mg kg^{-1} produce 65 per cent increase in survival, without cures (Brockman et al. 1975). By contrast, against variants of these leukemias selected for resistance to arabinosylcytosine (a phenomenon mediated by a deletion of deoxycytidine kinase), 3-deazauridine proved to be consistently curative. In clinical trials with this agent, modest activity was observed in several of the leukaemias, but solid tumours as a rule were refractory.

3-deazauridine is transported into the cell via the nucleoside carrier, phosphorylated by uridine/cytidine kinase, and then converted to 3-deazauridine 5′-triphosphate by the higher kinases of the pyrimidine series. McPartland and his colleagues (McPartland et al. 1974) were the first to demonstrate that it was the 5′-triphosphate of 3-deazauridine that was responsible for the inhibition of CTP synthetase and the fall in CTP pools which ensue upon exposure to the drug. Kinetic studies also established that this triphosphate was a competitive inhibitor of the enzyme with UTP as variable substrate, the K_i being 5×10^{-6} M (Brockman et al. 1975).

Cyclopentenyl cytosine is a newly synthesized, rationally designed nucleoside analogue of cytosine, joined to a carbocyclic cyclopentenyl ring in lieu of the customery β-D-ribofuranose moiety (Lim et al. 1984). It was hoped that the double bond of cyclopentenyl cytosine would confer high reactivity on the molecule, enabling it, in theory, to undergo covalent reactions with active sites on its target enzyme, CTP synthetase. Although this mode of action has yet to be demonstrated experimentally, it has been found that 100 nM cyclopentenyl cytosine causes prompt and dramatic falls in the CTP (and presumably dCTP) concentrations of cultured murine and human tumour cells (Glazer et al. 1985). By analogy with 3-deazauridine and carbodine (cyclopentanyl cytosine) (Shannon et al. 1981), it is presumed that this effect is mediated by the 5′-triphosphate of cyclopentenyl cytosine. Against the L1210 leukaemia, nine daily doses of cylopentenyl cytosine (1 mg kg^{-1}), produce a > 100 per cent increase in lifespan with 10 per cent cures (Moyer et al. 1986). Thus it can be concluded that this agent is roughly 100-fold more potent than 3-deazauridine and, in thera-peutic terms, substantially more effective. For these reasons, cyclopentenyl cytosine is being considered for clinical trials by the Division of Cancer Treatment of the National Cancer Institute.

Acivicin, discussed earlier as an inhibitor of CPS II, in its capacity as a reactive analogue of L-glutamine is also capable of inhibiting CTP synthetase (Jayaram *et al.* 1975; Weber *et al.* 1982). Indeed, of all the amidotransferases attacked by acivicin, this enzyme is pre-eminent in its sensitivity to the antibiotic (George Weber, personal communication). The inhibition engendered by acivi-cin, while initially competitive with L-glutamine, will probably proceed to a second irreversible stage, which inactivates the enzyme (Weber *et al.* 1982; Prajda 1986). As a consequence of this inhibition, CTP pools fall in most (but not all) experimental systems. Since 3-deazauridine or cyclopentenyl cytosine occupy sites distinct from those occupied by L-glutamine on CTP synthetase, it might be possible to achieve more profound or more durable inhibition of the enzyme by the conjoint use of these agents, or by the use of transition-state analogues employing elements of both compounds. Wholly unexplored thus far has been the use of analogues of ATP to interrupt the utilization of that nucleotide in the synthesis of CTP.

13.3 Conclusion

It has been the quest of a considerable number of investigations to develop specific inhibitors of *de novo* pyrimidine biosynthesis, and a substantial number (> 50) of compounds have been described that exert inhibitory activity against one or more of the pyrimidine biosynthetic enzymes *in vitro*. However, the present generation of drugs are, for the most part, without significant therapeu-tic value in humans, particularly in the management of neoplasia. The parent inhibitors are not site-specific, with the notable exception of PALA, and in no instances have they been demonstrated completely to block precursor flux through the pathway. It would appear that the use of present-day pyrimidine pathway inhibitors as single-agent therapies is not an optimal therapeutic strategy. However, the judicious use of these drugs in combination chemo-therapy offers encouraging possibilities, particularly when applied sequentially against the *de novo* pathway (Kensler *et al.* 1981b; Loh and Kufe 1981) or when used in combination with agents that inhibit the salvage pathway, thus effecting a total pyrimidine deprivation (Zhen *et al.* 1983; Karle *et al.* 1984; Moyer *et al.* 1985).

References

Ardalan, B., Kensler, T. W., Jayaram, H. N., Morrison, W., Choie, D. D., Chadwick, M., Liss, R., and Cooney, D. A. (1981). Long-term association of *N*-(phosphonacetyl)-L-aspartate with bone. *Cancer Res.*, **41**, 150–6.

Bennett, L. L., Jr., Smithers, D., Rose, L. M., Adamson, D. J., and Thomas, H. J. (1979). Inhibition of synthesis of pyrimidine nucleotides by 2-hydroxy-3(3,3-dichloroallyl)-1,4-naphthoquinone. *Cancer Res.*, **39**, 4868–74.

Brockman, R. W., Shaddix, S. C., Williams, M., Nelson, J. A., Rose, L. M., and Schabel, F. M., Jr. (1975). The mechanism of action of 3-deazauridine in tumor cells sensitive and resistant to arabinosylcytosine. *Ann. N Y Acad. Sci.*, **255.**, 501–521.

Buchanan, J. M. (1973). The amidotransferases. *Adv. Enzymol.*, **39**, 91–183.

Cadman, E. C., Dix, D. E., and Handschumacher, R. E. (1978). Clinical, biological and biochemical effects of pyrazofurin. *Cancer Res.*, **38.**, 682–8.

Chen, S.-F., Ruben, R. L., and Dexter, D. L. (1986). Mechanism of action of the novel anticancer agent 6-fluoro-2-(2′-fluoro-1,1′-biphenyl-4-yl)-3-methyl-4-quinoline-carboxylic acid sodium salt (NSC 368390): inhibition of *de novo* pyrimidine nucleotide biosynthesis. *Cancer Res.*, **46**, 5014–19.

Christopherson, R. I. and Jones, M. E. (1980). The effect of pH and inhibitors upon the catalytic activity of the dihydroorotase of multienzyme protein *pyrl-3* from mouse Ehrlich ascites carcinoma. *J. Biol. Chem.*, **255**, 3358–70.

Collins, K. D. and Stark, G. R. (1971). Aspartate transcarbamylase interaction with the transition state analogue N-(phosphonacetyl)-L-aspartate. *J. Biol. Chem.*, **246**, 6599–605.

Dahl, J. L., Way, J. L., and Parks, R. E., Jr. (1959). The enzymatic synthesis of 5-fluorouridine 5′-phosphate. *J. Biol. Chem.*, **234**, 2998–3002.

Dexter, D. L., Hesson, D. P., Ardecky, R. J., Rao, G. V., Tippett, D. L., Dusak, B. A., Paull, K. D., Plowman, J., DeLarco, B. M., Narayanan, V. L., and Forbes, M. (1985). Activity of a novel 4-quinolinecarboxylic acid, NSC 368390 [6-fluoro-2-(2′-fluoro-1,1′-biphenyl-4-yl)-3-methyl-4-quinolinecarboxylic acid sodium salt], against experimental tumors. *Cancer Res.*, **45**, 5563–8.

Dix, D. E., Lehman, C. P., Jakubowski, A., Moyer, J. D., and Handschumacher, R. E. (1979). Pyrazofurin metabolism; enzyme inhibition and resistance in L5178Y cells. *Cancer Res.*, **39**, 4485–90.

Dunlap, R. B. (1978). TMP synthetase from *Lactobacillus casei. Meth. Enzymol.*, **51**, 90–7.

Fernandez, D. J., Bertino, J. R., and Hynes, J. B. (1983). Biochemical and antitumor effects of 5,8-dideazaisopteroylglutamate, a unique quinazoline inhibitor of thymidylate synthetase. *Cancer Res.*, **43**, 1117–23.

Glazer, R. I., Knode, M. C., Lim, M.-I., and Marquez, V. E. (1985). Cyclopentenyl cytidine analogue. An inhibitor of cytidine triphosphate synthesis in human colon carcinoma cells. *Biochem. Pharmacol.*, **24**, 2535–9.

Heidelberger, C., Chaudhuri, N. K., Danneberg, P., Mooren, D., Griesbach, L., Duschinsky, R., Schnitzer, R. J., Pleven, E., and Scheiner, J. (1957). Fluorinated pyrimidines, a new class of tumour-inhibitory compounds. *Nature*, **179**, 663–6.

Heidelberger, C., Griesbach, L., Montag, B. J., Mooren, D., Cruz, O., Schnitzer, R. J., and Grunberg, E. (1958). Studies on fluorinated pyrimidines. II. Effects on transplanted tumors. *Cancer Res.* **18**, 305–17.

Hernandez, K., Pinkel, D., Lee, S., and Leone, L. (1969). Chemotherapy with 6-azauridine (NSC-32074) for patients with leukemia. *Cancer Chemother. Rep.*, **53**, 203–07.

Holmes, W. L. (1956). Studies on the mode of action of analogues of ortic acid: 6-uracilsulfonic acid, 6-uracil sulfonamide, and 6-uracil methyl sulfone. *J. Biol. Chem.*, **223**, 677–86.

Holmes, W. L. and Welch, A. D. (1956). Biologic studies of analogs of orotic acid: 6-uracil sulfonic acid, 6-uracilsulfonamide, and 6-uracil methyl sulfone. *Cancer Res.*, **16**, 251–7.

Hoogenrad, N. J. (1974). Reaction mechanism of aspartate transcarbamylase from mouse spleen. *Arch. Biochem. Biophys.*, **161**, 76–82.

Jaffee, J. J. and Cooper, J. R. (1958). Studies on 6-uracil methyl sulfone. II. Anti-tumor activity. *Cancer Res.*, **18**, 1089–93.

Jayaram, H. N. and Cooney, D. A. (1979). Analogs of L-aspartic acid in chemotherapy for cancer. *Cancer Treat. Rep.*, **63**, 1095–108.

Jayaram., H. N., Cooney, D. A., Ryan, J. A., Neil, G., Dion, R. L., and Bono, V. H. (1975). L-(αS, $5S$)-α-amino-3-chloro-4,5-dihydro-5-isoxazolacetic acid (NSC-163501): a new amino acid antibiotic with the properties of an antagonist of L-glutamine *Cancer Treat. Rep.*, **59**, 481–91.

Jayaram, H. N., Cooney, D. A., Vistica, D. T., Kariya, S., and Johnson, R. K. (1979). Mechanisms of sensitivity or resistance of murine tumors to *N*-(phosphonacetyl)-L-aspartate (PALA). *Cancer Treat. Rep.*, **63**, 1291–302.

Jones, M. E. (1980). Pyrimidine nucleotide biosynthesis in animals: genes, enzymes and regulation of UMP biosynthesis. *Ann. Rev. Biochem.*, **49**, 252–79.

Jones, T. R., Calvert, A. H., Jackman, A. L., Brown, S. J., Jones, M., and Harrap, K. R. (1980). A potent antitumor inhibitor of thymidylate synthetase. *Eur. J. Cancer*, **17**, 11–19.

Karle, J. M., Anderson, L. W., and Cysyk, R. L. (1984). Effect of plasma concentrations of uridine on pyrimidine biosynthesis in cultured L1210 cells. *J. Biol. Chem.*, **259**, 67–72.

Kempe, T. D., Swyryd, E. A., Bruist, M., and Stark, G. R. (1976). Stable mutants of mammalian cells that overproduce the first three enzymes of pyrimidine nucleotide biosynthesis. *Cell*, **9**, 541–50.

Kensler, T. W. and Cooney, D. A. (1981). Chemotherapeutic inhibitors of the enzymes of the *de novo* pyrimidine pathway. *Adv. Pharmac. Chemother.*, **18**, 273–352.

Kensler, T. W., Ehrlichman, C., Jayaram, H. N., Tyagi, A. K., Ardalan, B., and Cooney, D. A. (1980). Peripheral leukocytes as indicators of the enzymic effects of *N*-(phosphonacetyl)-L-aspartic acid on human L-aspartate transcarbamylase activity. *Cancer Treat. Rep.*, **64**, 967–73.

Kensler, T. W., Mutter, G., Hankerson, J. G., Reck, L. J., Harley, C., Han, N., Ardalan, B., Cysyk, R. J., Johnson, R. K., Jayaram, H. N., and Cooney, D. A. (1981a). Mechanism of resistance of variants of the Lewis lung carcinoma to *N*-(phosphonacetyl)-L-aspartic acid. *Cancer Res.*, **41**, 894–904.

Kensler, T. W., Reck, L. J., and Cooney, D. A. (1981b). Therapeutic effects of acivicin and *N*-(phosphonacetyl)-L-aspartic acid in a biochemically designed trial against a *N*-(phosphonacetyl)-L-aspartic acid-resistant variant of the Lewis lung carcinoma. *Cancer Res.*, **41**, 905–9.

Kensler, T. W., Jayaram, H. N., and Cooney, D. A. (1982). Effects of acivicin and PALA, singly and in combination, on *de novo* pyrimidine biosynthesis. *Adv. Enzyme Regul.*, **20**, 57–73.

Kensler, T. W., Schuller, H. M., Jayaram, H. N., and Cooney, D. A. (1988). Characterization of eleven important transplantable murine tumors from the standpoint of morphology, pyrimidine biosynthesis and responsiveness to pyrimidine antimetabolites. In *Progressive stages of neoplastic growth.* (ed. H. Kaiser) Vol. 2, pp. 145–56. Pergamon Press, Oxford.

Kisner, D. L., Kuhn, J. G., Weiss, G. R., Dorr, F. A., and Von Hoff, D. D. (1983). New anticancer drugs. In *Cancer chemotherapy. annual* (ed. H. M. Pinedo and B. A. Chabner), Vol. 5, pp. 120–60. Elsevier, New York.

Levine, R. L., Hoogenraad, N. J., and Kretchmer, N. (1974). A review: biological and clinical aspects of pyrimidine metabolism. *Pediat. Res.*, **8**, 724–34.

Lim, M.-I., Moyer, J. D., Cysyk, R. L., and Marquez, V. E. (1984). Cyclopentenyluridine and cyclopentenylcytidine analogues as inhibitors of uridine–cytidine kinase. *J. Med. Chem.*, **27**, 1536–8.

Livingston, R. B., Venditti, J. M., Cooney, D. A., and Carter, S. K. (1970). Glutamine antagonists in chemotherapy. *Adv. Pharmacol. Chemother.*, **8**, 57–120.

Loh, E. and Kufe, D. W. (1981). Synergistic effects with inhibitors of *de novo* pyrimidine synthesis, acivicin and *N*-(phosphonacetyl)-L-aspartic acid. *Cancer Res.*, **41**, 3419–23.

Loo, T. L., Benjamin, R. S., Lu, K., Benvenuto, J. A., Hall, S. W., and McKelvey, E. M. (1978). Metabolism and disposition of Baker's antifolate (NSC-139105), ftorafur (NSC-148958) and dichloroallyl lawsone (NSC-126771) in man. *Drug. Metab. Rev.*, **8**, 137–50.

McKelvey, E. M., Lomedico, M., Lu, K., Chadwick, M., and Loo, T. L. (1979). Dichloroallyl lawsone. *Clin. Pharmacol. Ther.*, **25**, 586–90.

McPartland, R. P., Wang, M. C., Bloch, A., and Weinfeld, H. (1974). Cytidine-5'-triphosphate synthetase as a target for inhibition by the antitumor agent 3-deazauridine. *Cancer Res.*, **34**, 3107–11.

Matherly, L. H., Barlowe, C. K., Phillips, V. M., and Goldman, I. D. (1986). The effects of 4-aminoantifolates on 5-formyltetrahydrofolate metabolism in L1210 cells. A biochemical basis for the selectivity of leucovorin rescue. *J. Biol. Chem.*, **262**, 710–17.

Matsuda, A., Yusuke, W., and Santi, D. V. (1978). 5-nitro-2'-deoxyuridylate: a mechanism-based inhibitor of thymidylate synthetase. *Biochem. Biophys. Res. Comm.*, **84**, 654–59.

Mori, M. and Tatibana, M. (1978). A multienzyme complex of carbamoyl-phosphate synthase (glutamine): aspartate transcarbamylase: dihydroorotase (rat ascites hepatoma and rat liver). *Meth. Enzymol.*, **51**, 111–21.

Moyer, J. D., Karle, J. M., Malinowski, N., Marquez, V. E., Salam, M. A., Malspeis, L., and Cysyk, R. L. (1985). Inhibition of uridine kinase and the salvage of uridine by modified pyrimidine nucleosides. *Mol. Pharmacol.*, **28**, 454–60.

Moyer, J. D., Malinowski, N. M., Treanor, S. P., and Marquez, V. E. (1986). Antitumor activity and biochemical effects of cyclopentenyl cytosine in mice. *Cancer Res.*, **46**, 3325–9.

Ohnuma, T., Roboz, J., Shapiro, M. L., and Holland, J. F. (1977). Pharmacological and biochemical effects of pyrazofurin in humans. *Cancer Res.*, **37**, 2043–9.

Olah, E., Lui, M. S., Tzeng, D. Y., and Weber, G. (1980). Phase and cell cycle specificity of pyrazofurin action. *Cancer Res.*, **40**, 2869–75.

Porter, R. W., Modebe, M. O., and Stark, G. R. (1969). Aspartate transcarbamylase: kinetic studies of the catalytic subunit. *J. Biol. Chem.*, **244**, 1846–51.

Potvin, B. W., Stern, H. J., May, S. R., Lam, G. F., and Krooth, R. S. (1978). Inhibition by barbituric acid and its derivatives of the enzymes in rat brain which participate in the synthesis of pyrimidine ribotides. *Biochem. Pharmacol.*, **27**, 655–65.

Prajda, N. (1986). Enzyme targets of antiglutamine agents in cancer chemotherapy. *Adv. Enzyme Reg.*, **24**, 207–23.

Rubin, R. J., Reynard, A., and Handschumacher, R. E. (1964). An analysis of the lack of drug synergism during sequential blockade of *de novo* pyrimidine biosynthesis. *Cancer Res.*, **24**, 1002–7.

Santi, D. V. (1981). Inhibition of thymidylate synthetase: mechanism, methods and metabolic consequences. *Molecular actions and targets for chemotherapeutic agents*, pp. 285–300. Academic Press, New York.

Shambaugh, G. E., III (1979). Pyrimidine biosynthesis. *Am. J. Clin. Nutr.*, **32**, 1290–7.

Shannon, W. H., Arnett, G., Westbrook, L., Shealy, Y. F., O'Dell, O. C. A., and Brockman, R. W. (1981). Evaluation of carbodine, the carbocyclic analog of cytidine and related carbocyclic analogs of pyrimidine nucleotides for antiviral activity against human influenza type A viruses. *Antimicrob. Agents Chemother.*, **20**, 769–76.

Shoaf, W. T. and Jones, M. E. (1973). Uridylic acid synthesis in Ehrlich ascites carcinoma.

Properties, subcellular distribution, and nature of enzyme complexes of the six biosynthetic enzymes. *Biochemistry*, **12**, 4039–51.

Traut, T. W. and Jones, M. E. (1977a). Inhibitors of orotate phosphoribosyltransferase and orotidine-5′-phosphate decarboxylase from mouse Ehrlich ascites cells: a procedure for analyzing the inhibition of a multi-enzyme complex. *Biochem. Pharmacol.*, **26**, 2291–6.

Traut, T. W. and Jones, M. E. (1977b). Kinetic and conformational studies of the orotate phosphoribosyltransferase: orotidine-5′-phosphate decarboxylase enzyme complex from mouse Ehrlich ascites cells. *J. Biol. Chem.*, **252**, 8374–81.

Tso, J. Y., Bower, S. G., and Zalkin, H. (1980). Mechanism of inactivation of glutamine amidotransferases by the antitumor drug L-(αS, 5S)-α-amino-3-chloro-4,5-dihydro-5-isoxazoleacetic acid (AT-125). *J. Biol. Chem.*, **255**, 6734–8.

Von Hoff, D. D., Rosencweig, M., and Muggia, F. M. (1979). New anticancer drugs. In *Cancer Chemotherapy. annual* (ed. H. Pinedo), Vol. 1, pp. 126–48. Elsevier, New York.

Weber, G., Pradja, N., Lui, M. S., Denton, J. E., Aoki, T., Sebolt, J., Zhen, Y.-S., Burt, M. E., Faderman, M. A., and Reardon, M. A. (1982). Multi-enzyme-targeted chemotherapy by acivicin and actinomycin. *Adv. Enzyme Reg.*, **20**, 75–96.

Weinfeld, H., Savage, C. R. and McPartland, R. P. (1978). CTP synthetase of bovine calf liver. *Meth. Enzymol.*, **51**, 84–90.

Worzalla, J. F., and Sweeney, M. J. (1980). Pyrazofurin inhibition of purine biosynthesis via 5-aminoimidazole-4-carboximide-1-β-D-ribofuranosyl 5′-monophosphate formyltransferase. *Cancer Res.*, **40**, 1482–5.

Yoshida, T., Stark, G. R., and Hoogenrad, N. J. (1974). Inhibition by N-(phosphonacetyl)-L-aspartate of aspartate transcarbamylase activity and drug-induced cell proliferation in mice. *J. Biol. Chem.*, **249**, 6951–5.

Zhen, Y.-S., Lui, M. S., and Weber, G. (1983). Effects of acivicin and dipyridamole on hepatoma 3924A cells. *Cancer Res.*, **43**, 1616–19.

14

Inhibitors of purine biosynthesis

J. A. Montgomery and L. L. Bennett, Jr.

14.1 Inhibitors of purine biosynthesis

Purines are synthesized in cells as their ribonucleoside-5′-monophosphates. Since this topic has been so extensively reviewed, only a brief outline is given herein. The *de novo* biosynthesis of inosinic acid and its conversion to adenylic and guanylic acids are depicted in Figs 14.1 and 14.2. The starting material for these pathways is 5′-phosphoribosyl-1-pyrophosphate (PRPP), which is also involved in the *de novo* synthesis of uridylic acid, in the so-called purine–pyrimidine salvage pathways, and in other phosphoribosyl transfer reactions. The formation of PRPP from ribose-5-phosphate and ATP is catalysed by ribose phosphate pyrophosphokinase. This enzyme, and the ones that are peculiar to the *de novo* purine ribonucleotide pathway and for which inhibitors are known, will be discussed below individually with their known inhibitors. The circled numbers behind the enzyme names correspond to the reactions they catalyse, as depicted in Figs 14.1 and 14.2. The enzymes for which there are no known inhibitors are not discussed. In addition, the enzymes of purine ribonucleotide interconversions and ribonucleotide diphosphate reductase, which are also important targets, are included. Since the enzymes of nucleic

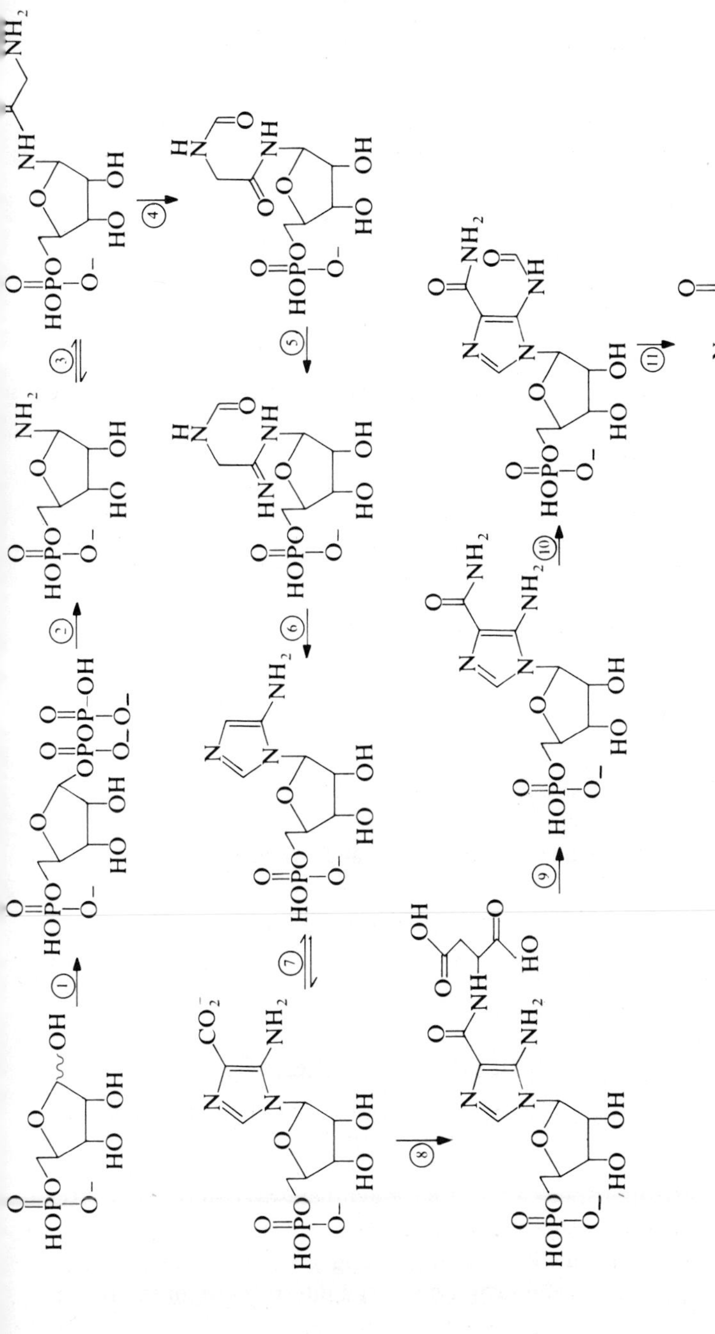

Fig. 14.1. The *de novo* synthesis of inosinic acid.

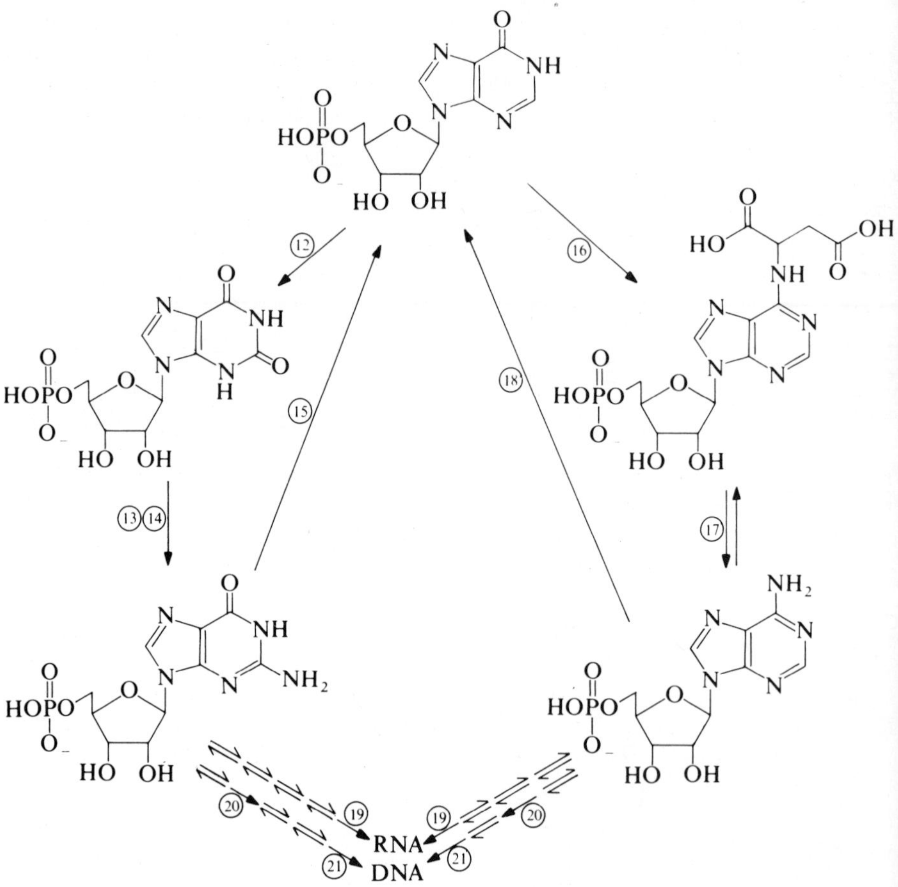

Fig. 14.2. Purine nucleotide interconversions and nucleic acid synthesis.

acid synthesis (i.e. the polymerases and related enzymes) are discussed in another chapter, they are only mentioned briefly here in connection with certain drugs that act on them.

14.1.1 Ribose phosphate pyrophosphokinase (EC 2.7.6.1) ①

$$ATP + \text{D-ribose-5-phosphate} \rightarrow AMP + \text{5-phospho-}\alpha\text{-D-ribose-1-diphosphate.}$$
$$(14.1)$$

Ribose phosphate pyrophosphokinase (PRPP synthetase) requires both Mg^{2+} and inorganic phosphate (Kornberg et al. 1955; Remy et al. 1955). MgATP is the true substrate of the reaction (Murray and Wong 1967; Switzer 1969) and a pyrophosphoryl-enzyme has been proposed as the intermediate in the reaction (Switzer 1968).

3'-Deoxyadenosine (cordycepin) inhibited ^{14}C-formate incorporation into nucleic acid purines and phosphoribosyl-formylglycinamide synthesis in the presence of diazooxonorleucine (DON) (Rottman and Guarino 1964). Its triphosphate inhibited the synthesis of adenine nucleotides from ^{14}C-adenine, ATP, and ribose-5-phosphate, but had no effect when 5-phosphoribosyl pyrophosphate (PRPP) replaced its precursors, leading to the conclusion that 3'-deoxyadenosine triphosphate is an inhibitor of PRPP synthetase (Overgaard-Hansen 1964). A similar experiment showed that 9-β-D-xylofuranosyladenine triphosphate inhibited PRPP synthetase activity in extracts of TA3 ascites cells (Ellis and LePage 1965). Later the effect of 3'-deoxyadenosine on PRPP accumulation was measured in L5178Y cells incubated with glucose. It caused a 70 per cent inhibition of this accumulation at a concentration of 0.28 mM. 2',3'-dideoxyadenosine, 2',3'-dideoxydidehydroadenosine, and 2',5'-dideoxyadenosine were also inhibitory but less potent. These latter results suggest that, at least in some cases, phosphorylation to analogue nucleotides is not necessary for inhibition of this enzyme. In this regard decoyinine and psicofuranine, which are not phosphorylated in cells, inhibited PRPP synthesis in extracts of *Streptococcus faecium* (Bloch and Nichol 1964) but not in Ehrlich ascites cells (Henderson and Khoo 1965). 9-β-D-arabinofuranosyladenine 5'-monophosphate (ara-AMP), which must be cleaved to the nucleoside before it can effectively enter cells, blocks the incorporation of adenine-8-^{14}C into nucleotides in intact erythrocytes (Becher and Schollmeyer 1983). Partially purified PRPP synthetase from erythrocytes was inhibited by ara-AMP in a non-competitive manner with respect to both MgATP and ribose-5-phosphate, although the effect appears to be of minimal importance for the vitality and survival of mammalian cells when therapeutic doses of the drug are administered. In combination with other inhibitors of nucleotide synthesis, however, it could be of some consequence.

Formycin, a C-nucleoside analogue of adenosine, blocked *de novo* purine nucleotide biosynthesis in Ehrlich ascites cells through inhibition of PRPP synthesis, but this did not occur in cells that did not phosphorylate formycin (Henderson *et al.* 1967). However, the formycin nucleotides have been effectively substituted for adenosine nucleotides in many enzymatic reactions and the compound is incorporated into RNA. The information available to date does not provide a clear understanding of the mechanism of its cytotoxicity or antiviral activity. 7-deaza-adenosine (tubercidin), another ring analogue of adenosine, inhibited the accumulation of PRPP and of phosphoribosyl-formylglycinamide in Ehrlich ascites cells (Henderson and Khoo 1965). Its inhibition of the growth of *Crithidia fasciculata* has been attributed to the inhibition of PRPP synthetase, based on the analysis of cell-free extracts of treated cells (Dewey *et al.* 1978).

Recent studies indicate that 6-(methylthio)purine ribonucleotide (MeMPRP), which behaves in many ways like an AMP analogue, is an inhibitor of highly purified erythrocyte PRPP synthetase. The inhibition appeared to be non-competitive with respect to both MgATP ($K_i = 1.34$ mM) and ribose-5-

phosphate ($K_i = 0.44$ mM). On the basis of the concentrations of MeMPR used in previous work on the inhibition of *de novo* purine ribonucleotide biosynthesis, it is likely that that pathway is more sensitive than PRPP synthesis to inhibition by metabolites of MeMPR (Yen *et al.* 1981).

It can be concluded that there are a number of adenosine analogues—with changes in the sugar moiety, the purine ring, or at the 6-position—that can inhibit PRPP synthetase. In most, but not all cases, it seems that metabolism to the nucleotides is a prerequisite for inhibition, although it is not clear whether *in vivo* the true inhibitor is the mono-, di-, or triphosphate, and it is possible that all three are involved. At the same time, it is clear that inhibition of this enzyme is not the most important site of action of at least two analogues, ara-A (or its monophosphate) and 6-(methylthio)purine ribonucleoside, and it may not be for others.

14.1.2   Amidophosphoribosyl transferase (EC 2.4.2.14) ②

L-glutamine + 5-phospho-α-D-ribose 1-diphosphate + H_2O =
5-phospho-β-D-ribosylamine + pyrophosphate + L-glutamate.   (14.2)

Amidophosphoribosyl transferase (amido-PRT) has been studied extensively because it catalyses the first reaction unique to the purine biosynthetic pathway and is the primary site of regulation of this pathway by the end products, purine ribonucleotides. Amido-PRTs have been isolated from a variety of sources (mammalian, microbial, and avian) and the properties of the enzymes from various sources are similar. The properties of the mammalian enzyme are discussed in a review by Holmes (1981), which should be consulted for documentation of the general statements that follow. Ammonia as well as glutamine can serve as a source of the amino group. Reported K_m or $S_{0.5}$ values are 0.14–0.64 mM for PRPP; 1.0–1.8 mM for glutamine; and 2.0–3.8 mM for ammonia. In controlling the activity of amido-PRT, the natural purine ribonucleotides act at an allosteric site to convert a low-molecular-weight active form of the enzyme to a high-molecular-weight inactive form. IMP, AMP, and GMP are all effective inhibitors. With enzymes from some sources, there appear to be separate binding sites for 6-aminopurine nucleotides and 6-oxypurine nucleotides, as shown by synergistic inhibition by combinations of the two species of nucleotide (Caskey *et al.* 1964; Nierlich and Magasanik 1965; Holmes *et al.* 1973; Messenger and Zalkin 1979), but in other preparations, this synergism was not observed (Hill and Bennett 1969; Nagy 1970; Wood and Seegmiller 1973).

Known inhibitors of amido-PRT include analogues of glutamine and analogues of the natural allosteric regulators.

14.1.2.1   *Inhibition by nucleotide analogues*
In intact cells, a large number of cytotoxic analogues of purines and purine nucleosides have been found to inhibit an early step of *de novo* purine synthesis;

these inhibitons may be the result of the nucleotide analogues simulating the action of the natural nucleotides as feedback inhibitors of amido-PRT. However, the inhibition cannot be conclusively ascribed to this action unless the alternative explanation, inhibition of synthesis of PRPP, is ruled out. In contrast to the large number of bases and nucleosides that have been evaluated in intact cells, only relatively few nucleotide analogues have been evaluated as inhibitors of isolated amido-PRT. Of these, the most effective was the 5′-phosphate of 6-(methylmercapto)purine ribonucleoside (MeMPR); others that were highly effective (as good or better than AMP) were 6-mercaptopurine (MP) ribonucleo-tide, 6-thioguanine (TG) ribonucleotide, 2-fluoroadenine ribonucleotide, tubercidin-5′-monophosphate, cordycepin-5′-phosphate and the ribonucleotide of allopurinol (McCollister *et al.* 1964; Rottman and Guarino 1964; Hill and Bennett 1969; Tay *et al.* 1969; Becher *et al.* 1978). Since the corresponding nucleosides or bases are inhibitors of *de novo* synthesis in intact cells (LePage and Jones 1961; Henderson 1963; Bennett and Smithers 1964; Brockman and Chumley 1965), it is probable that this inhibition results from the action of their nucleotides on amido-PRT. Additional correlation between the results with intact cells and those with the isolated enzyme was also seen in the synergistic effects between 6-amino- and 6-oxypurines (Henderson 1962; Grindey *et al.* 1976). With respect to modes of action, it is to be noted that purine analogues have multiple potential sites of inhibition and, with one exception, for none of these analogues is amido-PRT the exclusive or primary site of action. The exception is MeMPR for which there is good evidence that inhibition of amido-PRT is the action primarily responsible for its cytotoxicity (Bennett and Adamson 1970; Woods *et al.* 1978).

14.1.2.2   *Glutamine analogues*

Glutamine is a substrate for enzymes catalysing three reactions on the purine biosynthetic pathway, and analogues of glutamine might therefore be expected to inhibit this pathway at multiple points. The glutamine analogues of principal interest are *O*-diazoacetyl-L-serine(azaserine), 6-diazo-5-oxo-L-norleucine (DON), L-(αS, 5S)-α-amino-3-chloro-4,5-dihydro-5-isoazoleacetic acid (acivicin), and L-2-amino-4-oxo-5-chloropentanoic acid (CONV). All of these analogues contain chemically reactive groups; in inhibiting the amidotransferases, the analogues compete with glutamine for binding and, once bound, inactivate the enzyme by alkylation of a sulphydryl group (for reviews see Livingston *et al.* 1970; Buchanan 1973; Bennett 1975). These analogues are of importance in the history of drug design in that azaserine was the first recognized example of an active-site-directed irreversible inhibitor and the origin of this concept, which was elaborated by Baker (1967).

Although glutamine analogues could conceivably inhibit all of the three amidotransferases on the purine pathway, such general inhibition does not occur in intact cells because the various enzymes differ widely in their sensitivi-ties to these analogues. Amido-PRT appears to be less sensitive to inhibition than other amido transferases and in intact cells is not the primary site of inhibition by any of the analogues. Jayaram *et al.* (1975) examined all four analogues at concentrations of 1 mM, as inhibitors of glutamine amidotransferases in extracts of foetal rat liver: acivicin and azaserine gave no inhibition of amido-PRT, whereas DON and CONV gave complete inhibition. However, the enzyme is inhibited by high concentrations of azaserine; for amido-PRT from human placenta, the K_i for azaserine was 4 mM, whereas that for DON was 3.4 μM (King *et al.* 1978). For the enzyme from pigeon liver, the K_i for DON was 19 μM and that for azaserine was 4.2 mM (Hartman 1963). Amido-PRT from *Escherichia coli* was irreversibly inhibited by DON, which alkylated a cysteine residue at the NH_2-terminal (Tso *et al.* 1982). Despite this high sensitivity of amido-PRT to DON, the amidotransferase catalysing the conversion of formylglycinamide ribonucleotide to formylglycinamidine ribonucleotide in mammalian cells is even more sensitive, with the result that in intact cells, inhibition of amido-PRT is observed only at concentrations of DON in excess of those which inhibit purine synthesis by blocking the synthesis of formylglycinamidine ribonucleotide (Anderson and Brockman 1963). The reasons for the differences in sensitivities of the various amidotransferases are not understood; such knowledge might provide a basis for the design of a glutamine analogue with specificity for amido-PRT.

14.1.3. Phosphoribosylglycinamide formyltransferase (EC 2.1.2.2) ④

10-formyltetrahydrofolate + 5′-phosphoribosylglycinamide →
  tetrahydrofolate + 5′-phosphoribosyl-*N*-formylglycinamide.   (14.3)

Phosphoribosylglycinamide formyltransferase (GAR FTase) supplies the formyl group necessary for the eventual closure of the imidazole ring. Although the complicated interconversions of tetrahydrofolate cofactors caused confusion for many years, the specific one-carbon donor for this reaction was eventually identified as 10-formyltetrahydrofolic acid, the K_m of which varied from 9 to 15 μM with the source of the enzyme (chicken, Sarcoma 180, L1210). The K_m for GAR was 60 μM for the chicken enzyme and 17 μM for enzymes from the neoplastic cells. 5,8-dideaza-10-formyltetrahydrofolate and 5-deaza-10-formyltetrahydrofolate can also serve as cofactor for the reaction (Daubner and Benkovic 1985). On the other hand, 8-deaza-10-formylfolate is an inhibitor of the enzyme ($K_i = 4$ μM) (Smith *et al.* 1981). 11-formyl-7,8-dihydrohomofolate and 11-formyltetrahydrohomofolate both also inhibit GAR FTase (K_i values of 4 and 1 μM, respectively) (Slieker and Benkovic 1984).

5,10-dideazatetrahydrofolate (DDTHF) is a potent inhibitor of *de novo* purine biosynthesis and of the growth of L1210 cells in culture ($I_{50} = 20$–50 nM) (Moran *et al.* 1985). Growth inhibition was reversed by both hypoxanthine and 5-aminoimidazole-4-carboxamide. making GAR FTase the most likely target of DDTHF action, although its effects on the isolated enzyme have not been studied. Later it was shown to inhibit the formation of phosphoribosylformylglycinamide at the same concentration at which it inhibits cell growth (Beardsley *et al.* 1986). DDTHF shows activity against methotrexate-sensitive and resistant L1210 leukemia and a variety of solid tumours in rodents.

14.1.4 Phosphoribosylformylglycinamidine synthase (EC 6.3.5.3) ⑤

$$ATP + 5'\text{-phosphoribosylformylglycinamide (FGARP)}$$
$$+ \text{L-glutamine} + H_2O = AMP + \text{orthophosphate} +$$
$$5'\text{-phosphoribosylformylglycinamidine (FGAMRP)} +$$
$$\text{L-glutamate.} \qquad (14.4)$$

This reaction, which is the second point at which glutamine participates in the formation of an intermediate on the purine pathway, has been studied with enzymes from microbial (French *et al.* 1963), avian (Levenberg and Buchanan 1957; Levenberg *et al.* 1957; Melnick and Buchanan 1957; Mizobuchi and Buchanan 1968a, b; Mizobuchi *et al.* 1968), and mammalian sources (Chu and Henderson 1972a, b, c; Elliott and Weber 1985). Like the other glutamine amidotransferases on the pathway, the enzyme can use ammonia instead of glutamine. The mechanism of the reaction has been studied thoroughly in chicken liver by Buchanan and his associates (for review see Buchanan 1973), who proposed a mechanism that involves the following steps:

(1) glutamine reacts first with the enzyme to form a γ-glutamyl thioester; NH_3 is liberated and is transferred (without dissociation) to a second site;

(2) ATP or FGARP with Mg^{2+} bind randomly;

(3) the enzyme is phosphorylated by ATP but the resulting ADP is not dissociated;

(4) the carbonyl group in FGARP is attacked by NH_3 and loses its O-atom to the phosphate group;

(5) the products, FGAMRP, ADP, glutamate, and P_i are released.

For the enzyme from pigeon liver, the K_m values were: FGARP, 6.4×10^{-5} M and glutamine, 6.2×10^{-4} M (Levenberg *et al.* 1957); for the enzyme from Ehrlich cells, FGARP, 1.1×10^{-4} M and glutamine, 1.1×10^{-4} M (Chu and Henderson 1972b).

The only known inhibitors of this enzyme are analogues of glutamine. Of the three amidotransferases on the purine pathway, FGARP amidotransferase is uniquely sensitive to azaserine; in extracts of foetal rat liver, a 1 mM concentration of azaserine gave complete inhibition of FGARP amidotransferase and no inhibition of PRPP or XMP amidotransferases (Jayaram *et al.* 1975). The enzyme is even more sensitive to DON than to azaserine. For the amidotransferase from pigeon liver, the K_i values for azaserine and DON were 3.4×10^{-5} M and 1.1×10^{-6} M respectively (Levenberg *et al.* 1957); for the enzyme from

Ehrlich ascites cells, the values were 2.3×10^{-6} M and 4.0×10^{-7} M (Chu and Henderson 1972c). Acivicin and CONV also inhibited the enzyme in extracts of foetal rat liver (Jayaram *et al.* 1975). The K_i for inhibition of the enzyme from rat hepatoma by acivicin was 5×10^{-6} M (Elliott and Weber 1985). In intact cells, inhibition of FGARP amidotransferase is the primary site of inhibition of the purine pathway by both azaserine and DON, as evidenced by the accumulation of FGARP in bacterial, mammalian, and avian cells inhibited by these agents (see, among others, Greenlees and LePage 1956; Hartman *et al.* 1956; Tomisek *et al.* 1956; Henderson 1962; Tomisek and Reid 1962; Anderson and Brockman 1963). In intact cells, the primary sites of action of acivicin appear to be on XMP amidotransferase and UTP amidotransferase (Neil *et al.* 1979), but in an *in vivo* study with a rat hepatoma, FGARP amidotransferase was as sensitive to inactivation by acivicin as were XMP and UTP amidotransferases (Weber *et al.* 1984; Elliott and Weber 1985). The inactivation of FGARP amidotransferase by the glutamine analogues, like that of other amidotransferases, results from the alkylation of a cysteine residue. The reaction of the avian enzyme with azaserine was the first demonstration of this mode of inhibition (Dawid *et al.* 1963).

In addition to the glutamine analogues already considered, mention should be made of one other: albizziin (β-ureido-L-alanine), an analogue that was also useful in study of FGARP amidotransferase. This agent was found to inactivate the enzyme and to bind covalently to it in a 1:1 ratio (Schroeder *et al.* 1969). The most likely structure for the bound complex was considered to be $E—S—C—NH–CH_2—CHCOOH$, where the thio group is part of a cysteine

$$E—\underset{\underset{O}{\|}}{S—C}—NH–CH_2—\underset{\underset{NH_2}{|}}{CH}COOH$$

moiety. In forming such a complex, albizziin would act similarly to glutamine in that both molecules react with the enzyme to release a molecule of ammonia. However, the product from the reaction with glutamine is a thioester and that from the reaction with albizziin is a thiocarbamate. The reaction with albizziin is also distinct from those with azaserine, DON, and acivicin, all of which alkylate the sulphydryl group.

It would appear unlikely that types of inhibitor other than glutamine analogues will be found for this enzyme, because analogues of the other substrate, FGARP, presumably would have to be nucleotides and there is no apparent mechanism by which analogues of FGA or FGAR could be converted intracellularly to nucleotides. It is also unlikely that a glutamine analogue could be designed that could be more effective than azaserine, which has a low K_i, is specific, and is effective in a broad spectrum of cell types.

14.1.5   Adenylosuccinate lyase (EC 4.3.2.2) ⑨

1-(5-phosphoribosyl)-5-aminoimidazole-4-(*N*-succinocarboxamide) →
1-(5-phosphoribosyl)-5-aminoimidazole-4-carboxamide + fumarate   (14.5)

Adenylosuccinate ⇌ AMP + fumarate.   (14.6)

Phosphoribosylaminoimidazole succinocarboxamide (SAICAR) is cleaved reversibly to fumarate and phosphoribosylaminoimidazole carboxamide (AICAR), one of the well-characterized intermediates of the *de novo* pathway. The enzyme catalysing this reaction [eqn (14.5)] is called adenylosuccinate lyase, because it also cleaves, reversibly, adenylosuccinate to fumarate and adenylic acid [eqn (14.6)], an unusual circumstance that has given rise to two types of inhibitors of the enzyme – imidazole and purine derivatives. The reported K_m values for SAICAR vary from 5 to 8 μM and those for adenylosuccinate from 1 to 13 μM. L-alanosyl-5-aminoimidazole-4-carboxylic acid ribonucleotide (alanosyl-AICOR), a metabolite of L-alanosine, is not a substrate of the lyase but is a good inhibitor of the enzyme. The inhibition is of mixed type in both reactions catalysed by the enzyme with an IC_{50} of 18 μM, which is in the concentration range that alanosyl-AICOR accumulates in subjects receiving alanosine (Brand and Lowenstein 1978; Casey and Lowenstein 1986).

Another type of substrate analogue, adenylophosphonopropionate (N^6-(D,L-1-carboxy-2-phosphonoethyl)adenylic acid) inhibits adenylosuccinate lyase reversibly and competitively, with apparent K_i values between 5.4 and 86 nM, depending on the source of the enzyme. K_m/K_i ratios with adenylosuccinate as substrate fall in the range of 44–1350. The exceptionally high affinity of the enzyme for adenylophosphonopropionate appears to involve the dianion of the phosphonate group (Brand and Lowenstein 1978). Similarly, N^6-(L-1-carboxy-2-nitroethyl)-AMP inhibits the lyase but at pH 7 the K_m/K_i ratio is 1, rising to 65 at pH 8.6. Thus, the K_m/K_i ratio for the nitronate form of the analogue was estimated to be 28, indicating that this inhibitor is less potent than the phosphonate (Porter *et al.* 1983).

6-thioinosinic acid, an important metabolite of 6-mercaptopurine, inhibits several purine nucleotide metabolizing enzymes, including adenylosuccinate lyase. The K_i for this enzyme, however, is 3×10^{-4} M and the K_m/K_i ratio about 0.01 making it unlikely that this inhibition contributes significantly to the cytotoxicity, and therefore the anticancer activity, of 6-mercaptopurine (Elion 1967).

14.1.6 Phosphoribosylaminoimidazolecarboxamide formyltransferase (EC 2.1.2.3) ⑩

1-(5-phosphoribosyl)-5-aminoimidazole-4-carboxamide + N-10-formyltetrahydrofolate→

$$1\text{-}(5\text{-phosphoribosyl})\text{-}5\text{-formamidoimidazole-4-carboxamide}$$
$$+ \text{ tetrahydrofolic acid.} \qquad (14.7)$$

Phosphoribosylaminoimidazolecarboxamide formyltransferase (AICAR FTase) has been purified some 400-fold by a series of steps including an affinity column, but, inosinicase remains in a constant ratio to the transformylase activity and, presumably, is an additional property of the protein (Müller and Benkovic 1981). The enzyme is composed of two subunits of molecular weight 65 000 and in contrast to GAR FTase, is not subject to rapid proteolysis (Caperelli *et al.* 1980). Only one of a number of analogues of folic acid that have been studied inhibited the enzyme. Since this compound, 5-deaza-10-formylfolic acid, has a K_i of 38 μM despite the fact that it is not a tetrahydro analogue and does not have a polyglutamate side chain, it may be a good lead compound for the design of better inhibitors. At the same time, 5-deaza-10-formylfolic acid is a substrate for, rather than an inhibitor of, GAR transformylase.

14.1.7   IMP dehydrogenase (EC 1.1.1.205) ⑫

$$\text{Inosine } 5'\text{-phosphate} + \text{NAD}^+ + \text{H}_2\text{O} = \text{xanthosine } 5'\text{-phosphate} + \text{NADH.}   (14.8)$$

IMP dehydrogenase (IMP-DHO) catalyses the only reaction on the purine pathway *de novo* that involves an oxidation or reduction. IMP-DHOs isolated from a variety of sources have generally similar properties. For mammalian enzymes, the K_m values for IMP are in the range 11–30 μM; for NAD, the values are in the range 24–46 μM for enzymes from most sources but somewhat higher (154–254 μM) for enzymes from erythrocytes, leukaemic cells, and bone marrow cells (see references in the following discussion). The reaction is ordered with IMP the first substrate to be bound and XMP the last product to be released (Anderson and Sartorelli 1968; Brox and Hampton 1968; Holmes *et al.* 1974; Hupe *et al.* 1986).

The reaction catalysed by IMP-DHO occupies a strategic position on the purine pathway in that it is the first reaction leading specifically to guanine nucleotides; it appears to be a rate-limiting step and hence a potential target for chemotherapy (Jackson *et al.* 1975, 1977). The enzyme is subject to end-product inhibition by XMP and GMP, which are competitive with IMP, with K_i values in the range 30–800 μM (Anderson and Sartorelli 1969b; Holmes *et al.* 1974; Miller and Adamczyk 1976; Jackson *et al.* 1977; Okada *et al.* 1983).

The number and structural diversity of known inhibitors of IMP-DHO are greater than for any other enzyme on the *de novo* pathway (for review see Robins 1982). Inhibitors include analogues of the substrates (IMP and NAD), analogues of the end products (XMP and GMP), and mycophenolic acid, an agent that is not closely related structurally to the substrates.

14.1.7.1   *Analogues of IMP*

MP ribonucleotide (MPRP), the thio analogue of IMP, is a substrate for IMP-DHO from both bacterial and mammalian cells; the K_m values are 21–32 μM, about the same as those for IMP, but since the velocities are < 10 per cent that of IMP, MPRP may also be regarded as an inhibitor of the dehydrogenase

(Salser *et al.* 1960; Atkinson *et al.* 1963; Hampton and Nomura 1967; Miller and Adamczyk, 1976). The K_i value for IMP-DHO from Ehrlich ascites cells was 3.6 μM (Atkinson *et al.* 1963); from sarcoma cells, 20 μM (Miller and Adamcyzk 1976), and from *Aerobacter aerogenes* 140 μM (Hampton and Nomura 1967). MPRP inactivates the DHO from *A. aerogenes* apparently by formation of a disulphide bond with a sulfhydryl group at or near the active site (Hampton 1963; Hampton and Nomura 1967); inactivation of DHOs from mammalian sources has not been reported. Inhibition of IMP-DHO is not the primary site of action of MP, but the ability of MPRP to act as a substrate is essential to one of the toxic actions of MP, namely incorporation into DNA as TG (Paterson and Tidd 1975).

6-chloropurine ribonucleotide also inhibits IMP-DHO from both bacterial (Hampton 1963; Hampton and Nomura 1967; Brox and Hampton 1968) and mammalian (Anderson and Sartorelli 1969a) cells, and the inhibition is competitive with IMP. The enzyme from *A. aerogenes* is inactivated as the result of formation of a thioether bond with a cysteine residue of the enzyme (Brox and Hampton 1968). Inhibition of IMP-DHO adequately explains the metabolic effects of 6-chloropurine and 6-chloropurine ribonucleoside in intact cells and hence, apparently, is the primary site of action of these agents (Sartorelli and Booth 1960).

A number of derivatives of IMP containing variously substituted benzylthio groups at either the 2-or 8-positions had K_i or IC_{50} values $< 100 \mu$M, but none of them had K_i values lower than the K_m for IMP. Other members of the series with K_i values less than 100 μM were the 2—CH$_3$O— and 2—C$_6$H$_5$CH=CH— derivatives of IMP and a number of 8-C$_6$H$_5$CH$_2$S—derivatives of AMP with various substituents on the phenyl ring (Skibo and Meyer 1981; Wong and Meyer 1984). 8-AzaIMP is a competitive substrate for the dehydrogenase with a K_m of 42 μM, only slightly greater than that of IMP (Miller and Adamcyzk 1976). 2-AzaIMP, which obviously cannot be a substrate for the enzyme, is an inhibitor but not a potent one ($K_i = 66 \mu$M) (Bennett *et al.* 1985).

Another group of agents that inhibits IMP-DHO by virtue of their capacity to compete with IMP are nucleotides of certain 5-membered heterocycles: ribavirin-5′-phosphate (for review see Sidwell *et al.* 1979), the 5′-phosphate of bredinin (1-β-D-ribofuranosyl-5-hydroxyimidazole-4-carboxamide), and a nucleotide of 2-amino-1,3,4-thiadiazole (for review see Hill 1980), in which the point of attachment of the ribosyl group is uncertain but is probably to N-3 of the thiadiazole ring. Although these agents are related structurally to the imidazole intermediates occurring on the pathway (bredinin phosphate is in fact the deamination product of AICAR), they do not interfere at these steps. The K_i values for inhibition of IMP-DHO were: ribavirin-5′-phosphate, 0.27–4.18 μM (Streeter *et al.* 1973; Fuertes *et al.* 1974; Gebeyehu *et al.* 1985); bredinin-5′-phosphate 0.02 μM (Fukui *et al.* 1982); 2-amino-1,3,4-thiadiazole nucleotide, 0.1 μM (Nelson *et al.* 1977). IMP-DHO is also inhibited by the 5′-phosphates of tiazofurin (2-β-D-ribofuranosylthiazole-4-carboxamide) and the corresponding selenazole, with K_i values of 115–470 μM (Kuttan *et al.* 1982; Gebeyehu *et al.* 1985); the inhibition was non-competitive with IMP. The active forms of these last two agents are, however, the corresponding NAD analogues, which are much better inhibitors of the DHO than are the nucleoside monophosphates (see below).

14.1.7.2   *Analogues of XMP and GMP*

XMP and GMP exert feedback inhibition on IMP-DHO (see above), and certain analogues of these nucleotides simulate this end-product inhibition. The nucleotides of 8-azaxanthine, 8-azaguanine, arabinosylguanine, 2,6-diaminopurine, 6-thioxanthine, and 2'-deoxyxanthosine inhibited IMP-DHO from sarcoma 180 cells with K_i values not much different from that of GMP, and the inhibitions were competitive with IMP (Anderson and Sartorelli 1969b; Miller and Adamczyk 1976). Inhibition was also observed with the ribonucleotides of TG and 2-amino-6-chloropurine; these agents produced progressive inhibition as a result of formation of covalent bonds with the enzyme. Inactivation of IMP-DHO from *A. aerogenes* by 6-TGMP has also been observed (Hampton 1963). All of these agents have other sites of action and it does not appear that inhibition of IMP-DHO is a critical site of action for any of them with the exception of 2-amino-6-chloropurine, which has been observed to inhibit IMP-DHO in intact cells (Sartorelli *et al.* 1968). 3-Deaza-GMP inhibited IMP-DHO from *E. coli* and also inhibited the incorporation of hypoxanthine into XMP and guanine nucleotides in intact Ehrlich ascites cells (Streeter and Koyama 1976; Cook *et al.* 1978); the IC_{50} (1.2 μM) is the lowest reported for any GMP analogue. However, the significance of IMP-DHO as a site of action of 3-deazaguanine is questionable in view of a later study that failed to find any evidence for inhibition of IMP-DHO in a human lung adenocarcinoma cell line (Page *et al.* 1985).

14.1.7.3   *Oxanosine*

This guanosine analogue (5-amino-3-β-D-ribofuranosyl-3H-imidazo[4,5-*d*][1,3]oxazin-7-one) (Shimada *et al.* 1981) is considered separately because its mode of action is not entirely clear. It was found initially to be an inhibitor of GMP synthase from *E. coli* (see next section). Later investigations with mammalian cells showed that oxanosine specifically inhibited the synthesis of guanine nucleotides, that oxanosine monophosphate (but not oxanosine) inhibited IMP-DHO, and that neither the free nucleoside nor the phosphate inhibited GMP synthase (Uehara *et al.* 1985). Inhibition of IMP-DHO by the phosphate was 'nearly competitive' with IMP and the K_i was 1–5 μM. Thus it appears that there are species differences in the sensitivities of IMP-DHO and GMP synthase to this analogue and that in mammalian cells the nucleoside must be phosphorylated to exert its inhibitory activity.

14.1.7.4   *Analogues of NAD*

Three analogues of NAD are known that inhibit IMP-DHO; these are analogues in which nicotinamide is replaced by a thiazole, selenazole, or 1,3,4-thiadiazole moiety.

Tiazofurin (2-β-D-ribofuranosylthiazole-4-carboxamide) (Srivastava *et al.* 1977) and the corresponding selenazole analogue (Srivastava and Robins 1983) are metabolized in cells to the phosphates and to the NAD analogues; the latter are responsible for inhibition of synthesis of guanine nucleotides as a result of inhibition of IMP-DHO. These NAD analogues inhibit IMP-DHO at very low concentrations. The K_i values for enzymes from various mammalian sources were in the range 0.02-0.5 μM (Kuttan *et al.* 1982; Cooney *et al.* 1982; Streeter and Robins, 1983; Jayaram *et al.* 1983; Boritzky *et al.* 1985). Inhibition was non-competitive with NAD or IMP. In intact cells these agents produce effects consistent with inhibition of IMP-DHO, namely decreased pools of guanine nucleotides, increased pools of IMP, and toxicity reversible or preventable by guanine or guanosine (see in addition to references already cited; Streeter and Miller 1981; Jayaram *et al.* 1982a, b).

An NAD analogue in which a 2-amino-1,3,4-thiadiazole moiety replaced nicotinamide (point of attachment of the ribosyl group to the heterocycle undetermined) produced pseudoirreversible inhibition of IMP-DHO; the K_i was about 20 μM and the inhibition was non-competitive with both NAD and IMP (Nelson *et al.* 1977).

14.1.7.5   *Mycophenolic acid (MPA)*

[See Nichol (1975) and Sweeney (1977) for reviews.] Unlike the other agents that inhibit IMP-DHO, mycophenolic acid is not a nucleotide. MPA inhibits IMP-DHOs from a variety of mammalian sources, and there are some marked differences in the sensitivity of enzymes from the various sources. Sweeney (1977) and Sweeney *et al.* (1972) found, for the enzymes from Landschütz ascites cells and a human colon tumour, IC_{50} values of 2.5×10^{-8} M and 1.7×10^{-8} M respectively, but for those from some other rodent tumours the IC_{50} values were four orders of magnitude greater. The value for the enzyme from Landschütz tumour cells was about the same as that found by Franklin and Cook (1969), who also noted K_i values of the order of 10^{-8} M for enzymes from calf thymus and LS cells. A low K_i (12–16 nM) was also found for the enzyme from a Chinese hamster cell line (Huberman *et al.* 1981). IMP-DHO from *E. coli* was insensitive to MPA (Franklin and Cook 1969; Sweeney 1977), but that from a protozoan (*Eimeria tenella*) had the same order of sensitivity as that from mammalian cells (Hupe *et al.* 1986). Inhibition of IMP-DHO was of the mixed type for preparations from mammalian cells and uncompetitive for the enzyme from *Eimeria tenella*. In their kinetic analyses of the dehydrogenase from this protozoan, Hupe *et al.* (1986) obtained data consistent with binding of MPA to the enzyme–XMP complex but not to the enzyme–IMP complex, and proposed a mechanism in which MPA simulates the substrate inhibition by NAD. Since

IMP-DHO from bacteria is not subject to inhibition by NAD, whereas the enzymes from mammalian cells and *Eimeria tenella* are; this mechanism explains the insensitivity of bacterial IMP-DHO to MPA.

A number of studies have demonstrated specific inhibition by MPA of synthesis of guanine nucleotides in intact cells and MPA has been widely used to produce experimental deficiencies of guanine nucleotides (Smith and Henderson 1976; Cass *et al.* 1977; Lowe *et al.* 1977; Kaiser *et al.* 1980; Lee *et al.* 1985; Hupe *et al.* 1986). As noted in the next section, MPA has also been observed to inhibit GMP synthase in some cells, and the reduction of pools of guanine nucleotides might also be due, in part, to inhibition of this enzyme. No other sites of action are known for MPA; it thus appears to be an agent uniquely specific for inhibition of the synthesis of guanine nucleotides.

14.1.8   GMP synthase (glutamine hydrolysing) (EC 6.3.5.2) (13)

$$ATP + \text{xanthosine } 5'\text{-phosphate} + \text{L-glutamine} + H_2O = AMP + \text{pyrophosphate}$$
$$+ GMP + \text{L-glutamate}. \tag{14.9}$$

GMP synthase (for review see Buchanan 1973) catalyses the reaction shown above. Like the two other amidotransferases on the pathway, either ammonia or glutamine serves as a source of the amino group. The reaction involves activation of the 2-OH group of XMP by ATP (Lagerqvist 1958; Abrams and Bentley 1959). The K_m values for the enzyme from Ehrlich ascites cells were: glutamine 0.68 mM; NH_3 36 mM; XMP 3.6 μM; ATP 0.28 mM (Spector 1975). For the enzyme from *E. coli*: XMP 34–58 μM; glutamine 1 mM; NH_3 1 mM, (Zyk *et al.* 1969; Spector *et al.* 1974; Patel *et al.* 1975). Hydroxylamine can replace ammonia in the reaction leading to the formation of 2-*N*-hydroxy-XMP, which inactivates the enzyme (Fukuyama and Donovan 1968). Inhibitors of the enzyme include nucleotides, glutamine analogues, psicofuranine and related compounds, and mycophenolic acid.

14.1.8.1   *Nucleotides*

Several analogues of XMP—2′-dXMP, 8-azaXMP, 6-thio-XMP and araXMP—serve as substrates for the enzyme, and some have V_{max} values so low that they function as effective inhibitors (K_i for 6-thio-XMP = 5 μM) (Spector 1975). These nucleotides simulate the inhibition produced by the end product, GMP.

14.1.8.2   *Glutamine analogues*

All four of the principal glutamine analogues inhibit GMP synthase, but azaserine does so only at very high concentrations. In extracts of foetal rat liver, a 1 mM concentration of azaserine gave no inhibition whereas this concentration of DON, acivicin, or CONV produced complete inhibition (Jayaram *et al.* 1975). For the enzyme from calf thymus, the K_i for azaserine was 6.7 mM whereas that for DON was about 0.5 mM (Abrams and Bentley 1959). GMP synthase from *E. coli* was more sensitive to DON ($K_i = 35\ \mu$M) than the mammalian enzyme (Patel *et al.* 1977). GMP synthase is an important site of action of acivicin, the primary effects of which appear to be inhibition of synthesis of both GMP and CTP. (Neil *et al.* 1979; Lui *et al.* 1982).

14.1.8.3 *Adenosine analogues*

The most extensively studied inhibitors of GMP synthase are the nucleoside antibiotics, psicofuranine and decoyinine (for review see Nichol 1975). These nucleosides are specific inhibitors of this enzyme and are unusual in that they are active as such, i.e. without being phosphorylated. These analogues both have a hydroxymethyl group on the 1'-C atom, but this structural feature is not essential because other nucleosides without such a substituent are also active. Inhibition of both the bacterial and the mammalian enzymes are conditioned by the presence of PP_i, a product of the reaction. For the enzyme from *E. coli*, inhibition by nucleosides does not occur in the absence of prior binding of PP_i whereas for the mammalian enzyme, inhibition occurs in the absence of PP_i but is enhanced by its presence (Udaka and Moyed 1963; Zyk *et al.* 1969, 1970; Spector 1975; Spector and Beacham 1975; Spector *et al.* 1976). Nucleosides that inhibited the mammalian enzyme with K_i values $< 10\ \mu$M were: 2-fluoroadenosine, decoyinine, psicofuranine, and 2-chloroadenosine; nucleosides that inhibited the enzyme from *E. coli* with K_i values $< 10\ \mu$M were decoyinine, *N*-allyladenosine, adenosine, 5-methyladenosine, 2-fluoroadenosine, 8-azaadenosine, and 5'-deoxyadenosine. The influence of binding of substrates and products on inhibition by nucleosides is complex and the nature of the nucleoside binding is not completely understood. However, Spector *et al.* (1976) have observed that the binding of nucleosides is initially non-competitive with ATP but becomes competitive when PP_i is added; thus the binding appears to be at a site other than the active site and the results are consistent with it being at a regulatory site.

14.1.8.4 *Oxanosine*

This agent (see Section 14.1.7 on IMP-DHO) is an inhibitor of bacterial GMP synthase, competitive with XMP, with a K_i of 7.4×10^{-4} M (Yagisawa *et al.* 1982). However, neither oxanosine nor its 5'-monophosphate inhibited GMP synthase from mammalian cells, although (as noted in the preceding section) the 5'-monophosphate is a good inhibitor of IMP dehydrogenase (Uehara *et al.* 1985).

14.1.8.5 *Mycophenolic acid*

This agent has already been discussed above as an inhibitor of IMP dehydrogenase. It also inhibits GMP synthase but the relative importance of the two enzymes as sites of action is not entirely clear. Sweeney *et al.* (1972) found that the IC_{50} value for inhibition of the two enzymes from several tumours were about the same, and found a K_i for GMP synthase from Landschütz tumour cells of 8×10^{-8} M which was about the same as that reported by Franklin and Cook (1969) for inhibition of IMP dehydrogenase from the same source. MPA inhibited the synthase from *E. coli* but with a much higher K_i (3.7×10^{-5} M) (Spector and Beacham 1975), but did not inhibit the enzyme from Ehrlich ascites cells at a concentration of 4×10^{-4} M (Spector *et al.* 1976). In intact neuroblastoma cells, MPA produced a rapid inhibition of IMP dehydrogenase but no inhibition of GMP synthase (Cass *et al.* 1977). These results would suggest that even though the isolated IMP dehydrogenase and GMP synthase were equally sensitive to MPA, in whole cells IMP dehydrogenase is the primary site of action.

14.1.9   Adenylosuccinate synthetase (EC 6.3.4.4) (16)

$$GTP + IMP + \text{L-aspartate} \overset{M^{2+}}{\rightleftharpoons} GDP + HPO_4{}^{2-} + \text{adenylosuccinate}.$$

$$(14.10)$$

Adenylosuccinate synthetase, which catalyses the first step of the conversion of inosinic acid (IMP) to adenylic acid, requires GTP, IMP, aspartate, and a divalent cation (Stayton *et al.* 1983). Results from several studies suggest that the reaction involves the addition of aspartate to 6-phosphoryl-IMP to give a tetrahedral transition state. The substrate binding sites of adenylosuccinate synthetase are quite specific; only hydroxylamine substitutes for aspartate, and slight activity has been observed with alanosine (Tyagi and Cooney 1984). Inosinic acid probably binds as a dianion and the phosphoryl group is important to both binding and catalysis (Hampton and Chu 1970). Numerous inosinate analogues have been tested, but only 2'-deoxyinosinate and ara-hypoxanthine monophosphate were found to be substrates (Spector and Miller 1976). The enzymes from parasites such as *Leishmania donovani* and *Trypanosoma cruzi* have unusual specificity compared to the mammalian enzymes, accepting the inosinate analogues mentioned above and, in addition, 8-azainosinate, allopurinol ribonucleotide, and other ring analogues. Allopurinol ribonucleotide is formed from allopurinol in a number of protozoans and converted to 4-aminopyrazolo[3,4-*d*]pyrimidine ribonucleotide by adenylosuccinate synthetase and lyase. The resulting AMP analogue is converted to the triphosphate and incorporated into RNA, an event that is toxic to the protozoa. Since mammalian synthetases do not accept this compound, and certain other inosinate analogues, as substrates, all such analogues function as anti-leishmanial agents (Stayton *et al.* 1983).

It appears that the enzyme is subject to feedback and product inhibition by AMP, adenylosuccinate, GDP, and GMP. Three substrate analogues are known that may be important inhibitors, alanosine, hadacidin, and 6-mercaptopurine ribonucleotide. Hadacidin is a competitive inhibitor relative to aspartate with K_i values of 0.3–6.3 μM (Shigeura and Gordon 1962; Clark and Rudolph

1976; Markham and Reed 1977). This appears to be its only physiological action (Shigeura and Gordon 1962). Alanosine is metabolised in cells to L-alanosyl-5-amino-4-imidazodecarboxylic acid ribonucleotide, which is a competitive (with IMP) inhibitor with a K_i of 0.2 μM. This inhibition is probably responsible for the biological activity of alanosine (Tyagi and Cooney 1984), although inhibition of the lyase (see above) may also be important (Casey and Lowenstein 1986).

6-mercaptopurine ribonucleotide, the active metabolite of 6-mercaptopurine, an important anticancer agent, inhibits various nucleotide-metabolizing enzymes, including the synthetase. With the enzyme from mammalian sources, the inhibition appears similar to that of AMP, with interaction at both nucleotide binding sites. It is clear from the magnitude of the K_i values however, that this is not the major site of action of this drug, even though it may contribute to its activity (Elion 1967, 1969).

14.1.10   AMP deaminase (EC 3.5.4.6) (18)

$$AMP + H_2O = IMP + NH_3. \qquad (14.11)$$

AMP deaminase (AMP-DA) does not lie directly on the *de novo* pathway to nucleotides but is involved in interconversions of purine nucleotides. AMP-DA is a regulatory enzyme; it is stimulated by ATP and inhibited by GTP and accordingly has an essential role in regulating the pool sizes of the purine nucleotides. The enzyme is inhibited by inorganic phosphate and a number of other anions and is stimulated by monovalent cations. The K_m for AMP is high and for the enzyme from most sources falls in the range of 0.4–1.5 mM. Literature on AMP-DA has been reviewed by Zielke and Suelter (1971a) and by Stankiewicz (1978); the reader is referred to the first of these reviews for documentation of the unreferenced statements above. The reaction catalysed by AMP-DA is the same as that catalysed by adenosine deaminase (ADA), that is, the hydrolysis of the amino group of an adenine moiety, and the two enzymes are presumed to have similar mechanisms although the mechanism of AMP-DA has been investigated much less thoroughly than that of ADA. The deamination of adenosine by ADA proceeds by addition of H_2O across the 1,6-double bond to yield an intermediate from which NH_3 is released to form IMP (Agarwal 1982; Wolfenden 1976).

AMP-DA accepts as substrates a variety of analogues of AMP. The presence of a phosphate or other negative group at the 5'-position is required: 2'-AMP and 3'-AMP are not substrates (Zielke and Suelter 1971b). Substrate activity is retained if the 5'-phosphate group is replaced with sulphate, phosphoramidate, phosphorothiate, or methylphosphonate groups (Murray and Atkinson 1968; Zielke and Suelter 1971b; Ogasawara *et al.* 1975; Lazarus *et al.* 1979; Stankiewicz *et al.* 1980) or with a phosphonomethyl or a C-substituted phosphonomethyl group (Hampton *et al.* 1973, 1976); certain 5'-carboxy analogues also have activity as substrates (Meyer and Follman 1980). Like ADA (Zielke and Suelter 1971a), AMP-DA can catalyse the hydrolytic removal of 6-substituents other than amino, as shown with analogues in which the 6-amino group was replaced with methylamino or ethylamino (Zielke and Suelter 1971b), methoxamino (Donaldson *et al.* 1969), hydroxyamino (Stankiewicz *et al.* 1980) or chloro (Murray and Atkinson 1968) groups, and with 2-amino-6-chloropurine ribonucleotide (Bennett *et al.* 1984). Modification of the adenine moiety may lead to active or inactive analogues: the 5'-monophosphate of formycin A is a good substrate for AMP-DA but the 5'-phosphates of tubercidin and toyocamycin are devoid of activity (Zielke and Suelter 1971b; Stankiewicz *et al.* 1980). Substitution at the 1, 2, or 8-positions of AMP leads to loss of substrate activity (Murray and Atkinson 1968; Zielke and Suelter 1971b; Hampton *et al.* 1976; Stankiewicz *et al.* 1980). The 3'-hydroxy group appears to be more critical for substrate activity than the 2'-OH group, as is shown by the rates of deamination relative to AMP of 2'-dAMP (18.5 per cent), 3'-dAMP (0.22 per cent), ara-AMP (2.6 per cent) and xylo-AMP (0.0026 per cent) (Hampton and Sasaki 1973). That the 4'-O atom is not essential is indicated by the activity of the 5'-phosphates of the carbocyclic analogues, aristeromycin and neplanocin A (Bennett *et al.* 1986a).

By far the best inhibitors of AMP-DA are coformycin (CoF) and the 5'-phosphates of coformycin and 2'-deoxycoformycin (dCF) (Agarwal 1982). dCF and CoF and their phosphates may be regarded as analogues of the transition-state molecule in the deamination of adenosine or AMP in that the C-atom corresponding to the 6-C atom of adenosine or AMP is tetrahedral and contains a substituent OH group. The K_i values for dCF and CoF for ADA are 10^{-11}–10^{-12} M, and for AMP-DA are about 10^{-8} M for CoF and about 10^{-6} M for dCF (Agarwal and Parks 1977; Frieden *et al.* 1980; Ashby and Holmsen 1983). It is noteworthy that CoF is a very effective inhibitor, even though it is not a phosphate. As might be expected, the phosphates of CoF and dCF are even better than the nucleosides as inhibitors of AMP-DA, with K_i values in the range of 10^{-9}–10^{-11} M (Frieden *et al.* 1979; Frieden *et al.* 1980; Bzowska *et al.* 1985). As described below, there are other agents that inhibit isolated AMP-DA *in vitro*, but CoF is the only agent for which there is evidence for inhibition in intact cells. CoF has been shown to be an effective inhibitor of AMP-DA in platelets (Ashby *et al.* 1983). CoF also has been shown to modify the metabolism in L1210 cells of the carbocyclic analogue of adenosine and other 6-substituted carbocyclic purine nucleosides in a way that indicates inhibition of AMP-DA (Bennett *et al.* 1985, 1986b). Another analogue that may be regarded as a transition-state analogue and that is an active inhibitor is 1,6-dihydro-6-hydroxymethylpurine ribonucleotide. This agent, however, is much less effective ($K_i = 2.5$ μM) than CoF-5'-phosphate or CoF itself (Frieden *et al.* 1980).

Certain analogues of AMP, modified in the phosphate moiety and already mentioned above as substrates, are deaminated so slowly that they serve as competitive inhibitors; some have K_i values that are $< 100\ \mu M$, i.e. well below the K_m for AMP. These include 5'-C-acylaminomethyl-AMP derivatives, and phosphonate analogues in which the $H_2O_3POCH_2$ group of AMP is replaced by $H_2O_3PCH(R)CH_2$ (Hampton *et al.* 1976). The following AMP analogues that are modified at positions other than the phosphate moiety were also effective inhibitors: iso-AMP, $K_i = 12\ \mu M$ (Frieden *et al.* 1980) or 78 μM (Setlow and Lowenstein 1968); 2-hydroxy-AMP (33 per cent inhibition at 50 μM); 2-aminopurine ribonucleotide (47 per cent inhibition at 90 μM); and the N^1-oxide of 5'-AMP (51 per cent inhibition at 100 μM) (Stankiewicz *et al.* 1980); and purine ribonucleotide, $K_i = 6.5\ \mu M$ (Frieden *et al.* 1980). 3'-AMP was an inhibitor, but a very poor one ($K_i = 3 \times 10^{-3}$ M), Makarewicz 1969; Makarewicz and Stankiewicz 1974; Setlow and Lowenstein 1968).

AMP-DA is strongly inhibited by blue dextran 2000 and by certain fluorescein dyes (Yoshino *et al.* 1974; Yoshino and Kawamura 1978). In attempting to identify the moiety responsible for the activity of blue dextran, Yoshino *et al.* (1984) examined various naphthalene sulphonic acids as inhibitors. Several compounds had IC_{50} values less than 20 μM; the most potent was 7-anilino-1-naphthol-3-sulphonate ($IC_{50} = 8\ \mu M$). These agents apparently bind to an allosteric site.

In the course of investigating the role of fatty acids in regulating AMP-DA, Yoshino and co-workers noted the marked inhibition of the enzyme by coenzyme A esters of fatty acids and by certain fatty acids themselves (Yoshino *et al.* 1976, 1979; Yoshino and Murakami, 1981). The acyl-CoAs are structural analogues of AMP; apparently the non-polar part of the molecule is essential for strong inhibition of the deaminase. These observations are chiefly of interest with respect to the properties of the enzyme and its role in metabolism, but they also offer a possible basis for design of inhibitors.

14.1.11   Ribonucleoside diphosphate reductase (EC 1.17.4.1) [20]

ribonucleoside diphosphate + reduced thioredoxin $\longrightarrow$
2'-deoxyribonucleoside diphosphate + oxidized thioredoxin + H_2O

$$(14.12)$$

Deoxyribonucleotides are formed by a direct reduction of ribonucleotides. Ribonucleoside diphosphate reductase (RDPR) catalyses this first unique step in DNA synthesis and provides a balanced supply of the four deoxyribonucleotides (dADP, dGDP, TDP, and dCDP), although there is no evidence that the supply of these nucleotides, i.e. the activity of the reductase, by itself, regulates DNA synthesis. The enzyme is under exquisite allosteric control, which regulates both its overall activity and substrate specificity (Thelander and Reichard 1979). Most of the detailed mechanistic studies have been carried out on the *E. coli* enzyme, but in most respects the properties of highly purified preparations of the reductase from mammalian sources are similar. The active enzyme is a 1:1 complex of two non-identical subunits, proteins B1 and B2, each consisting of two identical or nearly identical polypeptide chains. Protein B1 binds both substrates and effectors with high affinities. The binding of individual substrates is strongly influenced by effectors, of which there are two classes, each with two sub-sites. Binding to one class influences overall activity of the reductase, with ATP giving an active enzyme and dATP giving an inactive enzyme. Binding to the second class directs the substrate specificity toward reduction of any one of the four ribonucleoside diphosphates. Specificity sites can bind dTTP and dGTP as well as ATP and dATP. The B2 subunit contains a free tyrosyl radical, stabilized by an iron centre consisting of two iron ions (Reichard and Ehrenberg 1983). In all probability, the radical participates in the catalytic process during substitution of the hydroxyl group by a hydrogen atom at C-2' of the ribonucleoside diphosphate. The tyrosyl radical is introduced in the presence of oxygen, while its absence favours removal, suggesting a regulating role for oxygen in DNA synthesis.

The diphosphates of 2'-chloro- and 2'-fluoro-2'-deoxyadenosines, as well as a number of similarly substituted uridines and cytidines, inactivate RDPR with the release of free base, halogen, and pyrophosphate (Thelander *et al.* 1976; Stubbe and Kozarich 1980; Stubbe *et al.* 1983). Evidence has been presented that the enzymatic reaction, with normal ribonucleoside diphosphates or these inhibitors, generates a 2'-deoxy-3'-keto-nucleoside (Ator and Stubbe 1985). In the case of an inhibitor, this nucleoside breaks down to the entities listed above and 2-methylene-3(2H)-furanone. This highly reactive Michael acceptor then alkylates the B1 protein, inactivating the enzyme (Harris *et al.* 1984). Although 2'-deoxy-2'-fluoroadenosine is rapidly deaminated by adenosine deaminase, it is converted to the triphosphate by Sarcoma 180 cells or human lymphocytes when given with pentostatin to prevent deamination (Stoeckler *et al.* 1982), but no additional information is available on its biological activity.

9-β-D-arabinofuranosyladenine (araA), as the di- or triphosphate, is an effective inhibitor of the reductase from Novikoff hepatoma cells with an I_{50} of 70 μM, whereas 1-β-D-arabinofuranosylcytosine is not (Moore and Cohen 1967). 9-β-D-arabinofuranosyl-2-fluoroadenine (F-araA), an analogue of araA highly resistant to adenosine deaminase (Montgomery and Hewson 1969), is a much more potent inhibitor of the reductase from both HeLa and L1210 cells (Tseng *et al.* 1982; White *et al.* 1982). It seems likely that this inhibition contributes to the anticancer and antiviral activity of these compounds, but the magnitude of this contribution is less certain, since araA is much more potent as an inhibitor of DNA polymerase α and F-araA is equally potent. To complicate matters further, araA is incorporated into DNA (Kufe *et al.* 1983) and F-araA into both DNA and RNA (Spriggs *et al.* 1986); this incorporation correlates well with the cytotoxicity of these compounds.

2-Chloro-, 2-bromo-, and 2-fluoro-2'-deoxyadenosine are all more potent inhibitors of the reductase from both HEp-2 cells and L1210 cells than the arabinonucleosides, with I_{50} values of 0.2, 1.0 and 4.0, μM, but they are also good inhibitors of DNA polymerase α and are probably incorporated into DNA. These compounds are cytotoxic and have *in vivo* anticancer activity (Montgomery 1986).

The inhibitors discussed thus far are analogues of the nucleoside diphosphate enzyme substrates or products thereof and they bind to protein B1 of the enzyme. There are other inhibitors, such as hydroxyurea and some of its analogues, guanazole, certain polyhydroxybenzohydroxamic acids, and a series of thiosemicarbazones, which inactivate the reductase by destroying the essential tyrosyl free radical. It has been proposed that hydroxyurea, guanazole, and the hydroxamic acids react with the free radical itself (Kjoller Larsson *et al.* 1982), whereas iron chelates of the thiosemicarbazones bind at the active site of the enzyme, and then the ferrous form of the chelate reacts with molecular oxygen in a redox process that, via a one-electron reduction, leads to destruction of the tyrosine radical (Thelander and Graslund 1983). The iron chelate of 1-formylisoquinoline thiosemicarbazone, with an I_{50} of 0.05 μM for the reductase from the Novikoff hepatoma, is one of the most potent known inhibitors of mammalian reductase (Moore *et al.* 1970).

Hydroxyurea is used to some extent in the management of human cancer (Dorr and Fritz 1980), but the thiosemicarbazones appear to be too toxic for human use, even though certain members of this class of compound have shown good anticancer, antiviral, and antiparasitic activity in animal systems (Agrawal and Sartorelli 1975).

References

Abrams, R. and Bentley, M. (1959). Biosynthesis of nucleic acid purines. III. Guanosine 5'-phosphate formation from xanthosine 5'-phosphate and L-glutamine. *Arch. Biochem. Biophys.*, **79**, 91–110.

Agarwal, R. P. (1982). Inhibition of adenosine deaminase. *Pharmacol. Ther.*, **17**, 399–429.

Agarwal, R. P. and Parks, R. E., Jr. (1977). Potent inhibition of muscle 5'-AMP deaminase by the nucleoside antibiotics coformycin and deoxycoformycin. *Biochem. Pharmacol.*, **26**, 663–6.

Agrawal, K. C. and Sartorelli, A. C. (1975). α-(N)-heterocyclic carboxaldehyde thiosemicarbazones. In *Antineoplastic and immunosuppressive agents* (ed. A. C. Sartorelli and D. G. Johns) Vol. II, pp. 793–807. Springer, Berlin.

Anderson, E. P. and Brockman, R. W. (1963). Biochemical effects of duazomycin A in the mouse plasma cell neoplasm 70429. *Biochem. Pharmacol.*, **12**, 1335–54.

Anderson, J. H. and Sartorelli, A. C. (1968). Inosinic acid dehydrogenase of Sarcoma 180 cells. *J. Biol. Chem.*, **243**, 4762–8.

Anderson, J. H. and Sartorelli, A. C. (1969a). Inhibition of inosinic acid dehydrogenase by 6-chloropurine nucleotide. *Biochem. Pharmacol.*, **18**, 2737–45.

Anderson, J. H. and Sartorelli, A. C. (1969b). Inhibition of inosinic acid dehydrogenase of Sarcoma 180 ascites cells by nucleotides and their analogs. *Biochem. Pharmacol.*, **18**, 2747–57.

Ashby, B. and Holmsen, H. (1983). Platelet AMP deaminase. *J. Biol. Chem.*, **258**, 3668–72.

Ashby, B., Wernick, E., and Holmsen, H. (1983). Coformycin inhibition of platelet AMP deaminase has no effect on thrombin-induced platelet secretion nor on glycolysis or glycogenolysis. *J. Biol. Chem.*, **258**, 321–5.

Atkinson, M. R., Morton, R. K., and Murray, A. W. (1963). Inhibition of inosine 5'-phosphate dehydrogenase from Ehrlich ascites-tumour cells by 6-thioinosine 5'-phosphate. *Biochem. J.*, **89**, 167–72.

Ator, M. A. and Stubbe, J. (1985). Mechanism of inactivation of *Escherichia coli* ribonucleotide reductase by 2'-chloro-2'-deoxyuridine 5'-diphosphate: evidence for generation of a 2'-deoxy-3'-ketonucleotide via a net 1,2 hydrogen shift. *Biochemistry*, **24**, 7214–21.

Baker, B. R. (1967). *Design of active site-directed irreversible enzyme inhibitors*. Wiley, New York.

Beardsley, G. P., Taylor, E. C., Shih, C., Poore, G. A., Grindey, G. B., and Moran, R. C. (1986). A new class of antifolates. 5,10-dideazatetrahydrofolic acid (DDATHF), an inhibitor of GAR transformylase with broad *in vivo* activity. *Proc. Am. Ass. Cancer Res. ASCO*, **27**, 259.

Becher, H. J. and Schollmeyer, P. (1983). Inhibition of salvage pathway enzymes by adenine arabinoside 5'-monophosphate (ara-AMP). *Klin. Wschr.* **61**, 751–7.

Becher, H., Weber, M., and Lohr, G. W. (1978). Purine nucleotide synthesis in normal and leukemic blood cells. *Klin. Wschr.*, **56**, 275–83.

Bennett, L. L., Jr. (1975). Glutamine antagonists. In *Antineoplastic and immunosuppressive agents* (ed., A. C. Sartorelli and D. G. Johns), Vol. II, pp. 484–511. Springer, Berlin.

Bennett, L. L., Jr. and Adamson, D. J. (1970). Reversal of the growth inhibitory effects of 6-methylthiopurine ribonucleoside. *Biochem. Pharmacol.*, **19**, 2172–6.

Bennett, L. L., Jr. and Smithers, D. (1964). Feedback inhibition of purine biosynthesis in H. Ep. #2 cells by adenine analogs. *Biochem. Pharmacol.*, **13**, 1331–9.

Bennett, L. L., Jr., Smithers, D., Rose, L. M., Adamson, D. J., and Brockman, R. W. (1984). Mode of action of 2-amino-6-chloro-1-deazapurine. *Biochem. Pharmacol.*, **33**, 261–71.

Bennett, L. L., Jr., Brockman, R. W., Rose, L. M., Allan, P. W., Shaddix, S. C., Shealy, Y. F., and Clayton, J. D. (1985a). Inhibition of utilization of hypoxanthine and guanine in cells treated with the carbocyclic analog of adenosine. *Mol. Pharmacol.*, **27**, 666–75.

Bennett, L. L., Jr., Smithers, D., Rose, L. M., Adamson, D. J., Shaddix, S. C., and Thomas, H. J. (1985b). Metabolism and metabolic effects of 2-azahypoxanthine and 2-azaadenosine. *Biochem. Pharmacol.*, **34**, 1293–304.

Bennett, L. L., Jr., Allan, P. W., Rose, L. M., Comber, R N., and Secrist, J. A., III (1986a). Differences in the metabolism and metabolic effects of the carbocyclic adenosine analogs, neplanocin A and aristeromycin. *Mol. Pharmacol.*, **29**, 383–90.

Bennett, L. L., Jr., Allan, P. W., Rose, L. M., and Shealy, Y. F. (1986b). Modes of action of carbocyclic nucleoside analogs. *Proc. Am. Ass. Cancer Res.*, **27**, 306.

Bloch, A. and Nichol, C. A. (1964). Inhibition of ribosephosphate pyrophosphokinase activity by decoyinine, an adenine nucleoside. *Biochem. Biophys. Res. Commun.*, **16**, 400–3.

Boritzki, T. J., Berry, D. A., Besserer, J. A., Cook, P. D., Fry, D. W., Leopold, W. R., and Jackson, R. C. (1985). Biochemical and antitumor activity of tiazofurin and its selenium analog (2-β-D-ribofuranosyl-4-selenazolecarboxamide). *Biochem. Pharmacol.*, **34**, 1109–14.

Brand, L. M. and Lowenstein, J. M. (1978). Inhibition of adenylosuccinase by adenylophosphonopropionate and related compounds. *Biochemistry*, **17**, 1365–70.

Brockman, R. W. and Chumley, S. (1965). Inhibition of formylglycinamide ribonucleotide synthesis in neoplastic cells by purines and analogs. *Biochim. Biophys. Acta*, **95**, 365–79.

Brox, L. W. and Hampton, A. (1968). Inosine 5′-phosphate dehydrogenase. Kinetic mechanism and evidence for selective reaction of the 6-chloro analog of inosine 5′-phosphate with a cysteine residue at the inosine 5′-phosphate site. *Biochemistry*, **7**, 2589–96.

Buchanan, J. M. (1973). The amidotransferases. *Adv. Enzymol.*, **39**, 91–183.

Bzowska, A., Lassota, P., and Shugar, D. (1985). Phosphorylation of coformycin and 2′-deoxycoformycin, and substrate and inhibitor properties of the nucleosides and nucleotides in several enzyme systems. *Z. Naturforsch.*, **40C**, 710–14.

Caperelli, C. A., Benkovic, P. A., Chettur, G., and Benkovic, S. J. (1980). Purification of a complex catalyzing folate cofactor synthesis and transformylation in *de novo* purine biosynthesis. *J. Biol. Chem.*, **255**, 1885–90.

Casey, P. J. and Lowenstein, J. M. (1986). Interaction of L-alanosyl-5-aminoimidazole-4-carboxylic acid ribonucleotide (alanosyl-AICOR) with adenylosuccinate lyase. *Fed. Proc. Fed. Am. Soc. Exp. Biol.*, **45**, 1932.

Caskey, C. T., Ashton, D. M., and Wyngaarden, J. B. (1964). The enzymology of feedback inhibition of glutamine phosphoribosylpyrophosphate amidotransferase by purine ribonucleotides. *J. Biol. Chem.*, **239**, 2570–9.

Cass, C. E., Lowe, J. K., Manchak, J. M., and Henderson, J. F. (1977). Biological effects of inhibition of guanine nucleotide synthesis by mycophenolic acid in cultured neuroblastoma cells. *Cancer Res.*, **37**, 3314–20.

Chu, S. Y. and Henderson, J. F. (1972a). Purification and properties of phosphoribosyl-formylglycineamidine synthetase of Ehrlich ascites tumor cells. *Can. J. Biochem.*, **50**, 484–9.

Chu, S. Y. and Henderson, J. F. (1972b). Kinetic studies of phosphoribosyl-formylglycine-amidine synthetase. *Can. J. Biochem.*, **50**, 490–500.

Chu, S. Y. and Henderson, J. F. (1972c). Inhibition of the phosphoribosylformylglycine-amidine synthetase of Ehrlich ascites tumor cells by glutamine analogues. *Biochem. Pharmacol.*, **21**, 401–6.

Clark, S. W. and Rudolph, F. B. (1976). Regulation of purine metabolism. Adenylosucci-nate synthetase from Novikoff ascites tumor cells. *Biochim. Biophys. Acta*, **437**, 87–93.

Cook, P. D., Allen, L. B., Streeter, D. G., Huffman, J. H., Sidwell, R. W., and Robins, R. K. (1978). Synthesis and antiviral and enzymatic studies of certain 3-deazaguanines and their imidazolecarboxamide precursors. *J. Med. Chem.*, **21**, 1212–18.

Cooney, D. A., Jayaram, H. N., Geheyehu, G., Betts, C. R., Kelley, J. A., Marquez, V. E., and Johns, D. G. (1982). The conversion of 2-β-D-ribofuranosylthiazole-4-carboxamide to an analogue of NAD with potent IMP dehydrogenase-inhibitory properties. *Biochem. Pharmacol.*, **31**, 2133–36.

Daubner, S. C. and Benkovic, S. J. (1985). Characterization of mammalian phosphoribos-ylglycineamide formyltransferase from transformed cells. *Cancer Res.* **45**, 4990–7.

Dawid, I. B., French, T. C., and Buchanan, J. M. (1963). Azaserine-reactive sulfhydryl group of 2-formamido-N-ribosylacetamide 5′-phosphate: L-glutamine amido-ligase (adenosine diphosphate). II. Degradation of azaserine-C^{14}-labeled enzyme. *J. Biol. Chem.*, **238**, 2178–85.

Dewey, V. C., Kidder, G. W., and Nolan, L. L. (1978). Mechanism of inhibition of *Crithidia fasciculata* by adenosine and adenosine analogs. *Biochem. Pharmacol.*, **27**, 1479–85.

Donaldson, G., Atkinson, M. R., and Murray, A. W. (1969). Synthesis and regulatory properties of an adenosine 5′-phosphate analogue, N^6-methoxyadenosine 5′-phosphate. *Biochim. Biophys. Acta*, **184**, 655–657.

Dorr, R. T. and Fritz, W. L. (1980). *Cancer chemotherapy handbook*. Elsevier, New York, pp. 468–471.

Elion, G. B. (1967). Biochemistry and pharmacology of purine analogues. *Fed. Proc. Fed. Am. Soc. Exp. Biol.*, **26**, 898–903.

Elion, G. B. (1969). Actions of purine analogs: enzyme specificity studies as a basis for interpretation and design. *Cancer Res.*, **29**, 2448–53.

Elliott, W. L., and Weber, G. (1985). *In vivo* inactivation of formylglycinamidine ribonucleotide synthetase in rat hepatoma. *Biochem. Pharmacol.*, **34**, 243–8.

Ellis, D. B. and LePage, G. A. (1965). Some inhibitory effects of 9-β-D-xylofuranosyladenine, an adenosine analog, on nucleotide metabolism in ascites tumor cells. *Mol. Pharmacol.*, **1**, 231–8.

Franklin, T. J. and Cook, J. M. (1969). The inhibition of nucleic acid synthesis by mycophenolic acid. *Biochem. J.*, **113**, 515–24.

French, T. C., Dawid, I. B., Day, R. A., and Buchanan, J. M. (1963). Azaserine-reactive sulfhydryl group of 2-formamido-N-ribosylacetamide 5'-phosphate:L-glutamine amido-ligase (adenosine diphosphate). I. Purification and properties of the enzyme from *Salmonella typhimurium* and the synthesis of L-azaserine-C[14]. *J. Biol. Chem.*, **238**, 2171–7.

Frieden, C., Gilbert, H. R., Miller, W. H., and Miller, R. L. (1979). Adenylate deaminase: potent inhibition by 2'-deoxycoformycin 5'-phosphate. *Biochem. Biophys. Res. Commun.*, **91**, 278–83.

Frieden, C., Kurz, L. C., and Gilbert, H. R. (1980). Adenosine deaminase and adenylate deaminase: Comparative kinetic studies with transition state and ground state analogue inhibitors. *Biochemistry*, **19**, 5303–9.

Fuertes, M., Witkowski, J. T., Streeter, D. G., and Robins, R. K. (1974). Synthesis and enzymatic activity of 1,2,4-triazole-3-carboxamide 6'-deoxyhomoribonucleoside-6'-phosphonic acid and related compounds. *J. Med. Chem.*, **17**, 642–5.

Fukui, M., Inaba, M., Tsukagoshi, S., and Sakurai, Y. (1982). New antitumor imidazole derivative, 5-carbamoyl-1H-imidazol-4-yl piperonylate, as an inhibitor of purine synthesis and its activation by adenine phosphoribosyltransferase. *Cancer. Res.*, **42**, 1098–102.

Fukuyama, T. T. and Donovan, K. L. (1968). Mechanism of hydroxylamine inhibition of xanthosine 5'-phosphate aminase. *J. Biol. Chem.*, **243**, 5798–801.

Gebeyehu, G., Marquez, V. E., Cott, A. V., Cooney, D. A., Kelley, J. A., Jayaram, H. N., Ahluwalia, G. S., Dion, R. L., Wilson, Y. A., and Johns, D. G. (1985). Ribavirin, tiazofurin, and selenazofurin: mononucleotides and nicotinamide adenine dinucleotide analogues. Synthesis, structure, and interactions with IMP dehydrogenase. *J. Med. Chem.*, **28**, 99–105.

Greenlees, J. and LePage, G. A. (1956). Purine biosynthesis and inhibitors in ascites cell tumors. *Cancer Res.*, **16**, 808–813.

Grindey, G. B., Lowe, J. K., Divekar, A. Y., and Hakala, M. T. (1976). Potentiation by guanine nucleosides of the growth-inhibitory effects of adenosine analogs on L1210 and Sarcoma 180 cells in culture. *Cancer Res.*, **36**, 379–83.

Hampton, A. (1963). Reactions of ribonucleotide derivatives of purine analogues at the catalytic site of inosine 5'-phosphate dehydrogenase. *J. Biol. Chem.*, **238**, 3068–74.

Hampton, A. and Chu, S. Y. (1970). Specific binding to adenylosuccinate synthetase of analogs of inosinic acid with nitrogen, sulfur, and carbon substituted for phosphate oxygen. *Biochim. Biophys. Acta*, **198**, 594–600.

Hampton, A. and Nomura, A. (1967). Inosine 5'-phosphate dehydrogenase. Site of inhibition by guanosine 5'-phosphate and of inactivation by 6-chloro- and 6-mercaptopurine ribonucleoside 5'-phosphates. *Biochemistry*, **6**, 679–89.

Hampton, A. and Sasaki, T. (1973). Substrate properties of 8,2'- and 8,3'-*O*-cycloderivatives of adenosine 5'-monophosphate with adenosine 5'-monophosphate utilizing enzymes. *Biochemistry*, **12**, 2188–91.

Hampton, A., Sasaki, T., and Paul, B. (1973). Synthesis of 6'-Cyano-6'-deoxyhomoadenosine-6'-phosphonic acid and its phosphoryl and pyrophosphoryl anhydrides and studies of their interactions with adenine nucleotide utilizing enzymes. *J. Am. Chem. Soc.*, **95**, 4404–14.

Hampton, A., Sasaki, T., Perini, F., Slotin, L. A., and Kappler, F. (1976). Design of substrate-site-directed irreversible inhibitors of adenosine 5'-phosphate aminohydrolase. Effect of substrate substituents on affinity for the substrate site. *J. Med. Chem.*, **19**, 1029–33.

Harris, G., Ator, M., and Stubbe, J. (1984). Mechanism of inactivation of *Escherichia coli* and *Lactobacillus leichmannii* ribonucleotide reductases by 2'-chloro-2'-deoxynucleotides: evidence for generation of 2'-methylene-3(2H)-furanone. *Biochemistry*, **23**, 5214–25.

Hartman, S. C. (1963). The interaction of 6-diazo-5-oxo-L-norleucine with phosphoribosyl pyrophosphate amidotransferase. *J. Biol. Chem.*, **238**, 3036–47.

Hartman, S. C., Levenberg, B., and Buchanan, J. M. (1956). Biosynthesis of the purines. XI. Structure, enzymatic synthesis, and metabolism of glycinamide ribotide and (α-*N*-formyl)-glycinamide ribotide. *J. Biol. Chem.*, **221**, 1057–70.

Henderson, J. F. (1962). Feedback inhibition of purine biosynthesis in ascites tumor cells. *J. Biol. Chem.*, **237**, 2631–5.

Henderson, J. F. (1963). Feedback inhibition of purine biosynthesis in ascites tumor cells by purine analogues. *Biochem. Pharmacol.*, **12**, 551–6.

Henderson, J. F. and Khoo, M. K. Y. (1965). On the mechanism of feedback inhibition of purine biosynthesis *de Novo* in ehrlich ascites tumor cells *in Vitro*. *J. Biol. Chem.*, **240**, 3104–9.

Henderson, J. F., Paterson, A. R. P., Caldwell, I. C., and Hori, M. (1967). Biochemical effects of formycin, an adenosine analog. *Cancer Res.*, **27**, 715–19.

Hill, D. L. (1980). Aminothiadiazoles. *Cancer Chemother. Pharmacol.*, **4**, 215–20.

Hill, D. L. and Bennett, L. L., Jr. (1969). Purification and properties of 5-phosphoribosyl pyrophosphate amidotransferase from adenocarcinoma 755 cells. *Biochemistry*, **8**, 122–30.

Holmes, E. W. (1981). Kinetic, physical, and regulatory properties of amidophosphoribosyltransferase. *Adv. Enz. Regul.*, **19**, 215–31.

Holmes, E. W., McDonald, J. A., McCord, J. M., Wyngaarden, J. B., and Kelley, W. N. (1973). Human glutamine phosphoribosylpyrophosphate amidotransferase. *J. Biol. Chem.*, **248**, 144–50.

Holmes, E. W., Pehlke, D. M., and Kelley, W. N. (1974). Human IMP dehydrogenase. Kinetics and regulatory properties. *Biochim. Biophys. Acta*, **364**, 209–17.

Huberman, E., McKeown, C. K., and Friedman, J. (1981). Mutagen-induced resistance to mycophenolic acid in hamster cells can be associated with increased inosine 5'-phosphate dehydrogenase activity. *Proc. Nat. Acad. Sci. USA*, **78**, 3151–4.

Hupe, D. J., Azzolina, B. A., and Behrens, N. D. (1986). IMP dehydrogenase from the intracellular parasitic protozoan *Eimeria tenella* and its inhibition by mycophenolic acid. *J. Biol. Chem.*, **261**, 8363–9.

Jackson, R. C., Morris, H. P., and Weber, G (1977). Partial purification, properties and regulation of inosine 5'-phosphate dehydrogenase in normal and malignant rat tissues. *Biochem. J.*, **166**, 1–10.

Jackson, R. C., Weber, G., and Morris, H. P. (1975). IMP dehydrogenase, an enzyme linked with proliferation and malignancy. *Nature (London)*, **256**, 331–3.

Jayaram, H. N., Cooney, D. A., Ryan, J. A., Neil, G., Dion, R. L., and Bono, V. H. (1975). L-[αS,5S]-α-amino-3-chloro-4,5-dihydro-5-isoxazoleacetic acid (NSC 163501): a new amino acid antibiotic with the properties of an antagonist of L-glutamine. *Cancer Chemother. Rep.*, Part I, **59**, 481–91.

Jayaram, H. N., Dion, R. L., Glazer, R. I., Johns, D. G., Robins, R. K., Srivastava, P. C., and Cooney, D. A. (1982a). Initial studies on the mechanism of action of a new oncolytic thiazole nucleoside, 2-β-D-ribofuranosylthiazole-4-carboxamide (NSC 286193). *Biochem. Pharmacol.*, **31**, 2371–80.

Jayaram, H. N., Smith, A. L., Glazer, R. I., Johns, D. G., and Cooney, D. A. (1982b). Studies on the mechanism of action of 2-β-D-ribofuranosylthiazole-4-carboxamide (NSC 286193)-II. Relationship between dose level and biochemical effects in P388 leukemia *in vivo*. *Biochem. Pharmacol.*, **31**, 3839–45.

Jayaram, H. N., Ahluwalia, G. S., Dion, R. L., Gebeyehu, G., Marquez, V. E., Kelley, J. A., Robins, R. K., Cooney, D. A., and Johns, D. G. (1983). Conversion of 2-β-D-ribofuranosylselenazole-4-carboxamide to an analogue of NAD with potent IMP dehydrogenase-inhibitory properties. *Biochem. Pharmacol.*, **32**, 2633–6.

Kaiser, W. A., Hermann, B., and Keppler, D. O. R. (1980). Selective guanosine phosphate deficiency in hepatoma cells induced by inhibitors of IMP dehydrogenase. *Hoppe-Seyler's Z. Physiol. Chem.*, **361**, 1503–10.

King, G. L., Bounous, C. G., and Holmes, E. W. (1978). Human placental amidophosphoribosyltransferase. *J. Biol. Chem.*, **253**, 3933–8.

Kjoller Larsen I., Sjöberg, B.-M., and Thelander, L. (1982). Characterization of the active site of ribonucleotide reductase of *Escherichia coli*, bacteriophage T4 and mammalian cells by inhibition studies with hydroxyurea analogues. *Eur. J. Biochem.*, **125**, 75–81.

Kornberg, A., Lieberman, I., and Simms, E. S. (1955). Enzymatic synthesis and properties of 5-phosphoribosylpyrophosphate. *J. Biol. Chem.*, **215**, 389–402.

Kufe, D. W., Major, P. P., Munroe, D., Egan, M., and Herrick, D. (1983). Relationship between incorporation of 9-β-D-arabinofuranosyladenine in L1210 DNA and cytotoxicity. *Cancer Res.*, **43**, 2000–4.

Kuttan, R., Robins, R. K., and Saunders, P. P. (1982). Inhibition of inosinate dehydrogenase by metabolites of 2-β-D-ribofuranosylthiazole-4-carboxyamide. *Biochem. Biophys. Res. Commun.*, **107**, 862–8.

Lagerqvist, U. (1958). Biosynthesis of guanosine 5'-phosphate. II. Amination of xanthosine 5'-phosphate by purified enzyme from pigeon liver. *J. Biol. Chem.*, **233**, 143–9.

Lazarus, R. A., Benkovic, P. A., and Benkovic, S. J. (1979). The synthesis and properties in enzymic reactions of substrate analogs containing the methylphosphonyl group. *Arch. Biochem. Biophys.*, **197**, 218–25.

Lee, H.-J., Pawlak, K., Nguyen, B. T., Robins, R. K., and Sadee, W. (1985). Biochemical differences among four inosinate dehydrogenase inhibitors, mycophenolic acid, ribavirin, tiazofurin, and selenazofurin, studied in mouse lymphoma cell culture. *Cancer Res.*, **45**, 5512–20.

LePage, G. A. and Jones, M. (1961). Purinethiols as feedback inhibitors of purine synthesis in ascites tumor cells. *Cancer Res.*, **21**, 642–9.

Levenberg, B. and Buchanan, J. M. (1957). Biosynthesis of the purines. XIII. Structure, enzymatic synthesis, and metabolism of (α-N-formyl)-glycinamidine ribotide. *J. Biol. Chem.*, **224**, 1019–27.

Levenberg, B., Melnick, I., and Buchanan, J. M. (1957). Biosynthesis of the purines. XV. The effect of aza-L-serine and 6-diazo-5-oxo-L-norleucine on inosinic acid biosynthesis de novo. *J. Biol. Chem.*, **225**, 163–76.

Lieberman, I. (1956). Enzymatic synthesis of adenosine-5'-phosphate from inosine-5'-phosphate. *J. Biol. Chem.*, **223**, 327–39.

Livingston, R. B., Venditti, J. M., Cooney, D. A., and Carter, S. K. (1970). Glutamine antagonists in chemotherapy. *Adv. Pharmacol. Chemother.*, **8**, 57–120.

Lowe, J. K., Brox, L., and Henderson, J. F. (1977). Consequences of inhibition of guanine nucleotide synthesis by mycophenolic acid and virazole. *Cancer Res.*, **37**, 736–43.

Lui, M. S., Kizaki, H., and Weber, G. (1982). Biochemical pharmacology of acivicin in rat hepatoma cells. *Biochem. Pharmacol.*, **31**, 3469–73.

McCollister, R. J., Gilbert, Jr., W. R., Ashton, D. M., and Wyngaarden, J. B. (1964). Pseudofeedback inhibition of purine synthesis by 6-mercaptopurine ribonucleotide and other purine analogues. *J. Biol. Chem.*, **239**, 1560–3.

Makarewicz, W. (1969). AMP-aminohydrolase in muscle of elasmobranch fish. Purification procedure and properties of the purified enzyme. *Comp. Biochem. Physiol.*, **29**, 1–26.

Makarewicz, W. and Stankiewicz, A. (1974). AMP-aminohydrolase of human skeletal muscle; partial purification and properties. *Biochem. Med.*, **10**, 180–97.

Markham, G. D. and Reed, G. H. (1977). Adenylosuccinate synthetase from *Azotobacter vinelandii*: purification, properties and steady-state kinetics. *Arch. Biochem. Biophys.* **184**, 24–35.

Melnick, I. and Buchanan, J. M. (1957). Biosynthesis of the purines. XIV. Conversion of (α-N-formyl)glycinamide ribotide to (α-N-formyl)glycinamidine ribotide; purification and requirements of the enzyme system. *J. Biol. Chem.*, **225**, 157–62.

Messenger, L. J. and Zalkin, H. (1979). Glutamine phosphoribosylpyrophosphate amidotransferase from *Escherichia coli*. *J. Biol. Chem.*, **254**, 3382–92.

Meyer, W. and Follmann, H. (1980). A study of the substrate and inhibitor specificities of AMP aminohydrolase, 5'-nucleotidase, and adenylate kinase with adenosine carboxylates of variable chain length. *Z. Naturforsch.*, **35C**, 273–8.

Miller, R. L. and Adamczyk, D. L. (1976). Inosine 5'-monophosphate dehydrogenase from Sarcoma 180 cells—substrate and inhibitor specificity. *Biochem. Pharmacol.*, **25**, 883–8.

Mizobuchi, K. and Buchanan, J. M. (1968a). Biosynthesis of the purines. XXIX. Purification and properties of formylglycinamide ribonucleotide amidotransferase from chicken liver. *J. Biol. Chem.*, **243**, 4842–52.

Mizobuchi, K. and Buchanan, J. M. (1968b). Biosynthesis of the purines. XXX. Isolation and characterization of formylglycinamide ribonucleotide amidotransferase–glutamyl complex. *J. Biol. Chem.*, **243**, 4853–62.

Mizobuchi, K., Kenyon, G. L., and Buchanan, J. M. (1968). Biosynthesis of the purines. XXXI. Binding of formylglycinamide ribonucleotide and adenosine triphosphate to formylglycinamide ribonucleotide amidotransferase. *J. Biol. Chem.*, **243**, 4863–77.

Montgomery, J. A. (1986). The design of chemotherapeutic agents. *Acc. Chem. Res.*, **19**, 293–300.

Montgomery, J. A. and Hewson, K. (1969). Nucleosides of 2-fluoroadenine. *J. Med. Chem.*, **12**, 498–504.

Moore, E. C. and Cohen, S. S. (1967). Effects of arabinonucleotides on ribonucleotide reduction by an enzyme system from rat tumor. *J. Biol. Chem.*, **242**, 2116–18.

Moore, E. C., Zedeck, M. S., Agrawal, K. C., and Sartorelli, A. C. (1970). Inhibition of ribonucleoside diphosphate reductase by 1-formylisoquinoline thiosemicarbazone and related compounds. *Biochemistry*, **9**, 4492–8.

Moran, R. G., Taylor, E. C., and Beardsley, G. P. (1985). 5,10-dideaza-5,6,7,8-tetrahydrofolic acid (DATHF), a potent antifolate inhibitory to *de novo* purine synthesis. *Proc. Am. Ass. Cancer Res. ASCO*, **26**, 231.

Müller, W. T. and Benkovic, S. J. (1981). On the purification and mechanism of action of

5-aminoimidazole-4-carboxamide-ribonucleotide transformylase from chicken liver. *Biochemistry*, **20**, 337–44.

Murray, A. W. and Atkinson, M. R. (1968). Adenosine 5'-phosphorothioate. A nucleotide analog that is a substrate, competitive inhibitor, or regulator of some enzymes that interact with adenosine 5'-phosphate. *Biochemistry*, **7**, 4023–9.

Murray, A. W. and Wong, P. C. L. (1967). 5-phosphoribosyl pyrophosphate synthetase from Ehrlich ascites-tumor cells: effect of magnesium and ATP concentration on the enzymic activity. *Biochem. Biophys. Res. Commun.*, **29**, 582–7.

Nagy, M. (1970). Regulation of the biosynthesis of purine nucleotides in *Schizosaccharomyces pombe*. I. Properties of the phosphoribosylpyrophosphate: glutamine amidotransferase of the wild strain and of a mutant desensitized towards feedback modifiers. *Biochim. Biophys. Acta*, **198**, 471–81.

Neil, G. L., Berger, A. E., McPartland, R. P., Grindey, G. B., and Bloch, A. (1979). Biochemical and pharmacological effects of the fermentation-derived antitumor agent, (αS,5S)-α-amino-3-chloro-4,5-dihydro-5-isoxazoleacetic acid (AT-125). *Cancer Res.*, **39**, 852–6.

Nelson, J. A., Rose, L. M., and Bennett, L. L., Jr. (1977). Mechanism of action of 2-amino-1,3,4-thiadiazole (NSC 4728). *Cancer Res.*, **37**, 182–7.

Nichol, C. A. (1975). Antibiotics resembling adenosine: tubercidin, toyocamycin, sangivamycin, formycin, psicofuranine and decoyinine. In *Antineoplastic and immunosuppressive agents*. (ed. A. C. Sartorelli and D. G. Johns), Vol. II, pp. 434–57. Springer, Berlin.

Nierlich, D. P. and Magasanik, B. (1965). Regulation of purine ribonucleotide synthesis by end product inhibition. The effect of adenine and guanine ribonucleotides on the 5'-phosphoribosyl-pyrophosphate amidotransferase of *Aerobacter aerogenes*. *J. Biol. Chem.*, **240**, 358–65.

Ogasawara, N., Goto, H., and Watanabe, T. (1975). Isozymes of rat AMP deaminase. *Biochim. Biophys. Acta*, **403**, 530–7.

Okada, M., Shimura, K., Shiraki, H., and Nakagawa, H. (1983). IMP dehydrogenase. II. Purification and properties of the enzyme from Yoshida sarcoma ascites tumor cells. *J. Biochem. (Tokyo)*, **94**, 1605–13.

Overgaard-Hansen, K. (1964). The inhibition of 5-phosphoribosyl-1-pyrophosphate formation by cordycepin triphosphate in extracts of Ehrlich ascites tumor cells. *Biochim. Biophys. Acta*, **80**, 504–7.

Page, T., Jacobsen, S. J., Smejkal, R. M., Scheele, J., Nyhan, W. L., Mangum, J. H., and Robins, R. K. (1985). Studies on the mechanism of cytotoxicity of 3-deazaguanosine in human cancer cells. *Cancer Chemother. Pharmacol.*, **15**, 59–62.

Patel, N., Moyed, H. S., and Kane, J. F. (1975). Xanthosine-5'-phosphate amidotransferase from *Escherichia coli*. *J. Biol. Chem.*, **250**, 2609–13.

Patel, N., Moyed, H. S., and Kane, J. F. (1977). Properties of xanthosine-5'-monophosphate-amidotransferase from *Escherichia coli*. *Arch. Biochem. Biophys.*, **178**, 652–61.

Paterson, A. R. P. and Tidd, D. M. (1975). 6-Thiopurines. In *Antineoplastic and immunosuppressive agents*, (ed. A. C. Sartorelli and D. G. Johns), Vol. II, pp. 384–403. Springer, Berlin.

Porter, D. J. T., Rudie, N. G., and Bright, H. J. (1983). Nitro analogs of substrates for adenylosuccinate synthetase and adenylosuccinate lyase. *Arch. Biochem. Biophys.*, **225**, 157–63.

Reichard, P. and Ehrenberg, A. (1983). Ribonucleotide reductase—a radical enzyme. *Science*, **221**, 514–19.

Remy, C. N., Remy, W. T., and Buchanan, J. M. (1955). Biosynthesis of the purines. VIII.

Enzymatic synthesis and utilization of α-5-phosphoribosylpyrophosphate. *J. Biol. Chem.*, **217**, 885–95.

Robins, R. K. (1982). Nucleoside and nucleotide inhibitors of inosine monophosphate (IMP) dehydrogenase as potential antitumor inhibitors. *Nucleosides Nucleotides*, **1**, 35–44.

Rottman, F. and Guarino, A. J. (1964). The inhibition of phosphoribosyl-pyrophosphate amidotransferase activity by cordycepin monophosphate. *Biochim. Biophys. Acta*, **89**, 465–72.

Salser, J. S., Hutchison, D. J., and Balis, M. E. (1960). Studies on the mechanism of action of 6-mercaptopurine in cell-free preparations. *J. Biol. Chem.*, **235**, 429–32.

Sartorelli, A. C. and Booth, B. A. (1960). Modifications in purine metabolism induced by 6-chloropurine. *Arch. Biochem. Biophys.*, **89**, 118–22.

Sartorelli, A. C., Anderson, J. H., and Booth, B. A. (1968). Alterations in purine nucleotide biosynthesis induced by 2-amino-6-chloropurine. *Biochem. Pharmacol.*, **17**, 37–44.

Schroeder, D. D., Allison, A. J., and Buchanan, J. M. (1969). Biosynthesis of the purines. XXXII. Effect of albizziin and other reagents on the activity of formylglycinamide ribonucleotide amidotransferase. *J. Biol. Chem.*, **244**, 5856–65.

Setlow, B. and Lowenstein, J. M. (1968). Adenylate deaminase. IV. Nucleotide specificity of the enzyme from calf brain with special reference to guanosine triphosphate. *J. Biol. Chem.*, **243**, 3409–15.

Shigeura, H. T. and Gordon, C. N. (1962). Hadacidin, a new inhibitor of purine biosynthesis. *J. Biol. Chem.*, **237**, 1932–6.

Shimada, W., Yagisawa, N., Naganawa, H., Takita, T., Hamada, M., Takeuchi, T., and Umezawa, H. (1981). Oxanosine, a novel nucleoside from actinomycetes. *J. Antibiot., Japan*, **34**, 1216–18.

Sidwell, R. W., Robins, R. K., and Hillyard, I. W. (1979). Ribavirin: an antiviral agent. *Pharmacol. Ther.*, **6**, 123–46.

Skibo, E. B., and Meyer, R. B., Jr. (1981). Inhibition of inosinic acid dehydrogenase by 8-substituted purine nucleotides. *J. Med. Chem.*, **24**, 1155–61.

Slieker, L. J. and Benkovic, S. J. (1984). Inhibition of HKSV28 cell growth by 5,11-methenyltetrahydrohomofolate. *Mol. Pharmacol.*, **25**, 294–302.

Smith, C. M. and Henderson, J. F. (1976). Relative importance of alternative pathways of purine nucleotide biosynthesis in Ehrlich ascites tumor cells *in vivo*. *Can. J. Biochem.*, **54**, 341–9.

Smith, G. K., Mueller, W. T., Benkovic, P. A., and Benkovic, S. J. (1981). On the cofactor specificity of glycinamide ribonucleotide and 5-aminoimidazole-4-carboxamide ribonucleotide transformylase from chicken liver. *Biochemistry*, **20**, 1241–5.

Spector, T. (1975). Studies with GMP synthetase from Ehrlich ascites cells. Purification, properties, and interactions with nucleotide analogs. *J. Biol. Chem.*, **250**, 7372–6.

Spector, T. and Beacham, L. M., III (1975). Guanosine monophophate synthetase from *Escherichia coli* B-96. Inhibition by nucleosides. *J. Biol. Chem.*, **250**, 3101–7.

Spector, T. and Miller, R. L. (1976). Mammalian adenylosuccinate synthetase. Nucleotide monophosphate substrates and inhibitors. *Biochim. Biophys. Acta*, **445**, 509–17.

Spector, T., Miller, R. L., Fyfe, J. A., and Krenitsky, T. A. (1974). GMP synthetase from *Escherichia coli B-96*. Interactions with substrate analogs. *Biochim. Biophys. Acta*, **370**, 585–91.

Spector, T., Jones, T. E. Krenitsky, T. A., and Harvey, R. J. (1976). Guanosine monophosphate synthetase from Ehrlich ascites cells. Multiple inhibition by pyrophosphate and nucleosides. *Biochim. Biophys. Acta*, **452**, 597–607.

Spriggs, D., Robbins, G., Mitchell, T., and Kufe, D. (1986). Incorporation of 9-β-D-arabinofuranosyl-2-fluoroadenine into HL-60 cellular RNA and DNA. *Biochem. Pharmacol.*, **35**, 247–52.

Srivastava, P. C., and Robins, R. K. (1983). Synthesis and antitumor activity of 2-β-D-ribofuranosylselenazole-4-carboxamide and related derivatives. *J. Med. Chem.*, **26**, 445–8.

Srivastava, P. C., Pickering, M. V., Allen, L. B., Streeter, D. G., Campbell, M. T., Witkowski, J. T., Sidwell, R. W., and Robins, R. K. (1977). Synthesis and antiviral activity of certain thiazole *C*-nucleosides. *J. Med. Chem.*, **20**, 256–62.

Stankiewicz, A. (1978). Dezaminaza AMP. *Post. Biochem.*, **24**, 243–64.

Stankiewicz, A., Spychala, J., and Makarewicz, W. (1980). Comparative studies on muscle AMP-deaminase. III. Substrate specificity of the enzymes from man, rabbit, rat, hen, frog, and pikeperch. *Comp. Biochem. Physiol.*, **66B**, 529–33.

Stayton, M. M., Rudolph, F. B. and Fromm, H. J. (1983). Regulation, genetics, and properties of adenylosuccinate synthetase: a review. *Curr. Top. Cell. Regul.*, **22**, 103–41.

Stoeckler, J. D., Bell, C. A., Parks, R. E. Jr., Chu, C. K., Fox, J. J., and Ikehara, M. (1982). C(2′)-substituted purine nucleoside analogs. Interactions with adenosine deaminase and purine nucleoside phosphorylase and formation of analog nucleotides. *Biochem. Pharmacol.*, **31**, 1723–8.

Streeter, D. G. and Koyama, H. H. P. (1976). Inhibition of purine nucleotide biosynthesis by 3-deazaguanine, its nucleoside and 5′-nucleotide. *Biochem. Pharmacol.*, **25**, 2413–15.

Streeter, D. G. and Miller, J. P. (1981). The *in vitro* inhibition of purine nucleotide biosynthesis by 2-β-D-ribofuranosylthiazole-4-carboxyamide. *Biochem. Biophys. Res. Commun.*, **103**, 1409–15.

Streeter, D. G. and Robins, R. K. (1983). Comparative *in vitro* studies of tiazofurin and a selenazole analog. *Biochem. Biophys. Res. Commun.*, **115**, 544–50.

Streeter, D. G., Witkowski, J. T., Khare, G. P., Sidwell, R. W., Bauer, R. J., Robins, R. K., and Simon, L. N. (1973). Mechanism of action of 1-β-D-ribofuranosyl-1,2,4-triazole-3-carboxamide (virazole), a new broad-spectrum antiviral agent. *Proc. Nat. Acad. Sci. USA*, **70**, 1174–8.

Stubbe, J. and Kozarich, J. W. (1980). Fluoride, pyrophosphate, and base release from 2′-deoxy-2′-fluoronucleoside 5′-diphosphates by ribonucleoside-diphosphate reductase. *J. Biol. Chem.*, **255**, 5511–13.

Stubbe, J., Ator, M. and Krenitsky, T. (1983). Mechanism of ribonucleoside diphosphate reductase from *Escherichia coli*. *J. Biol. Chem.*, **258**, 1625–30.

Sweeney, M. J. (1977). Mycophenolic acid and its mechanism of action in cancer and psoriasis. *J. Antibiot.*, *Japan*, **30**, S85–S92.

Sweeney, M. J., Hoffman, D. H., and Esterman, M. A. (1972). Metabolism and biochemistry of mycophenolic acid. *Cancer Res.*, **32**, 1803–9.

Switzer, R. L. (1968). Mechanism of phosphoribosylpyrophosphate synthetase: evidence for an enzyme–pyrophosphate intermediate. *Biochem. Biophys. Res. Commun.*, **32**, 320–5.

Switzer, R. L. (1969). Regulation and mechanism of phosphoribosylpyrophosphate synthetase. *J. Biol. Chem.*, **244**, 2854–63.

Tay, B. S., Lilley, R. McC., Murray, A. W., and Atkinson, M. R. (1969). Inhibition of phosphoribosyl pyrophosphate amidotransferase from Ehrlich ascites-tumour cells by thiopurine nucleotides. *Biochem. Pharmacol.*, **18**, 936–8.

Thelander, L. and Graslund, A. (1983). Mechanism of inhibition of mammalian ribonucleotide reductase by the iron chelate of 1-formylisoquinoline thiosemicarbazone. Destruction of the tyrosine free radical of the enzyme in an oxygen-requiring reaction. *J. Biol. Chem.*, **258**, 4063–6.

Thelander, L. and Reichard, P. (1979). Reduction of ribonucleotides. *Ann. Rev. Biochem.*, **48**, 133–58.

Thelander, L., Larsson, B., Hobbs, J., and Eckstein, F. (1976). Active site of ribonucleoside diphosphate reductase from *Escherichia coli. J. Biol. Chem.*, **251**, 1398–405.

Tomisek, A. J. and Reid, M. R. (1962). Chromatographic studies of purine metabolism. V. Inhibition mechanism of diazo-oxo-norleucine in wild-type and in diazo-oxo-norleucine-resistant *Excherichia coli. J. Biol. Chem.*, **237**, 807–11.

Tomisek, A. J., Kelley, H. J., and Skipper, H. E. (1956). Chromatographic studies of purine metabolism. I. The effect of azaserine on purine biosynthesis in *E. coli* using various C^{14}-labeled precursors. *Arch. Biochem. Biophys.*, **64**, 437–55.

Tseng, W.-C., Derse, D., Cheng, Y.-C, Brockman, R. W., and Bennett, L. L., Jr. (1982). *In vitro* biological activity of 9-β-D-arabinofuranosyl-2-fluoroadenine and the biochemical actions of its triphosphate on DNA polymerases and ribonucleotide reductase from HeLa cells. *Mol. Pharmacol.*, **21**, 474–7.

Tso, J. Y., Hermodson, M. A., and Zalkin, H. (1982). Glutamine phosphoribosylpyrophosphate amidotransferase from cloned *Escherichia coli purF*. NH$_2$-terminal amino acid sequence, identification of the glutamine site, and trace metal analysis. *J. Biol. Chem.*, **257**, 3532–6.

Tyagi, A. K. and Cooney, D. A. (1984). Biochemical pharmacology, metabolism, and mechanism of action of L-alanosine, a novel, natural antitumor agent. *Adv. Pharmacol. Chemother.*, **20**, 69–121.

Udaka, S. and Moyed, H. S. (1963). Inhibition of parental and mutant xanthosine 5'-phosphate aminases by psicofuranine. *J. Biol. Chem.*, **238**, 2797–803.

Uehara, Y., Hasegawa, M., Hori, M., and Umezawa, H. (1985). Increased sensitivity to oxanosine, a novel nucleoside antibiotic, of rat kidney cells upon expression of the integrated viral src gene. *Cancer Res.*, **45**, 5230–4.

Weber, G., Natsumeda, Y., Lui, M. S., Faderan, M. A., Liepnieks, J. J., and Elliott, W. L. (1984). Control of enzyme programs and nucleotide pattern in cancer cells by acivicin and tiazofurin. *Adv. Enz. Regul.*, **22**, 69–93.

White, E. L., Shaddix, S. C., Brockman, R. W., and Bennett, L. L., Jr. (1982). Comparison of the actions of 9-β-D-arabinofuranosyl-2-fluoroadenine and 9-β-D-arabinofuranosyladenine on target enzymes from mouse tumor cells. *Cancer Res.*, **42**, 2260–4.

Wolfenden, R. (1976). Transition state analog inhibitors and enzyme catalysis. *Ann. Rev. Biophys. Bioeng.*, **5**, 271–306.

Wong, C. G. and Meyer, R. B., Jr. (1984). Inhibitors of inosinic acid dehydrogenase. 2-substituted inosinic acids. *J. Med. Chem.*, **27**, 429–32.

Wood, A. W. and Seegmiller, J. E. (1973). Properties of 5-phosphoribosyl-1-pyrophosphate amidotransferase from human lymphoblasts. *J. Biol. Chem.*, **248**, 138–43.

Woods, R. A., Henderson, R. M. and Henderson, J. F. (1978). Consequences of inhibition of purine biosynthesis *de novo* by 6-methylmercaptopurine ribonucleoside in cultured lymphoma L5178Y cells. *Eur. J. Cancer.*, **14**, 765–70.

Yagisawa, N., Shimada, N., Takita, T., Ishizuka, M., Takeuchi, T., and Umezawa, H. (1982). Mode of action of oxanosine, a novel nucleoside antibiotic. *J. Antibiot. Japan*, **35**, 755–9.

Yen, R. C. K., Raivio, K. O., and Becker, M. A. (1981). Inhibition of phosphoribosylpyrophosphate synthesis in human fibroblasts by 6-methylthioinosinate. *J. Biol. Chem.*, **256**, 1839–45.

Yoshino, M. and Kawamura, Y. (1978). Inhibition of chicken erythrocyte AMP deaminase by tetraiodofluorescein compounds. *Biochim. Biophys. Acta*, **526**, 640–3.

Yoshino, M. and Murakami, K. (1981). *In vitro* and *in situ* studies on the inhibition of yeast AMP deaminase by fatty acids. *Biochim. Biophys. Acta*, **660**, 199–203.

Yoshino, M., Kawamura, Y., and Ogasawara, N. (1974). Inhibition of chicken erythrocyte AMP deaminase by blue Dextran 2000. *J. Biochem. (Tokyo)*, **75**, 1391–3.

Yoshino, M., Miyajima, E., and Tsushima, K. (1976). Inhibition of AMP deaminase of bovine brain and liver by fatty acyl-CoA derivatives. *FEBS Lett.*, **72**, 143–6.

Yoshino, M., Miyajima, E., and Tsushima, K. (1979). Kinetics of the interactions of AMP deaminase with fatty acids. *J. Biol. Chem.*, **254**, 1521–5.

Yoshino, M., Murakami K., and Kawamura, Y. (1984). Kinetics of the inhibition by naphtholsulfonate compounds of MAP deaminase from chicken erythrocytes. *Biochim. Biophys. Acta*, **791**, 364–9.

Zielke, C. L. and Suelter, C. H. (1971a). Purine, purine nucleoside, and purine nucleotide aminohydrolases. In *The enzymes* (ed. P. D. Boyer) Vol. 4, pp. 47–78. Academic Press, New York.

Zielke, C. L. and Suelter, C. H. (1971b). Substrate specificity and aspects of deamination catalyzed by rabbit muscle 5′-adenylic acid aminohydrolase. *J. Biol. Chem.*, **246**, 1313–17.

Zyk, N., Citri, N., and Moyed, H. S. (1969). Conformative response of xanthosine 5′-phosphate aminase. *Biochemistry*, **8**, 2787–94.

Zyk, N., Citri, N., and Moyed, H. S. (1970). Alteration of the conformative response and inhibition of xanthosine 5′-phosphate aminase by adenine glycosides. *Biochemistry*, **9**, 677–83.

15

Steroidal inhibitors of Na$^+$,K$^+$-ATPase

Kurt R. H. Repke, Werner Schönfeld,

Jürgen Weiland, Rudolf Megges, and

Arnulf Hache

The following remarks consist partly of matter of fact, and partly of opinion. The former will be permanent; the latter must vary with the detection of error, or the improvement of knowledge. I hazard them with diffidence, and hope they will be examined with candour.

William Withering (1785)

15.1   Statement of underlying medical problem

The cardiotonic steroids ('cardiac glycosides', 'digitalis compounds') are among the oldest groups of drugs used in medicine. They occur in a wide variety of plants and, in non-glycosidic form, in the poison of some toads. Their ability to increase the contractility of the heart muscle (their positive-inotropic action) and to inhibit atrioventricular impulse transmission keeps them among the most prescribed drugs even today, although they form, after the antibiotics, the group of compounds with the highest incidence of toxicity in general clinical use (Doering and König 1977).

Had the therapeutic value of digitalis glycosides not been popularized 200 years ago (Withering 1785), modern regulatory agencies would probably have judged this class of drugs too frequently toxic to approve their release for clinical use. Since Withering's time, countless patients suffering from dropsy as a consequence of congestive heart failure have been helped by cardiac glycosides; no doubt the death of countless others was hastened by this class of drugs. (Smith *et al.* 1984)

In all developed countries, cardiovascular disease has headed the list of causes of death for more than a half century. In the USA cardiovascular disease still accounts for more than 50 per cent of all deaths, and the total economic cost of cardiovascular disorders is estimated to be in excess of $ 60 billion annually (Levy and Moskowitz 1982). Cardiovascular disease is among the group for which the drugs now available are clearly inadequate to restore health or even minimize discomfort and disability (Weatherall 1982).

The cardiac glycosides will perhaps remain ideal for treating the (comparatively rare) tachycardic atrial fibrillation. They are not ideal for other types of heart failure.

Physicians are still waiting for one or more positive-inotropic substances with a broad therapeutic range and a reasonably long half-life, not inhibiting or rather enhancing impulse transmission and lacking dangerous arrhythmias. Such compounds may be manufactured some day by the pharmaceutic industry, but the answer probably will not be given by toads and flowers. (Kaufmann 1978)

The need for the synthetic development of cardiac glycosides with an improved therapeutic–toxic ratio is thus obvious. According to Thomas *et al.* (1974a), one of the factors limiting such studies are the difficulties inherent in the chemistry of the cardiac glycosides so that the work of 10 chemists might be insufficient to occupy the full time of one pharmacologist in synthesizing or screening a series of analogues respectively.

A further serious difficulty has been that the commonly preferred measurement of cat lethal toxicity, as extensively used by Chen (1963) does not provide sufficiently reliable data for the analysis of structure–activity relationships. In fact, Chen (1963) stressed the preliminary nature of his results (in part because of the variation of lethal potency as a function of speed of injection), and felt that each active substance deserves careful evaluation, from an enzymatic level to the whole animal. As pointed out by Brown and Thomas (1983, 1984), digitalis glycosides that have both a slow rate of interaction with the receptor and a high level of non-specific binding, show a reduced potency with the cat toxicity method owing to the non-equilibrium conditions always existing there. This tendency is obviously less in digitalis compounds, which react rapidly with the receptor or/and undergo minimal non-specific binding. These difficulties are common in the testing of cardiac glycosides in whole animals and can give rise to misleading conclusions about real potency and therapeutic ratio.

The discovery that Na^+,K^+-ATPase (EC 3.6.1.37) is the target (receptor) enzyme for cardiac glycosides (cf. Section 15.2.1) has allowed precise analysis under equilibrium conditions of the relationships between structure and activity at the molecular level in the absence of the above pharmacokinetic problems (Portius and Repke 1964; Repke and Portius 1966, 1971). In line with the interpretations of Brown and Thomas (1983, 1984), Figs. 15.1 and 15.2 show that the correlation between mean lethal dose and inhibitory potency for the target enzyme is:

(1) very poor for cardiac glycosides having a different but always slow interaction rate with Na^+,K^+-ATPase, and

(2) better for aglycones having a rapid action on both levels.

Another important factor for the deviations from linear correlation is the large variation in the extent of binding of glycoside and aglycone to blood proteins and other *in-vivo* sites of loss. In line with this reasoning, differences in the relative potency of some cardiac glycosides, revealed by determinations in whole animals and isolated cardiac preparations, could be explained by appropriate differences in their plasma-protein binding (Kobinger *et al.* 1970). For cardiac glycosides (aglycones) of different structure included in Figs. 15.1(15.2), the values for 50 per cent inhibition of Na^+,K^+-ATPase cover 3.5 (2.5) orders of magnitude, whereas the values for the mean lethal dose cover 1.5 (2) orders of magnitude. The differences in slopes of the regression lines prove that the reduction in potency discrimination on *in vivo* testing of cardiac glycosides is essentially caused by the non-equilibrium condition.

Finally, the recognition of Na^+,K^+-ATPase as the digitalis receptor enzyme has allowed the targetted research strategy to apply also in the cardiac glycoside field as a major promise of more rapid progress (Krenitsky and Elion 1982), as outlined in Sections 15.4 and 15.5 below.

15.2. Na^+,K^+-ATPase as digitalis receptor

15.2.1 Discovery of receptor function

The initiatory search of Repke and his group for the molecular point of digitalis attack started in 1959, from investigations of the metabolic fate and

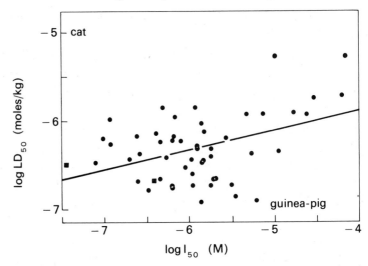

Fig. 15.1. Comparison of 53 cardiac glycosides with respect to Na^+,K^+-ATPase inhibitor potency (I_{50} = concentration needed for half-maximum inhibition of enzyme from guinea-pig cardiac muscle, determined according to Portius and Repke 1964) and cat toxicity (LD_{50} = mean lethal dose determined according to Chen 1963; the LD_{50} values are all from Chen and associates published in numerous papers between 1945 and 1970). Cardenolides (●); bufadienolides (■). The regression line has the form
$$\log LD_{50} = 0.221 \log I_{50} - 5.01 \text{ with } r = 0.409.$$

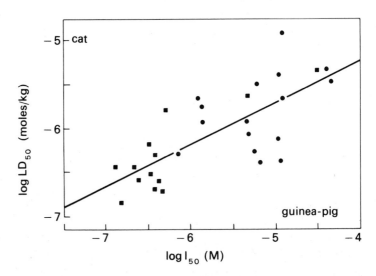

Fig. 15.2. Comparison of 29 aglycones with respect to Na^+,K^+-ATPase inhibitor potency and cat toxicity. The regression line has the form $\log LD_{50} = 0.474 \log I_{50} - 3.34$ with $r = 0.738$. For further explanations see Fig. 15.1.

mechanism of action of cardiac glycosides (Repke 1963). They yielded the following major conclusions:

(1) the cardiotonic steroids do not interfere with intermediate energy metabolism and do not influence in this way the economy of the muscle cell;

(2) the mechanism of action of cardiac glycosides is related to the nature and function of the digitalis receptor;

(3) the enzymes that effect the biotransformation of cardiotonic steroids in the animal body are not receptor enzymes;

(4) the Ca^{2+}-transporting ATPase of endoplasmic reticulum is not involved in digitalis action;

(5) the Na$^+$,K$^+$-ATPase appears to represent the digitalis receptor.

The last two preliminary conclusions were fully supported by the subsequent studies of Portius and Repke (1963), Repke and Portius (1963), Repke (1965), Repke et al. (1965), and Portius and Repke (1967), in which they extensively compared the many conditions under which digitalis compounds act on contractility, Na$^+$/K$^+$ pumping, and Na$^+$,K$^+$-ATPase activity. At each level, correlations were demonstrated with all 20 characteristics of digitalis action examined, e.g. locus of action, species differences of digitalis sensitivity, structure–activity relationships, ionic antagonisms and synergisms, cation requirements for action, time course for development of effects, dependence on specific functional states, influence of temperature, and range of effective digitalis concentrations.

Over the past 20 years, when Repke and associates had left this field of research, their findings have been confirmed and extended by various groups (Schwartz et al. 1974, 1975, 1982; Thomas et al. 1974a; Flasch and Heinz 1978; Michael et al. 1979; Akera 1981; Erdmann 1981; Brown et al. 1983; Smith et al. 1984).

15.2.2 Molecular mechanism of digitalis action

The mechanistic understanding of digitalis action requires assessment of the potential involvement of five cation-transport systems, the exploration of which was often effectively promoted by various seminal hypotheses put across by Wilbrandt as shown below.

15.2.2.1 Na$^+$/K$^+$ pump

Wilbrandt et al. (1953) accounted for the strong dependence of the cardiac action of cardiotonic steroids on contraction frequency by the hypothesis that the steroids interfere with ion transmembrane movements occurring during excitation and recovery. The incentive behind this suggestion was the knowledge that other steroids, especially corticosteroids, play an important role, possibly as cation carriers, in cation transport and homeostasis. In accordance with this hypothesis Schatzmann (1953), wishing, as stated in the introduction of his paper, to study the possible relationships between the actions of corticosteroids and cardiotonic steroids on the erythrocyte membrane, encountered a phenomenon that he considered might be responsible for the well-known K^+ loss from cardiac muscle during digitalis exposure, namely inhibitory digitalis action on Na^+/K^+ pumping in red blood cells. Schatzmann discussed this finding in terms of a carrier mechanism for Na^+/K^+ pumping, in which a cardiotonic steroid displaces a similarly structured carrier molecule, which may form complexes with Na^+ and K^+, from binding sites at an enzyme molecule involved.

Wilbrandt (1957), in support of his above hypothesis reported that corticosteroids antagonize the inhibitory action of cardiotonic steroids on Na^+/K^+ pumping. Wilbrandt (1963) consequently considered the possibility that the digitalis effect may be on the carrier part of Na^+,K^+-ATPase rather than on the enzyme protein. Portius and Repke (1969) showed, however, that corticosteroids do not attenuate digitalis-produced Na^+,K^+-ATPase inhibition. Their results appeared to exclude a functionally antagonistic competition between corticosteroids and cardenolides for binding to a common site on that enzyme. Thus the antagonistic action of corticosteroids and cardenolides found at higher levels of cellular organization (Wilbrandt and Weiss 1960) ought to have another point of attack.

In reviewing the cellular basis of cardiac glycoside action, Hajdu and Leonard (1959) concluded that the glycosides may increase contractility in the failing heart by causing a further decrease of intracellular K^+ concentration, $[K^+]_i$, without a corresponding increase in $[Na^+]_i$ but do not appear to have any direct effect on $[Ca^{2+}]_i$. Wilbrandt (1958), and Caviezel and Wilbrandt (1958) maintained, however, that $[Ca^{2+}]_i$ regulates contractility and that the inhibitory digitalis action on K^+ transport is not necessarily in conflict with that view if the inward transport of K^+ is coupled with the outward transport of Ca^{2+}, provided that Ca^{2+} displaces Na^+ from the pump. Portius and Repke (1967) actually demonstrated the supposed Na^+/Ca^{2+} competition for interaction with Na^+,K^+-ATPase which, however, was associated with an activating (Na^+) or inhibitory (Ca^{2+}) action on ATP hydrolysis by the enzyme. Although Schön *et al.* (1972) further showed that Ca^{2+} may replace Na^+ in promoting transphosphorylation from ATP, the Ca^{2+}-phosphoenzyme formed, unlike the Na^+-phosphoenzyme, was found to be insensitive to the dephosphorylating effect of K^+. The failure of K^+ to promote Ca^{2+}-phosphoenzyme turnover indicates that the Na^+/K^+ pump cannot alternatively operate as a Ca^{2+}/K^+ pump.

In an effort to unify his own data (Repke 1963) and data available in the literature up to mid-1963, Repke (1964) designed a hypothesis concerning the biochemical mode of digitalis action, now often called the 'sodium pump lag' hypothesis, as reviewed by Langer (1983). Key features of this hypothesis, which has been fully corroborated and considerably extended since 1964, are summarized below. During every action potential, Na^+ ions flow into the muscle cell, and K^+ ions flow out, down their concentration gradients. The transient increase in $[Na^+]_i$ that occurs at the inner surface of the plasma membrane near the Na^+ activation site of Na^+,K^+-ATPase, increases the number of pumping Na^+,K^+-ATPase molecules and enhances in this way the return pumping of Na^+ and K^+. The reserve capacity of the pump is so great that even with considerable increase of contraction frequency, Na^+ and K^+ homoeostasis will be maintained due to the recruitment of formerly resting Na^+/K^+ pumps. Nonetheless, the disposable pump reserve capacity will decrease with increasing contraction frequency. Digitalis interaction with Na^+,K^+-ATPase suppresses its pump activity and thus decreases the Na^+/K^+ pump potential of a cell. The positive and negative inotropic digitalis actions are evoked by moderate or large reductions of the required proportion of pumping Na^+,K^+-ATPase molecules per unit muscle cell. At lower digitalis concentrations, the actual contraction frequency determines whether there is no contractile response (characterized by full substitution of inhibited pump molecules from reserve capacity), a positive inotropic action (characterized by partial substitution of inhibited pump molecules leading to delayed, but still complete, return pumping of Na^+ and K^+ between contractions), or a negative inotropic effect (characterized by inadequate substitution of inhibited pump molecules resulting in negative cation balance with persistent Na^+ gain and K^+ loss). At higher digitalis concentrations, the gradual lowering of the working pump capacity with time, due to the slow formation of the inhibitory digitalis–enzyme complex (see Section 15.4.3.1), which eventually falls below the limit required for maintenance of cation homeostasis, underlies the turn from positive to negative inotropic action.

The key feature of Repke's hypothesis is that excitation–contraction coupling transients of $[Na^+]_i$ are determinants of $[Ca^{2+}]_i$ transients. This was deduced from analysis of experimental data available by 1963. Speed, magnitude and duration of $[Na^+]_i$ gain depend upon disposable working pump capacity. Positive inotropically-acting digitalis concentrations reduce the pump potential required, such that an instantaneous, greater, and more rapid net growth of $[Na^+]_i$ and, consequently, $[Ca^{2+}]_i$ via ion exchange (see Section 15.2.2.2) result. Negative inotropically-acting digitalis concentrations, that produce a persistent large increase in $[Na^+]_i$, cause a substantial uptake of Ca^{2+} from the extracellular space leading to sustained increase of $[Ca^{2+}]_i$.

As reviewed by Akera (1981), his computer simulation studies and experimental results support the concept that the Na^+ transient would be enhanced by moderate Na^+,K^+-ATPase inhibition. Barry et al. (1981) concluded from studies of digitalis actions on cellular Na^+, K^+, and Ca^{2+} content, Na^+/K^+ pumping, and contractile state of cultured heart cells, that their results are consistent with the hypothesis that the instantaneous Na^+/K^+ pumping rate is an important determinant of inotropic response in cardiac muscle. Their results are also compatible with the existence of sub-sarcolemmal space in which Na^+ activity at a given time in the contraction cycle is influenced by the outward trans-sarcolemmal Na^+ transport rate, the rate of Na^+ influx from the extracellular space, and the rate of exchange with other intracellular Na^+ pools. The findings showing that $[Ca^{2+}]_i$ returns to control levels when the Na^+/K^+ pump rate is back to normal, even though the cellular Na^+ content remains elevated, suggested to the authors that phasic changes in $[Na^+]_i$ in a region adjacent to the sarcolemma may be more important in modulating Ca^{2+} exchange than bulk cellular Na^+ content.

Recent studies using Na^+-selective microelectrodes established the essential role of an increase in the intracellular sodium ion activity, a_{Na}^i, in the action of digitalis at low and high concentrations (see Lee *et al.* 1985 and references therein). They showed that digitalis produces a parallel increase in a_{Na}^i and contractile force, and that these parameters remain closely correlated during the positive inotropic effect. Moreover, Lee *et al.* (1985) demonstrated that the effectiveness of inotropic digitalis action is related to enhanced Na^+/K^+ pumping due to elevated a_{Na}^i, which increases the number of working Na^+,K^+-ATPase molecules, but attenuates the reserve capacity (cf. below). Entry and accumulation of Na^+ in digitalis action occur partially through the sarcolemmal Na^+/H^+ exchanger so that amiloride derivatives, which block this exchanger, antagonize both therapeutic and toxic digitalis actions on cardiac cells (Lazdunski *et al.* 1985 and references therein).

In studies on the action of six cardiac glycosides on Na^+/K^+ pumping in Purkinje fibres, Achenbach *et al.* (1986) showed that the recruitment of resting Na^+,K^+-ATPase molecules from pump reserve can compensate for a reduction of up to 50 per cent in pump potential, while a fall of about 58 per cent leads to glycoside-produced onset of toxicity, pointing to the close link between pump inhibition and glycoside toxicity. According to Repke (1986), increases or decreases of $[Na^+]_i:[K^+]_i$ ratio in the neighbourhood of internal Na^+ activation sites of Na^+,K^+-ATPase molecules, whether occurring in excitation–contraction coupling or caused by drug exposure, play pacemaker roles in short-term autocontrol of the Na^+/K^+ pumping power of the cell. This control occurs through increases and decreases in the ratio between catalytically competent and incompetent conformers of Na^+,K^+-ATPase, $E_1 \cdot Na$ and $E_2 \cdot K$, respectively.

15.2.2.2 Na^+/Ca^{2+} exchanger

The discovery of Na^+/Ca^{2+} exchange across the plasma membrane of cardiac muscle cells involved several steps. Wilbrandt and Koller (1948) suggested that, in the regulation of cardiac contractility, Ca^{2+} and Na^+ ions compete for anionic groups at the membrane surface. Wilbrandt further showed (1955) that cardiac glycosides decelerate Ca^{2+} efflux from cardiac muscle cells. He interpreted this finding by assuming that the glycosides interfere with Ca^{2+} ion movement, which seems to occur, not only in the same direction as Na^+ ions, but also through the same mechanism, through affinity for the same carrier. Niedergerke (1963) found that Ca^{2+} uptake is increased after reduction of $[Na^+]_o$ and Ca^{2+} release is facilitated after normalization of $[Na^+]_o$. He interpreted these observations by assuming that the entry of Ca^{2+} ions into the cell occurs after their combination at the cell surface with carrier molecules whose presence is suggested by the Ca^{2+}–Na^+ antagonism. Reuter and Seitz (1968) suggested that the occurrence of a Na^+/Ca^{2+} exchange diffusion mechanism in the cardiac cell membrane accounts for the dependence on external Na^+ concentration of Ca^{2+} influx into and Ca^{2+} efflux from the cell, and that the downhill movement of Na^+ (or Ca^{2+}) ions can provide the free energy for uphill movement of Ca^{2+} (or Na^+) ions across the membrane. Eventually Glitsch et al. (1970) showed that an increase in $[Na^+]_i$, and hence a reduction or inversion of the Na^+ gradient, promotes Ca^{2+} influx into the cardiac muscle cell.

When three Na^+ ions move downhill and one Ca^{2+} ion moves uphill, Na^+/Ca^{2+} exchange can reduce a_{Ca}^i to 2.5 nM, as calculated by Reuter (1982) from measured extra- and intracellular Na^+ and Ca^{2+} ion activities. This is below the a_{Ca}^i value of 38 nM determined by Ca^{2+}-selective microelectrodes in cardiac sarcoplasm of resting muscle (Lee et al. 1980). Such $Na^+ : Ca^{2+}$ stoichiometry is supported by current generation during Na^+/Ca^{2+} exchange (Caroni et al. 1980), and the voltage sensitivity of the Ca^{2+} movement (Reeves and Hale 1984).

Thus, the operation mode of the Na^+/Ca^{2+} exchanger depends also on the membrane potential such that during heart muscle contraction, with the cell depolarized, Ca^{2+} will move inwards and during relaxation, with the cell repolarized, Ca^{2+} will move outwards (Cohen et al. 1982; Barry et al. 1985). The magnitude of the net $[Ca^{2+}]_i$ growth is strongly adjusted by the effective internal Na^+ concentration. This dependence is steepest between 10 and 40 mM $[Na^+]_i$ with a Hill coefficient of 3 (Frelin et al. 1984). This range of $[Na^+]_i$ may ensue from depolarization and Na^+/K^+ pumping in the sub-sarcolemmal space after excitation and recovery of the cell.

All this information taken together suggests that Na^+/Ca^{2+} exchanges are coupled through $[Na^+]_i$, with Na^+/K^+ pumping. Positive-inotropically active concentrations of cardiac glycosides reduce the pumping potential of the cell, resulting in increased $[Na^+]_i$ and, via the exchanger, in increased $[Ca^{2+}]_i$ through enhanced Ca^{2+} influx into and reduced Ca^{2+} efflux from the cell (Cohen et al. 1982; Barry et al. 1985).

Apart from cardiac sarcolemma, the Na^+/Ca^{2+} exchanger, which itself is insensitive to cardiac glycosides, occurs predominantly in the plasma membrane of brain and nerve cells; low exchange activity has also been reported for membrane preparations of kidney, skeletal muscle, small intestine, adrenal medulla, and liver, as reviewed by Blaustein (1974), Carafoli and Crompton (1978), and Philipson (1985). Such low capacity may explain the apparent absence of exchange in renal tubular epithelial cells (Schönfeld et al. 1984) and in embryonic skeletal muscle cells (Fosset et al. 1977).

15.2.2.3 Ca^{2+} channel

Excitation–contraction coupling in heart muscle requires an inward movement of Ca^{2+} across the sarcolemma, since in the relaxed state only a very small fraction of the total $[Ca^{2+}]_i$ is in ionic form in the myocardial fibres. Thus, the inward movement of calcium ions via the Ca^{2+} channel during depolarization can raise the amount of free internal calcium ions substantially in the vicinity of the membrane (Beeler and Reuter 1970). As stated by Carafoli and Crompton (1978), the quantity of this Ca^{2+} flux is insufficient for the Ca^{2+} requirement of muscle contraction, but it appears to be essential because it triggers the release of greater amounts of Ca^{2+} from the sarcoplasmic reticulum (cf. Section 15.2.2.4).

Cardiac glycosides increase the 'slow inward Ca^{2+} current' with a time course similar to the development of the positive inotropic effect (Marban and Tsien 1982). The link between these glycoside effects is the elevation of $[Na^+]_i$ due to attenuated Na^+/K^+ pumping. This results, via Na^+/Ca^{2+} exchange, in increased $[Ca^{2+}]_i$, which also positively regulates Ca^{2+} entry through the channel. Blockers of the Ca^{2+} channel such as nifedipine produce negative inotropic effects or reverse the toxic effects of higher digitalis concentrations (Nayler and Dresel 1984; Morgan 1985). Taken together, the available evidence suggests that digitalis actions on cardiac muscle include the enhancement of Ca^{2+} influx through the Ca^{2+} channel into the cell, although the primary effect is again the inhibition of Na^+,K^+-ATPase.

15.2.2.4   Sarcolemmal Ca^{2+} pump

While the Na^+/Ca^{2+} exchanger is not inherently directionally oriented, —the direction of net Ca^{2+} movements depends on both the magnitude of the Na^+ gradient and the direction of the electrical field—the ATP-driven Ca^{2+} pump extrudes Ca^{2+} from the cell independently of both quantities. As stated by Caroni et al. (1980), the V_{max} of the Na^+/Ca^{2+} exchange system is at least 30 times higher than that of the Ca^{2+}-transporting ATPase and qualifies the exchanger optimally as the system that operates whenever massive amounts of Ca^{2+} must be transported rapidly; the Ca^{2+}-ATPase could therefore be responsible for most of the Ca^{2+} ejection at rest (Caroni et al. 1980). The global role of the sarcolemmal Ca^{2+} pump in the regulation of $[Ca^{2+}]_i$ is estimated as minimal by Chapman et al. (1983), but of major importance by Barry and Smith (1984). In contrast to the sarcolemmal Na^+/K^+ pump, the Ca^{2+} pump in the cell membrane of all tissues studied is insensitive to cardiac glycosides.

15.2.2.5 Ca^{2+}-handling organelles

A perusal of the abundant pertinent literature suggests the following picture of the present state of knowledge on the role of sarcoplasmic reticulum and mitochondria in the regulation of $[Ca^{2+}]_i$. Ca^{2+} ions, entering the cardiac cell during the action potential through the Na^+/Ca^{2+} exchanger and the Ca^{2+} channel, serve as a trigger for the release of additional amounts of Ca^{2+} from the Ca^{2+}-loaded subsarcolemmal cisternae of sarcoplasmic reticulum. This process of Ca^{2+}-induced Ca^{2+} release places the cisternae in the role of an amplifier, responding by graded Ca^{2+} release according to the magnitude of Ca^{2+} entry and store. The rise in sarcoplasmic $[Ca^{2+}]$ initiates the final steps of excitation–contraction coupling in the myocardium. Relaxation occurs when the sarcoplasmic reticulum re-accumulates the released Ca^{2+} ions, thus decreasing $[Ca^{2+}]_i$ below the level required for contraction. Thus, this organelle is the major internal site of both Ca^{2+} release and removal during the contraction–relaxation cycle.

Via the mechanisms described in Sections 15.2.2.1–15.2.2.3, cardiac glycosides increase the amount of trigger Ca^{2+} and hence the amount of systolic free Ca^{2+} available for excitation–contraction coupling (Morgan 1985). In this way, the glycosides enhance the Ca^{2+} loading of the cisternae and, thus, the amount of Ca^{2+} available for subsequent excitation–contraction couplings. However, cardiac glycosides do not affect the time course of the Ca^{2+} transient and twitch tension development. This indicates that the digitalis-promoted increase in tension is fully accounted for by the increase in systolic free $[Ca^{2+}]_i$ without affecting the kinetics of subcellular Ca^{2+} handling and without increasing the Ca^{2+} sensitivity of the myofilaments.

The mitochondria have a lower Ca^{2+} affinity than the cisternae. Thus they do not play any role in the beat-to-beat regulation of sarcoplasmic $[Ca^{2+}]$ unless its concentration becomes extremely high. Since mitochondria have a high Ca^{2+}-accumulating capacity, they take up Ca^{2+} ions in digitalis-produced Ca^{2+} overload and so prevent an excessive rise in sarcoplasmic Ca^{2+} concentration (Chapman et al. 1983). The accompanying increases in $[Na^+]_i$ may also promote Ca^{2+} release from the mitochondria so that the state of Ca^{2+} overload of the cardiac cell may lead to a sustained increase of $[Ca^{2+}]_i$ or oscillatory movements of Ca^{2+} between the organelles and the sarcoplasm, so explaining certain arrhythmogenic digitalis effects (Kass et al. 1978).

In conclusion, cardiac glyosides exert only indirect effects on Ca^{2+}-handling by both types of organelle.

15.2.2.6 Implications for steroid testing and drug design

Since studies using relevant glycoside concentrations have failed to show primary effects on contractile or regulatory proteins, on intermediary metabolism or myocardial energetics, or on the Ca^{2+}-handling systems of cell membrane and intracellular organelles, investigative efforts in inhibitor testing and drug design may safely be focused on Na^+,K^+-ATPase as the target enzyme. As mentioned in Section 15.2.2.1, the magnitude and character of the final digitalis effect in beating heart muscle becomes multi-conditionally modulated such that a strict quantitative correlation between the degree of inhibition of isolated Na^+,K^+-ATPase and the size and type of in situ inotropic response cannot be regularly expected. This natural limitation has often been neglected, as partially discussed in Section 15.2.3, and has to be carefully considered in any attempt to extrapolate the in vitro data to in vivo responses (cf. Section 15.4.2).

15.2.3 Queries about receptor identity

15.2.3.1 *Inotropic digitalis action without inhibition of Na^+/K^+ pump?*

As repeatedly stated (e.g. Brown and Erdmann 1984a; Brown *et al.* 1985), cardiac glycosides can increase the contractile force of cardiac muscle with no apparent effect on Na^+/K^+ pumping as measured by uptake of $^{86}Rb^+$ (a K^+ analogue). This occurs when a proportion of Na^+/K^+ pump molecules are blocked by digitalis complex formation and thus $[Na^+]_i$ has increased to a higher steady level. This leads, as explained in Section 15.2.2.1, to a compensatory recruitment of resting Na^+,K^+-ATPase molecules from the pump reserve so that the overall pump rate in the steady state is essentially unchanged. The elevated $[Na^+]_i$ evokes, via Na^+/Ca^{2+} exchange, a rise of $[Ca^{2+}]_i$ and, hence, a positive inotropic effect. Measurements of $[Na^+]_i$ and tension have shown that tension depends on a steep relationship with $[Na^+]_i$ and, therefore, significant positive inotropy can be brought about by digitalis concentrations that produce only a small rise of $[Na^+]_i$ and an undetectably small decrease of Rb^+ uptake (Eisner *et al.* 1983).

As discussed by Cohen *et al.* (1982), previous attempts to correlate cell sodium content with inotropy of cardiac muscle have relied upon chemical measurements to estimate Na^+ concentration. These studies generally find that $[Na^+]_i$ in myocardium is 20–40 mM, while the intracellular Na^+ activity (a_{Na}^i), measured by using Na^+-selective microelectrodes, is about 8–9 mM (see e.g. Lee *et al.* 1985; Gretler 1985; Grupp *et al.* 1985). Inotropically active digitalis concentrations produce rises of only a few mmol in $[Na^+]_i$. Again, the dependence of tension on $[Na^+]_i$ is very steep and twitch tension is approximately proportional to $([Na^+]_i)^{3.2}$ (Blaustein 1985). A 1 mM increase in a_{Na}^i produces an increase of about 100 per cent in twitch magnitude (Wasserstrom *et al.* 1983; Grupp *et al.* 1985). Since such small changes in $[Na^+]_i$ might not be reliably detected by chemical analysis, the primary role of the rise in $[Na^+]_i$ in digitalis action was often denied in earlier studies (for some more recent references see Grupp *et al.* 1985).

In conclusion, pertinent literature data show no single proof for a lack of Na^+/K^+ pump inhibition in positive-inotropic digitalis action.

15.2.3.2 *Lack of correspondence between digitalis concentrations inhibiting Na^+,K^+-ATPase and enhancing contractility!*

Studies on a broad range of digitalis derivatives have shown significant correlations between their inhibitory potency and affinity for cardiac Na^+,K^+-ATPase on the one hand and their inotropic potency in cardiac muscle on the other (e.g. Haustein 1974; Flasch and Heinz 1978; Brown *et al.* 1983, 1985).

However, the cardiac muscle has been found to be approximately 10 times more sensitive than the enzyme to the various derivatives. Moreover, low glycoside concentrations that did not inhibit isolated Na^+,K^+-ATPase have been shown to increase a_{Na}^i and produce positive inotropy (Grupp *et al.* 1985).

There are two reasons for the apparent discrepancy:

1. A large enzyme reserve capacity exists in cardiac muscle, and the actual size of the reserve depends on beat frequency, which determines the magnitude of the inotropic digitalis effect (Reiter 1981). These factors are not compatible with a linear relationship between glycoside-occupancy of the enzyme and effect, which means that a significant inotropic response can be obtained when only a fraction of the total Na^+,K^+-ATPase population is occupied (cf. Rang 1971).

2. The outcome of a given digitalis-produced inhibition of Na^+,K^+-ATPase becomes amplified in cardiac muscle via Ca^{2+} release from the cisternae of sarcoplasmic reticulum (cf. Section 15.2.2.5).

The comparison between the Na^+,K^+-ATPases from cardiac and skeletal muscle with regard to their interaction with ouabain suggested to Pitts *et al.* (1977) that the lack of inotropic glycoside action on skeletal muscle is probably not due to failure to bind to and inhibit the Na^+/K^+ pump so that pump inhibition *per se* is not sufficient for development of the inotropic response. The authors therefore considered the possibility that the inotropic effect is not a consequence of inhibition of the pump (though this occurs), but results from a conformational change in the membrane as suggested by Gervais *et al.* (1977). The latter authors observed that ouabain alters the K_D for Ca^{2+} binding to Na^+,K^+-ATPase. However, skeletal muscle cells are reported by Fosset *et al.* (1977) to be devoid of the Na^+/Ca^{2+} exchange system. This would fully explain why the ouabain-elicited rise of a_{Na}^i does not promote Ca^{2+} entry (Frelin *et al.* 1984) and does not evoke a direct inotropic effect on skeletal muscle (Dénes and Greeff 1981). This clearly indicates that the development of the inotropic response requires the cooperation between the Na^+/K^+-pump and the Na^+/Ca^{2+} exchange system through the level of a_{Na}^i, as detailed in Section 15.2.2.2.

15.2.3.3 *Activation of Na^+,K^+-ATPase and Na^+/K^+ pump by cardiac glycosides?*

Very low glycoside concentrations were shown by Repke (1963) to increase or depress Na^+,K^+-ATPase activity when measured after short or continued exposure respectively. In 1965, Repke stated that 'stimulation' of the enzyme, which he could not regularly reproduce, might be caused by the release of an inhibitor or by a change in the physical state in the membrane-neighbourhood, but he doubted the specificity of this interaction since several non-digitalis compounds 'stimulated' ATPases of different origin in a similar manner. The biphasic digitalis action as a function of incubation time and inhibitor concentration has often been confirmed, but the mechanism of activation has remained unclear (Hamlyn *et al.* 1985 and references therein).

Noble (1980) and Godfraind (1985) reported on stimulation/disinhibition of the Na^+/K^+ pump in cardiac muscle by low digitalis concentrations. Lechat *et al.* (1983) showed that this response is mediated by a glycoside-evoked release of noradrenalin from the store in adrenergic nerve terminals. Catecholamines are known to enhance Na^+ influx and in this way a_{Na}^i, which leads to an increase of the fraction of catalytically competent conformers $(E_1 \cdot Na)$ of Na^+,K^+-ATPase from the reserve of catalytically incompetent conformers $(E_2 \cdot K)$ (cf. Repke 1986). This appears as a pump 'stimulation' before the new steady-state is reached. If cardiac glycosides at low concentration could increase molecular turnover number (this appears impossible, since Na^+,K^+-ATPase is a K system, as shown by Repke 1986), this would result in decreases in a_{Na}^i and eventually in negative inotropic effects. However, all concentrations of various digitalis compounds that were tested caused an increase in a_{Na}^i immediately before, or coincident with, a positive inotropic effect (Wasserstrom *et al.* 1983; Grupp *et al.* 1985, Lee *et al.* 1985 and references therein).

15.2.3.4 *More than one digitalis receptor?*

The newer experimental data evaluated in Sections 15.2.3.1–3 clearly support the hypothesis that Na^+,K^+-ATPase is the digitalis target enzyme and sole receptor. However, there are some findings that appear to require the existence of an additional, high-affinity receptor entity.

As reviewed by Noble (1980), Lüllmann and Peters (1979) and Schwartz and Adams (1980) supposed that an important direct effect of glycoside binding to the membrane Na^+,K^+-ATPase is perturbation of membrane structure, involving a rapidly exchanging Ca^{2+} store. In some way not yet clear, it is also supposed that this perturbation allows more Ca^{2+} to be released during excitation. It is this mechanism that is supposed to be most directly related to the increased force of contraction at very low cardiac glycoside concentrations. However, as reasoned by Kim *et al.* (1984), if the proposal that binding of digitalis to Na^+,K^+-ATPase causes release of Ca^{2+} from enzyme-associated sarcolemmal sites were true, and if binding of one digitalis molecule causes the release of a constant amount of Ca^{2+} per site irrespective of the number of binding sites present, then it might be expected that a greater amount of Ca^{2+} mobilization would occur in cells with increased numbers of Na^+,K^+-ATPase complexes and, consequently, there would be a greater inotropic response, contrary to observations. Kim *et al.* (1984) therefore rejected a mechanism of inotropic digitalis action based on altered Ca^{2+} binding properties of sarcolemmal sites due to cardiac glycoside binding to Na^+,K^+-ATPase.

As reviewed by Grupp *et al.* (1985), results from several laboratories have suggested that low and high concentrations of cardiac glycosides produce inotropic effects by different mechanisms. In particular, low concentrations produce their positive inotropic effects in the absence of Na^+/K^+ pump inhibition. However, the measurement of intracellular Na^+ activity and twitch tension of rat ventricular muscle during exposure to and wash-out of ouabain has shown that a_{Na}^i rises over the full range of ouabain concentrations that increase twitch tension. This finding indicates that in this cardiac muscle, as in others, the inotropic actions of even low ouabain concentrations are mediated by inhibition of Na$^+$/K$^+$ pumping.

Clearly, these insights do not exclude the possible involvement of Na$^+$,K$^+$-ATPase isozymes, which may strongly differ in digitalis affinity and can thus help to account for the reported biphasic dose–response curve in rat and guinea-pig cardiac muscle (Godfraind 1981; Schwartz *et al.* 1982). However, the coexistence of isozymes in the myocardium of both species showing high or low digitalis affinity is still being debated, as detailed in Section 15.3.5. Finally, the reported irregularities in digitalis concentration–binding curves (Erdmann 1985) and digitalis dose–response curves (Schwartz *et al.* 1982) could possibly also be based on the involvement of differently ligated enzyme conformers, which vary greatly in the kinetics of their interaction with digitalis compounds (Schwartz *et al.* 1982; Repke *et al.* 1984; Repke and Schönfeld 1984). These possibilities are not mutually exclusive, as discussed in Section 15.3.5.

15.2.4 Limitations in using Na$^+$,K$^+$-ATPase as a tool in drug design

Studies with the digitalis target enzyme are an indispensable tool in the search for the intrinsic i.e. pharmacokinetically unaltered, structure–activity relationships (Section 15.4.4). The quantitative nature and rapid generation of data by this approach are also ideal for guiding chemical synthesis. However, this targetted strategy is confronted by the pitfalls and complexities of various *in vivo* factors that influence the *in vivo* efficacy and selectivity of steroidal inhibitors of Na$^+$,K$^+$-ATPase and are unpredictable from the data obtained with the isolated enzyme.

15.2.4.1 *Receptor-independent mechanisms influencing efficacy*

Mechanisms influencing efficacy include various pharmacokinetic parameters, e.g. absorption, binding to various sites of loss (e.g. serum albumin), distribution in the body and tissues, penetration through the blood–brain barrier, bio-transformation, and excretion. A poor absorption from the intestinal tract can predictably be influenced by chemical modification of a glycoside such as gitoxin, that optimizes both the water and lipid solubility of the drug (Repke and Megges 1963). This was originally demonstrated with penta-acetylgitoxin, which shows poor efficacy (cf. Section 15.4.4.4), but in humans undergoes rapid enzymatic deacetylation after absorption, to form the highly active 16-acetylgitoxin (Haustein *et al.* 1978). The principle of optimization of solubility by chemical modification has since been successfully applied to digoxin and proscillaridin A (Kaiser 1971; Kurbjuweit 1971). Clearly, a pro-drug (for review see Stella and Himmelstein 1980) such as penta-acetylgitoxin cannot appropriately be tested with the isolated target enzyme.

The binding of cardiac glycosides and aglycones to serum albumin is very different, but can be qualitatively predicted by performing tests with the enzyme in the presence or absence of added albumin (Repke and Portius 1971).

The rate of metabolic inactivation of cardiac glycosides in human is in general extremely slow (for a short review see Wirth 1986). Hence, their *in vivo* efficacy will not be significantly overestimated in the enzymatic test. However, this does not apply to the rapidly inactivated aglycones (cf. Gold *et al.* 1969) so that their efficacy as determined on the isolated enzyme cannot easily be extrapolated to the *in vivo* efficacy.

15.2.4.2 *Receptor-independent mechanisms influencing specificity of action*

Steroidal inhibitors of Na^+,K^+-ATPase that are not derived from the lead structure (see Section 15.4.4.2) may additionally interfere with the function of other vital cellular systems. This is true for 3β-hydroxy-17β-formyl-$5\beta,14\alpha$-androstane-17-guanylhydrazone and chlormadinone acetate which, due to overriding detrimental actions on cardiac muscle contractility, do not produce positive inotropy (Section 15.4.4.2).

Although receptor discrimination in the body appears to be mainly determined in the recognition step, the uneven extracellular distribution of the drug in a given tissue due to selective accumulation may be effective as an additional determinant of specificity, as pointed out by Testa (1984).

Finally, the specificity of digitalis action depends on the concentration of target enzyme in the various tissues as well on the reserve capacity in Na^+/K^+ pump potential. Thus, the higher digitalis sensitivity of the conducting system in cardiac muscle, compared with the working myocardium, appears to be based on a lower density of Na^+/K^+ pumps in Purkinje fibres (Brown *et al.* 1985). Furthermore, the lack of digitalis sensitivity of skeletal muscle could (if the Na^+/Ca^{2+} exchanger is present although at low density: cf. Section 15.2.2.2) be related to excessive reserve capacity, amounting to 97 per cent in isolated skeletal muscle under resting conditions (Kjeldsen *et al.* 1985). Hence, even extensive enzyme inhibition by cardiac glycosides will produce little or no inotropic effect (Dénes and Greeff 1981), but will do so at high contraction frequency. On the other hand, the demand for a permanently high rate of Na^+/K^+ pumping in heart and brain may partially explain the preferential action of cardiac glycosides on these organs. Gillis and Quest (1980), in reviewing the role of the nervous system in the cardiovascular effects of digitalis, concluded that 'cardiac' glycosides might just as well be described as 'neural' glycosides.

15.2.4.3 *Conclusions*

As with any other targetted strategy (cf. Krenitsky and Elion 1982), the use of Na^+,K^+-ATPase as a tool consists of a cyclical improvement process involving the design, synthesis, and testing of inhibitors on the isolated enzyme. When inhibitors of suitable efficacy and specificity are discovered, they are evaluated in biological systems of increased complexity. However, if there is insufficient efficacy or selectivity, the biotransformation and pharmacokinetics of the inhibitor concerned will be studied in attempts to ascertain the basis for the inadequacy. The information obtained might point to the possibility of chemical modification of the inhibitor to improve its efficacy and selectivity.

15.3   The target enzyme

All facets of this broad topic have been discussed in great detail in various review articles on Na$^+$,K$^+$-ATPase (Robinson and Flashner 1979; Hobbs and Albers 1980; Cantley 1981; Schuurmans *et al.* 1981; Askari 1982; Jørgensen 1982; Kaplan 1985; Glynn 1985), as well in the proceedings of recent international conferences on Na$^+$,K$^+$-ATPase, (Hoffman and Forbush 1983; Glynn and Ellory 1985). Thus, only a brief summary of the pertinent fundamentals and a reference to some special aspects are given here.

15.3.1   Function

Na$^+$,K$^+$-ATPase is the enzymatic machinery in the Na$^+$/K$^+$ pump, which uses energy from hydrolysis of the terminal phosphoryl of one molecule of intracellular ATP to transport three Na$^+$ ions outwards and two K$^+$ ions inwards across the cell membrane against steep electrochemical gradients. Thus ATP, intracellular Na$^+$ ions, and extracellular K$^+$ ions may be viewed as substrates, and ADP, orthophosphate, extracellular Na$^+$ ions, and intracellular K$^+$ ions as products of the enzymatic process. The role of Na$^+$, K$^+$-ATPase in Na$^+$/K$^+$-pumping was established by the work of Post *et al.* (1960), and of Dunham and Glynn (1961). The basic functions of the Na$^+$/K$^+$ pump include:

(1) maintenance of transmembrane Na$^+$ and K$^+$ gradients over the plasma membrane, a prerequisite for the generation of the resting membrane potential and the action potential;

(2) generation of the transmembrane electrochemical potential gradient for Na$^+$ ions, which provides the energy for driving the uphill movement of Ca^{2+}, Cl$^-$, and H$^+$ ions, as well sugars and amino acids, through appropriately coupled transfer devices;

(3) maintenance of a high [K$^+$] environment, required for activity of many intracellular enzymes involved in energy generation and macromolecule synthesis.

Overall, the Na$^+$/K$^+$ pump plays an important role in the regulation of normal cellular homoeostasis, cell differentiation, and cell proliferation (Repke 1988).

15.3.2   Mechanism

As with all other cation-transporting ATPases, the mechanism by which Na$^+$,K$^+$-ATPase converts the scalar Gibbs energy of ATP into the vectorial coupled transmembrane transport of Na$^+$ and K$^+$ is essentially unknown. The current hypothesis on coupling between enzyme conformational changes and transport events, the so-called Albers–Post scheme, is the most popular. It is extensively treated by the authors listed above. As shown by Repke (1986), the processes proposed as final and initial steps of the hypothetical conformation change–transport coupling mechanism of Na$^+$,K$^+$-ATPase are alternatively fully suitable to be involved in the allosteric regulation of Na^+,K^+-ATPase activity and the Na^+/K^+ pump power. Repke (1986) has therefore concluded that the transphosphorylation-transport coupling hypothesis (Post *et al.* 1965; Taniguchi and Post 1975; Glynn and Karlish 1975) in its more advanced state (Repke 1977, 1982) deserves fresh consideration.

15.3.3   Occurrence

Na^+,K^+-ATPase has been found in the plasma membrane of nearly all eukaryotic cells, although its density per cell is very different, e.g., 2.7×10^2–1.2×10^3 in red blood cells and 5.2×10^6 in cardiac ventricular muscle (Michael *et al.* 1979). The highest density is found in tissues rich in cells specialized for Na^+ transport (e.g. the outer medulla of mammalian kidney) or in excitable tissues (e.g. the grey matter of the brain). Tissues of this type are commonly used for the preparation of pure Na^+,K^+-ATPase required for special purposes.

15.3.4   Structure

The total body of information derived from ultrastructural studies, radiation inactivation analyses, chemical cross-linking reactions, and detergent solubilization analyses strongly favours the conclusion that the Na^+,K^+-ATPase holoenzyme is an $\alpha_2\beta_2$-tetramer. Solubilization of the membrane-bound holoenzyme yields the α,β-protomer, as one of the major products; this protomer seems to retain some function-related properties of the holoenzyme. The diprotomeric structure has recently been confirmed by accurate determination of protein concentration and quantitative end-group analysis (Chetverin 1986). The β-glycopeptide ($M_r \approx 55\,000$) is without distinct functional significance. The α-polypeptide ($M_r \approx 100\,000$) spans the membrane with eight segments and carries one catalytic centre on the cytoplasmic extension and one digitalis binding matrix on the extracellular extension. According to Shull *et al.* (1985), the digitalis binding site is located at the extracellular junction of two transmembrane domains, which form a relatively hydrophobic cleft outside the membrane core. Studies with group-specific reagents suggest that no essential reactive tyrosine or tryptophan residue is present (Wallick *et al.* 1986).

15.3.5   Isozymes

The occurrence of Na^+,K^+-ATPase isozymes in various tissues or within one tissue of a given species has become apparent from studies performed using different analytical procedures where the results could not always be well correlated.

Fractionated antisera to purified Na^+,K^+-ATPase preparations revealed, apart from partial homology among the Na^+,K^+-ATPases from various sources, a significant antigenic organ difference, in the dog enzyme. This could indicate the existence of isozymes (McCans *et al.* 1975). Remarkably, the inhibitory effectiveness of the Na$^+$,K$^+$-ATPase antibodies was dependent to some extent on the ligation of the enzyme with its various effectors. Electrophoretic resolution of Na$^+$,K$^+$-ATPase preparations from brain of dog, mouse, and rat (Sweadner 1979) showed that the catalytic subunit occurs in a higher molecular weight form, termed $\alpha(+)$, and a lower molecular weight form, termed α. Sweadner showed that the $\alpha(+)$ form is present in the enzyme of axolemma (plasma membrane of myelinated axons), the α form in the enzyme of astrocytes (non-neuronal cells), of the renal medulla and cortex, and of skeletal and cardiac muscle (rat). Both forms are present in the synaptic plasma membrane of brain. Schellenberg *et al.* (1981) concluded from immunoreactivity studies that enzyme preparations from the brain of dog, rat, and from the human cerebral cortex, contain α and $\alpha(+)$ forms, while kidney enzyme preparations of dog and rat contain only the α form. The two forms do not show differences in proteolytic processing or in glycosylation, but are different in primary protein sequence (Sweadner and Gilkeson 1985). These authors also showed by application of antisera to α- and $\alpha(+)$-containing isozymes that the membranes from whole brain of all mammals tested (including rat, calf, cat, dog, guinea-pig, human, mouse, and rabbit) contained both $\alpha(+)$ and α subunits. McDonough and Schmitt (1985), utilizing antibodies for detection of the subunits, have traced the $\alpha(+)$ and α forms in enzyme preparations from guinea-pig brain, but not from cardiac muscle and kidney.

The possibility that the $\alpha(+)$- or α-subunit-containing Na$^+$,K$^+$-ATPase isozymes play different functional roles has not yet been settled. On the base of studies on rat adipocytes, Lytton *et al.* (1985) hypothesized that the $\alpha(+)$-isozyme represents a hormonally (insulin) regulated version of the enzyme. Sweadner (1985), although admitting this possibility, stated after thorough comparison of the enzymatic properties of the separated Na$^+$,K$^+$-ATPase isozymes that the largest difference between them is in their affinity for digitalis compounds. In the enzyme preparations from brain of rat, dog, and calf, the $\alpha(+)$-isozyme showed a 1000-fold, 100-fold and 300-fold higher affinity for strophanthidin (Sweadner 1979).

Unfortunately, however, the presence of $\alpha(+)$-or α-isozymes cannot generally be correlated with high or low digitalis affinity. Judging from pyrithiamine susceptibility and digitalis sensitivity of a part of Na$^+$,K$^+$-ATPase activity of membrane preparations from dog heart muscle, Matsuda *et al.* (1984) concluded that both the $\alpha(+)$- and α-isozyme are present. However, preparations from cardiac muscle of the similarly digitalis-sensitive ox and rabbit and of the digitalis-insensitive guinea-pig, mouse, and rat, all contain α-isozyme. The authors concluded that digitalis sensitivity is not always determined by the molecular form of the enzyme. In fact, Na$^+$,K$^+$-ATPase preparations from rat and dog renal medullae, with a 1000-fold difference in ouabain sensitivitiy, were shown to have similar subunit composition (Periyasami *et al.* 1983). Similarly, comparison of the catalytic subunit of Na$^+$,K$^+$-ATPase preparations from ouabain-resistant mutants and wild-type kidney cell lines by electrophoretic resolution did not reveal any difference in subunit size (Soderberg *et al.* 1983).

In retrospect, the occurrence of Na^+,K^+-ATPase isozymes in mammalian brain could explain the observed heterogeneities in digitalis interaction with cerebral enzyme preparations from ox, mouse, rat, guinea-pig, and hog. This is shown by the non-linear Scatchard and Hill plots (Taniguchi and Iida 1973; Erdmann and Schoner 1973a; Hansen 1976; Marks and Seeds 1978; Urayama and Nakao 1979) or the non-exponential dissociation rates of digitalis–enzyme complexes (Tobin *et al.* 1972; Choi and Akera 1977; Repke *et al.* 1984). However, identifying heterogeneities in digitalis interaction with cerebral Na^+,K^+-ATPase preparations depends on the composition and concentration of enzyme effectors present, so that under certain exposure conditions homogeneity appears (Erdmann and Schoner 1973a; Hansen 1976; Repke *et al.* 1984). As deduced by Repke *et al.* (1984), ATP and Na^+ promote the formation of a relaxed enzyme conformer, E_R, which allows rapid digitalis binding to and release from the enzyme, while Mg^{2+} and K^+ promote the formation of a tense conformer, E_T, which renders digitalis binding and release more difficult. Under physiological conditions, i.e. in the presence of ATP, Mg^{2+}, Na^+, and K^+, E_R and E_T symbolize enzyme states in which Na^+ or K^+, respectively, occupy the Na^+ activation sites at the intracellular enzyme surface. Thus, the position of the equilibrium $E_R \leftrightarrows E_T$ is a function of $[Na^+]_i : [K^+]_i$ ratio. Apparently ligation of the enzyme with Na^+ or K^+ induces changes in the flexibility and geometry of the digitalis-binding matrix, which become manifest in the kinetics of digitalis–enzyme interaction.

A cerebral enzyme preparation from hog, unlike a cardiac enzyme preparation, has been found to show the coexistence of both enzyme conformers under exposure to most effector combinations and concentrations (Repke *et al.* 1984). This possibly indicates the presence of isozymes with low and high digitalis affinity. However, this cannot be safely concluded from kinetic data, since even a cardiac enzyme preparation (which appears to contain α-isozyme only: see above) may be induced by appropriate effector exposure to form, like the cerebral enzyme preparation, both relaxed and tense enzyme conformers. The $E_R \leftrightarrows E_T$ response of a given population of Na^+,K^+-ATPase molecules to variations in effector ligation can be accounted for in terms of the occupancy of only two conformational states. In these states, the distribution of peptide chains is apparently restricted by cooperative transitions, such that the digitalis–enzyme complexes $E_R D$ and $E_T D$ reflect limiting cases of two highly cooperative protein transitions (Repke *et al.* 1984).

These considerations lead to the conclusion that the non-linear Scatchard plots for ouabain binding to cardiac enzyme preparations from rat (Erdmann *et al.* 1980; Noel and Godfraind 1984) and man (De Pover and Godfraind 1979; Erdmann 1985) can be accounted for by the coexistence of the two ligation-induced Na^+,K^+-ATPase conformers and would not necessarily indicate the presence of Na^+,K^+-ATPase isozymes. Actually, the presence or absence of a biphasic positive inotropic response of rat heart to ouabain has more recently been shown to be a function of the concentration of Ca^{2+} ions at the sarcolemma, the Na$^+$,K$^+$-ATPase of which contains only the α-subunit and loses its highly ouabain-sensitive portion when exposed to Ca^{2+} (Charlemagne et al. 1986; Grupp et al. 1986).

In conclusion, ongoing research on digitalis interaction with established Na$^+$,K$^+$-ATPase isozymes promises to yield a firm basis for the targetted design of digitalis derivatives with highly selective action.

15.4.   Steroidal inhibitors

15.4.1   Inhibitor classification

As reviewed by Schwartz et al. (1975) and Akera et al. (1981), many low-molecular weight, non-steroidal inhibitors of very different types have been studied which, however, seem to have been useful only for analysing various properties of Na$^+$,K$^+$-ATPase, rather than serving as prototypes for drug design. This is because they lack specificity for the target enzyme, which is the most prominent feature of 'digitalis' compounds (cardenolides and bufadienolides: for nomenclature see IUPAC–IUB rules, 1969).

The inhibitory action of digitalis compounds was initially explained by Middleton (1970) on the basis of their spatial similarity to the enzyme–ATP–ion complex. When the ADP portion has vacated the active site, it will leave a space into which the digitalis rings B and C fit such that the lactone ring carbonyl can interact with the phosphoenzyme phosphoryl group to form a mixed anhydride. This hypothesis is invalid, however, since digitalis binding to the enzyme does not require phosphoenzyme formation (Schwartz et al. 1968). Moreover, contrary to most of the well known reversible inhibitors of other enzymes, digitalis compounds do not compete with the substrate (ATP) for the catalytic site, but bind at an allosteric site about 74Å away (cf. Section 15.4.3.3).

Inhibitors that bind to the target enzyme at allosteric sites might be expected to resemble physiological allosteric regulators structurally. If so, it is still unsettled what endogenous compounds digitalis-like compounds will mimic this action (cf. Section 15.4.4.2).

Although the lactone ring structures of bufadienolides and cardenolides, α-pyrone, and γ-crotonolactone easily react with thiol compounds, no Michael addition reactions were observed with the butenolide ring of cardenolides (Jones and Middleton 1970; Malur and Repke 1970). Such a reaction is considered of little importance with respect to either cardiotonic or cardiotoxic properties.

In conclusion, digitalis compounds may be classified as allosteric, chemically inert inhibitors of Na$^+$,K$^+$-ATPase with an action not involving covalent bond formation. Remarkably, the allosteric site on the enzyme is initially not available but requires the change into a 'high-energy' enzyme conformation for its formation, while the inhibitory digitalis action requires an inhibitor-induced changeover into a 'low-energy' enzyme conformation (cf. Section 15.4.3.1).

15.4.2   Inhibitor testing

The methodology may be taken from the papers referred to in Section 15.4.4 so that here the discussion of inhibitor testing will be confined to an outline of some aspects that promise to be useful in future research. The basis of the following suggestions is the belief that the more closely testing conditions mimic the tissue situation existing in digitalis medication, the more likely they are to yield results of extrapolateable worth.

One prerequisite is the use of enzyme preparations from human tissues. The reason for this is that the well-known species differences in cardiac glycoside potency have recently been traced to species differences in complementarity of steroid binding sub-sites on Na^+,K^+-ATPase variants. Hence, estimates of the potency of new steroidal compounds obtained using guinea-pig enzyme variants (most commonly employed hitherto) or those of other animal species cannot readily be extrapolated either quantitatively or qualitatively to the human enzyme (Schönfeld et al. 1986b). Human necropsy specimens offer a rich and readily available source of Na^+,K^+-ATPase preparations. The cardiac and cerebral enzymes undergo only slow degradation between 6 and 24 h post mortem, and remain stable on storage in the frozen state.

When searching for digitalis derivatives with high selectivity, it is essential to choose tissue specimens suitable for the isolation of isozymes that potentially show differences in affinity to various digitalis derivatives (see Sweadner 1979; 1985). If this approach is followed, a high degree of purification in terms of specific catalytic activity is not necessary and may be even detrimental. The digitalis affinities of diverse enzyme variants have been found to be unaltered even after 1000-fold purification (Periyasami et al. 1983 and references therein). Extensive purification may lead to enzyme preparations that are not sufficiently stable during the necessarily long incubation periods at 37°C (Erdmann et al. 1976; Choi and Akera 1978).

Studies on the interaction between digitalis compounds and Na^+,K^+-ATPase have most often been performed using Mg^{2+} and orthophosphate (P_i) as supporting enzyme effectors. However, these conditions are unsuitable, because they do not occur in the cell (Akera et al. 1976), where free P_i is almost absent and most Mg^{2+} is bound to ATP and other nucleotides. Moreover, the digitalis–enzyme complex promoted by Mg^{2+} and P_i differs in stability, extent of enzyme inhibition, dependence of inhibition on cation concentration, and the absence of antagonism between Na^+ and K^+, from the digitalis–enzyme complex formed via phosphorylation by ATP (Schuurmans Stekhoven et al. 1976). The situation in the cell appears to be mimicked best in vitro by ATP-supported digitalis–enzyme complex formation modulated by the presence of Mg^{2+}, Na^+, and K^+ in various combinations and concentrations (cf. Repke and

Schönfeld 1984). A few hints have been noted of differences in the affinities of Na$^+$,K$^+$-ATPase isozymes for Mg^{2+} (Erdmann and Schoner 1973a; Periyasami et al. 1983) and for Na$^+$ relative to K$^+$ (Repke et al. 1984).

There is some need to standardize methods for testing cardiac glycosides with respect to determination of their K_i values, so that data from all researchers are suitable for integrated modelling. However, at present there are substantial variations in published values for the potency of some digitalis compounds, as shown by Brown and Thomas (1983).

15.4.3   Receptor kinetics and thermodynamics

15.4.3.1   Basic parameters

Drug–receptor interaction is often assumed to be a diffusion-controlled process, in that pharmacological effects are generally expected to be reflections of drug pharmacokinetics rather than being primarily determined by receptor kinetics (cf. van Ginneken 1977). Cardiac glycosides are clear exceptions to this rule. Because even after intravenous injection there is some latency period until the full effect is exerted, many researchers have argued that bioactivation is required for action; however, all identified biotransformations have been recognized as inactivating reactions (Repke 1963). Studies on the kinetics and thermodynamics of the interaction between cardiac Na$^+$,K$^+$-ATPase and digitalis compounds of very different structure have provided the correct explanation (Beer et al. 1988) as summarized below.

The reversible formation of inhibitory digitalis–enzyme complexes appears to proceed in two steps, like the reversible formation of productive substrate–enzyme complexes (Eigen and Hammes 1963), according to eqn. (15.1)

$$
\begin{array}{ccccc}
& \xrightarrow{\quad k_+ \quad} & & & \\
\mathrm{D+E} & \underset{k_{-\mathrm{d}}}{\overset{k_{+\mathrm{d}}}{\rightleftharpoons}} & \mathrm{D\!-\!\!-\!E} & \underset{k_{-\mathrm{is}}}{\overset{k_{+\mathrm{is}}}{\rightleftharpoons}} & \mathrm{D\cdot E} \qquad (15.1) \\
& \xleftarrow{\quad k_- \quad} & & &
\end{array}
$$

where D = free digitalis, E = enzyme in receptive state; D--E = non-inhibitive diffusive complex; D$\cdot$E = inhibitive isomerized complex; $k_{+\mathrm{d}}, k_{-\mathrm{d}}$ = diffusion rate constants; $k_{+\mathrm{is}}, k_{-\mathrm{is}}$ = isomerization rate constants; k_+ = observed forward rate contant; and k_- = observed reverse rate constant.

On the several-minute time scale on which measurements were made, k_+ and k_- are dominated by $k_{+\mathrm{is}}$ and $k_{-\mathrm{is}}$ through the conditions: $k_{+\mathrm{is}} \ll k_{-\mathrm{d}}$, and $k_{-\mathrm{is}} \ll k_{+\mathrm{d}}$, so that $k_+ \simeq k_{+\mathrm{is}}$, and $k_- \simeq k_{-\mathrm{is}}$. Compared with the diffusion rate constant of slowly diffusing reactants lying near $10^9 \mathrm{M}^{-1}\mathrm{s}^{-1}$ (Eigen and

Hammes 1963), the measured k_+ values were smaller by four to six orders of magnitude and the observed k_- values smaller by five to seven orders of magnitude (Beer *et al.* 1988), although quite close to the isomerization rate constant characterizing the conformational change in substrate–enzyme interactions ranging from $10^2 \, s^{-1}$ to $10^4 \, s^{-1}$ (cf. Hammes 1982). The slow rate of formation of the inhibitory digitalis–Na^+,K^+-ATPase complex appears partly to result therefore from the rare formation of a 'productive' diffusive complex with the enzyme in the receptive intermediary state. This traps the digitalis molecule in the appropriate rotational state and spatial position upon the binding matrix to isomerize into the inhibitory complex.

Independent support for the conclusion that the kinetic and energetic parameters of interaction are dominated by digitalis-induced conformational changes of enzyme protein came from findings that formation of the inhibitory complex is associated with a large gain in entropy and a substantial increment in enthalpy (Beer *et al.* 1988), whereas a diffusion-controlled interaction is characterized by a loss in entropy and no change in enthalpy (cf. Weber 1975; van Ginneken 1977). The k_+ and k_- parameters measured by Beer *et al.* (1988) can thus be taken as elementary rate constants, implying that the energetics derived from them reflect straightforwardly protein conformational changes characteristic for the digitalis derivative producing them. Evidently, then, the factor k_{-is}/k_{+is}, the equilibrium constant for the reversible conformational rearrangement $D\text{-}\text{-}E \rightleftharpoons D \cdot E$, is specific for the inhibitory combination of any digitalis derivative with any Na^+,K^+-ATPase variant (see below) and numerically equivalent to the apparent dissociation constant of $D \cdot E$.

The formation of the inhibitory isomerized complex between cardiac Na^+,K^+-ATPase and digitalis compounds is an endothermic, entropy-driven process in both hog and guinea-pig enzyme (Repke and Dittrich 1980; Beer *et al.* 1988). Compared with the 'digitalis-sensitive' hog enzyme, the Gibbs energy changes in the interaction between the less sensitive guinea-pig enzyme and digitoxin, ouabain or 16α-gitoxin are smaller by 5.6, 11.5, or 10.7 $kJ \, mol^{-1}$, respectively. The reduction of the $\Delta G^{\circ\prime}$ value results from a decrease of the component favourable $\Delta S^{\circ\prime}$ value which is but incompletely compensated for by a decrease of the component unfavourable $\Delta H^{\circ\prime}$ value. Judging from the difference in $\Delta G^{\circ\prime}$ values found with the two enzyme variants for the three glycosides, and from the diversity in the component $\Delta S^{\circ\prime}$ and $\Delta H^{\circ\prime}$ values, the interactive 'potential energy surface' (Eftink and Biltonen 1980) in the two enzyme variants appears to differ such that the favourable points of interaction are smaller or weaker in the guinea-pig enzyme (see also paragraph 15.4.2). In support of this conclusion, the transition-state thermodynamic values characterizing the interaction between hog or guinea-pig enzyme and the above digitalis compounds vary differently as a function of enzyme variant and inhibitor (Beer *et al.* 1988). In the guinea-pig enzyme variant, the $\Delta G^{\ddagger}_+$ values are lower or higher, and the component $\Delta H^{\ddagger}_+$ and $\Delta S^{\ddagger}_+$ values are also variable. Although the

$\Delta G^{\ddagger}_-$ values are consistently much lower, accounting for the low digitalis sensitivity of the guinea-pig enzyme, the $\Delta H^{\ddagger}_-$ and $\Delta S^{\ddagger}_-$ values likewise vary as a function of glycoside structure.

The complex formation between all digitalis compounds hitherto analysed, including ouabain, and *cycling* hog and guinea-pig Na$^+$,K$^+$-ATPase as initiated in the presence of ATP, Mg^{2+}, Na$^+$, and K$^+$, is an *endothermic*, entropy-driven process (Beer *et al.* 1988). However, the complex formation between ouabain and *non-cycling* beef cardiac Na$^+$,K$^+$-ATPase, as initiated in the presence of Mg^{2+} and orthophosphate, is an *exothermic*, essentially entropy-driven process (Erdmann and Schoner 1973b). Apparently caused by different ligations, the conformation changes of the enzyme upon formation of the inhibitory complex are somewhat different. Some of the digitalis derivatives studied with regard to their interaction with cycling hog cardiac Na$^+$,K$^+$-ATPase in the presence of ATP, Mg^{2+}, Na$^+$, and K$^+$ (Beer *et al.*, 1988) have also been examined for their interaction with non-cycling beef brain Na$^+$,K$^+$-ATPase in the presence of Mg^{2+} and orthophosphate (Clark *et al.* 1975). Under the latter conditions, the $\Delta G^{\circ\prime}$ values are on average -2.4 kJ/mole larger because either the $\Delta G^{\ddagger}_+$ values are smaller or the $\Delta G^{\ddagger}_-$ values are greater.

Taken together, the available pieces of evidence suggest that the basic thermodynamic characteristics in the interaction of digitalis compounds and Na$^+$,K$^+$-ATPase, i.e. dominant entropy gain in enzyme protein linked with high activation Gibbs energy, are independent of species and organ origin of the enzyme, although the nature of ligation (especially with respect to ATP, K$^+$, or orthophosphate) strongly modulates the thermodynamic quantities. These experiences allow some generalization of the reported findings, but call for the choice of *cycling* enzyme in studies aimed at extrapolating data to conditions existing *in vivo*.

The native structure of small globular proteins is stabilized by Gibbs energies ranging from -25 to -60 kJ mol^{-1} of protein (cf. Pfeil 1981). Thus, it is almost self-evident that the forces acting between proteins and ligands, when they are of the same order of magnitude, are very likely to influence intrapolypeptide interactions via energy transduction and produce the frequently observed structural and functional alterations (cf. Hinz 1983). The highest values of $\Delta G^{\circ\prime}$, $\Delta H^{\circ\prime}$ and $\Delta S^{\circ\prime}$ observed by Beer *et al.* (1988) in the interaction between proscillaridin A and hog cardiac Na$^+$,K$^+$-ATPase are -49.9 kJ mol^{-1}, 246 kJ mol^{-1}, and 956 J mol^{-1} K, respectively. Incidentally, rather similar thermodynamic quantities have been also found in the interaction of nicotine with the acetylcholine receptor (Maelicke *et al.* 1977). The character and magnitude of the thermodynamic quantities observed by Beer *et al.* (1988) strongly suggest that substantial conformational modifications of enzyme protein accompany formation of the inhibitory digitalis–Na$^+$,K$^+$-ATPase complex. A significant ouabain-induced structural change of Na$^+$,K$^+$-ATPase has also been derived from an increase in heat stability and decrease in transition width in the apparent heat capacity vs. temperature profile of ouabain–enzyme complex (Halsey *et al.* 1977), and from the change of α,α-subunit interaction in the α_2,β_2 oligomer revealed by chemical cross-linking (Huang and Askari 1980).

The chemical nature of the digitalis-receptive intermediary state of cycling Na^+,K^+-ATPase has not been yet identified (see review by Hansen 1984). The knowledge, however, that a large entropy gain in the enzyme protein is, irrespective of enzyme origin and ligation, the common denominator of the inhibitory action of all digitalis derivatives (see above), suggests that the thermodynamic essence of enzyme inactivation is relaxation of 'conformational energy' (negentropy strain, cf. Schrödinger 1967) of the enzyme protein which is the sum of the potential energy for all intrapolypeptide interactions and the Gibbs energy for all interactions involving structured water (cf. Scheraga 1971). Reciprocally, the common denominator of the digitalis-binding conformational state of the dephospho- and phosphoenzyme (Schwartz *et al.* 1968; Schönfeld *et al.* 1972) is then a high-energy conformation built up through binding of ATP, phosphorylation from ATP, and Mg^{2+} or Mn^{2+} complex formation with the enzyme.

As mentioned above, the formation of the inhibitory complexes between digitalis compounds and Na^+,K^+-ATPase variants is always an entropy-driven process. The inherent entropic disadvantage that renders binding of a flexible ligand to a macromolecule more difficult (cf. Eftink and Biltonen 1980) amounts, at 37°C, to 2.9 kJ mol^{-1} for the loss of each internal degree of conformational freedom and 61 kJ mol^{-1} for the loss of overall rotational and translational entropy (Andrews *et al.* 1984). These heavy entropy losses in the binding of digitalis to Na^+,K^+-ATPase are more than counterbalanced by even larger favourable entropy gains through conformational rearrangements in the structural framework of the receptor protein. That largely entropy-driven protein ligations mask entropy losses upon ligand binding is a more general experience (cf. Jencks 1980). Contrary to intuitive expectation, the reduction of internal conformational entropies by removal of the tridigitoxose side-chain or the butenolide side-chain from digitoxin does not increase but considerably reduces the entropy gains (Beer *et al.* 1988). This indicates that the observed $\Delta S^{\circ\prime}$ quantities are governed by the interaction mode of the digitalis derivatives with the interactive energy surface of Na^+,K^+-ATPase so that the binding of the tridigitoxose and the butenolide side-chains elicit additional entropy gains. Clearly, the loss of translational, external, and internal rotational entropies, which the compounds experience in the process of binding to the enzyme, is greatly mingled with the entropy gains in the enzyme protein that are thus correspondingly larger than the observed net $\Delta S^{\circ\prime}$ quantities.

Although the molecular mechanism underlying the inhibitory action of digitalis compounds on Na^+,K^+-ATPase appears to be quite uniform (see also Section 15.4.3.3), the digitalis receptor enzyme nevertheless emerges from thermodynamic analysis as a protein, the digitalis binding matrix of which can, in part, adapt to the moulding interaction with digitalis derivatives of widely different structure. The great range of associated thermodynamic equilibrium and activation values observed by Beer *et al.* (1988) implies a corresponding degree of conformational plasticity, which renders more difficult a three-dimensional modelling of the digitalis-binding matrix on the basis of the complementarity postulate as initially attempted (Repke and Portius 1966, 1971).

15.4.3.2 *Pharmacological corollaries*

A few examples may suffice to demonstrate that the interaction of digitalis derivatives with Na$^+$,K$^+$-ATPase shows a large spread of thermodynamic equilibrium and activation values as a function of their structure (Beer *et al.* 1988). The smallest values for Gibbs energy change ($\Delta G^{\circ\prime} = -25.8$ kJ mol^{-1}) and entropy gain ($\Delta S^{\circ\prime} = 159$ J mol^{-1} K) are observed with 3β-tridigitoxosyloxy-14-hydroxy-5β,14β-androstan-17-one, which structurally differs from digitoxin ($\Delta G^{\circ\prime} = -47.7$ kJ mol^{-1}, $\Delta S^{\circ\prime} = 439$ J mol^{-1} K) by the substitution of the carbonyl function for the C-17β lactone ring side-chain. The steroid ketone nevertheless produces as complete (100 per cent) an inhibitory action on the enzyme as any steroid lactone. Apparently, larger $\Delta G^{\circ\prime}$ and $\Delta S^{\circ\prime}$ values than those observed with the steroid ketone are essentially determining differences in receptor kinetics of the various compounds. For instance, the value of k_+ for the steroid lactone digitoxin, is 170 times larger than for its steroid ketone analogue (Beer *et al.* 1988). The kinetic superiority of the steroid lactone appears to result from its electrostatic anisotropy, characterized by lobes of strongly negative and positive potentials surrounding the lactone ring or the steroid nucleus, respectively (for potential map of digitoxigenin, see Repke 1985). This molecular dipole becomes orientated and attracted by the large receptor dipole, thus cancelling the translational and overall rotational entropy, and alleviating the entrance of the steroid lactone into the mouth of the receptor cleft (cf. Dittrich *et al.* 1983).

The potential-energy surface of the steroid lactones dominates not only the approach channel for the colliding partners, thus enhancing the formation of a correctly aligned and thus productive diffusive complex, but also determines at the equilibrium distance the mutual orientation and hence the interaction energy of the partners. This helps to account for the finding that the K'_D value for the steroid lactone is about 100 times smaller than that for the steroid ketone (Beer *et al.* 1988). As a reciprocal consequence, cardenolides carrying the lactone ring in the C-17α-position (and thus presenting a quite different electrostatic potential field to the receptor cleft) are devoid of an inhibitory effect on Na$^+$,K$^+$-ATPase and do not weaken the activity of the C17β-stereoisomers even when present in great excess (Repke 1965). In terms of the reaction model described by eqn (15.1), the C-17α-analogues do not even form the non-inhibitory encounter complex and, hence, cannot be used as competitive antagonists, i.e. possible antidotes.

Certain digitalis derivatives show a nearly linear correlation between activation and equilibrium Gibbs energy values in forming inhibitory isomerized complexes with Na^+,K^+-ATPase (Beer et al. 1988). Assuming the involvement of similar intermolecular, long-range orientating forces, their recognition by the receptor enzyme appears then to be governed by the close-range forces and geometrical limitations exerted by the interactive potential-energy surface. In other derivatives, the data points of which lie below or above the regression line, receptor-induced favourable or unfavourable orientation mechanisms, respectively, appear to play a dominant role in the recognition process and operate over distances where molecular contact does not yet (or no longer) occur. Such long-range orientation forces can thus significantly increase or decrease the frequency of productive encounters of digitalis derivatives with the recognition and binding matrix of the enzyme in the receptive state to form the diffusive complex, which is able to isomerize into the inhibitory complex. K^+ increases the activation energy barriers for formation of complexes between various digitalis compounds and Na^+,K^+-ATPase more than the barriers for dissociation, and so decreases their equilibrium Gibbs energies of interaction (Beer et al. 1988). The use of varied K^+ concentrations under otherwise similar conditions appears in part to explain why the K'_D or $\Delta G^{o\prime}$ values reported in the literature for the same compound often differ greatly. At any rate, the above findings appear to account for the observations that hyperkalaemia decreases digitalis uptake by cardiac muscle, whereas hypokalaemia increases myocardial digitalis uptake and the sensitivity of the myocardium to toxic digitalis actions (reviewed by Akera 1981).

A comparison of the thermodynamic quantities for digitoxigenin and digitoxin shows that energy barriers for the formation and dissociation of inhibited complexes with Na^+,K^+-ATPase and equilibrium Gibbs energies of interaction are significantly lower for the genin than for the glycoside (Beer et al. 1988). These findings allow a corresponding interpretation in thermodynamic terms of the clinical observation that with digitoxigenin the maximum effect is reached more quickly, the duration of the effect is shorter, and the degree of action is less than with digitoxin (Gold et al. 1969).

In conclusion, kinetic and thermodynamic parameters of the interaction between digitalis compounds and Na^+,K^+-ATPase appear to have an essential or even dominant role in the development, strength, and decline of their pharmacological actions. Consequently, determining the receptor parameters of digitalis derivatives is likely to provide a powerful tool in any targetted research on lead structure optimization (cf. Section 15.5).

15.4.3.3 Structural aspects

The interactive energy surface in Na^+,K^+-ATPase protein appears to be a cleft, approximately 20 Å deep, between two lobes of the catalytic α-chain, that becomes locked on cardiac glycoside binding so as to envelop the butenolide side-chain lying at the bottom of the cleft, the steroid nucleus, and the sugar next to the steroid nucleus, lying near the mouth of the cleft (Schönfeld et al. 1985).

The movement of large protein domains involves a negligible entropy gain (Jencks 1980). If so, the cleft closing on interaction with a cardiac glycoside cannot essentially contribute to the large entropy and enthalpy changes observed. Rather, it appears to act as a 'switching device' in eliciting the underlying peptide-chain rearrangements in the enzyme protein.

The digitalis-binding site cleft in the enzyme is known to be exposed on the external face of the membrane, and the catalytic centre, phosphorylatable from ATP, is exposed on the cytoplasmic side. The two sites, both on the α-peptide, are about 74 Å apart (cf. Carilli *et al.* 1982; Repke *et al.* 1983). The digitalis-binding cleft, probably including amino acid residues 307–312, is connected to the phosphorylation site, Asp-369, by an amino acid sequence that appears to be an important component of the energy-transducing system (Shull *et al.* 1985; Repke 1982). By transduction of digitalis-elicited relaxation of negentropy strain along this pathway, a geometric distortion of the catalytic centre could result, which would explain the lowered affinity for ATP (see Hansen 1984) and the suppression of phosphorylation by ATP (Sen *et al.* 1969; Schön *et al.* 1972). The resulting inhibition of Na$^+$/K$^+$ pumping is the initial event in the chain of events leading to inotropic digitalis action (see Section 15.2.2).

15.4.3.4 *Thermodynamic characteristics and nature of interactive forces*

On the basis of a large body of thermodynamic data for small ligand–protein interactions, Ross and Subramanian (1981) generalized that the strengthening of hydrogen bonds in the low dielectric macromolecular interior, and van der Waals' interactions introduced as a consequence of the hydrophobic effect, are the most important factors contributing to the *negative* quantities of $\Delta H^{\circ\prime}$ and $\Delta S^{\circ\prime}$ often observed, and hence to the stability of protein-association complexes. In the systems analysed by these authors, protein association reactions tend to become dominated by entropy *alone* at low temperature, but enthalpy-dominated at temperatures above 25°C, because the favourable contribution to $\Delta S^{\circ\prime}$ by hydrophobic association is diminished at higher temperatures. Eventually, the diminishing water structure at higher temperatures results in a fading out of the *positive* $\Delta S^{\circ\prime}$ quantity, which at low temperature indicates the participation of water at the surface, in the bulk phase or as sequestered water in the protein (cf. Lumry and Rajender 1970). The above-mentioned *negative* signs for bonding contributions to the $\Delta H^{\circ\prime}$ and $\Delta S^{\circ\prime}$ quantities, and their dependence on temperature (Ross and Subramanian 1981) differ from the temperature-independent *positive* signs of $\Delta H^{\circ\prime}$ and $\Delta S^{\circ\prime}$ quantities observed in the interaction between digitalis compounds and Na$^+$,K$^+$-ATPase (Beer *et al.* 1988). This disposes of remaining doubts (cf. Lumry and Rajender 1970) as to interpretation of the thermodynamic quantities in terms of digitalis-elicited, large changes in the conformation of the enzyme polypeptide chains.

The foregoing argument, however, does not exclude the more local involvement of van der Waals'–London dispersion forces (Repke and Portius 1966), hydrogen bonding (Portius and Repke 1964; Malur and Repke 1970) and dipole–dipole interaction (Dittrich *et al.* 1983). This is so because such forces, effective in the circumscribed interface between the two interacting molecules, could be overridden by much larger positive $\Delta H^{\circ\prime}$ and $\Delta S^{\circ\prime}$ quantities which appear to arise from digitalis-elicited relaxation of the 'high-energy' conformation of Na$^+$,K$^+$-ATPase into a 'low-energy' more stable conformation (Halsey *et al.* 1977) corresponding to a minimum of function (cf. Scheraga 1971). In conclusion, the nature of the local interactive forces probably cannot be derived from observed integral thermodynamic quantities.

15.4.4   Modelling of structure–activity relationships

Since the earliest study by Portius and Repke (1964), who analysed the inhibitory activity of 64 compounds on cardiac Na$^+$,K$^+$-ATPase, the enzyme has often been used as a tool to estimate the biological potency of digitalis derivatives. In a recent review of the scientific and patent literature, Güntert and Linde (1981) concluded that the structure–activity relationships are still obscure, although a number of individual features are known. Since 1981 some studies have been performed that appear to provide a partial insight to aid model building. In an investigation of 17 digitalis derivatives, Brown and Erdmann (1984b) corroborated the findings of Portius and Repke (1964) that modification to any part of the molecule can alter potency, and concluded that the whole molecule must bind to achieve maximal potency. From an analysis of the interaction of five digitalis genins with Na$^+$,K$^+$-ATPase, Ahmed *et al.* (1983) suggested that the position of the C-17 side-chain carbonyl oxygen in a given genin is the primary determinant of biological activity. Although From *et al.* (1984) felt that this relationship may prove to be a useful unifying structural model in further elucidation of the mechanism of digitalis–receptor interactions, they also stated that it is not possible to describe how the proposed model of carbonyl oxygen geometry and steroid complementariness and reactivity relates to receptor site fit, nor to derive data about the types of interactions and bonding at the enzyme receptor site that are important for activity (Rohrer *et al.* 1983).

These aims have been steadily pursued by our group since 1964, so the present integrated modelling is based on a wider organized body of information that includes the assessment of the inhibitory action of about 600 steroidal compounds on Na$^+$,K$^+$-ATPase from cardiac muscle of humans (Schönfeld *et al.* 1985), guinea-pig (Schönfeld *et al.* 1986b; Portius *et al.* to be published), and hog (Beer *et al.* 1988) as well as from human brain cortex (Schönfeld *et al.* 1985; Schönfeld *et al.* 1986a).

A brief summary has been given by Repke (1985). As mentioned in Section 15.4.2, the Na$^+$,K$^+$-ATPases from digitalis-insensitive species such as guinea-pig may show some peculiar relationships between structure and inhibitory potency of digitalis glycosides, but the statements in Sections 15.4.4.2–15.4.4.6 appear to be more generally valid.

15.4.4.1 *Extrathermodynamic procedure for modelling*

As the most promising approach to the design of new drugs, our primary aim has been the discovery of the lead structure in digitalis glycosides, i.e. the minimum structural requirement for specific receptor recognition and potent Na$^+$,K$^+$-ATPase inhibition. The priority given to the search for a lead structure is derived from the expectation that identification of the lead may provide a general mechanism of action and bear predictive and innovative potential. In our attempt to discover the lead structure, we have passed through the usual stages which increase the likelihood of success: random screening of the newly available compounds, non-random screening of naturally occurring representatives, chemical hunch for novel derivatives ('molecular roulette'), refinement of biochemical rationale (changeover from animal to human enzyme sources), and biochemically-inspired chemical modification (references to our work since 1964 are given above).

As a rational way of quantitatively correlating the potency and structure of digitalis compounds, we have proceeded to an extrathermodynamic analysis of the inhibitor constant (numerically equivalent to the dissociation constant, K'_D, of the inhibitor–enzyme complex) as detailed in papers by Schönfeld *et al.* (1985, 1986b), Beer *et al.* (1988) and Portius *et al.* (to be published). Essentially, the extrathermodynamic derivation of structure–action relationships is based on a division of the inhibitor molecule into substructural elements, the contribution of which to the integral Gibbs energy of interaction with Na$^+$,K$^+$-ATPase ($\Delta G^{\circ\prime} = RT\ln K'_D$) is to be evaluated. The $\Delta G^{\circ\prime}$ quantity is thus assumed to be the resultant of favourable and unfavourable energetic contributions of the individual structural elements. Hence, the procedure involves calculation of the $\delta\Delta G^{\circ\prime}$ value for a pair of compounds differing in only one structural feature to give the increment or decrement of $\Delta G^{\circ\prime}$ caused by the substructural variable concerned. Clearly, the successful applicability of this procedure rests on the high degree of inflexibility of the fully saturated steroid backbone in digitalis glycosides.

From the wealth of data collected, only the more essential findings relating to rational drug design will be summarized in the following sections.

15.4.4.2 *The steroid nucleus: lead structure and major determinant of specificity*

The lead structure in cardiac glycosides is their steroid nucleus which, as it meets the minimal receptor recognition requirement, cannot be replaced functionally by other structures and endows, in connection with suitable substituents at C-17 and C-3, the highest selectivity and potency in Na$^+$,K$^+$-ATPase inhibition (cf. Section 15.4.3.2).

The integral interaction energy of 3β-O-rhamnosyl-digitoxigenin and 3β-O-rhamnosyl-bufalin with the human cardiac and brain Na$^+$,K$^+$-ATPase is the additive property of the partial energy contributions of their structural components: the steroid nucleus 5β,14β-androstane-3β,14-diol, the butenolide or pentadienolide side-chain at C-17β, and the sugar side-chain at C-3β. This indicates a close fit between essential parts of the interfaces of the steroid nucleus and its binding sub-site on both enzymes, which does not become altered through the attachment of the voluminous side-chains at C-17β and C-3β.

The geometry of the steroid nucleus greatly determines the impact of the substituents at C-17β and C-3β on the overall interaction energy with Na$^+$,K$^+$-ATPase. So, for maximum potency, digitalis glycosides require a *cis*-(bent) junction of the C/D and A/B steroid rings, as present in the above cardiac glycosides. This steroid backbone geometry alone provides the spatial disposition of the lactone side-chain at C-17β in ring D and of the sugar side-chain at C-3β in ring A that is needed for receptor site fit at all, or for maximum receptor site fit, respectively. More specifically, flattening of the pertinent ring plane angles by conversion of a *cis*- to a *trans*-junction of the above rings or by introduction of a double bond from C-8 to C-14, C-14 to C-15, C-4 to C-5, or C-5 to C-6, annuls or depresses potency in the presence of side-chains at C-17β and C-3β. In the absence of those side-chains, ring flattening causes little reduction in potency, or may even increase it. The described interdependences between steroid geometry and interaction energy account for the paradox that the digitoxigenin isomer with a C/D and A/B *trans*-ring junction shows a lower interaction energy with Na$^+$,K$^+$-ATPase than is exhibited by progesterone (Portius and Repke 1969). In conclusion, the steroid binding sub-site in Na$^+$,K$^+$-ATPase can be isoenergetically occupied by certain steroids with both strongly bent or planar-extended geometry but planar steroids can only occupy the sub-site if there are no sterically hindering lactone side-chains at C-17β on ring D of the steroid skeleton. This knowledge raises the possibility that the 'endogenous digitalis' is a C/D *trans*-steroid (cf. Repke 1985, and below).

The C/D *cis*-ring junction, although not a prerequisite for inhibitory activity for steroids without a lactone ring at C-17β, is essential for the specificity of their pharmacological action. As shown by Gelbart and Thomas (1978), 3β,14-dihydroxy-17β-formyl-5β,14β-androstane 17-guanylhydrazone (C/D *cis*-ring junction) and 3β-hydroxy-17β-formyl-5β, 14α-androstane 17-guanylhydrazone (C/D *trans*-ring junction) exhibit about the same potency as Na$^+$,K$^+$-ATPase inhibitors, but the C/D *trans*-isomer also inhibits the digitalis-insensitive Mg^{2+}-ATPase. The C/D *cis*-isomer elicits a positive-inotropic effect on cardiac muscle, whereas the C/D *trans*-isomer gives only negative-inotropic effects through inhibition of mitochondrial respiration (Thomas *et al.* 1980). Thus, the C/D *cis*-ring junction confers specifity of action, whereas the guanylhydrazone side-chain confers on the steroid with a C/D *trans*-ring junction the non-specific ability to inhibit various ATPases. In a similar vein, progesterone-3,20-*bis*-guanylhydrazone strongly inhibits DNA and protein synthesis, while the cardiac glycoside ouabain does not (Langen and Repke 1966).

As reviewed by LaBella *et al.* (1985), some progesterone derivatives inhibit the Na$^+$/K$^+$ pump and Na$^+$,K$^+$-ATPase, and compete with ouabain for the same binding site on the enzyme. In contrast to ouabain, however, chlormadinone acetate, the most potent derivative identified so far, exerts primarily depressive effects on cardiac muscle. LaBella *et al.* feel that the absence of positive inotropy with chlormadinone acetate may reflect an additional cardiodepressant activity (as produced also by the precursor compound progesterone) that overrides any positive effect on contractility resulting from inhibition of the Na$^+$/K$^+$ pump. They nevertheless maintain the view that an endogenous steroid, metabolically transformed from C/D *trans*-into C/D *cis*-configuration, may be the natural ligand for Na$^+$,K$^+$-ATPase. However, this epimerization is not necessarily required.

As shown above, the cardiodepressant action of C/D *trans*-steroids may result from interference with an intracellular metabolic process. Should the cardiodepressant action of progesterone derivatives also result from an intracellular intervention, the sulphate or glucuronide conjugates of endogenous C/D *trans*-steroids (which do not easily penetrate the plasma membrane) could selectively occupy the extracellularly exposed digitalis binding site on the Na$^+$/K$^+$ pump and thus exert a positive-inotropic effect, not overridden by a cardiodepressant action. This concept was recently supported by the finding that glycosides of chlormadinol acetate, unlike the aglycone, produce lasting positive-inotropic actions (Weiland *et al.* 1987).

In summary, in digitalis glycosides 5β,14β-androstane-3β,14-diol is the lead structure, promising highest potency and specificity of action. 14β-androst-4-ene-3β,14-diol and, in part, 5α, 14β-androstane-3β,14-diol may act as almost equivalent lead structures, although the altered spatial disposition of the sugar side-chain at C-3β may reduce its contribution to the integral interaction energy. The introduction of a Δ^4-double bond produces a smaller loss of potency than the 5β- to 5α-conversion because the stereochemistry of rings A and B of the 3β-hydroxy-Δ^4-steroids bears a much closer resemblance to a 5β-steroid (A/B *cis*-fusion) than to a 5α-steroid (A/B *trans*-fusion) (see Tamm 1963). However, the C/D *cis*-configuration given in the above lead nuclei appears to be indispensable for specific cardiostimulant action. On the other hand, the selectivity in interacting with the Na$^+$/K$^+$ pump necessary for digitalis-like inotropic effects might possibly be conveyed to endogenous C/D *trans*-steroids through conjugation with sulphuric or glucuronic acid at the C-3β hydroxyl group.

15.4.4.3   *The C-17β lactone-side chain: major determinant of potency*

It has been suggested for many years that the lactone moiety of the cardiac glycoside molecule may be responsible for the positive-inotropic action (Bennett *et al.* 1958) or may represent the effective group (Portius and Repke 1964), the pharmacophoric structural element (Eberlein *et al.* 1974), the major functional group that elicits the inhibitory conformation change of Na$^+$,K$^+$-ATPase (Thomas *et al.* 1980), or the most essential functional group of cardiac glycosides (Güntert and Linde 1981). Some inconsistencies arising from these suggestions seemed to be overcome by the proposal of Fullerton *et al.* (1986) that the spatial disposition of the carbonyl oxygen in the lactone moiety is the major determinant of genin activity (for a critical evaluation of this over-simplification see Schönfeld *et al.* 1985).

The positive-inotropic action of some simple lactones on cat papillary muscle was described by Bennett *et al.* (1958). In cats, however, Chen *et al.* (1942) found no evidence indicative of any digitalis-like action. The cardiotonic effect of simple unsaturated lactones on isolated cardiac preparations rather appeared to be related to their potential for peroxide formation (Mendez 1944; Wenzel and Keplinger 1953), and their inhibitory potency on cyclic nucleotide phosphodiesterase (Némoz *et al.* 1982). At any rate, simple lactones not linked with the steroid lead (for instance those reported by Kahn 1957; Portius and Repke 1964; Malur and Repke 1970; Černy *et al.* 1983) are not potent inhibitors of Na^+,K^+-ATPase and the Na^+/K^+ pump, probably because they are not able to form a productive co.nplex and to elicit an inhibitory conformational change.

The Gibbs interaction energy of the lead steroid $5\beta,14\beta$-androstane-$3\beta,14$-diol with the human cardiac enzyme ($\Delta G^{\circ\prime} = -22.7\,\text{kJ mol}^{-1}$) increases through C-$17\beta$-attachment of the butenolide ring in the β-position by $-20.5\,\text{kJ mol}^{-1}$ or the pentadienolide ring in the γ-position by $-27.6\,\text{kJ mol}^{-1}$. This quantifies the importance of the lactone side-chain contribution to the molecular potency index $\Delta G^{\circ\prime}$. The butenolide side-chain can be isoenergetically replaced by certain open acrylic and crotonic acid esters as well as acrylnitriles (Eberlein *et al.* 1974; Thomas *et al.* 1974b; Theil *et al.* 1980). This confirmed the hypothesis put forward by Portius and Repke (1964) that all that is required to potentiate

the action of the lead steroid action is the atom arrangement $\overset{|}{\underset{/}{C}}=CH-\overset{|}{C}=O$

in the side-chain at C-17β. The lead steroids endowed with open side-chains will not be further considered here because they show, compared with cardenolides, an even higher conformational flexibility that renders the interpretation of structure–activity relationships still more difficult.

As reported by Hintsche *et al.* (1985), n.m.r. studies on the conformation in solution and X-ray crystal structure analyses have often revealed the coexistence of two conformations for the same cardenolide. In these conformations, due to rotation of the butenolide ring and the steroid nucleus about the linking single bond between C-20 and C-17β, either the C-21 protons or the C-22 proton of the butenolide ring are disposed opposite to C-14β-OH ('14,21-conformation' or '14,22-conformation', respectively). These findings led the authors to suggest that the potential energy of the two conformations is not much different, and that their interconversion is not prevented by too high a torsional energy barrier between the two low-energy conformations. This interpretation has been corroborated by theoretical calculation of the same parameters (Shamovskij *et al.* 1983; Höhne and Pfeiffer 1983; Fullerton *et al.* 1985). Hence, in biological systems, the two conformers of cardenolides can equilibrate such that the position of the equilibrium will be finally tipped in their interaction with the digitalis binding site of Na^+,K^+-ATPase (Hintsche *et al.* 1985).

The 14,22-conformation most often found in X-ray crystal structure analysis of cardenolide derivatives and erroneously regarded as a minimum energy conformation, has been suggested by Rohrer *et al.* (1979) as the receptor-preferred conformation, by reason of a correlation between the spatial disposition of the butenolide carbonyl oxygen in that conformation and the inhibitory action of a few digitoxigenin derivatives on Na$^+$,K$^+$-ATPase. The authors have denied the alternative 14,21-conformation as preferred by the receptor because the derivatives appeared in the correlation analysis as more active than could be explained by the dispositions of the pertinent carbonyl oxygen. In opposition to this view, Shamowskij *et al.* (1983) have deduced from theoretical studies on structure–activity relationships in cardenolides that the 14,21-conformer is the biologically active conformer.

Hintsche *et al.* (1985) reasoned that the close proximity of a cardenolide molecule to the asymmetric potential field determining the stereospecificity of the digitalis binding site of Na$^+$,K$^+$-ATPase must express itself in the conformation assumed by the cardenolide molecule when, as is probable, the energy required for conformational change to fit the binding site is small compared with the Gibbs energy of cardenolide binding. In an attempt to relate conformational variation to potency, they compared the conformational and inhibitory parameters of flexible cardenolides and semi-rigid derivatives, narrowed to 14,21- or 14,22-conformation by bulky substituents at C-22 or C-21, respectively. High potency is preserved in C-22-substituted cardenolides, in which the butenolide C-21 protons are placed in a minimum potential energy well close to C-14β-OH. Although, for instance, C-22-methyl-digitoxigenin and C-22-methyl-digitoxin did not appear to mimic completely the receptor-bound conformer of the two cardenolides (additional information in Schönfeld *et al.* 1985, 1986b), the findings nevertheless suggest that the 14,21 conformer is the receptor-bound conformer.

To define still more exactly the geometry of the cardenolide molecule in the binding site cleft, some derivatives have been studied in which the butenolide moiety and the steroid lead were covalently fixed in different geometric dispositions. However, the hitherto available derivatives (the Z- and E-$\Delta^{17(20)}$-digitoxigenin congeners; (21R)-14,21-epoxy-digitoxigenin; (21R)-16β,21a-epoxy-21-isopropyl-digitoxigenin 3-acetate; and 3β-acetoxy-14-hydroxy-5β,14β-pregn-16-en-21,16-lactone) showed a much lower potency than the precursor compounds. Of course, this could be due not only to fixation of the lactone ring in an unfavourable geometric disposition, but still more so to steric hindrance of tight fitting to the digitalis binding site by the disconfigurations. There is no simple way of distinguishing between these two possibilities. To yield useful information, rigid analogues are required that are as active as the most potent parent compounds. This aim will not be readily attained, since even rather small substituents at C-21 or C-22 often considerably depress the potency. Incidentally, the change in mutual arrangement of the butenolide and steroid moieties of digitoxigenin resulting from the insertion of a methyl group between C-17β and C-20 also drastically reduces potency (Lindig and Repke 1986). This appears to indicate a rather rigid spatial communication between the butenolide and steroid binding sub-sites of Na$^+$,K$^+$-ATPase.

The steroid lead, by eliciting the conversion of the high-energy conformation of Na$^+$,K$^+$-ATPase to the low-energy form (see Section 15.4.3.1) has full inhibitory capacity, i.e. produces 100 per cent inhibition at sufficiently high concentration. Its linkage with the lactone ring thus does not appear to involve a supplementary inhibition mechanism. The associated rise of the $\Delta G^{\circ\prime}$ value results from the increase of the composite favourable $\Delta S^{\circ\prime}$ value, which overrides the augmentation of the composite unfavourable $\Delta H^{\circ\prime}$ value. As reasoned in Section 15.4.3.1, these thermodynamic characteristics give no clue as to the nature of the binding forces evoked by the lactone side-chain.

The involvement of a hydrogen bond between the lactone carbonyl oxygen as H acceptor and a proximate NH residue from the binding sub-site as H donor has been suggested by Repke (1965) because this allows correlation of the fact that cardanolides, cardenolides, and bufadienolides show, in that order, an increased electron density on the carbonyl oxygen atom and hence an increased capacity in serving as H acceptor on the one hand, and an increased potency as Na$^+$,K$^+$-ATPase inhibitors on the other. However, a quantitative study with

(a)

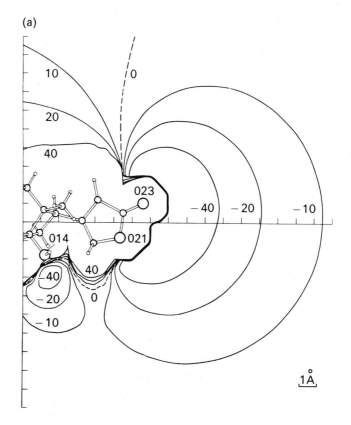

(b)

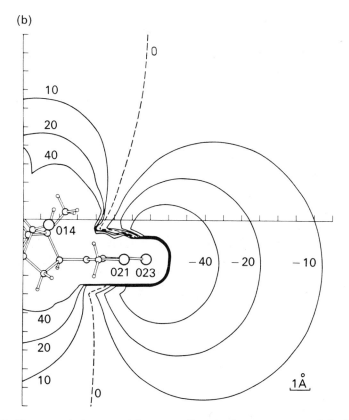

Fig. 15.3. Electrostatic isopotential contour lines in the outer space of the butenolide side-chain of digitoxigenin shown in 14/21-conformation with the torsional angle (C-16-C-17-C-20-C-21)=31.1°. The numerical values near the lines indicate the energy quantities (expressed in kJ mol^{-1}) that apply to the approach of a positive unit charge. The maps are: (a) for the plane that parallels that of the butenolide ring and crosses C-20, O-21, and O-23, and (b) for the plane that is vertical to the plane chosen in (a) and crosses O-23 and lies 1.9 Å above O-21. The wide lobe of negative potential around the butenolide oxygens O-21 and O-23 suggests the acceptor sites for hydrogen bonding. The electrostatic monopoles providing the potential maps were calculated by the Hückel–Del Re method with the appropriate parametrization given by Zakrzewska and Pullman (1985). The given energy quantities are for the aqueous medium and thus by about one order of magnitude lower than those recently calculated by Bohl and Süssmilch (1986) for the gas phase.

suitable model compounds, performed by Malur and Repke (1970), has made it clear that the superior potency of cardenolides compared with cardanolides is also due to a more favourable hydrogen bonding angle and bridge distance in the sterically fixed inhibitor binding to the enzyme. Shamowskij *et al.* (1983) corroborated these deductions in showing that the differences in charge density at the carbonyl oxygen in the pentadienolide, butenolide, and butanolide rings, although ranking in the same order as inhibitory potency, are comparatively small, and that the varied spatial dispositions of the carbonyl oxygens in these lactone side-chains dominate the H bonding strength and thus correlate roughly with biological activity. This conclusion has been confirmed by Bohl *et al.* (1984) using a somewhat different theoretical approach. Most recently, Fullerton *et al.* (1986) have suggested that the activity of three derivatives which are more powerful than their reference compound, digitoxigenin, may be accounted for by the strength of the hydrogen bond formed at the receptor.

Several pieces of independent information strongly suggest that the carbonyl oxygen in steroid lactones is not the sole or the major H acceptor. The strongly negative shells around the carbonyl and the bridge oxygen atoms in the electrostatic molecular potential map of digitoxigenin (see Fig. 15.3) point to the H acceptor capacity of both oxygen atoms. The net charges on carbonyl oxygen (-0.320 e) and bridge oxygen (-0.248 e) are not much different. Moreover, the two oxygens have often been identified as H acceptors (from secondary or tertiary hydroxyl groups of another cardenolide molecule or from solvent molecules) in X-ray crystal structure analyses. More specifically, the involvement of the bridge oxygen accounts for the findings that the β-attached butenolide side-chain can be almost isoenergetically replaced by β-furane, and that the exchange of the bridge oxygen by NH (Guzman *et al.* 1981) results in a substantial loss in potency, apparently because the substituted atom cannot serve as H acceptor. On the other hand, the findings that the β-butenolide side-chain can be energetically fully replaced by β-pyridine (the N is a very good H acceptor; see Malur and Repke 1970) or by β-pyridazine (Godfraind and Lutete 1979) favour the generalization that electron-rich hetero-atoms in various closed or open side-chains (e.g. the acrylnitrile derivative mentioned previously) may be involved in H bonding of the inhibitors to the enzyme. This being so, the great reductions of the interaction energy increment following replacement of the β-butenolide side-chain [by β-(20R)butanolide, β-(20S)butanolide, α-butenolide (as present in actodigin), γ-(20R)butenolide and γ-(20S)butenolide, or following the replacement of the γ-pentadieneamide side-chain by α-pentadieneamide] are then the consequence of associated unfavourable changes in spatial disposition of H acceptor oxygens, since the potential energy of the hydrogen bond (maximally up to -45 kJ mol^{-1}) is critically dependent on the distance between H acceptor and donor atoms.

Summing up, the dramatic increment of Gibbs interaction energy with Na$^+$,K$^+$-ATPase conveyed to the lead steroid through attachment of the β-butenolide or γ-pentadienolide side chain at C-17β, appears to originate essentially from hydrogen bonding to the lactone-residue binding sub-site of Na$^+$,K$^+$-ATPase. At the very least, alternative bonding force interpretations, such as the involvement of the side-chains in π-complex formation with enzyme phenyl groups (Wilson *et al.* 1970) cannot account for all the experimental findings mentioned above. The precise conformation of the conformationally flexible cardenolides and bufadienolides in the binding-site cleft of the Na$^+$,K$^+$-ATPase should finally be defined by synthesis of rigid congeners showing potencies as high or higher than the parent compounds.

15.4.4.4   *The C-3β-O-sugar side chain: major determinant of pharmacokinetics*

The paucity of available data comprising but small structural variations of the sugar substituent restrict modelling attempts within narrow limits. The approach to the problem is helped by the apparently very limited conformational freedom of the sugar proximate to the steroid nucleus (Fullerton *et al.* 1983, 1986; Hintsche and Megges 1986). More specifically, in the various hexoses, the bridge oxygen atom and the carbon 4′ in the pyranose ring (taken as reference points) will be assumed, in the following initial approximate interpretation of the data, to occupy similar positions in the sugar binding sub-site of Na$^+$,K$^+$-ATPase. This assumption is probably an over-simplication, as the apparent exceptions mentioned below seem to indicate.

The binding sub-site for the proximate sugar is localized near the mouth of the cardiac glycoside binding-site cleft in the enzyme. Studies with diazomalonyl derivatives of digitoxigenin-tridigitoxoside, -bisdigitoxoside, and -monodigitoxoside, in which the photo-activatable group is esterified to the 4′′′-, 4′′-, and 4′-hydroxyl groups, respectively, of the terminal sugars, have shown that the catalytic α-subunit is nearly exclusively labelled with the 4′-derivative and decreasingly less labelled with the 4′′- and 4′′′-derivatives due to the increasing distances from the steroid nucleus (Hall and Ruoho 1983). Likewise, ouabain substituted by the photo-activatable aryl nitrene group at the rhamnose side-chain also labels only the α-peptide; after limited tryptic cleavage, its 57 kDa and 45 kDa fragments are about equally labelled (Forbush 1983). This finding suggests that the labelled segments form two protein domains, which together make up the digitalis binding-site cleft. In line with the above reasoning, the usual order of inhibitory potency is aglycone-monosaccharide > -disaccharide > -trisaccharide > aglycone, indicating that the proximate sugar provides the optimal condition for maximum interaction with the sugar binding sub-site, and that any enlargement of the sugar side-chain decreases the potency. Therefore, the following discussion of structure–activity relationships will be confined to aglycone-monosaccharides.

The contribution of one particular sugar to the overall Gibbs interaction energy may vary considerably with the tissue and species origin of the Na$^+$,K$^+$-ATPase. The attachment of β-D-glucose to digitoxigenin has little effect on potency measured on guinea-pig cardiac enzyme (Table 15.1) or rat brain enzyme (Fullerton *et al.* 1980), but it considerably enhances the potency when determined on human cardiac enzyme (Table 15.1) or hog kidney enzyme (Fullerton *et al.* 1984). The conformational distribution of the glycosidic moiety has been postulated by Chiu and Watson (1985) to be the major determinant of the biological activity of cardenolide glycosides, such that compounds with a restricted conformational freedom should have a greater probability of binding to the receptor relative to those with a wider rotational freedom. This postulate does not generally apply. According to the above authors, digitoxigenin α-L-rhamnoside behaves in solution as a single conformational entity, whereas digitoxigenin β-D-digitoxoside exists as an equilibrium mixture of two or more sets of conformers. The latter conclusion now appears to be called into question as a result of the application of different techniques (Fullerton *et al.* 1986; Hintsche and Megges 1986). In fact, the receptor-enzyme preferences appear to be overriding. So, the most effective enhancers of digitoxigenin potency are β-D-digitoxose and α-L-rhamnose for the enzymes from guinea-pig or human heart muscle, respectively (Table 15.1). The following evaluations apply to the guinea-pig cardiac enzyme, for which most data are available.

The interaction energy increment, $\delta\Delta G^{\circ\prime}$, resulting from the attachment of a specific sugar to 3β-OH of a 5β-H-cardenolide, becomes regularly reduced through the introduction of a hydroxyl group at C-5 or a double bond between C-4 and C-5 (Table 15.2). Apparently, both structural modifications of the

Table 15.1   Effect of the attachment of sugars of varied structure to 3β-OH of some 5β-H cardenolides on the molecular potency index $\Delta G^{\circ\prime}$ determined by using Na^+,K^+-ATPase from muscle of human (h.h.) or guinea-pig heart (g.-p.h.)

Attached sugar[a]	$-\delta\Delta G^{\circ\prime}$ (kJ mol^{-1})	
	g.-p.h.	h.h.
α-L-mannose	0.3	ND[b]
2′,3′,4′-trideoxy-β-D-glycero-pentose (3′-tetrahydropyranyl ether)	0.8	ND
β-D-glucose	1.6	4.9
α-L-arabinofuranose	2.4	2.9
β-D-ribose	2.4	ND
(β-D-digitoxose)$_3$	3.2	4.9
α-L-thevetose (6′-deoxy-3′-O-methyl-α-L-glucose)	5.0	ND
α-L-rhamnose (6′-deoxy-α-L-mannose)	6.3	7.2
α-L-oleandrose (2′,6′-dideoxy-3′-O-methyl-α-L-mannose)	6.7	ND
β-D-cymarose (3′-O-methyl-β-D-digitoxose)	6.8	ND
β-D-digitoxose (2′,6′-dideoxy-β-D-ribose)	7.6	6.0

[a] Following Klyne's rule, the D-sugars were assigned to be attached in a β-glycosidic linkage, and the L-sugars in an α-glycosidic linkage. Zorbach and Bhat (1966) suggested that, irrespective of the configuration at C-1 of the pyranoside component, all cardenolides have conformations in which the aglycone residue is an equatorial substituent, thereby overriding all conformational effects imposed by substituents on the pyranoside ring. However, the α-L-rhamnose residue in proscillaridin A shows an axially disposed O-aglycone residue (Kubinyi *et al.* 1971), and this 1C-conformation may occur in 3β-O-α-L-rhamnosides of other cardiotonic steroids, too, because then two hydroxyl groups and the methyl group of rhamnose occupy the energetically favoured equatorial disposition.
[b] ND is not determined.

Table 15.2 Effect of the attachment of certain sugars to 3β-OH of varied aglycones on molecular potency index $\Delta G^{\circ\prime}$ determined by using Na$^+$,K$^+$-ATPase from guinea-pig heart muscle

Sugar attachment	$\delta\Delta G^{\circ\prime}$ (kJ mol^{-1})
β-D-ribose in 5β-H-cardenolide	-2.4
β-D-ribose in 5β-OH-cardenolide	-0.1
β-D-cymarose in 5β-H-cardenolide	-6.8
β-D-cymarose in 5β-OH-cardenolide	-2.8
β-D-glucose in 5β-H-cardenolide	-1.6
β-D-glucose in Δ^4-cardenolide	$+2.4$
α-L-rhamnose in 5β-H-bufadienolide	-5.3[a]
α-L-rhamnose in Δ^4-bufadienolide	-2.3[a]
β-D-digitoxose in 5β-H-cardenolide	-7.1
β-D-digitoxose in Δ^4-cardenolide	-5.2

[a] Enzyme from human heart muscle

steroid nucleus alter the spatial disposition of the sugar moiety and thus decrease their optimum fit into the sugar binding sub-site. In addition, the effect of a certain sugar on inotropic potency has been shown to vary dramatically when linked with either 5β-H- or 5α-H-cardenolides (Brown and Thomas 1984).

The attachment of the completely deoxygenated 3'-tetrahydropyranyl ether to the 3β-OH of digitoxigenin has a negligible effect on the interaction energy (Table 15.1). Apparently, the pyranyl ring makes no contribution of its own, but merely acts as a vehicle for carrying hydroxyl functions (Zorbach and Bhat, 1966). The tempting assumption that the potency becomes progressively enhanced with increased numbers of hydroxyl functions as potential H bond donors does not, however, apply. The examination of the data gathered in Tables 15.1 and 15.3 rather shows that the 'blockade' of the C-2'- and C-3'-hydroxyl groups by some chemical modifications does not essentially change the $\delta\Delta G^{\circ\prime}$ value, contributed by a particular sugar. The strong depressing effect on interaction energy of the C-3'-O-acetyl group is clearly caused by steric hindrance of binding due to the bulky substituent. Remarkably, the removal of the hydroxyl group from C-6' enormously enhances the $\delta\Delta G^{\circ\prime}$ value probably because it eliminates a thermodynamically unfavourable unpaired hydrogen bond donor. From the exclusion of the other hydroxyls as possible H donors, it follows that the equatorial hydroxyl group at C-4', present in the sugar components of all highly potent aglycone-monosaccharides, may serve as a partner in hydrogen bonding to the sugar binding sub-site. The amino group at C-4', then, could serve even better in this capacity. From different sets of data, similar conclusions have been derived concerning the unfavourable effect of a hydroxyl group at C-6', the favourable effect of an equatorial hydroxyl function at C-4', and the even more favourable impact of a (partially also equatorial)

Table 15.3 Effect of sugar modification in 3β-O-glycosides of 5βH-cardenolides on molecular potency index $\Delta G^{\circ\prime}$ determined by using Na^+,K^+-ATPase from guinea-pig heart muscle. A positive $\delta\Delta G^{\circ\prime}$ value indicates lessening of interaction energy.

Sugar modification	$\delta\Delta G^{\circ\prime}$ (kJ mol^{-1})
$3'$-O-methyl in rhamnose	$+0.3$
$4'\xi$-amino-$4'$-deoxy in rhamnose[a]	-4.8
$2',3'$-O-isopropylidene in rhamnose	-0.7
$4'$-dehydro-$2',3'$-O-isopropylidene in rhamnose	-0.5
$3'$-O-acetyl in (digitoxose)$_3$	$\sim +7.3$
$3''$-O-acetyl in (digitoxose)$_3$	-0.6
$3'''$-O-acetyl in (digitoxose)$_3$	$+1.7$
$4'''$-O-acetyl in (digitoxose)$_3$	$+0.2$
$3'$-,$3''$-,$3'''$-,$4'''$-tetra-O-acetyl in (digitoxose)$_3$	$\sim +10.4$
$3'$-,$3''$-,$3'''$-,$4'''$-tetra-O-formyl in (digitoxose)$_3$	$+3.1$

[a] The amino group presumably occurs in the thermodynamically preferred equatorial position as does the hydroxyl group in L-rhamnose; see also text.

amino group at C-$4'$ (in $4',6'$-dideoxygalactose and $4',6'$-dideoxyglucose) (Caldwell and Nash 1978; Brown *et al.* 1983; Brown and Thomas 1983; Fullerton *et al.* 1984).

The contribution of a particular sugar to the overall interaction energy with Na^+,K^+-ATPase can vary considerably with the configuration and conformation of the cardenolide-monosaccharides (Table 15.4). In fact, the interaction

Table 15.4 Effect of configuration and conformation of sugars in their attachment at 3β-OH of various 5βH-cardenolides on molecular potency index $\Delta G^{\circ\prime}$ determined by using Na^+,K^+-ATPase from guinea-pig heart muscle

Sugar attachment	$\delta\Delta G^{\circ\prime}$ (kJ mol^{-1})
3β-O-(α-L-rhamnosyl)digitoxigenin	-6.3
3β-O-(β-D-rhamnosyl)digitoxigenin	-2.3
3β-O-(α-D-rhamnosyl)digitoxigenin	$+4.3$
3β-O-(α-L-rhamnosyl)strophanthidin	-6.1
3β-O-(α-D-rhamnosyl)strophanthidin	-4.7
3β-O-(β-D-rhamnosyl)strophanthidin	-2.0
3β-O-(α-L-mannosyl)strophanthidin	-0.3
3β-O-(α-D-mannosyl)strophanthidin	$+1.1$
3β-O-(β-D-digitoxosyl)digitoxigenin	-4.3
3β-O-(α-D-digitoxosyl)digitoxigenin	-1.8

energy increments contributed by the α-L-rhamnosides of digitoxigenin and strophanthidin, when compared with their β-D-isomers are not as much greater as could be expected from their potential structural differences. A satisfactory explanation for this was given by Zorbach and Bhat (1966), who proposed a structural correspondence between the two isomers in as much as the aglycone component is always equatorially disposed, the two pyranose rings have the same chair form, and the order of substituents on the rings is the same. If so, the only difference between the α-L- and β-D-isomers is a reversal of configuration of the substituents on the pyranoid rings, which is tantamount to their 'vertical' displacement.

By contrast with the 'unnatural' α-D-isomers, the interaction energy contribution by the 'natural' α-L-rhamnosides and the α-L-mannoside can be superior but never unfavourable. More specifically, the $\delta\Delta G^{\circ\prime}$ value for α-L-rhamnosyl-digitoxigenin is more than $-10\ kJ\ mol^{-1}$ greater than that of the α-D-isomer. According to Zorbach and Bhat (1966), the aglycone moiety in both isomers is equatorially disposed and the pyranose ring has a chair form, but the order of substituents is reversed, accounting for the above disparity in the $\delta\Delta G^{\circ\prime}$ value. Remarkably, the impact of changes in configuration and conformation of cardenolide-monosaccharides with digitoxigenin is different from that with strophanthidin, implying an alteration in the sugar conformation by 5β-OH.

The types of sugar linkage present in the naturally occurring cardiac glycosides yield the highest potency. Any increase of $\Delta G^{\circ\prime}$ by glycosidation results from the requirement that the activation energy barrier for the formation of the inhibitory complex is smaller than for its decomposition (cf. Section 15.4.3.2). The prolonged half-life for these compounds is one reason for the convenient manner of cardiac glycoside medication, which allows many hours lapse between the doses.

Next to its importance in receptor kinetics, the sugar side-chain of cardiotonic steroids plays a major role in tuning in steroid kinetics in the animal body, as illustrated below. Glycosides show a higher uptake in cardiac muscle and aglycones inversely show a greater relative concentration in the brain, judged from studies on the distribution of digitoxigenin and digitoxin in the animal body (Repke 1963). This distribution pattern may help to explain why aglycones have a higher emetic and convulsive action than their parent glycosides (Chen et al. 1938). The hydroxyl group at C-3 is metabolically the most vulnerable substructure of cardioactive steroid lactones (Repke 1963). Inversion of 3β-OH into 3α-OH through the 3-keto intermediate and conjugation of the hydroxyl groups with glucuronic or sulphuric acid result in rapid inactivation of aglycones (Herrmann and Repke 1964a, b; Repke and Samuels 1964; Petersen et al. 1977). The linkage of 3β-OH with one or more suitable sugars is a very effective trick of nature to make cardioactive steroid lactones more resistant to bio-inactivation (Repke 1959; Lauterbach and Repke 1960; Herrmann and Repke 1964c). Thus, glycosides such as digitoxin and digoxin are more persistent in their action than their respective aglycones (Chen et al. 1938).

15.4.4.5 *Other substituents on the steroid nucleus: potency modulators*

The digitalis interaction matrix on Na^+,K^+-ATPase appears to be tailored to provide a snug complementary fit for the tight binding of 5β, 14β-androstan-3β, 14-diol, the steroid nucleus in digitoxin (Section 15.4.4.2). The tempting conclusion that the introduction of any substituent in the steroid nucleus leads to a loss in potency is only partially true.

Hydroxylation in positions 3α, 5β, 7β, 11β, 11α, 12β, 12α, 15β, 15α, 16β, 16α, or 17α leads to decrements in the interaction Gibbs energy of between 2 and $12\,kJ\,mol^{-1}$. Hydroxyl groups protruding from the α-surface of the steroid nucleus are, in general, not more detrimental to the interaction energy than those protruding from the β-surface. In most cases, the OH groups may be assumed to exist as unpaired hydrogen bond donors known to provide considerable driving energy for complex dissociation. The interpretation that the potency loss results from steric hindrance to a tight fit applies only with certainty for 12β-OH and 17α-OH, which when esterified with acetic or nitric acid show a further fall in interaction energy.

Remarkably, esterification of 3α-OH, 16β-OH, or 16α-OH with acetic acid, and 16β-OH or 16α-OH with nitric acid reverses the unfavourable effect of the previously mentioned hydroxyl groups or, in the latter two cases, leads to derivatives that are more potent than the parent deoxy compounds. This phenomenon may be accounted for by assuming that esterification of these OH groups not only eliminates unpaired H bond donors, but additionally provides very effective H bond acceptors. Clearly, in the neighbourhood of these hydroxyl groups, there is not a tight fit of the steroid nucleus with its binding sub-site.

The overall interaction energy becomes increased by introduction of a hydroxyl group in the 3β-position and by replacement of 3β-OH by 3β-NH_2. Interaction energy is strongly reduced by the replacement of 3β-OH by 3β-$N(CH_3)_2$ or of 3α-OH by 3α-NH_2. The favourable or unfavourable impact of the various structural modifications may be most simply interpreted in terms of providing or eliminating paired and unpaired H bond donors, respectively.

The hydroxyl group in position 14β, present in the steroid lead of cardiac glycosides, is not a prerequisite for inhibitory action but it moderately increases the interaction energy. The replacement of 14β-OH by 14β-NH_2 strongly enhances the potency of the precursor compound $(20R)$-3β-rhamnosyloxy-5β,14β-pregnane-14,20-diol. This effect may be caused by reinforced hydrogen bonding and/or strong ion-pair formation when 14β-NH_2 exists as 14β-NH_3^+ *in situ*.

Apart from the impact on receptor kinetics, introduction of a hydroxyl group in position 12β or 16β of digitoxin decreases its absorption from the intestinal tract, its binding to serum albumin, its uptake into the brain, and its rate of bioinactivation.

15.4.4.6 *Interpretative puzzles*

The fundamental basis of structure–activity analysis is the concept of additivity, where the sub-structures of a drug and their modifications are assumed to contribute to biological activity in an additive manner, each part of the structure being independent of all other variations in the molecule. The additivity postulate fully applies here to the individual energetic contributions made to the integral interaction Gibbs energy of digitoxigenin- or bufalin-rhamnoside by 5β,14β-androstane-3β,14-diol, the butenolide or pentadienolide side-chain at 17β, and the rhamnose side chain at 3β. These examples are rare exceptions to the rule that the structure of the precursor compounds, even in congeneric sets, more or less profoundly alters the impact of a certain structural modification on the global interaction energy. A few examples should illustrate these inter-relationships.

The result of attaching a butenolide ring at position 17β depends on the *cis*- (bent) or *trans*- (flat-extended) C/D ring-junction. The effect of introducing a particular sugar at 3β-OH also depends on the *cis*- or *trans*- A/B ring-junction as well as on the presence or absence of a methyl group in the 3α-position or of a hydroxyl function in the 5β-position. The shift of the butenolide attachment at position 17β of 5β,14β-androstane-3β,14-diol from the β- to the α-position changes the effect of glucosidation at 3β-OH from almost nil to strong enhancement of inhibitory potency (Fullerton *et al.* 1980). This indicates the interdependence between binding of the side-chains at 17β and 3β to their respective sub-sites (approximately 20 Å apart). The various sugar side-chains in the receptor-bound digitalis glycosides induce conformational changes of the steroid binding sub-site and consequently altered interactions with the steroid nuclei, such that the interaction energy decrement produced by a hydroxyl group at a certain position on the steroid skeleton is significantly smaller in the glycosides than in the respective aglycones. Even 3β-H and 3β-OH differentially change the spatial position of a cardenolide on the interactive potential energy surface such that with 3β-H, the bulky 3α-acetoxy group is compatible with high interaction energy, whereas with 3β-OH, the relatively small 3α-methyl group leads to a dramatic potency loss.

The available evidence favours the generalization that modification of any sub-structure may affect the reactivity of any other sub-structure, and that the extent and tendency of interaction between two sub-structures is quantifiable, but unpredictable from the knowledge obtainable through the extrathermodynamic approach alone. Moreover, the conformation of the digitalis-binding matrix of Na$^+$,K$^+$-ATPase may adjust to alterations in the shape of the various steroidal inhibitors, thus minimizing the total energy of the enzyme–inhibitor complex. Hence, the geometry of the binding sub-sites may be different for different derivatives even within the same related series of compounds.

In summary, digitalis glycosides of varied structures may interact with the binding matrix in whatever spatial orientation and adjusted conformation that will minimize the total Gibbs energy of the digitalis–enzyme–solvent system and hence maximize the interaction Gibbs energy of the digitalis derivative under consideration. Clearly, the problem still to be solved is to deduce the fundamental geometric and electrostatic characteristics of the digitalis-binding matrix from the accessible information on the interaction between 'flexible keys and

deformable locks', as defined by Roberts (1983) for ligand binding to dihydrofolate reductase. This clearly sets limits for modelling of the cardiac glycoside
receptor site on Na^+,K^+-ATPase by combining the pieces of information on
structure–activity relationships derived by Fullerton *et al.* (1986) from X-ray
crystallographic analyses, molecular mechanics, computer graphics, and biological determinations. The authors thus reservedly conclude that their
modelling studies 'are beginning to give a clear picture of the configurational and
conformational preferences of the receptor site for this most interesting group of
therapeutic agents'.

15.4.4.7 *Complementary tactics*

The extrathermodynamic approach, as applied in the foregoing sections, is
recognized as a rational way to a quantitative structure–activity analysis.
Although extrathermodynamic relationships do not directly follow from the
axioms of thermodynamics, they are still able to express in a simple way,
relationships between Gibbs energies and other thermodynamic qualities
(Section 15.4.3). However, the extrathermodynamic data only implicitly take into
consideration the three-dimensional geometry and electron density distribution
of the drugs. While the precise shape and charge-density distribution of the
digitalis-binding matrix is unknown, some of its characteristics can be deduced
indirectly by correlating, for a wide selection of digitalis derivatives, geometric
and electrostatic features of the molecule with receptor interaction kinetics.

As mentioned in Sections 15.4.4.2–15.4.4.5, rather minimal steric differences
between analogues can strongly reduce or even eliminate inhibitory potency.
This indicates a limited conformational flexibility of the peptide chains forming
the interactive energy surfaces. It is assumed that by characterizing the interaction parameters of a sufficient number of related compounds with Na^+,K^+-
ATPase, a mould of the volume occupied by the most active derivatives will
represent the shape of the adjusted binding matrix. Particularly valuable
information for demarcating the matrix boundaries can be deduced by
comparing the structural modifications that increase, reduce, or do not affect
potency.

The three-dimensional mapping of the adjusted matrix may be accomplished
by computing the combined occupied volume of conformationally characterized,
preferentially rigid analogues that bind with high affinity (Humblet and Marshall 1981). This will generate an 'enzyme-excluded' volume map, which defines
the enzyme area known to be available for binding of inhibitors structurally
related to digitalis compounds. Volume mapping of $5\beta(5\alpha),14\beta$-androstane
derivatives that possess the lead structure and thus the minimal structural
requirement for recognition but are nevertheless inactive, and superimposition of
their common sub-structures, allows determination of their unique volume
requirements that overlap the enzyme-excluded volume. Intersection of the
unique volume segments of the inactive analogues shows regions of unique

volume overlap for these derivatives and defines an 'enzyme-essential' region, i.e. a region required by the enzyme itself and not available for inhibitor binding. The contours of the enzyme-essential volume may be used to predict the chances of activity for new derivatives prior to their synthesis.

Clearly, steric fit is not the only parameter governing inhibitor–enzyme interaction. As mentioned in Section 15.4.3.2, cardenolides possess partial electrostatic charges that appear to match complementary charges on the digitalis-binding matrix. Knowledge of the electrostatic potential surface on the van der Waals' volume surface (Scrocco and Tomasi 1978) should prove very useful in analysing the interaction parameters of various derivatives with the enzyme, and in electrostatically mapping the digitalis-binding matrix by intersecting and overlaying the potentials of a large number of active and inactive analogues. By combining the shape assumed by the electrostatic molecular potential of different analogues in different plausible conformations, information may be gained about the shape of the charge–density distribution on the interactive surfaces, which determines the value of the electrostatic interaction energy.

To meet the many conditions operating in the physicochemical aspects of drug action, the substituent effects on the strength of interactions between drug and receptor are assumed in the Hansch type analysis of quantitative structure–activity relationships (QSAR) to be proportional to the corresponding values of Hammett σ, Taft E_S, Hansch π, and molar refractivity as reviewed by Martin (1981) (see also Chapter 2E). Since the geometry and infrastructure of the drug molecule, as far as the charge distribution is concerned, are not covered by this approach, its efficacy remains restricted to those series of drugs in which either the pharmacokinetics are a predominant factor for potency or, whose action does not require intricate complementarity between the drugs and their site of action (Ariëns 1969). In the field of digitalis derivatives, the QSAR equations may be useful for the design of analogues showing optimum values for intestinal absorption, serum protein binding, penetration into the brain, and biotransformation.

In conclusion, the power of the methods discussed in this section lies in their ability to generate a reasonable structural model of the digitalis-binding matrix for a fixed Na$^+$,K$^+$-ATPase variant based on the interaction parameters of suitably characterized digitalis structures. The model can then provide experimentally testable predictions of the potency of any new analogues designed. We may thus reach a general understanding of the structure–activity relationships for inhibition of an enzyme variant by digitalis derivatives where the inhibitor structure is varied and the isozyme remains the same. However, the inverse problem of understanding the molecular basis of the partially different structure–activity relationships when the Na$^+$,K$^+$-ATPase isozyme is varied and the inhibitor remains the same, has only just begun to be tackled (cf. Sections 15.4.2 and 15.5.1).

15.5. Strategy for rational design

Study of the properties of digitalis compounds at target enzyme level has hitherto mostly been confined to testing series of compounds for their interaction with a Na^+,K^+-ATPase from only one animal tissue under rather arbitrarily chosen incubation conditions. This approach has nevertheless considerably furthered the understanding of structure–activity relationships, eventually leading to discovery of the lead structure in cardiac glycosides as shown in Sections 15.4.3 and 15.4.4. However, lead structure optimization, aimed at the development of cardiotonic steroids with improved therapeutic qualities, requires the iterative establishment of a biochemical screening programme consisting of comparisons between several Na^+,K^+-ATPases from human digitalis target tissues with respect to their kinetics of interaction with digitalis derivatives. The development of such a screening programme may involve the search for isozymes and conformers of Na^+,K^+-ATPase as well as for digitalis derivatives that promise to reveal the basis for discrimination between potential target enzyme variants connected with the desired specificity of action. The usefulness of such a programme, outlined in Sections 15.5.1 to 15.5.3 below, may initially be probed by screening those digitalis derivatives for which an improved therapeutic range has been reported, e.g. cardanolide glycosides (Acheson et al. 1964), actodigin (Cagin et al. 1977 and references cited therein), 16α-gitoxin (Haustein 1980), (21R)-21-methyldigitoxigenin (Wiesner et al. 1984), or 3β-O-(β-D-glucosyl)-digitoxigenin (Einstein et al. 1986). The starting-point for a more detailed design of the screening programme is the in-depth consideration of the putative or established anatomical sites of toxic digitalis actions as well as the time course of desired and undesired effects.

As reviewed by Gillis and Quest (1986), extracardiac neural actions contribute to the inotropic and toxic effects seen in therapeutic digitalis application. The major determinant of the total amount of a digitalis compound that can be administered is the development of ventricular arrhythmias. The digitalis-induced increase in central, efferent sympathetic discharge plays an important role in the initiation of ventricular arrhythmias and in the genesis of arterial vaso-constriction. In experimental animals, the anatomical site of neural activation has been shown to be an area in the lower brain stem near the floor of the fourth ventricle (Somberg and Smith 1978). The proper site of neural activation appears to be an area lacking an effective blood–brain barrier as known for the area postrema (Mudge et al. 1978; Somberg et al. 1980). Thus, C1 spinal cord section provides true protection against overt digitalis toxicity (Somberg et al. 1978), increases the amount of digitalis needed to produce ventricular arrhythmias, and improves the toxic/inotropic and lethal/inotropic dose ratios (Pace and Gillis 1982). Remarkably, the neural effects appear to occur almost immediately after digitalis administration, whereas the direct inotropic cardiac actions require time to develop (Gillis and Quest 1986).

The concept of stereoelectronic complementarity, the lock and key concept of Emil Fischer (1894), has been invoked whenever there was a problem of molecular specificity. However, there is now a rapidly growing body of knowledge revealing the potential of kinetic modulation of receptor discrimination (Ninio and Chapeville 1980). In terms of Na$^+$,K$^+$-ATPase as a target enzyme, this means that the residence time of equipotent digitalis derivatives on the digitalis-binding matrix of various isozymes and conformers may considerably differ. Thus, when digitalis concentration near the external surface of Na$^+$,K$^+$-ATPase tends to fall off towards zero, the inhibitory complexes in one tissue may have already dissociated, whereas, in another tissue they may persist much longer. Within the screening programme, the comparative determination of association and dissociation rates in digitalis interaction with Na$^+$,K$^+$-ATPases of different anatomical origin will disclose the significance of kinetic mechanisms in target enzyme discrimination.

The knowledge obtained in the tentative screening stage will govern the choice of standardized conditions and the setting-up of the final screening programme, which will aim to reveal the specificity profile of the various test compounds. Initial studies with this aim have recently been performed (Schönfeld et al. 1986a, b).

15.5.1   Search for discriminating Na$^+$,K$^+$-ATPase isozymes

Minor differences in three-dimensional structure could cause isozymes to differ in their affinities for specific inhibitors, resulting in selective inhibition of a certain isozyme (Moss 1979). As reviewed in Section 15.3.5, Na$^+$,K$^+$-ATPase isozymes containing the α- or $\alpha(+)$-subunit forms occur in human whole brain and cerebral cortex. However, it remains to be settled whether the α-isozyme shows low and the $\alpha(+)$-isozyme high digitalis sensitivity, as demonstrated for these isozymes from some animal species. Moreover, the digitalis sensitivity of variant Na$^+$,K$^+$-ATPases may differ widely without easily traceable alternations of subunit composition.

This lack of knowledge requires a systematic search for Na$^+$,K$^+$-ATPases of differential digitalis sensitivity in areas of the human brain that have been shown to be involved in the genesis of neurally mediated digitalis toxicity. Such a search may be started by screening the specificity profile of selected digitalis derivatives with promising target enzyme discrimination (cf. Sections 15.5.0 and 15.5.3).

15.5.2   Search for discriminating Na$^+$,K$^+$-ATPase conformers

The selective binding of a drug to one of two conformational states of a receptor carries the necessary implication that the structure of the binding domain is different in the two conformations. This in turn must imply the strong probability that in a series of drug congeners, this will not represent a constant difference in binding energy; in other words, the structure–activity relationships will be different for the two conformations (Burgen 1981). These considerations also apply to Na$^+$,K$^+$-ATPase: the rather selective binding of digitoxin to one of two limit enzyme conformers appears to indicate that the stereoelectronic parameters of the digitalis binding matrix are different in the two conformers (Repke *et al.* 1984). The most interesting candidates for the in depth study are the E$_R$ and E$_T$ conformers of Na$^+$,K$^+$-ATPase, which are involved in the allosteric regulation of Na$^+$/K$^+$ pumping in the cell (Repke 1986). This may be viewed in the perspective that, according to Burgen (1981), the understanding of how drugs interact with regulatory processes provides a distinct path in the search for new drugs.

The existence of inhibitor-discriminating isozymes and discriminating conformers of Na$^+$,K$^+$-ATPase is not mutually exclusive. Isozymes may basically differ in their affinity to conformation-changing enzyme effectors, so that their discrimination may even depend on their suitable effector-ligation, as discussed in Section 15.3.5. In fact, the kinetics of interaction of ouabain or digitoxin with Na$^+$,K$^+$-ATPases from different tissues and species become differentially altered by changes in the composition and concentration of the enzyme effectors present (Schuurmans Stekhoven *et al.* 1976; Wallick *et al.* 1980; Repke *et al.* 1984). Unfortunately, all studies have hitherto been performed with classical digitalis glycosides so that the postulated discrimination of derivatives of widely differing structures by various enzyme conformers has not yet been established.

15.5.3 Search for discriminating digitalis derivatives

Synthetic lead structure optimization may first of all be confined to the side chains at C-17β and C-3β, since in general high potency in cardiac glycosides requires a snug fit of the steroid nucleus to the steroid binding sub-site of Na$^+$,K$^+$-ATPase (except in the region of C-16; cf. Section 15.4.4.2).

Cardenolides have a high conformational flexibility, due to rotation of the butenolide ring and the steroid skeleton about the C-17—C-20 single bond. This may facilitate their interaction with a number of isozymes or conformers of Na$^+$,K$^+$-ATPase. The attachment of bulky substituents at C-22 of the butenolide side-chain gives conformationally semi-rigid, potent cardenolide derivatives (Hintsche *et al.* 1985), which might preferentially interact with one isozyme or conformer. Studies on the relationship between conformational freedom and receptor specificity of steroid hormones have favoured the conclusions that conformational freedom may cause lack of receptor specificity (Delettré *et al.* 1980), whereas inflexibility may result in receptor discrimination and specific activity enhancement (Duax *et al.* 1975).

Both actodigin and 16α-gitoxin have been found to have highly favourable properties when tested on isolated heart preparations (Glicklich *et al.* 1975; Haustein 1980 and references cited therein). When studied in experimental animals, however, ventricular arrhythmias were elicited by actodigin easier, and by 16α-gitoxin less frequently than ouabain (Cagin *et al.* 1977; Haustein 1977). Apparently, the two synthetically differently modified cardiac glycosides significantly differ in their ability to induce an increase in central, efferent sympathetic discharge that initiates ventricular arrhythmias. Incidentally, 16α-gitoxin differs from digitoxin only by an additional hydroxyl group at C-16. This is reminiscent of the finding (Heubner 1940) that an additional hydroxyl group at C-16β, but not at C-12β, almost completely eliminates the cerebrotoxicity of digitoxigenin.

Contrary to the classical cardiac glycosides (ouabain, digoxin, and digitoxin), three highly polar synthetic derivatives [3β-O-(4'-amino-4',6'-dideoxy-β-D-galactopyranosyl)-digitoxigenin (ASI-222), digoxin-16'-β-D-glucuronide, and digitoxigenin-3-sulphate] do not cross the blood–brain barrier. Nevertheless, their therapeutic indices are significantly poorer than those of the classical drugs. In the production of cardiac arrhythmias elicited by these derivatives, a modulating role may be played by the area postrema in the central nervous system, known to be devoid of a blood–brain barrier. This view is supported by experiments showing that C1 spinal cord transection increases the dose of these compounds required to produce tachycardia. Thus, the area postrema may act for all the above inhibitors of Na$^+$,K$^+$-ATPase as a locus for digitalis-induced neural excitation, acting through autonomic pathways to facilitate the development of cardiac arrhythmias (Somberg et al. 1980).

Contrary to digoxin, 3β-O-(4'-amino-4',6'-dideoxy β-D-glucopyranosyl)-digitoxigenin (ASI-254) does not interact with peripheral or central sympathetic excitatory neural sites (Puryear et al. 1981), although its physicochemical properties should be very similar to those of ASI-222.

Taken together, available evidence suggests that it is not the purely physico-chemically determined accumulation in distinct parts of the nervous system, but the structure-dependent affinity to various target isozymes and conformers that governs the variant specificity profile of action seen with the different compounds.

In conclusion, one line of research, perhaps providing a class of cardiac glycosides with an improved therapeutic index, is the development of digitalis analogues that do not cause neural activation, which facilitates cardiotoxicity (Somberg et al. 1980).

15.5.4 Prospects of favourable outcome

According to Austel and Kutter (1978), the search for new cardiotonic steroids with an increased therapeutic range by structural modification of the classical cardiac glycosides is particularly risky. This sceptical judgement was essentially derived from two arguments.

1. Research by the pharmaceutical industry in the above direction was unsuccessful for about a decade. This lack of success has been interpreted by the authors as probably being due to an already insuperably high degree of optimization in the naturally occurring glycosides. This view, however, loses much of its weight when the following facts are taken into account:

(a) The synthetic modifications were guided by erroneous notions concerning the nature of the phamacophoric structure in cardiac glycosides (cf. Section 15.4.4.3) and thus showed features of a molecular roulette.

(b) The applied practice of using toxicity measurements in the initial assessment of potency of the derivatives does not allow accurate structure–activity analyses (cf. Section 15.1).

(c) The chances of finding a new lead by such random screening has been estimated to be as low as 1 in 4×10^7 for such a difficult field (Wooldrige 1977).

(d) After the lead structure in cardiac glycosides had been discovered through targetted research in 1985 (cf. Section 15.4.4.2), the question of the synthetic further development of cardiac glycosides has been resolved in the question of lead optimization, which may well be the most fruitful sector in drug development (Wooldridge 1977).

2. Separation of cardiotonic and cardiotoxic action appears unlikely because of the common molecular mechanism of their genesis (Eberlein 1978). This kind of argument is unintelligible simply because that separation has been and will remain impossible in any class of biologically active compounds. What is required clinically is an increase in the therapeutic range so as to increase the margin of safety on administration.

Starting from the new knowledge on the target enzyme and its steroidal inhibitors as well as information on the genesis of toxic side-effects, the development and refinement of a simple, sensitive, and specific biochemical screening procedure has become possible for the first time which promises accurate recognition of differences in the kinetics of interaction of digitalis derivatives with variant Na^+,K^+-ATPase isozymes and conformers. The full use of the screening system includes a cyclical improvement process involving the systematic design, synthesis, and testing of derivatives. When inhibitors with suitable selectivity and potency (in this order of priority) are found, they are evaluated in biological systems with increasingly higher organizational levels. If there is insufficient selectivity or activity, the metabolism and pharmacokinetics of the inhibitor is studied to ascertain the basis of such inadequacy. Hopefully, tailored inhibitors can thus be designed, but their applicability as drugs depends upon their pharmacokinetics and metabolism in humans.

When sufficient information has become available, this should be stored in data banks alongside data on chemical structure and biological activities. Multiparametric computer analysis, most promising in the form of the correspondence analysis as adopted by Doré et al. (1986) and practised by Raynaud et al. (1986), may then reveal new correlations and answer certain important questions, such as those raised by Raynaud et al. (1986) based on the results of screening more than 5000 compounds using 10 different membrane receptors.

The major development envisaged here is necessarily a long haul and involves extensive investment of resources in a concept, the therapeutic merit of which can be judged only at the end of the road (cf. Weatherall 1982).

The human mind is often so awkward and ill-regulated in the career of invention that it is at first diffident, and then despises itself. For it appears at first incredible that any such discovery should be made, and when it has been made, it appears incredible that it should so long escape man's research.

Francis Bacon, Novum Organum, Aphorism CX

Acknowledgement

We thank Mrs Manuela Büttner for her expert typing of the manuscript.

References

Achenbach, C., Daying, H., and Preisler, R. (1986). Electrophysiological assay of glycoside-induced sodium pump inhibition in isolated sheep heart Purkinje fibres at the onset of toxicity. In *Cardiac glycosides 1785–1985* (ed. E. Erdmann, K. Greeff, and J. C. Skou), pp. 79–86. Steinkopff Verlag, Darmstadt.

Acheson, G. H., Kahn JR., J. B., and Lipicky, R. J. (1964). A comparison of dihydro-ouabain, dihydrodigoxin, dihydrodigitoxin, 3-acetyl strophanthidin, erysimin, and ouabain given by continuous infusion into dogs. *Naunyn-Schmiedeberg's Arch. Exp. Path. Pharmakol.*, **248**, 247–60.

Ahmed, K., Rohrer, D. C., Fullerton, D. S., Deffo, T., Kitatsuji, E., and From, A. H. L. (1983). Interaction of (Na$^+$ + K$^+$)-ATPase and digitalis genins. A general model for inhibitory activity. *J. Biol. Chem.*, **258**, 8092–7.

Akera, T. (1981). Effects of cardiac glycosides on Na$^+$,K$^+$-ATPase. In *Cardiac glycosides, part I: experimental pharmacology* (ed. K. Greeff). Handbook of experimental pharmacology, Vol. 56/I, pp. 287–336. Springer, Berlin.

Akera, T., Ku, D., Tobin, T., and Brody, T. M. (1976). The complexes of ouabain with sodium- and potassium-activated adenosine triphosphatase formed with various ligands: relationship to the complex formed in the beating heart. *Mol. Pharmacol.*, **12**, 101–14.

Akera, T., Fox, A. L., and Greeff, K. (1981). Substances processing inotropic properties similar to cardiac glycosides. In *Cardiac glycosides, part I: experimental pharmacology* (ed. K. Greeff). Handbook of experimental pharmacology, Vol. 56/I, pp. 459–86. Springer, Berlin.

Andrews, P. R., Craik, D. J., and Martin, J. L. (1984). Functional group contributions to drug–receptor interactions. *J. Med. Chem.*, **27**, 1648–57.

Ariëns, E. J. (1969). Modulation of pharmacokinetics by modification of the various factors involved. *Farmaco Ed. Sci.*, **24**, 3–102.

Askari, A. (1982). Na$^+$,K$^+$-ATPase: relation of conformational transitions to function. *Mol. Cell. Biochem.*, **43**, 129–43.

Austel, V. and Kutter, E. (1978). Auffinden und Optimieren von Wirkstrukturen. In *Arzneimittelentwicklung: Grundlagen–Strategien–Perspektiven* (ed. E. Kutter), pp. 113–39. Georg Thieme, Stuttgart.

Barry, W. H. and Smith, T. W. (1984). Movement of Ca^{2+} across the sarcolemma: effects of abrupt exposure to zero external Na$^+$ concentration. *J. Mol. Cell. Cardiol.*, **16**, 155–64.

Barry, W. H., Hasin, Y., and Smith, T. W. (1985). Sodium pump inhibition, enhanced calcium influx via sodium–calcium exchange, and positive inotropic response in cultured heart cells. *Circ. Res.*, **56**, 231–41.

Barry, W. H., Biedert, S., Miura, D. S., and Smith, T. W. (1981). Changes in cellular Na$^+$,K$^+$, and Ca^{2+} contents, monovalent cation transport rate, and contractile state during washout of cardiac glycosides from cultured chick heart cells. *Circ. Res.*, **49**, 141–9.

Beeler, G. W. and Reuter, H. (1970). Membrane calcium current in ventricular myocardial fibres. *J. Physiol.*, **207**, 191–209.

Beer, J., Kunze, R., Herrmann, I., Portius, H. J., Mirsalichova, N. M., Abubakirov, N. K., and Repke, K. R. H. (1988). The thermodynamic essence of the reversible inactivation of Na$^+$/K$^+$-transporting ATPase by various digitalis derivatives is relaxation of enzyme conformational energy. *Biochim. Biophys. Acta*, **937**, 335–46.

Bennett, D. R., Andersen, K. S., Andersen, M. V., Robertson, D. N., and Chenoweth, M. B. (1958). Structure–activity analysis of the positive inotropic action of conjugated carbonyl compounds on the cat papillary muscle. *J. Pharmacol. Exp. Ther.*, **122**, 489–98.

Blaustein, M. P. (1974). The interrelationship between sodium and calcium fluxes across cell membranes. *Rev. Physiol. Biochem. Pharmacol.* **70**, 33–82.

Blaustein, M. P. (1985). The cellular basis of cardiotonic steroid action. *Trends Pharmacol. Sci.*, **6**, 289–92.

Bohl, M., Ponsold, K., and Reck, G. (1984). Quantitative structure–activity relationships of cardiotonic steroids using empirical molecular electrostatic potentials and semiempirical molecular orbital calculations. *J. Steroid Biochem.*, **21**, 373–9.

Bohl, M. and Süssmilch, R. (1986). Calculations on molecular structure and electrostatic potentials of cardiotonic steroids. *Eur. J. Med. Chem.*, **21**, 193–8.

Brown, L. and Erdmann, E. (1984a). A comparison of the effects of ouabain, dihydroouabain and 3α-methyldigitoxigenin glucoside on guinea pig left atria. *Arzneim.-Forsch.*, **34**, 204–8.

Brown, L. and Erdmann, E. (1984b). Binding of digitalis derivatives to beef, cat and human cardiac (Na$^+$ + K$^+$)-ATPase. Affinity and kinetic constants. *Arch. Int. Pharmacodynam.*, **271**, 229–40.

Brown, L. and Thomas, R. (1983). Comparison of the inotropic potencies of some synthetic and naturally occurring cardiac glycosides using isolated left atrium of guinea pig. *Arzneim.-Forsch.*, **33**, 814–17.

Brown, L. and Thomas, R. (1984). Comparison of the inotropic effects of some 5α-cardenolides on guinea pig left atria. *Arzneim.-Forsch.*, **34**, 572–4.

Brown, L., Erdmann, E., and Thomas, R. (1983). Digitalis structure–activity relationship analyses. Conclusions from indirect binding studies with cardiac (Na$^+$ + K$^+$)-ATPase. *Biochem. Pharmacol.*, **32**, 2767–74.

Brown, L., Hug, E., Wagner, G., and Erdmann, E. (1985). Comparison of ouabain receptors in sheep myocardium and Purkinje fibres. *Biochem. Pharmacol.*, **34**, 3701–10.

Burgen, A. S. V. (1981). Conformational changes and drug action. *Fed. Proc. Fed. Am. Soc. Exp. Biol.*, **40**, 2723–8.

Cagin, N. A., Somberg, J., Bounous, H., and Levitt, B. (1977). A comparison of actodigin and ouabain in cats. *Arch. Int. Pharmacodynam.*, **226**, 263–9.

Caldwell, R. W. and Nash, C. B. (1978). Comparison of the effects of aminosugar cardiac glycosides with ouabain and digoxin on Na$^+$,K$^+$-adenosine triphosphatase and cardiac contractile force. *J. Pharmacol. Exp. Ther.*, **204**, 141–8.

Cantley, L. C. (1981). Structure and mechanism of the (Na$^+$,K$^+$)-ATPase. In *Current topics in bioenergetics* (ed. D. R. Sanadi and L. P. Vernon), Vol. 11, pp. 201–37. Academic Press, London.

Carafoli, E. and Crompton, M. (1978). The regulation of intracellular calcium. In *Current topics in membranes and transport* (ed. F. Bronner and A. Kleinzeller), Vol. 10, pp. 151–216. Academic Press, New York.

Carilli, C. T., Farley, R. A., Perlman, D. M., and Cantley, L. C. (1982). The active site structure of Na$^+$- and K$^+$-stimulated ATPase. Location of a specific fluorescein isothiocyanate reactive site. *J. Biol. Chem.*, **257**, 5601–6.

Caroni, P., Reinlib, L., and Carafoli, E. (1980). Charge movements during the Na$^+$–Ca^{2+} exchange in heart sarcolemma vesicles. *Proc. Nat. Acad. Sci. USA*, **77**, 6354–8.

Caviezel, R. and Wilbrandt, W. (1958). Die Abhängigkeit der bleibenden Herzglykosid-wirkung von der Kalium- und Calciumkonzentration während der Glykosideinwir-kung auf das Herz. *Helv. Physiol. Acta*, **16**, 12–21.

Černý, I., Pouzar, V., Drašar, P., and Havel, M. (1983). Synthesis of 17β-steroidal 4-(2-butenolides). *Coll. Czech. Chem. Commun.*, **48**, 2064–71.

Chapman, R. A., Coray, A., and McGuigan, J. A. S. (1983). Sodium/calcium exchange in mammalian ventricular muscle: a study with sodium-sensitive micro-electrodes. *J. Physiol.*, **343**, 253–76.

Charlemagne, D., Mayoux, E., Preteseille, M., Maixent, J. M., Mouas, Ch., Swynghedauw, B., and Lelièvre, L. G. (1986). Digitalis receptors in normal and hypertrophied rat hearts. Differential effects of a Ca^{2+} free perfusion. In *Cardiac glycosides 1785–1985* (ed. E. Erdmann, K. Greeff and J. C. Skou), pp. 93–8. Steinkopff, Darmstadt.

Chen, K. K. (1963). Possibilities of further developments in the glycoside field by modifying the glycoside structure. In *New aspects of cardiac glycosides* (ed. W. Wilbrandt and P. Lindgren). Proceedings of the first international pharmacological meeting, Stockholm 1961, Vol. 3, pp. 27–43. Pergamon Press, Oxford.

Chen, K. K., Robbins, E. B., and Worth, H. (1938). The significance of sugar component in the molecule of cardiac glycosides. *J. Amer. Pharm. Ass.*, **27**, 189–95.

Chen, K. K., Steldt, F. A., Fried, J., and Elderfield, R. C. (1942). The action of simple lactones related to cardiac aglycones. *J. Pharmacol. Exp. Ther.*, **74**, 381–91.

Chetverin, A. B. (1986). Evidence for a diprotomeric structure of Na,K-ATPase. Accurate determination of protein concentration and quantitative end-group analysis. *FEBS Lett.*, **196**, 121–5.

Chiu, F. C. K. and Watson, T. R. (1985). Conformational factors in cardiac glycoside activity. *J. Med. Chem.*, **28**, 509–15.

Choi, Y. R. and Akera, T. (1977). Kinetics studies on the interaction between ouabain and (Na$^+$,K$^+$)-ATPase. *Biochim. Biophys. Acta*, **481**, 648–59.

Choi, Y. R. and Akera, T. (1978). Membrane (Na$^+$ + K$^+$)-ATPase of canine brain, heart and kidney. Tissue-dependent differences in kinetic properties and the influence of purification procedures. *Biochim. Biophys. Acta*, **508**, 313–27.

Clark, A. F., Swanson, P. D., and Stahl, W. L. (1975). Increase in dissociation rate constants of cardiotonic steroid-brain (Na$^+$ + K$^+$)-ATPase complexes by reduction of the unsaturated lactone. *J. Biol. Chem.*, **250**, 9355–9.

Cohen, C. J., Fozzard, H. A., and Sheu, S.-S. (1982). Increase in intracellular sodium activity during stimulation in mammalian cardiac muscle. *Circ. Res.*, **50**, 651–62.

Delettré, J., Mornon, J. P., Lepicard, G., Ojasoo, T., and Raynaud, J. P. (1980). Steroid flexibility and receptor specificity. *J. Steroid Biochem.*, **13**, 45–59.

Dénes, B. and Greeff, K. (1981). Effects of cardiac glycosides on skeletal muscle. In *Cardiac glycosides, part I: experimental pharmacology* (ed. K. Greeff). Handbook of experi-mental pharmacology, Vol. 56/I, pp. 517–32. Springer, Berlin.

De Pover, A. and Godfraind, T. (1979). Interaction of ouabain with (Na$^+$ + K$^+$)-ATPase from human heart and from guinea-pig heart. *Biochem. Pharmacol.*, **28**, 3051–6.

Dittrich, F., Berlin, P., Köpke, K., and Repke, K. R. H. (1983). Stereoelectronic interaction between cardiotonic steroids and Na,K-ATPase: molecular mechanism of digitalis action. In *Structure, mechanism and function of the Na/K pump* (ed. J. F. Hoffman and B. Forbush III) pp. 251–255. Current topics in membranes and transport, Vol. 19, Academic Press, New York.

Doering, W. and König, E. (1977). Digitalisintoxikation—Ursachen, Diagnose, Prophylaxe. *Dtsch. med. Wschr.*, **102**, 579–85.

Doré, J.-C., Gilbert, J., Ojasoo, T., and Raynaud, J.-P. (1986). Correspondence analysis applied to steroid receptor binding. *J. Med. Chem.*, **29**, 54–60.

Duax, W. L., Weeks, C. M., Rohrer, D. C., and Osawa, Y. (1975). Conformational studies of steroids: correlations with biological data. *J. Steroid Biochem.*, **6**, 195–200.

Dunham, E. T. and Glynn, I. M. (1961). Adenosinetriphosphatase activity and the active movements of alkali metal ions. *J. Physiol.*, **156**, 274–93.

Eberlein, W. (1978). Das molekulare Konzept der Pharmakonwirkung. In *Arzneimittelentwicklung: Grundlagen–Strategien–Perspektiven* (ed. E. Kutter), pp. 2–39. Georg Thieme, Stuttgart.

Eberlein, W., Heider, J., and Machleidt, H. (1974). Substitution des Butenolidringes von Herzglykosiden durch unverzweigte offenkettige π-Elektronensysteme. *Chem. Ber.*, **107**, 1275–84.

Eftink, M. and Biltonen, R. (1980). Thermodynamics of interacting biological systems. In *Biological microcalorimetry* (ed. A. E. Beezer), pp. 343–412. Academic Press, London.

Eigen, M. and Hammes, G. G. (1963). Elementary steps in enzyme reactions (as studied by relaxation spectrometry). In *Advances in enzymology* (ed. F. F. Nord), Vol. 25, pp. 1–38. Interscience, New York.

Einstein, R., Gray, P., Mihailidou, A., and Thomas, R. (1986). Can the therapeutic ratio of digitalis be improved? *J. Mol. Cell. Cardiol.*, **18**, (Suppl. 1), Abstr. 42.

Eisner, D. A., Vaughan-Jones, R. D., and Lederer, W. J. (1983). Letter to the editor. *Circ. Res.*, **53**, 834–5.

Erdmann, E. (1981). Influence of cardiac glycosides on their receptor. In *Cardiac glycosides, part I: experimental pharmacology* (ed. K. Greeff). Handbook of experimental pharmacology, Vol. 56/I, pp. 337–80. Springer Berlin.

Erdmann, E. (1985). Veränderung der Affinität und der Kapazität des Herzglykosidrezeptors. *Arzneimittel.-Forsch.* **35**, 1948–52.

Erdmann, E. and Schoner, W. (1973a). Ouabain–receptor interactions in $(Na^+ + K^+)$-ATPase preparations. II. Effect of cations and nucleotides on rate constants and dissociation constants. *Biochim. Biophys. Acta*, **330**, 302–15.

Erdmann, E. and Schoner, W. (1973b). Ouabain–receptor interactions in $(Na^+ + K^+)$-ATPase preparations from different tissues and species. Determination of kinetic constants and dissociation constants. *Biochim. Biophys. Acta*, **307**, 386–98.

Erdmann, E., Philipp, G., and Tanner, G. (1976). Ouabain–receptor interactions in $(Na^+ + K^+)$-ATPase preparations. A contribution to the problem of nonlinear Scatchard plots. *Biochim. Biophys. Acta*, **455**, 287–96.

Erdmann, E., Philipp, G., and Scholz, H. (1980). Cardiac glycoside receptor, $(Na^+ + K^+)$-ATPase activity and force of contraction in rat heart. *Biochem. Pharmacol.*, **29**, 3219–29.

Fischer, E. (1894). Einfluß der Configuration auf die Wirkung der Enzyme. *Ber. Dtsch. Chem. Ges.*, **27**, 2985–93.

Flasch, H. and Heinz, N. (1978). Correlation between inhibition of (Na^+, K^+)-membrane-ATPase and positive inotropic activity of cardenolides in isolated papillary muscles of guinea pig. *Naunyn-Schmiedeberg's Arch. Pharmacol.*, **304**, 37–44.

Forbush III, B. (1983). Cardiotonic steroid binding to Na,K-ATPase. In *Structure, mechanism and function of the Na/K pump* (ed. J. F. Hoffman and B. Forbush III).

Current topics in membranes and transport (ed. F. Bronner and A. Kleinzeller), Vol. 19, pp. 167–201. Academic Press, New York.

Fosset, M., De Barry, J., Lenoir, M.-C., and Lazdunski, M. (1977). Analysis of molecular aspects of Na$^+$ and Ca^{2+} uptakes by embryonic cardiac cells in culture. *J. Biol. Chem.*, **252**, 6112–7.

Frelin, C., Vigne, P., and Lazdunski, M. (1984). The role of the Na$^+$/H$^+$ exchange system in cardiac cells in relation to the control of internal Na$^+$ concentration. *J. Biol. Chem.*, **259**, 8880–5.

From, A. H. L., Fullerton, D. S., Deffo, T., Kitatsuji, E., Rohrer, D. C., and Ahmed, K. (1984). The inotropic activity of digitalis genins is dependent upon C(17) side-group carbonyl oxygen position. *J. Mol. Cell. Cardiol.*, **16**, 835–42.

Fullerton, D. S., Yoshioka, K., Rohrer, D. C., From, A. H. L., and Ahmed, K. (1980). A crystallographic, conformational energy, and biological study of actodigin (AY-22,241) and its genin. *Mol. Pharmacol.* **17**, 43–51.

Fullerton, D. S., Kitatsuji, E., Deffo, T., Rohrer, D. C., Ahmed, K., and From, A. H. L. (1983). Use of Prophet and MMS-X computer graphics in the study of the cardiac steroid receptor site of Na,K-ATPase. In *Structure, mechanism and function of the Na/K-pump* (ed. J. F. Hoffman and B. Forbush III). Current topics in membranes and transport (ed. F. Bronner and A. Kleinzeller), Vol. 19, pp. 257–64. Academic Press, New York.

Fullerton, D. S., Kihara, M., Deffo, T., Kitatsuji, E., Ahmed, K., Simat, B., From, A. H. L., and Rohrer, D. C. (1984). Cardiac glycosides. 1. A systematic study of digitoxigenin D-glycosides. *J. Med. Chem.*, **27**, 256–61.

Fullerton, D. S., Griffin, J. F., Rohrer, D. C., From, A. H. L., and Ahmed, K. (1985). Using computer graphics to study cardiac glycoside–receptor interactions. *Trends Pharmacol. Sci.*, **6**, 279–82.

Fullerton, D. S. Ahmed, K., From, A. H. L., McParland, R. H., Rohrer, D. C., and Griffin, J. F. (1986). Modelling the cardiac steroid receptor. In *Molecular graphics and drug design* (ed. A. S. V. Burgen, G. C. K. Roberts, and M. S. Tute), pp. 257–84. Elsevier, Amsterdam.

Gelbart, A. and Thomas, R. (1978). Cardenolide analogues. 7. Synthesis and biological activity of some new steroidal guanylhydrazones. *J. Med. Chem.*, **21**, 284–8.

Gervais, A., Lane, L. K., Anner, B. M., Lindenmayer, G. E., and Schwartz, A. (1977). A possible molecular mechanism of the action of digitalis. Ouabain action on calcium binding to sites associated with a purified sodium–potassium-activated adenosine triphosphatase from kidney. *Circ. Res.*, **40**, 8–14.

Gillis, R. A. and Quest, J. A. (1980). The role of the nervous system in the cardiovascular effects of digitalis. *Pharmacol. Rev.*, **31**, 19–97.

Gillis, R. A. and Quest, A. (1986). Extracardiac effects of cardiac glycosides. In *Cardiac glycosides 1785–1985* (ed. E. Erdmann, K. Greeff, and J. C. Skou), pp. 347–56. Steinkopff, Darmstadt.

Ginneken, C. A. M. van (1977). Kinetics of drug–receptor interaction. In *Kinetics of drug action* (ed. J. M. van Rossum). Handbook of experimental pharmacology, Vol. 47, pp. 357–411. Springer, Berlin.

Glicklich, J. I., Gaffney, R., Rosen, M. R., and Hoffman, B. F. (1975). Effects of AY-22,241(Actodigin) on electrical and mechanical activity of cardiac tissues. *Eur. J. Pharmacol.*, **32**, 1–9.

Glitsch, H. G., Reuter, H., and Scholz, H. (1970). The effect of the internal sodium concentration on calcium fluxes in isolated guinea-pig auricle. *J. Physiol. Lond.*, **209**, 25–43.

Glynn, I. M. (1985). The Na^+,K^+-transporting adenosine triphosphatase. In *The enzymes of biological membranes* (ed. A. N. Martonosi), Vol. 3, pp. 35–114. Plenum, New York.

Glynn, I. M. and Ellory, C., ed. (1985). *The sodium pump.* Proceedings of the fourth international conference on Na,K-ATPase. The Company of Biologists, Cambridge.

Glynn, I. M. and Karlish, S. J. D. (1975). The sodium pump. *Ann. Rev. Physiol.*, **37**, 13–55.

Godfraind, T. (1981). Stimulation and inhibition of the Na^+,K^+-pump by cardiac glycosides. In *Cardiac glycosides, part I: experimental pharmacology* (ed. K. Greeff). Handbook of experimental pharmacology, Vol. 56/I, pp. 381–93. Springer, Berlin.

Godfraind, T. (1985). Withering: 200 years is not enough. *Pharmacol. Sci.*, **6**, 360–3.

Godfraind, T. and Lutete, D. T. (1979). Inhibition by digoxin and SC 4453 of $(Na^+ + K^+)$-ATPase prepared from human heart, guinea-pig heart and guinea-pig brain. *Eur. J. Pharmacol.*, **60**, 329–36.

Gold, H., Kwit, N. T., Shane, S. J., and Dayrit, C. (1969). The role of the sugar component in cardiac glycosides on their action in patients with auricular fibrillation and congestive failure. *J. Clin. Pharmacol.*, **9**, 148–54.

Gretler, D. D. (1985). Strophanthidin and potassium on intracellular sodium activity in sheep heart. *J. Mol. Cell. Cardiol.*, **17**, 1105–13.

Grupp, G., Grupp, I. L., Hickerson, T., Lee, S. W., and Schwartz, A. (1986). Biphasic contractile response to ouabain: Species specific? Calcium dependent? Altered sensitivity? In *Cardiac glycosides 1785–1985* (ed. E. Erdmann, K. Greeff and J. C. Skou), pp. 99–108. Steinkopff, Darmstadt.

Grupp, I., Im, W.-B., Lee, C. O., Lee, S.-W., Pecker, M. S., and Schwartz, A. (1985). Relation of sodium pump inhibition to positive inotropy at low concentrations of ouabain in rat heart muscle. *J. Physiol.*, **360**, 149–60.

Güntert, T. W. and Linde, H. H. A. (1981). Chemistry and structure-activity relationships of cardioactive steroids. In *Cardiac glycosides, part I: experimental pharmacology* (ed. K. Greeff). Handbook of experimental pharmacology, Vol. 56/I, pp. 13–24. Springer, Berlin.

Guzman, A., Muchowski, J. M., Strosberg, A. M., and Sims, J. M. (1981). Replacement of butenolide moiety of digitoxigenin by cyclic Michael acceptor systems. *Can. J. Chem.*, **59**, 3241–7.

Hajdu, S. and Leonard, E. (1959). The cellular basis of cardiac glycoside action. *Pharmacol. Rev.*, **11**, 173–209.

Hall, C. C. and Ruoho, A. E. (1983). Photoaffinity labeling of the ouabain binding site of Na,K-ATPase. In *Structure, mechanism and function of the Na/K pump* (ed. J. F. Hoffman and B. Forbush III). Current topics in membranes and transport, Vol. 19, pp. 265–70. Academic Press, New York.

Halsey, J. F., Mountcastle, D. B., Takeguchi, C. A., Biltonen, R. L., and Lindenmayer, G. E. (1977). Detection of a ouabain-induced structural change in the sodium, potassium-adenosine triphosphatase. *Biochemistry*, **16**, 432–5.

Hamlyn, J. M., Cohen, N., Zyren, J., and Blaustein, M. P. (1985). Activating effects of low dose cardiotonic steroids on dog kidney Na,K-ATPase activity: role of endogenous inhibition. In *The sodium pump* (ed. I. Glynn and C. Ellory), pp. 667–73. The Company of Biologists, Cambridge.

Hammes, G. G. (1982). *Enzyme catalysis and regulation.* Academic Press, New York.

Hansen, O. (1976). Non-uniform populations of g-strophanthin binding sites of $(Na^+ + K^+)$-activated ATPase. Apparent conversion to uniformity by K^+. *Biochim. Biophys. Acta*, **433**, 383–92.

Hansen,O. (1984). Interaction of cardiac glycosides with (Na$^+$ + K$^+$)-activated ATPase. A biochemical link to digitalis-induced inotropy. *Pharmacol. Rev.*, **36**, 143–63.

Haustein, K.-O. (1974). Studies on cardioactive steroids. I. Structure–activity relationships on the isolated atrium. *Pharmacology*, **11**, 117–26.

Haustein, K.-O. (1977). Extraordinary cardiac effects of 16-epi-gitoxin in comparison to ouabain in cats and dogs. *Pharmacology*, **15**, 178–90.

Haustein, K.-O. (1980). 16α-Gitoxin. *Drugs of the future*, **5**, 187–8.

Haustein, K.-O., Pachaly, C., and Murawski, D. (1978). Pharmacokinetic investigations with ^{3}H-penta-acetyl-Gitoxin in volunteers and patients with respect to the occurrence of drug latentiation. *Int. J. Clin. Pharmacol.*, **16**, 285–9.

Herrmann, I. and Repke, K. R. H. (1964a). Epimerisierung und Hydroxylierung von digitaloiden Steroidlaktonen durch Fermente der Leber. *Naunyn-Schmiedeberg's Arch. Exp. Path. Pharmakol.*, **248**, 351–69.

Herrmann, I. and Repke, K. R. H. (1964b). Konjugation von Cardenolidgeninen mit Schwefelsäure oder Glukuronsäure. *Naunyn-Schmiedeberg's Arch. Exp. Path. Pharmakol.*, **248**, 370–86.

Herrmann, I. and Repke, K. R. H. (1964c). Entgiftungsgeschwindigkeit und Kumulation von Digitoxin bei verschiedenen Species. *Naunyn-Schmiedeberg's Arch. Exp. Path. Pharmakol.*, **247**, 19–34.

Heubner, W. (1940). Zur Frage der Digitaliskumulation. *Schweiz. Med. Wschr.*, **70**, 524–29.

Hintsche, R. and Megges, R. (1986). Konformation der Digitoxosereste des Digitoxins in Lösung. *Z. Chem.*, **26**, 439–41.

Hintsche, R., Megges, R., Pfeiffer, D., Portius, H. J., Schönfeld, W., and Repke, K. R. H. (1985). Biological potency and solution conformation of cardenolides determined by a new ^{1}H NMR method. *Eur. J. Med. Chem.*, **20**, 9–15.

Hinz, H.-J. (1983). Thermodynamics of protein–ligand interactions: calorimetric approaches. *Ann. Rev. Biophys. Bioeng.*, **12**, 285–317.

Hobbs, A. S. and Albers, R. W. (1980). The structure of proteins involved in active membrane transport. *Ann. Rev. Biophys. Bioeng.*, **9**, 259–91.

Hoffman, J. F. and Forbush III, B., ed. (1983). *Structure, mechanism, and function of the Na/K pump*. Current topics in membranes and transport (ed. F. Bronner and A. Kleinzeller), Vol. 19. Academic Press, New York.

Höhne, E. and Pfeiffer, D. (1983). Intramolecular steric interaction between steroid skeleton and lactone ring of steroids. *Stud. Biophys.*, **97**, 81–6.

Huang, W.-H. and Askari, A. (1980). Ouabain-induced changes in the tertiary and the quaternary conformations of (Na$^+$ + K$^+$)-activated adenosine triphosphatase. *Mol. Pharmacol.*, **18**, 53–6.

Humblet, C. and Marshall, G. R. (1981). Three-dimensional computer modeling as an aid to drug design. *Drug Dev. Res.*, **1**, 409–34.

IUPAC-IUB (1969). Revised tentative rules for nomenclature of steroids. *Biochemistry*, **8**, 2227–42.

Jencks, W. P. (1980). What everyone wanted to know about tight binding and enzyme catalysis, but never thought of asking. In *Chemical recognition in biology* (ed. F. Chapeville and A.-L. Haenni), pp. 3–25. Molecular biology, biochemistry and biophysics (ed. A. Kleinzeller, G. F. Springer and H. G. Wittmann), Vol. 32. Springer, Berlin.

Jones, J. B. and Middleton, H. W. (1970). Studies related to the mechanism of action of cardiac glycosides. On the reactions of thiols with unsaturated lactones and on the structure of the compound previously reported as ouabagenin. The preparation and properties of authentic ouabagenin. *Can. J. Chem.*, **48**, 3819–26.

Jørgensen, P. L. (1982). Mechanism of the Na^+,K^+ pump. Protein structure and conformations of the pure $(Na^+ + K^+)$-ATPase. *Biochim. Biophys. Acta*, **694**, 27–68.

Kahn, JR., J. B. (1957). Effects of various lactones and related compounds on cation transfer in incubated cold-stored human erythrocytes. *J. Pharmacol. Exp. Ther.*, **121**, 234–51.

Kaiser, F. (1971). Teilsynthetische Herzglykosid-Derivate mit verbesserter enteraler Wirksamkeit. *Planta Med.* (Suppl. 4), 52–60.

Kaplan, J. H. (1985). Ion movements through the sodium pump. *Ann. Rev. Physiol.*, **47**, 535–44.

Kass, R. S., Lederer, W. J., Tsien, R. W., and Weingart, R. (1978). Role of calcium ions in transient inward currents and aftercontractions induced by strophanthidin in cardiac Purkinje fibres. *J. Physiol. Lond.*, **281**, 187–208.

Kaufmann, G. (1978). Is there a need for new cardiac glycosides? For more blood level determinations? In *Cardiac glycosides* (ed. G. Bodem and H. J. Dengler), Part II, pp. 410–21. Springer, Berlin.

Kim, D., Marsh, J. D., Barry, W. H., and Smith, T. W. (1984). Effects of growth in low potassium medium or ouabain on membrane Na,K-ATPase, cation transport, and contractility in cultured chick heart cells. *Circ. Res.*, **55**, 39–48.

Kjeldsen, K., Nørgaard, A., and Clausen, T. (1985). Effects of ouabain, age and K-depletion on K-uptake in rat soleus muscle. *Pflügers Arch., Eur. J. Physiol.*, **404**, 365–73.

Kobinger, W., Wenzel, B. and Klupp, H. (1970). Beziehungen zwischen Herzwirkung, toxischer Wirkung und Plasmabindung bei Herzglykosiden. *Arzneim.-Forsch.*, **20**, 1862–5.

Krenitsky, T. A. and Elion, G. B. (1982). Enzymes as tools and targets in drug research. In *Strategy in drug research* (ed. J. A. Keverling Buisman), pp. 65–87. Elsevier, Amsterdam.

Kubinyi, H., Görlich, B., and Steidle, W. (1971). Acyl- und Alkylderivate des Proscillaridins. *Planta Med.*, (Suppl. 4). 127–31.

Kurbjuweit, H. G. (1971). Pharmakologische Untersuchungen mit neuen Scilla-Glykosiden. *Planta Med.*, (Suppl. 4), pp. 132–8.

LaBella, F. S., Bihler, I., Templeton, J., Kim, R.-S., Hnatowich, M., and Rohrer, D. (1985). Progesterone derivatives that bind to the digitalis receptor: effects on Na^+,K^+-ATPase and isolated tissues. *Fed. Proc. Fed. Am. Soc. Exp. Biol.*, **44**, 2806–11.

Langen, P. and Repke, K. R. H. (1966). Inhibition of DNA- and protein-synthesis of Ehrlich ascites tumour cells *in vitro* by pregnene-guanylhydrazones. *Acta Biol. Med. Germ.*, **17**, K15–19.

Langer, G. A. (1983). The 'sodium pump lag' revisited. *J. Mol. Cell. Cardiol.*, **15**, 647–51.

Lauterbach, F. and Repke, K. R. H. (1960). Die fermentative Abspaltung von D-Digitoxose, D-Cymarose und L-Thevetose aus Herzglykosiden durch Leberschnitte. *Naunyn-Schmiedeberg's Arch. Exp. Path. Pharmakol.*, **239**, 196–218.

Lazdunski, M., Frelin, C., and Vigne, P. (1985). The sodium/hydrogen exchange system in cardiac cells: its biochemical and pharmacological properties and its role in regulating internal concentrations of sodium and internal pH. *J. Mol. Cell. Cardiol.*, **17**, 1029–42.

Lechat, P., Malloy, C. R., and Smith, T. W. (1983). Active transport and inotropic state in guinea pig left atrium. *Circ. Res.*, **52**, 411–22.

Lee, C. O., Uhm, D. Y., and Dresdner, K. (1980). Sodium–calcium exchange in rabbit heart muscle cells: direct measurement of sarcoplasmic Ca^{2+} activity. *Science*, **209**, 699–701.

Lee, C. O., Abete, P., Pecker, M., Sonn, J. K., and Vassalle, M. (1985). Strophanthidin inotropy: role of intracellular sodium ion activity and sodium–calcium exchange. *J. Mol. Cell. Cardiol.*, **17**, 1043–53.

Levy, R. I. and Moskowitz, J. (1982). Cardiovascular research: decades of progress, a decade of promise. *Science*, **217**, 121–9.

Lindig, C. and Repke, K. R. H. (1986). Synthese von 3-(3β,14-Dihydroxy-5β,14β-androstan-17β-yl-methyl)-but-2-en-4-olid, eines homologen 5β,14β-Cardenolids. *J. Prakt. Chem.*, **328**, 695–704.

Lüllmann, H. and Peters, J. (1979). Action of cardiac glycosides on the excitation–contraction coupling in heart muscle. *Prog. Pharmacol.*, **2**, 1–57.

Lumry, R. and Rajender, S. (1970). Enthalpy–entropy compensation phenomena in water solutions of proteins and small molecules: an ubiquitous property of water. *Biopolymers*, **9**, 1125–7.

Lytton, J., Lin, J. C., and Guidotti, G. (1985). Identification of two molecular forms of (Na$^+$,K$^+$)-ATPase in rat adipocytes. Relation to insulin stimulation of the enzyme. *J. Biol. Chem.*, **260**, 1177–84.

McCans, J. L., Lindenmayer, G. E., Pitts, B. J. R., Ray, M. V., Raynor, B. D., Butler Jr., V. P., and Schwartz, A. (1975). Antigenic differences in (Na$^+$,K$^+$)-ATPase preparations isolated from various organs and species. *J. Biol. Chem.*, **250**, 7257–65.

McDonough, A. and Schmitt, C. (1985). Comparison of subunits of cardiac, brain, and kidney Na$^+$,K$^+$-ATPase. *Am. J. Physiol.*, **248**, C247–51.

Maelicke, A., Fulpius, B. W., Klett, R. P., and Reich, E. (1977). Acetylcholine receptor. Responses to drug binding. *J. Biol. Chem.*, **252**, 4811–30.

Malur, J. and Repke, K. R. H. (1970). Modelluntersuchungen über die Beteiligung einer Wasserstoff-Brückenbindung an der Komplexbildung zwischen Cardenolidverbindungen und Na$^+$ + K$^+$-aktivierter, Mg^{2+}-abhängiger Adenosintriphosphat-Phosphohydrolase. *Acta Biol. Med. Germ.*, **24**, K67–72.

Marban, E. and Tsien, R. W. (1982). Enhancement of calcium current during digitalis inotropy in mammalian heart: positive feed-back regulation by intracellular calcium? *J. Physiol.*, **329**, 589–614.

Marks, M. J. and Seeds, N. W. (1978). A heterogeneous ouabain–ATPase interaction in mouse brain. *Life Sci.*, **23**, 2735–44.

Martin, Y. C. (1981). A practitioner's perspective of the role of quantitative structure–activity analysis in medicinal chemistry. *J. Med. Chem.*, **24**, 229–37.

Matsuda, T., Iwata, H., and Cooper, J. R. (1984). Specific inactivation of α(+) molecular form of (Na$^+$ + K$^+$)-ATPase by pyrithiamin. *J. Biol. Chem.*, **259**, 3858–63.

Mendez, R. (1944). Pharmacology and chemistry of substances with cardiac activity. III. The effect of simple unsaturated lactones and t-butyl hydrogen peroxide on the isolated frog heart. *J. Pharmacol. Exp. Ther.*, **81**, 151–9.

Michael, L. H., Schwartz, A., and Wallick, E. T. (1979). Nature of the transport adenosine triphosphatase–digitalis complex: XIV. Inotropy and cardiac glycoside interaction with Na$^+$,K$^+$-ATPase of isolated cat papillary muscles. *Mol. Pharmacol.*, **16**, 135–46.

Middleton, H. W. (1970). Kinetics of monovalent ion activation of the (Na$^+$ + K$^+$)-dependent adenosine triphosphatase and a model for ion translocation and its inhibition by the cardiac glycosides. *Arch. Biochem. Biophys.*, **136**, 280–6.

Morgan, J. P. (1985). The effects of digitalis on intracellular calcium transients in mammalian working myocardium as detected with aequorin. *J. Mol. Cell. Cardiol.*, **17**, 1065–75.

Moss, D. W. (1979). *Isoenzyme analysis*. Analytical sciences monographs, No. 6. Chemical Society, London.

Mudge JR., G. H., Lloyd, B. L., Greenblatt, D. J., and Smith, T. W. (1978). Inotropic and toxic effects of a polar cardiac glycoside derivative in the dog. *Circ. Res.*, **43**, 847–53.

Nayler, W. G. and Dresel, P. E. (1984). Ca^{2+} and the sarcoplasmic reticulum. *J. Mol. Cell. Cardiol.*, **16**, 165–74.

Némoz, G., Prigent, A.-F., Picq, M., and Pacheco, H. (1982). Selective inhibition of separated forms of cyclic nucleotide phosphodiesterase from rat heart by some cardio- or vaso-active butenolide derivatives. *Biochem. Pharmacol.*, **31**, 3353–8.

Niedergerke, R. (1963). Movements of Ca in frog heart ventricles at rest and during contractures. *J. Physiol. Lond.*, **167**, 515–50.

Ninio, J. and Chapeville, F. (1980). Recognition: the kinetic concepts. In *Chemical recognition in biology* (ed. F. Chapeville and A.-L. Haenni), pp. 78–85. Springer, Berlin.

Noble, D. (1980). Mechanism of action of therapeutic levels of cardiac glycosides. *Cardiovasc. Res.*, **14**, 495–514.

Noel, F. and Godfraind, T. (1984). Heterogeneity of ouabain specific binding sites and $(Na^+ + K^+)$-ATPase inhibition in microsomes from rat heart. *Biochem. Pharmacol.*, **33**, 47–53.

Pace, D. G. and Gillis, R. A. (1982). Improvement of the toxic to inotropic dose ratio of digoxin by excluding central nervous system influences on the heart. *Arch. Int. Pharmacodynam.*, **255**, 103–16.

Periyasami, S. M., Huang, W.-H., and Askari, A. (1983). Origins of the different sensitivities of $(Na^+ + K^+)$-dependent adenosinetriphosphatase preparations to ouabain. *Comp. Biochem. Physiol.*, **76B**, 449–54.

Petersen, R., Flasch, H., and Heinz, N. (1977). Darstellung und Eigenschaften einiger Glukuronide und Sulfate von Cardenoliden und Cardenolidglykosiden. *Arzneim.-Forsch.*, **27**, 642–9.

Pfeil, W. (1981). The problem of the stability of globular proteins. *Mol. Cell. Biochem.*, **40**, 3–28.

Philipson, K. D. (1985). Sodium–calcium exchange in plasma membrane vesicles. *Ann. Rev. Physiol.*, **47**, 561–71.

Pitts, B. J. R., Wallick, E. T., van Winkle, W. B., Allen, J. C., and Schwartz, A. (1977). On the lack of inotropy of cardiac glycosides on skeletal muscle: a comparison of Na^+,K^+-ATPases from skeletal and cardiac muscle. *Arch. Biochem. Biophys.*, **184**, 431–40.

Portius, H. J. and Repke, K. R. H. (1963). Der Einfluß von Digitalis auf Adenosintriphosphatasen, die an der Einstellung der Ca^{++}-Konzentration in der Muskelzelle beteiligt sein können. *Acta Biol. Med. Germ.*, **11**, 829–41.

Portius, H. J. and Repke, K. R. H. (1964). Versuch einer Analyse der Beziehungen zwischen chemischer Struktur und Digitalis-ähnlicher Wirksamkeit auf der Rezeptorebene. *Arzneim.-Forsch.*, **14**, 1073–7.

Portius, H. J. and Repke, K. R. H. (1967). Eigenschaften und Funktion des $Na^+ + K^+$-aktivierten, Mg^{++}-abhängigen Adenosintriphosphat-Phosphohydrolase-Systems des Herzmuskels. *Acta Biol. Med. Germ.*, **19**, 907–38.

Portius, H. J. and Repke, K. R. H. (1969). Effect of steroids of different type on transport ATPase. In *Symposium über biochemische Aspekte der Steroidforschung* (ed. K. Schubert). Abhandlungen der Deutschen Akademie der Wissenschaften zu Berlin, Klasse für Medizin, No. 2, pp. 179–83. Akademie–Verlag, Berlin.

Post, R. L., Merritt, C. R., Kinsolving, C. R., and Albright, C. D. (1960). Membrane adenosine triphosphatase as a participant in the active transport of sodium and potassium in the human erythrocyte. *J. Biol. Chem.*, **235**, 1796–802.

Post, R. L., Sen, A. K., and Rosenthal, A. S. (1965). A phosphorylated intermediate in adenosine triphosphate-dependent sodium and potassium transport across kidney membranes. *J. Biol. Chem.*, **240**, 1437–45.

Puryear, S. K., Nash, C. B., and Caldwell, R. W. (1981). Effect of cardiac beta-adrenergic blockade or denervation on cardiotoxicity of digoxin and an aminosugar cardenolide. *J. Cardiovasc. Pharmacol.*, **3**, 113–27.

Rang, H. P. (1971). Drug receptors and their function. *Nature (London)*, **231**, 91–6.

Raynaud, J. P., Fortin, M., Hunt, P., Ojasoo, T., Doré, J. C., Surcouf, E., and Mornon, J. P. (1986). Approaches to drug development using receptors. In *The role of receptors in biology and medicine* (ed. A. M. Gotto Jr. and B. W. O'Malley), pp. 63–77. Raven Press, New York.

Reeves, J. P. and Hale, C. C. (1984). The stoichiometry of the cardiac sodium–calcium exchange system. *J. Biol. Chem.*, **259**, 7733–9.

Reiter, M. (1981). The positive inotropic action of cardioactive steroids on cardiac ventricular muscle. In *Cardiac glycosides, part I: experimental pharmacology* (ed. K. Greeff). Handbook of experimental pharmacology, Vol. 56/I, pp. 187–219. Springer, Berlin.

Repke, K. R. H. (1959). Die Bis- und Mono-digitoxoside des Digitoxigenins und Digoxigenins: Metaboliten des Digitoxins. *Naunyn-Schmiedeberg's Arch. Exp. Path. Pharmakol.*, **237**, 155–70.

Repke, K. R. H. (1963). Metabolism of cardiac glycosides. In *New aspects of cardiac glycosides* (ed. W. Wilbrandt and P. Lindgren). Proceedings of the first international pharmacological meeting, Stockholm 1961, Vol. 3, pp. 47–73. Pergamon Press, Oxford.

Repke, K. R. H. (1964). Über den biochemischen Wirkungsmodus von Digitalis. *Klin. Wschr.*, **42**, 157–65.

Repke, K. R. H. (1965). Effect of digitalis on membrane adenosine triphosphatase of cardiac muscle. In *Drugs and enzymes* (ed. B. B. Brodie, J. R. Gillette and R. Čapek). Proceedings of the second international pharmacological meeting, Prague 1963, Vol. 4. Pergamon Press, Oxford, pp. 65–87.

Repke, K. R. H. (1977). Concept on the link between chemical and electro-chemical free energies in (NaK)-ATPase transport function. In *Biochemistry of membrane transport*, FEBS symposium No. 42 (ed. G. Semenza and E. Carafoli), pp. 363–7. Springer, Berlin.

Repke, K. R. H. (1982). On the mechanism of energy release, transfer and utilization in Na,K-ATPase transport work: old ideas and new findings. In Transport ATPases (ed. E. Carafoli and A. Scarpa). *Ann. N.Y. Acad. Sci.*, **402**, 272–86.

Repke, K. R. H. (1985). New developments in cardiac glycoside structure–activity relationships. *Trends Pharmacol. Sci.*, **6**, 275–8.

Repke, K. R. H. (1986). A model for allosteric regulation of Na$^+$/K$^+$-transporting ATPase. *Biochim. Biophys. Acta*, **864**, 195–212.

Repke, K. R. H. (1988). The role of the Na$^+$/K$^+$ pump in normal and cancer cell proliferation. In *Basic and medical research on biomembranes* (ed. G. Benga and J. Tager). Springer, New York, in press.

Repke, K. R. H. and Dittrich, F. (1980). Thermodynamics of information transfer from cardiotonic steroids to receptor transport ATPase. *Trends Pharmacol. Sci.*, **1**, 398–402.

Repke, K. R. H. and Megges, R. (1963). Die Entwicklung eines neuen Herzglykosid-Präparats mit großer therapeutischer Breite (Penta-acetyl-gitoxin). *Dtsch. Gesundheitswesen*, **18**, 1325–33.

Repke, K. R. H. and Portius, H. J. (1963). Über die Identität der Ionenpumpen-ATPase in der Zellmembran des Herzmuskels mit einem Digitalis-Rezeptorenzym. *Experientia*, **19**, 452–8.

Repke, K. R. H. and Portius, H. J. (1966). Analysis of structure activity relationships in cardioactive compounds on the molecular level. In *Proceedings of the 25th international congress of pharmaceutical sciences*, Prague 1965. Scientiae Pharmaceuticae (ed. O. Hanč and J. Hubík), Vol. I, pp. 39–57. Butterworth, London.

Repke, K. R. H. and Portius, H. J. (1971). Molekularbiologische Wertbestimmung von Verbindungen des Digitalistyps. *Planta Med.*, (Suppl. 4), pp. 66–78.

Repke, K. R. H. and Samuels, L. T. (1964). Enzymatic basis for epimerization of cardiotonic steroids at carbon 3 in rat liver. *Biochemistry*, **3**, 689–95.

Repke, K. R. H. and Schönfeld, W. (1984). Na$^+$/K$^+$-ATPase as the digitalis receptor. *Trends Pharmacol. Sci.*, **5**, 393–7.

Repke, K. R. H., Est, M., and Portius, H. J. (1965). Über die Ursache der Speziesunterschiede in der Digitalisempfindlichkeit. *Biochem. Pharmacol.*, **14**, 1785–802.

Repke, K. R. H., Kott, M., and Vogel, F. (1983). Utmost cytoplasmic location of catalytic center in Na,K-motive ATPase disfavors Mitchell's phosphate–cation symport mechanism of Na/K transport across plasma membranes. *Biomed. Biochim. Acta*, **43**, 825–38.

Repke, K. R. H., Herrmann, I., and Portius, H. J. (1984). Interaction of cardiac glycosides and Na,K-ATPase is regulated by effector-controlled equilibrium between two limit enzyme conformers. *Biochem. Pharmacol.*, **33**, 2089–99.

Reuter, H. (1982). Na–Ca countertransport in cardiac muscle. In *Membranes and transport* (ed. A. N. Martonosi), Vol. 1, pp. 623–631. Plenum, New York.

Reuter, H. and Seitz, N. (1968). The dependence of calcium efflux from cardiac muscle on temperature and external ion composition. *J. Physiol. (London)*, **195**, 451–70.

Roberts, G. C. K. (1983). Flexible keys and deformable locks: ligand binding to dihydrofolate reductase. In *Quantitative approaches to drug design* (ed. J. C. Dearden), pp. 91–98. Elsevier, Amsterdam.

Robinson, J. D. and Flashner, M. S. (1979). The (Na$^+$ + K$^+$)-activated ATPase. Enzymatic and transport properties. *Biochim. Biophys. Acta*, **549**, 145–76.

Rohrer, D. C., Fullerton, D. S., Yoshioka, K., From, A. H. L., and Ahmed, K. (1979). Functional receptor mapping for modified cardenolides: use of the Prophet system. In *Computer-assisted drug design*. ACS symposium series, No. 112 (ed. E. C. Olson and R. E. Christoffersen), pp. 259–279. American Chemical Society, Washington D.C.

Rohrer, D. C., Fullerton, D. S., Yoshioka, K., Kitatsuji, E., Ahmed, K., and From, A. H. L. (1983). Structures of modified cardenolides. IV. [20S] 20(22)-dihydrodigitoxigenin analogues. *Acta Crystallogr.*, **B39**, 272–80.

Ross, P. D. and Subramanian, S. (1981). Thermodynamics of protein association reactions: forces contributing to stability. *Biochemistry*, **20**, 3096–102.

Schatzmann, H. J. (1953). Herzglykoside als Hemmstoffe für den aktiven Kalium- und Natriumtransport durch die Erythrozytenmembran. *Helv. Physiol. Acta*, **16**, 12–21.

Schellenberg, G. D., Pech, I. V., and Stahl, W. L. (1981). Immunoreactivity of subunits of the (Na$^+$ + K$^+$)-ATPase. Cross-reactivity of the $\alpha,\alpha+$ and β forms in different organs and species. *Biochim. Biophys. Acta*, **649**, 691–700.

Scheraga, H. E. (1971). Theoretical and experimental studies of conformations of polypeptides. *Chem. Rev.*, **71**, 195–217.

Schön, R., Schönfeld, W., Menke, K.-H., and Repke, K. R. H. (1972). Mechanism and role of Na$^+$/Ca^{2+} competition in (Na,K)-ATPase. *Acta Biol. Med. Germ.*, **29**, 643–59.

Schönfeld, W., Schön, R., Menke, K.-H., and Repke, K. R. H. (1972). Identification of conformational states of transport ATPase by kinetic analysis of ouabain binding. *Acta Biol. Med. Germ.*, **28**, 935–56.

Schönfeld, W., Menke, K.-H., Schönfeld, R., and Repke, K. R. H. (1984). Evidence against parallel operation of sodium/calcium antiport and ATP-driven calcium transport in plasma membrane vesicles from kidney tubule cells. *Biochim. Biophys. Acta*, **770**, 183–94.

Schönfeld, W., Weiland, J., Lindig, C., Masnyk, M., Kabat, M. M., Kurek, A., Wicha, J., and Repke, K. R. H. (1985). The lead structure in cardiac glycosides is 5β,14β-androstane-3β,14-diol. *Naunyn-Schmiedeberg's Arch. Pharmacol.*, **329**, 414–26.

Schönfeld, W., Weiland, J., and Repke, K. R. H. (1986a). Biochemical basis for the targeted synthesis of cardiac glycosides with selective action. In *Cardiac glycosides 1785–1985* (ed. E. Erdmann, K. Greeff and J. C. Skou), pp. 127–34. Steinkopff, Darmstadt.

Schönfeld, W., Schönfeld, R., Menke, K.-H., Weiland, J., and Repke, K. R. H. (1986b). Origin of differences of inhibitory potency of cardiac glycosides in Na$^+$/K$^+$-transporting ATPase from human cardiac muscle, human brain cortex and guinea-pig cardiac muscle. *Biochem. Pharmacol.*, **35**, 3221–31.

Schrödinger, E. (1967). *What is life?* University Press, Cambridge.

Schuurmans Stekhoven, F. and Bonting, S. L. (1981). Transport adenosine triphosphatases: properties and functions. *Physiol. Rev.*, **61**, 1–76.

Schuurmans Stekhoven, F., De Pont, J. J. H. H. M., and S. L. Bonting (1976). Studies on (Na$^+$ + K$^+$)-activated ATPase. XXXVII. Stabilization by cations of the enzyme-ouabain complex formed with Mg^{2+} and inorganic phosphate. *Biochim. Biophys. Acta*, **419**, 137–49.

Schwartz, A. and Adams, R. J. (1980). Studies on the digitalis receptor. *Circ. Res.*, **46**, 1154–60.

Schwartz, A., Matsui, H., and Laughter, A. H. (1968). Tritiated digoxin binding to (Na$^+$ + K$^+$)-activated adenosine triphosphatase: possible allosteric site. *Science*, **160**, 323–5.

Schwartz, A., Allen, J. C., van Winkle, W. B., and Munson, R. (1974). Further studies on the correlation between the inotropic action of ouabain and its interaction with the Na$^+$,K$^+$-adenosine triphosphatase: isolated perfused rabbit and cat hearts. *J. Pharmacol. Exp. Ther.*, **191**, 119–27.

Schwartz, A., Lindenmayer, G. E., and Allen, J. C. (1975). The sodium–potassium adenosine triphosphatase: pharmacological, physiological, and biochemical aspects. *Pharmacol. Rev.*, **27**, 3–134.

Schwartz, A., Whitmer, K., Grupp, G., Grupp, I., Adams, R. J., and Lee, S.-W. (1982). Mechanism of action of digitalis: is the Na,K-ATPase the pharmacological receptor? In *Transport-ATPases* (ed. E. Carafoli and A. Scarpa). *Ann. N.Y. Acad. Sci.*, **402**, 253–271.

Scrocco, E. and Tomasi, J. (1978). Electronic molecular structure, reactivity and inter-molecular forces: an heuristic interpretation by means of electrostatic molecular potentials. In *Advances in quantum chemistry* (ed. P.-O. Löwdin), Vol. 11, pp. 115–93. Academic Press, New York.

Sen, A. K., Tobin, T., and Post, R. L. (1969). A cycle for ouabain inhibition of sodium- and potassium-dependent adenosine triphosphatase. *J. Biol. Chem.*, **244**, 6596–604.

Shamovskij, I. L., Barenbojm, G. M., and Ovchinnikov, A. A. (1983). Theoretical study on structure–activity relationships in cardiotonic steroids (in Russian). *Bioorg. Khim.*, **9**, 1112–26.

Shull, G. E., Schwartz, A., and Lingrel, J. B. (1985). Amino-acid sequence of the catalytic subunit of the $(Na^+ + K^+)$-ATPase deduced from a complementary DNA. *Nature Lond.*, **316**, 691–5.

Smith, T. W., Antman, E. M., Friedman, P. L., Blatt, C. M., and Marsh, J. D. (1984). Digitalis glycosides: mechanisms and manifestations of toxicity. *Prog. Cardiovasc. Dis.* **26**, 413–41, 495–523, **27**, 21–56.

Soderberg, K., Rossi, B., Lazdunski, M., and Louvard, D. (1983). Characterization of ouabain-resistant mutants of kidney cell line, MDCK. *J. Biol. Chem.*, **258**, 12300–7.

Somberg, J. C. and Smith, T. W. (1978). Localization of the neurally mediated arrhythmogenic properties of digitalis. *Science*, **204**, 321–3.

Somberg, J. C., Risler, T., and Smith, T. W. (1978). Neural factors in digitalis toxicity: protective effect of C-1 spinal cord transection. *Am. J. Physiol.*, **235**, H531–6.

Somberg, J. C., Mudge JR., G. H., Risler, T., and Smith, T. W. (1980). Neurally mediated augmentation of arrhythmogenic properties of highly polar glycosides. *Am. J. Physiol.*, **238**, H202–8.

Stella, V. J. and Himmelstein, K. J. (1980). Prodrugs and site-specific drug delivery. *J. Med. Chem.*, **23**, 1275–82.

Sweadner, K. J. (1979). Two molecular forms of $(Na^+ + K^+)$-stimulated ATPase in brain. Separation and difference in affinity for strophanthidin. *J. Biol. Chem.*, **254**, 6060–7.

Sweadner, K. J. (1985). Enzymatic properties of separated isozymes of the Na,K-ATPase. Substrate affinities, kinetic cooperativity, and ion transport stoichiometry. *J. Biol. Chem.*, **260**, 11508–13.

Sweadner, K. J. and Gilkeson, R. C. (1985). Two isozymes of the Na,K-ATPase have distinct antigenic determinants. *J. Biol. Chem.*, **260**, 9016–22.

Tamm, C. (1963). The stereochemistry of the glycosides in relation to biological activity. In *New aspects of cardiac glycosides* (ed. W. Wilbrandt and P. Lindgren). Proceedings of the first international pharmacological meeting, Stockholm 1961, Vol. 3, pp. 11–26. Pergamon Press, Oxford.

Taniguchi, K. and Iida, S. (1973). The role of phospholipids in the binding of ouabain to sodium- and potassium-dependent adenosine triphosphatase. *Mol. Pharmacol.*, **9**, 350–9.

Taniguchi, K. and Post, R. L. (1975). Synthesis of adenosine triphosphate and exchange between inorganic phosphate and adenosine triphosphate in sodium and potassium ion transport adenosine triphosphatase. *J. Biol. Chem.*, **250**, 3010–18.

Testa, B. (1984). Drugs? Drug research? Advances in drug research? Musings of a medicinal chemist. In *Advances in drug research* (ed. B. Testa), Vol. 13, pp. 1–58. Academic Press, London.

Theil, F., Lindig, C., and Repke, K. R. H. (1980). Partialsynthesen von Cardenoliden und Cardenolid-Analogen. III. Synthese von Cardenolid-analogen β-Steroidyl-crotonsäuremethylestern. *J. Prakt. Chem.*, **322**, 1012–20.

Thomas, R., Boutagy, J., and Gelbart, A. (1974a). Synthesis and biological activity of semisynthetic digitalis analogs. *J. Pharm. Sci.*, **63**, 1649–83.

Thomas, R., Boutagy, J., and Gelbart, A. (1974b). Cardenolide analogs. V. Cardiotonic activity of semisynthetic analogs of digitoxigenin. *J. Pharmacol. Exp. Ther.*, **191**, 219–31.

Thomas, R., Brown, L., Boutagy, J., and Gelbart, A. (1980). The digitalis receptor. Inferences from structure–activity relationship studies. *Circ. Res.*, **46**, (Suppl. 1), 167–72.

Tobin, T., Henderson, R., and Sen, A. K. (1972). Species and tissue differences in the rate of dissociation of ouabain from $(Na^+ + K^+)$-ATPase. *Biochim. Biophys. Acta*, **274**, 551–5.

Urayama, O. and Nakao, M. (1979). Organ specificity of rat sodium- and potassium-activated adenosine triphosphatase. *J. Biochem.*, **86**, 1371–81.

Wallick, E. T., Kirley, T. L., and Schwartz, A. (1986). Structural studies on the cardiac glycoside receptor. In *Cardiac glycosides 1785–1985* (ed. E. Erdmann, K. Greeff, and J. C. Skou), pp. 27–53. Steinkopff, Darmstadt.

Wallick, E. T., Pitts, B. J. R., Lane, L. K., and Schwartz, A. (1980). A kinetic comparison of cardiac glycoside interactions with Na$^+$,K$^+$-ATPases from skeletal and cardiac muscle and from kidney. *Arch. Biochem. Biophys.*, **208**, 442–9.

Wasserstrom, J. A., Schwartz, D. J., and Fozzard, H. A. (1983). Relation between intracellular sodium and twitch tension in sheep cardiac Purkinje strands exposed to cardiac glycosides. *Circ. Res.*, **52**, 697–705.

Weatherall, M. (1982). An end to the search for new drugs? *Nature (London)*, **296**, 387–90.

Weber, G. (1975). Energetics of ligand binding to proteins. In *Advances in protein chemistry* (ed. C. B. Anfinsen, J. T. Edsall, and F. M. Richards), Vol. 29, pp. 1–83. Academic Press, New York.

Weiland, J., Schwabe, K., Hübler, D., Schönfeld, W., and Repke, K. R. H. (1987). Glycosidation of chlormadinol acetate alters its actions on Na$^+$/K$^+$-transporting ATPase and cardiac contractility: a contribution to the endogenous digitalis problem. *J. Enzyme Inhib.*, **2**, 31–6.

Wenzel, D. G. and Keplinger, M. L. (1953). Cardiac activity of unsaturated lactones as related to their theoretical peroxide formation. *J. Am. Pharm. Ass.*, **42**, 653–9.

Wiesner, K., Tsai, T. Y. R., Kumar, R., and Sivaramakrishnan, H. (1984). On cardioactive steroids, XV. A stereoselective synthesis of (21R)-21-methyldigitoxigenin, a fully active cardenolide with a wide margin of safety: a contribution to the topology of the digitalis receptors. *Helv. Chim. Acta*, **67**, 1128–35.

Wilbrandt, W. (1955). Zum Wirkungsmechanismus der Herzglykoside. *Schweiz. Med. Wschr.*, **85**, 315–20.

Wilbrandt, W. (1957). Permeabilität, aktiver Transport und Trägermechanismus. *Dtsch. Med. Wschr.*, **82**, 1153–8.

Wilbrandt, W. (1958). Zur Frage der Beziehungen zwischen Digitalis-und Kalziumwirkungen. *Wiener Med. Wschr.*, **108**, 809–14.

Wilbrandt, W. (1963). Introduction. In *New aspects of cardiac glycosides* (ed. W. Wilbrandt and P. Lindgren). Proceedings of the first international pharmacological meeting, Stockholm 1961, Vol. 3, pp. 3–9. Pergamon Press, Oxford.

Wilbrandt, W. and Koller, H. (1948). Die Calciumwirkung am Froschherzen als Funktion des Ionengleichgewichts zwischen Zellmembran und Umgebung. *Helv. Physiol. Acta*, **6**, 208–21.

Wilbrandt, W. and Weiss, E. M. (1960). Antagonismus zwischen Herzglykosid und Corticosteroiden am Froschhautpotential. *Arzneim.-Forsch.*, **10**, 409–12.

Wilbrandt, W., Brawand, K., and Witt, P. N. (1953). Die quantitative Abhängigkeit der Strophanthosidwirkung auf das Froschherz von der Tätigkeit des Herzens und von der Glykosidkonzentration. *Arch. Exp. Path. Pharmakol.*, **219**, 397–407.

Wilson, W. E., Sivitz, W. I., and Hanna, L. T. (1970). Inhibition of calf brain membranal sodium- and potassium-dependent adenosine triphosphatase by cardioactive sterols. A binding site model. *Mol. Pharmacol.*, **6**, 449–59.

Wirth, K. E. (1986). Relevant metabolism of cardiac glycosides. In *Cardiac glycosides 1785–1985* (ed. E. Erdmann, K. Greeff, and J. C. Skou), pp. 257–62. Steinkopff, Darmstadt.

Withering, W. (1785). *An account of the foxglove, and some of its medical uses: with practical remarks on dropsy, and other diseases.* G. G. J. and J. Robinson, London.

Wooldridge, K. R. H. (1977). Reducing the gamble in drug research. In *Medicinal Chemistry V* (ed. J. Matthieu), pp. 427–432. Elsevier, Amsterdam.

Zakrzewska, K. and Pullman, A. (1985). Optimized monopole expansions for the representation of the electrostatic properties of polypeptides and proteins. *J. Comput. Chem.*, **6**, 265–74.

Zorbach, W. W. and Bhat, K. V. (1966). Synthetic cardenolides. In *Advances in carbohydrate chemistry* (ed. M. L. Wolfrom), Vol. 21, pp. 273–321. Academic Press, New York.

16

Inhibitors of steroid biosynthesis

A. M. H. Brodie

16.1   Introduction

The biosynthesis of steroids occurs in the gonads to produce sex steroids and in the adrenals giving rise to glucocorticoids and mineralocorticoids. However, extra glandular production of some steroids also takes place in peripheral tissues. For example, aromatase, which converts androgens into oestrogens has been identified in a wide variety of tissues, such as adipose tissue, muscles, and some tumours.

A number of clinical situations exist in which steroid hormones, either in normal amounts or when produced in excess, have a role in the pathogenesis of disease. Thus, inhibition of the steroid-producing enzymes is a valuable means of treating these conditions. Until recently, however, there were relatively few inhibitors that were specific for any one steroidogenic enzyme. Most of these compounds inhibit steroid hydroxylation and interact with the cytochrome P-450 component of the enzymes. Cytochrome P-450 is a family of haem-containing proteins involved with oxidative reactions. However, the concentration of cytochrome P-450 is generally higher in the steroid-producing tissue of adrenal glands than in the liver and kidney.

In the last few years, several compounds have been identified that selectively inhibit aromatase. Since oestrogens are important in a variety of physiological processes and diseases (such as gynaecomastia, precocious puberty, and endometrial and breast cancer), selective inhibitors of aromatase are proving useful for both investigational and therapeutic purposes. Our studies on the development of these inhibitors form the framework of this chapter but inhibitors of other enzymes are also discussed to provide a more comprehensive review.

16.2 Biosynthesis of steroids

Steroid biosynthesis occurs either directly from acetate (Heard *et al.* 1955; Ryan and Smith 1961) mevalonate, squalene and cholesterol, or from blood-borne cholesterol. Hydroxylation must precede carbon–carbon cleavage; thus, the cholesterol side-chain is removed by hydroxylation first at C-20 and subsequently at C-22 to yield 20,22-dihydroxycholesterol. Cleavage then proceeds, mediated by the enzyme desmolase, yielding the immediate steroid precursor, pregnenolone (for further details of the biosynthetic steps, see Nes* and McKean 1977). Biosynthesis may occur via both the Δ^5 pathway, i.e. directly from pregnenolone, and the Δ^4 pathway, i.e. from progesterone. The latter is formed by dehydrogenation of the 3β-hydroxylation and isomerization of pregnenolone. Dehydrogenation at 3β is mediated by Δ^5-3β-hydroxysteroid dehydrogenase (3-HSD), which requires NAD^+ as the hydrogen acceptor in the removal of the hydrogen from the 3β-hydroxyl position. This reaction is followed by a shift of the double bond to the Δ^4 position by Δ^5-pregnene-3,20-dione isomerase.

Both pregnenolone and progesterone first undergo hydroxylation at the 17α-position. In the adrenal gland, 17α-hydroxyprogesterone and progesterone are hydroxylated at C-21 and subsequently at C-11 to yield glucocorticoids, cortisol, and/or corticosterone. The latter is thought to be further hydroxylated at C-18 to give aldosterone, the major mineralocorticoid. Carbon–carbon cleavage at C-17 of 17α-hydroxylated pregnenolone and progesterone by $C_{17,20}$-lyase yields C_{19} androgens.

Dehydroepiandrosterone (DHEA), the Δ^5 androgen, may be either reduced to form androstenediol and then converted by 3-HSD and isomerized to the Δ^4 androgen testosterone, or directly converted to 4-androstene-3,17-dione (Fig. 16.1). 17α-hydroxyprogesterone is converted directly to androstenedione. The androgens are further reduced via testosterone to dihydrotestosterone (5α and 5β) or converted to oestrogens. The 17-position oxido-reductions, i.e. androstenedione to testosterone and oestrone to oestradiol, are reversible reactions and thereby may play a regulatory role in controlling the amount of oestrogens produced by aromatization.

Aromatization of the androgens is a unique reaction in steroid biosynthesis and involves the loss of the angular C-19 methyl group and *cis* elimination of 1β- and 2β-hydrogens from androstenedione and testosterone to yield oestrone and oestradiol, respectively (Morato *et al.* 1962; Townsley and Brodie 1968; Brodie *et al.* 1969; Fishman and Guzik 1969). Androstenedione, or testosterone, is first monohydroxylated and then dihydroxylated at C-19. The second hydroxylation can be dehydrated to give the aldehyde. Oxidative dehydrogenation at C-1 and C-2 with expulsion of the C-19 moiety as formic acid then yields oestrone or oestradiol. Studies by Thompson and Siiteri (1974a) suggest that three hydroxylation steps are involved and that the third hydroxylation may be the rate-limiting step. A third hydroxylation at C-19 to give a 19-trihydroxy intermediate

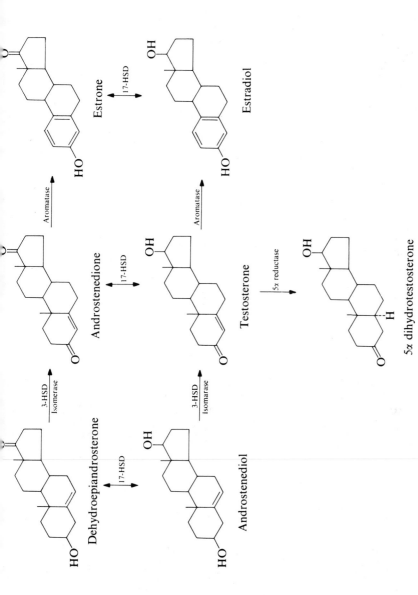

Fig. 16.1. Biosynthesis of androgens and oestrogens.

would be unlikely, however, due to severe conformational hindrance (Duax *et al.* 1976). One possibility is oxidative attack at C-1β (Brodie *et al.* 1969) or, alternatively, at C-2. Evidence from Goto and Fishman (1977) indicates that 2β-hydroxy-19-oxo-androstenedione is formed, which then rapidly converts to oestrone. This latter reaction occurs in aqueous solutions, suggesting that enzymatic catalysis need not be involved. 2β-hydroxy-19-oxo-androstenedione has been isolated from microsomal incubations of [1,2-^{3}H,^{14}C] androstenedione. When a specific antibody to 2β-hydroxy-19-oxygenated androgens was added to placental microsomal incubations together with [1,2-^{3}H-] androstenedione, there was a 50 per cent decrease in oestrogen formation (^{3}H$_2$O release) compared with controls (Hahn and Fishman 1984). These results are evidence in favour of the last and rate-determining hydroxylation in aromatization being at the C-2β position. However, studies by Akhtar *et al.* (1982) and Caspi *et al.* (1984) involving ^{18}O$_2$ incorporation suggest that the enzymatic formation of 2β-hydroxy-10β-formylandrostenedione and its non-enzymatic aromatization may not be an obligatory pathway.

The reducing equivalents for steroid hydroxylation or reductive reactions are supplied by the reduction of the oxidized form of nicotinamide adenine dinucleotide phosphate (NADP$^+$) by enzymes of the pentose phosphate pathway such as glucose-6-phosphate dehydrogenase, or by NADP$^+$-specific isocitrate dehydrogenase (McKerns 1969). In addition, hydroxylation reactions require an electron transport system, NADPH-cytochrome C reductase, non-haem iron, and cytochrome P-450, for oxygen activation and its specific introduction into various positions on the steroid molecule.

From tissue fractionation and electron microscopy studies, it appears that cholesterol in the cell reaches the inner membrane of the mitochondria, where side-chain cleavage takes place. Pregnenolone synthesized on the inner membrane then passes through the outer mitochondrial membrane and reaches the surface of the agranular endoplasmic reticulum, where it is converted to progesterone. Other transformations also probably take place in this region. It is supposed that the enzyme proteins are located together in an organized group in the endoplasmic reticulum. The manner of organization in the enzyme group is genetically determined (Tamaoki 1973). When the precursor reaches a group of these enzymes, multiple reactions are sequentially performed without expulsion of intermediates from the enzyme group until the final product is produced.

Recently, several of the steroidogenic enzymes have been purified and characterized. It is likely that the availability of the pure enzymes will provide added impetus to research on the biochemistry of steroidogenic enzymes and their role in physiology (Nakajin *et al.* 1984; Mendelson *et al.* 1985; Evans *et al.* 1986).

16.3   Inhibitors of steroid biosynthesis

16.3.1   Inhibitors of multiple steroidogenic enzymes

Steroid biosynthesis can be inhibited by a number of compounds which act on multiple enzymes. These compounds can be used to reduce adrenal steroids and produce a medical adrenalectomy. One such inhibitor is cyanoketone (2α-cyan-4,4,17 α-dimethylandrost-5-en-17β-ol-3-one), which is a competitive inhibitor of desmolase, the enzyme mediating cholesterol side-chain cleavage, 3-ketosteroid isomerase, 17-hydroxysteroid dehydrogenase, and aromatase (Schwarzel *et al.* 1973). In contrast, its potent action on 3α- and 3β-hydroxysteroid dehydrogenase (Goldman *et al.* 1965) is by non-competitive inhibition (Neville and Engel 1968). The cyano group appears to bind cytochrome a and haemoglobin and inhibits electron transfer, whereas the steroid moeity binds to cytochrome P-450. In addition, the compound binds to oestrogen receptors (K_i is 1.2×10^{-6} M in rat tissues; Wolfson *et al.* 1983). These actions may explain why cyanoketone has multiple effects *in vivo*.

Metyrapone has been shown to bind to P-450 enzymes including the adrenal side-chain cleavage enzymes and the 11β-hydroxylase. P-450$_{11\beta}$ can catalyse the 11β-, 18- and 19-hydroxylations of various steroids. However, P-450$_{11\beta}$ activity is usually characterized with the substrate 11-hydroxycorticosterone (DOC) (Watanuki *et al.* 1978). Metyrapone, 2-methyl-1,3-bis-3-pyridyl-1-propanone, is a potent competitive inhibitor of P-450$_{11\beta}$ activity. It is used clinically to test the ability of the pituitary to secrete ACTH in response to a decreased concentration of plasma cortisol and to control Cushing's disease (Donckier *et al.* 1986).

Spirolactone,   [3-(3-oxo-7-acetylthio-17β-hydroxy-4-androsten-17α-yl)pro-pionic acid lactone], an aldosterone antagonist, has been reported to decrease plasma testosterone levels, cause gynaecomastia, and be useful in the treatment of hirsutism. The compound was subsequently found to inhibit 17-hydroxylase by decreasing testicular microsomal cytochrome P-450. This results in impairment of testosterone biosynthesis (Menard *et al.* 1974). Spirolactone also inhibits binding of [³H]5α-dihydrotestosterone to the cytosolic and nuclear receptors of the rat ventral prostate. However, the compound had no effect on 5α-reductase even at 10^{-5} M (Corvol *et al.* 1975).

Aminoglutethimide (α-ethyl-α-*p*-aminophenylglutarimide, AG), is a non-steroidal inhibitor used to produce medical adrenalectomies. This compound was first introduced as an anticonvulsant but its use was restricted when it was realized that the compound causes adrenal insufficiency. AG is a competitive inhibitor of P-450 and interferes with desmolase, 11-hydroxylase, 21-hydroxylase, 18-hydroxylase, and aromatase (Chakraborty *et al.* 1972; Thompson and Siiteri 1974b).

AG is a mixture of D-, and L-stereoisomers. Salhanick and colleagues determined that the D-isomer was 30-fold more potent than the L-form for aromatase inhibition (Uzgris *et al.* 1977). The activity of the racemic mixture represents the amount of the D-isomer present (Uzgris *et al.* 1977; Whipple *et al.* 1978). The L-enantiomer is 15-fold more potent than the D-form with respect to inhibition of cholesterol side-chain cleavage. Although AG is not a selective inhibitor of oestrogen biosynthesis, it has been found to be a more potent inhibitor of aromatase than of the other steroid hydroxylases. Ten times the concentration of AG required to block aromatization, is needed to inhibit cholesterol side-chain cleavage. AG is now in use to reduce oestrogen formed in peripheral tissue by aromatization of adrenal androgens in post-menopausal breast cancer patients. Hydrocortisone is given concomitantly for glucocorticoid replacement. AG produces objective disease remission to the same extent as surgical adrenalectomy (Santen et al. 1981; Santen and Brodie 1982), thus establishing it as a useful agent in breast cancer treatment.

Modifications of aminoglutethimide are being investigated in order to improve aromatase inhibition but reduce inhibition of other enzymes, as well as reduce the somnolence-inducing side-effects. The arylamine group of AG appears to play a key role in inhibiting cytochrome P-450, while the glutarimide moiety may be responsible for the drug's depressant action on the central nervous system. Arylamine compounds such as 4-cyclohexylaniline, which lack this moiety, have been tested as aromatase inhibitors (Kellis and Vickery 1984). Although 4-cyclohexylaniline is several-fold less effective than AG, its inhibitory action suggests that the complex glutarimide ring and the chiral 3-ethyl substituent of D-aminoglutethimide are not required for binding to aromatase P-450.

Steele et al. (1986) recently compared inhibition of aromatase by AG with 4-(5,6,7,8-tetrahydroimidazol[1,5-a]pyridin-5-yl)benzonitrile. Using a substrate concentration of 1.2×10^{-7} M, the compound was 180 times more potent than AG, having an IC_{50} of 1.2×10^{-9} M compared to 2.2×10^{-7} M for AG. The compound was also effective in vivo in the rat in reducing the ovarian oestrogen content. The minimal effective dose was $2.6 \, \mu g \, kg^{-1}$ (p.o.) compared with $3.3 \, mg \, kg^{-1}$ (p.p.) for AG. The compound had no effect on adrenal weight, whereas AG induced adrenal atrophy, indicating interference with corticosterone secretion. These preliminary data suggest the compound is more potent and selective than AG as an aromatase inhibitor.

Several imidazole antimycotics—miconazole, clotrimazole, and ketoconazole—are reversible competitive inhibitors of placental microsomal cytochrome P-450, probably by interaction of an imidazole nitrogen with the haem protein. The IC_{50} for miconazole, the most potent inhibitor of aromatase in this series, was $0.6 \, \mu M$ versus $44 \, \mu M$ for aminoglutethimide. Miconazole is a relatively poor inhibitor of cholesterol side-chain cleavage, thus giving it some selectivity for aromatase (Mason et al. 1985).

5-bis(4-chlorophenyl)methylpyrimidine has also been reported to be a competitive non-steroidal aromatase inhibitor (Hirsch and Clemens 1985). The IC_{50} was $29 \, \mu M$ for placental aromatase. However, its activity relative to AG was not reported.

16.3.2 Selective inhibitors

In the last few years, there has been increasing interest in active-site-directed enzyme inhibitors. Inhibitors of this type are more specific for the enzyme and many are useful tools for investigating the enzyme's active site. They are likely to be valuable as drugs because of their selectivity and also because their interaction at the active site usually causes inactivation or irreversible inhibition of the enzyme; thus, they may have long-lasting effects *in vivo* (Sjoerdsma 1981).

16.3.2.1 *3β-hydroxysteroid dehydrogenase*

11α-bromoacetoxyprogesterone is an alkylating analogue of progesterone that behaves as an irreversible active-site-directed inhibitor of 3β-hydroxysteroid dehydrogenase (3-HSD) (Chikhaoui *et al.* 1983). 4-ethenylidene steroids have also been reported as inactivators of this enzyme. An advantage of blockade at the 3β-hydroxy-dehydrogenase step is that relatively innocuous precursors accumulate, while inhibition at later stages of steroidogenesis may result in the accumulation of or shunting to physiologically active intermediates. Thus, inhibition of 3-HSD will impair the production of cortisol by the zona fasciculata and of aldosterone by the zona glomerulosa. At the clinical level, trilostane (Potts *et al.* 1978) is effective in the treatment of primary aldosteronism, in reversing diuretic-induces hypokalaemia (Kem *et al.* 1980), in decreasing blood pressure in some patients with low renin hypertension (Liddle *et al.* 1976), and is useful in the treatment of Cushing's syndrome (Komanicky *et al.* 1978). Several methylated derivatives have increased ovarian/placental activity but decreased adrenal inhibition (Christiansen *et al.* 1984).

16.3.2.2 *Δ⁵-3-ketosteroid isomerase*

Studies on the active site of the bacterial Δ^5-3-ketosteroid isomerase have been carried out by Pollack and co-workers (Bevans *et al.* 1980), using two active-site-directed irreversible inhibitors, spiro-17β-oxiranyl-Δ^4-androstene-3-one(4β) and spiro-17β-oxiranyl oestra-1,3,5(10),6,8-pentaone-3-ol(5β), indicating two modes of binding of the steroid enzyme complexes. Other inhibitors have been reported by Balasubramanian and Robinson (1981) and Balasubramanian *et al.* (1982).

16.3.2.3 *17β-oestradiol and 20α-hydroxysteroid dehydrogenase*

In studies utilizing analogues of the 17β-propynyl-substituted progestin, Tobias *et al.* (1982) found that these inhibitors simultaneously inactivated both 17β-oestradiol dehydrogenase and 20α-hydroxysteroid dehydrogenase, which suggests bifunctional activity of a single enzyme-active site.

16.3.2.4 *5α-reductase*

5α-reductase converts testosterone to dihydrotestosterone (DHT), the bioactive androgen. This enzyme therefore plays a key role in growth regulation of the

prostate (Wilson, 1972; Sandberg, 1975; Isaacs and Coffey, 1979), and is considered a possible target site for therapeutic agents against prostatic cancer.
4-methyl-4-aza steroids are potent inhibitors of 5α-reductase. As an inhibitor of
prostatic tumour 5α-reductase, 17β-N,N-diethylcarbamoyl-4-methyl-aza-5α-
androstan-3-one (4-MA) is as effective as sodium 4-methyl-3-oxo-4-aza-5α-
pregnane-20(s)-carboxylate (4-MAPC). Inhibition of 5α-reductase activity by 4-
MAPC, but not by 4-MA, was accompanied by concomitant stimulation of 17β-
oxidation of testosterone. The effect of this would be to increase Δ^4-androstene-
dione, which presumably has a much weaker biological action on hormone-
dependent prostate growth (Kadohama et al. 1984). Other studies indicate that
4-MA may not be highly specific as it also inhibits 3-HSD and isomerase activity
(Cooke and Robaire 1986).

16.3.3 Aromatase inhibitors

Selective inhibitors of oestrogen biosynthesis may have the widest clinical
application of all steroid inhibitors, since oestrogen has a role in a number of
diseases. Because aromatization is unique in steroid biosynthesis, we envisaged
that inhibitors could be identified that would be more selective for aromatase
than for other steroid hydroxylases. Furthermore, aromatization is the last in
the series of steps in the biosynthetic progression from cholesterol to the
oestrogens. Therefore, blockade of this enzyme would not cause deprivation of
other essential steroids. Our rationale for the clinical use of aromatase inhibitors
is that compounds interacting with the aromatizing enzyme in all oestrogen-
synthesizing tissues could provide both selective and effective inhibition of
oestrogen production.

   In breast cancer, about 60 per cent of pre-menopausal and 75 per cent of post-
menopausal patients have hormone-dependent carcinomas (McGuire 1980), as
identified by the presence of oestrogen receptors (ER) in tumour biopsies.
Deprivation of oestrogen in such patients with metastatic disease results in
tumour regression that is objectively quantifiable and may often be long-lasting.

   Although oestrogens are produced primarily by the ovaries of young women,
after the menopause aromatization in extragonadal tissues (MacDonald et al.
1967; Longcope et al. 1978), such as fat and muscle, increases (Longcope 1971;
Hemsell et al. 1974) and becomes the main source of oestrogens. Some breast
tumours are reported to aromatize (Miller and Forrest 1974; Valera and Dao
1978; Abdul-Hajj et al. 1979) or produce oestrogens locally from oestrone
sulphate (Tseng et al. 1983; Santner et al. 1984). Even after hypophysectomy or
adrenalectomy, patients may continue to produce oestrogens in significant
amounts (Worgul et al. 1982). Therefore, a systemic method of treatment with
aromatase inhibitors could be a selective and effective means of lowering
oestrogen production from all sources and could be less traumatic than surgical
methods. Cytotoxic agents have not been found to be highly effective or to cure
breast cancer. Usually, oestrogen-controlling treatments are much less toxic

than chemotherapy and could be used to maximum effect in adjuvant therapy when the number of tumour cells is low. In addition, they can be administered for long periods and may be useful in combination therapy regimens. Recent evidence indicates that patients with oestrogen-receptor-positive tumours have a better prognosis and longer disease-free intervals. Thus, development of new oestrogen-controlling strategies for breast cancer is appropriate.

Endometrial cancer is highly correlated with obesity (Wynder *et al.* 1966). Not only does this increase the risk of surgery for these patients, but also the production of peripherally formed oestrogen is enhanced (Siiteri 1978). Treatment with aromatase inhibitors may be beneficial for this type of cancer also.

Endometriosis, idiopathic oligospermia, and gynaecomastia may be ameliorated by aromatase inhibitors. A number of recent reports also indicate that oestrogens are increased in benign prostatic hypertrophy and prostatic cancer. Studies are under investigation to determine whether inhibition of oestrogen production would be effective in these conditions.

Selective inhibition occurs with compounds that interfere with androgen aromatization on binding to the enzyme. In 1973, our group published the first report of inhibitors of this type as part of our programme to develop aromatase inhibitors for application to breast cancer treatment and contraception (Schwarzel *et al.* 1973). These studies are described below.

16.3.3.1 In vitro *studies with aromatase inhibitors*

Candidate inhibitors were evaluated by comparing the extent of aromatization in incubations of microsomes from aromatase-containing tissues. The conversion of androstenedione to oestrogen by the microsomal preparation can easily be estimated by measuring the loss of tritium from the C-1β and C-2β positions (Brodie *et al.* 1969) during aromatization of $[1,2^3H(70$ per cent $\beta)]$androstenedione. The tritium released as ^3H_2O is measured in the incubation medium after extraction of steroids by organic solvent (Thompson and Siiteri 1974a). Human placental microsomes were used initially as the source of aromatase (Schwarzel *et al.* 1973) and later a highly active microsomal preparation was developed from ovaries of rats stimulated with pregnant mares' serum gonadotropin (PMSG) (Brodie *et al.* 1976). Our studies of the two microsomal preparations suggest that subtle differences exist between the enzymes from the two sources. The ovarian microsomal preparation was considered more appropriate for predicting *in vivo* activity in the rat.

The inhibitors with greatest activity in both systems are 4-hydroxyandrostene-3,17-dione (4-OHA; Brodie *et al.* 1977), 4-acetoxyandrostene-3,17-dione (4-acetoxyA; Brodie *et al.* 1979), 1,4,6-androstatriene-3,17-dione (ATD), and 4-androstene-3,6,17-trione(A-trione) (Schwarzel *et al.* 1973; Brodie *et al.* 1982a). 4-OHA has been shown to have activity against human ovarian aromatase in granulosa cell cultures (Koos *et al.* 1986). All show Lineweaver–Burke plots typical of competitive inhibition (Brodie *et al.* 1977, 1982), which occurs rapidly in the presence of both substrate (androstenedione) and inhibitor. 4-

OHA, 4-acetoxy-A (Brodie *et al.* 1981; Covey and Hood 1981) ATD, and A-trione (Brodie *et al.* 1982b; Covey and Hood 1982) also cause slower time-dependent loss of enzyme activity which follows pseudo first-order kinetics in microsomes preincubated in the absence of substrate but in the presence of NADPH (Fig. 16.2). There was no loss of activity without added cofactors. Although 4-OHA caused the most rapid inactivation, the loss of activity with all three compounds was 10-fold slower in rat ovarian microsomes than in the placental system. Aromatase activity was not regained after washed micros-omes, preincubated with 4-OHA, had been allowed to stand for 18 h at 0°C followed by charcoal treatment and exhaustive washing to remove any residual inhibitor. These findings suggest that 4-OHA causes long-term inactivation (or irreversible inhibition) of aromatase.

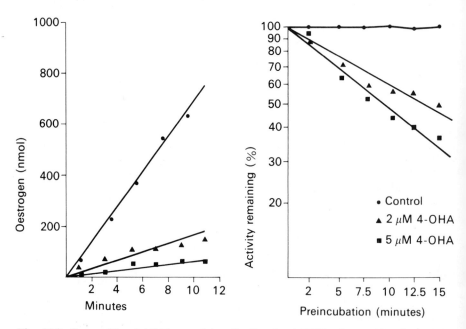

Fig. 16.2. Competitive inhibition and inactivation by 4-OHA of aromatase in human placental microsomes. Left panel shows competitive inhibition by 4-OHA in the presence of androstenedione. Right panel shows inactivation by preincubation of microsomes with 1 mM NADPH and 4-OHA at 37°C. After removal of 4-OHA with charcoal, aromatase activity was estimated from $[^3H_2O]$ released from incubation with $[1,2^3H]$-androstenedione for 30 min (Brodie *et al.* 1983).

Studies of structure–activity relationships indicate that $C_{19}17$-ketosteroids are the most potent inhibitors. Besides C-4, activity is also associated with substitution at a number of other sites. For example, 16α-bromoandrogens (reported by Bellino *et al.* 1976), 7-*p*-aminophenylthioandrostenedione (synthesized by Brueggermeier *et al.* 1978), and 1-methyl-1,4-androstadiene-3,17-dione (Henderson *et al.* 1986) are potent aromatase inhibitors but have not been studied in detail *in vivo*. Testololactone, a compound that has been used for breast cancer treatment for over 20 years (Segaloff *et al.* 1962) and has been subsequently reported to be an aromatase inhibitor (Siiteri and Thompson 1975) was found recently to cause aromatase inactivation, probably by virtue of the C-1 double bond (Johnston and Metcalf 1984). However, it has rather weak activity ($K_i = 750$ μM, $t_{1/2} = 21$ min) in placental microsomes compared to the above compounds (Johnston and Metcalf 1984).

Aromatase inactivation has also been reported to occur with the 10-propargyl analogue of androstenedione [10-(2-propynyl)oestr-4-ene-3,17-dione] in the placental system (Covey *et al.* 1981; Metcalf *et al.* 1981) and was confirmed by us in both the placental and rat ovarian systems (unpublished observations). Aromatase is inhibited approximately four times faster by 4-OHA than by the 10-propargyl analogue in *in vitro* preparations. On the other hand, the latter has a K_i of 4.5 nM with placental microsomes and has two to three times greater affinity for the active site of the enzyme than 4-OHA ($K_i = 10.2$ nM) (Johnston and Metcalf 1984). The 10-propargyl compound was designed to inactivate aromatase by binding covalently to the enzyme. Other inhibitors synthesized by these investigators (Johnston *et al.* 1984; Marcotte and Robinson 1983) are allenes, which probably lead to allene oxide intermediates via oxygen insertion by aromatase. These intermediates could alkylate either to the prosthetic haem or the surrounding enzymic protein, causing inactivation of the enzyme (Walsh 1982). Although the precise mechanisms by which 4-OHA, 4-acetoxyA, and ATD inactivate aromatase are unknown at present, their kinetics are similar to those of the allene compounds and suggest that they are mechanism-based enzyme inactivators.

16.3.3.2 In vivo *actions of aromatase inhibitors in animal models*

(a) *Inhibition of ovarian oestrogen secretion*
4-OHA, 4-acetoxyA, and ATD were evaluated further to determine whether they had activity against ovarian oestrogen biosynthesis *in vivo*. These studies were carried out in rats in which ovarian aromatase activity was stimulated by first priming the animals with PMSG over 11 days in order to overide hormone fluctuations during the oestrus cycle and maintain a constant oestrogen secretion. On day 12, the animals were injected with 4-OHA or ATD. At various times after injection, blood was first collected from the ovarian vein, and then microsomes were prepared from the ovaries. Aromatase activity in the ovarian microsomes was reduced to 20 per cent of the initial value within 8 h of injection and remained low for 24 h following injection of ATD and for 48 h following injection of 4-OHA. Oestrogen concentrations in the ovarian vein samples were also reduced by inhibitor treatment and remained low for about the same length

of time as aromatase activity. These findings suggest that enzyme inactivation is occurring in the ovary *in vivo* with both ATD (Brodie *et al.* 1982b) and 4-OHA (Brodie *et al.* 1981), since activity could not be increased by procedures designed to remove unbound 4-OHA.

In normal cycling rats, ovarian aromatase activity and oestrogen secretion during pro-oestrus are also inhibited markedly (at least 85 per cent) 3 h after an injection of 4-OHA, ATD, and 4-acetoxyA (Brodie *et al.* 1982b). Similar results have been obtained using PMSG-primed rats with the 10-propargyl compound (Puett *et al.* 1987).

(b) *Antitumour activity of aromatase inhibitors in the*
    7,12-dimethylbenz(a)anthracene (DMBA)-induced mammary
    carcinoma model

The DMBA-induced carcinoma model has been used extensively to study hormone-dependent mammary tumours. Although other hormones may be involved, the tumours are dependent on ovarian production of oestrogen. In this regard, the model is comparable to the pre-menopausal breast cancer patient. As shown in Fig. 16.3, daily injections of 4-OHA (50 mg kg^{-1} day^{-1}) caused

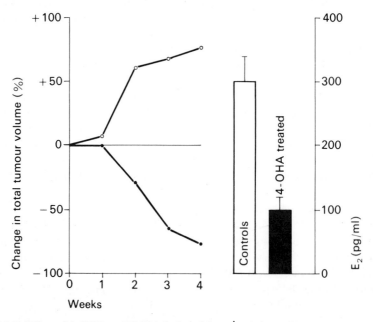

Fig. 16.3. Effect of 4-OHA on DMBA-induced, hormone-dependent mammary tumours of the rat. Key: (●) percentage change in total volume of thirteen tumours on six rats injected with 4-OHA (50 mg kg^{-1} day^{-1}) twice daily for four weeks; (○) tumours on five control rats injected twice daily with vehicle. At the end of treatment, blood was collected from each rat by ovarian vein cannulation for oestradiol (E$_2$) assay; controls were sampled during dioestrus (Brodie *et al.* 1984).

marked tumour regression (Brodie *et al.* 1977). Similiar results were obtained with 4-acetoxyA, ATD (Brodie *et al.* 1979, 1982a) and the 10-propargyl compound (Puett *et al.* 1987). After 4 weeks of 4-OHA treatment, the total tumour volume in the experimental group was reduced by about 80 per cent of the initial volume. At the end of 4 weeks of treatment, ovarian aromatase activity and oestrogen secretion were both markedly inhibited compared to controls.

(c) Inhibition of peripheral aromatization

Since extra-ovarian aromatization is an important source of oestrogens in post-menopausal breast cancer patients, we also studied the effects of 4-OHA and 4-acetoxyA on peripheral aromatase by measuring the conversion of androstene-dione to oestrone during constant infusion of [7-^{3}H]androstenedione and [4-^{14}C]oestrone. Male rhesus monkeys were used, since most of the circulating oestrogen in the male is of extragonadal origin. Each animal was infused under control conditions and during inhibitor treatment. 4-OHA was injected 18 h and then 3 h before infusion commenced. Peripheral aromatization was found to be undetectable in three of the four monkeys treated with 4-OHA and markedly reduced in the fourth animal. Treatment of two monkeys with 4-acetoxyA implants was also effective in reducing peripheral aromatization (Brodie and Longcope 1980).

(d) Clinical studies with aromatase inhibitors

As already discussed, aminoglutethimide has now been used in a number of clinical trials and investigations. These have been reviewed by Santen and colleagues (Santen *et al.* 1981; Santen and Brodie 1982). AG is effective in post-menopausal breast cancer patients and remission occurs in 40 per cent of unselected patients. The compound is active in some patients who have relapsed from tamoxifen, indicating that it can be used in addition to tamoxifen as well as an alternative treatment. Although somnolence is a side-effect of AG, recent studies with low dose AG (500 mg per day) indicate it to be as effective as the higher dose (1g per day) and better tolerated (Bonneterre *et al.* 1984).

Because of its greater potency *in vitro*, high efficacy in animal models and ease of synthesis, 4-OHA was chosen for the first clinical evaluation with a selective aromatase inhibitor (Coombes *et al.* 1984). All patients were post-menopausal women with advanced metastatic disease. A group of 52 patients received 500 mg 4-OHA i.m. weekly and 31 patients received 250 mg 4-OHA orally each day for the first month, then 500 mg daily thereafter (Goss *et al.* 1986). Figure 16.4 shows the decline in oestradiol levels following injection of 4-OHA.

Overall evaluation of 52 patients (Table 16.1) revealed that 14 (27 per cent) had objective complete (4) or partial (10) responses to treatment. In 10 (19 per cent) patients, the disease stabilized for at least 8 weeks on therapy, whereas the disease progressed in 28 (54 per cent) patients. Twenty-two patients were oestrogen-receptor (ER) positive, six of whom responded to 4-OHA, three had static disease, and 13 experienced progression of the disease. Three patients had

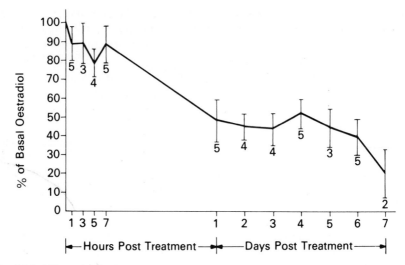

Fig. 16.4. Effect of a single dose of 500 mg 4-OHA on plasma oestradiol in five patients with breast cancer. The basal oestradiol for each patient was calculated by averaging seven pre-treatment values, and the post-treatment results were calculated as the percentage of the baseline. The mean of the percentage of baseline for the five patients is shown. Basal samples were obtained at four time points identical to those of samples obtained one day post-treatment. Results are shown as mean $\pm$ SD (Coombes *et al.* 1984).

ER negative tumours; one responded and two had progressive disease. Twenty-four patients had previously responded to endocrine therapy and seven of these responded to 4-OHA, while in three the disease stabilized. Responses seemed to occur most often in soft tissue and lymph nodes affected by breast cancer, with only one response in a visceral site. There were no responses in liver metastases of 11 patients affected. Four of 35 (11 per cent) patients with skeletal metastases responded, although bone pain was alleviated in five out of eight patients with this symptom.

There were few side-effects of treatment, the most significant being sterile abcesses and pain at the site of injection in about 10 per cent of patients receiving 500 mg 4-OHA i.m.

Eight (26 per cent) of 31 patients receiving oral 4-OHA showed evidence of partial response and 4 (13 per cent) showed stabilization of disease.

The results indicate that this aromatase inhibitor reduces plasma oestradiol levels and is effective in 50 per cent of patients who had previously relapsed during other endocrine therapies. In addition, 29 per cent of the patients responding to 4-OHA injections had not responded to prior tamoxifen treatment. Further studies are required to determine the most effective dose of 4-OHA and to compare its efficacy with current standard treatments.

In conclusion, a number of new compounds are now becoming available that are potent selective inhibitors of aromatase and of other steroidogenic enzymes.

Table 16.1 Response to 4-hydroxyandrostenedione according to oestrogen receptor status and previous response to endocrine therapy

	Response to 4-OHA				
	CR	PR	NC	PD	NA
Overall response	4	10	10	28	6
	14				
ER status					
positive	1	5	3	13	2
negative	0	1	0	2	0
unknown	3	4	7	13	4
Previous response to endocrine therapy					
Responders	2	5	3	14	3
Non-responders	2	2	3	9	0
No previous therapy or response not assessable	0	3	4	5	3

CR = complete response; PR = partial response; NC = no change; PD = progressive disease; NA = not assessable.

Fourteen patients responded to 4-OHA. Only one responder was known to have an ER-negative tumour. Four patients who had failed to respond to other therapies (tamoxifen in all cases) responded to 4-OHA.

These inhibitors could provide important contributions to the management of several hormone-dependent conditions.

*This chapter is dedicated to the memory of Dr. W. R. Nes who was my teacher, colleague, and friend.

References

Abdul-Hajj, Y. J., Iverson, R., and Kiang, D. T. (1979). Aromatization of androgens by human breast cancer. *Steroids*, **33**, 205–22.

Akhtar, M., Calder, M. R., Corina, D. L., and Wright, J. N. (1982). Mechanistic studies on C-19 demethylation in estrogen biosynthesis. *Biochem. J.*, 201, 569–80.

Balasubramanian, V. and Robinson, C. H. (1981). Irreversible inactivation of mammalian delta 5-3 beta-hydroxysteroid dehydrogenases by 5,10-secosteroids. Enzymatic oxidation of allenic alcohols to the corresponding allenic ketones. *Biochem. Biophys. Res. Commun.*, **101**, 495–501.

Balasubramanian, V., McDermott I. R., and Robinson C. H. (1982). 4-ethenylidene steroids as mechanism-based inactivators of 3β beta-hydroxysteroid dehydrogenases. *Steroids*, **40**, 109–19.

Bellino, N. F. L., Gilano, S. S. H., Eng, S. S., Osawa, Y., and Duax, W. L. (1976). Active-site inactivation of aromatase from human placental microsomes by brominated androgen derivatives. *Biochemistry*, **15**, 4730–6.

Bevins, C. L., Kayser R. H., Pollack R. M., Ekiko D. B., and Sadoff, S. (1980). Irreversible active-site-directed inhibition of delta 5-3-ketosteroid isomerase by steroidal 17-beta-oxiranes. Evidence for two modes of binding in steroid–enzyme complexes. *Biochem. Biophys. Res. Commun.*, **95**, 1131–7.

Bonneterre, J., Cappelacre, R., Mauriac, A., Chauvergne, J., Sevin, O., Rouesse, J., Metz, R. P. Arman, J. P., Fargeot, P., Tubiana, M., Clavel, R., Matieu, F., Gary-Bobo, J., and Coppens, H. (1984). Low doze aminoglutethimide in advanced breast cancer—preliminary report of a multicentre comparative trial. In *Aminoglutethimide as an aromatase inhibitor in the treatment of cancer* (ed. G. A. Nagel and R. H. Santen), pp. 104–8. Huber, Vienna.

Brodie, A. M. H. and Longcope, C. (1980). Inhibition of peripheral aromatization by aromatase inhibitors, 4-hydroxy and 4-acetoxy-androstenedione. *Endocrinology*, **106**, 19–21.

Brodie, A. M. H., Brodie, H. J., Garrett, W. M., Hendrickson, J. R., Marsh, D. A., and Tsai-Morris, C. H. (1982a). The effects of aromatase inhibitor 1,4,6-androstatriendione (ATD) on DMBA-induced mammary tumors in the rat and its mechanism of action *in vivo*. *Biochem. Pharmacol.*, **31**, 2017–23.

Brodie, A. M. H., Garrett, W. M., Hendrickson, J. R., and Tsai-Morris, C. H. (1982b). Effects of 4-hydroxyandrostenedione and other compounds in the DMBA breast carcinoma model. *Cancer Rés. Suppl.*, **42**, 3360s–4s.

Brodie, A. M. H., Garrett, W. M., Hendrickson, J. R., Tsai-Morris, C. H., Marcotte, P. A., and Robinson, C. H. (1981). Inactivation of aromatase *in vitro* by 4-hydroxyandrostenedione and 4-acetoxyandrostenedione and sustained effects *in vivo*. *Steroids*, **38**, 693–701.

Brodie, A. M. H., Garrett, W. M., Hendrickson, J. R., Tsai-Morris, C. H., and Williams, J. G. (1983). Aromatase inhibitors, Their pharmacology and application. *J. Steroid Biochem.*, **19**, 53–8.

Brodie, A. M. H., Garrett, W. M., Hendrickson, J. R., Tsai-Morris, C. H., and Wing, L. C. (1984). Aromatase inhibition; a new perspective in the treatment of breast cancers. In *Aminoglutethimide as an aromatase inhibitor on the treatment of cancer.* (ed G. A., Nagel and R. J. Santen), Vienna.

Brodie, A. M. H., Marsh, D. A., and Brodie, H. J. (1979). Aromatase inhibitors, IV. Regression of hormone-dependent, mammary tumors in the rat with 4-acetoxyandrostene-3,17-dione, *J. Steroid Biochem.*, **10**, 423–9.

Brodie, A. M. H., Schwarzel, W. C., and Brodie, H. J. (1976). Studies on the mechanism of estrogen biosynthesis in the rat ovary. *Steroid Biochem.*, **7**, 787–93.

Brodie, A. M. H., Schwarzel, W. C., Shaikh, A. A., and Brodie, H. J. (1977). The effect of an aromatase inhibitor, 4-hydroxy-4-androstene-3,17-dione, on estrogen-dependent processes in reproduction and breast cancer. *Endocrinology*, **10**, 1884–95.

Brodie, H. J., Kripalani, K. J., and Possanza, G. (1969). Studies on the mechanisms of estrogen biosynthesis. VI. The stereochemistry of hydrogen elimination of C-2 during aromatization. *J. Am. Chem. Soc.*, **91**, 1241–2.

Brueggermeier, R. W., Floyd, E. E., and Counsell, R. E. (1978). Synthesis and biochemical evaluation of inhibitors of estrogen biosynthesis. *J. Med. Chem.*, **21**, 1007–11.

Caspi, E., Wicha, J., Arunachalam, T., Nelson, P., and Spiteller, G. (1984). Estrogen biosynthesis. Concerning the obligatory intermediacy of 2β-hydroxy-10β-formylandrostene-4-ene-3,17-dione. *J. Am. Chem. Soc.*, **106**, 7282–3.

Chakraborty, J., Hopkins, R., and Parke, D. V. (1972). Inhibition studies in the aromatization of androstenedione by human placental microsome preparations. *Biochem. J.*, **130**, 190.

Chikhaoui, Y., Boussionux A. M., Nicolas, J. C., Descomps, B., and Crastes de Paulet, A. (1983). Active site-directed irreversible inhibition of 3-beta-hydroxysteroid dehydrogenase from human placenta. *J. Steroid Biochem.*, **19**, 1213–17.

Christiansen, R. G., Neumann, H. C., Salvador, U. J., Bell, M. R., Schane, H. P. Jr., Creange, J. E., Potts, G. O., and Anzalone, A. J. (1984). Steroidogenesis inhibitors. 1. Adrenal inhibitor and interceptive activity of Trilostane and related compounds. *J. Med. Chem.*, **27**, 928–31.

Cooke, G. M. and Robaire, B. (1986). The effects of diethyl-4-methyl-3-oxo-4-aza-5α-androstane-17β-carboxamide (4-MA) and (4R)-5,10-seco-19-norpregna-4,5-diene-3,10,20-trione (SECO) on androgen biosynthesis in the rat testis and epididymis. *J. Steroid Biochem.*, **24**, 877–86.

Coombes, R. C., Goss, P., Dowsett, M., Gazet, J. C., and Brodie, A. M. H. (1984). 4-Hydroxyandrostenedione treatment of postmenopausal patients with advanced breast cancer. *Lancet*, **ii**, 1237–9.

Corvol, P., Michaud, A., Menard, J., Freifeld, M., and Mahoudeau, J. (1975). Antiandrogenic effect of spirolactones: mechanism of action. *Endocrinology*, **97**, 52–8.

Covey, D. F. and Hood, W. F. (1981). Enzyme generated intermediates derived from 4-androstene-3,6,17-dione and 1,4,6-androstatriene-3,17,-dione cause a time-dependent decrease in human placental aromatase activity. *Endocrinology*, **108**, 1597–9.

Covey, D. F. and Hood., W. F. (1982). Aromatase enzyme catalysis is involved in the potent inhibition of estrogen biosynthesis caused by 4-acetoxy and 4-hydroxyandrostenedione. *Mol. Pharmacol*, **21**, 173–80.

Covey, D. F., Hood, W. F., and Parikh, V. D. (1981). 10β-propynyl-substituted steroids; mechanism-based enzyme-activated irreversible inhibitors of estrogen biosynthesis. *J. Biol. Chem.*, **256**, 1076–9.

Donckier, J., Burrin, J. M., Ramsay, I. D., and Joplin, G. F. (1986). Successful control of Cushing's disease in the elderly with long term metyrapone. *Postgrad. Med. J.*, **62**, 727–30.

Duax, W. L., Weeks, C. M., and Rohren, D. C. (1976). Crystal structure of steroids: molecular and biological function. *Recent Prog. Horm. Res.*, **32**, 81–116.

Evans, C. T., Ledesma, D. B., Schulz, T. Z., Simpson, E. R., and Mendelson, C. R. (1986). Isolation and characterization of a complementary DNA specific for human aromatase-system, cytochrome P-450 mRNA. *J. Biol. Chem.*, **83**, 6387–91.

Fishman, J. and Guzik, H. (1969). Stereochemistry of estrogen biosynthesis. *J. Am. Chem. Soc.*, **91**, 2805–6.

Goldman, A. S., Yakovac, W. C., and Bongiovanni, A. M. (1965). Persistent effects of a synthetic androstene derivative on activities of 3β-hydroxysteroid dehydrogenase and glucose-6-phosphate dehydrogenase in rats. *Endocrinology*, **77**, 1105–18.

Goss, P. E., Powles, T. J., Dowsett, M., Brodie A. M. H., and Coombes R. C. (1986). Treatment of advanced postmenopausal breast cancer with aromatase inhibitor, 4-hydroxyandrostenedione-Phase II report. *Cancer Res.*, **46**, 4823–6.

Goto, J. and Fishman, J. (1977). Participation of a nonenzyme transformation in the biosynthesis of estrogen from androgens. *Science*, **80**, 195–6.

Hahn, E. F. and Fishman, J. (1984). Immunological probe of estrogen biosynthesis. *J. Biol. Chem.*, **259**, 1689–94.

Heard, R. D. H., Jellink, P. H., and O'Donnell, V. J. (1955). Biogenesis of the estrogens: The conversion of testosterone-4^{14}C to estrogen in the pregnant mare. *Endocrinology*, **57**, 200–4.

Hemsell, D. L., Grodin, M. M., Brenner, P. F., Siitri, P. K., and MacDonald, P. C. (1974). Plasma precurors of estrogen. II. Correlation of the extent of conversion of plasma androstenedione to estrone with age. *J. Clin. Endocrinol. Metab.*, **38**, 476–9.

Henderson, D., Habenicht, U.-F., Nishino, Y., Kerb, U. L., and Eletreby, M. F. (1986). Aromatase inhibitors and benign prostatic hyperplasia. *J. Steroid Biochem.*, **25**, 867.

Hirsch, K. S. and Clemens, J. A. (1985). Effects of the non-steroidal aromatase inhibitor, LY 56110, on estrogen-dependent processes in the rat. 67th Endocrine Society Meeting, Baltimore, Abstract No. 447.

Isaacs, J. T. and Coffey, D. S. (1979). Androgenic control of prostatic growth regulation of steroid levels. UICC Tecnhical Reports Series, **48**, pp. 93–111.

Johnston, J. O. and Metcalf, B. W. (1984). Aromatase: a target enzyme in breast cancer In *Novel approaches to cancer chemotherapy* (ed. P. Sunkava), pp. 307–328. Academic Press, London.

Johnston, J. O., Wright, C. L. and Metcalf, B. W. (1984). Biochemical and endocrine properties of a mechanism based inhibitor of aromatase. *Endocrinology*, **115**, 776–85.

Kadohama, N., Carr, J. P., Murphy, G. P., and Sandberg, A. A. (1984). Selective inhibitor of prostatic tumor 5α-reductase by a 4-methyl-4-aza-steroid. *Cancer Res.*, **44**, 4947–54.

Kellis, J. T. and Vickery, L. E. (1984). Inhibition of estrogen synthetase (aromatase) by 4-cyclohexylaniline. *Endocrinology*, **114**, 2128–37.

Kem, D. C., Higgins, J. R., and Anh, N. (1980). The effect of adrenal blockade upon induced hypokalemia. 62nd Endocrine Society Meeting, Washington, DC, Abstract No. 496.

Komanicky, P., Spark, R. F., and Melby, J. C. (1978). Treatment of Cushing's Syndrome with trilostane (WIN 24 540), an inhibitor of adrenal steroid biosynthesis. *J. Clin. Endocrinol. Metab.*, **47**, 1042–51.

Koos, R. D., Lemaire, W. J., Hung, T. T., and Brodie, A. M. H. (1986). Effect of 4-hydroxyandrostenedione on aromatase activity in granulosa cells from preovulatory follicles of rats, rabbits and humans. *Steroids*, **45**, 143–50.

Liddle, G. W., Hollifield, J. W., Slaton, P. E., and Wilson, H. M. (1976). Effects of various adrenal inhibitors in low-renin essential hypertension. *J. Steroid Biochem.*, **7**, 937–40.

Longcope, C. (1971). Metabolic clearance and blood production rates of estrogen in postmenopausal women. *Am. J. Obstet. Gynecol.*, **111**, 778–1971.

Longcope, C., Pratt, J. H., Schneider, S. H., and Fineberg, S. E. (1978). Aromatization of androgens by muscle and adipose tissue *in vivo*. *J. Clin. Endocrinol. Metab.*, **46**, 146–52.

MacDonald, P. D., Rombaut, R. P. and Siiteri, P. K. (1967). Plasma precursors of estrogen. I. Extent of conversion of plasma Δ^4-androstenedione to estrone in normal males and nonpregnant normal, castrate and adrenalectomized females. *J. Clin. Endocrinol. Metab.*, **27**, 1103–11.

Marcotte, P. A. and Robinson, C. H. (1983). Synthesis and Evaluation of 10 β-substituted 4-estrene-3,17-diones as inhibitors of human placental microsomal aromatase. *Steroids*, **39**, 325–44.

Mason, J. I., Murray, B. A., Olcott, M., and Sheets, J. J. (1985). Imidazole antimycotics, inhibitors of steroid aromatase. *Biochem. Pharmacol.*, **34**, 1087–92.

McGuire, W. L. (1980). An update on estrogen and progesterone receptors in prognosis for primary and advanced breast cancer. In *Hormones and cancer* (ed. S. Iacobelli, R. J. B. King, H. R. Lidner, and M. E. Lippman), Vol. 15, pp. 337–43. Raven, New York.

McKerns, K. W. (1969). Studies on the regulation of ovarian function by gonadotropins. In: *The gonads*, (ed. K. W. McKerns), pp. 137–173. Appleton-Century-Crofts, New York.

Menard, R. H., Stripp, B., and Gillette, J. R. (1974). Spironolactone and testicular cytochrome P_{450}: decreased testosterone formation in several species and changes in hepatic drug metabolism. *Endocrinology*, **94**, 1628–36.

Mendelson, C. R., Wright, E. E., Evans, C. T., Porter, J. C., and Simpson, E. R. (1985). Preparation and characterization of polyclonal and monoclonal antibodies against human aromatase cytochrome P-450 (P-450$_{AROm}$) and their use in its purification. *Arch. Biochem. Biophys.*, **243**, 480–91.

Metcalf, B. E., Wright, C. L., Burkhart, J. P., and Johnston, J. O. (1981). Substrate-induced inactivation of aromatase by allenic and acetylenic steroids. *J. Am. Chem. Soc.*, **103**, 3221–2.

Miller, W. R. and Forrest, A. P. M. (1974). Oestradiol synthesis by a human breast carcinoma. *Lancet*, **ii**, 866–8.

Morato, T., Hayano, M., Dorfman, R. I., and Axelrod, L. R. (1962). The Intermediate steps in the biosynthesis of estrogens from androgens. *Biochem. Biophys. Res. Commun.*, **6**, 334–8.

Nakajin, S., Shinoda, M., Haniu, M., Shively, J. E., and Hall, P. F. (1984). C_{21} Steroid side chain cleavage enzyme from porcine adrenal microsomes. Purification and characterization of the 17α-hydroxylase/$C_{17,20}$-lyase cytochrome P-450. *J. Biol. Chem.*, **259**, 3971–6.

Nes, W. R., and McKean, M. L. (1977). *Biochemistry of steroids and other isopentenoids*. University Park Press, Baltimore.

Neville, M. A. and Engel, L. L. (1968). Inhibition of α- and β-hydroxysteroid dehydrogenases and steroid isomerases by substrate analogues. *J. Clin. Endocrinol.*, **28**, 49–60.

Potts, G. O., Creange, J. E., Harding, H. R, and Schane, H. P. (1978). Trilostane, an orally-active inhibitor of steroid biosynthesis. *Steroids*, **32**, 257–67.

Puett, D., Brandt, M., Covey, D. F., and Zimniski, S. J. (1986). Characterization of a potent inhibitor of aromatase: inhibition of the rat ovarian enzyme and regression of estrogen-dependent mammary tumors by 10-propargylestr-4-ene. In *Endocrinology and malignancy: basic and clinical issues* (ed. E. E. Baulieu, S. Iarobelli, and W. L. McGuire), pp. 278–89. Parthanon Publishing, Cornforth, UK.

Ryan, K. J. and Smith, O. W. (1961). Biogenesis of estrogen by the human ovary. *J. Biol. Chem.*, **236**, 705–9.

Sandberg, A. A. (1975). Potential test system for chemotherapeutic agents against prostatic cancer. *Vitam. Horm.*, **33**, 155–88.

Santen, R. J. and Brodie, A. M. H. (1982). Suppression of estrogen production as treatment of breast carcinoma: pharmacological and clinical studies with aromatase inhibitors. In *Clinics in oncology*, (ed. B. J. A. Furr), Vol. 1, pp. 77–130. Saunders, London.

Santen, R. J., Worgul, T. J., Samojlik, E., Interrante, A., Boucher, A. E., Lipton, A., Harvey, H. A., White, D. S., Smart, E., Cox, C., and Wells, S. S. (1981). Randomized trial comparing surgical adrenalectomy with aminoglutethimide plus hydrocortisone in women with advanced breast carcinoma. *New Engl. J. Med.*, **305**, 545–51.

Santner, S. J., Feil, P. D., and Santen, R. J. (1984). In situ estrogen production via the estrone sulfate pathway in breast tumors: relative importance versus the aromatase pathway. *J. Clin. Endocrinol. Metab.*, **59**, 29–33.

Schwarzel, W. C., Kruggel, W., and Brodie, H. J. (1973). Studies on the mechanism of estrogen biosynthesis. VII. The development of inhibitors of the enzyme system in human placenta. *Endocrinology*, **92**, 866–80.

Segaloff, A., Weeth, J. B., Meyer, K. K., Rongone, E. L., and Cunningham, G. (1962). Hormonal therapy in cancer of the breast XIX. Effect of oral administration of Δ^1-testololactone on clinical course and hormonal excretions. *Cancer*, **15**, 633–5.

Siiteri, P. K. (1978). Steroid hormones and endometrial cancer. *Cancer Res.*, **38**, 4360–6.

Siiteri, P. K. and Thompson, E. A. (1975). Studies of human placental aromatase. *J. Steroid. Biochem.* **6**, 317–22.

Sjoerdsma, A. (1981). Suicide inhibitors as potential drugs. *Clin. Pharmacol. Exp. Ther.* **30**, 3–22.

Steele, R. E., Mellor, L., Sawyer, W. K., Wasvary, J. M., and Browne, L. J. (1986). *In vitro* and *in vivo* inhibition of estrogen biosynthesis by a potent, selective, non-steroidal aromatase inhibitor CGS 16949A. 68th Endocrine Society Meeting, Anaheim, CA, Abstract No. 337.

Tamaoki, B. I., (1973). General review: steroidogenesis and cell structure, biochemical pursuit of site of steroid biosynthesis. *J. Steroid Biochem.*, **4**, 89–118.

Thompson, E. A. and Siiteri, P. K. (1974a). Utilization of oxygen and reduced nicotimanide adenine dinucleotide phosphate by human placental microsomes during aromatization of androstenedione. *J. Biol. Chem.*, **249**, 5362–72.

Tobias, B., Covey, D. F., and Strickler, R. C. (1982). Inactivation of human placental 17 beta-estradiol dehydrogenase and 20 alpha-hydroxysteroid dehydrogenase with active site-directed 17 beta-propynyl-substituted progestin analogs. *J. Biol. Chem.*, **257**, 2783–6.

Townsley, J. D., and Brodie, H. J. (1968). Studies on the mechanism of estrogen biosynthesis. III. The stereochemistry of aromatization of C_{19} and C_{18} steroids. *Biochemistry*, **7**, 33–40.

Tseng, L., Mazella, J., Lee, L. Y., and Stone, M. L. (1983). Estrogen sulfatase and estrogen sulfotransferase in human primary mammary carcinoma. *J. Steroid Biochem.*, **19**, 1413–17.

Uzgris, V. I., Whipple, C. A., and Salhanick, H. A. (1977). Stereoselective inhibition of cholesterol side chain cleavage by enantiomers of aminoglutethimide. *Endocrinology*, **101**, 89–92.

Varela, R. M. and Dao, T. L. (1978). Estrogen synthesis and estradiol binding by human mammary tumors. *Cancer Res.*, **38**, 2429–33.

Walsh, C. (1982). Suicide substrates: mechanism-based enzyme inactivators. *Tetrahedron*, **38**, 871–909.

Watanuki, M., Tilley, B. E., and Hall, P. F. (1978). Cytochrome P_{450} for 11β and 18-hydroxylase activities of bovine adrenocortical mitochondria. One enzyme or two? *Biochemistry*, **17**, 127–30.

Whipple, C. A., Colton, T., Strauss, J. M., Hourihan, J., and Salhanick, H. A. (1978). Comparison of luteolytic potencies of aminoglutethimide in the rabbit and rat. *Endocrinology*, **103**, 1605–10.

Wilson, J. D. (1972). Recent studies on the mechanism of action of testosterone. *New Engl. J. Med.*, **287**, 1284–91.

Wolfson, A. J., Richards, J. and Rotenstein, D. (1983). Cyanoketone competition with estradiol for binding to the cytosolic estrogen receptor. *J. Steroid Biochem.*, **19**, 1817–18.

Worgul, T. J., Santen, R. J., Samojlik, E., and Wells, S. A. (1982). How effective is surgical adrenalectomy in lowering steroid hormone concentrations? *J. Clin. Endocrinol. Metab.*, **54**, 22–6.

Wynder, E. L., Escher, G. C., and Mantel, N. (1966). An epidemiological investigation of cancer of the endometrium. *Cancer*, **19**, 489–520.

17

Inhibition of enzymes involved in bacterial cell wall synthesis

Jean-Marie Ghuysen, J. M. Frère,

B. Joris, J. Dusart, C. Duez,

M. Leyh-Bouille, M. Nguyen-Distèche,

J. Coyette, O. Dideberg, P. Charlier,

G. Dive, and J. Lamotte-Brasseur

523

17.1 Introduction

In the summer of 1928, Alexander Fleming gave the name penicillin to a mould broth filtrate that he obtained after growing a fungus, *Penicillium notatum*. Penicillin induced lysis of dividing bacteria, not of resting organisms, and was active against gram-positive bacteria, but not against a variety of gram-negative bacilli. In 1941, Howard W. Florey and Ernst B. Chain succeeded in partially purifying Fleming's mould juice and demonstrated its therapeutic value in humans. This event firmly established the concept of antibacterial chemotherapy and opened the antibiotic era in which we are living now (Wilson 1976; Abraham 1981).

Following the discovery of penicillin, the principles of bacterial cell wall biochemistry were progressively established. Early observations made by Joshua Lederberg that rod-shaped cells of *Escherichia coli* growing in a hypertonic medium changed into osmotically fragile spherical cells when penicillin was added to the culture, led to the conclusion that penicillin interfered with the synthesis of the bacterial wall. Thanks to the pioneering work of Milton R. J. Salton and others (Salton 1964; Rogers and Perkins 1968), it became clear that

(1) in all bacteria, the cytoplasmic membrane is covered by a layer of peptido-glycan;

(2) the integrity of the peptidoglycan is essential to keep the bacterial cell alive under ordinary hypotonic environmental conditions; and

(3) the peptidoglycan is the site of the lethal action of penicillin and other antibacterial agents.

In the late 1960s, the primary structure of the wall peptidoglycan was elucidated (Ghuysen 1968) and the pathway of wall peptidoglycan biosynthesis was unravelled (Blumberg and Strominger 1974).

17.2 Structure of the bacterial cell wall

17.2.1 The peptidoglycan

The wall peptidoglycan is a network structure and all the peptidoglycans are built on the same general pattern (Ghuysen 1968; Schleifer and Kandler 1972). Linear glycan strands of alternate β,1-4 linked N-acetylglucosamine (GlcNAc) and N-acetylmuramic acid (MurNAc) pyranoside residues are substituted through the D-lactyl group of N-acetylmuramic acid, by L-Ala-γ-D-Glu-L-Xaa-D-Ala tetrapeptide units, where L-Xaa is (most often) a diamino acid such as L-Lys or meso-A_2 pm. Peptide units substituting adjacent glycan chains are linked together by means of bridges that extend from the C-terminal D-alanine of a peptide to (most often) the ω amino group of the L-Xaa diamino acid residue of another peptide. The bridges either consist of a direct N^ω-(D-alanyl)-L-Xaa peptide bond [Fig. 17.1(a)] or are mediated by an additional amino acid residue or intervening peptide [Fig. 17.1(b)].

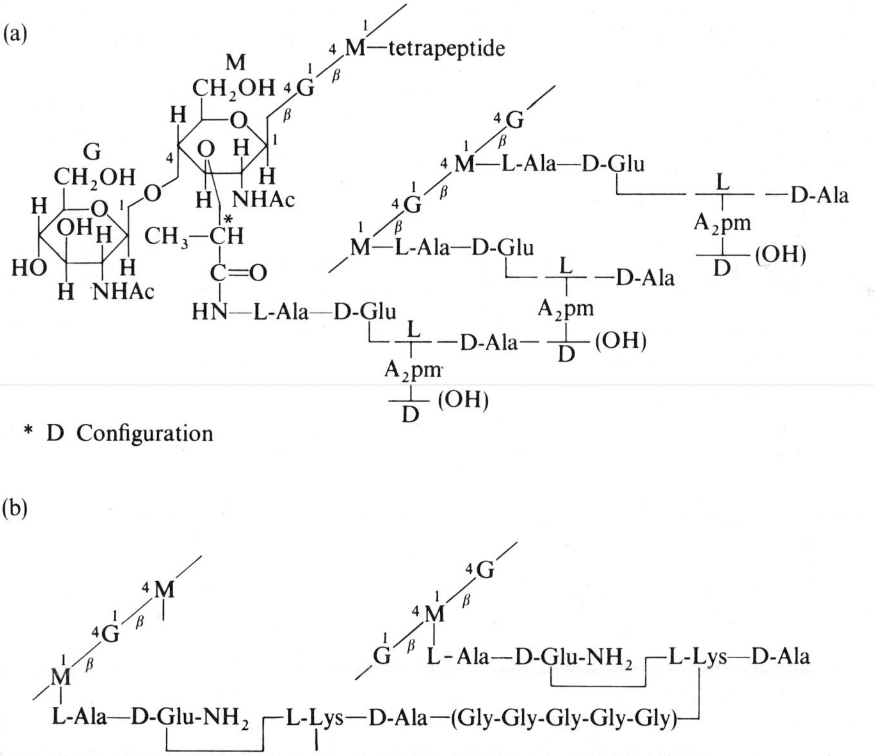

(a)

* D Configuration

(b)

Fig. 17.1. Wall peptidoglycans in *Escherichia coli* (a) and *Staphylococcus aureus* (b). G = N-acetylglucosamine; M = N-acetylmuramic acid.

17.2.2 Gram-positive bacteria

In gram-positive bacteria:

(1) the peptidoglycans have widely varying primary structures, particularly with respect to the nature and location of peptide bridges;

(2) shape and physical protection of the plasma membrane are entirely undertaken by the vast amount of multi-layered peptidoglycan that is present in the thick walls;

(3) the walls are highly permeable, with an exclusion limit for solutes of molecular mass of 70 000 or more; and

(4) the walls always contain anionic polymers, the structures and physiological functions of which have been discussed by Baddiley (1972), Wicken and Knox (1975), Ghuysen (1977), and Hancock and Baddiley (1985).

The teichoic acids are polymers containing 30 to 40 units of either glycerol or ribitol phosphate residues, variably substituted with glycosyl and D-alanine ester groups and attached by a glycerol phosphate to C_6 of N-acetylmuramic acid. In contrast, the teichuronic acids are phosphate-less, hexuronic acid-containing polymers. Peptidoglycan, teichoic acid, and teichuronic acid should be regarded as compounds of the same complex macromolecule. Yet growth conditions (phosphate limitation) may substantially alter the relative proportions of wall teichoic and teichuronic acids. These substitutions are phenotypical responses that necessitate an active system for wall turnover. Finally, the lipoteichoic acids are of the glycerol type and possess a glycolipid at one end of the molecule. While this lipid is part of the plasma membrane, the long polar chain of the polymer extends through the network of the wall peptidoglycan. The lipoteichoic acids (or their substitutes) appear to be indispensable; they are always produced even under growth conditions of phosphate limitation.

17.2.3 Gram-negative bacteria

In gram-negative bacteria:

(1) the primary structure of the peptidoglycan is uniform and D-alanyl-(D)-meso-A_2 pm linkages always serve as peptide bridges;

(2) the peptidoglycan forms a thin layer that is usually weakly cross-linked [Fig. 17.1(a)], and

(3) the peptidoglycan is covered by an outer membrane.

This additional membrane contributes to the mechanical strength of the cell envelope, provides the bacteria with an additional permeability barrier, and may be defined as a phospholipid–lipopolysaccharide–protein structure stabilized by Mg^{2+} cations (Fig. 17.2). Authoritative reviews on this subject have been presented by Inouye (1979), Lugtenberg and Van Alphen (1983), and Nikaido

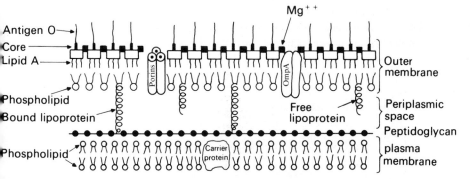

Fig. 17.2. The cell envelope of gram-negative bacteria.

and Vaara (1985). Features that are relevant to the present topic are summarized below.

The lipopolysaccharide molecules are composed of O-antigen chains that cover the exterior of the cell, a core that contains the characteristic L- or D-glycero-D-mannoheptose and 2-keto-3-deoxyoctonate, and a lipid A, the backbone of which is a disaccharide of D-glucosamine with the specific 3-D-hydroxymyristic acid in an amide linkage to the amino groups and with long-chain fatty acids in ester linkages to the hydroxyl groups (Lüderitz et al. 1982). While the lipopolysaccharide molecules are inserted by their lipid A in the outer leaflet of the outer membrane, the glycerophospholipid molecules are present mainly, if not exclusively, in the inner leaflet of the bilayer. As a consequence of this extremely asymmetric distribution, the basic continuum of the outer membrane is very poorly permeable to both hydrophobic and hydrophilic solutes.

Passage of nutrients through the outer membrane is made possible by specialized proteins called *porins*. The polypeptide backbone of the porins is arranged in an anti parallel β-pleated sheet structure and the β-strands (average length 10–12 residues) are oriented nearly normal to the membrane plane (Kleffel et al. 1985). These structures form water-filled trans-membrane channels through which diffusion of hydrophilic substances occur with, usually, an exclusion limit of 600–900 daltons. Porins form three channels on the outer surface of the cell and merge into a single channel at the periplasmic face (Engel et al. 1985). They are peptidoglycan-associated proteins, a term meant to emphasize that separation of the protein from the peptidoglycan requires drastic treatments such as extraction with hot sodium dodecylsulphate. The properties of the pores are determined by the nature of the constituent porin; these properties relate to the permeability efficiency for uncharged molecules and the effects of electrical charges and lipophilicity of the solutes.

In gram-negative bacteria, β-lactamase molecules are 'concentrated' in the periplasmic compartment. Diminishing the rate of penetration of β-lactam molecules through the porin channels is an important mechanism of resistance, at least against those antibiotics that show high susceptibility to β-lactamase. Indeed, their extremely rapid degradation must be counteracted by bringing in new molecules at a very rapid rate. The degree of protection that the outer membrane affords to bacteria against the toxic effects of β-lactam antibiotics has been studied in detail (Nikaido et al. 1983; Nikaido and Vaara 1985; Yoshimura and Nikaido 1985).

The gram-negative bacteria manufacture several major proteins other than the porins for export to the outer membrane. Some of these proteins contain fatty acids at the amino terminus (Fig. 17.3). One fatty acid is bound as an amide to the amino group of a cysteine and two other fatty acids occur as esters of the hydroxyl groups of S-glyceryl cysteine. The 56 amino acid-containing lipoprotein of E. coli occurs both in a free form and in covalent linkage with the underlying peptidoglycan. Statistically, one lipoprotein is bound to every tenth to twelfth peptidoglycan unit. The linkage is an amide bond between the ε-amino group of the lysine residue at the carboxyl terminus of the protein and the carboxyl group at the L-centre of the meso-A_2 pm of the peptidoglycan unit (i.e. where a D-alanine residue occurs in a conventional tetrapeptide unit).

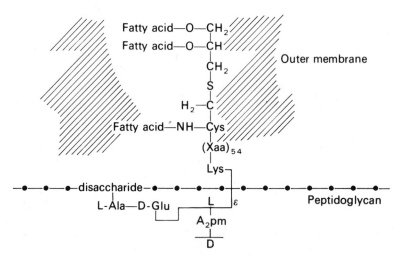

Fig. 17.3. The peptidoglycan-bound, 56 amino acid-containing lipoprotein of E. coli.

Altogether, the lipoproteins, major proteins, lipopolysaccharides, and peptidoglycan are important for the integrity of the cell envelope of gram-negative bacteria. The peptidoglycan is possibly a hydrated gel filling most of the periplasmic compartment (Hobot et al. 1984) and discontinuities of the peptidoglycan structure may allow fusion between the plasma and outer membranes. About 200–400 adhesion zones are seen in a growing cell of E. coli. These areas have been biochemically characterized, at least to some extent (Bayer et al. 1982;

Bayer and Bayer 1985). Some of these zones present themselves as annuli that surround the cell body (MacAlister *et al.* 1983).

17.2.4 Peptidoglycan markers

Gram-positive and gram-negative bacteria possess chemical groups (Fig. 17.4) that are markers of both peptidoglycan synthesis and penicillin action. In *E. coli*, the glycan chains are terminated by a non-reducible 1,6-anhydro-*N*-acetylmur-amic acid [Fig. 17.4(a)]. These groups, made by intramolecular transglycosyl-ation, may be regarded as punctuation marks indicating terminations of glycan polymerization. Moreover, representatives of gram-positive and gram-negative bacterial species have *O*-acetyl groups ester-linked to C_6 of *N*-acetylmuramic acid (with or without anhydro-muramyl residues). 6-*O*-acetyl, *N*-acetylmuramic acid [Fig. 17.4(b)] confers resistance to lysozyme. *O*-acetyl modification of the peptidoglycan in *Proteus* (Gmeiner and Kroll 1981) and *Neisseria gonorrhoeae* (Dougherty, 1983a; Lear and Perkins, 1983) is a process that is largely if not wholly post-synthetic.

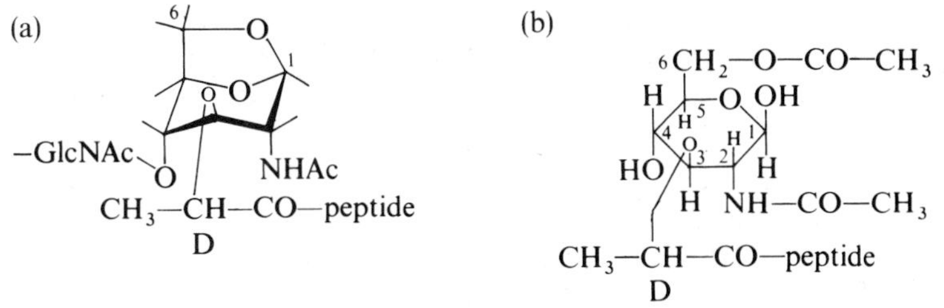

Fig. 17.4. Peptidoglycan markers: 1,6-anhydro-*N*-acetylmuramic acid (a) and *O*-acetyl, *N*-acetylmuramic acid (b).
References: (a) Höltje *et al.* (1975); Taylor *et al.* (1975). (b) Abrams (1958); Brumfitt *et al.* (1958); Tipper *et al.* (1965); Tipper and Strominger (1966); Fleck *et al.* (1971); Martin *et al.* (1973); Coyette *et al.* (1978); Martin and Gmeiner (1979); Blundell *et al.* (1980); Dougherty (1983a; 1985a,b); Gmeiner *et al.* (1982); Glauner and Schwarz (1983); Blundell and Perkins (1985).

17.3 Biosynthesis of bacterial cell wall

17.3.1 The peptidoglycan matrix (Fig. 17.5 and Table 17.1).

Wall peptidoglycan synthesis rests upon:

1. Manufacture in the cytoplasm of the two nucleotides UDP-GlcNAc and UDP-MurNAc-L-Ala-γ-D-Glu-L-Xaa-D-Ala-D-Ala (reactions 1–10 in Fig. 17.5).

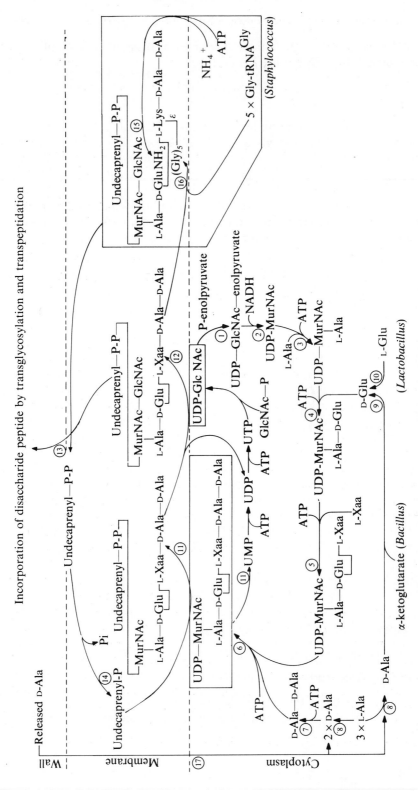

Fig. 17.5. Wall peptidoglycan biosynthesis. Cytoplasmic and lipid cycles.

2. Formation, from these precursors, of lipid $\text{P---P} \underset{\alpha \ \text{peptide}}{\overset{1 \ \overset{\text{MurNAc}}{|} \ 4}{\text{---}}} \underset{\beta}{\overset{1}{\text{---}}} \text{GlcNAc}$ pepti-

doglycan units, where the lipid carrier is a C_{55} polyisoprenoid alcohol (reactions 11–14);

3. If necessary, amidation of some carboxylate groupings (reaction 15) and/or addition of that (or those) additional amino acid residue(s) destined to serve as peptide bridges (reaction 16). These reactions may take place at the level of the UDP–MurNAc-pentapeptide precursor or at the level of the disaccharide–pentapeptide lipid intermediate.

4. Incorporation of the newly formed disaccharide peptide units, as they emerge from the cytoplasmic membrane, into the pre-existing wall peptidoglycan.

Incorporation of lipid-transported disaccharide peptide units requires the action of several membrane-bound enzymes. Transglycosylases catalyse extension of the glycan strands. In representatives of gram-positive bacterial species, chains consisting of multiple disaccharide peptide units grow on the lipid carrier by addition of new disaccharide peptide units at the reducing terminus of the lengthening chain (Fig. 17.6) and the nascent peptidoglycan strands are then transferred to the pre-existing peptidoglycan (see refs 38–45 in footnote of Table 17.1). In other organisms such as *E. coli*, the lipid-transported disaccharide peptide units appear to be incorporated directly without first existing as a soluble, nascent intermediate (Burman and Park 1983). Whatever the process, connection between the newly formed and pre-existing peptidoglycan materials is made by peptide cross-linking.

DNA-template-directed protein synthesis, where a peptide bond is made at the expense of ATP, proceeds via conversion of the carbonyl donor co-substrate to an ester-linked intermediate followed by attack on the carbonyl carbon of the ester intermediate by the amino acceptor co-substrate. These principles apply to peptidoglycan synthesis. However, several mechanisms are involved, none of which is ribosome-mediated. Except for the addition of five glycine residues to the ε-amino group of the L-lysine residue of the peptide unit of *Staphylococcus aureus* (reaction 16 in Fig. 17.5), the ester-linked intermediate is not an aminoacyl-tRNA.

Peptide bond formation in reactions 3, 4, 5, 6, and 7 rely on the action of specific water-soluble ligases (ADP). For reaction 7, it has been proposed (Fig. 17.7) that, (i) an ordered sequence of D-Ala binding in the active site of the D-Ala-D-Ala ligase (ADP) takes place (first the donor, then the acceptor), (ii) an ester-linked D-alanyl intermediate is formed at the enzyme's donor site at the expense of ATP, and (iii) the intermediate undergoes nucleophilic attack by the amino group of the D-Ala co-substrate bound at the enzyme's acceptor site (Neuhaus and Hammes 1981). In turn, closure of the interpeptide bonds by transpeptidation is a transfer reaction that involves the *C*-terminal D-alanyl-D-alanine sequence of the peptidoglycan precursor acting as carbonyl donor, and an amino group of the pre-existing peptidoglycan acting as acceptor. This reaction

Table 17.1 Main enzymes involved in the cytoplasmic (reactions 1–10 in Fig. 17.5) and lipid (reactions 11–16 in Fig. 17.5) cycles of wall peptidoglycan synthesis

Reaction	Enzyme	Structural gene (in *E. coli*)	Reference
1	Phosphoenolpyruvate:UDP-GlcNAc 2-enoyl-1-carboxyethyl transferase (enolpyruvate transferase) EC 2.5.1.7	murA	1–4
2	UDP-MurNAc:NADP$^+$ 1-carboxyethyl oxydoreductase (UDP-GlcNAc-enolpyruvate reductase) EC 1.3.1.xx	mrbA	5–8
3	UDP-MurNAc:L-Ala ligase (ADP) EC 6.3.2.8	murC	9–12
4	UDP-MurNAc-L-Ala:D-Glu ligase (ADP) EC 6.3.2.9	murD	9,13–14
5	UDP-MurNAc-L-Ala-D-Glu:meso-A$_2$pm ligase (ADP) EC 6.3.2.13	murE	10–12,15
	UDP-MurNAc-L-Ala-D-Glu:L-Lys ligase (ADP) EC 6.3.2.7	—	9–16
6	UDP-MurNAc-L-Ala-γ-D-Glu-L-Xaa:D-Ala-D-Ala ligase (ADP) Ec 6.3.2.10	murF	10, 12, 17–19
7	D-Ala:D-Ala ligase (ADP) EC 6.3.2.4.	ddl	12, 13, 17, 20–22
8	Alanine racemase EC 5.1.1.1	alr	19, 23–31
9	D-amino acid transaminase EC 2.6.1.21		32–33
10	Glutamic acid racemase EC 5.1.1		34
11	UDP-MurNAc-pentapeptide:undecaprenyl phosphate phospho-MurNAc-pentapeptide transferase (phospho-MurNAc-pentapeptide transferase) EC 2.7.8.13		35

12	UDP-GlcNAc:undecaprenyl-diphospho-MurNAc-pentapeptide N-acetylglucosaminyl transferase (N-acetylglucosaminyl transferase) EC 2.4.1.xx	36–37
13	Undecaprenyl-diphospho-disaccharide peptide: peptidoglycan disaccharide transferase (transglycosylase) Ec 2.4.1.xx	38–46
14	Undecaprenyl diphosphate phospho-hydrolase (undecaprenyl disphosphatase) EC 3.6.1.xx	47
15	Undecaprenyl-diphospho-disaccharide-pentapeptide:ammoniac ligase (ADP) (amide synthetase) EC 6.3.1.xx	48
16	Glycyl-ARN$_t$: undecaprenyl-diphospho-disaccharide-pentapeptide N^ε-glycyl transferase (glycyl transferase) EC 2.3.2.xx	49

1. Cassidy and Kahan (1973). 2. Venkateswaran, et al. (1973). 3. Wickus and Strominger (1973). 4. Wu and Venkateswaran (1974). 5. Anwar and Vlaovic (1979). 6. Taku et al. (1970). 7. Wickus et al. (1973). 8. Miyakawa et al. (1973). 9. Ito and Strominger (1962a). 10. Lugtenberg and van Schijndel-van Dam (1972). 11. Mizuno et al. (1973). 12. Wijsman (1972a). 13. Lutkenhaus and Wu (1980). 14. Nathenson et al. (1964). 15. Mizuno and Ito (1968). 16. Ito and Strominger (1964). 17. Ito and Strominger 1962b.18. Neuhaus and Struve (1965). 19. Oppenheim and Patchornick 1974. 20. Lugtenberg and van Schijndel-van Dam (1972, 1973). 21. Neuhaus (1962a). 22. Neuhaus (1962b). 23.Adams (1976). 24. Johnston and Diven (1969). 25. Johnston et al. (1966). 26. Lambert and Neuhaus (1972). 27. Rosso et al. (1969). 28. Roze and Strominger (1966). 29. Shen et al. (1983). 30. Wood and Gunsalus (1951). 31. Wijsman (1972b). 32. Soper and Manning (1981). 33. Soper et al. (1979). 34. Glaser (1960). 35. Neuhaus (1971). 36. Taku and Fan (1976a), 37. Taku and Fan (1976b). 38. Ward and Perkins (1973). 39. Ward and Perkins (1974). 40. Elliott et al. (1975a). 41. Elliott et al. (1975b). 42. Taku and Fan (1979). 43. Van Heijenoort et al. (1978). 44. Park and Matsuhashi 1984. 45. Park et al. (1985). 46. Burman and Park (1983). 47. Goldman and Strominger (1972). 48. Siewert and Strominger (1968). 49. Katz et al. (1967).

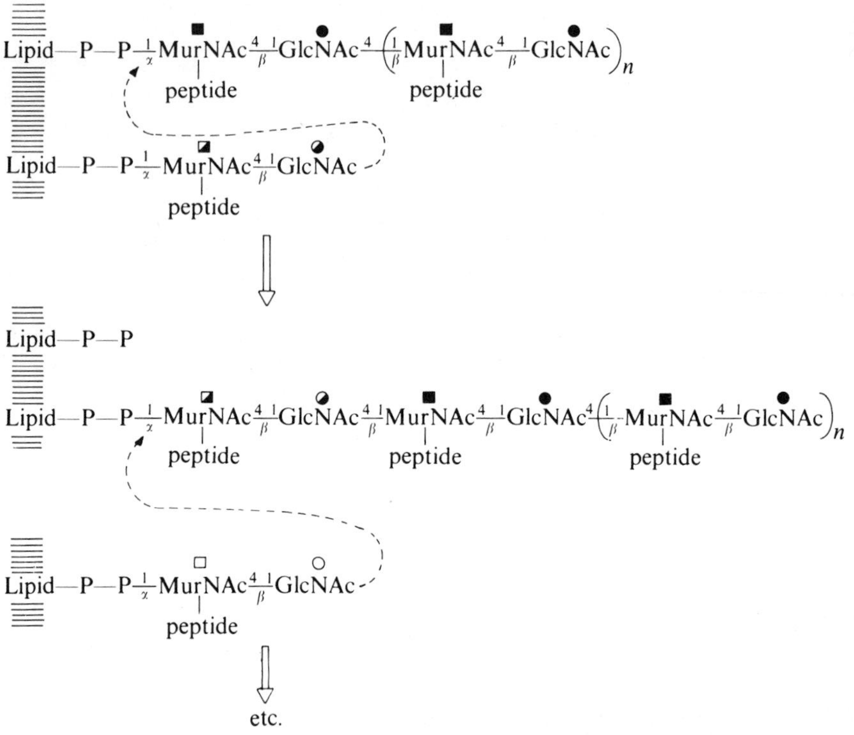

Lipid—P—P—$\frac{1}{\alpha}$MurNAc$\frac{4}{\beta}\frac{1}{}$GlcNAc$\frac{4}{}$$\left(\frac{1}{\beta}$MurNAc$\frac{4}{\beta}\frac{1}{}$GlcNAc$\right)_n$

        peptide   peptide

Lipid—P—P—$\frac{1}{\alpha}$-MurNAc$\frac{4}{\beta}\frac{1}{}$GlcNAc

        peptide

Lipid—P—P

Lipid—P—P—$\frac{1}{\alpha}$MurNAc$\frac{4}{\beta}\frac{1}{}$GlcNAc$\frac{4}{\beta}\frac{1}{}$MurNAc$\frac{4}{\beta}\frac{1}{}$GlcNAc$\frac{4}{}$$\left(\frac{1}{\beta}$-MurNAc$\frac{4}{\beta}\frac{1}{}$GlcNAc$\right)_n$

     peptide   peptide   peptide

Lipid—P—P—$\frac{1}{\alpha}$-MurNAc$\frac{4}{\beta}\frac{1}{}$GlcNAc

        peptide

etc.

Fig. 17.6. Glycan chain elongation during peptidoglycan synthesis.

is discussed in detail in an ensuing section of this chapter (see Figs. 17.12, 17.13). It proceeds by conversion of the carbonyl donor to a short-lived ester-linked acyl enzyme (with release of the C-terminal D-alanine) and attack of the acyl enzyme by the amino acceptor (with synthesis of a new interpeptide bond). Transpeptidation does not require any input of energy but is made at the expense of a preformed D-Ala-D-Ala peptide bond, the synthesis of which is catalysed in the cytoplasm by a ligase (ADP) with accompanying hydrolysis of one molecule of ATP (Fig. 17.7).

The C_{55}-polyisoprenoid alcohol phosphate is an essential component of the machinery responsible for the assembly and export of the disaccharide peptide units. In gram-negative bacteria, this lipid carrier is partitioned between peptidoglycan and lipopolysaccharide synthesis. The O-antigens are polymerized on the lipid carrier through a reaction sequence analogous to that leading to the formation of the peptidoglycan units. Transfer of completed O-antigen chains to the preformed core-lipid A then occurs within the plasma membrane itself. After the two components are joined, the complete lipopolysaccharide molecules are translocated into the outer membrane through the adhesion zones mentioned

$$\text{Ligase} + 2 \text{ D-Ala} + \text{ATP}$$

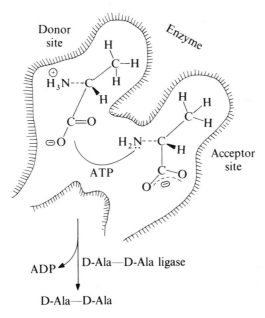

Fig. 17.7. Schematic view of the D-Ala: D-Ala ligase (ADP)-catalysed synthesis of D-Ala-D-Ala.

above and distributed over the entire surface of the cell within the outer leaflet of the outer membrane (for a recent review, see Lüderitz *et al.* 1982).

17.3.2 Peptidoglycan appendages: teichoic acids and lipoproteins

The biosynthesis of teichoic acid and its linkage unit has been reviewed by Hancock and Baddiley (1985). Suffice it here to say that the wall teichoic acids are synthesized through a three-stage process which, in essence, is also similar to that of the peptidoglycan; however, the lipid carrier is different. From CDP-glycerol and CDP-ribitol, the cytoplasmic precursors, synthesis proceeds by sequential transfer of the polyol phosphate residues to a membrane lipoteichoic acid carrier. These transfers are transphosphorylation reactions, and CMP is released. In turn, incorporation of the side-chain sugars onto the polyolphosphate backbone is made by transglycosylation from UDP-glucose or UDP-*N*-acetylglucosamine to the hydroxyl groups of the polyol, with release of UDP. Newly synthesized teichoic acid is attached to the nascent peptidoglycan while the latter polymer is itself in the process of being incorporated into the pre-existing wall peptidoglycan. Inhibition of peptidoglycan cross-linking by penicillin causes the release of nascent teichoic acid in the growth medium just as it causes the release of nascent peptidoglycan; the two excreted polymers are not linked to each other (Fischer and Tomasz 1984; Barrett *et al.* 1984).

Non-cytoplasmic proteins are manufactured in plasma membrane-bound polysomes in the form of precursors that contain characteristic signal peptides. Co-translational or post-translational transfer across the plasma membrane may occur (Silhavy *et al.* 1983; Randall and Hardy 1984; Scarborough 1985; Pugsley and Schwartz 1985). In addition to that provided by the signal sequence, information for export and proper localization are present in the mature part of the exported protein (Freudl *et al.* 1985). The signal sequences of several lipoproteins of gram-negative bacteria are shown in Fig. 17.8 and compared with the signal sequences of the penicillin binding protein no. 3 of *E. coli* and the membrane-associated β-lactamases of the gram-positive *Bacillus licheniformis* and *S. aureus*. The putative pathway of peptidoglycan-linked lipoprotein synthesis is shown in Fig. 17.9. The conserved amino acid stretch Leu-Ala-Gly-Cys in the signal sequence of the precursor form of the lipoprotein is recognized by the prolipoprotein glyceryl transferase and *O*-acyl transferase to form a glyceride-prolipoprotein which, in turn, is processed proteolytically by a prolipoprotein signal peptidase. It has been proposed—but neither proved nor disproved—that attachment of free lipoprotein to the peptidoglycan is catalysed by a (penicillin-insensitive) L,D-transpeptidase present in the periplasmic compartment (reaction 6 in Fig. 17.9).

17.3.3 Roles of autolysins in wall synthesis and toxic effects of wall inhibitors

All bacteria possess peptidoglycan autolysins. These enzymes hydrolyse bonds in the glycan strands (glycosidases) at the junction between glycan strands and peptide units (*N*-acetylmuramyl-L-alanine amidases) or in several places in the peptide moiety (peptidases). They may be associated with the membrane, concentrated in the periplasmic space, fixed on the wall, or excreted in the growth medium. They play important roles in various cellular events (cell septation, wall turnover, sporulation) and are actively involved in bacterial growth itself (by creating new insertion sites and permitting wall remodelling during the life cycle). Some are specifically localized in the region of dividing septum (Daneo-Moore and Shockman 1977; Shockman and Barrett 1983).

The primary effect of inhibition of peptidoglycan synthesis is inhibition of cellular growth (bacteriostatic effect) and is not lethal *per se*. However, it initiates a chain of secondary events that abolish protein and RNA/DNA synthesis and affect the specific activity and/or cellular control of the autolysins. Penicillin-induced lysis of staphylococci has been related to the punching of holes into the wall at predictable sites and these perforations have been attributed to the lytic activity of vesicular structures named 'murosomes' (Giesbrecht *et al.* 1985). Bulgecin, a metabolite of *Pseudomonas acidophilia*, is, by itself, deprived of antibacterial activity. In concert with β-lactam antibiotics, it induces the formation of bulges and enhances β-lactam lytic effect (Imada *et al.* 1982).

Peptidoglycan lipoproteins

E. coli. (1)
$$-20 \qquad\qquad\qquad\qquad\qquad\qquad\qquad\qquad\qquad\qquad +1$$
Met Lys Ala Thr Lys Leu Val Leu Gly Ala Val Ile   Leu Gly Ser Thr Leu Leu Ala Gly Cys Ser Ser Asn Ala

S. marcescens (2)
$$-20 \qquad\qquad\qquad\qquad\qquad\qquad\qquad\qquad\qquad\qquad +1$$
Met Asn Arg Thr Lys Leu Val Leu Gly Ala Val Ile   Leu Gly Ser Thr Leu Leu Ala Gly Cys Ser Ser Asn Ala

E. amylovora (3)
$$-20 \qquad\qquad\qquad\qquad\qquad\qquad\qquad\qquad\qquad\qquad +1$$
Met Asn Arg Thr Lys Leu Val Leu Gly Ala Val Ile   Leu Gly Ser Thr Leu Leu Ala Gly Cys Ser Ser Asn Ala

M. morganii (4)
$$-19 \qquad\qquad\qquad\qquad\qquad\qquad\qquad\qquad\qquad\qquad +1$$
Met Gly Arg Ser Lys Ile   Val Leu Gly Ala Val Val Leu Ala Ser   Ala Leu Leu Ala Gly Cys Ser Ser Asn Ala

P. mirabilis (4)
$$+1$$
Met Lys Ala . . . Lys Ile   Val Leu Gly Ala Val Ile   Leu Ala Ser Gly Leu Leu Ala Gly Cys Ser Ser Ser Asn

E. coli Penicillin binding protein no. 3 (5)
$$-29 \qquad\qquad\qquad\qquad\qquad\qquad\qquad\qquad\qquad\qquad\qquad +1$$
Met Lys Ala Ala Ala Lys Thr Gln Lys Pro Lys Arg Gln Glu Glu His Ala Asn Phe Ile Ser Trp Arg Phe Ala Leu Leu Cys Gly Cys Ile Leu Leu Ala

β-Lactamases

B. licheniformis (6)
$$-26 \qquad\qquad\qquad\qquad\qquad\qquad\qquad\qquad\qquad\qquad\qquad +1$$
Met Lys Leu Trp Phe Ser Thr Leu Lys Leu Lys Lys Ala Ala Ala Val Leu Leu Phe Ser Cys Val Ala Leu Ala Gly Cys Ala Asn Asn Gln

S. aureus (7)
$$-16$$
Met Lys Lys Leu Ile Phe Leu Ile Val Ile Ala Leu Val Leu Ser Ala Cys Asn Ser Asn Ser

Fig. 17.8. Signal sequences of bacterial cell envelope proteins.
References: 1. Nakamura and Inouye (1979). 2. Nakamura and Inouye (1980). 3. Yamagata *et al.* (1981). 4. Huang *et al.* (1983). 5. Nakamura *et al.* (1983). 6. Neugebaure *et al.* (1981). 7. McLaughlin *et al.* (1981). For signal sequences of other lipoprotein precursors, see also Ogata *et al.* (1982). Hakkaart *et al.* (1981). Cavard *et al.* (1985); Cole *et al.* (1985).

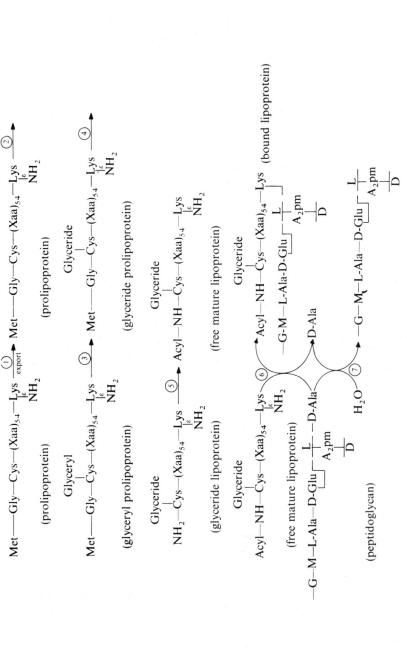

Fig. 17.9. Putative pathway of biosynthesis of the peptidoglycan-linked lipoprotein in *E. coli* and site of action of globomycin.

Reactions 1–5 leading to the synthesis of free mature lipoprotein are catalysed by: the machinery for export through the plasma membrane (1), a phosphatidyl-glycerol glyceryl transferase (2), a phospholipid acyl transferase (3), the signal peptidase (3), a phospholipid acyl transferase (4), and a phospholipid acyl transferase (5). Reaction 4 (maturation of the glyceride prolipoprotein) is inhibited by globomycin. The LD-transpeptidase-catalysed

Alterations at the level of presumed 'effector molecules' that normally link the synthesis of the wall peptidoglycan and the synthesis and/or functioning of the autolysins (and other essential biopolymers) may result in tolerance to wall inhibitors. Phenotypically or genotypically acquired resistance to cellular autolysis does not cause an increased resistance to growth inhibition by the wall inhibitors but is accompanied by an increased resistance to killing and cellular lysis by these agents. Tolerance, as first seen in pneumococci (Tomasz *et al.* 1970; Tomasz 1979), can be defined as diminished and/or delayed killing by growth-inhibiting concentrations of the antibiotic. Tolerance of β-lactam antibiotics is not a laboratory curiosity; it has been observed with clinical isolates of staphylococci, *Streptococcus mutans*, and group B streptococci (Kim *et al.* 1979). Unexpectedly, tolerance toward a given wall inhibitor is not invariably accompanied by tolerance to other wall inhibitors.

17.4   Wall inhibitors

17.4.1   Fosfomycin (Fig. 17.10)

Synthesis of UDP-MurNAc involves transfer of a three-carbon unit from 2-phosphoenolpyruvate with formation of the pyruvate enol ether of UDP-GlcNAc (reaction 1 in Fig. 17.5), followed by reduction of the pyruvate enol ether (reaction 2). Fosfomycin, or L-*cis*-1,2-epoxypropyl phosphonic acid, inactivates the transferase of reaction 1 by derivatization of a cysteine residue at the enzyme's active site. The reaction is enzyme-catalysed, as is the formation of the intermediate enzyme–phosphoenolpyruvate (Cassidy and Kahan 1973; Kahan *et al.* 1974). Fosfomycin penetrates inside the cell by utilizing the L-α-glycerophosphate transport system. Loss of this system is the primary cause of emergence of resistant strains (Lèon *et al.* 1985). Plasmid-mediated fosfomycin resistance by intracellular enzymatic modification of the antibiotic has also been described (Llaneza *et al.* 1985).

17.4.2   Alanine analogues (Neuhaus and Hammes 1981) (Fig. 17.10)

17.4.2.1.   *Reaction 8 of Fig. 17.5*

D-alanine is formed by racemization of L-alanine. Some alanine analogues (*O*-carbamoyl-L-serine; *O*-acetyl-L-serine; acrylate; 2-bromopropionate) are competitive inhibitors of the racemase. Other analogues form Schiff bases with the pyridoxal phosphate cofactor and inactivate the enzyme irreversibly. This latter process involves alkylation of a nucleophile in the enzyme's active site (β-chloro-D- or L-alanine; β-fluoro-D- or L-alanine; *O*-acetyl-D-serine; *O*-carbamoyl-D-serine; D-vinylglycine; β-trifluoro-D,L-alanine) or oxime formation with the pyridoxal phosphate cofactor (β-aminoxy-D-alanine; D-cycloserine). Variations

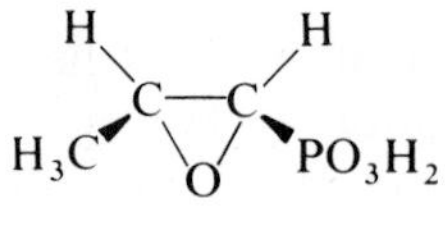

fosfomycin 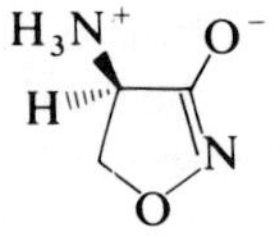   D-cycloserine 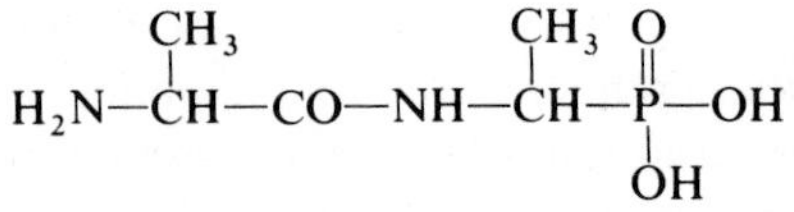   L-alanyl-L-1-aminoethylphosphonic
acid (alaphosphin)

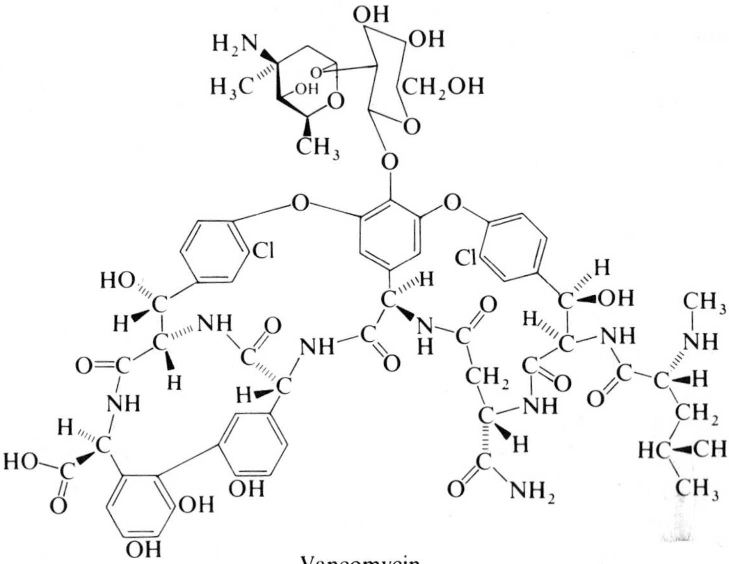

Vancomycin

Fig. 17.10. Structure of wall inhibitors used as chemotherapeutic agents.

may be observed depending on the origin of the enzyme. Thus L-1-aminoethylphosphonic acid competitively inhibits the racemases of *E. coli* and *Pseudomonas aeruginosa* and it inactivates irreversibly those from *S. aureus* and *Streptococcus faecium*.

17.4.2.2. *Reactions 9 and 10 of Fig. 17.5*

D-glutamic acid is formed by racemization of L-glutamic acid (as it occurs in lactobacilli) or, more frequently, by transamination of D-alanine and α-ketoglutarate (for example in gram-positive bacilli). D-amino acid transaminases are also pyridoxal phosphate-containing enzymes. They are inhibited by D-cycloserine, β-chloro-D-alanine and D-vinylglycine.

17.4.2.3 *Reactions 3–7 of Fig. 17.5*

Each of these reactions is catalysed by a specific ligase (ADP). A putative mechanism of action of the D-Ala:D-Ala ligase (ADP) is shown in Fig. 17.7. This enzyme (of *S. faecium*) has a high specificity for a D-alanine at the *N*-terminal site and a low specificity for D-amino acids at the *C*-terminal site and thus is able to catalyse synthesis of a wide variety of mixed dipeptides such as D-Ala-D-Ser, D-Ala-D-Abu, etc. Conversely, the UDP-MurNAc-L-Ala-γ-D-Glu-L-Lys:D-Ala-D-Ala ligase (ADP) (also from *S. faecium*) has no strict requirement for the *N*-terminal residue of the dipeptide to be added and D,D-dipeptides of the type D-alanine analogue–D-alanine have been considered as a method for the incorporation of analogues into the penultimate position of the pentapeptide subunit. D-cycloserine inhibits the D-alanine:D-alanine ligase (ADP) (reaction 7). It competes with D-alanine at both sites of the enzyme but with a higher affinity for the donor site than for the acceptor site. L-1-aminoethylphosphonic acid (the primary action of which is at the level of the alanine racemase) has a second mode of action, which is competition with L-alanine for the ligase (ADP) of reaction 3, the resulting nucleotide UDP-MurNAc-L-Ala(P) not being utilized by the UDP-MurNAc-L-Ala:D-glutamic acid ligase (ADP). Finally, high concentrations of glycine and D-serine (which induce growth inhibition and spheroplast or protoplast formation) cause a decrease in peptidoglycan cross-linking and accumulation of a family of UDP-MurNAc-pentapeptides with partial replacement of both enantiomers of alanine by the analogue. Replacement of D-alanine at the penultimate position of the precursor exerts the greatest inhibitory effect on cross-linked peptidoglycan synthesis.

Part of the (moderate) success achieved with D-cycloserine and L-1-aminoethylphosphonic acid as chemotherapeutic agents can be correlated with an efficient active transport of these agents. D-cycloserine accumulates in the cell via the D-alanine–glycine transport system (reaction 17 in Fig. 17.5). The key to the use of L-1-aminoethylphosphonic acid is the active transport and intracellular hydrolysis of either a dipeptide (for example alaphosphin) or an oligopeptide that contains the alanine analogue (these peptides are designated collectively as phosphonopeptides). L-1-aminoethylphosphonic acid that is not linked in a peptide shows no substantial uptake or antibacterial activity (Atherton *et al.* 1983).

17.4.3 Inhibitors of the lipid cycle

The lipid carrier plays a role in peptidoglycan synthesis similar to that of dolichol in the biosynthesis of the glycoproteins in the eukaryotes. The wall inhibitors that act at the level of the lipid cycle lack selective toxicity. However, these compounds have been extremely useful in the study of the process of disaccharide peptide synthesis and assembly. Depending on the case, they inhibit a membrane-bound enzyme target or immobilize an enzyme substrate in an inactive form.

17.4.3.1 *Reaction 11 (Fig. 17.5)*

The phospho-MurNAc-pentapeptide transferase possesses binding sites that recognize both the nucleotide and peptide regions of the substrate and has a specificity that is complementary to that of the ligases (ADP) discussed above. The enzyme is sensitive to detergents. In the presence of dodecylamine, the intermediate enzyme-P-MurNAc-pentapeptide undergoes hydrolysis, i.e. the transphosphorylase functions as a pyrophosphatase. Several liponucleosides such as tunicamycin (Duksin and Mahomey 1982; Eckardt 1983) and lipopoly-peptides such as amphymycin (Bodansky et al. 1973) inhibit the reaction. Tunicamycin binds irreversibly to the transferase; it is a general inhibitor of the formation of polyprenyl-P–P–GlcNAc and polyprenyl–P–P–MurNAc.

17.4.3.2   Reaction 12 (Fig. 17.5)

Nisin (Gross and Morell 1971) and subtilin (Gross et al. 1973) are polypeptides containing 34 and 32 amino acid residues, respectively, with 5 S–S bridges. They form, with the undecaprenyl-P–P–MurNAc-pentapeptide, complexes that have no acceptor activity for the enzyme-catalysed transfer of N-acetylglucosamine from UDP-GlcNAc.

17.4.3.3   Reaction 13 (Fig. 17.5)

Release of both the completed disaccharide peptide unit and the lipid carrier in the form of a pyrophosphate derivative is made by transglycosylation. This reaction is the target of phosphoglycolipids such as moenomycin (Welzel et al. 1981) and lipopeptolides such as enduracidins (Iwasaki et al. 1973).

17.4.3.4   Reaction 14 (Fig 17.5)

Bacitracin derives its antibacterial activity from its ability to form a strong complex with the C_{55}-isoprenyl pyrophosphate (association constant: 1×10^6 M^{-1}). In its presence, dephosphorylation of the lipid carrier does not occur and a new lipid cycle cannot begin (Storm 1974). Bacitracin A is a cyclic polypeptide with a peptide side-chain and a thiazolidine ring formed between the L-cysteine and L-isoleucine residues at the N-terminal of the acyclic peptide side chain. The free amino group of L-isoleucine is adjacent to the thiazolidine ring and is essential for antibacterial activity.

17.4.4   Vancomycin and ristocetin (Fig. 17.10)

Vancomycin and ristocetin A are glycopeptides (Williams et al. 1980). The active part of vancomycin is an heptapeptide that forms a tricyclic structure by three phenol-oxidative coupling reactions. A similar aglycone occurs in ristocetin A, except that N-methyl-D-leucine and L-aspartic acid that are present in vancomy-cin are replaced by two aromatic amino acids that enable a fourth oxidative phenol coupling, with formation of a tetracyclic structure. The extraordinary feature of these compounds is that their three-dimensional structures create a cavity that binds C-terminal D-alanyl-D-alanine-terminated peptides with high selectivity and affinity (Gale et al. 1981; Williams et al. 1983). Vancomycin and ristocetin freeze the peptidoglycan precursors as they emerge from the plasma membrane in an inert state, and prevent their incorporation in the wall sacculus. The association constants for the peptidoglycan precursor analogue Ac_2-L-Lys–D-Ala–D-Ala are 1.5×10^{-6} M^{-1} and 0.59×10^{-6} M^{-1} with vancomycin and ristocetin, respectively. The outer membrane of the gram-negative bacteria affords a high degree of protection against these agents. But vancomycin has found a place in therapeutics for treating antibiotic-induced enterocolitis associated with *Clostridium difficile*, and in treating the increasingly large number of serious methicillin and nafcillin-resistant staphylococcal infections. Resistance to vancomycin among gram-positive cocci is a rare event. Indeed, drastic changes in the structure of the peptidoglycan would have to occur to prevent combination with the antibiotic. Yet infections caused by vancomycin-resistant *Streptococcus sanguis* have been reported (Shlaes *et al.* 1984).

17.4.5 β-lactam antibiotics (Fig. 17.11)

The β-lactam antibiotics represent a large family of molecules the single common structural feature of which is the possession of a β-lactam ring (Fig. 17.11). As a class, they consist of the penicillins (**1**), Δ^3-cephalosporins (**2**), cephamycins (**3**), oxapenams (clavulanic acid; **4**), carbapenems (thienamycin; **5**), and monobactams (nocardicin A; **6**). Fungi invented the penams and 3-cephems (**1–3**), streptomyces the oxapenams and carbapenems (**4–5**), and soil eubacteria the monocyclic β-lactam compounds (**6**). Many of these compounds have been rendered more effective and their resistance to β-lactamase action has been increased by modifications of the R and R′ side-chains. The semi- or totally synthetic compounds 6-β-amidinopenam mecillinam (**7**), oxacephem (**8**), the penems (**9**) and novel types of monocyclic β-lactam compounds such as SQ 26776 or azthreonam (**10**) have also been made. Δ^2-cephalosporins (**11**) were also synthesized but none of them has ever been reported to have appreciable antibacterial activity. Thousands of β-lactam compounds have been made, the design being essentially achieved by trial and error. About 30 have found a place in medicine. They are the most powerful tools in the armoury of modern antibacterial chemotherapy. As discussed below, they interfere with the last stages of wall peptidoglycan metabolism by disturbing the peptidoglycan cross-linking enzyme machinery.

17.4.6 Globomycin

The prolipoprotein signal peptidase (Figs 17.8 and 17.9) is extremely sensitive to inhibition by the cyclic antibiotic globomycin. Treatment of *E. coli* with globomycin causes spheroplast formation and accumulation of the glyceride-containing precursor of the lipoprotein. The prolipoprotein is translocated across the plasma membrane, interacts with the outer membrane but, at the same time, it remains attached to the plasma membrane in such a way that the

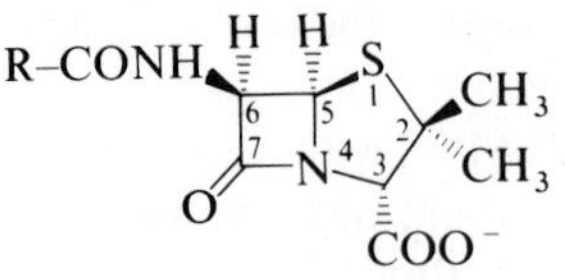

Fig. 17.11. (continued)

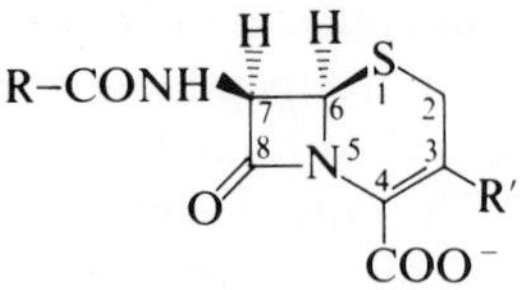

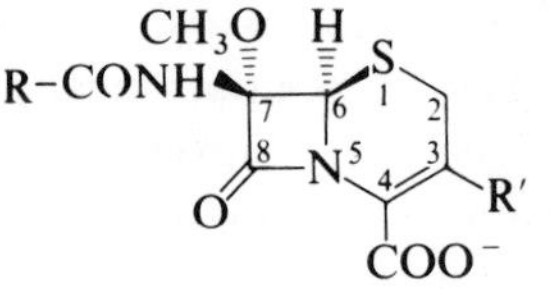

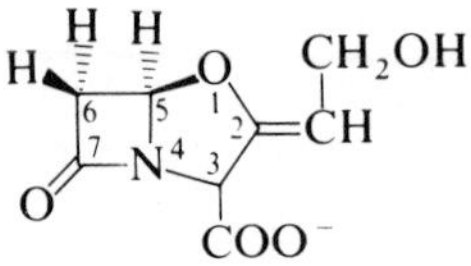

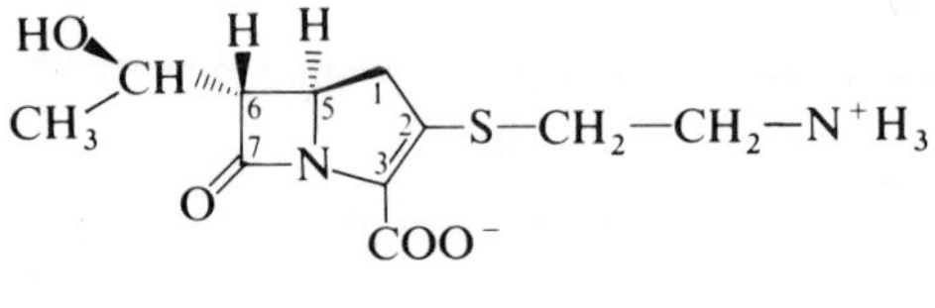

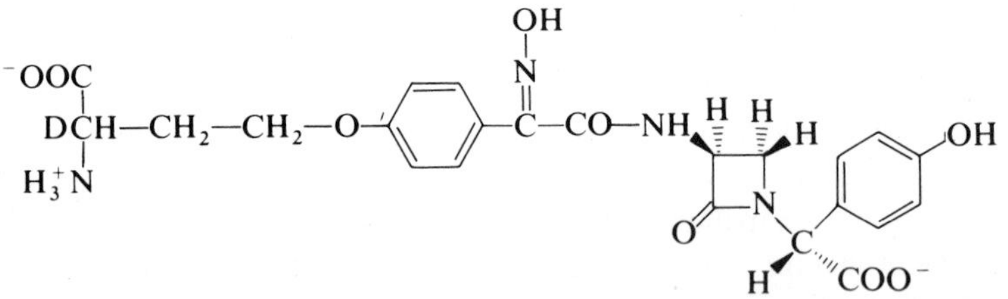

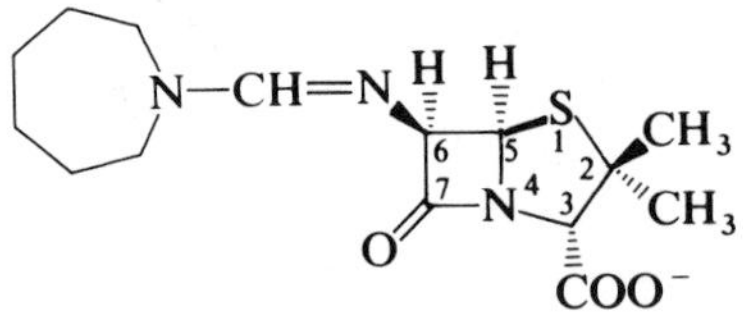

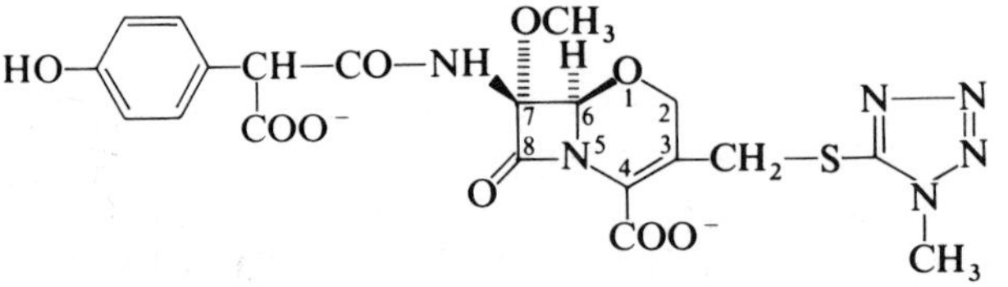

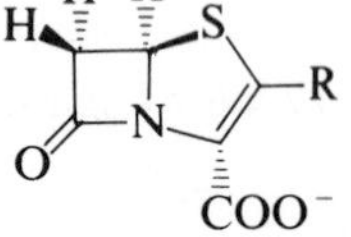

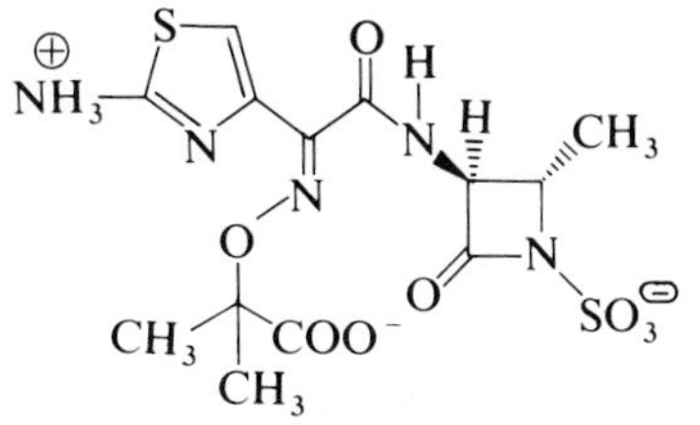

Fig. 17.11. Classes of β-lactam antibiotics.

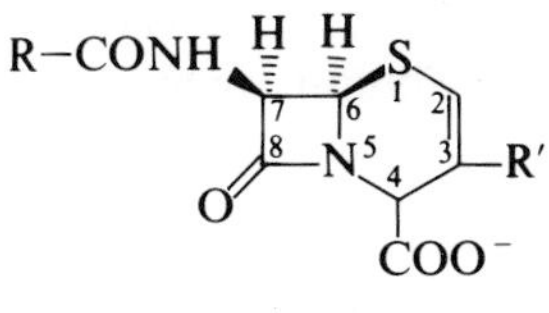

amino-terminal portion of the signal peptide containing two lysine residues is left inside the cytoplasm (Inukai and Inouye 1983; Lee *et al.* 1983).

17.5 Penicillin binding proteins

17.5.1 Multiplicity of penicillin binding proteins

In 1965, Tipper and Strominger proposed that killing of susceptible bacteria by penicillin was due to the inhibition of peptide cross-linking between peptidoglycan strands and that the inactivation of the relevant membrane-bound transpeptidase was a suicide process. The enzyme, mistaking the antibiotic molecule for a D-alanyl-D-alanine-terminated peptide, undergoes acylation and gives rise to a stable penicilloyl enzyme. The transpeptidase thus behaves as a 'penicillin binding protein' (PBP). As the research was progressing, the unitary transpeptidase model of penicillin action had to be revised (Spratt 1983; Waxman and Strominger 1983; Frère and Joris 1985). Indeed

(1) all the bacteria possess multiple PBPs of molecular mass ranging from 25 000 to 100 000 or more;

(2) each bacterial species has its own specific assortment of PBPs (currently numbered in order of decreasing molecular mass) from perhaps only one (Canepari *et al.* 1985) to seven or more (Spratt, 1983); and

(3) the several PBPs present in a single bacterial cell may fulfil distinct cellular functions, do not exhibit the same degree of essentiality, and show widely varying sensitivity to β-lactam antibiotics.

Upon reaction with radioactive β-lactam compounds, the PBPs form adducts that are stable enough to be submitted to polyacrylamide gel electrophoresis in the presence of sodium dodecylsulphate and to be visualized by fluorography of the gel. They are bound to the plasma membrane. PBPs 5 and 6 of *E. coli* are secreted through the plasma membrane until synthesis of a hydrophobic carboxyl terminal peptide prevents their complete release in the periplasm (Pratt *et al.* 1981). The plasma membrane, which is the only cell tegument of the stable protoplast L-forms of *Proteus*, has a PBP pattern essentially similar to that of the normal bacterium except, for the lack of PBP4, which is excreted during growth in the culture medium (Ghuysen *et al.* 1986). Depending on the procedure used to separate the plasma and outer membranes of *E. coli*, PBPs may undergo partitioning, to a varying extent, between the two membrane fractions. Barbas *et al.* (1986) have suggested that in *E. coli*, the PBPs reside in special membranous structures, possibly related to the adhesion zones mentioned above. In this respect, one should mention that the precursor form of PBP3 has a signal peptide and the mature PBP3 an *N*-terminal cysteine residue that are analogous to those found in lipoproteins (Fig. 17.8).

17.5.2 Multiplicity of physiological lesions caused by β-lactam antibiotics

Defining a 'killing target' to β-lactam antibiotics is difficult, sometimes elusive. In *E. coli*, the low-M_r PBPs 4, 5, and 6 are not of prime importance for the killing action of the β-lactam antibiotics and are not essential for bacterial growth. Yet dacA and dacC mutations that affect proteins 5 and 6, respectively, result in supersensitivity to several β-lactam antibiotics, and cells genetically modified to overproduce protein 5 grow as osmotically stable spheres (Spratt 1983). Derivatization of protein 2 by reaction with mecillinam (which is specific in binding exclusively to this PBP over a thousand-fold concentration range) results in the growth of *E. coli* as spherical cells for several generations. Selective binding to protein 3, in particular by the monobactam azthreonam (Fig. 17.11, **10**) (Sykes and Philips 1981), causes inhibition of cell division and formation of filamentous cells. Deletions of the ponA and ponB genes that totally impair the physiological functions of PBP1A and PBP1B have been studied by Kato *et al.* (1985) and Yousif *et al.* (1985). The deletion of the ponA gene has no significant effect on the cell growth rate, morphology, and sensitivity to a range of β-lactam antibiotics. The deletion of the ponB gene is only slightly deleterious, causing some reduction of the growth rate and supersensitivity to β-lactam antibiotics. The absence of either PBP1A or PBP1B is tolerable under laboratory conditions, but double mutants lacking both proteins are not viable and binding of several 3-cephems such as cephaloridine to both proteins 1A and 1B causes rapid cellular death and lysis. Protein 1A and protein 1B probably have compensatory roles in peptidoglycan synthesis. Their amino acid sequences show 30 per cent identity (providing that two large gaps are introduced in the PBP1B sequence). In contrast, PBPs 1A/1B, PBP3 and PBP5 lack homology except for two short regions, one of which includes the penicillin-binding site (Broome-Smith *et al.* 1985).

In the gram-positive bacteria, few PBPs have been identified as being related, directly or indirectly, to cellular morphological events. In *Clostridium perfringens*, the four lowest-M_r-PBPs of the six present in this species become virtually saturated with benzylpenicillin when the organism is grown in the presence of a penicillin concentration sufficient to cause filamentation of the entire population

(Williamson and Ward 1982). In *S. faecium* ATCC9790 (which possesses seven PBPs), binding of the 3-cephem cefotaxime to PBPs 2 and/or 3 also affects cell septation: septa continue to be initiated but they never reach completion (Coyette *et al.* 1983).

Comparison between the bacterial growth inhibitory effectiveness of a β-lactam antibiotic and the concentration needed to complex some percentage (i.e. 50 or 90 percent) of one or more of the PBPs present in the bacterial cell has produced reasonable correlations in some cases. But in many others, this type of study has failed to establish such a relationship. When growing (lysis-defective) *Streptococcus pneumoniae* are exposed to various concentrations of benzylpenicillin over extended periods of time, complete complexation of any or all PBPs is not required for the cessation of culture growth (Williamson and Tomasz 1985). Remarkably, when the pneumococcal cultures begin to show the first symptom of growth inhibition, each PBP has always reached a characteristic degree of saturation. At this 'threshold antibiotic dose', which depends on both the penicillin concentration and the length of exposure, the PBPs left in a free form can no longer sustain the normal rate of wall synthesis. The antibacterial effect of penicillin arises from a summation of the inactivation of several PBPs or from the abnormal relative concentrations of free PBPs in the antibiotic-treated cells.

17.5.3 Multiplicity of modes of intrinsic resistance to β-lactam antibiotics

Several mechanisms of resistance to β-lactams are known (Wiedemann and Ghuysen 1983). They may involve the following.

17.5.3.1 *Modification of a single, essential PBP*

An example is PBP1 in *Clostridium perfringens* (Williamson 1983) or PBP2 in *N. gonorrhoeae* (Dougherty 1983b). This results in a decreased affinity for the β-lactam antibiotic.

17.5.3.2 *Overproduction of a particular PBP that has a low affinity for the drug*

The penicillin-sensitive strain of *S. faecium* possesses a highly penicillin-resistant PBP5. This particular PBP is produced in much larger amounts in the resistant strains, where it seems to be capable of taking over the functions of the other PBPs (Fontana *et al.* 1983). Conversely, Rev14 hypersusceptible mutants (derived from a highly resistant strain) lack PBP5. They resemble the parent with respect to cell morphology, growth rate, and autolytic activity (Fontana *et al.* 1985).

17.5.3.3 *Acquisition of a new PBP that has a low affinity for the antibiotic*

Methicillin-resistant clinical isolates of *S. aureus* possess a 'new', resistant PBP2' that is not present in the sensitive strains, the amount of which is regulated by growth conditions (Reynolds and Brown 1985). PBP2' is the only PBP still present in an uncomplexed state when the resistant strains are grown in media containing concentrations of β-lactam antibiotics sufficient to kill the sensitive strains. PBP2' presumably functions as the sole active PBP. However, growth of the resistant strains in media containing large concentrations of the β-lactam antibiotic is not as rapid as normal growth of sensitive strains, and the resistant cells are enlarged, suggesting that not all the physiological functions of PBPs 1, 2, and 3 can be compensated for by PBP2'.

17.5.3.4 *Profound alterations in the PBP pattern*

Clinical isolates of (β-lactamase-non producing) strains of *S. pneumoniae*, with increasing levels of resistance to penicillin exhibit different PBP patterns. Using the DNA of one of the resistant strains and the sensitive strain as recipient, the high level of penicillin resistance can be transmitted only in a stepwise fashion by several rounds of genetic transformation. Increasing resistance is paralleled by gradual changes, shifting from the pattern of sensitive strains toward the pattern of resistant strains. These gradual modifications involve four of the five pneumococci PBPs (Hakenbeck *et al.* 1980; Zighelboim and Tomasz 1980). Note that such PBP pattern changes are seen in a bacterial species where, as explained above, cell growth inhibition by penicillin always occurs at a consistent pattern of percentage PBP saturation.

17.5.4 Multiplicity of biochemical lesions caused by β-lactam antibiotics

There has been a widely held view that the biochemical lesion caused by β-lactam antibiotic action is a lower degree of peptidoglycan interpeptide cross-linking. In fact, the picture is much more complex; many observations reveal a complex interplay between PBPs and the close interdependency that exists between the peptidoglycan, its substituents and appendages and both the plasma and outer membranes.

In the penicillin-susceptible strains of *N. gonorrhoeae*, PBP2—which is the target for the physiological events leading to cell death—is involved, directly or indirectly, in peptidoglycan *O*-acetylation (Dougherty 1985a,b). Benzylpenicillin, at the minimal growth inhibitory concentration, primarily affects PBP2 and causes a sharp decrease in *O*-acetylation; it is only at higher penicillin concentrations that, in turn, PBP1 is affected and that a markedly decreased extent of peptide cross-linking is observed. The resistance mediated by penA decreases the affinity of PBP2 for penicillin to a point at which PBP1 becomes the most susceptible target. Whether PBP2 has acetylase activity or synthesizes some structural features in the peptidoglycan which act as recognition or acceptor sites for the acetylase is not known. Similarly, the functions of the *O*-acetyl groups are hypothetical; they might serve as substrate-level controls on the active autolysin system that is present in the gonococci.

At those concentrations that induce cell filamentation in *E. coli*, benzylpenicillin enhances the attachment of newly synthesized peptidoglycan units and increases the degree of peptide cross-linking. Similar effects are seen with mecillinam at those concentrations that induce conversion of *E. coli* into round cells. But, at the same time, mecillinam reduces the average glycan chain length of the peptidoglycan to about half its normal value (as estimated by measuring the amounts of anhydromuramic acid residue; Essig *et al.* 1982; Ghuysen *et al.* 1986).

When compared with normal bacteria, the benzylpenicillin-induced unstable spheroplast L-forms of *Proteus mirabilis* have reduced amounts of lipopolysaccharide and total protein in the outer membrane. The peptidoglycan shows only a slight decrease in overall extent of peptide cross-linking, a large decrease in degree of *O*-acetylation of *N*-acetylmuramic acid, and has appreciable amounts of tripeptide units to which no lipoprotein is attached. This latter defect suggests that an indirect consequence of penicillin action might be the conversion of the putative L,D-transpeptidase (reaction 6 in Fig. 17.9) into an L,D-carboxypeptidase (reaction 7). The reduced assortment of PBPs left in a free form in the spheroplasts is probably responsible for the continued synthesis of a cross-linked (but defective) peptidoglycan. Cefoxitin complements the action of benzylpenicillin at the level of the PBPs. In combination, the two antibiotics effectively inhibit L-form growth and, in parallel to this, cause a 50 per cent decrease of peptide cross-linking in the peptidoglycan (for a more complete discussion on *Proteus* L-forms, see Ghuysen *et al.* 1986).

Finally, mention must be made of alterations in the phospholipid composition of the plasma membrane itself in response to changes induced by β-lactam antibiotics (and other wall inhibitors) in the cell wall (Kariyama 1982; Rozgonyi *et al.* 1980).

17.5.6   Multiplicity of catalysed reactions

In spite of their diversity, the PBPs to which catalytic activity could be assigned behave as D,D-peptidases: they catalyse attack of peptide bonds that are located between two carbon atoms having the D-configuration, in an α-position to a free carboxylate (Fig. 17.12). However, depending on whether the nucleophilic acceptor of the transfer reaction is the ω amino group of another peptide or water, the catalysed reaction leads to an increased (Fig. 17.12a) or a decreased [Fig. 17.12(b, c)] level of peptidoglycan cross-linking. Hydrolysis of D-alanyl-D-alanine-terminated peptides [Fig. 17.12(b)] limits the amount of carbonyl donors available for transpeptidation. Hydrolysis of D-alanyl-(D)-meso-diaminopimelic acid linkages (previously made by transpeptidation, as it occurs in *E. coli*) produces new amino acceptor sites in the wall peptidoglycan (Fig. 17.12(c)]. Hence, depending on the reaction(s) catalysed by, and the drug susceptibility of, the PBP target(s), varying biochemical and physiological lesions are expected to be caused by β-lactam antibiotic action.

The PBPs 4, 5, and 6 of *E. coli* (and the low-M_r PBPs of several other organisms) function primarily as D,D-carboxypeptidases and, with a lower efficacy, as D,D-transpeptidases, the two reactions occurring on a competitive

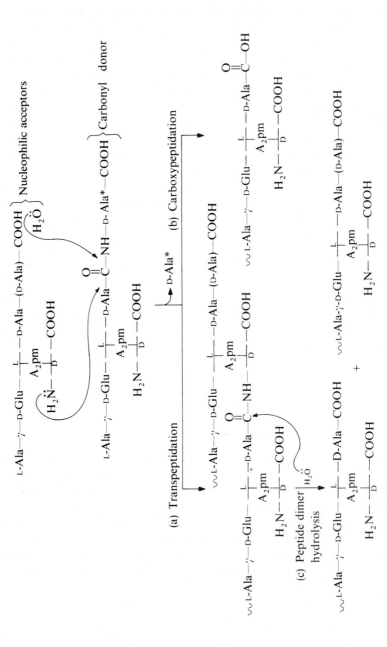

Fig. 17.12. D,D-peptidase-catalysed transpeptidation (a), carboxypeptidation (b), and peptide dimer hydrolysis (c) during wall peptidoglycan metabolism in *E. coli.*

basis. The high-M_r PBPs 1A, 1B, and 3 function, to all appearances, as strict transpeptidases but, as shown by the reaction products that they generate upon incubation with the lipid-linked precursor GlcNAc-MurNAc (pentapeptide)–diphosphoryl-undecaprenol, each of these PBPs also possesses a penicillin-insensitive (but moenomycin-sensitive) transglycosylase active site (Matsuhashi *et al.* 1982). In these assays, no peptidoglycan material is present at the onset of the incubation; these 'non-natural' conditions may explain, in part, the low turnover number, $0.01\,s^{-1}$ or less, of the catalysed reactions. The penicillin-binding (transpeptidase) site is located in the *C*-terminal domain of PBP3 (i.e. within amino acids 240–588). Indeed, removal by gene fusion of the NH_2-terminal 240 amino acids which presumably contain the transglycosylase site, results in a truncated protein that has an unaltered penicillin binding capacity but a much reduced stability (Hedge and Spratt 1984).

The presence in *E. coli* of bifunctional enzymes catalysing in concert transglycosylation and transpeptidation reactions may be related to the mode of incorporation of the newly formed disaccharide-peptide units in the wall peptidoglycan, a process which, in this organism, apparently proceeds without prior synthesis of nascent chains. Yet, *E. coli* also possesses a (relatively insensitive moenomycin) glycan polymerase, which does not bind penicillin, and a not insignificant part of the peptidoglycan synthesis may be sustained by this enzyme in cooperation with an as yet unelucidated peptide cross-linking enzyme (Hara and Suzuki 1984). Similarly, the major transglycosylases of *S. aureus* and *Micrococcus luteus* (Park and Matsuhashi 1984) and *S. pneumoniae* (Park *et al.* 1985) are not penicillin-binding proteins.

17.6   Active sites of D,D-peptidases/penicillin binding proteins

17.6.1   Kinetics of catalysed acyl transfer reactions

The D,D-peptidases/PBPs operate by an acyl enzyme mechanism in which an enzyme's active-site serine residue is involved (Frère *et al.* 1976; Broome-Smith *et al.* 1985; Houba-Herin *et al.* 1986). Giving E = D,D-peptidase/PBP; D = R-D-Ala-D-Ala-terminated or β-lactam carbonyl donor; HY = nucleophilic acceptor (i.e. water or a suitable amino compound NH_2—R); $E \cdot D$ = Michaelis complex; E—D* = serine ester-linked acyl (R-D-alanyl, penicilloyl, cephalosporoyl, etc.) enzyme; P_1 = the leaving group of the enzyme acylation step; P_2 = the second reaction product; K = dissociation constant (M) of the Michaelis complex; k_{+2} and k_{+3} = first-order rate constants (s^{-1}), the D,D-peptidases/PBPs-catalysed reactions on R-D-Ala-D-Ala-terminated carbonyl donors are

$$E + D \underset{K}{\rightleftharpoons} E \cdot D \underset{P_1}{\xrightarrow{k_{+2}}} E\text{—}D^* \underset{HY}{\xrightarrow{k_{+3}}} E + P_2 \qquad (17.1)$$

where P_1 is the released D-alanine and P_2 is R-D-Ala-Y.

In essence, eqn. (17.1) applies to the interactions with the β-lactam antibiotics. These compounds are recognized as carbonyl donor analogues but the endocyclic nature of the scissile amide bond has two consequences:

(i) the leaving group P_1 remains part of the acyl enzyme and does not diffuse away from the enzyme's active site and

(ii) k_{+3} has, in principle, a very small value so that the reaction flux stops, at least for a long time, at the level of the acyl (penicilloyl, cephalosporoyl, etc.) enzyme. Hence, eqn. (17.1) becomes,

$$E + D \underset{}{\overset{K}{\rightleftharpoons}} E \cdot D \xrightarrow{k_{+2}} E - D^* \underset{HY}{\xrightarrow{k_{+3}}} E + P_2 \qquad (17.2)$$

with $k_{+3} \ll k_{+2}$. The β-lactam antibiotics are suicide substrates or mechanism-based inactivators of the D,D-peptidases/PBPs.

The kinetics of the catalysed acyl transfer reactions eqns. (17.1) and (17.2) has been reviewed by Ghuysen *et al.* (1986). Three features are especially relevant to the present discussion.

At a given concentration of the carbonyl donor and at the steady-state of the reaction, the ratio of total D,D-peptidase/PBP (i.e. $[E_0]$) to acyl enzyme (i.e. $[E-D^*]_{ss}$) is,

$$[E_0]/[E-D^*]_{ss} = 1 + (k_{+3}/k_{+2}) + (Kk_{+3}/k_{+2}[D]) \qquad (17.3)$$

which for $k_{+3} \ll k_{+2}$ simplifies to

$$[E_0]/[E-D^*]_{ss} = 1 + (Kk_{+3}/k_{+2}[D]). \qquad (17.4)$$

The time necessary for the acyl enzyme to reach a certain percentage of its steady-state level is,

$$t = -\ln\left(1 - \frac{[E-D^*]}{[E-D^*]_{ss}}\right) \bigg/ (k_{+3} + k_a) \qquad (17.5)$$

where k_a, i.e. the pseudo-first-order rate constant of acyl enzyme formation at a given $[D]$ value, is equal to $k_{+2}/\{1 + (K/[D])\}$.

For $[D] \ll K$ and $k_a \gg k_{+3}$, the product of the carbonyl donor concentration ($[D]_{0.5}$) by the incubation time ($t_{0.5}$) that are necessary to achieve 50 per cent of enzyme/PBP acylation is

$$([D]t_{0.5}) = 0.69 \, K/k_{+2} \qquad (17.6)$$

Note that k_{+2}/K is the second-order rate constant of enzyme acylation.

The following sections illustrate the principles summarized above. Figure 17.13 shows how hydrolysis and dimerization of a meso-A_2pm-D-Ala–D-Ala-terminated peptidoglycan unit [Fig. 17.12(a, b)] proceed. Figure 17.14 shows how the D,D-peptidases/PBPs are inactivated by β-lactam antibiotics. In this discussion, reference is often made to the D,D-peptidases/PBPs produced by *Streptomyces* R61 and K15, respectively. These enzymes cleave with high efficiency the C-terminal linkage in the amide carbonyl donor analogue Ac$_2$-L-

Lys-D-Ala-D-Ala but differ with respect to their susceptibility to β-lactam antibiotics and the effects that amino compounds exert on the fate and rate of consumption of the carbonyl donor. These enzymes (and others) have been used as models for the purpose of defining the properties and functioning of the D,D-peptidases/PBPs' active sites. For recent reviews, see Ghuysen *et al.* (1984) and Frère and Joris (1985).

17.6.2 Interaction with D-Ala-D-Ala terminated carbonyl donors [eqn. (17.1) and Fig. 17.13]

17.6.2.1 *The K step*

Initial recognition, binding energy, and proper alignment with regard to the active-site serine residue and other functional groups rely on the complementation of at least three enzyme sub-sites (S_1', S_1, and S_2) by the carbonyl donor. Enzyme activity requires a D-Ala at the penultimate position, being decreased but not abolished when Gly or a D-amino acid other than D-Ala occurs at the C-terminus [for example, a residue possessing a bulky side-chain as shown in Fig. 17.12(c)]. Activity also requires a long-side chain at the L-centre. The design of sub-site S_2 is enzyme-specific; it reflects structural features of the peptidoglycan interpeptide bridges. Complementation of subsites S_1', S_1, and S_2 is probably a minimum requirement; D,D-peptidases/PBPs may exist which possess additional subsites. As deduced from gene analysis, the primary structures of the D,D-peptidases/PBPs 1A, 1B, 3, and 5 of *E. coli* and that of the *Streptomyces* R61 are known (Broome-Smith *et al.* 1985; Broome-Smith *et al.* 1983; Nakamura *et al.* 1983; Duez *et al.* 1987). Remarkably, lysine always occurs at the third position on the carbonyl side of the active-site serine (Ser-X-X-Lys). Most likely, this lysine also contributes to the formation of the Michaelis complex by charge-pairing with the terminal carboxylate of the carbonyl donor. In agreement with this view, protonation of a group on the enzyme with pK 9–9.5 greatly increases the efficacy of the initial binding to the *Streptomyces* R61 D,D-peptidase (Varetto *et al.* 1987).

17.6.2.2 *The k_{+2} step*

Once positioned in the enzyme's donor site, the carbonyl donor launches a series of reactions which leads to acyl enzyme formation and release of the leaving group D-Ala. Amino acid side-chains (which are as yet unidentified) must collaborate with the active-site serine residue in order to achieve polarization of the carbonyl group and proton donation to the nitrogen atom of the carbonyl donor's scissile bond. The *Streptomyces* R61 D,D-peptidase shows no sign of an imidazole group with p$K \cong 7$ as occurs in chymotrypsin and if a negatively charged carboxylate takes part in the process, its pK should be lower than 5 (Varetto *et al.* 1987). The efficacy of the overall rate of enzyme acylation (k_{+2}/K) rests upon rather high K values (0.1–10 mM) that are compensated by high k_{+2}

Serine D.D-peptidase + *meso*-A$_2$pm—D-Ala—D-Ala—terminated peptide

values. As discussed by Fersht (1985), rate maximization is best achieved by enzymes which have evolved to bind substrates weakly.

17.6.2.3 *The k_{+3} step*

Partitioning of the enzyme activity between hydrolysis and transpeptidation reflects competition between water and an amino acceptor NH_2—R at the level of the acyl enzyme. The process is highly efficient: the reaction flux is from substrate(s) to product(s); no or little acyl enzyme accumulates ($k_{+3} >$ or $\gg k_{+2}$). Transpeptidation is not a trivial reaction. *In vitro* assays, millimolar concentrations of a suitable amino compound successively compete with 55.5 M H_2O (Frère *et al.* 1973). The enzymes' amino acceptor sites exhibit distinct specificity profiles and these differences also reflect distinct structural features in the wall peptidoglycans. Deprotonation of the amino compound bound to the enzyme's acceptor site is enzyme-catalysed. With the *Streptomyces* R61 D,D-peptidase, a group with $pK \cong 7$ appears to be involved in the process (Frère *et al.* 1973).

The high-M_r PBPs of *E. coli* have low catalytic activities in *in vitro* systems and function as strict transpeptidases (i.e. apparently, water cannot attack the acyl enzyme; see above). The D,D-peptidase of *Streptomyces* K15 may offer a possible explanation to these puzzling observations (Nguyen-Distèche, Leyh-Bouille, Pirlot, Frère, and Ghuysen 1986). The *Streptomyces* K15 enzyme-catalysed acyl transfer reactions—though in essence identical with those shown in Fig.17.13—are peculiar in several respects. In water, the D-Ala that is released during the enzyme acylation step is effectively re-utilized as acceptor for the enzyme deacylation step. As a consequence, the acceptor activity of water is suppressed, hydrolysis of the carbonyl donor is prevented and the enzyme is seemingly 'silent' (though it turns over with a k_{cat} of 0.11 s^{-1}). Addition to the reaction mixture of a suitable amino compound (structurally related to the wall peptidoglycan) that competes successfully with the endogenously released D-Ala drastically changes the situation. The carbonyl donor is now quantitatively converted into the corresponding transpeptidated product, and the D,D-peptidase functions as a strict transpeptidase with a k_{cat} value of 0.55 s^{-1}. Experimental evidence shows that the amino compound not only acts as an alternate nucleophile at the level of the acyl enzyme (as shown in Fig. 17.13) but

Fig. 17.13. Covalent catalysis by an active-site serine D,D-peptidase via formation of a serine ester-linked acyl enzyme. (a) Hydrolysis of a meso-A_2pm-D-Ala–DAla--terminated peptide unit by carboxypeptidation. (b) Conversion of a meso-A_2pm-D-Ala-D-Ala-terminated peptide into a peptide dimer by transpeptidation. R—$\ddot{N}H_2$ at the enzyme's acceptor site is the amino group located on the D centre of meso-A_2pm of another peptide. K = dissociation constant; k_{+2} and k_{+3} = first-order rate constants.

Exploration of the active sites of the D,D-peptidases/PBPs of *Streptomyces* R61 and K15 has been made using distinct molecular entities as carbonyl donor (Ac$_2$-L-Lys-D-Ala-D-Ala, in which case the acetylated lysine side-chain complements the enzyme's subsite S_2) and amino acceptor (Gly-Gly or Gly-L-Ala).

enhances the efficacy with which the carbonyl donor acylates the enzyme's active site serine.

Finally, one should note that D,D-peptidases/PBPs function as esterases on certain D-alanyl-OCHR-COO$^-$-terminated ester carbonyl donors, for example Ac$_2$-L-Lys-D-Ala-D-lactate, phenylacetyl-D-Ala–D-mandelate and phenylacetyl-glycyl-D-mandelate (Pratt and Govardhan 1984; Pratt et al. 1985; Nguyen-Distèche et al. 1986). Given that the leaving group of the enzyme acylation step is D-lactate or D-mandelate, instead of D-Ala, eqn. (17.1) applies and the reaction flux proceeds as shown in Fig. 17.13.

17.6.4   Interaction with β-lactam carbonyl donors (eqn. (17.2) and Fig. 17.14).

Central to the inactivation of the D,D-peptidases/PBPs by the β-lactam anti-biotics is the ability of these agents to immobilize the enzymes as acyl enzyme (low k_{+3} values).

As shown in Fig. 17.14, the enzyme deacylation step may be a complex branched pathway. An amino compound, known to be an effective acceptor in the transfer reaction involving an R-D-Ala-D-Ala-terminated carbonyl donor, has no effect on the rate of breakdown of the acyl enzyme formed by reaction with a bicyclic or monocyclic β-lactam compound. Access of the amino acceptor to or functioning of the enzyme's acceptor site is prevented. However, the acyl enzyme may undergo rearrangements that destabilize the serine ester linkage (Frère et al. 1978). Rupture of the C_5–C_6 bond in the benzylpenicilloyl enzyme and protonation of C_6 release the leaving group (which gives rise to N-formyl-D-penicillamine) and the newly-formed phenylacetylglycyl enzyme then breaks down immediately with transfer of the phenylacetylglycyl moiety to water and, if present, an amino acceptor. Note that this phenylacetylglycyl enzyme intermedi-ate is identical to the acyl enzyme formed by reaction with the acyclic ester carbonyl donor phenylacetylglycyl-D-mandelate. With the Streptomyces R61 DD-peptidase, direct attack of the benzylpenicilloyl enzyme by OH$^-$ ions and formation of benzylpenicilloate increase as the pH of the reaction mixture increases. The second-order rate constant for the reaction is about 4 M^{-1}s^{-1}, a value that is not much higher than that observed (0.7 M^{-1}s^{-1}) for the hydrol-ysis of α-methylpenicilloate by OH$^-$ ions. In contrast, the rate of release of phenylacetylglycine is pH-independent between pH 5 and 10, showing that rupture of the C—C bond is rate-determining ($\cong 1 \times 10^{-4}$s^{-1}) within this range of pH (Varetto et al. 1987).

In the process of inactivation of the D,D-peptidases/PBPs by the β-lactam antibiotics, two concepts are of major importance. The first one relates to the percentage of enzyme which is immobilized at the steady state of the reaction. The higher the second-order rate constant of enzyme acylation (k_{+2}/K; M^{-1}s^{-1}) and the smaller the first-order rate constant of acyl enzyme breakdown (k_{+3}; s^{-1}), the lower the β-lactam compound concentration ([D]) for which the term Kk_{+3}/k_{+2} [D] of eqn. 17.4 becomes negligible. When this

Serine DD-peptidase and β-lactamase + benzylpenicillin

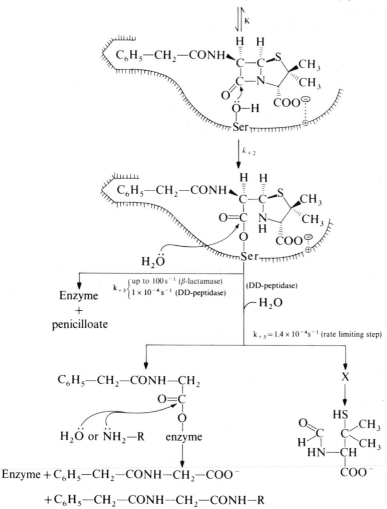

Fig. 17.14. Interaction between benzylpenicillin and active-site serine D,D-peptidases, and β-lactamases.

With the D,D-peptidases, breakdown of the benzylpenicilloyl enzyme is a branched pathway (hydrolysis and fragmentation). The indicated k_{+3} values refer to the interaction with the *Streptomyces* R61 D,D-peptidase (see text).

term is smaller than 0.01, virtually all the D,D-peptidase/PBP is immobilized as acyl enzyme at the steady state of the reaction. The second concept relates to the time required to reach the steady state [eqn. (17.5)]. Assume that (i) k_{+3} is sufficiently small to confer on the acyl enzyme a half-life (i.e. $0.69/k_{+3}$) much larger than the generation time of the bacterium; (ii) a 1 μM β-lactam antibiotic concentration (i.e. roughly 0.5 μg ml^{-1}) in the blood of humans can be achieved by oral administration of the drug and (iii) the drug permeates freely through the bacterial cell envelope and is not destroyed by β-lactamase action. Then the inactivating efficacy of a β-lactam antibiotic for a D,D-peptidase/PBP depends only on the k_{+2}/K value. Giving $[D] = 1\ \mu$M, $K = 1$ mM (i.e. $\gg [D]$), $k_{+3} = 1 \times 10^{-4}\ \text{s}^{-1}$ (half-life of the acyl enzyme: 125 min), and varying k_{+2} values such that $k_{+2}/K = 10$, 100, 1000 and 10 000 M^{-1} s^{-1}, respectively, it follows from eqns. (17.4) and (17.5) that

(1) the enzyme is acylated by 9.1, 50, 90.9 and 99 per cent at the steady-state of the reaction;

(2) it takes 698 min, 384 min, 70 min, and 7.6 min for the reaction to reach 99 per cent of the steady-state; and

(3) in 30 min (supposed to be the generation time of the bacterium), 1.6, 15.1, 78.4 and 99 per cent of the enzyme is acylated.

The values of k_{+2}/K and k_{+3} (and sometimes the individual values of K and k_{+2}) can be estimated accurately (Ghuysen *et al.* 1986; Leyh-Bouille *et al.* 1986). Moreover, it seems that many of the published β-lactam antibiotic concentrations ($[D]_{0.5}$) at which a PBP is saturated by 50 percent in a given time have been obtained under conditions such that $[D] \ll K$ and $k_a \gg k_{+3}$. Hence, introducing these $[D]_{0.5}$ values in eqn. (17.6) may give at least rough estimates of the values of the second-order rate constant of PBP acylation, thus permitting study of the structure–activity relationships.

17.6.4 Structure–activity relationships

For a long time, β-lactam antibiotic activity was attributed to the inherent strain of the four-membered ring and reduced amide resonance due to the lack of normal planar arrangement assumed to be necessary for the stabilization of the nitrogen long pair (Woodward 1980). Recently, chemists themselves have cast doubt on this 'dogma'. Most bicyclic β-lactam antibiotics do not exhibit exceptional chemical reactivity, and monocyclic β-lactam compounds (where the nitrogen atom is planar) with suitable electron-withdrawing substitutents may be as reactive as bicyclic ones (Page 1984). In fact, the 'goodness of fit' of the β-lactam molecules to the active sites of D,D-peptidases/PBPs is the primary parameter that governs their inactivating potency (Frère *et al.* 1982).

Although the scissile bonds in the R–D–Ala–D–Ala-terminated peptides and β-lactam compounds are functionally equivalent, in that they are susceptible to attack by the active-site serine, the efficacy of the enzyme acylation step shows wide variations, depending on both the D,D-peptidase/PBP and the carbonyl donor. The bicyclic benzylpenicillin is not necessarily a better acylating agent than the acyclic tripeptide Ac$_2$–L–Lys–D–Ala-D–Ala (Leyh-Bouille *et al.* 1986) and k_{+2}/K values ranging from $10\ \mathrm{M}^{-1}\mathrm{s}^{-1}$ or less to $1\,000\,000\ \mathrm{M}^{-1}\mathrm{s}^{-1}$ or more have been observed (for examples, see Ghuysen *et al.* 1984; Frère and Joris 1985). These variations must reflect differences in modes of binding to the enzymes' active sites and enzyme/PBP–ligand associations of widely varying productiveness.

Both partners—the enzymes and the ligands—play essential and complementing roles. 'Slight' remodelling of the active site of a D,D-peptidase/PBP may produce a bacterial strain with a substantial level of resistance to certain β-lactam antibiotics. Single amino acid substitutions in the *E. coli* PBP3 have such profound effects (Hedge and Spratt 1985a,b). 'Slight' structural modifications in selected peptide and β-lactam conformers result, as revealed by the calculation of their electrostatic potentials, in drastic alterations in the spatial disposition and strength of the positive and negative potentials that surround the carbonyl group of the scissile bond. These potentials are, most likely, important pharmacophores that govern the rate of enzyme acylation (Lamotte-Brasseur *et al.* 1984).

17.6.5   Functional similarities and evolutionary relationship between active-site serine D,D-peptidases/PBPs and β-lactamases

β-Lactamases and inhibitors are discussed in Chapter 4 by R. F. Pratt. The following points are relevant to the present analysis.

The majority of the known β-lactamases are active-site serine enzymes. They are devoid of peptidase activity but, in complete analogy with the active-site serine D,D-peptidases, they catalyse, with varying efficiency, hydrolysis of acyclic D-alanyl-O-CHR-COO$^-$-terminated ester carbonyl donors (see above) and the presence of alternate nucleophiles causes partitioning of β-lactamase activity at the level of the acyl enzyme (Knott-Hunziker *et al.* 1982; Pratt and Govardhan 1984; Pratt *et al.* 1985). Moreover, the active-site serine β-lactamase-catalysed hydrolysis of β-lactam compounds is a three-step process that obeys eqn. (17.2) and proceeds as shown in Fig. 17.14. In principle, the acyl enzyme is short-lived ($k_{+3} = 10$–$100\ \mathrm{s}^{-1}$) but this property is far from being general. The acyl enzyme formed with β-lactam compounds such as cefoxitin, clavulanate, penicillanate sulphone, and 6-β-bromo(iodo)penicillanate, may be long-lived or may rearrange itself in an inactive, stable α,β-unsaturated adduct, thus conferring on these compounds the property to inactivate the β-lactamases.

Gene analysis and establishment of complete amino acid sequences (Ambler 1980; Jaurin and Grundström 1981; Dale *et al.* 1985; Lindberg and Normark 1986) show that the active-site serine in the β-lactamases is flanked by a lysine at the third position of its carbonyl side and by a phenylalanine at the fourth position of its amino side (Phe-X-X-X-Ser-X-X-Lys). Hence, the tetrad Ser-X-X-Lys is conserved in all the active-site serine β-lactamases and D,D-peptidases/PBPs studied so far. Note that a phenylalanine situated as shown above is also present in both the PBP3 of *E. coli* and the D,D-peptidase/PBP of *Streptomyces* R61, but not in the *E. coli* PBPs 1A, 1B, and 5.

X-ray analysis of the active-site serine β-lactamase of class A of *B. licheniformis* (at a 3.5 Å resolution; Kelly *et al.* 1986) and the active-site serine D,D-peptidase/PBP of *Streptomyces* R61 (at a 2.8 Å resolution; Kelly *et al.* 1985) has made it possible to compare the path of each of the polypeptide chains through the elements of secondary structure. Although the two enzymes lack overall similarity in their primary structures except for a small number of conserved amino acids (9 out of 25) around the active-site serine (Duez *et al.* 1987; Neugebauer *et al.* 1981), the matching of the α-helices and strands of β-sheet is so marked between the two structures that it is impossible to argue against a close evolutionary relationship (Fig. 17.15). A similar conclusion has been reached by Samraoui *et al.* (1986) with the *Bacillus cereus* β-lactamase, also of class A. Conversion of a penicillin-binding D,D-peptidase into a penicillin-hydrolysing β-lactamase by divergent evolution has resulted in almost complete disappearance of the similarity in primary structures but almost complete conservation of three-dimensional folding with structural changes affecting only the relatively compact catalytic area. The *Streptomyces* R61 D,D-peptidase and the β-lactamases of class C show higher similarity in their amino acid sequences. The class C β-lactamases may share all of the tertiary structural features that are common to the class A β-lactamases and the *Streptomyces* R61 D,D-peptidase.

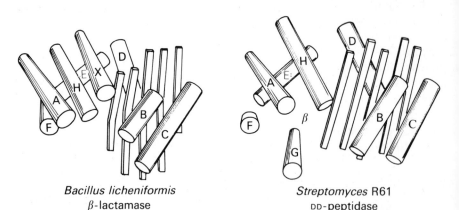

Bacillus licheniformis
β-lactamase

Streptomyces R61
DD-peptidase

Fig. 17.15. Secondary structure elements in *Bacillus licheniformis* β-lactamase of class A and *Streptomyces* R61 D,D-peptidase. Each structure contains a β-sheet composed of five strands of similar length protected on the front face by two helices and by one helix on the back face. Seven of the eight helices in the D,D-peptidase structure are identified with seven helices in the β-lactamase structure. However, helix G of the D,D-peptidase has no corresponding helix in the β-lactamase and there is a well-defined helix X in the β-lactamase that lies at the top of the helical cluster and crosses the edge of the β-sheet. The penicillin binding (D,D-peptidase) active site in the *Streptomyces* R61 enzyme is flanked on one side by the beginning of helix A, at the rear by the β-sheet, and at the bottom by helix G. From Kelly *et al.* (1986). Reprinted with permission.

17.6.6   On the existence of zinc-dependent D,D-peptidases and β-lactamases

One zinc-dependent D,D-peptidase (from *Streptomyces albus* G) and at least two zinc-dependent β-lactamases are known. They do not operate by an acyl enzyme mechanism. The metallo-D,D-peptidase catalyses only carboxypeptidation reactions, is a powerful peptidoglycan hydrolase (Leyh-Bouille *et al.* 1970), shows very low susceptibility to β-lactam compounds, and does not behave as a PBP (unless very drastic conditions are used). *E. coli* also possesses a peptidoglycan-hydrolysing D,D-peptidase that is not susceptible to β-lactam antibiotics (Keck and Schwarz 1979). The three-dimensional structure at 2.5 Å resolution (Dideberg *et al.* 1982; Charlier *et al.* 1984) and amino acid sequence (Joris *et al.* 1983) of the *Streptomyces* zinc-dependent D,D-peptidase are known. Its counterpart, the zinc-dependent β-lactamase II of *B. cereus* (of known primary structure; Ambler *et al.* 1985; Hussain *et al.* 1985) has been crystallized. The metallo D,D-peptidase and β-lactamase lack amino acid sequence homology. Further studies will show whether or not they have three-dimensional relationships.

17.7.   Concluding remarks and future prospects

Recent studies have brought closer the final goal of precise understanding, at the atomic level, of the catalytic properties of the D,D-peptidases and β-lactamases and their molecular interactions with ligands. Site-directed mutagenesis, X-ray crystallography, molecular graphics, and theoretical chemistry should lead to the rational design of novel types of inactivators—not necessarily possessing a β-lactam ring—of these two important groups of enzymes.

Addendum

For recent papers dealing with the three-dimensional structure of and the evolutionary relationship between the active-site serine D,D-peptidase/PBPs and β-lactamases, see:

Dideberg, O., Charlier, P., Wéry, J. P., Dehottay, P., Dusart, J., Erpicum, T., Frère, J. M., and Ghuysen, J. M. (1987). The crystal structure of the β-lactamase of *Streptomyces albus* G at 0.3 nm resolution. *Biochem. J.*, **245**, 911–13.

Herzberg, O. and Moult, J. (1987). Bacterial resistance to β-lactam antibiotics: crystal structure of β-lactamase from *Staphylococcus aureus* PC1 at 2.5 Å resolution. *Science*, **236**, 694–701.

Joris, B., Ghuysen, J. M., Dive, G., Renard, A., Dideberg, O., Charlier, P., Frère, J. M., Kelly, J. A., Boyington, J. C., Moews, P. C., and Knox, J. R. (1988). The active-site serine penicillin-recognized enzymes as members of the *Streptomyces* R61 DD-peptidase family. *Biochem. J.*, **250**, 313–24.

Acknowledgements

The work in Liège is supported by contracts with the Fonds National de la Recherche Scientifique, Brussels, the Belgian Government, Brussels, and the Ministère des Technologies nouvelles, Région wallonne, Brussels.

References

Abrams, A. (1958). O-acetyl groups in the cell wall of *Streptococcus faecalis*. *J. Biol. Chem.*, **230**, 949–59.

Abraham, E. P. (1981). The β-lactam antibiotics. *Sci. Am.*, **244**, 64–74.

Adams, E. (1976). Catalytic aspects of enzymatic racemization. *Adv. Enzymol.*, **44**, 69–138.

Ambler, R. P. (1980). The structure of β-lactamases. *Phil. Trans. R. Soc.*, **B289**, 321–31.

Ambler, R. P., Daniel, M., Fleming, J., Hermoso, J. M., Pang, C., and Waley, S. G. (1985). The amino acid sequence of the zinc-requiring β-lactamase II from the bacterium *Bacillus cereus* 569. *FEBS Lett.*, **189**, 207–11.

Anwar, R. A. and Vlaovic, M. (1979). Purification of UDP-N-acetylenol-pyruvoyl glucosamine reductase from *Escherichia coli* by affinity chromatography, its subunit structure and the absence of flavin as the prosthetic group. *Can. J. Biochem.*, **57**, 188–96.

Atherton, F. R., Hall, M. J., Hassall, C. H., Lambert, R. W., Lloyd, W. J., Lord, A. V., Ringrose, P. S., and Westmacott, D. (1983). Phosphonopeptides as substrates for peptide transport systems and peptidases of *Escherichia coli*. *Antimicrob. Agents Chemother.*, **24**, 522–8.

Baddiley, J. (1972). Teichoic acids in cell walls and membranes of bacteria. *Essays Biochem.*, **8**, 35–77.

Barbas, J. A., Diaz, J., Rodriguez-Tebar, A., and Vazquez, D. (1986). Specific location of penicillin-binding proteins within the cell envelope of *Escherichia coli*. *J. Bacteriol.*, **165**, 269–75.

Barrett, J. F., Schramm, V. L., and Shockman, G. D. (1984). Hydrolysis of soluble, linear, un-cross-linked peptidoglycans by endogenous bacterial N-acetylmuramylhydrolases. *J. Bacteriol.*, **159**, 520–6.

Bayer, M. H. and Bayer, M. E. (1985). Phosphoglycerides and phospholipase C in membrane fractions of *Escherichia coli* B. *J. Bacteriol.*, **162**, 50–4.

Bayer, M. H., Costello, G. P., and Bayer, M. E. (1982). Isolation and partial characterization of membrane vesicles carrying markers of membrane adhesion sites. *J. Bacteriol.*, **149**, 758–69.

Blumberg, P. M. and Strominger, J. L. (1974). Interaction of penicillin with the bacterial wall : penicillin binding proteins and penicillin-sensitive enzymes. *Bacteriol. Rev.*, **38**, 291–335.

Blundell, J. K. and Perkins, H. R. (1985). The peptidoglycan of *Neisseria gonorrhoeae*, with or without O-acetyl groups, contains anhydromuramyl residues. *J. Gen. Microbiol.*, **131**, 3397–400.

Blundell, J. K., Smith, G. J., and Perkins, H. R. (1980). The peptidoglycan of *Neisseria gonorrhoeae* : O-acetyl groups and lysozyme sensitivity. *FEMS Microbiol. Lett.*, **9**, 259–61.

Bodansky, M., Sigler, G. F., and Bodansky, A. (1973). Structure of the peptide antibiotic amphomycin. *J. Am. Chem. Soc.*, **95**, 2352–7.

Broome-Smith, J. K., Edelman, A., and Spratt, B. G. (1983). Sequence of penicillin-binding protein 5 of *Escherichia coli*. In *The target of penicillin* (ed. R. Hakenbeck, J. V. Höltje, and H. Labischinski), pp. 403–8. de Gruyter, Berlin.

Broome-Smith, J. K., Hedge, P. J., and Spratt, B. G. (1985). Production of thiol-penicillin-binding protein 3 of *Escherichia coli* using a two-primer method of site-directed mutagenesis. *EMBO J.*, **4**, 231–5.

Broome-Smith, J. K., Edelman, A., Yousif, S., and Spratt, B. G. (1985). The nucleotide sequences of the *ponA* and *ponB* genes encoding penicillin-binding proteins 1A and 1B of *Escherichia coli* K12. *Eur. J. Biochem.*, **147**, 437–46.

Brumfitt, W., Wardlaw, A. C., and Park, J. T. (1958). Development of lysozyme-resistance in *Micrococcus lysodeikticus* and its association with an increased O-acetyl content of the cell wall. *Nature Lond.*, **181**, 1783–4.

Burman, L. G. and Park, J. T. (1983). Changes in the composition of *Escherichia coli* murein as it ages during exponential growth. *J. Bact.*, **155**, 447–53.

Canepari, P., Varaldo, P. E., Fontana, R., and Satta, G. (1985). Different staphylococcal species contain various numbers of penicillin-binding proteins ranging from four (*Staphylococcus aureus*) to only one (*Staphylococcus hyicus*). *J. Bacteriol.*, **163**, 796–8.

Cassidy, P. J. and Kahan, F. M. (1973). A stable enzyme-phosphoenolpyruvate intermediate in the synthesis of uridine-5′diphospho-N-acetyl-2-amino-2-deoxy glucose 3-O-enolpyruvyl ether. *Biochemistry*, **12**, 1364–74.

Cavard, D., Lloubès, R., Morlon, J., Chartier, M. and Lazdunski, M. (1985). Lysis protein encoded by plasmid ColA-CA31. Gene sequence and export. *Mol. Gen. Genet.*, **199**, 95–100.

Charlier, P., Dideberg, O., Jamoulle, J. C., Frère, J. M., Ghuysen, J. M., Dive, G., and Lamotte-Brasseur, J. (1984). Active-site directed inactivators of the Zn^{2+} D-alanyl-D-alanine-cleaving carboxypeptidase of *Streptomyces albus* G. *Biochem. J.*, **219**, 763–72.

Cole, S. T., Saint-Joanis, B., and Pugsley, A. P. (1985). Molecular characterisation of the colicin E2 operon and identification of its products. *Mol. Gen. Genet.*, **198**, 465–72.

Coyette, J., Ghuysen, J. M., and Fontana, R. (1978). Structure of the walls of *Lactobacillus acidophilus* strain 63 AM Gasser. *Biochemistry*, **9**, 2935–43.

Coyette, J., Somzé, A., Briquet, J. J., and Ghuysen, J. M. (1983). Function of penicillin binding protein 3 in *Streptococcus faecium*. In *The target of penicillin* (ed. R. Hakenbeck, J. V. Höltje, and H. Labischinski), pp. 523–30. de Gruyter, Berlin.

Dale, J. W., Godwin, D., Mossakowska, D., Stephenson, P., and Wall, S. (1985). Sequence of the OXA-2-β-lactamase: comparison with other penicillin-reactive enzymes. *FEBS Lett.*, **191**, 39–44.

Daneo-Moore, L. and Shockman, G. D. (1977). The bacterial cell surface in growth and division. In *The synthesis, assembly and turnover of cell surface components* (ed. G. Poste and G. L. Nicolson) pp. 599–715. Elsevier/North-Holland, Amsterdam.

Dideberg, O., Charlier, P., Dive, G., Joris, B., Frère, J. M., and Ghuysen, J. M. (1982). Structure at 2.5 Å resolution of a Zn^{2+}-containing D-alanyl-D-alanine-cleaving carboxypeptidase. *Nature Lond.*, **299**, 469–70.

Dougherty, T. J. (1983a). Synthesis and modification of the peptidoglycan in *Neisseria gonorrhoeae*. *FEMS Microbiol. Lett.*, **17**, 51–3.

Dougherty, T. J. (1983b). Peptidoglycan biosynthesis in *Neisseria gonorrhoeae* strains sensitive and intrinsically resistant to β-lactam antibiotics. *J. Bacteriol.*, **153**, 429–35.

Dougherty, T. J. (1985a). Analysis of *Neisseria gonorrhoeae* peptidoglycan by reverse-phase high pressure liquid chromatography. *J. Bacteriol.*, **163**, 69–74.

Dougherty, T. J. (1985b). Involvement of a change of penicillin target and peptidoglycan structure in low level resistance to β-lactam antibiotics in *Neisseria gonorrhoeae*. *Antimicrob. Agents Chemother.*, **28**, 90–5.

Duez, C., Piron-Fraipont, C., Joris, B., Dusart, J., Urdea, M. S., Martial, J. A., Frère, J. M., and Ghuysen, J. M. (1987). Primary sequence of the *Streptomyces* R61 extracellular D,D-peptidase a. Cloning into *Streptomyces lividans* and nucleotide sequence of the gene, *Eur. J. Biochem*, **162**, 509–18.

Duksin, D. and Mahomey, W. C. (1982). Relationships of the structure and biological activity in the natural homologues of tunicamycin. *J. Biol. Chem.*, **257**, 3105–9.

Eckardt, K. (1983). Tunicamycins, streptovirudins and corynetoxins, a special subclass of nucleoside antibiotics. *J. Nat. Prod.*, **46**, 544–50.

Elliott, T. S. J., Ward, J. B., and Rogers, H. J. (1975a). The formation of cell wall polymers by reverting protoplasts of *Bacillus licheniformis* 6346 His. *J. Bacteriol.*, **124**, 623–32.

Elliott, T. S. J., Ward, J. B., Wyrick, P. B., and Rogers, H. J. (1975b). An ultrastructural study of the reversion of protoplasts of *Bacillus licheniformis* His⁻ to bacilli. *J. Bacteriol.*, **124**, 905–17.

Engel, A., Massalski, A., Schindler, H., Dorset, D. L., and Rosenbusch, J. P. (1985). Porin channel triplets merge into single outlets in *Escherichia coli* outer membranes. *Nature Lond.*, **317**, 643–5.

Essig, P., Martin, H. H., and Gmeiner, J. (1982). Murein and lipopolysaccharide biosynthesis in synchronized cells of *Escherichia coli* K12 and the effect of penicillin G, mecillinam and nalidixic acid. *Arch. Microbiol.*, **132**, 245–50.

Fersht, A. (1985). *Enzyme structure and mechanism*, pp. 325–30. Freeman, San Francisco.

Fischer, H. and Tomasz, A. (1984). Production and release of peptidoglycan and wall teichoic acid polymers in pneumococci treated with β-lactam antibiotics. *J. Bacteriol.*, **157**, 507–13.

Fleck, J., Mock, M., Minck, R., and Ghuysen, J. M. (1971). The cell envelope in *Proteus vulgaris* P18. Isolation and characterization of the peptidoglycan component. *Biochim. Biophys. Acta*, **233**, 489–503.

Fontana, R., Cerini, R., Longoni, P., Grossato, A., and Canepari, P. (1983). Identification of a streptococcal penicillin-binding protein that reacts very slowly with penicillin. *J. Bacteriol.*, **155**, 1343–50.

Fontana, R., Grossato, A., Rossi, L., Rong Cheng, Y., and Satta, G. (1985). Transition from resistance to hypersusceptibility to β-lactam antibiotics associated with loss of a low-affinity penicillin-binding protein in a *Streptococcus faecium* mutant highly resistant to penicillin. *Antimicrob. Agent. Chemother.*, **28**, 678–83.

Frère, J. M. and Joris, B. (1985). Penicillin-sensitive enzymes in peptidoglycan synthesis. *CRC Critical Reviews in Microbiology*, **11**, 299–396.

Frère, J. M., Ghuysen, J. M., and De Graeve, J. (1978). Fragmentation of penicillin catalysed by the exocellular D,D-carboxypeptidase–transpeptidase of *Streptomyces* R61. Isotopic study of hydrogen fixation on carbon 6. *FEBS Lett.*, **88**, 147–50.

Frère, J. M., Duez, C., Ghuysen, J. M., and Vandekerckhove, J. (1976). Occurrence of a serine residue in the penicillin-binding site of the exocellular D,D-carboxypeptidase–transpeptidase from *Streptomyces* R61. *FEBS Lett.*, **70**, 257–60.

Frère, J. M., Ghuysen, J. M., Perkins, H. R., and Nieto, M. (1973). Kinetics of concomitant transfer and hydrolysis reactions catalysed by the exocellular D,D-carboxypeptidase–transpeptidase of *Streptomyces* R61. *Biochem. J.*, **135**, 483–92.

Frère, J. M., Kelly, J. A., Klein, D., Ghuysen, J. M., Claes, P., and Vanderhaeghe, H. (1982). Δ²- and Δ³-Cephalosporins, penicillanate and 6-unsubstituted penems. Intrinsic reactivity and interaction with β-lactamases and D-alanyl-D-alanine-cleaving serine peptidases. *Biochem. J.*, **203**, 223–34.

Freudl, R., Schwarz, H., Klose, M., Movva, N. R., and Henning, U. (1985). The nature of information, required for export and sorting, present within the outer membrane protein OmpA of *Escherichia coli* K12. *EMBO J.*, **4**, 3593–8.

Gale, E. F., Cundliffe, E., Reynolds, P. E., Richmond, M. H., and Waring, M. J. (1981). *The molecular basis of antibiotic action* (2nd edn). pp. 144–61. Wiley, London.

Ghuysen, J. M. (1968). Use of bacteriolytic enzymes in determination of wall structure and the role in cell metabolism. *Bacteriol. Rev.*, **32**, 425–64.

Ghuysen, J. M. (1977). Biosynthesis and assembly of bacterial cell walls. In *The synthesis, assembly and turnover of cell surface components* (ed. G. Poste and G. L. Nicolson), pp. 463–595. Elsevier/North-Holland, Amsterdam.

Ghuysen, J. M., Nguyen-Distèche, M., and Rousset, A. (1986). β-lactam-induced *Proteus* L-forms. In *The bacterial L-forms* (ed. S. Madoff), Vol. 15, pp. 127–62. Marcel Dekker, New York.

Ghuysen, J. M., Frère, J. M., Leyh-Bouille, M., Nguyen-Distèche, M., and Coyette, J. (1986). Active-site serine D-alanyl-D-alanine-cleaving peptidase-catalysed acyl transfer reactions. Procedures for studying the penicillin-binding proteins of bacterial plasma membranes. *Biochem. J.*, **235**, 159–169.

Ghuysen, J. M., Frère, J. M., Leyh-Bouille, M., Nguyen-Distèche, M., Coyette, J., Dusart, J., Joris, B., Duez, C., Dideberg, O., Charlier, P., Dive, G., and Lamotte-Brasseur, J. (1984). Bacterial wall peptidoglycan, D,D-peptidases and β-lactam antibiotics. *Scand. J. Infect. Dis.*, **42**, 17–37.

Giesbrecht, P., Labischinski, H., and Wecke, J. (1985). A special morphogenetic wall defect and the subsequent activity of 'murosomes' as the very reason for penicillin-induced bacteriolysis in staphylococci. *Arch. Microbiol.*, **141**, 315–24.

Glaser, L. (1960). Glutamic acid racemase from *Lactobacillus arabinosus*. *J. Biol. Chem.*, **235**, 2095–8.

Glauner, B. and Schwarz, U. (1983). The analysis of murein composition with high pressure liquid chromatography. In *The target of penicillin* (ed. R. Hakenbeck, J. V. Höltje, and H. Labischinski), pp. 29–34. de Gruyter, Berlin.

Gmeiner, J. and Kroll, H. P. (1981). Murein biosynthesis and O-acetylation of N-acetylmuramic acid during the cell division cycle of *Proteus mirabilis*. *Eur. J. Biochem.*, **117**, 171–7.

Gmeiner, J., Essig, P., and Martin, H. H. (1982). Characterization of minor fragments after digestion of *Escherichia coli* murein with endo-N,O-diacetylmuramidase from *Chalaropsis*, and determination of glycan chain length. *FEBS Lett.*, **138**, 109–12.

Goldman, R. and Strominger, J. L. (1972). Biosynthesis of the peptidoglycan of bacterial cell walls. XXVI. Purification and properties of C_{55}-isoprenyl pyrophosphate phosphatase from *Micrococcus lysodeikticus*. *J. Biol. Chem.*, **247**, 5116–22.

Gross, E. and Morell, J. L. (1971). Structure of nisin. *J. Am. Chem. Soc.*, **93**, 4634–7.

Gross, E., Kilz, H. H., and Nebelin, E. (1973). Subtilin VI. Die Struktur des Subtilins. *Hoppe-Seyler's Z. Physiol. Chem.*, **35**, 810–12.

Hakenbeck, R., Tarpay, M., and Tomasz, A. (1980). Multiple changes of penicillin-binding proteins in penicillin-resistant clinical isolates of *Streptococcus pneumoniae*. *Antimicrob. Agents Chemother.*, **17**, 364–71.

Hakkaart, M. J. J., Veltkamp, E., and Nijkamp, H. J. J. (1981). Protein H encoded by plasmid Clo DF13 involved in lysis of the bacterial host. I. Localisation of the gene and identification and sub-cellular localisation of the gene H product. *Mol. Gen. Genet.*, **183**, 318–25.

Hancock, J. C. and Baddiley, J. (1985). In *The enzymes and biological membranes* (ed. A. N. Martonosi) (2nd edn), Vol. 2, pp. 279–307. Plenum, New York.

Hara, H. and Suzuki, H. (1984). A novel glycan polymerase that synthesizes uncross-linked peptidoglycan in *Escherichia coli*. *FEBS Lett.*, **168**, 155–60.

Hedge, P. J. and Spratt, B. G. (1984). A gene fusion that localizes the penicillin-domain of penicillin-binding protein 3 of *Escherichia coli*. *FEBS Lett.*, **176**, 179–84.

Hedge, P. J. and Spratt, B. G. (1985a). Resistance to β-lactam antibiotics by re-modelling the active site of an *E. coli* penicillin-binding protein. *Nature Lond.*, **318**, 478–80.

Hedge, P. J. and Spratt, B. G. (1985b). Amino acid substitutions that reduce the affinity of penicillin-binding protein 3 of *Escherichia coli* for cephalexin. *Eur. J. Biochem.*, **161**, 111–21.

Hobot, J. A., Carlemalm, E., Welliger, W., and Kellenberger, E. (1984). Periplasmic gel: new concept resulting from the reinvestigation of bacterial cell envelope ultrastructure by new methods. *J. Bacteriol.*, **160**, 143–52.

Höltje, J. V., Mirelman, D., Sharon, N., and Schwarz, U. (1975). A novel type of murein transglycosylase in *Escherichia coli*. *J. Bacteriol.*, **124**, 1067–76.

Houba-Herin, N., Hara, H., Inouye, M., and Hirota, Y. (1986). Binding of penicillin to thiol-penicillin-binding protein 3 of *Escherichia coli* : identification of its active site. *Mol. Gen. Genet.*, **201**, 499–504.

Huang, Y.-X., Ching, G., and Inouye, M. (1983). Comparison of the lipoprotein gene among the *Enterobacteriaceae*. DNA sequence of *Morganella morganii* lipoprotein gene and its expression in *Escherichia coli*. *J. Biol. Chem.*, **258**, 8139–45.

Hussain, M., Carlino, A., Madonna, M. J., and Lampen, J. O. (1985). Cloning and sequencing of the metallothioprotein *β*-lactamase II gene of *Bacillus cereus* 569/H in *Escherichia coli*. *J. Bacteriol.*, **164**, 223–9.

Imada, A., Kintaka, K., Nakao, M., and Shinagawa (1982). Bulgecin, a bacterial metabolite which in concert with *β*-lactam antibiotics, causes bulge formation. *J. Antibiot.*, **35**, 1400–3.

Inouye, M. (1979). *Bacterial outer membranes : biosynthesis and functions*. Wiley Interscience, London.

Inukai, M. and Inouye, M. (1983). Association of the prolipoprotein accumulated in the presence of globomycin with the outer membrane of *Escherichia coli*. *Eur. J. Biochem.*, **130**, 27–32.

Ito, E. and Strominger, J. L. (1962a). Enzymatic synthesis of the peptide in bacterial uridine nucleotides. I. Enzymatic addition of L-alanine, D-glutamic acid and L-lysine. *J. Biol. Chem.*, **237**, 2689–95.

Ito, E. and Strominger, J. L. (1962b). Enzymatic synthesis of the peptide in bacterial uridine nucleotides. II. Enzymatic synthesis and addition of D-alanyl-D-alanine. *J. Biol. Chem.*, **237**, 2696–703.

Ito, E. and Strominger, J. L. (1964). Enzymatic synthesis of the peptide in bacterial uridine nucleotides. III. Purification and properties of L-lysine-adding enzyme. *J. Biol. Chem.*, **239**, 210–4.

Iwasaki, H., Horii, S., Asai, M., Mizuno, K., Uenayagi, J., and Miyaka, A. (1973). Enduracidin, a new antibiotic. Structures of enduracidins A and B. *Chem. Pharm. Bull.*, (Tokyo) **21**, 1184–91.

Jaurin, B. and Grundström, T. (1981). AmpC cephalosporinase of *Escherichia coli* K12 has a different evolutionary origin from that of *β*-lactamases of the penicillinase type. *Proc. Nat. Acad. Sci. USA*, **78**, 4897–901.

Johnston, M. M. and Diven, W. F. (1969). Studies on amino acid racemases. I. Partial purification and properties of the alanine racemase from *Lactobacillus fermenti*. *J. Biol. Chem.*, **244**, 5414–20.

Johnston, R. B., Scholz, J. J., Diven, W. F., and Shepard, S. (1966). Some further studies on the purification and mechanism of action of alanine racemase from *Bacillus subtilis*. In *Pyridoxal catalysis : enzymes and model systems* (ed. E. E. Snell, A. E. Braunstein, E. S. Severin, and Y. M. Torshinsky), pp. 537–45. Wiley Interscience, New York.

Joris, B., Van Beeumen, J., Casagrande, F., Gerday, Ch., Frère, J. M., and Ghuysen, J. M. (1983). The complete amino acid sequence of the Zn^{2+}-containing D-alanine-D-alanine-cleaving carboxypeptidase of *Streptomyces albus* G. *Eur. J. Biochem.*, **130**, 53–69.

Kahan, F. M., Kahan, J. S., Cassidy, P. J., and Kropp, H. (1974). The mechanism of action of fosfomycin. *Ann. N.Y. Acad. Sci.*, **235**, 364–86.

Kariyama, R. (1982). Increase of cardiolipin content in *Staphylococcus aureus* by the use of antibiotics affecting the cell wall. *J. Antibiotics*, **35**, 1700–4.

Kato, J. I., Suzuki, H., and Hirota, Y. (1985). Dispensability of either penicillin-binding protein-1a or -1b involved in the essential process for cell elongation in *Escherichia coli*. *Mol. Gen. Genet.*, **200**, 272–7.

Katz, W., Matsuhashi, M., Dietrich, C. P., and Strominger, J. L. (1967). Biosynthesis of the peptidoglycan of bacterial cell walls. IV. Incorporation of glycine in *Micrococcus lysodeikticus*. *J. Biol. Chem.*, **242**, 3207–17.

Keck, W. and Schwarz, U. (1979). *Escherichia coli* murein-D,D-endopeptidase insensitive to *β*-lactam antibiotics. *J. Bacteriol.*, **139**, 770–4.

Kelly, J. A., Knox, J. R., Moews, P. C., Hite, G. J., Bartolone, J. B., Zhao, H., Joris, B.,

Frère, J. M., and Ghuysen, J. M. (1985). 2.8 Å Structure of penicillin-sensitive D-alanyl-carboxypeptidase-transpeptidase from *Streptomyces* R61 and complexes with β-lactams. *J. Biol. Chem.*, **260**, 6449–58.

Kelly, J. A., Dideberg, O., Charlier, P., Wéry, J. P., Libert, M., Moews, P. C., Knox, J. R., Duez, C., Fraipont, C., Joris, B., Dusart, J., Frère, J. M., and Ghuysen, J. M. (1986). On the origin of bacterial resistance to penicillin. Comparison of a β-lactamase and a penicillin target. *Science*, **231**, 1429–31.

Kim, K. S., Yoshimori, R. N., Imagawa, D. T., and Bascom, F. A. (1979). Importance of medium in demonstrating penicillin tolerance by group B Streptococci. *Antimicrob. Agents Chemother.*, **16**, 214–6.

Kleffel, B., Garavito, R. M., Baumeister, W., and Rosenbusch, J. P. (1985). Secondary structure of a channel-forming protein : porin from *E. coli* outer membranes. *EMBO J.*, **4**, 1589–92.

Knott-Hunziker, V., Petursson, S., Waley, S. G., Jaurin, B., and Grundström, T. (1982). The acyl-enzyme mechanism of β-lactamase action. *Biochem. J.*, **207**, 315–22.

Lambert, M. P. and Neuhaus, F. C. (1972). Mechanism of D-cycloserine action : alanine racemase from *Escherichia coli* W. *J. Bacteriol.*, **110**, 978–87.

Lamotte-Brasseur, J., Dive, G., and Ghuysen, J. M. (1984). On the structural analogy between D-alanyl-D-alanine terminated peptides and β-lactam antibiotics. *Eur. J. Med. Chem.*, **19**, 319–30.

Lear, A. L. and Perkins, H. R. (1983). Degrees of *O*-acetylation and cross-linking of the peptidoglycan of *Neisseria gonorrhoeae* during growth. *J. Gen. Microbiol.*, **129**, 885–8.

Lee, N., Yamagata, H., and Inouye, M. (1983). Inhibition of secretion of a mutant lipoprotein across the cytoplasmic membrane by the wild-type lipoprotein of the *Escherichia coli* outer membrane. *J. Bacteriol.*, **155**, 407–11.

Léon, J., Garcia-Lobo, J. M., Navas, J., and Ortiz, J. M. (1985). Fosfomycin causes transient lysis in *Escherichia coli* strains carrying fosfomycin-resistance plasmids. *J. Gen. Microbiol.*, **131**, 3255–60.

Leyh-Bouille, M., Nguyen-Distèche, M., Pirlot, S., Veithen, A., Bourguignon, C., and Ghuysen, J. M. (1986). *Streptomyces* K15 D,D-peptidase-catalysed reaction with suicide β-lactam carbonyl donors. *Biochem. J.*, **235**, 177–82.

Leyh-Bouille, M., Ghuysen, J. M., Bonaly, R., Nieto, N., Perkins, H. R., Schleifer, K. H., and Kandler, O. (1970). Substrate requirements of the Streptomyces albus G D,D-carboxypeptidase. *Biochemistry*, **9**, 2961–71.

Lindberg, F. and Normark, S. (1986). Sequence of the *Citrobacter freundii* 0560 chromosomal ampC β-lactamase gene. *Eur. J. Biochem.*, **156**, 441–5.

Llaneza, J., Villar, C. J., Salas, J. A., Suarez, J. E., Mendoza, M. C., and Hardisson, C. (1985). Plasmid-mediated fosfomycin resistance is due to enzymatic modification of the antibiotic. *Antimicrob. Agents Chemother.*, **28**, 163–4.

Lüderitz, O., Freudenberg, M. A., Galanos, C., Lehmann, V., Rietschel, E. T., and Shaw, D. H. (1982). Lipopolysaccharides of gram-negative bacteria. *Current Topics Membr. Transp.*, **17**, 79–151.

Lugtenberg, B. and Van Alphen, L. (1983). Molecular architecture and functioning of the outer membrane of *Escherichia coli* and other gram-negative bacteria. *Biochim. Biophys. Acta*, **737**, 51–115.

Lugtenberg, E. J. J. and van Schijndel-van Dam, A. (1972). Temperature-sensitive mutants of *Escherichia coli* K12 with low activities of the L-alanine-adding enzyme and the D-alanyl-D-alanine adding enzyme. *J. Bacteriol.*, **110**, 35–40.

Lugtenberg, E. J. J. and van Schijndel-van Dam, A. (1973). Temperature-sensitive mutant of *Escherichia coli* K12 with an impaired D-alanyl:D-alanine ligase. *J. Bacteriol.*, **113**, 96–104.

Lutkenhaus, J. F. and Wu, H. C. (1980). Determination of transcriptional units and gene products from the ftsA region of *Escherichia coli*. *J. Bacteriol.*, **143**, 1281–8.

MacAlister, T. J., MacDonald, B., and Rothfield, L. I. (1983). The periseptal annulus: an organelle associated with cell division in gram-negative bacteria. *Proc. Nat. Acad. Sci. USA*, **80**, 1372–6.

Martin, H. H. and Gmeiner, J. (1979). Modification of peptidoglycan structure by penicillin action in cell walls of *Proteus mirabilis*. *Eur. J. Biochem.*, **95**, 487–95.

Martin, J. P., Fleck, J., Mock, M., and Ghuysen, J. M. (1973). The wall peptidoglycans of *Neisseria perflava*, *Moraxella glucidolytica*, *Pseudomonas alcaligenes* and *Proteus vulgaris* P18. *Eur. J. Biochem.*, **38**, 301–6.

Matsuhashi, M., Ishino, F., Tamaki, S., Nakajima-Iijima, S., Tomioka, S., Nakagawa, J. I., Hirata, A., Spratt, B. G., Tsuruoka, T., Inouye, S., and Yamada, Y. (1982). Mechanism of action of β-lactam antibiotics: inhibition of peptidoglycan transpeptidases and novel mechanisms of action. In *Trends in antibiotic research* (eds. A. L. Demain, T. Hata, and C. R. Hutchinson), pp. 99–114. Japan Antibiotics Research Association, Tokyo.

McLaughlin, J. R., Murray, C. L., and Rabinowitz, J. C. (1981). Unique features in the ribosome binding site sequence of the gram-positive *Staphylococcus aureus* β-lactamase gene. *J. Biol. Chem.*, **256**, 11283–91.

Miyakawa, T., Matsuzawa, H., Matsuhashi, M., and Sugino, Y. (1973). Cell wall peptidoglycan mutants of *Escherichia coli* K12: existence of two clusters of genes, *mra* and *mrb*, for cell wall peptidoglycan biosynthesis. *J. Bacteriol.*, **112**, 950–8.

Mizuno, Y. and Ito, E. (1968). Purification and properties of uridine diphosphate N-acetylmuramyl-L-alanyl-D-glutamate: *meso*-2,6-diaminopimelate ligase. *J. Biol. Chem.*, **243**, 2665–72.

Mizuno, Y., Yaegashi, M., and Ito, E. (1973). Purification and properties of uridine diphosphate N-acetylmuramate: L-alanine ligase. *J. Biochem. (Tokyo)*, **74**, 525–38.

Nakamura, K. and Inouye, M. (1979). DNA sequence of the gene for the outer membrane lipoprotein of *Escherichia coli*: an extremely AT-rich promoter. *Cell*, **18**, 1109–17.

Nakamura, K. and Inouye, M. (1980). DNA sequence of the *Serratia marcescens* lipoprotein gene. *Proc. Nat. Acad. Sci. USA*, **77**, 1369–73.

Nakamura, M., Maruyama, I. N., Soma, M., Kato, J., Suzuki, H., and Hirota, Y. (1983). On the process of cellular division of *Escherichia coli*. *Mol. Gen. Genet.*, **191**, 1–9.

Nathenson, S. G., Strominger, J. L., and Ito, E. (1964). Enzymatic synthesis of the peptide in bacterial uridine nucleotides. IV. Purification and properties of D-glutamic acid adding enzyme. *J. Biol. Chem.*, **239**, 1773–6.

Neugebauer, K., Sprengel, R., and Schaller, H. (1981). Penicillinase from *Bacillus licheniformis*: nucleotide sequence of the gene and implications for the biosynthesis of a secretory protein in a gram-positive bacterium. *Nucleic Acids Res.*, **9**, 2577–88.

Neuhaus, F. C. (1962a). Enzymatic synthesis of D-alanyl-D-alanine. I. Purification and properties of D-alanyl-D-alanine synthetase. *J. Biol. Chem.*, **237**, 778–86.

Neuhaus, F. C. (1962b). The enzymic synthesis of D-alanyl-D-alanine. II. Kinetic studies on D-alanyl-D-alanine synthetase. *J. Biol. Chem.*, **237**, 3128–35.

Neuhaus, F. C. (1971). Initial translocation reaction in the biosynthesis of peptidoglycan by bacterial membranes. *Acc. Chem. Res.*, **4**, 297–303.

Neuhaus, F. C. and Hammes, W. P. (1981). Inhibition of cell wall biosynthesis by analogues of alanine. *Pharmacol. Ther.*, **14**, 265–319.

Neuhaus, F. C. and Struve, W. G. (1965). Enzymatic synthesis of analogs of cell-wall precursor. I. Kinetics and specificity of uridine diphospho-N-acetylmuramyl-L-alanyl-

D-glutamyl-L-lysine: D-alanyl-D-alanine ligase (adenosine diphosphate) from *Streptococcus faecalis* R. *Biochemistry*, **4**, 120–31.

Nguyen-Distèche, M., Leyh-Bouille, M., Pirlot, S., Frère, J. M., and Ghuysen, J. M. (1986). *Streptomyces* K15 D,D-peptidase-catalysed reactions with ester and amide carbonyl donors. *Biochem. J.*, **235**, 167–76.

Nikaido, H. and Vaara, M. (1985). Molecular basis of bacterial outer permeability. *Microbiol. Rev.*, **49**, 1–32.

Nikaido, H., Rosenberg, E. Y. and J. Foulds (1983). Porin channels in *Escherichia coli*: studies with β-lactams on intact cells. *J. Bacteriol.*, **153**, 232–40.

Ogata, R. T., Winters, C., and Levine, R. P. (1982). Nucleotide sequence analysis of the complement resistance gene from plasmid R 100. *J. Bacteriol.*, **151**, 819–27.

Oppenheim, B. and Patchornik, A. (1974). Formation of D-alanyl-D-alanine and D-alanine from UDP-MurNAc-L-Ala-D-iso Glu-L-Lys-D-Ala-D-Ala by extracts of *Staphylococcus aureus* and *Streptococcus faecalis*. *FEBS Lett.*, **48**, 172–5.

Page, M. I. (1984). The mechanisms of reactions of β-lactam antibiotics. *Acc. Chem. Res.*, **17**, 144–51.

Park, W. and Matsuhashi, M. (1984). *Staphylococcus aureus* and *Micrococcus luteus* peptidoglycan transglycosylases that are not penicillin-binding proteins. *J. Bacteriol.*, **157**, 538–44.

Park, W., Seto, H., Hakenbeck, R., and Matsuhashi, M. (1985). Major peptidoglycan transglycosylase activity in *Streptococcus pneumoniae* that is not a penicillin-binding protein. *FEMS Microbiol. Lett.*, **27**, 45–8.

Pratt, R. F. and Govardhan, C. P. (1984). β-lactamase-catalysed hydrolysis of acyclic depsipeptides and acyl transfer to specific amino acid acceptors. *Proc. Nat. Acad. Sci. USA*, **81**, 1302–6.

Pratt, R. F., Faraci, W. S., and Govardhan, C. P. (1985). A direct spectrophotometric assay for D-alanine carboxypeptidases and for the esterase activity of β-lactamases. *Anal. Biochem.*, **144**, 204–6.

Pratt, J. M., Holland, I. B., and Spratt, B. G. (1981). Precursor forms of penicillin binding proteins 5 and 6 of *E. coli* cytoplasmic membrane. *Nature Lond.*, **293**, 307–9.

Pugsley, A. P. and Schwartz, M. (1985). Export and secretion of proteins by bacteria. *FEMS Microbiol. Rev.*, **32**, 3–38.

Randall, L. L. and Hardy, S. (1984) Export of protein in bacteria. *Microbiol. Rev.*, **48**, 290–8.

Reynolds, P. E. and Brown, D. F. J. (1985). Penicillin-binding proteins of β-lactam resistant strains of *Staphylococcus aureus*. Effect of growth conditions. *FEBS Lett.*, **192**, 28–32.

Rogers, H. J. and Perkins, H. R. (1968). *Cell walls and membranes*. Spon, London.

Rosso, G., Takashima, K., and Adams, E. (1969). Coenzyme content of purified alanine racemase from *Pseudomonas*. *Biochem. Biophys. Res. Commun.*, **34**, 134–40.

Roze, U. and Strominger, J. L. (1966). Alanine racemase from *Staphylococcus aureus*: conformation of its substrates and its inhibitor, D-cycloserine. *Mol. Pharmacol.*, **2**, 92–4.

Rozgonyi, F., Kiss, J., Jékel, P., and Vaczi, L. (1980). Effect of methicillin on the phospholipid of methicillin *Staphylococcus aureus*. *Acta Microbiol. Acad. Sci. Hung.*, **27**, 31–40.

Salton, M. R. J. (1964). *The bacterial cell wall*. Elsevier/North-Holland, New York.

Samraoui, B., Sutton, B. J., Todd, R. J., Artymiuk, P. J., Waley, S. G., and Philips, D. C. (1986). Tertiary structural similarity between a class A β-lactamase and a penicillin-sensitive D-alanyl carboxypeptidase-transpeptidase. *Nature (London)*, **320**, 378–80.

Scarborough, G. A. (1985). Binding energy, conformational change and the mechanism of transmembrane solute movements. *Microbiol. Rev.*, **49**, 214–31.

Schleifer, K. H. and Kandler, O. (1972). Peptidoglycan types of bacterial cell walls and their taxonomic implications. *Bacteriol. Rev.*, **36**, 407–77.

Shen, S. J., Floss, H. G., Kumagai, H., Yamada, H., Esaki, N., Soda, K., Wasserman, S. A., and Walsh, C. (1983). Mechanism of pyridoxal phosphate-dependent enzymatic amino acid racemization. *Chem. Commun.*, 1983, 82–3.

Shlaes, D. M., Marino, J., and Jacobs, M. R. (1984). Infection caused by vancomycin-resistant *Streptococcus sanguis* II. *Antimicrob. Agents Chemother.*, **25**, 527–8.

Shockman, G. D. and Barrett, J. F. (1983). Structure, function and assembly of cell walls of gram-positive bacteria. *Ann. Rev. Microbiol.*, **37**, 501–27.

Siewert, G. and Strominger, J. L. (1968). Biosynthesis of the peptidoglycan of bacterial cell walls. XI. Formation of the *iso*glutamine amide group in the cell walls of *Staphylococcus aureus*. *J. Biol. Chem.*, **243**, 783–91.

Silhavy, T., Benson, S. A., and Emr, S. D. (1983). Mechanisms of protein localization. *Microbiol. Rev.*, **47**, 313–44.

Soper, T. S. and Manning, J. M. (1981). Different modes of action of inhibitors of bacterial D-amino acid transaminase. *J. Biol. Chem.*, **256**, 4263–8.

Soper, T. S., Jones, W. M., and Manning, J. M. (1979). Effects of substrates on the selective modification of the cysteinyl residues of D-amino acid transaminase. *J. Biol. Chem.*, **254**, 10901–5.

Spratt, B. G. (1983). Penicillin binding proteins and the future of β-lactam antibiotics. *J. Gen. Microbiol.*, **129**, 1247–60.

Storm, D. R. (1974). Mechanism of bacitracin action: a specific lipid-peptide interaction. *Ann. N.Y. Acad. Sci.*, **235**, 387–98.

Sykes, R. B. and Philips, I. (1981). Azthreonam, a synthetic monobactam. *J. Antimicrob. Chemother.*, **8**, (suppl. E), 1–149.

Taku, A. and Fan, D. P. (1976a). Purification and properties of a protein factor stimulating peptidoglycan synthesis in toluene and LiCl-treated *Bacillus megaterium* cells. *J. Biol. Chem.*, **251**, 1889–95.

Taku, A. and Fan, D. P. (1976b). Identification of an isolated protein essential for peptidoglycan synthesis as the *N*-acetylglucosaminyl transferase. *J. Biol. Chem.*, **251**, 6154–6.

Taku, A. and Fan, D. P. (1979). Dissociation and reconstitution of membranes synthesizing the peptidoglycan of *Bacillus megaterium*. A protein factor for the polymerization step. *J. Biol. Chem.*, **254**, 3991–9.

Taku, A., Gunetileke, K. C., and Anwar, R. A. (1970). Biosynthesis of uridine diphospho *N*-acetylmuramic acid. III. Purification and properties of UDP-*N*-acetylenolpyruvyl glucosamine reductase. *J. Biol. Chem.*, **245**, 5012–6.

Taylor, A., Das, B. C., and Van Heijenoort, J. (1975). Bacterial cell wall peptidoglycan fragments produced by phage λ or Vi II endolysin and containing 1,6-anhydro-*N*-acetylmuramic acid. *Eur. J. Biochem.*, **53**, 47–54.

Tipper, D. J. and Strominger, J. L. (1965). Mechanism of action of penicillins: a proposal based on their structural similarity to acyl-D-alanyl-D-alanine. *Proc. Nat. Acad. Sci. USA*, **54**, 1133–41.

Tipper, D. J. and Strominger, J. L. (1966). Isolation of 4-0-β-*N*-acetylmuramyl-*N*-acetylglucosamine and 4-*O*-β-N,6-O-diacetyl muramyl-*N*-acetylglucosamine and the structure of the cell wall polysaccharide of *Staphylococcus aureus*. *Biochem. Biophys. Res. Commun.*, **22**, 48–56.

Tipper, D. J., Ghuysen, J. M., and Strominger, J. L. (1965). Structure of the cell wall of

Staphylococcus aureus, strain Copenhagen. III. Further studies of the disaccharides. *Biochemistry*, **4**, 468–73.

Tomasz, A. (1979). The mechanism of the irreversible antimicrobial effects of penicillins: how the β-lactam antibiotics, kill and lyse bacteria. *Ann. Rev. Microbiol.*, **33**, 113–37.

Tomasz, A., Albeno, A., and Zarato, E. (1970). Multiple antibiotic resistance in a bacterium with suppressed autolytic system. *Nature Lond.*, **227**, 138–40.

Van Heijenoort, Y., Derrien, M., and Van Heijenoort, J. (1978). Polymerization by transglycosylation in the biosynthesis of the peptidoglycan of *Escherichia coli* K12 and its inhibition by antibiotics. *FEBS Lett.*, **89**, 141–4.

Varetto, L., Frère, J. M., Nguyen-Distèche, M., Ghuysen, J. M., and Houssier, C. (1987). The pH-dependence of the active-site serine D,D-peptidase of *Streptomyces* R61. *Eur. J. Biochem.*, **162**, 525–31.

Venkateswaran, P. S., Lugtenberg, E. J., and Wu, H. C. (1973). Inhibition of phosphoenol-pyruvate: uridine diphosphate *N*-acetylglucosamine enolpyruvyl transferase by uridine diphosphate *N*-acetylmuramyl peptides. *Biochim. Biophys. Acta*, **293**, 570–4.

Ward, J. B. and Perkins, H. R. (1973). The direction of glycan synthesis in a bacterial peptidoglycan. *Biochem. J.*, **135**, 721–8.

Ward, J. B. and Perkins, H. R. (1974). Peptidoglycan biosynthesis by preparations from *Bacillus licheniformis*: crosslinking of newly synthesized chains to preformed cell wall. *Biochem. J.*, **139**, 781–4.

Waxman, D. J. and Strominger, J. L. (1983). Penicillin-binding proteins and the mechanism of action of β-lactam antibiotics. *Ann. Rev. Biochem.*, **52**, 825–69.

Welzel, P., Witteler, F. J., Müller, D., and Riemer, W. (1981). Structure of the antibiotic meonomycin A. *Angew. Chem. Int. Ed.*, **20**, 121–3.

Wicken, A. J. and Knox, K. W. (1975). Lipoteichoic acids: a new class of bacterial antigen. *Science*, **187**, 1161–7.

Wickus, G. G. and Strominger, J. L. (1973). Partial purification and properties of the pyruvate: uridine-diphospho-*N*-acetylglucosamine transferase from *Staphylococcus epidermidis*. *J. Bacteriol.*, **113**, 287–90.

Wickus, G. G., Rubenstein, P. A., Warth, A. D., and Strominger, J. L. (1973). Partial purification and some properties of UDP-*N*-acetylglucosamine enolpyruvate reductase from *Staphylococcus epidermidis*. *J. Bacteriol.*, **113**, 291–4.

Wiedemann, B. and Ghuysen, J. M. (1983). Symposium: mechanisms of resistance to β-lactam antibiotics. In Proceedings 13th International Congress of Chemotherapy. Vienna, 28 August–2 September, 1983. (ed K. H. Spitzy and K. Karrer), Part 12, pp. 12/1–42.

Wijsman, H. J. W. (1972a). A genetic map of several mutations affecting the mucopeptide layer of *Escherichia coli*. *Genet. Res.*, **20**, 65–74.

Wijsman, H. J. W. (1972b). The characterization of an alanine racemase mutant of *Escherichia coli*. *Genet. Res.*, **20**, 269–77.

Williams, D. H., Rajananda, V., Williamson, M. P., and Bojesen, G. (1980). The vancomycin and ristocetin group of antibiotics. In *Topics in antibiotic chemistry* (ed. P. Sammes), Vol. 5, pp. 119–59. Horwood, Chichester.

Williams, D. H., Williamson, M. P., Butcher, D. W., and Hammond, S. J. (1983). Detailed binding sites of the antibiotics vancomycin and ristocetin A: determination of intermolecular distances in antibiotic/substrate complexes by use of the time-dependent NOE. *J. Am. Chem. Soc.*, **105**, 1332–39.

Williamson, R. (1983). Resistance of *Clostridium perfringens* to β-lactam antibiotics mediated by a decreased affinity of a single essential penicillin-binding protein. *J. Gen. Microbiol.*, **129**, 2339–42.

Williamson, R. and Tomasz, A. (1985). Inhibition of cell wall synthesis and acylation of the penicillin binding proteins during prolonged exposure of growing *Streptococcus pneumoniae* to benzylpenicillin. *Eur. J. Biochem.*, **151**, 475–83.

Williamson, R. and Ward, J. B. (1982). Benzylpenicillin-induced filament formation of *Clostridium perfringens*. *J. Gen. Microbiol.*, **128**, 3025–35.

Wilson, D. (1976). *Penicillin in perspective*. Knopf, New York.

Wood, W. A. and Gunsalus, I. C. (1951). D-alanine formation: a racemase in *Streptococcus faecalis*. *J. Biol. Chem.*, **190**, 403–16.

Woodward, R. B. (1980). Penems and related substances. *Phil. Trans. R. Soc.*, **B289**, 239–50.

Wu, H. C. and Venkateswaran, P. S. (1974). Fosfomycin-resistant mutant of *Escherichia coli*. *Ann. N.Y. Acad. Sci. USA*, **235**, 587–92.

Yamagata, H., Nakamura, K., and Inouye, M. (1981). Comparison of the lipoprotein gene among the *Enterobacteriaceae*. DNA sequence of *Erwinia amylovora* lipoprotein gene. *J. Biol. Chem.*, **256**, 2194–8.

Yoshimura, F. and Nikaido, H. (1985). Diffusion of β-lactam antibiotics through the porin channels of *Escherichia coli* K15. *Antimicrob. Agents Chemother.*, **27**, 84–92.

Yousif, S. Y., Broome-Smith, J. K., and Spratt, B. G. (1985). Lysis of *Escherichia coli* by β-lactam antibiotics: deletion analysis of the role of penicillin-binding proteins 1A and 1B. *J. Gen. Microbiol.*, **131**, 2839–45.

Zighelboim, S. and Tomasz, A. (1980). Penicillin binding proteins of multiply antibiotic-resistant South-African strains of *Streptococcus pneumoniae*. *Antimicrob. Agents Chemother.*, **17**, 434–42.

18

Inhibition of proteinases

Section 18A

Proteinases: potential role in health and disease

W. H. Hörl

Proteinases act as catalysts in numerous biological processes. They participate in the digestion of food, formation of blood clots, fibrinolysis, and activation of the complement system. They are involved in the activation of various hormones and in the degradation of endogenous proteins within cells, particularly in the lysosomes.

18A.1 Classification of proteinases

Proteinases are not classified according to their origin or physiological function, but on the basis of their catalytic mechanisms, since knowledge of catalytic function at the active site is initially more informative than the substrate is. Hartley (1960) suggested a division into four groups, serine, thiol, acid, and metallo-proteinases. Some minor modifications have been proposed by Barrett (1980), who suggested cysteine instead of thiol and aspartic instead of carboxyl (acid) proteinases.

18A.1.1 Serine proteinases

The serine proteinases form the largest group; more than 50 are known in mammals. In plasma, some of them occur as coagulation factors and complement components. Among cellular serine proteinases, elastase and cathepsin G from polymorphonuclear (PMN) leucocytes are the best known (see Chapter 18C). Plasminogen activator is also a very important cellular serine proteinase (see Chapter 18D). Serine proteinases are inhibited by diisopropyl fluorophosphate. Some naturally occurring higher molecular weight inhibitors, such as soya bean trypsin inhibitor and aprotinin, are specific for certain groups or sub-groups of serine proteinases.

18A.1.2 Cysteine proteinases

The catalytic activity of cysteine proteinases is dependent on the thiol group of a cysteine residue. The best known is cathepsin B. Cathepsins H, L, and N have also been isolated recently. There is also a calcium-dependent cysteine proteinase that occurs in muscle and other tissues. The active site of the cysteine proteinases can be blocked by iodoacetate and disulphides.

18A.1.3 Aspartic proteinases

Pepsin is the best known acid proteinase. Carboxyl groups are involved in the catalytic mechanism. It is now known that these groups are aspartic acid residues. Cathepsin D is the major cellular aspartic proteinase and is identical to the gastric enzyme. Renin is also an aspartic proteinase. Pepstatin, which is produced by various streptomyces, seems to be the most effective inactivator.

18A.1.4 Metallo-proteinases

Zinc is naturally present in the active site of the metallo-proteinase enzyme. Metallo-proteinases are also activated by calcium. This group includes leucocyte collagenase, macrophage elastase, and a kidney microvillus enzyme. The metallo-proteinases are inhibited by chelating agents such as EDTA and 1,10-phenanthroline, and by dithiothreitol (for review see Heidland et al. 1983).

18.2 White blood cell proteinases

Neutrophil granulocytes contain a broad variety of agents that are involved in defence against and digestion of invading microorganisms. These include elastase, cathepsin G (formerly called chymotrypsin-like enzyme), proteinase-3, and collagenase. Neutral proteinases are stored within the azurophil granules (elastase and cathepsin G) and specific granules (latent forms of collagenase). In addition, two acid proteinases, cathepsin B and cathepsin D, are found in the azurophil granules and C-particles.

Lysosomal proteinases are not restricted to the intracellular compartment. They are readily released extracellularly during cell death, phagocytosis, exposure to antigen–antibody complexes, foreign bodies (extracorporal circulation during haemodialysis or open heart surgery), complement components, and toxic substances such as endotoxins or uraemic toxins. Under pathological conditions, massive proteinase release may occur. This results in tissue injury (vasculitis, necrotizing arteritis, arthritis, emphysema, proteinuria) and in degradation of plasma proteins, if the activities of the controlling proteinase inhibitor in plasma and tissue are insufficient.

Granulocyte elastase is probably largely responsible for tissue death both because of its broad substrate specificity and because of its abundance in the PMN leucocytes. This cationic protein degrades various plasma proteins such as transferrin, immunoglobulins, clotting factors, and fibronectin. Intravenous injection of human leucocyte elastase in green monkeys or endotoxin administration in dogs induced a marked drop in several clotting factors, including fibrinogen, and produced an increase in fibrinogen degradation products and severe bleeding complications. Some types of disseminated intravascular coagulation may therefore be partly due to direct proteolysis caused by PMN leucocytes. Elastase also causes a limited degradation of the third and fifth complement factors of human complement, digests solubilized elastin from tendon, lung, and basement membrane as well as proteoglycan subunits and native collagen (for review see Heidland *et al.* 1983).

Plasma levels of granulocyte elastase complexed with α_1-proteinase inhibitor (E–α_1 PI) increase during hemodialysis. Cellulose hydrate membrane caused a maximal increase of the E–α_1 PI levels (1659.0 ± 256.8 ng ml^{-1}). Patients dialysed with polyacrylonitrile dialysers failed to exhibit comparable E–α_1 PI values (237.8 ± 22.9 ng ml^{-1}). Patients dialysed with polysulphone dialyzers also displayed only very modest increases in their plasma E–α_1 PI levels. During haemodialysis, plasma E–α_1 PI values rose to a peak of 643.0 ± 174.7 ng ml^{-1} in patients on polymethylmethacrylate dialysers, to 557.5 ± 120.0 ng ml^{-1} on cuprophan dialysers, but only 381.9 ± 54.0 ng ml^{-1} on ethylene-vinyl alcohol copolymer dialysers. It was concluded that the degree of PMN leucocyte stimulation depends on the nature of the dialyser membrane material (Hörl *et al.* 1985).

In patients without pre-operative infection, operative trauma was followed by an increase in E–α_1 PI level upto three times the normal value. Patients suffering from pre-operative infections already showed clearly elevated pre-operative E–α_1 PI levels. Immediately after surgery, a slight decrease was observed, probably due to elimination of the focus of infection. At the onset of septicaemia, a highly significant increase in E–α_1 PI levels, up to 10-fold could be detected. E–α_1 PI levels of septicaemic patients who recovered showed a clear tendency towards normal values. In patients with persisting septicaemia, high levels of E–α_1 PI were measured until death supervened (Fritz *et al.* 1984).

Granulocyte cathepsin G is a cationic protein with microbicidal properties.

Migration and phagocytosis of PMN leucocytes are stimulated by cathepsin G. It has broad substrate affinity, similar to that of pancreatic chymotrypsin. It hydrolyses cartilage proteoglycans and degrades insoluble collagen. Cathepsin G is only weakly active on human lung elastin. However, the enzyme appears to degrade the microfibrillar component of the lung rapidly. *In vitro*, several clotting factors are irreversibly destroyed by a concentration far below the saturation level of the plasma antiproteinase. Cathepsin G also cleaves complement fractions C3, C5, and C1q. Cathepsin G from human neutrophils generates angiotensin II directly from angiotensinogen.

Granulocyte collagenase cleaves native solubilized collagen into TC_a and TC_b fragments. The neutral protease shows preference for Type I collagen, acts on proteoglycans, and has fibrinolytic activity. Granulocyte collagenase leads to immunochemical conversion of complement C3. In rheumatoid arthritis, a relationship between granulocyte collagenase and cartilage destruction has been observed.

Cathepsin D is present in lysosomes and has been purified from PMN leucocytes. This acid proteinase degrades cartilage proteoglycans and cleaves leucokininogens (for review, see Heidland *et al.* 1983).

18A.3   Proteases and hormones

Proteases can potentially regulate hormone availability by, (1) intracellular conversion of precursor hormones to active hormones, (2) degradation of hormone in the cell prior to secretion, (3) facilitation of release of hormone from the cell, (4) activation or inactivation of hormone in the circulation, and (5) degradation of hormone in target tissue. Crinophagy, the increased intracellular degradation of hormones, presumably by lysosomal proteases, may be an important physiological mechanism regulting the amount of hormone available for cellular secretion. Extracellular degradation occurs in blood, target organs, liver and kidney.

The conversion of PreProPTH (PrePro parathyroid hormone) to ProPTH occurs cotranslationally, and is presumably activated by proteases localized in the endoplasmatic reticulum. ProPTH is converted to the intact PTH-(1-84) by the action of trypsin. Proteases involved in peptide hormone biosynthesis are the endopeptidases, trypsin, cathepsin B, cathepsin D, plasmin, glandular kallikrein, carboxypeptidase B, and aminopeptidases.

Pre-proinsulin is converted to pro-insulin and then to insulin and C-peptide. A trypsin-like enzyme cleaves off C-peptide at the arginine–glutamine and arginine–glycine bonds, leaving the A and B chains of insulin connected by two disulphide bridges. A carboxypeptidase B-like enzyme then cleaves the two carboxyterminal arginines from the B chain, which is necessary for the secreted insulin to have full biological activity.

Pro-renin can be activated *in vitro* by low pH, prostaglandins, and a variety of proteases including trypsin, pepsin, plasmin, plasma and glandular kallikrein, and cathepsins B, D, and H. Large amounts of inactive renin (pro-renin) have been observed in patients with renin-secreting tumors and in diabetic patients with nephropathy and hyporeninaemic hypoaldosteronism. It was suggested that impaired prostaglandin production leads to inactivation of lysosomal enzymes, this preventing activation of renin (for review see Hsueh 1984).

Enkephalin-containing polypeptides have been described in different organs such as adrenal medulla, intestinal mucosa and brain as potential intermediary products of the larger pro-encephalin precursor. The pro-encephalin can be converted to [met]-encephalin by sequential action of trypsin and carboxypeptidase B activities.

18.4 Proteinases in malnutrition

Nutrient deprivation is the best-studied condition of protein catabolism. Increased mobilization of amino acids stored in tissue proteins can supply important precursors for hepatic or renal gluconeogenesis and substrates for direct oxidation, particularly in clinical situations where metabolic needs increase and/or intake of food stuffs may be reduced. It has been suggested that increased utilization of fatty acids and ketone bodies in prolonged fasting limits net protein catabolism. Additionally, administration of carbohydrates to a fasting organism has long been known to spare body protein (for review, see Goldberg and St John 1976).

Liver protein loss and recovery in response to caloric deprivation and refeeding occur without significant changes in intracellular protein synthesis, suggesting that protein degradation is the primary site of regulation. Proteolysis in the isolated mammalian liver is highly responsive to a number of regulatory agents, including amino acids, insulin, and glucagon. As shown by Mortimore and Schworer (1980), a complete physiological mixture of amino acids is a highly effective inhibitor of proteolysis. Proteolysis was inhibited by 75 per cent at normal (1 ×) plasma amino acid levels and suppressed to basal level at twice their concentration and greater. It was suggested that free amino acids serve as an important non-hormonal regulator of liver protein degradation providing a basis for a feedback of proteolysis (Mortimore and Schworer 1980).

Glucagon clearly stimulates proteolysis. The effects, however, are also strongly affected by amino acids. It has been shown that proteolysis is virtually abolished at a concentration greater than a four-fold plasma amino acid level (Schworer and Mortimore 1979). Quite possibly, glucagon stimulates proteolysis because of depletion of intracellular gluconeogenic amino acids, probably as a direct consequence of its action on gluconeogenic and other pathways.

Protein synthesis and degradation in muscle are particularly sensitive to malnutrition. For example, feeding a lysine-deficient diet for one week to a chick caused rapid muscle protein degradation compared with a well-fed chick of the same age, while protein synthesis was not very different.

Myofibrillar alkaline proteinase activity was measured by Lernau et al. (1980)

in myofibrillar preparations obtained from abdominal wall muscles of patients undergoing surgery. Patients with inflammatory diseases such as acute appendicitis, cholecystitis, and septic amputation had a two-fold increase in enzymatic activity compared with control patients. A fourfold rise in proteinase activity was observed in patients suffering from malignant tumours, while patients with a benign obstruction of the pylorus or small intestine who received no nutrition for at least 10 days prior to surgery exhibited an almost 10-fold increase in enzymatic activity. Such activity, however, was within the range of that for control patients following prolonged total parenteral nutrition with a solution containing amino acids, glucose, and lipids (Lernau *et al.* 1980).

18A.5   Proteinases in catabolic states

Clowes *et al.* (1983) reported that acutely traumatized or septic catabolic non-uraemic patients may have increased serum levels of a peptide that promotes muscle protein degradation when assayed *in vitro*. Baracos *et al.* (1983) have identified a polypeptide from human leucocytes that appears to be identical to interleucin-1, it causes fever and enhances protein degradation in rat muscle. The pyrogen also dramatically stimulates muscle synthesis of prostaglandin E_2, which promotes protein breakdown in this tissue. Inhibition of prostaglandin E_2 synthesis with indomethacin or the use of an inhibitor of lysosomal thiol proteases block the stimulatory effects of this leucocytic pyrogen on muscle protein degradation (Baracos *et al.* 1983). Alternatively, indomethacin blocked the release of prostaglandin E_2 but did not reduce the accelerated muscle proteolysis in the perfused hemicorpus of acutely uraemic rats. Burn injury stimulates prostaglandin E_2 release and protein degradation in rat skeletal muscle. However, when prostaglandin E_2 synthesis is blocked, the enhanced rate of protein degradation does not fall (for review, see Feinstein and Kopple 1985).

Proteolytic activity of plasma ultrafiltrates obtained from patients with acute and chronic renal failure was characterized using phosphorylase kinase as substrate. A predominant splitting of the γ-subunit of the enzyme was observed *in vitro*. This splitting could be inhibited by EDTA, suggesting the action of a metallo-proteinase (Hörl *et al.* 1986). Increased urinary proteinase activity was measured following traumatic injuries. Proteolytic activity was higher in septicaemic compared with non-septicaemic patients. Patients with sepsis and acute renal failure showed higher urinary proteinase activity than those with sepsis and normal kidney function. The digestion pattern of phosphorylase kinase suggests the presence of different urinary proteases in patients with trauma, sepsis, or acute renal failure (Wanner *et al.* 1986).

The degradation of ^{125}I-labelled parathyroid hormone (PTH) *in vitro* has been investigated in order to test the hypothesis that proteolytic degradation of PTH is related to the hypocalcaemia associated with acute pancreatitis. It has been demonstrated that trypsin bound to the plasma protease inhibitor, α_2-macroglobulin, rapidly degrades PTH and destroys its biological activity *in vitro* in a kidney cortex adenyl cyclase assay system. Substantial PTH-degrading activity was also detected in serum samples obtained from patients with severe acute pancreatitis (Brodrick *et al.* 1981).

Acute haemorrhagic-necrotizing pancreatitis was induced by retrograde intraductal injection of 10 per cent sodium taurocholate in piglets. Total kininogen concentration in plasma decreased continously after taurocholate injection. The highest loss was found in the penultimate period. Differentiation into effects on high and low molecular weight kininogen showed a higher consumption of high molecular weight kininogen (80 per cent loss) compared with low molecular weight kininogen (60 per cent loss), indicating strong liberation of kinins. These potent vasoactive peptides increase local capillary permeability, resulting in continuous ascitic fluid production and finally hypovolemic shock (Kortmann *et al.* 1984). Recent studies by Müller-Esterl *et al.* (1985) have shown that kininogens are potent inhibitors of cysteine proteinases.

18A.6 Proteinases and lung

One of the earliest phenomenona occurring during adult respiratory distress syndrome (ARDS) is the microvascular stasis of granulocytes. Aggregated PMN leucocytes may release mediators into the lung, i.e. free toxic radicals or proteolytic enzymes and hence contribute to the genesis of the syndrome. High levels of neutrophil elastolytic activity were found by Lee *et al.* (1981) in the bronchial lavage fluid of ARDS patients. In experimental studies on ARDS, infused elastase or thrombin caused progressive respiratory failure with prompt increase in pulmonary vascular resistance and high proteolytic activity selectively in the lung. Similar results, however, were obtained in agranulocytotic minipigs. Therefore, elastase is only one of several mediators that may cause experimentally-induced ARDS, even in the absence of granulocytes (Stokke *et al.* 1985).

Gadek *et al.* (1979) showed collagenase activity in the lower respiratory tract of patients with idiopathic pulmonary fibrosis (IPF). It was concluded that in IPF the collagen of the lung is subjected to sustained lysis, followed by disordered resynthesis, and that the presence of active collagenase in the lower respiratory tract is a specific feature of the alveolitis associated with this disease (Gadek *et al.* 1979). Alveolar macrophages are capable of interacting with a variety of inflammatory and immune stimuli, including immunoglobins, complement, proteases, microorganisms, and non-infectious particulates, all of which have been implicated as possible aetiological agents for interstitial lung disorders (for review, see Crystal *et al.* 1981).

Cigarette smoking is a major risk factor in the development of pulmonary emphysema, a chronic disorder thought to be caused by an excess of neutrophil elastase activity in the lung parenchyma. An increased number of neutrophils is present in the lung of cigarette smokers. It was suggested that cigarette smoke may attract neutrophils to the lung by stimulating alveolar macrophages to release a potent chemotactic factor for neutrophils (Hunninghake and Crystal 1983).

References

Baracos, V., Rodemann, P., Dinarello, C. A., and Goldberg, A. L. (1983). Stimulation of muscle protein degradation and prostaglandin E_2 release by leucocytic pyrogen (interleukin-1). *New Engl. J. Med.*, **308**, 553–8.

Barrett, A. J. (1980). The classification of proteinases. In *Protein degradation in health and disease* (Ciba Foundation Symposium 75) pp. 1–13. Excerpta Medica, Amsterdam.

Brodrick, J. W., Largman, C., Ray, S. B., and Geokas, M. C. (1981). Proteolysis of parathyroid hormone *in vitro* by sera from acute pancreatitis patients. *Proc. Soc. Exp. Biol. Med.*, **167**, 588–96.

Clowes, G. H., George, B. C., Villee, C. A., and Saravis, C. A. (1983). Muscle proteolysis induced by a circulating peptide in patients with sepsis or trauma. *New Engl. J. Med.*, **308**, 545–52.

Crystal, R. G., Gadek, J. E., Ferrans, V. J., Fulmer, J. D., Line, B. R., and Hunninghake, G. W. (1981). Interstitial lung disease: current concepts of pathogenesis, staging and therapy. *Am. J. Med.*, **70**, 542–68.

Feinstein, E. I. and Kopple, J. D. (1985). Severe wasting and malnutrition in a patient undergoing maintenance dialysis. *Am. J. Nephrol.*, **5**, 398–405.

Fritz, H., Jochum, M., Duswald, K.-H., Dittmer, H., Kortmann, H., Neumann, S., and Lang, H. (1984). Granulocyte proteinases as mediators of unspecific proteolysis in inflammation: a review. In *Selected topics in clinical enzymology* (ed. D. M. Goldberg and M. Werner) pp. 305–28. Walter de Gruyter, Berlin.

Gadek, J. E., Kelman, J. A., Fells, G., Weinberger, S. E., Horwitz, A. L., Reynolds, H. Y., Fulmer, J. D., and Crystal, R. G. (1979). Collagenase in the lower respiratory tract of patients with ideopathic pulmonary fibrosis. *New Engl. J. Med.*, **301**, 737–42.

Goldberg, A. L. and St. John, A. C. (1976). Intracellular protein degradation in mammalian and bacterial cells. Part. 2. *Ann. Rev. Biochem.*, **45**, 747–803.

Hartley, B. S. (1960). Proteolytic enzymes. *Ann. Rev. Biochem.*, **29**, 45–72.

Heidland, A., Hörl, W. H., Heller, N., Heine, H., Neumann, S., and Heidbreder, E. (1983). Proteolytic enzymes and catabolism: enhanced release of granulocyte proteinases in uremic intoxication and during hemodialysis. *Kidney Int.*, **24**, (Suppl. 16), S27–36.

Hörl, W. H., Steinhauer, H. B., and Schollmeyer, P. (1985). Plasma levels of granulocyte elastase during hemodialysis: effects of different dialyzer membranes. *Kidney Int.*, **28**, 791–96.

Hörl, W. H., Wanner, C., Thaiss, F., and Schollmeyer, P. (1986). Detection of a metalloproteinase in patients with acute and chronic renal failure. *Am. J. Nephrol.*, **6**, 6–13.

Hsueh, W. A. (1984). Proteases in hormone production and metabolism. In *Proteases: potential role in health and disease* (ed. W. H. Hörl and A. Heidland), pp. 141–51. Plenum, New York.

Hunninghake, G. W., and Crystal, R. G. (1983). Cigarette smoking and lung destruction. Accumulation of neutrophils in the lungs of cigarette smokers. *Am. Rev. Respir. Dis.*, **128**, 833–8.

Kortmann, H., Fink, E., and Bönner, G. (1984). The influence of the kallikrein-kinin system in the development of the pancreatic shock. In *Proteases: Potential role in health and disease* (ed. W. H. Hörl and A. Heidland) pp. 495–503. Plenum, New York.

Lee, C. T., Fein, A. M., Lippmann, M., Holtzman, H., Kimbel, P., and Weinbaum, G. (1981). Elastolytic activity in pulmonary lavage fluid from patients with adult respiratory distress syndrome. *New Engl. J. Med.*, **304**, 192–6.

Lernau, O. Z., Nissan, S., Neufeld, B., and Mayer, M. (1980). Myofibrillar protease activity in muscle tissue from patients with catabolic conditions. *Eur. J. Clin. Invest.*, **10**, 357–61.

Mortimore, G. E. and Schworer, C. M. (1980). Application of liver perfusion as in vitro model in studies of intracellular protein degradation. In *Protein degradation in health and disease* (Ciba Foundation Symposium No. 75), pp. 281–305, Excerpta Medica, Amsterdam.

Müller-Esterl, W., Fritz, H., Machleidt, W., Ritonja, A., Kotnik, M., Turk, V., Kellermann, J., and Lottspeich, F. (1985). Human plasma kininogens are identical with α-cysteine proteinase inhibitors. Evidence from immunological, enzymological and sequence data. *FEBS Lett.*, **182**, 310–14.

Schworer, C. M. and Mortimore, G. E. (1979). Glucagon-induced autophagy and proteolysis in rat liver: Mediation by selective deprivation of intracellular amino acids. *Proc. Nat. Acad. Sci. USA*, **76**, 3169–73.

Stokke, T., Burchardi, H., Hensel, I., and Hörl, W. H. (1985). Experimental studies on the adult respiratory distress syndrome: Effects of induced DIC; granulocytes and elastase in mini pigs. *Eur. J. Clin. Invest.*, **15**, 415–21.

Wanner, C., Schollmeyer, P., and Hörl, W. H. (1986). Urinary proteinase activity in patients with multiple traumatic injuries, sepsis or acute renal failure. *J. Lab. Clin. Med.*, **108**, 224–9.

Section 18B

Serpins: Engineered re-targeting of plasma proteinase inhibitors

P. M. George and R. W. Carrell

18B.1   Introduction

At least 10 per cent of the protein content of human plasma is formed by proteinase inhibitors (Travis and Salvesen 1983), the majority being members of the recently identified superfamily of serine proteinase inhibitors, the serpins (Hunt and Dayhoff 1980; Carrell and Travis 1985; Carrell and Boswell 1986). Members of this family are widely distributed and include the egg protein ovalbumin, as well as plant (Hejgaard *et al.* 1985) and viral (Upton *et al.* 1986) proteins. However, the major group of serpins is composed of plasma inhibitors, most of which have evolved specialized roles as regulators of the inflammatory cascades (Boswell and Carrell 1987). Each of these cascades, including coagulation, complement activation, and kinin release, involves precisely targeted serine proteinases and is regulated by an appropriately specialized inhibitor. For example, thrombin is inhibited by antithrombin, plasmin by antiplasmin, and C1s by C1-inhibitor (details and full nomenclature, Table 18B.1).

Table 18B.1 Reactive centres and targets of serpins

Inhibitor	P_2	P_1	P'_1	P'_2	P'_3	P'_4	Target
α_1-antitrypsin	Pro	Met	Ser	Ile	Pro	Pro	Elastase
Antithrombin-III	Gly	Arg	Ser	Leu	Asn	Pro	Thrombin
Heparin cofactor II	Pro	Leu	Ser	Thr	Gln	Val	Thrombin
Cl-inhibitor	Ala	Arg	Thr	Leu	Leu	Val	Clr, Cls
α_1-antichymotrypsin	Leu	Leu	Ser	Ala	Leu	Val	Cathepsin G
α_2-antiplasmin	Ser	Arg	Met	Ser	Leu	Ser	Plasmin

Table heading: Reactive centre sequence (spanning P_2 through P'_4 columns)

This specificity of control has opened therapeutic possibilities and has prompted efforts to design recombinant serpins. The potential of the engineered serpins followed from the demonstration that a single mutation is sufficient to convert alpha$_1$-antitrypsin, the plasma inhibitor of leucocyte elastase, to what is functionally antithrombin, i.e. an inhibitor of thrombin (Owen *et al.* 1983). Subsequently, the use of recombinant techniques (Rosenberg *et al.* 1984; Courtney *et al.* 1985) has produced a range of variants with different inhibitory specificities. These engineered serpins have a potential use not only as plasma replacements in genetic deficiency but also as agents for specific intervention in the inflammatory cascades (Carrell 1984, 1986a).

18B.2 Structure

The serpins are relatively small glycoproteins (M_r 40 000–100 000) composed of a single polypeptide chain (Carrell and Boswell, 1986). Alignment of the sequence of the major plasma serpins gives a 30 per cent homology indicating a common derivation, with an evolutionary divergence over some 500 million years. The conserved areas of sequence show that the family shares a common tertiary structure as a highly ordered globular protein. This structure can be deduced from that of alpha$_1$-antitrypsin (called here antitrypsin) which has been crystallized in a modified, cleaved, form (Loeberman *et al.* 1984). The crystal structure shows 30 per cent helical structure and 40 per cent pleated sheets, with two deduced disordered regions: an external peptide loop containing the reactive centre of the molecule, and an amino-terminal freely-structured tail. Not surprisingly, it is these two exposed structures that show the greatest variation in sequence; the reactive centre loop because it conveys individual inhibitory specificity, and the N-terminal tail because it provides binding and other specificities to each serpin.

The reactive centre of the inhibitor is exposed exteriorly in such a way as to provide a substrate bait for the target proteinase (Fig. 18B.1). This bait is principally formed by two amino acids, the P_1–P_1' residues (Table 18B.1) characteristically X-Ser, where X is the amino acid that defines the prime specificity: thus antithrombin has a P_1–P_1' Arg-Ser and traps proteinases, such as thrombin, that cleave at an arginyl-serine bond; similarly, antitrypsin has a Met-Ser and traps serine proteinases, such as leucocyte elastase, that cleave at a methionyl-serine bond.

The attractiveness of the reactive centre as a substrate bait for the target enzyme is believed to be enhanced (Loebermann *et al.* 1984) by the strain placed

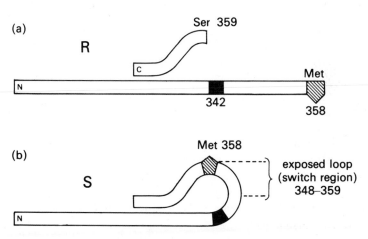

Fig. 18B.1. The structure of the serpins is based on the cleaved relaxed (R) form of alpha$_1$-antitrypsin shown diagrammatically in (a). The native stressed (S) form has to be reconstituted by a deduced exposed loop which hinges on residue 342 (b). This loop is accessible to proteinases and acts as an irreversible switch as well as bait for the target proteinase.

on the exposed loop. This loop of 12–16 amino acids holds the serpin molecule in a stressed S conformation, with the strain being transmitted to the critical P_1–P_1' bond. Cleavage at the reactive centre, or elsewhere in the loop, results in the formation of the relaxed, but inactive, R form of the molecule (Carrell and Owen 1985). The serpins, therefore, readily undergo a change from the meta-stable native inhibitor to an inactive cleaved form. This S–R transformation provides a switch by which the serpins can be irreversibly inactivated: physiologically this is utilized by the neutrophil leucocyte, which secretes proteinases to inactivate inhibitors in the region surrounding an inflammatory locus; pathologically the loop switch is cleaved by snake venom proteinases (Kress *et al.* 1979) and by the metalloproteinases of invasive bacteria, e.g. *Pseudomonas aeruginosa* (Morihara *et al.* 1984).

18B.3   Mechanism of inhibition

Inhibition of serine proteinases by serpins is essentially irreversible (Beatty *et al.* 1982) and results in the formation of a 1:1 enzyme inhibitor complex that is stable to boiling in sodium dodecyl sulphate (Moroi and Yamasaki 1974). The complex is believed to be structurally equivalent to an intermediate in the normal serine proteinase–substrate pathway. The inhibitor presents a putative cleavage site, the P_1–P_1' bond that neatly fits but does not leave the active site of the enzyme.

Boswell has summarized the mechanism of inhibition (Carrell and Boswell 1986) in terms of the known serine proteinase–substrate cleavage mechanism (Kraut 1977). The first step is a close approach of enzyme and substrate to form the hydrogen-bonded Michaelis complex. The distortion induced by binding to the enzyme forces the carbonyl carbon of the scissile bond from the trigonal to tetrahedral geometry. The oxygen of the proteinase serine can then make a nucleophilic attack on the carbon to give the tetrahedral complex. This readily collapses to give the acyl enzyme, in which the enzyme is covalently bonded to the proteinase by an ester bond. The carboxy terminal segment of the substrate is then released and, in turn, the acyl enzyme is readily hydrolysed to give a recycling of the intact proteinase.

However, the reaction of the proteinase with the inhibitor differs from that with the substrate in that the reaction stops at the stage of initial complex formation. It is likely that the distortion of the P_1–P_1' bond, as a result of stress on the exposed loop, favours a conformation which matches that of the intermediate state. The evidence suggests the complex is stabilized as the tetrahedral intermediate since it is dissociable, albeit slowly, back to the native inhibitor and proteinase (Beatty *et al.* 1982). But the complex also dissociates, under denaturing conditions, to give the forward reaction with formation of the inhibitor–acyl enzyme complex and release of the carboxy terminal leaving peptide. So the exact form of the proteinase inhibitor complex must await X-ray diffraction studies. However, although there are several good diffraction maps of serine proteinase complexes with other (non-serpin) inhibitors, the most recent being that of neutrophil elastase with ovomucoid inhibitor (Bode *et al.* 1986), there are as yet no reports of successful crystallization of a serpin–proteinase complex.

18B.4 Therapeutic requirements

Interest in the serpins has focused on alpha$_1$-antitrypsin, the inhibitor present in highest concentration in human plasma. Although it is named alpha$_1$-antitrypsin, its physiological target is leucocyte elastase (Travis and Salvesen 1983), and for this reason it is alternatively called alpha$_1$-proteinase inhibitor. Here the historical name is retained, abbreviated to antitrypsin.

Leucocyte elastase attacks collagen as well as elastin, so antitrypsin, as the prime inhibitor of elastase, functions as a protective agent for connective tissue. This protective role of antitrypsin has motivated interest in its synthesis by recombinant techniques, as a potential therapeutic agent. Antitrypsin has also become the obvious candidate for engineered mutations at the reactive site, with the aim of providing therapeutic agents with specified inhibitory activity.

18B.4.1 Genetic deficiency of antitrypsin

Medical interest in antitrypsin originated with Laurell and Eriksson's observation in 1963 of a frequent genetic deficiency of the inhibitor associated with the premature onset of degenerative lung disease. About 1:1000 people of Northern European extraction carry two mutant genes that make them effectively homozygous for antitrypsin deficiency. The consequent decrease in plasma concentration of inhibitor to 30 per cent or less makes the elastic tissue of the lungs vulnerable to the elastase released by neutrophil leucocytes. Thus inflammation, as in respiratory infections, is accompanied by localized, irreversible destruction of lung tissue. The cumulative effect of this destruction over a period of years results in a crippling loss of lung elasticity, a disease process known as emphysema (Gadek and Crystal 1982; Carrell 1986b).

The genetic deficiency of antitrypsin is readily detectable and since the lung damage does not become significant until early adult life, there is a case for the prophylactic administration of replacement antitrypsin. The problems involved in this are reviewed in an editorial in the *The Lancet* in 1985. Replacement therapy is a daunting prospect as 4 g of antitrypsin is required intravenously each week for a period of many years. Trials are already under way, using plasma fractionated antitrypsin, but supplies could not possibly meet even a proportion of the total potential requirement of 20 or more tonnes a year in Western Europe and the USA. This requirement has prompted the production of recombinant antitrypsin, but the logistics of both individual and bulk supply has raised alternative strategies. In particular, long-term therapy becomes much more practicable with lower molecular weight elastase inhibitors that can be given orally or by aerosol (see following, Section C). In addition, the need for long-term therapy has been questioned, with the alternative proposal that intravenous replacement antitrypsin should instead be used only intermittently, to cover periods of accelerated damage, as for example during minor respiratory infections. For this short-term use of antitrypsin, there would be advantages in using the modified recombinant forms designed to function at the site of damage, i.e. in proximity to leucocytes. These measures of 'topping-up' plasma antitrypsin at times of crisis, together with the important preventive precautions of avoidance of smoking and polluted environs, provide the most practicable approach to ensuring long-term respiratory health.

18B.4.2   Acquired deficiency, white cells and smoking

The study of the lung disease associated with genetic deficiency of antitrypsin has opened up the wider concept of a proteinase–antiproteinase balance in the lung; and of the disruption of this balance as a general mechanism for the development of emphysema, particularly the emphysema of the habitual smoker (Lieberman 1976). Even moderate cigarette smoking causes a remarkable acceleration of lung disease in individuals with antitrypsin deficiency. It seems likely that the same process is also at play in the normal individual who develops emphysema as a result of excessive smoking. As a corollary, therapeutic agents designed for the treatment of antitrypsin deficiency should also be applicable to the treatment of emphysema due primarily to smoking. Hence the interest in the development of effective plasma or alveolar elastase inhibitors.

Cigarette smoke has a number of effects (Janoff 1983), but two measurable consequences in the lung are an increase in the number of white cells and a decrease in the activity of antitrypsin as an elastase inhibitor. The two effects are related, as the loss of activity is thought to be principally due to increased leucocyte and macrophage populations in the lungs of the smoker. These cells possess mechanisms for the inactivation of serpins within their immediate vicinity, a necessary requirement to allow their own proteinases to break down tissue at an inflammatory site.

Leucocytes release oxygen radicals, which can reversibly oxidize the reactive centre methionine of antitrypsin to the much more bulky methionine sulphoxide (Johnson and Travis 1979). The oxidized methionine is too large to fit the active centre of neutrophil elastase readily, and the antitrypsin loses its ability to inhibit elastase. Leucocytes and macrophages also release other proteinases that can catalytically cleave the exposed loop of antitrypsin (Fig. 18B.1), thereby inactivating it as an inhibitor. These two mechanisms are physiological but become pathological when there is excessive white cell activity, as in the heavy smoker, to give an accumulation of focal damage resulting eventually in clinically evident emphysema. The progress of this tissue damage will obviously be accelerated by the presence of a genetic deficiency of antitrypsin.

It follows that the ideal recombinant antitrypsin for intermittent therapy should be designed to function at the site of focal destruction and, hence, resist inactivation by leucocytes and macrophages. In design terms, this means an oxidation-resistant replacement for the reactive centre methionine and an adjacent sequence modified to minimize loop cleavage.

18B.4.3 Antithrombin deficiency and the shock syndromes

Several of the serpins play important roles in coagulation, notably antithrombin, the principle natural inhibitor of coagulation. Even a heterozygous deficiency of antithrombin is sufficient to predispose to repeated thrombotic episodes, which often justify lifelong treatment with anticoagulants. Recently, it has been recognized that there is also an acquired deficiency of antithrombin which is a frequent accompaniment of severe trauma or infection (Duswald et al. 1985). Large scale tissue damage or fulminant infections produce a systemic activation of leucocytes with the resultant release of both oxygen radicals and a mixture of proteinases. The oxygen radicals oxidize antitrypsin and the proteinases can irreversibly inactivate it by cleavage of its reactive centre loop. The oxidation of antitrypsin allows the unhindered activity of released leucocyte elastase which catalytically cleaves and inactivates antithrombin and other clotting factors (Fig. 18B.2). As a consequence, there is a complete derangement of the balanced cascades of coagulation to give disseminated intravascular coagulation and the shock syndromes (Carrell and Owen 1985).

Replacement therapy with plasma concentrates of antithrombin has been used for the treatment of both genetic and acquired deficiencies (Blauhut et al. 1985; Hanada et al. 1985). However, antithrombin fractionation from plasma is expensive and antithrombin has a relatively short half-life in the circulation. This has raised interest in the use of antithrombin homologues, modelled on the natural Pittsburgh mutant of antitrypsin (see later) with an arginine rather than methionine at the reactive centre. These promise to provide an effective thrombin inhibitor with the advantage of a longer half-life in circulation and a reactive loop less susceptible to inactivation by elastase (Carrell 1986a).

18B.5 Design and production of recombinant serpins design

It is easier to state the requirements for the redesign of the individual serpins than to define the precise structural changes necessary to achieve them. A first aim is to be able to specify the inhibitory activity of each engineered serpin, i.e. to redesign the reactive centre. A second aim is to be able to minimize inactivation by leucocytes and exogenous proteinases, principally by modification of the flanking sequences that form the reactive centre loop.

The first aim, the specification of inhibitory activity, seems the most readily achievable, certainly insofar as it is determined by the structure of the reactive centre. However, this will not be the whole answer, as part of the specificity of inhibition is dependent on interactions between complementary surfaces of the

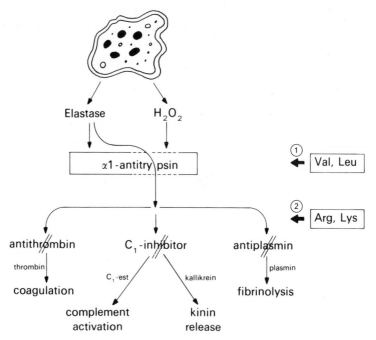

Fig. 18B.2 Neutrophil leucocytes and the shock syndromes. Scheme showing alpha$_1$-antitrypsin as prime inhibitor of neutrophil elastase but subject to inactivation by oxidation. This allows elastase to cleave and inactivate other tissue serpins with, on a massive scale, the triggering of the inflammatory cascades as seen in the acute shock syndromes. Intervention with recombinant mutants could take place as oxidation-resistant analogues of alpha$_1$-antitrypsin (valine or leucine mutants) and as cleavage-resistant analogues of the other serpins (arginine or lysine mutants).

proteinase and inhibitor (Clark Bock *et al.* 1986). These cannot be defined in detail until there are crystallographic data on the proteinase–inhibitor complex.

Fortunately, we know from the finding of the natural Pittsburgh mutant, and subsequent work with other recombinant variants, that specificity is primarily defined by the single P_1 centre residue or better still the P_2–P_1 residues (Table 18B.1). Antitrypsin inhibits serine proteinases that cleave at methionine residues but even more specifically those that cleave after a Pro-Met sequence, and antithrombin inhibits those that cleave after a Gly-Arg. Thus a knowledge of substrate specificity of the cognate protease provides a basis for the selection of the P_2–P_1 residues of a recombinant inhibitor. Our knowledge beyond this is largely confined to observations with other mutants, mostly engineered, and constructed on a largely empirical basis (although guided by experience with synthetic substrates: see Powers and Zimmerman in Chapter 18C). The specificity and K_{ass} for these mutant serpins is summarized in Tables 18B.2 and 18B.3.

Table 18B.2 Proteinase–inhibitor association constants: mutants compared to normal serpins

Serpin P_2-P_1-P'_1	Plasma antitrypsin Pro-MET-Ser	Pittsburg antitrypsin Pro-Arg-Ser	Valine recombinant Pro-Val-Ser	Antithrombin GLy-ARG-Ser	Cl-inhibitor Ala-ARG-Thr
Proteinase					
Human neutrophil elastase	7×10^7	2×10^3	2×10^7	Nil	—
Porcine pancreatic elastase	1×10^5	Nil	1×10^6	Nil	—
Porcine pancreatic trypsin	4×10^4	7×10^6	Nil	2×10^6	—
Human thrombin	5×10^6	3×10^5	Nil	$1 \times 10^{6*}$	—
Human kallikrein	7×10^1	1×10^5	—	3×10^6	2×10^4
Human Xa	2×10^2	2×10^4	Nil	—	
Human XIa	7×10^1	1×10^5	—	2×10^2	2×10^2
Human XIIf	Nil	8×10^2	—	5×10^1	3×10^4
Human plasmin	2×10^2	2×10^5	Nil	1×10^4	—
Human cathepsin G	4×10^5	2×10^4	7×10^2	Nil	—

* With heparin.
Unpublished results, authors' laboratory, and from Scott *et al.* (1986); Matheson *et al.* (1986).

Table 18B.3 Reactive centre: engineered and natural mutants

	P_4	P_3	P_2	P_1	P'_1	P'_2	P'_3	P'_4	P'_5	Inhibits	Oxidation
α₁-antitrypsin	Ala	Ile	Pro	Met	Ser	Ile	Pro	Pro	Glu	elastase	+
Pittsburgh variant	Ala	Ile	Pro	*Arg*	Ser	Ile	Pro	Pro	Glu	thrombin	−
Val-recombinant	Ala	Ile	Pro	*Val*	Ser	Ile	Pro	Pro	Glu	elastase	−
Ile-recombinant	Ala	Ile	Pro	*Ile*	Ser	Ile	Pro	Pro	Glu	Cat G. elastase	−
P₃ala-recombinant	Ala	*Ala*	Pro	*Val*	Ser	Ile	Pro	Pro	Glu	non-functional	
P₁cys-recombinant	Ala	Ile	Pro	*Cys*	Ser	Ile	Pro	Pro	Glu	elastase	
P₂cys-recombinant	Ala	Ile	*Cys*	Met	Ser	Ile	Pro	Pro	Glu	non-functional	
Ala-recombinant	Ala	Ile	Pro	*Ala*	Ser	Ile	Pro	Pro	Glu	elastase	−
Christchurch variant	Ala	Ile	Pro	Met	Ser	Ile	Pro	Pro	*Lys*	elastase	+
P₃–P'₃-recombinant	Ala	*Ala*	*Gly*	*Arg*	*Ser*	*Leu*	*Asn*	Pro	Glu	non-functional	−
P₁–P'₃ variants	Ala	Ile	Pro	*Arg*	*Ser*	*Leu*	*Asn*	Pro	Glu	thrombin	−
Antithrombin	Ile	Ala	Gly	Arg	Ser	Leu	Asn	Pro	Asn	thrombin	−
Denver variant	Ile	Ala	Gly	Arg	*Leu*	Leu	Asn	Pro	Asn	non-functional	

18B.5.1 The Pittsburgh variant

The finding that a fatal bleeding disorder (Lewis *et al.* 1978) is due to a mutation of the P_1 methionine of antitrypsin to arginine confirmed the importance of this single residue as a determinant of *in vivo* as well as *in vitro* function (Owen *et al.* 1983). The Pittsburgh mutant has a complete loss of inhibitory activity to pancreatic elastase 10^4-fold decrease in K_{ass} for neutrophil elastase. The K_{ass} for thrombin is increased by 10^5 to an equivalence with heparin-activated antithrombin (Travis *et al.* 1986). It is also a potent inhibitor of plasmin and the contact proteinases, and is the most effective known inhibitor of kallikrein (Scott *et al.* 1986).

18B.5.2 Other natural variants

The common Z variant of antitrypsin 342 Glu-Lys (Jeppsson 1976) has a two-fold decrease in the K_{ass} for neutrophil elastase (Ogushi *et al.* 1986). However, it is likely that this reflects an overall perturbation in structure rather than a local reactive centre effect since the mutation is well separated, in steric terms, from the reactive centre. It is also unlikely to be due to a simple charge effect, since the same substitution much nearer to the reactive centre, in antitrypsin Christchurch 363 Glu-Lys, does not alter the kinetics of inhibition (Brennan and Carrell 1986). This last result also implies that residue 363, at the P_5 position, lies outside the region that determines specificity. However, not surprisingly, the P'_1 residue is critical to inhibitory function as demonstrated in the mutant antithrombin Denver 394 Ser–Leu, where there is a complete loss of inhibitory activity (Sambrano *et al.* 1986).

18B.5.3 The recombinant variants

The development of the recombinant variants of antitrypsin, their properties, and specificities, have been reviewed in detail by Jallat *et al.* (1986) and Carrell (1986b).

The production of a range of engineered variants occurred independently at several commercial genetic engineering laboratories, the leading contributions coming from the Chiron Corporation, USA, with a yeast based expression system (Rosenberg *et al.* 1984), and from Transgene SA (France), with *Escherichia coli* based production (Courtney *et al.* 1985).

In both the *E. coli* and yeast systems, antitrypsin is obtained as 10–15 per cent of the cytosolic protein and is not glycosylated. Comparison of the recombinant antitrypsins with their plasma equivalents, i.e. the 358 methionine recombinant versus normal antitrypsin, or 358 arginine versus the Pittsburgh antitrypsin, shows that glycosylation is not necessary for inhibitory function. There is no significant difference between the specificity or inhibitory kinetics of the glycosylated plasma proteins and their non-glycosylated recombinant derivatives. The absence of glycosylation does, however, dramatically decrease their circulatory half-life. In rabbits this is seen as a reduction from 50 h to 8 h with most of the recombinant protein appearing in the urine as active inhibitor. This increase in glomerular filtration probably reflects the smaller size and reduced negative charge of the recombinants (Travis *et al.* 1985).

Recombinant antitrypsins have several potential antigenic sites not present in the plasma protein. Antigenicity could arise either due to induced alterations at the reactive centre or to areas exposed by the absence of oligosaccharide side chains. This is not expected to be a problem and the possible presence of contaminating proteins from the yeast or *E. coli* expression system is a greater concern (*Lancet*, Editorial 1985).

The recombinant variants of antitrypsin which have been made to date are of three main types; oxidation-resistant antielastases, antithrombins and other variants designed to examine the structural requirements for residues adjacent to the reactive centre. The properties and modified centre sequences are summarized in Tables 18B.2 and 18B.3.

The oxidation-resistant variants have P_1 valine, alanine, leucine, or isoleucine at position 358. They are all potent inhibitors of neutrophil elastase and are not inactivated by oxidant exposure. The potential therapeutic use of these inhibitors has been demonstrated in a model system, mimicking the inflammatory process, in which neutrophils are activated and digest connective tissue collagen (George *et al.* 1984). In this system, normal antitrypsin is inactivated by oxidation of its 358 methionine and inhibition of digestion only occurs in the presence of high concentrations of antitrypsin. However, the recombinant with 358 valine is not inactivated and inhibits digestion at 10-fold lower concentrations compared to normal antitrypsin. Similarly, the 358 valine variant is resistant to inactivation by cigarette smoke and chemical oxidants (Janoff *et al.* 1986). Thus, this group of oxidation-resistant elastase inhibitors has potential therapeutic use in preventing both focal and systematic proteolysis during inflammation, i.e. as a covering treatment during acute episodes in developing emphysema or as a prophylactic agent in the prevention of disseminated intravascular coagulation and the shock syndromes (Fig. 18B.2).

The antithrombin homologues all have P_1 arginine and in addition recombinant antitrypsins have been produced with sequences P_1 to P_3' (George *et al.* 1986) and P_3 to P_3' (Jallat *et al.* 1986) identical to antithrombin (Table 18B.3). The recombinant with only P_1 arginine has specificity and inhibitory kinetics virtually identical to that of its human equivalent antitrypsin Pittsburgh. It does not require heparin activation, has a circulatory half-life of about 8h, and in contrast to antithrombin is resistant to cleavage by elastase. Further modifications to give P_1 to P_3' identical to antithrombin-III do not significantly alter its properties but inhibition is lost with the additional changes of P_2 glycine and P_3 alanine. This indicates the structural importance of the P_2 proline in antitrypsin; the P_3 alanine is not as critical but still of probable importance in defining the reactive centre, as a recombinant with P_3 alanine and P_1 valine is a poor elastase inhibitor (Jallat *et al.* 1986).

A variant with P_2 cysteine was also inactive and did not react with polyclonal antiserum to antitrypsin. Another variant, with P_1 cysteine, forms disulphide linked dimers but has inhibitory activity when reduced with mercaptoethanol (Matheson et al. 1986). Modification of this cysteine with ethylenimine produces a lysine analogue that is active as an inhibitor of trypsin and plasmin, implying that a P_1 lysine variant would be a selective plasmin inhibitor.

18B.6 Conclusions

Although the tertiary structure of the native serpins is not yet known, it is possible to make a range of recombinant variants of alpha$_1$-antitrypsin with differing inhibitory specificities. These variants are potentially useful as oxidation-resistant elastase inhibitors for use as plasma supplements in the treatment of genetic antitrypsin deficiency or for prophylactic therapy against the shock syndromes. The antithrombin homologues have therapeutic potential for the treatment of established septic shock and disseminated intravascular coagulation as well as in the replacement therapy of congenital antithrombin deficiency to cover periods of trauma such as surgery. The recombinant Pittsburgh homologue could be used instead of antithrombin concentrates and has the advantages that it is not inactivated by neutrophil elastase, it does not require heparin activation, and it has a short circulatory half-life. Structural modifications to date have been based on the known primary specificity of the various proteinases but it is clear that other, more distant, residues are also important in the selective complexing of proteinase and inhibitor. There is reason for confidence that it will be possible to design and produce variants of antitrypsin and the other plasma serpins, which will allow the specific inhibition of each of the inflammatory cascades.

References

Beatty, K., Travis, J., and Bieth, J. (1982). The effect of alpha$_2$-macroglobulin on the interaction of alpha$_1$-proteinase inhibitor with porcine trypsin. *Biochim. Biophys. Acta*, **704**, 221–6.

Blauhut, B., Kramar, H., Vinazzer, H., and Bergman, H. (1985). Substitution of antithrombin III in shock and DIC: a randomised study. *Thromb. Res.*, **30**, 81–9.

Bode, W., Wei, A-Z., Huber, R., Meyer, E., Travis, J., and Neumann, S. (1986). X-ray crystal structure of the complex of human leukocyte elastase (PMN elastase) and the third domain of the turkey ovomucoid inhibitor. *EMBO J.*, **5**, 2453–8.

Boswell, D. R. and Carrell, R. W. (1987). Clinical aspects of the serpins—a family of plasma proteinase inhibitors. In *Clinical immunology* (ed. R. A. Thompson), pp. 1–17. Churchill Livingstone, Edinburgh.

Brennan, S. O. and Carrell, R. W. (1986). Alpha$_1$-antitrypsin Christchurch; 363 Glu–Lys: mutation at the P'_5 position does not affect inhibitory activity. *Biochim. Biophys. Acta*, **837**, 13–19.

Carrell, R. W. (1984). Therapy by instant evolution. News and views. *Nature Lond.*, **312**, 14.

Carrell, R. W. (1986a) Reactive centre variants of alpha$_1$-antitrypsin. A range of anti-inflammatory reagents. *Biotechnol. Genet. Eng. Rev.*, **4**, 291–309.

Carrell, R. W. (1986b). Alpha$_1$-antitrypsin: molecular pathology, leukocytes and tissue damage. *J. Clin. Invest.*, **78**, 1427–31.

Carrell, R. W. and Boswell, D. R. (1986). Serpins: the superfamily of plasma serine proteinase inhibitors. In *Proteinase inhibitors* (ed. A. Barrett and G. Salvesen). Elsevier, Amsterdam.

Carrell, R. W. and Owen, M. C. (1985). Plakalbumin, alpha$_1$-antitrypsin, antithrombin and the mechanism of inflammatory thrombosis. *Nature (London)*, **317**, 730–2.

Carrell, R. W. and Travis, J. (1985). Alpha$_1$-antithrypsin and the serpins: variation and countervariation. *Trends Biochem. Sci.*, **10**, 20–4.

Clark Bock, S., Skriver, K., Nielsen, E., Thogersen, H-C., Wiman, B., Donaldson, V. H., Eddy, R. L., Marrinan, J., Radziejewska, E., Huber, R., Shows, T. B., and Magnusson, S. (1986). Human Cl inhibitor: primary structure, cDNA cloning, and chromosomal localization. *Biochemistry*, **25**, 4292–301.

Courtney, M., Jallat, S., Tessier, L. H., Beneventa, A., Crystal, R. G., and Lecocq, J. P. (1985). Synthesis in *E. coli* of alpha$_1$-antitrypsin variants of therapeutic potential for emphysema and thrombosis. *Nature (London)*, **313**, 149–51.

Duswald, K-H., Jochum, M., Schramm, W., and Fritz, H. (1985). Released granulocytic elastase: an indicator of pathobiochemical alterations in septicemia after abdominal surgery. *Surgery*, **98**, 892–9.

Gadek, J. E. and Crystal, R. G. (1982). Alpha$_1$-antitrypsin deficiency. In *The metabolic basis of inherited disease* (5th edn) (ed. J. B. Stanbury, J. B. Wyngaarden, D. S. Frederickson, J. L. Goldstein, and M. S. Brown), pp. 1450–67. McGraw-Hill, New York.

George, P. M., Vissers, M. C. M., Travis, J., Winterbourn, C. C., and Carrell, R. W. (1984). A genetically engineered mutant of alpha$_1$-antitrypsin protects connective tissue from neutrophil damage and may be useful in lung disease. *Lancet*, **ii**, 1426–28.

George, P., Pemberton, P., Bathurst, I., Carrell, R., Gibson, A., Rosenberg, S., Hallewell, R., and Barr, P. (1987). Characterisation of antithrombins produced by mutagenesis of human alpha$_1$-antitrypsin in yeast. In *Developments in biological standardisation*, Vol. 67, (ed. P. Schiff and W. Hennessen), pp. 73–5. Karger, Basel.

Hanada, T., Abe, T., and Takita, H. (1985). Antithrombin III concentrates for treatment of disseminated intravascular coagulation in children. *Am. J. Pediatr. Hematol. Oncol.* **7**, 3–8.

Hejgaard, J., Rasmussen, S. K., Brandt, A., and Svendson, J. (1985). Sequence homology between barley endosperm protein and protease inhibitors of the alpha$_1$-antitrypsin family. *FEBS Lett.* **180**, 89–94.

Hunt, L. T. and Dayhoff, M. O. (1980). A surprising new protein superfamily containing ovalbumin, antithrombin-III and alpha$_1$-proteinase inhibitor. *Biochem. Biophys. Res. Commun.*, **95**, 864–971.

Jallat, S., Carvallo, D., Tessier, L. H., Roecklin, D., Roitsch, C., Ogushi, F., Crystal, R. G., and Courtney, M. (1986). Altered specificities of genetically engineered alpha$_1$-antitrypsin variants. *Protein Eng.*, **1**, 29–35.

Janoff, A. (1983). Biochemical links between cigarette smoking and pulmonary emphysema. *J. Appl. Physiol.*, **55**, 282–93.

Janoff, A., George-Nascimento, C., and Rozenberg, S. (1986). A genetically engineered, mutant human alpha-1-proteinase-inhibitor is more resistant than the normal inhibitor to oxidative inactivation by chemicals, enzymes, cells, and cigarette smoke. *Am. Rev. Resp. Dis.*, **133** (in press).

Jeppsson, J-O. (1976). Amino acid substitution Glu–Lys in alpha$_1$-antitrypsin PiZ. *FEBS Lett.*, **65**, 195–7.

Johnson, D. and Travis, J. (1979) The oxidative inactivation of human alpha$_1$-proteinase inhibitor. *J. Biol. Chem.*, **254**, 4022–6.

Kraut, J. (1977). Serine proteases structure and mechanism of catalysis. *Ann. Rev. Biochem.*, **46**, 331–58.

Kress, L. F., Kurecki, T., Chan, S. K., and Laskowski, M. (1979). Characterization of the inactive fragment resulting from limited proteolysis of human alpha$_1$-proteinase inhibitor by *Crotalus adamanteus* proteinase II. *J. Biol. Chem.*, **254**, 5317–20.

Lancet Editorial (1985). Treatment for alpha$_1$-antitrypsin deficiency. *Lancet*, **ii**, 812–13.

Laurell, C-B. and Eriksson, S. (1963). The electrophoretic alpha$_1$-globulin pattern of serum in alpha$_1$-antitrypsin deficiency. *Scand. J. Clin. Lab. Invest.*, **15**, 132–40.

Lewis, J. H., Iammarino, R. M., Spero, J. A., and Hasiba, U. (1978). Antithrombin Pittsburgh: an alpha$_1$-antitrypsin variant causing hemorrhagic disease. *Blood*, **51**, 129–37.

Lieberman, J. (1976). Elastase, collagenase, emphysema and alpha$_1$-antitrypsin deficiency. *Chest*, **70**, 62–7.

Loebermann, H., Tokuoka, R., Deisenhofer, J., and Huber, R. (1984). Human alpha$_1$-proteinase inhibitor: crystal structure analysis of two crystal modifications, molecular model and preliminary analysis of the implications for function. *J. Mol. Biol.*, **177**, 531–56.

Matheson, N. R., Gibson, H. L., Hallewell, R. A., Barr, P. J., and Travis, J. (1986). Recombinant DNA-derived forms of human alpha$_1$-proteinase inhibitor. Studies on the alanine 358 and cysteine 358 substituted mutants. *J. Biol. Chem.*, **261**, 10404–9.

Morihara, K., Tsuzuki, H., Harada, M., and Iwata, T. (1984). Purification of human alpha$_1$-proteinase inhibitor and its inactivation by Pseudomonas aeruginosa elastase. *J. Biochem.*, **95**, 795–804.

Moroi, M. and Yamasaki, M. (1974). Mechanism of interaction of bovine trypsin with human alpha$_1$-antitrypsin. *Biochim. Biophys. Acta*, **359**, 130–41.

Ogushi, F., Fells, G., Hubbard, R., Straus, S., and Crystal, R. G. (1986). *Am. Rev. Respir. Dis.*, **133**, (Suppl.) A218.

Owen, M. C., Brennan, S. O., Lewis, J. H., and Carrell, R. W. (1983). Mutation of antitrypsin to antithrombin alpha$_1$-antitrypsin Pittsburgh (358 Met–Arg), a fatal bleeding disorder. *New Engl. J. Med.*, **309**, 694–8.

Rosenberg, S., Barr, P. J., Najarin, R. C., and Hallewell, R. A. (1984). Synthesis in yeast of a functional oxidation-resistant mutant of human alpha$_1$-antitrypsin. *Nature (London)*, **312**, 77–80.

Sambrano, T. E., Jacobson, L. J., Reeve, E. B., Manco-Johnson, M. J., and Hathaway, W. E. (1986). Abnormal antithrombin-III with defective serine proteinase binding (antithrombin-III-Denver). *J. Clin. Invest.*, **77**, 887–93.

Scott, C., Carrell, R., Glaser, C., Lewis, J., and Colman, R. (1986). Alpha$_1$-antitrypsin Pittsburgh: a potent inhibitor of human plasma factor Ia, kallikrein and factor XII$_f$. *J. Clin. Invest.*, **77**, 631–4.

Travis, J. and Salvesen, G. S. (1983). Human plasma proteinase inhibitors. *Ann. Rev. Biochem.*, **52**, 655–709.

Travis, J., Owen, M. C., George, P. M., Carrell, R. W., Rosenberg, S., Hallewell, R. A., and Barr, P. J. (1985). Isolation and properties of recombinant DNA produced variants of human alpha$_1$-proteinase inhibitor. *J. Biol. Chem.*, **260**, 4384–9.

Travis, J., George, P., and Carrell, R. W. (1986). The specificity of human alpha$_1$-proteinase inhibitor is determined by a single reactive site amino acid. *Hoppe-Seyler's, Z. Biol. Chem.*, **367**, 853–9.

Upton, C., Carrell, R. W., and McFadden, G. (1986). A novel member of the serpin superfamily is encoded on a circular plasmid-like DNA species isolated from rabbit cells. *FEBS Lett.*, **1**, 115–20.

Section 18C

Inhibitors of elastases, chymases, and cathepsin G

James C. Powers and Morris Zimmerman

18C.1   Introduction

This chapter will cover inhibitors of elastase, of both pancreatic and human leucocyte origin; inhibitors of the chymases, present in mast cells; and inhibitors of cathepsin G, the chymotryptic-like protease of the human neutrophil.

Human leucocyte (HL) elastase (EC 3.4.21.11) has been studied extensively recently, because of its involvement in a wide variety of pathological states (Zimmerman 1979; Briggaman *et al.* 1984; Stein *et al.* 1985; Bonney and Smith 1986), including pulmonary emphysema (Janoff 1985a, b), rheumatoid arthritis, adult respiratory distress syndrome (Weiland *et al.* 1986), infantile respiratory distress syndrome (Merritt *et al.* 1983), glomerulonephritis, pancreatitis

(Lungarella *et al.* 1985), cystic fibrosis (Suter *et al.* 1984), atherosclerosis, and psoriasis. HL elastase has the ability to attack a broad range of natural proteins, particularly those of connective tissue, and its natural substrates include elastin, collagen, fibronectin, type IV collagen, basement membrane proteoglycans, fibrinogen, complement components, various plasma protease inhibitors, and immunoglobulins (Baici *et al.* 1982). Pancreatic elastase is stored as an inactive zymogen form until secreted into the intestine, where it presumably is a digestive enzyme. If activated in the pancreas, as in acute pancreatitis, it can destroy the structure of the organ, with dire consequences. Most of the studies on pancreatic elastase have been performed with the extensively studied enzyme of porcine pancreas (PP), although human pancreatic elastases have been described.

Cathepsin G (EC 3.4.21.20) is present in amounts equal to HL elastase in the neutrophil but its normal function or role in pathology is much less clear. Although cathepsin G has no specific function that has been fully characterized, it can produce angiotensin I directly from kininogen (Reilly *et al* 1982; Wintroub *et al.* 1984) and can assist elastase in degrading some components of connective tissue, particularly proteoglycan. The chymases (EC 3.4.21.—) are also chymotrypsin-like serine proteinases, and a number of functions have been ascribed to these enzymes (Dahlmann *et al.* 1983; Gervasoni *et al.* 1986). Two chymases from rat mast cells have been extensively characterized (Woodbury and Neurath 1980), but enzymes from human skin and lung mast cells have also been studied (Vartio *et al.* 1981; Schechter 1983; Kido *et al.* 1985; Wintroub *et al.* 1986). Mast cell chymase is released upon stimulation of mast cells under the same conditions that release histamine. The enzyme may enhance allergic responses and participate with polymorphonuclear (PMN) enzymes in the lesions that characterize psoriasis.

The mast cell and leucocyte proteinases are stored in granules and are generally only released into the environment in response to inflammatory stimuli. The release of these proteinases into areas where the inhibitors which would normally control their action are not present or are inactivated can lead to pathological changes. Thus synthetic inhibitors of these enzymes should have considerable therapeutic potential. In particular, the unusually broad natural substrate specificity of HL elastase and its involvement in a number of disease states has made it the principal target of those presently designing inhibitors of these proteinases.

18C.2   Serine proteinase mechanism and inhibitor design

The rational design of synthetic inhibitors requires an understanding both of the catalytic mechanism and the substrate specificity of the chosen enzyme. Fig. 18C.1 shows three important steps in the serine proteinase mechanism that are often utilized by inhibitor designers. The catalytic apparatus of a serine proteinase consists of a triad (Ser-195, His-57, and Asp-102) with the serine and histidine residues being by far the most frequent inhibitor targets. After forma-

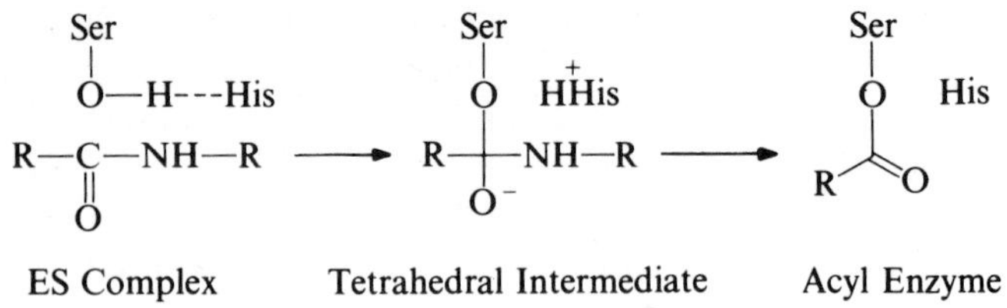

$$
\begin{array}{ccccc}
\overset{\displaystyle\text{Ser}}{|} & & \overset{\displaystyle\text{Ser}}{|} & & \overset{\displaystyle\text{Ser}}{|} \\
\text{O--H---His} & & \text{O} \quad \overset{+}{\text{HHis}} & & \text{O} \qquad \text{His} \\
\text{R--C--NH--R} & \longrightarrow & \text{R}\overset{|}{\underset{|}{\text{---}}}\text{NH--R} & \longrightarrow & \\
\overset{|}{\underset{\displaystyle\text{O}}{\|}} & & \underset{\displaystyle\text{O}^-}{} & & \\
\end{array}
$$

ES Complex   Tetrahedral Intermediate   Acyl Enzyme

Fig. 18C.1 Important steps in the serine proteinase mechanism. The catalytic residues are histidine-57 and serine-195. Aspartic acid-102 is not shown.

tion of the E. S complex, the serine attacks the substrate carbonyl to give a tetrahedral adduct which is stabilized by hydrogen bonding to peptide backbone NH groups in the oxyanion hole. Decomposition of this intermediate yields an acyl enzyme, which is subsequently hydrolysed to the carboxylic acid product.

The specificity of a serine protease is determined by the exact nature of the substrate binding regions. Most inhibitors utilize the primary substrate binding site (S_1), but extended peptide inhibitors often make use of interactions with secondary substrate binding sites (S_2, S_3, S_1', etc.; nomenclature of Schechter and Berger 1967). Closely related serine proteinases differ markedly in their ability to accept specific extended peptide structures and use of secondary subsites is an excellent way to increase the specificity of inhibitors.

18C.3   Classical reversible inhibitors and transition state analogues

The most potent inhibitors in this group are carbonyl or boronic acid derivatives of peptides, which form transition-state-resembling complexes with serine proteinases. There is in addition another group of inhibitors containing long alkyl chains, which make moderately powerful inhibitors of HL elastase.

18.3.1   Peptide aldehydes and ketones

Many substrate analogues in which the carbonyl of the scissile amide bond of a peptide has been replaced by an aldehyde or ketone moiety are potent reversible inhibitors of elastase. Elastatinal (Fig. 18C.2), a fermentation product isolated from A *actinomycetes* (Umezawa *et al.* 1973; Okura *et al.* 1975), contains a terminal alaninal residue and is a good inhibitor of elastases. The K_i values for inhibition of PP elastase and HL elastase are 0.24 μM and 50–80 μM, respectively (Feinstein *et al.* 1976; Umezawa and Aoyagi 1977; Zimmerman and Ashe 1977). The relative potency towards these related enzymes is consistent with their primary specificities: the leucocyte enzyme prefers valine residues over alanine residues at P_1, while the pancreatic enzyme prefers alanine over valine.

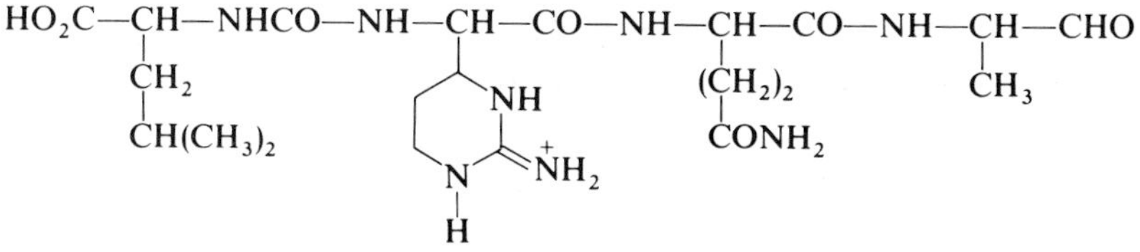

$$HO_2C-CH-NHCO-NH-CH-CO-NH-CH-CO-NH-CH-CHO$$

(structure diagram)

with substituents: CH_2, $CH(CH_3)_2$ on first carbon; NH ring, $N-H$, $\overset{+}{N}H_2$ on the pyrimidine; $(CH_2)_2$, $CONH_2$; CH_3.

Fig. 18C.2 Structure of elastatinal.

Synthetic peptide aldehydes containing valinal or alaninal residues are potent inhibitors of HL and PP elastase. Valinal derivatives such as $AdSO_2$-Lys (Suc)-Pro-Val-H, $AdSO_2$-Lys(Suc)-Ala-Val-H, and $AdSO_2$-Lys(4-carboxybenzoyl)-Val-H ($AdSO_2$- = 1-adamantanesulphonyl, Val-H = $-NHCH (CHMe_2) CHO$) are excellent inhibitors of HL elastase and have IC_{50} values of 0.08, 0.1, and 0.8 μM, respectively (Hassall *et al.* 1985). The compounds had no overt toxicity and significantly inhibited the development of emphysema in animal studies. A patent of similar aldehydes has recently appeared (Dutta *et al.* 1985).

Thompson (1973) initially proposed that inhibition of PP elastase by some tight-binding synthetic peptide aldehydes (Ac-Pro-Ala-Pro-Ala-H, $K_i = 0.8$ μM, Ala-H = $-NHCH(CH_3)CHO$) was the result of formation of a hemiacetal linkage between the aldehyde carbonyl of the inhibitor and the active site serine (Fig. 18C.3). The finding that peptide aldehydes bind to elastase orders of magnitude more tightly than the corresponding amide substrates suggests that aldehydes are transition-state analogues. The tetrahedral structure has been conclusively proven, together with other serine proteinases such as chymotrypsin by nuclear magnetic resonance and X-ray crystallographic studies.

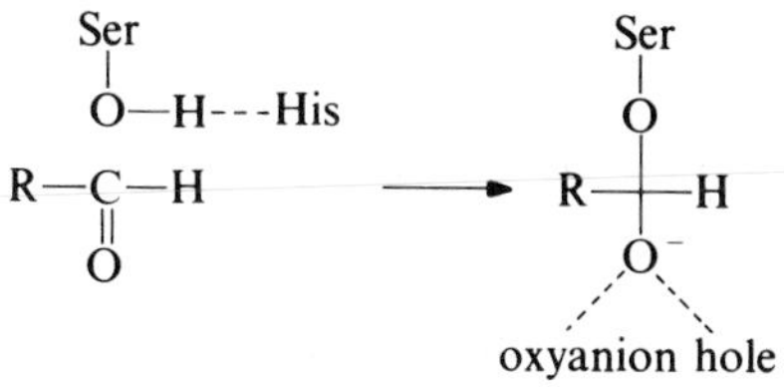

(reaction scheme)

Ser
|
O—H---His   →   Ser
                          |
R—C—H   O
   ‖ |
   O   R—+—H
                          |
                          O⁻
                       oxyanion hole

Fig. 18C.3 Structure of the tetrahedral adduct formed upon binding of peptide aldehydes to the active site of serine proteinases.

Chymostain (Umezawa *et al.* 1970), a relative of elastinal that contains a P_1 Phe-H residue, inhibits a wide variety of chymotrypsin-like enzymes including human cathepsin G ($K_i = 0.28$ μM), human skin chymase (0.017 μM), rat mast cell protease I (0.026 μM) and rat mast cell protease II (0.56 μM) (Powers *et al.* 1985). A number of synthetic peptide aldehydes containing P_1 Phe-H residues have been prepared, but none have yet been tested with chymases.

Peptide α-ketoester and ketone inhibitors have been described as inhibitors of HL and PP elastase (Hori *et al.* 1985). While the ketones are only moderate inhibitors, the α-ketoesters are quite potent and Z-Ala-Ala-D,L-Abu-CO$_2$Bzl (Abu-CO$_2$Bzl = —NHCH(n-Pr)CO—CO$_2$Bzl) had K_i values of 0.09 and 0.08 μM, respectively, with HL and PP elastase. The ester portion of the inhibitor was proposed to be interacting with the S_1' sub-site of elastase.

18.3.2   Peptide boronic acids

Trigonal boron compounds contain a vacant 2p orbital that easily reacts with nucleophiles such as alkoxide or imidazole to give a tetrahedral boron adduct. This characteristic led a number of investigators to postulate that alkyl and aryl boronic acids could bind at the active site of serine proteases, forming a tetahedral transition-state-like structure (Fig. 18C.4) similar to that observed with aldehydes. Peptides containing C-terminal α-aminoalkylboronic acid residues and an extended peptide moiety that can be tailored to bind specifically to one enzyme or to a group of closely related enzymes are several orders of magnitude more potent than simple alkyl or arylboronic acid inhibitors.

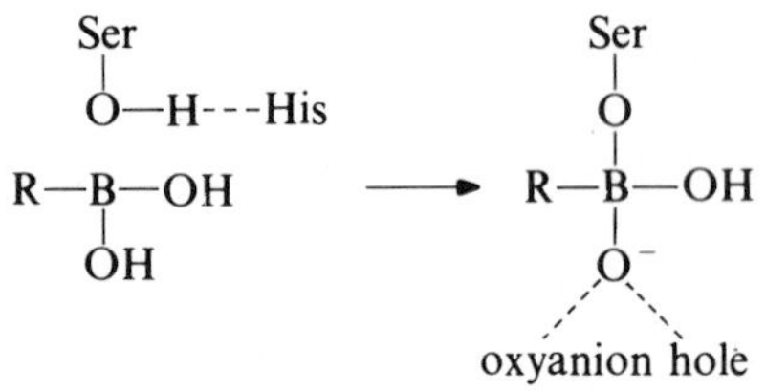

Fig. 18C.4 Structure of the tetrahedral adduct formed upon binding of boronic acid inhibitors to the active site of serine proteinases.

The K_i values for inhibition by some peptide boronic acids of human leucocyte (HL) elastase, porcine pancreatic (PP) elastase, cathepsin G, and chymotrypsin are shown in Table 18C.1 (Kettner and Shenvi 1984). The abbreviation Boro-Aaa is used to indicate the structure in which the carboxyl group of an amino acid residue (Aaa) is replaced by a boronic acid functional group. These structures are some of the most potent reversible inhibitors yet reported for these enzymes. The results clearly show the preference of elastases for P_1 Val and Ala residues, while cathepsin G prefer P_1 Phe residues. The extended peptide structure is critical for optimal inhibition, since the amino-acid derivative N-acetyl-Boro-Phe is greater than four orders of magnitude less active towards chymotrypsin than the best extended peptide boronic acid.

With the most potent peptide boronic acid inhibitors of elastases, inhibition is time-dependent and probably occurs by a two-step mechanism (Kettner and

Table 18C.1 Inhibition of serine proteinases by peptide boronic acid derivatives[a]

Proteinase	Inhibitor	K_i (nM) initial	K_i (nM) final
HL elastase	R-Boro-Phe	350	
	R-Boro-Val	15	0.57
	R-Boro-Ala	79	
PP elastase	R-Boro-Phe	270	
	R-Boro-Val	30	0.25
	R-Boro-Ala	18	0.32
Cathepsin G	R-Boro-Phe	21	
	R-Boro-Val	74000	
	R-Boro-Ala	113000	

[a] pH 7.5; R = MeO-Suc-Ala-Ala-Pro.

Shenvi 1984). A relatively weak enzyme inhibitor complex E·I (K_i = 3–30 nM) is rapidly formed upon addition of enzyme to a mixture of substrate and inhibitor. This E·I complex undergoes a slow conversion to a more tightly bound complex (E·I*, K_i = 0.16–0.6 nM). The rate constants for this conversion vary from 0.009 to 0.026 s^{-1} according to the enzyme and inhibitor concerned. This slow conversion of E·I to E·I* may reflect the formation of the tetrahedral adduct or a reorganization in the active site structure during inhibitor binding.

18C.3.3 Other reversible inhibitors

Several cyclic peptides that contain the reactive site sequence of α_1-proteinase inhibitor have been designed for human leucocyte elastase (Powers et al. 1981). The termini of the reactive site related peptides were linked together by one of three bridging groups, which varied from the very flexible ε-aminocaproyl (Aca) group to a very rigid 3-Abz-3-Abz (3-Abz = 3-aminobenzoyl) group. The best inhibitor was cyclo (-Ala-Leu-Pro-Met-Thr-Leu-3-Abz-3-Abz-) with K_i = 0.39 mM.

Trifluoroacetyl peptides and trifluoroacetyldipeptide anilides (Renaud et al. 1983) are reversible inhibitors of HL and PP elastase. The best HL elastase inhibitor is CF_3CO-Lys-Leu-NHC_6H_4-4-$CH(CH_3)_2$ with K_i = 0.3 μM, while the most potent PP elastase inhibitor is CF_3CO-Lys-Ala-NHC_6H_4-4-CF_3 with K_i = 0.09 μM. Without exception, PP elastase is inhibited more effectively than HL elastase by the structures.

The structure of the CF_3CO-Lys-Ala-NHC_6H_4-4-CF_3 complex with PP elastase complex has been determined by X-ray crystallography at a resolution of 0.25 nm (Hughes et al. 1982). The trifluoroacetyl group occupies the S_1 binding site and forms a hydrogen bond with the NH group of Ser-214. Several additional hydrogen bonds exist between the inhibitor and enzyme residues 214–16. The aromatic ring of the inhibitor lies in a hydrophobic pocket made up by the side-chains of Trp-172 and Phe-215. A 0.35 nm resolution structure of the binding of CH_3CH_2CO-Ala-Pro-NHC_5H_9 (C_5H_9 = cyclopentyl) to PP elastase has also been reported (Hassall *et al.* 1979). The binding mode is also in the vicinity of residues 214–16, with the cyclopentyl group lying between Phe-215 and Gln-192 and the N-terminal group in the region of Trp-172 and Thr-179.

Depsipeptide azaalanine (Aala, —NHNMeCO—) derivatives containing C-terminal lactamide groups (HO—$CHMeCONH_2$) are good reversible inhibitors of HL and PP elastase (K_i values = 22 to 40 μM with HL elastase) and are resistant to hydrolysis by the enzyme (Dorn *et al.* 1977). The most potent PP elastase inhibitor was Ac-Pro-Ala-Pro-Aala—O—$CHMeCONH_2$, with K_I = 0.45 μM, and the most reactive HL elastase inhibitor was Ac-Pro-Ala-Pro-Aala—O—CHMeCO—NH—CH_2Ph, with K_i = 22 μM. The corresponding lactyl esters inhibited only the porcine enzyme.

HL elastase is markedly inhibited by *cis*-unsaturated fatty acids, whereas other serine proteinases are totally unaffected. Oleic acid (K_i = 9μM) is the most potent inhibitor. Inhibition was chain-length dependent, dropping rapidly going from the C_{18} acid to C_{14}, and was absolutely dependent on the configuration— the *trans* isomer, elaidic acid, had no activity. PP elastase was not inhibited (Ashe and Zimmerman 1977). Inhibition of rat mast cell chymase by fatty acids has also been reported (Kido *et al.* 1984). In this case the C_{18} saturated fatty acid also inhibits, but elaidic acid is less active.

Oleoyl peptides or peptide aldehydes are more potent inhibitors of HL elastase (oleoyl-Ala-Ala-Pro-Ala, K_i = 5.8 μM; oleoyl-Ala-Ala-Pro-Ala-H, K_i = 0.07 μM) than the corresponding unblocked peptides, but the fatty acid residue also introduces activity toward PP elastase. The suggestion has been made that such compounds are bifunctional inhibitors, inhibiting elastolysis by binding both to elastin and elastase (Hornebeck *et al.* 1985).

Elasnin is a novel HL elastase inhibitor that has been isolated from *Streptomyces noboritoensis* (Ohno *et al.* 1978; Omura *et al.* 1979). It is a moderate inhibitor of HL elastase (IC_{50} = 3.3 μM, Ohno *et al.* 1978; K_i = 140 μM, Spencer *et al.* 1985) and PP elastase (IC_{50} = 77 μM). Elasnin, an alkyl substituted 2-hydroxy-4-pyrone, is a highly lipophilic material and may interact with the same hydrophobic binding site in HL elastase as fatty acids. Several synthetic 2-hydroxy-4-pyrones (or 4-hydroxy-2-pyrones) are also moderate inhibitors of HL elastase (Groutas *et al.* 1984, 1985c; Spenser *et al.* 1985).

18C.4 Active site-directed irreversible inhibitors

18C.4.1 Peptide chloromethyl ketones

Peptide (or amino acid) chloromethyl ketones are perhaps the most well understood class of irreversible serine proteinase inhibitors discussed here (see Powers 1977 for review). The mechanism of inactivation involves recognition of the peptide moiety by the enzyme, reaction of the active site serine with the carbonyl of the chloromethyl ketone to give a tetrahedral structure, and alkylation of the nitrogen of the imidazole ring of the active site histidine residue (Fig. 18C.5). A β-sheet antiparallel hydrogen bonding interaction is formed between the peptide chain of the inhibitor and the peptide backbone of residues 214, 215, and 216 in the extended substrate binding region of the enzyme.

The rate constants for inactivation of HL and PP elastase by several highly specific and reactive peptide chloromethyl ketone inhibitors are shown in Table 18C.2 (Tuhy and Powers 1975; Powers et al. 1977). The RCO-Ala-Ala-Pro-Val–CH$_2$Cl sequence proved to be the best for both enzymes when RCO = Suc—or MeO—Suc—. Until recently, MeO-Suc-Ala-Ala-Pro-Val-CH$_2$Cl was one of the most potent irreversible elastase inhibitors known (k_{obsd}/[I] = 1560 M^{-1}s^{-1}). This peptide chloromethyl ketone is quite specific and does not react with cathepsin G and several chymases. The best inhibitors of cathepsin G and chymases are Z-Gly-Leu-Phe-CH$_2$Cl and Boc-Gly-Leu-Phe-CH$_2$Cl (Powers et al. 1977, 1985; Yoshida et al. 1980). Z-Gly-Leu-Phe-CH$_2$Cl is specific and does not react with HL elastase.

The problem of delivering chloroketone inhibitors selectively to the lung has been approached by using human albumin microspheres (HAM) which are non-toxic, non-antigenic, and because of their unique size are trapped in the

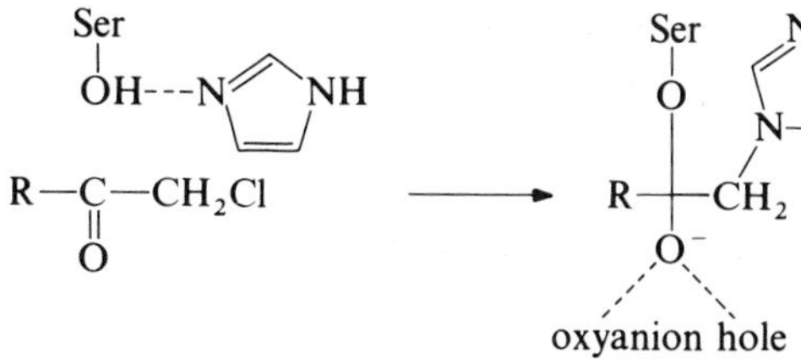

Fig. 18C.5 Structure of a serine proteinase inhibited by a peptide chloromethyl ketone.

Table 18C.2 Inhibition of elastases by peptide chloromethyl ketones

Chloromethyl ketone Inhibitor	k_{obsd}/[I] (M^{-1} s^{-1})	
	HL elastase	PP elastase
MeO-Suc-Ala-Ala-Pro-Val-CH$_2$Cl	1560[a]	55[a]
Suc-Ala-Ala-Pro-Val-CH$_2$Cl	1400[a]	73[a]
Ac-Ala-Ala-Pro-Val-CH$_2$Cl	219[a]	35[a]
CF$_3$CO-Ala-Ala-Ala-Ala-CH$_2$Cl	1.0[b]	60[b]
Ac-Lys-Ala-Ala-Ala-Ala-CH$_2$Cl	56	100[b]
CF$_3$CO-Lys-Ala-Ala-Ala-Ala-CH$_2$Cl	34	74[b]

[a] Data of Powers et al. 1977.
[b] Data of Lestienne et al. 1979.

pulmonary capillary bed after intravenous injection. HAM derivatives with Ala-Ala-Pro-Val-CH$_2$Cl covalently bound through the amino group of the P$_4$ alanine residue have been shown to be taken up rapidly and exclusively by the lungs when injected into rats (Martodam *et al.* 1979). Half of the modified HAM remained in the lungs with a half-life of 17 days.

18C.4.2   Sulphonyl fluorides

Sulphonyl fluorides inhibit serine proteinases by formation of a covalent sulfonyl bond with the γ-oxygen of Ser-195. A crystal structure of tosyl-elastase has been reported (Watson *et al.* 1970; Shotton and Watson 1970). It is likely that one sulphonyl oxygen atom forms hydrogen bonds with hydrogen bond donors in the oxyanion hole.

The $k_{obsd}/[I]$ values for inactivation of HL elastase and PP elastase by phenylmethanesulphonyl fluoride and some substituted benzenesulphonyl fluoride derivatives are shown in Table 18C.3 (Lively and Powers 1978; Yoshimura *et al.* 1982). The best HL elastase inhibitors in this series contain a perfluoroacyl-amino substituent *ortho* to the sulphonyl fluoride moiety. Reactivity is dependent upon the size of the fluoroalkyl structure, with the CF$_3$CF$_2$CONH– group being optimum. With PP elastase, the trifluoroacetyl derivative gives optimal inactivation. The *N*-acetylamino derivative is a poor inhibitor of both elastases, suggesting that the perfluoro group interacts with a hydrophobic site on the enzyme. The kinetic results are consistent with the binding mode shown in Fig. 18C.6, where the perfluoroacetylamino moiety occupies the S$_1$ sub-site of the enzyme and the amino NH is hydrogen bonded to the enzyme, possibly with the backbone carbonyl of Ser-214. The pentafluoropropionyl derivative is a very specific inhibitor of elastases and inhibits cathepsin G and chymotrypsin from 40 to 100 times more slowly.

A number of sulphonyl fluorides have been investigated as inhibitors for cathepsin G and chymases (Lively and Powers 1978; Yoshimura *et al.* 1982;

Table 18C.3   Inactivation of HL elastase and PP elastase by substituted sulphonyl fluorides

Sulfonyl fluoride inhibitor	$[k_{obsd}/[I]\ (M^{-1}s^{-1})]$	
	HL elastase	PP elastase
Phenylmethanesulphonyl fluoride	21	2.7
2-(CF$_3$CONH)—C$_6$H$_4$SO$_2$F	590	2300
2-(CF$_3$CF$_2$CONH)—C$_6$H$_4$SO$_2$F	1700	1300
2-(CF$_3$CF$_2$CF$_2$CONH)—C$_6$H$_4$SO$_2$F	1400	62
3-(Z—NHCH$_2$CH$_2$CONH)-C$_6$H$_4$SO$_2$F	220	6

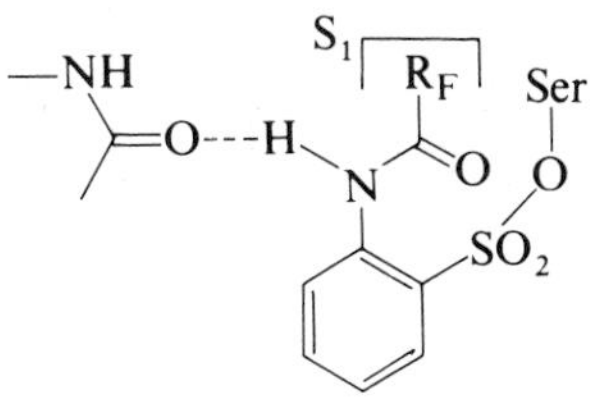

Fig. 18C.6 Structure of elastase inhibited by 2-fluoroacylaminobenzenesulphonyl fluoride.

Powers *et al.* 1985). One of the best is 2-(Z–NHCH$_2$CONH)–C$_6$H$_4$–SO$_2$F (Z = benzyloxycarbonyl) which inhibits rat mast cell protease I ($k_{obsd}/[I]$ = 2500 M^{-1}s^{-1}), rat mast cell proteinase II (270 M^{-1}s^{-1}), human skin chymase (1800 M^{-1}s^{-1}), and cathepsin G (81 M^{-1}s^{-1}).

18C.4.3 Acylating agents

A variety of structures including heterocyclic compounds, simple acyl esters and amides, azapeptides, and isocyanates will acylate the active site serine of elastase and other serine proteinases. In many cases the acyl enzymes formed are unstable and rapidly deacylate. However, geometric or electronic effects can often impart great stability to specific acylated serine proteinases and the parent acylating agent for all practical purposes should then be considered to be an irreversible inhibitor.

Some of the most interesting serine proteinase acylating agents are heterocyclic structures. These include N-substituted saccharins (Zimmerman *et al.* 1980; Ashe *et al.* 1981), benzoxazin-4-ones (Teshima *et al.* 1982; Hedstrom *et al.* 1984) 3-alkoxy-4-chloroisocoumarins (Harper and Powers 1985), isatoic anhydride (Moorman and Abeles 1982), β-lactams (Doherty *et al.* 1984, 1985a, b), isobenzofuranones (Hemmi *et al.* 1985), and oxazine-2,6-diones (Weidmann and Abeles 1984). While these structures are sometimes referred to as mechanism-based or suicide inactivators (See Chapter 2C), we prefer to call them *acylating agents*, since they typically do not contain latent reactive functional groups. The heterocyclic structures are unusual in that they often give rise to extremely stable enzyme–inhibitor complexes, deacylating with rate constants that are orders of magnitude lower than those of typical substrates.

18.4.4.1 *N-acyl saccharins, N-acylbenzoisothiazolinones and N-aryl saccharins*

N-acylbenzoisothiazolinones and their *S*-dioxides (acyl saccharins, Fig. 18C.7, R = acyl) are inhibitors of HL elastase and cathepsin G (Zimmerman *et al.* 1980). The most potent inhibitors have IC$_{50}$ values in the micromolar range. The inhibition mechanism was shown to involve cleavage of the CO—N bond of the heterocyclic ring by the active site serine to form an acyl enzyme (Fig. 18C.7). Studies using ^{35}S-labelled *N*-furoylsaccharin indicated that the saccharin portion of the inhibitors became covalently and stoichiometrically bound to both HL and PP elastase upon acylation. Both derivatives regain activity extremely slowly at neutral pH, with the half-life of the *N*-furoyl derivative of HL elastase being 137 h at pH 7.

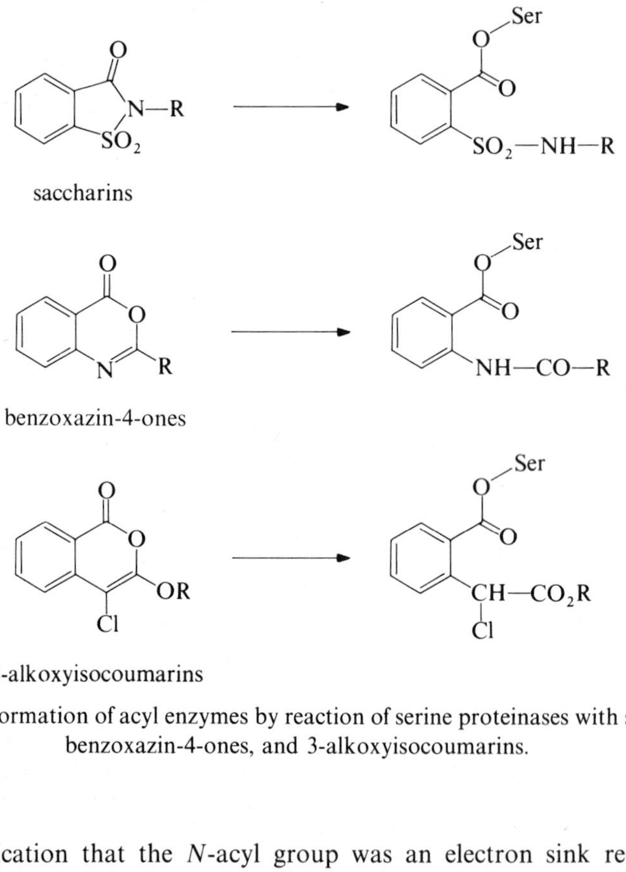

saccharins

benzoxazin-4-ones

3-alkoxyisocoumarins

Fig. 18C.7 Formation of acyl enzymes by reaction of serine proteinases with saccharins, benzoxazin-4-ones, and 3-alkoxyisocoumarins.

The implication that the *N*-acyl group was an electron sink required to activate the CO—N bond of the heterocycle led to the synthesis of a variety of substituted N-aryl saccharins (Fig. 18C.7, R = aryl) and *N*-arylbenzoisothiazol-inones (Ashe *et al.* 1981). None of the latter were inhibitors as expected, but substitution of the aromatic ring of the *N*-arylsaccharin with electron-withdrawing groups led to the inhibition of HL elastase. The inhibition was slowly reversible which is evidence for an acyl enzyme structure. Unfortunately, the acyl enzymes derived from these structures are significantly more unstable than those obtained with *N*-acyl saccharins.

18C.4.3.2 *Benzoxazin-4-ones*

Substituted benzoxazin-4-ones (Fig. 18C.7) are potent inhibitors of HL elastase, PP elastase, and cathepsin G, while similarly substitute quinazolin-4-ones and phthalimides are potent and specific inhibitors of HL elastase (Teshima *et al.* 1982). The K_i values obtained from initial rate measurements ranged from 0.01 to 1100 μM. Inhibitor potency was related to both the electrophilicity of the heterocyclic carbonyl group and to the structure of the 2-substituent. The most potent HL elastase inhibitor ($K_i = 0.09$ μM) has a 2-heptafluoropropyl substituent. It appears that the 2-substituent interacts with the S_1 sub-site of the enzyme. No evidence for enzyme-catalysed ring opening was obtained in the initial study, where catalytic quantities of enzyme (10^{-8}–10^{-9} M) were used, but later studies with chymotrypsin (Hedstrom *et al.* 1984) and HL elastase (Harper and Powers 1985) showed that at least some of the more reactive inhibitors were forming acyl enzymes (Fig. 18C.7).

18C.4.3.3 *3-Alkoxy-4-chloroisocoumarins*

3-Alkoxy-4-chloroisocoumarins (Fig. 18C.7) and 3-alkoxy-4-chloro-7-nitroisocoumarins are potent acylating agents for a variety of serine proteinases including elastases and chymotrypsin-like enzymes (Harper and Powers 1984, 1985). The most reactive compounds have $k_{obsd}/[I]$ values as high as 46 000 $M^{-1} s^{-1}$. The reactivity towards a particular enzyme is dependent upon the structure of the 3-alkoxy group. For instance, HL elastase is inactivated most rapidly by the 4-chloro-3-ethoxyisocoumarin ($k_{obsd}/[I] = 43 000$ $M^{-1} s^{-1}$) and reacts with the 3-benzyloxy derivative about 30-fold more slowly. Similarly, chymotrypsin-like enzymes react most rapidly with the 3-benzyloxy derivatives [$k_{obsd}/[I] = 46 000$ $M^{-1} s^{-1}$ for rat mast cell proteinase I with 4-chloro-3-(4-fluorobenzyloxy)isocoumarin]. Since this reactivity matches the primary specificity of the various serine proteinases, the results suggest that the 3-alkoxy group is interacting with the S_1 sub-site of the enzyme.

18C.4.3.4 *Azapeptides*

Aza-amino acids are analogues of amino acids in which the α-methine has been replaced by a nitrogen atom [—NHN(R)CO—]. Peptides containing P_1 aza-amino acid residues (azapeptides) and good leaving groups (—ONp, —OCH$_2$CF$_3$, —OPh) react with elastase to form stable acyl enzymes (Fig. 18C.8). The acyl derivative is a carbazate and is much more stable toward nucleophilic attack by water than the ester formed from normal substrates. Interaction of the side chain substituent with the S_1 pocket of the enzyme is another factor that affects the stability of the acyl enzyme. Azapeptides with poor leaving groups do not acylate serine proteinases, but simply act as reversible inhibitors (Dorn *et al.* 1977).

HL and PP elastase were instantly acylated by the azapeptide Ac-Ala-Ala-Aaa-ONp, where Aaa = Aala, Aval, Anva, Aleu, or Anle (Powers and Gupton 1977; Powers *et al.* 1984). The Aleu and Anle derivatives were quite stable

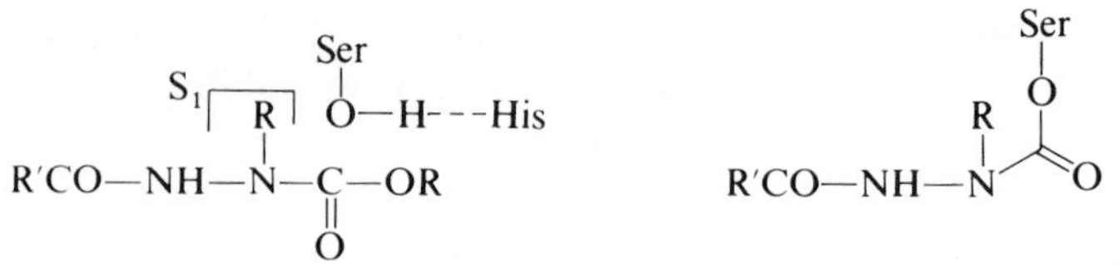

Fig. 18C.8 Formation of a carbazyl derivative of a serine proteinase upon reaction with an azapeptide ester.

toward deacylation at pH 6, while the other derivatives deacylated at various rates. Cathepsin G was inhibited by Ac-Ala-Aphe-ONp and the tripeptide Anle, Aleu, and Aval derivatives, but not with the Aala derivative, which was specific for elastase. In contrast Ac-Ala-Aphe-ONp was specific for cathepsin G and did not react with elastase (Gupton *et al.* 1984). The limited stability of azapeptides toward hydrolysis has thus far limited their utility in animal studies.

18C.4.3.5 *Carbamates and isocyanates*

Carbamates, isocyanates, and related structures react with serine proteinases to give carbamate derivatives at the active site serine. Alkyl isocyanates inhibit PP elastase by reaction at the active site serine to form *N*-alkyl carbamyl derivatives (Brown and Wold 1973a, b). The reagents show some specificity. Elastase does not react with octyl isocyanate (a good chymotrypsin inhibitor), but is inactivated by stoichiometric reaction with butyl isocyanate. Neither isocyanate reacts with trypsin. The selectivity of the alkyl isocyanates with the three proteinases is consistent with their known substrate specificities.

Several amino acid urea derivatives of the general structure (1-imidazolyl)—CO—NH—CH(R)—CO_2Me are time-dependent inactivators of PP elastase and HL elastase (Groutas *et al.* 1985b) and probably yield carbamyl derivatives with the active site serine upon displacement of imidazole. Although the inhibitors can be considered to be latent isocyanates, the mechanism of inhibition has not yet been studied thoroughly enough to discount a direct carbamylation reaction. A wide range of D- and L-amino acid derivatives were examined. *N*-(1H-imidazol-1-ylcarbonyl)norvaline methyl ester is the most effective inactivator of both PP elastase $(k_2/K_i = 6.3 \text{ M}^{-1}\text{s}^{-1})$ and HL elastase $(k_2/K_i = 500 \text{ M}^{-1}\text{s}^{-1})$ at pH 6.5. Acylated PP elastase is stable for more than 24 h. The L-methionine derivative is selective for HL elastase and does not react with PP elastase. Simple alkyl imidazole-*N*-carboxamides (Groutas *et al.* 1980) are less reactive than the amino acid derivatives towards PP elastase $(k_2/K_i = 2.4 \text{ M}^{-1}\text{s}^{-1})$.

Another class of carbamylating agents, *N*-sulphocarbonyl amino acid esters $-O_3S$—CO—NHCH(R)CO_2Me] have recently been reported as specific inactivators of HL elastase (Groutas *et al.* 1985a). Of the amino acid derivatives examined, *N*-(sulphocarbonyl)-L-norleucine methyl ester was the most reactive

$(k_2/K_i = 920 \text{ M}^{-1}\text{s}^{-1}$ at pH 7.2). The carbamoyl enzyme regains activity slowly (10 percent at 7 h). The norvaline derivative did not inactivate chymotrypsin or PP elastase.

Two tripeptide carbamate esters, MeO-Suc-Ala-Ala-Pro-CH$_2$N-(CHMe$_2$)CO—ONp and MeO-Suc-Ala-Ala-Pro-CH$_2$N(CHMe$_2$)CO—OPh, are inhibitors of PP elastase with K_i values of 42 and 30 μM, respectively (Tsuji *et al.* 1984). Preliminary experiments indicate that the inhibitors may be forming the carbamyl derivative MeO-Suc-Ala-Ala-Pro-CH$_2$N(CHMe$_2$)CO—O-Ser-195 upon reaction with the active site serine.

18C.5 Mechanism-based inactivators

The potential for use of mechanism-based serine proteinase inactivators *in vivo* has excited considerable interest in the field. These inhibitors have also been called suicide inhibitors, k_{cat} inhibitors or enzyme-activated inhibitors. The interaction of such an inactivator with the enzyme's active site results in the unmasking of a reactive function present in the inhibitor molecule, which can then react with an active site residue to give an irreversibly inactivated enzyme. In theory, the requirement that enzymatic catalysis must occur prior to the inactivation event should make such inhibitors more selective than other structures that contain intact reactive moieties. Thus far, several electrophilic groups including quinone methides, alkyl nitrosoamines, halo ketones, allenes, acid chlorides, and quinonimine methides have been incorporated into cyclic structures capable of reacting with serine proteinases. Most of the structures described thus far react initially with Ser-195 to give an acyl enzyme, while the reactive group is simultaneous unmasked.

18C.5.1 Chloropyrones and chloroisocoumarins (masked acid chlorides)

Two groups of heterocycles that contain masked acid chlorides have been reported as mechanism-based inactivators of elastase. Chloroisocoumarins are one of the first classes of mechanism-based inhibitors to be reported for HL elastase (Harper *et al.* 1983, 1985). In addition to a masked acid chloride function, these structures contain a fused benzene ring system, a characteristic of saccharin and benzoxazinone inhibitors of HL elastase. 3,4-dichloroisocoumarin is a general serine proteinase inactivator but is somewhat selective towards HL elastase ($k_{obsd}/[I] = 8900 \text{ M}^{-1}\text{s}^{-1}$).

Enzyme-catalysed isocoumarin ring opening occurs concurrently with inactivation. Proton release studies suggest that the 3-chloroisocoumarins form a diacylated enzyme structure (Fig. 18C.9, lower left) upon inactivation of chymotrypsin. A monoacylated enzyme in which the acid chloride has been hydrolysed to the carboxylic acid cannot be ruled out. Such an acyl enzyme (Fig. 18C.9, lower right) could be stabilized by a salt link between the carboxylate of the

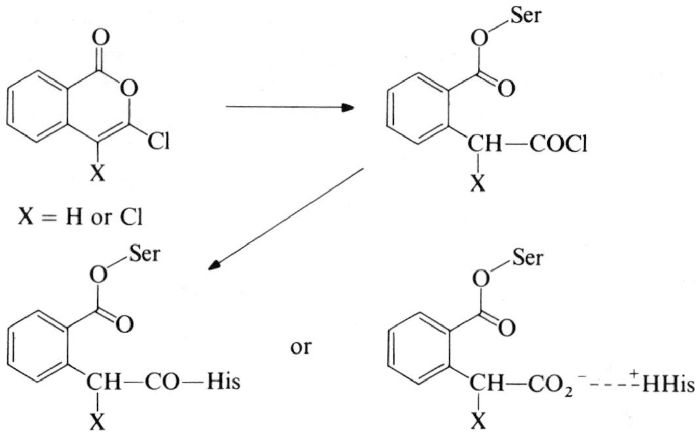

Fig. 18C.9 Inhibition of serine proteinases by 3-chloroisocoumarins.

inhibitor and the protonated His-57. PP elastase is inactivated but quite poorly by substituted 6-chloro-2-pyrones (Westkaemper and Abeles 1983).

18C.5.2   7-amino-4-chloroisocoumarins

Substituted 3-alkoxy-7-amino-4-chloroisocoumarins (Fig. 18C.10) are potent inactivators of elastase and chymases (Harper and Powers 1984, 1985). The dependence of inactivation rates on the structure of the 3-alkoxy substituent indicates strongly that this substituent interacts with the S_1 sub-site of the enzyme. For example, one of the most reactive HL elastase inhibitor, 7-amino-4-chloro-3-methoxyisocoumarin ($k_{obsd}/[I] = 9400$ $M^{-1}s^{-1}$), has a relatively small alkyl substituent, while the best rat mast cell proteinase I inhibitor ($k_{obsd}/[I] = 910$ $M^{-1}s^{-1}$) has a bulky aromatic substituent [3-(2-phenylethyl)]. In addition to being quite reactive, these 7-amino-4-chloroisocoumarins are also very efficient inactivators, often having small partition ratios. Enzymatic ring opening is required for inactivation and the inactivated enzymes are extremely stable to reactivation after removal of excess inhibitor. For example, HL and PP elastase inactivated by 7-amino-3-ethoxy-4-chloroisocoumarin regained no detectable activity upon standing after dialysis.

The available evidence points to the inactivation mechanism shown in Fig. 18C.10. Enzyme acylation results in the formation of a 4-quinonimine methide, which can react with an enzyme nucleophile (probably His-57) to give an irreversibly inhibited enzyme structure (Fig. 18C.10, middle right) or with a solvent nucleophile to give a stable acyl enzyme (Fig. 18C.10, bottom right). Partial reactivation (42 per cent at pH 7.5) by hydroxylamine suggests a partitioning between the two enzyme–inhibitor complexes, with 58 per cent

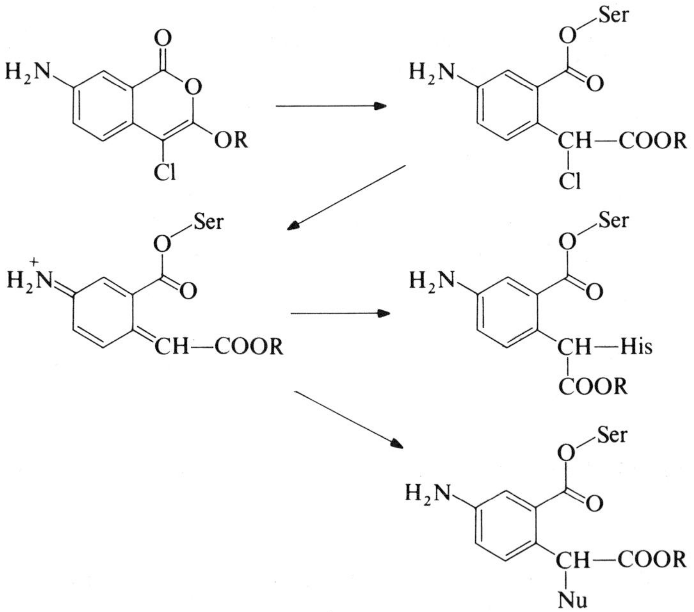

Fig. 18C.10 Mechanism of inhibition of elastases and chymases by 3-alkoxy-7-amino-4-chloroisocoumarins.

being the non-reactivatable complex, probably containing an alkylated histidine residue. Both the 7-amino and 4-chloro groups are required for formation of a stable inactivated enzyme and isocoumarins, which lack these features, deacylate fairly rapidly (Harper and Powers 1985).

The crystal structure of PP elastase inactivated by 7-amino-4-chloro-3-methoxyisocoumarin has been solved at pH 5 in 0.1 M acetate buffer at a resolution of 0.18 nm (Meyer *et al.* 1985). A single ester linkage is formed between the inhibitor and the active site serine residue and an acetate solvent molecule has added stereospecifically to the quinonimine methide intermediate (Fig. 18C.10, Nu = OCOCH$_3$). A hydrogen bond exists between the imidazole ring of His-57 and the carbomethoxy group of the covalently bound inhibitor molecule. The acetate moiety occupies the S$_1$ sub-site. This inactivated elastase molecule can be reactivated by the addition of hydroxylamine, although quite slowly (Harper and Powers 1985).

18C.5.3 Ynenol lactones (masked allenyl ketones)

Benzyl substituted ynenol tetrahydro-2-furanones and tetrahydro-2-pyranone are extremely potent inactivators of HL elastase (Tam *et al.* 1984). PP elastase was also inactivated, but at a much lower rate. The most reactive inactivator of

HL elastase is a 3-benzyl ynenol tetrahydrofuranone, which has a k_2/K_i value of $28\,000\ \mathrm{M}^{-1}\,\mathrm{s}^{-1}$. Inactivation of HL elastase by this inactivator is quite efficient and has a partition coefficient of 1.5. The proposed mechanism involves acylation of the active site serine with the release of a reactive allene ketone moiety, which can alkylate an active site nucleophile to give an irreversibly inactivated enzyme (Fig. 18C.11). The site of alkylation has not yet been identified.

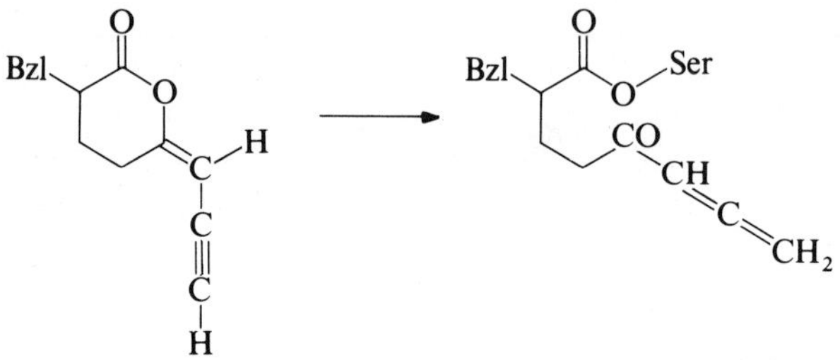

Fig. 18C.11 Mechanism of inhibition of serine proteinases by ynenol lactones.

18C.6   Animal studies

Thus far, elastase inhibitors have been tested in animal models of emphysema and in inflammation models, but no animal studies have yet been carried out with chymase inhibitors. Most of the emphysema research has been performed in hamsters, although some studies with other rodents have been reported. The primary method of induction of the lung destruction, which in many respects is similar to that seen in clinical emphysema, has been the intra-tracheal administration of pancreatic or leucocyte elastase or papain preparations with elastolytic activity. The read-out has primarily involved measurement of the destruction of the alveolar walls of the lung by measuring the distance between these walls, although other parameters have been utilized. The route of inhibitor administration has varied.

Kleinerman et al. (1980) measured the effect of intraperitoneal administration of the tetrapeptide chloromethyl ketone Ac-Ala-Ala-Pro-Ala-CH$_2$Cl on the induction of emphysema by intratracheal elastase and demonstrated inhibition. Similar results have been obtained with Suc-Ala-Ala-Pro-Val-CH$_2$Cl (Stone et al. 1981). The tetrapeptide chloromethyl ketone MeO-Suc-Ala-Ala-Pro-Val-CH$_2$Cl can be delivered orally and still show an inhibitory effect on intratracheal induction of emphysema by elastase (Janoff and Dearing 1980). Administration of the same inhibitor by aerosol also inhibited the induction of emphysema (Tarjan et al. 1983). Thus, the irreversible chloromethyl ketone elastase inhibitors have been shown to inhibit the induction of emphysema; however, their eventual therapeutic use is problematical because of potential toxicity and high reactivity with nucleophiles.

Furoyl saccharin has been evaluated for its ability to prevent the development of emphysematous lesions in the hamster model. Although somewhat unexpected, because of the instability of the compound by some routes of administration, this acylating inhibitor has prevented the induction of emphysema by intratracheal elastase (Martorana *et al.* 1985; Lungarella *et al.* 1986); by intratracheal papain (Zimmerman 1979), and in a model of lung damage consequent to the induction of experimental pancreatitis (Lungarella *et al.* 1985). This is the first non-peptide to be effective in preventing the development of experimental emphysema.

A number of peptide aldehyde derivatives have also been studied *in vivo*. Hassall *et al.* (1985) demonstrated the activity of a valinal derivative in preventing the lung hemorrhage induced by i.t. administration of human leucocyte elastase. This damage is elastase mediated (D. F. Fletcher, personal communication).

18.7 Perspectives

There are still questions as to the validity of animal disease models induced by the protease for which a particular inhibitor is designed. Survival of the inhibitor in the target tissue may indeed be all that is being measured by the model; as such this is not much different from a pre-mix experiment, particularly for irreversible or long-lived inhibitors. Since it is presumed that in those models for PMN proteinase-mediated disease the released proteinases are doing the damage, better systems for causing recruitment to target tissues and release of the proteolytic enzymes by inflammatory stimuli should be developed.

The clinical utility of a proteinase inhibitor for chronic destructive pulmonary disease such as emphysema and ARDS depends on a reliable biochemical readout of tissue damage and/or evidence that free, uninhibited enzyme has been present. Such biochemical markers for the disease are essential for following the outcome of therapeutic intervention, particularly with long-term diseases like emphysema. Some assays for elastase-generated fragments of elastin have been reported but are not yet sensitive enough. It was recently reported that a specific bond in fibrinogen is cleaved by human leucocyte elastase, and determination of the resulting peptide in blood correlates well with the presumptive or determined presence of free elastase in areas of tissue destruction (Weitz, J., personal communication). Such assays will be essential for the rapid evaluation of elastase inhibitor therapy in humans.

The fact that a wide variety of heterocyclic compounds can act as suicide or mechanism-based inhibitors of elastase and other serine proteinases leads one to believe that these readily synthesized inhibitors will be used as therapeutic agents in humans in the near future. It is clear that elastase inhibitors have been essential in uncovering the nature of the active site of elastases and their role in normal and pathological physiology. In the future, the development of similar knowledge about the properties of both the chymases and cathepsin G may help in determining whether they are involved in causing pathological states and whether they would also be suitable targets for therapeutic intervention.

References

Ashe, B. M. and Zimmerman, M. (1977). Specific inhibition of human granulocyte elastase by *cis*-unsaturated fatty acids and activation by the corresponding alcohols. *Biochem. Biophys. Res. Commun.*, **75**, 194–9.

Ashe, B. M., Clark, R. L., Jones, H., and Zimmerman, M. (1981). Selective inhibition of human leukocyte elastase and bovine α-chymotrypsin by novel heterocycles. *J. Biol. Chem.*, **256**, 11603–6.

Baici, A., Salgam, P., Cohen, G., Fehr, K., and A. Boni (1982). Action of collagenase and elastase from human polymorphonuclear leukocytes on human articular cartilage. *Rheumatol. Int.*, **2**, 11–16.

Bonney, R. J. and R. J. Smith (1986). Evidence for the role of neutral proteases in chronic inflammatory diseases in humans. *Adv. Inflamm. Res.*, **11**, 127–33.

Briggaman, R. A., Schechter, N. M., Fraki, J., and Lazarus, G. S. (1984). Degradation of the epidermal-dermal junction by proteolytic enzymes from human skin and human polymorphonuclear leukocytes. *J. Exp. Med.*, **160**, 1027–42.

Brown, W. E. and Wold, F. (1973a). Alkyl isocyanates as active-site-specific reagents for serine proteases. Reaction properties. *Biochemistry*, **12**, 828–34.

Brown, W. E. and Wold, F. (1973b). Alkyl isocyanates as active-site-specific reagents for serine proteases. Identification of the active-site serine as the site of reaction. *Biochemistry*, **12**, 835–40.

Dahlmann, B., Kuehn, L., and H. Reinauer (1983). Susceptibility of muscle soluble proteins to degradation by mast cell chymase. *Biochim. Biophys. Acta*, **761**, 23–33.

Doherty, J. B., Zimmerman, M., and Ashe, B. M. (1984). Thienamycin derivatives as anti-inflammatory agents. US. Patent No. 4 465 687.

Doherty, J. B., Zimmerman, M., and Ashe, B. M. (1985a). 1-Carbapenem-3-carboxylic esters as anti-inflammatory agents. US Patent No. 4 493 839.

Doherty, J. B., Zimmerman, M., and Ashe, B. M. (1985b). N-Carboxylthienamycin esters and analogs thereof as anti-inflammatory agents. US. Patent No. 4 495 197.

Dorn, B. P., Zimmerman, M., Yang, S. S., Yurewicz, E. C., Ashe, B. M., Frankshun, R., and Jones, H. (1977). Protease inhibitors. I. Inhibitors of elastase. *J. Med. Chem.*, **20**, 1464–8.

Dutta, A. S., Stein, R. L., Trainor, D. A., and Wildonger, R. A. (1985). Proline derivatives. European Patent Applied for, EP 124 317. *Chem. Abstr.*, **102**, 185502f.

Feinstein, G., Malemud, C. J., and Janoff, A. (1976). The inhibition of human leukocyte elastase and chymotrypsin-like protease by elastatinal and chymostatin. *Biochim. Biophys. Acta*, **429**, 925–32.

Gervasoni, Jr., J. E., Conrad, D. H., Hugli, T. E., Schwartz, L. B., and Ruddy, S. (1986). Degradation of human anaphylotoxin C3a by rat peritoneal mast cells: a role for the secretory granule enzyme chymase and heparin proteoglycan. *J. Immunol.*, **136**, 285–92.

Groutas, W. C., Badger, R. C., Ocain, T. D., Felker, D., Frankson, J., and Theodorakis, M. (1980). Mechanism based inhibitors of elastase. *Biochem. Biophys. Res. Commun.*, **95**, 1890–4.

Groutas, W. C., Abrams, W. R., Carroll, R. T., Moi, M. K., Miller, K. E., and Margolis, M. T. (1984). Specific inhibition of human leukocyte elastase by substituted alpha-pyrones. *Experimentia*, **40**, 361–2.

Groutas, W. C., Brubaker, M. J., Zandler, M. E., Stanga, M. A., Huang, T. L., Castrisos, J. C., and Crowley, J. P. (1985a). Sulfonate salts of amino acids: novel inhibitors of the serine proteinases. *Biochem. Biophys. Res. Commun.*, **128**, 90–3.

Groutas, W. C., Abrams, W. R., Theodorakis, M. C., Kasper, A. M., Rude, S. A., Badger, R. C., Ocain, T. D., Miller, K. E., Moi, M. K., Brubaker, M. J., Davis, K. S., and Zandler, M. E. (1985b). Amino acid derived latent isocyanates: irreversible inactivators of porcine pancreatic elastase and human leukocyte elastase. *J. Med. Chem.*, **28**, 204–9.

Groutas, W. C., Stanga, M. A., Brubaker, M. J., Huang, T. L., Moi, M. K., and Carroll, R. T. (1985c). Substituted 2-pyrones, 2-pyridones, and other congeners of elasnin as potential agents for the treatment of chronic obstructive lung diseases. *J. Med. Chem.*, **28**, 1106–9.

Gupton, B. F., Carroll, D. L., Tuhy, P. M., Kam, C-M., and Powers, J. C. (1984). Reaction of azapeptides with chymotrypsin-like enzymes. New inhibitors and active site titrants for chymotrypsin A$_x$, substilisin BPN′, subtilisin carlsberg, and human leukocyte cathepsin G. *J. Biol. Chem.*, **259**, 4279–87.

Harper, J. W. and Powers, J. C. (1984). 3-Alkoxy-7-amino-4-chloroisocoumarins: a new class of suicide substrates for serine proteases. *J. Am. Chem. Soc.*, **106**, 7618–19.

Harper, J. W. and Powers, J. C. (1985). Reaction of serine proteases with substituted 3-alkoxy-4-chloroisocoumarins and 3-alkoxy-7-amino-4-chloroisocoumarins. New reactive mechanism based inhibitors. *Biochemistry*, **24**, 7200–13.

Harper, J. W., Hemmi, K., and Powers, J. C. (1983). New mechanism-based serine protease inhibitors: inhibition of human leukocyte elastase, porcine pancreatic elastase, human leukocyte cathepsin G and chymotrypsin by 3-chloroisocoumarin and 3,3-dichloroaphthalide. *J. Am. Chem. Soc.*, **105**, 6518–20.

Harper, J. W., Hemmi, K., and Powers, J. C. (1985). Reaction of serine proteases with substituted isocoumarins: discovery of 3,4-dichloroisocoumarin, a new general mechanism based serine protease inhibitor. *Biochemistry*, **24**, 1831–41.

Hassall, C. H., Johnson, W. H., and Roberts, N. A. (1979). Some novel inhibitors of porcine pancreatic elastase. *Bioorg. Chem.*, **8**, 299–309.

Hassall, C. H., Johnson, W. H., Kennedy, A. J., and Roberts, N. A. (1985). A new class of inhibitors of human leucocyte elastase. *FEBS Lett.*, **183**, 201–5.

Hedstrom, L., Moorman, A. R., Dobbs, J., and Abeles, R. H. (1984). Suicide inactivation of chymotrypsin by benzoxazinones. *Biochemistry*, **23**, 1753–9.

Hemmi, K., Harper, J. W., and Powers, J. C. (1985). Inhibition of human leukocyte elastase, cathepsin G, chymotrypsin A$_x$ and porcine pancreatic elastase with substituted isobenzofuranones and benzopyranediones. *Biochemistry*, **24**, 1841–48.

Hori, H., Yasutake, A., Minematsu, Y., and Powers, J. C. (1985). Inhibition of human leukocyte elastase, porcine pancreatic elastase and cathepsin G by peptide ketones. In *Peptides: structure and function. Proceedings of the Ninth American Peptide Symposium* (ed. C. M. Debers, V. J. Hruby, and K. D. Kopple), pp. 819–22. Pierce Chemical, Rockford, IL.

Hornebeck, W., Moczar, E., Szecsi, J., and Robert, L. (1985). Fatty acid peptide derivatives as model compounds to protect elastin against degradation by elastases. *Biochem. Pharmacol.*, **34**, 3315–21.

Hughes, D. L., Sieker, L. C., Bieth, J., and Dimicoli, J.-L. (1982). Crystallographic study of the binding of a trifluoroacetyl dipeptide anilide inhibitor with elastase. *J. Mol. Biol.*, **162**, 645–8.

Janoff, A. (1985a). Elastases and emphysema—current assessment of the protease–antiprotease hypothesis. *Am. Rev. Respir. Dis.*, **132**, 417–33.

Janoff, A. (1985b). Elastase in tissue injury. *Ann. Rev. Med.*, **36**, 207–16.

Janoff, A. and Dearing, R. (1980). Prevention of elastase induced experimental emphysema by oral administration of a synthetic elastase inhibitor. *Am. Rev. Respir. Dis.*, **121**, 1025–9.

Kettner, C. A. and Shenvi, A. B. (1984). Inhibition of the serine proteases leukocyte elastase, pancreatic elastase, cathepsin G, and chymotrypsin by peptide boronic acids. *J. Biol. Chem.*, **259**, 15106–14.

Kido, H., Fukusen, N., and Katunuma, N. (1984). Inhibition of chymase activity by long chain fatty acids. *Arch. Biochem. Biophys.*, **230**, 610–14.

Kido, H., Fukusen, N., and Katunuma, N. (1985). Chymotrypsin- and trypsin-type serine proteases in rat mast cells: properties and functions. *Arch. Biochem. Biophys.*, **239**, 436–3.

Kleinerman, J., Ranga, V., Rynbrandt, D., Ip, M. P. C., Sorensen, J., and Powers, J. C. (1980). The effect of the specific elastase inhibitor, alanylalanylprolylalanine chloromethylketone, on elastase-induced emphysema. *Am. Rev. Respir. Dis.*, **121**, 381–7.

Lestienne, P., Dimicoli, J-L., Renaud, A., and Bieth, J. G. (1979). Inhibition of human leukocyte elastase by acetyl and trifluoroacetyl oligopeptide chloromethylketones. *J. Biol. Chem.*, **254**, 5219–21.

Lively, M. O. and Powers, J. C. (1978). Specificity and reactivity of human granulocyte elastase and cathepsin G, porcine pancreatic elastase, bovine chymotrypsin and trypsin towards inhibition with sulfonyl fluorides. *Biochim. Biophys. Acta*, **525**, 171–9.

Lungarella, G., Gardi, C., de Santi, M. M., and Luzi, P. (1985). Pulmonary vascular injury in pancreatitis: evidence for a major role played by pancreatic elastase. *Exp. Mol. Pathol.*, **42**, 44–59.

Lungarella, G., Gardi, Fonzi, L., Comparini, L., Share, N. N., Zimmerman, M., and Martorana, P. A. (1986). Effect of the novel synthetic protease inhibitor furoyl saccharin on elastase-induced emphysema in rabbits and hamsters. *Exp. Lung Res.*, **11**, 35–47.

Martodam, R. R., Twumasi, D. Y., Liener, I. E., Powers, J. C., Nishino, N., and Krejcarek, G. (1979). Albumin microspheres as carrier of an inhibitor of leukocyte elastase: potential therapeutic agent for emphysema. *Proc. Nat. Acad. Sci. USA.*, **76**, 2128–32.

Martorana, P. A., Share, N. N., and Zimmerman, M. (1985). The effect of furoyl saccharin, a novel non-peptidic acylating protease inhibitor, on experimental emphysema in the hamster. *Eur. J. Respir. Dis.*, **66**, 297–301.

Merritt, T. A., Cochrane, C. G., Holcomb, K., Bohl, B., Hallman, M., Strayer, D., Edwards III, D. K., and Gluck, L. (1983). Elastase and alpha$_1$-proteinase inhibitor activity in tracheal aspirates during respiratory distress syndrome. *J. Clin. Invest.*, **72**, 658–66.

Meyer, Jr., E. F., Presta, L. G., and Radhakrishnan, R. (1985). Stereospecific reaction of 3-methoxy-4-chloro-7-aminisocoumarin with crystalline porcine pancreatic elastase. *J. Am. Chem. Soc.*, **107**, 4091–3.

Moorman, A. R. and Abeles, R. H. (1982). A new class of serine protease inactivators based on isatoic anhydride. *J. Am. Chem. Soc.*, **104**, 6780–7.

Ohno, H., Saheki, T., Awaya, J., Nakagawa, A., and Omura, S. (1978). Isolation and characterization of elasnin, a new human granulocyte elastase inhibitor produced by a strain of Streptomyces. *J. Antibiot.* **31**, 1116–23.

Okura, A., Morishima, H., Takita, T., Aoyagi, T., Takeuchi, T., and Umezawa, H. (1975). The structure of elastatinal, an elastase inhibitor of microbial origin. *J. Antibiot.*, **28**, 337–9.

Omura, S., Nakagawa, A., and Ohno, H. (1979). Structure of elasnin, a novel elastase inhibitor. *J. Am. Chem. Soc.*, **101**, 4386–8.

Powers, J. C. (1977). Haloketone inhibitors of proteolytic enzymes. In *Chemistry and biochemistry of amino acids, peptides, and proteins* (ed. B. Weinstein), Vol. 4, pp. 65–178. Marcel Dekker, New York.

Powers, J. C. and Gupton, B. F. (1977). Reaction of serine proteases with aza-amino acid and azapeptide derivatives. *Met. Enzymol.*, **46**, 208–16.

Powers, J. C., Gupton, B. F., Harley, A. D., Nishino, N., and Whitley, R. J. (1977). Specificity of porcine pancreatic elastase, human leukocyte elastase, and cathepsin G. Inhibition with peptide chloromethyl ketones. *Biochim. Biophys. Acta*, **485**, 158–66.

Powers, J. C., Yasutake, A., Nishino, N., Gupton, B. F., and Kam, C-M. (1981). Synthetic elastase inhibitors and their role in the treatment of disease. In *Peptides: synthesis–structure–function, Proceedings of the Seventh American Peptide Symposium* (ed. D. H. Rich and E. Gross) pp. 391–9. Pierce Chemical., Rockford, IL,.

Powers, J. C., Boone, R., Carroll, D. C., Gupton, B. F., Kam, C-M., Nishino, N., Sakamoto, M., and Tuhy, P. M. (1984). Reaction of azapeptides with human leukocyte elastase and porcine pancreatic elastase. New inhibitors and active site titrants. *J. Biol. Chem.*, **259**, 4288–94.

Powers, J. C., Tanaka, T., Harper, J. W., Minematsu, Y., Barker, L., Lincoln, D., Crumley, K. V., Fraki, Y., Schechter, N. M., Lazarus, G. S., Nakajima, K., Nakashino, K., Neurath, H., and Woodbury, R. G. (1985). Mammalian chymotrypsin-like enzymes. Comparative reactivities of rat mast cell proteases, human and dog skin chymases, and human cathepsin G with 4-nitroanilide substrates, and peptide chloromethyl ketone and sulfonyl fluoride inhibitors. *Biochemistry*, **24**, 2048–58.

Reilly, C. F., Tewksbury, D. A., Schechter, N. M., and Travis, J. (1982). Rapid conversion of angiotensin I to angiotensin II by neutrophil and mast cell proteinases. *J. Biol. Chem.*, **257**, 8619–22.

Renaud, A., Lestienne, P., Hughes, D. L., Bieth, J. G., and Dimicoli, J-L. (1983). Mapping the S'subsites of porcine pancreatic and human leukocyte elastases. *J. Biol. Chem.*, **258**, 8312–16.

Schechter, I. and Berger, A. (1967). On the size of the active site in proteases. I. Papain. *Biochem. Biophys. Res. Commun.*, **27**, 157–62.

Schechter, N. M., Fraki, J. E., Geesin, J. C., and Lazarus, G. S. (1983). Human skin chymotryptic proteinase—isolation and relation to cathepsin G and rat mast cell proteinase I. *J. Biol. Chem.*, **258**, 2973–8.

Shotton, D. M. and Watson, H. C. (1970). Three dimensional structure of tosylelastase. *Nature*, **225**, 811–16.

Spencer, R. W., Copp, L. J., and Pfister, J. R. (1985). Inhibition of human leukocyte elastase, porcine pancreatic elastase, and chymotrypsin by elasnin and other 4-hydroxy-2-pyrones. *J. Med. Chem.*, **28**, 1828–32.

Stein, R. L., Trainor, D. A., and Wildonger, R. A. (1985). Neutrophil elastase. *Ann. Rep. Med. Chem.*, **20**, 237–46.

Stone, P. J., Lucey, E. C., Calore, J. D., Snider, G. L., Franzblau, C., Castillo, M. J., and Powers, J. C. (1981). The moderation of elastase-induced emphysema in the hamster by intratracheal pretreatment or post-treatment with succinyl alanyl alanyl prolyl valine chloromethyl ketone. *Am. Rev. Resp. Dis.*, **124**, 56–9.

Suter, S., Schaad, U. B., Roux, L., Nydegger, U. E., and Waldvogel, F. A. (1984). Granulocyte neutral proteases and pseudomonas elastase as possible causes of airway damage in patients with cystic fibrosis. *J. Infect. Dis.*, **149**, 523–31.

Tam, T. F., Spencer, R. W., Thomas, E. M., Copp, L. J., and Krantz, A. (1984). Novel suicide inhibitors of serine proteinases. Inactivation of human leukocyte elastase by ynenol lactones. *J. Am. Chem. Soc.*, **106**, 6849–51.

Tarjan, E., Peto, L., Appel, J., and Tolnay, P. (1983). Prevention of elastase-induced emphysema by aerosol administration of a specific synthetic elastase inhibitor. *Eur. J. Respir. Dis.*, **64**, 442–8.

Teshima, T., Griffin, J. C., and Powers, J. C. (1982). A new class of heterocyclic serine protease inhibitors. Inhibition of human leukocyte elastase, porcine pancreatic elastase, cathepsin G, and bovine chymotrypsin A by substituted benzoxazinones, quinazolines and anthranilates. *J. Biol. Chem.*, **257**, 5085–91.

Thompson, R. C. (1973). Use of peptide aldehydes to generate transition-state analogs of elastase. *Biochemistry*, **12**, 47–51.

Tsuji, K., Agha, B. J., Shinogi, M., and Digenis, G. A. (1984). Peptidyl carbamate esters: a new class of specific elastase inhibitors. *Biochem. Biophys. Res. Commun.*, **122**, 571–6.

Tuhy, P. M. and Powers, J. C. (1975). Inhibition of human leukocyte elastase by peptide chloromethylketones. *FEBS Lett.*, **50**, 359–61.

Umezawa, H. and Aoyagi, T. (1977). Activities of proteinase inhibitors of microbial origin. In *Proteinases in mammalian cells and tissues* (ed. A.. Barrett) pp. 637–62. Elsevier/North Holland, Amsterdam.

Umezawa, H. Aoyagi, T., Morishima, H., Kunimoto, S., Matsuzaki, M., Hamad, M., and Takenchi, T. (1970). Chymostatin, a new chymotrypsin inhibitor produced by actinomycetes. *J. Antibiot.*, **23**, 425–30.

Umezawa, H., Aoyagi, T., Okura, A., Marishima, H., Takeuchi, T., and Okami, Y. (1973). Elastatinal, a new elastase inhibitor produced by actinomycetes. *J. Antibiot.*, **26**, 787–9.

Vartio, T., Seppa, H., and Vaheri, A. (1981). Susceptibility of soluble and matrix fibronectins to degradation by tissue proteinases, mast cell chymase and cathepsin G. *J. Biol. Chem.*, **256**, 471–7.

Watson, H. C., Shotton, D. M., Cox, J. M., and Muirhead, H. (1970). Three-dimensional fourier synthesis of tosyl-elastase at 3.5 Å resolution. *Nature, Lond.*, **225**, 806–11.

Weidman, B. and Abeles, R. H. (1984). Mechanism of inactivitation of chymotrypsin by butyl-3H-1,3-oxazine-2,6-dione. *Biochemistry*, **23**, 2373–6.

Weiland, J. E., Davis, W. B., Holter, J. F., Mohammed, J. R., Dorinsky, P. M., and Gadek, J. E. (1986). Lung neutrophils in the adult respiratory distress syndrome—clinical and pathophysiologic significance. *Am. Rev. Respir. Dis.*, **133**, 218–25.

Westkaemper, R. B. and Abeles, R. H. (1983). Novel inactivators of serine proteases based on 6-chloro-2-pyrone. *Biochemistry*, **22**, 3256–84.

Wintroub, B. U., Klickstein, L. B., Dzau, V. J., and Watt, K. W. K. (1984). Granulocyte–angiotensin system. Identification of angiotensinogen as the plasma protein substrate of leucocyte cathepsin G. *Biochemistry*, **23**, 227–32.

Wintroub, B. U., Kaempfer, C. E., Schechter, N. M., and Proud, D. (1986). A human lung mast cell chymotrypsin-like enzyme. Identification and partial characterization. *J. Clin. Invest.*, **77**, 196–201.

Woodbury, R. G. and Neurath, H. (1980). Structure, specificity and localization of serine proteases of connective tissue. *FEBS Lett.* **114**, 189–96.

Yoshida, N., Everitt, M. T., Neurath, H., Woodbury, R. G., and Powers, J. C. (1980). Substrate specificity of two chymotrypsin-like proteases from rat mast cells. Studies with peptide 4-nitroanilides and comparison with cathepsin G. *Biochemistry*, **19**, 5799–804.

Yoshimura, T., Barker, L. N., and Powers, J. C. (1982). Specificity and reactivity of human leukocyte elastase, porcine pancreatic elastase, human granulocyte cathepsin G, and bovine chymotrypsin with arylsulfonyl fluorides. *J. Biol. Chem.*, **257**, 5077–84.

Zimmerman, M. (1979). Role of proteinases from leukocytes in inflammation. In *Bio-*

logical function of proteinases (ed. by H. Holzer and H. Tschesche), pp. 186–95. Springer, New York.

Zimmerman, M. and Ashe, B. M. (1977). Substrate specifity of the elastase and the chymotrypsin-like enzyme of the human granulocyte. *Biochim. Biophys. Acta*, **480**, 241–5.

Zimmerman, M., Morman, H., Mulvey, D., Jones, H., Frankshun, R., and Ashe, B. M. (1980). Inhibition of elastase and other serine proteases by heterocyclic acylating agents. *J. Biol. Chem.*, **255**, 9848–51.

Section 18D

Inhibitors of trypsin and trypsin-like enzymes with a physiological role

Fritz Markwardt and Jörg Stürzebecher

18D.1   General aspects

Serine proteinases are proteolytic enzymes characterized by a reactive serine residue in the catalytic mechanism. The trypsin family includes serine proteinases that attack at peptide bonds following an arginine or lysine residue. Of physiological importance are trypsin-like enzymes that are involved in the processes of coagulation, fibrinolysis, kinin liberation, and complement activation as well as fertilization and digestion. Figure 18D.1 gives a schematic representation of the interlinked reactions of the enzymes participating in the plasma effector systems.

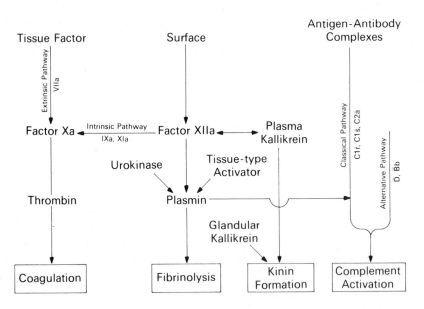

Fig. 18D.1 Role of some trypsin-like proteinases in the blood effector systems.

18D.1.1   Structural features participating in catalysis

Nowadays we have a clear conception of the various functional groups involved in the binding of substrate to enzyme and the catalytic events that occur in the active site during peptide bond hydrolysis. The charge relay system postulated by Blow *et al.* (1969) is the most important feature in the active site of serine proteinases. It consists of the side-chain imidazole of His-57, the carboxylate of Asp-102, and the reactive hydroxyl of Ser-195, and enables the oxygen atom of the serine to participate in the catalysis as a strong nucleophile. Following formation of the enzyme–substrate complex, a tetrahedral intermediate is formed by nucleophilic attack of the hydroxyl group of Ser-195. It is stabilized by hydrogen bonds between the carbonyl oxygen and the NH groups of Gly-193 and Ser-195 of the oxyanion binding site. In the next step, the tetrahedral intermediate breaks down to the acyl enzyme and liberates the leaving group. Deacylation of the acyl enzyme is the reverse of the initial reaction (Kraut 1977).

Further binding sites contribute to the binding of the polypeptide substrate to the enzyme. The side-chain specificity site is the structural base for the specificity of trypsin-like enzymes for basic amino acids. It consists of a pocket with the Asp-189 residue at the bottom (specificity pocket, primary substrate binding site), which forms an ion pair with the side-chain of basic amino acids. Two polypeptide binding sites (secondary substrate binding sites) are located at both sides of the specificity pocket; one of them interacts with substrate on its acyl-group side, the other binds to the leaving-group side of the substrate. Essential substrate binding sites outside the active centre are known only in the case of plasmin. These so-called lysine-binding sites are involved in the binding of the substrate fibrin and of the inhibitor α_2-antiplasmin to plasmin (Wiman and Wallén 1977; Morris and Castellino 1983; Christensen 1984).

18D.1.2 Design of inhibitors based on substrate structure

Modification of substrates is a common principle for the development of inhibitors. For obvious reasons, a classical reversible inhibitor possesses high affinity only when it imitates the substrate, whereby it is enabled to occupy essential substrate binding sites. Covalent bond formation between enzyme and inhibitor is a further way to enhance inhibitory activity. However, high affinity for the enzyme meets only one of the requirements for an inhibitor. With a view to using inhibitors as drugs, they should selectively inactivate the target enzyme.

Using examples of various types of inhibitor of trypsin and related enzymes, those structural features will be discussed that enable a synthetic, low molecular weight compound to occupy different substrate binding sites and/or interact with the catalytic mechanism.

18D.1.2.1 *Inhibitors occupying the specificity pocket*

These inhibitors must possess or imitate the amino- or guanidinoalkyl side chain of Lys and Arg. Consequently, the first competitive inhibitor of trypsin, $N\alpha$-tosylagmatine, was obtained by decarboxylation of the substrate $N\alpha$-tosyl-L-arginine methyl ester (Lorand and Rule 1961). However, the affinity of alkylamines and alkylguanidines for the trypsin-like enzymes is low (Inagami and York 1968), while aromatic ring structures with a side-chain basic group possess comparatively high affinity (Mares-Guia and Shaw 1965; Geratz *et al.* 1979). In designing inhibitors, phenylguanidine (Fig. 18D.2, **1**) and benzamidine (Fig. 18D.3, **5**) are the key building blocks besides arginine. The binding of benzamidine in the specificity pocket was demonstrated by X-ray crystal structure analysis (Bode and Schwager 1975).

18D.1.2.2 *Inhibitors interacting with the active site serine*

Di-isopropylphosphorofluoridate (DFP) and phenylmethanesulphonyl fluoride (PMSF) react not only with the active site serine hydroxyl of trypsin-like enzymes, but also with that of other proteinases and esterases. Among the

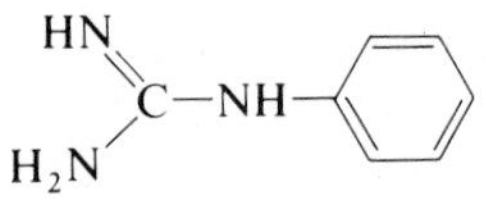

Fig. 18D.2 Structures of inhibitors derived from phenylguanidine.

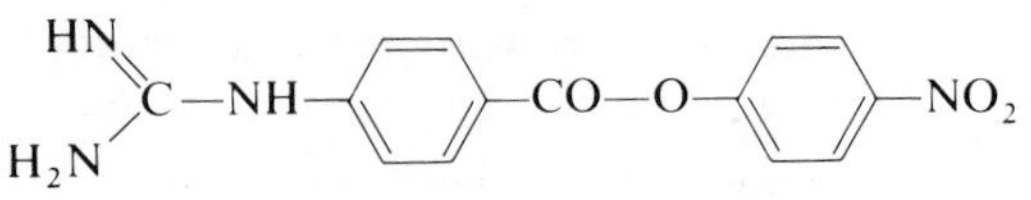

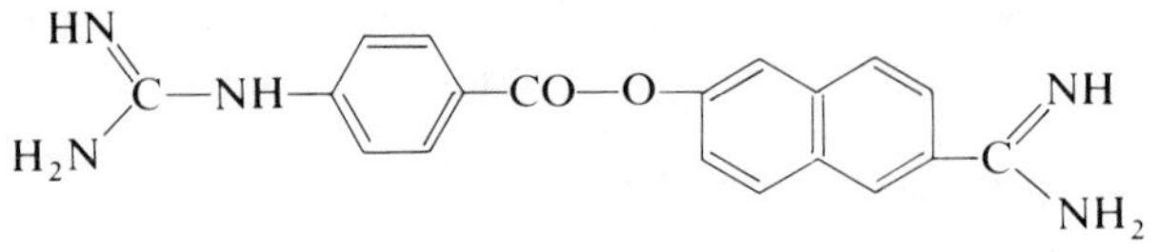

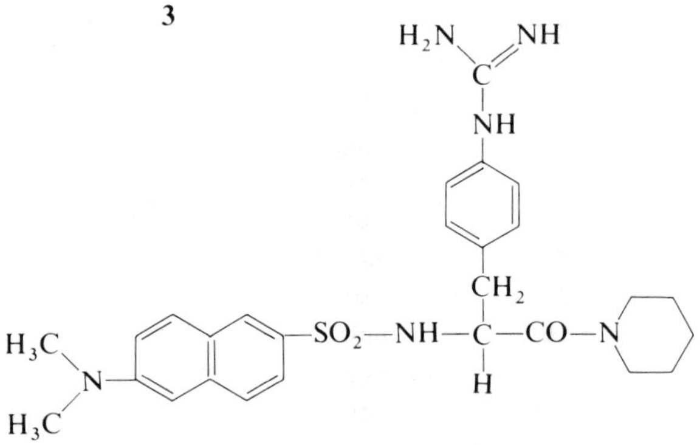

organic phosphorus compounds, specific inhibitors of trypsin-like enzymes have not been found (Ooms and van Dijk 1966). Variation of the structure of PMSF, especially introduction of a cationic group into the aromatic nucleus, enhances the inhibitory activity. Sulphonyl fluorides with a benzamidine moiety have the highest inhibitory potency (Markwardt et al. 1971c; Laura et al. 1980). Sulphonation of the active site serine of trypsin-like enzymes is also achieved by the nitrophenyl esters of benzenesulphonic and phenylmethanesulphonic acids with a cationic group. The reactivity and selectivity of most compounds are low (Markwardt et al. 1973; Wong and Shaw 1974; Wong et al. 1978).

Trypsin and related enzymes are acylated at Ser-195 by esters of guanidino and amidinobenzoic acids (Chase and Shaw 1969; Markwardt et al. 1973), but not by esters of amidinophenylalkylcarboxylic acids (Walsmann et al. 1974). p-nitrophenyl p'-guanidinobenzoate (p-NPGB, Fig. 18D.2, 2) has the highest affinity and reactivity. With p-NPGB and related esters, the acyl enzyme is formed so rapidly that liberation of stoichiometric amounts of nitrophenol allows titration of the active site of these enzymes (Chase and Shaw 1970; Coleman et al. 1976). Among the inhibitors with a benzamidine moiety, 4-

amidinophenyl esters of carboxylic acids that possess the structure of 'inverse substrates' are most reactive (Markwardt *et al.* 1972; Tanizawa *et al.* 1977). By the use of 4-amidinophenyl esters of substituted benzoic acids (Fig. 18D.3, **7**), acyl enzyme intermediates with different deacylation rates can be designed.

Peptide aldehydes with a C-terminal Arg-H inhibit trypsin-like enzymes via a transition-state mechanism, as has been shown for the inhibition of trypsin by leupeptin (Kuramochi *et al.* 1979). Among the tripeptide aldehydes, D-Phe-Pro-Arg-H and Boc-D-Phe-Pro-Arg-H are the most potent inhibitors of trypsin and related enzymes (Bajusz *et al.* 1978, 1982).

Similarly characteristic of reversible inhibitors, specific interactions with the active site serine hydroxyl account for the high inhibitory activity of benzami-

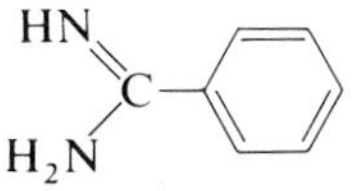

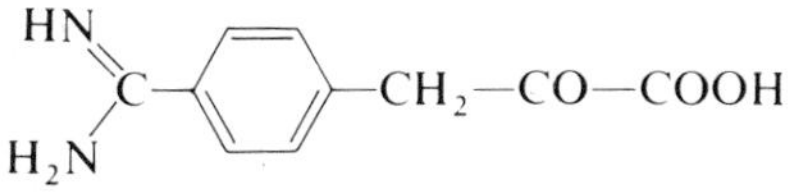

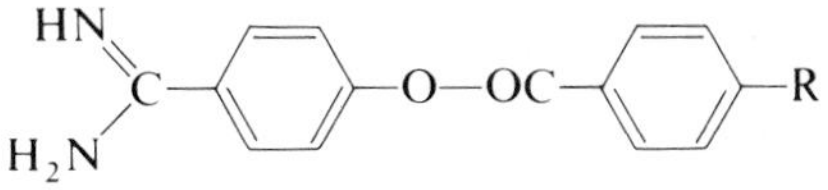

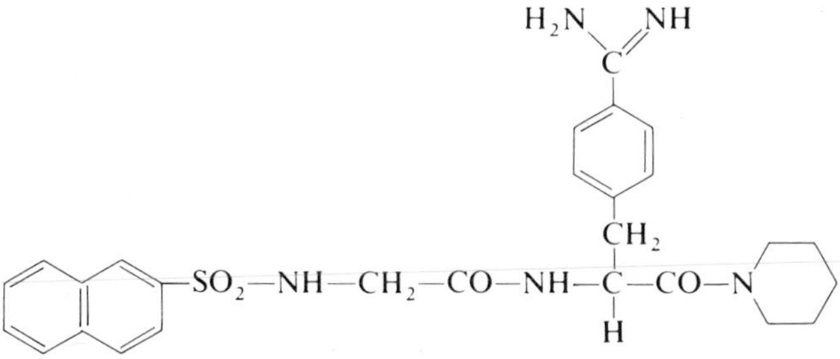

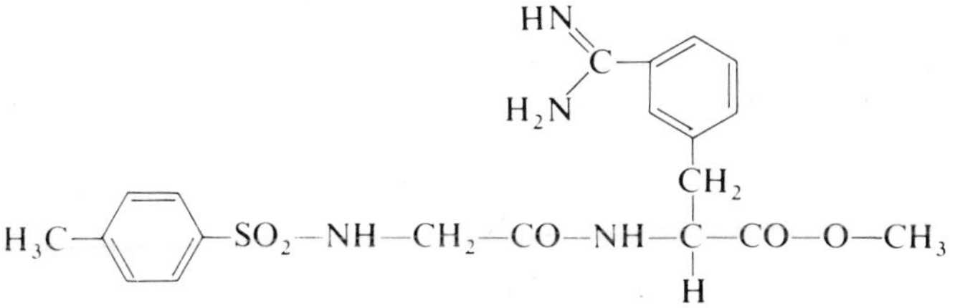

Fig. 18D.3 Structures of inhibitors derived from benzamidine.

dines with a keto group. Based on QSAR it has been postulated that a polarized carbonyl group might be attacked by the nucleophilic serine hydroxyl to give a tetrahedral arrangement (Stürzebecher *et al.* 1976b). Recently this concept was confirmed by X-ray crystal structure analysis (Walter and Bode 1983) and kinetic studies (Tanizawa *et al.* 1985). In Table 18D.1, derivatives of ω-amidino-phenyl-α-aminoalkylcarboxylic acids are listed as an example of an important group of benzamidines in which interactions between the carbonyl function and the serine hydroxyl group contribute much to the binding energy. Two structural features influence the inhibitory potency and selectivity of these α-amino acids: the distance between the amidino group and the carbonyl function, and the polarity of the carbonyl function.

18D.2.1.3 *Inhibitors interacting with the active site histidine*

The first irreversible inhibitor found to react only with trypsin-like enzymes was Tos-LysCH$_2$Cl (TLCK), which alkylates the active centre histidine (Shaw *et al.* 1965). Tos-ArgCH$_2$Cl (TACK) is more potent than TLCK for the inactivation of trypsin (Yoshida *et al.* 1973). Selective inactivation of individual trypsin-like proteinases is achieved only by using the approach of incorporating part of the sequence of the physiological substrate into the chloromethyl ketone (Kettner and Shaw 1981a; see Chapter 2B, this volume).

18D.2.1.4 *Inhibitors imitating the acyl-group side of the substrate*

Serine proteinases that are trypsin-like in primary specificity show a significant degree of sequence homology with trypsin. However, a great number of these proteinases differ from trypsin in that they are highly selective for one or two peptide bonds of their physiological substrate (Table 18D.2). It appears that the amino acid sequence, specifically the P_1, P_2, and P_3 residues, of the physiological substrate, contribute to the selectivity of the proteinases. Supporting this suggestion, peptides of lysine and arginine chloromethyl ketone were shown to be more reactive and more selective inhibitors than TLCK and TACK (see Chapter 2B). This is true of inhibitors of thrombin, factor Xa, urokinase, and kallikreins, while the selectivity for enzymes that hydrolyse multiple bonds in protein substrates is low (Table 18D.3).

Many derivatives of benzamidine were prepared with the object of obtaining reversible inhibitors able to occupy secondary substrate binding sites. QSAR shows that inhibitory potency depends on hydrophobic properties, the electron-donating potency of the substituents and the polarity of the carbonyl function (Stürzebecher *et al.* 1976b; Stürzebecher and Walsmann 1978; Andrews *et al.* 1978; Labes and Hagen 1979). However, no selective inhibitors of individual enzymes were found.

18D.1.2.5 *Inhibitors imitating the leaving-group side of the substrate*

Only a few peptide inhibitors are known that imitate the departing group. Ganu and Shaw (1981) have reported a small series of depsipeptides of *p*-guanidino-

Table 18D.1 Inhibition of trypsin-like enzymes by Nα-tosylated cyclic amides (piperidides or morpholides) and anilides of ω-amidinophenyl-α-aminoalkylcarboxylic acids (Stürzebecher 1981; Stürzebecher et al. 1981a,b; 1982; 1986a,d)

n	R_1	R_2	R_3	R_4	K_i (µmol l^{-1})						
					Trypsin	Thrombin	Factor Xa	Plasmin	Urokinase	Glandular kallikrein	Acrosin
0	H	Am	$CH_2CH_2-O-CH_2CH_2$		0.58	7.1	12	18	19	>1000	0.55
0	Am	H	$CH_2CH_2CH_2CH_2CH_2$		550	61	122	>1000	>1000	550	6.2
1	H	Am	$CH_2CH_2CH_2CH_2CH_2$		1.2	0.34	15	12	25	590	0.51
1	Am	H	$CH_2CH_2CH_2CH_2CH_2$		64	2.3	73	>1000	>1000	38	10.0
2	Am	H	$CH_2CH_2CH_2CH_2CH_2$		37	80	29	230	410	520	11.4
3	H	Am	$CH_2CH_2-O-CH_2CH_2$		3.0	0.06	3.6	35	94	220	0.56
3	Am	H	$CH_2CH_2CH_2CH_2CH_2$		7.0	0.36	19	92	28	87	0.50
1	Am	H	C_6H_5	H	31	100	120	410	240	170	3.1
2	Am	H	C_6H_5	H	0.34	40	12	2.3	35	39	0.50
3	H	Am	C_6H_5	H	1.7	3.7	0.36	29	74	60	0.72
3	Am	H	C_6H_5	H	4.1	16	4.0	34	6.5	77	0.08

Table 18D.2 Sequences at physiological substrate cleavage sites of trypsin-like enzymes

Enzyme	Substrate	Acyl group -P_4 -P_3 -P_2-P_1 ↓	Leaving group P'_1-P'_2-
Trypsin		multiple—bonds	
Thrombin	Fibrinogen αA-chain	-Gly-Gly-Val-Arg—Gly-Pro-	
	Prothrombin	-Val-Ile -Pro-Arg—Ser-Gly-	
	Factor XIII	-Gly-Val-Pro-Arg—Gly-Val-	
Factor Xa	Prothrombin	-Ile -Glu-Gly-Arg—Thr-Ser-	
		-Ile -Glu-Gly-Arg—Ile-Ser-	
Plasmin	Fibrin	multiple Lys—bonds	
Urokinase	Plasminogen	-Lys-Pro-Gly-Arg—Val-Val-	
		-Ser-Pro-Phe-Arg—Ser-Val-	
Plasma kallikrein	Kininogen	-Ser-Leu-Met-Lys—Arg-Pro-	
		-Ser-Pro-Phe-Arg—Ser-Val-	
Glandular kallikrein	Kininogen	-Ser-Leu-Met—Lys-Arg-	
Acrosin		multiple—bonds	

benzoic acid with low reactivity and selectivity. Obviously, the importance of those parts of the inhibitor imitating the leaving-group side consists in polarizing the carbonyl function rather than in occupying the substrate binding site. This is demonstrated in the acylation of trypsin by 4-amidinophenyl benzoates. There exists a linear correlation between rate of acylation and inductive effect of the alcohol residue of the benzoic acid ester (Markwardt *et al.* 1972). QSAR shows that the carbonyl substituent influences the polarity of the carbonyl group and thus the inhibitory activity of benzamidines with a keto group (Stürzebecher *et al.* 1976b). Moreover, due to this dependence upon the polarity of the carbonyl function of derivatives of ω-amidinophenyl-α-aminoalkylcarboxylic acids induced by different amide residues, individual enzymes may even be inhibited selectively. Thus, certain cyclic amides of ω-amidinophenyl-α-aminoalkylcarboxylic acids are selective thrombin inhibitors, while other primary amides of this type are selective inhibitors of trypsin, plasmin, or factor Xa (Table 18D.1).

18D.1.2.6 *Inhibitors binding to the enzyme outside the active site*
Compounds containing a benzamidine moiety linked to a phenylsulphonyl-fluoride moiety by a long-chain bridging group inhibit trypsin-like enzymes irreversibly. These compounds do not sulphonate the active centre serine but an amino acid residue outside the active site (Baker and Cory 1971; Cory *et al.* 1977).

Table 18D.3 Comparison of the susceptibility of trypsin and related enzymes to inactivation by peptide chloromethyl ketones (Kettner and Shaw 1981a,b; Kettner et al. 1978, 1980; Collen et al. 1980.)

Compound	$10^4 \times k_{app} \times I^{-1} (l\ mol^{-1}\ min^{-1})$							
	Trypsin	Thrombin	Factor Xa	Plasmin	Urokinase	Plasma kallikrein	Glandular kallikrein	Acrosin
Tos-LysCH$_2$Cl	0.076	0.0004		0.001	0.00002			0.04
Ala-Phe-LysCH$_2$Cl	3.6		0.03	21	0.0003	7.4	0.020	0.88
D-Val-Phe-LysCH$_2$Cl	66	3.2	0.66	150	0.0018			
Ala-Phe-ArgCH$_2$Cl	36	0.17	2.22	7.83	0.0059	440	0.34	28
Dns-Ala-Phe-ArgCH$_2$Cl			49	95		566		
Pro-Phe-ArgCH$_2$Cl	6.0	0.12	1.33	1.86	0.0015	140	0.79	5.2
Ser-Pro-Phe-ArgCH$_2$Cl						150	0.65	
Phe-Ser-Pro-Phe-ArgCH$_2$Cl						140	4.20	
D-Phe-Phe-ArgCH$_2$Cl		45	19.3	36.7		2320	18	
Gly-Val-ArgCH$_2$Cl	42	1.9	0.04	0.05	0.017	1.6	0.0031	48
Val-Pro-ArgCH$_2$Cl	430	54	0.28	0.31	0.54	2.9	0.0039	160
Ile-Pro-ArgCH$_2$Cl	450	42	0.34	0.27	0.39	2.0	0.0028	240
D-Phe-Pro-ArgCH$_2$Cl	70	69000	27.2	4.3	0.62	47.5	0.27	
Pro-Gly-ArgCH$_2$Cl	87	1.2	2.0	0.11	0.79	3.3	0.0029	67
Ac-Gly-Gly-ArgCH$_2$Cl	620	0.74	5.6	0.053	2.6	1.4	0.0005	27
Glu-Gly-ArgCH$_2$Cl		2.2	16	1.0	20.4	15.8	0.0009	370
Ile-Glu-Gly-ArgCH$_2$Cl		3.0	190	0.45		28.6	0.0004	380
Dns-Glu-Gly-ArgCH$_2$Cl	1100	26	2200	28.6	4.8	141	0.18	510

The potency of bis-benzamidines has been explained by the fact that the second amidino moiety interacts with a second cationic binding site beyond the specificity pocket. Presumably, this view cannot be applied to trypsin, thrombin, and plasmin, since compounds whose second amidino moiety is removed or replaced by a nitro group possess the same inhibitory activity (Geratz and Tidwell 1977; Walsmann *et al.* 1979).

In this context, it is noteworthy that ω-aminocarboxylic acids occupy the lysine-binding sites located in the kringle structures of plasmin(ogen).

18D.2 Inhibitors of trypsin

A great number of compounds are known that inactivate trypsin as well as related enzymes. Obviously trypsin, which hydrolyses multiple bonds, does not possess specific secondary binding sites. For instance, chloromethyl ketones (Table 18D.3) and benzamidine derivatives (Table 18D.1) are potent trypsin inhibitors; however, they also inhibit related enzymes. Only a few inhibitors are known that inactivate trypsin selectively. An outstanding example is bis-(5-amidino-2-benzimidazolyl)methane, with a K_i value of 1.7×10^{-8} M (Tidwell *et al.* 1978). Several benzamidines with a γ-keto group and 4-amidinoanilides of ω-phenyl-α-aminovaleric acid cause preferential inhibition of trypsin (Stürzebecher *et al.* 1976c, 1984b).

Trypsin is generated in the intestine by activation of trypsinogen released from the pancreas. It serves as the activator of all the other zymogens of pancreatic tissue. Thus, inhibition of trypsin has broad consequences in terms of the formation of the endopeptidase and exopeptidase components of pancreatic juice. Synthetic trypsin inhibitors such as guanidino compounds and benzamidine derivatives prevent the autocatalytic activation of trypsinogen and the activation of zymogens in pancreatic homogenate (Trettin and Mix 1965; Geratz 1966; Markwardt *et al.* 1974b). The carboethoxyphenyl ester of ε-guanidinocaproic acid (FOY, gabexate mesilate; Fig. 18D.4, **13**) has been the only synthetic inhibitor used in the treatment of pancreatitis for several years. FOY inhibits trypsin and related enzymes (Muramatu and Fujii 1972; Saitoh 1982). In this context it has to be mentioned that aprotinin, a polypeptide inhibitor from bovine organs, is used in clinical practice for treatment of pancreatitis and hyperproteolytic states.

On the other hand, animal experiments have shown that trypsin inhibitors stimulate pancreatic function. A single intragastric administration of benzamidine derivatives in rats causes an immediate secretory response resulting in release of zymogens, while feeding the inhibitor for a prolonged period of time induces enlargement of the pancreas and a marked increase in trypsinogen content (Geratz 1969). Similar observations have been made in chicks and rabbits with natural trypsin inhibitors from legumes (Rackis 1965; Garlich and Nesheim 1966).

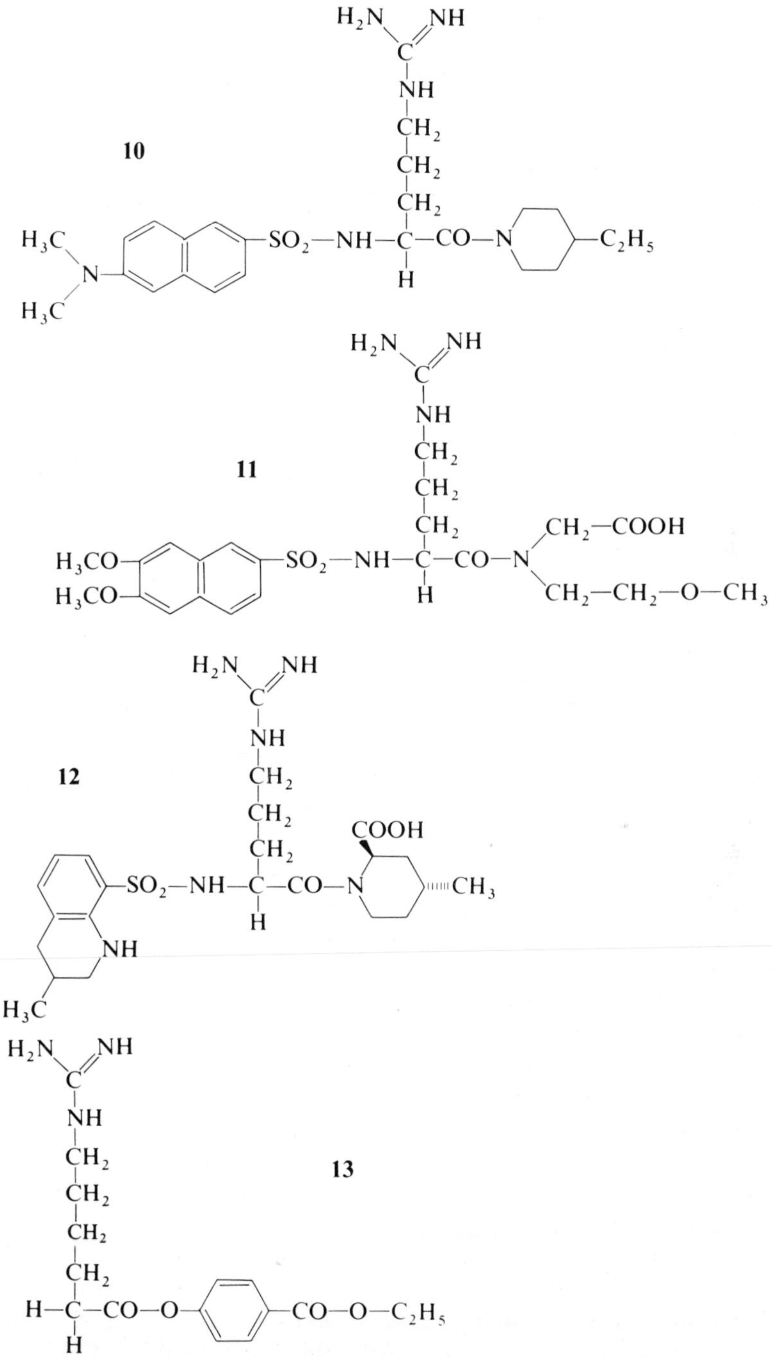

Fig. 18D.4 Structures of inhibitors derived from arginine.

18D.3   Inhibitors of proteinases of the coagulation system

Coagulation of blood is the visible result of a chain of reactions induced and maintained by specific proteolytic enzymes (Fig. 18D.1). Serine proteinases of the trypsin family are involved in the intrinsic (factors XIIa, XIa, IXa) and extrinsic (factor VIIa) pathway. Both lead to activation of factor X, which in turn activates prothrombin to the fibrinogen-converting enzyme thrombin.

Inhibitors of blood clotting enzymes are of therapeutic interest since they are potential anticoagulants. Due to the possiblity of oral administration and their direct action they present alternatives to the heparin- and coumarin-type anticoagulants (Markwardt 1980).

18D.3.1   Inhibitors of thrombin

Three types of inhibitor have been developed that inhibit thrombin selectively: peptide inhibitors modelled after natural substrates, derivatives of arginine, and derivative of 4-amidinophenylalanine. Recently, thrombin inhibitors have been reviewed in detail (Stürzebecher 1984).

18D.3.1.1   *Peptide inhibitors*

Peptide esters and amides, as well as chloromethyl ketones and aldehydes corresponding to the thrombin-sensitive Gly-Val-Arg-sequence of fibrinogen, are less effective inhibitors (Blombäck *et al.* 1969; Liem *et al.* 1971; Bajusz *et al.* 1978). Analogues of the factor XIII (Val-Pro-Arg) and prothrombin cleavage site (Ile-Pro-Arg) are more reactive and selective inhibitors of thrombin (Dorman *et al.* 1972; Kettner and Shaw 1977; Table 18D.3). However, the effective sequence in inhibitors is D-Phe-Pro-Arg, combining the Pro-Arg of factor XIII and the prothrombin sequence with D-Phe, which imitates the P_9 Phe of fibrinopeptide A (Marsh *et al.* 1982). The corresponding tripeptide aldehydes D-Phe-Pro-Arg-H and Boc-D-Phe-Pro-Arg-H possess particularly high antithrombin activity (Bajusz *et al.* 1978); however, they also inhibit other trypsin-like serine proteinases (Fareed *et al.* 1981). The time-dependency of thrombin inactivation suggests formation of a covalent hemiacetal adduct similar to the tetrahedral intermediate, which is assumed to appear during substrate hydrolysis (Stürzebecher 1984). The anticoagulant effect of these argininals was assessed in animal experiments (Tremoli *et al.* 1981; Bagdy *et al.* 1982; Mattsson *et al.* 1982; Markwardt *et al.* 1983).

D-Phe-Pro-ArgCH_2Cl is the most powerful and selective inhibitor to inactivate thrombin irreversibly (Kettner and Shaw 1979a). The second-order rate constant for inactivation of thrombin is three to five orders of magnitude higher than that for inhibition of other trypsin-like proteinases (Table 18D.3). The anticoagulant and antithrombotic effects of the compound have been demonstrated (Hauptmann and Markwardt 1980). D-Phe-Pro-ArgCH_2Cl is an efficient inhibitor of intravascular coagulation induced by thrombin, thromboplastin (Collen *et al.* 1982; Markwardt *et al.* 1983) or snake venom (Schaeffer *et al.* 1984).

Esters and amides and the agmatine derivative of D-Phe-Pro-Arg-OH are competitive inhibitors of thrombin, with K_i values in the micromolar range. Their anticoagulant activity is low (Mattsson *et al.* 1982; Bajusz 1984).

18D.3.1.2 *Arginine derivatives*

Starting from the synthetic substrate $N\alpha$-tosyl-L-arginine methyl ester, Okamoto and co-workers extensively varied the carbonyl and $N\alpha$-substituents and designed reversible thrombin inhibitors having a potent and highly selective action. Among the cyclic amides with a $N\alpha$-dansyl residue, the most effective compound is $N\alpha$-dansyl-L-arginine 4-ethylpiperidinamide (OM 205, DAPA; Fig. 18D.4, **10**) with a K_i of 3.7×10^{-8} M (Hijikata *et al.* 1979; Kikumoto *et al.* 1980b; Okamoto *et al.* 1980). Exchange of the $N\alpha$-dansyl group for a substituted arylsulphonyl residue and introduction of a carboxyl group into the amide component yielded compounds with similar antithrombin activity (Kikumoto *et al.* 1980a, b). These compounds have lower toxicity and more favourable pharmacokinetic properties when compared to the $N\alpha$-dansyl-L-arginine amides. The anticoagulant and antithrombotic effects of $N\alpha$-(6,7-dimethoxynaphthalene-2-sulphonyl)-L-arginyl(N-methoxyethyl)glycine (OM 407; Fig. 18D.4, **11**) were demonstrated *in vitro* and *in vivo* (Ikoma *et al.* 1980; Ohtsu *et al.* 1980). The most potent OM-inhibitor is (2R,4R)-4-methyl-1-[$N\alpha$-(3-methyl-1,2,3,4-tetrahydro-8-quinoline sulphonyl)-L-arginyl]-2-piperidine-carboxylic acid (OM 805, MD 805, MCI 9038; Fig. 18D.4, **12**), with a K_i of 1.9 $\times 10^{-8}$ M. The antithrombin activity depends decisively on the stereochemistry of the 4-methyl-2-piperidinecarboxylic acid moiety (Okamoto *et al.* 1981; Kikumoto *et al.* 1984). OM 805 has low toxicity and is a highly effective antithrombotic substance (Kumada and Abiko 1981). Recently, its successful use in humans has been reported (Kosaki *et al.* 1983; Yamada 1983).

18D.3.1.3 *Benzamidines*

Despite extensive variation of the structure of ordinary benzamidines, success has not been achieved in obtaining selective inhibitors. However, among the ordinary benzamidines, 4-amidinophenylpyruvic acid (APPA, Fig. 18D.3, **6**) is an outstanding inhibitor (Markwardt *et al.* 1974c). Due to its low toxicity and favourable pharmacokinetic properties, particularly enteric absorption and slow elimination, it was the first thrombin inhibitor to be thoroughly investigated *in vivo* (Markwardt and Klöcking 1972; Markwardt *et al.* 1979). Its anticoagulant and antithrombotic effects have been demonstrated by its prevention of experimental thrombosis and disseminated intravascular coagulation (Markwardt *et al.* 1977; Hauptmann 1982).

Selective competitive thrombin inhibitors with a benzamidine moiety have been found among the derivatives of $N\alpha$-substituted ω-amidinophenyl-α-amino-alkylcarboxylic acids (Table 18D.1). In particular, the cyclic amides of 4-

amidinophenylalanine possess high affinity for thrombin (Markwardt *et al.* 1980; Stürzebecher *et al.* 1981a). Compounds of this type bind selectively and tightly to thrombin when amino acids are included in the link to the α-nitrogen of 4-amidinophenylalanine. Nα-(2-naphthylsulphonylglycyl)-4-amidino-phenylalanine piperidinamide (α-NAPAP, Fig. 18D.3, **8**), possesses the highest affinity for thrombin (K_i 6×10^{-9} M) ever to be reported for a synthetic inhibitor (Stürzebecher *et al.* 1983). Amides of 4-amidinophenylalanine with Pro in the P_2-position have low affinity for thrombin, although their structure is isosteric to the thrombin-sensitive Pro-Arg sequence (Stürzebecher *et al.* 1987).

Nα-arylsulphonylated cyclic amides of 3- and 4-amidinophenylalanine are potent anticoagulants *in vitro* and *in vivo*. They prevent the formation of experimental venous thrombi and thrombin-induced microthrombosis. The anticoagulant and antithrombotic effect of α-NAPAP corresponds to its pronounced antithrombin activity (Hauptmann *et al.* 1980, 1985; Markwardt *et al.* 1983; Kaiser *et al.* 1985).

Effective, non-specific thrombin inhibitors have been found among compounds with two benzamidine moieties, K_i values being in the micromolar range. The antithrombin activity of bis-benzamidines increases with the length and bulkiness of the central chain (Geratz *et al.* 1973; 1976; Walsmann *et al.* 1976). This is also true of tris- and tetra-benzamidines, with K_i values of 1×10^{-6} M (Tidwell *et al.* 1976; Ferroni *et al.* 1984). Due to their toxicity and rapid elimination, bis-benzamidines are not suitable as anticoagulants for *in vivo* use (Hauptmann *et al.* 1976).

18D.3.1.4   *Inhibitors with other structures*

Several amidino-bearing aromatic ring structures are more tightly bound to thrombin than benzamidine (Geratz *et al.* 1979). Systematic substitutions have been carried out only with β-naphthamidines, the K_i values of the most potent compounds being in the micromolar range (Wagner *et al.* 1977; Walsmann *et al.* 1978). 2-(6-amidino)naphthyl 4'-guanidinobenzoate (FUT-175; Fig 18D.2, **3**) possesses antithrombin and anticoagulant activity (Fujii and Hitomi 1981; Hitomi *et al.* 1985).

Among the inhibitors with a guanidinoalkyl moiety, esters of ε-guanidinocaproic acid have high inhibitory activity against trypsin-like enzymes. The carboethoxyphenyl ester (FOY; Fig. 18D.4, **8**) inhibits thrombin with a K_i of 9.7 $\times 10^{-7}$ M (Muramatu and Fujii 1972; Ohno *et al.* 1980). FOY has an extremely short half-life in blood. It exerts anticoagulant and antithrombotic effects *in vivo* only when administered as a continuous infusion (Ohno *et al.* 1981; Taenaka *et al.* 1982; Oedekoven *et al.* 1984).

Derivatives of 4-guanidinophenylalanine are selective competitive inhibitors of thrombin (Claeson *et al.* 1983). The K_i values of Nα-tosylated (S-2576) and Nα-dansylated 4-guanidinophenylalanine piperidinamide (S-2581; Fig. 18D.2, **4**) are of the same order of magnitude as those of the isosteric 4-amidinophenylalanine derivatives (Stürzebecher *et al.* 1984a).

18D.3.2 Inhibitors of factor Xa

Although factor Xa plays a central role in blood coagulation (Fig. 18D.1), its inhibition has been less extensively studied than that of thrombin.

Among a large series of benzamidines, derivatives with aromatic substituents in the 3-position are potent and relatively selective inhibitors of factor Xa (Stürzebecher et al. 1976a; Robison et al. 1980). QSAR has revealed the importance of hydrophobic interactions (Stürzebecher and Walsmann 1978). 3-amidino derivatives more efficiently inhibit the factor Xa-catalysed formation of thrombin and the overall plasma coagulation than inhibitors of thrombin (Hauptmann et al. 1978).

Comparatively potent inhibitors of factor Xa are the anilides of 3-amidino-phenyl-α-aminovaleric acid (Table 18D.1). $N\alpha$-arylsulphonylaminoacylated derivatives of 3-amidinophenylalanine are selective inhibitors (Stürzebecher et al. 1988c). A representative compound of this type is $N\alpha$-tosyl-glycyl-3-amidinophenylalanine methyl ester (K_i 8.4×10^{-7} M; Fig. 18D.3, 9).

Several bis-benzamidines are tight-binding inhibitors of factor Xa, with K_i values in the range of 10^{-8} M (Stürzebecher et al. 1980, 1986d). Amidino-substituted heterocycles have higher affinity for factor Xa than benzamidine (Geratz et al. 1979). With the aid of bis-amidino derivatives of this type it was shown that inhibition of factor Xa is more significant for overall anticoagulant effects than inhibition of thrombin. In vivo experiments with 1,2-di-(5-amidino-2-benzofuranyl) ethane have shown that an inhibitor of factor Xa is able to prolong the partial thromboplastin time in pigs (Geratz and Tidwell 1978; Tidwell et al. 1980).

Potent and selective inhibitors that alkylate factor Xa irreversibly are chloromethyl ketones, that imitate the factor Xa-sensitive sequence in prothrombin (Tables 18D.2, 18D.3). In a series of chloromethyl ketones, Kettner and Shaw (1981b) found Ile-Glu-Gly-ArgCH$_2$Cl to be a potent inhibitor. The most reactive inhibitor was obtained by substitution of Ile in P$_4$ for a dansyl residue. In contrast to the chloromethyl ketones, peptide aldehydes corresponding to the Ile-Glu-Gly-Arg-sequence possess low affinity for factor Xa (Bajusz et al. 1982).

18D.3.3 Inhibitors of other blood-clotting enzymes

The first enzyme that is activated in the intrinsic pathway of blood clotting is factor XII (Fig. 18D.1). High molecular weight (HMW) kininogen and plasma kallikrein participate in its activation so that inhibitors of plasma kallikrein may influence the early phase of clotting. For various inhibitors of trypsin-like enzymes anti-factor XIIa activity has been demonstrated, such as with leupeptin, DAPA, D-Phe-Pro-Arg-H, and Boc-D-Phe-Pro-Arg-H (Fareed et al. 1981; Rattnoff 1981). Factor XIIa, which hydrolyses the kallikrein substrate D-Pro-Phe-Arg-pNA, is inhibited by the corresponding amides and esters (Fareed et al. 1981) and by D-Pro-Phe-ArgCH$_2$Cl (Silverberg and Kaplan 1982). 4-amidinophenyl derivatives with hydrophobic residues and derivatives of 4-amidino-phenyl-α-aminobutyric acid are competitive inhibitors of factor XIIa (Stürzebe-cher *et al.* 1986b).

Factors, XIa, IXa, and VIIa are inhibited by benzamidine and *p*-aminobenz-amidine (Jesty and Nemerson 1974; Silverberg *et al.* 1977; Byrne *et al.* 1980) and can be isolated by affinity chromatography on benzamidine agarose. It seems reasonable to assume that more complex benzamidines will be found to be more potent inhibitors of these enzymes. Irreversible inhibition of factor IXa and factor VIIa by chloromethyl ketones corresponding to the factor Xa-sensitive sequence Glu-Gly-Arg has been reported (Zur *et al.* 1982; Lollar and Fass 1984). Activated protein C, which inhibits coagulation by inactivating factors V and VIII, is inactivated by chloromethyl ketones with Pro or Phe at P_2 and a D-amino acid in the P_3 position (Lijnen *et al.* 1984; Stone and Hofsteenge 1985).

18D.4   Inhibitors of proteinases of the fibrinolytic system

The resolution of fibrin, the end-product of blood coagulation, in the organism involves the conversion of plasminogen into plasmin catalysed by plasminogen activators and the subsequent degradation of fibrin by plasmin (Fig 18D.1). Like trypsin, plasmin is able to digest a number of protein substrates, yet its physiological action *in vivo* is practically restricted to fibrin. Recent studies have shown that the so-called lysine-binding sites involved in the binding of plasmin-ogen to fibrin account for this specificity (Morris and Castellino 1983; Christen-sen 1984). The major plasminogen activators belong to two trypsin-like enzyme groups, a urokinase-type activator and a tissue-type activator, with different structures and properties. A further activator may be formed following the activation of clotting factor XII; this requires the presence of kallikrein and HMW kininogen.

18D.4.1   Inhibitors of plasmin

Two types of plasmin inhibitor occupying different binding sites may be distinguished: active-site-directed inhibitors, which inhibit the plasmin-cata-lysed hydrolysis of fibrin and of non-physiological substrates, and the analogues of L-lysine, the specific antifibrinolytic effect of which results from interactions with the lysine-binding sites of plasminogen and plasmin.

18D.4.1.1   *Active-site-directed inhibitors*

Plasmin hydrolyses multiple bonds in fibrin. In consequence, arginine chloro-methyl ketones that are able to distinguish plasmin from other trypsin-like proteinases have not been obtained (Table 18D.3). However, plasmin has a preference for lysine chloromethyl ketones (Kettner and Shaw 1978; Collen *et al.* 1980) and arginine chloromethyl ketones containing a P_2 Phe (Kettner and Shaw 1981a). This is also true of tripeptide aldehydes. Aldehydes containing

Lys-H at P_1 and Phe at P_2 are good inhibitors of the plasmin–fibrin reaction (Bajusz *et al.* 1982).

Benzamidines with a keto group (Stürzebecher *et al.* 1976c), derivatives of ω-amidinophenyl-α-aminobutyric acid (Table 18D.1), naphthamidines (Walsmann *et al.* 1978), bis-benzamidines (Walsmann *et al.* 1976; Geratz 1971, 1973), and amidino-substituted heterocyclic compounds (Geratz *et al.* 1981) are reversible inhibitors of plasmin (K_i in micromolar range) that also inhibit the lysis of plasma clots. Selective inhibitors of plasmin have not been found. The antifibrinolytic effect of 4-amidinophenylpyruvic acid (Markwardt *et al.* 1970) and pentamidine (Geratz 1971) has been demonstrated *in vivo* . Active-site-directed plasmin inhibitors of the benzamidine type inhibit generalized secondary fibrin(ogen)olysis more effectively than ω-aminocarboxylic acids (Markwardt 1981).

18D.4.1.2 *Lysine-binding-site directed inhibitors*

ε-aminocaproic acid (EACA) was the first representative of antifibrinolytic agents used in clinical practice (Abe and Sato 1958; Okamoto *et al.* 1959). Further search for more potent antifibrinolytic compounds than EACA led to the identification of cyclic ω-aminocarboxylic acids with higher inhibitory activity. These are *p*-aminomethylbenzoic acid (PAMBA) (Lohmann *et al.* 1963; Markwardt *et al.* 1964), the *trans*-isomer of 4-aminomethylcyclohexanecarboxylic acid (AMCHA), named tranexamic acid (AMCA) (Okamoto *et al.* 1964), and bicyclic and polycyclic aminocarboxylic acids (Baumgarten *et al.* 1969). Synthesizing variants of these structures allowed structure–activity relationships to be derived. Inhibitory activity is attributable to the distance between the essential amino and carboxyl groups (Markwardt 1978). The ω-aminocarboxylic acids are potent inhibitors of the plasmin–fibrin reaction and influence plasminogen activation. However, they inhibit the plasmin-catalysed hydrolysis of synthetic substrates weakly and in a non-competitive manner. It has, therefore been assumed that they interact with binding sites beyond the active site (Landmann 1973; Christensen 1978). These regions, the so-called lysine-binding sites, have been identified in plasminogen and plasmin (Wiman and Wallén 1977).

Shortly after the discovery of its antifibrinolytic properties, EACA was used in the therapy of hyperfibrinolytic states. In subsequent years, this drug has been replaced by PAMBA and AMCA. Their pharmacology and clinical uses have been described in great detail (Markwardt 1978; Ogston 1984).

18D.4.2 Inhibitors of plasminogen activators

Several peptide chloromethyl ketones are effective in the inactivation of urokinase. However, they are poorly reactive when compared to labels of other proteinases (Table 18D.3). Pro-Gly-ArgCH$_2$Cl, a reagent corresponding to the urokinase cleavage site in plasminogen, and Glu-Gly containing arginine chloromethyl ketones, are the most effective labels of this series (Kettner and Shaw 1979b). Urokinase is susceptible to inhibition by derivatives of benzamidine and naphthamidine (Stürzebecher and Markwardt 1978) as well as by amidino-substituted heterocyclic compounds (Geratz and Cheng 1975; Geratz et al. 1981). Several of these compounds are effective in the inhibition of urokinase-induced plasminogen activation. The ω-aminocarboxylic acids are weak inhibitors of urokinase (Landmann 1973).

Only chloromethyl ketones have been tested for their ability to inhibit tissue-type plasminogen activator. Glu-Gly-Arg-containing compounds are highly reactive; however, they are not selective for the activator from HeLa cells (Coleman et al. 1979). Urokinase and tissue-type plasminogen activator can be differentiated on the basis of their inhibitory spectrum towards chloromethyl ketones containing a D-amino acid at P_3 (Lijnen et al. 1984).

18D.5   Inhibitors of kallikreins

Plasma kallikrein and glandular kallikrein differ in their properties, specificity and physiological function. Plasma kallikrein liberates bradykinin from kininogen following specific cleavage at a Lys-Arg and an Arg-Ser bond. Similarly, glandular kallikrein splits the Arg-Ser bond. However, the second cleavage occurs at a Met-Lys bond of kininogen, whereby kallidin is released. The cleavage sites of other substrates of plasma kallikrein (factor XII, pro-renin) or glandular kallikrein are not known.

18D.5.1   Inhibitors of plasma kallikrein

The chloromethyl ketone, Pro-Phe-ArgCH$_2$Cl, corresponding to the C-terminal of bradykinin, is a selective inhibitor of plasma kallikrein (Table 18D.3). In comparison, reagents imitating P_4 and P_5 of kininogen are not more reactive. The compound with a P_3 D-Phe is the most potent inhibitor of plasma kallikrein; however, it is less selective than Pro-Phe-ArgCH$_2$Cl (Kettner and Shaw 1978, 1981a).

Esters and amides containing the D-Pro-Phe-Arg-sequence exert inhibitory action toward plasma kallikrein (Fareed et al. 1981). Benzamidine derivatives are reversible inhibitors of this enzyme. Among them, 4-amidinophenylpyruvic acid and derivatives of 4-amidinophenyl-α-aminobutyric acid are the most potent. They inhibit kinin liberation induced by plasma kallikrein in vitro and in vivo. Several 4-guanidinobenzoates and 4-amidinophenyl esters are able to acylate plasma kallikrein (Markwardt et al. 1971a, b,1974a; Stürzebecher et al. 1988b).

18D.5.2   Inhibitors of glandular kallikreins

As with plasma kallikrein, chloromethyl ketones with a P_1 Arg and P_2 Phe are the most effective inhibitors of glandular kallikrein (Kettner et al. 1980). However, they are more reactive with plasma kallikrein than with glandular kallikrein isolated from urine (Table 18D.3). Among the derivatives of benzamidine, compounds with two or more benzamidine moieties are potent inhibitors (Geratz *et al.* 1976; Ferroni *et al.* 1984). The most potent and selective glandular kallikrein inhibitor, a tris-benzamidine, has a K_i value of 2.4×10^8 M (Tidwell *et al.* 1976). Derivatives of 4-amidinophenylalanine distinguish glandular kallikrein from plasma kallikrein (Stürzebecher *et al.* 1988a). 4-amidinophenyl benzoates (Fig. 18D.3, **7**) acylate the enzyme at the active site serine hydroxyl. Acylkallikrein behaves like a pro-drug *in vivo* (Markwardt *et al.* 1984).

18D.6 Inhibitors of proteinases of the complement system

The complement system is a humoral effector involved in the immunological defence of the body. In a variety of physiological and pathological conditions, activation of the complement system occurs. In several disorders, the disease state is associated with activation of the complement system. It is, therefore, believed that inhibition of complement activation is likely to arrest the disease process. Trypsin-like serine proteinases are involved in complement activation; C1r̄, C1s̄, and C2ā participate in the classical pathway, D̄ and Bb̄ in the alternative pathway. Therefore, proteinase inhibitors have stimulated growing interest for inhibition of complement activation (Asghar 1984).

Baker and co-workers were the first to study the inhibition of complement activation by substituted benzamidines (Baker and Cory 1969; Baker and Erickson 1969). Compounds containing a benzamidine moiety linked to a phenylsulphonylfluoride moiety by a bridging group have comparatively high inhibitory activity. They inhibit total complement and most of them inhibit C1 (Baker and Cory 1971; Bing *et al.* 1974). QSAR have been formulated by Hansch and Yoshimoto (1974). Benzamidines containing hydrophobic substituents and bis-benzamidines are relatively potent inhibitors of total complement activity (Bing 1970; Hauptmann and Markwardt 1977; Otterness *et al.* 1978). Several bis-benzamidines inhibit C1r̄ and C1s̄ with K_i values of 1×10^{-4} M (Asghar *et al.* 1973). They also inhibit the alternative pathway (Asghar and Cormane 1976). Amidinophenyl and amidinonaphthyl esters inhibit C1r̄ and C1s̄ as well as complement-mediated haemolysis at micromolar concentrations (Yaegashi *et al.* 1984; Aoyama *et al.* 1985). The most potent inhibitor of this type is 2-(6-amidino)naphthyl 4'-guanidinobenzoate (FUT-175; Fig. 18D.2, **3**). It inhibits the proteinases of the classical and alternative pathway and has effects on various complement-mediated reactions *in vivo* (Fujii and Hitomi 1981; Fujii *et al.* 1983; Aoyama *et al.* 1984). However, FUT-175 and related compounds are nonselective inhibitors of complement (Hitomi *et al.* 1985). This is also true of derivatives of phenylguanidine (Okutome *et al.* 1984).

18D.7   Inhibitors of proteinases involved in reproduction

Although a great number of proteolytic enzymes have been demonstrated to be present in the reproductive tract of mammals, acrosin is the only trypsin-like enzyme that has been definitely characterized with regard to its properties and physiological function. Acrosin is found in the spermatozoa of vertebrates and enables the sperm to penetrate into the ovum by digestion of the zona pellucida. Consequently, the idea of using inhibitors of acrosin as contraceptive agents has been put forward.

Benzamidine and several derivatives are competitive inhibitors of acrosin. Benzyl-4-amidinophenyl ethers, keto compounds, and derivatives of 4-amidino-phenyl-α-aminovaleric acid (Table 18D.1) are the most potent and comparatively selective inhibitors (Parrish *et al.* 1978; Stürzebecher and Markwardt 1980; Stürzebecher 1981). Acrosin is also inhibited by bis-benzamidines (Bhattacharyya *et al.* 1976; Parrish *et al.* 1978) Peptide chloromethyl ketones are highly effective in inhibiting the enzyme (Table 18D.3). A comparison of the reactivity of acrosin and trypsin with the reagents suggests that binding sites of either proteinase are very similar (Kettner *et al.* 1978). Various studies have demonstrated the inhibition of fertilization *in vivo* by inhibitors of acrosin such as Tos-LysCH$_2$Cl (Zaneveld *et al.* 1970), 4-amidinobenzamidine (Fraser 1982), and other derivatives of benzamidine and 4-guanidinobenzoates (Müller-Esterl *et al.* 1983). Anti-fertility activity of activated amino acid esters is assumed to be caused by inhibition of acrosin or other acrosomal enzymes (Hall *et al.* 1979). An undesired side-effect of acrosin inhibition might be the inhibition of other trypsin-like enzymes found in the female reproductive tract. However, inhibition of further proteinases involved in fertilization is desirable from the viewpoint of contraception. Such proteinases are involved in the initiation of blastocyst implantation, which is inhibited by proteinase inhibitors (Denker 1978).

18D.8   Concluding remarks

Proteinase inhibitors are potential drugs for the control of physiologically important, proteinase-mediated processes. Since endogenous and naturally occurring inhibitors are high molecular weight polypeptides, their therapeutic use is limited because of their pharmacokinetics, especially with regard to distribution, gastrointestinal absorption, and immunogenic properties. Therefore, extensive searches have been made for synthetic, low molecular weight inhibitors. Selectivity for the target enzyme and low toxicity are important requirements for their therapeutic use. It is essential that their pharmacokinetic properties are adapted to the mode of action of the extracellular proteinases. Such enzymes are not present in active form in the blood but are activated by physiological and pathophysiological stimuli. Their substrates are permanently present. Therefore, such inhibitors are only able to interfere with the enzyme–substrate reaction occurring in blood if present at adequate concentrations for a prolonged period of time. In this context, the question arises whether irreversible or reversible inhibitors are more suited for *in vivo* use. Irreversible inhibitors block the target enzyme permanently by covalent binding. However, they react not only with the target enzyme but also with other constituents of blood and tissue, because they possess a reactive alkylating or acylating function. This undesired reactivity is not present in mechanism-based inactivators. Unfortunately, no potent inhibitors of this type are available for trypsin-like enzymes. Therefore, reversible, tight-binding inhibitors with high selectivity are preferred, although constant administration of the drug is necessary since dissociation of the enzyme–inhibitor complex and restoration of enzymatic activity may occur (Smith 1978).

Up to now, most of the synthetic inhibitors of trypsin-like enzymes have been designed with a view to obtaining compounds with pronounced inhibitory activity. Much work has yet to be done to obtain drugs that fulfil the above-mentioned requirements.

Acknowledgements

We thank Dr Jörg Hauptmann for his critical reading of the manuscript. Special thanks are given to Mrs Margot Gerstberger for indispensable help in the preparation of the manuscript.

References

Abe, T. and Sato, A. (1958). Inhibitory activity of ε-aminocaproic acid upon fibrinolysis. *Acta Haematol. Jap.*, **21**, 305–13.

Andrews, J. M., Roman, D. P., and Bing, D. H. (1978). Inhibition of four human serine proteinases by substituted benzamidines. *J. Med. Chem.*, **21**, 1202–7.

Aoyama, T., Ino, Y., Ozeki, M., Oda, M., Sato, T., Koshiyama, Y., Suzuki, S., and Fujita, M. (1984). Pharmacological studies of FUT-175, nafamstat mesilate. I. Inhibition of protease activity in *in vitro* and *in vivo* experiments. *Jap. J. Pharmacol.*, **35**, 203–27.

Aoyama, T., Okutome, T., Nakayama. T., Yaegashi, T., Matsui, R., Nunomura, S., Kurumi, M., Sakurai, Y., and Fujii, S. (1985). Synthesis and structure–activity study of protease inhibitors. IV. Amidinonaphthols and related acyl derivatives. *Chem. Pharm. Bull.*, **33**, 1458–71.

Asghar, S. S. (1984). Pharmacological manipulation of complement system. *Pharmacol. Rev.*, **36**, 223–44.

Asghar, S. S. and Cormane, R. H. (1976). Interaction of the B-determinant of the third component of complement with amidino compounds. *Immunochemistry*, **13**, 975–8.

Asghar, S. S., Pondman, K. W., and Cormane, R. H. (1973). Inhibition of C1r̄, C1s̄ and generation of C1s̄ by amidino compounds. *Biochim. Biophys. Acta*, **317**, 539–48.

Bagdy, D., Barabás, D., Széll, E., and Bajusz, S. (1982). Über die biochemische Pharmakologie einiger Tripeptidaldehyde. *Folia Haematol. (Leipzig)*, **109**, 22–32.

Bajusz, S. (1984). Interaction of trypsin-like enzymes with small inhibitors. *Symp. Biol. Hung.*, **25**, 278–97.

Bajusz, S., Barabás, E., Tolnay, P., Széll, E., and Bagdy, D. (1978). Inhibition of thrombin and trypsin by tripeptide aldehydes. *Int. J. Peptide Protein Res.*, **12**, 217–21.

Bajusz, S., Széll, E., Barabás, E., and Bagdy, D. (1982). Design and synthesis of peptide inhibitors of blood coagulation. *Folia Haematol. (Leipzig)*, **109**, 16–21.

Baker, B. R. and Cory, M. (1969). Irreversible enzyme inhibitors. CLXV. Proteolytic enzymes. XV. Inhibition of guinea pig complement by derivatives of *m*-phenoxyprop-oxybenzamidine. *J. Med. Chem.*, **12**, 1053–6.

Baker, B. R. and Cory, M. (1971). Irreversible enzyme inhibitors. 186. Irreversible inhibitors of the C'1a component of complement derived from *m*-(phenoxyproxy)benzamidine by bridging to a terminal sulfonyl fluoride. *J. Med. Chem.*, **14**, 805–8.

Baker, B. R. and Erickson, E. H. (1969). Irreversible enzyme inhibitors. CLII. Proteolytic enzymes. X. Inhibition of guinea pig complement by substituted benzamidines. *J. Med. Chem.*, **12**, 408–14.

Baumgarten, W., Priester, L. I., Stiller, D. W., Duncan, A. E. W., Ciminera, J. L., and Loeffler, L. J. (1969). 4-Aminomethylbicyclo [2.2.2]-octane-1-carboxylic acid, a new potent antifibrinolytic agent. Its evaluation by *in vitro* assay procedures. *Thromb. Diath. Haemorrh.*, **22**, 263–72.

Bhattacharyya, A. K., Zaneveld, L. J. D., Dragoje, B. M., Schumacher, G. F. B., and Travis, J. (1976). Inhibition of human sperm acrosin by synthetic agents. *J. Reprod. Fert.*, **47**, 97–100.

Bing, D. H. (1970). Inhibition of guinea pig complement by aromatic amidine and guanidine compounds. *J. Immunol.*, **105**, 1289–90.

Bing, D. H., Cory, M., and Doll, M. (1974). The inactivation of human C1 by benzami-dine and pyridinium sulfonylfluorides. *J. Immunol.*, **113**, 584–90.

Blombäck, B., Blombäck, M., Olsson, P., Svendsen, L., and Åberg, G. (1969). Synthetic peptides with anticoagulant and vasodilating activity. *Scand. J. Clin. Lab. Invest.*, **24**, (Suppl. 107), 59–64.

Blow, D. M., Birktoft. J. J., and Hartley, B. S. (1969). Role of a buried acid group in the mechanism of action of chymotrypsin. *Nature. Lond.*, **221**, 337–40.

Bode, W. and Schwager, P. (1975). The refined crystal structure of bovine β-trypsin at 1.8 Å resolution. II. Crystallographic refinement, calcium binding site, benzamidine binding site and active site at pH 7.0. *J. Mol. Biol.*, **98**, 693–717.

Byrne, R., Link, R. P., and Castellino, F. J. (1980). A kinetic evaluation of activated bovine blood coagulation factor IX toward synthetic substrates. *J. Biol. Chem.*, **255**, 5336–41.

Chase, T. and Shaw, E. (1969). Comparison of the esterase activities of trypsin, plasmin, and thrombin on guanidinobenzoate esters. Titration of the enzymes. *Biochemistry*, **8**, 2212–24.

Chase, T. and Shaw, E. (1970). Titration of trypsin, plasmin, and thrombin with *p*-nitrophenyl *p'*-guanidinobenzoate HCl. *Meth. Enzym.*, **19**, 20–7.

Christensen, U. (1978). Allosteric effects of some antifibrinolytic amino acids on the catalytic activity of human plasmin. *Biochim. Biophys. Acta*, **526**, 194–201.

Christensen, U. (1984). The AH-site of plasminogen and two C-terminal fragments. A weak lysine-binding site preferring ligands not carrying a free carboxylic function. *Biochem. J.*, **223**, 413–21.

Claeson, G., Gustavsson, S., and Mattsson, C. (1983). New derivatives of *p*-guanidino-phenylalanine as potent reversible inhibitors of thrombin. *Thromb. Haemostas.*, **50**, 53.

Coleman, P. L., Latham, H. G., and Shaw, E. N. (1976). Some sensitive methods for the assay of trypsin-like enzymes. *Meth. Enzym.*, **45**, 12–26.

Coleman. P., Kettner, C., and Shaw, E. (1979). Inactivation of the plasminogen activator from HeLa cells by peptides of arginine chloromethyl ketone. *Biochim. Biophys. Acta*, **569**, 41–51.

Collen, D., Lijnen, H. R., de Cock, F., Durieux, J. P., and Loffet, A. (1980). Kinetic properties of tripeptide lysyl chloromethylketones and lysyl *p*-nitroanilide derivatives towards trypsin-like serine proteinases. *Biochim. Biophys. Acta*, **615**, 158–66.

Collen, D., Matsuo, O., Stassen, J. M., Kettner, C., and Shaw, E. (1982). *In vivo* studies of a synthetic inhibitor of thrombin. *J. Lab. Clin. Med.*, **99**, 76–83.

Cory, M., Andrews, J. M., and Bing, D. H. (1977). Design of exo affinity labeling reagents. *Meth. Enzym.*, **44**, 115–30.

Denker, H.-W. (1978). The role of trophoblastic factors in implantation. In *Novel aspects of reproductive physiology* (ed. C. H. Spilman, J. W. Wilks), pp. 181–212. Spectrum, New York.

Dorman, L. C., Cheng, R. C., and Marshall, F. N. (1972). Mechanism of thrombin action on fibrinogen; activity of thrombin toward human α(A)-fibrinogen peptides. In *Chemistry and biology of peptides*, pp. 455–9. Ann Arbor Science Publishers, Ann Arbor, MI.

Fareed, J., Messmore, H. L., Kindel, G., and Balis, J. U. (1981). Inhibition of serine proteinases by low molecular weight peptides and their derivatives. *Ann. N.Y. Acad. Sci.*, **370**, 765–84.

Ferroni, R., Menegatti, E., Guarneri, M., Taddeo, U., Bolognesi, M., Ascenzi, P., and Amiconi, G. (1984). Aromatic tetra-amidines: synthesis of halo-derivatives and their antiproteolytic activity. *Farmaco*, **39**, 901–9.

Fraser, L. R. (1982). *p*-aminobenzamidine, an acrosin inhibitor, inhibits mouse sperm penetration of the zona pellucida but not the acrosome reaction. *J. Reprod. Fertil.*, **65**, 185–94.

Fujii, S. and Hitomi, Y. (1981). New synthetic inhibitors of C1r̄, C1 esterase, thrombin, plasmin, kallikrein and trypsin. *Biochim. Biophys. Acta*, **661**, 342–5.

Fujii, S., Hitomi, Y., Kakai, Y., Ikari, N., Hirado, M., and Niinobe, M. (1983). Synthetic inhibitors of proteases in blood. In *Proteinase inhibitors. Medical and biological aspects* (ed. N. Katunuma, H. Umezawa and H. Holzer), pp. 37–44. Japan Scientific Press, Tokyo/Springer, Berlin.

Ganu, V. S. and Shaw, E. (1981). Inactivation of trypsin-like proteases by depsipeptides of p-guanidinobenzoic acid. *J. Med. Chem.*, **24**, 698–700.

Garlich, J. D. and Nesheim, M. C. (1966). Relationship of fractions of soybeans and a crystalline soybean trypsin inhibitor to the effects of feeding unheated soybean meal to chicks. *J. Nutr.*, **88**, 100–10.

Geratz, J. D. (1966). *p*-aminobenzamidine as inhibitor of trypsinogen activation. *Experientia*, **22**, 73–4.

Geratz, J. D. (1969). Secretory stimulation of the rat pancreas by *p*-aminobenzamidine. *Am. J. Physiol.*, **216**, 812–7.

Geratz, J. D. (1971). Inhibition of coagulation and fibrinolysis by aromatic amidino compounds. An *in vitro* and *in vivo* study. *Thromb. Diath. Haemorrh.*, **25**, 391–404.

Geratz, J. D. (1973). Structure–activity relationships for the inhibition of plasmin and plasminogen activation by aromatic diamidines and a study of the effect of plasma proteins on the inhibition process. *Thromb. Diath. Haemorrh.*, **29**, 154–67.

Geratz, J. D. and Cheng, M. C. -F. (1975). The inhibition of urokinase by aromatic diamidines. *Thromb. Diath. Haemorrh.*, **33**, 230–43.

Geratz, J. D. and Tidwell, R. R. (1977). The development of competitive reversible thrombin inhibitors. In *Chemistry and biology of thrombin* (ed. R. L. Lundblad, J. W. Fenton II, and K. G. Mann), pp. 179–96. Ann Arbor Science Publishers, Ann Arbor, MI.

Geratz, J. D. and Tidwell, R. R. (1978). Current concepts on action of synthetic thrombin inhibitors. *Haemostasis*, **7**, 170–6.

Geratz, J. D., Whitmore, A. C., Cheng, M. C.-F., and Piantadosi, C. (1973). Diamidino-α,ω-diphenoxyälkanes. Structure–activity relationships for the inhibition of thrombin, pancreatic kallikrein, and trypsin. *J. Med. Chem.*, **16**, 970–5.

Geratz, J. D., Cheng, M. C.-F., and Tidwell, R. R. (1976). Novel bis(benzamidino) compounds with an aromatic central link. Inhibitors of thrombin, pancreatic kallikrein, trypsin, and complement. *J. Med. Chem.*, **19**, 634–9.

Geratz, J. D., Stevens, F. M., Polakoski, K. L., Parrish, R. F., and Tidwell, R. R. (1979). Amidino-substituted aromatic heterocycles as probes of the specificity pocket of trypsin-like proteases. *Arch. Biochem. Biophys.*, **197**, 551–9.

Geratz, J. D., Shaver, S. R., and Tidwell, R. R. (1981). Inhibitory effect of amidino-substituted heterocyclic compounds on the amidase activity of plasmin and of high and low molecular weight urokinase and on urokinase-induced plasminogen activation. *Thromb. Res.*, **24**, 73–83.

Hall, I. H., Drew, J. H., Sajadi, Z., and Loeffler, L. J. (1979). Antifertility and antiproteolytic activity of activated N-carbobenzoxy amino acid esters. *J. Pharm. Sci.*, **68**, 696–8.

Hansch, C. and Yoshimoto, M. (1974). Structure–activity relationships in immunochemistry. 2. Inhibition of complement by benzamidines. *J. Med. Chem.*, **17**, 1160–7.

Hauptmann, J. (1982). Pharmacology of benzamidine-type thrombin inhibitors. *Folia Haematol. (Leipzig)*, **109**, 89–97.

Hauptmann, J. and Markwardt, F. (1977). Inhibition of the haemolytic complement activity by derivatives of benzamidine. *Biochem. Pharmacol.*, **26**, 325–9.

Hauptmann, J. and Markwardt, F. (1980). Studies on the anticoagulant and antithrombotic action of an irreversible thrombin inhibitor. *Thromb. Res.*, **20**, 347–51.

Hauptmann, J., Hoffmann, J., and Markwardt, F. (1976). Zur Wirkung von aromatischen Bisamidinen auf Blutgerinnungs- und Fibrinolysevorgänge. *Acta Biol. Med. Germ.*, **35**, 635–44.

Hauptmann, J., Markwardt, F., and Walsmann, P. (1978). Synthetic inhibitors of serine proteinases. XVI. Influence of 3- and 4-amidinobenzyl derivatives on the formation and action of thrombin. *Thromb. Res.*, **12**, 735–44.

Hauptmann, J., Kaiser, B., Markwardt, F., and Nowak, G. (1980). Anticoagulant and antithrombotic action of novel specific inhibitors of thrombin. *Thromb. Haemostas.*, **43**, 118–23.

Hauptmann, J., Kaiser, B., and Markwardt, F. (1985). Anticoagulant action of synthetic tight binding inhibitors of thrombin *in vitro* and *in vivo*. *Thromb. Res.*, **39**, 771–5.

Hijikata, A., Okamoto, S., Kikumoto, R., and Tamao, Y. (1979). Kinetic studies on the selectivity of a synthetic thrombin-inhibitor using synthetic peptide substrates. *Thromb. Haemostas.*, **42**, 1039–45.

Hitomi, Y., Ikari, N., and Fujii, S. (1985). Inhibitory effect of a new synthetic protease inhibitor (FUT-175) on the coagulation system. *Haemostasis*, **15**, 164–8.

Ikoma, H., Ohtsu, K., Tamao, Y., Kikumoto, R., Mori, E., Funahara, Y., and Okamoto, S. (1980). Effect of a potent thrombin inhibitor, No. 407, on novel experimental thrombosis generated by acetic acid. *Kobe J. Med. Sci.*, **26**, 33–45.

Inagami, T. and York, S. S. (1968). Effect of alkylguanidines and alkylamines on trypsin catalysis. *Biochemistry (New York)*, **7**, 4045–52.

Jesty, J. and Nemerson, Y. (1974). Purification of factor VII from bovine plasma. Reaction with tissue factor and activation of factor X. *J. Biol. Chem.*, **249**, 509–16.

Kaiser, B., Hauptmann, J., Weiss, A., and Markwardt, F. (1985). Pharmacological characterization of a new highly effective synthetic thrombin inhibitor. *Biomed. Biochim. Acta*, **44**, 1201–10.

Kettner, C. and Shaw, E. (1977). The selective inactivation of thrombin by peptides of arginine chloromethyl ketone. In *Chemistry and biology of thrombin* (ed. R. L. Lundblad, J. W. Fenton II, and K. G. Mann), pp. 129–43. Ann Arbor Science Publishers, Ann Arbor, MI.

Kettner, C. and Shaw, E. (1978). Synthesis of peptides of arginine chloromethyl ketone. Selective inactivation of human plasma kallikrein. *Biochemistry*, **17**, 4778–84.

Kettner, C. and Shaw, E. (1979a). D-Phe-Pro-ArgCH$_2$Cl—a selective affinity label for thrombin. *Thromb. Res.*, **14**, 969–73.

Kettner, C. and Shaw, E. (1979b). The susceptibility of urokinase to affinity labeling by peptides of arginine chloromethyl ketone. *Biochim. Biophys. Acta*, **569**, 31–40.

Kettner, C. and Shaw, E. (1981a). Inactivation of trypsin-like enzymes with peptides of arginine chloromethyl ketone. *Meth. Enzym.*, **80**, 826–42.

Kettner, C. and Shaw, E. (1981b). The selective affinity labeling of factor X$_a$ by peptides of arginine chloromethyl ketone. *Thromb. Res.*, **22**, 645–52.

Kettner, C., Springhorn, S., Shaw, E., Müller, W., and Fritz, H. (1978). Inactivation of boar acrosin by peptidyl-arginyl-chloromethanes. Comparison of the reactivity of acrosin, trypsin and thrombin. *Hoppe-Seyler's Z. Physiol. Chem.*, **359**, 1183–91.

Kettner, C., Mirabelli, C., Pierce, J. V., and Shaw, E. (1980). Active site mapping of human and rat urinary kallikreins by peptidyl chloromethyl ketones. *Arch. Biochem. Biophys.*, **202**, 420–30.

Kikumoto, R., Tamao, Y., Ohkubo, K., Tezuka, T., Tonomura, S., Okamoto, S., and Hijikata, A. (1980a). Thrombin inhibitors. 3. Carboxyl-containing amide derivatives of Nα-substituted L-arginine. *J. Med. Chem.*, **23**, 1293–9.

Kikumoto, R., Tamao, Y., Ohkubo, K., Tezuka, T., Tonomura, S., Okamoto, S., Funahara, Y., and Hijikata, A. (1980b). Thrombin inhibitors. 2. Amide derivatives of Nα-substituted L-arginine. *J. Med. Chem.*, **23**, 830–6.

Kikumoto, R., Tamao, Y., Tezuka, T., Tonomura, S., Hara, H., Ninomiya, K., Hijikata, A., and Okamoto, S. (1984). Selective inhibition of thrombin by (2R,4R)-4-methyl-1-{N^2[(3-methyl-1,2,3,4-tetrahydro-8-quinolinyl)   sulfonyl]-L-arginyl}-2-piperidine-carboxylic acid. *Biochemistry*, **23**, 85–90.

Kosaki, G., Kambayashi, J., and Imaoka, S. (1983). Application of a synthetic serine protease inhibitor in the treatment of DIC. *Bibl. Haematol.*, **43**, 317–32.

Kraut, J. (1977). Serine proteases: structure and mechanism of catalysis. *Ann. Rev. Biochem.*, **46**, 331–58.

Kumada, T. and Abiko, Y. (1981). Comparative study on heparin and a synthetic thrombin inhibitor No. 805 (MD-805) in experimental antithrombin III-deficient animals. *Thromb. Res.*, **24**, 285–98.

Kuramochi, H., Nakata, H., and Ishii, S. (1979). Mechanism of association of a specific aldehyde inhibitor, leupeptin, with bovine trypsin. *J. Biochem. (Tokyo)*, **86**, 1403–10.

Labes, D. and Hagen, V. (1979). Hansch-Analyse der Hemmwirkung von 3- und 4-substituierten Benzamidinen gegenüber Thrombin, Plasmin und Trypsin. *Pharmazie*, **34**, 649–53.

Landmann, H. (1973). Studies on the mechanism of action of synthetic antifibrinolytics. A comparison with the action of derivatives of benzamidine on the fibrinolytic process. *Thromb. Diath. Haemorrh.*, **29**, 253–75.

Laura, R., Robison, D. J., and Bing, D. H. (1980). (p-amidinophenyl)-methanesulfonyl fluoride, an irreversible inhibitor of serine proteases. *Biochemistry (New York)*, **19**, 4859–64.

Liem, R. K. H., Andreatta, R. H., and Scheraga, H. A. (1971). Mechanism of action of thrombin on fibrinogen. II. Kinetics of hydrolysis of fibrinogen-like peptides by thrombin and trypsin. *Arch. Biochem. Biophys.*, **147**, 201–13.

Lijnen, H. R., Uytterhoeven, M., and Collen, D. (1984). Inhibition of trypsin-like serine proteinases by tripeptide arginyl and lysyl chloromethylketones. *Thromb. Res.*, **34**, 431–7.

Lohmann, K., Markwardt, F., and Landmann, H. (1963). Über neue Hemmstoffe der Fibrinolyse. *Naturwissenschaften*, **50**, 502.

Lollar, P. and Fass, D. N. (1984). Inhibition of activated porcine factor IX by dansyl-glutamyl-glycyl-arginyl-chloromethylketone. *Arch. Biochem. Biophys.*, **233**, 438–46.

Lorand, L. and Rule, N. G. (1961). Inhibition of proteolytic enzymes by decarboxylated amino acid derivatives. Effect of toluenesulphonyl (tosyl-)agmatine (4-toluenesulphon-aminobutylguanidin) on thrombin and trypsin. *Nature*, **190**, 722.

Mares-Guia, M. and Shaw, E. (1965). Studies on the active center of trypsin. *J. Biol. Chem.*, **240**, 1579–85.

Markwardt, F. (1978). Synthetic inhibitors of fibrinolysis. In *Handbook of experimental pharmacology*, Vol. 46, *Fibrinolytics and antifibrinolytics* (ed. F. Markwardt), pp. 512–77. Springer, Berlin.

Markwardt, F. (1980). Pharmacological control of blood coagulation by synthetic, low-molecular-weight inhibitors of clotting enzymes. A new concept of anticoagulants. *Trends Pharmacol. Sci.*, **1**, 153–7.

Markwardt, F. (1981). Synthetic inhibitors of fibrinolysis. In *Progress in fibrinolysis* (ed. J. F. Davidson, I. M. Nilsson, and B. Åstedt), Vol. 5, pp. 178–83. Churchill Livingstone, Edinburgh.

Markwardt, F. and Klöcking, H.-P. (1972). The antithrombotic effect of synthetic thrombin inhibitors. *Thromb. Res.*, **1**, 243–52.

Markwardt, F., Haustein, K.-O., and Klöcking, H.-P. (1964). Die pharmakologische Charakterisierung des neuen Antifibrinolytikums p-Aminomethylbenzoesäure (PAMBA). *Arch. Int. Pharmacodynam.*, **152**, 223–33.

Markwardt, F., Klöcking, H.-P., and Nowak, G. (1970). Antithrombin- und Antiplasmin-wirkung von 4-Amidinophenylbrenztraubensäure (APPA) *in vivo*. *Thromb. Diath. Haemorrh.*, **24**, 240–7.

Markwardt, F., Drawert, J., and Walsmann, P. (1971a). Einfluß von Benzamidinderivaten auf die Aktivität von Serum- und Pankreaskallikrein. *Acta Biol. Med. Germ.*, **26**, 123–8.

Markwardt, F., Klöcking, H.-P., and Nowak, G. (1971b). Hemmung der Kininbildung im Blut durch p-Amidinophenylbrenztraubensäure. *Experientia*, **27**, 812–3.

Markwardt, F., Walsmann, P., Richter, M., Klöcking, H.-P., Drawert, J., and Landmann, H. (1971c). Aminoalkylbenzolsulfofluoride als Fermentinhibitoren. *Pharmazie*, **26**, 401–4.

Markwardt, F., Wagner, G., Walsmann, P., Horn, H., and Stürzebecher, J. (1972). Inhibition of trypsin and thrombin by amidinophenyl esters of aromatic carboxylic acids. *Acta Biol. Med. Germ.*, **28**, K19–25.

Markwardt, F., Walsmann, P., Stürzebecher, J., Landmann, H., and Wagner, G. (1973). Synthetische Inhibitoren der Serinproteinasen. 1. Mitteilung: Über die Hemmung von Trypsin, Plasmin und Thrombin durch Ester der Amidino- und Guanidinobenzoe-säure. *Pharmazie*, **28**, 326–30.

Markwardt, F., Drawert, J., and Walsmann, P. (1974a). Synthetic low molecular weight inhibitors of serum kallikrein. *Biochem. Pharmacol.*, **23**, 2247–56.

Markwardt, F., Walsmann, P., and Hofmann, J. (1974b). Über den Einfluß synthetischer Proteinaseninhibitoren auf die Wirkung und Aktivierung proteolytischer Enzyme des Pankreas. *Acta Biol. Med. Germ.*, **32**, 433–9.

Markwardt, F., Richter, P., Stürzebecher, J., Wagner, G., and Walsmann, P. (1974c). Synthetische Inhibitoren der Serinproteinasen. 6. Mitteilung: Über die Hemmung von Trypsin, Plasmin und Thrombin durch Phenylbrenztraubensäuren mit verschiedenen basischen Gruppen. *Acta Biol. Med. Germ.*, **33**, K1–7.

Markwardt, F., Nowak, G., and Hoffmann, J. (1977). The influence of drugs on disseminated intravascular coagulation (DIC). II. Effects of naturally occurring and synthetic thrombin inhibitors. *Thromb. Res.*, **11**, 275–83.

Markwardt, F., Hauptmann, J., Richter, M., and Richter, P. (1979). Tierexperimentelle Untersuchungen zur Pharmakokinetik von 4-Amidinophenylbrenztraubensäure (APPA). *Pharmazie*, **34**, 178–81.

Markwardt, F., Wagner, G., Stürzebecher, J., and Walsmann, P. (1980). $N\alpha$-arylsulfonyl-ω-(4-amidino-phenyl)-α-aminoalkylcarboxylic acid amides—novel selective inhibitors of thrombin. *Thromb. Res.*, **17**, 425–31.

Markwardt, F., Nowak, G., and Hoffmann, J. (1983). Comparative studies on thrombin inhibitors in experimental microthrombosis. *Thromb. Haemostas.*, **49**, 235–7.

Markwardt, F., Stürzebecher, J., and Müller, H. (1984). Acyl-kallikrein; a delivery system for the kinin-liberating enzyme. *Experientia*, **40**, 373–4.

Marsh, H. C., Meinwald, Y. C., Lee, S., and Scheraga, H. A. (1982). Mechanism of action of thrombin on fibrinogen. Direct evidence for the involvement of phenylalanine at position P_9. *Biochemistry (New York)*, **24**, 6167–71.

Mattsson, Ch., Ericsson, E., and Nilsson, S. (1982). Anti-coagulant and anti-thrombotic effects of some protease inhibitors. *Folia Haematol. (Leipzig)*, **109**, 43–51.

Morris, J. P. and Castellino, F. J. (1983). The role of lysine binding sites of human plasmin in the hydrolysis of human fibrinogen. *Biochim. Biophys. Acta*, **744**, 99–104.

Müller-Esterl, W., Wendt, V., Leidl, W., Dann, O., Shaw, E., Wagner, G., and Fritz, H. (1983). Intra-acrosomal inhibition of boar acrosin by synthetic proteinase inhibitors. *J. Reprod. Fertil.*, **67**, 13–8.

Muramatu, M. and Fujii, S. (1972). Inhibitory effects of ω-guanidino acid esters on trypsin, plasmin, plasma kallikrein and thrombin. *Biochim. Biophys. Acta*, **268**, 221–4.

Oedekoven, B., Bey, R., Mottaghy, K., and Schmid-Schönbein, H. (1984). Gabexate mesilate (FOY[(R)]) as an anticoagulant in extracorporeal circulation in dogs and sheep. *Thromb. Haemostas.*, **52**, 329–32.

Ogston, D. (1984). *Antifibrinolytic drugs: chemistry, pharmacology and clinical usage.* Wiley, Chichester.

Ohno, H., Kambayashi, J., Chang, S. W., and Kosaki, G. (1981). FOY: [Ethyl *p*-(6-guanidinohexanoyloxy)benzoate]methanesulfonate as a serine proteinase inhibitor. II. *In vivo* effect on coagulo-fibrinolytic system in comparison with heparin or aprotinin. *Thromb. Res.*, **24**, 445–52.

Ohno, H., Kosaki, G., Kambayashi, J., Imaoka, S., and Hirata, F. (1980). FOY: [Ethyl *p*-(6-guanidinohexanoyloxy)benzoate]methanesulfonate as a serine proteinase inhibitor. I. Inhibition of thrombin and factor Xa *in vitro*. *Thromb. Res.*, **19**, 579–88.

Ohtsu, K., Tamao, Y., Kikumoto, R., Ikezawa, K., Hijikata, A., and Okamoto, S. (1980). Effects of a potent thrombin inhibitor, No. 407, on DIC models *Kobe J. Med. Sci.*, **26**, 61–71.

Okamoto, S., Nakajima, T., Okamoto, U., Watanabe, H., Iguchi, Y., Igawa, T., Chien, C.-C., and Hayashi, T. (1959). A suppressing effect of ε-amino-n-caproic acid on the bleeding of dogs, produced with the activation of plasmin in circulatory blood. *Keio J. Med.*, **8**, 247–66.

Okamoto, S., Sato, S., Takada, Y., and Okamoto, U. (1964). An active isomer (*trans* form) of AMCHA and its antifibrinolytic (antiplasminic) action *in vitro* and *in vivo*. *Keio J. Med.*, **13**, 177–85.

Okamoto, S., Kinjo, K., Hijikata, A., Kikumoto, R., Tamao, Y., Ohkubo, K., and Tonomura, S. (1980). Thrombin inhibitors. 1. Ester derivatives of $N\alpha$-(arylsulfonyl)-L-arginine. *J. Med. Chem.*, **23**, 827–30.

Okamoto, S., Hijikata, A., Kikumoto, R., Tonomura, S., Hara, H., Ninomiya, K., Maruyama, A., Sugano, M., and Tamao, Y. (1981). Potent inhibition of thrombin by the newly synthesized arginine derivative No. 805: the importance of the stereo-structure of its hydrophobic carboxamide portion. *Biochem. Biophys. Res. Commun.*, **101**, 440–6.

Okutome, T. Kawamura, H., Taira, S., Nakayama, T., Nunomura, S., Kurumi, M., Sakurai, Y., Aoyama, T., and Fujii, S. (1984). Synthesis and structure–activity study of protease inhibitors. I. (Guanidinophenyl)propionate and guanidinocinnamate de-rivatives. *Chem. Pharm. Bull.*, **32**, 1854–65.

Ooms, A. J. J. and van Dijk, C. (1966). The reaction of organophosphorus compounds with hydrolytic enzymes. III. The inhibition of chymotrypsin and trypsin. *Biochem. Pharmacol.*, **15**, 1361–77.

Otterness, I. G., Torchia, A. J., and Doshan, H. D. (1978). Complement inhibition by amidines and guanidines—*in vivo* and *in vitro* results. *Biochem. Pharmacol*, **27**, 1873–8.

Parrish, R. F., Straus, J. W., Paulson, J. D., Polakoski, K. L., Tidwell, R. R., Geratz, J. D., and Stevens, F. M. (1978). Structure–activity relationships for the inhibition of acrosin by benzamidine derivatives. *J. Med. Chem.*, **21**, 1132–6.

Rackis, J. J. (1965). Physiological properties of soybean trypsin inhibitors and their relationship to pancreatic hypertrophy and growth inhibition of rats. *Fed. Proc. Fed. Am. Soc. Exp. Biol.*, **24**, 1488–93.

Ratnoff, O. D. (1981). Studies on the inhibition of ellagic acid-activated Hageman factor (factor XII) and Hageman factor fragments. *Blood*, **57**, 55–8.

Robison, D. J., Furie, B., Furie, B. C., and Bing, D. H. (1980). Active site of bovine factor Xa. Characterisation using substituted benzamidines as competitive inhibitors and affinity-labeling reagents. *J. Biol. Chem.*, **255**, 2014–21.

Saitoh, Y. (1982). Review of clinical results with gabexate mesilate (FOY) in Japan. In *Proteinasen-Inhibition* (ed. K.-H.Grözinger, A. Schrey, and R. W. Wabnitz), pp. 108–22. Wolf, Munich.

Schaeffer, R. C. Jr., Chilton, S.-M., Hadden, T. J., and Carlson, R. W. (1984). Pulmonary fibrin microembolism with Echis carinatus venom in dogs: effect of a synthetic thrombin inhibitor. *J. Appl. Physiol.*, **57**, 1824–8.

Shaw, E., Mares-Guia, M., and Cohen, W. (1965). Evidence for an active-center histidine in trypsin through use of a specific reagent, 1-chloro-3-tosylamido-7-amino-2-heptanone, the chloromethyl ketone derived from $N\alpha$-tosyl-L-lysine. *Biochemistry*, **4**, 2219–24.

Silverberg, M. and Kaplan, A. P. (1982). Enzymatic activities of activated and zymogen forms of human Hageman factor (factor XII). *Blood*, **60**, 64–70.

Silverberg, S. A., Nemerson, Y., and Zur, M. (1977). Kinetics of the activation of bovine coagulation factor X by components of the extrinsic pathway. *J. Biol. Chem.*, **252**, 8481–8.

Smith, H. J. (1978). Perspectives in the design of small molecule enzyme inhibitors as useful drugs. *J. Theor. Biol.*, **73**, 531–8.

Stone, S. R. and Hofsteenge, J. (1985). Specificity of activated human protein C. *Biochem. J.*, **230**, 497–502.

Stürzebecher, J. (1981). Inhibition of acrosin by benzamidines. *Acta Biol. Med. Germ.*, **40**, 1519–22.

Stürzebecher, J. (1984). Inhibitors of thrombin. In *The Thrombin* (ed. R. Machovich), Vol. 1, pp. 131–60. CRC Press, Boca Raton.

Stürzebecher, J. and Markwardt, F. (1978). Synthetische Inhibitoren der Serinproteinasen. 17. Mitteilung: Einfluß von Benzamidinderivaten auf die Aktivität der Urokinase und den Ablauf der Fibrinolyse. *Pharmazie*, **33**, 600–2.

Stürzebecher, J. and Markwardt, F. (1980). Synthetic inhibitors of serine proteinases. 22. Inhibition of acrosin by benzamidine derivatives. *Hoppe-Seyler's Z. Physiol. Chem.*, **361**, 25–9.

Stürzebecher, J. and Walsmann, P. (1978). Quantitative Struktur-Wirkungs-Beziehungen bei der Hemmung von Thrombin und Gerinnungsfaktor Xa durch Benzamidinderivate. *Abh. Akad. Wiss. Math. Naturwiss. Techn.*, **2N**, 111–5.

Stürzebecher, J., Markwardt, F., and Walsmann, P. (1976a). Synthetic inhibitors of serine proteinases. XIV. Inhibition of factor Xa by derivatives of benzamidine. *Thromb. Res.*, **9**, 637–46.

Stürzebecher, J., Markwardt, F., Wagner, G., and Walsmann, P. (1976b). Synthetische Hemmstoffe der Serinproteinasen. 13. Quantitative Struktur-Wirkungs-Beziehungen bei der Hemmung von Trypsin, Plasmin und Thrombin durch 4-Amidinophenylverbindungen mit Ketonstruktur. *Acta Biol. Med. Germ.*, **35**, 1665–76.

Stürzebecher, J., Markwardt, F., Richter, P., Voigt, B., Wagner, G., and Walsmann, P. (1976c). Synthetische Inhibitoren der Serinproteinasen. 8. Mitteilung: über die Hemmung von Trypsin, Plasmin und Thrombin durch Amidinophenylverbindungen mit Ketonstruktur. *Pharmazie*, **31**, 458–61.

Stürzebecher, J., Markwardt, F., and Walsmann, P. (1980). Synthetic inhibitors of serine proteinases. XXIII. Inhibition of factor Xa by diamidines. *Thromb. Res.*, **17**, 545–8.

Stürzebecher, J., Horn, H., Markwardt, F., Wagner, G., and Walsmann, P. (1981a). Synthetische Inhibitoren der Serinproteinasen. 25. Mitteilung: Hemmung von Trypsin, Plasmin und Thrombin durch Amide Nα-arylsulfonylierter Amidinophenylalanine und 3-Amidinophenyl-3-amino-propionsäuren. *Pharmazie*, **36**, 639–41.

Stürzebecher, J., Markwardt, F., Voigt, B., Wagner, G., and Walsmann, P. (1981b). Synthetische Inhibitoren der Serinproteinasen. 24. Mitteilung: Hemmung von Trypsin, Plasmin und Thrombin durch cyclische Amide Nα-arylsulfonylierter Amidinophenylglycine. *Pharmazie*, **36**, 501–2.

Stürzebecher, J., Markwardt, F., Vieweg, H., Wagner, G., and Walsmann, P. (1982). Synthetische Inhibitoren der Serinproteinasen. 26. Mitteilung: Hemmung von Trypsin, Plasmin und Thrombin durch Amide Nα-arylsulfonylierter 2-Amino-4-(4-amidinophenyl)-buttersäure und 2-Amino-5-amidinophenylvaleriansäuren. *Pharmazie*, **37**, 281–3.

Stürzebecher, J., Markwardt, F., Voigt, B., Wagner, G., and Walsmann, P. (1983). Cyclic amides of Nα-arylsulfonylaminoacylated 4-amidinophenylalanine—tight binding inhibitors of thrombin. *Thromb. Res.*, **29**, 635–42.

Stürzebecher, J., Walsmann, P., Voigt, B., and Wagner, G. (1984a). Inhibition of bovine and human thrombins by derivatives of benzamidine. *Thromb. Res.*, **36**, 457–65.

Stürzebecher, J., Markwardt, F., Vieweg, H., Wagner, G., and Walsmann, P. (1984b). Synthetische Inhibitoren der Serinproteinasen. 31. Mitteilung: Über die Hemmwirkung isomerer Verbindungen von Nα-arylsulfonylierten ω-Amidinophenyl-α-aminoalkyl-carbonsäureamiden gegenüber Trypsin, Plasmin und Thrombin. *Pharmazie*, **39**, 411–3.

Stürzebecher, J., Markwardt, F., Walsmann, P., Voigt, B., and Wagner, G. (1987). Synthetische Inhibitoren der Serinproteinasen. 32. Mitteilung: Hemmung von Trypsin, Plasmin und Thrombin durch Amide des Nα-substituierten 4-Amidinophenylalanins. Einfluß verschiedener Aminosäuren und Schutzgruppen im Nα-Rest auf die Inhibitoraktivität. *Pharmazie*, **42**, 114–6.

Stürzebecher, J., Müller, H., and Markwardt, F. (1988a). Inhibition of glandular kallikrein by benzamidine derivatives. *J. Enzyme Inhib.*, in press.

Stürzebecher, J., Stürzebecher, U., and Markwardt, F. (1988b). Inhibition of activated factor XII and plasma kallikrein by benzamidine derivatives. *Thromb. Res.*, in press.

Stürzebecher, J., Stürzebecher, U., Vieweg, H., Wagner, G., Hauptmann, J., and Markwardt, F. (1988c). Synthetic inhibitors of factor Xa and thrombin—comparison of the anticoagulant efficiency. *Thromb. Res.*, in press.

Taenaka, N., Shimada, Y., Hirata, T., Nishijima, M., and Yoshiya, I. (1982). New approach to regional anticoagulation in haemodialysis using gabexate mesilate (FOY). *Clin. Care Med.*, **10**, 773–5.

Tanizawa, K., Kasaba, Y., and Kanaoka, Y. (1977). 'Inverse substrates' for trypsin. Efficient enzymatic hydrolysis of certain esters with a cationic center in the leaving group. *J. Am. Chem. Soc.*, **99**, 4485–8.

Tanizawa, K., Kanaoka, Y., Wos, J. D., and Lawson, W. B. (1985). Transition-state inhibition of thrombin and trypsin by amidinophenylpyruvates. *Biol. Chem. Hoppe-Seyler*, **366**, 871–8.

Tidwell, R. R., Fox, L. L., and Geratz, J. D. (1976). Aromatic tris-amidines. A new class of highly active inhibitors of trypsin-like proteases. *Biochim. Biophys. Acta*, **445**, 729–38.

Tidwell, R. R., Geratz, J. D., Dann, O., Volz, G., Zeh, D., and Loewe, H. (1978). Diarylamidine derivatives with one or both of the aryl moieties consisting of an indole or indole-like ring. Inhibitors of arginine-specific esteroproteases. *J. Med. Chem.*, **21**, 613–23.

Tidwell, R. R., Webster, W. P., Shaver, S. R., and Geratz, J. D. (1980). Strategies for anticoagulation with synthetic protease inhibitors. Xa inhibitors versus thrombin inhibitors. *Thromb. Res.*, **19**, 339–49.

Tremoli, E., Morazzoni, G., Maderna, P., Colli, S., and Paoletti, R. (1981). Studies on the antithrombotic action of Boc-D-Phe-Pro-Arg-H (Gyki 14, 451). *Thromb. Res.*, **23**, 549–53.

Trettin, H.-J. and Mix, H. (1965). Hemmung der Pankreas-Zymogenaktivierung durch Guanidinverbindungen. *Hoppe-Seyler's Z. Physiol. Chem.*, **340**, 24–30.

Wagner, G., Lischke, I., Markwardt, F., Richter, P., Stürzebecher, J., and Walsmann, P. (1977). Synthetische Inhibitoren der Serinproteinasen. 15. Mitteilung: Über die Anti-trypsin-, Antiplasmin-und Antithrombinwirkung von 2-Amidino-6-alkoxy- und -ar-alkoxynaphthalinen. *Pharmazie*, **32**, 761–3.

Walsmann, P., Markwardt, F., Richter, P., Stürzebecher, J., Wagner, G., and Landmann, H. (1974). Synthetische Inhibitoren von Serinproteinasen. 2. Mitteilung: Über die Hemmwirkung von Homologen der Amidinobenzoesäuren und ihrer Ester gegenüber Trypsin, Plasmin und Thrombin. *Pharmazie*, **29**, 333–6.

Walsmann, P., Horn, H., Markwardt, F., Richter, P., Stürzebecher, J., Vieweg, H., and Wagner, G. (1976). Synthetische Inhibitoren der Serinproteinasen. 11. Mitteilung: über die Hemmung von Trypsin, Plasmin und Thrombin durch neue Bisamidinoverbindungen. *Acta Biol. Med. Germ.*, **35**, K1–8.

Walsmann, P., Markwardt, F., Stürzebecher, J., Voigt, B., and Wagner, G. (1978).

Synthetische Inhibitoren der Serinproteinasen. 18. Mitteilung: Hemmung von Trypsin, Plasmin und Thrombin durch Derivate des Naphthamidins mit Ketonstruktur. *Pharmazie*, **33**, 760–1.

Walsmann, P., Markwardt, F., Stürzebecher, J., Vieweg, H., and Wagner, G. (1979). Synthetische Inhibitoren der Serinproteinasen. 21. Mitteilung: Untersuchungen über die Beziehungen zwischen Struktur und Wirkung bei Bisamidinen. *Pharmazie*, **34**, 837–9.

Walter, J. and Bode, W. (1983). The X-ray crystal structure analysis of the refined complex formed by bovine trypsin and *p*-amidinophenylpyruvate at 1.4 Å resolution. *Hoppe-Seyler's Z. Physiol. Chem.*, **364**, 949–59.

Wiman, B. and Wallén, P. (1977). The specific interaction between plasminogen and fibrin. A physiological role of the lysine binding site in plasminogen. *Thromb. Res.*, **10**, 213–22.

Wong, S.-C. and Shaw, E. (1974). Differences in active center reactivity of trypsin homologs. Specific inactivation of thrombin by nitrophenyl p-amidinophenylmethanesulfonate. *Archs Biochem. Biophys.*, **161**, 536–43.

Wong, S.-C., Green, G. D. J., and Shaw, E. (1978). Inactivation of trypsin-like proteases by sulfonylation. Variation of positively charged group and inhibitor length. *J. Med. Chem.*, **21**, 456–9.

Yamada, K. (1983). A clinical trial of MD-805, a synthetic thrombin inhibitor, for the treatment of DIC. *Bibl. Haematol.*, **43**, 343–4.

Yaegashi, T., Nunomura, S., Okutome, T., Nakayama, T., Kurumi, M., Sakurai, Y., Aoyama, T., and Fujii, S. (1984). Synthesis and structure-activity study of protease inhibitors. III. Amidinophenols and their benzoyl esters. *Chem. Pharm. Bull.*, **32**, 4466–77.

Yoshida, N., Sasaki, A., and Inouye, K. (1973). Active site of trypsin-like enzyme from *Streptomyces erythreus*. Specific inactivation by new chloromethyl ketones derived from N^α-dinitrophenyl-L-lysine and N^α-tosyl-L-arginine. *Biochim. Biophys. Acta*, **321**, 615–23.

Zaneveld, L. J. D., Robertson, R. T., and Williams, W. L. (1970). Synthetic enzyme inhibitors as antifertility agents. *FEBS Lett.*, **11**, 345–7.

Zur, M., Radcliffe, R. D., Oberdick, J., and Nemerson, Y. (1982). The dual role of factor VII in blood coagulation. Initiation and inhibition of a proteolytic system by a zymogen. *J. Biol. Chem.*, **257**, 5623–31.

Development of selective inhibitors of calmodulin-dependent phosphodiesterase and adenylate cyclase

Benjamin Weiss, Walter C. Prozialeck,
and Jill M. Roberts-Lewis

19.1 Introduction

Since the initial isolation of cyclic 3′,5′-adenosine monophosphate (cyclic AMP) by Sutherland and Rall (1958), investigators have been attempting to elucidate its physiological functions and to develop means for selectively altering its concentration in tissue. This task has not been easy, for cyclic AMP and other more recently discovered cyclic nucleotides have been shown to influence biological events as varied as muscle contraction, endocrine function, and neurotransmission, and as fundamental as cellular differentiation and division. Therefore, agents that alter the synthesis or biodegradation of cyclic nucleotides would be predicted to have profound, yet relatively indiscriminate effects.

Nevertheless, because of the important roles cyclic nucleotides play in biological processes, numerous attempts have been made to alter their intracellular concentration selectively, with the hope of producing selective biological effects.

The monographs and reviews that have already been published summarizing the biological actions of cyclic nucleotides are legion (see Sutherland and Rall 1960; Robison *et al.* 1968, 1971a, b; Weiss and Kidman 1969; Rall *et al.* 1969; Greengard and Costa 1970; Jost and Rickenberg 1971; Chasin 1972; Greengard and Robison 1972–86; Birnbaumer 1973; Bitensky and Gorman 1973; Kahn and Lands 1973; Abou-Sabe 1976; Friedman 1976; Daly 1977; Greengard 1978; Nathanson and Kebabian 1982; Bonnet 1983), and several books and monographs have been published reviewing the efforts to develop therapeutically effective agents that act by modulating the concentration or actions of cyclic AMP or other cyclic nucleotides (Breckenridge 1970; Weinryb *et al.* 1972; Amer and McKinney 1973; Schultz and Gratzner 1973; Braun *et al.* 1974; Smith 1974; Weiss 1975a, b; Weiss and Fertel 1977; Weiss and Hait 1977; Folco and Paoletti 1978; Cehovic and Robison 1979; Palmer 1983; Hidaka *et al.* 1984). In this review, we will focus our attention on cyclic AMP, mentioning the other cyclic nucleotides only in passing, and will concentrate further only on certain aspects of the enzyme systems that govern its intracellular concentration—those aspects that we feel hold the most promise for leading toward drugs having relatively selective actions.

There are several approaches that may be taken towards selectively altering the concentration of cyclic nucleotides in tissue. Advantage may be taken of the fact that the properties of adenylate cyclase, the enzyme that catalyses the biosynthesis of cyclic AMP, are quite different from those of guanylate cyclase, the enzyme responsible for the biosynthesis of cyclic GMP (Murad *et al.* 1981; Garbers and Radany 1981). For example, agents like fluoride, cholera toxin, and forskolin have been shown to activate adenylate cyclase but not guanylate cyclase (Murad *et al.* 1981; Garbers and Radany 1981; Gerzer *et al.* 1981). Unfortunately, there are relatively few agents that selectively inhibit these enzymes.

Much more progress has been made in finding drugs that inhibit phosphodiesterase, the enzyme that catalyses the hydrolysis of the cyclic nucleotides. The possibility of developing selective phosphodiesterase inhibitors was enhanced by the discovery that phosphodiesterase is not a simple molecular entity, but rather exists in a variety of forms having different molecular weights, kinetic properties, electrophoretic properties, substrate specificities and, most important from the present standpoint, different sensitivities to drugs (see below). Indeed, the finding that the different forms of phosphodiesterase are differentially distributed in tissue, combined with the fact that these enzyme forms can be inhibited relatively selectively, suggests that it may be possible to alter the concentration of cyclic nucleotides in one tissue but not in another.

There are a number of mechanisms by which drugs may alter the activity of phosphodiesterase (see Weiss and Hait 1977; Strada and Thompson 1984). The most obvious is by competing with the substrate, as has been shown with the methylxanthines. However, since the substrate sites on the different forms of phosphodiesterase are probably quite similar, this type of inhibition is not likely to provide a great deal of selectivity. Non-competitive inhibition of phosphodiesterase has also been reported, but this also has not proved to be particularly selective. Another mechanism is through an action at an allosteric site on the enzyme. Thus, cyclic GMP has been shown to alter the activity of cyclic AMP phosphodiesterase by acting at an allosteric site on cyclic AMP phosphodiesterase (Weiss and Hait 1977).

A more selective means of altering the activity of one of the forms of phosphodiesterase stemmed from the finding that there is an endogenous activator of phosphodiesterase present in tissue (Cheung 1970). This activator, termed calmodulin, was shown to be dependent on the presence of calcium for its biological activity (Kakiuchi and Yamazaki 1970). Early studies suggested that calmodulin was highly selective in that it could activate one of the forms of phosphodiesterase many-fold while having no effect on other forms of the enzyme (Uzunov and Weiss 1972). This observation led to the discovery that by inhibiting calmodulin, a discrete molecular form of phosphodiesterase could be inhibited (Weiss 1973). Since the calmodulin-sensitive form of phosphodiesterase is differentially distributed, or even absent in some cells (Uzunov et al. 1974), calmodulin inhibitors might alter the concentration of cyclic nucleotides in specific tissues and be potentially useful therapeutic agents (Hait and Lazo 1986).

However, calmodulin itself proved to lack specificity. A few years after the report that this calcium-binding protein could activate one of the forms of phosphodiesterase, calmodulin was shown to activate one of the forms of adenylate cyclase (Cheung et al. 1975; Brostrom et al. 1975; Brostom et al. 1977; Gnegy et al. 1984), and shortly thereafter it was reported to activate several other enzymes as well, including Ca^{2+}-ATPase (Levin and Weiss 1980), tryptophan hydroxylase (Kuhn et al. 1980), tyrosine hydroxylase (Yamauchi et al. 1981), guanylate cyclase (Nagao et al. 1979) and a number of protein kinases (Schulman and Greengard 1978; Payne and Soderling 1980; Smilowitz et al. 1981; Kochhar et al. 1986).

As far as cyclic nucleotide metabolism is concerned, by inhibiting calmodulin activity one would be blocking the biosynthesis of cyclic AMP (by inhibiting the calmodulin-sensitive adenylate cyclase) as well as its hydrolysis (by inhibiting calmodulin-sensitive phosphodiesterase). Therefore, it would be difficult to predict what the net result on the concentration of cyclic AMP would be. However, if the relative activities of these two enzyme forms in tissue were known, it might be possible to predict the net effect of inhibiting calmodulin on the levels of cyclic AMP. For example, inhibiting calmodulin activity in a tissue with little calmodulin-sensitive adenylate cyclase but abundant calmodulin-sensitive phosphodiesterase should increase the concentration of cyclic AMP. By contrast, in a tissue with a high activity of calmodulin-sensitive adenylate cyclase but a low activity of calmodulin-sensitive phosphodiesterase, a calmodulin inhibitor should reduce the levels of cyclic AMP by preferentially inhibiting its synthesis. As yet, insufficient information is available concerning the relative distribution of these enzymes to take advantage of this possibility. This represents an area for future research.

The possibility of selectively altering the concentration of cyclic nucleotides in tissue has been promoted by the recent finding suggesting that it might be possible to develop agents that act not on calmodulin itself but rather on the calmodulin-binding site of calmodulin-dependent enzymes (Prozialeck et al. 1983; Newton and Klee 1984; Guerini et al. 1984; Weiss et al. 1985). This type of compound may be more selective in changing cyclic nucleotide levels because it might preferentially inhibit one calmodulin-dependent enzyme over another.

The following sections describe the properties of the enzymes responsible for regulating cyclic nucleotide concentrations in cells and some of the attempts to inhibit them with selective pharmacological agents. The general properties of phosphodiesterase (Strada and Thompson 1984) and phosphodiesterase inhibitors (see above for references) have already been considered in great detail. Therefore, discussion of this topic will be limited to the properties of the calmodulin-sensitive form of phosphodiesterase and to those compounds that have been shown to inhibit this particular form of the enzyme, either by acting directly on calmodulin or by acting on the calmodulin binding site of the enzyme (see also reviews by Weiss et al. 1980; Weiss and Prozialeck 1984; Thermos and Weiss 1985; Hait and Lazo 1986).

Less attention has been paid to inhibitors of adenylate cyclase; like phosphodiesterase, adenylate cyclase also exists in more than one form, one being sensitive to calmodulin and another being insensitive to this calcium binding protein (Cheung et al. 1975). In addition, the adenylate cyclase system is quite complex, consisting of several interrelated components: a receptor, guanyl nucleotide binding proteins, and a catalytic portion (Cooper and Seamon 1985). This very complexity affords us the opportunity of selectively altering its activity. Accordingly, we will consider this important area of investigation in a more comprehensive manner, reviewing the properties of this adenylate cyclase and pointing out the efforts that have been made to take advantage of the multiple levels of regulation of the adenylate cyclase complex.

19.2 General properties of calmodulin

Calmodulin is a highly acidic (pI = 4.2), relatively small (16.2 Da) protein that is found in high concentrations in all eukaryotic cells. It is highly conserved throughout the phylogenetic scale, as evidenced by the fact that calmodulins from various species, though not identical, are structurally quite similar (Klee and Vanaman 1982). Calmodulin consists of four domains, each of which can bind one atom of calcium. When calcium binds to calmodulin, it alters its tertiary structure, exposing more hydrophobic residues and causing it to assume a more helical conformation. These structural changes allow calmodulin to interact with and activate a number of calcium-dependent enzymes (Liu and Cheung 1976; LaPorte *et al.* 1980; Cox 1984). These conformational changes also allow calmodulin to interact with other calcium binding proteins as well as with a number of pharmacological agents and peptides, many of which inhibit the actions of calmodulin (see below).

Accordingly, calmodulin, like cyclic AMP, appears to be a phylogenetically ancient and fundamental regulator that modulates a wide variety of calcium-dependent processes as diverse and basic as muscular contraction, neuronal transmission, and cellular growth and differentiation (see Means *et al.* 1982; Klee and Vanaman 1982: Brown *et al.* 1985). Interestingly, calmodulin is involved in the regulation of the two enzymes that control the biosynthesis and biodegradation of cyclic AMP. Therefore, the activity of calmodulin will to a large extent determine the intracellular concentration and biological activity of cyclic AMP. Obviously, pharmacological agents that interfere with the action of calmodulin should have profound effects on cyclic nucleotide levels and may serve as novel compounds for altering biological processes.

19.3 Phosphodiesterase

19.3.1 General properties of calmodulin-sensitive phosphodiesterase

Calmodulin-sensitive phosphodiesterase is a soluble enzyme that is functionally, immunologically, and genetically distinct from other forms of phosphodiesterase (for reviews, see Appelman *et al.* 1982; Klee and Vanaman 1982; Strada *et al.* 1984; Krinks *et al.* 1984; Hurwitz *et al.* 1984). It can be separated from calmodulin and from other forms of phosphodiesterase by a variety of techniques including preparative polyacrylamide gel electrophoresis (Uzunov and Weiss 1972), DEAE cellulose anion exchange chromatograph (Appelman *et al.* 1982), and Ca^{2+}-dependent affinity chromatography on calmodulin-Sepharose (Sharma *et al.* 1983). Insofar as the nomenclature is concerned, the enzyme has been referred to by a variety of names, such as Peak I, Peak II, F II, PDE I, etc., which are based on its pattern of elution from electrophoretic or chromatographic columns.

From a functional standpoint, the distinguishing characteristic of this particular phosphodiesterase is that it requires both Ca^{2+} and calmodulin for maximal activity (Kakiuchi and Yamazaki 1970; Uzunov and Weiss 1972; Teo and Wang 1973). In the absence of Ca^{2+} or calmodulin, the enzyme displays a low level of activity that varies depending on its source and method of preparation. Upon the addition of optimal concentrations of Ca^{2+} and calmodulin, the maximal activity (V_{max}) of the enzyme is increased 10- to 60-fold (Uzunov and Weiss 1972; Klee *et al.* 1979; Sharma *et al.* 1980; Cox *et al.* 1981; Krinks *et al.* 1984). The enzyme can metabolize both cyclic AMP and cyclic GMP, although it has a much greater affinity for the latter; in the presence of Ca^{2+} and calmodulin, the K_m for cyclic GMP is $5–10 \times 10^{-6}$ M whereas the K_m for cyclic AMP is usually greater than 1×10^{-4} M. However, at saturating concentrations of substrate, the enzyme can metabolize cyclic AMP faster than cyclic GMP (Brostrom and Wolff 1976; Ho *et al.* 1977; Klee *et al.* 1979).

Calmodulin-sensitive phosphodiesterase appears to be widely distributed throughout the animal kingdom (for reviews see Klee and Vanaman 1982; Appelman *et al.* 1982). Enzyme activity has been detected in a variety of mammalian tissues including brain (Cheung 1970; Kakiuchi *et al.* 1975), heart (Kakiuchi *et al.* 1975), blood vessels (Wells *et al.* 1975), platelets (Hidaka and Endo 1984), liver (Kakiuchi *et al.* 1975), and others (Smoake *et al.* 1974; Sitaramayya *et al.* 1978; Brown 1980; Sugden and Ashcroft 1981; Appelman *et al.* 1982). The highest levels of activity are present in brain (Smoake *et al.* 1974; Kakiuchi *et al.* 1975), which is often used as a source of the enzyme for biochemical studies. In brain, the levels of enzyme activity vary from region to region, with the highest activity being found in the striatum and the cerebral cortex (Egrie *et al.* 1977; Greenberg *et al.* 1978). It should be noted that the distribution of the calmodulin-sensitive phosphodiesterase does not exactly parallel the distribution of calmodulin (Smoake *et al.* 1974), or other forms of phosphodiesterase (Appelman *et al.* 1982). Furthermore, calmodulin and the enzyme exhibit different patterns of development (Strada *et al.* 1974; Smoake *et al.* 1974).

In general, samples of calmodulin-sensitive phosphodiesterase from various sources exhibit similar biochemical and physicochemical properties (Klee and Vanaman 1982). Most studies in this area have focused on the bovine brain enzyme. In its native state, this enzyme exists as a dimer, composed of two identical subunits each having a molecular weight of approximately 60 000 (Klee *et al.* 1979; Sharma *et al.* 1980; Klee and Vanaman 1982). Studies showing that limited proteolysis of the enzyme by trypsin causes a marked increase in enzyme activity, accompanied by a loss in sensitivity to calmodulin, indicate that each of the subunits contains two functional domains, a catalytic domain that binds various cyclic nucleotide substrates, and a regulatory domain that binds calmodulin (Tucker *et al.* 1981; Gietzen *et al.* 1982; Krinks *et al.* 1984).

Figure 19.1 shows the mechanism for the activation of phosphodiesterase by Ca^{2+} and calmodulin. In the absence of calmodulin, the regulatory domain exerts an inhibitory effect on the catalytic domain, masking the catalytic site and thereby maintaining the enzyme in a relatively inactive state. The activation of the enzyme involves the sequential binding of three to four Ca^{2+} ions to calmodulin followed by the binding of the Ca^{2+}–calmodulin complex to the calmodulin binding sites of regulatory domains on each of the two subunits (Fig. 19.1, 'non-activated phosphodiesterase'). The interaction of the Ca^{2+}–calmodulin complex with these sites causes a change in the conformation of the enzyme and removes the inhibitory influence of the regulatory domain. This results in the exposure of additional catalytic sites on the enzyme and leads to an increase in the affinity of the enzyme for its cyclic nucleotide substrates, and thereby increases enzyme activity (Fig. 19.1, 'activated phosphodiesterase').

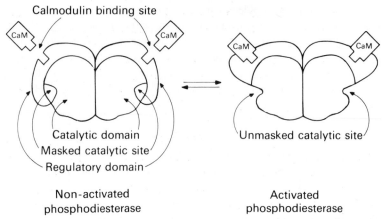

Activation of phosphodiesterase by calcium–calmodulin

Non-activated phosphodiesterase

Activated phosphodiesterase

Fig. 19.1. Schematic illustration of the activation of phosphodiesterase by the calcium–calmodulin complex (CaM). See text for details.

19.3.2   Mechanisms for inhibiting calmodulin sensitive phosphodiesterase

There are a variety of mechanisms by which drugs could inhibit the calmodulin-sensitive form of phosphodiesterase. Agents might act by:

(1) reducing the availability of Ca^{2+} (this could be accomplished by inhibiting the entry of Ca^{2+} into cells, by inhibiting its release from intracellular pools, or by chelating it);

(2) binding to calmodulin and altering its ability to bind Ca^{2+};

(3) binding to the Ca^{2+}–calmodulin complex and modifying its activity;

(4) binding to the calmodulin-recognition site on phosphodiesterase and thereby preventing interaction of the Ca^{2+}–calmodulin complex with the enzyme;

(5) interacting with the catalytic portion of the enzyme; and

(6) interacting with the ternary Ca^{2+}–calmodulin–enzyme complex.

Agents that act by each of these mechanisms are discussed in more detail below.

19.3.2.1   *Agents that alter the availability of Ca^{2+}*

Examples of agents that act by this mechanism include the Ca^{2+}-chelators such as EGTA, which bind directly to Ca^{2+}, and the Ca^{2+}-entry blockers such as nifedipine, which inhibit the influx of extracellular Ca^{2+}. Although it is clear that such agents could indirectly affect the activity of the calmodulin-sensitive phosphodiesterase, they would probably exhibit little specificity for this enzyme. For example, Ca^{2+}-chelators would inhibit all of the biochemical effects of Ca^{2+}, not just its interaction with calmodulin and phosphodiesterase. Likewise, the Ca^{2+}-entry blockers would inhibit all of the intracellular effects of Ca^{2+}. Interestingly, several Ca^{2+}-entry blockers have been shown to interact directly with calmodulin-sensitive phosphodiesterase (Epstein et al. 1982; Norman et al. 1983) and/or the Ca^{2+}–calmodulin complex (Bostrom et al. 1981; Johnson 1983; Thayer and Fairhurst 1983; see also below).

19.3.2.2 *Agents that interact with calmodulin and alter its ability to bind Ca^{2+}*

Agents in this category might act by binding directly to the Ca^{2+} binding sites on calmodulin or by binding to some other site on the molecule and thereby inducing changes in the Ca^{2+} binding regions. A variety of di- and trivalent cations including Al^{3+}, Cd^{2+}, Hg^{2+}, La^{3+}, Mg^{2+}, Mn^{2+}, Pb^{2+}, Sr^{2+}, Tb^{3+}, and Zn^{2+} have been shown to interact with calmodulin (Teo and Wang 1973); Lin et al. 1974; Cox and Harrison 1983; Siegel and Haug 1983; Chao et al. 1984; Mills and Johnson 1985). However, it is not clear whether these agents act primarily to mimic or to antagonize the effects of Ca^{2+}. For example, it has been reported that Cd^{2+}, Hg^{2+}, and Pb^{2+} and several other metals interact with calmodulin in the same manner that Ca^{2+} does; they compete with Ca^{2+} for binding sites on calmodulin and mimic the effect of Ca^{2+} in activating calmodulin-sensitive phosphodiesterase (Chao et al. 1984). However, other studies have shown that some of these agents, particularly Cd^{2+} and Hg^{2+}, interact with calmodulin in a fashion that is different from Ca^{2+} (Mills and Johnson 1985), and that they actually inhibit the activation of calmodulin-stimulated phosphodiesterase (Cox and Harrison 1983; Richardt et al. 1985). Whether any of the toxic effects of these metals result from an interaction with calmodulin or calmodulin-sensitive enzymes such as phosphodiesterase remains to be seen. It is also not known whether these agents can differentially affect various calmodulin-sensitive enzymes.

19.3.2.3 *Agents that interact with the Ca^{2+}–calmodulin complex*

A wide variety of agents belonging to diverse chemical and pharmacological classes have been shown to inhibit the calmodulin induced activation of phosphodiesterase by interacting with the Ca^{2+}–calmodulin complex (for reviews, see Prozialeck 1983; Prozialeck and Weiss 1985). Most of the agents in this category are 'selective' phosphodiesterase inhibitors only in the sense that they inhibit the calmodulin-sensitive form of phosphodiesterase without affecting other phosphodiesterase isozymes (Weiss et al. 1974; Weiss 1975a). They are 'non-selective' in the sense that they inhibit the effects of calmodulin on many other enzyme systems (Weiss and Wallace 1980). Several of these calmodulin-binding drugs such as the phenothiazines (chlorpromazine (**1**) and trifluoperazine (**2**)), the naphthalenesulphonamide W-7 (**3**), and the miconazole derivative

Chlorpromazine ($C_{17}H_{19}ClN_2S$)
1

Trifluoperazine ($C_{21}H_{24}F_3N_3S$)
2

W-7 ($C_{16}H_{21}ClN_2O_2S$)
3

Calmidazolium ($C_{25}H_{23}Cl_6N_2O$)
4

calmidazolium (**4**) are commonly referred to as 'calmodulin antagonists' and have been used extensively in studies on the physiological and biochemical functions of calmodulin. It should be noted that several recent findings indicate that it may be possible to develop calmodulin-binding drugs that could selectively inhibit one calmodulin-sensitive enzyme, such as phosphodiesterase, but not another. These findings are discussed in subsequent sections of this chapter.

The phenothiazine antipsychotics were the first drugs that were shown to inhibit the calmodulin-sensitive form of phosphodiesterase selectively. Studies in the early 1970s showed that phenothiazine antipsychotics inhibited only one of the forms of phosphodiesterase that could be isolated from brain tissue by polyacrylamide gel electrophoresis (Weiss 1973; Weiss et al. 1974). Of particular interest was the fact that this was the same form of phosphodiesterase that was activated by Ca^{2+} and calmodulin (Uzunov and Weiss 1972). Subsequent studies showed that the mechanism by which phenothiazines inhibited this calmodulin-sensitive form of phosphodiesterase was by binding to calmodulin and not by interacting with the enzyme itself (Levin and Weiss 1976; 1977; Weiss and Levin 1978).

The phenothiazines bind to two distinct classes of sites on calmodulin: a class of saturatable, high-affinity, Ca^{2+}-dependent sites, and a class of low-affinity, Ca^{2+}-independent sites (Levin and Weiss 1977, 1979). The Ca^{2+}-dependent sites appear to be the biochemically important sites, since there is an excellent correlation between the Ca^{2+}-dependent binding of various drugs and their ability to inhibit the calmodulin-induced activation of phosphodiesterase (Levin and Weiss 1979). There are two or three Ca^{2+}-dependent drug-binding sites per calmodulin molecule, with the most potent agents displaying dissociation constants of $1 \times 10^{-5}M$ or less (Levin and Weiss 1979; Weiss et al. 1980). Results of structure–activity studies have shown that the binding of phenothiazines to calmodulin involves two kinds of attachments; a hydrophobic interaction between the phenothiazine nucleus and a non-polar region of calmodulin and an electrostatic interaction between a positively charged amino group on the drug and a negatively charged residue on calmodulin (Weiss et al. 1982; Prozialeck and Weiss 1982; Prozialeck 1984).

At present, the exact location of the drug binding site on calmodulin and the mechanism by which drug binding alters the interaction between calmodulin and phosphodiesterase are not totally understood. Results of n.m.r. and fluorescence spectroscopy studies have shown that phenothiazine-like drugs interact with methionine and phenylalanine residues between the second and third Ca^{2+}-binding domains of calmodulin (La Porte et al. 1980; Tanaka and Hidaka 1980; Klevit et al. 1981; Krebs and Carafoli 1982; Dalgarno et al. 1984). These hydrophobic residues are exposed when Ca^{2+} binds to calmodulin, and they are thought to serve as an interface for the binding of calmodulin to target enzymes such as phosphodiesterase. It has been suggested that the phenothiazines compete with the enzyme for these binding sites. When the sites are occupied by drug molecules, the enzyme can no longer bind to calmodulin and thus cannot be activated (La Porte et al. 1980; Tanaka and Hidaka 1980; Gietzen et al. 1982). Although this model is consistent with the finding that phenothiazines decrease the affinity of calmodulin for its target enzymes (LaPorte et al. 1980; Malnoe et al. 1982; Tanaka et al. 1983), recent studies showing that certain covalently linked phenothiazine calmodulin adducts are still able to interact with phosphodiesterase (Prozialeck et al. 1983; Newton et al. 1983; Newton and Klee 1984), indicate that the phenothiazines and phosphodiesterase may bind to different sites on calmodulin.

Besides the phenothiazines, a variety of other agents belonging to diverse pharmacological and chemical classes have also been shown to interact with the Ca^{2+}–calmodulin complex and inhibit the calmodulin-induced activation of phosphodiesterase (see Table 19.1). Many of these seemingly unrelated agents can compete with phenothiazines for binding sites on calmodulin, whereas other agents, such as the dihydropyridines and certain neuropeptides, cannot. Interestingly, the agents that interact with the phenothiazine binding site display certain structural similarities; all are amphiphilic amines containing a large hydrophobic region separated from a charged amino group by four or more atoms. These compounds apparently bind to calmodulin through a combination of hydrophobic and ionic interactions in much the same manner as do the phenothiazines.

Table 19.1   Pharmacological classes of drugs that inhibit calmodulin by binding to the Ca^{2+}–calmodulin complex

Class	References
Alpha-adrenergic antagonists	Watanabe and West 1982; Earl *et al.* 1984
Antianginal agents	Bostrom *et al.* 1981; Epstein *et al.* 1982
Anti-anxiety agents	Levin and Weiss 1979
Antidepressants	Levin and Weiss 1979
Antidiarrhoeals	Zavecz *et al.* 1982
Antihistaminics	Levin and Weiss 1976, 1979
Antipsychotics	Levin and Weiss 1976, 1977, 1979
Cancer chemotherapeuticals	Katoh *et al.* 1981; Watanabe and West 1982
Local anesthetics	Tanaka and Hidaka 1981; Volpi *et al.* 1981
Neuropeptides	Malencik and Anderson 1982, 1983; Sellinger-Barnette and Weiss 1982, 1984
Insect venom peptides	Comte *et al.* 1983; Sellinger-Barnette and Weiss 1984
Smooth muscle relaxants	Hidaka *et al.* 1980, 1981
Miscellaneous agents	
Calmidazolium (R 24 571)	Van Belle 1981
Compound 48/80	Gietzen *et al.* 1983
Cyclosporin A	Colombani *et al.* 1985
DDT	Hagmann 1982
Triton X-100	Sharma and Wang 1981

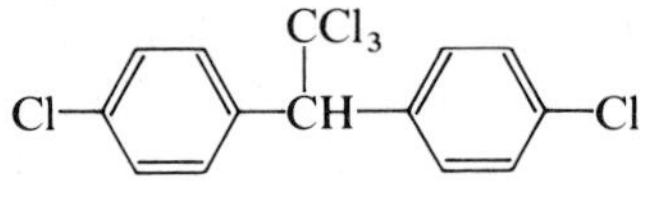

DDT

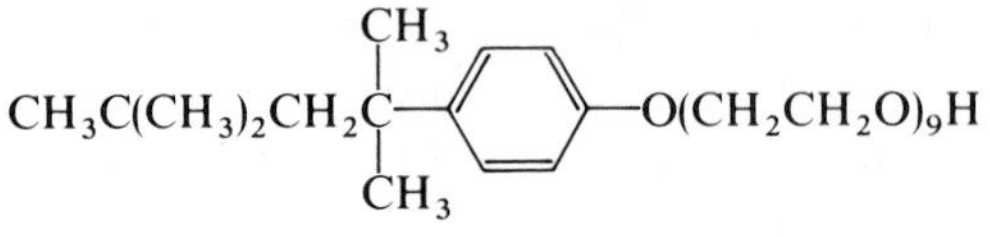

Triton X-100

It should be noted that certain agents such as Triton X-100 or DDT can bind to calmodulin and inhibit phosphodiesterase activity even though they are structurally quite different from the agents described above. For the most part, it is not known whether these compounds interact with the same sites on calmodulin as the phenothiazines do (Sharma and Wang 1981; Hagmann 1982). Several recent studies have shown that calmodulin may contain different classes of drug binding site (Johnson 1983; Inagaki and Hidaka 1984; Mills *et al.* 1985). For example, felodipine, a 1,4-dihydropyridine derivative, binds to a different site on calmodulin than do the phenothiazines, although there may be cooperative interactions between the two types of drug binding site (Johnson 1983; Mills *et al.* 1985).

In addition to synthetic drugs, there are several naturally occurring compounds that interact with the Ca^{2+}–calmodulin complex to inhibit phosphodiesterase activation. These include a group of calmodulin-binding proteins and a variety of peptides (Sellinger Barnette and Weiss 1982, 1984, 1985; Malencik and Anderson 1982, 1983; Cox *et al.* 1985; DeGrado *et al.* 1985). Certain neuropeptides and insect venom peptides are among the most potent calmodulin inhibitors yet discovered. Some of them are orders of magnitude more potent than the most potent antipsychotic drugs. Mellitin inhibits calmodulin-stimulated phosphodiesterase activity without affecting basal activity of the enzyme. The IC_{50} value of mellitin is approximately 2×10^{-7}M and its K_i is 3×10^{-8} M. Therefore, this compound is about 50 times more potent than trifluoperazine in inhibiting calmodulin activity. When mellitin is acetylated, its anticalmodulin activity decreases approximately five-fold. Since acetylation of the lysine residues in mellitin does not substantially alter the molecule's hydrophobicity but does decrease its net positive charge, these results again show the importance of ionic interactions between calmodulin inhibitors and calmodulin (Sellinger-Barnette and Weiss 1984). Competitive binding studies indicate that peptides such as mellitin and β-endorphin interact with different sites on calmodulin than the phenothiazines, although there may be some overlap between peptide and phenothiazine binding sites (Giedroc *et al.* 1985). This finding, that certain neuropeptides inhibit calmodulin-sensitive phosphodiesterase, suggests that these or perhaps some as yet undiscovered peptides may function as endogenous regulators of the enzyme and may themselves provide potential sites for pharmacological intervention.

Early studies showed that binding to calmodulin of phenothiazines and related agents is a reversible process, since the binding could be reversed by removing Ca^{2+} or by dialysing against an excess of competing drug (Levin and Weiss 1977; Weiss and Wallace 1980). However, more recent findings have shown that some agents can bind irreversibly to calmodulin under certain conditions. Upon irradiation with ultra-violet light (Weiss *et al.* 1980; Prozialeck *et al.* 1981) or treatment with peroxidase–hydrogen peroxide (Weiss *et al.* 1980; Grossman *et al.* 1985), chlorpromazine and trifluoperazine bind irreversibly to calmodulin, presumably through free-radical mechanisms. Recently, several agents, including the alkylating alpha adrenergic antagonists, phenoxybenzamine, and dibenamine (Earl *et al.* 1984; Lukas *et al.* 1985; Ciminó and Weiss, 1988) and the alkylating phenothiazines, fluphenazine-nitrogen mustard (5)

Fluphenazine-N-mustard ($C_{22}H_{25}ClF_3N_3S$)

5

(Weiss *et al.* 1984; Winkler *et al.* 1987) and norchlorpromazine isothiocyanate (Newton *et al.* 1983; Newton and Klee 1984), have been shown to bind irreversibly to calmodulin even in the absence of u.v. irradiation or oxidative enzymes. In each of the cases described above, irreversible binding of the drug resulted in irreversible inactivation of calmodulin, i.e. calmodulin that had been irreversibly linked to the drugs could not activate calmodulin-sensitive phosphodiesterase, although in some instances the drug–calmodulin adducts could still interact with the enzyme and inhibit its activation by native calmodulin (Prozialeck *et al.* 1983; Newton *et al.* 1983; Newton and Klee 1984; Newton *et al.* 1985). The implications of these findings are discussed below.

19.3.2.4   *Agents that interact with calmodulin-binding sites on phosphodiesterase*

So far, relatively little attention has been given to developing agents that bind to the calmodulin recognition sites on phosphodiesterase. However, recent findings suggest that these sites may prove useful for pharmacological intervention. As was noted previously, upon irradiation with u.v. light, the phenothiazine antipsychotics, chlorpromazine and trifluoperazine, bind irreversibly to calmodulin and inactivate it, as shown by the fact that the phenothiazine–calmodulin complex cannot activate calmodulin-sensitive phosphodiesterase (Prozialeck *et al.* 1981). Although the precise mechanism by which this irreversible binding leads to the inactivation of calmodulin is not known, only two possibilities seem likely: either the drug–calmodulin complex is not able to bind to the calmodulin recognition site on the calmodulin-sensitive enzyme, or else the complex can bind to the enzyme but is unable to induce the conformational changes necessary for activation of the enzyme. If the drug–calmodulin complex can bind to the calmodulin-recognition site, it should be able to prevent native calmodulin from binding to the enzyme and thereby inhibit activation of the enzyme by calmodulin. Studies on the effects of the chlorpromazine–calmodulin complex (CPZ–CM) on the activation of phosphodiesterase by native calmodulin are shown in Fig. 19.2. Calmodulin that had been linked to chlorpromazine by ultraviolet irradiation (CPZ–CM) had no effect on basal phosphodiesterase activity but did inhibit enzyme activation by native calmodulin in a concentration-dependent manner ($IC_{50} = 450$ ng per sample). Another study showed that CPZ–CM increased the activation constant (K_a) for the interaction of calmodulin with phosphodiesterase but did not affect maximal enzyme activation (V_{max}) by calmodulin. Neither calmodulin nor CPZ–CM altered the K_m for the interaction between phosphodiesterase and cyclic AMP (Prozialeck *et al.* 1983). The most likely explanation for these findings is that the CPZ–CM complex inhibits the calmodulin-induced activation of phosphodiesterase by competing with calmodulin for recognition sites on the enzyme. Similar findings and conclusions have recently been reported by others (Newton *et al.* 1983; Newton and Klee 1984), who showed that the irreversible complex of norchlorpromazine isothiocyanate with calmodulin (CAPP–CM) could inhibit the calmodulin-induced activation of phosphodiesterase in a competitive manner,

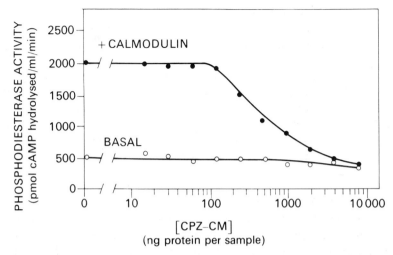

Fig. 19.2. Inhibition of the calmodulin-induced activation of phosphodiesterase by chlorpromazine-linked calmodulin.

Chlorpromazine-linked calmodulin (CPZ–CM) was prepared by irradiating purified bovine brain calmodulin with ultra-violet light ($\lambda_{max} = 366$ nm), in the presence of 100 μM chlorpromazine and 100 μM CaCl$_2$. The sample was then dialysed extensively to remove reversibly bound chlorpromazine. Phosphodiesterase activity was measured in the absence and presence of calmodulin (1 unit; approximately 10 nM) with and without varied amounts of CPZ–CM in a final volume of 125 μl (Weiss *et al.* 1972). Each point represents the mean value of three samples.

apparently by competing with calmodulin for binding sites on the enzyme. In another study, these same investigators showed that residues 78–148 of calmodulin, which failed to activate phosphodiesterase, prevented the calmodulin-induced activation of the enzyme through the same mechanism (Newton *et al.* 1984).

These findings suggest that it may be possible to develop a new class of calmodulin inhibitors that are directed at calmodulin recognition sites on calmodulin-sensitive enzymes. Since there is good evidence (see below) that various calmodulin-sensitive enzymes may have somewhat different calmodulin recognition sites, it may be possible to develop agents that would inhibit one enzyme but not another. Preliminary results suggest that this may, in fact, be a fruitful approach to developing more selective agents. As may be seen in Fig. 19.3, the CPZ–CM complex does not inhibit the calmodulin-induced activation of Ca^{2+}–ATPase even at concentrations that completely block the activation of phosphodiesterase by calmodulin. In a similar manner, the CAPP–CM complex inhibits the calmodulin-induced activation of phosphodiesterase, but acts as a partial agonist on the calmodulin-sensitive phosphatase, calcineurin (Newton and Klee 1984), and as a full agonist on calmodulin-sensitive glycogen synthase kinase and phosphorylase kinase (Newton *et al.* 1985).

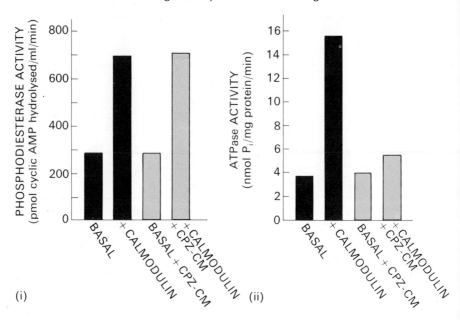

Fig. 19.3. Effects of chlorpromazine-linked calmodulin (CPZ–CM) on the activity of calmodulin-sensitive phosphodiesterase and Ca^{2+}-ATPase.

The CPZ–CM complex was prepared by irradiating purified bovine brain calmodulin with ultra-violet light in the presence of 150 μM chlorpromazine and 100 μM $CaCl_2$. To remove free chlorpromazine, the sample was dialysed extensively. Phosphodiesterase activity was measured by the luciferin–luciferase method (Weiss *et al.* 1972), using 400 μM cyclic AMP as substrate, in the absence and presence of calmodulin (1 unit; approximately 80 ng ml^{-1}) and/or CPZ–CM (15 μg ml^{-1}). Each point represents the mean value of three samples. Ca^{2+}-ATPase activity was determined in human erythrocyte membranes by a modified form of the procedure of Luthra (1982). Where indicated, samples contained calmodulin (100 ng ml^{-1}) and/or CPZ–CM (30 μg ml^{-1}). The reaction was started by adding ATP (final concentration of 2×10^{-3} M) and the samples were incubated at 37°C for 2 h. The reaction was stopped and inorganic phosphate was determined by the method of Baginski *et al.* (1967). Ca^{2+}-ATPase activity was calculated by subtracting the activity seen in the absence of Ca^{2+} (i.e. in the presence of EGTA) from that seen in the presence of Ca^{2+}. Values represent the mean of three replicate samples.

19.3.2.5   *Agents that act on the catalytic domain of phosphodiesterase*

A vast array of compounds inhibit the different forms of phosphodiesterase by interacting with their catalytic domains (for reviews see Weinryb *et al.* 1972; Chasin and Harris 1976; Weiss and Fertel 1977; Weiss and Hait 1977; Appelman *et al.* 1982; Weishaar *et al.* 1985). Included among them are the classical phosphodiesterase inhibitors such as the methylxanthines and papaverine.

These agents interact directly with the catalytic site on phosphodiesterase and competitively interfere with the binding of the cyclic nucleotide substrates (Butcher and Sutherland 1962; Weiss *et al.* 1974; Weiss 1975a; Chasin and Harris 1976). Although they do inhibit calmodulin-stimulated phosphodiesterase, they are non-selective because they inhibit the non-stimulated form of the enzyme as well as the calmodulin-stimulated form (Lin *et al.* 1974; Weiss *et al.* 1974; Weiss 1975a). Furthermore, they are equally as potent in inhibiting calmodulin-insensitive forms of the enzyme (Weiss 1975a; Weishaar *et al.* 1985).

Despite the lack of specificity of most compounds in this category, there is some evidence that certain agents can exert selective effects on the calmodulin-sensitive form of phosphodiesterase. In the mid 1970s Wells and his co-workers noted that certain xanthine derivatives, particularly 1-methyl-3-isobutylxanthine (MIX) (**6**), were slightly more potent at inhibiting a calmodulin-sensitive phosphodiesterase from pig coronary arteries than a calmodulin-insensitive phosphodiesterase from the same tissue (Wells *et al.* 1975). Subsequent studies showed that the selectivity of MIX could be enhanced by adding alkyl or arylalkyl substituents at position 7, or alkyl substituents at position 8 (Garst *et al.* 1976; Kramer *et al.* 1977; Wells *et al.* 1981). The most selective of these agents was up to 30 times more potent as an inhibitor of calmodulin-sensitive phosphodiesterase than as an inhibitor calmodulin-insensitive forms of the enzyme.

1-Methyl-3-isobutylxanthine($C_{11}H_{14}N_4O_2$)

6

Besides these xanthine analogues, several other agents have recently been shown to interact with and selectively inhibit the calmodulin-sensitive form of phosphodiesterase. Bergstrand *et al.* (1977) showed that the antiallergic compounds zaprinast (M & B 22948) and 6-*n*-butyl-2,8-dicarboxy-4-tetrahydro-1,7-phenanthroline (ICI 74197) were more potent at inhibiting a low K_m, cyclic GMP-specific form of phosphodiesterase (Fraction I) from human lung than they were at inhibiting two other isozymes (Fraction II and Fraction III). Zaprinast in particular displayed a high degree of selectivity; its IC_{50} for inhibition of the Fraction I enzyme was 1.1×10^{-6}, whereas its IC_{50} values for the inhibition of the Fraction II and Fraction III enzymes were 1.7 and 2.3 $\times 10^{-4}$ M, respectively. It should be noted that although these investigators did not specifically examine the effects of calmodulin on the Fraction I phospho-diesterase, the enzyme displayed chromatographic properties and substrate specificities that it was a calmodulin-insensitive form of phospho-diesterase.

Recently, Hidaka and his co-workers (Hidaka *et al.* 1984; Hidaka and Endo 1984) have shown that the compounds HA-558 (**7**) and TCV-3B (vinpocetin) (**8**) selectively inhibit a calmodulin-sensitive phosphodiesterase (F II) from platelets. Both agents were over 50 times more potent at inhibiting the F II enzyme than at inhibiting a cyclic GMP-dependent isozyme (F I) and a cyclic AMP-dependent isozyme (F III). These agents differed from the calmodulin-binding drug W-7 in that they were equally potent at inhibiting the basal and calmodul-in-activated forms of the FII enzyme. This latter observation suggests that HA-558 and TCV-3B act by binding directly to phosphodiesterase itself and not by interacting with calmodulin.

HA 558 ($C_{29}H_{32}N_5O_3S$)
7

Vinpocetine ($C_{22}H_{26}N_2O_2$)
8

Nifedipine ($C_{17}H_{18}N_2O_6$)
9

Felodipine ($C_{18}H_{19}Cl_2NO_4$)
10

The 1,4-dihydropyridines are a particularly interesting group of phosphodies-terase inhibitors. Although these agents were originally developed as Ca^{2+}-entry blockers, several of them have been shown to inhibit the calmodulin-induced activation of phosphodiesterase. Epstein *et al.* (1982) showed that nimodipine and nicardipine inhibited various forms of cyclic AMP phospho-diesterase from rat tissues in a manner that was competitive with respect to cyclic AMP. Although these agents displayed similar potencies for inhibiting calmodulin-sensitive and insensitive forms of the enzyme, they were two- to five-fold more potent against the activated state of the calmodulin-sensitive phosphodiesterase than they were against the basal state of the same enzyme. It should be noted that another Ca^{2+}-entry blocker, verapamil (structurally-related to papaverine), was 30–100 times more potent against calmodulin-insensitive forms of phosphodiesterase than against the calmodulin-sensitive enzyme. In a more recent study, Norman et al. (1983) reported that the 1,4-dihydropyridines nifedipine (9) and felodipine (10) inhibited a calmodulin-sensitive cyclic AMP phosphodiesterase (Form I) from bovine heart with IC_{50} values of 1.3 and 1.6×10^{-6} M, respectively, but were much less potent in inhibiting a calmodulin-insensitive phosphodiesterase (Form II) from the same tissue. The reason for the slightly different results from these two laboratories is not clear but it may be related to the different techniques used to isolate the enzymes and to the fact that different species were used as a source of enzyme.

Although the evidence described above indicates that the dihydropyridines inhibit calmodulin-sensitive phosphodiesterase by interacting with the enzyme itself, there is some evidence that certain of these agents also interact with calmodulin. Results of n.m.r. (Bostrom et al. 1981) and fluorescence spectroscopy (Johnson 1983) studies indicate that felodipine binds directly to calmodulin. Of particular interest is the fact that felodipine interacts with a different site on calmodulin than the phenothiazines do, although the two binding sites can allosterically influence each other (Johnson 1983; Mills et al. 1985). It should be noted that direct ligand binding studies indicate that not all 1,4-dihydropyridines are able to interact with calmodulin, and the pharmacological significance of the interaction of some of these agents with calmodulin is questionable (Thayer and Fairhurst 1983; Janis and Triggle 1983).

19.3.3   Approaches to developing selective inhibitors of calmodulin-sensitive phosphodiesterase

Any efforts to develop selective inhibitors of calmodulin-sensitive phosphodiesterase should take advantage of those features that are unique to this enzyme. Since calmodulin-sensitive phosphodiesterase can be distinguished from other forms of phosphodiesterase by its substrate specificity and its sensitivity to calmodulin, efforts to develop more selective agents should focus on altering the interaction of the substrate with the catalytic site on the enzyme or on altering the interaction between calmodulin and the enzyme.

With regard to developing selective agents that act on the catalytic domain, structure–activity studies clearly show that it is possible to enhance the potency of inhibitors toward the calmodulin-sensitive phosphodiesterase while decreasing their potency toward other phosphodiesterase isozymes (Kramer et al. 1977; Wells et al. 1981; Hidaka et al. 1984; Hidaka and Endo 1984). Further structure-studies such as these should lead to the development of even more selective agents.

A more novel approach to developing selective inhibitors would be to focus on agents that directly modify the interaction between calmodulin and the enzyme. That this may be a successful approach is shown by the fact that calmodulin-binding drugs such as the phenothiazines inhibit the calmodulin-sensitive enzyme without affecting other forms of the enzyme. Unfortunately, all of the calmodulin-binding drugs that have been described thus far inhibit the effects of calmodulin on its other target enzymes and thus are not specific phosphodiesterase inhibitors. This problem of poor specificity is compounded by the fact that most of the calmodulin-binding drugs that are currently available interact with biochemical sites other than calmodulin and can produce non-specific alterations in membrane structure.

Despite these problems, recent findings suggest that it might be possible to develop calmodulin antagonists that selectively inhibit calmodulin-sensitive phosphodiesterase but not other enzymes. For example, although the same general region of the calmodulin molecule is involved in binding to many different enzymes, the structural requirements for this interaction may be more stringent for some enzymes than for others (Klee 1980; Klee and Vanaman 1982). Various enzymes display different affinities for the Ca^{2+}–calmodulin complex (Klee 1980; Klee and Vanaman 1982) or may require calmodulin in different degrees of calcium occupancy for activity (Klee and Vanaman 1982; Huang et al. 1981; Cox et al. 1982; Blumenthal and Stull 1980), although the significance of these differences is still controversial (Klee and Vanaman 1982; Cox et al. 1982). Other studies have shown that the various calmodulin–sensitive enzymes exhibit different sensitivities to inhibition by calmodulin-binding drugs such as the phenothiazines (Hidaka et al. 1980; Van Belle 1981).

The findings showing that different regions of the calmodulin molecule are involved in the activation of various enzymes (Newton et al. 1984) and that different classes of drugs interact at more than one site on calmodulin (Inagaki and Hidaka 1984; Mills et al. 1985; Giedroc et al. 1985) suggest that it may be possible to develop calmodulin-binding drugs that prevent the interaction of calmodulin with one enzyme but not with others.

The recent findings that certain covalently linked phenothiazine–calmodulin adducts and calmodulin fragments can interact with phosphodiesterase and competitively inhibit its activation by calmodulin without affecting certain other calmodulin-sensitive enzymes suggest that it may be possible to develop a new class of phosphodiesterase inhibitors specifically directed against the calmodulin-recognition site on the enzyme.

It should be noted that the phenothiazine–calmodulin adducts and calmodulin fragments that have been shown to inhibit phosphodiesterase would probably not penetrate cell membranes very well. Therefore, they might not inhibit calmodulin-sensitive enzymes in intact cells or tissues. However, such agents might be very useful in cell-free systems or in systems where they can be introduced directly into cells. In addition, they would serve as a useful starting point for the systematic development of agents that might be useful *in vivo*.

19.4   Adenylate cyclase

19.4.1   General properties of adenylate cyclase

Adenylate cyclase belongs to a unique class of membrane-bound enzymes that are functionally coupled to receptors for hormones and neurotransmitters. These enzymes are physiologically regulated by extracellular hormones and transmitters, and are thus involved in mediating cell-to-cell communication by catalysing the formation of an intracellular second messenger in response to an extracellular 'signal' (Robison *et al.* 1971a).

Upon activation, adenylate cyclase catalyses the conversion of adenosine triphosphate (ATP) to cyclic adenosine monophosphate (cyclic AMP) (Rall and Sutherland 1962). Cyclic AMP activates a cyclic AMP-dependent protein kinase, which phosphorylates a wide variety of cellular components involved in the metabolic activity of the cell. This action of cyclic AMP thus represents the first step in a cascade of intracellular biochemical reactions resulting in the amplification and physiological expression of a hormonal message (Kuo and Greengard 1969; Krebs 1972).

Adenylate cyclase is found in virtually every tissue of higher organisms and is particularly abundant in brain (Klainer *et al.* 1962; Sutherland *et al.* 1962). The adenylate cyclase system consists of at least three types of interdependent components (see Fig. 19.4): outward-facing membrane-bound receptors for agents such as hormones or neurotransmitters (R_s and R_i), guanyl nucleotide binding proteins on the inside of the membrane (N_s and N_i), and a catalytic subunit (C), also located on the inside surface of the membrane (Ross and Gilman 1980; Rodbell 1980). Specific receptors may either activate (R_s) or inhibit (R_i) the catalytic subunit. This stimulation or inhibition results in receptor coupling to one of two distinct guanyl nucleotide binding proteins, designated N_s or N_i, (Limbird 1981; Cooper 1982; Codina *et al.* 1984; Gilman 1984). These components may move about within the fluid matrix of the membrane, and it is thought that the catalytic subunit may be shared by more than one receptor–guanyl nucleotide binding protein complex (see Schramm and Selinger 1984).

Both the stimulatory (N_s) and inhibitory (N_i) guanyl nucleotide binding proteins are oligomeric proteins composed of an alpha, a beta, and a gamma subunit, with molecular masses of about 45 (N_s alpha), 41 (N_i alpha), 35 (beta) and 5–10 (gamma) kilodaltons (Manning and Gilman 1983; Hildebrandt *et al.* 1984). The two guanyl nucleotide binding proteins, which have been purified to homogeneity (Northup *et al.* 1980; Bokoch *et al.* 1984), differ only in the alpha subunit, or guanyl nucleotide binding moiety; beta and gamma subunits appear to be identical for both proteins. The distinct alpha subunits of the stimulatory

Activation of inhibition of adenylate cyclase

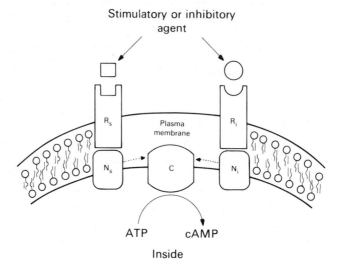

Fig. 19.4. Schematic illustration of the receptor-mediated regulation of adenylate cyclase activity. See text for details. R_s = stimulatory receptor; R_i = inhibitory receptor; N_s = stimulatory guanyl nucleotide binding protein; N_i = inhibitory guanyl nucleotide binding protein; C = catalytic subunit of adenylate cyclase.

and inhibitory guanyl nucleotide binding proteins can be selectively ADP-ribosylated by cholera, or *Bordetella pertussis* toxins, respectively (Cassel and Selinger 1977; Gill and Meren 1978; Katada and Ui 1982). These toxins have proven to be valuable tools for defining and characterizing the alpha subunits of the guanyl nucleotide binding proteins.

Pfeuffer *et al.* (1985) have recently purified the catalytic subunit of adenylate cyclase about 60 000-fold from rabbit myocardial membranes, revealing a molecular mass of about 150 kDa. These investigators have noted that the large molecular weight and the binding of this protein to wheatgerm lectin indicate that it may be a glycoprotein that actually spans the entire plasma membrane. However, little is known about the structure or nature of the specific sites that regulate intrinsic enzyme activity. Catalytic subunits from both *Escherichia coli* (Aiba *et al.* 1984) and yeast (Casperson *et al.* 1985; Kataoka *et al.* 1985) have now been sequenced from complementary DNA clones, and were found to differ substantially. Given such findings, it seems unlikely that information about the structure of the prokaryotic subunits will reveal useful insights into the structure of the catalytic subunits (s) of adenylate cyclase in eukaryotic cells.

The activation or inhibition of adenylate cyclase is thought to be regulated according to the mechanisms depicted in Fig. 19.4. Neurotransmitter or hormone binds to the receptor at the cell surface (R_s or R_i), promoting an association of receptor with a guanyl nucleotide binding protein, resulting in the displacement of bound guanosine diphosphate (GDP) by guanosine triphosphate (GTP) on the alpha subunit of the guanyl nucleotide binding protein (N_s or N_i). This leads to a dissociation of alpha from beta/gamma subunits of the guanyl nucleotide binding proteins in an Mg^{2+}-dependent manner, and the association of the alpha subunit of the stimulatory guanyl nucleotide binding protein (N_s) with the catalytic subunit (C). This reaction greatly increases the affinity of adenylate cyclase for magnesium, resulting in the direct activation of the catalytic moiety (C) by the alpha subunit of N_s (for reviews see Schramm and Selinger 1984; Ross and Gilman 1980). On the other hand, activated inhibitory guanyl nucleotide binding protein (N_i) can reverse this increase in affinity for magnesium (Bockaert and Sebben-Perez 1983; Jakobs et al. 1983).

Guanyl nucleotide and magnesium are required for activation of either guanyl nucleotide binding proteins (N_s or N_i); however, N_i exhibits a 1000-fold greater sensitivity to magnesium, and requires five to ten times more GTP for activation than does N_s (Jakobs et al. 1984a). Although the exact mechanism by which the inhibitory guanyl nucleotide binding protein mediates the inhibition of adenylate cyclase has not been resolved, an indirect inhibition of catalytic activity may be effected by re-association of the free beta/gamma subunits of the inhibitory guanyl nucleotide binding protein (N_i) with the alpha subunits of the stimulatory guanyl nucleotide binding protein (N_s) (Smigel et al. 1984). Alternatively, it has been suggested that the alpha subunit of N_i might directly inhibit the catalytic subunit (C) (Jakobs et al. 1984a). Recently, the inhibitory guanyl nucleotide binding protein has been shown to facilitate the stimulatory receptor-mediated activation of adenylate cyclase above the activation by GTP in a reconstituted phospholipid vesicle system (Cerione et al. 1985). These results suggest that the inhibitory guanyl nucleotide binding protein may be involved in modulating both maximal agonist-induced stimulation of adenylate cyclase activity, as well as the inhibition of this activity. It has also been shown that the inhibitory guanyl nucleotide binding protein can be phosphorylated by protein kinase C (Katada et al. 1985), and that selective inactivation of this protein by the Bordetella pertussis toxin results in a decrement of receptor-mediated inositol phospholipid breakdown in the absence of changes in cyclic AMP metabolism (Nakamura and Ui 1983). These findings suggest the possibility that in some systems, the inhibitory guanyl nucleotide binding protein might exert its primary effects through phosphatidylinositol turnover, and play an indirect or secondary role in the inhibition of adenylate cyclase activity. Indeed, it is possible that the soluble, dissociated alpha subunits of the guanyl nucleotide binding proteins, subject to various intracellular modifications such as phosphorylation, may interact with effector systems other than adenylate cyclase (Gilman 1984; Rodbell 1985).

The stimulatory or inhibitory activation cycle is apparently 'turned off' through the hormone-stimulated hydrolysis of GTP by a GTPase activity associated with the guanyl nucleotide binding proteins (Brandt et al. 1983). This results in binding of GDP to the guanyl nucleotide binding protein and termination of the activation or inhibition of catalytic activity by the dissociated components (Cassel and Selinger 1976). Sodium ions also attenuate the activation of the stimulatory or inhibitory guanyl nucleotide binding proteins through an as yet undesignated site present in both systems (Jakobs *et al.* 1984b). Alterations in the lipid microenvironment of plasma membranes can result in changes in adenylate cyclase activity due to facilitation or inhibition of coupling between receptor and catalytic subunit (Helmreich and Elson 1984). This suggests that receptors or guanyl nucleotide binding proteins may move about independently in the plasma membrane, coupling via 'collision', or some other means induced by a physiological/pharmacological stimulus (DeLean *et al.* 1980; Neufeld *et al.* 1980; Levitzki 1982).

19.4.2   Activation of adenylate cyclase by calmodulin

One of the important endogenous modulators of adenylate cyclase activity is the calcium-binding protein calmodulin. Calmodulin-stimulated adenylate cyclase activity has been demonstrated in many tissues (see MacNeil *et al.* 1985 for review). Stimulation of adenylate cyclase by calmodulin is calcium-dependent over a narrow range of relatively low calcium ion concentrations (e.g. 10^{-8} to 10^{-7} M free calcium ion; see MacNeil *et al.* 1985). Higher concentrations of calcium ion inhibit adenylate cyclase activity. Interestingly, concentrations of calcium ion that inhibit adenylate cyclase stimulate other Ca^{2+}-dependent enzymes, such as phosphodiesterase, which requires micromolar concentrations of calcium ion for activation (Potter *et al.* 1980 and see Cheung and Storm 1982; MacNeil *et al.* 1985). This suggests that alterations in the concentration or distribution of free calcium could have profound effects on the intracellular concentration of cyclic AMP. Concentrations of free calcium ion which are thought to be present in the resting cell are optimal for calmodulin-stimulated adenylate cyclase activity (10^{-7} M or less), whereas the higher concentrations of calcium ion which are optimal for calmodulin-stimulated phosphodiesterase activity (10^{-7} to 10^{-5}), and which would inhibit adenylate cyclase activity, occur only transiently after hormone or neurotransmitter stimulation (Kretsinger 1979; Borle 1981).

While the stimulation of adenylate cyclase activity by calcium ion in a given tissue appears to be conferred by endogenous calmodulin (Brostrom *et al.* 1975; Cheung *et al.* 1975), the inhibition of this activity at higher (micromolar) concentrations of calcium is apparently independent of calmodulin. This suggests that calcium may have a direct effect on adenylate cyclase activity, or that this Ca^{2+}-dependent inhibition may be mediated by some factor other than calmodulin.

The mechanism by which calmodulin activates adenylate cyclase is not yet understood; the available evidence suggests that the interaction of calmodulin and the various components of the adenylate cyclase system is extremely complex. As with phosphodiesterase, adenylate cyclase also appears to exist in at least two forms, one being sensitive to calmodulin, the other insensitive (Brostrom *et al.* 1977, 1978; Treisman *et al.* 1983). A number of studies suggest that calmodulin acts directly at the catalytic subunit of the enzyme. Calmodulin can activate an isolated or detergent-solubilized guanyl nucleotide-insensitive catalytic unit of brain adenylate cyclase (Salter *et al.* 1981; Sano *et al.* 1983), and several investigators have shown that GTP is not required for calmodulin-stimulated enzyme activity in both neural and non-neural tissue (Le Donne and Coffee 1980; Heideman *et al.* 1982; Seamon and Daly 1982; Pinkus *et al.* 1983). Moreover, studies showing that elevated temperatures differentially inhibit guanyl nucleotide- and calmodulin-stimulated adenylate cyclase activities suggest that guanyl nucleotides and calmodulin are acting at different sites on the enzyme complex (Malnoe *et al.* 1983).

Other studies, however, suggest that calmodulin can interact at the level of the guanyl nucleotide binding protein. In neural tissues it has been shown that the sensitivity of adenylate cyclase to activation by neurotransmitters is increased by the calcium–calmodulin complex (Gnegy and Treisman 1981; Gnegy *et al.* 1984), and synergistic effects between calmodulin- and guanyl nucleotide-stimulated adenylate cyclase activities have been reported (Heideman *et al.* 1982; Treisman *et al.* 1983). Furthermore, in a partially purified calmodulin- and guanyl nucleotide-insensitive adenylate cyclase preparation from brain, both sensitivities were restored upon reconstitution with a membrane preparation containing guanyl nucleotide binding protein. Under these conditions, the calmodulin sensitivity of this enzyme activity was only seen in the presence of guanyl nucleotide (Toscano *et al.* 1979). There are also data from brain suggesting that guanyl nucleotide and calmodulin compete for a single component of adenylate cyclase (Treisman *et al.* 1983). Finally, there is evidence that calmodulin may also be involved in guanyl nucleotide-induced inhibition of adenylate cyclase activity in brain (Girardot *et al.* 1983).

Thus, it appears that calmodulin may act at the guanyl nucleotide binding protein or the catalytic subunit of adenylate cyclase, or both, in a manner that has yet to be elucidated.

19.4.3   Strategies for inhibiting adenylate cyclase activity

Because of the ternary composition of the adenylate cyclase system, there are multiple sites at which a drug might act to inhibit the enzyme activity (see Fig. 19.4). The possibility of specifically manipulating adenylate cyclase activity through any one or combination of these sites provides a potential for greater selectivity of drug action, particularly as there already exists an endogenous mechanism for inhibition as well as activation of adenylate cyclase activity. As illustrated in Fig. 19.4, potential targets for drug-induced inhibition of adenylate cyclase activity include the receptor (R_s or R_i), the guanyl nucleotide binding protein (N_s or N_i), the catalytic subunit (C), or calmodulin. Each of these is discussed in turn below.

19.4.3.1   *Inhibition of receptor-mediated adenylate cyclase activity*

Adenylate cyclase activity may be inhibited by the use of selective ligands that directly stimulate receptors negatively coupled to adenylate cyclase (R_i), or antagonize receptors positively coupled to adenylate cyclase (R_s), or both. Furthermore, chronic or persistent treatment with (R_s) receptor agonists leads to desensitization or down-regulation of receptor-stimulated adenylate cyclase activity in many systems (Perkins and Harden 1984; Sibley and Lefkowitz 1985). Thus, it is also possible to decrease adenylate cyclase activity by desensitization through the continuous exposure of the stimulatory receptor to agonist. Some examples of these drugs, and the receptor subtypes upon with they act, are shown in Table 19.2.

Table 19.2   Representative list of receptor subtypes and their prototypical agonists and antagonists that are positively or negatively coupled to adenylate cyclase through stimulatory guanyl nucleotide (N_s) or inhibitory guanyl nucleotide (N_i) binding proteins.

Hormone or Neurotransmitter	Receptor sub-type	Drugs	
		Agonist	Antagonist
Receptors coupled to N_s			
DA	D_1	SKF 38393	SCH 23390
NA = ADR	Beta$_1$	Hydroxybenzyl-isoproterenol	Dihydroalprenolol
ADR > NA	Beta$_2$	Salbutamol	Hydroxybenzylpindolol
AD	A_2	2-chloro-adenosine	1,3-dipropyl-8-(*p*-carboxyl)xanthine
HA	H_2	—	Cimetidine
Receptors Coupled to N_i			
Da	D_2	LY 171555	Sulpiride
NA > ADR	Alpha$_2$	Clonidine	Yohimbine
AD	A_1	N^6-*R*-Cyclohexyladenosine	1,3-dipropyl-8-phenyl-xanthine
OP	Delta	D-Pen^2,D-Pen^5-enkephalin	ICI-154,129

Other receptor sub-types that appear to be coupled to adenylate cyclase have been described, but are less well characterized. The ligands listed above may exhibit only relative selectivity for their receptor sub-types.

A dashed line indicates that a selective ligand has not yet been identified. Relative potencies of neurotransmitters at a given receptor are indicated by = or > signs. DA = dopamine; NA = noradrenalin. ADR = adrenalin; AD = adenosine; HA = histamine; OP = opiates.

The advantage of altering adenylate cyclase activity by modulating the receptor component of the enzyme is that it is possible to manipulate a discrete, functional neurotransmitter or hormone system without inducing global changes in adenylate cyclase activity. Moreover, such treatments can readily be applid *in vivo*.

Another strategy for inhibiting adenylate cyclase activity is through the use of agents that affect coupling of the receptor to the guanyl nucleotide binding protein (N). The lipid and cholesterol composition of the plasma membrane is a primary determinant of receptor–guanyl nucleotide binding protein coupling efficacy (Helmreich and Elson 1984). Manipulations of membrane fluidity or structure through alterations in composition of the lipid bilayer can result in a decrease in the coupling of receptor to stimulatory guanyl nucleotide binding protein. For example, treatment of membranes with the polyene antibiotics filipin (11) or amphotericin B (12), both of which complex with membrane cholesterol, result in a decrease in hormone-stimulated adenylate cyclase activity (DeKruijiff *et al.* 1974; Puchwein *et al.* 1974). Futhermore, procedures that either elevate or decrease cholesterol concentration in plasma membranes lead to an inhibition of hormone-stimulated adenylate cyclase

Filipin (C$_{35}$H$_{58}$O$_{11}$)
11

Amphotericin B (C$_4$H$_{73}$NO$_{17}$)
12

activity (Whetton *et al.* 1983 a, b). Purified ganglioside preparations inhibit hormone and NaF-stimulated adenylate cyclase activity in human thyroid membranes, depending upon the position of sialic acid residues (Dacremont *et al.* 1984). These findings suggest the possibility that endogenous gangliosides within cell membranes may modulate adenylate cyclase activity *in vivo* (Dacremont *et al.* 1984). Local anaesthetics, such as lidocaine (**13**) and procainamide (**14**), have also been reported to influence brain adenylate cyclase activity through presumed alterations in the state of membrane microviscosity (Illiano *et al.* 1980, 1983).

Lidocaine ($C_{14}H_{22}N_2O$)
13

procainamide-HCl ($C_{13}H_{22}ClN_3O$)
14

19.4.3.2 *Inhibition of guanyl nucleotide-mediated adenylate cyclase activity*

Factors that selectively promote the dissociation of the alpha and beta/gamma subunits of the inhibitory guanyl nucleotide binding protein (N_i), or inhibit the dissociation of the stimulatory protein (N_s), should lead to increased inhibitory activity of adenylate cyclase. The activation of both N_s and N_i is magnesium-dependent; however, magnesium requirements differ for the two guanyl nucleotide binding proteins, with N_i exhibiting a 1000-fold higher affinity for magnesium than N_s (Jakobs *et al.* 1984a). Moreover, the inhibitory guanyl nucleotide binding protein (N_i) is activated at about five- to ten-fold greater concentrations of GTP than the stimulatory protein (N_s) (Jakobs *et al.* 1984a). Thus, it might be possible to titrate selectively low magnesium and high GTP concentrations to enhance the activation of N_i preferentially over that of N_s. This approach might be particularly effective when combined with a stimulatory receptor antagonist to 'silence' stimulatory guanyl nucleotide-mediated activity.

Since displacement of GDP by GTP is the critical reaction step in the activation of the stimulatory guanyl nucleotide binding protein (N_s), one means of arresting this reaction is through the binding of stable, slowly reversible GDP analogues to the guanyl nucleotide binding site. Thus, compounds such as GDP-beta-s (Jakobs 1983), or the *N*-chloroacetylhydrazones of oxoGTP and oxoGDP (Perfilyeva *et al.* 1985) have been used to substitute for GDP, and prevent the GTP-induced activation of N_s.

Similarly, the selective stimulation of GTPase activity associated with the stimulatory guanyl nucleotide binding protein (N_s) would also lead to a faster inactivation of N_s, with a subsequent overall decline in adenylate cyclase activity. It has been postulated that some inhibitory neurotransmitters may exert their effects by stimulating a GTPase associated with the stimulatory guanyl nucleotide binding protein (Koski and Klee 1981). However, it now appears that this inhibitory hormone-stimulated GTPase activity is, in fact, associated with the inhibitory guanyl nucleotide binding protein (Jakobs and Schultz 1983).

Activation of the guanyl nucleotide binding proteins may also be prevented by treating intact cells or membranes with the sulphydryl alkylating agent N-ethylmaleimide (NEM) (15). A critical sulphydryl group involved in the activation of adenylate cyclase is thought to be located directly on the alpha subunit of the guanyl nucleotide binding protein near the GTP binding site. It is believed that this region is exposed by a conformational change in the guanyl nucleotide binding protein when hormone or neurotransmitter is bound to the receptor (Heidenreich et al. 1982; Suen et al. 1982). Although the inhibitory guanyl nucleotide binding protein (N_i) is more sensitive to NEM than the stimulatory protein (N_s) (Harden et al. 1982; Jakobs et al. 1982), if NEM were used in the presence of an inhibitory receptor antagonist, it should be possible to protect N_i from inactivation by NEM, and impair the function of N_s directly.

N-ethylmaleimide ($C_6H_2NO_2$)

15

Another strategy for inhibiting the stimulatory guanyl nucleotide binding protein has evolved because both stimulatory and inhibitory proteins have been purified to homogeneity (Northup et al. 1980; Bokoch et al. 1984; Codina et al. 1984). The purification of these proteins creates the possibility of developing selective antibodies against them, which could be used for in vivo immunoneutralization experiments. The immunoneutralization approach has already proved successful in demonstrating inhibition of the activity of a number of neural peptides and proteins (Cheramy et al. 1978; Rapport et al. 1978; Rivier et al. 1982; Wright et al. 1982). A related strategy is based on the ability of complementary nucleic acids to hybridize to mRNA and thus inhibit the translation of encoded protein (Mizuno et al. 1984; Izant and Weintraub 1985; Melton 1985). This approach, which has been used to inhibit selectively the translation of diverse proteins, including globin, thymidine kinase, and beta-galactosidase (Pestka et al. 1984; Izant and Weintraub 1985; Melton 1985), requires the complementary nucleic acid sequence and the ability to transfect the nucleic acid probe into the cell. A first step in this direction has been the recent cloning of complementary DNA for the alpha subunit of N_s mRNA, as well as the development of an antibody against this protein subunit (Mumby *et al.* 1986; Robishaw *et al.* 1986).

19.4.3.3   *Inhibition of the catalytic subunit of adenylate cyclase*

The design of agents that directly and specifically inhibit the catalytic subunit of mammalian adenylate cyclase is hampered by a paucity of information. The enzyme requires manganese or magnesium ion for activation [independent of the magnesium ion requirement for activation of (N)] (Garbers and Johnson 1975; Neer 1979; Cech and Maguire 1982; Jakobs *et al.* 1984a), and it may be that high concentrations of calcium ion inhibit adenylate cyclase activity through competitive interactions with this metal binding site (Steer and Levitzki 1975; Mahaffee and Ontjes 1980; Lasker *et al.* 1982; Piascik *et al.* 1985). Adenosine diphosphate (ADP) interacts competitively with substrate, ATP, to inhibit catalytic activity, as does 2,3-dialdehyde-ATP, an inhibition which is rendered irreversible following reduction with Na—CNBH$_3$ (Westcott *et al.* 1980). The polyphenolic binaphthalene-dialdehyde, gossypol (**16**), also inhibits adenylate cyclase activity in a concentration-dependent, reversible manner, through competitive interaction with the ATP binding site on the catalytic subunit (Olgiati *et al.* 1984).

Gossypol (C$_{30}$H$_{30}$O$_8$)
16

Adenosine, or adenosine analogues such as dideoxyadenosine, inhibit stimulated adenylate cyclase activity non-competitively with respect to metal ion–ATP substrate (Londos and Preston 1977; Johnson *et al.* 1979; Wolff *et al.* 1981). The low-affinity inhibitory site involved in this reaction appears to be located on or near the catalytic subunit designated the 'P-site' (Premont *et al.* 1979). This site is distinct from the high affinity inhibitory receptor for adenosine ('A$_1$'; see Table 19.2). Inhibition of hormone and guanyl nucleotide-stimulated activity by adenosine at the 'P-site' is metal ion-dependent and is accompanied by a 20-fold increase in the affinity of adenylate cyclase for divalent cations (Johnson 1982).

19.4.3.3 *Inhibition of calmodulin-stimulated adenylate cyclase activity*

The inhibition of calmodulin-stimulated adenylate cyclase activity may be achieved by limiting the availability of calcium ion for binding to calmodulin or by using agents that bind directly to calmodulin, thus altering its biological activity. These strategies have been discussed in detail in the preceding section on phosphodiesterase.

Alternatively, the use of agents that bind directly to the calmodulin-binding site of adenylate cyclase would be a more specific approach. Unfortunately, as discussed above, the exact binding domain of calmodulin on the adenylate cyclase complex is not known. Efforts to isolate the calmodulin-dependent form of adenylate cyclase are continuing (Andreason *et al.* 1983), but the design of a compound that directly inhibits this form of adenylate cyclase must await further characterization of the enzyme.

19.4.4 Agents that inhibit adenylate cyclase at unspecified sites

There exist a number of compounds that inhibit adenylate cyclase activity through as yet undetermined mechanisms. The following is a discussion of some of these agents.

19.4.4.1 *Monovalent cations*

Monovalent cations, particularly sodium and lithium, facilitate inhibition of adenylate cyclase activity in some systems (see Jakobs *et al.* 1981; Cooper 1982). The inhibitory effect of sodium appears to derive from the attenuation of activation of both stimulatory and inhibitory guanyl nucleotide binding proteins (N_s and N_i) (Jakobs *et al.* 1984b). This action of sodium ions appears to be at a site other than the receptor or alpha subunits of N_s or N_i. It appears that sodium may be acting on the beta subunits, or on the catalytic subunit directly (Limbird and Speck 1983; Jakobs *et al.* 1984b). Lithium, a drug with unique therapeutic actions in the treatment of affective disorders, inhibits adenylate cyclase activity in many hormone and neurotransmitter systems (Dousa and Hechter 1970; Baastrup 1980; Geisler *et al.* 1985). There is some evidence that lithium, like sodium, may inhibit the activities of both stimulatory and inhibitory guanyl nucleotide binding proteins (Murphy *et al.* 1973). However, it does not appear that lithium is acting directly on either the guanyl nucleotide binding proteins or on the catalytic subunit of adenylate cyclase (Andersen and Geisler 1984). Lithium also inhibits calmodulin-stimulated adenylate cyclase activity at concentrations lower than are required for inhibition of neurotransmitter-stimulated activity (Geisler *et al.* 1985).

Iodide inhibits stimulation of adenylate cyclase activity by TSH, PGE_1, cholera toxin, and forskolin in thyroid cells (Van Sande and Dumont 1973; Rapoport *et al.* 1975; Helden *et al.* 1985). It is thought that this action of iodide may be caused by the iodination of an adenylate cyclase component or another organic compound that exerts its inhibitory effects at or near the catalytic subunit (Van Sande and Dumont 1973; Rapoport *et al.* 1976). This modification of adenylate cyclase activity is unique to thyroid cells, due to their dependence on iodide metabolism. However, analogous mechanisms of inhibition may occur in other tissue types.

19.4.4.2 *Divalent cations*

As discussed above, divalent (metal) cation is essential for adenylate cyclase activation. Therefore EGTA may be used to inhibit this activity, provided the chelator can gain access to a hydrophobic region of the membrane bilayer that is not normally exposed in intact membranes (Neer and Echeverria 1981). Sulakhe and Hoehn (1984) have described two EGTA-sensitive metal ion binding or interaction sites in brain membranes that produce divergent effects on adenylate cyclase activity. Interactions of both sites with Mn^{2+} result in stimulation of adenylate cyclase activity. Yet Co^{2+}, Ca^{2+}, and Sr^{2+} inhibit enzyme activity at the low-affinity site (II), and stimulate activity at the high affinity site (I). The low-affinity, inhibitory site may be located on (N), whereas the high-affinity, stimulatory site may be present in the hydrophobic region of the catalytic subunit, or possibly on calmodulin.

Sc^{3+}, which has a similar ionic radius to Mg^{2+} but an increased charge, has also been used as an Mg^{2+} antagonist, producing inhibition of beta-adrenergic receptor-stimulated adenylate cyclase activity in S49 lymphoma cells (Maguire 1982). The site of action of this ion appeared to be at the Mg^{2+} site on the catalytic subunit of adenylate cyclase.

19.4.4.3 *Other compounds*

Halothane has been shown to inhibit catecholamine-stimulated adenylate cyclase activity in heart (Bernstein *et al.* 1984). This inhibition is dependent upon the presence of a soluble, endogenous factor other than GTP that can be reversibly separated from the adenylate cyclase complex. A specific halothane binding site has been localized in a hydrophobic region within the enzyme complex; it appears to be a binding site for purine bases (Sachsenheimer *et al.* 1977). Thus, the cytosolic factor(s) required for halothane inhibition of adenylate cyclase activity may act by promoting the binding of halothane to these sites within the enzyme complex.

Protamine, the antitumour agent, inhibits guanyl nucleotide- and hormone-stimulated adenylate cyclase activity in liver plasma membranes through a direct action on the enzyme (Kiss and Zamfirova 1983). These effects are thought to be related to the toxic but not to the therapeutic effects of protamine in the treatment of tumour growth.

Cannabimimetic compounds also inhibit hormone-stimulated adenylate cyclase activity in cultured neuroblastoma cell membranes (Howlett 1984). This inhibition appears to be regulated through mechanisms similar to those involved in a receptor-mediated process involving an inhibitory guanyl nucleotide binding protein; however, a specific receptor for these compounds has not yet been identified (Howlett 1985; Howlett et al. 1986).

Other 'non-specific' inhibitors of adenylate cyclase activity include a cycloalkyl compound, RMI 12330A (17) (Wiech et al. 1978), and an adenine analogue, SQ 22536 (18) (Harris et al. 1979). The former compound is also a potent inhibitor of phosphodiesterase, as well as of other enzymes that are dependent on magnesium (Grupp et al. 1980; Hunt and Evans 1980).

RMI 12330 A.
17

SQ 22536 [9(tetrahydro-2-furyl)adenine]
18

19.4.5   Theoretical considerations

The physiological significance of endogenous systems or factors that inhibit the activation of adenylate cyclase is currently the subject of vigorous investigation. Presumably, the regional control of cyclic AMP levels through the interaction of both stimulatory and inhibitory adenylate cyclase systems is an important determinant of a particular functional response. Unfortunately, when cyclic AMP levels are measured in heterogeneous tissue homogenates, information about different cellular or subcellular compartments is lost and often the determination of cyclic AMP levels in a whole tissue homogenate does not correlate with other physiological events. Thus, a key to understanding the functional consequences of alterations in adenylate cyclase activity may lie in developing more selective methods for measuring regional changes in enzyme activity within a subcellular compartment of a specific cell type. Similarly, the rational control of this activity may depend upon developing treatments that are selective for a particular level or functional compartment of adenylate cyclase activity. Although most of the inhibitory agents described here are relatively non-specific, it may be possible to enhance the selectivity or efficacy of treatment through a combination of two or more inhibitors. For example, a sub-threshold dose of a non-specific inhibitor of adenylate cyclase activity used in combination with a sub-threshold dose of a selective inhibitory receptor agonist (or stimulatory receptor antagonist) might result in a more complete and selective inhibition of adenylate cyclase activity coupled to a particular receptor system than either treatment alone. Moreover, by combining sub-threshold doses of different inhibitors, it might also be possible to avoid toxic side-effects induced by the administration of high doses of a single inhibitor.

Many of the compounds discussed in this chapter are of limited usefulness *in vivo* because they cannot permeate intact cells. A possible strategy for delivering these drugs to their appropriate targets *in vivo* involves encapsulating the drugs in liposomes (Gregoriadis 1979; Harsch *et al.* 1981). Using this method, the drug is transferred into the cell via endocytosis of the liposome. Moreover, the liposomes may be targeted for specific cell types by attaching to the liposomal membranes antibodies directed against specific cell-surface antigens (Harsch *et al.* 1981; Leserman *et al.* 1981). Thus, it may be possible to deliver an otherwise toxic or impermeable adenylate cyclase or phosphodiesterase inhibitor into a specific cell type, such as a spleen cell, to achieve a tissue-selective inhibition of enzyme activity.

Acknowledgements

This work was supported by funds awarded by the National Institutes of Health (GM 34334), the National Institute of Mental Health (MH 42148) and the Department of Public Welfare, Commonwealth of Pennsylvania.

References

Abou-Sabe, M. (ed). (1976). *Cyclic nucleotides and the regulation of cell growth.* Dowden, Hutchinson & Ross, Stroudsburg, Pa.

Aiba, H, Mori, K., Tanaka, M., Ooi, T., Roy, A., and Danchin, A. (1984). The complete nucleotide sequence of the adenylate cyclase gene of *Escherichia coli. Nucl. Acids Res.,* **12**, 9427–9440.

Amer, M. S. and McKinney, G. R. (1973). Possibilities for drug development based on the cyclic AMP system. *Life Sci.,* **13**, 753–67.

Andersen, P. H. and Geisler, A. (1984). Lithium inhibition of forskolin-stimulated adenylate cyclase. *Neuropsychobiology,* **12**, 1–3.

Andreason, T. J., Heideman, W., Rosenberg, G. B., and Storm, D. R. (1983). Photoaffinity labelling of brain adenylate cyclase preparations with azido [^{125}I]calmodulin. *Fed. Proc. Fed. Am. Soc. Exp. Biol.,* **42**, 1852.

Appelman, M. M., Ariano, M. A., Takemoto, D. J., and Whitson, R. H. (1982). Cyclic nucleotide phosphodiesterases. *Handbook of experimental pharmacology. Cyclic nucleotides I* (ed. J. A. Nathanson and J. W. Kebabian), vol. 58, pp. 261–300. Springer, Berlin.

Baastrup, P. C. (1980). Lithium in the prophylactic treatment of recurrent affective disorders. In *Handbook of lithium therapy* (ed. F. N. Johnson), pp. 26–38. MTP Press, London.

Baginski, E. S., Foa, P. P., and Zak, B. (1967). Microdetermination of inorganic phosphate, phospholipids, and total phosphate in biologic materials. *Clin. Chem.,* **13**, 326–32.

Bergstrand, H., Kristoffersson, J., Lundquist, B., and Schurmann, A. (1977). Effects of antiallergic agents, compound 48/80 and some reference inhibitors on the activity of partially purified human lung tissue adenosine cyclic 3′,5′-monophosphate and guanosine cyclic 3′,5′-monophosphate phosphodiesterases. *Mol. Pharmacol.*, **13**, 38–43.

Bernstein, K. J., Verosky, M., and Triner, L. (1984). Halothane inhibition of canine myocardial adenylated cyclase—modulation by endogenous factors. *Anesth. Analg.*, **63**, 285–9.

Birnbaumer, L. (1973). Hormone-sensitive adenylyl cyclases: useful models for studying hormone receptor functions in cell-free systems. *Biochim. Biophys. Acta*, **300**, 129–58.

Bitensky, M. W. and Gorman R. E. (1973). Cellular responses to cyclic AMP. *Prog. Biophys.*, **26**, 411–61.

Blumenthal, D. K. and Stull, J. T. (1980). Activation of skeletal muscle myosin light chain kinase by calcium $(2+)$ and calmodulin. *Biochemistry*, **19**, 5608–14.

Bockaert, J. and Sebben-Perez, M. (1983). Adenylate cyclase inhibition by hormones. The Mg^{2+} hypothesis. *FEBS Lett.*, **161**, 113–16.

Bokoch, G. M., Katada, T., Northup, J. K., Ui, M., and Gilman, A. G. (1984). Purification and properties of the inhibitory nucleotide-binding component of adenylate cyclase. *J. Biol. Chem.*, **259**, 3560–7.

Bonnet, K. A. (1983). Cyclic nucleotide metabolism. *Handbook of neurochemistry* (2nd edn), Vol 4 *Enzymes in the nervous system* (ed. A. Lajtha), Plenum, New York. pp. 331–366.

Borle, A. B. (1981). Control, modulation and regulation of cell calcium. *Rev. Physiol. Biochem. Pharmacol.*, **90**, 13–153.

Bostrom, S. L., Ljung, B., Mardh, S., Forsen, S., and Thulin, E. (1981). Interaction of the antihypertensive drug felodipine with calmodulin. *Nature (London)*, **292**, 777–8.

Brandt, D. R., Asano, T., Pederson, S. E., and Ross, E. M. (1983). Reconstitution of catecholamine-stimulated guanosine triphosphatase activity. *Biochemistry*, **22**, 4357–62.

Braun, W., Lichtenstein, L. M., and Parker, C. W., (1974). *Cyclic AMP, cell growth, and the immune response*. Springer, New York.

Breckenridge, B. McL. (1970). Cyclic AMP and drug action. *Ann. Rev. Pharmacol.*, **10**, 19–34.

Brostrom, C. O. and Wolff, D. J. (1976). Calcium-dependent cyclic nucleotide phosphodiesterase from brain: comparison of adenosine 3′,5′-monophosphate and guanosine 3′5′-monophosphate as substrates. *Arch. Biochem. Biophys.*, **172**, 301–11.

Brostrom, C. O., Huang, Y. C., Breckenridge, B. M., and Wolff, D. J. (1975). Identification of a calcium-binding protein as a calcium-dependent regulator of brain adenylate cyclase. *Proc. Nat. Acad. Sci. USA*, **72**, 64–8.

Brostrom, C. O., Brostrom, M. A., and Wolff, D. J. (1977). Calcium-dependent adenylate cyclase from rat cerebral cortex: reversible activation by sodium fluoride. *J. Biol. Chem.*, **252**, 5677–85.

Brostrom, M. A., Brostrom, C. O., and Wolff, D. J. (1978). Calcium-dependent adenylate cyclase from rat cerebral cortex: activation by guanine nucleotides. *Arch. Biochem. Biophys.*, **191**, 341–50.

Brown, E. M. (1980). Calcium – regulated phosphodiesterase in bovine parathyroid cells. *Endocrinology*, **107**, 1998–2003.

Brown, B. L., Walker, S. W., and Tomlinson, S. (1985). Calcium calmodulin and hormone secretion. *Clin. Endocrinol.*, **23**, 201–18.

Butcher, R. W. and Sutherland, E. W. (1962). Adenosine 3′5′-phosphate in biological materials I: purification and properties of cyclic 3′,5′-nucleotide phosphodiesterase and use of this enzyme to characterize adenosine 3',5'-phosphate in human urine. *J. Biol. Chem.*, **237**, 1244–50.

Casperson, G. F., Walker, N., and Bourne, H. R. (1985). Isolation of the gene encoding adenylate cyclase in *Saccharomyces cerevisiae. Proc. Nat. Acad. Sci. USA*, **82**, 5060–3.

Cassel, D. and Selinger, Z. (1976). Catecholamine stimulated GTPase activity in turkey erythrocyte membranes. *Biochim. Biophys. Acta*, **452**, 538–45.

Cassel, D. and Selinger, Z. (1977). Mechanism of adenylate cyclase activation by cholera toxin: inhibition of GTP hydrolysis at the regulatory site. *Proc. Nat. Acad. Sci. USA*, **74**, 3307–11.

Cech, S. Y. and Maguire, M. E. (1982). Magnesium regulation of the beta-receptor–adenylate cyclase complex I. Effects of manganese on receptor binding and cyclase activation. *Mol. Pharmacol.*, **22**, 267–73.

Cehovic, G. and Robison, G. A., ed. (1979). *Cyclic nucleotides and therapeutic perspectives.* Pergamon Press, New York.

Cerione, R. A., Staniszewski, C., Caron, M. G., Lefkowitz, R. J., Codina, J., and Birnbaumer, L. (1985). A role for N_i in the hormonal stimulation of adenylate cyclase. *Nature (London)*, **318**, 293–5.

Chao, S.-H., Suzuki, Y., Zysk, J. R., and Cheung, W. Y. (1984). Activation of calmodulin by various metal cations as a function of ionic radius. *Mol. Pharmacol.*, **26**, 75–82.

Chasin, M., ed. (1972). *Methods in cyclic nucleotide research.* Marcel Dekker, New York.

Chasin, M., and Harris, D. N. (1976). Inhibitors and activators of cyclic nucleotide phosphodiesterase. *Adv. Cyclic Nucleotide Res.*, **7**, 225–64.

Cheramy, A., Michelot, R., Leviel, V., Nieoullon, A., and Glowinski, J. (1978). Effect of the immunoneutralization of substance P in the cat substantia nigra on the release of dopamine from dendrites and terminals of dopaminergic neurons. *Brain Res.*, **155**, 404–8.

Cheung, W. Y. (1970). Cyclic 3',5'-nucleotide phosphodiesterase: demonstration of an activator. *Biochem. Biophys. Res. Commun.*, **38**, 533–538.

Cheung, W. Y. and Storm, D. R. (1982). Calmodulin regulation of cyclic AMP metabolism. In *Handbook of experimental pharmacology* (ed. J. A. Nathanson and J. W. Kebabian), Vol. 58, pp. 301–23. Springer, New York.

Cheúng, W. Y., Bradham, L. S., Lynch, T. J., Lin, Y. M., and Tallant, E. A. (1975). Protein activator of cyclic 3',5'-nucleotide phosphodiesterase of bovine or rat brain also activates its adenylate cyclase. *Biochem. Biophys. Res. Commun.*, **66**, 1055–62.

Ciminó M, and Weiss, B. (1988). Characteristics of the binding of phenoxybenzamine to calmodulin. *Biochem. Pharmacol.*, in press.

Codina, J., Hildebrandt, J. D., Sekura, R. D., Birnbaumer, M., Bryan, J., Manclark, R., Lyengar, R., and Birnbaumer, L. (1984). N_s and N_i, the stimulatory and inhibitory regulatory components of adenylate cyclases. *J. Biol. Chem.*, **259**, 5781–6.

Colombani, P. M. Robb, A., and Hess, A. D. (1985). Cyclosporin A binding to calmodulin: a possible site of action on T lymphocytes. *Science*, **228**, 337–9.

Comte, M., Maulet, Y., and Cox, J. A. (1983). Ca^{2+}-dependent high–affinity complex formation between calmodulin and melittin. *Biochem. J.*, **209**, 269–72.

Cooper, D. M. F. (1982). Bimodal regulation of adenylate cyclase. *FEBS Lett.*, **138**, 157–63.

Cooper, D. M. F. and Seamon, K. B. (ed.) (1985). Dual regulation of adenylate cyclase. In *Advances in cyclic nucleotide and protein phosphorylation research*, Vol. 19. Raven, New York.

Cox, J. A. (1984). Sequential events in calmodulin on binding with calcium and interaction with target enzymes. *Fed. Proc. Fed. Am. Soc. Exp. Biol.*, **43**, 3000–4.

Cox, J. L. and Harrison, S. D. (1983) Correlation of metal toxicity with *in vitro* calmodulin inhibition. *Biochem. Biophys. Res. Commun.*, **115**, 106–111.

Cox, J. A., Malnoe, A., and Stein, E. A. (1981). Regulation of brain cyclic nucleotide phosphodiesterase by calmodulin: a quantitative analysis. *J. Biol. Chem.*, **256**, 3218–22.

Cox, J. A., Comte, M., and Stein, E. A. (1982). Activation of human erythrocyte Ca^{2+}-dependent Mg^{2+}-activated ATPase by calmodulin and calcium: quantitative analysis. *Proc. Nat. Acad. Sci. USA*, **79**, 4265–9.

Cox, J. A., Comte, M., Fitton, J. E., and DeGrado, W. F. (1985). The interaction of calmodulin with amphiphilic peptides. *J. Biol. Chem.*, **260**, 2527–34.

Dacremont, G., DeBaets, M., Kaufman, J. M., Elewaut, A., and Vermeulen, A. (1984). Inhibition of adenylate cyclase activity of human thyroid membranes by gangliosides. *Biochim. Biophys. Acta*, **770**, 142–7.

Dalgarno, D. C., Klevit, R. E., Levine, B. A., Scott, G. M. M., Williams, R. J. P., Gergely, J., Grabarek, Z., Leavis, P. C., Grand, R. J. A., and Drabikowski, W. (1984). The nature of the trifluoperazine binding sites on calmodulin and troponin-C. *Biochim. Biophys. Acta*, **791**, 164–172.

Daly, J. (1977). *Cyclic nucleotides in the nervous system.* Plenum, New York.

DeGrado, W. F., Prendergast, F. G., Wolfe, H. R., and Cox, J. A. (1985). The design, synthesis and characterization of tight-binding inhibitors of calmodulin. *J. Cell. Biochem.*, **29**, 83–93.

DeKruijiff, B., Gerritsen, W. J., Oerlemans, A., Demel, R. A., and Van Deenen, L. L. M. (1974). Polyene antibiotic-sterol interactions in membranes of *Acholeplasma laidlawii* cells and lecithin liposomes I. Specificity of the membrane permeability changes induced by the polyene antibiotics. *Biochim. Biophys. Acta*, **339**, 30–43.

DeLean, A., Stadel, J. M., and Lefkowitz, R. J. (1980). A ternary complex model explains the agonist-specific binding properties of the adenylate-cyclase coupled beta-adrenergic receptor. *J. Biol. Chem.*, **255**, 7108–17.

Dousa, T. P. and Hechter, O. (1970). Lithium and brain adenylate cyclase. *Lancet*, **i**, 834–5.

Earl, C. Q., Prozialeck, W. C., and Weiss, B. (1984). Interaction of alpha adrenergic antagonists with calmodulin. *Life Sci.*, **35**, 525–34.

Egrie, J. C., Campbell, J. A., Flangas, A. L., and Siegel, F. L. (1977). Regional, cellular and subcellular distribution of calcium-activated cyclic nucleotide phosphodiesterase and calcium-dependent regulator in porcine brain. *J. Neurochem.*, **28**, 1207–13.

Epstein, P. M., Fiss, K., Hachisu, R., and Andrenyak, D. M. (1982). Interaction of calcium antagonists with cyclic AMP phosphodiesterases and calmodulin. *Biochem. Biophys. Res. Commun.*, **105**, 1142–9.

Folco, G. and Paoletti, R., ed. (1978). *Molecular biology and pharmacology of cyclic nucleotides.* Elsevier-North Holland, Amsterdam.

Friedman, D. L. (1976). Role of cyclic nucleotides in cell growth and differentiation. *Physiol. Rev.*, **56**, 652–708.

Garbers, D. L. and Johnson, R. A. (1975). Metal and metal–ATP interactions with brain and cardiac adenylate cyclase. *J. Biol. Chem.*, **250**, 8449–56.

Garbers, D. L. and Radany, E. W. (1981). Characteristics of the soluble and particulate forms of guanylate cyclase. In *Advances in cyclic nucleotide research* (ed. J. Dumont, P. Greengard and G. A. Robison), Vol. 14, pp. 241–54. Raven Press, New York.

Garst, J. E., Kramer, G. L., Wu, Y. J., and Wells, J. N. (1976). Inhibition of separated forms of phosphodiesterases from pig coronary arteries by uracils and by 7-substituted derivatives of 1-methyl-1,3-isobutylxanthine. *J. Med. Chem.*, **19**, 499–503.

Geisler, A., Klysner, R., and Andersen, P. H. (1985). Influence of lithium *in vitro* and in *vivo* on the catecholamine-sensitive cerebral adenylate cyclase systems. *Acta Pharmacol. Toxicol.*, **56**, (Suppl. 1), 80–97.

Gerzer, R., Hofmann, F., Bohme, E., Ivanova, K., Spies, C. and Schultz, G. (1981). Purification of soluble guanylate cyclase without loss of stimulation by sodium nitroprusside. In *Advances in cyclic nucleotide research* (ed. J. Dumont, P. Greengard, and G. A. Robison), Vol. 14, pp. 255–61. Raven Press, New York.

Giedroc, D. P., Keravis, T. M., Staros, J. V., Ling, N., Wells, J. N., and Puett, D. (1985). Functional properties of covalent beta-endorphin peptide/calmodulin complexes: chlorpromazine binding and phosphodiesterase activation. *Biochemistry*, **24**, 1203–11.

Gietzen, K., Delgado, E. S., and Bader, H. (1983). Compound 48/80: a powerful and specific inhibition of calmodulin-dependent Ca^{2+}-transport ATPase. *IRCS Med. Sci. Biochem.*, **11**, 12–13.

Gietzen, K., Sadorf, I., and Bader, H., (1982). A model for the regulation of the calmodulin-dependent enzymes erythrocyte Ca^{2+}-transport ATPase and brain phosphodiesterase by activators and inhibitors. *Biochem. J.*, **207**, 541–8.

Gill, D. M. and Meren, R. (1978). ADP-ribosylation of membrane proteins catalyzed by cholera toxin: basis for the activation of adenylate cyclase. *Proc. Nat. Acad. Sci. USA*, **75**, 3050–4.

Gilman, A. G. (1984). G proteins and dual control of adenylate cyclase. *Cell*, **36**, 577–9.

Girardot, J.-M., Kempf, J., and Cooper, D. M. F. (1983). Role of calmodulin in the effect of guanyl nucleotides on rat hippocampal adenylate cyclase: involvement of adenosine and opiates. *J. Neurochem.*, **41**, 848–59.

Gnegy, M. E. and Treisman, G. (1981). Effect of calmodulin on dopamine-sensitive adenylate cyclase activity in rat striatal membranes. *Mol. Pharmacol.*, **19**, 256–63.

Gnegy, M. E., Muirhead, N., Roberts-Lewis, J. M., and Treisman, G. (1984). Calmodulin stimulates adenylate cyclase activity and increases dopamine activation in bovine retina. *J. Neurosci.*, **4**, 2712–17.

Greenberg, L. H., Troyer, E., Ferrendelli, J. A., and Weiss, B. (1978). Enzymatic regulation of the concentration of cyclic GMP in mouse brain. *Neuropharmacology*, **17**, 737–45.

Greengard, P. (1978). *Cyclic nucleotides, phosphorylated proteins, and neuronal function.* Raven Press, New York.

Greengard, P. and Costa, E. (1970). *Role of cyclic AMP in cell function.* Raven Press, New York.

Greengard, P. and Robison, G. A., ed. (1972–86). *Advances in cyclic nucleotide research* Vols 1–20. Raven, New York.

Gregoriadis, G. (ed) (1979). *Drug carriers in biology and medicine.* Academic Press, London.

Grossman, S. L., Saporito, M. S., and Prozialeck, W. C., (1985). Interaction of enzymatically-generated phenothiazine free radicals with calmodulin. *Fed. Proc. Fed. Am. Soc. Exp. Biol.*, **44**, 726.

Grupp, G., Grupp, I. L., Johnson, C. L., Matlib, M. A., Rouslin, W., Schwartz, A., Wallick, E. T., Wang, T., and Wisler, P. (1980). Effects of RMI 12330A, a new inhibitor of adenylate cyclase on myocardial function and subcellular activity. *Br. J. Pharmacol.*, **70**, 429–42.

Guerini, D., Krebs, J., and Carafoli, E. (1984). Stimulation of the purified erythrocyte Ca^{2+}-ATPase by tryptic fragments of calmodulin. *J. Biol. Chem.*, **259**, 15172–7.

Hagmann, J. (1982). Inhibition of calmodulin-stimulated cyclic nucleotide phosphodiesterase by the insecticide DDT. *FEBS Lett.*, **143**, 52–4.

Hait, W. N. and Lazo, J. S. (1986). Calmodulin: a potential target for cancer chemotherapeutic agents. *J. Clin. Oncol.*, **4**, 994–1012.

Harden, T. K., Scheer, A. G., and Smith, M. H. (1982). Differential modification of the interaction of cardiac muscarinic cholinergic and beta-adrenergic receptors with a guanine nucleotide binding component(s). *Mol. Pharmacol.*, **21**, 570–80.

Harris, D. N., Asaad, M. M., Phillips, M. B., Goldenberg, H. J., and Antonaccio, M. J. (1979). Inhibition of adenylate cyclases in human blood platelets by 9-substituted adenine derivatives. *J. Cyclic Nucleotide Res.*, **5**, 125–34.

Harsch, M., Walther, P., and Weder, H. G. (1981). Targeting of monoclonal antibody-coated liposomes to sheep and red blood cells. *Biochem. Biophys. Res. Comm.*, **103**, 1069–76.

Heideman, W., Weirman, B. M., and Storm, D. R. (1982). GTP is not required for calmodulin stimulation of bovine brain adenylate cyclase. *Proc. Nat. Acad. Sci. USA*, **79**, 1462–5.

Heidenreich, K. H., Weiland, G. A., and Molinoff, P. B. (1982). Effects of magnesium and N-ethylmaleimide on the binding of ^{3}H-hydroxybenzylisoproterenol to beta-adrenergic receptors. *J. Biol. Chem.*, **257**, 804–10.

Helden, N.-E., Karlsson, F. A., and Westermark, B. (1985). Inhibition of cyclic AMP formation by iodide in suspension cultures of porcine thyroid follicle cells. *Mol. Cell Endocrinol.*, **41**, 61–7.

Helmreich, E. J. M. and Elson, E. L. (1984). Mobility of proteins and lipids in membranes. *Adv. cyclic nucleotide prot. phosphor. res.*, **18**, 1–61.

Hidaka, H. and Endo, T. (1984). Selective inhibitors of three forms of cyclic nucleotide phosphodiesterase-basic and potential clinical applications. *Adv. Cyclic Nucleotide Res.*, **16**, 245–59.

Hidaka, H., Yamaki, T., Naka, M., Tanaka, T., Hayashi, H., and Kobayashi, R. (1980). Calcium-regulated modulator protein interacting agents inhibit smooth muscle calcium-stimulated protein kinase and ATPase. *Mol. Pharmacol.*, **17**, 66–72.

Hidaka, H., Asano, M. and Tanaka, T. (1981). Activity–structure relationship of calmodulin antagonists: naphthalenesulfonamide derivatives. *Mol. Pharmacol.*, **20**, 571–8.

Hidaka, H., Tanaka, T., and Itoh, H. (1984). Selective inhibitors of three forms of cyclic nucleotide phosphodiesterases. *Trends Pharmacol. Sci.*, 237–9.

Hildebrandt, J. D., Codina, J., Risinger, R., and Birnbaumer, L. (1984). Identification of a (gamma) subunit associated with adenylate cyclase regulatory proteins N_s and N_i. *J. Biol. Chem.*, **259**, 2039–42.

Ho, H. C., Wirch, E., Stevens, F. C., and Wang, J. H. (1977). Purification of a Ca^{2+}-activatable cyclic nucleotide phosphodiesterase from bovine heart by specific interaction with its Ca^{2+}-dependent modulator protein. *J. Biol. Chem.*, **252**, 43–50.

Howlett, A. C. (1984). Inhibition of neuroblastoma adenylate cyclase by cannabinoid compounds. *Life Sci.*, **35**, 1803–10.

Howlett, A. C. (1985). Cannabinoid inhibition of adenylate cyclase. Biochemistry of the response in neuroblastoma cell membranes. *Mol. Pharmacol.*, **27**, 429–36.

Howlett, A. C., Qualy, J. M., and Khachatrian, L. L. (1986). Involvement of G_i in the inhibition of adenylate cyclase by cannabimimetic drugs. *Mol. Pharmacol.*, **29**, 307–13.

Huang, C. Y., Chau, V., Chock, P. B., Wang, J. H., and Sharma, R. K. (1981). Mechanism of activation of cyclic nucleotide phosphodiesterase: requirement of the binding of four Ca^{2+} to calmodulin for activation. *Proc. Nat. Acad. Sci. USA*, **78**, 871–4.

Hunt, N. H. and Evans, T. (1980). RMI 12330A, an inhibitor of cyclic nucleotide phosphodiesterases and adenylate cyclase in kidney preparations. *Biochim. Biophys. Acta*, **613**, 499–506.

Hurwitz, R. L., Hansen, R. S., Harrison, S. A., Martins, T. J., Mumby, M. C., and Beavo, J.

A. (1984). Immunologic approaches to the study of cyclic nucleotide phosphodiesterases. *Adv. Cyclic Nucleotide Prot. Phosphor. Res.*, **16**, 89–106.

Illiano, G., DiDonato, A., Galderisi, R., Chiosi, E., and Paolissi, G. (1980). Membrane stabilizing factors and membrane lipid microviscosity: the effects of local anesthetics. *Ital. J. Biochem.*, **29**, 463–5.

Illiano, G., Chiosi, E., Draetta, G. F., and Laurenza, A. (1983). Relationship between the fluidity of the membrane lipids and the activity of the membrane-bound proteins: the effects of lidocaine on the adenylate cyclase activity of rat myocardium. *Gen. Pharmacol.*, **14**, 669–72.

Inagaki, M. and Hidaka, H. (1984). Two types of calmodulin antagonists: a structurally related interaction. *Pharmacology*, **29**, 75–84.

Izant, J. G. and Weintraub, H. (1985). Constitutive and conditional suppression of exogenous and endogenous genes by anti-sense RNA. *Science*, **229**, 345–52.

Jakobs, K. H. (1983). Determination of the turn-off reaction for the epinephrine-inhibited human platelet adenylate cyclase. *Eur. J. Biochem.*, **132**, 125–30.

Jakobs, K. H. and Schultz, G. (1983). Occurrence of a hormonesensitive inhibitory coupling component of the adenylate cyclase in S49 lymphoma cyc- variants. *Proc. Nat. Acad. Sci. USA*, **80**, 3899–902.

Jakobs, K. H., Aktories, K., and Schultz, G. (1981). Inhibition of adenylate cylase by hormones and neurotransmitters. *Adv. Cyclic Nucleotide Prot. Phosphor. Res.*, **14**, 173–87.

Jakobs, K. H., Lasch, P., Aktories, K., Minuth, M., and Schultz, G. (1982). Uncoupling of alpha-adrenoreceptor-mediated inhibition of human platelet adenylate cyclase by N-ethylmaleimide. *J. Biol. Chem.*, **257**, 2829–33.

Jakobs, K. H., Gehring, U., Gaugler, B., Pfeuffer, T., and Schultz, G. (1983). Occurrence of an inhibitory guanine nucleotidebinding regulatory component of the adenylate cyclase sytem in cyc- variants of S49 lymphoma cells. *Eur. J. Biochem.*, **130**, 605–11.

Jakobs, K. H., Aktories, K., and Schultz, G. (1984a). Mechanisms and components involved in adenylate cyclase inhibition by hormones. *Adv. Cyclic Nucleotide Prot. Phosphor. Res.*, **17**, 135–43.

Jakobs, K. H., Minuth, M., and Aktories, K. (1984b). Sodium regulation of hormonesensitive adenylate cyclase *J. Receptor Res.*, **4**, 443–58.

Janis, R. A. and Triggle, D. J. (1983). New developments in CA^{2+} channel antagonists. *J. Med. Chem.*, **26**, 775–85.

Johnson, J. D. (1983). Allosteric interactions among drug binding sites on calmodulin. *Biochem. Biophys. Res. Commun.*, **112**, 787–93.

Johnson, R. A. (1982). An approach to the identification of adenosine's inhibitory site on adenylate cyclase. *FEBS Lett.*, **140**, 80–4.

Johnson, R. A., Saur, W., and Jakobs, K. H. (1979). Effects of prostaglandin E_1 and adenosine on metal and metal–ATP kinetics of platelet adenylate cyclase. *J. Biol. Chem.*, **254**, 1094–101.

Jost, J.-P. and Rickenberg, H. V. (1971). Cyclic AMP. *Ann. Rev. Biochem.*, **40**, 741–74.

Kahn, R. H. and Lands, W. E. M., (ed.) (1973). *Prostaglandins and cyclic AMP*. Academic Press, New York.

Kakiuchi, S. and Yamazaki, R. (1970). Calcium dependent phosphodiesterase activity and its activating factor (PAF) from brain. *Biochem. Biophys. Res. Commun.*, **41**, 1104–10.

Kakiuchi, S., Yamazaki, R., Teshima, Y., Uenishi, K., and Miyamoto, E. (1975). Multiple cyclic nucleotide phosphodiesterase activities from rat tissues and occurrence of a calcium-plus-magnesium-ion-dependent phosphodiesterase and its protein activator.

Biochem. J., **146**, 109–20.

Katada, T. and Ui, M. (1982). Direct modification of the membrane adenylate cyclase system by islet-activating protein due to ADP-ribosylation of a membrane protein. *Proc. Nat. Acad. Sci. USA*, **79**, 3129–33.

Katada, T., Gilman, A. G., Watanabe, Y., Bauer, S., and Jakobs, K. H. (1985). Protein kinase C phosphorylates the inhibitory guanine-nucleotide-binding regulatory component and apparently suppresses its function in hormonal inhibition of adenylate cyclase. *Eur. J. Biochem.*, **151**, 431–7.

Kataoka, T., Broek, D., and Wigler, M. (1985). DNA sequence and characterization of the *S. cerevisiae* gene encoding adenylate cyclase. *Cell*, **43**, 493–505.

Katoh, N., Wise, B. C., Wrenn, R. W., and Kuo, J. F. (1981). Inhibition by adriamycin of calmodulin-sensitive and phospholipid-sensitive calcium-dependent phosphorylation of endogenous proteins from heart. *Biochem. J.*, **198**, 199–205.

Kiss, Z. and Zamfirova, R. (1983). Protamine inhibits adenylate cyclase activity: a possible reason for the toxicity of protamine. *Experientia*, **39**, 1381–2.

Klainer, L. M., Chi, Y.-M., Freidberg, S. L., Rall, T. W., and Sutherland, E. W. (1962). Adenylate cyclase IV: The effects of neurohormones on the formation of adenosine 3′, 5′-phosphate. *J. Biol. Chem.*, **237**, 1239–43.

Klee, C. B. (1980). Calmodulin: structure-function relationships. In *Calcium and cell function* (ed. W. Y. Cheung), Vol. 1, pp. 59–77. Academic Press, New York.

Klee, C. B. and Vanaman, T. C. (1982). Calmodulin. *Adv. Prot. Chem.*, **35**, 213–321.

Klee, C. B., Crouch, T. H., and Krinks, M. H. (1979). Subunit structure and catalytic properties of bovine brain Ca^{2+}-dependent cyclic nucleotide phosphodiesterase. *Biochemistry*, **18**, 722–9.

Klevit, R. E., Levine, B. A., and Williams R. J. P. (1981). A study of calmodulin and its interaction with trifluoperazine by high resolution ^{1}H NMR spectroscopy. *FEBS Lett.*, **123**, 25–9.

Kochhar, S., Kochhar, V. K., and Sane, P. V. (1986). Isolation, characterization and regulation of isoenzymes of aspartate kinase differentially sensitive to calmodulin from spinach leaves. *Biochem. Biophys. Acta*, **880**, 220–6.

Koski, G. and Klee, W. A. (1981). Opiates inhibit adenylate cyclase by stimulating GTP hydrolysis. *Proc. Nat. Acad. Sci. USA*, **78**, 4185–9.

Kramer, G. L., Garst, J. E., Mitchel, S. S., and Wells, J. N. (1977). Selective inhibition of cyclic nucleotide phosphodiesterases by analogues of 1-methyl-3-isobutylxanthine. *Biochemistry*, **16**, 3316–21.

Krebs, E. G. (1972). Protein kinases. *Curr. Top. Cell Regul.*, **5**, 99–133.

Krebs, J. and Carafoli, E. (1982). Influence of Ca^{2+} and trifluoperazine on the structure of calmodulin: a ^{1}H-nuclear magnetic resonance study. *Eur. J. Biochem.*, **124**, 619–27.

Kretsinger, R. H. (1979). The informational role of calcium in the cytosol. *Adv. Cyclic Nucleotide Res.*, **11**, 1–26.

Krinks, M. H., Haiech, J., Rhoads, A., and Klee, C. B. (1984). Reversible and irreversible activation of cyclic nucleotide phosphodiesterase: separation of the regulatory and catalytic domains by limited proteolysis. *Adv. Cyclic Nucleotide Protein Phosphor. Res.*, **16**, 31–47.

Kuhn, D. M., O'Callagan, J. P., and Lovenberg, W. (1980). The role of calmodulin in the activation of tryptophan hydroxylase by phosphorylating conditions. *Ann. N. Y. Acad. Sci.*, **356**, 399.

Kuo., J. F. and Greengard, P. (1969). Cyclic nucleotide-dependent protein kinases. IV. Widespread occurance of adenosine 3′, 5′-monophosphate-dependent protein kinase in various tissues and phyla of the animal kingdom. *Proc. Nat. Acad. Sci.*, **64**, 1349–55.

La Porte, D. C., Wierman, B. M., and Storm, D. R. (1980). Calcium-induced exposure of a hydrophobic surface on calmodulin. *Biochemistry*, **19**, 3814–3819.

Lasker, R. D., Downs, R. W. Jr., and Aurbach, G. D. (1982). Calcium inhibition of adenylate cyclase: studies in turkey erythrocytes and S49 cyc- cell membranes. *Arch. Biochem. Biophys.*, **216**, 345–55.

LeDonne, N. C. and Coffee, C. J. (1980). Evidence for calmodulin sensitive adenylate cyclase in bovine adrenal medulla. *Ann. N. Y. Acad. Sci.*, **356**, 402–3.

Leserman, L. D., Machy, P., and Barbet, J. (1981). Cell-specific transfer from liposomes bearing monoclonal antibodies. *Nature (London)*, **293**, 226–8.

Levin, R. M. and Weiss, B. (1976). Mechanism by which psychotropic drugs inhibit adenosine cyclic 3′, 5′-monophosphate phosphodiesterase of brain. *Mol. Pharmacol.*, **12**, 581–9.

Levin, R. M. and Weiss, B. (1977). Binding of trifluoperazine to the calcium-dependent activator of cyclic nucleotide phosphodiesterase. *Mol. Pharmacol.* **13**, 690–7.

Levin, R. M. and Weiss, B. (1979). Selective binding of antipsychotics and other psychoactive agents to the calcium-dependent activator of cyclic nucleotide phosphodiesterase. *J. Pharmacol. Exp. Ther.*, **208**, 454–9.

Levin, R. M. and Weiss, B. (1980). Inhibition by trifluoperazine of calmodulin-induced activation of ATPase activity of rat erythrocyte. *Neuropharmacology*, **19**, 169–74.

Levitzki, A. (1982). Activation and inhibition of adenylate cyclase by hormones: mechanistic aspects. *Trends Pharmacol., Sci.*, **5**, 203–8.

Limbird, L. E. (1981). Activation and attenuation of adenylate cyclase. The role of GTP-binding proteins as macromolecular messengers in receptor-cyclase coupling. *Biochem. J.*, **195**, 1–13.

Limbird, L. E. and Speck, J. K. (1983). *N*-ethylmaleimide, elevated temperature, and digitonin solubilization eliminate guanine nucleotide but not sodium effects on human platelet alpha-2-adrenergic receptor–agonist interactions. *J. Cyclic Nucleotide Protein. Phosphor.*, **9**, 191–201.

Lin, Y. M., Liu, Y. P., and Cheung, W. Y. (1974). Cyclic 3′, 5′-nucleotide phosphodiesterase: purification, characterization and active form of the protein activator from bovine brain. *J. Biol. Chem.* **249**, 4943–4954.

Liu, Y. P. and Cheung, W. Y. (1976). Cyclic 3′,5′-nucleotide phosphodiesterase: Ca^{2+} confers more helical conformation to the protein activator. *Biochem. J.*, **251**, 4193–8.

Londos, C. and Preston, M. S. (1977). Regulation by glucagon and divalent cations of inhibition of hepatic adenylate cyclase by adenosine. *J. Biol. Chem.*, **252**, 5951–6.

Lukas, T. J., Marshak, D. R., and Watterson, D. M. (1985). Drug–protein interactions: isolation and characterization of covalent adducts of phenoxybenzamine and calmodulin. *Biochemistry*, **24**, 151–7.

Luthra, M. G. (1982). Trifluoperazine inhibition of calmodulin-sensitive Ca^{2+}-ATPase and calmodulin-insensitive (Na^{+} and K^{+}) and Mg^{2+}-ATPase activities of human and rat red blood cells. *Biochim. Biophys. Acta*, **692**, 271–7.

MacNeil, S., Lakey, T. and Tomlinson, S. (1985). Calmodulin regulation of adenylate cyclase activity. *Cell Calcium*, **6**, 213–26.

Maguire, M. E. (1982). Magnesium regulation of the beta-receptor–adenylate cyclase complex, II. Sc^{3+} as a Mg^{2+} antagonist. *Mol. Pharmacol.*, **22**, 274–80.

Mahaffee, D. D. and Ontjes, D. A. (1980). The role of calcium in the control of adrenal adenylate cyclase. Enhancement of enzyme activation by guanyl-5′-yl imidodiphosphate. *J. Biol. Chem.*, **255**, 1565–71.

Malencik, D. A. and Anderson, S. R. (1982). Binding of simple peptides, hormones and neurotransmitters by calmodulin. *Biochemistry*, **21**, 3480–6.

Malencik, D. A. and Anderson, S. R. (1983). Binding of hormones and neuropeptides by calmodulin. *Biochemistry*, **22**, 1995–2001.

Malnoe, A., Cox, J. A., and Stein, E. A. (1982). Ca^{2+}-dependent regulation of calmodulin binding and adenylate cyclase activation in bovine cerebellar membranes. *Biochim. Biophys. Acta*, **714**, 84–92.

Malnoe, A., Stein, E. A., and Cox, J. A. (1983). Synergistic activation of bovine cerebellum adenylate cyclase by calmodulin and beta-adrenergic agonists. *Neurochem. Int.*, **5**, 65–72.

Manning, D. R. and Gilman, A. G. (1983). The regulatory components of adenylate cyclase and transducin: a family of structurally homologous guanine nucleotide binding proteins. *J. Biol. Chem.*, **258**, 7059–63.

Means, A. R., Tash, J. S., and Chafouleas, J. G. (1982). Physiological implications of the presence, distribution, and regulation of calmodulin in eukaryotic cells. *Physiol. Rev.*, **62**, 1–39.

Melton, D. A. (1985). Injected anti-sense RNAs specifically block messenger RNA translation *in vivo*. *Proc. Nat. Acad. Sci. USA*, **82**, 144–8.

Mills, J. S. and Johnson, J. D. (1985). Metal ions as allosteric regulators of calmodulin. *J. Biol. Chem.*, **260**, 15100–5.

Mills, J. S., Bailey, B., and Johnson, J. D. (1985). Cooperativity among calmodulin's drug binding sites. *Biochemistry*, **24**, 4897–902.

Mizuno, T., Chou, M.-Y., and Inouye, M. (1984). A unique mechanism regulating gene expression: translational inhibition by a complementary RNA transcript (micRNA). *Proc. Nat. Acad. Sci. USA*, **81**, 1966–70.

Mumby, S. M., Kahn, R. A., Manning, B. R., and Gilman, A. G. (1986). Antisera of designed specificity for subunits of guanine nucleotide-binding regulatory proteins. *Proc. Nat. Acad. Sci. USA*, **83**, 265–9.

Murad, F., Lewicki, J. A., Brandwein, H. J., Mittal, C. K., and Waldman, S. A. (1981). Guanylate cyclase: Purification, properties, free radical activation, radiolabeling, and preparation of hybridoma antibodies. In *Advances in cyclic nucleotide research* (ed. J. Dumont, P. Greengard, and G. A. Robison), Vol. 14, pp. 229–39. Raven Press, New York.

Murphy, D. L., Donelly, C., and Moskowitz, J. (1973). Inhibition by lithium of prostaglandin E_1 and norepinephrine effects on cyclic adenosine monophosphate production in human platelets. *Clin. Pharmacol. Ther.*, **14**, 810–14.

Nagao, S., Suzuki, Y., Watanabe, Y., and Nozawa, Y. (1979). Activation by a calcium-binding protein of guanylate cyclase in *Tetrahymena pyriformis*. *Biochem. Biophys. Res. Commun.*, **90**, 261–8.

Nakamura, T. and Ui, M. (1983). Suppression of passive anaphylaxis by pertussis toxin, and islet-activating protein, as a result of inhibition of histamine release from mast cells. *Biochem. Pharmacol.* **32**, 3435–41.

Nathanson, J. A. and Kebabian, J. W. (1982). *Cyclic Nucleotides, I. Biochemistry*, Springer, New York.

Neer, E. J. (1979). Interaction of soluble brain adenylate cyclase with manganese. *J. Biol. Chem.*, **254**, 2089–96.

Neer, E. J. and Echeverria, D. (1981). Effect of Triton X-100 and alamethicin on the susceptibility of brain adenylate cyclase to EGTA inhibition. *Biochem. Pharmacol.*, **30**, 2488–91.

Neufeld, G., Schramm, M. and Weinberg, N. (1980). Hybridization of adenylate cyclase components by membrane fusion and the effect of selective digestion by trypsin. *J. Biol. Chem.*, **255**, 9268–74.

Newton, D. L. and Klee, C. B. (1984). CAPP-calmodulin: a potent competetive inhibitor of calmodulin actions. *FEBS Lett.*, **165**, 269–72.

Newton, D. L., Burke, T. R., Rice, K. C., and Klee, C. B. (1983). Calcium ion dependent covalent modification of calmodulin with norchlorpromazine isothiocyanate. *Biochemistry*, **22**, 5472–6.

Newton, D. L., Oldewurtel, M. D., Krinks, M. H., Shiloach, J., and Klee, C. B. (1984). Agonist and antagonist properties of calmodulin fragments. *J. Biol. Chem.*, **259**, 4419–26.

Newton, D., Klee, C., Woodgett, J., and Cohen, P. (1985). Selective effects of CAPP$_1$/calmodulin on its target proteins. *Biochim. Biophys. Acta*, **845**, 533–9.

Norman, J. A., Ansell, J., and Phillips, M. A. (1983). Dihydropyridine Ca^{2+} entry blockers selectively inhibit peak I cyclic AMP phosphodiesterase. *Eur. J. Pharmacol.*, **93**, 107–12.

Northup, J. K., Sternweis, P. C., Smigel, M. D., Schleifer, L. S., Ross, E. M., and Gilman, A. G. (1980). Purification of the regulatory component of adenylate cyclase. *Proc. Nat. Acad. Sci. USA*, **77**, 6516–20.

Olgiati, K. L., Toscano, D. G., Atkins, W. M., and Toscano, W. A. Jr. (1984). Gossypol inhibition of adenylate cyclase. *Arch. Biochem. Biophys.*, **231**, 411–15.

Palmer, G. C. (1983). Effects of psychoactive drugs on cyclic nucleotides in the central nervous system. *Prog. Neurobiol.* **21**, 1–133.

Payne, M. E. and Soderling, T. R. (1980). Calmodulin-dependent glycogen synthase kinase. *J. Biol. Chem.*, **255**, 8054–6.

Perfilyeva, E. A., Skurat, A. V., Yurkova, M. S., Khropov, Y. V., Bulargina, T. V., and Severin, E. S. (1985). N-chloroacetylhydrazone of oxo-GTP irreversibly inhibits the activating function of GTP-binding protein coupled with adenylate cyclase. *Biochem. Int.*, **11**, 1–9.

Perkins, J. P. and Harden, T. K. (1984). Mechanisms of desensitization of beta-adrenergic receptors. In *Proceedings of the Ninth International Congress on Pharmacology* (ed. J. F. Mitchell, W. Paton, and P. Turner), pp. 85–90. Macmillan, London,

Pestka, S., Daugherty, B. L., Jung, V., Hotta, K., and Pestka, R. K. (1984). Anti-mRNA: specific inhibition of translation of single mRNA molecules. *Proc. Nat. Acad. Sci. USA*, **81**, 7525–8.

Pfeuffer, E., Dreher, R.-M., Metzger, H., and Pfeuffer, T. (1985). Catalytic subunit of adenylate cyclase: purification and identification by affinity crosslinking. *Proc. Nat. Acad. Sci., USA*, **82**, 3086–90.

Piascik, M. T., Addison, B., and Babich, M. (1985). Ca^{2+}-dependent inhibition of smooth muscle adenylate cyclase activity. *Arch. Biochem. Biophys.*, **241**, 28–35.

Pinkus, L. M., Sulimovici, S., Susser, F. I., and Roginsky, M. S. (1983). Involvement of calmodulin in the regulation of adenylate cyclase activity in guinea-pig enterocytes. *Biochim. Biophys. Acta*, 762, 552–9.

Potter, J. D., Piascik, M. T., Wisler, P. L., Robertson, S. P., and Johnson, C. L. (1980). Calcium dependent regulation of brain and cardiac muscle adenylate cyclase. *Ann. N.Y. Acad. Sci.*, **356**, 220–31.

Premont, J., Guillon, G., and Bockaert, J. (1979). Specific Mg^{2+} and adenosine sites involved in a bireactant mechanism for adenylate cyclase inhibition and their probable localization on this enzyme's catalytic component. *Biochem. Biophys. Res. Commun.*, **90**, 513–19.

Prozialeck, W. C. (1983). Structure–activity relationships of calmodulin antagonists. *Ann. Rep. Med. Chem.*, **18**, 203–12.

Prozialeck, W. C. (1984). Interaction of quaternary phenothiazine salts with calmodulin. *J. Pharmacol. Exp. Ther.*, **231**, 473–9.

Prozialeck, W. C. and Weiss, B. (1982). Inhibition of calmodulin by phenothiazines and related drugs: structure-activity relationships. *J. Pharmacol. Exp. Ther.*, **222**, 509–16.

Prozialeck, W. C. and Weiss, B. (1985). Mechanisms of Pharmacologically altering calmodulin activity. In *Calcium in biological systems* (ed. R. P. Rubin, G. B. Weiss, and J. W. Putney) pp. 255–264. Plenum, New York.

Prozialeck, W. C., Cimino, M., and Weiss, B. (1981). Photoaffinity labeling of calmodulin by phenothiazine antipsychotics. *Mol. Pharmacol.*, **19**, 264–9.

Prozialeck, W. C., Wallace, T. L., and Weiss, B. (1983). Chlorpromazine-linked calmodulin: a novel calmodulin antagonist. *Fed. Proc. Fed. Am. Soc. Exp. Biol.*, **42**, 1087.

Puchwein, G., Pfeuffer, T., and Helmreich, E. J. M. (1974). Uncoupling catecholamine activation of pigeon erthrocyte membrane adenylate cyclase by fillipin. *J. Biol. Chem.*, **249**, 3232–40.

Rall, T. W. and Sutherland, E. W. (1962). Adenyl cyclase. II. The enzymatically catalyzed formation of adenosine triphosphate. *J. Biol. Chem.*, **237**, 1228–32.

Rall, T. W., Rodbell, M., and Condliffe, P. (eds) (1969). *The role of adenyl cyclase and cyclic 3',5'-AMP in biological systems*. Fogarty International Center, Bethesda.

Rapoport, B., West, M. N., and Ingbar, S. H. (1975). Inhibitory effects of dietary iodine on the thyroid adenylate cyclase response to thyrotropin in the hypophysectomized rat. *J. Clin. Invest.*, **56**, 516–19.

Rapoport, B., West, M. N., and Ingbar, S. H. (1976). On the mechanisms of inhibition by iodine of the thyroid adenylate cyclase response to thyrotropic hormone. *Endocrinology*, **99**, 11–22.

Rapport, M. M., Darpiak, S. E., and Mahadik, S. P. (1978). Biological activities of antibodies injected into the brain. *Fedn. Proc. Fed. Am. Soc. Ezp. Biol.*, **38**, 2391–6.

Richardt, G., Federolf, G., and Habermann, E. (1985). The interaction of aluminum and other metal ions with calcium–calmodulin-dependent phosphodiesterase. *Arch. Toxicol.*, **57**, 257–9.

Rivier, C., Rivier, J., and Vale, W. (1982). Inhibition of adrenocorticotropic hormone secretion in the rat by immunoneutralization of corticotropin-releasing factor. *Science*, **218**, 377–8.

Robishaw, J. D., Russell, D. W., Harris, B. A., Smigel, M. D., and Gilman, A. G. (1986). Deduced primary structure of the alpha subunit of the GTP-binding stimulatory protein of adenylate cyclase. *Proc. Nat. Acad. Sci. USA.*, **83**, 1251–5.

Robison, G. A., Butcher, R. W., and Sutherland, E. W. (1968). Cyclic AMP. Ann. Rev. Biochem., **37**, 149–73.

Robison, G. A., Butcher, R. W., and Sutherland, E. W. (1971a). *Cyclic AMP*. Academic Press, New York.

Robison, G. A., Nahas, G. G., and Triner, L. (eds) (1971b). *Cyclic AMP and cell function*. New York Academy of Sciences, New York.

Rodbell, M. (1980). The role of hormone receptors and GTP-regulatory proteins in membrane transduction. *Nature (London)*, **284**, 17–22.

Rodbell, M. (1985). Programmable messengers: a new theory of hormone action. *Trends Biochem. Sci.*, **12**, 461–4.

Ross, E. M. and Gilman, A. G. (1980). Biochemical properties of hormone-sensitive cyclase. *Ann. Rev. Biochem.*, **49**, 533–64.

Sachsenheimer, W., Pai, E. F., Schulz, G. E., and Schirmer, R. H. (1977). Halothane binds in the adenine-specific niche of crystalline adenylate kinase. *FEBS Lett.*, **79**, 310–12.

Salter, R. S., Krinks, M. H., Klee, C. B., and Neer, E. J. (1981). Calmodulin activates the isolated catalytic unit of brain adenylate cyclase. *J. Biol. Chem.*, **256**, 9830–3.

Sano, M., Yamazaki, Y., and Mitzutani, A. (1983). Detergent extraction of a regulatory subunit of brain adenylate cyclase and its sensitivity to calmodulin and forskolin. *Biochem. Int.*, **7**, 463–9.

Schramm, M. and Selinger, Z. (1984). Message transmission: receptor controlled adenylate cyclase system. *Science*, **225**, 1350–6.

Schulman, H. and Greengard, P. (1978). Stimulation of brain membrane protein phosphorylation by calcium and an endogenous heat stable protein. *Nature (London)*, **271**, 478–9.

Schultz, J. and Gratzner, H. G., ed. (1973). *The role of cyclic nucleotides in carcinogenesis.* Academic Press, New York.

Seamon, K. B. and Daly, J. W. (1982). Calmodulin stimulation of adenylate cyclase in rat brain membranes does not require GTP. *Life Sci.*, **30**, 1457–64.

Sellinger-Barnette, M. and Weiss, B. (1982). Interaction of beta-endorphin and other opioid peptides with calmodulin. *Mol. Pharmacol.*, **21**, 86–91.

Sellinger-Barnette, M. and Weiss, B. (1984). Interaction of various peptides with calmodulin. *Adv. Cyclic Nucleotide Protein Phosphor. Res.*, **16**, 261–76.

Sellinger-Barnette, M. and Weiss, B. (1985). Inhibition calmodulin-stimulated phosphodiesterase activity by vasoactive intestinal peptide. *J. Neurochem.*, **45**, 640–3.

Sharma, R. K. and Wang, J. H. (1981). Inhibition of calmodulin-activated cyclic nucleotide phosphodiesterase by Triton X-100. *Biochem. Biophys. Res. Commun.*, **100**, 710–15.

Sharma, R. K., Wang, T. H., Wirch, E., and Wang, J. H. (1980). Purification and properties of bovine brain calmodulin-dependent cyclic nucleotide phosphodiesterase. *J. Biol. Chem.*, **255**, 5916–23.

Sharma, R. K., Taylor, W. A., and Wang, J. H. (1983). Use of calmodulin affinity chromatography for purification of specific calmodulin-dependent enzymes. *Meth. Enzymol.*, **102**, 210–19.

Sibley, D. R. and Lefkowitz, R. J. (1985). Molecular mechanisms of receptor desensitization using the beta-adrenergic receptor coupled adenylate cyclase system as a model. *Nature (London)*, **317**, 124–9.

Siegel, N. and Haug, A. (1983). Aluminum interaction with calmodulin: evidence for altered structure and function from optical and enzymatic studies. *Biochim. Biophys. Acta*, **744**, 36–45.

Sitaramayya, A., Campbell, J. A., and Siegel, F. L. (1978). Adrenal medullary cyclic nucleotide phosphodiesterase-regulatory properties of three enzyme activities. *J. Neurochem.*, **30**, 1281–5.

Smigel, M., Katada, T., Northup, J. K., Bokoch, G. M., Ui, M. and Gilman, A. G. (1984). Mechanisms of guanine nucleotide-mediated regulation of adenylate cyclase activity. *Adv. Cyclic Nucleotide Protein Phosphor. Res.*, **17**, 1–19.

Smilowitz, H., Hadjian, R. A., Dwyer, J., and Feinstein, M. B. (1981). Regulation of acetylcholine receptor phosphorylation by calcium and calmodulin. *Proc. Nat. Acad. Sci. USA*, **78**, 4708–12.

Smith, C. G. (1974). The cyclic AMP system and drug development. *Adv. Enzyme Reg.*, **12**, 187–203.

Smoake, J. A., Song, S.-Y., and Cheung, W. Y. (1974). Cyclic 3′,5′ nucleotide phosphodiesterase: distribution and developmental changes of the enzyme and its protein activator factor in mammalian tissues. *Biochim. Biophys. Acta*, **341**, 402–11.

Steer, M. L. and Levitzki, A. (1975). The control of adenylate cyclase by calcium in turkey erythrocyte ghosts. *J. Biol. Chem.*, **250**, 2080–4.

Strada, S. J. and Thompson, W. J., ed. (1984). Cyclic nucleotide phosphodiesterases. *Adv. Cyclic Nucleotide Protein Phosphor. Res.*, **16**.

Strada, S. J., Uzunov, P., and Weiss, B. (1974). Ontogenetic development of a phospho-diesterase activator and the multiple forms of cyclic AMP phosphodiesterase of rat brain. *J. Neurochem.*, **23**, 1097–103.

Strada, S. J., Martin, M. W., and Thompson, W. J. (1984). General properties of multiple molecular forms of cyclic nucleotide phosphodiesterase. *Adv. Cyclic Nucleotide Protein Phosphor. Res.*, **16**, 13–29.

Suen, E. T., Kwan, P. K. C., and Clement-Cormier, Y. C. (1982). Selective effects of an essential sulfhydril group on the activation of dopamine- and guanine nucleotide-sensitive adenylate cyclase. *Mol. Pharmacol.*, **22**, 595–601.

Sugden, M. C. and Ashcroft, S. J. H. (1981). Cyclic nucleotide phosphodiesterase of rat pancreatic islets. *Biochem. J.*, **197**, 459–64.

Sulakhe, P. V. and Hoehn, E. K. (1984). Interaction of EGTA with a hydrophobic region inhibits particulate adenylate cyclase from rat cerebral cortex: a study of an EGTA-inhibitable enzyme by using alamethicin. *Int. J. Biochem.*, **16**, 1029–35.

Sutherland, E. W. and Rall, T. W. (1958). Fractionation and characterization of a cyclic adenine ribonucleotide formed by tissue particles. *J. Biol. Chem.*, **232**, 1077–91.

Sutherland, E. W. and Rall, T. W. (1960). The relation of adenosine-3',5'-phosphate and phosphorylase to the actions of catecholamines and other hormones. *Pharmacol. Rev.*, **12**, 265–99.

Sutherland, E. W., Rall, T. W., and Menon, T. (1962). Adenyl cyclase. I. Distribution, preparation and properties. *J. Biol. Chem.*, **237**, 1220–7.

Tanaka, T. and Hidaka, H. (1980). Hydrophobic regions function in calmodulin–enzyme interactions. *J. Biol. Chem.*, **255**, 11078–80.

Tanaka, T. and Hidaka, H. (1981). Interaction of local anesthetics with calmodulin. *Biochem. Biophys. Res. Commun.*, **101**, 447–53.

Tanaka, T., Ohmura, T., and Hidaka, H. (1983). Calmodulin antagonists' binding sites on calmodulin. *Pharmacology*, **26**, 249–257.

Teo, T. S. and Wang, J. H. (1973). Mechanism of activation of a cyclic adenosine 3',5'-monophosphate phosphodiesterase from bovine heart by calcium ions: identification of the protein activator as a Ca^{2+} binding protein. *J. Biol. Chem.*, **248**, 5950–5.

Thayer, S. A. and Fairhurst, A. S. (1983). The interaction of dihydropyridine calcium channel blockers with calmodulin and calmodulin inhibitors. *Mol. Pharmacol.*, **24**, 6–9.

Thermos, K. and Weiss, B. (1985). Calmodulin: Function and Pharmacological Regulation. In *Calcium metabolism and cell physiology* (ed. A. Agnoli, P. L. Canonico, G. Milhaud, and U. Scapagnini) pp. 26–37. John Libbey, London.

Toscano, W. A., Wescott, K. R., LaPorte, D. C., and Storm, D. R. (1979). Evidence for a dissociable protein subunit required for calmodulin stimulation of brain adenylate cyclase. *Biochemistry*, **76**, 5582–6.

Treisman, G., Bagley, S., and Gnegy, M. E. (1983). Calmodulin-sensitive and calmodulin-insensitive components of adenylate cyclase activity in rate striatum have differential responsiveness to guanyl nucleotides. *J. Neurochem.*, **41**, 1398–406.

Tucker, M. M., Robinson, Jr., J. B., and Stellwagen, E. (1981). The effect of proteolysis on the calmodulin activation of cyclic nucleotide phosphodiesterase. *J. Biol. Chem.*, **256**, 9051–8.

Uzunov, P. and Weiss, B. (1972). Separation of multiple molecular forms of cyclic adenosine 3',5'-monophosphate phosphodiesterase in rat cerebellum by polyacrylamide gel electrophoresis. *Biochim. Biophys. Acta*, **284**, 220–6.

Uzunov, P., Shein, H. M. and Weiss, B. (1974). Multiple forms of cyclic 3',5'-AMP phosphodiesterase rat cerebrum and cloned astrocytoma and neuroblastoma cells. *Neuropharmacology*, **13**, 377–91.

Van Belle, H. (1981). R24571: a potent inhibitor of calmodulin activated enzymes. *Cell. Calcium*, **2**, 483–94.

Van Sande, J. and Dumont, J. E. (1973). Effects of thyrotropin, prostaglandin E_1 and iodide on cyclic $3',5'$-AMP concentration in dog thyroid slices. *Biochim. Biophys. Acta*, **313**, 320–8.

Volpi, M., Sha'afi, R. I., Epstein, P. M., Andrenyak, D. M., and Feinstein, M. B. (1981). Local anesthetics, mepacrine and propranolol are antagonists of calmodulin. *Proc. Nat. Acad. Sci. USA*, **78**, 795–9.

Watanabe, K. and West, W. L. (1982). Calmodulin, activated cyclic nucleotide phosphodiesterase, microtubules, and vinca alkaloids. *Fed. Proc. Fed. Am. Soc. Exp. Biol.*, **41**, 2292–9.

Weinryb, I., Chasin, M., Free, C. A., Harris, D. N., Goldenberg, H., Michel, I. M., Paik, V. S., Phillips, M., Samaniego, S., and Hess, S. M. (1972). Effects of therapeutic agents on cyclic AMP metabolism *in vitro*. *J. Pharm. Sci.*, **61**, 1556–7.

Weishaar, R. E., Cain, M. H., and Bristol, J. A. (1985). A new generation of phosphodiesterase inhibitors: multiple molecular forms of phosphodiesterase and the potential for drug selectivity. *J. Med. Chem.*, **28**, 537–45.

Weiss, B. (1973). Selective regulation of the multiple forms of cyclic nucleotide phosphodiesterase by norepinephrine and other agents. In *Frontiers and catecholamine research* (ed. E. Usdin and S. Snyder), pp. 327–33. Pergamon Press, New York.

Weiss, B. (1975a). Differential activation and inhibition of the multiple forms of cyclic nucleotide phosphodiesterase. *Adv. Cyclic Nucleotide Res.*, **5**, 195–211.

Weiss, B., ed. (1975b). *Cyclic nucleotides in disease*. University Park Press, Baltimore.

Weiss, B., and Fertel, R. (1977). Pharmacologic control of the synthesis and metabolism of cyclic nucleotides. *Adv. Pharmacol. Chemother.*, **14**, 189–283.

Weiss, B. and Hait, W. N. (1977). Selective cyclic nucleotide phosphodiesterase inhibitors as potential therapeutic agents. *Ann. Rev. Pharmacol. Toxicol.*, **17**, 441–77.

Weiss, B. and Kidman, A. D. (1969). Neurobiological significance of cyclic $3',5'$-adenosine monophosphate. *Adv. Biochem. Psychopharmacol.*, **1**, 131–64.

Weiss, B. and Levin, R. M. (1978). Mechanism for selectively inhibiting the activation of cyclic nucleotide phosphodiesterase and adenylate cyclase by antipsychotic agents. *Adv. Cyclic Nucleotide Res.*, **9**, 285–303.

Weiss, B. and Prozialeck, W. C. (1984). Pharmacological inhibition of calmodulin-dependent processes. In: *Mechanisms of hepatocyte injury and cell death*; Falk Symposium No. 38. (ed. D. Keppler and H. Popper), pp. 337–75. MTP Press, Hingham, MA.

Weiss, B. and Wallace, T. L. (1980). Mechanisms and Pharmacological implications of altering calmodulin activity. In *Calcium and cell function* (ed. W. Y. Cheung), Vol. 1, pp. 329–79. Academic Press, New York.

Weiss, B., Lehne, R., and Strada, S. J. (1972). A rapid microassay of adenosine $3',5'$-monophosphate phosphodiesterase activity. *Anal. Biochem.* **45**, 222–35.

Weiss, B., Fertel, R., Figlin, R., and Uznov, P. (1974). Selective alteration of the activity of the multiple forms of adenosine $3',5'$-monophosphate phosphodiesterase of rat cerebrum. *Mol. Pharmacol*, **10**, 615–25.

Weiss, B., Prozialeck, W. C., Cimino, M., Barnette, M., and Wallace, T. L. (1980). Pharmacological regulation of calmodulin. *Ann. N. Y. Acad. Sci.*, **356**, 319–45.

Weiss, B., Prozialeck, W. C., and Wallace, T. L. (1982). Interaction of drugs with calmodulin: biochemical, pharmacological and clinical implications. *Biochem. Pharmacol.*, **31**, 2217–26.

Weiss, B., Barnette, M., Paikowsky, S., and Kaiser, C. (1984). Irreversible inhibition of calmodulin (CM) activity by fluphenazine-N-mustard (FNM). *Fed. Proc. Fed. Am. Soc. Exp. Biol.*, **43**, 765.

Weiss, B., Sellinger-Barnette, M., Winkler, J. D., Schechter, L. E., and Prozialeck, W. C. (1985). Calmodulin antagonist: structure activity relationships. In *Calmodulin antagonists and cellular physiology* (ed. H. Hidaka and D. J. Hartshorne) pp. 45–61. Academic Press, New York.

Wells, J. N., Garst, J. E., and Kramer, G. L. (1981). Inhibition of separated forms of cyclic nucleotide phosphodiesterase from pig coronary arteries by 1,3-disubstituted and 1,3,8-trisubstituted xanthines. *J. Med. Chem.*, **24**, 954–8.

Wells, J. N., Wu, Y. J., Baird, C. E., and Hardman, J. G. (1975). Phosphodiesterases from porcine coronary arteries: inhibition of separated forms by xanthines, papaverine and cyclic nucleotides. *Mol. Pharmacol.*, **11**, 775–83.

Westcott, K. R., Olwin, B. B., and Storm, D. R. (1980). Inhibition of adenylate cyclase by the 2',3'-dialdehyde of adenosine triphosphate. *J. Biol. Chem.*, **225**, 8767–71.

Whetton, A. D., Gordon, L. M., and Houslay, M. D. (1983a). Elevated membrane cholesterol concentrations inhibit glucagon-stimulated adenylate cyclase. *Biochem. J.*, **210**, 437–49.

Whetton, A. D., Gordon, L. M., and Houslay, M. D. (1983b). Adenylate cyclase is inhibited upon depletion of plasma-membrane cholesterol. *Biochem. J.*, **212**, 331–8.

Wiech, N. L., Siegel, B. W., and Hogan, A. C. (1978). RMI 12330A: an inhibitor of adenylate cyclase activity. *Adv. Cyclic Nucleotide Protein Phosphor. Res.*, **9**, 736.

Winkler, J. D., Thermos, K., and Weiss, B. (1987). Differential effects of fluphenazine-N-mustard on calmodulin activity as on D_1 and D_2 dopaminergic responses. *Psychopharmacology*, **92**, 285–91.

Wolff, J., Londos, C., and Cooper, D. M. F. (1981). Adenosine receptors and the regulation of adenylate cyclase. *Adv. Cyclic Nucleotide. Res.*, **14**, 199–214.

Wright, L. J., Feinstein, A., Heap, R. B., Saunders, J. C., Bennett, R. C., and Wang, M.-Y. (1982). Progesterone monoclonal antibody blocks pregnancy in mice. *Nature (London)*, **295**, 415–17.

Yamauchi, T., Nakata, H., and Fujisawa, H. (1981). A new activator protein that activates tryptophan 5-mono-oxygenase and tyrosine 3-mono-oxygenase in the presence of Ca^{2+}-calmodulin dependent protein kinase. *J. Biol. Chem.*, **256**, 5404–9.

Zavecz, J. H., Jackson, T. E., Limp, G. L., and Yellin, T. O. (1982). Relationship between anti-diarrheal activity and binding to calmodulin. *Eur. J. Pharmacol.*, **78**, 375–7.

Inhibitors of carbonic anhydrase

Sven Lindskog and Per J. Wistrand

20.1   Carbonic anhydrase

20.1.1   Introduction

Carbonic anhydrase (CA; EC 4.2.1.1) is a zinc metalloenzyme catalyzing the reversible hydration of carbon dioxide:

$$CO_2 + H_2O \rightleftharpoons HCO_3^- + H^+$$

(Pocker and Sarkanen 1978; Lindskog 1983). The enzyme can also catalyse a variety of other reactions, for example the hydration of aldehydes and the hydrolysis of certain esters, including p-nitrophenyl acetate. However, all known physiological functions of CA are believed to result from catalysis of CO_2/HCO_3^- interconversion (Maren 1967).

There are two major groups of CA inhibitors, monovalent anions and sulphonamides. The most efficient anionic inhibitors are 'metal poisons', such as CN^- and SH^-, but the enzyme is also inhibited by anions that are not normally strong metal ligands, for example, NO_3^- and ClO_4^-. The most powerful and specific inhibitors are certain aromatic and heterocyclic sulphonamides. Such inhibitors are used therapeutically, particularly in the treatment of glaucoma (Wistrand 1984b), but they are also valuable tools in studies of the physiological roles of the enzyme and of structure–function relationships at the molecular level (Maren 1967; Lindskog 1983). Only this type of inhibitor will be discussed here. Several excellent reviews on this subject are available (Bar 1963; Maren 1967, 1976; Coleman 1975; Maren and Sanyal 1983; Friedland and Maren 1984).

Three genetically and immunologically distinct cytosolic forms of CA have been described in higher vertebrates (mammals, birds, and reptiles). They are designated CA I (previously CA B), CA II (previously CA C) and CA III. These isozymes have different kinetic and inhibitor-binding properties, but they have homologous structures and have probably arisen through duplications of an ancestral CA gene at least 300 million years ago (Tashian et al. 1983; Hewett-Emmett et al. 1984). In humans, the genes encoding these isozymes are all located on chromosome 8 (Venta et al. 1983; Butterworth et al. 1985; Edwards et al. 1985).

Other soluble forms of CA have been found in mitochondria from certain tissues (Dodgson et al. 1980; Vincent and Silverman 1982) and in the parotid saliva from some mammals (Fernley et al. 1979; Feldstein and Silverman 1984). Membrane-bound forms have been reported from several tissues, for example human renal tubular cells (McKinley and Whitney 1976; Wistrand 1979), bovine lung (Whitney and Briggle 1982), and rat brain (Sapirstein et al. 1984). Reported immunological properties and amino acid composition data indicate, as reviewed by Wistrand (1984a), that at least some of these forms of CA are genetically distinct from the cytosolic isozymes.

20.1.2 Distribution in the human body

The various forms of CA are differently distributed in tissues. Certain cells contain more than one form, while other cells have a single form (see Tashian et al. 1984).

CA II is found in erythrocytes and in a variety of cells secreting H^+ or HCO_3^- and/or OH^- (Parsons 1982). The enzyme purified from kidney cortex and medulla has been shown to be identical to red cell CA II (Wistrand et al. 1975). The evidence for the presence of CA II in other tissues where inhibitors exert their therapeutic effects, for example in ciliary processes, choroid plexus, and glial cells, is based on inhibition characteristics and immunological reactivity.

CA I is found together with CA II in erythrocytes. Next to haemoglobin, it is the most abundant protein in these cells, where the levels have been found to be under hormonal control by the thyroid gland (Anker and Mondrup 1974). Results of immunohistochemical studies indicate its presence in certain surface epithelial cells in the ileum and colon (Lönnerholm et al. 1985) and in the endothelium of the capillaries and the cornea (Wistrand et al. 1986).

CA III is the most abundant soluble protein in skeletal muscle where it is present in the slow, red fibres (Riley et al. 1982; Shima et al. 1983; Moyle et al. 1984). Only trace amounts have been detected in other tissues (Jeffery et al. 1980; Kato and Mokuno 1984).

The membrane-bound form has been found in the brush-border and/or basolateral membranes of various epithelial cells in the kidney and gastro-intestinal tract (Lönnerholm *et al.* 1985).

20.1.3 Catalytic activity and physiological role

CA II is one of the most efficient of all known enzymes, with a maximal CO_2 hydration turnover number of $1 \times 10^6 \, s^{-1}$ at $25°C$ (Lindskog 1983). The K_m values for CO_2 and HCO_3^- are above the tissue concentrations of these substrates. In red cells, the role of CA II is to facilitate CO_2 transport by catalysing the hydration of CO_2 in the tissue capillaries and the reverse reaction in the capillaries of the lung (Maren 1967; Swenson and Maren 1978). Its role in secretory cells appears to be to provide an adequate supply of H^+, OH^- or HCO_3^- by rapidly responding to perturbations of the CO_2/HCO_3^- equilibrium in the cytosol.

Recently a CA II deficiency in erythrocytes was found in the autosomal recessive syndrome of osteopetrosis with renal tubular acidosis and cerebral calcification (Tashian *et al.* 1984; Sly *et al.* 1985). It was inferred that lack of CA II in osteoclasts, renal tubular cells, and glial cells would be the primary defect in this syndrome, but this remains to be proven (Maren 1985).

CA I is less active than CA II, but its maximal CO_2 hydration turnover number is still appreciable, about $1.5 \times 10^5 \, s^{-1}$ at $25°C$ (Lindskog 1983). Its physiological role has not yet been defined, but it has been suggested that it is involved in the absorption and subsequent metabolism of substances formed during fermentation by microorganisms in the intestine (Carter and Parsons 1971). Individuals homozygous for a red cell CA I deficiency showed no symptoms of disease (Kendall and Tashian 1977). It is not known if these subjects also lack non-erythrocyte CA I.

CA III is the least active of the soluble CA isozymes with a CO_2 hydration turnover number of about $3 \times 10^3 \, s^{-1}$ at $25°C$ (Sanyal 1984; Engberg *et al.* 1985). Sulphonamide inhibitors bind 10^2–10^4 times less strongly to CA III than to CA I or CA II (Sanyal *et al.* 1982). In fact, this was initially described as a 'sulphonamide-resistant' form in livers of male rats (Maren *et al.* 1966; King *et al.* 1974) where its levels are under hormonal control (Shiels *et al.* 1983). The physiological function of CA III is unclear, but its role in muscle might be to facilitate the diffusion of metabolic CO_2 to the capillaries (cf. Kawashiro and Scheid 1976).

There is experimental evidence indicating that the membrane-bound kidney enzyme is involved in the reabsorption of bicarbonate in the proximal tubule (Lucci *et al.* 1983). The mitochondrial enzyme in liver has been suggested as being involved in the process of substrate availability for urea synthesis (Dodgson *et al.* 1983; Carter *et al.* 1984; Häussinger and Gerok 1985).

20.1.4   Structure and mechanism of action

The amino acid sequences of human CA I ($M_r = 28\,850$), CA II ($M_r = 29\,300$) and CA III ($M_r = 29\,500$) show extensive homologies (Fig. 20.1). The crystal structures of human CA I and CA II have been determined to 2 Å resolution (Liljas *et al.* 1972; Kannan *et al.* 1975; Notstrand *et al.* 1975). The two isozymes have homologous folding patterns. The molecular dimensions are about $41 \times 41 \times 47$ Å^3. The active site is located in a conical cavity about 15 Å wide at the entrance and about 16 Å deep. The zinc ion is near the bottom of the cavity. It is liganded to three imidazole groups from His-94, His-96, and His-119. A fourth ligand, presumably H_2O (or OH^-), completes an almost regular tetrahedral coordination geometry. The metal-ion ligands are hydrogen-bonded to protein groups as indicated in Fig. 20.2. One part of the active-site surface has essentially hydrophilic amino acid side-chains, including residues 7, 64, 65, 67, 92, 106, 199, and 200, while another part has mainly hydrophobic side-chains from residues 91, 121, 131, 141, 143, 198, 207, and 209. The ligands and the residues linked to them by hydrogen bonds are invariant in all sequenced CAs, I, II, and III (Lindskog 1983; Hewett-Emmett *et al.* 1984), suggesting that the metal ion centre has the same structure in all the cytosolic isozymes. However, there is considerable variation among other active-site residues. It is believed that residues 64, 67, and 200 are particularly important for the fine tuning of catalytic properties (Lindskog 1983; Lindskog *et al.* 1984).

In all the CA isozymes, the basic catalytic step in CO_2 hydration is thought to be a nucleophilic attack of a zinc-bound OH^- on CO_2 to produce a HCO_3^- ion, which is then displaced from the metal ion by H_2O (Fig. 20.3). This step is not rate-limiting in CA II, but in a well-buffered solution the slowest step is probably an intramolecular transfer of H^+ from the metal-bound H_2O to His-64, thus regenerating OH^-. The rapid release of H^+ from His-64 to the reaction medium requires the participation of buffer molecules (Lindskog 1983; Silverman and Vincent 1983; Lindskog *et al.* 1984). In CA I, His-200 and, possibly, His 67 have been assumed to serve as 'proton transfer groups' (Lindskog *et al.* 1984). CA III has no titratable active-site histidines. Still, there is evidence that a H^+ transfer step rather than CO_2/HCO_3^- interconversion limits the rate of catalysis (Kararli and Silverman 1985).

20.2   Sulphonamides

20.2.1   Interaction with the enzyme

There is overwhelming crystallographic and spectroscopic evidence that sulphonamides bind to the metal ion in the CA isozymes (Kannan *et al.* 1977; Lindskog 1983). The inhibitors are coordinated via the N atom of the sulphonamide group as shown by the ^{113}Cd-^{15}N spin–spin coupling in the ^{113}Cd n.m.r. spectrum of the ^{15}N-benzenesulphonamide complex of ^{113}Cd(II)-substituted bovine CA II (Evelhoch *et al.* 1981) and supported by the ^{15}N chemical shift of

Design of Enzyme Inhibitors as Drugs

```
         1                                                              50
                 *                                        *
CA I     ASPDWGYDDKNGPEQWSKLYPIANGNNQSPVDIKTSETKHDTSLKPISVS
CA II      SHHWGYGKHNGPEHWHKDFPIAKGERQSPVDIDTHTAKYDPSLKPLSVS
CA III     AKEWGYASHNGPDHWHELFPNAKGENQSPIELHTKDIRHDPSLQPWSVS

                               ** *                         ** * *  100
CA I     YNPATAKEIINVGHSFHVNFEDNDNRSVLKGGPFSDSYRLFQFHFHWGST
CA II    YDQATSLRILNNGHAFNVEFDDSQDKAVLKGGPLDGTYRLIQFHFHWGSL
CA III   YDGGSAKTILNNGKTCRVVFDDTYDRSMLRGGPLPGPYRLRQFHLHWGSS

                      **      * * *            *          * *   150
CA I     NEHGSEHTVDGVKYSAELHVAHWNSAKYSSLAEAASKADGLAVIGVLMKV
CA II    DGQGSEHTVDKKKYAAELHLVHWNT-KYGDFGKAVQQPDGLAVLGIFLKV
CA III   DDHGSEHTVDGVKYAAELHLVHWNP-KYNTFKEALKQRDGIAVIGIFLKI

                                                    *    ***200
CA I     GEANPKLQKVLDALQAIKTKGKRAPFTNFDPSTLLPSSLDFWTYPGSLTH
CA II    GSAKPGLQKVVDVLDSIKTKGKSADFTNFDPRGLLPESLDYWTYPGSLTT
CA III   GHENGEFQIFLDALDKIKTKGKEAPFTKFDPSCLFPACRDYWTYQGSFTT

                   * *                                   *    250
CA I     PPLYESVTWIICKESISVSSEQLAQFRSLLSNVEGDNAVPMQHNNRPTQP
CA II    PPLLECVTWIVLKEPISVSSEQVLKFRKLNFNGEGEPEELMVDNWRPAQP
CA III   PPCEECIVWLLLKEPMTVSSDQMAKLRSLLSSAENEPPVPLVSNWRPPQP


CA I     LKGRTVRASF
CA II    LKNRQIKASFK
CA III   INNRVVRASFK
```

Fig. 20.1. Amino acid sequences of human CA I (Andersson *et al.* 1972; Lin and Deutsch 1973), CA II (Henderson *et al.* 1976), and CA III (Lloyd *et al.* 1986). The α-amino groups are acetylated (Marriq *et al.* 1965). Active-site residues mentioned in the text or shown in Fig. 20.2 are marked by asterisks.

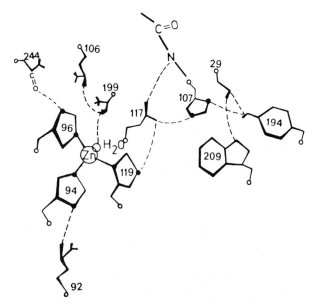

Fig. 20.2. A schematic drawing of the hydrogen-bond network around the metal-ion centre in human CA I and CA II. From Notstrand *et al.* (1975), with permission.

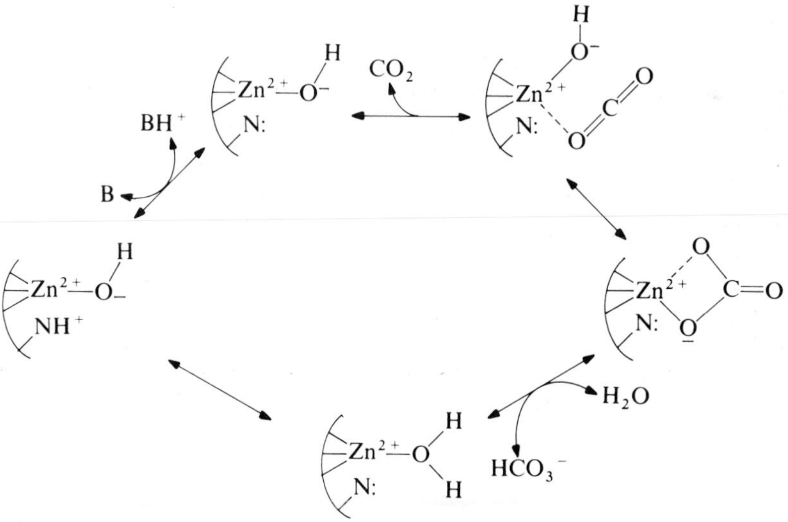

Fig. 20.3. A simplified scheme of the catalytic mechanism of CA II including an intramolecular H^+ transfer between the metal-ion centre and His-64 (symbolized by —N:) and a buffer-dependent step. See Lindskog (1983), Lindskog *et al.* (1984) and Silverman and Vincent (1983) for further details.

the corresponding complex with native human CA I (Kanamori and Roberts 1983). A variety of spectroscopic measurements have shown that the inhibitors are bound as anions, $R\text{---}SO_2NH^-$ (Chen and Kernohan 1967; King and Burgen 1970; Kumar *et al.* 1976; Kanamori and Roberts 1983). This is consistent with the (affinity constant)/pH profiles, which are bell-shaped (Fig. 20.4) and can, formally, be rationalized in terms of competition between OH^- and $R\text{--}SO_2NH^-$ for a metal ion coordination site (Kernohan 1966; Lindskog and Thorslund 1968). Thus, the affinity is controlled by the pK_a values of the $\text{---}SO_2NH_2$ group and of $Zn(II)\text{--}OH_2$ in the active centre.

In addition, the sulphonamide group interacts with the active site by hydrogen bonds between the NH entity and the side-chain oxygen atom of Thr-199 and between one of the oxygen atoms and the peptide NH group of the same amino acid (Kannan *et al.* 1977; Eriksson *et al.* 1986). The other oxygen atom of the sulphonamide group is near the metal ion at a distance of about 3 Å. The thiadiazole ring and the acetylamido side chain of acetazolamide (see Table 20.3) are located in the hydrophobic part of the active site. The position of this inhibitor in the active site of human CA II, shown in Fig. 20.5, was obtained after refinement of the crystal structure by molecular mechanics calculations (Vedani and Dunitz 1985), and seems to be consistent with the crystallographically refined structure (Eriksson *et al.* 1986). In addition to the metal ion and Thr-199, the side chains of the hydrophobic residues Ile-91, Val-121, Phe-131, and Leu-198, as well as that of Gln-92, are close to the bound inhibitor molecule. Höltje and Simon (1984) calculated interaction energies for the binding of some inhibitors to human CA II. They report that the dominating contribution to these energies comes from Gln-92, His-94, Val-121, Phe-131, Leu-198, and Thr-199. The importance of the hydrophobic part of the active site has been further emphasized in model-building studies (Vedani and Meyer 1984; Hansch *et al.* 1985).

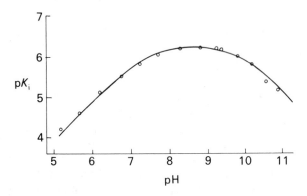

Fig. 20.4. pH dependence of the affinity (expressed as $pK_i = -\log K_i$) of bovine CA II for benzenesulphonamide ($pK_a = 10.1$). From Kernohan (1966), with permission.

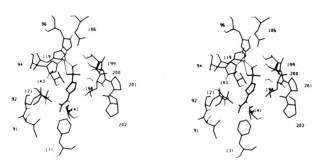

Fig. 20.5. Stereoscopic view of the active centre of human CA II with bound acetazolamide. The zinc ion is represented by a sphere. Bonds from O and N atoms to H or Zn are drawn light. The inhibitor molecule is drawn enhanced. Note that the inhibitor is drawn as $R-SO_2NH_2$ rather than as $R-SO_2NH^-$ (see text). From Vedani and Dunitz (1985) with permission.

In comparison with most other carbonic anhydrase inhibitors, sulphonamides equilibrate rather slowly with the enzyme. Thus, rates of sulphonamide binding can be measured by stopped-flow techniques (Kernohan 1966; Taylor *et al.* 1970a). The pH dependence of the affinity constant is reflected in a marked pH dependence of the apparent association rate constant, while the dissociation rate constant is independent of pH (Taylor *et al.* 1970b; King and Maren 1974). King and Burgen (1976) found that metal-depleted apoCA II has a weak, pH-independent affinity for sulphonamides. This observation led to the proposal of a two-step mechanism for the reaction with holoenzyme. The first step involves the formation of a loose complex, similar to that formed with apoenzyme, independently of the ionization states of $R-SO_2NH_2$ and $Zn(II)-OH_2$ and not involving the metal ion. The second step depends on the ionization states of these groups and results in a stabilization of the complex by the formation of the $R-SO_2NH^- -Zn(II)$ bond.

20.2.2 Structure–activity relationships

Substitution at the nitrogen atom of the sulphonamide group normally leads to a drastic reduction of the inhibitory power (Mann and Keilin 1940; Krebs 1948). King and Burgen (1976) found that 4-nitrobenzenesulphonacetamide binds to human CA II in a pH-independent manner with 10^4 times lower affinity than unsubstituted 4-nitrobenzene sulphonamide. The sulphonacetamide did not perturb the absorption spectrum of the Co(II)-substituted enzyme, strongly suggesting that this compound does not bind to the metal ion. Thus, it appears that the interaction of the N-substituted sulphonamide with the active centre is analogous to that of a potent inhibitor with the apoenzyme. However, the inactivity of N-substituted sulphonamides is not a general rule. It was recently shown (Blackburn et al. 1985) that N-hydroxybenzenesulphonamides are potent inhibitors. Evidence from ^{111}Cd and ^{15}N n.m.r. studies showed that these compounds bind to the metal ion in the same manner as the unsubstituted sulphonamides.

The first systematic effort to characterize relations between sulphonamide structure and inhibitory power was presented by Bar (1963). Since then several papers on quantitative structure–activity relationships have appeared (Kakeya et al. 1969a, c; Shinagawa and Shinagawa 1974; Subbarao and Bray, 1979; Testa and Purcell, 1978; Kishida 1978; Kishida and Manabe 1980; Kumar et al. 1981; De Benedetti et al. 1985; Hansch et al. 1985). All these studies concern CA II from human or bovine red cells. A variety of empirical or quantum-mechanical parameters have been used to estimate the importance of electronic and/or steric factors and/or the lipophilicities of the inhibitor molecules. The conclusions vary considerably and, to a large extent, this seems to depend on the choice of parameters, which has often been made to illustrate one particular property of the inhibitors.

However, it has been shown in a number of these studies that a high affinity is favoured by the withdrawal of electrons from the sulphonamide group, thus increasing its acidity (Kakeya et al. 1969c; De Benedetti et al. 1985; Hansch et al. 1985). This is well understood from a structural point of view, since the inhibitors are bound in their ionized forms. This electronic effect also rationalizes the very weak inhibitory power of aliphatic sulphonamides (Krebs 1948; Maren and Wiley 1968). It is interesting to note that the importance of the sulphonamide pK_a was suggested previously by Miller et al. (1950) and that they recognized that other factors must also be important.

Considering that the binding site includes a hydrophobic part of the active centre, it is not surprising that it has been claimed that one of these additional factors is the lipophilicity of the inhibitor. Steric restraints have also been reported. In particular, 2-substituted benzenesulphonamides are less potent inhibitors of CA II than predicted on the basis of their electronic and lipophilic properties alone (Kakeya et al. 1969c; Kishida and Manabe 1980; Hansch et al. 1985).

Using the data of King and Burgen (1976), Hansch et al. (1985) derived the following relationship for a set of benzenesulphonamides having substituents of various size and hydrophobicity in the 2-, 3-, and 4-positions, respectively:

$$\log K = 1.55\sigma + 0.64 \log P - 2.07 I_1 - 3.28 I_2 + 6.94 \qquad (20.1)$$

In eqn (20.1) K (M^{-1}) is the affinity constant, σ is the Hammett electronic substituent constant, P is the octanol/water partition coefficient, and I_1 and I_2 are indicator variables (with values 0 or 1) for 3- and 2-substituents, respectively. The negative coefficients with I_1 and I_2 imply steric hindrance by these substituents to the extent that 3- and 2-substituted inhibitors have about 100 and 2000 times lower affinity, respectively, than the equivalent 4-substituted inhibitors.

Kakeya *et al.* (1969c) also used Hammett's σ constants and the octanol/water partition coefficient to analyse the inhibitory powers of a series of substituted benzenesulphonamides. However, they used substituents with smaller size than in the King and Burgen (1976) series. The coefficients with σ and log P found by Kakeya *et al.* (1969c) were only about half the magnitude of those in eqn (20.1). In addition, one can estimate from their data that 3-substituted derivatives showed very little steric hindrance, corresponding to less than a two-fold decrease of affinity, while 2-substituted inhibitors deviated significantly from 4-substituted compounds but by less than a factor of 10. Although Kakeya *et al.* (1969c) used a different assay method from that of King and Burgen (1976) and bovine CA II rather than the human isozyme, we feel that the results of the structure–activity analyses of the two series of inhibitors are significantly different. This seems to imply that some factor, presumably related to molecular size, has been neglected (see Testa and Purcell 1978; Kumar *et al.* 1981).

20.2.3 Therapeutic use

20.2.3.1 *General aspects*
Inhibition of CA II reduces electrolyte and fluid secretion in several tissues in a way that can be used therapeutically (Maren 1967). However, inhibition of the other forms has not yet been shown to evoke physiological effects of therapeutic value. Only the sulphonamide type of inhibitors have been found to be useful clinically, because they are highly potent, selective, and reversible. For inhibitors with a K_i of 10^{-8} M, a plasma concentration of 10 μM of freely diffusible inhibitor is required for maximal physiological response in most organs. Such concentrations are generated by doses of about 3–5 mg kg^{-1} body weight (Fig. 20.7). Therefore, the use of less potent inhibitors would be impractical due to the high doses needed. Several studies in animals and man have shown that the physiological response is closely correlated with the degree of enzyme inhibition (Maren 1963) provided the factors of drug distribution and disposition are taken into account (Wistrand *et al.* 1960). If the inhibitor in plasma is assumed to be in diffusion equilibrium with the enzyme inside the cell, it can be calculated from the K_i and the plasma concentration that CA II is inhibited by 99 per cent or more at half-maximal physiological response. CA II therefore appears to be in about 100-fold excess of physiological needs. This appears to be true for all tissues tested. It should be noted that maximal enzyme inhibition can never block the physiological activity completely due to the ongoing uncatalysed hydration of CO_2.

Table 20.1 gives the various disorders where sulphonamide inhibitors have been used. All effects can be ascribed to the inhibition of CA II in the respective

Table 20.1 The use of carbonic anhydrase inhibitors in clinical medicine and the probable mechanism of action (from Wistrand 1984b)

Disorder	Mechanism of action[a]	Reference
Glaucoma	Reduction of aqueous humour flow	Becker 1954
Edema	Renal excretion of sodium	Maren 1967
Hydrocephalus	Reduction of CSF formation	Vogh 1980
Menière's disease	Reduction of endolymph formation?	Brookes and Booth 1984
Minor motor seizures	Metabolic acidosis (effect on CNS?)	Woodbury 1980
Mountain sickness	Imposition of metabolic acidosis on respiratory alkalosis. Other causes?	Larson et al. 1982
Central sleep apnea	Reduction plasma HCO_3^- and respiratory stimulation	White et al. 1982
Obstructive lung disease	Reduction of plasma HCO_3^- and respiratory stimulation	Häcki et al. 1983
Hypokalaemic periodic paralysis	Metabolic acidosis reduces flux of K^+ into skeletal muscle	Vroom et al. 1975
Hyperkalaemic periodic paralysis	Renal loss of K^+	Griggs et al. 1978
Gastric and duodenal ulcer	Reduction of gastric HCl secretion	Puşcaş 1984
Toxicity due to acidic drug nor metabolites	Alkalinization of urine	Maren 1968

[a] Renal effects are due to inhibition of CA II, and probably of membrane-bound CA in tubular cells. Other effects are due to inhibition of CA II in epithelia of ciliary processes (glaucoma), choroid plexus (hydrocephalus), cochlea, and saccus endolymphaticus (Menière's disease).

organs. Moreover, many of the side-effects observed (Table 20.2) are probably also due to inhibition of CA II primarily in the kidney, gastrointestinal tract, and brain. The therapeutic index for the presently used inhibitors is therefore low, as exemplified for acetazolamide in Fig. 20.6. Nearly 50 per cent of glaucoma patients have to abandon therapy because of side-effects and compliance when using azetazolamide, the most widely used inhibitor, has accordingly been shown to be low (Alward and Wilensky 1981). The main problem in designing new inhibitors against CA II is, therefore, to make them more organ-selective by adjusting the pharmacokinetic properties while maintaining an inhibitory power of $K_i \leqslant 10^{-8}$ M. There are only a few systematic studies available where the physical and chemical properties of sulphonamides have been related to pharmacokinetic parameters (Wistrand et al. 1960; Maren et al. 1983). They show that changes in lipophilicity and aqueous solubility affect these parameters, as would be expected from the rules of general pharmacology.

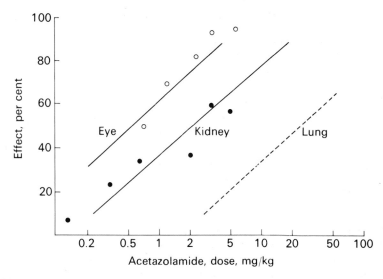

Fig. 20.6. Relation between doses of acetazolamide and the effects on eye pressure, renal total bicarbonate excretion, and respiration in humans. The curve for the ocular effects is from experiments with continuous i.v. infusions where eye pressures were recorded at different levels of steady-state plasma concentrations. The renal effects were recorded after single oral doses. The curve for the respiratory effect is from theoretical and experimental data showing that effects start to appear at i.v. doses between 7.5 and 15 mg kg^{-1}. From Wistrand (1984b), with permission.

Besides selecting the optimal pharmacokinetic parameters to target the inhibitor to the enzyme in a given tissue, it would also be desirable to design inhibitors that are more selective against CA II. Acetazolamide is about 20 times less active against CA I, which should make tissues like the erythrocytes and the cornea, which contain CA I as well as CA II (Wistrand *et al.* 1986), relatively resistant to inhibition by this compound as compared to the other clinically used inhibitors (Table 20.3) which are equally active against both these isozymes. This resistance of CA I towards acetazolamide probably explains the relatively large doses of acetazolamide needed to elicit an effect on respiration, as illustrated in Fig. 20.6.

20.2.3.2 *Kidney*

Apart from use as a mild diuretic, many of the other clinical uses of sulphonamide inhibitors depend on the establishment of a metabolic acidosis as a result of inhibition of CA II in the renal tubular cells (Table 20.1). The renal effects correlate well with the inhibitory activity of the enzyme and with the degree of accumulation in proximal tubules (cf. Maren 1968). The early goal (cf. Beyer and Baer 1961) was to get an inhibitor with good oral absorption, high specific

Table 20.2   Side-effects of carbonic anhydrase inhibitors and the probable mechanism of action

Side-effect	Mechanism of action[a]	Reference
Malaise type		
Nausea		
Fatigue		
Depression	CNS effect and/or metabolic	Lichter *et al.* 1978
Anorexia	acidosis?	Epstein and Grant 1979
Weight loss		
Loss of libido		
Gastro-intestinal type		
Gastritis	Reduction of gastric alkaline secretion	
Abdominal cramping	Reduction of fluid reabsorption	Wistrand 1984b
Diarrhoea	in small and large intestine?	
Other		
Shortness of breath	Respiratory acidosis	Block and Rostand 1978
Paresthesia	Effect on CNS or peripheral nerves?	
Flat taste	Effect on taste buds?	Friedland and Maren 1984
Renal stone formation	Reduced citrate excretion	Kass *et al.* 1981
Transient myopia	Retinal oedema?	Beasley 1962
Aplastic anaemia	Idiosyncratic	Werblin *et al.* 1979

[a] Malaise type of side-effects are probably due to inhibition of CA II in the kidney and CNS (glial cells) and gastro-intestinal type to inhibition of CA II in surface epithelial cells of ventricle and intestine.

inhibitory activity, high urine/plasma concentration ratio, and low erythrocyte/ plasma concentration ratio. The inhibitor which best fits these criteria today is benzolamide (Table 20.3). Being a relatively strong acid it accumulates in the renal cortex 40 times over the concentration in plasma by the organic anion transport system, making it more than 10 times as potent as acetazolamide (Travis 1969). Due to its low lipophilicity, it diffuses slowly into red cells, ciliary processes and brain, and 10 to 20-fold and 12-fold higher doses are required to elicit ocular and respiratory effects, respectively. The use of this inhibitor will therefore avoid the threat of respiratory failure in patients with pre-existing pulmonary deficit and respiratory acidosis (Platts and Hanley 1956). One disadvantage of benzolamide is its relatively low gastrointestinal absorption and its rapid elimination from plasma. However, benzolamide should be the drug of choice for eliciting renal effects and it is unfortunate that it still belongs to the list of so called 'orphan' drugs (Maren 1979).

A quantitative structure–activity relationship between physicochemical properties of carbonic anhydrase inhibitors and their natriuretic effects has been given by Kakeya *et al.* (1969b).

20.2.3.3 *Eye*

Glaucoma is the major indication for the use of these inhibitors. In Sweden as many as 95 per cent of prescriptions for these inhibitors are for this use (Wistrand 1984b). By inhibition of CA II in the ciliary processes, the secretion of sodium bicarbonate and fluid is diminished, reducing the aqueous humour flow and intra-ocular pressure (Maren 1974). In Fig. 20.7, it is seen that more than 99 per cent inhibition of CA II in the ciliary epithelium is required to reach maximal pressure-lowering effect, accomplished by a plasma concentration of 10 μM of acetazolamide at steady state. The pressure response is directly related to inhibitory activity, provided the drug has access to the ciliary epithelium (Wistrand *et al.* 1960). Benzolamide-type of inhibitors with a low pK_a and lipid solubility penetrate poorly into the ciliary epithelium and are therefore not active. Moreover they are probably also transported out of the aqueous humour by the organic anion transport system present in the ciliary epithelium. Acetazolamide is the drug mostly used. One important disadvantage of this drug, however, is its tendency to elicit malaise type of symptoms (Table 20.2), which probably to some extent are related to the development of metabolic acidosis secondary to the renal effects. The therapeutic index is also relatively low since it takes a dose only about twice as high to elicit a renal response as compared to the eye pressure effect (Fig. 20.6). It should be stressed that these effects were seen after different types of administration, intravenous infusion and oral, and it is possible that the therapeutic index is still lower since experiments in dogs indicate that renal and ocular effects are elicited by approximately the same dose of acetazoleamide (Maren 1979). There are no studies in humans, where organ effects have been compared under strict steady-state conditions. However, the use of more lipid-soluble inhibitors like methazolamide, dichlorphenamide, and ethoxzolamide (Table 20.3), which do not accumulate inside the tubular cells, dissociates the ocular and renal effects. On the other hand, increased lipid solubility enhances the passage of acetazolamide into the brain and tends to give stronger CNS effects, probably as a result of the inhibition of CA II in the glial cells. This is perhaps another factor behind the malaise type of symptoms. Actually, ethoxzolamide, which is the most lipid-soluble agent, appears to have the highest incidence of intolerable side-effects of this type (Lichter *et al.* 1978). The ideal inhibitor seems therefore to be one that is less lipid soluble than acetazolamide but is still not accumulated by the renal proximal tubules. This agent would be predicted to have less CNS and renal effects.

20.2.3.4 *Topical inhibitors for use in glaucoma*

Carbonic anhydrase inhibitors have been known for sometime to be active after their local application to gastric mucosa, kidney, ciliary epithelium, and choroid

Table 20.3 Properties of clinically used or investigated carbonic anhydrase inhibitors (adapted from Wistrand et al. 1960 and Friedland and Maren 1984)

Name	Structure	$10^9 \times K_i$ (M)[a]	pKa_1	Ether–buffer (pH 7.4) partition	Unbound plasma concentration (per cent)[b]	Plasma half-life $t_{\frac{1}{2}}$ (h)
Acetazolamide	$CH_3-C(=O)-N(H)-$ [thiadiazole] $-SO_2NH_2$	6	7.4	0.14	5	4
Methazolamide	$CH_3-C(=O)-N(CH_3)-$ [thiadiazole] $-SO_2NH_2$	8	7.2	0.62	45	15
Ethoxzolamide	C_2H_5O- [benzothiazole] $-SO_2NH_2$	1	8.1	140	4	6
Dichlorphenamide	Cl, Cl [benzene] $-SO_2NH_2, -SO_2NH_2$	18	8.3	11	—	2
Benzolamide	[phenyl]$-SO_2-N(H)-$ [thiadiazole] $-SO_2NH_2$	1	3.2	0.001	4	2

| NSD 3004 | | | 12 | 9.2 | 7[c] | <5 | 28 |

[a] Against pure CA II in hydration and barbital buffer at 0°C.
[b] At plasma concentrations 1–10 $\mu g\,ml^{-1}$.
[c] Dodecanol–water.

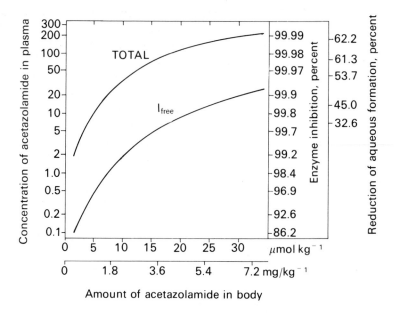

Fig. 20.7. The relation between the total amounts of acetazolamide in the human body, the total and free (I_{free}) plasma concentration, the degree of enzyme (CA II) inhibition in the ciliary epithelium, and the effect on aqueous humour formation at steady state. From Wistrand (1969), with permission.

plexus. Recently, several groups of investigators have reported on the successful development of inhibitors which after topical application to the cornea will reach the epithelium of the ciliary processes to inhibit CA II and thereby reduce aqueous humour flow and eye pressure. Three modes of approach have been used. One way has been the synthesis of an inhibitor with a proper balance of lipophilic and hydrophilic properties (Maren *et al.* 1983), as exemplified by the 6-hydroxy and 6-chloro analogues of ethoxzolamide (Schoenwald *et al.* 1984) and by the 5-trifluormethyl derivative of methazolamide (Stein *et al.* 1983; Bar-Ilan *et al* 1984). A second mode has been the esterification of a suitable inhibitor to form a pro-drug that would penetrate the cornea and then be hydrolysed to an active inhibitor. This approach is exemplified by the *O*-pivaloyl ester of 6-hydroxybenzothiazole-2-sulphonamide (Sugrue *et al.* 1985). A third approach has been to incorporate the inhibitor in a gel vehicle, which would prolong the corneal contact time (Lewis *et al.* 1984). At present, the most promising approach seems to be the use of an esterified inhibitor in a gel vehicle. This seems to allow the instillation of the inhibitor in the form of eye drops.

20.2.3.5 *CNS*

Inhibition of CA II in the glial cells of the brain is probably the cause of the anticonvulsant effect of those inhibitors that can penetrate the blood–brain barrier (Woodbury 1980). Again, there is a good correlation between carbonic anhydrase inhibitory activity and potency of these drugs. However, respiratory and possibly also metabolic acidosis due to the simultaneous inhibition of red cell and renal enzymes, respectively, could also be the cause of, or add to, the effect. Increasing the lipophilicity of the inhibitors appears to dissociate the anticonvulsant effect from the renal effect. Thus, methazolamide and ethoxzolamide have been found to be more potent as anticonvulsants than acetazolamide. When exhibiting marked anticonvulsant activity, they have only weak diuretic activity, while the opposite relationship between the two effects is found with acetazolamide. With NSD 3004 (Lund *et al.* 1971), a highly lipophilic drug (Table 20.3), a strong anticonvulsant effect was actually seen without any effect on the kidney and on the ocular pressure. Unfortunately, due to the strong binding to CA I in the red cells NSD 3004 could not be marketed. Similar principles for design of inhibitors with anticonvulsant and cerebral vasodilatory activities have been applied by Barnish *et al.* (1981). The ideal anticonvulsant of this kind would seem to be an inhibitor similar to NSD 3004 but having a low affinity for CA I, which would avoid long-term binding to red cells.

20.2.3.6 *Gastric mucosa*

Acetazolamide has been claimed to be useful in the treatment of gastric and duodenal ulcers due to its lowering of the secretion of HCl by the gastroparietal cells (Puşcaş 1984). The more lipophilic inhibitors like ethoxzolamide and NSD 3004 are more potent than acetazolamide (Lund *et al.* 1971; Maren 1984) but have not yet been tried clinically for this indication. However, side-effects in the form of gastritis and diarrhoea are common (Table 20.2) and are probably explained by inhibition of CA II in the protective alkali-secreting cells of the gastric mucosa and of the fluid-absorbing cells of the small and large intestine. The problem is therefore to design an inhibitor that can be targeted to the parietal cells without affecting the carbonic anhydrase-containing surface epithelial cells of the gastrointestinal tract.

20.2.3.7 *Choroid-plexus and cochlea*

Acetazolamide has been used in the treatment of hydrocephalus and Menière's disease. The same type of inhibitor as used in the treatment of glaucoma, i.e. similar to methazolamide, should probably be chosen for this indication. Benzolamide has been shown to be only weakly active in reducing cerebrospinal fluid production.

20.2.4 Design of new inhibitors

A number of sulphonamides inhibiting CA II with a $K_i \leqslant 10^{-8}$ M are presently available for clinical use (Table 20.3). Thus, there is no apparent need in clinical medicine for new compounds that are even better CA II inhibitors. Instead, the design of future inhibitors should be directed towards finding those compounds that are organ-selective as well as isozyme-selective. A drug with a better CA II selectivity than acetazolamide (see section 20.2.3.1.) would probably have therapeutic value. Since the present therapeutic use of CA inhibitors is based solely on the physiological functions of isozyme II, no clinical needs for CA I- or CA III-selective inhibitors can yet be defined. However, to elucidate the physiological roles of these isozymes in various tissues, such selective inhibitors would be of great value, particularly as the isozymes are found together in the same cells in some tissues (CA I and CA II in red cells, corneal endothelium and in some epithelial cells in the intestine) or as the only isozyme in adjacent epithelial cells containing either CA I or CA II (as is the case in colon and caecum). In the brain, CA I is found in the capillary endothelial cells and CA II in the glial cells nearby.

Very few data are available on the isozyme specificity of sulphonamides. The most CA I-selective inhibitor reported so far is 2-nitro-4-cyanobenzene-sulphonamide (Taylor *et al.* 1970a), which has about 40 times higher affinity for CA I than for CA II. The most efficient sulphonamide inhibitor of CA III known is chlorzolamide (5-[2-chlorophenyl]-1,3,4-thiadiazole-2-sulphonamide), with $K_i \approx 10^{-7}$ M (Sanyal *et al.* 1982), but it inhibits CA I and CA II even more strongly. Karlmark *et al.* (1979) have described two inhibitors of the membrane-bound renal tubular cell CA, a derivative of benzolamide covalently attached to dextran and a benzenesulphonamide having a quaternary ammonium group in the 4-position. These inhibitors do not penetrate the membrane and were used to show that the active site of this enzyme form is located on the exterior, luminal side of the brush-border membrane. By selectively inhibiting the enzyme by the dextran-coupled inhibitor, it could, moreover, be shown (Lucci *et al.* 1983) that this enzyme of the brush-border membranes of the renal tubules is involved in the reabsorption of bicarbonate.

References

Alward, P. D. and Wilensky, J. T. (1981). Determination of acetazolamide compliance in patients with glaucoma. *Arch. Ophthalmol.*, **99**, 1973–6.

Andersson, B., Nyman, P. O., and Strid, L. (1972). Amino acid sequence of human erythrocyte carbonic anhydrase B. *Biochem. Biophys. Res. Commun.*, **48**, 670–7.

Anker, N. and Mondrup, M. (1974). Carbonic anhydrase isoenzyme B in erythrocytes of subjects with thyroid disorders. *Clin. Chim. Acta*, **54**, 277–82.

Bar, D. (1963). Inhibiteurs de l' anhydrase carbonique. *Actual. Pharmacol.*, **15**, 1–44.

Bar-Ilan, A., Pessah, N. I., and Maren, T. H. (1984). The effects of carbonic anhydrase inhibitors on aqueous humor chemistry and dynamics. *Invest. Ophthalmol. Vis. Sci.*, **25**, 1198–205.

Barnish, I. T., Cross, P. E., Dickinson, R. P., Parry, M. J., and Randall, M. J. (1981). Cerebrovasodilatation through selective inhibition of the enzyme carbonic anhydrase. 3. 5-(arylthio)-, 5-(arylsulfinyl)-, and 5-(arylsulfonyl)-thiophene-2-sulfonamides. *J. Med. Chem.*, **24**, 959–64.

Beasley, F. J. (1962). Transient myopia and retinal edema during ethoxzolamide (Cardrase) therapy. *Arch. Ophthalmol.*, **68**, 490–1.

Becker, B. (1954). Diamox and the therapy of glaucoma. *Am. J. Opthalmol.*, **38**, 16–17.

Beyer, K. H. and Baer, J. E. (1961) Physiological basis for the action of newer diuretic agents. *Pharmacol. Rev.*, **13**, 517–62.

Blackburn, G. M., Mann, B. E., Taylor, B. F., and Worral, A. F. (1985). A nuclear magnetic resonance study of the binding of novel *N*-hydroxybenzenesulphonamide carbonic anhydrase inhibitors to native and cadmium-111-substituted carbonic anhydrase. *Eur. J. Biochem.*, **153**, 553–8.

Block, E. R. and Rostand, R. A. (1978). Carbonic anhydrase inhibition in glaucoma: Hazard or benefit for the chronic lunger? *Surv. Ophthalmol.*, **23**, 169–72.

Brookes, G. B. and Booth, J. B. (1984). Oral acetazolamide in Menière's disease. *J. Laryngol. Otol.* **98**, 1087–95.

Butterworth, P., Barlow, J., Konialis, C., Povey, S., and Edwards, Y. H. (1985). The assignment of human erythrocyte carbonic anhydrase CA1 to chromosome 8. *Cytogenet. Cell Genet.*, **40**, 597.

Carter, M. J. and Parsons, D. S. (1971). The isoenzymes of carbonic anhydrase: tissue, subcellular distribution and functional significance with particular reference to the intestinal tract. *J. Physiol. (London)*, **215**, 71–94.

Carter, N. D., Chegwidden, W. R., Hewett-Emmett, D., Jeffery, S., Shiels, A., and Tashian, R. E. (1984). Novel inhibition of carbonic anhydrase isozymes I, II and III by carbamoyl phosphate. *FEBS Lett.*, **165**, 197–200.

Chen, R. F. and Kernohan, J. C. (1967). Combination of bovine carbonic anhydrase with a fluorescent sulfonamide. *J. Biol. Chem.*, **242**, 5813–23.

Coleman, J. E. (1975). Chemical reactions of sulfonamides with carbonic anhydrase. *Ann. Rev. Pharmacol.* **15**, 221–42.

De Benedetti, P. G., Menziani, M. C. and Frassineti, C. (1985). A quantum chemical QSAR study of carbonic anhydrase inhibition by sulfonamides. *Quant. Struct. Act. Relat.*, **4**, 23–8.

Dodgson, S. J., Forster, R. E., II, Storey, B. T., and Mela, L. (1980). Mitochondrial carbonic anhydrase. *Proc. Nat. Acad. Sci. USA*, **77**, 5562–6.

Dodgson, S. J., Forster, R. E., II, Schwed, D. A. and Storey, B. T. (1983). Contribution of matrix carbonic anhydrase to citrulline synthesis in isolated guinea pig liver mitochondria. *J. Biol. Chem.*, **258**, 7696–701.

Edwards, Y. H., Lloyd, J., Parker, M., and Povey, S. (1985). Human muscle specific carbonic anhydrase CA-3 is on chromosome 8. *Cytogenet. Cell Genet.*, **40**, 621.

Engberg, P., Millqvist, E., Pohl, G., and Lindskog, S. (1985). Purification and some properties of carbonic anhydrase from bovine skeletal muscle. *Arch. Biochem. Biophys.*, **241**, 628–38.

Epstein, D. L. and Grant, W. M. (1979). Management of carbonic anhydrase inhibitor side effects. In *Symposium on ocular therapy* (ed. J. H. Leopold and R. P. Burns), Vol. 2, pp. 51–64. Wiley, New York.

Eriksson, E. A., Jones, T. A., and Liljas, A. (1986). Crystallographic studies of human carbonic anhydrase II (HCA II). In *Zinc enzymes* (ed. I. Bertini, C. Luchinat, W. Maret, and M. Zeppezauer), pp. 317–28. Birkhäuser, Basel.

Evelhoch, J. L., Bocian, D. F., and Sudmeier, J. L. (1981). Evidence for direct metal–nitrogen binding in aromatic sulfonamide complexes of cadmium(II)-substituted carbonic anhydrases by cadmium-113 nuclear magnetic resonance. *Biochemistry*, **20**, 4951–4.

Feldstein, J. B. and Silverman, D. N. (1984). Purification and characterization of carbonic anhydrase from the saliva of the rat. *J. Biol. Chem.*, **259**, 5447–53.

Fernley, R. T., Wright, R. D., and Coghlan, J. P. (1979). A novel carbonic anhydrase from the ovine parotid gland. *FEBS Lett.*, **105**, 299–302.

Friedland, B. R. and Maren, T. H. (1984). Carbonic anhydrase: pharmacology of inhibitors and treatment of glaucoma. *Handb. Exp. Pharmacol.*, **69**, 279–309.

Griggs, R. C., Moxley, III, R. T., Riggs, J. E., and Engel, W. K. (1978). Effects of acetazolamide on myotonia. *Ann. Neurol.*, **3**, 531–7.

Häcki, M. A., Waldeck, G., and Brändli, O. (1983). Acetazolamid bei hyperkapnischer chronischer obstruktiver Lungenkrankheit—eine Renaissance? *Schweiz. Med. Wschr.*, **113**, 110–14.

Hansch, C., McClarin, J., Klein, T., and Langridge, R. (1985). A quantitative structure-activity relationship and molecular graphics study of carbonic anhydrase inhibitors. *Mol. Pharmacol.*, **27**, 493–8.

Häussinger, D. and Gerok, W. (1985). Hepatic urea synthesis and pH regulation. Role of CO_2, HCO_3^-, pH and the activity of carbonic anhydrase. *Eur. J. Biochem.*, **152**, 381–6.

Henderson, L. E., Henriksson, D., and Nyman, P. O. (1976). Primary structure of human carbonic anhydrase C. *J. Biol. Chem.*, **251**, 5457–63.

Hewett-Emmett, D., Hopkins, P. J., Tashian, R. E., and Czelusniak, J. (1984). Origins and molecular evolution of the carbonic anhydrase isozymes. *Ann. N. Y. Acad. Sci.*, **429**, 338–58.

Höltje, H. D. and Simon, H. (1984). Theoretische Untersuchungen zu Wechselwirkungen zwischen Pharmaka und Rezeptormodellen, 4. Mitt. Der Sulfonamidinhibitor-Humanerythrozyte-Carboanhydrase C-Komplex. *Arch. Pharm. (Weinheim)* **317**, 506–16.

Jeffery, S., Edwards, Y., and Carter, N. (1980). Distribution of CA III in fetal and adult human tissue. *Biochem. Genet.*, **18**, 843–9.

Kakeya, N., Aoki, M., Kamada, A., and Yata, N. (1969a). Biological activities of drugs. VI. Structure–activity relationship of sulfonamide carbonic anhydrase inhibitors (1). *Chem. Pharm. Bull. (Tokyo)*, **17**, 1010–18.

Kakeya, N., Yata, N., Kamada, A., and Aoki, M. (1969b). Biological activities of drugs. VII. Structure–activity relationship of sulfonamide carbonic anhydrase inhibitors. (2). *Chem. Pharm. Bull. (Tokyo)*, **17**, 2000–7.

Kakeya, N., Yata, N., Kamada, A., and Aoki, M. (1969c). Biological activities of drugs. VIII. Structure-activity relationship of sulfonamide carbonic anhydrase inhibitors. (3). *Chem. Pharm. Bull. (Tokyo)* **17**, 2558–64.

Kanamori, K. and Roberts, J. D. (1983). Nitrogen-15 nuclear magnetic resonance study of benzensulfonamide and cyanate binding to carbonic anhydrase. *Biochemistry*, **22**, 2658–64.

Kannan, K. K., Notstrand, B., Fridborg, K., Lövgren, S., Ohlsson, A., and Petef, M. (1975). Crystal structure of human erythrocyte carbonic anhydrase B. Three-dimensional structure at nominal 2.2-Å resolution. *Proc. Nat. Acad. Sci. USA*, **72**, 51–5.

Kannan, K. K., Vaara, I., Notstrand, B., Lövgren, S., Borell, A., Fridborg, K., and Petef, M. (1977). Structure and function of carbonic anhydrase: Comparative studies of sulfonamide binding to human erythrocyte carbonic anhydrases B and C. In *Drug action at the molecular level* (ed. G. C. K. Roberts), pp. 73–91. University Park Press, Baltimore.

Kararli, T. and Silverman, D. N. (1985). Inhibition of the hydration of CO_2 catalyzed by carbonic anhydrase III from cat muscle. *J. Biol. Chem.*, **260**, 3884–9.

Karlmark, B., Ågerup, B., and Wistrand, P. J. (1979). Renal proximal tubular acidification. Role of brush-border and cytoplasmic carbonic anhydrase. *Acta Physiol. Scand.*, **106**, 145–50.

Kass, M. A., Kolker, A. E., Gordon, M., Goldberg, I., Gieser, D. K., Krupin, T. and Becker, B. (1981). Acetazolamide and urolithiasis. *Ophthalmology*, **88**, 261–5.

Kato, K. and Mokuno, K. (1984). Distribution of immunoreactive carbonic anhydrase III in various human tissues determined by a senstitive enzyme immunoassay method. *Clin. Chim. Acta*, **141**, 169–77.

Kawashiro, T. and Scheid, P. (1976). Measurement of Krogh's diffusion constant of CO_2 in respiring muscle at various CO_2 levels: evidence for facilitated diffusion. *Pflügers Arch. Ges. Physiol.*, **362**, 127–33.

Kendall, A. G. and Tashian, R. E. (1977). Erythrocyte carbonic anhydrase I: Inherited deficiency in humans. *Science*, **197**, 471–2.

Kernohan, J. C. (1966). A method for studying the kinetics of the inhibition of carbonic anhydrase by sulphonamides. *Biochim. Biophys. Acta*, **118**, 405–12.

King, R. W. and Burgen, A. S. V. (1970). Sulphonamide complexes of human carbonic anhydrases. Ultraviolet difference spectroscopy. *Biochim. Biophys. Acta*, **207**, 278–85.

King, R. W. and Burgen, A. S. V. (1976). Kinetic aspects of structure–activity relations: the binding of sulphonamides to carbonic anhydrase. *Proc. R. Soc.*, **B193**, 107–25.

King, R. W. and Maren, T. H. (1974). Kinetics of complex formation between carbonic anhydrase B and heterocyclic sulfonamides. *Mol. Pharmacol.*, **10**, 344–8.

King, R. W., Garg, L. C., Huckson, J., and Maren, T. H. (1974). Isolation and partial characterization of sulfonamide-resistant carbonic anhydrases from the liver of the male rat. *Mol. Pharmacol.*, **10**, 335–43.

Kishida, K. (1978). 1,3,4-thiadiazole-5-sulfonamides as carbonic anhydrase inhibitors: relationship between their electronic and hydrophobic stuctures and their inhibitory activity. *Chem. Pharm. Bull.* (*Tokyo*), **26**, 1049–53.

Kishida, K. and Manabe, R. (1980). The role of hydrophobicity of the substituted groups of dichlorphenamide in the development of carbonic anhydrase inhibition. *Med. J. Osaka Univ.*, **30**, 95–100.

Krebs, H. A. (1948). Inhibition of carbonic anhydrase by sulphonamides. *Biochem. J.*, **43**, 525–8.

Kumar, K., King, R. W., and Carey, P. R. (1976). Resonance Raman studies on some carbonic anhydrase–aromatic sulfonamide complexes. *Biochemistry*, **15**, 2195–202.

Kumar, K., Bindal, M. C., Singh, P., and Gupta, S. P. (1981). Effect of molecular size on carbonic anhydrase inhibition by sulfonamides. *Int. J. Quantum Chem.*, **20**, 123–9.

Larson, E. B., Roach, R. C., Schoene, R. B., and Hornbein, T. F. (1982). Acute mountain sickness and acetazolamide. Clinical efficacy and effect on ventilation. *J. Am. Med. Ass.*, **248**, 328–32.

Lewis, R. A., Schoenwald, R. D., Eller, M. G., Barfknecht, C. F., and Phelps, C. D. (1984). Ethoxzolamide analogue gel. A topical carbonic anhydrase inhibitor. *Arch. Ophthalmol.*, **102**, 1821–4.

Lichter, P. R., Newman, L. P., Wheeler, N. C., and Beall, O. V. (1978). Patient tolerence to carbonic anhydrase inhibitors. *Am. J. Ophthalmol.*, **85**, 495–502.

Liljas, A., Kannan, K. K., Bergstén, P. C., Waara, I., Fridborg, K., Strandberg, B., Carlbom, U., Järup, L., Lövgren, S., Petef, M. (1972). Crystal structure of human carbonic anhydrase C. *Nature, New Biol.*, **235**, 131–7.

Lin, K.-T. D. and Deutsch, H. F. (1973). Human carbonic anhydrases. XI. Complete primary structure of carbonic anhydrase B. *J. Biol. Chem.*, **248**, 1885–93.

Lindskog, S. (1983). Carbonic anhydrase. In *Zinc enzymes* (ed. T. G. Spiro), pp. 77–121. Wiley, New York.

Lindskog, S. and Thorslund, A. (1968). On the interaction of bovine cobalt carbonic anhydrase with sulfonamides. *Eur. J. Biochem.*, **3**, 453–60.

Lindskog, S., Engberg, P., Forsman, C., Ibrahim, S. A., Jonsson, B.-H., Simonsson, S., and Tibell, L. (1984). Kinetics and mechanism of carbonic anhydrase isoenzymes. *Ann. N. Y. Acad. Sci.*, **429**, 61–75.

Lloyd, J., McMillan, S., Hopkinson, D., and Edwards, Y. H. (1986). Nucleotide sequence and derived amino acid sequence of a cDNA encoding human muscle carbonic anhydrase. *Gene*, **41**, 233–9.

Lönnerholm, G., Selking, Ö., and Wistrand, P. J. (1985). Amount and distribution of carbonic anhydrases I and II in the gastrointestinal tract. *Gastroenterology*, **88**, 1151–61.

Lucci, M. S., Tinker, J. T., Weiner, J. M., and DuBose, Jr., T. D. (1983). Function of proximal tubule carbonic anhydrase defined by selective inhibition. *Am. J. Physiol.*, **245**, F443–9.

Lund, J., Pedersen, H. E., Olsen, P. Z., and Hvidberg, E. F. (1971). Early human studies of a new carbonic anhydrase inhibitor (NSD 3004) with anticonvulsant properties. *Clin. Pharmacol. Ther.*, **12**, 902–12.

Mann, T. and Keilin, D. (1940). Sulphanilamide as a specific inhibitor of carbonic anhydrase. *Nature (London)*, **146**, 164–5.

Maren, T. H. (1963). The relation between enzyme inhibition and physiological response in the carbonic anhydrase system. *J. Pharmacol. Exp. Ther.*, **139**, 140–53.

Maren, T. H. (1967). Carbonic anydrase: Chemistry, physiology, and inhibition. *Physiol. Rev.*, **47**, 595–781.

Maren, T. H. (1968). Renal carbonic anhydrase and the pharmacology of sulfonamide inhibitors. In *Handbook of experimental pharmacology* (ed. H. Herken), Vol. 24, pp. 195–256. Springer, Berlin.

Maren, T. H. (1974). HCO_3^- formation in aqueous humor: mechanism and relation to the treatment of glaucoma. *Invest. Ophthalmol.*, **13**, 479–84.

Maren, T. H. (1976). Relations between structure and biological activity of sulfonamides. *Ann. Rev. Pharmacol. Toxicol.*, **16**, 309–27.

Maren, T. H. (1979). Benzolamide: a renal carbonic anhydrase inhibitor. In *Orphan drugs* (ed. F. E. Karch), pp. 273–84. Marcel Dekker, New York.

Maren, T. H. (1984). The general physiology of reactions catalyzed by carbonic anhydrase and their inhibition by sulfonamides. *Ann. N. Y. Acad. Sci.*, **429**, 568–79.

Maren, T. H. (1985). Carbonic anhydrase. *New Engl. J. Med.*, **313**, 179–80.

Maren, T. H. and Sanyal, G. (1983). The activity of sulfonamides and anions against the carbonic anhydrases of animals, plants, and bacteria. *Ann. Rev. Pharmacol. Toxicol.*, **23**, 439–59.

Maren, T. H. and Wiley, C. E. (1968). The *in vitro* activity of sulfonamides against red cell carbonic anhydrases. Effect of ionic and substrate variation on the hydration reaction. *J. Med. Chem.*, **11**, 228–32.

Maren, T. H., Ellison, A. C., Fellner, S. K., and Graham, W. B. (1966). A study of hepatic carbonic anhydrase. *Mol. Pharmacol.*, **2**, 144–57.

Maren, T. H., Jankowska L., Sanyal, G., and Edelhauser, H. F. (1983). The transcorneal permeability of sulfonamide carbonic anhydrase inhibitors and their effect on aqueous humour secretion. *Exp. Eye Res.*, **36**, 457–80.

Marriq, C., Luccioni, F., and Laurent, G. (1965). Présence de radicaux acétyle dans les anhydrases carboniques érythrocytaires humaines et caractérisation d'un peptide N-terminal acétylé dans l'enzyme B. *Biochim. Biophys. Acta*, **105**, 606–8.

McKinley, D. N. and Whitney, P. L. (1976). Particulate carbonic anhydrase in homogenates of human kidney. *Biochim. Biophys. Acta*, **445**, 780–90.

Miller, W. H., Dessert, A. M., and Roblin, R. O., Jr. (1950). Heterocyclic sulfonamides as carbonic anhydrase inhibitors. *J. Am. Chem. Soc.*, **72**, 4893–6.

Moyle, S., Jeffery, S., and Carter, N. D. (1984). Localization of human muscle carbonic anhydrase isozymes using immunofluorescence. *J. Histochem. Cytochem.*, **32**, 1262–4.

Notstrand, B., Vaara, I., and Kannan, K. K. (1975). Structural relationship of human erythrocyte carbonic anhydrase isozymes B and C. *Isozymes*, **1**, 575–99.

Parsons, D. S. (1982). Role of anions and carbonic anhydrase in epithelia. *Phil. Trans. R. Soc. London* **B299**, 369–81.

Platts, M. M. and Hanley, T. (1956). The effect of the carbonic anhydrase inhibitor acetazolamide on chronic respiratory acidosis. *Acta Med. Scand.*, **154**, 53–60.

Pocker, Y. and Sarkanen, S. (1978). Carbonic anhydrase: structure, catalytic versatility, and inhibition. *Adv. Enzymol.*, **47**, 149–274.

Puşcaş, I. (1984). Treatment of gastroduodenal ulcers with carbonic-anhydrase inhibitors. *Ann. N. Y. Acad. Sci.*, **429**, 587–91.

Riley, D. A., Ellis, S., and Bain, J. (1982). Carbonic anhydrase activity in skeletal muscle fiber types, axons, spindles, and capillaries of rat soleus and extensor digitarum longus muscles. *J. Histochem. Cytochem.*, **30**, 1275–88.

Sanyal, G. (1984). The carbon dioxide hydration activity of the sulfonamide-resistant carbonic anhydrase from the liver of male rat: pH independence of the steady-state kinetics. *Arch. Biochem. Biophys.*, **234**, 576–9.

Sanyal, G., Swenson, E. R., Pessah, N. I., and Maren, T. H. (1982). The carbon dioxide hydration activity of skeletal muscle carbonic anhydrase. *Mol. Pharmacol.*, **22**, 211–20.

Sapirstein, V. S., Strocchi, P., and Gilbert, J. (1984). Properties and function of brain carbonic anhydrase. *Ann. N. Y. Acad. Sci.*, **429**, 481–93.

Schoenwald, R. D., Eller, M. G., Dixson, J. A., and Barfknecht, C. F. (1984). Topical carbonic anhydrase inhibitors. *J. Med. Chem.*, **27**, 810–12.

Shiels, A., Jeffery, S., Phillips, I. R., Shephard, E. A., Wilson, C. A., and Carter, N. D. (1983). Sexual differentiation of rat liver carbonic anhydrase III. *Biochim. Biophys. Acta*, **760**, 335–42.

Shima, K., Tashiro, K., Hibi, N., Tsukada, Y., and Hirai, H. (1983). Carbonic anhydrase III immunohistochemical localization in human skeletal muscle. *Acta Neuropathol.*, **59**, 237–9.

Shinagawa, Y. and Shinagawa, Y. (1974). Hückel MO studies on diuretics and carbonic anhydrase inhibitors. *Int. J. Quantum Chem. Quantum Biol. Symp.*, **1**, 169–78.

Silverman, D. N. and Vincent, S. H. (1983). Proton transfer in the catalytic mechanism of carbonic anhydrase. *CRC Crit. Rev. Biochem.*, **14**, 207–55.

Sly, W. S., Whyte, M. P., Sundaram, V., Tashian, R. E., Hewett-Emmett, D., Guibaud, P., Vainsel, M., Baluarte, H. J., Gruskin, A., Al-Mosawi, M., Sakati, N., and Ohlsson, A. (1985). Carbonic anhydrase II deficiency in 12 families with the autosomal recessive syndrome of osteopetrosis with renal tubular acidosis and cerebral calcification. *New Engl. J. Med.*, **313**, 139–45.

Stein, A., Pinke, R., Krupin, T., Glaab, E., Podos, S. M., Serle, J., and Maren, T. H. (1983). The effect of topically administered carbonic anhydrase inhibitors on aqueous humor dynamics in rabbits. *Am. J. Ophthalmol.*, **95**, 222–8.

Subbarao, S. N. and Bray, P. J. (1979). Correlation of carbonic anhydrase inhibitory activities of benzenesulfonamides with the data obtained by the use of nitrogen-14 nuclear quadrupole resonance. *J. Med. Chem.*, **22**, 111–14.

Sugrue, M. F., Gautheron, P., Schmitt, C., Viader, M. P., Conquet, P., Smith, R. L., Share, N. N., and Stone, C. A. (1985). On the pharmacology of L-645, 151: a topically effective ocular hypotensive carbonic anhydrase inhibitor. *J. Pharmacol. Exp. Ther.*, **232**, 534–40.

Swenson, E. R. and Maren, T. H. (1978). A quantitative analysis of CO_2 transport at rest and during maximal exercise. *Respir. Physiol.*, **35**, 129–59.

Tashian, R. E., Hewett-Emmett, D., and Goodman, M. (1983). The evolution and genetics of carbonic anhydrases I, II, and III. *Isozymes*, **7**, 79–100.

Tashian, R. E., Hewett-Emmett, D., Dodgson, S. J., Forster, R. E., II, and Sly, W. S. (1984). The value of inherited deficiencies of human carbonic anhydrase isozymes in understanding their cellular roles. *Ann. N. Y. Acad. Sci.*, **429**, 262–75.

Taylor, P. W., King, R. W., and Burgen, A. S. V. (1970a) Kinetics of complex formation between human carbonic anhydrases and aromatic sulfonamides. *Biochemistry*, **9**, 2638–45.

Taylor, P. W., King, R. W., and Burgen, A. S. V. (1970b) Influence of pH on the kinetics of complex formation between aromatic sulfonamides and human carbonic anhydrase. *Biochemistry*, **9**, 3894–902.

Testa, B. and Purcell, W. P. (1978). A QSAR study of sulfonamide binding to carbonic anhydrase as test of steric models. *Eur. J. Med. Chem. Chim. Ther.*, **13**, 509–14.

Travis, D. M. (1969). Renal carbonic anhydrase inhibition by benzolamide (CL 11, 366) in man. *J. Pharmacol. Exp. Ther.*, **167**, 253–60.

Vedani, A. and Dunitz, J. D. (1985). Lone-pair directionality in hydrogen-bond potential functions for molecular mechanics calculations: the inhibition of human carbonic anhydrase II by sulfonamides. *J. Am. Chem. Soc.*, **107**, 7653–8.

Vedani, A. and Meyer, E. F., Jr. (1984). Structure–activity relationships of sulfonamide drugs and human carbonic anhydrase C: modeling of inhibitor molecules into the receptor site of the enzyme with an interactive computer graphics display. *J. Pharm. Sci.*, **73**, 352–8.

Venta, P. J., Shows, T. B., Curtis, P. J., and Tashian, R. E. (1983). Polymorphic gene for human carbonic anhydrase II: a molecular disease marker located on chromosome 8. *Proc. Nat. Acad. Sci. USA.*, **80**, 4437–40.

Vincent, S. H. and Silverman, D. N. (1982). Carbonic anhydrase activity in mitochondria from rat liver. *J. Biol. Chem.*, **257**, 6850–5.

Vogh, B. P. (1980). The relation of choroid plexus carbonic anhydrase activity to cerebrospinal fluid formation: study of three inhibitors in cat, with extrapolation to man. *J. Pharmacol. Exp. Ther.*, **213**, 321–31.

Vroom, F. Q., Jarrell, M. A., and Maren, T. H. (1975). Acetazolamide treatment of hypokalemic periodic paralysis. *Arch. Neurol.*, **32**, 385–92.

Werblin, T. P., Pollack, J. P., and Liss, R. A. (1979). Aplastic anemia and agranulocytosis in patients using methazolamide for glaucoma. *J. Am. Med. Ass.*, **241**, 2817–18.

White, D. P., Zwillich, C. W., Pickett, C. K., Douglas, N. J., Findley, L. J., and Weil, J. V. (1982). Central sleep apnea. Improvement with acetazolamide therapy. *Arch. Int. Med.*, **142**, 1816–19.

Whitney, P. L. and Briggle, T. V. (1982). Membrane-associated carbonic anhydrase purified from bovine lung. *J. Biol. Chem.*, **257**, 12056–9.

Wistrand, P. J. (1969). Pharmacokinetics and pharmacodynamics of acetazolamide in relation to its use in the treatment of glaucoma. In *Pharmacology and pharmacokinetics* (ed. T. Teorell, R. L. Dedrick, and P. G. Condliffe), pp. 191–4. Plenum, New York.

Wistrand, P. J. (1979). Renal membrane-bound carbonic anhydrase. Purification and properties. *J. Med. Sci. (Uppsala)*, *Suppl.* **26**, 75.

Wistrand, P. J. (1984a). Properties of membrane-bound carbonic anhydrase. *Ann. N. Y. Acad. Sci.*, **429**, 195–206.

Wistrand, P. J. (1984b). The use of carbonic anhydrase inhibitors in ophthalmology and clinical medicine. *Ann. N. Y. Acad. Sci.*, **429**, 609–19.

Wistrand, P. J., Rawls, J. A., and Maren, T. H. (1960). Sulfonamide carbonic anhydrase inhibitors and intra-ocular pressure in rabbits. *Acta Pharmacol. Toxicol.*, **17**, 337–55.

Wistrand, P. J., Lindahl, S., and Wåhlstrand, T. (1975). Human renal carbonic anhydrase. Purification and properties. *Eur. J. Biochem.*, **57**, 189–95.

Wistrand, P. J., Schenholm, M., and Lönnerholm, G. (1986). Carbonic anhydrase isoenzymes CA-I and CA-II in the human eye. *Invest. Ophthalmol. Vis. Sci.*, **27**, 419–28.

Woodbury, D. M. (1980). Carbonic anhydrase inhibitors. In *Antiepileptic drugs: mechanism of action* (ed. G. H. Glaser, J. K. Penry, and D. M. Woodbury), pp. 617–33. Raven Press, New York.

21

Inhibition of intracellular methyl transfer and aminopropyl transfer reactions by analogues of substrates, products, and transition states

James K. Coward

21.1   Introduction

Enzyme-catalysed alkyl transfer reactions are involved in a myriad of important metabolic processes within the cell. The principal alkyl donors are the electrophilic sulphonium compounds, S-adenosyl-L-methionine (SAM) and its decarboxylated derivative (dcSAM). The biosynthesis of these substrates and their utilization as intracellular alkylating agents are shown in eqn. (21.1). In this series of reactions the role of SAM is that of a methylating agent for a host of cellular nucleophiles. In contrast, the role of dcSAM is that of an aminopropyl donor by which putrescine (Put) is converted sequentially to spermidine (Spd) and spermine (Spm). The nucleoside products of these reactions are S-adenosyl-L-homocysteine (SAH) and 5′-deoxy-5′-methylthioadenosine (MTA). Each is degraded by specific enzyme-catalysed reactions which salvage homocysteine

$$Met + ATP \xrightarrow[\begin{array}{c}\uparrow\\ PPP\end{array}]{\;\; 3Pi\;\;} SAM \longrightarrow dcSAM \begin{array}{c} \nearrow \; Spm + MTA \\ \searrow \; Spd + MTA \end{array} \begin{array}{c} \searrow \\ \nearrow \end{array} Met + Ade$$

$$\begin{array}{c} HNuc \searrow \\ \downarrow \; CH_3Nuc + H^- \\ SAH \\ \uparrow \\ \downarrow \\ Ado + Hcy \end{array} \qquad Put$$

(21.1)

(Hcy) from SAH or synthesize new methionine (Met) from MTA, and release respectively the purine nucleoside, adenosine (Ado) or the purine base, adenine (Ade). Thus, purines and amino acids derived from SAH and MTA are re-introduced into the cellular pools. The discussion in this chapter will focus on inhibitors, both naturally-occurring and synthetic, of the alkyltransferases and of the degradative enzymes S-adenosylhomocysteine hydrolase (SAHase) and MTA phosphorylase. Where appropriate, enzyme mechanism data will be presented to provide a basis for inhibitor design.

21.2 Methyltransferases—structure and mechanism

To date, the most thoroughly studied methyltranferase is catechol O-meth-yltransferase (COMT), an enzyme that catalyses the inactivation of a large number of catecholamine neurotransmitters, hormones, and catechol steroids (Guldberg and Marsden 1975; Borchardt 1980a). The enzyme is available from a variety of sources, the most widely used being rat liver. Mechanistic studies of the COMT-catalysed reaction utilizing steady-state kinetics techniques (Coward et al. 1973; Hegazi et al. 1979; Rivett and Roth 1982) and stereochemical probes (Woodard et al. 1980) have reached the conclusion that sequential binding of the substrates leads to a ternary complex in which nucleophilic attack by one of the catechol oxygens on the methyl carbon at SAM leads to meta-and/or para-O-methylation depending on the catechol substrate (Wu et al. 1984; Thakker et al. 1986). Kinetic studies on related model reactions have provided evidence for general base catalysis of this S_N2 reaction (Knipe et al. 1982). The question of whether the sequential binding of substrates is random (Coward et al. 1973) or ordered, with SAM binding prior to the catechol (Rivett and Roth 1982), is not yet resolved.

Several substrate analogues bearing (photo) chemically reactive groups have been synthesized and used to probe the structure of COMT. Studies with catecholamine analogues bearing alkylating moieties have revealed the presence of two different nucleophiles at or near the catecholamine binding site

(Borchardt and Thakker 1975). In addition, reaction of the enzyme with radiolabelled *N*-ethylmaleimide indicates the presence of three nucleophilic groups, only two of which are required for enzyme activity. Protection experiments support the hypothesis that the two critical nucleophiles are those which react with the catecholamine affinity labels (Borchardt and Thakker 1976). A methylase photoaffinity reagent, 8-azido-SAM, has been prepared by enzyme-catalysed reaction of 8-azido-ATP and methionine (Kaiser *et al.* 1983). Light-dependent covalent labelling of COMT by the reagent has been demonstrated, but the precise location of the labelled site on the protein has not yet been determined. Crystals of COMT suitable for structural studies by X-ray diffraction have not been reported.

Mechanistic studies on other SAM-dependent methyl transfer reactions have been reported, but none has been studied as completely as the reaction catalysed by COMT. The results of stereochemical studies of methylation reactions using methionine or SAM chiral in the methyl group are on record (Arigoni 1978; Floss and Tsai 1979). The reactions investigated all proceeded with net inversion of configuration at the chiral methyl group, indicative of a single-displacement mechanism such as is observed with the COMT-catalysed reaction. The methylation of cytosine residues in DNA has, on the surface, many mechanistic similarities to the well-studied reductive methylation of 2′-deoxyuridylate by 5,10-methylenetetrahydrofolate catalysed by thymidylate synthase (Santi *et al.* 1983). Thus, one would expect an addition–elimination mechanism involving attack at C-6 of dUMP by a nucleophilic residue on the enzyme resulting in methylation at C-5, followed by elimination of a proton at C-5 and the enzyme nucleophile at C-6 to regenerate the 5,6 double bond. Such a mechanism appears to operate in the unusual folate-dependent formation of ribothymidine residues in tRNA isolated from *S. faecalis* and *B. subtilis* (Delk *et al.* 1976, 1979, 1980.)

21.3   Methyltransferases—inhibitors

Nearly all SAM-dependent methyltransferases are inhibited by the common thioether product SAH (**1a**) (Ueland, 1982). Several laboratories have used the fact as a basis for the design of synthetic inhibitors of this class of enzymes (Coward and Crooks 1979; Borchardt 1980b). Analogues of SAH have been synthesized and investigated as inhibitors of isolated methylases, as well as inhibitors of methylation *in vitro* using selected cell culture systems. In addition, natural products related to SAH, such as sinefungin and A9145C (Fuller and Nagarajan 1978; Pugh *et al.* 1978) have been investigated in a similar manner. Of the large number of compounds studied with isolated methylases (Coward and Crooks 1979; Borchardt 1980b), two have emerged for examination in cultured mammalian cells. The 7-deaza analogue of SAH, *S*-tubercidinylhomocysteine (**1b**), is a metabolically stable drug (Crooks *et al.* 1979) that has been shown to inhibit tRNA methylation in PHA-stimulated rat lymphocytes (Chang and

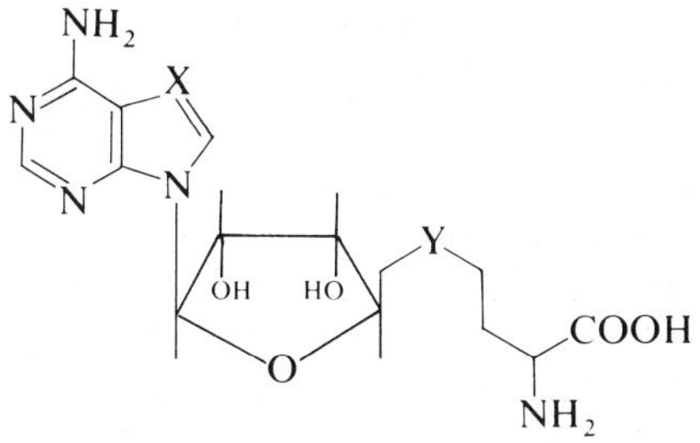

1

(a) X = N, Y = S; SAH

(b) X = CH, Y = S; c^7SAH, STH

(c) X = N, Y = (+)CHNH$_2$; sinefungin

Coward 1975), dopamine methylation in neuroblastoma cells (Michelot *et al.* 1977), mRNA methylation in Novikoff hepatoma cells (Kaehler *et al.* 1977, 1979; Camper *et al.* 1983), and phospholipid methylation in isolated rat hepatocytes (Schanche *et al.* 1982). The aim of this type of research is to correlate specific methylation reactions with cellular processes of interest. In the case of mRNA methylation, inhibition of N^6-methyladenosine (m^6A) formation by c^7SAH results in a lag in the cytoplasmic appearance of mature mRNA in HeLa cells (Camper *et al.* 1983). These data suggest a role for m^6A in either the nuclear processing of primary RNA transcripts or in the transport of mature mRNA from the nucleus to the cytoplasm.

A second SAH analogue effective *in vitro* is sinefungin (1c) an antifungal antibiotic isolated from *S. griseolus*, and a potent inhibitor of certain methyltransferases, most notably mRNA methylases and protein carboxy *O*-methyltransferases. Thus, sinefungin has been shown to inhibit vaccinia virus replication and viral mRNA methylation (7-methylguanine and 2'-*O*-methyl nucleoside moieties in the RNA 5'-cap structure) in infected L cells (Pugh *et al.* 1978). Sinefungin has been shown also to inhibit protein carboxy *O*-methylation in extracts derived from calf thymus and lysed rat hypothalamic synaptosomes, but not intact synaptosomes (Borchardt *et al.* 1981).

The use of SAH analogues as drugs to inhibit methylation reactions *in vitro* or *in vivo* is limited by the transport barrier presented by the cell membrane. Thus, SAH is not transported well by mammalian cells (Walker and Duerre 1975), and no intact material is found intracellularly in murine neuroblastoma cells (Crooks *et al.* 1979), rat hepatocytes (Aarbakke and Ueland 1981), or Novikoff heptoma cells (Coward *et al.* 1983) following incubation with 8-[^{14}C]SAH. Rapid hydrolysis of SAH, catalysed by the enzyme *S*-adenosylhomocysteine hydrolase (SAHase), leads to the accumulation of nucleosides and nucleotides derived from adenosine and inosine (Crooks *et al.* 1979). In contrast, c^7SAH

(STH; **1b**), is not metabolized in these cells (Crooks *et al.* 1979; Coward *et al.* 1983), but the rate and extent of drug uptake is very low (Coward *et al.* 1983). For these reasons, it is not surprising that high concentrations of c^7AdoHcy are required in order to observe inhibition of methyl transfer reactions *in vitro*. It should be noted that plasma membranes from rat hepatocytes apparently bind c^7AdoHcy well (Aarbakke *et al.* 1982), and phospholipid methylation in these cell membranes is dramatically inhibited at low drug concentrations (Schanche *et al.* 1981, 1982). Transport of sinefungin has not been studied extensively, but the range of biological activities observed with this antibiotic suggest that it is transported well by a variety of cells (however, see Borchardt *et al.* 1981). The lack of radio-labelled sinefungin has precluded transport and metabolism studies which could help address the mechanism of action of this interesting drug. The fact that sinefungin is a δ-substituted ornithine derivative suggests that it may be transported by an amino-acid transport system. It is because of these transport problems that investigators have sought to modulate intracellular SAH levels by inhibition of SAHase using a variety of adenosine analogues. This will be discussed in more detail in a subsequent section.

In addition to the SAH analogues just discussed, one can imagine the use of substrate analogues, i.e. variable nucleophile or SAM analoges, as potentially effective methyltransferase inhibitors. Unfortunately, most of the work with analogues of the variable nucleophile, e.g. a catecholamine derivative for COMT, has not distinguished between compounds which act as alternative substrates to yield a product with unknown biological properties, and those which act as inhibitors to decrease the rate of reaction for all substrates. One notable exception, and a very important example of this approach, is the use of 5-azacytidine to inhibit DNA methylation. As noted above, the mechanism of action of this enzyme, by analogy with thymidylate synthase, probably involves the steps shown in eqn. (21.2). In the case of 5-azacytidine-containing DNA ($X = N$), the rate of expulsion of the enzyme from C-6 is markedly reduced so that a stable complex between the methyltransferase and DNA can be isolated (Santi *et al.*, 1984; Christman *et al.*, 1985; Friedman, 1985). Similar results have been observed with 5-fluorouracil-containing tRNA and a tRNA methyltransferase, (D. V. Santi, personal communication), an even more striking analogy

(a) $X = CH$
(b) $X = N$

$$(21.2)$$

with the well-established mechanism of 5-fluorodeoxyuridylate inhibition of thymidylate synthase (Pogolotti and Santi 1977).

Analogues of the non-varied substrate, SAM, have been synthesized. Most of these molecules have structural modification in the purine, sugar, or amino acid moieties, which lead to poor binding to the enzyme (Borchardt 1980a). Recently, the synthesis of an analogue in which $\overset{+}{N}HCH_3$ replaces the $\overset{+}{S}CH_3$ of SAM has been published (Davis et al. 1983, 1985). No biochemical data were reported, but the desmethyl compound, an SAH analogue in which —NH— replaces —S—, has been shown to be a very poor inhibitor of several methylases (Chang and Coward 1976). In any event, rat liver membranes are impermeable to exogenous SAM (Hoffman et al. 1980), and it is questionable whether SAM analogues that retain net positive charge would be taken up by cells.

Finally, the use of inhibitors of SAM synthetase such as cycloleucine (Sufrin et al. 1981) has been suggested as a method for inhibiting intracellular methyl transfer reactions. This drug has been used to inhibit mRNA methylation in two cases (Caboche and Bachellerie 1977; Dimock and Stoltzfus 1977). A concern about the use of SAM synthetase inhibitors, in addition to the high concentrations required, is the fact that any drug that blocks the synthesis of SAM would presumably affect the levels of dcSAM in the cell, and therefore affect polyamine biosynthesis. Although the use of a more potent inhibitor of SAM synthetase, L-2-amino-4-methoxy-cis-but-3-enoic acid (L-cis-AMB), has been reported to lead to no changes in polyamine levels (Porter et al. 1984), the same paper reported a marked increase in the activity of SAM decarboxylase activity in cells treated with 0.4 mM L-cis-AMB. Therefore, more complete studies on the effects of SAM synthetase inhibitors on the complex series of reactions involved in polyamine biosynthesis and metabolism must be carried out before drawing conclusions about the validity of using this class of drugs specifically to affect intracellular methyl transfer reactions.

21.4 S-adenosylhomocysteine hydrolase—structure and mechanism

Relief of SAH inhibition of SAM-dependent methyltransferases is provided by two enzyme-catalysed reactions. In prokaryotes, SAH nucleosidase catalyses cleavage of the glycosidic bond, leading to adenine and ribosylhomocysteine (Duerre 1962). In eukaryotes, reversible cleavage of the 5'-thioether bond of SAH is effected in a reaction catalyzed by SAH hydrolase (DeLaHaba and Cantoni 1959). The latter enzyme is of most interest in the context of drug design research with mammalian cells, and the discussion which follows will be restricted to that enzyme. SAH hydrolase (EC 3.3.1.1) has been purified to homogeneity and crystallization of the enzyme has been reported (Richards et al. 1978) but structural studies with the crystalline enzyme have not been described. The mechanism of action of SAHase has been elucidated in elegant studies by Palmer and Abeles (1979). The simple hydrolysis of a thioether such as SAH is not likely to occur in aqueous media, and the thermodynamically favoured reaction (DeLaHaba and Cantoni 1959) in the synthetic direction is difficult to imagine occurring without prior activation of the 5'-hydroxyl of adenosine to provide a better leaving group. Therefore, the discovery that the hydrolase is an $NAD^+/NADH$-dependent enzyme led Palmer and Abeles (1976) to propose the mechanism shown in eqn (21.3), for which they have provided a considerable body of supportive data (Palmer and Abeles 1979). Additional mechanistic details on this reaction have been provided by Sinhababu *et al.* (1985), and by Parry and Askonas (1985). These studies respectively demonstrated partially rate-limiting hydride transfer from C-3' of SAH to NAD^+ in the critical initial redox activation step of eqn. (21.3), and established the *syn* stereochemistry of both elimination of RSH or H_2O and subsequent nucleophilic attack at the 4',5'-olefin.

$$(21.3)$$

In terms of drug design, this mechanism suggests several interesting possibilities. The oxidative elimination of RS^- (hydrolytic direction) or OH^- (synthetic direction) leads to a common α,β-unsaturated ketone (3'-keto-4',5'-dehydroadenosine), which could undergo nucleophilic attack by the enzyme. This scheme has many of the characteristics of the well-studied 'suicide' inactivation of several pyridoxal-phosphate-dependent enzymes by amino acid analogues (Walsh 1982). Inactivation of SAH hydrolase by 2'-deoxyadenosine (Hershfield 1979; Abeles *et al.* 1980, 1982)) and adenine arabinoside (Hershfield 1979) is in accord with this proposal in that both compounds are bound tightly to the enzyme as indicated by gel filtration experiments. However, only free adenine is isolated following denaturation (Abeles *et al.* 1980) or dialysis (Hershfield *et al.*

1982) of the inhibited enzyme. These results suggest the facile β-elimination of adenine from the intermediate 3'-ketonucleoside (Pfitzner and Moffatt 1963). Some aspects of the scheme shown in eqn. (21.3) require further investigation in terms of the inactivators. There are apparent conflicting data in the literature on the interaction of MTA with SAHase (Palmer and Abeles 1979; Hershfield 1979; Ferro *et al.* 1981). The mechanism of eqn. (21.3) would predict formation of the same α,β-unsaturated ketonucleoside from MTA (R = CH$_3$) and SAH (R = CH$_2$CH$_2$CH(NH$_2$)CO$_2$H) only if MTA is able to bind to the enzyme and become oxidized to the 3'-keto derivative. Data from Palmer and Abeles (1979) indicate that this oxidation reaction does not occur with MTA as the substrate. Hershfield (1979) and Ferro *et al.* (1981) report that SAH hydrolase is inactivated by MTA in a time-dependent manner, but Hershfield *et al.* (1982) indicate that this inactivation does not lead to release of adenine or a decrease in enzyme-bound NAD$^+$, the oxidant required for oxidation of the 3'-OH of the substrate in the Palmer–Abeles mechanism [eqn. (21.3)]. These data suggest that MTA, and perhaps other nucleosides (Hershfield *et al.* 1982; Chiang *et al.* 1981), inactivate SAH hydrolase by a different mechanism than a suicide-type based on eqn. (21.3). It should be noted that the reversible nature of the reaction catalyzed by SAH hydrolase allows for assay of the enzyme in either the hydrolytic or synthetic direction. The inactivation experiments just described generally have been carried out using various assays of the enzyme in the synthetic direction. The assay in the hydrolytic direction employs adenosine deaminase in the reaction in order to remove adenosine as it is liberated. Use of this assay is precluded when studying adenosine derivatives as potential inactivators, but it would be reassuring to know that the inactivation kinetics and mechanism do not differ in the hydrolytic vs synthetic reaction; i.e. MTA vs 2'-deoxyadenosine.

SAHase is also inactivated by cAMP, a process in which NAD$^+$ is released from the enzyme with concomitant loss of enzyme activity (Hohman *et al.* 1985). This differs from the inactivation by 2'-deoxyadenosine where, as noted above, oxidation of the 3'-OH is required [eqn. (21.3)] and enzyme-bound NAD$^+$ is reduced to NADH, thus inactivating the enzyme. While the inactivation by both cAMP and 2'-deoxyadenosine can be reversed by addition of NAD$^+$, the detailed mechanism of inactivation must be different. Photoaffinity labelling experiments using 8-azidoadenosine and 8-azido-cAMP indicate that both molecules bind to the same region of the SAHase protein (Aiyar and Hershfield 1985). The physiological significance of SAHase inactivation by naturally occuring adenosine nucleosides is not yet understood.

21.5   *S*-adenosylhomocysteine hydrolase—inhibitors

As noted above, the problems associated with transport of SAH and its analogues in mammalian cells have led several groups of investigators to develop inhibitors of SAH hydrolase. In this way, it is proposed that intracellular methyl transfer reactions will be inhibited by the increased concentration of SAH as hydrolytic degradation is blocked. This approach is appealing because there are extensive data in the literature concerning the transport of nucleosides across cell membranes and scores of adenosine analogues available as potential inhibitors. Unfortunately, there is one serious drawback to this approach. The probability is high that these nucleoside analogues, with a free 5'-OH, will be phosphorylated by one or more nucleoside kinases during long-term exposure in the cell. Therefore, it may be difficult to separate biological effects due to inhibition of methylation from those due to fraudulent nucleotide formation common to a myriad of cytotoxic nucleosides.

The earliest systematic study of SAHase inhibitors is that of Chiang et al. (1977). These authors screened a wide variety of AdoHcy analogues and noted some modest inhibitors of the enzyme. Of most interest was the fact that 3-deaza SAH (c^{3}SAH), an excellent substrate, gave rise to an extremely inhibitory product, 3-deazaadenosine (c^{3}Ado). This discovery was followed by a series of papers in which nucleosides were screened for activity as competitive inhibitors (Guranowski et al. 1981; Montgomery et al. 1982) or inactivators (Chiang et al. 1981; Kim et al. 1985). Some extremely potent inhibitors of SAHase have emerged from this work, notably ($\pm$)aristeromycin (carbocyclic adenosine C-Ado) with $K_i = 5 \times 10^{-9}$ M and 3-deaza-($\pm$)aristeromycin (c^{3}CAdo) with $K_i = 1-3 \times 10^{-9}$ M. These values are nearly three orders of magnitude lower than obtained for c^{3}Ado ($K_i = 1-4 \times 10^{-6}$ M).

Adenine arabinoside (AraA), 2'-deoxyadenosine (2'-dAdo), 3-deaza-adenosine (c^{3}Ado) and its carbocyclic analogue, c^{3}CAdo, have been studied for their ability to inhibit SAH hydrolase in intact cells. Studies with these drugs include the inactivation and reactivation of the enzyme in cells treated with AraA (Helland and Ueland 1982), thus indicating a reversible inactivation in vitro, as noted above [eqn (21.3)] for the isolated enzyme. In addition, inactivation of SAHase in 2'-dAdo-treated T-lymphoblasts has been reported (Kefford et al. 1982). Among the competitive inhibitors, 3-deaza-($\pm$)aristeromycin (c^{3}CAdo) has been investigated as an antiviral agent (Montgomery et al. 1982) and as an inhibitor of chemotaxis in macrophages (Alksamit et al. 1982). The most extensive work on cellular effects of SAHase inhibitors has been done with c^{3}Ado (Stopford et al. 1985, and references therein). As noted above, a concern with biological studies using these nucleosides is that metabolism to the corresponding nucleotide might cause difficulty in interpreting the data. Early studies with c^{3}Ado as an inhibitor of virus replication (Bader et al. 1978) indicated that no nucleotides could be detected in chick embryo cells treated with [^{14}C]c^{3}Ado. More recent work by Zimmerman et al. (1984) indicate that alterations in leukocyte functions caused by c^{3}Ado are not due to alterations in intracellular SAH levels, but rather are associated with alterations in microfilament structure. In this work, the authors detected small but significant metabolism of c^{3}Ado to the corresponding nucleotides. These recent results and those of Sung and Silverstein (1985) suggest that caution should be used in interpreting results using nucleoside inhibitors of SAHase pending thorough examinations of drug metabolism and the use of alternative hydrolase inhibitors (Stopford *et al.*, 1985).

An unusual nucleoside which has been shown to be a potent SAHase inhibitor is the antitumor antibiotic, neplanocin A, [eqn (21.4), **2**] (Borchardt *et al.* 1984). Although the chemical details of this inhibition have not yet been elucidated, one can extrapolate from the Palmer–Abeles mechanism [eqn (21.3)] to the reactions shown in eqn (21.4) showing the conversion of neplanocin first to an electrophilic α,β-unsaturated ketone, perhaps followed by a slower, *cis* β-elimination of adenine to yield a substituted cyclopentadieneone. Both of these

$$(21.4)$$

unsaturated ketones would be capable of inactivating the enzyme. In addition, it has been shown that neplanocin A can be converted to *S*-neplanocylmethionine (SNM) (Keller and Borchardt 1984; Glazer and Knode 1984), via the intermediate nucleotide triphosphate (Glazer and Knode 1984; Saunders *et al.* 1985). Furthermore, it has been shown by Saunders *et al.* (1985) that the accumulation of neplanocin triphosphate observed in wild-type Chinese hamster ovary (CHO) cells is not observed in an adenosine kinase-deficient cell line, whereas cytotoxicity of neplanocin A is observed at similar drug concentrations in both the wild-type and mutant cells. Earlier studies had demonstrated the ability of a wide variety of adenosine analogues to form the corresponding SAM and SAH analogues in human erythrocytes and/or mouse lymphocytes (Zimmerman *et al.* 1979, 1980). In the case of cells treated with neplanocin A, it is not yet clear whether the newly formed SNM is converted to *S*-neplanocylhomocysteine (SNH). Reports on the ability of SNM to act as a methyl donor indicate that it is a substrate for purified COMT (Keller and Borchardt 1984) but not for crude lysates from L cells containing phospholipid and protein carboxymethyltransferases (Keller *et al.* 1985). Additional studies with (bio)synthetic SNM with isolated enzymes will be required, since it is known that SNM is further metabolized in two cell systems studied to date (Keller *et al.* 1985; Linevsky *et al.* 1985). SNM is not a substrate for SAM decarboxylase, nor does it inhibit that enzyme (Keller *et al.* 1985). Neplanocin A leads to an increase in intracellular SAH in mouse L929 cells (Borchardt *et al.* 1984) but not in a human colon carcinoma cell line (HT-29) (Glazer and Knode 1984) or a human promyelocytic leukaemia cell line (HL-60) (Linevsky *et al.* 1985). One would expect an accumulation of SAH in cells treated with an SAHase inhibitor as potent as neplanocin A (Borchardt *et al.* 1984; Whaun *et al.* 1986). Inhibition of RNA methylation has been invoked as the basis for the observed antiviral activity of neplanocin A (Borchardt *et al.* 1984), and also for its effect on HL-60 cell differentiation and expression of c-myc mRNA (Linevsky *et al.* 1985). Detailed analyses of RNA methylation patterns in the absence and presence of this drug have not yet been reported, and any conclusions regarding the role of mRNA methylation in the observed biological responses must await such analyses.

It should be noted that other inhibitors of SAHase such as adenosine dialdehyde (Hoffman 1980) and acyclic analogues of adenosine (Holy *et al.* 1985) have been studied for their ability to block methyl transfer reactions in whole cells. Thus, adenosine dialdehyde has been shown to inactivate SAHase from mouse L929 cells rapidly (Bartel and Borchardt 1984), and to inhibit both lipid methylation and protein carboxylmethylation in those cells as a result of an increased concentration of SAH brought about by the drug. Similarly, several acyclic analogues of adenosine have been studied in isolated rat hepatocytes (Schanche *et al.* 1984) and have been shown to inhibit intracellular methylations by increasing the intracellular concentration of SAH. An interesting correlation between SAH hydrolase inhibitory activity and antiviral activity has been reported for many of the drugs discussed in this section (DeClerq and Cools 1985).

21.6   Aminopropyltransferases—structure and mechanism

The aminopropyltransferases, spermidine synthase [putrescine aminopropyltransferase (PAPT)] and spermine synthase [spermidine aminopropyltransferase (SAPT)], catalyse two key reactions in polyamine biosynthesis, as shown in eqn. (21.5) (Williams-Ashman and Pegg 1981). Several studies of the steady-state kinetics for both the PAPT- and SAPT-catalyzed reactions have been reported. In the case of PAPT isolated from *E. coli*, a non-sequential ('ping–pong') kinetic mechanism was suggested by the results (Zappia *et al.* 1980). Unfortunately, the

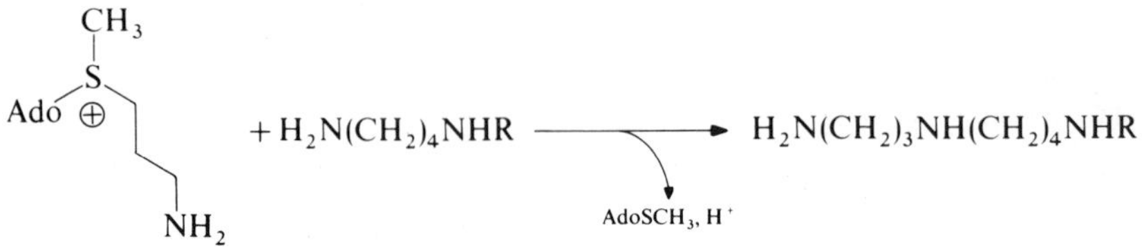

$$+ \ H_2N(CH_2)_4NHR \longrightarrow H_2N(CH_2)_3NH(CH_2)_4NHR$$

AdoSCH$_3$, H$^+$

(a) PAPT, R = H
(b) SAPT, R = $(CH_2)_3NH_2$

(21.5)

presence of a contaminating MTA nucleosidase activity in the enzyme preparation precluded a complete study of product inhibition kinetics. In contrast, kinetics studies on PAPT (Raina *et al.* 1984) and SAPT (Pajula 1983) from bovine brain indicate that a sequential kinetic mechanism is operative. In principle, these opposing conclusions based on enzyme kinetics studies can be resolved by an investigation of the stereochemical course of the reaction, as illustrated by the stereochemical literature on methyl transfer (Floss and Tsai 1979; Arigoni 1978) and phosphoryl transfer (Knowles 1980; Frey 1982) reactions.

Recent stereochemical studies of the PAPT reaction have utilized either a mixture of chiral $[3, 4-^2H_2]$ methionines (3) in biosynthetic feeding experiments (*E. coli*) (Golding and Nassereddin 1985b), or have used stereoselectively synthesized chiral $[^2H]$dcSAM enantiomers (4) as substrates for partially purified *E. coli* PAPT (Orr *et al.* 1988). Both of these investigations used high-field ^1H-n.m.r. in order to establish the relative (Golding and Nassereddin 1985a) or absolute (Pontoni *et al.* 1983) stereochemistry of the products isolated from 3 and 4, respectively. The ^1H-n.m.r. (400 MHz) spectra of a mixture of hexahydropyrimidines ultimately derived from 3 are considerably more complex than the 500 MHz spectra of each purified isomer of N_1,N_8-bisboc spermidine-N_5-(−)camphanamide ultimately derived from a single isomer of 4. In the research that used 3 in *E. coli* feeding experiments, selected decoupling experiments and computer simulation of a portion of the complex spectra aided in peak assignments, and led to the conclusion that the aminopropyl transfer reaction in *intact E. coli* proceeds with net inversion of configuration at the methylene of interest (3, C-4) (Golding and Nassereddin 1985b). This is in accord with similar stereochemical studies on methyl transfer reactions (Floss and Tsai 1979; Arigoni 1978). Simultaneous studies using purified *R*- and *S*-enantiomers of 4 come to the same conclusion. Inspection of the ^1H-n.m.r. spectra of the spermidine camphanamides ultimately derived from *R*-4 and *S*-4, and comparison with stereospecifically synthesized standards (Pontoni *et al.* 1983), lead to the conclusion that the reaction proceeds with net inversion of configuration at the methylene at interest (4, —SCHD—) (Orr *et al.* 1988).

3   4

21.7   Aminopropyltransferases—inhibitors

As is the case with the methyltransferases discussed above, product inhibition is an important feature of both the PAPT and SAPT reactions. 5'-Deoxy-5'-methylthioadenosine (MTA) is a potent product inhibitor of both reactions (Bowman *et al.* 1973; Pajula and Raina 1979; Hibasami *et al.* 1980). In addition, marked substrate inhibition by dcSAM has been observed in the reaction catalysed by PAPT (Coward *et al.* 1977; *Zappia et al.* 1980; Hibasami *et al.* 1980; Samejima and Yamanoha 1982; Raina *et al.* 1983) but not in the reaction catalysed by SAPT (Pajula 1983). This type of inhibition by dcSAM is a complicating factor in any analysis of the enzyme kinetics, but is probably not of great physiological significance because of the high concentration of dcSAM required for inhibition. Some analogues of dcSAM (Samejima and Nakazawa 1980; Samejima and Yamanoha 1982; Raina *et al.* 1984) and MTA (Hibasami *et al.* 1980; Carteni-Farina *et al.* 1984) have been studied as inhibitors of isolated PAPT and SAPT.

There are not extensive data on the use of compounds of this type to modulate polyamine biosynthesis in intact cells. Pegg *et al.* (1981) have shown that MTA and its 7-deaza analogue (c^7AdoSMe or MTT) inhibit both spermidine and spermine biosynthesis in SV40-transformed 3T3 mouse embryo fibroblasts (SV-3T3 cells). A related molecule, 5'-isobutylthioadenosine (SIBA), also inhibits spermidine and spermine biosynthesis in those cells. It is important to note, however, that the concentrations of MTA and SIBA required for inhibition of spermidine and spermine biosynthesis and, also, inhibition of cell growth, were considerably higher than the concentrations of MTT required. Both MTA and SIBA are substrates for the degradative enzyme MTA phosphorylase, as will be discussed in a later section. MTT, designed as a metabolically stable analogue of MTA (Coward *et al.* 1977), is not metabolized *in vitro* under conditions in which MTA is extensively degraded (Coward *et al.* 1983). Thus, despite the fact the MTA analogues such as MTT are poorly transported across mammalian cell membranes (Coward *et al.* 1983), low intracellular concentrations of metabolically stable MTA analogues are effective as inhibitors of aminopropyl transfer reactions *in vitro*. That the inhibition of polyamine biosynthesis is not the basis of the observed cytotoxicity is suggested by the fact that addition of both spermidine and MTT to the cultures did not prevent inhibition of cell growth by MTT. Several additional studies on the effects of MTA and its analogues on cell growth will be discussed in the section on MTA phosphorylase.

Recently, the *S*-methyl derivative of MTA, AdoSMe$_2^+$, has been shown to be a strong inhibitor of spermine synthase (Pegg and Coward 1985), in addition to its previously demonstrated activity as an inhibitor of SAM decarboxylase (Kolb *et al.* 1982; Pegg and Jacobs 1983). Despite the fact that it is a fully charged sulphonium salt, AdoSMe$_2^+$ appears to be readily transported across the cell membrane, at least in SV-3T3 cells, and to affect spermine biosynthesis markedly in those cells. This readily synthesized molecule should prove to be useful in other cell culture systems, although its inhibitory activity against SAM decarboxylase must be kept in mind in interpreting the *in vitro* data.

21.8 MTA phosphorylase—methionine, adenine, and cell growth

The product inhibition by MTA of isolated PAPT and SAPT is not considered to be a significant regulatory mechanism in the cell because of the rapid phosphorolytic or hydrolytic cleavage at the purine–ribose bond of MTA. This reaction, catalysed by MTA phosphorylase (EC 2.4.2.28) in eukaryotes and MTA nucleosidase (EC 3.2.2.16) in prokaryotes, results in the release of one mole of adenine per mole of MTA, and is now thought to be a major source of adenine in the cell (Kamatani and Carson 1981). The other portion of MTA, 5-deoxy-5-methylthioribose or its 1-phosphate (MTRP), is then converted to methionine in an unusual series of reactions summarized in eqn (21.6) (Schlenk 1983). The detailed mechanism of this series of reactions is not known (Backlund *et al.* 1982a), but several fractions have been isolated from rat liver homogenates that catalyse different reactions of eqn (21.6) (Trackman and Abeles 1983). In addition, certain clones of cultured human tumour cells (colon carcinoma) have the ability to carry out *only* the phosphorylytic cleavage of MTA to MTRP, and have allowed the characterization of one of the rat liver fractions as catalysing the conversion of MTRP to the ribulose derivative (Ghoda *et al.* 1984). Several cell lines will grow in the absence of exogenous methionine if MTA is provided in its place (Backlund and Smith 1982b; Carson *et al.* 1983). Thus, it appears that MTA degradation has a major role in providing two critical nutrients for cell growth: adenine and methionine.

$$\text{MTRP} \xrightarrow[\text{P}_i,\ HCO_2H]{} CH_3SCH_2CH_2CCO_2H \longrightarrow CH_3SCH_2CH_2CHCO_2H \tag{21.6}$$

Several MTA phosphorylase inhibitors and alternative substrates have been used recently to study the role of MTA in cell growth. It is beyond the scope of this chapter to review the large body of literature that has accumulated on this subject in recent years (Williams-Ashman *et al.* 1982), since most investigators agree that MTA cytotoxicity is not directly a result of inhibition of intracellular aminopropyl transfer reactions (Pegg *et al.* 1981; Raina *et al.* 1982; Riscoe *et al.*

1984). The critical role of MTA phosphorylase in rapidly removing this cyto-toxic material is indicated by the fact that MTA is lethal to cells deficient in this enzyme (Kamatani *et al.* 1981). These results suggested the use of inhibitors of *de novo* purine biosynthesis, together with MTA as the only exogenous source of purines, selectively to kill human malignant tumour cell lines deficient in MTA phosphorylase. The selective killing of MTA phosphorylase-negative cells by azaserine or methotrexate in the presence or absence of MTA and the preven-tion of that cytotoxicity by MTA in several MTA phosphorylase-containing cell lines was clearly demonstrated (Kamatani *et al.* 1981).

   Alternatively, MTA analogues have been investigated as possible depot forms of fraudulent purines and/or amino acids in cells containing MTA phosphoryl-ase (Parks *et al.* 1982). A large number of MTA analogues (Montgomery *et al.* 1974) have been studied in cells containing MTA phosphorylase and in cells deficient in that enzyme. Evidence for the conversion of MTA analogues to cytotoxic nucleotides and/or cytotoxic carbohydrate analogues has been pre-sented (Parks *et al.* 1982). Another MTA analogue, SIBA (*S*-isobutylthioadeno-sine), is an alternative substrate for MTA phosphorylase (Carteni-Farina 1979; Savarese *et al.* 1979; Pegg *et al.* 1981; Kamatani *et al.* 1982), but was originally synthesized and studied as an SAH analogue capable of inhibiting SAM-dependent methyltransferases. SIBA has only very weak inhibitory activity against isolated methyltransferases (Legraverend *et al.* 1977; Raies *et al.* 1976). This is not surprising since it has been known for many years that MTA is not an effective inhibitor of isolated methyltransferases (Zappia *et al.* 1969; Coward and Sweet 1972). Thus, any biological effects of the metabolically labile MTA analogue, SIBA, are probably best explained not by a direct inhibition of intracellular methyl transfer reactions but rather by MTA-like effects, perhaps leading to an indirect inhibition of methylation reactions.

21.9 Multi-substrate adduct inhibitors of methyltransferases and aminopropyltransferases

Product inhibition of SAM-dependent methyltransferases by SAH, and of dcSAM-dependent aminopropyltransferases by MTA, has led to the study of a large number of synthetic and naturally occurring nucleoside derivatives as potential inhibitors of selected isolated enzymes and of specific alkyl transfer reactions *in vitro* and *in vivo*. Aside from the transport and metabolism problems noted above in the use of SAH and MTA analogues, a major weakness in this approach is in the inherent lack of specificity to be expected. SAH is a strong inhibitor of all SAM-dependent methyltransferases studied to date, with the exception of glycine *N*-methyltransferase, which is regulated by interaction with folate derivatives (Wagner *et al.* 1985). Similarly, both spermidine synthase (PAPT) and spermine synthase (SAPT) are strongly inhibited by the common product, MTA. Therefore, it is not surprising that very little specificity is seen with most analogues of SAH (Coward and Crooks 1979; Borchardt 1980b), or with MTT, the most widely studied MTA analogue (Pegg *et al.* 1981; Raina *et al* 1982). In order to address this problem, the use of multi-substrate adduct (MSA) inhibitors (Heller *et al.* 1975) has been suggested (Coward 1979). In this bisubstrate variant of the more well-known transition-state analogues (Wolfenden 1976; Jencks 1975; see also Chapter 2A), the thermodynamic cost of bringing two substrates together at the enzyme active site is avoided by the formation of a stable, covalent bond between their surrogates in the MSA inhibitor. From theoretical considerations (Wolfenden 1976; Jencks 1975), one would expect the MSA inhibitor to be an extremely potent and specific inhibitor of any selected bisubstrate enzyme. This approach has been investigated with two methyltransferases, COMT (Anderson *et al.* 1981; Lever *et al.* 1984) and an indole *N*-methyltransferase (INMT) (Benghiat and Crooks 1983). For COMT, the adduct (**5**) was the synthetic target, but only **6** and **7** were synthesized and shown to be very weak inhibitors ($K_i = 0.5–0.8$ mM) of the enzyme (Anderson *et al.* 1981). In a more recent study, Lever *et al.* (1984) synthesized a series of related compounds of general type **8**; these also were only weak inhibitors of COMT. In both studies, the corresponding thioethers were even weaker COMT inhibitors. The compounds synthesized and evaluated as INMT inhibitors, **9** and **10**, also lacked the third large sulphur ligand involved in the proposed transition state and therefore, as with **6–8**, cannot be considered optimal candidates as MSA inhibitors. Nonetheless, **9** ($K_i = 12$ μM) and **10** ($I_{50} = 0.56$ mM) were inhibitors of INMT, and the more potent S-adenosyl sulphonium derivative (**9**) was shown to be inactive against COMT, thus demonstrating the desired enzyme specificity. The thioether precursors of **9** and **10** were inactive as INMT inhibitors, as noted also in the COMT research described above. These initial results have provided useful lead compounds for further investigation, and permit optimism about obtaining more potent inhibitors in molecules containing the relevant structural moieties of the proposed transition states, e.g. **5**.

The aminopropyltransferases, PAPT and SAPT, offered a case in which the third ligand in the proposed MSA inhibitor, **11**, would be a methyl group, rather than the more bulky ligands of **5**. Thus, synthesis of the thioether precursors

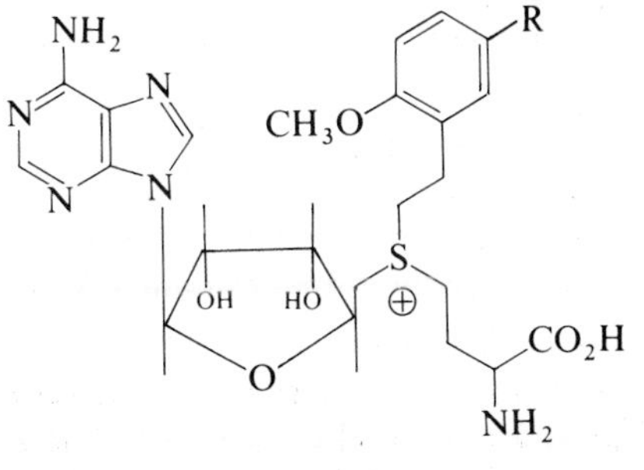

5

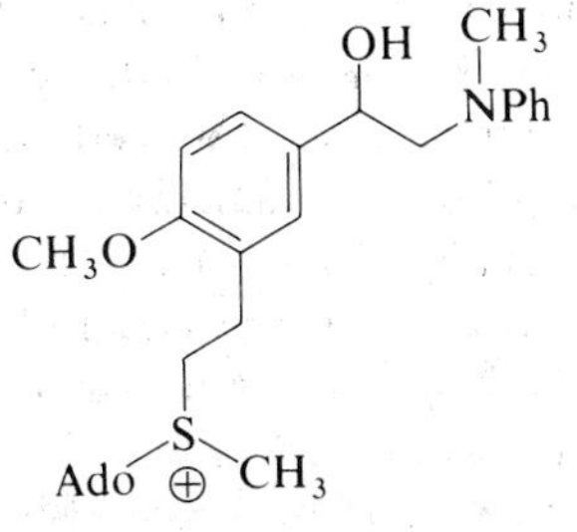

6

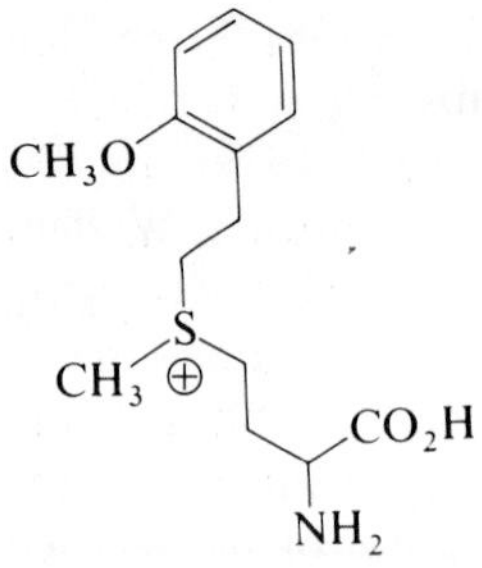

7

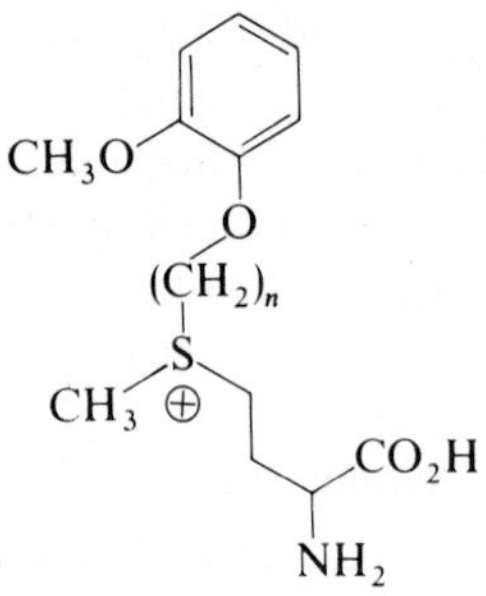

8

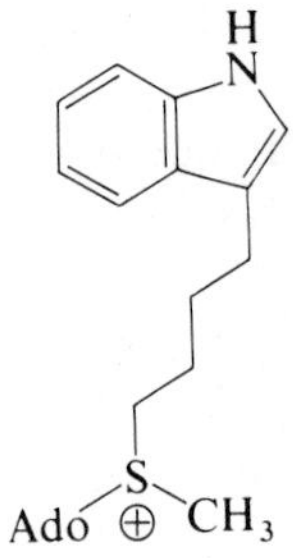

9

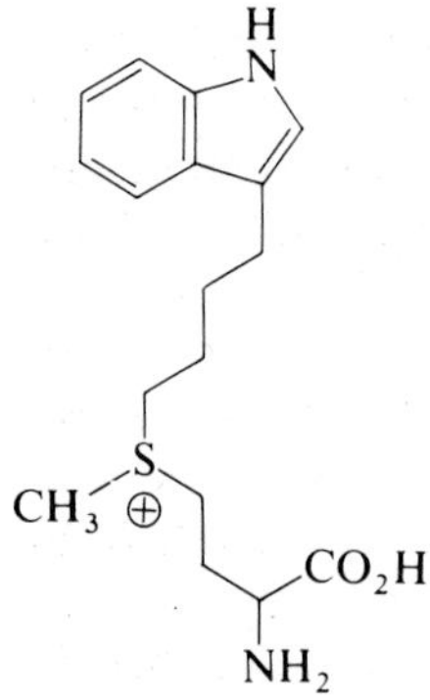

10

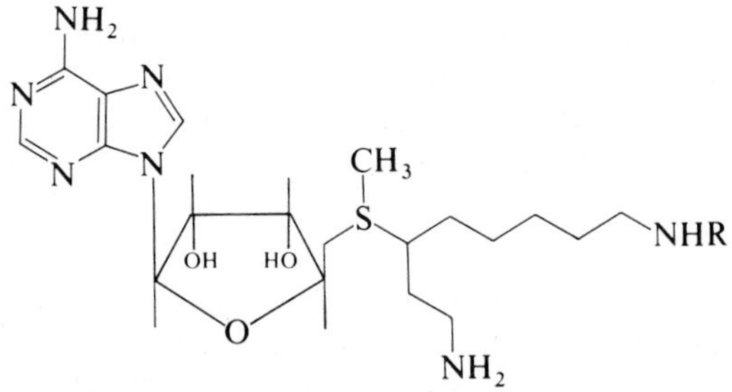

11

(a) R = H
(b) R = $(CH_2)_3NH_2$

followed by methylation should afford the desired adducts, **11a** and **11b**. Synthesis of **11a** and the corresponding thioether, S-adenosyl-1,8-diamino-3-thiooctane (AdoDATO) has been reported by Tang *et al.* (1981). Although **11a** was a good inhibitor of PAPT, the thioether proved to be an extremely potent and specific PAPT inhibitor (Tang *et al.* 1980). Appropriate control compounds (e.g. 1,8-desamino derivatives) were weak inhibitors, thus indicating that the groups required for binding of substrates were required for binding of the MSA inhibitor. AdoDATO has been studied as an inhibitor of polyamine biosynthesis in SV-3T3 cells and rat hepatoma cells (Pegg *et al.* 1982). As expected from the inhibition data obtained with isolated enzymes, treatment of the cells with AdoDATO resulted in a dose-dependent decrease in intracellular spermidine levels and a concomitant increase in putrescine resulting from the PAPT block. Surprisingly, spermine levels also increased in a dose-dependent manner. Since AdoDATO had only weak inhibitory activity against isolated spermine synthase, the observed effects of AdoDATO on intracellular spermine biosynthesis were difficult to explain until it was determined that the intracellular levels of dc SAM had increased up to 100-fold during treatment with AdoDATO. Thus, any spermidine synthesized in the presence of AdoDATO would have available large amounts of the aminopropyl donor, dcSAM, and would be readily converted to spermine. There is another undesired aspect of this apparent derepression of SAM decarboxylase. AdoDATO is less effective in the presence of higher amounts of dcSAM (Pegg and Coward 1981), as expected with a molecule binding to the enzyme at sites normally occupied by the substrates undergoing reaction. Thus, as the intracellular dcSAM increases in response to decreasel spermidine biosynthesis, the drug (AdoDATO) becomes less effective as an inhibitor of PAPT, leading to increased amounts of putrescine conversion to spermidine, and ultimately to spermine.

In order to test this hypothesis, a potent inactivator of ornithine decarboxylase (Orn-DC), α-difluoromethylornithine (DFMO) (Metcalf *et al.* 1978), was used to block putrescine formation from ornithine. The combination of DFMO + Ado-DATO led to a marked (*c.* 75 per cent) inhibition of spermine biosynthesis, together with the expected decrease in putrescine and spermidine biosynthesis (Pegg *et al.* 1982). These data provide support to the hypothesis outlined above for the increased synthesis of spermine in cells treated with AdoDATO alone.

The synthesis of the thioether corresponding to **11b**, *S*-adenosyl-1,12-diamino-8-aza-3-thiododecane (AdoDATAD) has recently been completed, and preliminary results indicate that this compound is a potent and specific inhibitor of SAPT. Preliminary studies with AdoDATAD *in vitro* indicate that it is an effective inhibitor of spermine biosynthesis in intact cells (A. E. Pegg and J. K. Coward, unpublished results). As there are now available potent and specific inhibitors of all three enzymes in the pathway putrescine→spermidine →spermine, future research should better be able to address the role of polyamines in cell physiology

21.10 Conclusions

Research over the past 15 years has resulted in a series of useful inhibitors of intracellular methyl transfer and aminopropyl transfer reactions. While problems associated with drug transport, metabolism, and specificity are still apparent, progress has been made to minimize these. Considering the large amount of literature data available on the involvement of methylation reactions (Hoffman 1984) and polyamine biosynthesis (Janne *et al.* 1978) in disease states, one should be optimistic about the ultimate utility of inhibitors of the alkyltransferase class of enzymes as clinically useful drugs. They have already proven to be extremely useful as biochemical and pharmacological tools.

References*

Aarbakke, J., and Ueland P. M. (1981). Interaction of *S*-adenosylhomocysteine with isolated rat hepatocytes. *Mol. Pharmacol.*, **19**, 463–9.
Aarbakke, J., Ueland, P. M., and Bessesen, A. (1982). Binding of *S*-adenosylhomocysteine

to isolated rat hepatocytes and purified plasma membranes from rat liver. In *Biochemistry of S-adenosylmethionine and related compounds* (ed. E. Usdin, R. T. Borchardt, and C. R. Creveling), pp. 679–82. Macmillan, London.

Abeles, R. H., Fish, S., and Lapinskas, B. (1982). S-adenosylhomocysteinase: mechanism of inactivation by 2′-deoxyadenosine and interaction with other nucleosides. *Biochemistry*, **21**, 5557–62.

Abeles, R. H., Tashjian, A. H., Jr., and Fish, S. (1980). The mechanism of inactivation of S-adenosylhomocysteinase by 2′-deoxyadenosine. *Biochem. Biophys. Res. Commun.*, **95**, 612–17.

Aiyar, V. N., and Hershfield, M. S. (1985). Covalent labelling of ligand binding sites of human placental S-adenosylhomocysteine hydrolase with 8-azido derivatives of adenosine and cyclic AMP. *Biochem. J.*, **232**, 643–50.

Alksamit, R. A., Falk, W., and Cantoni, G. L. (1982). Inhibition of chemotaxis by S-3-deazaadenosylhomocysteine in mouse macrophage cell line. *J. Biol. Chem.*, **257**, 621–5.

Anderson, G. L., Bussolotti, D. L., and Coward, J. K. (1981). Synthesis and evaluation of some stable multisubstrate adducts as inhibitors of catechol O-methyltransferase. *J. Med. Chem.*, **24**, 1271–7.

Arigoni, D. (1978). Stereochemical studies of enzyme C-methylations. In *Molecular interactions and activity in proteins*. Ciba Foundation Symposium No. 60, pp. 243–61. Excerpta Medica, Amsterdam.

Backlund, P. S., Jr., Chang, C. P., and Smith, R. A. (1982a). Identification of 2-keto-4-methylthiobutyrate as an intermediate compound in methionine synthesis from 5′-methylthioadenosine. *J. Biol. Chem.*, **257**, 4196–202.

Backlund, P. S., Jr., and Smith, R. A. (1982b). 5′-methylthioadenosine metabolism and methionine synthesis in mammalian cells grown in culture. *Biochem. Biophys. Res. Commun.*, **108**, 687–95.

Bader, J. P., Brown, N. R., Chiang, P. K., and Cantoni, G. L. (1978). 3-deazaadenosine, an inhibitor of adenosylhomocysteine hydrolase, inhibits reproduction of Rous sarcoma virus and transformation of chick embryo cells. *Virology*, **89**, 494–505.

Bartel, R. L. and Borchardt, R. T. (1984). Effects of adenosine-dialdehyde on S-adenosylhomocysteine hydrolase and S-adenosylmethionine-dependent transmethylations in mouse L929 cells. *Mol. Pharmacol.*, **25**, 418–24.

Benghiat, E. and Crooks, P. A. (1983). Multisubstrate adducts as potential inhibitors of S-adenosylmethionine dependent methylases: Inhibition of indole N-methyltransferase by (5′-deoxyadenosyl)-[3-(3-indolyl)prop-1-yl]methylsulfonium and (5′-deoxyadenosyl)-[4-(3-indolyl)but-1-yl]methylsulfonium salts. *J. Med. Chem.*, **26**, 1470–7.

Borchardt, R. T. (1980a). N- and O-methylation. In *Enzymatic basis of detoxification* (ed. W. B. Jakoby), Vol. 2, pp 43–62. Academic Press, New York.

Borchardt, R. T. (1980b). s-adenosyl-L-methionine-dependent macromolecule methyltransferases: potential targets for the design of chemotherapeutic agents. *J. Med. Chem.*, **23**, 347–57.

Borchardt, R. T. and Thakker, D. R. (1975). Affinity labeling of catechol O-methyltransferase by N-haloacetyl derivatives of 3,5-dimethoxy-4-hydroxyphenylethylamine and 3,4-dimethoxy-5-hydroxyphenylethylamines. Kinetics of inactivation. *Biochemistry*, **14**, 4543–51.

Borchardt, R. T. and Thakker, D. R. (1976). Evidence for sulfhydryl groups at the active site of catechol O-methyltransferase. *Biochim. Biophys. Acta*, **445**, 598–609.

Borchardt, R. T., Kuonen, D., Huber, J. A., and Moorman, A. (1981). Inhibition of calf thymus and rat hypothalmic synaptosomal protein carboxymethyltransferase by analogues of S-adenosylhomocysteine. *Mol. Pharmacol.*, **21**, 181–6.

Borchardt, R. T., Keller, B. T., and Patel-Thombre, U. (1984). Neplanocin A. A potent inhibitor of S-adenosylhomocysteine hydrolase and of vaccinia virus replication in mouse L929 cells. *J. Biol. Chem.*, **259**, 4353–8.

Bowman, W. H., Tabor, C. W., and Tabor, H. (1973). Spermidine biosynthesis. Purification and properties of propylamine transferase from *Escherichia coli. J. Biol. Chem.*, **248**, 2480–6.

Caboche, M. and Bachellerie, J.-P. (1977). RNA methylation and control of eukaryotic RNA biosynthesis. Effects of cycloleucine, a specific inhibitor of methylation, on ribosomal RNA maturation. *Eur. J. Biochem.*, **74**, 19–29.

Camper, S. A., Albers, R. J., Coward, J. K., and Rottman, F. M. (1983). Effect of undermethylation on mRNA cytoplasmic appearance and half-life. *Mol. Cell. Biol.*, **4**, 538–43.

Carson, D. A., Willis, E. H., and Kamatani, N. (1983). Metabolism to methionine and growth stimulation by 5′-methylthioadenosine and 5′-methylthioinosine in mammalian cells. *Biochem. Biophys. Res. Commun.*, **112**, 391–7.

Carteni-Farina, M., Cacciapuoti, G., Porcelli, M., Della Ragione, F., Lancieri, M., Geraci, G., and Zappia, V. (1984). Studies on the metabolic effects of methylthioformycin. *Biochim. Biophys. Acta*, **805**, 158–64.

Carteni-Farina, M., Della Ragione, F., Ragosta, G., Oliva, A., and Zappia, V. (1979). Studies on the metabolism of 5′-isobutylthioadenosine (SIBA). Phosphorolytic cleavage by methylthioadenosine phosphorylase. *FEBS Lett.*, **104**, 266–70.

Chang, C.-D. and Coward, J. K. (1975). Effect of S-adenosylhomocysteine and S-tubercidinylhomocysteine on transfer ribonucleic acid methylation in phytohemaglutinin-stimulated lymphocytes. *Mol. Pharmacol.*, **11**, 701–7.

Chang, C.-D. and Coward, J. K. (1976). Analogues of S-adenosylhomocysteine as potential inhibitors of biological transmethylation. Synthesis of analogues with modifications at the 5′-thioether linkage. *J. Med. Chem.*, **19**, 684–91.

Chiang, P. K., Guranowski, A., and Segall, J. E. (1981). Irreversible inhibition of S-adenosylhomocysteine hydrolase by nucleoside analogs. *Arch. Biochem. Biophys.*, **207**, 175–84.

Chiang, P. K., Richards, H. H., and Cantoni, G. L. (1977). S-adenosyl-L-homocysteine hydrolase: analogues of S-adenosyl-L-homocysteine as potential inhibitors. *Mol. Pharmacol.*, **13**, 939–47.

Christman, J., Schneiderman, N., and Acs, G. (1985). Formation of highly stable complexes between 5-azacytosine-substituted DNA and specific non-histone proteins. *J. Biol. Chem.*, **260**, 4059–68.

Coward, J. K. (1979). The synthesis of transition-state analogues as potential specific inhibitors of group transfer enzymes. *Dev. Biochem.*, **6**, 13–26.

Coward, J. K. and Crooks, P. A. (1979). *In vitro* and *in vivo* effects of S-tubercidinylhomocysteine: a physiologically stable methylase inhibitor. In *Transmethylation* (ed. E. Usdin, R. T. Borchardt, and C. R. Creveling) pp. 215–24. Elsevier-North Holland, New York.

Coward, J. K. and Sweet, W. D. (1972). Analogs of S-adenosylhomocysteine as potential inhibitors of biological transmethylation. Synthesis and biological activity of homocysteine derivatives bridged to adenine. *J. Med. Chem.*, **15**, 381–4.

Coward, J. K., Slisz, E. P., and Wu, F. Y.-H. (1973). Kinetic studies on catechol O-methyltransferase. Product inhibition and the nature of the catechol binding site. *Biochemistry*, **12**, 2291–7.

Coward, J. K., Motola, N. C., and Moyer, J. D. (1977). Polyamine biosynthesis in rat prostate. Substrate and inhibitor properties of 7-deaza analogues of decarboxylated S-adenosylmethionine and 5′-methylthioadenosine. *J. Med. Chem.*, **20**, 500–5.

Coward, J. K., Chaudhari, P. R., Kwiat, M. A., and Hluboky, M. (1983). Transport and metabolism of adenosine 5'-thioethers and 7-deaza (tubercidin) analogs in Novikoff hepatoma cells. *Fed. Proc. Fed. Am. Soc. Exp. Biol.*, **42**, 2011.

Crooks, P. A., Dreyer, R. N., and Coward, J. K. (1979). Metabolism of S-adenosylhomocysteine and S-tubercidinylhomocysteine in neuroblastoma cells. *Biochemistry*, **18**, 2601–9.

Davis, M., Dudman, N. P., and White, H. F. (1983). The synthesis of the N-methyl analogue of S-adenosylmethionine: NMR observation of diastereomers. *Aust. J. Chem.*, **36**, 1623–7.

Davis, M., Dudman, N. P., and White, H. F. (1985). Preparation of (S)-3-azidodihydrofuran-2(3H)-one (α-azidobutyrolactone), a useful chiral synthon. *Aust. J. Chem.*, **38**, 621–4.

DeClercq, E., and Cools, M. (1985). Antiviral potency of adenosine analogs: Correlation with inhibition of S-adenosylhomocysteine hydrolase. *Biochem. Biophys. Res. Commun.*, **129**, 306–11.

DeLaHaba, G. and Cantoni, G. L. (1959). The enzymatic synthesis of S-adenosyl-L-homocysteine from adenosine and homocysteine. *J. Biol. Chem.*, **234**, 603–8.

Delk, A. S., Romeo, J. M., Nagle, D. P., Jr., and Rabinowitz, J. C. (1976). Biosynthesis of ribothymidine in the transfer RNA of *Streptococcus faecalis* and *Bacillus subtilus*. *J. Biol. Chem.*, **251**, 7649–56.

Delk, A. S., Nagle, D. P., Jr., Rabinowitz, J. C., and Straub, K. M. (1979). The methylenetetrahydrofolate-mediated biosynthesis of ribothymidine in the transfer-RNA of *Streptococcus faecalis*: Incorporation of hydrogen from solvent into the methyl moiety. *Biochem. Biophys. Res. Commun.*, **86**, 244–51.

Delk, A. S., Nagle, D. P., Jr., and Rabinowitz, J. C. (1980). Methylenetetrahydrofolate-dependent biosynthesis of ribothymidine in transfer RNA of *Streptococcus faecalis*. *J. Biol. Chem.*, **255**, 4387–90.

Dimock, K. and Stoltzfus, C. M. (1977). Sequence specificity of internal methylation in B77 avian sarcoma virus RNA subunits. *Biochemistry*, **16**, 471–8.

Duerre, J. A. (1962). A hydrolytic nucleosidase acting on S-adenosylhomocysteine and 5'-methylthioadenosine. *J. Biol. Chem.*, **237**, 3737–41.

Ferro, A. J., Vandenbark, A. A., and MacDonald, M. R. (1981). Inactivation of S-adenosylhomocysteine hydrolase by 5'-deoxy-5'-methylthioadenosine. *Biochem. Biophys. Res. Commun.*, **100**, 523–31.

Floss, H. G. and Tsai, M.-D. (1979). Chiral methyl groups. *Adv. Enzymol.*, **50**, 243–302.

Frey, P. A. (1982). Stereochemistry of enzymatic reactions of phosphates. *Tetrahedron*, **38**, 1541–67.

Friedman, S. (1985). The irreversible binding of azacytosine-containing DNA fragments to bacterial DNA (cytosine-5) methyltransferases. *J. Biol. Chem.*, **260**, 5698–705.

Fuller, R. W. and Nagarajan, R. (1978). Inhibition of methyl transferases by some new analogs of S-adenosylhomocysteine. *Biochem. Pharmacol.*, **27**, 1981–3.

Ghoda, L. Y., Savarese, T. M., Dexter, D. L., Parks, R. E., Jr., Trackman, P. C., and Abeles, R. H. (1984). Characterization of a defect in the pathway for converting 5'-deoxy-5'-methylthioadenosine to methionine in a subline of a cultured-heterogeneous human colon carcinoma. *J. Biol. Chem.*, **259**, 6715–19.

Glazer, R. I. and Knode, M. C. (1984). Neplanocin A. A cyclopentyl analog of adenosine with specificity for inhibiting RNA methylation. *J. Biol. Chem.*, **259**, 12964–9.

Golding, B. T. and Nassereddin, I. K. (1985a). The biosynthesis of spermidine. Part 2: Preparation and study by ¹H nmr spectroscopy of hexahydropyrimidines from spermidine and propane-1,3-diamines. *J. Chem. Soc. Perkin I*, 2011–15.

Golding, B. T. and Nassereddin, I. K. (1985b). The biosynthesis of spermidine. Part 3: The stereochemistry of the formation of the N-CH$_2$ group in the biosynthesis of spermidine. *J. Chem. Soc. Perkin I*, 2017–24.

Guldberg, H. C. and Marsden, C. A. (1975). Catechol *O*-methyltransferase: pharmacological aspects and physiological role. *Pharmacol. Rev.*, **27**, 135–206.

Guranowski, A., Montgomery, J. A., Cantoni, G. L., and Chiang, P. K. (1981). Adenosine analogues as substrates and inhibitors of *S*-adenosylhomocysteine hydrolase. *Biochemistry*, **20**, 110–15.

Hegazi, M. F., Borchardt, R. T., and Schowen, R. L. (1979). α-deuterium and carbon-13 isotope effects for methyl transfer catalyzed by catechol *O*-methyltransferase. S$_N$2-like transition state. *J. Am. Chem. Soc.*, **101**, 4359–65.

Helland, S. and Ueland, P. M. (1982). Reactivation of *S*-adenosylhomocysteine hydrolase activity in cells exposed to 9-β-D-arabinofuranosyladenine. *Cancer Res.*, **42**, 2861–6.

Heller, J. S., Canellakis, E. S., Bussolotti, D. L., and Coward, J. K. (1975). Stable multisubstrate adducts as enzyme inhibitors. Potent inhibition of ornithine decarboxylate by *N*-(5'-phospyridoxyl)-ornithine. *Biochim. Biophys. Acta*, **403**, 197–207.

Hershfield, M. S. (1979). Apparent suicide inactivation of human lymphoblast *S*-adenosylhomocysteine hydrolase by 2'-deoxyadenosine and adenine arabinoside. *J. Biol. Chem.*, **254**, 22–5.

Hershfield, M. S., Small, W. C., Premakumar, R., Bagnara, A. S., and Fetter, J. E. (1982). Inactivation of *S*-adenosylhomocysteine hydrolase: mechanism and occurence *in vivo* in disorders of purine nucleoside catabolism. In *Biochemistry of S-adenosylmethionine and related compounds*. (ed. E. Usdin, R. T. Borchardt, and C. R. Creveling), pp. 657–65. Macmillan, London.

Hibasami, H., Borchardt, R. T., Chen, S. Y., Coward, J. K., and Pegg, A. E. (1980). Studies of inhibition of rat spermidine synthase and spermine synthase. *Biochem. J.*, **187**, 419–28.

Hoffman, D. R., Marion, D. W., Cornatzer, W. E., and Duerre, J. A. (1980). *S*-adenosylmethionine and *S*-adenosylhomocysteine metabolism in isolated rat liver. *J. Biol. Chem.*, **255**, 10822–7.

Hoffman, R. M. (1984). Altered methionine metabolism, DNA methylation and oncogene expression in carcinogenesis. *Biochim. Biophys. Acta*, **738**, 49–87.

Hoffman, J. L. (1980). The role of transmethylation in mouse liver as measured by trapping *S*-adenosylhomocysteine. *Arch. Biochem. Biophys.*, **205**, 132–5.

Hohman, R. J., Guitton, M. C., and Veron, M. (1985). Inactivation of *S*-adenosyl-L-homocysteine hydrolase by cAMP results from dissociation of enzyme-bound NAD$^+$. *Proc. Nat. Acad. Sci. USA*, **82**, 4578–81.

Holy, A. Votruba, I., and DeClercq, E. (1985). Structure–activity studies on open chain analogs of nucleosides. Inhibition of *S*-adenosylhomocysteine hydrolase and antiviral activity 1. Neutral open-chain analogues. *Coll. Czech. Chem. Commun.*, **50**, 245–61; 262–79.

Janne, J., Poso, H., and Raina, A. (1978). Polyamines in rapid growth and cancer. *Biochim. Biophys. Acta*, **473**, 241–93.

Jencks, W. P. (1975). Binding energy, specificity, and enzymic catalysis: the Circe effect. *Adv. Enzymol.*, **43**, 219–410.

Kaehler, M., Coward, J., and Rottman, F. (1977). *In vivo* inhibition of Novikoff cytoplasmic messenger RNA methylation by *S*-tubercidinyl homocysteine. *Biochemistry*, **16**, 5770–5.

Kaehler, M., Coward, J., and Rottman, F. (1979). Cytoplasmic location of under-methylated messenger RNA in Novikoff cells. *Nucleic Acid Res.*, **6**, 1161–75.

Kaiser, I. L., Klandianos, D. M., Van Kirk, E. A., and Haley, B. E. (1983). Photoaffinity labeling of catechol *O*-methyltransferase with 8-azido-*S*-adenosylmethione. *J. Biol. Chem.*, **258**, 1747–51.

Kamatani, N. and Carson, D. A. (1981). Dependence of adenine production upon polyamine synthesis in cultured human lymphoblasts. *Biochim. Biophys. Acta*, **675**, 344–50.

Kamatani, N., Nelson-Rees, W. A., and Carson, D. A. (1981). Selective killing of human malignant cell lines deficient in methylthioadenosine phosphorylase, a purine meta-bolic enzyme. *Proc. Nat. Acad. Sci. USA*, **78**, 1219–23.

Kamatani, N., Willis, E. H., and Carson, D. A. (1982). Sequential metabolism of 5′-isobutylthioadenosine by methylthioadenosine phosphorylase and purine-nucleoside phosphorylase in viable human cells. *Biochem. Biophys. Res. Commun.*, **104**, 1335–42.

Kefford, R. F., Helmer, M. A., and Fox, R. M. (1982). *S*-adenosylhomocysteine hydrolase inhibition in deoxyadenosine-treated human T-lymphoblasts and resting peripheral blood lymphocytes. *Cancer Res.*, **42**, 3822–7.

Keller, B. T. and Borchardt, R. T. (1984). Metabolic conversion of neplanocin A to *S*-neplanocylmethionine in mouse L929 cells. *Biochem. Biophys. Res. Commun.*, **120**, 131–7.

Keller, B. T., Clark, R. S., Pegg, A. E., and Borchardt, R. T. (1985). Purification and characterization of some metabolic effects of *S*-neplanocylmethionine. *Mol. Pharma-col.*, **28**, 364–70.

Kim, I. Y., Zhang, C.-Y., Cantoni, G. L., Montogomery, J. A., and Chiang, P. K. (1985). Inactivation of *S*-adenosylhomocysteine hydrolase by nucleosides. *Biochim. Biophys. Acta*, **829**, 150–5.

Knipe, J. O., Vasquez, P. J., and Coward, J. K. (1982). Methylase models: studies on general base vs nucleophilic catalysis in the intramolecular alkylation of phenols. *J. Am. Chem. Soc.*, **104**, 3202–9.

Knowles, J. (1980). Enzyme-catalyzed phosphoryl transfer reactions. *Ann. Rev. Biochem.*, **49**, 877–919.

Kolb, M., Danzin, C., Barth, J., and Claverie, N. (1982). Synthesis and biochemical properties of chemically stable product analogues of the reaction catalyzed by *S*-adenosyl-L-methionine decarboxylase. *J. Med. Chem.*, **25**, 550–6.

Legraverend, M., Ibanez, S., Blanchard, P., Enouf, J., Lawrence, F., Robert-Gero, M., and Lederer, E. (1977). Structure–activity relationship of *S*-adenosylhomocysteine analog-ues. Effect on oncogenic virus-induced cell transformation and on methylation of macromolecules. *Eur. J. Med. Chem.*, **12**, 105–8.

Lever, O. W., Jr., Hyman, C., and White, H. L. (1984). Synthesis of bridged catechol-homocysteine derivatives as potential inhibitors of catechol *O*-methyltransferase. *J. Pharm. Sci.*, **73**, 1241–4.

Linevsky, J., Cohen, M. B., Hartman, K. D., Knode, M. C., and Glazer, R. I. (1985). Effect of neplanocin A on differentiation, nucleic acid methylation, and c-myc mRNA expression in human promyelocytic leukemia cells. *Mol. Pharmacol.*, **28**, 45–50.

Metcalf, B. W., Bey, P., Danzin, C., Jung, M. J., Casara, P., and Vevert, J. P. (1978). Catalytic irreversible inhibition of mammalian ornithine decarboxylase (EC 4.1.1.17) by substrate and product analogues. *J. Am. Chem. Soc.*, **100**, 2551–3.

Michelot, R. J., Lesko, N., Stout, R. W., and Coward, J. K. (1977). Effect of *S*-adenosylhomocysteine and *S*-tubercidinylhomocysteine on catecholamine metabolism in neuroblastoma cells. *Mol. Pharmacol.*, **13**, 368–73.

Montgomery, J. A., Clayton, S. J., Thomas, H. J., Shannon, W. M., Arnett, G., Bodner, A. J., Kion, I.-K., Cantoni, G. L., and Chiang, P. K. (1982). Carbocylic analog of 3-deazaadenosine: a novel antiviral agent using S-adenosylhomocysteine hydrolase as a pharmacological target. *J. Med. Chem.*, **25**, 626–9.

Montgomery, J. A., Shortnacy, A. T., and Thomas, H. J. (1974). Analogs of 5'-deoxy-5'-(methylthio)adenosine. *J. Med. Chem.*, **17**, 1197–207.

Orr, G. R., Kullberg, D. W., Pontoni, G., Gould, S. J., and Coward, J. K. (1988). The synthesis of chirally deuterated S-adenosylmethylthiopropylamines and spermidines. Elucidation of the stereochemical course of putrescine aminopropyltransferase (spermidine synthase). *J. Am. Chem. Soc.*, in press.

Pajula, R.-L. (1983). Kinetic properties of spermine synthase from bovine brain. *Biochem. J.*, **215**, 669–76.

Pajula, R.-L. and Raina, A. (1979). Methylthioadenosine: a potent inhibitor of spermine synthase from bovine brain. *FEBS Lett.*, **99**, 343–5.

Palmer, J. L. and Abeles, R. H. (1976). Mechanism of enzymatic thioether formation. Mechanism of action of S-adenosylhomocysteinase. *J. Biol. Chem.*, **251**, 5817–19.

Palmer, J. L. and Abeles, R. H. (1979). The mechanism of action of S-adenosylhomocysteinase. *J. Biol. Chem.*, **254**, 1217–26.

Parks, R. E., Jr., Savarase, T. M., and Chu, S.-H. (1982). Analogues of 5'-methylthioadenosine as potential chemotherapeutic agents. In *New approaches to the design of antineoplastic agents* (ed. T. Bardos and T. Kalman) pp. 141–56. Elsevier, Amsterdam.

Parry, R. J. and Askonas, L. J. (1985). Studies of enzyme stereochemistry. Elucidation of the stereochemistry of the reaction catalyzed by S-adenosylhomocysteine hydrolase. *J. Am. Chem. Soc.*, **107**, 1417–18.

Pegg, A. E. and Coward, J. K. (1981). Inhibition of aminopropyltransferases. *Adv. Polyamine Res.*, **3**, 153–61.

Pegg, A. E. and Coward, J. K. (1985). Growth of mammalian cells in the absence of the accumulation of spermine. *Biochem. Biophys. Res. Commun.*, **133**, 82–89.

Pegg, A. E. and Jacobs, G. (1983). Comparison of inhibitors of S-adenosylmethionine decarboxylase from different species. *Biochem. J.*, **213**, 495–502.

Pegg, A. E., Tang, K.-C., and Coward, J. K. (1982). Effects of S-adenosyl-1,8-diamino-3-thiooctane on polyamine metabolism. *Biochemistry*, **21**, 5082–9.

Pegg, A. E., Borchardt, R. T., and Coward, J. K. (1981). Effects of inhibitors of spermidine and spermine synthesis on polyamine concentrations and growth of transformed mouse fibroblasts. *Biochem. J.*, **194**, 79–89.

Pfitzner, K. E. and Moffatt, J. G. (1963). The synthesis of nucleoside 5'-aldehydes. *J. Am. Chem. Soc.*, **85**, 3027.

Pogolotti, A. and Santi, D. V. (1977). The catalytic mechanism of thymidylate synthetase. *Bioorgan. Chem.*, **1**, 277–311.

Pontoni, G., Coward, J. K., Orr, G. R., and Gould, S. J. (1983). Stereochemical studies on enzyme-catalyzed alkyltransfer reactions. An nmr method for distinguishing between the two prochiral hydrogens at C-1' of spermidine. *Tetrahedron Lett.*, **24**, 151–4.

Porter, C. W., Sufrin, J. R., and Keith, D. D. (1984). Growth inhibition by methionine analog inhibitors of S-adenosylmethionine biosynthesis in the absence of polyamine depletion *Biochem. Biophys. Res. Commun.*, **122**, 350–7.

Pugh, C. S. G., Borchardt, R. T., and Stone, H. O. (1978). Sinefungin, a potent inhibitor of virion mRNA (guanine-7-) methyltransferase, mRNA (nucleoside-2'-) methyltransferase, and viral multiplication, *J. Biol. Chem.*, **253**, 4075–7.

Raies, A., Lawrence, F., Robert-Gero, M., Locke, M., and Cramer, R. (1976). Effect of 5'-deoxy-5'-isobutyl adenosine on polyoma virus replication. *FEBS Lett.*, **72**, 48–52.

Raina, A., Tuomi, K., and Pajula, R.-L. (1982). Inhibition of the synthesis of polyamines and macromolecules by 5'-methylthioadenosine and 5'-alkylthiotubercidins in BHK21 cells. *Biochem. J.*, **204**, 697–703.

Raina, A., Eloranta, T., Hyvonen, T., and Pajula, R.-L. (1983). Mammalian propylamine transferases. *Adv. Polyamine Res.*, **4**, 245–53.

Raina, A., Hyvonen, T., Eloranta, T., Voutilainen, M., Samejima, K., and Yamanoha, B. (1984). Polyamine synthesis in mammalian tissues. Isolation and characterization of spermidine synthase from bovine brain. *Biochem. J.*, **219**, 991–1000.

Richards, H. H., Chiang, P. K., and Cantoni, G. L. (1978). Adenosylhomocysteine hydrolase. Crystallization of the purified enzyme and its properties. *J. Biol. Chem.*, **253**, 4476–80.

Riscoe, M. K., Tower, P. A., and Ferro, A. J. (1984). Mechanism of action of 5'-methylthioadenosine in S49 cells. *Biochem. Pharmacol.*, **33**, 3639–43.

Rivett, A. J. and Roth, J. A. (1982). Kinetic studies on the *O*-methylation of dopamine by human brain membrane-bound catechol *O*-methyltransferase. *Biochemistry*, **21**, 1740–2.

Samejima, K. and Nakazawa, Y. (1980). Action of decarboxylated S-adenosylmethionine analogs in the spermidine-synthesizing system from rat prostate. *Arch. Biochem. Biophys.*, **201**, 241–6.

Samejima, K. and Yamanoha, B. (1982). Purification of spermidine synthase from rat ventral prostate by affinity chromatography on immobilized S-adenosyl(5')-3-thiopropylamine. *Arch. Biochem. Biophys.*, **216**, 213–22.

Santi, D. V., Garrett, C. E., and Barr, P. J. (1983). On the mechanism of inhibition of DNA-cytosine methyltransferases by cytosine analogs. *Cell.*, **33**, 9–10.

Santi, D. V., Norment, A., and Garrett, C. E. (1984). Covalent bond formation between a DNA-cytosine methyltransferase and DNA containing 5-azacytosine. *Proc. Nat. Acad. Sci. USA.*, **81**, 6993–7.

Savarese, T. M., Crabtree, G. W., and Parks, R. E., Jr. (1979). Reaction of 5'-deoxyadenosine and related analogs with the 5'-methylthioadenosine cleaving enzyme of sarcoma 180 cells. A possible chemotherapeutic target enzyme. *Biochem. Pharmacol.*, **28**, 2227–30.

Saunders, P. P., Tan, M.-T., and Robins, R. K. (1985). Metabolism and action of neplanocin A in Chinese hamster ovary cells. *Biochem. Pharmacol.*, **34**, 2749–54.

Schanche, J.-S., Schanche, T., and Ueland, P. M. (1981). Inhibition of phospholipid methyltransferase(s) from rat liver plasma membranes by analogues of S-adenosylhomocysteine. *Mol. Pharmacol.*, **20**, 631–6.

Schanche, J.-S., Schanche, T., and Ueland, P. M. (1982). Inhibition of phospholipid methylation in isolated rat hepatocytes by analogues of adenosine and S-adenosylhomocysteine. *Biochim. Biophys. Acta*, **721**, 399–407.

Schanche, J.-S., Schanche, T., Ueland, P. M., Holy, A., and Votruba, I. (1984). The effect of aliphatic adenine analogues on S-adenosylhomocysteine and S-adenosylhomocysteine hydrolase in intact rat hepatocytes. *Mol. Pharmacol.*, **26**, 553–8.

Schlenk, F. (1983). Methylthioadenosine. *Adv. Enzymol.*, **54**, 195–265.

Sinhababu, A. K., Bartel, R. L., Pochopin, N., and Borchardt, R. T. (1985). Mechanism of action of S-adenosyl-L-homocysteine hydrolase. Measurement of kinetic isotope effects using adenosine-3'-d and S-adenosyl-L-homocysteine-3'-d as substrates. *J. Am. Chem. Soc.*, **107**, 7628–32.

Stopford, C. R., Wolberg, G., Prus, K. L., Reynolds, V. R., and Zimmerman, T. P. (1985). 3-Deazaadenosine-induced disorganization of macrophage microfilaments. *Proc. Nat. Acad. Sci. USA*, **82**, 4060–64.

Sufrin, J. R., Dunn, D. A., and Marshall, G. R. (1981). Steric mapping of the L-methionine binding site of ATP: L-methionine binding site of ATP: L-methionine S-adenosyltransferase. *Mol. Pharmacol.*, **19**, 307–13.

Sung, S.-S. J. and Silverstein, S. C. (1985). Inhibition of macrophage phagocytosis by methylation inhibitors. *J. Biol. Chem.*, **260**, 546–554.

Tang, K.-C., Pegg, A. E., and Coward, J. K. (1980). Specific and potent inhibition of spermidine synthase by the transition-state analog, S-adenosyl-3-thio-1,8-diaminooctane. *Biochem. Biophys. Res. Commun.*, **96**, 1371–7.

Tang, K.-C., Mariuzza, R., and Coward, J. K. (1981). Synthesis and evaluation of some stable multisubstrate adducts of spermidine synthase. *J. Med. Chem.*, **24**, 1277–84.

Thakker, D. R., Boehlert, C., Kirk, K. L., Antkowiak, R., and Creveling, C. R. (1986). Regioselectivity of catechol-O-methyltransferase. The effect of pH of the site of O-methylation of fluorinated norepinephrines. *J. Biol. Chem.*, **261**, 178–84.

Trackman, P. C. and Abeles, R. H. (1983). Methionine synthesis from 5'-S-methylthioadenosine. Resolution of enzyme activities and identification of 1-phospho-5'-S-methylthiooribulose. *J. Biol. Chem.*, **258**, 6717–20.

Ueland, P. M. (1982). Pharmacological and biochemical aspects of S-adenosylhomocysteine and S-adenosylhomocysteine hydrolase. *Pharmacol. Rev.*, **34**, 223–53.

Wagner, C., Briggs, W. T., and Cook, R. J. (1985). Inhibition of glycine N-methyltransferase activity by folate derivatives: Implications for regulation of methyl group metabolism. *Biochem. Biophys. Res. Commun.*, **127**, 746–52.

Walsh, C. (1982). Suicide substrates. Mechanism-based enzyme inactivators. *Tetrahedron*, **38**, 871–909.

Walker, R. D. and Duerre, J. A. (1975). S-adenosylhomocysteine metabolism in various species. *Can. J. Biochem.*, **53**, 312–19.

Whaun, J. M., Miura, G. A., Brown, N. D., Gordon, R. K., and Chiang, P. K. (1986). Antimalarial activity of neplanocin A with perturbations in the metabolism of purines, polyamines and S-adenosylmethionine. *J. Pharmacol. Exp. Ther.*, **236**, 277–83.

Williams-Ashman, H. G. and Pegg, A. E. (1981). Aminopropyl group transfers in polyamine biosynthesis. In *Polyamines in biology and medicine* (ed. D. R. Morris and L. J. Marton) pp. 43–73. Marcel Dekker, New York.

Williams-Ashman, H. G., Seidenfeld, J., and Galletti (1982). Trends in the biochemical pharmacology of 5'-deoxy-5'-methylthioadenosine. *Biochem. Pharmacol.*, **31**, 277–88.

Wolfenden, R. (1976). Transition state analog inhibitors and enzyme catalysis. *Ann. Rev. Biophys. Bioeng.*, **5**, 271–306.

Woodard, R. W., Tsai, M.-D., Floss, H. G., Crooks, P. A., and Coward, J. K. (1980). Stereochemical course of the transmethylation catalyzed by catechol O-methyltransferase. *J. Biol. Chem.*, **255**, 9124–7.

Wu, S.-E., Huskey, W. P., Borchardt, R. T., and Schowen, R. L. (1984). Different isotope effects for parallel pathways of enzyme-catalyzed transmethylation. *J. Am. Chem. Soc.*, **106**, 5762–3.

Zappia, V., Cacciapuoti, G., Pontoni, G., and Oliva, A. (1980). Mechanism of propylamine transfer reactions. Kinetic and inhibition studies on spermidine synthase from *Escherichia coli*. *J. Biol. Chem.*, **255**, 7276–80.

Zappia, V., Zydeck-Cwick, C. R., and Schlenk, F. (1969). The specificity of S-adenosylmethionine derivatives in methyl transfer reactions. *J. Biol. Chem.*, **244**, 4499–509.

Zimmerman, T. P., Deeprose, R. D., Wolberg, G., and Duncan, G. S. (1979). Metabolic formation of nucleoside-modified analogues of S-adenosylmethionine. *Biochem. Biophys. Res. Commun.*, **91**, 997–1004.

Zimmerman, T. P., Iannone, M., and Wolberg, G. (1984). 3-deazaadenosine. *S*-adenosylhomocysteine hydrolase-independent mechanism of action in mouse lymphocytes. *J. Biol. Chem.*, **259**, 1122–6.

Zimmerman, T. P., Wolberg, G., Duncan, G. S., and Elion, G. B. (1980). Adenosine analogs as substrates and inhibitors of *S*-adenosylhomocysteine hydrolase in intact lymphocytes. *Biochemistry*, **19**, 2252–9.

* Literature survey complete to end of 1985.

Inhibitors of some other target enzymes as potential clinical agents

H J Smith

Section 22A
Dopamine β-hydroxylase inhibitors

22A.1   Characteristics of the enzyme

Dopamine β-hydroxylase [3,4-dihydroxyphenylethylamine ascorbate: O_2 oxido-reductase (β-hydroxylating) or dopamine β-monooxygenase; DBH] is respons-ible for the conversion of dopamine into noradrenalin in the catecholamine biosynthetic chain (Molinoff and Axelrod 1971). It is found in both soluble and membrane-bound forms in the granulated vesicles of adrenal medulla chromaf-fin cells as well as in synaptic vesicles in the peripheral and central sympathetic nerve terminals (Levitt et al. 1965; Hortnagl et al. 1972). It also exists in various body fluids such as serum and cerebrospinal fluid, being released during nervous activity (de Potter et al. 1969). The literature concerning DBH has been extensively reviewed (Kaufman and Friedman 1965; Skotland and Ljones 1979a Weinshilboum 1979; Rosenberg and Lovenberg 1980) together with shorter reviews (Geffen and Livett 1971; Molinoff and Axelrod 1971; Nagatsu 1973; Kaufmann 1974; Vanneste and Zuberbuehler 1974; Winkler 1976; Nagatsu 1977).

The soluble form of DBH from bovine adrenal medulla has been purified by several groups, (e.g Walker et al. 1977; Colombo et al. 1984d). The enzyme is a glycoprotein and has a molecular weight of 290 000 (Friedman and Kaufman 1965). Amino acid and carbohydrate analyses for homogeneous enzyme, pro-vided by different groups, have given variable results (see Rosenberg and Lovenberg 1980). The enzyme is generally regarded as a tetramer consisting of four identical sub units, M_r 77 000, the degree of association being pH-depen-dent over the range pH 5.0–5.7. This pH range spans the normal environment of the enzyme in the interior of the secretory vesicles (Saxena *et al.* 1985). DBH utilizes three substrates, molecular oxygen, an electron donor, and the organic compound to be hydroxylated:

$$\text{dopamine} + \text{ascorbate} + O_2 \xrightarrow{\text{DBH}} \text{noradrenalin} + \text{hydroascorbate} + H_2O$$

$$(22A.1)$$

Ascorbic acid is the most efficient electron donor, although others are known, and is endogenous to the chromaffin granules (Terland and Flatmark 1975).

The enzyme displays a lack of substrate specificity, catalysing the hydroxylation of a variety of both 2- and aryl-substituted phenylethylamines, (Kaufman and Friedman 1965; May *et al.* 1981; Klinman and Krueger 1982), as well as the benzylic oxidation of groups such as olefines (May *et al.* 1983; Colombo and Villafranca 1984), aldehydes, and sulphides (May *et al.* 1981; May and Phillips 1980). The enzyme is activated by many dicarboxylic anions and a mechanism for fumarate-activation has been suggested (Ahn and Klinman 1983).

DBH is a copper-dependent enzyme. Various workers have shown that it contains from two to ten copper atoms per tetramer (see Skotland and Ljones 1979a,b, for summary), although more recent work indicates eight copper atoms per tetramer (Ash *et al.* 1984; Klinman *et al.* 1984) for maximal activity. The discrepancies arising here are probably related to distinguishing between essential metal ion and non-essential yet tightly bound ion, as well as losses occuring during purification. Both coppers per subunit are required for full activity of the enzyme, but appear magnetically non interactive. Evidence from EPR studies suggests that a change in the oxidation of the copper occurs during catalysis (Blumberg *et al.* 1965; Friedman and Kaufman 1965).

$$E(Cu^{2+}).\,NE.\,H_2O \xrightarrow{k_7} E$$

$$(22A.2)$$

The minimal kinetic mechanism for random addition of dopamine (DM) and oxygen to DBH followed by catalytic and product release steps is shown in eqn (22A.2) (Ahn and Klinman 1983). A random kinetic mechanism has been shown for the addition of oxygen and phenylethylamine substrates at high pH (6.6) and this changes to a predominantly ordered mechanism at low pH (4.5) or in the presence of fumarate, where phenylethylamine binds prior to oxygen (Ahn and

Klinman 1983; Miller and Klinman 1985). In the catalysed reaction, two protons and two electrons (from ascorbate) are consumed for each turnover of the substrate. Studies of the pH-dependence of initial rate parameters (V_{max} and V_{max}/K_m) and their primary isotope effects show that at least two ionizable residues are involved in catalysis: B1, pK_a 5.6–5.8, which probably acts as a general-acid catalyst prior to benzylic C—H bond cleavage; and B2, pK_a 5.2–5.4, which in the protonated form facilitates, but is not required for, product release. Further studies (Miller and Klinman 1985), using a combination of secondary kinetic isotope effects and structure–reactivity correlations within para-substituted phenylethylamines, have indicated C–H bond cleavage prior to C–O bond formation, the substrate-derived intermediate probably being a radical. This suggestion of a radical mechanism supercedes earlier considerations of an ionic (Friedman and Kaufman 1965) or free radical mechanism (Blumberg *et al.* 1965), as discussed by Rosenberg and Lovenberg (1980), and Skottland and Ljones (1979a). The mechanism proposed by Miller and Klinman (1985) is shown in eqn (22A.3).

$$(22A.3)$$

Homolysis of the —O—O— bond of the Cu(II)—OOH species, [formed by general acid protonation (reduction) by B1 of oxygen bound to the reduced form of the enzyme], and C—H homolysis (from substrate), occur in a concerted fashion, the energy from the latter providing the energy for the former. Recombination of substrate and peroxide-derived radical intermediates formed give the Cu(II)–alkoxide product complex, which slowly breaks down (catalysed by B2) to yield free enzyme and products.

## 22A.2	Inhibitors

### 22A.2.1	Early work

There has been considerable interest in the development of potent inhibitors of DBH, either as tools to manipulate endogenous levels of brain or peripheral noradrenalin in pharmacological studies, or as potential drugs for the treatment of hypertension.

The inhibitors available up to 1980 have been summarized by Rosenberg and Lovenberg (1980), who classified them as competitive or non-competitive inhibitors in terms of their effect on either the ascorbate (A) or phenylethylamine (P) substrate. Competitive inhibitors include picolinic acids (A), aromatic thioureas (P), benzyloxylamine (P), ascorbate-2-sulphate (A), and hydroquinone. Non-competitive inhibitors include diethyldithiocarbonate (P and A), aquayamycin (P), histidine (P), hydralazine (P), and prazosin. A great number of DBH inhibitors are known or suspected metal-chelating agents, whilst others are analogues based on the phenylethylamine substrate. These types of inhibitors lack selectivity: the most notable examples are fusaric acid, which has been studied in the clinic for the treatment of hypertension (Hidaka 1971; Piesche *et al.* 1983), and disulfiram (probably after reduction to diethydithiocarbamate), which is an effective inhibitor of endogenous noradrenalin synthesis in the intact animal (Goldstein 1966).

2-mercapto-1-methylimidazole has been shown (Rosenberg 1983) to be an uncompetitive inhibitor (ascorbate) or mixed type inhibitor (tyramine) of the enzyme. Although an efficient Cu^{++}-chelator, the compound does not exert its action by removal of essential copper, since it interacts exclusively with the reduced form of the enzyme.

Diethylpyrocarbonate completely inactivates the enzyme, with a loss of approximately 1.7 histidine residues per protein monomer. The correlation of activity loss with histidine modification supports the view that histidine participates in the catalytic function of the enzyme (Sams and Matthews 1984).

Bleomycin, a powerful, reversible inhibitor of DBH, irreversibly inhibits the enzyme after brief exposure of the bleomycin–DBH mixture to light (> 300 nm) (Ratwatte and Douglas 1983).

Inhibition of dopamine β-hydroxylase *in vitro* by reversible inhibitors is not necessarily translatable to the *in vivo* situation, since DBH is not the first enzyme in the biosynthetic pathway, nor does it catalyse the rate-controlling step, this role belonging to tyrosine-3-monooxygenase (Spector *et al.* 1964). The stress on development of specific DBH inhibitors as useful clinical agents has shifted to studies on mechanism-based inactivators, where near-complete irreversible inhibition of the enzyme would effectively block noradrenalin biosynthesis with little interaction with other systems and without the appearance of undesirable side-effects or toxic symptoms.

22A.2.2   Recent work with mainly mechanism-based inactivators

In a series of papers, Colombo and Villafranca's group (Baldoni and Villafranca 1980; Colombo *et al.* 1984 a,b,c) have described the inactivation of DBH by benzyl cyanides, the first class of compounds to inactivate DBH under catalytic conditions.

Although DBH is inactivated by several substituted benzyl cyanides in a turnover-dependent manner in the presence of ascorbate and oxygen, the kinetic mechanism for the inactivation is complex and not solely due to formation of covalent adduct. Using [ring-^{3}H]p-hydroxybenzyl cyanide (pHBCN) and K^{14}CN, the general reaction pathway for benzyl cyanide inactivation was unravelled and is shown in eqn (22A.4). pHBCN initially complexes with the enzyme and is converted to p-hydroxymandelonitrile (pHMN). During the catalysed reaction, partial irreversible inhibition of the enzyme occurs [pathway (b)] together with tightly bound reversible inhibition. The latter is due to release of cyanide at the active site, from the enzyme-catalysed breakdown of the enzyme–pHMN complex [pathway (c)], which binds to the essential copper [pathway (d)]. The cyanide inhibition complex is reactivatable at low pH and contains no tritium label. Under extended incubation periods, the product of the reaction, pHMN, decomposes spontaneously in the solution and the build-up of CN$^-$ gives additional inhibition of the enzyme through pathway (a).

The partitioning between pathways (b) and (c) at high oxygen concentration (ie. 100 per cent) and short incubation periods, as measured by tritium incorporation, is in the ratio 1:3, assuming four active sites per tetramer.

$$[^3H]E_{\text{inact.}}$$
$$\uparrow (b)$$
$$E+[^3H]pHBCN \rightleftharpoons (E.[^3H]pHBCN) \rightarrow E[^3H]pHMN \rightleftharpoons E+[^3H]pHMN$$
$$\downarrow (c) \qquad\qquad \updownarrow$$
$$E.[^3H]pHBA.CN \quad {}_{(a)}\diagdown CN^- +[^3H]pHBA$$
$$\updownarrow (d)$$
$$[^3H]pHBA +[E.CN]_{\text{inact.}}$$

$$(22A.4)$$

2-bromo-3-(p-hydroxyphenyl)-1-propene (**1**) is a substrate of DBH, being converted to the product (**2**) in the presence of oxygen and ascorbate (Rajashek-har *et al.* 1984; Colombo *et al.* 1984d). Irreversible inactivation of the enzyme also occurs in a time-dependent manner, the partition ratio ($K_{\text{cat}}/K_{\text{inact}}$) being 36. Evidence that the inactivation process was linked to the enzymatic conversion of (**1**) to an enzyme-bound intermediate or product was demonstrated. 1-phenyl-1-propyne (**3**) (Colombo and Villafranca 1984) exhibits all the characteristics of a mechanism-based inhibitor of DBH except that, being a more effective

1   2   3

inactivator of the enzyme with a partition ratio very low or even unity, no product (ie. the diol) is detectable in the reaction medium.

Preincubation of DBH with β-chlorophenylethylamine (4) under turnover conditions leads to a time-dependent loss of enzyme activity consistent with a mechanism-based inactivation once in every 12 000 turnovers (Klinman and Krueger 1982). The mechanism of the inhibition reaction is not clear, since the product of the reaction, α-aminoacetophenone, does not inhibit the enzyme except in the absence of ascorbate.

4   5

Mechanism-based inactivation of DBH by the olefinic substrate 1-phenyl-1-aminomethylethene (5) has been observed (May et al. 1983). The product of the reaction (after acid work-up) was 2,3-dihydroxy-2-phenylpropylamine, and the partition ratio was 750 (see Colombo et al. 1984d). The reaction may proceed during epoxidation through a radical or cationic intermediate, probably leading to both epoxide formation and alkylations, as accepted for olefinic substrates for the highly non-specific p-450 oxygenation system.

Evidence for a radical mechanism in the mechanism-based inactivation by aryl-substituted 3-phenylpropenes [6; see eqn (22A.5)] has been presented (Fitzpatrick et al. 1985). A plot of K_{inact}/K_{O_2} versus σ^+ for these compounds had $\rho = -1.2$, which was within the expected range for a radical reaction. Replacement of the benzylic hydrogens in 6 with deuterium results in a kinetic isotope effect of 2.0 on K_{inact}/K_{O_2}. It has no effect on the partition ratio V_{max}/K_{inact}, consistent with a stepwise mechanism for hydrogen abstraction and oxygen insertion (cf. Miller and Klinman 1985, mentioned earlier), with reaction of a common intermediate in the hydroxylation reaction or the inhibition reaction with the enzyme. The proposed mechanism for the reaction [eqn. (22A.5)] postulates formation of a resonance-stabilized benzylic radical that is either hydroxylated to the product of the reaction or reacts with a group on the enzyme leading to inactivation.

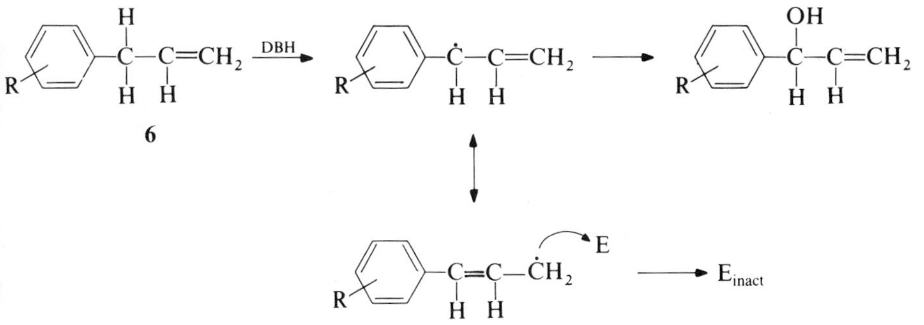

(22A.5)

The 3-phenylpropynes (**7**) and benzylcyclopropanes (**8**) are also mechanism-based inactivators of DBH (Fitzpatrick and Villafranca 1985), showing how advantage can be taken of the broad specificity of the enzyme in the design of inhibitors, and a similar radical mechanism has been suggested for their action.

Despite the progressive increase in activity as mechanism-base inactivators, the previously described compounds, with K_I values in the millimolar potency range, have not been reported to possess antihypertensive activity *in vivo*. The required breakthrough came with work described by Bargar *et al.* (1986). They showed that replacement of the phenyl ring by a heterocyclic ring in **5** gave a series of allylamines (**9**) where K_{cat}/K_I was dramatically increased and, for **9a**, was 1000-fold greater than for **5**. k_{cat} was little influenced by the nature of the heterocyclic ring, position (2- or 3-) of the allylamine moiety on the ring, side-chain substitution, or amine alkylation. However, these same changes greatly influenced the affinity of the compounds for the enzyme, the relative affinities of **9** (a–d) being 60:6:1:5. These compounds had anti-hypertensive activity when administered intraperitoneally to spontaneously hypertensive rats. Prolonged dose-related effects were noted with **9a** and **9d**.

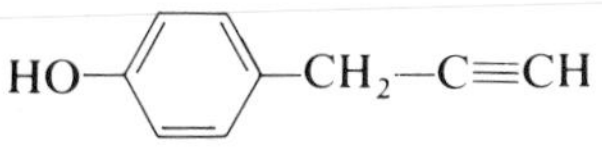

7

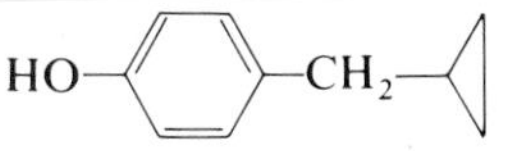

8

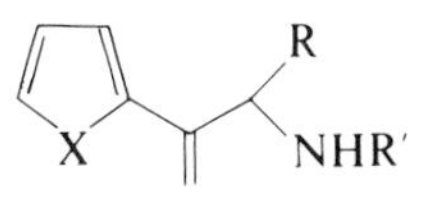

9

(a) X = S; R = R′ = H
(b) X = S; R = CH₃; R′ = H
(c) X = S; R = H; R′ = CH₃
(d) X = O; R = R′ = H

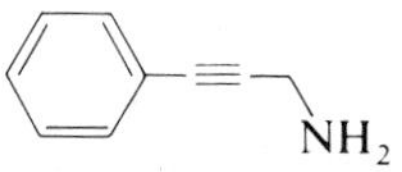

10

The 3-phenylpropargylamine (**10**) was as equipotent an inhibitor of the enzyme as (**9a**), being bound 2000-fold more tightly than the deaminated analogue but possessing a similar k_{cat}. It had a short-acting anti-hypertensive effect and was toxic. Padgette *et al.* (1985) have also found **10** to be a potent time-dependent inhibitor of DBH.

Recently, Kruse *et al.* (1986a) have described a new class of *reversible* DBH inhibitor based on 1-(4-hydroxybenzyl) imidazole-2-thiol (**11**) which, by incorporating a phenylethylamine substrate mimic and an oxygen mimic in a single molecule, act as multi-substrate inhibitors and accordingly bind 10^5–10^6 times more tightly to the enzyme than a tyramine substrate. The weaker inhibitors, **12** and **13**, which mimic the oxygen and phenylethylamine substrates, were shown to be mutually exclusive in binding at the active site of the DBH (Cu^+) enzyme, which suggests a much smaller inter-site distance than originally suggested. Inhibitors based on **11** produce substantial rapid antihypertensive effects *in vivo* when administered orally to spontaneously hypertensive rats (Kruse *et al.* 1986b). One of these compounds is currently being examined as a potential antihypertensive drug.

Hydrazines have been shown to inhibit a wide variety of redox-active proteins, and Fitzpatrick and Villafranca (1986) have extended these studies to DBH, to probe the identity of protein residues in the vicinity of the copper ions at the active site. DBH is inactivated by phenylhydrazine, methyl hydrazine, and phenylethylhydrazine in accordance with the production of a hydrazine cation radical, which undergoes homolytic cleavage of the C—N bond to generate a carbon-centred radical. This reacts with the enzyme, resulting in inactivation:

$$E\text{-}Cu^{2+} + RNHNH_2 \rightarrow E\text{—}Cu^+ + R\text{–}\overset{\cdot +}{N}\text{–}NH_2 \xrightarrow{\quad N_2H_2 \quad}$$

$$E\text{–}Cu^+ + R^{\cdot} \rightarrow E\text{—}R_{inact} \tag{22A.6}$$

Benzylhydrazine behaves as a mechanism-based inactivator of DBH, probably in accordance with eqn. (22A.7) where inactivation is due to abstraction of an electron from nitrogen instead of abstraction of a hydrogen atom from the benzylic carbon as occurs in the alternative hydroxylation reaction of benzyl hydrazine.

$$(22A.7)$$

Evidence for these conclusions comes from studies with deuterated benzyl-hydrazine, where the rate of hydrogen abstraction was decreased by a factor equal to the intrinsic isotope effect, with no effect on abstraction of an electron from the nitrogen, so resulting in a decrease in the partition ratio. This observation is in contrast with that noted earlier for 3-(*p*-hydroxyphenyl)propene (6), where with a common intermediate, no isotope effect is seen upon the partition ratio.

In summary, mechanism-based inactivators and reversible inhibitors of DBH have recently appeared that exert an anti-hypertensive effect in suitable animal models. The successful translation of these properties to humans would introduce a new type of anti-hypertensive agent to take its place alongside the existing renin or angiotensin-converting enzyme inhibitors in current use or being developed for this disease.

References

Ahn, N. and Klinman, J. P. (1983). Mechanism of modulation of dopamine β-mono-oxygenase by pH and fumarate as deduced from initial rate and primary deuterium isotope effect studies. *Biochemistry*, **22**, 3096–106.

Ash. D. E., Papadopoulos, N. J., Colombo, G., and Villafranca, J. J. (1984). Kinetic and spectroscopic studies on the interaction of copper with dopamine β-hydroxylase. *J. Biol. Chem.*, **259**, 3395–8.

Baldoni, J. M. and Villafranca, J. J. (1980). Dopamine β-hydroxylase inactivation by a suicide substrate *J. Biol. Chem.*, **255**, 8987–90.

Bargar, T. M., Broersma, R. J., Creemer, L. C., McCarthy, J. R., Hornsperger, J. M., Palfreyman, M. G., Wagner, J., and Jung, M. J. (1986). Unsaturated heterocyclic amines as potent time dependent inhibitors of dopamine β-hydroxylase. *J. Med. Chem.*, **29**, 315–17.

Blumberg, W. E., Goldstein, M., Lauber, E., and Peisach, J. (1965). Magnetic resonance studies on the mechanism of the enzymatic β-hydroxylation of 3,4-dihydroxyphenyl-ethylamine. *Biochim. Biophys. Acta*, **99**, 187–90.

Colombo, G. and Villafranca, J. J. (1984). An acetylenic mechanism-based inhibitor of dopamine β-hydroxylase. *J. Biol. Chem.*, **259**, 15017–20.

Colombo, G., Giedroc, D. P., Rajashekhar, B., and Villafranca, J. J. (1984b). Alternate substrates of dopamine β-hydroxylase. Inhibition by benzyl cyanides and reactivation of inhibited enzyme. *J. Biol. Chem.*, **259**, 1601–6.

Colombo, G., Rajashekhar, B., Ash, D. E., and Villafranca, J. J. (1984c). Alternate substrates of dopamine β-hydroxylase. Stoichiometry of the inactivation reaction with benzyl cyanides and spectroscopic investigations. *J. Biol. Chem.*, **259**, 1607–15.

Colombo, G., Rajashekhar, B., Giedroc, D. P., and Villafranca, J. J. (1984a). Alternate substrates of dopamine β-hydroxylase. Kinetic investigations of benzyl cyanides as substrates and inhibitors *J. Biol. Chem.*, **259**, 1593–600.

Colombo, G., Rajashekhar, B., Giedroc, D. P., and Villafranca, J. J. (1984d). Mechanism-based inhibitors of dopamine β-hydroxylase: Inhibition by 2-bromo-3-(p-hydroxy-phenyl)-1-propene. *Biochemistry*, **23**, 3590–8.

Fitzpatrick, P. F., Flory, D. R., and Villafranca, J. J. (1985). 3-phenylpropenes as mechanism-based inhibitors of dopamine β-hydroxylase: evidence for a radical mechanism. *Biochemistry*, **24**, 2108–14.

Fitzpatrick, P. F. and Villafranca, J. J. (1985). Mechanism-based inhibitors of dopamine β-hydroxylase containing acetylenic or cyclopropyl groups. *J. Am. Chem. Soc.*, **107**, 5022–3.

Fitzpatrick, P. F. and Villafranca, J. J. (1986). The mechanism of inactivation of dopamine β-hydroxylase by hydrazines. *J. Biol. Chem.*, **261**, 4510–18.

Friedman, S. and Kaufman, S. (1965). 3,4-dihydroxyphenylethylamine β-hydroxylase: physical properties, copper content and the role of copper in the catalytic activity. *J. Biol. Chem.*, **240**, 4763–73.

Geffen, L. B. and Livett, B. G. (1971). Synaptic vesicles in sympathetic neurons. *Physiol. Rev.*, **51**, 98–157.

Goldstein, M. (1966). Inhibition of norepinephrine biosynthesis at the dopamine-β-hydroxylation stage.*Pharmacol. Rev.*, **18**, 77–82.

Hidaka, H. (1971). Fusaric (5-butylpicolinic acid), an inhibitor of dopamine β-hydroxylase, affects serotonin and noradrenaline. *Nature (London)*, **231**, 54–5.

Hortnagl, H., Winkler, H., and Lochs, H. (1972). Membrane proteins of chromaffin granules. *Biochem. J.*, **129**, 187–95.

Kaufman, S. (1974). Dopamine-beta-hydroxylase. *J. Psychiatr. Res.*, **11**, 303–16.

Kaufman, S. and Friedman, S. (1965). Dopamine-β-hydroxylase. *Pharmacol. Rev.*, **17**, 71–100.

Klinman, J. P. and Krueger, M. (1982). Dopamine β-hydroxylase: activity and inhibition in the presence of β-substituted phenethylamines. *Biochemistry*, **21**, 67–75.

Klinman, J. P. Krueger, M., Brenner, M., and Edmonson, D. E. (1984). Evidence for two copper atoms/subunit in dopamine β-monooxygenase catalysis. *J. Biol. Chem.*, **259**, 3399–402.

Kruse, L. I., DeWolf, W. E., Chambers, P. A., and Goodhart, P. J. (1986a). Design and kinetic characterisation of multisubstrate inhibitors of dopamine β-hydroxylase. *Biochemistry*, **25**, 7271–8.

Kruse, L. I., Kaiser, C., DeWolf, W. E., Frazee, J. S., Erickson, R. N., Ezekiel, M., Ohlstein, E. H., Ruffolo, R. R., and Berkowitz, B. A. (1986b). Substituted 1-benzylimidazole-2-thiols as potent and orally active inhibitors of dopamine β-hydroxylase. *J. Med. Chem.*, **29**, 887–9.

Levitt, M., Spector, S., Sjoerdsma, A., and Udenfriend, S. (1965). Elucidation of the rate-limiting step in norepinephrine biosynthesis in the perfused guinea pig heart. *J. Pharmacol. Exp. Ther.*, **148**, 1–8.

May, S. W., Mueller, P. W., Padgette, S. R., Herman, H. H., and Phillips, R. S. (1983). Dopamine-β-hydroxylase: suicide inhibition by the novel olefinic substrate, 1-phenyl-1-aminomethylethene. *Biochem. Biophys. Res. Commun.*, **110**, 161–168.

May, S. W. and Phillips, R. S. (1980). Asymmetric sulfoxidation by dopamine β-hydroxylase, an oxygenase heretofore considered specific for methylene hydroxylation. *J. Am. Chem. Soc.*, **102**, 5981–3.

May, S. W., Phillips, R. S., Mueller, P. W., and Herman, H. H. (1981). Dopamine β-hydroxylase. Comparative specificities and mechanisms of the oxygenation reactions. *J. Biol. Chem.*, **256**, 8470–5.

Miller, S. M, and Klinman, J. P. (1985). Secondary isotope effects and structure–reactivity correlations in the dopamine β-monooxygenase reaction: evidence for a chemical mechanism. *Biochemistry*, **24**, 2114–27.

Molinoff, P. B. and Axelrod, J. (1971). Biochemistry of catecholamines. *Ann. Rev. Biochem.*, **40**, 465–500.

Nagatsu, T. (1973). Dopamine-β-hydroxylase (DBH). In *Biochemistry of catecholamines*, pp. 60–74. University Park Press, Baltimore.

Nagatsu, T. (1977). Dopamine β-hydroxylase in blood and cerebrospinal fluid. *Trends Biochem. Sci.*, **2**, 217–19.

Padgette, S. R., Wimalasena, K., Herman, H. H., Sirimanne, S. R., and May, S. W. (1985). Olefine oxygenation and N-dealkylation by dopamine β-monooxygenase: catalysis and mechanism-based inhibition. *Biochemistry*, **24**, 5826–39.

Piesche, L., Hilse, H., Oehlke, J., Schrötter, E., and Oehme, P. (1983). Substituted picolinic acids as DBH [dopamine β-hydroxylase] inhibitors. Inhibition of dopamine β-hydroxylase and antihypertensive action. *Pharmazie*, **38**, 335–8.

Potter, W. P. de., De Schaepdryver, A. F., Moerman, E. J., and Smith, A. D. (1969). Evidence for the release of vesicle-proteins together with noradrenaline upon stimulation of the splenic nerve. *J. Physiol. (Lond.)*, **204**, 102P–4P.

Rajashekhar, B., Fitzpatrick, P. F., Colombo, G., and Villafranca, J. J. (1984). Synthesis of several 2-substituted 3-(p-hydroxyphenyl)-1-propenes and their characterisation as mechanism-based inhibitors of dopamine β-hydroxylase. *J. Biol. Chem.*, **259**, 6925–30.

Ratwatte, H. A. M. and Douglas, K. T. (1983). Photolabelling of dopamine-β-hydroxylase by bleomycin. *Biochem. Biophys. Res. Commun.*, **112**, 273–8.

Rosenberg, R. C. and Lovenberg, W. (1980). Dopamine β-hydroxylase. In *Essays in neurochemistry and neuropharmacology*, (ed. M. B. H. Youdin, W. Lovenberg, D. F. Sharman, and J. R. Lagnado), vol. 4., pp. 163–209 Wiley, New York.

Rosenberg, R. C. Inhibition of dopamine β-hydroxylase by 2-mercapto-1-methylimidazole (1983). *Biochim. Biophys. Acta*, **749**, 276–80.

Sams, C. F. and Matthews, K. S. (1984). Chemical modification of dopamine β-hydroxylase. *Biochim. Biophys. Acta*, **787**, 61–70.

Saxena, A., Hensley, P., Osborne, J. C. Jr., and Fleming, P. J. (1985). The pH-dependent subunit dissociation and catalytic activity of bovine dopamine β-hydroxylase. *J. Biol. Chem.*, **260**, 3386–92.

Skotland, T. and Ljones, T. (1979a). Dopamine β-monooxygenase: Structure, mechanism and properties of the enzyme-bound copper. *Inorg. Perspect. Biol. Med.*, **2**, 151–80.

Skotland, T. and Ljones, T. (1979b). The enzyme-bound copper of dopamine β-monoxygenase. *Eur. J. Biochem.*, **94**, 145–51.

Spector, S., Sjoerdsma, A., and Udenfriend, S. (1964). Blockade of endogenous norephedrine synthesis by α-methyltyrosine, an inhibitor of tyrosine hydroxylase. *J. Pharmacol.*, **147**, 86–95.

Terland, O. and Flatmark, T. (1975). Ascorbate as a natural constituent of chromaffin granules from the bovine adrenal medulla. *FEBS Lett.*, **59**, 52–6.

Vanneste, W. H. and Zuberbuehler, A. (1974). Copper-containing oxygenases. In *Molecular mechanisms of oxygen activation* (ed. O. Hayaishi), pp. 371–404. Academic Press, New York.

Walker, G. A., Kon, H., and Lovenberg, W. (1977). An investigation of the copper site(s) of dopamine β-hydroxylase by electron paramagnetic resonance. *Biochim. Biophys. Acta*, **482**, 309–22.

Winkler, H. (1976). The composition of adrenal chromaffin granules: and assessment of controversial results. *Neuroscience*, **1**, 65–80.

Weinshilboum, R. M, (1979). Serum dopamine β-hydroxylase *Pharmacol. Rev.*, **30**, 133–65.

Section 22B

α-amylase inhibitors

22B.1   Characteristics of the enzyme

α-amylases (α 1→4-glucan 4-glucanohydrolase, EC 3.2.1.1)catalyse the hydrolysis of α 1→4-linked glucose polymers to give hydrolytic products with the α-configuration (cf. β-amylases). The enzyme from plant and animal (Thoma *et al.* 1971) bacterial and fungal (Takagi *et al.* 1971) and human sources (Zakowski and Bruns 1984; Duchassaing *et al.* 1984) has been reviewed. In mammals, the salivary gland and pancreas are the main source of α-amylase, which is used for the initial steps in the degradation of dietary starch. Different α-amylases are evolved during germination in cereals and consist of a number of isoenzymes (Machaiah and Vakil 1984).

α-amylase from hog pancreas (Danielsson, 1947) has a molecular weight of 45 000; that from human saliva has a molecular weight of 55 200 (or 69 000). The latter occurs as several isoenzymes (see Zakowski and Bruns 1984) and has an optimum pH near neutrality (in the presence of chloride ion) (Greenwood and Milne 1968), and is probably dependent on calcium for activity (see Thoma *et al.* 1971).

Cleavage of the C_1–$O_4{}^1$ bond occurs by endo-attack; digestion of amylose, the linear glucose polymer of starch containing only α-1,4-linkages, gives a mixture of maltose, maltotriose and other dextrins. α-1,6 linkages are not hydrolysed by amylase, and the digestion of amylopectin, the branched-chain component of starch, yields products called *limit dextrins*, containing un-hydrolysed α-1,6-linkages. The specificity site of porcine pancreatic enzyme is considered to be composed of five sub-sites with the catalytic site between sub-sites II and III (Robyt and French 1970b). By analogy with the sub-site energy contour for lysozyme and its substrates, the effect of chain length of the saccharide on Michaelis parameters has been rationalized (Thoma *et al.* 1971). In long chains there is a greater probability than in short chains that a bond will lie across the catalytic site. This accounts for the greater enzyme affinity for longer chains. With very short chains, a high proportion of non-productive complexes are formed. Porcine pancreatic α-amylase and others bring about a number (Robyt and French 1967) of subsequent attacks on a bound substrate before the chain is released and the process is then repeated on another chain. These subsequent attacks occur in the direction towards the non-reducing end of the substrate (Robyt and French 1970a). More recently, Prodanov *et al.* (1984), using maltooligosaccharides as substrates rather than starch, have proposed a modified model to fit the action pattern. The effect of modified α-$D(1\rightarrow4)$-glucans on sub-site binding has been discussed by Braun *et al.* (1985).

The amino acid sequence of porcine pancreatic α-amylase, a peptide with a long single chain of 496 residues, has been reported (Pasero *et al.* 1981, 1983). The three-dimensional structure has been determined at 0.5 nm resolution (Payan *et al.* 1980). The enzyme has a 3nm-long cleft, which can accommodate five glucose units. Crystallography of substrate analogues has indicated two binding sites; one in the cleft and the other on the surface of the molecule.

22B.2   Inhibitors

Many naturally occuring inhibitors of α-amylase from a wide variety of sources are known (see Marshall 1975, Frels and Rupnow 1984 for reviews). Protein-aceous inhibitors occur in buckwheat malt, oat seeds, mangoes, *Colocasia esculenta* tubers, wheat, rye, and *Phaseolus vulgaris* (kidney beans). α-amylases from different sources, i.e. saliva, pancreas, fungus, bacteria, *Helix pomatia*, insect (*Tenebrio molitor*), may show differences in susceptibility to inhibition by the specific proteinaceous inhibitors. Work has shown that a large number of proteins in the wheat albumin fraction display inhibitory activity towards many α-amylases from different origins (Deponte *et al.* 1976). These differences may be classified into three families with M_r 60 000, 24 000, and 12 000. The inhibitors with M_r 24 000 act on mammalian and insect α-amylases, whereas those with M_r 12 000 act only on insect amylases. Little is known about the specificity of the M_r 60 000 family. The two most characterized inhibitors of α-amylase are those from wheat and kidney bean.

The situation regarding the number of α-amylase inhibitors in wheat and their relationship is not clear, since at least six proteins with inhibitory activity have been reported (Shainkin and Birk 1970; Saunders and Lang 1973; Silano *et al.* 1973; O'Donnel and McGeeney 1976; Granum and Whitaker 1977; Maeda *et al.* 1985). The inhibitor fractions have been differentiated mainly on the basis of electrophoretic mobility on polyacrylamide gel, pI, and M_r, although the quoted

M_r values are dependent on the method used and this has led to difficulty in comparison of results between workers. Purification of the wheat inhibitor has yielded two forms designated AmI_1, and AmI_2, with molecular weights 18 000 and 26 000 respectively (Shainkin and Birk 1970), which differed in specificity and other properties. Strumeyer and Fisher (1973) have reported a single inhibitor with molecular weight 55 000. Fractionation of albumins from kernels of haploid wheat gave an albumin fraction (molecular weight 23 800) that inhibited salivary and pancreatic α-amylases and was considered to correspond to AmI_2 and also to consist of two subunits, one of which was AMI_1 (Silano et al. 1973). Saunders and Lang (1973) reported the separation of two albumin proteins (I and II) with inhibitory activity. These had molecular weights of 20 000 and 21 000, respectively, and distinctly different pI values from the inhibitor isolated by Silano. All these three inhibitors acted in an uncompetitive fashion against pancreatic α-amylase.

The inhibition of α-amylase by the wheat inhibitors AmI_1 and AmI_2 was markedly greater after preincubation of the enzyme with inhibitor, followed by addition of substrate, than after preincubation of substrate with inhibitor followed by enzyme. Addition of substrate did not reverse the inhibition seen. O'Donnell and McGeeney (1976) have isolated four inhibitors of α-amylase from wheat. One inhibitor was purified and found to be 100-fold more specific for human salivary amylase than for human pancreatic amylase. It had M_r 21 000, electrophoretic mobility 0.19 (bromophenol blue $= 1$), and was considered to correspond to AmI_2 (Silano et al. 1973), inhibitor I (Saunders and Lang 1973) and inhibitor III (Petrucci et al. 1974).

Granum and Whitaker (1977) purified three α-amylase inhibitors from wheat, designated 0.19 (M_r 24 000), 0.28 (M_r 18 500), and 0.55 (M_r 30 000) on the basis of their relative electrophoretic mobilities on polyacrylamide. They differed in their activity against α-amylase from different sources. The 0.19 inhibitor was active against human salivary and hog pancreatic enzyme but not against bacterial or fungal enzyme. The 0.28 inhibitor was weakly active only against human salivary α-amylase, and the 0.55 inhibitor was only active against human salivary α-amylase. The 0.28 inhibitor probably corresponds with the AmI_1 inhibitor (Silano et al. 1973; Shainkin and Birk 1970). The 0.55 inhibitor may be closely related to the 0.19 inhibitor. The amino acid sequence of the 0.19 inhibitor from wheat kernel has been established (Maeda et al. 1985), as well as that of a new inhibitor, designated 0.53 on the basis of its electrophoretic mobility (Maeda et al. 1983). The 0.53 inhibitor has 500 times more activity towards human salivary amylase than towards human pancreatic amylase.

Specific proteinaceous inhibitors of α-amylase are widespread in kidney beans (Phaseolus vulgaris). The inhibitor from white kidney bean has been obtained in a high state of purity (Marshall and Lauda 1975) and named phaseolamin. It was originally isolated in crude form by Jaffé and his co-workers (Hernandez and Jaffé 1968; Jaffé et al. 1973) after attempts to identify the factor responsible for impaired starch digestion in rats fed on diets of uncooked kidney beans (Jaffé and Lette 1968). The pure inhibitor has a molecular weight of 45 000–50 000 and is a glycoprotein containing about 10 per cent carbohydrate. Inhibitory activity is irreversibly destroyed after heating in solution (pH 4) for 10 min at 100°C. Experiments with hog pancreatic α-amylase showed that inhibition is dependent on the duration of interaction between the enzyme and inhibitor as well as the pH and temperature of the media. Optimum pH for inhibition is pH 5.5 and inhibition occurs more rapidly at 37°C than at lower temperatures. Substrate does not reverse inhibition but prevents inhibition where there is no preincubation stage between inhibitor and enzyme. The stoichiometry of the interaction is 1:1 and complex formation between inhibitor and enzyme was shown using gel filtration. The inhibitor is specific for animal α-amylases. More recently a second inhibitor, which is heat-labile, has been isolated (Cinco et al. 1985).

Red kidney bean contains a single inhibitor, M_r 49 000 (Powers and Whitaker, 1977a, b; Cinco et al. 1985), probably containing four subunits of three different types. It forms a 1:1 stoichiometric complex with porcine pancreatic amylase, leading to complete loss of activity on starch. The slow rate of complex formation has been interpreted as indicative of a conformational change after reversible complex formation (Powers and Whitaker 1977b; cf. Tanizaki and Lajola 1985, with black bean inhibitor). The structural features of the carbohydrate moiety of the glycoprotein have been examined (Wilcox and Whitaker 1984).

Black bean contains two α-amylase inhibitors (Frels and Rupnow 1984). These have been purified to homogeneity and designated I-1 and I-2. These inhibitors have molecular weights of 49 000 and 47 000, and pI values of 4.93 and 4.86, respectively. I-2 is more resistant to heat denaturation than I-1. Electrophoresis of I-1 resulted in two major carbohydrate-containing bands with molecular weights of 32 000–34 000 and 15 500–17 000, whereas I-2 gave a major carbohydrate-containing band with molecular weight 15 000–17 000 and several minor bands. These inhibitors differ from the red kidney bean inhibitor which was resolved into three major carbohydrate-containing bands with molecular weight below 17 000.

22B.3   Pharmacology of α-amylase inhibitors

The presence of high levels of α-amylase inhibitors in legumes and cereals constituting common foodstuffs has raised the possibility that these inhibitors could have an effect in impairing starch digestion. It seemed likely that proteolysis of the proteinaceous inhibitors by pepsin would render them orally inactive (Kneen and Sandstedt 1946) and their action would be restricted to salivary α-amylase. Black bean inhibitor has since been shown to be stable to digestion (Lajolo et al. 1984). However, early findings in animal experiments have confirmed the in vivo activity of the wheat inhibitor in modulating carbohydrate digestion (Marshall 1975; Lang et al. 1974) and the bean α-amylase inhibitor was also considered to be active in vivo (Jaffé and Lette 1968;

Moreno 1971). Although these findings have implications on the nutritional value of wheat-based feeds for animal and human consumption (Marshall 1975), the main interest here is in the therapeutic application of α-amylase protein-aceous inhibitors in diabetes, and as dietetic agents for obese subjects.

Diabetes mellitus can be ameliorated by diet, insulin therapy, or oral therapy with hypoglycaemic agent. Even so, complications develop that can effect the eyes, nerves, kidneys, and arteries, making diabetics much more susceptible to these diseases than non-diabetics (Brownlee and Cerami 1981). α-amylase in-hibitors would allow diabetic individuals to eat a moderate amount of starch and thus mimic the effects of dieting. They would also help to reduce high post-prandial blood glucose levels (200mg per 100ml) often associated with re-tinopathy (Bennett et al. 1976).

Puls and co-workers (see Puls et al. 1983, 1984, for review) have studied the effect of a fractionated proteinaceous α-amylase wheat inhibitor on post-prandial blood glucose in rats fed on raw starch. BAY D7791 brought about a dose-dependent flattening of the post-prandial blood glucose increment, an effect confirmed in dogs and healthy volunteers as well as in obese and diabetic persons. The inhibitor was not effective in similar loading tests on rats using glucose, sucrose, or maltose, confirming that its action was brought about by inhibition of pancreatic amylase. In similar experiments on rats using cooked starch, the effect of the inhibitor was very weak and it was suggested that the boiling process destroyed the membrane of the starch grain, giving the α-amylase easier access to the chains of amylose and amylopectin. More potent inhibitors (BAY E4609) were discovered from microorganisms, the main compo-nent of the mixture being acarviosine (14) linked to 7–30 glucose units.

(14) $m + n = 7$–30

When evidence was obtained that for a combination of starch and glucose BAY E4609 did not reduce the post-prandial blood glucose or increase insulin levels in carbohydrate loading tests on animals and humans, a search for sucrase inhibitors was initiated. Derivatives of acarviosine with much fewer glucose units (ie. $m + n = 2$, acarbose, BAY G5421) displayed weak inhibitory effects on amylase inhibition but strong in vivo effects in starch loading tests on rats. This effect was due to very strong inhibitory effects on maltase, dextrinase, and glucoamylase i.e. those enzymes responsible for the breakdown of the oligosacc-harides formed from the α-amylase breakdown of starch. Acarbose is a competi-tive inhibitor of sucrase ($K_i = 0.26$ μM) and has been shown in healthy volunteers to reduce the increase in post-prandial blood glucose levels by 50 per cent after administration of either sucrose and/or cooked starch (Puls *et al.* 1977; Hillebrand *et al.* 1982). It increases the metabolic control of patients suffering from diabetes mellitus, as was shown by reduced hyperglycaemia and glucosuria (Creutzfeldt 1982).

More recently, semi-synthetic derivatives of 1-deoxynojirimycin (BAY M1099 and BAY 01248) have been found to be small-molecule inhibitors of sucrase as well as maltase, which bring about a reduction in food consumption, body weight gain, and fat pads in rats (see Puls *et al.* 1984 for review).

Amylase inhibitor from red kidney beans, after removal of toxic components, has been marketed commercially in the USA and to a lesser extent in Europe as a 'starch blocker' for obese persons who find difficulty in limiting their consumption of carbohydrate. It has been estimated that 10 million starch-blocking tablets, of 119 different brands, are consumed weekly in America (Anon 1982).

Acute testing of several of these commercial products, at the indicated levels, with healthy volunteers showed that, despite earlier reports from animals experiments, they had no action on blood glucose levels, insulin response, breath hydrogen (Carlson *et al.* 1983; Hollenbeck *et al.* 1983) or calorie utilization (Bo-Linn *et al.* 1982). A recent report has indicated that an inhibitor obtained from a black bean variety was able to reduce hyperglycaemia, in rats in a dose-dependent manner following the ingestion of a starch meal. This inhibitor could also reduce growth when the feed was a calorie-deficient diet based on raw starch (Lajolo *et al.* 1984). It was concluded that the smoothing effect on serum glucose caused by the inhibitor could be potentially useful, but as a weight-reducing agent the effect was too small to be useful.

Layer *et al.* (1985), using a more purified bean-derived α-amylase inhibitor, have shown in humans that it effectively decreased the *in vitro* digestion of dietary starch in a dose-dependent manner and rapidly inhibited (94–99 percent) intraluminal amylase activity. They concluded that commercial amylase inhibitors failed to decrease starch digestion *in vivo* because they had insufficient anti-amylase activity.

In summary, α-amylase inhibitors have not yet realized their potential as therapeutic agents in diabetes or as dietetic agents for obese subjects. Continuing research will establish whether these aims can be wholly achieved.

References

Anon, (1982). Much interest in new 'starch blockers'. *Pharm. J.*, **229**, 124.

Bennett, P. H., Rushforth, N. B., Miller, M. and Le-Compte, P. M. (1976). Epidemiologic studies of diabetes in the Pima Indians. *Rec. Progr. Horm. Res.*, **32**, 333–76.

Bo-Linn, G. W. Santa Ana, C. A., Morawski, S. G., and Fordtran, J. S. (1982). Starch blockers—their effect on calorie absorption from a high starch meal. *New Engl. J. Med.*, **307**, 1413–16.

Brownlee, M. and Cerami, A. (1981). The Biochemistry of the complications of diabetes mellitus. *Ann. Rev. Biochem.*, **50**, 385–432.

Braun, P. J., French, D., and Robyt, J. F. (1985). The effect of substrate modification on porcine pancreatic α-amylase subsite binding: hydrolysis of substrates containing 2-deoxy-D-glucose and 2-amino-2-deoxy-D-glucose. *Arch. Biochem. Biophys.*, **242**, 231–9.

Carlson, G. L., Li, B. U. K., Bass, P., and Olsen, W. A. (1983). A bean alpha-amylase inhibitor formulation (starch blocker) is ineffective in man. *Science*, **219**, 393–5.

Cinco, F. J., Frels, J. M., Holt, D. L., and Rupnow, J. H. (1985). Determination of the number and heat stability of α-amylase inhibitors in white and red kidney bean (*Phaseolus vulgaris*) *J. Food Sci.*, **50**, 533–4.

Creutzfeldt, W. (1982). Antiobesity activity of pluronic L-101. In *Effects on carbohydrate and fat metabolism*, (ed. W. Creutzfeldt), International Congress Series 594. Excerpta Medica, Amsterdam.

Danielsson, C. E. (1947). Molecular weight of α-amylase. *Nature* (*London.*), 160, 899.

Deponte, R., Parlamenti, R., Petriucci, T., Silano, V., and Tomasi, M. (1976). Albumin α-amylase inhibitor families from wheat flour. *Cereal Chem.*, **53**, 805–20.

Duchassaing, D., Cambillau, M., and Paris, M. (1984). Isoamylases. *Pharm. Biol.* **18**, No. 153, 325–37.

Frels, J. M. and Rupnow, J. H. (1984). Purification and partial characterization of two α-amylase inhibitors from black bean (*Phaseolus vulgaris*). *J. Food Biochem.*, **8**, 281–301.

Granum, P. E., and Whitaker, J. R. (1977). Purification and characterization of α-amylase inhibitors in wheat (*Triticum aestivum* var Anza). *J. Food Biochem.*, **1**, 385–401.

Greenwood, C. T. and Milne, E. A. (1968). Starch degrading and synthesising enzymes. A discussion of their properties and action pattern. In *Advances in carbohydrate chemistry* (ed. M. L. Wolfrom and R. S. Tipsom). **23**, 281–366.

Hernandez, A. and Jaffé, W. G. (1968). Inhibitor of pancreatic amylase from beans (*Phaseolus vulgaris*). *Acta Cient. Venez.*, **19**, 183–5.

Hillebrand, I., Boehme, K., Frank, G., Fink, H., and Berchtold, P. (1982). Effect of the glucosidase inhibitor acarbose on postprandial blood glucose, serum insulin and triglyceride levels in normal and overweight subjects. In *First International Symposium on Acarbose*, (ed. W. Creutzfeldt), pp. 191–4. Excerpta Medica, Amsterdam.

Hollenbeck, C. B., Coulston, A. M., Quan, R., Becker, T. R., Vreman, H. J., Stevenson, D. K., and Reaven, G. M. (1983). Effect of a commercial starch blocker preparation on carbohydrate digestion and absorption: *in vivo* and *in vitro* studies. *Am. J. Clin. Nutr.*, **38**, 498–503.

Jaffé, W. G. and Lette, C. L. V. (1968). Heat-labile growth-inhibiting factors in beans (*Phaseolus vulgaris*). *J. Nutr.*, **94**, 203–10.

Jaffé, W. G., Moreno, R., and Wallis, V. (1973). Amylase inhibitors in Legume seeds. *Nutr. Rep. Int.*, **7**, 169–74.

Kneen, E. and Sandstedt, R. M. (1946). Distribution and general properties of an amylase inhibitor in cereals. *Arch. Biochem. Biophys.*, **9**, 235–49.

Lajolo, F. M., Filho, J. M., and Menezes, E. W. (1984). Effect of a bean (*Phaseolus vulgaris*) α-amylase inhibitor on starch utilization. *Nutr. Rep. Int.*, **30**, 45–54.

Lang, J. A., Chang-Hum, L. E. Reyes, P. S., and Briggs, G. M. (1974). Interference of starch metabolism by α-amylase inhibitors. *Fed. Proc.*, *Fed. Am. Soc. Exp. Biol.*, **33**, 718.

Layer, P., Carlson, G. L. and DiMagno, E. P. (1985). Partially purified white bean amylase inhibitor reduces starch digestion *in vitro* and inactivates intraduodenal amylase in humans. *Gastroenterology*, **88**, 1895–902.

Machaiah, J. P. and Vakil, U. K. (1984). Isolation and partial characterisation of α-amylase components evolved during early wheat germination. *J. Biosci.*, **6**, 47–59.

Maeda, K., Kakabayashi, S. and Matsubara, H. (1985). Complete amino acid sequence of an α-amylase inhibitor in wheat kernel (0.19-inhibitor). *Biochim. Biophys. Acta*, **828**, 213–21.

Maeda, K., Hase, T., and Matsubara, H. (1983). Complete amino acid sequence of an α-amylase inhibitor in wheat kernel. *Biochim. Biophys. Acta*, **743**, 52–7.

Marshall, J. J. (1975). α-amylase inhibitors from plants. In *Physiological effects of food carbohydrates*. (ed. A Jeans and J. Hodge), ACS symposium series 15, pp. 244–66. American Chemical Society, Washington, D. C.

Marshall, J. J. and Lauda, C. M. (1975). Purification and properties of phaseolamin, an inhibitor of α-amylase, from the kidney bean, *Phaseolus vulgaris*. *J. Biol. Chem.*, 250, 8030–7.

Moreno, G. R. (1971). Thesis, Central University of Caracas.

Mutzbauer, H. and Schulz, G. V. (1965). Die Bestimmung der molekularen konstanten von α-amylase aus humanspeichel. *Biochem. Biophys. Acta*, **102**, 526–32.

O'Donnell, M. D., and McGeeney, K. F. (1976). Purification and properties of an α-amylase inhibitor from wheat. *Biochim. Biophys. Acta*, **422**, 159–69.

Pasero, L., Abadie, B., Chicheportiche, Y., Mazzei, Y., Moinier, D., Bizzozero, J. P., Fougereau, M., and Marchis-Mouren, G. (1981). Porcine pancreatic α-amylase I: sequence between the 35th and 410th amino acid. *Biochimie*, **63**, 71–6.

Pasero, L., Mazzei, Y., Abadie, B., Moinier, D., Fougereau, M., and Marchis-Mouren, G. (1983). Localisation of the two free thiol groups in the porcine pancreatic α-amylase I sequence. *Biochem. Biophys. Res. Commun.*, **110**, 726–32.

Payan, F., Haser, R., Pierrot, M., Frey, M., Astier, J. P., Abadie, B., Duee, E., and Buisson, G. (1980). The three-dimensional structure of α-amylase from porcine pancreas at 5 Å resolution. *Acta Crystallogr.*, **B36**, 416–21.

Petrucci, T., Tomasi, M., Cantagalli, P., and Silano, V. (1974). Comparison of wheat albumin inhibitors of α-amylase and trypsin. *Phytochemistry*, **13**, 2487–95.

Powers, J. R. and Whitaker, J. R. (1977b). Effect of several experimental parameters on combination of red kidney bean (*Phaseolus vulgaris*) α-amylase inhibitor with porcine pancreatic α-amylase. *J. Food Biochem.*, **1**, 239–60.

Powers, J. R. and Whitaker, J. R. (1977a). Purification and some physical and chemical properties of red kidney bean (*Phaseolus vulgaris*) α-amylase inhibitor. *J. Food Biochem.*, **1**, 217–38.

Prodanov, E., Seigner, C., and Marchis-Mouren, G. (1984). Subsite profile of the active centre of porcine pancreatic α-amylase. Kinetic studies using maltooligosaccharides as substrates. *Biochem. Biophys. Res. Commun.*, **122**, 75–81.

Puls, W., Keup, U., Krause, H. P., Thomas, G., and Hoffmeister, F. (1977). Glucosidase inhibition. A new approach to the treatment of diabetes, obesity and hyperlipoproteinaemia. *Naturwissenschaften*, **64**, 536–7.

Puls, W., Bischoff, H., and Schutt, H., (1983). Pharmacology of amylase and glucosidase inhibitors. In *Delaying absorption and therapeutic principles of metabolism* (ed. W. Creutzfeldt and K. R. Foelsch), pp. 70–8. Thiene, Stuttgart.

Puls, W., Krause, H. P., Muller, L., Schutt, H., Sitt, R., and Thomas, G. (1984). Inhibitors of the rate of carbohydrate and lipid absorption by the intestine. *Int. J. Obesity*, **8**, 181–90.

Robyt, J. F. and French, D. (1967). Multiple attack hypothesis of α-amylase action: action of porcine pancreatic, human salivary, and *Aspergillus oryzae* α-amylases. *Archs. Biochem. Biophys.*, **122**, 8–16.

Robyt, J. F. and French. D. (1970a). Multiple attack and polarity of action of porcine pancreatic α-amylase. *Arch. Biochem. Biophys*, **138**, 662–70.

Robyt, J. F. and French. D. (1970b). The action pattern of porcine pancreatic α-amylase in relationship to the substrate binding site of the enzyme. *J. Biol. Chem.*, **245**, 3917–27.

Saunders, R. M. and Lang, J. A. (1973). α-amylase inhibitors in *Triticum aestivum*. Purification and physical chemical properties. *Phytochemistry*, **12**, 1237–41.

Shainkin, R. and Birk, Y. (1970). α-amylase inhibitors from wheat. Isolation and characterisation. *Biochem. Biophys. Acta.* **221**, 502–13.

Silano, V., Pocchiari, F., and Kasarda, D. D. (1973). Physical characteristation of α-amylase inhibitors from wheat. *Biochim. Biophys. Acta*, **317**, 139–48.

Strumeyer, D. H. and Fisher, B. R. (1973). Purification and characterisation of an amylase inhibitor from wheat gliadin. *Fed. Proc. Fed. Am. Soc. Exp., Biol.*, **32**, 624 (Abst. 2310).

Takagi, T., Toda, H. and Isemura, T. (1971). Bacterial and mold amylases. In *The enzymes*, (3rd edn) (ed. P. D. Boyer) Vol. 5 pp. 235–71. Academic Press, New York.

Tanizaki, M. M. and Lajolo, F. M. (1985). Kinetics of the interaction of pancreatic α-amylase with a kidney bean (*Phaseolus vulgaris*) amylase inhibitor. *J. Food Biochem.*, **9**, 71–89.

Thoma, J. A., Spradlin, J. E., and Dygert, S (1971). Plant and animal amylases. In *The enzymes* (3rd edn), (ed. P. D. Boyer), Vol. 5, pp. 115–189. Academic Press, New York.

Wilcox, E. R. and Whitaker, J. R. (1984). Structural features of red kidney bean α-amylase inhibitor important in binding with α-amylase. *J. Food Biochem.*, **8**, 189–213.

Zakowski, J. J. and Bruns, D. E. (1984) Biochemistry of human alpha amylase isoenzymes. *CRC Crit. Rev. Clin. Lab. Sci.*, **21**, 283–322.

Section 22C
Xanthine oxidase inhibitors

22C.1 Characteristics of the enzyme

Xanthine oxidase (xanthine:O_2 oxidoreductase, EC 1.2.3.2) catalyses the hydroxylation of many purine substrates and, in mammals, converts hypoxanthine to xanthine and then uric acid. It has been extensively reviewed by Bray (1963, 1975) and Massey (1973). Xanthine oxidase is widely distributed in mammals and is readily available from cow's milk. It has been obtained in crystalline form (Avis *et al.* 1956a, b). Early preparations of the enzyme contained inactive enzyme where an essential sulphur atom was lost during treatment with cyanide ('desulpho' enzyme), and inactive 'demolybdo' enzyme where the molybdenum content was reduced (see review by Bray 1975). Milk xanthine oxidase, free from the demolybdo form, contains FAD, molybdenum, iron, and acid-labile sulphur in the ratio 1:1:4:4 (see Bhattacharyya *et al.* 1983; Hart *et al.* 1970). It has an average molecular weight of 283 000 and consists of two identical, independent active-site systems, each containing one molybdenum atom, one FAD, and one each of two different two-ion-two-labile-sulphur centres, as discussed by Bray (1975). Recently, Nishino and Tsushima (1986), using affinity chromatography and folate as affinity ligand, have demonstrated that there are three enzyme species due to different combinations of inactive and active monomers in the dimer and that there is no interaction between the two subunits.

Xanthine oxidase has a wide substrate specificity pattern and the milk enzyme oxidizes more than 50 compounds at measurable rates at physiological pH (Krenitsky et al. 1972). The specificity of the enzyme with regard to electron acceptors (e.g. oxygen, methylene blue, 2,6-dichlorophenol-indophenol, triphenyltetrazolium chloride, ferricyanide, nitrate, cytochrome C, etc.) is also low.

The mechanism of action of the catalysed hydroxylation of xanthine by the milk enzyme has been extensively studied using e.p.r. This technique has been used particularly to monitor changes in the valency state of molybdenum at the active site (see Olsen et al. 1974; Bray 1975, 1980a, b; Bray et al. 1979; Malthouse et al. 1981; Bhattacharyya et al. 1983; George and Bray 1983). A reaction mechanism (simplified) suggested by Bray and co-workers (Bray et al. 1979) is shown in Fig. 22C.1 and is based on an earlier scheme proposed by Olson et al. (1974).

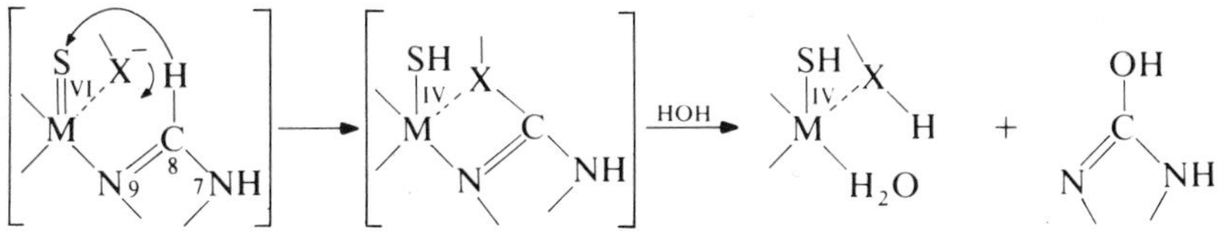

Michaelis complex

Fig. 22C.1 Reduction of molybdenum during xanthine oxidase-catalysed hydrolysis of xanthine (simplified after Bray et al. 1979).

In the Michaelis complex in which the substrate is coordinated, via its N-9 position, to the anion binding site in the enzyme (Bergmann and Levene 1976; Gutteridge et al. 1978), the undefined nucleophile, X, forms a covalent bond to the C-8 carbon of the xanthine with transfer of a proton to the proton-accepting sulphur atom and a pair of electrons to the molybdenum (i.e. hydride ion transfer). The intermediate then breaks down by hydrolysis to the product of the reaction. This is a simplistic account of the mechanism, which has been discussed in detail by Bray et al. (1979) and Malthouse et al. (1981). Reoxidation of the enzyme occurs through transfer of the two electrons received from the substrate. The reoxidation of the Mo, the flavin, and the two iron–sulphur centres is very rapid, according to the redox potential of these four centres, with release of product and reoxidation of the enzyme occurring by oxygen reacting with the reduced flavin (see Bhattacharyya et al. 1983; Hille and Massey 1986).

Xanthine oxidase has been shown in vitro to be capable of mobilizing the antitumour action of mitomycin C (15) although it is not clear how important the contribution made by the enzyme is in vivo. Mitomycin C has been

extensively studied for its antibacterial and anticancer activity since its discovery. Schwartz (1962) and Iyer and Szybalski (1964) found that the compound
is activated by biological reductive systems and that the activated form covalently binds and cross-links DNA (Iyer and Szybalski 1963; Weissbach and Lisio
1965). The metabolites have since been identified (Tomasz and Lipman 1981) as
2,7-diaminomitosene (**16**, R = H) and its *cis*- and *trans*-hydroxylated (**16**,
R = OH) and phosphorylated derivatives (**16**, R = OPO$_3$H$_2$). Pan *et al.* (1984)
have studied the formation of these metabolites from mitomycin C by reduction
with xanthine oxidase (+NADH) or NADP cytochrome P-450 reductase
(+NADPH) under anaerobic conditions. The proposed mechanism involves a
one-electron transfer to mitomycin C to form a semiquinone radical ion, leading
to elimination of methanol to form a stabilized radical (**17**). In the cell this
undergoes nucleophilic (Nu) attack on the aziridine ring to give the metabolites
or adducts noted, presumably with DNA. Regeneration of the quinone can
occur with molecular oxygen or another scavenger. Secondary activation of
monofunctionally bound mitomycin C, through a second anaerobic free-radical
semiquinone step, can occur (although the metabolites of such steps have not yet
been identified), to yield bifunctional adducts where the DNA is cross-linked. A
second series of aerobic reactions, which parallel the anaerobic activation
pathway, may be possible. Here flavoenzyme-catalysed free-radical transfer to
oxygen occurs to produce the cytotoxic agent's superoxide and hydroxyl radical,
with continuous cycling of the hydroquinone formed to semiquinone anion.

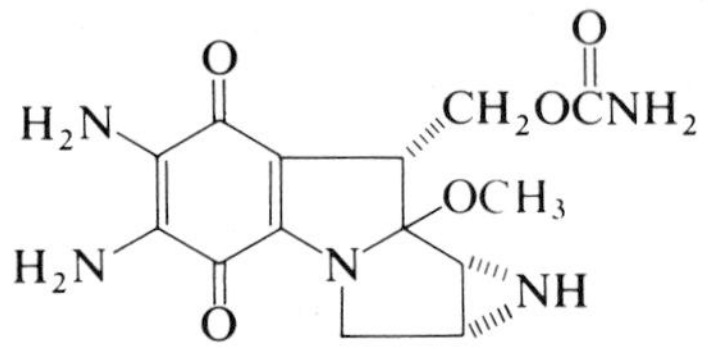

15 Mitomycin C

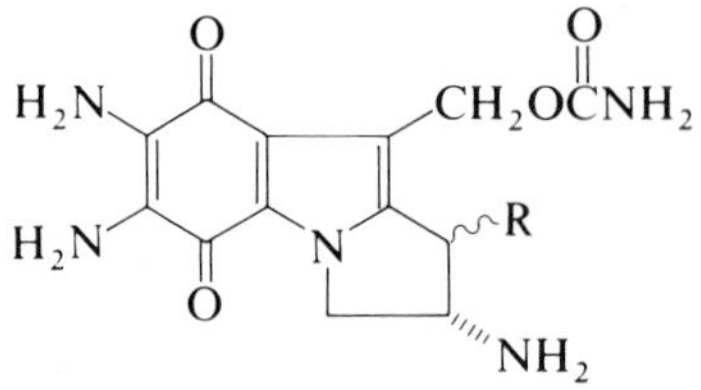

16

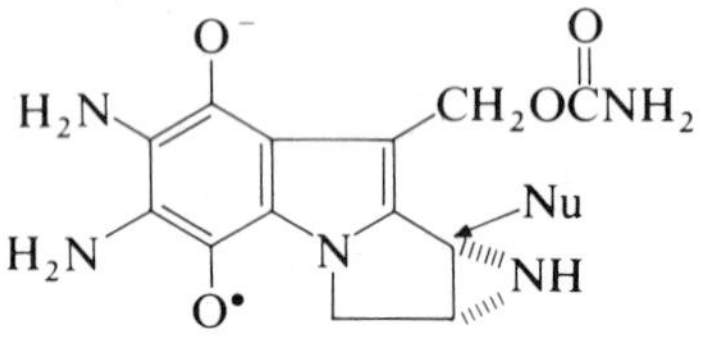

17

22C.2   Inhibitors

Many competitive, reversible inhibitors of xanthine oxidase have been described
(see Bray 1963 for review). Many are modelled on substrates or products of the

catalysed reaction, e.g. urea and guanidine, salicylate, and 2,4-diamino-6-hydroxy-s-triazine (ammeline), the latter being a fairly potent inhibitor. Chemical modifiers of the enzyme, e.g. thiol and carbonyl reagents, metal complexing and chelating agents, are not described here (see Bray 1975). Three particularly potent inhibitors are 2-amino-4-hydroxy-pteridine-6-aldehyde (pterine aldehyde; Lowry *et al.* 1949, see later), purine-6-aldehyde; (Gilbert 1964), and allopurinol [18; 4-hydroxypyrazolo (3,4-*d*)-pyrimidine]. Allopurinol is a substrate of the enzyme being converted to alloxanthine (oxipurinol, 19), which is

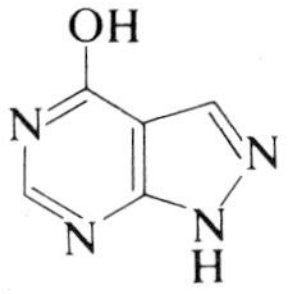

18 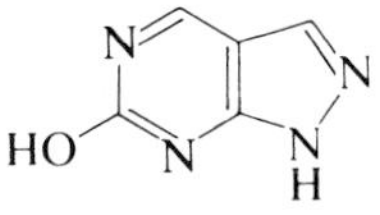   19

firmly bound in the molar ratio 1:1 to the reduced form of the molybdenum at the active site, leading to inhibition of the enzyme (Elion 1966; Massey *et al.* 1970). The potency of allopurinol as an inhibitor is reflected in its low K_i value of 6×10^{-10} M (Spector and Johns 1970). The structure of the inhibitory complex of alloxanthine and the enzyme has been suggested from e.p.r. studies (Hawkes *et al.* 1984). Alloxanthine reacts with reduced xanthine oxidase in a rapid reversible manner ($K_i \sim 1 \mu$M) followed by a second much slower step ($K = 0.006$ s^{-1}) with a reverse rate constant that is extremely small. The slow step may involve nucleophilic attack on molybdenum by the alloxanthine nitrogen atom at the 2-position with loss of oxygen from the molybdenum as water [eqn (22C.1)].

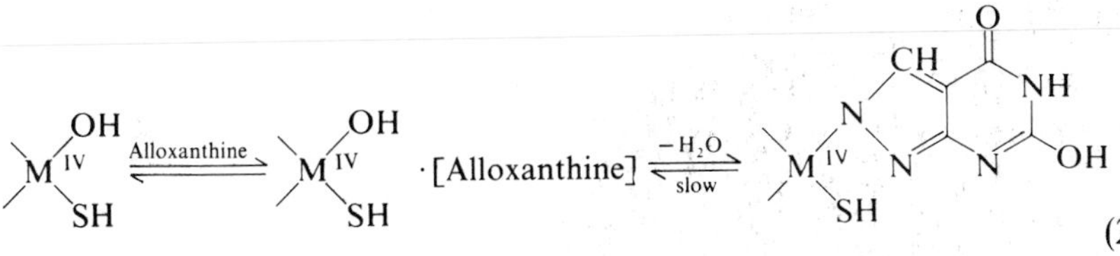

(22C.1)

Other disubstituted allopurine derivatives also bind to the reduced enzyme in a manner similar to that for alloxanthine (Massey *et al.* 1970), e.g. 4,6-dimercapto allopurine. These allopurine derivatives also react slowly with the desulpho-enzyme (Edmondson *et al.* 1972) in contrast to allopurinol, indicating the proximity of sulphur to the molybdenum site in the native enzyme.

Allopurinol, first synthesized as a potential antitumour agent, is widely used in the treatment of gout (see Yu 1974 for review). Gout is caused by the deposition in the joints of uric acid, which is formed by the hydroxylation by xanthine oxidase of the naturally occurring purines hypoxanthine and xanthine. Inhibition of the enzyme leads to increased excretion of these purines. Allopurinol has a biological half-life of 2–3h whereas the inhibitor oxipurinol, has a much longer biological half-life in humans (18–30h), with a renal clearance rate much slower than allopurinol but much faster than that of uric acid (Elion *et al.* 1968). Clinically, a combined programme of allopurinol with uricosuric agents such as probenecid or sulphinpyrazole, which increase clearance of oxipurinol, results in more rapid mobilisation of deposits. Increased clearance of oxipurinol, although leading to decreased inhibition of the enzyme, is counteracted by allopurinol being able to increase the biological half-life of probenecid (Tjandramaga *et al.* 1972).

Allopurinol has also been tried (Elion *et al.* 1963) as an adjuvant drug to enhance the antitumour potency of 6-mercaptopurine, which is converted to 6-thiouric acid by xanthine oxidase leading to decreased plasma levels of the 6-mercaptopurine.

Many different types of analogue have been synthesized in an attempt to increase the potency of the parent drug. Substituted pyrrolo (2,3-*d*) pyrimidine-2,4-diones (**20**) have been shown to have low inhibitory potency towards milk xanthine oxidase (Betlach and Sowell 1982).

20 R = C₆H₅ or CH₃

3-substituted 5,7-dihydroxypyrazolo [1,5-*a*]pyrimidines are potent reversible (non-competitive or mixed type) inhibitors of the enzyme when the 3-substituent is an aryl group. Some of these compounds have demonstrated K_i values two orders of magnitude lower than that for allopurinol (mixed type) (Springer *et al.* 1976). 3-hydroxy-1-nitrophenyl-1*H*-pyrazolo [4,3-*c*] pyridines, as well as the [3,4-*b*] isomers (which are devoid of nitrogen in either the 7- or 5-position, respectively, of allopurinol), are weak inhibitors of rat liver xanthine oxidase (Parmar *et al.* 1972, 1974). 4-Hydroxypyrazolo [3,4-*b*] pyridine-5-carboxylic acids substituted with a 1-aryl substituent showed potent inhibitory properties approaching those of allopurinol (Chu and Lynch, 1975).

Following the observation (Komai and Massey 1969) that iodoacetamide irreversibly inactivates xanthine oxidase under catalytic conditions by C(4a)-alkylation of the reduced functional FAD cofactor, Skibo (1986) has developed a benzimidazole (**21**) as a more potent inhibitor of this type. Whereas allopurinol and related compounds act at or near the hydroxypurine site of the enzyme, these non-purine-like inhibitors bind in the vicinity of the FAD cofactor and would have the advantage, if developed as drugs, of not interfering with other aspects of purine metabolism after conversion to nucleotides and nucleosides (see references cited in Skibo 1986).

Substituted 2-pyridylimidazopyridines and 2-pyridylbenzimidazoles have been shown to be inhibitors of xanthine oxidase (Baldwin *et al.* 1977). 2-(4-pyridyl)-4,5-dicyanomidazole (**22a**) and 2-(4-pyridyl)-4-nitroimidazole (**22b**) were at least an order of magnitude more potent than allopurinol.

Following the observation that 7-arylpteridine-4-ones (**23**) are good substrates of xanthine oxidase yet 6-phenylpteridine-4-one is a poor substrate and acts as an effective competitive inhibitor of the enzyme, the inhibitory properties of the 6-substituted compounds have been examined (Naeff and Van der Plas 1985). The most active compounds in a series of 13 studied were **24a** and **24b**, which inhibited xanthine oxidase about 40 times more effectively than allopurinol. The aryl substituent enhances the binding of the compound by interacting with a hydrophobic region in the active site, as reported for aryl-substituted purines (Baker and Wood 1967, 1968; Baker *et al.* 1968). QSAR analysis of the inhibitory effect of the compounds, using as parameters the minimum van der Waals' width (B1) and molar refraction (MR) for the *para*-substituents, showed that bulky rod-shaped substituents (i.e. n-butyl) did not reduce the effectiveness of the inhibition, whereas bulky spherical substituents (i.e.—I) did.

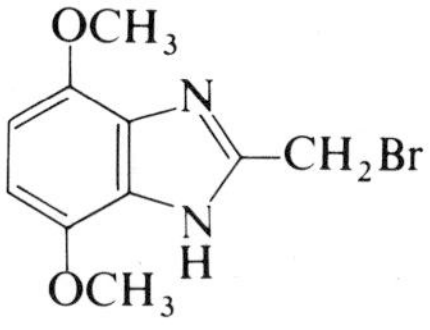

21

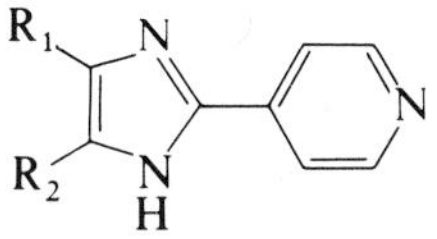

22

(a) $R_1 = R_2 = CN$

(b) $R_1 = H$; $R_2 = NO_2$

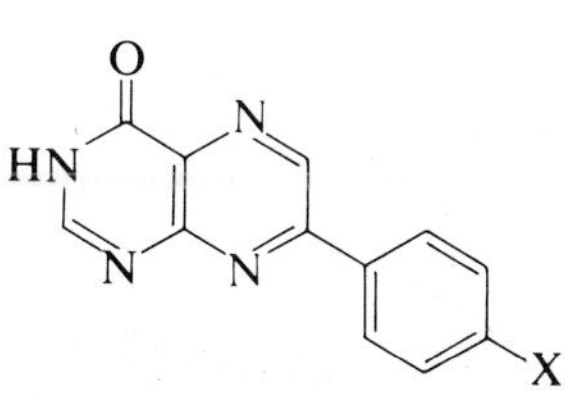

23

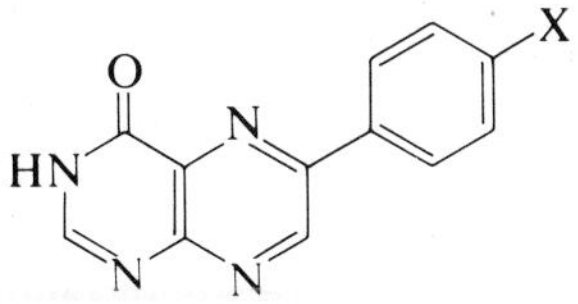

24

(a) X = H

(b) $X = nC_4H_9$

(c) X = I

8-bromoxanthine ($K_i = 0.4$ mM) is an inhibitor of xanthine oxidase (Hille and Stewart 1984) and exerts its action by binding to the reduced form of the enzyme at the molybdenum (Mo^{iv}) centre. X-ray absorption spectroscopy indicates that the bromine atom is approximately 4 Å from the molybdenum atom, which leads to the interpretation that the imidazole moiety of the purine provides additional binding at the site of the reduced enzyme rather than at the pyrimidine nucleus.

In summary, it appears unlikely that the other potent inhibitors described here based on the pyrimidine and other heterocyclic structures will displace allopurinol from its well-established position as a clinical agent in the treatment of gout unless it can be shown that they have a comparable *in vivo* activity and either possess a superior pharmacokinetic profile or have less potential to interfere with purine metabolism after conversion to nucleotides and nucleosides.

Folate compounds and the folate analogue amethopterin are potent reversible inhibitors of xanthine oxidase (bovine spleen), tetrahydrofolic acid (slow binding), and 2-amino-4-hydroxypteridine being the most potent inhibitors yet discovered for mammalian xanthine oxidase, being several times more potent than allopurinol (Lewis *et al.* 1984). A claim that folic acid is an extremely potent inhibitor of the enzyme was subsequently refuted by Spector and Ferone (1984), who found that inhibitory effect was due to slow-binding inhibition produced by pterin aldehyde, shown to be present in commercial samples of folic acid as a spontaneously produced photolytic breakdown product. Early studies with pterin aldehyde (Lowry *et al.* 1949) showed that its K_i value (0.6 nM) compares well with that for oxipurinol, which is the active species generated from allopurinol, a clinically useful drug in the treatment of gout (see earlier). However, folic acid (with its pterin aldehyde contaminant) has no effect on serum uric acid levels, presumably due to the known conversion of the aldehyde to its corresponding acid by xanthine oxidase; the acid only weakly inhibits the enzyme (Lowry *et al.* 1949). It has subsequently been shown (Nishino and Tsushima 1986) that pure folic acid is a competitive inhibitor of xanthine oxidase ($K_i = 4.2 \times 10^{-5}$ M).

Various aliphatic and pyridinecarboxaldehydes, but not aryl aldehydes, are inhibitors of xanthine oxidase. The inhibited enzyme is reactivated spontaneously on removal of excess aldehyde (Morpeth and Bray 1984).

References

Avis, P. G., Bergel, F., Bray, R. C., James, D. W. F. and Shooter, K. V. (1956a). Cellular constituents. The chemistry of xanthine oxidase. Part II. The homogeneity of crystalline metalloflavoprotein fractions. *J. Chem. Soc.*, 1212–19.

Avis, P. G., Bergel, F., and Bray, R. C. (1956b). Cellular constituents. The chemistry of xanthine oxidase. Part III. Estimations of the co-factors and the catalytic activities of enzyme fractions from cow's milk. *J. Chem. Soc.*, 1219–26.

Baker, B. R. and Wood, W. F. (1967). Irreversible enzyme inhibitors. CII. On the mode of phenyl binding of 9-phenylguanine to guanine deaminase and xanthine oxidase. *J. Med. Chem.*, **10**, 1101–5.

Baker, B. R. and Wood, W. F. (1968). Irreversible enzyme inhibitors, CXXII. On the nature and dimensions of the hydrophobic bonding region of guanine deaminase and xanthine oxidase *J. Med. Chem.*, **11**, 644–9.

Baker, B. R., Wood, W. F., and Kozma, J. A. (1968). Irreversible enzyme inhibitors. CXXVI. Hydrocarbon interaction with xanthine oxidase by phenyl substituents on purines and pyrazolo-[3,4-*d*] pyrimidines. *J. Med. Chem.*, **11**, 661–6.

Baldwin, J. J., Lumma, P. K., Novello, F. C., Ponticello, G. S., and Sprague, J. M. (1977). 2-pyridylimidazoles as inhibitors of xanthine oxidase. *J. Med. Chem.*, **20**, 1189–93.

Bergmann, F. and Levene, L. (1976). Oxidation of *N*-methyl substituted hypoxanthines, xanthines, purine-6,8-diones and the corresponding 6-thioxo derivatives by bovine milk xanthine oxidase. Biochem. Biophys. Acta, **429**, 672–88.

Betlach, C. J. and Sowell, J. W. (1982). The antitumour and mammalian xanthine oxidase inhibitory activity of 5-methyl-6-substituted pyrrolo (2,3-*d*) pyrimidine-2,4-diones. *J. Pharm. Sci.*, **71**, 269–70.

Bhattacharyya, A., Tollin, G., Davis, M., and Edmonson, D. E. (1983). Laser flash photolysis studies of intramolecular electron transfer in milk xanthine oxidase. *Biochemistry*, **22**, 5270–9.

Bray, R. C. (1963). Xanthine oxidase. In *The enzymes* (2nd edn) (ed. P. D. Boyer, H. Lardy, and K. Myrback) Vol. 7, pp. 533–56. Academic Press, New York.

Bray, R. C. (1975). Molybdenum iron-sulphur flavin hydroxylases and related enzymes. In *The enzymes* (3rd edn) (ed. P. D. Boyer), Vol. 12, pp. 299–419. Academic Press, New York.

Bray, R. C. (1980a). The reactions and the structures of molybdenum centers in enzymes. In *Adv. Enzymol. Relat. Areas Mol. Biol.*, **51**, 107–65.

Bray, R. C. (1980b). EPR of molybdenum-containing enzymes. In *Biological magnetic resonance*, (ed. L. J. Berliner and J. Reuben), Vol. 2, pp. 45–84, Plenum, New York.

Bray, R. C., Gutteridge, S., Stotter, D. A., and Tanner, S. J. (1979). The mechanism of action of xanthine oxidase. The relationship between the rapid and very rapid molybdenum electron-paramagnetic resonance signals *Biochem. J.*, **177**, 357–60.

Chu, I. and Lynch, B. M. (1975). Synthesis and biological evaluation of xanthine oxidase inhibitors. Pyrazolo [3,4-*d*] pyrimidines and pyrazolo [3,4-*b*] pyridines. *J. Med. Chem.*, **18**, 161–5.

Edmondson, D., Massey, V., Palmer, G., Beacham, L. M., and Elion, G. B. (1972). The resolution of active and inactive xanthine oxidase by affinity chromatography. *J. Biol. Chem.*, **247**, 1597–604.

Elion, G. B. (1966). Enzymatic and metabolic studies with allopurinol. *Ann. Rheum. Dis. Suppl.*, **25**, 608–14.

Elion, G. B., Callahan, S., Nathan, H., Bieber, S., Rundles, R. W., and Hitchings, G. H. (1963). Potentiation by inhibition of drug degradation: 6-substituted purines and xanthine oxidase. *Biochem. Pharmacol.*, **12**, 85–93.

Elion, G. B., Yu, T. F., Gutman, A. B., and Hitchings, G. H. (1968). Renal clearance of oxipurinol, the chief metabolite of allopurinol. *Am. J. Med.*, **45**, 69–77.

George, G. N. and Bray, R. C. (1983). Formation of the inhibitory complex of *p*-mercuribenzoate with xanthine oxidase, evaluation of hyperfine and quadrupole couplings of mercury to molybdenum(V) from the electron paramagnetic resonance spectrum and structure of the complex. *Biochemistry*, **22**, 5443–52.

Gilbert, D. A. (1964). The chemistry of xanthine oxidase. 10. The inhibition of the bovine enzyme by purine-6-aldehyde. *Biochem. J.*, **93**, 214–19.

Gutteridge, S., Tanner, S. J., and Bray, R. C. (1978). The molybdenum centre of native xanthine oxidase. Evidence for proton transfer from substrates to the centre and for existence of an anion-binding site. *Biochem. J.*, **175**, 869–78.

Hart, L. I., McGartoll, M. A., Chapman, H. R., and Bray, R. C. (1970). The composition of milk xanthine oxidase. *Biochem. J.*, **116**, 851–64.

Hawkes, T. R., George, G. N., and Bray, R. C. (1984). The Structure of the inhibitory complex of alloxanthine (1H-pyrazolo (3,4-*d*) pyrimidine-4,6-diol) with the molybdenum centre of xanthine oxidase from electron-paramagnetic-resonance spectroscopy. *Biochem. J.*, **218**, 961–8.

Hille, R. and Massey, V. (1986). The equilibration of reducing equivalents within milk xanthine oxidase. *J. Biol. Chem.*, **261**, 1241–7.

Hille, R. and Stewart, R. C. (1984). The inhibition of xanthine oxidase by 8-bromoxanthine. *J. Biol. Chem.*, **259**, 1570–6.

Iyer, V. N. and Szybalski, W. (1963). A molecular mechanism of mitomycin action: linking of complementary DNA strands. *Proc. Nat. Acad. Sci. USA*, **50**, 355–62.

Iyer, V. N. and Szybalski, W. (1964). Mitomycins and porfiromycin: chemical mechanism of activation and cross-linking of DNA. *Science*, **145**, 55–8.

Komai, H. and Massey. V. (1969). Flavin-free xanthine oxidase. *Fed. Proc. Fed. Am. Soc. Exp. Biol.*, **28**, 868 (Abstr. 3418).

Krenitsky, T. A., Niel, S. M., Elion, G. B., and Hitchings, G. H. (1972). A comparison of the specificities of xanthine oxidase and aldehyde oxidase. *Arch. Biochem. Biophys.*, **150**, 585–99.

Lewis, A. S., Murphy, L., McCalla, C., Fleary, M., and Purcell, S. (1984). Inhibition of mammalian xanthine oxidase by folate compounds and amethopterin. *J. Biol. Chem.*, **259**, 12–15.

Lowry, O. H., Bessey, O. A., and Crawford, E. J., (1949). Pterine oxidase. *J. Biol. Chem.*, **180**, 399–410.

Malthouse, J. P. G., George, G. N., Lowe, D. J., and Bray, R. C. (1981). Coupling of [^{33}S] sulphur to molybdenum (V) in different reduced forms of xanthine oxidase. *Biochem. J.*, **199**, 629–37.

Massey, V. (1973). Iron–sulphur flavoprotein hydroxylases. In *Iron–sulphur proteins*, (ed. W. Lovenberg), pp. 301–360. Academic press, New York.

Massey, V., Komai, H., Palmer, G., and Elion, G. B. (1970). On the mechanism of inactivation of xanthine oxidase by allopurinol and other pyrazolo [3,4-*d*] pyrimidines. *J. Biol. Chem.*, **245**, 2837–44.

Morpeth, F. F. and Bray, R. C. (1984). Inhibition of xanthine oxidase by various aldehydes. *Biochemistry*, **23**, 1332–8.

Naeff, H. S. D. and Van der Plas, H. C. (1985). Synthesis and quantitative structure–activity relationship (QSAR) analysis of some novel xanthine oxidase inhibitors: 6-(*para*-substituted phenyl)–pteridine-4-ones. *Quant. Struct. Act. Relat.*, **4**, 161–6.

Nishino, T. and Tsushima, K. (1986). Interaction of milk xanthine oxidase with folic acid. Inhibition of milk xanthine oxidase by folic acid and separation of the enzyme into two fractions on sepharose 4B/folate gel. *J. Biol. Chem.*, **261**, 11242–6.

Olson, J. S., Ballou, D. P., Palmer, G., and Massey, V. (1974). The mechanism of action of xanthine oxidase. *J. Biol. Chem.*, **249**, 4363–82.

Pan, S. S., Andrews, P. A., Glover, C. J., and Bachur, N. R. (1984). Reductive activation of mitomycin C and mitomycin C metabolites catalyzed by NADPH-cytochrome P-450 reductase and xanthine oxidase. *J. Biol. Chem.*, **259**, 959–66.

Parmer, S. S., Dwivedi, C., and Ali, B. (1972). Selective inhibition of xanthine-oxidase by

3-hydroxy-1-nitrophenyl-1*H*-pyrazolo [4,3-*c*] pyridines. *J. Pharm. Sci.*, **61**, 179–82.

Parmer, S. S., Pandey, B. R., Dwivedi, C., and Ali, B. (1974). 3-Hydroxy-1-nitrophenyl-1*H*-pyrazolo [3,4-*b*] pyridines as selective inhibitors of rat liver xanthine oxidase. *J. Med. Chem.*, **17**, 1031–3.

Schwartz, H. S. (1962). Pharmacology of mitomycin C: III. *In vitro* metabolism by rat liver. *J. Pharmacol. Exp. Ther.*, **136**, 250–8.

Skibo, E. B. (1986). Non competitive and irreversible inhibition of xanthine oxidase by benzimidazole analogues acting at the functional flavin adenine dinucleotide co-factor. *Biochemistry*, **25**, 4189–94.

Spector, T. and Ferone, R. (1984). Folic acid does not inactivate xanthine oxidase. *J. Biol. Chem.*, **259**, 10784–6.

Spector, T. and Johns, D. G. (1970). Stoichiometric inhibition of reduced xanthine oxidase by hydroxypyrazolo [3,4-*d*] pyrimidines. *J. Biol. Chem.*, **245**, 5079–85.

Springer, R. H., Dimmitt, M. K., Novinson, T., O'Brien, D. E., Robins, R. K., Simon, L. N., and Miller, J. P. (1976). Synthesis and enzymic activity of some novel xanthine oxidase inhibitors. 3-substituted 5,7-dihydroxy[1,5-*a*]pyrimidines. *J. Med. Chem.*, **19**, 291–6.

Tomasz, M. and Lipman, R. (1981). Reductive metabolism and alkylating activity of mitomycin C induced by rat liver microsomes. *Biochemistry*, **20**, 5056–61.

Tjandramaga, T. B., Cucinell, S. A., Israel, Z. H., Perel, J. M., Dayton, P. G., Yu, T. F., and Gutman, A. B. (1972). Observations on the disposition of probenecid in patients receiving allopurinol. *Pharmacology*, **8**, 259–72.

Weissbach, A. and Lisio, A. (1965). Alkylation of nucleic acids by mitomycin C and porfiromycin. *Biochemistry*, **4**, 196–206.

Yu, T. F. (1974). Milestones in the treatment of gout. *Am. J. Med.*, **56**, 676–85.

Section 22D
5α-reductase inhibitors

22D.1   Characteristics of the enzyme
22D.2   Dihydrotestosterone and its physiological role
22D.3   Prostatic cancer
22D.4   Inhibitors of 5α-reductase
References

22D.1   Characteristics of the enzyme

5α-reductase (NADPH: Δ^4-3-oxosteroid-5α-oxido-reductase) is a membrane-bound enzyme responsible for converting the androgen testosterone (T) to 5α-dihydrotestosterone (DHT), as well as other Δ^4-3-oxosteroids to their 5α-dihydro derivatives. It occurs in bacteria and many animals; in humans and the rat, it is found in liver, lung, prostate, seminal vesicle, epididymis, and skin. The enzyme is unstable *in vitro* at 25°C, has a molecular weight of 250 000–350 000 and pH optimum of about 6.6 (see Petrow and Padilla 1984, for review). Inhibition and other studies have indicated that the enzymes from the prostate of the rat, dog and human are different (Liang *et al.* 1985).

22D.2 Dihydrotestosterone and its physiological role

Whereas T is the androgen responsible for androgen action in skeletal muscle, for sexual behaviour, for Wolffian duct differentiation, and for normal development of seminal vesicles, vas deferens, and epididymis, DHT is the key androgen governing normal growth of the genitalia and prostate, as shown by histological studies on the human embryo. Studies on male human pseudo-hermaphrodites with 5α-reductase deficiency show that although normal male characteristics and a normal testosterone plasma level are present in these subjects, there is a small or absent prostate associated with a very small conversion of T to DHT (Imperato-McGinley *et al.* 1974) due to 5α-reductase deficiency (Walsh *et al.* 1974). Administration of DHT to these subjects results in prostatic growth. These studies establish DHT rather than T as the essential hormone for normal prostate growth.

Testosterone, produced by the testes, is transported in the blood by a steroid binding β-globulin and, after entering the prostatic cell (prolactin may have an effect here; Sandberg 1981), is converted to DHT in the extranuclear compartment. DHT then binds to the androgen receptor (R_{DHT}) in the cytoplasm (see Rossini and Liao 1982; Janne and Bardin 1984 for reviews). The DHT–receptor complex then migrates from the cytoplasm to the nucleus and interacts with nuclear chromatin, possibly at a specific site (Barrack 1982), to stimulate RNA synthesis. This results in formation of specific proteins, including 5α-reductase along with other cellular components (Sandberg and Kadohama 1984). A comparison of enzyme activity and receptor binding activity for T as well as DHT leads to the view that there are interrelational regulatory mechanisms between androgen receptors and 5α-reductase (Herkner *et al.* 1986). The role of androgen in basic maintenance and proliferation of prostate epithelial cells is less conclusive. Whereas prolactin has been suggested for this role, it has recently been demonstrated that the androgen-independent proliferation of isolated epithelial cells from rat androgen-responsive prostate tumours and androgen-dependent normal prostate of rat and human requires growth factors known as prostatropins which are concentrated in neural tissue (McKeehan *et al.* 1984; Chaproniere and McKeehan 1986; Crabb *et al.* 1986).

Skin metabolises T to DHT very effectively (Sansone and Reisner 1971) and DHT has been implicated in acne (Sansone and Reisner 1971), female hirsutism (Kuttenn *et al.* 1977; see Brooks 1986) and male-pattern baldness (Bingham and Shaw 1973), where affected areas have elevated DHT levels or 5α-reductase activity. 5α-reductase activity in skin has been correlated with serum levels of 3α,17β-androstanediol glucuronide (a metabolite of DHT) and hirsutism in women (Paulson *et al.* 1986). DHT has also been implicated in benign prostate hyperplasia (BPH) and prostate cancer. BPH is a common disease in older men and there is increasing evidence that a major role is played by a shift in the oestrogen–androgen balance in favour of oestrogens (see Habenicht et al. 1986). Consequently, much interest has been shown in the development of inhibitors of 5α-reductase which may be useful in minimizing these androgen-responsive conditions. However, the treatment of normal males for acne and alopecia must not be associated with interference with receptor action, since this can result in a feminizing effect, inducing gynaecomastia and loss of libido.

22D.3 Prostatic cancer

At the time of discovery, prostatic cancer is usually metastatic and < 10 per cent of patients are suitable for curative total prostatectomy. In the treatment of prostatic cancer, elimination of androgen support forms the basis for endocrine therapy of the early hormone-dependent phase of the disease, since approximately 80 per cent of prostate cancers are androgen-sensitive. Removal of the testes (orchiectomy) or chronic therapy with oestrogens have undesirable aspects and provide only temporary remission during the early phase of the cancer. However, complete adrenal androgen blockade with aminoglutethimide after relapse following castration has given a 33 per cent response rate (see Geller and Albert 1985). An alternative approach using inhibitors of 5α-reductase has been suggested (see Kadohama et al. 1984a; Petrow and Padilla 1984), possibly as combined therapy with androgen receptor binding antagonists (cyproterone acetate, flutamide, anandron) or LHRH agonists and antagonists (Sandberg and Kadohama 1984). The 5α-reductase inhibitors should show little agonist activity at the androgen receptor, although an antagonist action would be reinforcing.

The well-differentiated cells found in the early stages of prostate cancer biochemically resemble normal prostate cells and the majority are hormone-responsive. As the malignancy progresses, the cells lose their differentiation and hormone dependence. These changes are accompanied by loss of R_{DHT} (Kliman et al. 1978) and diminished ability to synthesize DHT (Shain et al. 1977), with a shift in the metabolism of testosterone by the oxidative pathway to the weaker androgen, androstenedione (Morfin et al. 1977; Smith et al. 1983). Although 5α-reductase activity, mainly present in the stromal cells (Cowan et al. 1977), is elevated in BPH (Siiteri and Wilson 1970; Geller et al. 1976; Meikle et al. 1981) compared with normal tissue, the general view that its activity in cancerous tissue is decreased has been challenged by Kadohama et al. (1984a) from studies on organic culture explants. These studies have shown that malignant cells from rat prostate have testosterone-metabolizing capacity at levels higher than in hyperplastic tissue, probably due to a lowered K_m value for the enzyme.

Consequently, it has been argued (Petrow and Padilla 1984) that partial elimination of DHT from the prostate cell by inhibition of 5α-reductase, with the expected maintenance of R_{DHT} levels to guard against development of an autonomous cell population, is a reversible, flexible therapy for prolongation of patient life during the endocrine-responsive phase of the disease without withdrawal of testosterone support.

22D.4   Inhibitors of 5α-reductase

4-aza steroids have proved to be potent inhibitors of 5α-reductase (see Brooks 1986 for review). One of the most potent competitive reversible inhibitors of 5α-reductase known is 4-MA (**25**, 17β,N,N-diethylcarbamoyl-4-methyl-4-aza-5α -androst-3-one, also known as DMAA), which strongly inhibits the rat prostate enzyme *in vitro* ($K_i = 5.0$ nM; Liang and Heiss 1981) and *in vivo* (Brooks *et al.* 1981) as well as the enzyme from human genital skin fibroblasts in culture ($K_i = 5.5$ nM, Leshin and Wilson 1982; $K_i = 15$ nM, Berkovitz *et al.* 1984). In intact male rats, on treatment with 4-MA, prostatic concentrations of T and DHT were raised and lowered, respectively. In castrated male rats injected with either T propionate (TP) or DHT propionate (DHTP), there was a marked reduction in prostatic concentration of DHT in the TP injected animals alone. These results are consistent with the view that 4-MA acts by inhibiting 5α-reductase *in vivo*. At higher doses of 4-MA, the concentration of DHT in the prostates of animals receiving TP or DHTP was lowered. This suggested that higher doses of 4-MA may have reduced androgen uptake or retention, an effect not associated with 5α-reductase (Brooks *et al.* 1981). This view is supported by the observation that 4-MA has moderate affinity only for the prostate cytosol androgen receptor, being 1000-fold lower than that of DHT (Liang and Heiss 1981).

4-MA produces a significant reduction in the rate of tumour progression in the Nobel rat model of prostatic adenocarcinoma (Kadohama *et al.* 1985).

25 4-MA

Modification of the structure of 4-MA (Liang *et al.* 1984) to the 4-desmethyl 17β-N,N-diethylcarbamoyl or 4-desmethyl 17β-N,N-disopropylcarbamoyl analogue gives potent inhibitors of the rat prostate enzyme ($K_i = 29$ and 12.6 nM, respectively) that have little affinity for the androgen receptor. 2′,3′-α-tetrahydrofuran-2′-spiro-17(4-aza-5α-androstan-3-one) and its 4-N-CH₃ analogue are also good inhibitors of the enzyme, with some affinity for the androgen receptor. When fibroblasts from human genital skin were incubated with T and 4-MA, the nuclear uptake of DHT decreased in parallel with 5α-reductase activity in the expected manner (Berkovitz *et al.* 1984). However, these studies raised the possibility that a sufficiently critical mass of androgen receptor-bound DHT and T may still reach the nuclei of some androgen-dependent tissues.

4-MAPC (**26**; sodium 4-methyl-3-oxo-4-aza-5α -pregnane-20(*S*) carboxylate) is an inhibitor of prostatic tumour 5α-reductase, equally as effective as 4-MA (Kadohama *et al.* 1984a). Concomitant stimulation of 17β-oxidation of testosterone was also observed in human prostatic carcinoma and BPH and in a region of the rat prostate. 4-MAPC caused retardation of tumour progression in Noble rats bearing androgen-responsive adenocarcinoma (Kadohama *et al.* 1984b). 4-MAPC increased tumour volume-doubling time to values similar to those for female and castrated rats. This finding indicated that androgen-responsive cells of the tumour were sensitive to the inhibitory effect of the inhibitor. 4-MAPC has a low affinity for the rat prostatic cytosol 8S androgen receptor (Kadohama *et al.* 1984a).

26 4-MAPC

Weintraub *et al.* (1985) have described another 4-azasteroid, the urethane 20-(hydroxymethyl)-4-methyl-4-aza-2-oxo-5α-pregnan-3-one, as an inhibitor ($K_i = 1.2 \times 10^{-7}$ M) of rat prostate microsomal enzyme. Many other 3-oxo-4-aza steroids have been prepared (Rasmusson *et al.* 1984, 1986) that show a wide range of potency as inhibitors of rat prostate and human 5α-reductase. The primary structural modifications were changes in the A ring and substituents attached to the C-17 position of the steroid nucleus. A-ring modifications included 1α-CN, 1α-CH$_3$, 1α, 2α-CH$_2$, 2β-F, 2-aza, ring expansion, and contraction. The 17β-substituent was varied to include a wide range of polar and semi-polar groups with different degrees of extension and branching. Structure–activity relationships showed that receptor binding was decreased when the A-ring 4-nitrogen was not substituted and a 17β-side-chain of low affinity (17β-OH $> $17β-CH$_2$COOEt $> $17β-COOCH$_3 > $17β-CONH$_2$) was present. Enhanced 5α-reductase inhibition of both human and rat enzyme was observed when the C-17 side-chain incorporated a semi-polar group with lipophilic substituents. Structural requirements for inhibition of the human enzyme were found to be more demanding than those for the rat enzyme.

The 4-aza steroids are considered to be transition-state analogues of 5α-reductase. During addition of the 5α-hydrogen atom from NADPH on reduction of a substrate, the transition-state structure has a 3-enolic form derived from the double bond at the 4–5 position. The conformation of Ring A in the transition state (half-chair or envelope) is mimicked by the 3-oxo-4-aza steroid, thus accounting for the high potency ($K_i = c.$ 10^{-9} M) of some of these inhibitors (Liang et al. 1984). The lack of or decrease in binding at the androgen receptor has also been explained in terms of the geometry of ring A and the bulky nature of the 17β-group.

6-methylene-4-pregnene-3,20-dione (27a) and its 17-acetoxy derivative (27b) have been reported as mechanism-based inactivators that irreversibly inhibit the enzyme in vitro (Petrow et al. 1981). The K_i of 27b is 1.25×10^{-6} M and the k_{cat} value is 4.8×10^{-3} s^{-1}. Compound 27a is an active antiprostatic agent in the rat (Petrow et al. 1982), but 27b is only weakly active. Extension of these studies to the 4-androsten-3-one nucleus showed that 6-methylenetestosterone has reduced activity, whereas its 17-acetate has 70 per cent of the inhibitory activity of progesterone (Petrow et al. 1983).

MacIndoe et al. (1984) have examined 27b and 6-methylenetestosterone 17-acetate as inhibitors of 5α-reductase from rat prostate and from MCF-human breast cancer cells and homogenates.

Of the other derivatives examined, the 17β-allyloxy compound (28) showed moderate activity, whereas the 17α-chloro compound (29) was a strong inhibitor. In vivo studies showed that 29 did not inhibit 5α-reductase in rat prostatic explants in tissue culture and that 6-methylenetestosterone acetate in the intact rat had androgenic properties.

Further modification of the 6-substituent of progesterone to the 6β-ethynyl derivative (30) gave an inactive compound but the allene (31) had 20 per cent of the inhibitory potency of progesterone (in the presence and absence of NADPH) and appeared to be an active-site-directed irreversible inhibitor.

The requirement for activity in the 6-methylene-4-en-3-one series, as shown by the structure–activity relationships, appears to be associated with an un-

27 (a) R = H
    (b) R = OCOCH$_3$

28 R = O·CH$_2$·CH = CH$_2$; R′ = H
29 R = H; R′ = Cl

30 R = −C ≡ CH
31 R = = C = CH$_2$

substituted terminal methylene group at C-6 and a C-17 substituent containing a carbonyl residue not less than 11 Å from the carbonyl group at C-3. It was concluded that the enzyme active site possesses a hydrophobic pocket to accommodate the 6-methylene group and that this contains a nucleophilic group within bonding distance of the 6-methylene terminal (Petrow et al. 1983).

Robaire et al. (1977) have shown that the allenic 3-oxo-5,10-seco steroid (**32**; SECO) is an irreversible inhibitor of rat epididymal 5α-reductase, and Voigt et al. (1978) found that it prevented the growth-promoting effect of TP on the flank organs of female hamsters. SECO is a more specific inhibitor of 5α-reductase than 4-MA, and at concentrations inhibiting the epididymal enzyme it does not, like 4-MA, affect the conversion of pregnenolone to testosterone via the 4-ene-3-oxo-pathway (Cooke and Robaire 1986). The interference by 4-MA in this pathway may be through inhibition of 3β-hydroxysteroid:NAD (P)$^+$ oxidoreductase (EC 1.1.1.51) and 3β-hydroxysteroid dehydrogenase isomerase (EC 5.3.3.1).

(5α,20-R)-4-diazo-21-hydroxy-20-methyl pregnan-3-one (**33**; RMI 18 341) is a mechanism-based inactivator of 5α-reductase (Blohm et al. 1980) with $K_i = 3.5 \times 10^{-8}$ M and $k_{cat} = 7.1 \times 10^4 \, \text{s}^{-1}$. When administered in vivo to prepubertally castrated male rat, maintained thereafter on T, it blocked growth of the ventral prostrate but did not prevent the action of administered DHT or the muscle growth-promoting effects of T (Blohm et al. 1985).

32 SECO   33

The proposed mechanism of inactivation assumes that the inhibitor represents an analogue of the enol intermediate formed after initial hydrogen addition at C-5 in the normal substrate reaction pathway. Subsequent protonation at C-4 in the expected manner for the substrate reaction leads with **33** to the formation of a reactive diazonium species, which forms a covalent bond at C-4 with a nucleophile at the active site.

A number of 4-chlorosubstituted steroids based on the androstane, cholestane, and pregnane nucleus have been examined as inhibitors of the enzyme. The 4-chloro derivative of 17α-hydroxyprogesterone was found to be a potent inhibitor of the rat and human (BPH) prostate enzyme in organ culture (Sandberg and Kadohama 1984).

Several 16β-alkyl testosterones or nortestosterones have been shown to be weak inhibitors of the enzyme, including the anti-androgen 16β-ethyl-19-nortestosterone (TSAA-291, Sudo *et al.* 1981).

6β-Methoxy-9β,10α-pregna-4,6-diene-3,20-dione (Ro 6-1963) is an inhibitor of 5α-reductase from male rat liver microsomes (Graef and Golf 1976).

Progesterone and norethindrone, as well as other synthetic progestational compounds commonly used in oral contraception, have been examined as inhibitors of 5α-reductase activity in genital skin fibroblasts. This was in response to the suggestion that an increase in the incidence of hypospadias in industrialized countries in the past decade may be related to inhibition of 5α-reductase leading to a deficiency of DHT. Norethindrone was a weak inhibitor with one-tenth the potency of progesterone (Dean and Winter 1984) and the other compounds were inactive, which does not support this contention.

Progesterone, androst-4-en-3-one-17β-carboxylic acid (17βC), and its methyl ester (17β ME) are inhibitors of 5α-reductase *in vitro* but have no effect *in vivo* on T and DHT levels in intact rats (Brooks *et al.* 1981). However, Voigt and Hsia (1973) have reported that topical application of 17βC to the flank organ of female hamsters prevented the TP-induced growth of that gland. The growth of the flank organ was uninfluenced by 17βC or 17β ME when the animals were treated with DHT. These results are in accord with the 5α-reductase-inhibiting property of 17βC.

Permixon, an extract of the plant *Serenoa repens* B and a new treatment for BPH, has been shown to be an antagonist of the cytosolic androgen receptor in rat prostate (Carilla *et al.* 1984) and in human foreskin fibroblasts (Sultan *et al.* 1984). A more recent finding is that it is a specific inhibitor of rat ventral prostate 5α-reductase ($IC_{50} = 88.2$ μg ml^{-1}) (Briley *et al.* 1984).

A series of non-steroidal 5α-reductase inhibitors based on the parent structure **(34)** and **(35)** have been described in the patent literature (Arai *et al.* 1985a, b).

The 5α-reductase inhibitors, lansic acid, lansiosides A, B, and C from the pericarp of *Lansium domesticum*, endogenous to Malaysia, have been reported in the patent literature to be effective in controlling male-hormone-type baldness, acne, and prostatic hypertrophy (Miyamoto and Miyamoto 1985).

In summary, a number of steroidal inhibitors, particularly 4-aza-steroids,

34

35

have been found in recent years to possess excellent inhibitory effects against 5α-reductase, both *in vitro* and *in vivo*. Several of these compounds show little or no affinity for the androgen receptor of the rat prostate cytosol, reduce the growth-promoting effects of T on the prostate of castrated rats, reduce DHT concentration in acutely treated rats and dogs, and bring about a reduction in the size of the prostate in chronically treated rats and dogs. The use of these compounds in the clinic for the treatment of prostatic cancer in humans, as well as other DHT-mediated conditions, is eagerly awaited.

References

Arai, Y., Toda, M., and Miyamoto, T. (1985a). Anilide derivatives as pharmacetuticals, J. P. 60, 146, 855 [85,146,855], 2 August 1985. (CA 104, 33890).

Arai, Y., Toda, M., and Miyamoto, T. (1985b). Ketone compounds, J.P. 60,142,941 [85,142,941] 29th July 1985 (CA **104**, 109340).

Barrack, E. R. (1982). The nuclear matrix in steroid hormone action. In, *The Nuclear envelope and the nuclear matrix*, Wistar Symposium Series, Vol. 2, pp. 247–58. Alan Liss, New York.

Berkovitz, G. D., Brown, T. R., and Migeon, C. J. (1984). Inhibition of 5α-reductase activity and alteration of nuclear testosterone. Dihydrotestosterone ratio in human genital skin fibroblasts. *J. Andrology*, **5**, 171–5.

Bingham, K. D. and Shaw, D. A. (1973). The metabolism of testosterone by human male scalp skin. *J. Endocrinol.*, **57**, 111–21.

Blohm, T. R., Metcalf, B. W., Laughlin, M. E., Sjoerdsma, A., and Schatzman, G. L. (1980). Inhibition of testosterone 5 α-reductase by a proposed enzyme-activated, active site-directed inhibitor. *Biochem. Biophys. Res. Commun.*, **95**, 273–80.

Blohm, T. R., Laughlin, M. E., and Weintraub, P. M. (1985). Pharmacologic induction of 5α-reductase deficiency in the postnatal rat. *Pharmacologist*, **27**, 273 (Abstr. 862).

Briley, M., Carilla, E., and Roger, A. (1984). Inhibitory effect of permixon on testosterone-5α-reductase activity of the rat ventral prostate. *Br. J. Pharmacol.*, **83**, 401P.

Brooks, J. R. (1986). Treatment of hirsutism with 5α-reductase inhibitors. *Clin. Endocrinol. Metab.*, **15**, 391–405.

Brooks, J. R., Baptista, E. M., Berman, C., Ham, E. A. Hichens, M., Johnston, D. B. R., Primka, R. L., Rasmusson, G. H., Reynolds, G. F., Schmitt, S. M., and Arth, G. E. (1981). Response of rat ventral prostate to a new and novel 5α-reductase inhibitor. *Endocrinology*, **109**, 830–6.

Carilla, E., Briley, M., Fauran, F., Sultan, Ch., and Duvilliers, C. (1984). Binding of permixon, a new treatment for prostatic benign hyperplasia, to the cytosolic androgen receptor in the rat prostate. *J. Steroid Biochem.*, **20**, 521–3.

Chaproniere, D. M. and McKeehan, W. L. (1986). Serial culture of single adult human prostatic epithelial cells in serum-free medium containing low calcium and a new growth factor from bovine brain. *Cancer Res.*, **46**, 819–24.

Cooke, G. M. and Robaire, B. (1986). The effects of diethyl-4-methyl-3-oxo-4-aza-5α-androstane-17β-carboxamide (4-MA) and (4R)-5,10-seco-19-norpregna-4,5-diene-3,10,20-trione (SECO) on androgen biosynthesis in the rat testis and epididymis. *J. Steroid. Biochem.*, **24**, 877–86.

Cowan, R. A., Cowan, S. K., Grant., J. K., and Elder, H. Y. (1977). Biochemical investigations of separated epithelium and stroma from benign hyperplastic prostatic tissue. *J. Endocrinol.*, **74**, 111–20.

Crabb, J. W., Armes, L. G., Carr, S. A., Johnson, C. M., Roberts, G. D., Bordoli, R. S., and McKeehan, W. L. (1986). Complete primary structure of prostatropin, a prostate epithelial cell growth factor. *Biochemistry*, **25**, 4988–93.

Dean, H. J. and Winter, J. S. D. (1984). The effect of five synthetic progestational compounds on 5α-reductase activity in genital skin fibroblast monolayers. *Steroids*, **43**, 13–23.

Geller, J. and Albert, J. D. (1985). Adrenal androgen blockade in relapsed prostate cancer. *Eur. J. Cancer Clin. Oncol.*, **21**, 1127–31.

Geller, J., Albert, J., Lopez, D., Geller, S., and Niwayama, G. (1976). Comparison of androgen metabolites in benign prostatic hypertrophy (BPH) and normal prostate. *J. Clin. Endocrinol. Metab.*, **43**, 686–88.

Graef, V. and Golf, S. W. (1976). Effect of 6β-methoxy,9β,10α-pregna-4,6-diene-3,20 dione (Ro6-1963) on the steroidal reductases in rat liver. *Experientia*, **32**, 1250–51.

Habenicht, U. F., Schwarz, K., Schweikert, H. U., Neumann, F., and El Etreby, M. F. (1986). Development of a model for the induction of estrogen-related prostatic hyperplasia in the dog and its response to the aromatase inhibitor 4-hydroxy-4-androstene-3,17-dione: preliminary results. *The prostate*, **8**, 181–94.

Herkner, K., Swoboda, W., Hoeller, B., and Goedl, U. (1986). Molecular biology of androgen action: testosterone/dihydrotestosterone receptor and androgen 5α-reductase in the human foreskin. *J. Steroid. Biochem.*, **24**, 239–43.

Imperato-McGinley, J., Guerrero, L., Gautier, T., and Peterson, R. E. (1974). Steroid 5α-reductase deficiency in man: an inherited form of male pseudohermaphroditism. *Science*, **186**, 1213–15.

Janne, O. A. and Bardin, C. W. (1984). Androgen and antiandrogen receptor binding. *Ann. Rev. Physiol.*, **46**, 107–18.

Kadohama, N., Karr, J. P., Murphy, G. P., and Sandberg, A. A. (1984a). Selective inhibition of prostatic tumor 5α-reductase by a 4-methyl-4-azasteroid. *Cancer Res.*, **44**, 4947–54.

Kadohama, N., Wakisaka, M., Karr, J. P., Murphy, G. P., and Sandberg, A. A., (1984b). Growth suppression of the noble rat prostatic tumour by 4-methyl-4-azasteroidal inhibitors of 5-α-reductase. *Proc. Am. Ass. Cancer. Res.*, **25**, 209 (Abstr. 827).

Kadohama, N., Wakisaka, M., Kim, U., Karr, J. P., Murphy, G. P., and Sandberg, A. A. (1985). Retardation of prostate tumour progression in the Noble rat by 4-methyl-4-aza-steroidal inhibitors of 5α-reductase. *J. Nat. Cancer. Inst.*, **74**, 475–86.

Kliman, B., Prout, G. R., McLaughlin, R. A., Daly, J. J., and Griffin, P. P. (1978). Altered androgen metabolism in metastatic prostate cancer. *J. Urol.*, **119**, 623–6.

Kuttenn, F., Mowszowicz, I., Shaison, G., and Mauvais-Jarvis P. (1977). Androgen production and skin metabolism in hirsutism. *J. Endocrinol.*, **75**, 83–91.

Leshin, M. and Wilson, J. D. (1982). Inhibition of steroid 5α-reductase from human skin fibroblasts by 17β-N,N-diethylcarbamoyl-4-methyl-4-aza-5α-androstan-3-one. *J. Steroid Biochem.*, **17**, 245–50.

Liang, T. and Heiss C. E. (1981). Inhibition of 5α-reductase, receptor binding, and nuclear uptake of androgens in the prostate by a 4-methyl-4-aza-steroid. *J. Biol. Chem.*, **256**, 7998–8005.

Liang, T., Heiss, C. E., Cheung, A. H. Reynolds, G. F., and Rasmusson, G. H. (1984). 4-azasteroidal 5α-reductase inhibitors without affinity for the androgen receptor. *J. Biol. Chem.*, **259**, 734–9.

Liang, T., Cascieri, M. A., Cheung, A. H., Reynolds, G. F., and Rasmusson, G. H. (1985). Species differences in prostatic steroid 5α-reductases of rat, dog and human. *Endocrinol.*, **117**, 571–9.

MacIndoe, J. H., West, E. R., and Petrow, V. (1984). Comparative studies of 5α-reductase inhibitors within MCF-7 human breast cancer cells. *J. Steroid Biochem.*, **20**, 1095–100.

McKeehan, W. L., Adams, P. S., and Rosser, M. P. (1984). Direct mitogenic effects of insulin, epidermal growth factor, glucocorticoid, cholera toxin, unknown pituitary factors and possibly prolactin, but not androgen, on normal rat prostate epithelial cells in serum-free, primary cell culture. *Cancer. Res.*, **44**, 1998–2010.

Meikle, A. W., Collier, E. S., Stringham, J. D., Fang, S. M., and Taylor, G. N. (1981). Elevated intranuclear dihydrotestosterone in prostatic hyperplasia of aging dogs. *J. Steroid. Biochem.*, **14**, 331–5.

Miyamoto, T. and Miyamoto, T. (1985). 5α-reductase inhibitors from *lansium domesticum*. J.P. 60, 243,020 [85,243,020]. 3 December, 1985 (C.A. **104**, 213249)

Morfin, R. F., Leav, I., Charles, J. F., Carvazos, L. F., Ofner, P., and Floch, H. H. (1977). Correlative study of the morphology and C_{19}-steroid metabolism of benign and cancerous human prostatic tissue. *Cancer (Philadelphia)*, **39**, 1517–34.

Paulson, R. J., Serafini, P. C., Catalino, J. A. and Lobo, R. A. (1986). Measurements of 3α,17β-androstanediol glucuronide in serum and urine and the correlation with skin 5α-reductase activity. *Fertil. steril.*, **46**, 222–6.

Petrow, V. and Padilla, G. M. (1984). 5α-reductase and prostatic cancer. In *Novel approaches to cancer chemotherapy* (ed. P. S. Sunkara), pp. 269–305. Academic Press, London.

Petrow, V., Wang, Y., Lack, L., and Sandberg, A. (1981). Prostatic cancer. 1.6-methylene-4-pregnen-3-ones as irreversible inhibitors of rat prostatic Δ^4-3-ketosteroid 5α-reductase. *Steroids*, **38**, 121–140.

Petrow, V., Padilla, G. M., Kendle, K., and Tantawi, A. (1982). Inhibition of prostatic growth in rats by 6-methylene-4-pregnene-3,20-dione. *J. Endocrinol.*, **95**, 311–13.

Petrow, V., Wang, Y. S., Lack, L. Sandberg, A., Kadohama, N., and Kendle, K. (1983). Prostatic cancer-11. Inhibitors of rat prostatic 4-ene-3-ketosteroid 5α-reductase derived from 6-methylene-4-androsten-3-ones. *J. Steroid Biochem.*, **19**, 1491–502.

Rasmusson, G. H., Reynolds, G. F., Utne, T., Jobson, R. B., Primka, R. L., Berman, C., and Brooks, J. R. (1984). Azasteroids as inhibitors of rat prostatic 5α-reductase. *J. Med. Chem.*, **27**, 1690–701.

Rasmusson, G. H., Reynolds, G. F., Steinberg, N. G., Walton, E., Patel, G. F., Liang, T., Cacieri, M. A., Cheung, A. H., Brooks, J. R., and Berman, C. (1986). Azasteroids: structure–activity relationships for inhibition of 5α-reductase and of androgen receptor binding. *J. Med. Chem.*, **29**, 2298–315.

Robaire, B., Covey, D. F., Robinson, C. H., and Ewing, L. L. (1977). Selective inhibition of rat epididymal steroid Δ^4-5α-reductase by conjugated allenic 3-oxo-5,10-secosteroids. *J. Steroid Biochem.*, **8**, 307–10.

Rossini, G. P. and Liao, S. (1982). Intracellular inactivation, reactivation and dynamic status of prostate androgen receptors. *Biochem. J.*, **208**, 383–92.

Sandberg, A. A. (1981). Some experimental results with prolactin: an overview of effects on the prostate. In *The prostatic cell: structure and function. Part B.* (ed. G. P. Murphy, A. A. Sandberg and J. P. Karr), pp. 55–62. Alan Liss., New York.

Sandberg, A. A. and Kadohama, N. (1984). Enzymatic and receptor systems as targets for therapy of prostatic cancer. In *Progress in cancer research and therapy* (ed. F. Bresciani, R. King, J. B. Roger, M. E. Lippman, M. Namer, and J. P. Raynaud) pp. 477–89. Raven Press, New York.

Sansone, G. L. and Reisner, R. M. (1971). Differential rates of conversion of testosterone to dihydrotestosterone in acne and in normal human skin—a possible pathogenic factor in acne. *J. Invest. Dermatol.*, **56**, 366–72.

Shain, S. A., McCullough, B., Nitchuk, M., and Boesel, R. W. (1977). Prostate carcinogenesis in the AXC rat. *Oncology*, **34**, 114–22.

Siiteri, P. K. and Wilson, J. D. (1970). Dihydrotestosterone in prostatic hypertrophy. I. The formation and content of dihydrotestosterone in the hypertrophic prostate of man. *J. Clin. Invest.*, **49**, 1737–45.

Smith, C. B., Masters, J. R. W., Metcalfe, S. A., and Ghanadian, R. (1983). Androgen metabolism by human prostatic tumours in organ culture. *Eur. J. Cancer Clin. Oncol.*, **19**, 929–34.

Sudo, K., Yoshida, K., Akinaga, Y., and Nakayama, R. (1981). 5α-reduction of an antiandrogen TSAA-291, 16β-ethyl-17β-hydroxy-4-estren-3-one, by nuclear 5α-reductase in rat prostates. *Steroids*, **38**, 55–71.

Sultan, C. Terraza, A., Devillier, C., Carilla, E., Briley, M., Loire, C., and Descomps, B. (1984). Inhibition of androgen metabolism and binding by a liposterolic extract of 'Serenoa Repens B' in human foreskin fibroblasts. *J. Steroid Biochem.*, **20**, 515–19.

Voigt, W. and Hsia, S. L. (1973). The antiandrogenic action of 4-androsten-3-one-17β-carboxylic acid and its methyl ester on hamster flank organ. *Endocrinol.*, **92**, 1216–22.

Voigt, W., Castro, A., Covey, D. F., and Robinson, C. H. (1978). Inhibition of testosterone 5α-reductase by antiandrogenicity of allenic 3-keto-5,10-secosteroids. *Acta Endocrinol.*, **87**, 668–72.

Walsh, P. C., Madden, J. D., Harrod, M. J., Goldstein, J. L., MacDonald, P. C., and Wilson, J. D. (1974). Familial incomplete male pseudohermaphroditism, type 2. Decreased dihydro-testosterone formation in pseudovaginal perineoscrotal hypospadias. *New Engl. J. Med.*, **291**, 944–9.

Weintraub, P. M., Blohm, T. R., and Laughlin, M. (1985). Preparation of 20-(hydroxymethyl)-4-methyl-4-aza-2-oxo-5α-pregnan-3-one as an inhibitor of testosterone 5α-reductase. *J. Med. Chem.*, **28**, 831–3.

Section 22E
Histidine decarboxylase inhibitors

22E.1   Characteristics of the enzyme
22E.2   Inhibitors of the mammalian enzyme
References

22E.1   Characteristics of the enzyme

Histidine decarboxylase (L-histidine carboxylase, EC 4.1. 1.22) specifically decarboxylates L-histidine to histamine and CO_2 and is widely distributed in animals and microorganisms (Boeker and Snell 1972.) High activity is found in the gastric mucosa of many mammalian species (Hakanson 1970) and the enzyme plays a role in gastric function, since gastric decarboxylase activity is related to the concentration of circulating gastrin (Hakanson *et al.* 1974). Animal studies have shown that histidine decarboxylase is responsible for histamine biosynthesis *in vivo* (Levine and Noll 1969) and the nonspecific L-aromatic amino acid decarboxylase (AADC) has little influence. The mammalian enzyme is dependent on covalently bound pyridoxal phosphate and is relatively unstable compared with the pyruvoyl-dependent bacterial enzyme (see later). Gastric histidine decarboxylase exists in three major forms with pI values of 5.90, 5.60, and 5.35, similar molecular weights (95 000), and the same optimum pH (6.8) and K_m value (0.15–0.21 mM) for histidine (Savany and Cronenberger 1982). The enzyme from rat liver has M_r 110 000 and is a dimer with pI 5.1 (Taguchi *et al.* 1984).

Among bacteria, the decarboxylase is found most commonly among intestinal micro-organisms (Eggerth 1939). The enzyme from the bacteria *Morganella morganii* and *Klebsiella pneumoniae* is pyridoxal phosphate-dependent, has $M_r c.$ 170 000, and consists of four identical subunits ($M_r c.$ 43 000). The sequence of the *M. morganii* enzyme has been elucidated and the lysine (Lys-232) that binds pyridoxal phosphate has been established (Vaaler *et al.* 1986). Interest in this enzyme stems from its greater stability and availability than the human enzyme, which it resembles in many respects. The enzyme has been purified and crystallized from *Micrococcus* (Mardashev *et al.* 1967) and *Lactobacillus* 30a (Riley and Snell 1968, 1970). The *Lactobacillus* 30a enzyme differs from mammalian enzyme (Tran and Snyder 1981) in that a pyruvoyl residue is covalently bound at the active site. The enzyme consists of a hexamer that contains six each of two dissimilar subunits (α and β) (Hackert *et al.* 1981). The larger α-subunit ($M_r \approx 28\,000$) (Huynh *et al.* 1984a,b) and smaller ($M_r = 8\,840$) β-subunit (Vaaler *et al.* 1982) sequences are known, as well as the enzyme's three-dimensional structure (0.3 nM; Parks *et al.* 1983, 1985). The enzyme is formed from a pyruvate-free pro-enzyme where the identical hexameric chains are cleaved at a single serine–serine bond by an unusual intramolecular reaction (Recsei *et al.* 1983; Huynh and Snell 1986a).

22E.2   Inhibitors of the mammalian enzyme

Histamine possesses many pharmacological actions including dilatation of the cardiovascular system, contraction of smooth muscle, and regulation of gastric acid secretion. It is also considered to be implicated in some human disease processes such as anaphylaxis/allergy/hypersensitivity, atherosclerosis, and the inflammatory response (Shepherd and Mackay 1967; Green 1970; Hollis and Markle 1974; see Douglas 1980).

Some of the effects of histamine, such as bronchoconstriction and gut contraction, are mediated by one type of receptor, the H_1-receptor. Other effects, notably gastric secretion, are initiated through H_2-receptors. Drugs have been developed that selectively interfere with the action of histamine at its H_1-, or H_2-receptors, such as the tertiary amine antihistamines (Ash and Schild 1966; H_1 receptor) and cimetidine (H_2 receptor; see Ganellin 1981 for review). Interest has been shown in the development of a new type of antihistamine drug, which would block the biosynthesis of histamine through inhibition of the decarboxylase enzymes and so allow a study of the physiological and pharmacological role of histamine at its sites of action in the body.

A number of inhibitors synthesized during early work have been reviewed (Shepherd and Mackay 1967; Levine and Noll 1969). Brocresine (36; NSD-1055) is the most extensively studied of a class of oxyamine compounds that are potent inhibitors of the enzyme (as well as AADC) (Reid and Shepherd 1963; Levine *et al.* 1965; Ellenbogen *et al.* 1969) and inhibit the decarboxylase *in vivo* in humans (Levine and Noll 1969). The hydrazine derivative of histidine (37; MK-785) is also a potent inhibitor *in vivo* (Levine *et al.* 1965), the enantiomers differing seven-fold in inhibitory activity (See Duggan *et al.* 1984). Semicarbazide (38) inhibits histidine decarboxylase *in vivo* but also inhibits another pyridoxal phosphate-dependent enzyme, diamine oxidase. Part of the inhibition exerted by 36, 37, and 38 is due to reaction with the aldehyde moiety of the pyridoxal phosphate coenzyme. Compound (36) forms an oxime that is itself an inhibitor of histamine decarboxylase.

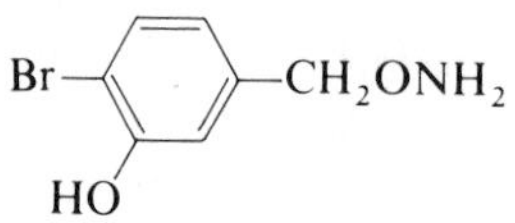

36

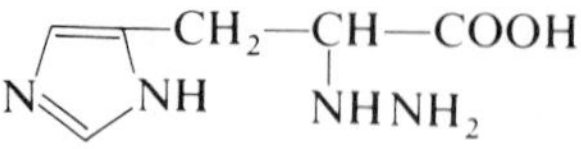

37

38

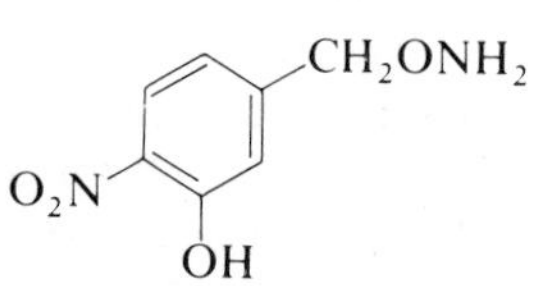

39

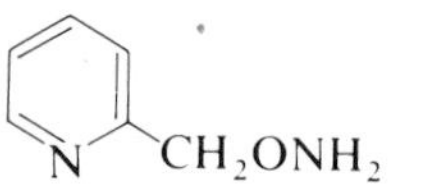

40

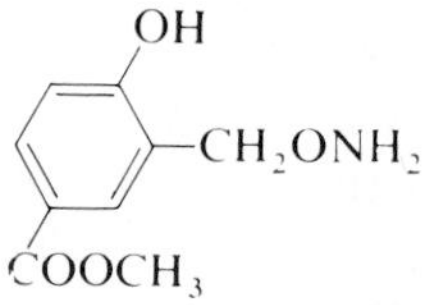

41

A number of other benzyloxyamines, as well as pyridylmethoxyamines, have been found to have high inhibitory activity against AADC and histamine decarboxylase (Huszti *et al.* 1973a). The most active compound is 3-hydroxy-4-nitrobenzyloxyamine (**39**), which has IC_{50} values of 0.3 μM and 0.6 μM for AADC and gastric histamine decarboxylase, respectively. Pyridyl-2-methoxyamine (**40**) is less inhibitory than **39** *in vitro* [$IC_{50} = 5$ μM (AADC), 1 μM (HD)]. Inhibition of diamine oxidase occurred to some extent with all the inhibitors studied (e.g. **39**; $IC_{50} = 60$ μM). 3-Nitrobenzoxyamine was a potent inhibitor of histidine decarboxylase ($IC_{50} = 50$ μM) with less activity towards AADC ($IC_{50} = 0.1$ mM). *In vivo* studies with **39** showed a decreased level of histamine both in stomach and in lungs, whereas **40** selectively lowered the level of histamine in the lungs.

2-Hydroxy-5-carbomethoxybenzyloxyamine (**41**), a further development of this work (Huszti *et al.* 1973b), was also a potent inhibitor of histidine decarboxylase [$K_i = 0.1$ μM for histidine, with inhibition of AADC ($K_i = 5$ μM for 5-HT)].

Kinetic studies showed reversible and competitive inhibition relative to both substrate and coenzyme and it was suggested that although the inhibitory effect of the compound was partly directed on the coenzyme (forming a pyridoxal phosphate inactivator complex), the main action was in displacing pyridoxal phosphate from the apoenzyme.

In vivo, **41** proved to be highly active in decreasing the levels of histamine in stomach and lungs, and it was non-toxic in repeated treatments. Preliminary pharmacological studies indicate potential clinical usefulness in the treatment of rheumatoid arthritis and histamine-induced bronchospasm.

The non-specificity of these inhibitors limits their usefulness as drugs or even as research tools. Non-carbonyl reagent inhibitors to date, such as α-methyl histidine (**42**), are relatively weak inhibitors (i.e. 1 mM, 40 per cent inhibition; De Graw *et al.* 1977). Another difficulty associated with transfer of *in vitro* activity to the *in vivo* situation for reversible/irreversible inhibitors is that frequent dosing would be required since the turnover of histidine decarboxylase in gastric mucosa is very rapid ($t_{1/2} = 100$–126 min) and in liver and lung it may also be very rapid (Beaven *et al.* 1968; Levine and Noll 1969; Dismukes and Snyder 1974).

The first reversible, potent, near-*specific* inhibitor of histidine decarboxylase discovered was 4-(4-imidazolyl)-3-amino-2-butanone (**43**) (1 mM; 87 per cent inhibition), with little activity towards AADC (2.5 mM; 10 per cent inhibition) (Smissman and Weis 1971). This compound (**43**) (McN-A-1293) was a more potent inhibitor than α-methylhistidine but less potent than brocresine (WSD-1055) (Taylor *et al.* 1973). Administration of **43** to rats in their feed resulted in 55 per cent inhibition of gastric histidine decarboxylase, while gastric AADC was only slightly inhibited (17 per cent). At doses seven-fold higher than α-FMH (see later) in normal rats, it failed to achieve significant reduction on gastric histidine decarboxylase levels (Duggan *et al.* 1984).

An analogue of **43**, 4-(4-imidazolylmethyl)-2,5-dimethyloxazole (**44**), had slightly lower potency (1 mM; 56 per cent inhibition). In both compounds, the function in histidine to be decarboxylated is replaced by a nondecarboxylating function. Further modifications on this theme led to histidine hydroxamic acid **45**, a potent inhibitor of the enzyme (0.3 mM; 81 per cent inhibition) but with appreciable inhibitory properties towards AADC (42 per cent inhibition) (Smissman and Warner 1972). D,L-dopahydroxamic acid was a non-specific potent inhibitor of both systems. Further modification (Smissman *et al.* 1976) of the carboxyl and amino groups in histidine gave the 2,2-dimethyl-4-imidazolidinone (**46**), which was a less potent inhibitor (5 mM; 44 per cent inhibition) with some inhibitory activity towards tyrosine decarboxylase (27 per cent inhibition). The methyl ester of L-histidine has been shown (Kelley *et al.* 1977b) to be an excellent inhibitor of the enzyme (4 μM; 50 per cent inhibition; $K_i = 1.8 \times 10^{-6}$ M) but the structural requirements of the inhibitor are very specific since homologation of the ester group or alkyl substitution on the α-carbon leads to reduction in activity. Substitution of a β-alkyl group on the methyl ester (or acid) is also associated with complete loss of activity (Kelley *et al.* 1977a; De Graw *et al.* 1977). L-histidine methyl ester has been reported to cause irreversible inhibition of histidine decarboxylase from *Micrococcus sp.* (Mardashev *et al.* 1968) and *Lactobacillus* 30a (Lane *et al.* 1976) by forming a Schiff's base with the essential pyruvoyl moiety of the enzyme (Huynh and Snell 1986b).

More recently, the search for inhibitors of histidine decarboxylase has extended to mechanism-based inactivators with their expected more specific action and greater efficiency in reducing enzyme levels through their irreversible action (necessary attributes in a prospective drug in view of the fast turnover rate of the enzyme and the necessity to preserve other pyridoxal-phosphate-dependent enzymes essential to the well-being of the body). Histidine decarboxylase inhibitors of this type have been described in some detail in Chapter 8 and are only briefly mentioned here.

α-Chloromethylhistidine (**47**; Lippert *et al.* 1979), α-ethynylhistamine (**48**; Holbert and Metcalf, 1984) and trifluoromethylhistamine (**49**; Metcalf *et al.* 1984) are time-dependent inhibitors of animal histidine decarboxylase, although the mechanism of inactivation is not clear (see Chapter 8).

(*S*)-α-Fluoromethylhistidine (**50**; α-FMH; IC_{50}, 8×10^{-6} M; Duggan *et al.* 1984) is a mechanism-based inactivator of mammalian histidine decarboxylase (Kollonitsch *et al.* 1978). These authors also claimed that the less potent (*R*)- and (*S*)-forms of α-fluoromethyl histamine (**51**; IC_{50}, 1×10^{-3} and 9×10^{-5}, respectively) were time-dependent inactivators, but this claim has been refuted (see Chapter 8).

α-FMH irreversibly inhibits mammalian histidine decarboxylase in a time-dependent manner, with a low partition ratio between inactivated enzyme and product (histamine), since the latter is not detectable (Duggan *et al.* 1984). *In vivo* work (Duggan *et al.* 1984) showed a reduction of whole-body histidine decarboxylase activity that was time-dependent. Concomitant reduction in histamine levels was also seen in the rapid-turnover pools of stomach and brain and, on chronic administration, the slow-turnover pool of the mastcells. α-FMH did not inhibit AADC action *in vivo*. The histamine-catabolizing enzymes diamine oxidase and histamine-*N*-methyl transferase were not affected by α-FMH at a concentration more than 100-fold in excess of its IC_{50} for histamine formation.

α-FMH does not inhibit the pyruvoyl-dependent histidine decarboxylase from *Lactobacillus* 30a, but it inactivates the pyridoxal phosphate-dependent

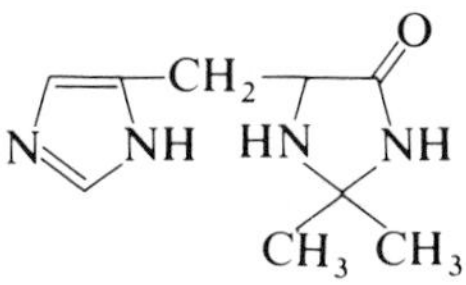

46

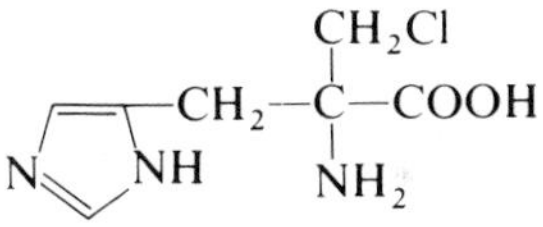

47

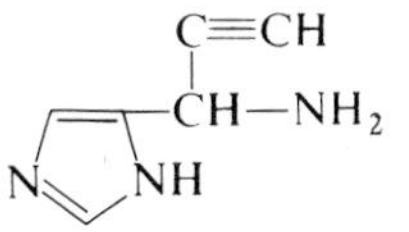

48

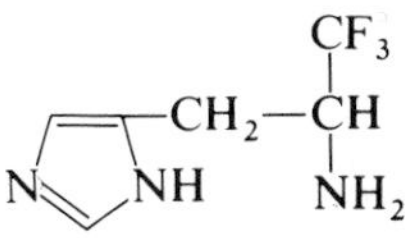

49

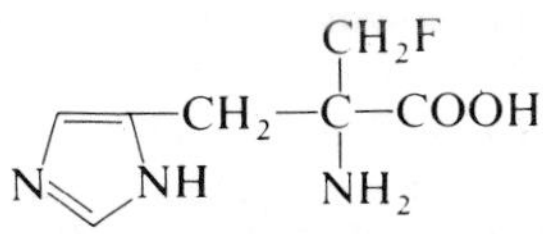

50

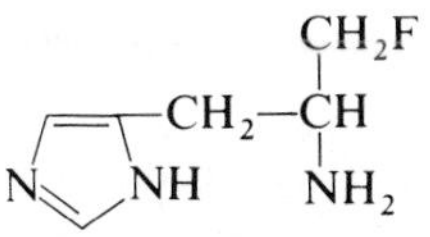

51

enzyme from *M. morganii*. The reaction has a 1:1 stoichiometry and the adduct formed with the coenzyme binds to Ser-322 by a postulated complex mechanism (Hayashi *et al.* 1986).

In summary, α-FMH seems the best prospect to date for the development of a potent, specific, rapid irreversible inhibitor of the mammalian enzyme that would prove useful in the treatment of duodenal and gastric ulcer. However, the successful launching of such a drug into the clinical area covered efficiently by the current H_2 antagonists would require more than resolve on the part of the manufacturer and it seems more likely that such compounds would be used as tools in elucidating the role of histidine at its physiological sites.

References

Ash, A. S. F. and Schild, H. O. (1966). Receptors mediating some actions of histamine. *Br. J. Pharmacol. Chemother.*, **27**, 427–39.

Beaven, M. A., Horakova, Z., Severs, W. B., and Brodie, B. B. (1968). Selective labeling of histamine in rat gastric mucosa: Application to measurement of turnover rate. *J. Pharmacol. Exp. Ther.*, **161**, 320–8.

Boeker, E. A. and Snell, E. E. (1972). Amino acid decarboxylases. In *The enzymes* (ed. P. D. Boyer), Vol. 6, pp. 217–253. Academic Press, New York.

DeGraw, J. I., Engstrom, J., Ellis, M., and Johnson, H. L. (1977). Potential histidine decarboxylase inhibitors α-and β-substituted histidine analogues. *J. Med. Chem.*, **20**, 1671–4.

Dismukes, K. and Snyder, S. H. (1974). Histamine turnover in rat brain. *Brain Res.*, **78**, 467–81.

Douglas, W. W. (1980). Autacoids. In *Goodman and Gilman's the pharmacological basis of therapeutics* (6th edn) (ed. A. G. Gilman, L. S. Goodman, and A. Gilman), pp. 608–646. Macmillan, New York.

Duggan, D. E., Hooke, K. F., and Maycock, A. L. (1984). Inhibition of histamine synthesis *in vitro* and *in vivo* by S-α-fluromethylhistidine. *Biochem. Pharmacol.*, **33**, 4003–9.

Eggerth, A. H. (1939). The production of histamine in bacterial cultures. *J. Bacteriol.*, **37**, 205–22.

Ellenbogen, L., Markley, E., and Taylor, R. J. (1969). Inhibition of histidine decarboxylase by benzyl and aliphatic aminooxyamines. *Biochem. Pharmacol.*, **18**, 683–5.

Ganellin, R. (1981). Medicinal chemistry and dynamic structure–activity analysis in the discovery of drugs acting at histamine H_2 receptors. *J. Med. Chem.*, **24**, 913–20.

Green, J. P. (1970). Histamine. In *Medicinal chemistry* (3rd edn) (ed. A. Burger), Part II, pp. 1633–42. Wiley-Interscience, New York.

Hackert, M. L., Meador, W. E., Oliver, R. M., Salmon, J. B. Recsei, P. A., and Snell, E. E. (1981). Crystallisation and subunit structure of histidine decarboxylase from *Lactobacillus 30a*. *J. Biol. Chem.*, **256**, 687–90.

Hakanson, R. (1970). New aspects of the formation and function of histamine, 5-hydroxytryptamine and dopamine in gastric mucosa. Properties of enterochromaffin and enterochromaffin like cells. Properties of mammalian histamine-forming enzymes. *Acta Physiol. Scand* (Suppl. 340), 77–134.

Hakanson, R., Kroesen, J. H., Liedberg, G., Oscarson, J., Rehfeld, J. F., and Stadil, F. (1974). Correlation between serum gastrin concentration and rat stomach histidine decarboxylase activity. *J. Physiol*, **243**, 483–98.

Hayashi, H., Tanase, S. and Snell, E. E. (1986). Pyridoxal 5′-phosphate-dependent histidine decarboxylase. Inactivation by α-fluoromethylhistidine and comparative sequences at the inhibitor and coenzyme-binding sites. *J. Biol. Chem.*, **261**, 11003–9.

Holbert, G. W. and Metcalf, B. W. (1984). Synthesis of α-ethynylhistamine, an inactivator of histidine decarboxylase. *Tetrahedron*, **40**, 1141–4.

Hollis, T. M. and Markle, R. A. (1974). Aortic endothelial histidine decarboxylase activity in experimental atherosclerosis. *Fed. Proc. Fed. Am. Soc. Exp. Biol.*, **33**, 624 (Abstr. 2341).

Huszti, Z., Kasztreiner, E., Kurti, M., Fekete, M., and Borsy, J. (1973b). 2-hydroxy-5-carbomethoxybenzyloxyamine: a new potent inhibitor of histidine decarboxylase. *Biochem. Pharmacol.*, **22**, 2253–65.

Huszti, Z., Kasztreiner, E., Szilagyi, G., Kosary, J., and Borsy, J. (1973a). Decarboxylase inhibition and structure–activity relationship studies with some newly synthesized benzyloxyamine and pyridylmethoxyamine derivatives. *Biochem. Pharmacol.*, **22**, 2267–75.

Huynh, Q. K., Vaaler, G. L., Recsei, P. A., and Snell, E. E. (1984a). Histidine decarboxylase of *Lactobacillus* 30a. Sequences of the cyanogen bromide peptides from the α-chain. *J. Biol. Chem.*, **259**, 2826–32.

Huynh, Q. K., Recsei, P. A., Vaaler, G. L., and Snell, E. E. (1984b). Histidine decarboxylase of *Lactobacillus* 30a. Sequences of the overlapping peptides, the complete α-chain, and prohistidine decarboxylase. *J. Biol. Chem.*, **259**, 2833–9.

Huynh, Q. K. and Snell, E. E. (1986a). Histidine decarboxylase of *Lactobacillus* 30a. Hydroxylamine cleavage of the seryl–seryl bond at the activation site of prohistidine decarboxylase. *J. Biol. Chem.*, **261**, 1521–4.

Huynh, Q. K. and Snell, E. E. (1986b). Pyruvoyl-dependent histidine decarboxylase from *Lactobacillus* 30a. Covalent modifications of aspartic acid 191, lysine 155, and the pyruvoyl group. *J. Biol. Chem.*, **261**, 4389–94.

Kelley, J. L., Miller, C. A., and White, H. L. (1977b). Inhibition of histidine decarboxylase. Derivatives of histidine. *J. Med. Chem.*, **20**, 506–9.

Kelley, J. L., Miller, C. A., and McLean, E. W. (1977a). Attempted inhibition of histidine decarboxylase with β-alkyl analogues of histidine. *J. Med. Chem.*, **20**, 721–3.

Kollonitsch, J., Patchett, A. A., Marburg, S., Maycock, A. L., Perkins, L. M. Doldouras, G. A., Duggan, D. E., and Aster, S. D. (1978). Selective inhibitors of biosynthesis of aminergic neurotransmitters. *Nature (London)* **274**, 906–8.

Lane, R. S. Manning, J. M., and Snell, E. E. (1976). Histidine decarboxylase of *Lactobacillus* 30a: Inactivation and active-site labeling by L-histidine methyl ester. *Biochemistry*, **15**, 4180–5.

Levine, R. J. and Noll, W. W. (1969). Histidine decarboxylase and its inhibition. *Ann. N. Y. Acad. Sci.*, **166**, 246–56.

Levine, R. J., Sato, T. L., and Sjoerdsma, A. (1965). Inhibition of histamine synthesis in the rat by α-hydrazino analog of histidine and 4-bromo-3-hydroxybenzyloxyamine. *Biochem. Pharmacol.*, **14**, 139–49.

Lippert, B., Bey, P., Van Dorsselaer, V., Vevert, J. P., Danzin, C., Ribereau-Gayon, G, and Jung, M. J. (1979). Selective irreversible inhibition of mammalian histidine decarboxylase by α-chloromethyl histidine. *Agents Actions*, **9**, 38–9.

Mardashev, S. R., Siomina, L. A., Prozorovskii, V. N. and Sokhina, A. M. (1967). N-terminal amino acid sequence in histidine decarboxylase. *Biokhimiya*, **32**, 761–5.

Mardashev, S. R., Siomina, L. A., Dabagov, N. S., and Gonchar, N. A. (1968). Studies on bacterial L-histidine decarboxylase. In *pyridoxal catalysis: enzymes and model systems*. (ed. E. E. Snell, A. E. Braunstein, E. S. Severin, and Yu. M. Torchinsky), p. 451–67. Wiley-Interscience, New York.

Metcalf, B. W., Holbert, G. W., and Lippert, B. J. (1984). α-trifluoromethylhistamine: a mechanism-based inhibitor of mammalian histidine decarboxylase. *Bioorg. Chem.*, **12**, 91–7.

Parks, E. H., Clinger, K., and Hackert, M. L. (1983). The molecular symmetry of histidine decarboxylase and prohistidine decarboxylase by rotation-function analysis. *Acta Crystallogr. B: Struct. Sci.*, **B39**, 490–4.

Parks, E. H., Ernst, S. R., Hamlin, R., Xuong, Ng. H., and Hackert, M. L. (1985). Structure determination of histidine decarboxylase from *Lactobacillus* 30a to 3.0Å resolution. *J. Mol. Biol.*, **182**, 455–65.

Recsei, P. A., Huynh, Q. K., and Snell, E. E. (1983). Conversion of prohistidine decarboxylase to histidine decarboxylase: peptide chain cleavage by non hydrolytic serinolysis. *Proc. Natn. Acad. Sci. USA*, **80**, 973–7.

Reid, J. D. and Shepherd, D. M. (1963). Inhibition of histidine decarboxylases. *Life. Sci.*, **2**, 5–8.

Riley W. D. and Snell, E. E. (1968). Histidine decarboxylase of *Lactobacillus* 30a. IV. The presence of covalently bound pyruvate as the prosthetic group. *Biochemistry*, **7**, 3520–8.

Riley W. D. and Snell, E. E., (1970). Histidine decarboxylase of *Lactobacillus* 30a. V. Origin of enzyme-bound pyruvate and separation of nonidentical subunits. *Biochemistry*, **9**, 1485–91.

Savany, A. and Cronenberger, L. (1982). Isolation and properties of multiple forms of histidine decarboxylase from rat gastric mucosa. *Biochem. J.*, **205**, 405–12.

Shepherd, D. M. and Mackay, D. (1967). The histidine decarboxylases. In *Progress in medicinal chemistry*, (ed. G. P. Ellis, and G. B. West), pp. 199–250. Butterworths, London.

Smissman, E. E. and Weis, J. A. (1971). Specificity in enzyme inhibition. 1. Synthesis of 4-(4-imidazolyl)-3-amino-2-butanone, 4-(4-imidazolyl)-3-acetamido-2-butanone, and 4-(4-Imidazolylmethyl)-2,5-dimethyloxazole for assay as inhibitors of histidine decarboxylases. *J. Med. Chem.*, **14**, 945–7.

Smissman, E. E. and Warner, V. D. (1972). Specificity in enzyme inhibition. 2. α-amino-hydroxamic acids as inhibitors of histidine decarboxylase and 3,4-dihydroxyphenylalanine decarboxylase. *J. Med. Chem.*, **15**, 681–4.

Smissman, E. E., Inloes, R. L., and El-Antably, S. (1976). Specificity in enzyme inhibition. 3. Synthesis of 5-substituted 2,2-dimethyl-4-imidazolidinones as inhibitors of tyrosine decarboxylase and histidine decarboxylase. *J. Med. Chem.*, **19**, 161–3.

Taguchi, Y., Watanabe, T., Kubota, H., Hiyashi, H., and Wada, H. (1984). Purification of histidine decarboxylase from the liver of fetal rats and its immunochemical and immunohistochemical characterisation. *J. Biol. Chem.*, **259**, 5214–21.

Taylor, R. J., Leinweber, F. J., and Braun, G. A. (1973). 4-imidazolyl-3-amino-2-butanone (McN-A-1293). A new specific inhibitor of histidine decarboxylase. *Biochem. Pharmacol.*, **22**, 2299–310.

Tran, V. T. and Snyder, S. H. (1981). Histidine decarboxylase. Purification from fetal rat liver, immunologic properties, and histochemical localisation in brain and stomach. *J. Biol. Chem.*, **256**, 680–6.

Vaaler, G. L., Recsei, P. A., Fox, J. L., and Snell, E. E. (1982). Histidine decarboxylase of *Lactobacillus* 30a. Comparative sequences of the β-chain from wild type and mutant enzymes. *J. Biol. Chem.*, **257**, 12770–4.

Vaaler, G. L., Brasch, M. A., and Snell, E. E. (1986). Pyridoxal 5′-phosphate-dependent histidine decarboxylase. *J. Biol. Chem.*, **261**, 11010–14.

Index